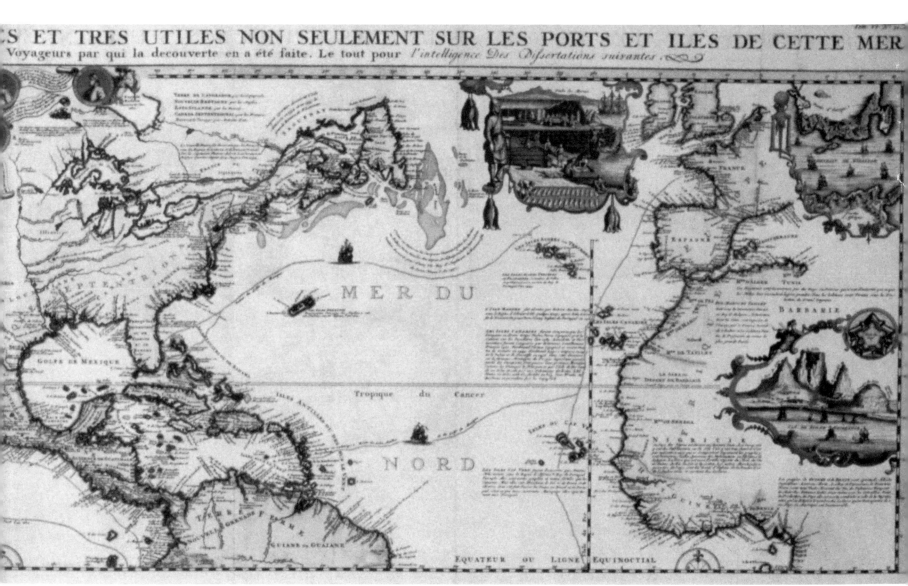

Henri Chatelaine Map, 1719
Carte Tres Curieuse De La Mer Du Sud, Contenant Des Remarques Nouvelles Et Tres Utiles Non Seulement Sur Les Ports Et Iles De Cette Mer

Dear Misha + Michael,

May you enjoy a
lifetime of love and happiness
and
may you enjoy many wonderful
meals together and with family
and friends.

Sincerely,
Cindy Hardin
9/17/05

"The Oysterman," 1933 by Fonville Winans. Courtesy of James and Meriget Turner, Fonville Winans Collection.
With appreciation to Steve Kleinpeter, Southern Photographic Images, featuring the Fonville Winans Collection, www.spiart.com.

Library of Congress Card Catalog Number: 2003108987

ISBN 0-9704457-1-7

First Printing: December 2004
Second Printing: January 2005

This book is also available on CD-ROM. If the book or CD-ROM is not available at your local bookstore, copies may be ordered directly from:

Chef John Folse & Company
2517 S. Philippe Avenue
Gonzales, LA 70737
225-644-6000
www.jfolse.com

Other cookbooks available by Chef John Folse include:

The Evolution of Cajun & Creole Cuisine

Chef John Folse's Plantation Celebrations

Chef John Folse's Louisiana Sampler

Something Old & Something New

Hot Beignets & Warm Boudoirs

Designer: John Lee Smith, Smith Communications
Typefaces: Myriad Pro, Albertus, Bernhard, English Vivace, Futura and Arial
Software: Adobe Creative Suite Professional
Hardware: PC Power 512
Printed and bound in Canada by Friesens Corporation

THE ENCYCLOPEDIA OF CAJUN & CREOLE CUISINE

Chef John D. Folse, CEC, AAC

CHEF JOHN FOLSE
& COMPANY
PUBLISHING

GONZALES, LOUISIANA

Chef John D. Folse, CEC, AAC

John Folse, born in St. James Parish in 1946, learned early that the secrets of Cajun cooking lay in the unique ingredients of Louisiana's swamp floor pantry. Folse seasoned these raw ingredients with his passion for Louisiana culture and cuisine, and from his cast iron pots emerged Chef John Folse & Company.

When Folse opened Lafitte's Landing Restaurant in 1978 in Donaldsonville, he set out to market his restaurant by taking "a taste of Louisiana" worldwide. He introduced Louisiana's indigenous cuisine to Japan in 1985, Beijing in 1986 and Hong Kong and Paris in 1987. In 1988 Folse made international headlines with the opening of "Lafitte's Landing East" in Moscow during the Presidential Summit between Ronald Reagan and Mikhail Gorbachev. In 1989 Folse was the first non-Italian chef to create the Vatican State Dinner in Rome. Promotional restaurants also included London in 1991 and 1993, Bogota in 1991, Taipei in 1992 and 1994 and Seoul in 1994. In 1988 the Louisiana Sales and Marketing Executives named Folse "*Louisiana's Marketing Ambassador to the World*" and the Louisiana Legislature gave him the title of "*Louisiana's Culinary Ambassador to the World.*"

The international success of Folse's cornerstone property, Lafitte's Landing Restaurant, spawned the incorporation of several other Chef John Folse & Company properties. White Oak Plantation in 1986 established Folse's catering and events management division. Chef John Folse & Company Publishing, since 1989 has produced seven cookbooks and numerous works by other authors. "*A Taste of Louisiana*" is Folse's international television series produced by Louisiana Public Broadcasting since 1990. Chef John Folse & Company Manufacturing, since 1991, is one of the few chef-owned food manufacturing companies in America producing custom manufactured

Chef John Folse stands outside the 2-seater outhouse at Nonc Paul's Camp, Cabanocey Plantation, St. James, La.

foods for the retail and foodservice industry. A new USDA manufacturing facility opened in 2004. The Chef John Folse Culinary Institute at Nicholls State University in Thibodaux, La., opened in October 1994 and is dedicated to the preservation of Louisiana's rich culinary and cultural heritage. In 2003 the institute broke ground on the new Ruth U. Fertel Culinary Arts Building. In August 1996, Folse began broadcasting his radio cooking show, "*Stirrin' It Up.*" In 2001, "*Stirrin' It Up*" expanded to a television cooking segment during the 5 p.m. newscast on WAFB-TV Channel 9, the Baton Rouge CBS affiliate.

Exceptional Endings, the pastry division, was launched in 1996 to create specialty desserts, pastries and savories. In May 1999 Folse opened his former Donaldsonville home as the new Lafitte's Landing Restaurant at Bittersweet Plantation offering fine dining and bed and breakfast accommodations. He has expanded on the catering services of White Oak Plantation, which better fulfills the special events needs of clients both regionally and nationally. In 2002 Bittersweet Plantation Dairy opened offering a full line of fresh and aged cheeses. In 2004, Bittersweet Plantation Dairy's cow's milk triple cream fromages, Fleur de Teche and Fleur de Lis, both won awards at the American Cheese Society Conference in Wisconsin. Fleur de Lis won a gold medal at the World Cheese Awards in London.

Folse has received numerous national and international accolades. In 1987 the Louisiana Restaurant Association named him "*Louisiana Restaurateur of the Year.*" In 1989, *Nation's Restaurant News* inducted Lafitte's Landing Restaurant into its "*Fine Dining Hall of Fame.*" In 1990 the American Culinary Federation named Folse the "*National Chef of the Year.*" In 1992 Johnson & Wales University in Providence, R.I., recognized Folse with an honorary doctorate of Culinary Arts as did Baltimore International Culinary College in 1995. In 1994 he assumed the role as national president of the American Culinary Federation, the largest

John Folse's parents, Royley Folse and Therese Zeringue, on their wedding day in 1941.

organization of professional chefs in America. The ACF Louisiana chapter inducted Folse into their *"Chef's Hall of Fame" in 1999.* In 1995 Folse was one of 50 people recognized in *Nation's Restaurant News'* "*Profiles of Power.*" In 1996 Lafitte's Landing Restaurant

As evident by his birth certificate, when John Folse was born his father's occupation was "trapper."

11. City or Town — (If outside city or town limits write RURAL)		13. Parish
St. James, La (Rural)		St. J
15. Street Number— if rural indicate location		16. Give
Rural		St
17. Full Name of Father		18. Color or
Antoine Royley Folse		w
20. Occupation of Father	21. Industry or Business	22. Birthp
Self employed	Trapper	Va
23. Full Maiden Name of Mother		24. Color c
Therese Marie Zeringue		w
26. Occupation of Mother	27. Industry or Business	28. Birthp
Housewife	Home	W
29. Total Number of Children (Exclude this Child)	30. No. now living (Exclude this Child)	31. No. bo
3	2	
I certify that the above stated information is true and correct to the best of my knowledge	33. Signature of Parent or Other Informant	
	Antoine	

received the Award of Excellence from Distinguished Restaurants of North America (DiRōNA). Folse served two terms as DiRōNA Chairman, and he was inducted into the Hall of Fame in 2003. He served on the Dairy Management, Inc. Cheese Advisory Panel from 2003-2004. In 1998 Chef John Folse & Company Manufacturing received the TGI Friday's Inc. Procurement Product Development Award for assisting in the development of Friday's Jack Daniels® Glaze. In 1998 *Food Arts* magazine awarded Folse the "Silver Spoon Award" for his sterling performance and contributions to the foodservice industry. In 1999 the Research Chefs Association named Chef John Folse & Company "*Pioneers in Culinology*" because of the efforts of Folse's culinary research team. In 2001 Folse was elected to RCA's Board of Directors and became vice president in 2003. In November 1999 the Acadiana Chapter of the American Culinary Federation inducted Folse into the Louisiana Chef's Hall of Fame for his lifetime contributions to the promotion of Louisiana cuisine. Folse received the Antonin Careme Medal in November 2000.

Twenty-five years of culinary excellence later, Folse is still adding ingredients to the corporate gumbo he calls Chef John Folse &

John Folse with his father and siblings in the late 1950s. Back row, left to right: Jerry, Ruth, Daddy, John, Royley. Second row, left to right: Carroll and Phyllis. Bottom row, left to right: Philip and Larry.

Company. He continues to share his culinary talents and expertise with students and the public, promoting Cajun and Creole cuisine worldwide. Folse's endeavors are as diverse as the Louisiana landscape, and he would not want it any other way.

The Team

A project of this magnitude requires the efforts of many dedicated professionals. I was privileged to have a team who poured their hearts and souls into ensuring the success of this project. From the research, writing and editing to the photography and design, my expectations were exceeded at every turn.

Chef John Folse

Michaela York, researcher/writer

When Chef John Folse was founding Lafitte's Landing Restaurant in 1978, Michaela was eating homemade ice cream sandwiches on her grandparents' front porch steps while singing "My Louisiana." Little did she know that the passion instilled by her grandparents for Louisiana would prepare her to research and write the state's culinary history, which Folse was already exploring.

While the research process was still in its infancy, Michaela realized discussing Louisiana's culinary history was impossible without understanding why and how these cultures came to this New World frontier. Nothing was more exhilarating than reading the journals of early explorers and the letters of Sister Marie Madeleine Hachard, who inadvertently recorded one of the best food accounts of 1700s Louisiana while writing to her father.

After combing Louisiana's libraries and archives for two years in search of every snippet of food history obtainable, Michaela discovered the riveting tale of the Louisiana she sang about as a child. The story of the "Land of Louis" was not a drab regurgitation of history, but a provocative tale flavored by the nuances of the coureurs-de-bois, concubines and cassette girls.

Michaela graduated from Northeast Louisiana University in 1991 with a Bachelor of Arts in Journalism. In 1996 she received her Master of Mass Communication degree from Louisiana State University. In addition to researching and writing Folse's *Hot Beignets & Warm Boudoirs*, Michaela assisted Sister Lillian McCormack with her memoir, *God Writes His Miracles for the Other Side of the Shadow*. Additionally, Michaela has two published children's books, *Mr. Oodle MaDoodle Discovers Today* and *Mr. Oodle MaDoodle's Time Around the World*. Michaela serves as director of communications for Chef John Folse & Company where she has been employed since 1997.

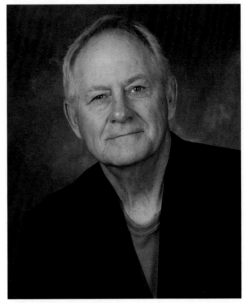

John Lee Smith, designer

John Lee Smith, president of Smith Communications, has more than three decades of design and communications experience. He received a Bachelor of Arts in Commercial Art from North Texas State University and was certified by The Famous Artist School in Westport, Conn. He has won numerous awards for design and art direction including best of shows on a national level. His clients are diverse and located from coast to coast. John was born in Tonkawa, Okla., and moved to Dallas to begin his career in advertising. Though he has resided in Louisiana for 20 years, after designing this book, he feels a deeper appreciation for Louisiana's culture.

John resides in Baton Rouge, La., with his wife of 37 years, Linda, and three daughters, Tiffiny, Amanda and Emily.

Karen Stassi, researcher/writer

Karen grew up eating Creole food in a house bordered by sugarcane fields. Not in Louisiana, but in her birthplace of Trinidad. She traveled extensively, eventually exchanging Trinidadian citizenship for British. After completing her bachelor's degree at Wesleyan University, Karen followed her parents to Louisiana. The mix of cultures, delicious food and "joie de vivre" felt like home. Karen received a master's degree in journalism from Louisiana State University in 1990. She became an American citizen while serving in the U.S. Naval Reserve. Karen worked as a writer and editor for 14 years, with stints at Peter Mayer Advertising and Business and Legal Reports before joining Chef John Folse & Company in 2004.

Karen lives in Prairieville, La., with her husband, John, and their sons Joe and Andrew. They all enjoy cooking, which should come as no surprise—their family background includes five of the seven nations.

Christy Lill, editor

Christy Lill was the copy editor and editor for both her high school and college yearbooks. She graduated from Louisiana State University with a Bachelor of Arts in Mass Communication in December 2003, and a week later she interviewed for the position with Chef John Folse & Company. After visiting a New Orleans restaurant and writing about its history, she landed the job and began writing pieces for the Lagniappe chapter. Christy soon asked if she could play a larger role in the editing process, and she began editing recipes. Along the way she had semiweekly meetings with the designer, which turned into daily meetings toward the end of the project, and she was handed the task of selecting photographs and planning photo shoots. Where some would have been overwhelmed with all of the responsibilities, Christy relished every moment.

Christy was born in St. Petersburg, Fla., but grew up in Houma, La. She moved to Baton Rouge in the fall of 1999 and still resides in the capital city.

Abbie Cataldo, editor

Abbie Cataldo was born and raised in Donaldsonville, La., where Bayou Lafourche meets the Mississippi River. Her Italian-Cajun background along with the influence of great cooks such as her mother and grandmothers has given her insight into and appreciation for South Louisiana cuisine.

Abbie graduated from Louisiana State University in 2002 with a Bachelor of Arts degree in Mass Communication. While at LSU she also pursued her passion for photography and graphic design.

Abbie joined Chef John Folse & Company in May 2003 to work on *The Encyclopedia of Cajun & Creole Cuisine*. She assisted in recipe selection and editing. When not busy with the cookbook, Abbie was immersed in the communications functions of the company, including advertising, design and web management.

Ron Manville, photographer

Ron Manville is a culinary, travel and lifestyle photographer who has photographed 15 cookbooks. *The Bread Baker's Apprentice: Mastering the Art of Extraordinary Bread* by Peter Reinhart won both the 2002 International Association of Culinary Professionals (IACP) and James Beard awards for Cookbook of the Year. *The Secrets of Baking: Simple Techniques for Sophisticated Desserts* by Sherry Yard won the 2003 James Beard Award. This is the third book Ron has photographed for Chef John Folse.

Ron lives in Rhode Island with his wife, Christine, and children, Sarah and Joel. His work can be viewed on his Web site, www.ronmanville. com.

David Gallent, photographer

A native of Baton Rouge, La., David Gallent received an early education in cooking. Early on he learned to appreciate the unique foods and flavors of South Louisiana. This love of food created a curiosity that led to the professional kitchen. He attended the Culinary Institute of America at Hyde Park, N.Y., where he received an education in culinary arts and learned food photography through a student job. After graduating, he worked in the test kitchens and photo studios of Oxmoor House in Birmingham, Ala. In 2002 he moved back to Louisiana where he started his food photography company, The Media Chef. Through a chance meeting with Chef John Folse, he joined the cookbook team and began work on *The Encyclopedia of Cajun & Creole Cuisine*.

Contents

Foreword

What gives one the right to assume the task of authoring an encyclopedia? Is it scholarly attributes? Is it by virtue of being an authority on the subject? Or, is it just pure, outright arrogance? Well, in my particular case, it is none of the three. I feel instead that it is a combination of birthright and obligation. Surely, I should explain.

Five generations of Folse's ago, in 1720, Jean Jacob Foltz, a shoemaker from Ramstein in the Palatinate walked west from the Rhine River to Orleans and then to Port Louis at L'Orient, France. It was there that he boarded a sailing ship for his voyage to Louisiana. While it is unclear on what ship he embarked, the November 14, 1720 manifest of *Les Deux Freres* listed a Jean Gorge Fols and his wife Julienne. Of the 4,000 Germans who signed up as indentured servants under contract to John Law's Company of the Indies, the Fols' were two of just 1,000 who eventually made the voyage overseas. More than 3,000 perished or returned to their homeland. After arriving in Louisiana, the Germans settled 25 miles upriver from New Orleans on the westbank at present-day Hahnville.

Between 1755 and 1760 the first wave of Acadians were arriving on Louisiana's shores from Nova Scotia. The Spanish government of Louisiana welcomed these bedraggled refugees and settled them upriver from the Germans in present-day St. James Parish.

During this same period, Antoine, a grandson of Johann Jacob Foltz, was born. We assume given the various languages and dialects in Louisiana that Jean Jacob Foltz and Johann Jacob Foltz were one and the same. Less than four decades later, Antoine left the river and founded Vacherie Folse on Lac Des Allemands or "Lake of the Germans."

In the late 1800s my grandfather Louisey Folse was born in the town of Vacherie. In 1914 he and my grandmother became the proud parents of my dad, Royley, on those very same banks of Lac Des Allemands.

I guess if one word were to describe my German heritage it would be tenacity. When I reflect on the perils my ancestors faced, their commitment to food, cultural preservation, faith, family and dedication to God, I am inspired to share their story nearly 300 years later. However, it was in the process of exploring my German heritage that I discovered there was so much more to the story of Louisiana than the blend of French and German culture I already knew so well.

Indeed, numerous other cultures arrived in this land fleeing famine, war and homeland hostilities while seeking opportunity, religious freedom, adventure and prosperity. They came from many nations: France, Nova Scotia, Spain, Africa, England, Germany and Italy. They came in great numbers and small, from large established countries to tiny island nations. Some arrived from Ireland as early as 1803. Many more came between 1830 and 1860, fleeing the Irish Potato Famine. Several thousand Croatians from the Dalmatian Coast arrived in the 18th century and began settling the Gulf Coast. Their fishing communities soon grew around Empire, Buras and Port Sulphur. A community of Hungarians settled around Springfield and Albany in the 1890s. Many aspects of their culture are still practiced there today including an archaic version of the Hungarian language. The Vietnamese arrived after the Vietnam War. They were fishermen and farmers in the old country and took up those roles here including shrimping, boat building and net mending. Fabulous Vietnamese groceries were opened to cater to enduring food traditions. Immigrants from Belgium, Czechoslovakia, China, Lebanon,

Greece and even the Philippines migrated to this great Bayou State. All of these cultures and more joined the Native Americans who were well established in Louisiana centuries before the first settlers arrived. Needless to say, it was not long before these cultures merged through trade, social interaction and of course, marriage.

A term was created to describe the children of the intermarriage of many of these cultures born on Louisiana soil. The word was "Creole." Few words in American English are as misunderstood or as frequently misused. The term "Creole" is believed to have derived from the Latin word "creare" meaning "to create." Originating in the Western Hemisphere, the term "Creole" was used around 1590 by Father de Acosta, a Spanish priest, to distinguish newborn West Indies children from everyone else. Eventually, it was used to describe everything in Louisiana from vegetables to furniture and even the state itself, which became known as the "Creole State."

Numerous writers and historians over the years have tried diligently to define Creole. Today, with 300 years of their vision and expertise, we now know and can clearly debate that the Creole is defined as anyone born on Louisiana soil from the intermarriage of Europeans, Africans and Native Americans who contributed significantly to the culture and cuisine of Louisiana. The key word here is significantly! Even though many important cultures still seek refuge on our rich shores today, it was those that significantly impacted our way of life, language, food, customs, music, and even the stories we tell that by definition are considered Creole. And who were those significant cultures? They were the Native Americans who shared their knowledge of this land with us; the French who first claimed this land for colonization under "The Sun King," Louis XIV; the Spanish who first explored Louisiana and eventually received it as a gift from France; the Africans who arrived on these shores against their will in slavery, but who contributed greatly to our culture and especially our cuisine; the Germans who saved the city of New Orleans from starvation with their great knowledge of farming; the English who arrived here from New England to establish themselves in the rolling hills of the Felicianas; and the Italians, the last of our Creoles, who came to work on the sugar plantations after the Civil War and became dock workers, strawberry farmers and ultimately, helped build Louisiana's food empire. These are the mixtures; these are the Creoles.

I cannot study the story of the Germans without telling the stories of all Louisiana's Creole cultures including the Acadian refugees from Nova Scotia who became the Cajuns, with their own unique food and customs. This book is my attempt to encapsulate in 850 pages, Louisiana's 300 years of history.

There are others who may see Louisiana's history and cuisine more broadly or more narrowly, but it is my position that seven nations, the Native Americans, France, Spain, Germany, England, Africa and Italy, were the most significant contributors in this impossible to replicate experiment that we call Cajun and Creole cuisine. Of course, as you read this encyclopedia you will come to see that Cajun and Creole cuisine was not created or invented; it was a process of evolution and adaptation. Who's to say that it will not continue to evolve, incorporating aspects of the Asian, Middle Eastern or Latin American cultures that now thrive here or perhaps of those that have not yet arrived? I truly hope it does. It is exactly that kind of adaptability and change along with a strong sense of history that makes Cajun and Creole cuisine so exciting, so fun to prepare and so delicious.

Louisiana:
Her Story

Sunset over Bear Bayou
CC Lockwood

Native America

La Salle taking possession of Louisiana and the Mississippi River

1720 Colonial Louisiana, Mississippi River and Native American tribes

POVERTY POINT

When Columbus sailed to America, Native Americans had been living in Louisiana for more than 3,500 years. While the general view is that Native Americans were primarily hunters and gatherers, archeological evidence suggests that a thriving trade economy existed in Louisiana at the same time Ramses II was ruling Egypt, Moses was leading the Israelites from bondage and the Phoenicians were trading along the Mediterranean. As yet, Rome had not been founded. Much of the evidence for this comes from a massive earthwork in northeastern Louisiana, near present-day Delhi, known as Poverty Point. First reported in 1873 by Samuel Lockett, this prehistoric, permanent village of sophisticated dwellers existed on a bluff overlooking swamplands of the Mississippi River. Aerial photographs reveal that the Poverty Point site was comprised of ridges and embankments forming a semi-circular enclosure bound on the east by a bluff. Radiocarbon dating places the site approximately 2,000 years before the birth of Christ.

The Poverty Point culture existed in the Lower Mississippi Valley between 2000 and 700 B.C. and stretched from near the junction of the Mississippi and Arkansas rivers to the Gulf Coast. The area encompassed parts of Louisiana, Arkansas and Mississippi and influenced areas as far away as Florida, Tennessee and Missouri.

A hallmark of the Poverty Point culture was long-distance trading. Evidence suggests that trade was conducted throughout the Ouachita, Ozark and Appalachian mountains as well as the Upper Mississippi Valley and Great Lakes regions. This culture thrived between 1500 and 700 B.C. when the supreme province and capital town of the entire area was Poverty Point. All the trade lines converged here.

The scattered peoples of the Poverty Point population clusters were linked by waterways that connected to the Mississippi River. Native Americans traveled this maze of

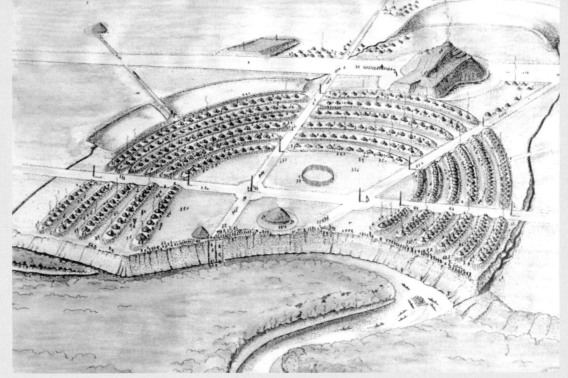

Poverty Point

waterways in dugout canoes, the forerunners of the French pirogues. The canoes, made of cypress, cottonwood or black walnut, were protected from drying and splitting by bringing them ashore and stuffing them with wet Spanish moss. Sometimes, the canoes were simply sunk in shallow water for protection.

Houses were small, circular structures about 13 to 15 feet in diameter. The Native Americans built mounds around their town including a huge mound in the shape of a bird with outstretched wings and tail. Pits at the site suggest there may have existed a municipal water system or perhaps fishponds or "farms" where fish could be kept until needed. Surprisingly, the complex Poverty Point culture seems to have developed without agriculture. Because excavations at Poverty Point failed to reveal corn, beans or squash, doubt exists that these people were farmers at all. There was probably no need, because this area teemed with wild plants, game and fish, providing a bountiful, year-round harvest without cultivation. Hunting implements of the Poverty Point Native Americans included javelins, atlatls and plummets. They also had crude cleavers and knives.

Perhaps most fascinating was the peoples' ingenious use of hearths and earth ovens for cooking. The earth oven was a hole dug in the ground to which hot baked clay objects were added. These small clay cooking balls were molded to create different styles. Experiments have proven that the shape of the clay object determined the intensity and duration of temperatures inside the pit, thus they could regulate heat and cooking conditions. The clay

cooking balls were cylindrical, cross-grooved, biconical grooved, biconical plain and melon-shaped. These earth ovens also allowed for firewood conservation, an important consideration for a permanent settlement.

Throwing the atlatl

EUROPEAN EXPLORERS & LOUISIANA'S NATIVE AMERICAN NATIONS

Louisiana's story began with the Native Americans and Christopher Columbus' discovery of the New World in 1492, which ignited tremendous interest among European nations and explorers. Another Italian sailing for Spain, Amerigo Vespucci, America's namesake, followed Columbus' lead and may have sailed the coast of the Gulf of Mexico as early as 1497. Twenty-two years later Alonzo Alvarez de Pineda traveled the extent of the Gulf Coast and back again, likely sailing into Mobile Bay where he observed many Native American villages. The first descriptions of Louisiana Native Americans came from the accounts kept by voyagers of Hernando de Soto who may have traveled into present-day Louisiana in March 1542.

Additional valuable records of the Native Americans came from the voyages of Father Zenobius Membre and Henri Joutel. Other notable explorers include Frenchmen Louis Joliet and Father Jacques Marquette who descended the

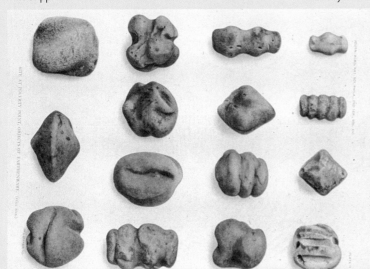

Poverty Point cooking stones

Mississippi River in 1673. Five years later, Rene Robert Cavelier de La Salle traveled the Mississippi River to its mouth and in 1682 claimed the country for France. Four years later, Henri de Tonti, La Salle's lieutenant, repeated the course and in 1699 Pierre Le Moyne, Sieur d'Iberville sailed upriver to the Houmas (also known as Ouma, Oumas and Houma) people's town on the bluff lands of the Mississippi River at present-day Angola. From these early explorers' documentation come descriptions of the six Native American nations that comprised Louisiana in 1700. The Atakapa, Caddo, Tunica, Natchez, Muskogean and Chitimacha shared a common language.

The Atakapa people lived in the coastal marshes of present-day southwestern Louisiana, extending from upper Bayou Teche to the Sabine River and from the Gulf of Mexico to present-day Alexandria. The Atakapa tribe included the Opelousa band that was located near present-day Opelousas. The Atakapa people lived at times on the upper Bayou Teche, lower Vermilion River, near Plaquemine Brule, near Lake Arthur on the Mermentau River, on western Grand Lake, on lower Bayou Nezpique, on Bayou Queue de Tortue and on Lacassine Island. They also lived along Calcasieu River and the lakes around Lake Charles.

Louisiana's Caddo people included the Kadohadacho tribe living near present-day Shreveport; the Natchitoches near Natchitoches; the Yatasi near Coushatta; the Adai near Robeline; the Doustioni near Campti; and the Ouachita near Columbia.

The Tunica tribes of Koroa and Yazoo were located on high ground along the Yazoo River near present-day Vicksburg, Miss.

The Natchez speakers were of three tribes: the Taensa, the Avoyel and the Natchez. The Taensa lived on the western end of Lake St. Joseph and on the Tensas River near present-day Clayton in Concordia Parish. The Avoyel had villages at present-day Marksville and Alexandria.

There were seven small tribes known as Muskogean. They were sporadically located along the Mississippi River's banks from the Red River southward and occupied the margins of the Florida Parishes above New Orleans. These tribes included the Houmas, known by their tribal symbol, the red crawfish. The Bayougoula, known by their tribal symbol, the alligator, lived on the modern site of Bayou Goula. Little is known of the other Muskogean speaking tribes including the Acolapissa, Mugulasha, Okelousa, Quinapisa and Tangipahoa.

The Chitimacha comprised three tribes of nearly 4,000 people. Most of their villages were on Bayou Teche, Grand Lake, Butte la Rose, Grand River and at the mouth of Bayou Plaquemine. The Washa occupied upper Bayou Lafourche near today's Labadieville with settlements extending to the Gulf Coast and along the lower Mississippi. In 1739, they established a village near the Côte des Allemands post on the banks of the Mississippi River. The Chawasha's earliest known village was on Bayou Lafourche below the main Washa settlement. They lived along the lower Mississippi River to the mouth as well.

SPORTSMAN'S PARADISE

Before agriculture, hunting was the primary food source for the interior Louisiana tribes. Domesticated animals were virtually unknown to the indigenous people, but they had a sacred relationship with animals because of their dependence upon them for nourishment. After the kill, hunters thanked their prey. The Choctaw even said prayers over their bounty.

Many believe that Native Americans might have been the first wildlife conservationists. They thinned out sick animals, burned the forest to kill ticks and vermin and planted wild plant seeds for animals to eat. One Choctaw chief even regulated deer hunting.

Though hunting was possible year-round, certain times of year were devoted to game hunting. There was a "short run" between crop planting and harvesting. After the harvest season, families moved away from the populated areas to hunting camps where the game was more plentiful.

The white-tailed deer was the Native Americans' favorite prey. They tracked the deer, killed it from stands and even slept in the deer's bed while it fed only to kill it upon the animal's return. Often, Native Americans, especially the Natchitoches, engaged in "still-hunting" or "stalking." They wore a deer's skinned-out head and shoulders while

1753 Louisiana map of numerous Native American tribes

Communal hunt

The Native Americans also hunted buffalo and made use of the entire animal. Clothing and blankets were made from the hides. The fine wool of a male buffalo was spun into thread to make loincloths or was used for mattresses. The suet was made into tallow cakes to sell or trade with the Europeans, and the sinew was used as bowstrings. They also pulled the sinew into strings to sew their hide shoes. The horns made spoons, and bones became punches and awls.

If the bison meat was not immediately eaten, it was cut into flat pieces and smoked over a grill made of forked sticks and green cane about three feet off the ground. It remained over the fire until the exterior was roasted and very dry. According to Jean-Bernard Bossu, who published accounts of his mid-1700s travels through North America, the buffalo meat was also preserved using salt.

Members of de Soto's expedition described Louisiana bison on their journey, and La Salle observed the indigenous people hunting them south of New Orleans along a bayou called Terre aux Boeufs. A group of Frenchmen killed 23 bison near Bayou Manchac in 1705.

Bears were also hunted for their hides, meat, and especially for their grease or oil. Other wild game enjoyed in the Native American diet included raccoons, cottontail and swamp rabbits, squirrels, beavers and otters. Bossu described four types of squirrels in Louisiana including black, red, gray and flying squirrels. These animals were caught using a variety of hunting techniques including the deadfall, nets, snares, traps, bows, blowguns and darts. Sharpened poles were used to hunt alligators. These poles were thrust down the alligators' throats. Then, the alligator was turned over to expose its vulnerable side. Alligators are slaughtered similarly today.

The Native Americans also consumed muskrats, beavers, wasps, beetles, locusts, lizards and porpoises. Opossum was not generally eaten, though at least one diary entry by Bossu indicates that he ate opossum on several occasions. He compared opossum to the size and taste of a suckling pig.

Birds, including turkey, passenger pigeons, sandhill cranes and quail, were eaten as well as a variety of waterfowl. Ducks and geese were caught in shallow water. Nets were often draped across a slough, so that ducks could be frightened into them and killed with arrows or clubs. Geese were caught by hand when hunters lay silently in the marsh waiting for the bird to approach. Wounded birds were used as decoys to catch the ibis, or gros bec, or they were clubbed at night. Bossu was most fascinated with wood ducks, which perched in trees with webbed feet that had claws. They nested in tree trunks that leaned over

making deer calls to approach the game near its watering hole. The disguise was then dropped and the prey killed with a bow and arrow.

The Natchez conducted communal hunts. They would sight a deer and about a hundred hunters would form a crescent surrounding the deer, driving it from side to side until it fell in exhaustion. The Atakapa ran deer to exhaustion and also used fire to bring game into the open.

The Native Americans field dressed deer and dried the meat to reduce its weight for the voyage home. The meat was cut into long strips along the muscle, especially from

the deer's back and shoulders. Roasts, rib cuts and shoulder steaks were cut similar to the way hunters cut meat today.

The entire deer, meat, skeleton, brain, tongue, liver and heart, was consumed. The mandible, antlers, hooves, toes, leg bones, scapulae and ribs were used for tools and jewelry. The radius, ulna and femur bones yielded marrow. Bones were made into fishhooks, awls, needles and knives. If not eaten, the brain was used to tan the hide. Other tanning solutions consisted of eggs and squirrel or rabbit brains. When smoked over smoldering bark or corncobs, the hide became virtually waterproof.

Nature Morte: **Hare and Birds**

rivers and lakes. He believed these were the best ducks to eat because they fed on acorns and beechnuts. Bossu also described egrets, pelicans, geese, bustards, teals and water hens. He described an Arkancas technique for hunting waterfowl in which tame or stuffed birds were placed on the water as decoys. When other birds landed, young Native Americans swam under the water, grabbed the birds by the feet, hooked them to their loincloths by the head and brought them home alive. These birds' wings were clipped, and they were kept in cages to eat when food was scarce.

It does not seem that Native Americans domesticated wild animals, though some small animals may have been tamed. A few vague reports suggest that dogs were used to hold game at bay. One or more native dogs were eaten, perhaps on ceremonial occasions. Interestingly, the tribes did not eat their tribal symbol animals. For example, the Houmas, recognized by the red crawfish, would not have consumed it. Likewise, the Koasati would not have eaten the deer and turkey.

As in Louisiana today, fish and shellfish were abundant.

Native Louisianians enjoyed freshwater finfish including gar, choupique (or grindle), catfish, paddlefish, sunfish, bass, eel, pike, sac-a-lait (or white crappie), sturgeon, sardine, gizzard shad and buffalofish.

Shallow coastal waters and bays provided drum, croaker, speckled trout, redfish, flounder and mullet. Generally, Native Americans were not equipped for saltwater fishing, though records indicate that sharks were captured. The Atakapa used sharks' teeth as a prized trade item. Occasionally, small whales were used, though these probably washed ashore. Fish were caught with hooks, lines, rabbit-vine hoop nets, cone-shaped traps made of wooden slats, trotlines (which the Acolapissa created) and weirs (built by the Natchez). Under torchlights of fat pine and dried cane, fish were speared in shallow water at night. Sometimes Native Americans poisoned fish using horse chestnuts (or buckeyes), root of the devil's shoestring (or catgut), green hickory nuts or walnut hulls. The crushed vegetable poison was stirred into the water, paralyzing the fish's gills, so they floated to the top. Another fishing practice called the bec croche was used. Native Americans waded in shallow water to muddy the pool, which

T.2.p.67

Pichou.

Boeuf Sauvage.

Explorer's interpretation of the Louisiana wildcat and buffalo

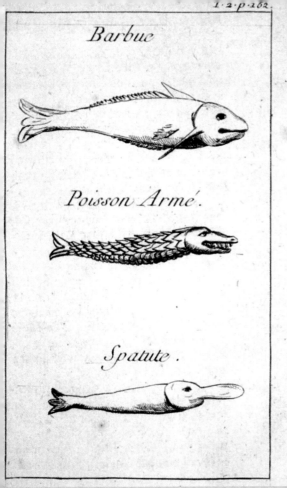

Early explorer illustrates catfish, choupique and spoonbill catfish

NATIVE AMERICAN AGRICULTURE

Native Louisiana tribesmen were farmers, hunters and fishermen who lived by the changing seasons. In spring they fished, harvested wild fruits, cleared fields and planted. Summer meant watching the crops and gathering seeds and mussels. The arrival of new corn prompted celebrations and great ceremonies honoring the sacred plant. (These events were equivalent to New Year's celebrations today.) The harvest festival came in autumn, when the migratory waterfowl returned and nuts were collected. Long hunts and journeys to collect salt were necessary. Indian men ate parched, smoke-dried cornmeal mixed with water when traveling. In winter, food was less available, so meals were meager.

Agriculture influenced where the Native Americans settled. In order to grow crops, they lived in areas with rich, fertile soil and natural levees to prevent flooding.

Corn, beans and squash, which came from Mexico, were staples of Native American agriculture except for the coastal tribes. Summer squash and pumpkins (round and crookneck) were known by 1000 B.C. Squash arrived in the Mississippi Valley long before corn and beans and might have been part of an agriculture that included growing native plants such as sunflowers, amaranth or pigweed, goosefoot or lamb's quarters, giant ragweed, marsh elder and tobacco. When corn and beans were introduced, native plants were less important. Cultivated beans included navy, red kidney and pinto, which could be eaten green as snap beans.

There were three major varieties of corn: Tropical Flint, Northern or Eastern Flint and Dent. Flint corn was white, red, blue or yellow with hard kernels. Dent corn was white with pink spots and corrugated kernels. The "great corn" was the Eastern or Northern Flint that was planted after the wild fruits ripened, so the birds were drawn away. "Great corn" was harvested in September to make fine white flour.

Preparation of the ground, planting and harvesting were community projects. Equipment included hoes with blades crafted from bison shoulder bones, fish bones, stones or shells. Once the men coarsely broke the ground, the women planted several grains of corn and a few beans into shallow holes. As the corn grew, the beans climbed the stalks. Earth was heaped around the stalk creating a hill. Squash, beans, gourds or melons could be planted between these little hills eliminating the need to hoe or weed and to prevent erosion. Some tribes forbade the planting of corn with other crops, so a separate field would have been reserved for the corn. Women and children stood on scaffolding to guard the fields from birds, deer, rabbits and other wildlife. They lived in nearby structures to keep watch day and night.

Gourds were a useful crop, because these provided dippers, ladles, cups, bowls, birdhouses, rattles and masks. Besides the large crop fields, which were divided into family plots, the Native Americans kept kitchen gardens at individual dwellings.

deprived the fish of oxygen. The fish could then be taken by hand. The Koasati reportedly caught fish using ritual songs. If the fish were not consumed immediately, they were smoked and dried over a low fire for later use. The flat-bottomed Lafitte skiffs from the Houmas area are used to navigate shallow waters along the Gulf Coast. They are considered one of the Native Americans' contributions to Louisiana's culture.

Oysters were abundant in the lakes next to Lake Pontchartrain. The Natchez traveled to the Mississippi's mouth to gather oysters, which they preserved by smoking. Though limited archaeological evidence supports oyster consumption, there was also heavy use of brackish-water clams. Their popularity probably stemmed from the ease of gathering them from the bottoms of lakes and bays, while oysters had to be pried from reefs.

Lake Pontchartrain and the Mississippi River provided shrimp. The native Louisianians caught mussels and crawfish from freshwater streams and lakes. Bossu described frogs of extraordinary size that croaked louder than a bellowing bull. He also discovered what is believed to be king crab as he journeyed from Mobile to New Orleans. Crabs were available in both fresh and salt water. Though kitchen refuse heaps show only traces of crawfish, crabs and shrimp, enough historical references exist to suggest that they were popular foods. Native Americans also consumed turtles, terrapins, alligators and even snakes.

Harvests were marked by a great feast of nearly continuous eating. Corn was prepared in every way they knew. Medicine men gathered the people at the harvest of new corn, usually in July or August, for a ceremony called "posketa" or "bosketa." They drank the "Black Drink," which was called "asi" by the Muskogean speakers and "La Cassine" by the French. This tea, brewed from a variety of holly, caused vomiting, a ritual cleansing of the body and mind before the new corn could be eaten. This cleansing ritual was common for the Koasati people as well.

During the Corn Feast the Tunica practiced a ritual feeding of the dead. Boys from each family carried packets of corn folded in shucks to family graves.

Harvested corn was often dried and stored in granaries, corncribs, earth silos or homes. Sometimes it was ground and stored for later use. The "great corn" of the later harvest was often half-boiled and dried over a fire or in the sun.

Native Americans were excellent cooks, preparing food by boiling, broiling, frying, roasting, baking and parching. While large animals were dressed before cooking, smaller animals were cooked whole. Meat was never eaten raw. Soups, porridges, mush and stews, often combining a number of ingredients, were daily fare. The Natchez were said to have had 42 ways to prepare corn. Green corn was roasted or boiled. Hominy was eaten alone or cracked into soup. Grits were eaten as well as sagamite, a porridge of boiled, husked corn and bean flour. They also made an unfermented drink of finely ground corn and water. There

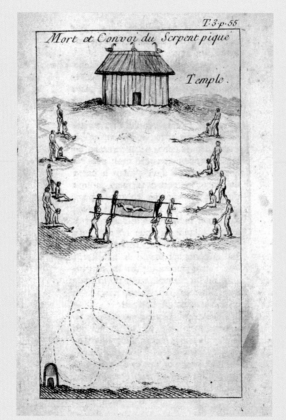

Page du Pratz-Native American funeral

were dishes of stewed meat; squash and beans; pumpkins cut into spiral slices and slowly dried over a fire; boiled mussels and oysters; and soups thickened with cornmeal. Often, Native Americans sucked green cornstalks for sugar.

Bread accompanied most meals. Corn, pounded and sifted to a fine meal, was the primary ingredient, but Native American cooks also made bread from persimmons, acorns and other nutmeats, wild sweet potatoes, cane seeds, sunflower seeds, chestnuts and boiled beans. The persimmon bread was often dried and used on long journeys. Breads were baked, fried or rolled into balls and boiled. There were cakes, pones, ashcakes, fritters or dumplings. The Caddo and Choctaw sometimes boiled bread wrapped in cornhusks, similar to tamales.

It was not uncommon for Native Americans to prepare special meals for important guests. Bossu recalled that the Akancas fed him a wooden porringer of sagamite, which consisted of crushed corn cooked with boiled turkey. He was served broiled venison cutlets and smoked bear tongues. He ate native fruit and drank cassine. On another occasion the Peoria village in the Illinois Territory served him persimmon bread, bear paws and beaver tails.

He ate dog, side courses of corn meal with maple syrup and dried blueberries for dessert. Bossu reported that the Native Americans treated him to wild ducks, which tasted as good as the ducklings he had eaten in Rouen on his way to Le Havre. These ducks fed on wild oats and were best when eaten at the beginning of winter. The Akancas gave him a gift of wild oat flour in a deerskin bag, which he used in pancakes and gruel. Bossu reported that two valuable plants other than tobacco grew in Louisiana: indigo and cotton. He also believed that saffron would grow easily in Louisiana's highlands.

The Native American pantry included bear's oil, pigeon oil, deer suet and acorn oil. Salt was procured through trade and expeditions to the Caddo country. The Natchitoches, who were major salt producers, created three-pound cakes for trade. They gathered salt-encrusted earth, placed it in suspended baskets and poured water through it to extract the salt. Boiling evaporated the water, which produced the mineral. The Native Americans did not use the coastal salt domes in the 1700s, though both prehistoric and modern tribes mined them. Most Louisiana Native Americans preferred to obtain salt by seawater evaporation. Amazingly, native Louisianians were making sea salt in the 1700s, which chefs today have rediscovered and purchase for as much as $40 a pound.

Native women ground corn in mortars and pestles. With large cedar or hickory paddles they stirred pots of corn soup called sofke or chawaka. Generally, Native Americans ate with their hands, though pottery, wooden bowls and wooden, shell or horn spoons were used with soup. Conch shells were used as dippers, particularly in rituals to drink

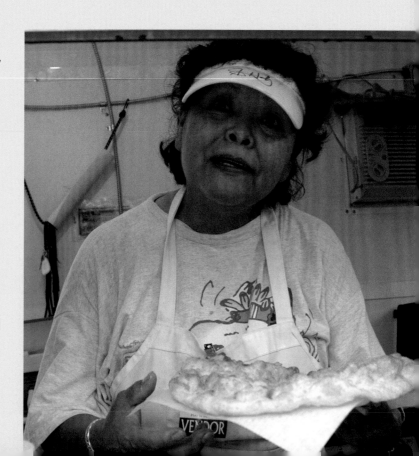

the "Black Drink" or "La Cassine" from the common pot. The sacred conch dippers were often engraved with mythical symbols. Nuts, corn and oil were stored in jars that could hold as much as 50 pints of bear oil. There were stone and clay vessels for cooking, though the Caddo boiled food in water heated in suspended deerskins. They also had plates, pitchers and bottles.

Women cooked in the morning, preparing enough food for several families. Meals were not eaten at set times, but served in common pots so villagers could eat when they were hungry. During planting or harvesting seasons, mid-morning meals might have been eaten after the day's tasks were begun. Another meal was served at night at the conclusion of the day's activities. If game or a good catch of fish were obtained, immediate feasting ensued.

The Native Americans ate together only on special occasions, such as feasts, or when involved in group activities. Generally, men and women ate separately and men and boys were always served first.

WILD PLANT FOODS

The abundant supply of wild plant foods, game and fish delayed the acceptance of agriculture among the Native Americans. Their greatest reason for ultimately accepting agriculture was because it provided stored food, especially corn, which could be used on trading trips, during hunts and warfare. It was convenient when they travelled not to have to search for something to eat.

Though the indigenous people became good farmers, they did not abandon their natural pantry, which was an important supplement to their crops.

A great variety of wild plant foods were available to the Native Americans in the Lower Mississippi Valley. They used approximately 250 edible wild root plants such as groundnuts, wild sweet potatoes, arrowhead, Jerusalem artichokes, wild morning glory and smilax. A reddish jelly could be made by pulverizing smilax root and boiling it. The Native Americans enjoyed wild fruits and berries including maypops, mayhaws, plums, wild grapes, persimmons, mulberries, hackberries, dewberries, strawberries, blackberries and pawpaws. They preserved these fruits by sun drying them. Native Americans gathered and stored acorns, chestnuts, chinquapins, walnuts, pecans, hickory nuts, pond-lily nuts and honey locust beans, which were sucked for a molasses-like substance. These nuts and sunflower seeds were eaten raw, parched, boiled or roasted. Live oak acorns were popular because they contained less tannic acid than other acorns. The meat of hickory nuts was ground on stone mortars then boiled into oil for cooking. Some Native Americans made pecan oil to use in corn meal mush.

LOUISIANA NAMES OF NATIVE AMERICAN ORIGIN

WORD	LANGUAGE	ENGLISH MEANING
Abita Springs	Choctaw	fountain; source; head, as of a watercourse
Acadia	Micmac	the place where something abounds
Atakapa	Choctaw	eater of human flesh
Atchafalaya	Choctaw	long river
Avoyelles	Choctaw	flint people or nation of the rocks
Bayou	Choctaw	river, creek, bayou
Bayou Goula	Choctaw	bayou or river people
Bogalusa	Choctaw	Black Creek
Bogue Chitto	Choctaw	Big Creek
Caddo	Caddo	chief; principal
Calcasieu	Atakapa	crying eagle
Catahoula	Choctaw	beloved lake
Choupique	Choctaw	mudfish or grinnel
Coushatta	Choctaw	white reed brake
Houmas	Choctaw	red
Istrouma	Choctaw	red pole
Kabahannossé	Choctaw	clearing where mallard ducks roost
Kisatchie	Choctaw	reed brake river
Manchac	Choctaw	rear entrance
*Mississippi	Algonquian	great water
Natchez	Chetimacha	hurrying man or warrior
Natchez	Mobilian	away from
Natchitoches	Caddo	pawpaws or pawpaw eaters
Nottoway	Algonquian	rattlesnakes
Okaloosa	Choctaw	black water
Opelousas	Choctaw	black legs or black hair
Osceola	Creek	black drink singer
Ouachita	Uncertain	big cat river, big cow river, big river, silver water, male deer or country of large buffaloes
Panola	Choctaw	cotton
Plaquemine	Illinois	persimmon
Ponchatoula	Choctaw	falling hair or hanging hair
Powhatan	Algonquian	hill of the medicine man
Shongaloo	Choctaw	cypress tree
Tangipahoa	Choctaw	cornstalk gatherers or corncob
Tchefuncta	Choctaw	chinquapin
Tchoupitoulas	Choctaw	those who live at the river
Tickfaw	Choctaw	pine rest
Tioga	Iroquois	anything between two others; at the forks of rivers
Tunica	Tunica	the people
Yupon	Catawba	tree, shrub

Louisiana native persimmons

*One of the Native American variations for the name of the Mississippi River was "Malbanchya" or "Malbanchia." This Choctaw word is translated to mean "a place of foreign languages." The name was first applied to the Lower Mississippi and then to the city of New Orleans. The Native Americans looked at both as places where foreign languages were spoken.

Sassafras leaves

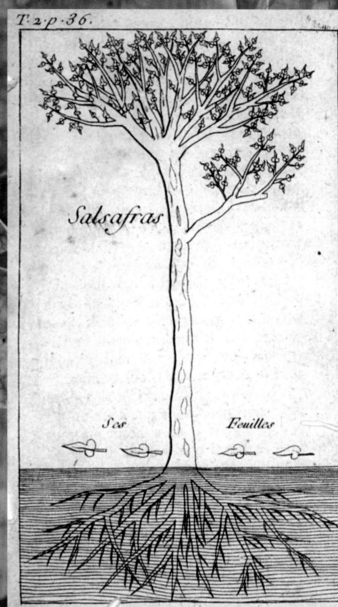

T. 2. p. 36.

Salsafras

Ses   Feuilles

Early sketch of a sassafras tree

Lionel Key grinding sassafras leaves for filé powder

Wild seed-bearing plants included but were not limited to palmetto, cane, cockspur grass and wild rice. Palmetto hearts, wild peas and puffballs were also used. Mushrooms were rarely consumed. The Poverty Point settlers ate the seeds of the honey locust, goosefoot, knotweed and doveweed. Filé, pounded sassafras leaves, was also an important ingredient to Louisiana's indigenous people.

Native Americans gathered wild plant foods at varying times and in different amounts. For a month each year the Tunica lived on wild persimmons, and the Atakapa traveled inland annually to live for a time on prickly pear fruit. Native Americans harvested wild foods using baskets, digging sticks and paddles. Sometimes nuts, roots and seeds were stored for later use. Seeds of the best fruits were selected, saved and planted where the native people thought they would grow well, thereby increasing the quality and quantity of even the wild plants.

Besides the wild plants' nutritional value, plant stems, blooms, bark, leaves and roots were used medicinally. Each had specific purposes and was categorized by color and origin. Native Americans valued medicinal herbs more than gold. Even in the 1930s, a Houmas medicine

man identified 79 plant cures. Herbalists carefully observed nature and noted that gathering medicinal herbs was critical to season and time of day. Medicines were generally made into teas, though poultices were created from items such as ground ivy. Sweet gum balm was believed to cure wounds, ulcers and consumption,

Coushatta Indians long-needle pine baskets

open obstructions and relieve colic. Willow-bark tea was the equivalent of aspirin. Warm smoke blown into the ear could treat an earache. Bossu reported that persimmons were a great remedy for dysentery and the bloody flux. Powdered persimmon seeds and water were believed to cure kidney stones. Once the combination stood for a

Louisiana Indian women weaving cane baskets, 1923

day, it was strained through a cloth, then consumed. A glassful was taken before meals to cure the stones. Bossu also reported that the acacia tree bore a gummy fruit, which contained seeds resembling beans and that the Native Americans used them as a laxative. He also said that gensing root made an excellent cough syrup, and jalap, rhubarb, smilax, snakeroot, sarsaparilla and St.-John's-wort made excellent oils to heal wounds. According to Bossu, pregnant women pulverized rattlesnake rattles and swallowed the powder to give birth without pain. Rattlesnake grease made ointment for rheumatic pains; fine white opossum fat cured hemorrhoids; and down from the carrion crow stopped bleeding. Sassafras trees were also used for medicine. Cassina was an excellent diuretic, and the Choctaws treated upset stomachs with mayapple medicine. To clean teeth and gums the Native Americans chewed the cut, peeled ends of black-gum twigs. As Native American herbalists fused into French culture, their cures and remedies passed to subsequent generations. These French-speaking, native Louisianian herbalists or physicians became known as a "traiteur" or "traiteuse." Even today, these healers can be found living in the towns located along Louisiana's bayous and swamps.

THE DEMISE OF LOUISIANA'S NATIVE AMERICAN NATIONS

De Soto's arrival in 1542 marked the beginning of drastic change for Louisiana's native cultures. With the Europeans' arrival, some tribes nearly abandoned agriculture for hunting. By the mid-1700s, the influx of European hide traders transformed many tribesmen into professional hide hunters. Only then were deer wasted and hunted for skins rather than for food and materials.

Around 1730 Jean Baptiste le Moyne, Sieur de Bienville wrote a report on the Louisiana tribes. (This was between his second and third term as governor of the province.) He calculated that the French could do an annual business with the native people of 50,000 deer skins, not counting pelts from the Sioux, Missouries, Illinois, Miami and others. During the 1800s one Koasati hunter sold almost 300 deerskins at Natchitoches.

The Europeans shipped these hides to France, Spain and England to make hats and footwear. When tribesmen began commercial hunting, territorial disputes developed, crop cycles were disrupted and the Native Americans became dependent upon Europeans for material goods.

White men brought alcoholism and disease, which spread quickly to the Native American population.

Iberville's prospectus for settling Louisiana

Louisiana Native American powwow, Marksville

Bienville wrote, "It was not without grief that I reached the point where I became master over all these different nations of such barbaric nature and opposite character, and who nearly all have their own particular language. One can easily see what difficulties I had in working, and the risks I took in laying the foundations of this colony and the upholding of it to the present time."

As they paid less attention to agriculture, the native people lost their farmlands. Many became mercenary warriors, traders, hunters, prostitutes, trappers and even prisoners or slaves. It was then that they had to barter for or buy their food.

As early as 1700 the European impact on the tribes was apparent. The people became increasingly migratory and armed conflict erupted among the lesser tribes proving their lack of unity. Tribes were displaced from their homeland not just by European settlers but by warring nations as well. Whole Native American towns were destroyed, sometimes completely eliminating the tribes.

Some small tribes moved near New Orleans seeking protection near the French settlement. Others faded into extinction or were absorbed into other nations. The

Houmas became pantribal by accepting many individual Native Americans. It is believed that the Acolapissa, Bayougoula, Quinapisa, Mugulasha, Tangipahoa and Okelousa eventually joined with the Houmas.

By the 1800s tribes moved to isolated swamps and pinewoods. Native American hunters supplemented planters' meat supplies, tracked runaway slaves and

provided entertainment for guests with demonstrations of stickball games and traditional dances.

Native American trade remained important throughout the latter half of the 1800s especially in the developing European centers at Natchitoches, Natchez, New Orleans, Opelousas and present-day Monroe. The men provided blowguns, smoke-tanned skins, game and wild honey.

Indian Gumbo sellers, French Market, New Orleans

Native American women sold cane baskets, herbs and remedies. A New Orleans market near Bayou St. John was known as the "Indian market," and Native American goods were sold in the French market as well. Often, stores required clerks to speak Native American languages and stocked items including pipe tomahawks, glass beads and silver ornaments.

Eventually, Native Americans accepted jobs as day laborers preferring work in the forests. Some families became sharecroppers, which they equated to slavery. The Native Americans were poverty-stricken, worked long hours, suffered from exposure and were often in close contact with non-indigenous people. Many died of tuberculosis, smallpox, measles and influenza. In the 1900s, the Native Americans earned wages, sharecropping disappeared and government assistance programs developed.

According to the Louisiana Office of Indian Affairs, there are currently nine recognized tribes in Louisiana including the Choctaw-Apache Community of Ebarb in Zwolle; the Adai Caddo Tribe in Robeline; the Four Winds Cherokee Tribe in Leesville; the Clifton Choctaw Tribe in Clifton; the Jena Band of Choctaw in Jena; the Tunica-Biloxi Tribe in Marksville; the Coushatta Tribe in Elton; the Chitimacha Tribe in Charenton; and the United Houmas Nation in Golden Meadow.

In Louisiana there are three Native American tribes that have gaming compacts with the state: the Chitimacha Tribe of Louisiana, which operates Cypress Bayou Casino in Charenton; the Coushatta Tribe of Louisiana, which operates Grand Casino Coushatta in Kinder; and the Tunica-Biloxi Tribe of Louisiana, which operates Grand Casino Avoyelles in Marksville. These casinos operate based on

the National Indian Regulation Act of 1988. According to the Regulation of Indian Gaming website (www.indiangaming.com) the tribes are very protective of their integrity where gaming is concerned. In fact, the tribal governments regulate gaming on their reservations with their own commissions. Though the federal government is allowed to help oversee the gaming, states have limited roles in gaming regulation based on what has been negotiated in the compacts.

Knowing that the Native Americans once commanded Louisiana's wilderness and all the natural resources therein, it is ironic that gaming is now considered the most precious economic resource they ever had.

LA PIERRE FOLLE DE VACHERIE OR THE MAD STONE OF VACHERIE

The Gravois and Webre families were among the first settlers of the Lake Des Allemands area in present-day St. James Parish. According to local legend, a cottonmouth moccasin bit Mrs. Gravois' hand while she gathered cabbage from her garden. Her head and extremities swelled immediately from the venom. A Native American neighbor helped by placing a black stone, about the size of a man's thumb, over the oozing puncture wounds to which it stuck almost magnetically. When all the poison was absorbed into the stone, it fell off the wound and was washed in a pan of water. By the next morning, Mrs. Gravois was completely healed. Several months later the Native American became ill. The Gravois and Webre families nursed him back to health. Upon his departure, he gave them the healing stone, his most treasured possession.

For more than 200 years, the Gravois and Webre families have kept the stone, which is renowned in the community for its ability to extract poison from snake and spider bites. Estimates suggest that the stone has been used 4,000 to 5,000 times.

Although the stone's origin is unknown, many believe it came from the heart of a white deer. Others believe the stone is an enterolith, a small, hard formation from a deer's intestine with osmotic properties, that cause fluids to pass from one thing to another. Legendary "mad stones" have been reported throughout history. Through the years, the stone has diminished and broken into four pieces, the largest being quarter-sized.

Royley Folse, Sr., my dad, used the "mad stone" when he was only 12 years old to remove venom from his forearm. Daddy was running muskrat trap lines in the swamp with his father when a cottonmouth struck him. He and my grandfather walked to Earnest Gravois' home where the "keeper of the stone" washed the wound, removed an imbedded fang from Daddy's arm and applied the stone to the oozing wound. The stone stuck to the wound for about 30 minutes, then fell off. The stone was washed in water to remove the poison and was reapplied twice more until all of the poison had been extracted from his arm. Though Daddy had doubted the "mad stone's" ability, he became an adamant believer in its power.

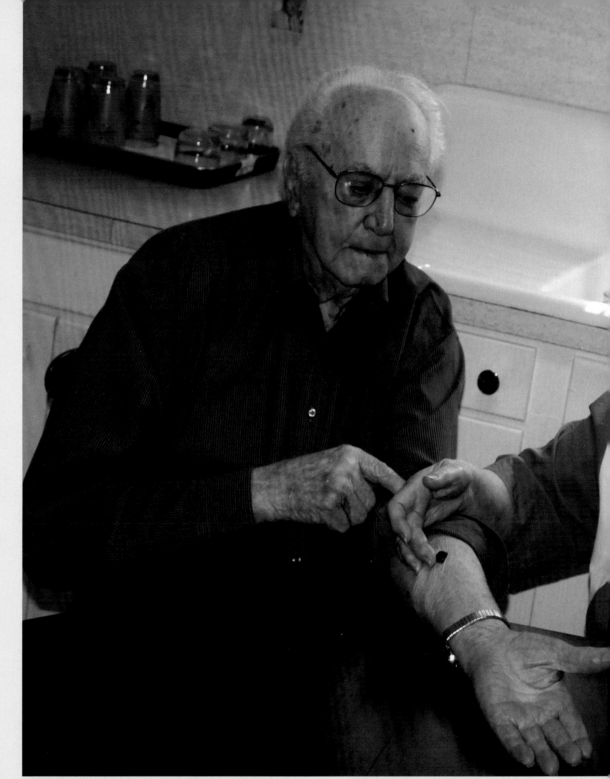

Royley Folse, Sr, demonstrates using the Mad Stone of Vacherie

Fragments of the Mad Stone of Vacherie

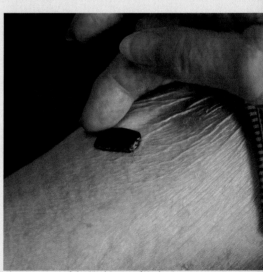

Close-up view of the Mad Stone of Vacherie

France

La Salle at the mouth of the Mississippi River

Louis XIV, The Sun King

Searching for a westward route to the rich Indies, Christopher Columbus, a Genoan mapmaker sailing under Spain's flag, landed in the Caribbean in 1492. By 1504, he had explored the Gulf of Mexico and the mainland of Central and South America. Some accounts suggest that he mapped the Gulf's northern rim indicating a Great River, possibly the Mississippi. There begins the early, civilized history of the future Louisiana Territory.

Columbus' discoveries led others to North America, the Mississippi River and La Louisiane. In the early 1500s Amerigo Vespucci, an Italian explorer sailing under Spain's flag, published a pamphlet entitled *Mundus Novus* explaining his belief that Columbus had reached a New World, not India. When the Institute at Saint-Dié in Lorraine reprinted the work in 1507, a map of the New World was included. Martin Waldseemüller, a noted

German mapmaker and geographer of the Institute, believed Vespucci had discovered a fourth continent. Not seeing why anyone would object to naming the continent for Amerigo, the land became America, the Latin feminine form of Americus. (Both Europe and Asia were named for women as well.)

By the end of the 16th century, Spain had a lock on the Gulf region, and the future Louisiana Territory, but exhibited more interest in the treasures of the South American continent. The Gulf region, although explored heavily, lacked golden treasures and stood somewhat ignored, but not forgotten. Although a century passed, the race was soon on again in earnest with Spain, France and England focused on the Gulf's northern rim and the future Louisiana Territory.

The 17th century ushered in history's Era of Colonization, though it would be mid-century before the roots of conquest and settlement flourished. New places grew across the landscape: New Spain, New France, New England, New Netherlands, New Amsterdam and New Scotland or Nova Scotia.

Significant to Louisiana's history was the birth in 1638 of Louis XIV, "Le Roi du Soleil" or "The Sun King." Louisiana's namesake reigned for 72 years directing from afar America's most epic adventures and discoveries, not the least of which included explorations of the Mississippi River Valley by Marquette and Jolliet in 1673. In 1680, he instructed the missionary, Father Louis Hennepin, to travel the Mississippi River to its mouth and live among the native tribes. Hennepin discovered Bayou Lafourche, the river's western branch. Other North American explorers for

MARQUETTE AND JOLIET DISCOVER THE MISSISSIPPI.

Renee-Robert Cavalier, Sieur de La Salle

King Louis included the Italian soldier Henri de Tonti, "Iron Hand," and Pierre Le Moyne, Sieur d'Iberville. The French-Canadian, Renee-Robert Cavalier, Sieur de La Salle, is officially recognized as the first to discover the Mississippi River's mouth and to claim the Louisiana Territory, naming it La Louisiane for France on April 9, 1682. Because of La Salle's discovery, he was proclaimed "the Columbus of the Mississippi Valley; the blazer of the virgin Mississippi trail." La Louisiane bordered the English Colonies of the East Coast from the Gulf of Mexico to Canada. The Rocky Mountains and New Spain (Mexico) were its western and southern boundaries. La Louisiane was a country unto itself with "The Sun King" its sovereign master.

Although unquestionably loyal to France, La Salle allegedly had his own ambitions for the newly claimed territory and New Spain just south of the border. New Spain had made many Spaniards wealthy with its stolen golden treasures. La Salle returned to Canada to set about the task of becoming wealthy by colonizing La Louisiane while plundering gold-laden Spanish ships in the Gulf. He returned to France and received a King's commission to settle a colony near the Mississippi's mouth. Curiously, this was where La Salle's alleged dark and obscure intent was best illustrated. His mapmaker, Jean-Baptiste Louis Franquelin, placed the mouth of the Mississippi River at Matagorda Bay, just north of modern-day Corpus Christi, Texas, 500 miles west of the actual location.

With nearly 300 settlers, 50 soldiers, a dozen or so gentlemen and five priests, La Salle sailed from France in July 1684. Ironically, Spanish privateers captured one of his four ships. La Salle missed the Mississippi's mouth and landed at Matagorda Bay, conceivably completing his deliberate plan. Ultimately, his plan failed and in 1687 he was murdered by his own men somewhere near the modern-day Louisiana-Texas line. Regardless of his uncertain intent, he lay dead in the new country he had dedicated his life to studying and exploring.

From 1682 to 1698, the northern rim of the Gulf became the target of Spain, France and England. The first nation

La Salle claims the Mississippi River for France

to colonize would be the first nation to dominate the vast new land. The jewel of the Gulf was today's Pensacola Bay. Spain desperately tried to claim a foothold, but nothing succeeded until word reached the Spanish court that Louis XIV planned to establish colonies on both sides of the River Mechisippi (Mississippi).

Celebrated French-Canadian soldier and adventurer, Pierre Le Moyne, Sieur d'Iberville, led the French expedition.

Born in 1661, Iberville was the third of eleven sons of the wealthy merchant, Charles Le Moyne, native of Dieppe, France. Iberville entered the French navy and rose rapidly in command. He fought the English successfully in northern Canada and Hudson Bay. Considered one of Canada's greatest heroes, he was affectionately known as "the Cid of New France." Iberville chose his younger brother, Jean-Baptiste Le Moyne, Sieur de Bienville, then only 20 years old, to join him on the adventure. Bienville ultimately founded New Orleans and became one of Louisiana's first governors.

Iberville traveled to the French port La Rochelle to organize the La Louisiane colonizing expedition. He secured two frigates and two supply ships and assembled two companies of marines. On October 24, 1698, the fleet sailed for the Gulf of Mexico. On December 4, they made port at Santo Domingo where Iberville acquired the services of the celebrated buccaneer, Laurent de Graaf, to maneuver through the Gulf waters.

On January 26, 1699, Iberville anchored near present-day Pensacola Bay. Because of France's colonization interests, Spain had built a crude fort, establishing a foothold at the most coveted of the northern Gulf harbors. Though Iberville had hoped to establish a French colony there, he concluded that this was not the Mississippi River La Salle had described. On January 30, he sailed west, anchoring the next day near

The Murder of LaSalle

P. LE MOYNE
E. S. D'YBERVILLE

Pierre Le Moyne, Sieur d'Iberville

to seal their important alliance. These articles astounded the indigenous people. The French also gave them better tools such as picks, shovels and axes. In return, the Native Americans instructed the French in the best ways to farm the land. Iberville hoped his amicable French policy toward these people would help them avoid the mistakes the English and Spanish made.

On February 27, Iberville set out with his lieutenant, Sieur de Sauvole, his brother, a priest and 48 men with provisions for 20 days to rediscover the Great River, which the Native Americans called Michisippi. They sailed cautiously through the Chandeleur Islands of Mississippi Sound under wind, rain and rough seas.

From the Gulf of Mexico, the Mississippi River's mouth was nearly invisible even at close proximity. In the 16th century the Spanish named the river "Rio del Escondido" or "Hidden River." They also called it "Rio del Palizado" for what they thought were fallen trees forming a type of palisade blocking the river's entrance from view.

present-day Mobile. After several days in the shallow waters of Mobile Bay, Iberville determined this was not the Mississippi either.

Sailing farther west the French fleet anchored at Ship Island, 10 miles offshore. On February 13, Iberville and 11 men crossed to the mainland setting up camp at Biloxi. Iberville wrote, "We see many plum trees, tracks of turkeys, partridges, hares like in France, and some rather good oysters."

Here, Iberville first contacted the Biloxi tribe, also known as Annochy and Moctobi, who were associated with the Pascagoula people. He mentions the Chozeta (Choctaw) and neighboring tribes including the Mougoulasha, Bayougoula and Quinipissa. Iberville did not hesitate to

share the Native Americans' customs. He smoked the calumet or peace pipe to prove his friendship. As a sign of honor, he allowed sand to be rubbed over his face and those of his officers. Everyone participated in the three-day ceremony that ensued upon their arrival in any village. The Native Americans would sing, dance and sink a Maypole on the third day. Iberville was carried ceremoniously on a Native American's shoulders to the Maypole for continued dancing.

After these celebrations the French gave the Native Americans mirrors, combs, beads, shirts, hats, rings and assorted items

T. v. 105.

Marche du Calumet de Paix.

Dancing calumet

Heavy rain and a north wind complicated the voyage as night approached on March 2, 1699. Iberville and his men searched desperately for any landing that would prevent their perishing. Then, quite accidentally, they rediscovered the mouth of the Mississippi River. In his journal Iberville wrote, "Drawing near to some rocks I became aware of a river. I passed between the rocks in heavy seas and 12 feet of water. When I got closer I found it was fresh and a very strong current. Here was the Palisade River, rightly named, its mouth completely obstructed by rocks. We ascended one and a half leagues of which the land is low, covered with reeds 10 feet tall, and made camp among the reeds. It is cold but not freezing. The water quite muddy and white."

On Tuesday, March 3rd, 1699, Louisiana's first Mardi Gras was religiously observed. At 12 leagues (about 36 miles) from the river's mouth, at a westward bend, Iberville and his crew spent their second night on the right ascending bank. He noted, "We have given the name Mardi Gras to this point."

By March 17 the explorers had ventured upriver to an area of bluffs on the Mississippi's east side. A stream there divided the Houmas and Bayougoula hunting grounds. A tall maypole stood on the bank with no limbs, painted red, with several fish heads and bear bones tied to it as a sacrifice. This "red stick" was probably used as both a boundary marker and for ceremonial purposes. Iberville called this place "Baton Rouge" or "red stick," the present site of Louisiana's capital city.

With the rediscovery of the mouth of the river, French colonization of Louisiana began. Forts were established throughout the Louisiana Territory. Initially, the capital was established at Fort Louis of Mobile in 1701. In 1714, Louisiana's first colony, the Natchitoches post was established. Finally in 1718, Bienville founded New Orleans, naming it for Philippe, duc d'Orléans.

The mouth of the Mississippi River was blocked. Ocean-going vessels could not proceed upriver from the Gulf of Mexico. In 1723, His Royal Highness established a 10,000-livre reward for the person who could find the method to dredge the bar and open the river to navigation. (The usual method for estimating equivalent currency values today is to multiply by 60.) Eventually, through much difficulty the task was accomplished.

Louisiana was governed alternately by the crown and chartered proprietors. These proprietors contracted with the crown for administration of the colony and a trade monopoly in exchange for settlers and slaves to supply the colony with goods. Antoine Crozat was Louisiana's

Philippe II, duc d'Orleans

first proprietor from 1712 – 1717. Upon his resignation, the crown turned the colony over to John Law, a Scottish financier, banker and speculator, but more importantly, a gambler and an outlaw, who became a good friend of the duc d'Orléans. He created the Company of the West and obtained a 25-year charter to develop the agriculture of the colony and to populate the territory in record time. He attracted investors in his Louisiana scheme, while planning to make a fortune for himself. His plan became known as the "Mississippi Bubble." In 1719, Law

created the corporation called the Company of the Indies to govern Louisiana and began populating the territory with prostitutes and prisoners. By 1720, his plan failed miserably and he fled Paris. With the bursting of the "Mississippi Bubble," Louisiana suffered its first political debacle. On December 23, 1721, the Company of the Indies ordered that the general office of the administration of Louisiana be moved to New Orleans. In 1723, the capital of Louisiana was officially moved from Biloxi to New Orleans. In 1731, the Company of the Indies turned the colony back over to the crown of France, who administered it until 1763, when Louisiana was turned over to Spain.

THE ORIGINAL COLONY

In August 1704, Nicolas de La Salle, commissary of the navy, reported the census of Louisiana from Fort Louis. The buildings belonging to the King included a fort, a one-story house, a storehouse, a house serving as a church, a one-story guard house, a shop for the forge, a shop for gunsmithery, a small shop of piles where barks and small vessels parked and a hall to make bricks. There were two 50-ton barks, three ship's boats and seven wooden pirogues. The town was comprised of 190 arpents of land. An arpent was a French unit of land area equivalent to about 0.85 acre. There were 80 one-story wooden houses covered with palmetto leaves or straw, built in a straight line along the streets. In the colony there were 180 men bearing arms, one Jesuit, three priests and 27 French families. In the families there were three girls and seven boys from one to 10 years old. There were six young Indian slave boys from 12 to 18 years old and five Indian slave girls from 15 to 20 years old. The animals included nine oxen (five belonging to the King, four to private persons), 14 cows, four bulls (one belonging to the King), five calves, about 100 pigs, three kids and 400 hens.

By 1708, Nicolas de La Salle reported 122 men in the garrison including staff officers, soldiers, sailors, warehouse clerks, priests, workmen, a Canadian interpreter and cabin boys. There were 24 colonists, 28 women, 25 children and 80 Native American slaves. In all, the colony had 279 people plus six sick persons and 60 Canadian backwoodsmen living in the Native American village. The livestock had multiplied, so there were 50 milk cows, 40 calves, four bulls, eight oxen (four belonging to the King), 1,400 pigs and sows and about 2,000 chickens.

France's primary interest in this new colony was to have an outlet for the fur trade in the upper Mississippi Valley. The coureurs-de-bois, or Canadian backwoodsmen, were trappers. Most of these men were single and preferred to live a crude, unsettled lifestyle, much like the native people. They did not cultivate the land, preferring to live on what they hunted. They were not well regarded by the religious or the "society" from France and did little to help the colony succeed. These men received goods from the lower colony, which they traded at the Illinois for exorbitant sums that amounted to stealing. However disagreeable, these men furnished the colony with furs, bear oil and meat.

As early as 1729, exclusive hunting agreements were negotiated with individual Canadian trappers on condition that they bring the pelts to New Orleans to trade with the Company. The pelts, which were to be good winter skins, were valued as follows.

Beaver skins	34 sous a pound
Deer skins	34 sous a pound
Raccoon skins	15 sous each
Stag & doeskins, dressed	5 livres each
Forest wolves' skins	50 sous
Fox and wildcat skins	40 sous
Bear skins, large	5 livres
Otter skins, large & black	4 livres

Duc d'Orleans feeding coins to John Law

EQUIVALENT MONEY VALUES TABLE

1 piastre	=	1 dollar
8 escalins	=	1 dollar
8 reals	=	1 dollar
5 livres	=	1 dollar
5 francs	=	1 dollar
1 sou	=	1 cent
1 picayune	=	6 cents
1 escalin	=	12 ½ cents
1 ecu	=	60 cents

The usual method for estimating equivalent currency values today is to multiply by 60.

English Turn
In September 1699, Bienville convinced an English captain that the French were in complete control of the Mississippi River. The English turned back and that point in the river is still known today as English Turn.

Jean-Baptiste Le Moyne, Sieur de Bienville

RATIONS FROM FRANCE

The colonists feared starvation and depended on the Native Americans for corn, beans and to help them hunt and fish for food. Bienville developed great relations with the indigenous people. He spoke their languages and invited them to eat with him when they traveled during their hunts. Often, the Native Americans traveled 40 or 50 leagues on these hunting trips, but carried no provisions. They were grateful to eat with Bienville, and especially enjoyed the bread he served. In fact, 50 hundredweight of flour at a time was requested from France as presents for the Native Americans. Many colonists suspected Bienville used Company bread to feed his servants not the Native American chiefs.

Ships from France carried provisions such as flour, beef, bacon and salt. Items such as vegetables, butter, oil and vinegar were sent, but often spoiled in transit, because of the many months required to travel the distance from France to Louisiana. Trade relations developed with Havana and islands such as Martinique and Santo Domingo where

BIENVILLE'S WILL

In 1765, prior to his death in Paris on March 7, 1768, Bienville recorded his last will and testament. He had no wife or children and his siblings were all deceased. To the poor of his parish he bequeathed 1,000 livres. He requested that 300 Masses be said for the repose of his soul. To his valet he left an annual pension of 200 livres for the remainder of his life, 150 livres in the Hotel de Ville securities, his wardrobe including all clothing and the bed and bedding where the valet slept.

To his cook Bienville left 300 livres. To the cook's daughter, Marguerite, he left 50 francs. He left 200 francs to the lackey and 100 livres to the coachman.

To his grandnephew, Payan de Noyan, he remitted a 10,000-livre loan and left him a diamond. To the boy's father he left a diamond worth 1500 livres. To another nephew he left a diamond. To Iberville's two granddaughters (and his grandnieces) he left two diamonds.

Bienville's only epitaph is the church record of his death and burial, but his Louisiana legacy lives on.

supplies, provisions and medicines could be obtained. Ships from these islands brought bacon, flour, sugar, tobacco, cocoa, molasses and casks of wine. Chickens could be obtained from Mississippi, while flour and corn were borrowed from the Spanish. They tried desperately

to multiply the herds, but the colonists were forced to slaughter livestock to feed the sick.

Though the soldiers and some workmen received rations as part of their pay, these provisions did not always arrive

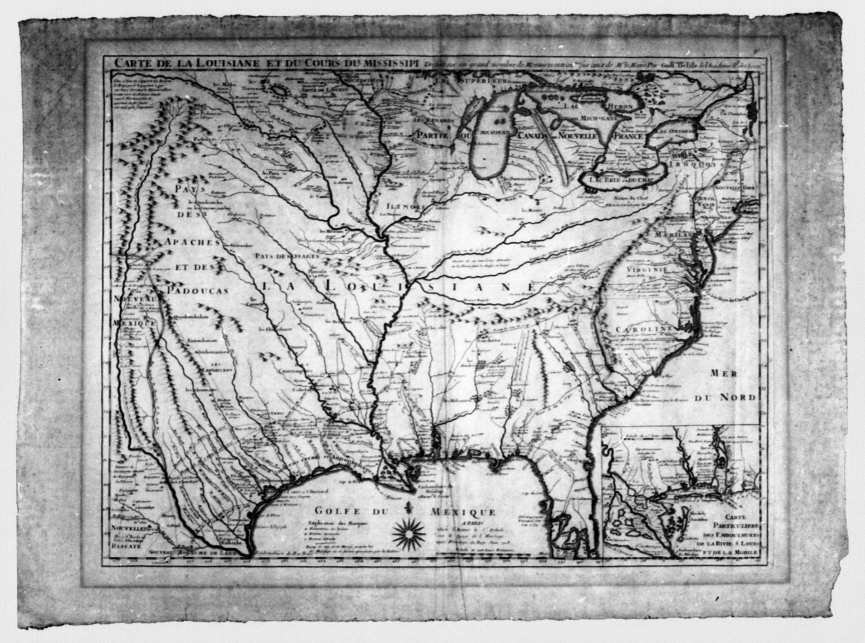

1718 mother map of Louisiana

THE PETTICOAT INSURRECTION

Charles Etienne de Nivelles, a lieutenant of Bienville, took an active part in quelling the "petticoat insurrection," a rebellion of the women who were dissatisfied with the settler's diet of Indian corn.

According to legend, in 1718 the women of New Orleans knew very little about the strange, indigenous foods of this new land. They marched in protest to Governor Bienville's house banging utensils on their black, cast iron pots, demanding that he hear their grievances. Being an outstanding diplomat, Bienville sent his housekeeper, Madame Langlois (his mother's cousin), to live with the Native Americans for about six weeks. From the Native Americans she learned to cook Louisiana's native foods. She flavored dishes by adding bay leaves, boiled whole ears of corn and learned to stuff squirrel with pecans and spices.

Corn Macque Choux

She prepared succotash, a delicious combination of corn and butterbeans. Upon her return to the city, she educated the New Orleans ladies in what must have been the first culinary school in North America. Even today, Madame Langlois is considered the "mother of Creole cooking."

in a timely fashion, in the quantity promised or in the quality to which they were accustomed. The soldiers could trade flour and brandy received from France for other necessities such as livestock and fresh meat. Therefore, they complained when they received inferior goods from home. Not surprisingly, the soldiers, workmen and colonists suffered disease, because they lacked proper food and clothes. Many times they traded food to buy clothes and shoes. If meat was not available from France, they received the equivalent in powder and ammunition. With these items they traded with the Native Americans for food. In 1716, many French soldiers deserted to Pensacola for better provisions.

While the officers and soldiers received rations as pay, the settlers received limited food supplies. In 1701, officials gave rations only to those settlers who were the "most necessary" to the colony and only to prevent them from returning to France. Settlers were expected to provide for themselves, especially with the fertile soil and abundant wild game and fish, yet they remained dependent on the supply vessels. Because families could not buy rations elsewhere, they were allowed to purchase items from the storehouses. However, they paid as much as 25% above the prices in France. To make matters worse, the Company limited how much they could earn on the pelts they traded. Food scarcity and limited funds resulted in exorbitant prices on colonial goods. Venison was so outrageously priced that many could not afford it. Therefore, in 1721, the Council of Commerce in Biloxi standardized venison prices. An entire deer would be sold for 16 livres, half a deer for eight livres and a quarter deer for four livres. Wine and brandy were priced exorbitantly as well, so the Council ordered that no brandy could be sold for more than four livres a pot and no wine above 40 sous a pot. A failure to comply with these price scales resulted in imprisonment or fines. Similarly, in 1722, the Superior Council of Louisiana set Company prices for the goods available at the shop. Selling wine, brandy or flour above the Company's prices was forbidden. Goods were established at the following prices:

Buffalo Beef	8 sous a pound
French Beef	10 sous a pound
1/4 deer	4 livres
Poultry	3 livres a piece
Eggs	50 sous a dozen

The Council also mandated pricing at the canteen, which distributed goods from 6 o'clock in the morning until 7 o'clock at night. Drinking at the canteen was forbidden. Samples were drawn from each keg or hogshead in case complaints arose of adulterated beverages. Beverage prices were:

Sou

Brandy	3 livres a pot
Red Wine	30 sous a pot
White Wine	20 sous a pot

Because food and provisions were highly sought after, the warehouses were kept in stellar fashion. However, in 1723, complaints raged against warehouse keepers who lived as lords with many slaves, good food, houses and furniture though they had arrived in the colony poor. Corruption reigned. The warehouse keepers pillaged and stole provisions and allowed merchandise to be damaged

while making excessive profits. Even officers obtained goods such as wine, sugar and soap not for personal use, but to sell to others. Officers requested that the Company send beverages and 5,000 to 6,000 quarts of flour to stop the unlawful profiteering and to prevent colonists from returning to France. By 1728, the warehouses were arranged "as in the most famous shops in Paris."

Because rations were so precious, it is interesting to note a letter from Commissioner Jacques de La Chaise dated 1723 in which he stated that rations were given to useless women and children who caused disorder. The women had pox, ruined the sailors and should be ordered to the interior to live with the native people.

As time passed and the colony grew, the complaints stayed the same. In 1725, the Council of Louisiana registered a complaint with the Company of the Indies that the goods they sent arrived in terrible condition, partly because they were not packaged properly. Two-thirds of the inferior wine soured and leaked during transport. Of the 609 large casks of olive oil, nearly half had leaked out. Other items were damaged or useless including writing paper, guns, carriage windows, embroidered coats and iron tools. They requested drums, glass panes and walnut oil for painting. By 1726, a shop carried a variety of goods except items that were always rare in the colony such as flour, wine, brandy, shirts, shoes, soap and coffee. In 1728, brandy, wine, flour, meat, dry goods and medicines were still needed.

FOOD IN THE COLONY

While colonists needed food and supplies from France, it was vital that they become self-sufficient in the New World. Fortunately, Louisiana offered fertile soil, three growing seasons and abundant wild fruit, game, fish and seafood. The early colonists found that Louisiana's soil was similar to that of Bordeaux. Plum trees grew, peaches were abundant and grapes from France, which had been seen and eaten, grew well along with several wild varieties. Quality fish were abundant and colonists made salt. Though the indigenous people had salt, the French obviously believed that salt was scarce in the colony. Salt was usually sent from France for food preservation. As late as 1723, salt was still extremely rare and individuals were selling it for as much as 60 sous or three livres a pound.

Though many early colonial writers painted bleak pictures of colonists living on crushed and boiled corn with a piece of meat, others stated that there was no fear of dying from hunger. Corn, buffalo and deer were abundant. Sauvole mentioned serving deer soup to missionaries and offering lettuce salad to Iberville before he departed for the Old World. The colonists planted corn and a variety of vegetables. The first years of cultivation were extremely

Henri de Tonti, the "Iron Hand"

the goods being produced, food was expensive and brandy scarce. There was no butcher's meat and the chickens cost as much as three livres and 12 sous a piece and eggs 50 sous a dozen. Just five years later, a handful of peas cost 50 to 60 sous, a watermelon three livres, an egg 16 – 18 sous and bear oil was 10 – 12 livres a pot.

The colonists planted gardens, which included sorrel and parsley. There were fig, pear, apple and plum trees as well as grapevines, French melons and pumpkins. Even olive trees grew in Louisiana with fruit similar to that of Provence. De La Chaise planned to have a colonist grow and tend the olive trees as was done in Provence to make the Louisiana olives sweeter. As early as 1706, Bienville demanded that everyone plant land, so they would not be dependent on France for supplies.

In 1728 a place was reserved for a market in the front of the city with room for a slaughterhouse. The colony was settling with high hopes for the crops. Fruit trees such as russet apples, small red apples, fennel-apples, peaches, apricots, pears, cherries, red currants, olives, plums and raspberries were shipped for planting. The Illinois country supplied the lower colony with a considerable amount of flour and bacon. Butcher's meat sold for eight sous, and many believed that within two years, provisions might be priced lower in the colony than in France.

Professional cooks lived in the colony as early as 1706. Records indicate that a colonial settler had a cook, allowing one to surmise that many others had cooks as well. A cook of Tonti's named Delaunay was mentioned who lived at the Accanas post with a carpenter. According to the census, there were artisan bakers as early as 1722.

productive, which allowed them to live comfortably while raising poultry and pigs. Cows were raised easily with no cost for feed, plus they provided milk. The colonists sold chickens, milk, fruit, cheese and corn to the Spanish in Pensacola who paid handsomely for the goods. In 1713, a hen sold for one piastre, a pound of butter for one piastre and a dozen eggs for 40 sous.

Lamothe Cadillac, then governor of Louisiana, desperately wanted the leadership of France to stop this trade, because he thought it enslaved the French to the Spanish. He did not want the French to go to Pensacola to trade nor did he want the Spanish in the Louisiana colony. Ironically, by 1725, the Superior Council of Louisiana reserved a store of goods to trade with the Spanish, which eventually included the sale of Negroes. They wanted the Spanish to

come to New Orleans to buy and trade goods, but did not want individuals conducting business with the Spaniards. A baker was put in irons because he secretly baked and sold bread to the Spanish for three reals a pound. By 1727, the French government hoped to carry on commerce of 100,000 piastres a year with the Spanish. From the Spanish, the French obtained meat, cattle, even chocolate.

Early attempts at wheat cultivation on land located between the Mississippi River and Lake Pontchartrain failed because of the fogs, but by 1717 the colonists grew tobacco, rice, indigo, silk, vegetables and fruits of all kinds. Hardworking farmers were still needed in the colony to raise great quantities of livestock on the meadows and pastures. While cattle, deer and other animals were plentiful, sheep were also requested from France. Despite

LETTERS FROM SISTER MARIE MADELEINE HACHARD

Perhaps one of the best colonial food accounts came from Sister Marie Madeleine Hachard, an Ursuline nun who arrived in 1727 with 10 other nuns, plus two servants from Rouen, France. They traveled aboard *La Gironde*, which was loaded with sheep and 500 chickens for sustenance during the voyage. They ate rice cooked in water, beans seasoned with lard because there was no butter, biscuits, salted beef and bacon, though it was too horrible to consume. They drank water, but were limited to a half pint per day. En route, they stopped at the Island of Madeira where they received gifts of lemons, salads and preserves.

She wrote to her father upon arrival. "I can assure you that I can hardly believe that I am at the Mississippi; there is as much politeness and magnificence here as in France and the use of cloth of gold and velvet is very common, even though it is three times as expensive here as in Rouen. Bread costs ten sols per pound here and is made of Indian, or sometimes Turkish, cornmeal. Eggs are 45 to 50 sols

1719 map by Homanno, Io.

a dozen and milk is 14 sols for a pot of half the measure of France. We eat meat, fish, peas, and wild beans and many fruits and vegetables, like pineapples, which are

the most excellent of fruit, watermelons, sweet potatoes, apples, which are very much like the russets of France, figs, pecans, cashew nuts, which when eaten stick in the throat, and "giranmons," a kind of pumpkin. Even so there are a thousand other fruits which have not yet come to my knowledge.

"In fact, we live on wild beef, deer, swans, geese and wild turkeys, rabbits, chickens, ducks, teals, pheasants, partridges, quail and other fowl and game of different kinds. The rivers are teeming with enormous fish, especially the brill, which is an excellent fish, rays, carps, salmon and an infinity of other fish which are unknown in France. Milk chocolate and coffee are much used here. A lady of this country gave us a goodly supply and we take some every day. We eat meat here three days a week during Lent and during the rest of the year meat can be eaten on Saturdays here, just as on the Island of Santo Domingo. We are getting remarkably used to the wild food of this country. We eat a bread which is half rice and half wheat. There is here a wild grape that is larger than our French grape and does not grow in a bunch. It is served in a dish like a prune. Rice cooked in milk is very common

Ursuline Convent

and we eat it often along with sagamite, which is made from Indian corn that has been ground in a mortar and then boiled in water with butter or bacon fat. Everyone in Louisiana considers this an excellent dish."

Sister Hachard went on to describe the Mississippi River, the moderate winters that lasted only three months and fertile lands that yielded several crops a year. She described a number of trees including mulberries, chestnuts, figs, almonds, walnuts, lemons, oranges and pomegranates. She said, "If the land were cultivated there would be no better in the world, but for that it would have to be otherwise inhabited and France would have to send workmen of all trades. A man working only two days a week digging the ground and planting wheat would harvest more than he would need to feed himself all year, but, the majority of the people here live an idleness and apply themselves only to hunting and fishing. The Company of the Indies does much business in furs, beavers and other merchandise with the savages, the majority of whom are very sociable."

Sister Hachard also wrote to her father that in the summer, "We eat little meat as it is slaughtered only twice a week and is not easy to preserve. Hunting is done about 10 leagues from our city and lasts all winter which here begins in October. Many wild oxen are taken and brought here to New Orleans and nearby areas. We buy this meat for three sols a pound, the same as deer, which is better than the beef and mutton you eat in Rouen.

"Wild ducks are very cheap. Teals, water-hen, geese and other fowl and game are also very common, but we do not buy it as we do not wish to indulge in delicacies. Really, it is a charming country all winter and in summer the fish are plentiful

and good. There are oysters and carps of prodigious size and delicious flavor. As for the other fish, there are none in France like them. They are large monster fish that are fairly good. We also eat watermelons and French melons and sweet potatoes which are large roots that are cooked in the coals like chestnuts. They even taste somewhat like chestnuts but are much sweeter, very soft and very good. All this, my dear Father, is exactly like I am telling you — I do not tell you anything that I have not yet personally experienced. Many other kinds of meat, fish and vegetables are eaten here but I have not yet tasted them so I cannot tell you of their goodness.

"Regarding the fruits of the country, there are many that we do not care for but the peaches and figs are very excellent and abundant. We are sent so many of them from the nearby plantations that we make them into preserves and jelly. Blackberry jelly is particularly good. Reverend Father de Beaubois has the finest garden in the city. It is full of orange trees which bear as beautiful and as sweet an orange as those of Cape Francis. He gave us about 300 sour ones which we preserved. Thanks to God, we have never yet lacked anything. Our Reverend Father carefully sees to it that we are provided with food."

In time, the nuns kept a poultry yard and a garden at their convent. They received gifts from the colonists including "two cows with their calves, a sow with her little ones, some chickens and muscovy ducks. All of these have helped to start up our barnyard. We also have some turkeys and geese in it. The inhabitants, seeing that we do not wish to take money to instruct our day students, are filled with gratitude and help us in every way they can."

COLONISTS

Strong, healthy settlers willing to work were critical for the survival of the colony. Requests were repeatedly sent to France asking for hardworking men and women who could arrive with tools to clear, plow, plant and harvest the land. Plus, these colonists needed a two-year food supply, otherwise they were just more mouths to feed. In 1713, it was decided that only useful workmen should be maintained and given food rations. The requested French workmen included a baker to prepare bread for the officers and garrison. He was provided one year's supply of flour, a six months supply of salt pork, and it was suggested that he be paid 360 livres a year. Also, if the wives and children of the workmen were requested, they should be sent to keep the workmen in the colony.

FILLES A LA CASSETTE.

The coureurs-de-bois, or Canadian backwoodsmen, were trappers

Peasants were requested to teach colonists how to cultivate the land. Unfortunately, many married and settled people lived an idle and lazy lifestyle. They had an abundance of fish and game, so saw no need to clear and work the ground. Laboring settlers were desperately needed for the colony to grow and thrive.

Girls were requested annually, though they needed provisions to sustain them until they married. The hope was that men, particularly the coureurs-de-bois, would marry these girls, settle down and work to support their families. After the first female-laden ships arrived, a letter was sent that it was not necessary to send Parisian girls. In fact, the colony needed farmers' daughters "who (were) rid of vain show and vanity or else those who (were) not acquainted with it at all." At one point 40 good farmers were requested who had the largest number of daughters, sisters and nieces.

In September 1704, approximately 27 girls arrived in Louisiana from Paris and Rochefort aboard the *Pelican* with the sole purpose of marrying to help settle the colony. The bishop screened these girls determining them virtuous, pious and accustomed to labor and diligence. Among the girls were a pastry cook's daughters eager to seize free passage for his family to the New World.

In February 1728, the Company sent another boatload of virtuous girls ready for marriage. Each was provided with a little trunk (cassette) of clothing, thus earning them the nickname, "The Cassette Girls." Many believed it an honor and mark of good breeding to be a descendant of these early colonists.

MORALITY OF THE COLONY

As for religion and morality in the colony, Father Raphael observed in 1725 that it was so little advanced that he scarcely thought it had begun. In the early days of settlement the clergy tolerated things not tolerable in established countries. Father Raphael observed that "the commands of God and of the church were transgressed with so much license that it seemed that they were no longer binding when they had crossed the seas."

Perhaps, things would have been better had there been churches where the faithful could gather. Originally, Mass was said in the kitchen of the little house where Father Raphael and the Capuchins lived. Only about 20 people fit in the small room. Fortunately, they were given a larger house in which Mass could be said, but everyone had to bring his own chair. Pews were made for colonists to rent, but this caused more disruption, when certain ladies became offended, because they were not given the opportunity to purchase the front pews. Interestingly, in November 1725 the Superior Council decreed that talking in church during divine service was prohibited. Apparently, a woman had disrupted Mass by talking, but when the priest threatened to put her out of the church, she refused. Father Raphael felt the disorder could only be fixed with the assistance of the "secular arm." Unfortunately, the officers caused the greatest scandals. Sieur de Louboey maintained a scandalous relation with Madame Garnier. De Louboey and Garnier had one child together, and she became pregnant with a second. Father Raphael observed that "both of them take a sort of pride in their

St. Louis Cathedral in New Orleans' Jackson Square

concubinage, walk about together and live as familiarly in the sight of everybody as if they were living in a legitimate marriage." De Louboey further scandalized the priest following the sermon on Good Friday, when he left as everyone else prepared to adore the cross.

Also vexing were the Canadians and unmarried soldiers who kept female Native American slaves insisting they were needed to cook and keep the cabins. Somehow, these slaves were nearly always with child or nursing. The priests were outraged at the masters for creating these "half breeds," and encouraged them to keep male native slaves and either marry the native women or sell them to the islands.

Apparently, many women of "bad life" lived in the colony. Many became pregnant, but refused to name the father, so the Company was obliged to feed the child. In 1728, the Ursuline Nuns established a correction room at their convent where these disreputable and publicly scandalous women could be kept.

Sister Hachard found the morals of the lay people quite corrupt and scandalous. She wrote, "not only do debauchery, lack of faith and all other vices reign here more than elsewhere, but they reign with an immeasurable abundance! As for the girls of bad conduct, they are watched closely and severely punished by being placed on a wooden horse and flogged by all the soldiers of the Regiment that guards our city." She said, "While the women ignore facts pertaining to their salvation, they ignore nothing when it comes to vanity. The luxury in this city is such that one can distinguish no one; everyone is of equal magnificence. Most of the women and their families are reduced to living only on sagamite, a sort of gruel. However, not withstanding the expense, they are dressed in velvets and damasks covered with ribbons, materials which are regularly sold in this country for three times their cost in France. The women here, as elsewhere, use red and white paint and patches, too, to cover the wrinkles in their faces. The devil here possesses a large empire, but this does not discourage us from the hope of destroying him, with God's love."

THE END OF THE FRENCH COLONIAL PERIOD

By the end of the 1720s, life in the fledgling colony was more tranquil than in days past. Those who opposed colonial establishment were settling down. Even the officers and other malcontents asked for land to cultivate, requested Negroes and seemed sorry in not having done this before.

Unfortunately, even by the end of the 1750s, France still spent a tremendous amount of money on the colony with precious little revenue in return. From 1758-1761 France sent no supplies to Louisiana and letters from the crown were scarce. Expenses mounted annually, and the colony was not profitable. The population was less than 7,500 after 50 years of colonization. Officials wrote to France that most of the inhabitants of New Orleans were lazy, insubordinate, drank too much and were bankrupt. With an unprosperous New World colony and mounting troubles at home, France abandoned colonial Louisiana. With the secret Treaty of Fontainebleau in 1762, Spain possessed colonial Louisiana and the Spanish colonial era of Louisiana history began.

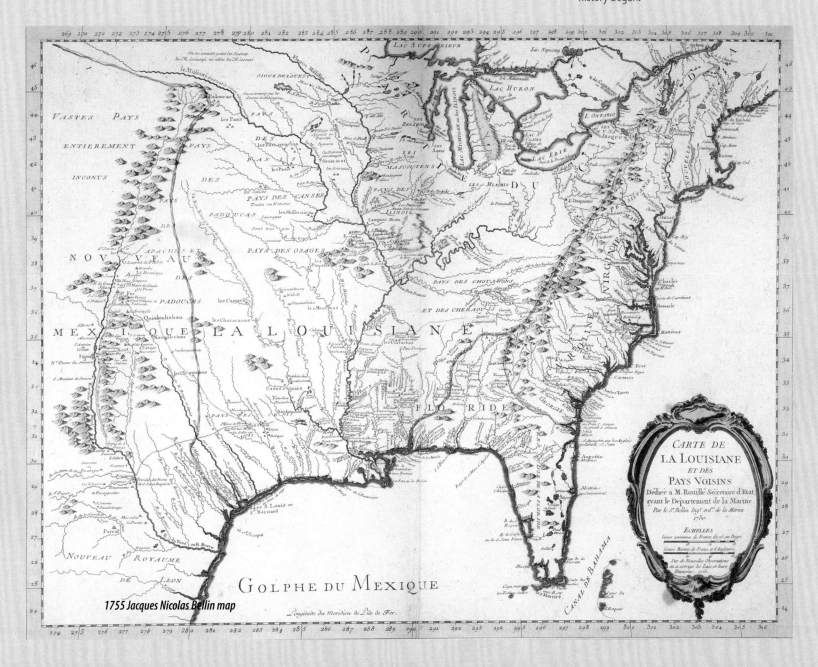

1755 Jacques Nicolas Bellin map

Early Acadia

Reading the Deportation Order

HISTORY AND EXPULSION OF THE ACADIAN PEOPLE

The history of Louisiana's Acadian settlers, or "Cajuns," began in the 15th century with New World exploration. In 1497, the Genoan mapmaker and voyager, Giovanni Caboto, claimed the region northeast of present-day Maine for England. Though Caboto mysteriously disappeared before the area could be settled, England continued to unofficially claim the territory. In fact, his voyage gave England claim to North America and led to the founding of the English Colonies.

A little more than 25 years later, Giovanni da Verrazanno, an Italian explorer sailing under the French flag, claimed the same region northeast of Maine and named it "L'Acadie" or "Acadia." Most historians believe the name L'Acadie came from the Greek, "Arcadia," a mountainous area celebrated as the home of contented, pastoral people. Others think "Acadia" derived from the Micmac Indian word, "akade," meaning "fertile fields." Neither France nor England settled Acadia for 80 years. By 1605, Samuel de

Champlain and Pierre du Guast, Frenchmen from the Loire Valley, had charted Acadia's coastline and founded Port-Royal, the first permanent settlement north of the Gulf of Mexico. Port-Royal predated the Jamestown settlement by two years and the Pilgrims' landing at Plymouth Rock by 15 years. Over the next three decades, Acadia became a destination for thousands of French pioneers. Family names in Acadia included Arceneaux, Aucoin, Bergeron, Blanchard, Boudreaux, Bourg, Bourgeois, Breaux, Clouatre, Comeaux, Cormier, Daigle, Dubreuil, Dugas, Foret, Gaudet, Gautreau, Giroir, Guidry, Guilbeau, Hebert, Lambert, Landry, Lanoux, Latour, LeBlanc, Marchand, Martin, Melancon, Michel, Peltier, Poirier, Prejean, Richard,

Robichaux, Roy, Savoie, Saunier, Templet, Theriot, Thibaut and Thibodeaux.

In 1613, Samuel Argall, an Englishman who commanded a ship to Jamestown in 1609, destroyed the Port-Royal colony. Thus began the Anglo-French controversy over Acadia. England desired the area because of trading opportunities and rich fishing grounds. England's King James I, formerly Scotland's James VI, was disgusted by France's success on what he considered his land. He sent Scottish settlers to reclaim the region and named it Nova Scotia or New Scotland. From that point control of Acadia or Nova Scotia changed almost with the seasons.

"That your Lands & Tenements, Cattle of all Kinds and Live Stock of all Sortes are Forfitted to the Crown with all other your Effects Saving your Money & Household goods and you your Selves to be removed from that his Province." From the Deportation Order issued by Lieutenant Colonel John Winslow

Despite harsh colonizing conditions and the harsher turmoil of contested dominion and war, the Acadians survived and flourished. They were an independent, hardworking, agricultural people with an incredible faith. Acadia's population grew from nearly 400 settlers in 1670 to nearly 900 by 1686. Settlement spread from Port-Royal up the Bay of Fundy to Minas Basin, Cobequid Bay and around Cape Chignecto to Beaubassin.

By 1690, the Acadians were trapped in a colonial power struggle in which they had little interest. Following attacks on New England by French troops from Canada, William Phipps led a Massachusetts expedition to capture Port-Royal. A naval blockade and further attacks by the English finally led to the capture of Port-Royal on October 13, 1710. A British garrison was established and the town renamed Annapolis Royal in honor of Great Britain's Queen Anne. The Treaty of Utrecht in 1713 established Acadia as a British possession and officially changed the name to Nova Scotia. France retained Isle Royale (Cape Breton Island) and Isle Saint Jean (Prince Edward Island). According to

the treaty, the Acadians could move or they could become British subjects by pledging an oath of allegiance. Most swore the oath on three conditions: 1) religious freedom 2) neutrality in war, and 3) the right to emigrate. Governor Richard Philips accepted their oaths. Interestingly, the Acadians were forbidden to build boats or to sell their property or cattle. The British wanted the Acadians to remain because they could shield Micmac Indian attacks and provide labor and food for the garrison.

Three decades of peace ensued. The population grew from 2,900 in 1714 to 8,000 by 1739. By the 1740s, the French and British were fighting again for control of Nova Scotia. Thousands of Acadians moved to the nearest French Canadian territories. English Lieutenant Governor Charles Lawrence decided to disperse the remaining Acadians throughout the New England Colonies, because they refused to take the oath of allegiance without stipulation. This cleared the way for British settlers to populate Nova Scotia.

Deportation responsibilities were given to Colonel Robert Monckton, Major John Handfield and Lieutenant Colonel John Winslow. Winslow arrived in Grand Pré, Nova Scotia on August 19, 1755 establishing his headquarters at the church. In reply to his summons more than 400 Acadian men and boys arrived by September 5, and were declared prisoners. By November 1 they and 1,100 more of their comrades were shipped to Maryland, Pennsylvania and Virginia. This procedure was repeated in village after village. Acadian men and boys were summoned, imprisoned and promptly deported on overcrowded vessels to ports unknown. Many died because of the filth on the ships and poor seaport accommodations. Many refused to work once they settled claiming they were prisoners of war.

Acadian priests and leaders were arrested and some murdered. The English burned homes, churches, mills, crops and confiscated livestock. In two parishes alone 686 homes, 11 mills and two churches were destroyed. Thriving Acadian villages vanished.

Ships take Acadians into exile

Settlements are burned

ACADIAN EXILES IN LOUISIANA

Uprooted, hopeless and cruelly banished, the Acadians were plunged into poverty overnight. Families were torn apart, some never to meet again. A nation was annihilated. Confusion and desperation reigned. The Acadians were left with few possessions and no country to call home, with French heritage as their only crime.

Interestingly, the Acadians were sent to British possessions rather than to their motherland or French colonies. It was also strange that the deportation happened years after the English conquered Acadia. In autumn 1755, more than 6,000 Acadians were victims of Le Grande Derangement, which lasted until 1763. In total, more than 10,000 Acadians, 75 percent of the entire population, were deported, though many escaped to Canada, Isle Saint Jean or hid in northern New Brunswick. The last Acadians deported from Nova Scotia sailed from Halifax to Boston. However, the Massachusetts Assembly rejected them and sent them home. During the 1760s, approximately 8,000 New Englanders moved to Nova Scotia to occupy Acadian lands, completing Lawrence's original command that the area be repopulated with English colonists.

Most of the Acadian exiles of 1755 were scattered throughout the English Colonies to Massachusetts, Connecticut, New York, Pennsylvania, Maryland, North Carolina, South Carolina, Virginia and Georgia. Virginia, however, refused to accept the Acadians and shipped them to England where they lived until the end of the Seven Years War. Then, they returned to France. The New England colonists did not want to financially support the Acadians and disliked them because they were Catholic and French. Many feared the Acadians would join in slave uprisings. Many Acadians went to the West Indies islands of Saint Domingue, Guadeloupe and Martinique. Approximately 3,500 were deported to France. The French government unsuccessfully attempted to establish Acadian colonies in Brittany, Belle-Isle-en-Mer, Poitou, Corsica, French Guiana, Santo Domingo and the Falkland Islands. Many Frenchmen resented the Acadians because they received government pensions and land.

According to undocumented accounts, the first Acadians reached Louisiana as early as 1755 settling at Cabahanocer (Cabanocey) in present-day St. James Parish on the west bank of the Mississippi River. Also undocumented is the claim that the Acadians arrived in 1756 settling near today's St. Martinville. According to the Mouton Legend, the Mouton brothers settled at Tabiscania in 1756 near present-day St. John Parish.

SITE OF
FIRST ACADIAN SETTLERS
IN LOUISIANA
···
Refugees came overland 1756-57.
In vicinity was 1762 grant to
Jacques Cantrelle, Sr. of France
after whom Church and Parish were
named. Section once included in
Les Oumas, Eveche of Quebéc.

However, a document known as the Aubry letter written in 1763 stated, "I saw the arrival of 60 Acadian families from Sainte Domingue but did not foresee the many to follow to make Louisiana the New Acadia. 300 are on the Mississippi. We do not speak of them in hundreds anymore, but in thousands. It is our duty not to abandon them."

In fact, in 1764 approximately 600 Acadians arrived in Louisiana via the French West Indies.

The 1765 Maxent List documented Acadians at St. Jacques des Cabahanocer, Lafourche des Tchitimacha and St. Gabriel des Iberville, the present-day parishes of St. James, Ascension and Iberville, respectively. St. James Parish was known as the First Acadian Coast; Ascension as the Second Acadian Coast; and Iberville as the Third Acadian Coast. These were Louisiana's first official Acadian settlements. The families listed were Arceneaux, Bergeron, Bourgeois, Cormier, Dugas, Guidry, Guilbeau, LeBlanc, Martin, Poirier, Roy and Saunier.

The 1766 Gordon journal stated, "The colony 20 leagues (60 miles) above New Orleans consists of just-planted, poor Acadians on each side of the river. With them are Houma and Alibamu natives." Estimates indicate that 200 additional Acadians made Louisiana their home in 1766.

Like L'Acadie a century before, Louisiana's Acadian Coast became the exiles' destination. By the early 1780s, Louisiana was home to almost a thousand Acadians

Country Estate

arriving from New England and the West Indies. In 1785, Louisiana's Spanish government welcomed Acadians gathered in France since 1763. Nearly, 1,600 Acadians sailed on seven ships bound for Louisiana's swamps and prairies. The Acadian Coast became their last refuge. Upon arrival, authorities gave them land, cattle and tools for building and farming. Rations of corn were provided to each person, and each family received an ax, hoe, sickle, spade, two hens, a cock and a two-month old pig. Each head of a family also received a shotgun. Sufficient food was delivered from the rations at military posts to enable the Acadians to survive until the first crop was harvested. The Acadians flourished, and many penniless refugees amassed fortunes by the 19th century.

The arrival of the Acadians in Louisiana

Tony Kristicevich, 1939

FOODS OF NOVA SCOTIA

Like many early colonists, the Acadians were farmers. They settled along the banks of the tidal rivers building dykes for protection against the tides. From rich, fertile soil the Acadians cultivated wheat, rye and vegetables. These self-sufficient people raised poultry, sheep, pigs and cattle. Their cows were a small breed producing little milk, so butter and cheese were sparse. Mutton and pork were salted for winter use.

In Acadia, wild game and fish were plentiful. The Acadians savored beaver, porcupine, rabbit, moose, caribou and bear, and they particularly liked shad. The native tribes taught the Acadians to glean a living from the land including making maple sugar and syrup.

The Acadians collected, dried and stored wild fruits and berries, especially strawberries and blueberries, for winter use. Every farm had an orchard. In fact, the first apple trees were brought to Acadia from Normandy around 1606. The Acadians made apple cider and spruce beer, which was not only a delicacy but healthy as well. Wine and hard liquor were relatively unknown.

Generally, food was prepared in large iron kettles over an open hearth. Soups, chowders and stews were common fare. Every village had a centrally located outdoor brick oven where each family baked bread.

The Acadians were simple people who expected little and were satisfied with less. Family was the most important aspect of their lives followed by community. When a young couple married, the entire community helped establish them. The men helped clear the land to build a log house. Those who could afford it gave cattle, hogs and poultry as gifts. Generally, the bride's mother gave the couple a feather bed as a wedding present.

Because of their prosperity, the Second Acadian Coast became known as the "Golden Coast" of Louisiana. Later, the Acadians settled and populated many South Louisiana towns and much of the Gulf Coast from the mouth of the Mississippi River to Texas. Today, approximately half of the world's estimated two million Acadians live in Louisiana. Louisiana's Acadian descendants are called "Cajuns," an American slang word for "Acadian."

A once banished race, Cajuns endured hardships through vitality, ingenuity and faith. Many ancestral traditions have been preserved through the pride Cajuns find in their heritage. Today, these survivors are indeed, a "contented, pastoral people" of Louisiana's "fertile fields."

L'ORDRE DU BON TEMPS

"The Order of the Good Time," the first social club in America, was originally established at Port-Royal by Samuel de Champlain in 1606. The purpose of the club was to provide entertainment and satisfy hearty appetites during the long, harsh Acadian winter. There were 15 gentlemen in the company and each took a turn being host for the day.

The host designed his menu based on the day's hunt. Generally, the men enjoyed huge moose or caribou roasts as well as smaller game such as beaver, porcupine and rabbits. In fact, moose meat and beaver's tail were highly regarded for their tenderness and delicate flavors. Waterfowl, ruffled grouse, partridge and other birds were plentiful.

Trout, cod and lobsters were speared through the ice for the dinner fare as well.

The men competed to provide the most sumptuous meal for their comrades. If the day's hunt was not as successful as hoped, the host traded with local tribesmen for sufficient fare. Usually, these Micmac Indians joined in the elaborate banquet. That evening, the host wore the Insignia of the Order and paraded in grandeur to the dining hall with each comrade carrying a delectable platter of food. Once the meal was enjoyed, the men told stories and sang. A toast with wine completed the evening's events and the Insignia of the Order was passed to the successor. Thus began America's first "gourmet's club" in Acadia.

NOVA SCOTIA ACADIAN COOKING BECOMES LOUISIANA CAJUN COOKING

The exiled Acadians easily adapted to their Louisiana home. The only real difference between Nova Scotia and Louisiana was the change from the harsh Northern winters to hot, humid Southern summers. Wild game and fish were plentiful, as were nuts, berries and fruits. The soil was rich and fertile with three fabulous growing seasons. The Acadians settled in either Louisiana's abundant swamplands or on the open prairies.

Similar to Louisiana cuisine, Nova Scotia cooking represented a mélange of cultures. Their dishes were derived from the pots of the native Indians, French,

DEMYSTIFYING CAJUN COOKING: IS IT HOT OR NOT?

Cajun cooking is reputed to be very spicy. Generally, the cuisine is more piquant than most European counterparts, but when prepared correctly the spices heighten the flavor of soups, vegetables, meats and seafood without overwhelming the dish. Spices and fresh herbs add flavor and dimension to Cajun cooking. Basic Cajun flavorings are most often associated with the use of the "trinity" and the "pope." In Louisiana cooking, the "trinity" is classified as onions, celery and bell pepper while garlic is referred to as the "pope," because a single garlic pod resembles the miter or headgear worn by the Holy Father. Both are fitting descriptions created by a culture that is predominantly Catholic. If a dish is overseasoned or too hot and spicy for the average palate, it is not representative of true Cajun cooking.

Tonging, Grand Isle, La., 1938

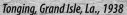

Augustine woman pounding rice, 1892

41

Trapper's cabin

English, Germans, New Englanders, Irish, Scottish and Africans. The dishes the Acadians enjoyed in Nova Scotia were much the same as those prepared in Louisiana, most often with a simple ingredient change. Boiled lobster, lobster chowder and lobster stew easily gave way to boiled crawfish, crawfish bisque and crawfish étouffée. Soups such as potato, bean, pumpkin, cabbage and eel were brought to Louisiana as were oyster stew, corn chowder bisque and fish chowder. The fish teaming in the Gulf of Mexico rivaled the fish varieties of the Atlantic waters. Fried smelts became fried catfish or pan-fried striped bass; baked stuffed fish changed to crabmeat-stuffed flounder; baked shad gave way to herb-baked large mouth bass; codfish balls metamorphosed into catfish and garfish boulettes; planked salmon was transformed into planked redfish; scallops baked in their shells became oysters baked on the half shell; clam pie became oyster pie; and ultimately, raw oysters were just as cold, salty and delectable in Louisiana as those from Cobequid Bay.

In Louisiana, as in Nova Scotia, pigs and cows were slaughtered during the winter months for fresh meat, which was also preserved by salting, smoking or pickling. Lard was rendered, sausages made, blood puddings and head cheese created. No part of the animal was wasted. Louisiana's cuisine was enhanced with the Acadian's chicken fricot, rappe pie, roasted wild duck, roasted goose, venison pot roast and rabbit fricassée.

Vegetables important to the Acadians of Nova Scotia were popular with the Acadians of Louisiana as well. Potatoes, turnips, cabbage, corn, wild greens, broad beans and lima beans were important in the Acadians' diets. Seasonal fruit and berry pies were made as well as pumpkin and squash pies. In Louisiana, sweet potato pie became a favorite. In Nova Scotia, stale bread was used to create bread pudding, which is now a Louisiana staple.

The food of Louisiana's Cajuns was harvested from the swamp floor pantry and consisted of what they could hunt, catch or grow. Louisiana's bayous provided crawfish, alligators, frogs and a wide variety of fish. The coastal marshes provided the Cajuns with ducks, geese and game birds on their migratory routes from Canada to South America. The saltwater of the Gulf of Mexico provided shrimp, oysters, crabs and more fish for their cast iron pots. The Cajuns grew large gardens of sweet potatoes, Creole tomatoes, squashes, eggplant, okra and a great variety of other fruits and vegetables. Without a doubt, the new Acadiana in Louisiana provided fields as fertile and harvests as abundant as those the exiles had known in their former L'Acadie.

The Acadians remained virtually isolated until the mid-1970s, though they had lived in Louisiana for two centuries. Two things focused attention on their saga and their cooking. First, an interstate highway was constructed across the Atchafalaya Basin creating a shortcut between New Orleans and the heart of Cajun Country. Secondly, "blackening," an untraditional method of cooking created in the early 1980s, brought Louisiana Cajun cooking to the world's attention. In blackening, both sides of the food (usually redfish or other firm fish or meat) are coated with a spice mixture and then seared in a white-hot cast iron skillet with little or no fat. The burned spices form a crust that seals in the natural juices while creating an incomparable texture and bite to the food. Within a few years Cajun cooking spread beyond Louisiana's borders and a Cajun food craze swept the world. As a result, redfish was placed on the endangered species list for years.

CAJUN VS. CREOLE CUISINE: WHAT'S THE DIFFERENCE?

Today, Louisiana Cajun cooking is best defined as a style of cuisine based on country French cooking, which evolved around indigenous ingredients. Generally, Cajun cooking is hearty, rustic country fare created as a family project. Cajun cooking is home-style cuisine served over or with cooked white rice. Most often it is found simmering in a cast iron pot with its main ingredients harvested from the abundance of the land, swamps, bayous and streams.

In comparison, Creole cuisine is a more sophisticated cousin. Creole is the cuisine of cooks and chefs and is based on European techniques. Wine- or liquor-based sauces often enhance the subtle, delicate flavors. Though Creole cuisine has French roots as well, it has been greatly influenced by other cultures including Native America, Spain, Germany, England, Africa and Italy. In general, Creole cooking is more sophisticated fare.

Evangeline at memorial church in Grand-Pré, Nova Scotia

Henry Wadsworth Longfellow mentioned the Acadian Coast in his 1847 epic poem, Evangeline: "Into the golden Mississippi floated Acadians. A band of exiles, a nation scattered, bound by common belief and misfortune. Men, women and children guided by hope, seeking the Acadian Coast."

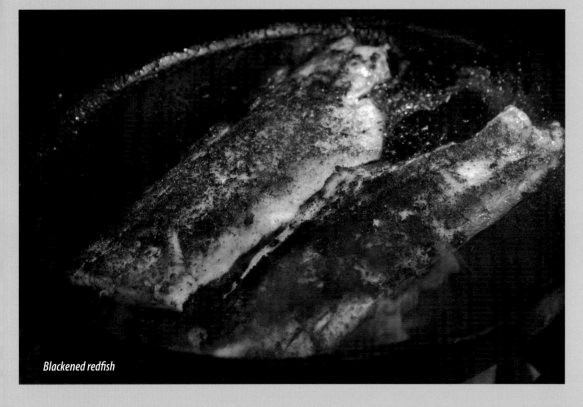

Blackened redfish

Hernando de Soto discovers the Mississippi

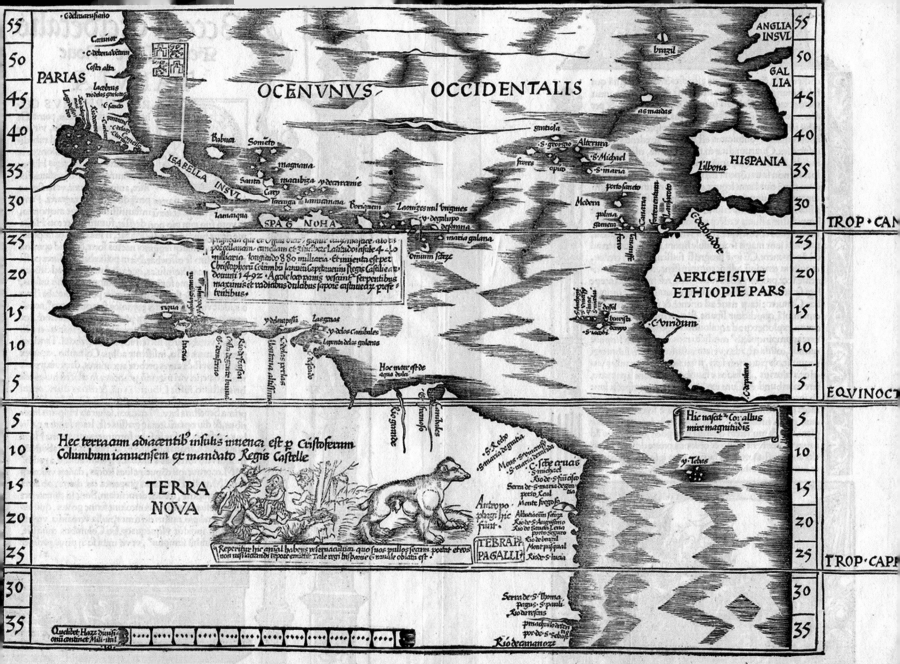

Though the French first colonized Louisiana, the Spanish conquistadors explored and mapped the land as early as the 1500s. Spain's period of glory, when she was "mistress of the world and queen of the ocean," began with the reign of Queen Isabella and King Ferdinand in the latter part of the 15th century. Known together as "the Catholic Kings," Isabella and Ferdinand's driving ambition led to the recapture of Spain from the Moors, the Inquisition and the ruthless expulsion of Spanish Jews with confiscation of their wealth and property. However, Isabella and Ferdinand are probably best remembered for sponsoring Christopher Columbus' voyage that ultimately led to the discovery of the New World.

With Columbus' discovery, the dominant powers (Spain, England, France and Portugal) rushed to conquer the new land. Spain, in its empire-building period, firmly established influence in the Americas and along the Gulf of Mexico corridor.

In 1501, Alberto Cantino first mapped the Gulf region

Hernando de Soto's burial

and was perhaps the first European to visit the Mississippi River. In 1504, Hernando Cortez sailed the Gulf and had conquered Mexico by 1521. Treasure ships returned to Spain laden with gold and silver.

Juan Ponce de Leon, known for his legendary Fountain of Youth, claimed La Florida in 1512. De Leon led the first official Spanish exploration of the Gulf region. Though his 1521 Calusa settlement failed, he probably explored the future Louisiana Territory. Panfilo de Narvaez organized an overland expedition to the New World in 1527. He met disaster after disaster in his mission to possess Florida. After nearly a decade of wandering, five of the 600 men reached Mexico. One of them, Alvar Nunez Cabeza de Vaca, who spent years as an Indian slave in Louisiana, wrote a narrative about the expedition describing Louisiana's coastline.

Hernando de Soto was the first to be officially recognized as the discoverer of the Mississippi River in 1541. Unfortunately, he died of fever during the exploration. He was unceremoniously buried in the Mississippi River to hide his death from the Native American tribes, so they could not desecrate his body. According to legend, de Soto was buried in a log, which sunk to the bottom of the river to prevent his body from floating to the surface. De Soto's lieutenant, Luis de Moscoso, led the expedition down the river noting in his journal that it took 17 days to reach the Gulf and complaining of "swift, high waters."

Alonso Alvarez de Pineda drew the oldest surviving maps depicting the Gulf region. Barely a sketch, the 1519 map outlined the Gulf and what was apparently the Mississippi River, known then as "Rio del Espiritu Santo." The 1524 Cortez map depicted a great river, which the native people called "Michi Sipi." The 1584 Chaves map did the same. Low lands, high waters, reeds, rushes and mud banks made the Mississippi River nearly invisible from the Gulf,

even at close proximity. Because of this, the Spaniards called the river "Rio del Escondido" or "Hidden River." They also referred to it as "Rio del Palizada" for what they considered fallen trees forming a palisade blocking the river's entrance from view.

The 17th century became the era of colonization in North America and successful settlements were finally established in the Gulf region. In the 16th century, at least a dozen settlements failed. For many, death seemed to be a welcome relief from starvation, inclement weather and brutal native tribes. The most notable settlement in the Gulf region was that of America's oldest city, St. Augustine, Fla., founded by Menendez de Aviles in 1565.

Though the Spanish acquired geographical knowledge of the Louisiana Territory, their exploration ceased. The French arrived and claimed the land for Louis XIV. Not until 1762 did Spain again claim the land they explored in the 1500s.

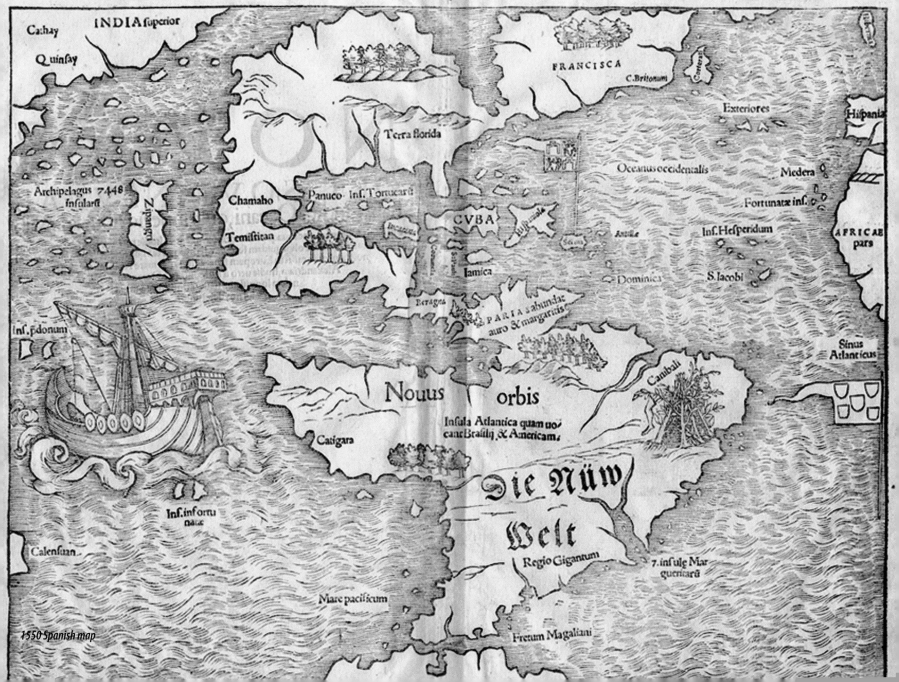

1550 Spanish map

SPANISH COLONIAL LOUISIANA

With the secret Treaty of Fontainebleau in 1762, Spain acquired Louisiana from France, thus owning the entire Southwest. Although transferred in 1762, the colonists did not learn of the deed until October 1764. Suddenly living under Spanish rule rather than French, the inhabitants of New Orleans felt devastated and betrayed. In 1764, King Louis XV of France agreed with Spain that French soldiers in New Orleans would enlist in Spain's army. The independent-minded colonists objected and petitioned King Louis to revoke the order, but he refused, because they were no longer his concern.

In fact, the Louisiana colony had never been profitable and by 1756 the cost of the colony was exorbitant. France received precious little revenue for its investment. Expenses mounted; the population stagnated at fewer than 7,500 people after 50 years of settlement; the inhabitants were lazy and insubordinate; they drank too much and nearly three-quarters of them were bankrupt. In 1758, France ceased sending colonial supplies and even discontinued correspondence.

It became evident during the French and Indian War that France would lose Canada to England. Because France was unable to protect and provide for Louisiana, France gave Louisiana to Spain rather than lose it to the British. However, the Spanish were not interested in acquiring the Louisiana colony, until they declared war on England in early 1762. When the English captured Havana from Spain in August, Spain realized Louisiana might be an important bargaining chip. While the colony would be expensive, it might develop into a profitable venture. Plus, the location of the colony was important to the defense of the Spanish colonial empire. There was an excellent port and if Spain

Don Antonio de Ulloa, Louisiana's first Spanish governor

DON ALESSANDRO O'REILLY

did not secure Louisiana, it might fall to Great Britain. In France, only a few protested, including the philosopher Voltaire. He wrote that he could not conceive how Frenchmen could abandon "the most beautiful climate on the earth, from which one may have tobacco, silk, indigo, a thousand useful products." He said if he had not just built a new estate, "I would go and establish myself in Louisiana."

Though Spain ruled Louisiana from 1762-1803, the French controlled and governed the colony until Don Antonio de Ulloa arrived as the first Spanish governor in March 1766. His less than warm reception escalated into open rebellion in 1768, when he fled for his life by ship. The city's Supreme Council wrote a letter reaffirming allegiance to France. The Spaniards countered by sending Don Alejandro O'Reilly, an Irish-born, soldier of fortune, to stop the rebellion. He arrived with 20 ships and 2,000 soldiers, which were more men than lived in New Orleans at the time. O'Reilly arrested and shot the more vocal opponents of the revolt, though he pardoned everyone except the leaders. Known as "Bloody O'Reilly," the French Creoles never forgave him. O'Reilly abolished the Supreme Council, substituting a Cabildo or Spanish governing body that maintained law and order in the community. O'Reilly replaced French laws with Spanish laws and ultimately founded Louisiana's Spanish regime. Don Luis de Unzaga y Amezaga replaced him as governor and married a French Creole woman. He did not enforce Spanish laws as stringently as other Spanish governors.

In 1776, Don Bernardo de Galvez became governor of the Spanish colony. Galvez married a Creole woman and like his predecessor, was lax in enforcing the strict Spanish economic regulations that required trade with only Spain and Havana. Though Spain was officially neutral in the American Revolution, Galvez aided the Americans. In fact, he and his Spanish military helped ensure the success of the American revolutionaries.

In May 1779, Spain declared war against Great Britain. Immediately, the English planned an attack on New Orleans. Galvez led his troops to victory in the British strongholds of Baton Rouge, Mobile and Pensacola. Because he worked so hard for the colony by leading the French Creoles to brilliant military victories over the British, they soon forgot Galvez was a Spaniard. In 1785, he was named Captain-General of Louisiana, Cuba and Florida, as well as Viceroy of Mexico. A statue of him still stands at the foot of Canal Street in New Orleans.

Don Esteban Rodriguez Miro was the next Spanish governor who also married a Creole named Marie Celeste Elenore de McCarty. During Miro's tenure, many additional Acadians came to Louisiana, joining those who had arrived following their exile from Acadia by the English. The Spanish welcomed the Acadians who were considered ideal settlers, because they were Catholic, small farmers, poor and anti-British. The Acadians were sent upriver from New Orleans to settle, so they could provide a buffer against the English living in the areas around Baton Rouge. The Acadians were industrious and hardworking. They cleared and planted land, provided food for New Orleans markets and helped with communication along the Mississippi. Land was given to them in small concessions at specific locations along the Mississippi. Rations of corn were provided to each person, and each family received an ax, hoe, sickle, spade, two hens, a cock and a two-month old pig. Each head of a family also received a shotgun. Sufficient food was delivered from the rations at military posts to enable the Acadians to survive until the first crop was harvested.

This was all in keeping with Miro's policy of making Louisiana a stronger colony. He promoted immigration, kept the Native Americans at peace and increased trade and commerce. The French seemed to have no recognizable Native American policy beyond furnishing a limited number of gifts and inferior trading goods. The Spanish, however, tried to protect the Indians, made treaties with the tribes and regularly gave them large amounts of gifts.

The new trade regulations under the Spanish administrators allowed for the promotion of trade and commerce. It was not long before Louisiana trading posts were making a good profit and New Orleans was a busy port city.

The great fire of New Orleans in 1788 destroyed more than 800 buildings. A strong blowing wind coupled with orders given in Spanish that the French Creoles could not understand wreaked havoc on the settlement. New building codes followed that utilized solid, fireproof construction, creating the dominate Spanish appearance of the French Quarter today. The Spanish patios, or inner courtyards, along with shady arcades and cooling fountains were all Spanish design. By the time the French returned in the early 1800s, New Orleans looked like a Spanish town with tile roofs, stucco, wrought iron balcony railings and Spanish street names. The Cabildo, St. Louis Cathedral and the Presbyter exemplified typical Spanish architecture. Two other fires destroyed most of the remaining French architectural influence. The only surviving French colonial building is the Ursuline Convent on Chartres Street, which was completed in 1751.

Don Francisco Luis Hector, Baron de Carondelet, became governor in 1791. He developed the city's first lighting system and a bilingual, night police force. To meet the costs of the watchmen and the streetlights, Carondelet levied a tax on every chimney. He had engineers design fortification plans for New Orleans, while repairing old ones. In 1797, the Baron de Carondelet was promoted to a high position in the Spanish government at Quito, Ecuador.

Don Bernardo de Galvez

Don Esteban Rodriguez Miro

Don Francisco Luis Hector, Baron de Carondelet

The people of Louisiana regretted his leaving, because he had protected their rights and treated everyone fairly. He had conducted a strong and businesslike administration and was one of the greatest of Louisiana's colonial governors.

Gayoso de Lemos, Casa Calvo and Salcedo were the next governors during which there was much unrest. Brigadier General Juan Manuel de Salcedo served as governor until November 30, 1803, when he officially returned Louisiana to the French prior to the Louisiana Purchase by the United States.

When Spain acquired Louisiana in 1762, it was a small unprofitable colony of less than 7,500 inhabitants. Apart from New Orleans, it had only a few small villages along the Mississippi and other rivers. By the end of Spanish rule, Louisiana was a large and prosperous colony with more than 50,000 inhabitants, 30,000 of whom lived along the lower Mississippi and in New Orleans. Economic progress had been slow prior to 1762. Some French governors had been more interested in making fortunes for themselves

than in providing good government. The Spanish governors had generally been hardworking, intelligent and honest and the Spanish systems of government and administration of justice had been efficient and fair to all. Under Spanish rule, settlers from many countries had established farms, villages and towns in Louisiana and a better means of communication had been organized.

Though Louisiana colonists lived under Spanish rule, they refused to speak Spanish; there was never a Spanish language newspaper; and the language of commerce was French. Spaniards stationed in New Orleans were primarily single men, many of whom married French women, learned to speak French and raised French-speaking children. These children became French Creoles, not Spanish Creoles. Spanish cultural and architectural influences were absorbed into mainstream French life in New Orleans. In this way, the Spaniards left few traces of their period of colonial rule. However, they did leave their spirit of chivalry, a few laws and geographic names. Though the French in Louisiana never fully adopted Spanish ways and customs, they owed a greater debt of gratitude to Spain than to their mother country.

THE CANARY ISLANDERS

Don Bernardo de Galvez's father, Matias de Galvez, was governor and lieutenant of the King of the Canary Islands. This chain of 13 islands, located about 60 miles off the coast of Morocco, consists of seven inhabited islands including Fuerteventura, Lanzarote, Gran Canaria, Hierro, Tenerife, La Palma and Gomera. The Canaries were explored and colonized in the 1300s and became the first colonial territory of the Spanish empire. Because these islands fell directly in the path of the trade winds that pushed sailing vessels toward the Americas, it was a pivotal port. In fact, the Canary Islands were Columbus' last stop before discovering the New World.

Galvez recruited Canary Islanders to help protect and settle the Louisiana colony. The first Isleños (Canary Islanders) arrived in Louisiana in 1778 and continued to come until 1783. They were strategically settled in four locations around New Orleans to guard approaches to the city. The first settlement was Galveztown, located just below Baton Rouge. The other settlements were Valenzuela, located along Bayou Lafourche; Barataria, located along Bayou des Familles in Jefferson Parish; and La Concepcion, later San Bernardo de Galvez, located in St. Bernard Parish along Bayou Terre-aux-Boeufs. Bayougoulas, a fifth settlement, was planned but never completed. Today, most Louisianians who can trace their heritage to Spain are the remaining descendants of Canary Island fisherman who settled in St. Bernard Parish. Elderly Isleños still speak an archaic Spanish dialect brought to Louisiana more than two centuries ago.

NATCHITOCHES

When Mexico was conquered and settled by the Spanish and Mexico City was established as the capital of New Spain, expeditions were sent to conquer new land for the King of Spain. In all directions from Mexico City, ranchos, missions and presidios (prisons) were established. Spanish conquistadors and clerics explored these regions. Franciscan friars attempted to convert the Indians to Catholicism. Aside from the duties of the Spanish missions to help spread the Catholic faith, they were also observation and trading posts of the Spaniards. Spain gradually pushed settlements into Texas and western Louisiana. All roads leading from these establishments back to Mexico City to the Viceroy, who was the direct representative of the King, were called "El Camino Real" or "The Road to the King."

In 1714, the French governor Cadillac called upon Louis Juchereau de St. Denis to establish a post in northwest Louisiana to stop Spanish infiltration from Texas at the Sabine River. Natchitoches was established and became the oldest permanently inhabited area in the Louisiana Purchase territory and the oldest town in the state of Louisiana, including New Orleans. An earlier Spanish

expedition had established a settlement at Los Adais, capital of the Texas country, just 15 miles west of French Natchitoches. Because of the close proximity of these two settlements, some conflict was inevitable. After considerable correspondence between the Spanish and French leaders, an indefinite boundary somewhat east of the Sabine River was accepted by both sides.

Because the French and Spanish were backwoods neighbors for nearly 50 years, the inhabitants of Natchitoches were little affected by the news in the autumn of 1764 that their province had been given to

"In 1779 Governor Bernardo de Galvez explained to his uncle that 'persons of distinction' resisted service in the militia where they were compelled to stand in rank next to their shoemakers and barbers. Galvez, sympathizing with the plight of the elite, created a cavalry troop for this class. The caribiniers would now ride while the common sort walked."

Chef David Harris making bread at the Rural Life Museum, Baton Rouge, La.

between the French and Spanish of this area. In fact, even St. Denis married a Spaniard. On a trip to trade goods on the Rio Grande, he was taken prisoner by the Spanish Commandant. During the weeks that passed, St. Denis fell in love with the Commandant's granddaughter, Manuela. After a long courtship, the girl's father at last gave his consent to the marriage, and in 1716 Senorita Manuela de Sanchez y Ramon became the bride of St. Denis.

During the Spanish regime in Louisiana, Los Adais was abandoned and the site of government moved to Natchitoches. The "El Camino Real" began in Mexico City and ended at the north end of Front Street in Natchitoches. Even today, Natchitoches' architecture, place names, traditions and customs reflect the Spanish influence in the area.

FOOD IN NEW ORLEANS DURING THE SPANISH REGIME

As during the French colonial period, the city suffered serious food shortages. Undesirable items such as rum, molasses, sugar, adulterated and spoiled oils and raisins arrived from Havana rather than the needed clothes, food and agricultural tools. Items from Europe were outrageously priced, so contraband trade developed rapidly. In 1772, 1779 and 1781, the Cabildo used city funds to purchase foodstuffs.

In 1796, conditions were so dire that supplies were requested from Havana and Vera Cruz. John McDonogh, New Orleans businessman and future philanthropist, chartered his boat to carry the merchandise. United States merchants were invited to send flour to New Orleans. Corn was obtained and rice purchased in case of future scarcity. Cabildo members nearly donned baker's caps and aprons themselves in their stringent efforts to stretch the existing flour, and rice supplies. They closely supervised food experiments that mixed rice and flour to bake into edible versions of bread.

Ultimately, coffee and flour were imported from America. Furniture, linens, hats, laces, jewelry, silks, glassware and olive oil arrived from France. England supplied hardware, fine cloths and manufactured goods, especially of cotton. Wine and whiskey were imported as well as condiments such as brandied fruits, sausages, pickles and anchovies. Merchandising and shipping formed the nucleus of economic life in New Orleans.

During the Spanish regime, the streets of New Orleans were muddy, filled with holes and unlighted for most of the period. Often, floodwaters spilled over the levees, leaving dead fish as a breeding ground for disease and stench. Markets existed in the city, though they stank and were badly ventilated. Rubbish and dead fish were thrown on the quays adding to the city's sanitation problems.

As the city grew, tradesmen were needed including bakers, butchers, tailors, carpenters, candlestick makers and a variety of other skilled laborers. New Orleans became home to pastry cooks, confectioners, tavern owners and innkeepers. Many men of the city were hunters and fishermen, while others rowed the mail boats. There were city slaves selling their garden surplus. Native Americans peddled vegetables, fish, blankets and trinkets on the levees. As the port and market of New Orleans grew, transients including sailors and boatmen increasingly blended into the town's inhabitants.

Flour was a rare and much sought after commodity. Often, Cabildo subcommittees stormed through the warehouses seeking and destroying spoiled flour often by throwing it into the river. In June 1777, a sanitary inspector was appointed, because the flour was so wretched that illness was caused from the baked bread.

The bakers thrived in the city. Standard practice maintained mixing good flour with cheaply bought rancid and inferior flour, then selling the product as fresh bread. It was not uncommon for retailers to sell bread short weight. In 1773, a gauger was appointed to protect against abuses in the weighing and measuring of foodstuffs. During shortages, merchants met vessels carrying the flour, purchased the merchandise, then held it for high prices. In 1793, bread prices were fixed based on the price of flour with the Cabildo posting official prices weekly throughout the Spanish period. Monthly, 600 barrels of flour were needed so that each citizen could obtain just under a pound of bread daily.

The butchers flourished. Everyone in the Louisiana colony ate meat, which was plentiful and cheap. In fact, it was written that, "No country on earth eats more of it . . . little pieces of bread are served with great pieces of meat; the

the King of Spain. Even though there were conflicts over boundaries and contraband trade, in the evenings and on holidays a unique hospitality existed between the two cultures. For many years Natchitoches was without a regular priest, so the people depended upon the Spanish fathers from Los Adais to perform their religious services. Records show that there were many intermarriages

Old Spanish trail

amount the children eat would frighten a European." Beef retailed for six sols a pound and was usually sold out by 8 or 9 o'clock in the morning. Good pork and inferior mutton could be bought for one escalin. (See Table of Equivalent Money Values in French section.) Veal, game and poultry such as turkeys and chickens were fairly cheap. Salt meat from the Illinois cattle was inexpensive as was fish such as perch, pike, sturgeon, eels and carp. Those of lesser means generally ate carp, because a 10- to 12-pound fish only cost one escalin. Oysters, crawfish and shrimp were available as well.

Prior to the Spanish regime in Louisiana, meat was supplied to the city by hunting parties operating in the Natchez area or through salt beef imports from the French West Indies, which originated in the English Colonies and Ireland. To increase meat supplies and encourage herd development in the 1770s, the Cabildo granted a meat market monopoly. Competitive bids were taken with interested parties submitting a sum and suggested quantity, price and location of the slaughter sheds. The primary contractor acted as lessee of the butcher shops of the central meat market. By 1789, the Cabildo discontinued the contract system and established a free meat market. Livestock raisers and butchers negotiated their own sales terms, though the Cabildo retained a tax of three reals per head of cattle sold in the city.

The Cabildo established retail prices for beef and pork, supervised and policed the operation of the central meat market where the butchers rented stalls and tried to keep the pens and slaughter sheds outside the city limits. Generally, adequate meat supplies at moderate prices were assured, plus a revenue of more than 4,000 piastres annually was guaranteed. During the late 1790s, the butchers' tax was increased to support the streetlights, when residents refused to pay a chimney tax for the same purpose. Butchers were unhappy about the increased tax rate, but it was better than the threat of a meat monopoly.

Vegetables in the Spanish colonial period were scarce and exorbitantly priced. New Orleans depended on Des Allemands, the German community located 40 miles upriver, to supply vegetables, eggs and butter, though the latter was difficult to obtain. In 1798, the Cabildo sympathized with vegetable retailers who protested the weekly tax on their stands. The council acted against itinerant peddlers who littered the levees and sold spoiled foods of unknown origin.

Because olive oil was scarce, it was imported. Bear's oil was obtained from the Native Americans. In January 1771 the Cabildo released a memorandum stating that bear fat could be taxed three reals, instead of two and one-half. The tavern keeping business was lucrative and nearly

The Cabildo in New Orleans' Jackson Square

monopolized by the Catalans. The crowded taverns were located at every cross street and the taps flowed incessantly. Large wine imports coupled with great demand and fixed pricing by the tavern keepers made many of them rich. Though thrifty and industrious people, they were considered inferior by the Creoles.

There were inns, boardinghouses and hotels, which were fairly good though highly priced, because of expensive provisions, taxes and a questionable demand. The city had a sugar refinery and 12 distilleries, which produced considerable amounts of tafia.

24,000 pesos to purchase 3,000 barrels of flour, thus beginning the American commercial invasion of New Orleans. Floods engulfed New Orleans and devastated farmlands. In August, September and October 1794, hurricanes ravished the colony, ruined crops and destroyed buildings and shipping. That same year another fire destroyed most of the French colonial structures that remained as well as the flour reserve. In autumn 1796, yellow fever epidemics hit the city. Many fled to the countryside, Barataria or at least to the other side of the river. The extreme number of fatalities inspired innovative precautions, which included wearing garlic and camphor, burning tar and using hartshorn and vinegar. The hartshorn and vinegar combination was sprinkled around the rooms and over the servants.

Thankfully, the Spanish government provided relief following these disasters. The Cabildo authorized agents to purchase food supplies. Rice was obtained for the colony and flour was requisitioned from the merchants, distributed to the city's bakers, then sold to the inhabitants.

The Cabildo influenced the daily economic life of the town. Taxes were passed establishing a permanent revenue base for city improvements. During O'Reilly's administration, nearly $2,000 was given to the Cabildo annually in tax revenue. The French administration's anchorage tax on vessels was maintained by the Spanish for the upkeep of the levees and harbor. Each barrel of tafia imported at New Orleans was taxed one piastre, later raised to two. Taverns, billiard halls and rooming houses were taxed. Bakers paid a tax on each barrel of flour used. These taxes along with the tax on the butchers supported the streetlighting system. Intermittently, operational licenses were required of dancehalls, vegetable and fish stands and for auctioneers, river pilots and other professions. Fees were charged by the public gauger, port warden and other officers for the salaries of civil servants. By 1776, the revenue from cabaret owners alone surpassed the total city budget of 1770.

The Cabildo oversaw construction and repair of roads, bridges and levees; port regulation; city lighting; sanitation; police and fire protection; and regulation of the food market. The most difficult task facing the Cabildo was regulating the market place to guarantee an edible food supply at equitable prices for the producer, manufacturer and consumer. The Cabildo set prices, inspected for quality and assured the use of standard weights and measures. They also worked to ensure that food shortages did not benefit monopolists at the expense of the public welfare.

In 1798, Gayoso de Lemos issued a succession of edicts to improve the streets and rid the city of disease. Henceforth, swine could not be raised or kept in the city. Citizens were responsible for the walks fronting their property

THE CABILDO

The Cabildo, which was fairly efficient, encountered monumental tasks of governance. A severe economic depression characterized the first years of Spanish rule. Wars detained municipal progress, cut off food supplies and threatened the city with economic deprivation. In 1788, a fire destroyed New Orleans. Miro had to discontinue the daily rations of rice issued to 200 families. He and the Cabildo alleviated food supply issues by obtaining flour, medicines and other needed items from Philadelphia. Three ships were sent to Philadelphia with

Spanish architecture

Dining in a New Orleans courtyard

means "land of salt" in the Phoenician language. On the west coast the Phoenicians built another city known today as Cadiz. Here, they planted olive trees and vineyards. The vineyards produced the sherry of Spain, which is still world famous, and in time, the olive trees made Spain the world's largest producer of olive oil.

The Moors, another of Spain's conquerors, had a definite impact on the country's cuisine. They brought spices from the Orient including cinnamon, cumin, saffron and cloves. The Moors brought rice, almonds and sugarcane. In fact, the southern coast of Spain has many sugar plantations, and Spanish pastries are syrupy sweet as are those of the Near East.

Undeniably, ingredients from the Americas influenced the cuisine of the Old World. When Columbus and his men returned home, they ushered in the modern era of the Spanish kitchen. Before Columbus, Europe lived without the tomato, potato, chocolate and vanilla. There were no green beans, chili peppers, bell peppers, corn or peanuts.

Natchitoches meat pies

There were also many introductions to the New World from Europe. The Spanish and Portuguese brought seasonings, spice plants, black-eyed peas, onions, watermelons, European grape varieties, herbs and citrus fruits not to mention farm animals such as cattle, goats, pigs and sheep. The result was a new family of cuisine and regionalism in which Spanish ideas mixed with Aztec and Incan practices. Though much of this took centuries to evolve, Columbus was indirectly the initiator of this delectable cuisine.

In the written records of his voyages, Columbus brought with him bread, wine, meat and

and had to keep them swept as well as sprinkled during the summer. Dirty water could not be poured into the gutters and throwing leather trimmings, shavings, tailor's remnants and oyster shells in the roadway was prohibited.

During this period the city government and its contractors employed slaves for construction jobs. Slaves were hired out as coachmen, cooks, gardeners, maids, stevedores, teamsters, draymen and garbage collectors. Many peddled goods on the levees and street corners despite city ordinances. Though Miro ordered that black women abstain from licentious lifestyles, many became prostitutes, competing with their white counterparts.

SPANISH FOOD
Spain itself was a conquered land. Not only did the vast resources of metals attract the Phoenicians, but also the rich sources of salt, which were as precious in the ancient world as gold. In fact, the present-day city of Malaga

fish. After the discovery of the West Indies, he began exchanging foodstuffs with the inhabitants such as molasses for fruit and other plants. On the first voyage, food specimens were collected and much attention was paid to unfamiliar foods. Horticultural experiments were conducted with seeds brought from Europe. Spring melon, cucumber, Old World squash and radishes flourished, though onions, lettuce and scallions initially failed.

Spanish cooking is characterized by the use of olive oil, pimiento, paprika, garlic, onions, tomatoes, a generous use of parsley and an occasional orange flavor in meat and poultry dishes. Contrary to popular belief, the cuisine of Spain is not hot. It is one of Spain's paradoxes that a country largely responsible for providing pepper and other spices to the Western World should have produced a cuisine that uses so little spice. Occasionally, a pinch of cayenne may appear in a recipe, but even black pepper is used sparingly. The confusion arises because many people call Mexican food Spanish, which it is not.

Many of the Europeans who came to Louisiana brought their cooks or chefs. Four of the Spanish governors, Ulloa, Unzaga, Galvez and Salcedo were from the Andalusian area in southern Spain. Andalusian foods have an almost Oriental flavor with the extensive use of spices such as

Paella

Caldo

No. 672. Cotton Levee, Canal St.

cinnamon, cumin, saffron and cloves. Fruits are used in meat or rice dishes and in sauces. Red beans came to the New World from Andalusia as did, incidentally, wrought iron gateways, overhanging balconies and enclosed courtyards.

Miro was from Catalonia in northeast Spain where the food resembled that of southern France. The countryside had lush vineyards, rich black soil and acres of well-tended fruit trees. Fish cooked in tomato sauce was traditionally served on Christmas Eve in Catalonia.

In the center of Spain is Madrid, the Castilian area that was the birthplace of many conquistadors as well as Queen Isabella. The cuisine of the Castilians is simple and hearty with few sauces, but much garlic and onions.

Galicia, in the northwest area of Spain above Portugal, was the homeland of Gayoso de Lemos. It is known for caldo, a broth of turnip greens, potatoes, white beans, salted pork, onions and smoked pork. Empanadas, which are elaborate Spanish turnovers filled with chopped meat, usually beef, chopped fruit such as peaches or raisins, vegetables, olives and sometimes hard-boiled eggs, have long been a specialty of Galicia. Natchitoches is known for its meat pies, which are turnovers filled with ground meat and seasonings. The original Louisiana version is believed to have been developed by the Natchitoches Indians and improved upon by the Spanish.

Paella, native to Valencia though made all over Spain, is the country's most famous dish. It is made with meat and fish mixed with rice, vegetables and seasonings including saffron. The top is decoratively finished with red pepper, which has been fried a minute in oil, shrimp, green vegetables and mussels or clams in their open shells. Paella was first cooked outdoors over open fires, and many cooks maintain that is the best way to prepare it even today. It is probable that paella is the forerunner of one of Louisiana's most famous dishes, jambalaya. The Creole name jambalaya is derived from the French word for ham, jambon, and the African word for rice, yaya. The dish is truly a merging of cultures.

Without contradiction, many of Louisiana's most famous dishes and most famous ingredients are direct descendants of culinary masterpieces from our earliest inhabitants. Even the mirliton, also called vegetable pear or chayote squash, came to Louisiana from the Canary Islands.

DAWNING OF THE LOUISIANA PURCHASE
During the final years of Spanish domination, New Orleans had transformed from the backwater village it had been to an up and coming port city. Trade in New Orleans' port founded the city's mercantile prosperity. Tobacco and indigo were Louisiana's staple crops with great possibilities emerging in cotton and sugar. By the beginning of the 1800s, New Orleans' merchants were well aware of their

strategic position with a great harbor and port facilities.

At the time of the Louisiana Purchase, the industry of New Orleans was comprised of a number of sawmills and distilleries. In the suburbs there were two cotton mills, a sugar refinery and a small rice mill. There were also plants manufacturing hair powder, vermicelli and small shot.

When the Americans took possession of New Orleans, bakers were still adulterating flour, peddlers were still selling their wares on the levee and tavern owners were in cahoots to fix the price of wine. An ordinary day's wage was about four escalins or 50 cents. Half of the daily wage of a laborer or artisan helper was spent to purchase a loaf of bread and a pound of meat. Living was expensive and few could afford to live in comfort.

By 1803, the population of New Orleans had grown to 8,000 inhabitants with some estimates as high as 11,000, because of immigration to the colony. Few Native Americans remained and most citizens were of European, American or African descent.

Africa

Cooking shrimps

"Until the lion writes its own story, the tale of the hunt will always glorify the hunter." African proverb

WEST AFRICAN SLAVES

Senegambia, the region of Africa located between the Senegal and Gambia rivers, was home to two-thirds of the slaves brought to Louisiana by the French slave trade. The French were established slave traders in Senegambia long before the slave trade to Louisiana began. In 1664, they monopolized this industry in the Senegambian region with established trading posts at Gorée, St. Louis and Galam (Fort St. Joseph).

During the 1720s the Company of the Indies, which organized the slave trade to Louisiana, focused their efforts in Senegal where they had exclusive trading rights. Despite this they faced strong competition from the Dutch, English, Portuguese and African slave traders.

Gorée, the best port in the Senegal concession, served as the main warehouse of slaves. From here, slaves from all the trading posts departed for America. As early as 1719, 450 slaves arrived in the Louisiana colony from the Bight of Benin. Additional slaves came from this area in 1721 (834 slaves) and in 1728 (464 slaves).

The first slave ship from Senegal, *Le Ruby*, arrived in Louisiana in July 1720. Between that year and 1723, more than 500 slaves came from Senegambia. In 1721, 294 slaves arrived from the Congo and Angola regions.

Between 1726 and 1731 nearly all of the Company's slave trade voyages were bound for Louisiana. During these years, 12 slave ships arrived in Louisiana from Senegambia and one from the Bight of Benin. More than half of Louisiana's slaves arrived from Senegambia during these five years. The last Senegambian slave ship arrived in 1743 and was a privately financed voyage.

Because of Senegal River floods, the Senegal Valley was fertile. The people cultivated rice, corn, tobacco, indigo, cotton and several varieties of peas. Interestingly, these same crops were growing in Louisiana. African farmers also grew melons, vegetables and collected salt from the mouth of the Senegal River.

On the prairie lands of the Senegal region there were sheep, cows, goats and fowl including partridges, guineas, wood pigeons, sea and migratory birds. The natives hunted and ate wild game.

The Senegalese were talented goldsmiths, silversmiths, blacksmiths, coppersmiths, horseshoe and arms makers. They crafted knives, hatchets, axes and blades. Generally, they worked in groups of no less than three people and maintained a relaxed, informal manner. Work was social and ceremonial.

Nude gangs with lightweight, long-handled, crescent-shaped spades worked the fields. A lord, who supervised the fieldwork, walked ahead of the group with individuals called "griots" singing and loudly beating drums. The lord, wearing a sword on his side and carrying a whip, sang and gestured with the griots. The griots' song dictated the speed and tenacity of the work.

Senegambian women threshed rice, corn and millet. They made couscous and other foods and drinks, spun cotton, made clothes, dyed thread and cloth, cultivated tobacco and grains, cleaned the huts, cared for the animals and collected wood and water. Additionally, the women chased away the mosquitoes when their husbands were conversing.

By the early 18th century, natives living along the Senegal River and in the areas to the east and south were Muslims. The people of the Mandinga kingdom were the most

THE RETURN OF THE CAPTURED AFRICANS.

Return of the captured Africans

devout. The blacks living between the Gambia River and Guinea were idolaters, while others were believed to be savages with no religion. The Mandinga drank no wine or liquor; they observed fasting for Ramadan; they worked hard to cultivate the land; they raised cattle, sheep, goats and fowl, but no pigs. These people enjoyed commerce and long voyages. They loved and helped each other and the only captives they had were those being punished for a crime. They were polite, witty, perceptive and most could read and write the Arab language. They made charms called gris-gris. They treated their women poorly and practiced female circumcision. Many native men had multiple wives.

The Isle of St. Louis and the territory at and to the south of the mouth of the Senegal River was known as The Kingdom of the Wolofs. The French men living at St. Louis were attracted to the dark-skinned Wolof women. In fact, many lived in straw huts with these women who "cooked and cleaned" for them. To stop this behavior, the men were required to eat at the fort and attend morning and evening prayers, or they would not receive liquor distributed at the end of Mass. In 1724, young Parisian girls were requested for marriage to these workers and sailors to prevent their return to France.

During the 1720s few Wolof people were sent to Louisiana. However, the French colonists called those who arrived Senegalese, though they retained the Wolof designation among themselves. The French preferred the dark-skinned Wolof people, because they believed they were of the purest blood. They were considered the best slaves for home use, especially because they were not as resistant to heat or as skilled at tilling the soil. They were more faithful, easily learned skills and were proud and good commanders of other blacks.

During the 1720s neither the Fulbe people living along the middle of the Senegal River nor the Mandinga sold their people or allowed others to sell their people into slavery. However, the Mandinga were prominent slave traders and sold the Bambara who lived on the upper Senegal River. During the 1720s the Bambara warred among their own kingdoms. Many were slaves of the king or were captured by their own people and sold into slavery. The slave trade peaked when war raged in Bambarana.

1840 map of West Africa

WEST AFRICA.

Between 1727 and 1729, about 1000 slaves were sent from Galam to St. Louis annually. Bambara slaves also came from the post near the mouth of the Gambia River. Slave raiding in Bambarana was an organized institution. An association of hunters became slave raiders. Warfare booty included enslaved people and became the property of the hunters. Not all of these slaves were sent to the New World. Some captives remained in their homeland while others were sent to desert or interior markets.

Large numbers of Bambara people were transported to Louisiana where they were considered the best Africans for labor. These Africans were robust, intelligent, obedient and good-natured. They rarely ran away or revolted. They worked hard as long as they were properly fed. Agriculture was their principal labor and millet and sorghum were their major crops.

In the Senegal concession, the Bambara became domestics and were used as guides, interpreters and reinforcements for European troops. They were brave, loyal and skillful warriors. An oral history tradition existed among the Bambara, which bards presented as legends and myths. Bambaran conversation was peppered with proverbs. Wisdom was handed down from generation to generation and historical information preserved.

The success of French colonial Louisiana was based not only on African labor but also on African knowledge of rice cultivation. Slave traders selected and purchased blacks who knew how to cultivate rice. They also obtained barrels of seed rice. By 1720 rice became an important food staple and an abundant crop along the Mississippi River.

Indigo grew wild in Senegambia as well as Louisiana. It is reasonable to assume that the Africans were instrumental in sharing their knowledge of indigo processing. The slaves were highly regarded for their vast knowledge of herbal medicine as well.

Upon their arrival the slaves worked to clear and cultivate the land, dig ditches and build drainage systems. They built levees, buildings, fences and cut trees and wood. The Company slaves worked on fortifications, as sailors and navigators, city guards and gathered fresh water, food and supplies for the garrison. They worked in the general storehouse, the hospital and marine headquarters.

SLAVE LIFE IN LOUISIANA

The reproachable act of human bondage has stained mankind's history through the ages. Exploiting races of intelligent, cultured people and treating them as beasts of burden was a grievous indignity for all humankind. While the imprisoned suffered hardships and, at times, severe consequences for "misbehavior," Louisiana's history would be incomplete without the Africans' culinary and cultural legacy to the state.

The majority of Louisiana's slaves were from regions of West Africa, which represented the high and complex

Sale of estates, pictures and slaves in the rotunda

SLAVE QUARTERS AT

PLANTATION SLAVES
Records Taken From Inventory of J. T. Roman's Estate –
April 1848 Filed at St. James Parish Courthouse

HOUSE SLAVES – 20 INCLUDING CHILDREN

Deteville (34 yrs.)	$1,045
Simon (18 yrs.) Son of Antoinette	$1,000
Méanna (34 yrs.) – Mulatress seamstress with her 5 children:	
Charles (10 yrs.), Raphael (7 yrs.), Rosalie (5 yrs.),	
Elizabeth (2 yrs.) Genevieve (10 mos.), estimated together at	$1,500
Anna (45 yrs.) Negress laundress	$900
Rose (36 yrs.) – With her two children:	
Nicholas (3), Céleste (10 mos.), estimated together at	$1,000
Mary (25 yrs.) – American Mulatress	$900
Bijou (11 yrs.)	$600
Rosine (15 yrs.) – Mulatress	$800
Therese (10 yrs.)	$400
Marine (12 yrs.) – Creole Negress	$600
Hyacinthe (35 yrs.) – Cook	$1,000
Julian (19 yrs.) – Creole Negro shoemaker	$1,000
Antoinette (50 yrs.) – Creole Negress laundress	$200

FIELD SLAVES – 93 INCLUDING CHILDREN

Léandre (63 yrs.) – Creole Negro field boss & driver	$500
Avril (35 yrs.) – Creole Negro teamster & laborer	$1,000
Paris (35 yrs.) – Creole Negro teamster & laborer	$1,000
Pret-á-boire "ready-to-drink" (46 yrs.) – Teamster & laborer	$500
Jack (39 yrs.) – American Negro	$800
Mars (44 yrs.) – Creole Negro teamster & laborer	$800
Mandrin (49 yrs.) – Creole Negro teamster & laborer	$900
Toni (24 yrs.) – Creole Negro teamster & laborer	$1,000
Do (21 yrs.) – Creole Negro teamster & laborer	$1,000
John (46 yrs.) – American Negro cooper (cask/barrel maker)	$1,000
Mohamet (34 yrs.) – Creole Negro teamster & laborer	$1,000
Isaac (30 yrs.) – American Negro cooper	$900
Cary (22 yrs.) – American Negro	$800
William (28 yrs.) – American Negro	$800
Madison (55 yrs.) – American Negro	$300
Anthony (49 yrs.) – American Negro	$800
Daniel (40 yrs.) – American Negro	$400
Hiram (42 yrs.) – American Negro blacksmith	$1,200
Mercury (64 yrs.) – African Negro	$100
Argus (27 yrs.) – Creole Negro mason	$1,200
Gognon (24 yrs.) – Creole Negro teamster & laborer	$800
Bacchus (36 yrs.) Creole Negro teamster & laborer	$1,000
Antoine (38 yrs.) – Creole Negro gardener/expert grafter of pecan trees	$1,000
Lovelace (23 yrs.) – Creole Negro teamster & laborer	$1,000
Prince (34 yrs.) – Mulatto carpenter	$1,500
Henry (44 yrs.) – African Negro	$500
Ellick (21 yrs.) – Creole Negro teamster & laborer	$1,000
Moses (49 yrs.) – American Negro	$400
Lazarre (35 yrs.) – Creole Negro carpenter	$1,300
Joe Tucker (44 yrs.) – American Negro	$800
Billy (44 yrs.) – American Negro	$600
Adonis (37 yrs.) – Creole Negro teamster & laborer	$400
Charley (54 yrs.) – American Negro	$600
Louis (62 yrs.) – African Negro (one armed)	$50
Codjo (40 yrs.) – African Negro	$100
Joseph (30 yrs.) – Creole Negro	$500
Alexis (28 yrs.) – Creole Negro	$500

Slave inventory from Oak Alley Plantation, Vacherie

Albert (25 yrs.) – American Negro	$800
Onuré (54 yrs.) – African Negro	$50
Tobi (60 yrs.) – Creole Negro (sickly)	$25
Adeline (52 yrs.) – Creole Negress	$50
Froisine (32 yrs.) – Creole Negress & her 3 children: Bazile (6 yrs.),	
Paul (3 yrs.), Ursule (15 mos.), estimated together at:	$1,000
Félonise (12 yrs.)	$700
Emelia (30 yrs.) – American Mulatress & her 2 children:	
Pauline (5 yrs.) & Nancy (3 yrs.), estimated together at	$900
Flore (32 yrs.) – Creole Negress & her 3 children: Vincent (7 yrs.),	
Mannette (4 yrs.), Thomas (18 mos.), estimated together at	$1,000
Félicité (12 yrs.)	$400
Françoise (28 yrs.) – Creole Negress & her 3 children: Lézin (9 yrs.),	
Jules (7 yrs.), Laviolette (2 yrs.), estimated together at	$1,300
Cloé (25 yrs.) – Creole Negress & her 4 children:	
Maurice (9 yrs.), Thisbé (7 yrs.), Henriette (4 yrs.)	
& Madeleine (2 yrs.) estimated together at	$1,300
Mathilde (28 yrs.) – American Negress & her child	
Victorine (19 mos.), estimated together at	$700
Hélène (12 yrs.) – Little Negress	$400
Sarah (35 yrs.) – American Negress & her child	
Charlotte (5 yrs.), estimated together at	$200
Thalie (30 yrs.) – Creole Negress & her child	
Justine (7 yrs.) estimated together at:	$400
César (12 yrs.) – Little Negro	$500
Zéphyrin (12 yrs.); Raymond (10 yrs.); Zélie (5 yrs.) – 3 orphans,	
estimated together at	$1,000
Cybelle (40 yrs.) – Creole Negress & her 4 children:	
George (9 yrs.), André (5 yrs.), Jessy (3 yrs.), Michel (11 mos.),	
estimated together at:	$1,100
Joseph (12 yrs.)	$500
Kitty (10 yrs.)	$500
Bertheline (30 yrs.) – Creole Negress	$600
Servilie (45 yrs.) – Creole Negress	$500
Marguerite (35 yrs.)	$300
Jenny (55 yrs.) – American Negress	$300
Angèle (20 yrs.) – Creole Negress	$600
Augustine (59 yrs.) – Creole Negress	$200
Marie (69 yrs.) – Cook for the Negroes	$50
Celestine (18 yrs.) – Creole Negress	$600
Mary Jane (20 yrs.) – American Negress	$600
Suzanne (50 yrs.) – African Negress	$50
Louisa (15 yrs.) – Creole Negress	$25
Désiré (14 yrs.) – Young Negress	$600

TOTAL 113 SLAVES INCLUDING CHILDREN

SLAVE DEFINITIONS

African Negro/Negress – Born in Africa (

American Negro/Negress – Born in Ameri

Creole Negro/Negress – Born in the West
of African (Old World) parents.

Mulatto – From the Spanish & Portuguese
meaning mixed breed. Child of Negro and
Mulattress refers to a female of mixed herit

---

field peas, syrup, rice, fruit and berries. Occasionally, slaves enjoyed milk, honey and molasses. Though slaves were seldom given coffee, they improvised by making coffee from roasted okra, corn, cowpeas or sweet potatoes sweetened with molasses or sorghum.

Traditionally, Africans lived off the land, and the Louisiana frontier provided slaves an ample supply of game and fish, which masters encouraged them to catch to supplement their diets. Slaves ate bowfin, mudfish, drum, gar and catfish. Boiled catfish were enjoyed and catfish head stew was a delicacy. In the spring, slaves caught crawfish by the bushel, and many caught and ate crabs, too. Slaves hunted squirrel, turkey, duck, rabbit, venison and bear. This wild game contributed not only to the slave's table, but the master's as well. At night, slaves hunted raccoons, but nothing was as tasty as roasted opossum.

Many slaves prepared their own meals with their rationed foods. Cornmeal was mixed with water, placed on a hoe blade and baked in the fireplace ashes to create "hoecakes." Sweet potatoes and green corn were cooked in the coals while fresh meat was roasted on a makeshift spit. Most slaves either boiled or fried their food, because usually only one cooking utensil was available. Some owners preferred central kitchens where food was prepared for

---

civilizations of the continent. A West African culture existed and was transported with these bondsmen across the Atlantic. Though the slaves were generally illiterate and non-mechanical, their culture was comparable to the European Middle Ages. Theirs was an agricultural society not unlike that of Louisiana. In fact, early Louisiana settlers respected the Africans agricultural knowledge and specifically requested slaves familiar with rice cultivation.

As early as 1706, Louisiana colonists asked for Negroes to clear and cultivate the land. Though enslaved Indians worked well, they deserted easily. Many colonists suggested exchanging Indian slaves in the American islands for Negroes. Bienville arranged with Santo Domingo traders to exchange two Indians for one Negro slave. By 1709, a few black slaves lived in Louisiana, but by 1721, 680 blacks lived in New Orleans and Mobile.

During the antebellum period, the slave labor force grew. Slave owners quickly learned that mistreated, ill-clad, malnourished slaves became ill and were rendered less

productive or useless. A healthy, productive work force was directly proportional to a healthy, profitable bottom line. Africans were valuable, expensive assets as exemplified in plantation property inventories like those exhibited at Oak Alley Plantation in St. James Parish.

Generally, masters allotted each adult slave a half pound of salt pork and a quart of cornmeal daily. Though some planters issued food each day, others portioned food weekly. Not only did slaves have salt meat, occasionally there was fresh pork or beef. Not surprisingly, slaves received the less desirable cuts. Seasonally, root vegetables such as turnips or sweet potatoes might be rationed as well as cabbage,

---

BY HEWLETT & RASPILLER,
On Saturday, 14th April, inst.
At 1-2 12 o'clock, at Hewlett's Exchange,
WILL BE SOLD,
24 HEAD OF SLAVES,

Lately belonging to the Estate of Jno. Erwin, of the parish of Iberville. These Slaves have been for more than 10 years in the country, and are all well acclimated, and accustomed to all kinds of work on a Sugar Plantation. There are among them a first rate cooper, a first rate brick maker, and an excellent hostler and coachman. They will be sold chiefly in families.

TERMS-----One year's credit, payable in notes endorsed to the satisfaction of the vendor, and bearing mortgage until final payment. Sales to be passed before Carlisle Pollock, Esq. at the expense of the purchasers.

Fielding,	aged 27 years,	field hand,	
Sally,	aged 24 do.	field hand and cook,	15..
Levi,	aged 26 years,	cooper and field hand.	
Aggy,	do. 24 do.	house servant and field hand.	2100
James, do.	6 do.		
Emeline,	8 do.		
Stephen,	3 do.		
Priscilly,	1 do.		
Bill,	aged 24 years,	field hand,	
Leah,	do. 22 do.	field hand,	1600
Rosette,	do. 3 do.		
Infant child.			
Alfred,	aged 22 years,	brick maker, servant and field hand,	2800
Charlotte, do. 20 years,		house servant and field hand,	1800
Infant.			
Forrester,	aged 41 years,	hostler, house servant and field hand.	
Mary,	aged 22 years,	field hand and cook.	1400
Infant.			
Harry,	aged 24 years,	field hand,	
Charity,	aged 24 years,	field hand,	800
Polly,	aged 22 years,	house servant and seamstress,	
Sam,	aged 2 years,		
Bedford,	aged 14 years,	field hand,	700
Mahaly,	aged 12 years,	field hand,	500
			1100

Slave auction advertisement

everyone to prevent waste and mishandling. Children, however, were slopped like hogs from a communal trough. Commonly, they ate milk or buttermilk and corn bread, most without having washed their hands before diving into the food bucket. Crumbled corn bread covered with peas or vegetables and potlikker (broth) were common fare for children.

Many slaves kept small gardens. Others raised pigs, cows for milk and butter, and chickens, which also provided fresh eggs. Their supplemental vegetables, eggs and chickens were sold in nearby cities to earn a little income. Often, they peddled their goods to the cooks aboard steamboats. Slaves also cooked small items to sell outside St. Louis Cathedral such as pralines, pies and cala or rice cakes. Many slaves strolled the levy selling their foodstuffs, while men sold oysters from the shell to passersby.

Many slaves were off on Saturday afternoons and everyone rested on Sundays, except during the grinding season on sugar plantations. With the master's permission a slave could work for others to earn extra money to buy knives, fishing nets, bandannas, cloth, petticoats, whiskey and wine. Some saved their earnings to purchase freedom.

African slaves cooked, worked in homes, fields and at various trades. They were already familiar with the foods they prepared such as greens, maize, beans, okra, rice, fish, fowl and pork. A good cook gardened, pickled, brewed, baked, washed, ironed and sewed.

In Louisiana, slaves were regarded for their cooking abilities. In 1860, a French and English speaking slave named Gracieuse was sold at a New Orleans auction as one of the city's best Creole cooks. Other slaves were touted as confectioners and candy makers. New Orleans' French citizenry trained many slaves in French cookery while some black men obtained culinary training in Paris. Most African men cooked for inns, hotels and ships.

On large plantations there were two types of cooks: the field hand cook and the big house cook. The slave owners' cooks prepared an incredible variety of foods including guinea fowl, turkey, geese, partridge, quail, pheasant and pigeon. They prepared pork, beef, veal, mutton and venison. Tables were filled with fresh fish, crawfish, oysters, crab, shrimp and turtle. The plantation gardens produced asparagus, celery, cauliflower, eggplant, beets, lettuce, parsnips, pears, beans, radishes, melons and mirliton, and

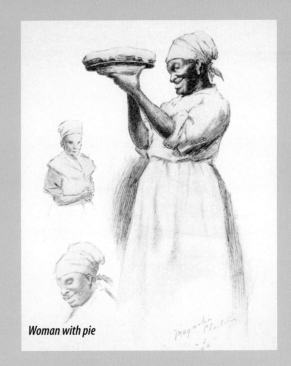

Woman with pie

there were orchards of fresh oranges, plums and peaches as well as groves of pecans.

There was a great deal of variety in how slaves dressed. Generally, men were given two cotton shirts, two pair of cotton pants and straw hats for summer. Women received

Brother Jones

Old South-relics of slavery

visit their wives on Wednesdays and Saturdays after work. Mothers and children less than 10 years old could not be sold separately. Disabled or aged slaves who had children could select a child to be sold with at public sales.

Favored blacks attended balls, orations, political debates and horse races. They helped in house-raisings and logrollings and participated in the celebrations that followed.

two cotton dresses. Winter wear included denim or blanket overcoats and heavy horsehide shoes for men and women. In the winter men wore wool caps, while women wore headscarves year-round.

In the early part of the 19th century housing for both slaves and planters was primitive. As frontier conditions improved, so did housing. Generally, slave houses had plank floors, a brick chimney and a shingle roof with no loft or storage space. Clothes hung on pins. Each house was furnished with a bedstead, cotton mattress and bedclothes. Other furnishings might include tin buckets, pots, kettles, chairs, wooden spoons and tables. Slaves crafted much of their furnishings. Some cabins were constructed of planks fitted together with rags and mud, clapboard roofs, stick and mud chimneys and an earthen floor. Slave cabins were generally located near a forest and spring, so they could easily obtain firewood and drinking water. On large plantations, slave quarters were lined up one after the other in rows opposite each other.

For slaves, marriage held no legal status. Husbands and wives could be sold with no regard for their relationship. A ceremony was usually held when a man and woman decided to live together. Sometimes this simply entailed obtaining the master's permission or "jumping over a broomstick," a curious marital ceremony among slaves. At other times, a religious ceremony was held with either a Negro preacher or a Catholic priest presiding. It was preferable for slaves to marry someone from their own plantation. Otherwise, husbands were generally allowed to

Laborer's cottage at Columbia Plantation

Baptism in the river

SPIRITUALS

Influenced by the African culture, slaves endured their troubled lives by singing spirituals. Through song they expressed their joys, sorrows, hopes and dreams while recording history.

Spirituals were created and sung by individuals and groups more often while working than in church. Field slaves inevitably sung the popular period songs while they worked. New songs developed from bits of old songs with new tunes and lyrics. "Corn ditties," precursors of spirituals, were sung in the late 1700s. The most notable spirituals described slaves as the chosen people providing them with comfort that God was with them and that freedom would come.

Songs were created from books of the Old Testament as well as revelations of the New Testament. As God delivered the Israelites from Egyptian slavery, so too would the Africans find deliverance from slavery. Some spirituals referred to the Underground Railroad and "Jordan," the country on the northern side of the Ohio River.

After the Civil War, many former slaves did not want to remember the past, so the prevalence of spirituals waned. However, in the early 1870s the Fisk University Jubilee Singers revived spirituals as a method of fundraising for one of the first universities for African-Americans.

Even today, spirituals allow listeners to understand the joys and sorrows of the slaves' lives. Black gospel music draws heavily from traditional slave spirituals.

Slave cabin interior, Rural Life Museum, Baton Rouge

Man cooking meat

Christmas was a great holiday for slaves. On cotton plantations fieldwork stopped the day before Christmas Eve and generally did not resume until New Year's Eve. Slaves were given as much or more free time on sugar plantations, but only after grinding was completed, which could delay the holiday until late January. On Christmas Eve, a dinner and ball were held for slaves. Sometimes, plantation owners hosted the gathering for slaves of several plantations with alternate hosts annually. Outdoor tables were laden with meat and vegetables. If the feast was not prepared in the plantation kitchen, it was cooked in trenches dug for the occasion. Wood was burned in the trench to create glowing coals over which chickens, ducks, turkeys, pigs and wild oxen were roasted. Flour was provided for biscuits and preserves for tarts and pies. It was not uncommon for white people to watch the festivities.

An all-night dance followed the dinner. Slaves provided the music or sometimes black musicians were hired for the occasion. Some slave musicians earned extra money by playing for white dances. In fact, the Shreveport Ethiopian Band was an institution.

Customarily, slaves gathered outside the big house on Christmas morning to receive gifts from the plantation owner. Women received bright handkerchiefs and calico dresses. Men received hats and perhaps a small sum of money. Children received candy. Adults were given passes during the Christmas holiday to travel where they pleased, within reason.

Wise masters encouraged music, dancing and occasionally hosted big suppers and dances at seasons other than Christmas. Others opposed such gatherings, because they feared slaves would plot insurrections.

Human bondage is reprehensible and must be acknowledged as a cruel chapter in Louisiana's history as well as that of the nation. Though slaves toiled long hours with rigorous discipline, it seems they were adequately fed, clothed, housed and received primitive medical care not unlike that of their owners. Still, no approval of human bondage is suggested. History is simply recorded more frequently by the captor than by the captive.

THE CODE NOIR

King Louis XIV of France initially issued "The Code Noir" or "The Black Code" in an edict dated March 1685. Subsequent decrees modified the provisions, but the first document established the main criteria for policing slavery until 1789. For the most part, the code defined conditions of slavery and established harsh controls over the enslaved.

The Code Noir of Louisiana given at Versailles in March 1724 maintained that all slaves and overseers be Roman Catholic. Everyone in the Louisiana colony was obliged to regularly observe Sundays and Feast Days. No one worked on those days including slaves. Violations could result in fines, punishment of the master or even confiscation of the slaves.

White subjects were forbidden to marry blacks. Pastors, priests, missionaries and ship chaplains were forbidden to conduct marriage ceremonies between whites and blacks. Whites, freed blacks and blacks born free were forbidden to live in concubinage with slaves. A master had to consent to a slave's marriage. Curates were forbidden to marry slaves, if the master's consent had not been acquired. Children born of slaves were slaves. If different masters owned the slave parents, the children belonged to the female slave's master. If a slave man married a freewoman, the children were free. If the father was free and the mother a slave, the children were slaves.

Masters had to bury baptized slaves in holy ground in designated cemeteries. Slaves not baptized were buried that night in a field near the place they died.

SAINT DOMINGUE SLAVE REVOLTS

During its French colonial period, Haiti was known as the colony of Saint Domingue. The eastern Spanish colony was called Santo Domingo. Some combined the two and referred to the French colony as San Domingue. Following independence in 1804, Haiti emerged. Haiti exists in the western one-third of the Caribbean island, Hispaniola, which is shared with the Dominican Republic. Haiti and the United States were countries born from European colonization and became the first independent nations of the modern Western Hemisphere.

From earliest exploration, Saint Domingue was an important port of call for fuel and supplies en route to the New World and the Louisiana colony. During the 1790s and early 1800s, Saint Domingue was a crucial port for United States merchant ships bringing manufactured goods to the area in return for rum, molasses and tropical goods.

Jean Etienne de Boré

Slave rebellions began on the sugar plantations of northern Saint Domingue in 1791. By 1798, Toussaint Louverture, a former slave turned general, had great influence in the Saint Domingue colony and served as governor-general. A mulatto leader and Louverture rival, Andre Rigaud controlled Saint Domingue's southern region. France feared Louverture's power and spurred the rivalry, which resulted in civil war. The United States assisted Louverture to prevent Rigaud from expanding the slave revolt to Jamaica and other Caribbean colonies.

The Saint Domingue slave revolts caused fear among plantation owners, slaveholders and leaders of the southern United States who worried that these revolts might spread to the North American mainland. The revolts caused uneasiness in Louisiana, where abortive slave uprisings resulted in more stringent slave laws in New Orleans.

In 1802, Napoleon sent troops to Saint Domingue to annihilate the government of the blacks and re-assert French power over the colony. The United States feared that if Napoleon succeeded in re-establishing French control in Saint Domingue, then his forces might easily move to the French colony of Louisiana. Once in Louisiana, the ambitious Napoleon might try to conquer the United States.

However, by 1803, Louverture and his army of former slaves defeated Napoleon's troops pushing them back to France, not on to Louisiana. Perhaps not coincidentally, in that same year the United States negotiated the Louisiana Purchase, acquiring France's vast North American territory.

Louisiana became the destination of many Saint Domingue refugees escaping the revolutionary upheaval in their homeland. Arriving in three immigrant waves, these whites, people of color and slaves contributed greatly to Louisiana's development in the early 19th century. During the last decade of the 1790s and the first decade of the 1800s, at least 10,000 Saint Domingue immigrants arrived in Louisiana, virtually doubling the French-speaking population. These immigrants were divided more or less equally among whites, people of color and slaves.

During the mid-1790s in New Orleans, Jean Etienne de Boré successfully granulated cane juice, which revolutionized the sugarcane industry making its cultivation economically viable in Louisiana. During the same period expert planters from Saint Domingue arrived with new sugarcane varieties. Within a few years sugar had replaced indigo as the principal export from Louisiana's southern plantations. Between 1796 and 1804 Louisiana sugarcane plantations increased from a struggling handful to at least 81 thriving operations. As sugar plantations grew, so did the need for slaves. Between 1799 and 1804 the number of African slaves in Louisiana increased from about 17,000 to 70,000, many entering the Louisiana colony via Saint Domingue, Martinique and Guadeloupe.

by a slave against a free person was to be severely punished.

Slaves could not be tortured or racked, only bound and beaten with rods or cords, if the master believed the slave deserved such punishment. Masters and overseers who killed or mutilated slaves were to be criminally charged according to the atrocity.

Slaves were personal property. However, if the same master owned a husband, his wife and their prepubescent children, the family was not to be sold separately.

Freemen of color worked in various occupations. Some were artisans, businessmen, farmers or slave-owning plantation masters. Many became wealthy and were treated as fellow businessmen by the Creoles while others were subject to contempt. For example, a Creole plantation owner might transact business with a freeman of color, but he would not eat a meal with him. For this reason, many gens de couleur moved to France and formed a colony of expatriates.

The femmes de couleur were prohibited by law from marrying white men and prejudice discouraged marriage to black men. Laws and codes dictated their social behavior. In 1788, 1,500 free, unmarried women of color lived in houses near the Ramparts. The quadroon women's reputation was so notorious that Spanish Governor Don Esteban Rodriguez Miro passed an ordinance making it an offense for the femmes de couleur to appear during the day wearing jewels, plumes or silk. Additionally, they were ordered to comb their hair flat or cover their hair if it was combed high. Many believe the order backfired, because the tignons worn by the quadroons framed their faces rather than disguised their beauty.

Few women of color married men of mixed race. Most often they became mistresses to the white Creole men in a system called "placage." The men chose their mistresses at the famous Quadroon Balls, which were the top New Orleans social events.

Slaves were forbidden to have firearms or large sticks.

Slaves belonging to different masters were forbidden to gather in a crowd including weddings. Gatherings in the masters' homes were not permitted. If a master permitted such an assembly, the master was punished.

Masters had to give written permission for slaves to sell anything in a market including provisions, fruits, vegetables, firewood, herbs or grain. Markets had two people appointed to examine

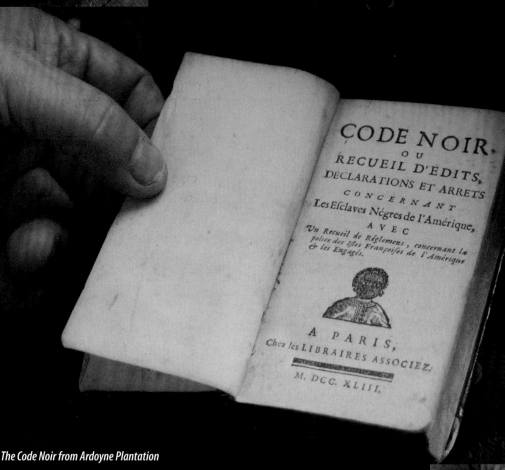

The Code Noir from Ardoyne Plantation

the slaves' goods and written permission notes. If a slave did not have the required permission papers, his goods were confiscated.

Masters had to furnish food and clothes for their slaves. Brandy could not be given to slaves in place of food and clothing. If a slave was given a day to work for himself, the master was still responsible for the slave's food and subsistence. Slaves could report their master to the Procurator General of the Superior Council of Louisiana, if they were not properly fed and clothed.

Any slave who struck his master, mistress or their children was punished by death. Any abuse or assault committed

FREEMEN AND WOMEN OF COLOR

Even before the Civil War, New Orleans and Louisiana were home to a sizable population of free men and women of mixed race. The first record of a free black in New Orleans dates from 1722. Legal documents referred to the men as "gens de couleur" and women as "femmes de couleur." An elaborate caste system existed among these people based on skin color. A mulatto was the offspring of a black person and a white person. A griffe was the offspring of a mulatto and a black. A quadroon was the offspring of a mulatto and a white. An octoroon was the offspring of a quadroon and a white. Other terms were used such as "os rouge," if the person had Native American ancestry.

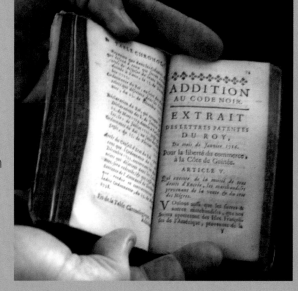

QUADROON BALLS AND QUADROON WOMEN

The quadroon balls originated in Spanish Louisiana at the end of the 1700s and endured nearly 100 years. Following the War Between the States, the balls degenerated into shabby, ill-mannered affairs with none of the prior elegance and decorum.

"Bal de Cordon Bleu" was the first "coming-out" ball hosted by quadroon mothers to introduce their young, beautiful daughters to white, aristocratic men. Guests were always white men, because white women would not dare attend. Nor were men of questionable color welcome. Admission was two dollars, more than the cost of any other public dance. The gay, lavish balls were well worth the price. Quadroon balls were held nearly every night between October and Ash Wednesday. Freewomen of color, once the white men's mistresses, hosted the balls honoring their illegitimate daughters. Not until the Americans moved to New Orleans did the events become known as quadroon balls. The Salle d'Orleans, a ballroom adjoining the Orleans Theatre, was the debut site.

Sister Henriette Delille

The lovely, refined quadroon women dressed extravagantly in fashionable gowns. Mothers chaperoned and if a man wished to speak to a lady, he must first obtain her mother's permission. Like white mothers, quadroon mothers objected to unwise arrangements.

Quadroon mothers have been criticized for selling their daughters like slaves and bartering them into concubinage. Under the circumstances, the mothers did the best they could for their daughters and acted in what they considered their best interests. Ironically, white girls often had less choice choosing a husband than quadroons had choosing a lover. Quadroon women did not have to accept any man. If she found someone she liked, then the gentleman met with her mother to make proper arrangements. Usually, it was agreed that the girl would have a small cottage, usually on or near Rue de Rampart. There was a financial arrangement for her and any children born from the relationship. The man did not visit the girl alone until the house was completed. Once the arrangement was made, the girl was referred to as a

"placée." This was an honorable betrothal with a secure future for the girl. Some arrangements lasted a short time while others endured years or a lifetime. When the man married, he might discontinue the relationship. It was not unusual to see a man's white family in the opera box and his quadroon family in the balcony. A Creole gentleman always provided for his illegitimate children who were reared piously by their mothers and often educated abroad. Quadroon women usually had slaves, cooks, maids to fix their hair and errand boys. Quadroons cherished by the richest, most honorable and important men were believed to possess jewels and wealth.

If the relationship ended, the quadroon kept her financial settlement and often went into business as a dressmaker, hairdresser, or she may have owned and operated a boarding house. Many were yellow fever nurses. Though some quadroons committed suicide when their lovers abandoned them, others lived as "widows" or moved to the country. Some married black men after their white lovers rejected them.

At her bedroom altar, the quadroon mother prayed that God would send kind protectors for her beautiful daughters. Small sins of the flesh rarely interfered with piety.

Henriette Delille was born in 1813 to a New Orleans aristocrat, Jean Baptiste Delille-Sarpy, and his quadroon mistress, Pouponne Dias. Like most young quadroon women, Delille was trained to have a refined taste in music, to dance gracefully and to be conversant in French literature. Her mother taught her nursing skills and how to prepare herbal medicines. As a teenager, Delille attended quadroon balls to meet the aristocracy in an effort to become someone's mistress.

At one of the balls she met Sister St. Marthe Fontier, a French nun of the Dames Hospitlier religious order. Never having met a religious, Delille was impressed by her dedication to God, her vows and acts of charity. With the assistance of free people of color in New Orleans, Sister St. Marthe purchased land on Barracks Street where she opened a Catholic girls' school. The school became the nucleus for missionary activities among free and slave Negroes. At night, Sister St. Marthe taught classes in morals and faith to adults. During the day, young girls learned religion and trained to be teachers. At 14, Delille began to teach at the Catholic school.

Orleans Theater, which later became the motherhouse of the Sisters of the Holy Family

Delille became engrossed in her work not only teaching but also visiting the sick, the elderly and helping to feed the city's poor. Often, she went to the Ursuline Convent chapel to offer daily devotions. Though her family tried to persuade her to abandon her work and choose a lover, Delille chose celibacy. Public recognition of her mixed ancestry and association with blacks vexed her family, who passed as white, causing her mother to suffer a nervous breakdown.

When Delille was declared of legal age, she sold her property and founded a community of Negro nuns with the assistance of a French woman, Marie Jeanne Aliquot. On November 21, 1836, Aliquot, Delille and eight black women became the Sisters of the Presentation, changing their name a few years later to the Sisters of the Holy Family. Their motto was "To be of one heart and one soul." They cared for the sick, the poor and taught freemen. Ironically, the Salle d'Orleans, the location of the quadroon balls, became the motherhouse of the Sisters of the Holy Family.

Today, the sisters have missions in Louisiana, California, Texas, Washington, D.C. and Belize, Central America. They still teach, care for the elderly and run schools for disadvantaged children.

Indigenous foods of West Africa

WEST AFRICAN COOKERY AND ITS INFLUENCE ON LOUISIANA CUISINE

Cultural and food exchanges have occurred through the centuries and often, determining food origin is difficult if not impossible. Most scientists believe that Africa was the birthplace of man. If true, then man's first meal must have been eaten in Africa.

By 6000 B.C. Africans lived in urban, farming communities. They had developed cotton and oil producing plants, which were introduced to the Egyptians. They grew rice, millet, sorghum, peanuts, watermelon, yams, oil palm and sesame. By the 17th century, Portugal had introduced maize to West Africa, though artwork on Nigerian pottery dating from 1100 A.D. suggests that maize could have been grown long before Portugal's recorded entrance.

Indigenous to West Africa were yams, peas, beans, rice, peanuts, sesame, pumpkins, melons including watermelon, okra, eggplant, palm oil, mangoes, yellow plums, cashew nuts and coffee. From the Americas, West Africa obtained capsicums, tomatoes, pineapples, sweet potatoes, corn, cassava, avocados and papayas. Arab caravans from North Africa brought wheat, onions, citrus fruits and dates while merchants from the Far East brought plantains, bananas, sugarcane, ginger and coconut.

Peanuts, okra, cowpeas (particularly black-eyed peas) and sesame arrived in America either directly from Africa with the slaves or via America's flourishing trade with the West Indies. These foods were ideal for the voyage to the New World, because they remained edible long after the harvest. The slave gardens of the American South flourished with these plants providing the Africans with familiar foods they could grow with no expense to their owners. Today, these four foods initially considered the diet of a servant class are well established in the American diet.

Though peanuts originated in South America, they arrived in North America from Africa, perhaps via the West Indies. Portuguese and Spanish traders brought peanuts to the Old World and fed them to their slaves. Even today in Africa, peanuts are ground smoothly to coat meat and fish for enhanced flavor. One could suppose that the Louisiana method of encrusting meat and fish in smoothly ground pecans could be an adaptation of this African technique.

In West Africa, okra was a popular vegetable prized for its thickening ability. "Gumbo," the African word for okra, became the name of Louisiana's most famous soup, which is generally made with okra, seafood and/or poultry. Some believe that a French adaptation of their traditional bouillabaisse when combined with okra and thickened with roux became Louisiana gumbo. In early New Orleans it was not uncommon to see black women hawking gumbo and steamed rice in the city's markets.

West Africans add peas and dried beans to soups and stews to supplement fish and meat. Black-eyed peas, a popular Southern dish, are always served on New Year's Day in Louisiana for health in the New Year. One of the most famous dishes of Southern cooking and a staple of many Confederate War soldiers was hoppin' John, a combination of black-eyed peas and rice.

Rice, indigenous to West Africa, first arrived in Charleston,

South Carolina from Madagascar around 1685. A staple of the African diet, rice is used for breakfast and to create "rice water," a porridge-like pudding similar to Louisiana's rice pudding. As in Africa, rice is served in Louisiana with stews and soups, and rice flour is used as a thickening agent. "Moimoi" or "koose," a favorite African dish, is served in Louisiana as red beans and rice.

African slaves brought sesame, the oldest herb known to mankind, to America. While the British cultivated sesame to create a substitute for olive oil, the slaves ate sesame raw, toasted or boiled in soup. Sesame was baked in bread, boiled with greens or used to enrich broth. Seeds were pounded into a butter or paste to eat on bread or hominy grits. Slaves planted sesame in their gardens for good luck.

In Africa, watermelon was a food and water source. Slaves probably brought seeds to plant in the New World, though European colonists were growing watermelons abundantly in the New England Colonies by 1630.

Yams, West Africa's oldest cultivated crop, were a staple of many West African people. The English word "yam" is derived from the original African word. In West Africa, yams were peeled, washed and boiled in salt water to serve as an accompaniment to meat or fish. Sometimes yams were sliced or cubed, then deep fried in peanut oil. Traditionally, yams were stewed with smoke-dried shrimp, onions and other seasonings.

Black pepper, which originated in Sumatra, was once the coin of tributes, taxes and dowries, though it is used sparingly in African cooking today. Interestingly, early traders named the West African Coast between Freetown and Cape Palmas the "pepper coast," because of the Melegueta or "grains of paradise" found there. As early as 1364 African pepper was exported to France.

Africa's ancient gold, slave and pepper coast located along the Atlantic seaboard was the ancestral homeland of most African-Americans. Though slave owners may have tried to erase African cultural influences, the cooks inevitably left an indelible mark on the palates of their captors. Louisiana cuisine descended from the many cultures that settled the state with West Africa contributing significantly to the regional flavors prevalent in Louisiana today. Africans were the principal cooks in New Orleans and influenced the cuisine of Louisiana with their native foodways. Though introduced by the Spanish, jambalaya had been prepared using ham only. Easily surmised is that Africans would have added shrimp, chicken and crab to create Creole jambalaya. African cooks are credited with creating such dishes as gumbo z'herbes and chicken gumbo. Slave cooks were gifted culinarians with natural instincts in herb and spice use. Traditionally, African cooking methods favored

deep frying and long stewing, both prevalent techniques in Louisiana cooking, though roasting, steaming, baking, boiling and broiling were used daily as well.

Like Southerners, West Africans enjoyed great quantities of greens cooked slowly with a little meat and pepper. Though bitterleaf was consumed in Africa, turnip greens made a nice substitute in the New World.

Corn was a Native American food, but early traders and explorers took it to Africa. By the time slaves arrived, corn was a staple in their diet and was cooked in porridges, breads, pancakes and side dishes. White cornmeal and grits are still Louisiana staples. African corn and bean cakes became hush puppies in American cuisine.

In West Africa, chicken was a dish for festive occasions, honored guests and traditional meals. In Louisiana, popular Sunday meals still consist of fried, stewed or smothered chicken. In Africa, chicken was most commonly stewed and served over boiled yams or rice, or a chicken soup was created to serve over fufu. Fufu is created by first boiling cassava, yams or cocoyams until tender. The cooked vegetables are pounded until smooth, placed in bowls, then served with soup atop the sticky vegetable mixture.

Barracuda, mackerel, cod, tuna, herring, shad, tarpon, shark, sea catfish, stingray and sawfish were eaten daily in West Africa either fresh, fried, dried, salted, baked, broiled or smoked. Lobsters, shrimp, crabs, clams and oysters were not uncommon, especially for coastal tribes. Dried shrimp and powdered crawfish were used for flavoring. As in Africa, Louisiana teemed with fresh fish and seafood. A favorite African dish, deep-fried fish balls with tomato sauce, is still a favorite Louisiana dish called catfish boulettes in sauce piquante.

Stews and soups, which stretch meat and fish to make a little go a long way, are popular West African dishes but

figure into the Louisiana diet as well. While plantains, bananas, coconuts and mangoes were common to West Africa, substitutions in Louisiana were apples, peaches and pecans. Like Louisianians, West Africans spent a great deal of time planting, harvesting, cooking, eating, selling and talking about food. Interestingly, the greeting for a returning African traveler was not, "Did you have a good time?" The greeting was, "Have you eaten well?"

Uncomplicated West African cooking was characterized by the generous use of hot chili or capsicum peppers, great amounts of oil and mashed vegetables and seeds for thickening. Pepper in highly seasoned African food enhanced, never concealed, the flavor of the other ingredients.

While Louisianians favor the "trinity" (onions, bell pepper and celery) in cooking, Africans prefer "the ingredients" (onions, hot chili or capsicum peppers and tomatoes). Almost every main dish features this flavoring.

SOUL FOOD

The term became popular among urban blacks in the 1960s to describe foods eaten by Southern slaves. Soul food exemplified the skill of the African cook who created masterful dishes from pork scraps, weeds and leftovers considered unfit for consumption. Some believe that the special taste of soul food came not from the ingredients, but from the heart and soul the cook stirred into the pot. Interestingly, soul food derived not from Africa, but from frontier experiences and English and Native American influences and was eaten by farmers and poor whites as well.

Soul food

HON. P. B. S. PINCHBACK,
EX-LIEUT. GOVERNOR.

The roster of accomplished Louisiana African-American musicians, artists, writers, politicians, and perhaps most importantly, chefs and cooks is lengthy. Names such as Leah Chase, Michael Roussel, Austin Leslie, Nathaniel Burton, Raymond Thomas, Sr., Annie Laura Squalls, Louis Evans, Charles Bailey, Henry Carr, Rosa Barganier, Malcolm Ross, Larry Williamson, Sherman Crayton, Louise Joshua, Letitia Parker, Rochester Anderson and Charles Kirkland will be savored through history. These and hundreds of others have been Louisiana's most notable cooks.

Sadly, the names of many African cooks are lost in history. Because Africans were considered property, only first names were recorded, if noted at all. Advertisements such as one in the *New-Orleans* on May 13, 1835 eagerly noted the culinary attributes of slaves. Sarah, a 45-year-old mulatto, was a good cook accustomed to housework and nursing the sick. Dennis, her 24-year-old son, was a "first-rate cook and steward." Chloe, 36, was a good cook as was 24-year-old Nancy and 22-year-old Fanny.

Besides great cooks, Louisiana gave birth to notable African-American musicians including jazz trumpeter and bandleader, Joseph "King" Oliver; trumpet player and jazz legend, Louis Armstrong; band leader, Claiborne Williams; "Gospel Queen," Mahalia Jackson; New Orleans

rhythm and blues legend, "Fats" Domino; king of zydeco, Rockin' Dopsie; "Zydeco's Royal Family," Rockin' Dopsie, Jr. & The Zydeco Twisters; the embodiment of New Orleans rhythm and blues, Professor Longhair; "Inventor of Jazz,""Jelly Roll" Morton; Rockin' Sidney; and Dr. Isaac Greggs, band director, Southern University, Baton Rouge. Huddie Ledbetter, better known as "Leadbelly," was born in Mooringsport, La. Leadbelly sang his way to freedom from Texas' Sugarland prison and Louisiana's Angola penitentiary. Famous Leadbelly songs include "Goodnight Irene,""Midnight Special,""Fannin Street" and children's songs such as "Skip to My Lou."

A few of Louisiana's famous artists of African origin include internationally-renown sculptor, Frank Hayden; Mitchell Peter Lafrance who created a distinct pattern and style of carving and painting duck decoys; and Clementine Hunter, who was the most outstanding primitive painter since Grandma Moses. Hunter, who lived most of her life on Melrose Plantation near Natchitoches, La., worked first in the fields, then as the cook at the big house before devoting her time to painting. Author Ernest Gaines, who wrote *The Autobiography of Miss Jane Pittman* and *A Lesson Before Dying* among several others, was born near New Roads, La., and still resides in the state today.

Others of note include Dr. Louis Charles Roudanez who was born in 1823 in St. James Parish. A successful doctor with both black and white patients, Roudanez was a civil rights activist, community leader and philanthropist. He and his brother are credited with founding *L'Tribune de la Nouvelle Orleans*, the first black daily newspaper published in the nation.

Pierre Landry, born on a plantation in Ascension Parish in 1841, was a confectioner and cook. He served as chief pastry man at Houmas Plantation and moved to Donaldsonville after obtaining his freedom. In 1868, he was elected mayor of Donaldsonville and was subsequently elected president of the Ascension Parish Police Jury. He was a member of the school board, appointed tax collector by the governor and was elected to Louisiana's Senate and House of Representatives.

Charles Edmund Nash, born in Opelousas in 1844, was the first black man seated in Congress from Louisiana. Though J. Willis Menard and Pinckney Benton Stewart Pinchback were both elected to Congress prior to Nash, they were never seated.

In 1872, P. B. S. Pinchback, the son of a slave woman and a wealthy white planter from Mississippi, became the first black governor of Louisiana as well as the first black governor of an American state. He served for 36 days from December 9, 1872 to the inauguration of W. P. Kellogg on January 13, 1873. As a leader of the Louisiana Republican party, Pinchback held or claimed offices including state senator, president pro tempore of the senate and acting lieutenant governor, de facto director of the New Orleans schools and police force, governor, U.S. representative and U.S. senator.

NORBERT RILLIEUX
1806 - 1894

AFRICAN-AMERICANS

Marie Thereze Carmelite Anty Metoyer, granddaughter of Marie Thérèse Coincoin

One of the nation's greatest sugar chemists and inventors was Norbert Rillieux, born in 1806 in New Orleans to Vincent Rillieux, a French planter, engineer and inventor, and Constance Vivant, one of Rillieux's slaves. Pere Antoine, the chaplain at St. Louis Cathedral, baptized him in St. Louis Cathedral.

Norbert Rillieux, a freeman of color, was educated in Paris, France, at L'Ecole Centrale where he studied evaporating engineering. It was not unusual for well-to-do Louisiana quadroons to be educated in France. Rillieux showed a rare aptitude for engineering at an early age. By 24, he was an instructor in applied mechanics at L'Ecole Centrale and published a series of papers on steam engine work and steam economy.

Upon his return to New Orleans he designed and patented an evaporating pan in 1846, which enclosed a series of condensing coils in vacuum chambers. This invention removed much of the hand labor from the sugar refining process, saved fuel because the juice boiled at lower temperatures and produced a superior end product. Rillieux's invention revolutionized sugar refining, while protecting slaves from the dangerous, crude, back-breaking labor of ladling boiling cane juice from one scalding kettle to another. Rillieux's device, which increased sugar production and reduced operating costs, was widely used on sugar plantations in Louisiana, Mexico, the West Indies and Cuba.

Though Rillieux was one of the most sought after engineers in Louisiana, his African blood prevented his being entertained at plantation owner's homes. As he conducted consultation visits from plantation to plantation, a special house with slave servants was provided for him. Though Rillieux did not acknowledge suffering racial injustices, it is highly probable that he was subjected to restrictions and indignities, which may have influenced his decision to return to France to live.

For a while Rillieux appeared to have lost interest in sugar machinery and studied Egyptology. On an 1880 trip to Paris, Duncan Kenner, a leading Louisiana sugar planter, visited Rillieux who was deciphering hieroglyphics at the Bibliotheque Nationale. Inevitably, passions triumph. At 75 years old Rillieux returned to the problems of evaporation and sugar machinery. In 1881 he patented a system for heating juice with vapors in multiple effect, which became universal practice in sugarcane factories.

Rillieux died in 1894 and was buried in Paris, France, in the churchyard of Pere La Chaise. Today, evaporation in multiple effect is used not only in the sugar industry but also in the manufacture of condensed milk, soap, gelatin, glue and in the recovery of waste liquors in distilleries and paper factories.

Also important to the sugar industry was Leonard Julien who was born in Modeste, La., in 1910. Julien invented the sugarcane-planting machine in 1964, which led to the first successful mechanical sugarcane planter.

Another ambitious African-American was Marie Thérèse Coincoin who became a plantation and slave owner and matriarch of a family of 14. Born in 1742, Coincoin was a slave of Louis Juchereau de St. Denis, the first commandant of the Natchitoches post. Coincoin and several of her children were sold to Frenchman Thomas Pierre Metoyer with whom she lived in public concubinage for approximately two decades. Together they had 10 children.

In 1786, Metoyer and Coincoin's relationship ended. Metoyer gave Coincoin the land he had bequeathed to their children and paid her a lifetime stipend of 120 piastres annually, which he felt was sufficient to provide for the family's basic needs. Eventually, Metoyer freed all of his children.

Coincoin and her sons established Melrose Plantation. She worked alongside her slaves to clear land, build roads and fences and plant tobacco and other crops. Coincoin also trapped wild bears and sent their grease to market in large jars. Bear grease was a valuable commodity in Europe where it was used for coaches, wagons and artillery. A 1792 shipment record includes clearance for tobacco, 300 hides and two barrels of grease. Eventually, she and her

Marie Laveau

sons controlled more than 50 slaves who worked 2,000 acres.

Despite Metoyer's marriage in 1788 to a woman of his background and race, he and Coincoin had founded a unique colony of people. Proud descendants of the Creoles of Cane River still live in the area today.

Though little is known definitively about Marie Laveau, the legendary Voodoo Queen of New Orleans, it is believed that she was born around 1794 to Charles Laveau, a wealthy white planter, and Darcantel Marguerite, a slave. Whether she was born in Saint Domingue or New Orleans is uncertain, but she lived in the city by 1809. A freewoman of color with African, Indian, French and Spanish blood, Laveau became the most famous and most powerful Voodoo Queen in the world. Though feared by many, she was highly respected and held rituals behind St. Louis Cathedral where she attended daily Mass.

Laveau was a hairdresser who visited the homes of wealthy white women. She became the first commercial Voodoo Queen and thrived financially. In fact, she obtained her house on Rue St. Anne after successfully freeing a client's son of a murder charge by secretly placing charms throughout the courtroom.

In 1819, she married Jacques Paris who mysteriously disappeared soon after their vows. A few years later Louis Glapion moved in with the "Widow Paris" who gave birth to 15 children. Their daughter, Marie Philomene Laveau

Voodoo dance

Glapion, had an uncanny resemblance to her mother and became nearly as powerful as a Voodoo priestess. Because of her daughter's practice, Laveau seemed to appear in more than one place at a time and became ageless.

Though Laveau was adept at a multitude of charms and potions, her real power came from an extensive network of spies. New Orleans' elite spoke of confidential matters in front of their slaves and servants who respectfully reported to Laveau. For that reason, Laveau seemed to have a magical knowledge of the political and social power in New Orleans.

Reportedly, Laveau practiced rituals on the banks of Bayou St. John every June 23, St. John's Eve. Occasionally, ceremonies were held at her cottage, Maison Blanche, on the shores of Lake Pontchartrain.

Late in life, Laveau stopped practicing Voodoo and became devoted solely to Catholicism. Pere Antoine was her friend. Though she weaved spells and charms, she also helped the sick, injured and downtrodden.

Many believe Laveau is buried in St. Louis Cemetery No. 1 and still has an active clientele. To obtain Laveau's assistance, believers place their right foot against the bottom of her tomb, make three "X" marks with red brick, place their hand over the marks, close their eyes and rub the tomb three times with their foot. Other rituals include knocking on the grave, lighting candles and bringing coin or candy gifts.

Voodoo, as it is known today, was born in Haiti during the European colonization of Hispaniola and is a fusion of beliefs and rituals from various African ethnic groups. This Afro-Caribbean religion mixed the practices of groups such as the Fon, the Nago, the Ibos, Dahomeans, Congos, Senegalese, Haussars, Caplaous, Mondungues, Angolese, Libyans, Ethiopians and the Malgaches. "Voodoo" comes from the West African word "vodun," meaning spirit. The Bambara people who came to Louisiana as slaves were superstitious and believed in charms called "gris-gris." The word "gris-gris" comes from the Mande, "gerregerys," meaning a harmful charm.

Voodoo practitioners believe that nothing happens by accident and that everything affects something else. Everyone is part of a whole, therefore, what you do to another, you do to yourself, because you are the same. The Voodoo society also believes that God is manifest through the spirits of ancestors who bring good or harm and must be honored ceremonially. A sacred cycle exists between the living and the dead.

Rituals include prayers, drumming, dancing, singing and animal sacrifice. Serpents figure prominently in Voodoo. Spirits, called Loa, can possess participants during ceremonies who then relay advice, warnings and desires. The Voodoo priest or priestess, through divine aid, helps those seeking advice, spiritual guidance or healing.

Public perception suggests that Voodoo is evil. However, there are spells for healing, love, purification and joyous celebration. Spirits can be invoked to bring harmony, peace, birth, rebirth, luck, material happiness and renewed health. Voodoo is powerful for those who believe.

Le Pere Antoine de Sedella

MEMORIES OF MARY

There are few things that can dull the anguish of the untimely death of a young wife and mother. My family had Mary Ferchaud. Affectionately known in the black community as "Miss Sister," she was more like a mother to us. This angel of mercy believed she was called by God to help our father Royley Folse raise his eight young children when our mother Therese died in 1955. It took Mary two weeks to decide to knock on our father's door and announce, "Mr. Royley, you need me to help you raise them children." It took 20 years for us to discover why she was driven to dedicate her life to our family.

After ushering us all safely, and very well-fed, into adulthood, Mary revealed that she had encountered our mother, very pregnant and hanging out laundry on the clothesline, just one day before she died. Mary remembered commenting to Therese that she had a lot of work to do washing laundry for all those children. Therese replied, "You're right Mary. If something ever happens to me, I sure hope somebody would help Royley take care of all my babies." The very next day, she died in childbirth. Over the next two weeks Mary became convinced that her conversation with our mother had been a sign from God that she should be the one to help raise the Folse children.

Mary did not take holy assignments lightly. For the next 20 years she devoted her life to feeding, clothing and most importantly, loving us like we were her own. Our father worked hard and earned little, but we never wanted for anything, especially at mealtimes. Mary was a wonder in the kitchen. She used patience, love and skill to transform simple ingredients into Cajun and Creole classics. Luckily, we had a one-acre vegetable garden, raised pigs and chickens and had access to an abundant supply of fish, shrimp, crawfish and wild game. Perhaps because we ate like royalty, or perhaps because Mary never made it seem like a chore to cook for us, we all grew up with a love of cooking and of the hearty, flavorful food Mary created.

We'll never know if our mother knew she was selecting our guardian angel during a chat over a clothesline, but she sure did a good job. And though we claim Mary as our own, it is important to note that while she cared for us, she was still a devoted wife to her husband, Eugene, and a loving mother and doting grandmother to her own family. When Mary died in 1998, she had five children, Autimese, Ora Lee, Lena, Elsie and Vera, 21 grandchildren, 36 great-grandchildren and seven great-great-grandchildren. It brings a smile to my face to imagine that Mary inspired that many people to love and cook the way she did.

Mary Ferchaud

THE CABIN RESTAURANT

Saint Rose Philippine Duchesne, born in Grenoble, France, in 1769, was a nun of the Society of the Sacred Heart of Jesus. In 1818, she came to the United States and became Mother Superior of the Ladies of the Sacred Heart in Missouri. She founded a number of convent schools including Sacred Heart Convent in Grand Coteau. Before she died in 1852, she helped establish a Catholic school for white children in St. James Parish. In 1867, her order added a school for children of newly freed black slaves. St. Joseph's School in Convent was the first Louisiana school for black children. One of the school's buildings is now part of The Cabin Restaurant in Burnside, La., near Gonzales, and is listed on the National Register of Historic Places. Saint Rose was canonized in 1988.

The Cabin Restaurant, Burnside

THE BATTLE OF FORT BUTLER

The 1st Louisiana Infantry (Union) built Fort Butler, a star-shaped earthen fortification, at the juncture of the Mississippi River and Bayou Lafourche at Donaldsonville, La. Erected between November 1862 and February 1863, a large number of freed slaves from the area helped in the construction.

The Battle of Fort Butler, fought during a rare nighttime engagement in late June 1863, was a stunning defeat for the Confederacy. Confederate eyewitnesses claimed that blacks fought alongside Union soldiers during the struggle. The Battle of Fort Butler marked the first Union victory in the War Between the States using black participants.

Currently, the Fort Butler Foundation is working to excavate the grounds at the battle site, so that a portion of the fort can be reconstructed and a museum built honoring those brave soldiers who fought and died during the struggle.

AFRICAN-AMERICAN COOKS IN THE CIVIL WAR

Military genius acknowledges that successful soldiers are not just well equipped on the battlefield; they must also be well fed. Both Union and Confederate generals understood that they needed to provide tasty provisions prepared by capable cooks for their soldiers. The armies of both the North and the South hired black cooks. Most of the Confederate cooks were slaves. The government designated four cooks per company and paid each $15 per month plus clothing. Affluent Confederate soldiers brought their Negro servants to war with them. These slaves cleaned the quarters, washed clothes, groomed uniforms, polished swords, ran errands, secured rations, cut hair and groomed the animals. Some even participated in battle. However, as the fighting grew desperate and the rations grew short, many slaves were sent home.

THE DONALDSONVILLE CANNONEERS

Formed in 1779, the Donaldsonville Cannoneers fought with General Andrew Jackson at the Battle of New Orleans. During the Civil War they fought with General Robert E. Lee's Army of Northern Virginia and were the first cannon battery to arrive at the Battle of Gettysburg. Pictured in this re-creation photo are, from left to right, Andrew Capone, Mike Marshall, August Bradford, Glenn Falgoust, Dwayne Dupre (drummer), Jimmy Johnson, Glen Dupre, Andre Jacobs, Johnny Hooper, Don Melancon and Leonard Simoneaux.

Abraham Lincoln

THE IRONY OF THE EMANCIPATION PROCLAMATION

Issued by President Abraham Lincoln to free slaves, the Emancipation Proclamation became effective on January 1, 1863. A little known fact is that the proclamation did not free all slaves — just the ones in the Confederacy. Slaves in the sugar region of Louisiana, however, were not freed by the Emancipation Proclamation including those in the parishes of St. Bernard, Plaquemines, Jefferson, St. John, St. Charles, St. James, Ascension, Assumption, Terre Bonne, Lafourche, St. Mary, St. Martin and Orleans, including the city of New Orleans.

Slaveholding states that did not secede from the Union and territories under federal occupation were exempt from the Emancipation Proclamation, therefore slavery was still legal in America, but only in the Union and Union-occupied areas.

Jules Dickerson, alias Jules Dixon, was identified as a corporal in the Civil War from Company B, 80th United States Colored Volunteer Infantry. He was originally from St. James Parish.

Germany

John Law's propaganda poster

Leon: Schenk Fecit   Pet: Schenk Exc: Amst.

Mre JEAN LAW CONer DU ROY EN TOUS CES CONils CONTROLEUR
GNAL DES FINANCES en 1720.

Sous l'Auguste et Sage Regence | LAW consommé dans l'art de regir la finance
D'un Prince aimant la bonne foy: | Trouve l'art d'enrichir les sujets et le Roy.

John Law

POPULATING LOUISIANA

After Iberville's 1699 discoveries, years passed without any serious settlement in the Louisiana colony. Under Louis XIV, France had been at war since the late 17th century and could not devote time or resources to overseas colonization. In 1712, however, Antoine Crozat gained control of Louisiana with intentions to colonize the region. After five years and only 400 colonists, he relinquished his monopoly to the Company of the West, headquartered in L'Orient, France.

King Louis XIV died in 1715 leaving his five-year-old great-grandson, Louis XV, to rule under the regent, Philippe, duc d'Orléans. France was near economic collapse because of the "Sun King's" disastrous policies. Desperate to redirect France, the regent employed the Scottish financier, John Law, as president of the Company, now called the Company of the Indies. Law was a notorious gambler and promoter bent on making his fortune using France's fragile economy as the means to his goal.

First, he created the Bank of France and circulated paper money to cure the country's economic ills. This bold move could succeed only with complete public trust. With France lacking the necessary resources for this purpose, Law saw Louisiana as an innovative product to collateralize his plan, though he would first have to populate the territory.

The first obstacle was France's strict policy that decreed only French Catholics could colonize overseas possessions to prevent "foreigners" from endangering French control. Law, a non-Catholic and a foreigner, lured settlers by proclaiming the virtues of Louisiana through an intensive campaign. Unfortunately, only a small number of people responded. Desperate for settlers, the Company began populating the colony with vagrants, prostitutes and criminals. From 1719 to 1720, almost 1,200 derelicts were kidnapped from French streets and shipped to the colony. The French were outraged and stopped the process after only one year of execution. These derelict colonists were ill prepared for the harsh life in Louisiana and died in droves. With pressure mounting to implement Law's plan, the regent decided to allow foreigners, including Germans, into French colonies.

As early as 1717, a plan to send German Catholic colonists to Louisiana was proposed by Jean-Pierre Purry, a Swiss businessman active in France. His plan suggested sending only Germans and Swiss of good character. Purry's plan caught Law's attention, when it was published in Holland. With the decree now reversed, Law moved to appoint Purry director of the Company. Quickly implementing the plan, Law recruited greater numbers of Germans and Swiss than expected. Now, as France's Minister of Finance, he hoped to send thousands of Germans to Louisiana. Law propagandized Louisiana as a semitropical paradise. A document entitled *The Magnificent Country of Louisiana* was printed in Leipzig and distributed in Germany and Switzerland. The colony was described as a land of gold and silver; a land of herbs and plants for apothecaries; a land of healing remedies and infallible cures for the fruits of love. The Germans, who wanted freedom and relief from war, were severely misled and fell as easy prey. In some cases, entire villages headed by their mayors began migration to this promised land of plenty.

THE GERMAN RECRUITS

Though it is unknown how many responded, historian J. Hanno Deiler estimated that 12,000 Germans were recruited. Other historians estimated 10,000 Germans were recruited while other estimates were 6,000 and 3,000. The Germans began moving in spring 1720. A letter by Elizabeth Charlotte, Duchess of Lorraine, noted the passage of 75 German families through Lorraine. The newspaper *Nouveau Mercure* cited, "Seventy German Families passed Toul bound for Orleans and Louisiana."

In all, 520 families, or 3,991 individuals, signed up as indentured agricultural servants under contract to the Company. Once settled, they were obligated to sell their produce to the Company and to purchase necessities at fixed Company prices.

The Germans walked west to Orleans, then to Port Louis at L'Orient, France, on the Atlantic Ocean. Most completed the 60-day, 1,000-mile journey by July and were placed under the command of Edouard de Rigby, a Company director. At L'Orient the ships were not ready and shelter and provisions were scarce. The Company established a temporary tent encampment around nearby fountains for a water source. Nearly a year passed before the Germans departed for Louisiana. Unsanitary conditions prevailed

Gegenwärtiger Zustand
derer
Finantzen
von Franckreich,
Worinnen
die bißherigen Unternehmungen
des Herrn LAW,
Insonderheit aber
die Historie der Königlichen Banco,
der Indianischen nach Mississipi handeln-
den Compagnie, und die in dem Müntz-
wesen gemachte Veränderungen,
Aus denen hiervon eingelauffenen Nach-
richten, mit allerhand Reflexions über dieses
neue Systema angeführt und erläutert
werden;
Als ein ander Theil
der Beschreibung
des
MISSISSIPISchen Handels,
und SUPPLEMENT
zu der
Europäischen FAMA.
Leipzig, 1720.
bey Joh. Friedrich Gleditschens seel. Sohn.

Law's advertisement of Louisiana to the Germans

and epidemic diseases claimed hundreds. So many died, particularly children, they were buried in mass graves. Approximately 2,000 perished while awaiting transport to Louisiana. Some returned to Germany to escape the contagious maladies. Relatively few, 1,000 or more, actually sailed for the New World.

The 7,500-mile voyage took them from Port Louis at L'Orient to the Canary Islands off North Africa down to the New World port of entry on the West Indies island of Saint Domingue. From here they sailed into the Gulf of Mexico to Ship Island, their final port of entry. By long boat or barge they were ferried 10 miles to Biloxi where they waited to be moved into the interior.

The first ship, *Les Deux Freres*, departed for Louisiana in November 1720 arriving in March 1721. Though 230 Germans sailed, 100 died at sea or in foreign ports.

The *Garonne* set sail in January 1721 with 210 Germans. Because of sickness, it returned to port and sailed again February 27, reaching Saint Domingue in late April where it was captured by pirates and held for six weeks. It is thought the ship reached Louisiana in early 1722 after a year at sea and 160 casualties.

The *Charente* supposedly departed in February 1721 with 245 Germans, but returned to L'Orient. These Germans probably transferred to the *Portefaix*, which sailed in March with 330 Germans and Swiss. They arrived in June after an uneventful crossing. The most notable passenger aboard was the Swiss officer and future German leader, Charles Friederick D'Arensbourg.

The *Saint-André* departed on May 5, 1721 with 158 aboard and the *Durance* departed a day later with 108 passengers.

On May 20 the regent issued an order halting the project. The 600 Germans still living in the temporary camp at L'Orient were paid 20 livres each to aid them in the ordered return home. Because of this order it is unlikely that the *Saône* sailed in July, though a passenger list exists. Some historians believe the ship sailed and reached Louisiana in November.

Of those recruited for settlement in Louisiana, roughly 400 were Swiss. Of these, only 200 sailed, not as indentured servants, but as skilled worker-soldiers. One group departed L'Orient in November 1720 on the *Mutine*. Another sailed with the Germans on Les *Deux Freres*. A final group left in April 1721 aboard the *Venus*.

Of the 4,000 recruits, it is believed more than 2,000 died at L'Orient and only about 1,000 actually departed. Some 600 probably returned to their homeland or remained in France. About 700 of the 1,000 who sailed, arrived in Louisiana. These individuals lived for months on the Gulf beaches exposed to the elements and plagued by famine. Many died from eating unknown plants. D'Artaguette, Louisiana's administrative officer, stated, "More than half perished because of their long stay on the barren coast." In June and July, some 200 died of disease and starvation at Biloxi. More would have died if not for the help of the Biloxi, Pascagoula, Choctaw and Mobile people who provided corn and venison.

THE GERMAN COAST: NEW ORLEANS' GARDEN

In April, Bienville moved some of the Germans up the Mississippi River to New Orleans on the small ship *Dromedaire*. Others moved 400 miles to Law's Arkansas concession. They settled and cleared land at the confluence of the Arkansas and Mississippi rivers unaware that Law had gone bankrupt and fled France. When the news arrived about Law, the majority returned to New Orleans demanding a better settlement region than the Arkansas or a return to Germany.

Bienville and D'Arensbourg met. The 300 remaining Germans were relocated to the Mississippi's west bank, 25 miles above New Orleans near modern-day Hahnville. The area had been cleared and cultivated by the Taensa and Ouachas people. Charlevoix, a Jesuit priest, described the land as, "The most beautiful with the best soils." In January and February 1722, the Germans arrived and the area became known almost immediately as the "German Coast" or "Côte Des Allemands." The Germans settled not as indentured servants but as habitants, a status that did not offer ownership immediately, but would in the future. They were still required to sell their surplus produce to the Company at predetermined prices. Ultimately, it was hoped that these German settlers could help feed the New Orleans colonists.

With the hardships the Germans had already endured, now they dealt with Louisiana's subtropical climate, hurricanes, floods, Native Americans, insects and snakes. With the help of Company laborers, the Germans built homes and established four tiny villages called Hoffen,

Marienthal, Augsburg and Karlstein. According to the May 1722 census, only 247 Germans, barely six percent of the original 4,000, lived in the settlement. Of these, 40 percent were children. The Germans owned no livestock or draft animals, but still they planted the land with grains and vegetables provided by the Company.

Colony officials expected an abundant, rich harvest that first year. The industrious, determined, productive Germans delivered. The first crops were tobacco, corn, rice, beans, peas and other vegetables. Tobacco was a cash crop for the Company. The

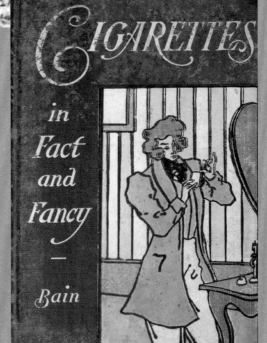

Perique tobacco field in Paulina, 1920s

food crops sustained the Germans and surpluses were sold to the Company for New Orleans.

However that same year, a devastating hurricane hit Louisiana. Two of the German villages flooded and 41 Germans died. After that, the Germans built their homes on high ground next to the Mississippi River. Over time, the German Coast stretched for miles along the great River Road establishing many present-day communities.

Despite obstacles, by 1724 the Germans supplied New Orleans' produce. They cultivated 115 arpents of land and harvested 612 barrels of rice as well as a wide variety of vegetables. They had 51 hogs and 12 cows, an important step toward self-sufficiency. German agriculture was so critical to New

Orleans' survival, a law was passed to safeguard the supply. French authorities described the Germans as, "Devoted, hardworking people who are esteemed for their honesty, their morality and their devotion to the land." The German Coast was called the "Garden of the Capital." According to historical records, the Germans saved the city of New Orleans from famine twice. By 1732 the Germans supplied the New Orleans market with vegetables, herbs, butter, eggs, poultry and other commodities. By 1744 they brought apples, plums, pears, figs, sweet potatoes, melons, artichokes, cabbage and various greens. Their accomplishments encouraged French authorities to request more German colonists, because they were the best settlers.

The 56 surviving German families originated from the German Rhineland, the Palatinate, Alsace, Lorraine, Württemberg, Frankfurt, Speyer, Mainz, Switzerland, Strassburg, Swabia, Siliesia, Baden, Bavaria, Augsburg, Cologne, Franconia, Saxony, Hungary and Sweden. Most were Catholic with some Lutherans, Calvinists and Zwinglians. Many German descendants still live on the original German Coast in St. Charles, St. James and St. John the Baptist parishes. Family names include Waguespack, Schexnayder, Troxclair, Zeringue, Oubre, Tregre, Webre, Folse, Toups, Matherne, Haydel, Reynard, Leche, Vicknair, Labranche, Stahl, Lambert, Rome and Hymel.

Though the Germans prospered, the Company of the Indies was bankrupt. The French Crown regained direct control of the Louisiana colony. Some historians believe France's extreme financial losses influenced their ultimate decision to transfer Louisiana to Spain.

By 1769 there were 186 German farms with 1,268 inhabitants and 3,588 cattle, horses, sheep and hogs. Living among the Germans were 52 French families, 90 Canadian families and 12 foreign families.

Back row, left to right: Lawrence Fabacher, Anthony Fabacher, Louis Fabacher, Barbara Fabacher, John Fabacher, Peter Fabacher and Albert Fabacher. Front row, left to right: Franz Joseph Fabacher, Jr., Madeline Frey Fabacher, Madeline Fabacher, Jr., Jacob Fabacher, Aloysius Fabacher and Joseph Fabacher, Sr.

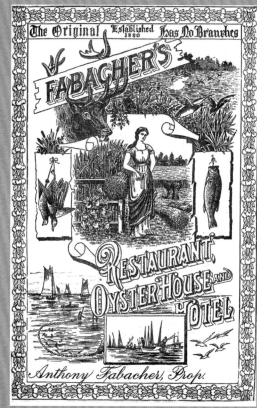

Fabacher family restaurant menu

WAVES OF GERMAN IMMIGRATION

Germans immigrated to Louisiana again in the 19th century in three waves. From 1820 – 1850, they came following the Napoleonic Wars. Many of these were

indentured servants who worked on farms and plantations. The second wave of German immigrants arrived in New Orleans between the 1840s and 1850s after fleeing Germany's civil war. Most were skilled professionals such as physicians, engineers and lawyers who introduced the Crescent City to German music and architecture and

built numerous breweries, churches and theaters. They helped build city streets and waterworks. In 1853, 53,000 Germans arrived in New Orleans, the United States' second leading port of entry. Though more than half of these immigrants moved to other states, 25,000 Germans made Louisiana their home.

The final wave of German immigration began in 1864, peaked in 1882 and declined dramatically by 1898. Almost three million Germans, primarily industrial workers, came through New Orleans en route to other areas of the country.

Also noteworthy to German settlement in Louisiana is Germantown, the 1835 religious colony founded by followers of Count Leon seven miles northeast of present-day Minden. The colony operated under a communal system for 37 years. The original kitchen, dining hall and one cabin remain as well as a replica smokehouse and blacksmith shop.

"The Search" by Wanda Kendrick Ballard. After losing her husband, Count Leon, and many other German immigrants to yellow fever in the swamp lands near Campti, the Countess Elisa Leon and her children searched for a healthier place to live.

Likewise, a small group of Germans who arrived in Louisiana in the late 19th century established the Fabacher and Robert's Cove communities in present-day Acadia Parish in southwestern Louisiana. Cheap land and the future railroad attracted them to the area. Though the Fabacher settlers dispersed, the Robert's Cove community still exists. Many German traditions including the celebration of German religious holidays are preserved in this small community.

HISTORY OF GERMAN FOODS

In the latter part of the 1st century, Tacitus, a Roman historian, wrote *Germania* in which he referred to German food as simple. Ancient Germans lived on gruels; breads made of oats, barley and millet; milk and cheeses; wild fruits and berries; and game and fowl. Change occurred over the first 10 centuries, because of Rome's influence. Charlemagne, who united most of Europe into a single Christian community in 800, taught the people how to plant herb gardens and vineyards and instructed people on food usage per meal.

During the Middle Ages, Germany's food was differentiated from the rest of Europe solely based on regional resources. Open-fire, spit-roasted beef and whole oxen were culinary masterpieces of the day. Smaller meat dishes included kidneys prepared with onions and raisins in a pungent wine sauce. Salt pork, sausages and black puddings were enjoyed. Kings and nobles feasted on dishes of hart (deer), wild boar and pheasant. Geese and apple stuffings were popular as were chickens. Roasted peacock prepared with caraway and other spices and doused with egg yolk was highly prized on the medieval table. Fish such as carp, pike

Mrs. Florence Gravois making Petit Gâteaux

Charles Francois Cambre in front of his bakery shop, 1902-03

and flatfish were prepared in various ways from roasting on a spit to stewing with raisins, pepper, honey and brine.

Foods of the medieval table contained spices imported from the Orient, which signified a person's wealth. Spices were a luxury, a preservative and a means of masking the taste of spoiled foods. Nürnberg's greatness was built on the spice trade and rich merchants were known as Pfeffersacke or "pepper bags."

Beer, cider and milk were the preferred beverages. The wealthy also enjoyed wine, which was often served hot and spiced.

The Germans cherished sweets. They used honey in their heavily spiced and scented pastries and confections, because sugar was rare and expensive. Cookies were formed in wooden molds in the shapes of castles, warriors and animals. Recipes from 1350 explain the making of sour cherry or apple fritters and how to crystallize rose leaves.

At meals, kings and dukes served Charlemagne. After Charlemagne dined, the kings and dukes were served by their counts and chief vassals who were then served by

their subordinates. Thus, Charlemagne instituted the policy of dignitaries being served by their inferiors. Often, the lowliest did not dine before midnight. Though people ate with their fingers, table manners were rigid.

Formal banquets offering numerous courses and dishes highlighted the Middle Ages. The great banquets of Medieval Germany featured the Schauessen or "foods for show." These splendid dishes included whole lambs, calves and deer ornamented with gold or silver. Pheasants, swans and peacocks were prepared in their full plumage with gilded beaks and feet. These grand outdoor banquets lasted as long as five hours and included entertainment between courses. A meal truly became a work of art. The common people were not forgotten. When Maximilian I became King of Germany in 1486, whole oxen were roasted for everyone in the marketplace. Whole roasted lambs, fish and hares were tossed to the people from the palace windows where the king dined.

As the Middle Ages ended and the Renaissance began, German cities expanded and grew in their rigid structure. Most citizens belonged to monopolistic craft guilds. These artisan societies controlled every aspect of the individual's work and regulated every trade and profession, including

Choucroute Garni

As the Renaissance progressed, fine cooking and feasting trickled down to the rising middle class. Foods consumed included beer soup spiced with pepper and ginger, turtle soup, sausages, lamb with kale, veal with saffron, roast venison with garlic and onions, venison baked in a crust, lark pies, stews of lampreys, preserved beaver legs, roast boar, spice cakes, ham, breads including those with caraway and fennel, boiled fish, spiced wine, beer varieties, a cream of almonds, cheeses and marzipan.

food production and distribution. Many poor people living in the heavily populated German cities did not have kitchens, so they purchased cooked foods including boiled and roasted meats from the Garküchen. The guild organizations were so strict that cooks who ran these establishments could not slaughter the animals they prepared. Likewise, bakers could not grind their own flour. The kitchens were subdivided into those allowing the cooks to boil, roast, fry or bake. This subdivision of kitchen duties was the beginning of the kitchen brigade that was firmly established by Antoine Careme and his student Auguste Escoffier centuries later.

POTATOES

The potato did not initially find favor with the Germans, because many believed it caused leprosy. Though Frederick the Great coerced the peasants of eastern Germany to raise potatoes, they refused to eat them. It was not until His Majesty dined on potatoes publicly on a balcony in Breslau that the peasants were convinced that they were harmless. Ironically, during the course of the 1700s, the potato was an indispensable food item for the commoner who referred to them as "earth apples" or "ground pears." Today, Germans serve potatoes boiled, stuffed, mashed, baked and fried. Potatoes are served in sauerkraut, salads, soups, pancakes and dumplings and are sometimes eaten at every meal, every day of the week.

Shredding cabbage

Cookbooks included the popular 15th century *Küchenmaysterey* or *Mastery of the Kitchen*. Published in Nürnberg in 1485, it was originally written for a nobleman's kitchen and remained in print for 200 years. The five parts of the book dealt with fast-day foods, meats, baked and fried foods, sauces and vinegar and wine. One recipe recommendation was to cook fish and crayfish in wine rather than beer or vinegar. Vegetable recipes included turnips, spinach, peas and sauerkraut.

In 1652, Paul Fürst of Nürnberg wrote a culinary manual, which included instructions on how to set a table and tips on interesting napkin folding. The manual included carving instructions, which had become a fine art during the Renaissance. There were specific methods to carve a goose, pheasant, duck, hare, rabbit, boar, pig, lamb and fish. Even desserts such as marzipan, Torten, candies, melons, oranges and other fruit had special carving instructions. A calendar of seasonal foods, guidance for the preparation of formal banquets and table manners and etiquette were also included in the manual.

The Thirty Years' War from 1618 to 1648 devastated Germany. Prompted by religious antagonism between Protestants and Catholics and territorial ambitions of princes, Germany starved. More than a generation after the war ended, a third of Northern Germany's farmland was still untilled. The people ate dogs, cats, rats, acorns and grass. People of the Rhineland died with grass in their mouths. In 1618, Germany's population was 21 million. By 1648, it was less than 13 ½ million.

Gradually, Germany recuperated and became influenced by the kings of France, especially Louis XIV. Food became sophisticated. Handwritten German cookbooks circulated between families and courts and contained recipes for pie of hare, squabs served with a salad of chervil and cucumber and venison stew sauced with capers. Desserts were refined from the spiced honey cakes to yeast pastries, egg-and-almond cakes and Torten. The cookbooks revealed the influence of Chef La Varenne who reformed French cooking in the 17th century.

By the end of the 1600s, class differences in living habits, food choices, cooking styles and eating habits were rigid. In contrast, the aristocratic food and drink of the 18th century included recipes for rose or violet sugar, capons stuffed with oysters or cooked with almonds and a variety of cakes and sweetmeats.

Coffee, chocolate and tea were a passion and led to the establishment of coffee rooms and pastry shops.

Germany was greatly influenced by France during this period. In fact, Frederick the Great of Prussia preferred to speak French and imported French cooks and a master chef named Noël. Frederick the Great was a fussy eater and offered numerous suggestions before his food was cooked, then made notes on his menu card as he dined to discuss with the chef later. Though he preferred simple foods such as herring, green peas, eel pie and ham with cabbage, he liked it hot and piquant, insisting on more and varied spices.

By the end of the 18th century, peasants, workers and the poor lived and ate simply on traditional dishes of kraut and bacon, lentils and peas, and dumplings. During the 1800s, German food became simpler and developed into the style most familiar today, though the upper class tables kept a strong French influence.

FOODS OF LOUISIANA'S GERMANS

Until unification in 1871, Germany was a loose grouping of tribes, fiefdoms, townships, dukedoms, principalities and small kingdoms. Invaders constantly waged war on the Germans, devastating their homes and leaving their rich fields a vast wasteland. Not surprisingly, many Germans immigrated to the New World.

In 1681, William Penn, an English Quaker who visited the Rhineland four years previous, invited all the inhabitants of that area to live on his new land grant in America. His adopted land offered plentiful, rich soil where peace reigned and everyone worshipped God as he wished under laws they established and administered. By 1776, nearly half of Pennsylvania's residents were Germans from the Palatinate. These immigrants were farmers, scholars, ministers, lawyers, artisans, printers, weavers, potters, turners and gunsmiths. These religious immigrants were passionate about music, color and decoration. Most of their recipes were for good, substantial dishes, the recipes for which were preserved by word of mouth.

Stella Guedry and her teacher friends from New Orleans on an outing in Norco in Joseph Lovetro's vegetable truck, 1920

Similarly, the Germans who settled in Louisiana in the 1720s were primarily from the southern area of Germany including places such as Alsace, Lorraine, the Palatinate, Wurttemberg, Strassburg, Baden, Bavaria and Augsburg. Southern Germany was known for cattle and dairy farms; wheat, grain and white wine fields; and

VACHERIE FOLSE

Foltz, the German surname that was changed in Louisiana to Folse, originated in the Ramstein and Kaiserslautern areas of Germany. One of the earliest mentions of the Foltz name was found in 1656, when Petter Voltz was referred to as the Hohenecken miller. Petter's son, Philipp Volz, was a forester in the Hohenecken woods in 1675. It is theorized that Philipp's son was Johann Adam Volz, the father of the future German Coast settler, Johann Jacobum Foltz.

Though it is unclear on what ship Johann Jacobum Foltz traveled to Louisiana, the 1724 census of the German villages at Les Allemands in present-day St. Charles Parish between Taft and Hahnville recorded a Jean Jacob Foltz. Because the record keepers of that era were casual about name spellings and often applied French versions of German names, lineages are difficult to verify. For example, the November 14, 1720 manifest of *Les Deux Freres* also recorded the name of Jean Gorge Fols and his wife Julienne.

According to the census, Jean Jacob Foltz was 26 years old and a native of Ramstein in the Palatinate. He was a Roman Catholic shoemaker with a wife and a one-year-old child. Jean Jacob had been living for two years on four arpents of land on which he had harvested seven barrels of rice in 1724, though he was ill all summer. The 1722 hurricane affected Jean Jacob's harvest as did a flood in 1724 resulting from an overflow of the Mississippi River. On May 12, 1725, Jean Jacob asked the Superior Council for an advance of rice because his land flooded the previous year. He died on June 10, 1746.

Antoine Folse, the grandson of Johann Jacob Foltz, founded Vacherie Folse. Antoine was born on the German Coast between 1755 and 1760 at Edgard. Around 1796, he, his wife and children moved to his cow ranch, or Vacherie, on the ridges bordering the west side of Lac Des Allemands. Antoine held his land by permission of the Spanish authorities and possibly by a Spanish land grant. Folse's land tract was comprised of 7,500 superficial arpents and was bounded on the east and north by the lake, on the south by bayous Boeuf and Cabahanose, and on the west by vacant lands and the bayous Tigre, Chevreuil, Le Ha Ha and Heron. Antoine Folse cultivated 640 arpents of his land. This area was later the territory of Golden Star Plantation and the Steib Settlement of Vacherie.

ame Elizabeth Kettenring Dutrey Begue with her husband, Hypolite Begue

barley grown for the breweries to make beer. Their cooking was simple, hearty, one-dish combinations. Though their recipes, like those of the Pennsylvania Germans, were transmitted by word of mouth from one generation to the next, it is not difficult to determine the foods they enjoyed based on the lifestyles they led and their legacy, which lingers on the German Coast of Louisiana today. These cattlemen, butchers, dairymen, gardeners and brewmasters thrived on Louisiana's swamp floor pantry, which provided wild game as well as abundant fruits and vegetables.

Not surprisingly, Louisiana's Germans were perhaps best known for their ability to create incredible gardens. For 30 generations, the Germans of the Rhenish Palatinate cultivated gardens, orchards and vineyards and were the envy of the world. The Rhineland was the garden spot of Germany where chestnuts, peaches, apricots, figs, almonds and lemons flourished. With three great growing seasons, the land of Louisiana suited these farmers well and soon

with jellies, preserves, vegetables and dried fruits and berries for lean months of the year.

The German diet included greens and edible wild plants. Often, Germans foraged for greens in the pastures and along fence rows. Interestingly, the Germans brought a traditional dish to Louisiana of greens served on "Maundy Thursday" or "Green Thursday" of Holy Week. The German custom was to prepare a dish containing seven different greens, or a seven-herb soup, to remain healthy throughout the year. In Louisiana, this German tradition has been adapted and is still celebrated on Holy Thursday with the preparation of gumbo verde or gumbo des herbes. An odd number of greens including mustard greens, collards, turnip tops, beet tops, parsley, spinach and purslane flavored with salt pork must be used in the pot for luck. In years past, cooks in New Orleans gathered greens from the neutral grounds to flavor the gumbo verde. Today, Leah Chase of Dooky Chase in New Orleans is famous for her Creole version of this traditional German dish.

Many German Coast descendants remember shredding and salting cabbages in large barrels for traditional sauerkraut making. In Rhenish and Palatine homes, a pot of soup remained on the hearth where beef, pork, poultry or vegetable and herb scraps were deposited to create a unique and flavorful dish. These hearty, one-dish meals reflected the seasonal foods. The Germans of Louisiana would have prepared similar soups of vegetables, corn, potato or beans as well as wild game and sausage. Cattle raising and butchering were also German contributions to Louisiana. In their smokehouses hung venison, sausage, beef and hams. Rabbit pie, roasted duck or roasted squab resulted from wild game hunts. Like many other cultures, the Germans celebrated the boucherie, or the butchering of the pigs, in the winter months. This laborious task provided fresh meat as well as smoked and salted meats for families' use in the summer. This strenuous task was made less difficult and

Turnip washing, LaPlace, 1936. Workers were paid 10 cents per hour and sometimes worked 17 hours a day at peak season.

Louisiana's swamps and bayou lands were transformed into a veritable Eden. The Germans tilled the fields, planted kitchen gardens and immediately reaped splendid harvests. Even today, ancient German planting traditions survive in Louisiana such as planting the summer garden on Good Friday. The settlers cultivated vegetables they had known in Germany, but grew new ones as well. The Germans' gardens likely included leaf lettuce, onions, radishes, cabbage, beans, tomatoes, corn, peppers, celery, endive and a variety of root vegetables. Though they grew wheat and barley in Germany, they quickly adapted to rice and sweet potato crops in Louisiana. Mint and herbs grew in the kitchen garden and were used fresh, though some were dried and stored for later use. Important herbs may have included garlic, horseradish, thyme, sweet marjoram, coriander, caraway, fennel and rosemary. An industrious people, they filled their cupboards and pantries

Packing carrots at the A. Montz Ice Plant, LaPlace, 1930s. Left to right: Mrs. Denis Madere, Mrs. Hilda Webre Triche, Beatrice Webre, Willie Webre and C. F. Woodley, vegetable inspector.

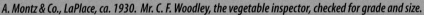
A. Montz & Co., LaPlace, ca. 1930. Mr. C. F. Woodley, the vegetable inspector, checked for grade and size.

enjoyable, because many families participated. Everyone was assigned a task from fire stoker, to bristle scraper, to boudin maker. Before dawn, large cauldrons of scalding water were prepared over hot, open fires. A 300- to 800-pound pig was slaughtered by cutting the jugular vein. The blood was gathered for making red boudin. The pig was scalded and the bristles removed, which were sold later to brush manufacturers. Then, the pig was strung from a tree. The women removed and cleaned the intestines, which became the sausage casing. The pig was then cut and quartered into chops, spareribs, roasts and bacon. Portions of the pig were smoked or salted, while sections were reserved for families' immediate use. The skin was made into pork cracklins and the fat was rendered into lard. In the German household, pig lard or bacon fat was used for cooking, not olive oil. Inedible portions of the pig were used to make soap.

During the festivities, families enjoyed music, home brewed beer and fresh pork. Usually grillades, boudin, fresh sausage and ponce (stuffed pig's stomach) were served as well as debris, a rich stew made with the organ meat of the pig and served over rice. At the end of the day, everyone went home with their families' portion of the slaughter. This activity was repeated nearly every weekend during the slaughtering months of December, January and February.

An ingenious people, the Germans created dishes such as meat and seafood filled vegetables. They created rice and meat dressings as well as sweet farre dressing using yams or rice, ground meat and pork.

Traditionally, Germans were dairymen. Records indicate that the French sent cattle to the German Coast and the industrious Germans sent butter, cheese and fresh meat back to New Orleans. Though the Germans did not have springhouses, many dug deep wells, in which their milk, butter and eggs were suspended. The water table from the

As soon as the first cold spell of autumn hit the river parishes, residents knew that "boucherie" time was imminent.

1930s boucherie at the home of Charles Troxler in Taft

Mississippi River kept these perishable foods cool.

The concept of outdoor bake ovens of the Rhineland and Palatinate was brought to the New World. Traditionally, baking was done once weekly, usually on Friday. Breads were baked in the back of the oven while pies and cakes were cooked simultaneously in the oven front for shorter bake times. German pies known as Obstkuchen were large, wagon-wheel flats made of yeast dough. Cherries, apples, plums, peaches and other seasonal fruits were placed atop the dough and baked. It is likely that the German Coast settlers created pies such as strawberry, blackberry, raspberry, elderberry, custard, cheese, crookneck squash (jurdimon) and mincemeat.

On Shrove Tuesday, or Mardi Gras, Germans traditionally ate Fassnachts, which were doughnuts sprinkled with sugar. Though it is not believed that the Germans developed the beignet, they obviously had a beignet-type dessert in their culture.

Christmas was the height of baking season. Every German home was fragrant with spice as fresh fruit pies, breads, cakes, cookies, nuts and fruitcakes were pulled from the oven. Only at Christmas were precious items such as almonds, raisins, currants, citron and orange peel used in baking.

The German tradition of cutting cookies into various shapes and designs lives on in Louisiana today. The old cutters and molds that once fashioned stars, sheep, shepherds, camels and St. Nicholas have been replaced by aluminum cookie cutters, but the "Petit Gâteaux" as they are known, are still exchanged between households up and down the river at Christmas. Now, as then, Christmas Eve is a major day of celebration. For weeks young boys prepare bonfires on the riverbanks using driftwood and cane, which are lit on Christmas Eve to guide Santa Claus or Papa Noel into Bayou Country.

The Germans came from a wine-producing region of Germany that was also known for beer and cider. Not surprisingly, Germans along the River Road made cherry bounce, beer, homemade fruit wines from persimmons, Muscadines, black cherries, blackberries, strawberries and peaches, as well as cordials and fruit ratafias. These homemade wines and cordials were enjoyed with guests particularly during Christmas and New Year celebrations. Additionally, coffee was a popular beverage and is still served in many German homes with every meal.

England

Back row, left to right: George Shotwell, Isabell Bowman, Sarah Bowman, Sarah Turnbull Bowman (Daniel and Martha's daughter), James Bowman (Sarah's husband); Front row, left to right: Nina Bowman, Martha Bowman Fort and her infant son, William Fort III, Martha Turnbull and Corrie Bowman.

ENGLISH MIGRATION TO COLONIAL AMERICA

The earliest English settlers to North America arrived in Jamestown, Va., in 1607. By 1620, the Pilgrims were colonizing Plymouth, Mass. These pioneers, the first to arrive on America's shores seeking religious freedom, were followed by four large waves of English-speaking colonists arriving between 1620 and 1775.

The Puritans constituted the first mass migration from England and were the first religious exiles to reach the English Colonies. Similar to the Pilgrims, they came from the east of England settling in Massachusetts between 1629 and 1640. Since the 1550s, England had been racked by religious tensions between the Church of England and Catholicism. The Puritans were anti-Catholic and viewed the Anglican Church as a corruption of true Protestantism with too many remnants of the Catholic faith. They wanted purity in the Anglican Church with each man having the right to worship God individually. The Puritans stressed a strong work ethic and scrutinized others for signs of waywardness.

The second immigrant group came from the south of England and was similar to the Jamestown colonists. A small number were Royalist elite while the greater faction were indentured servants. They settled in Virginia between 1642 and 1725.

The third wave of colonists came from the northern midlands of England and Wales and settled the Delaware River Valley between 1675 and 1725.

Finally, the Scotch-Irish arrived from the borders of northern Britain and Northern Ireland. They were primarily Presbyterian and settled the Appalachian backcountry of the southern colonies from 1718 to 1775.

While all groups were English speaking and primarily shared a Protestant faith, each had its own form of religion, spoke in a unique dialect and had specified social rankings. They built homes in different styles, held different business and farming views and had specific ideas about public order, power and freedom. The unique characteristics of each colonist group can still be recognized in various parts of America today.

King James I supported the colonization of America, because it offered the opportunity to obtain wealth, which the Spanish had proven existed in the Americas. Plus, this was a great opportunity to get rid of the most radical Puritan minorities. English migration to America occurred over a period of time and was a direct reflection of political turmoil and religious persecution in the mother country. The greatest Puritan migration occurred under King Charles

I (1625-1649). The Royalists and Catholics migrated to the southern English Colonies, when Oliver Cromwell served as Lord Protector of England during the Republican Period (1649-1658). Following the persecution of Quakers under the Test Act of 1673, William Penn created a plan for a Quaker colony in the New World, which led to Quaker settlements in western New Jersey and Pennsylvania. Finally, the persecution and repression that followed the failed Scottish Rebellions of 1715 and 1746 caused many Scots and Scotch-Irish to flee to the colonies during this same period.

Unlike the French in Louisiana, English immigrants came in family groups with women and girls making up almost half of the colonists. The English immigrants were highly skilled craftsmen, merchants, farmers, agricultural workers and laborers, many with some level of education. Because reading holy scripture was a foundation of the Puritans' religious beliefs, it is believed that most who came to America could read. Because of the great number of diaries, journals and letters written by officers and soldiers, English society, in general, appeared to be literate. Likewise, even those living in backcountry homes owned collections of books such as primers, prayer books, handbooks on farming, medicine, mathematics and surveying, definite indications of educated people.

ENGLISH COLONIAL FRONTIER FOODS

Frontier women cooked and preserved food, planted vegetable gardens, cleaned, sewed, washed and mended clothes. Of all chores, preparing and preserving food consumed most of the colonial housewife's time. Vegetable gardens grew close to their homes in raised beds. They planted native pumpkin, squash and melon crops as well as fruit trees.

The Native Americans taught colonists about native foods. The settlers learned to bake beans in earthen dishes buried in ashes; made sugar from maple tree sap for candy; and pounded corn into meal for simple cakes. One of the first crops introduced to New England was field peas, which were served hot or cold, boiled or baked at any meal.

Women milked in the morning, so breakfast was usually leftovers or previously prepared foods. A typical breakfast was toasted bread, cheese, leftover meat or vegetables and milk in the summer months. Lunch, the primary daily meal, reflected the season's bounty. Spring was the leanest season. Eel pie flavored with winter savory might be served. Wild onions, dandelions and skunk cabbage were welcome additions to a depleted pantry and a dwindling larder of turnips, parsnips and carrots. Summer meals might include leek soup and garden greens. Often, fresh eggs, milk and a fruit or berry tart might be added to the evening meal. Autumn meals included pork or goose with

Prime rib of beef

apples. Winter foods were typically boiled meats with sauces and preserved produce. Typically, meals consisted of boiled, stewed or steamed meats and fish served with peas, cornmeal cakes, puddings and wild berries. Supper was a simple meal of leftovers, because there was no refrigeration. Bread and cheese were served at supper and the broth from boiled meat could be made into a pottage by adding oatmeal or barley.

Colonial kitchens were either a room in the house, which was also used as the dining area, living area or perhaps a bedroom, or there was a separate kitchen and workspace for chores. Cooking was done in the fireplace on suspended pots, or coals were raked onto the hearth to create a cooking station. Much of the cooking and household chores such as soap and candle making were done outside where lighting was better. Each fireplace burned 15 to 20 cords of wood annually.

Generally, beer or cider accompanied meals. Expert craftsmen brewed "strong" beer each October. Housewives made "small" beer, a milder beverage, for immediate consumption. Beer was brewed using ingredients such as pine chips, pine buds, hemlock, fir leaves, roasted corn, dried apple skins, sassafras roots and bran. Making cider preserved the apple harvest. The liquid from the pressed fruit fermented in the cellar until it was mildly alcoholic. Tavern cider was more alcoholic, because sugar was added during fermentation.

Housewives gifted in preserving seasonal bounty were tremendous blessings. Winter and spring meals depended on their ingenuity, which meant comfort or starvation. They made summer milk into cheeses. They stored vegetables such as beets, cabbage, carrots, onions, parsnips, potatoes, radishes, turnips and winter squash in cellars or barrels packed with straw to prevent spoilage. Corn, beans and peas were dried. Squash, apples and pumpkins were cut into thin slices, peeled, threaded and dried. Beer was made from the apple and pumpkin skins. Cabbage was made into sauerkraut. Apple butter and sauces were created from fruits and vegetables.

Herb gardens were also important to colonial housewives. Parsley, skirret and sorrel were used for "sallets." Cooked herbs served hot or cold with oil and vinegar dressing accompanied many dishes. Herbs were used to season salted meats. Often, garden herbs were medicinal. Hyssop mixed with honey was cough syrup. Yarrow placed on wounds stopped bleeding. Savory treated colic. Tea from marjoram leaves relieved spasms, colic and indigestion. Chewing marjoram leaves relieved toothaches, and mixing the leaves with honey lessened bruising. The Native Americans taught colonists to use native plants and herbs for remedies, pesticides and dyes. According to early records and seed lists, essential herbs included angelica, basil, burnett, dill, fennel, hyssop, marjoram, parsley, rosemary, savory, thyme and tansey.

Other colonial crops included wheat, rye, barley, flax, hay and tobacco. Both the colonials and the Native Americans improved the soil by using seaweed, clam and oyster shells, fish, ashes and bone meal.

Autumn meant slaughtering. Men butchered the large animals, while women handled small pigs. Pork, the mainstay of the colonial diet, was pickled, salted and smoked. Brined pork was jarred and stored in the dairy where it was cool. Salted bacon slabs were smoked in chimneys. The colonials also raised cattle, sheep, goats and horses.

Once weekly the housewife baked in the outdoor oven or the fireplace oven. If there were no ovens, iron kettles were used. Brown bread was created from a mixture of wheat and corn and became a mainstay of the New Englander's diet. Wheat flour was saved for special occasions and to decorate the top crust of pies.

Colonial settlers adapted their cooking methods to American frontier foods. Though grain, potatoes and meat, other than wild game, were scarce upon arrival, the settlers found that leeks and nettles seasoned venison and bear meat well. Native plants such as watercress, milkweed shoots and dandelions were boiled with wild game. Chestnuts, hickory nuts, butternuts, walnuts and acorns seasoned wild meat as well. The settlers found American venison tastier than that of England, and it was "full of gravy, like fat young beef." Fish and fowl were plentiful. Grapes, gooseberries, cranberries, currants, blueberries, strawberries, raspberries and blackberries were eaten fresh or made into tarts. Cranberries made excellent sauce for venison, turkeys and other fowl and were preferred to gooseberries and cherries for tarts.

THE FRENCH AND INDIAN WAR: PIVOTAL POINT FOR INTERNATIONAL POWER IN AMERICA

At the onset of the French and Indian War, also known as the Seven Years War, the 13 English Colonies had a population estimated at 1.3 million. The war began in America's Ohio Valley in 1754. At the time, North America was a mass colonization effort of the English, French and Spanish, so the American conflict sparked international campaigns. War erupted in Europe in 1756 and rapidly spread around the globe.

In North America, the English captured Cape Breton in Canada from the French in 1758 and continued the Acadian expulsion known as Le Grande Derangement. By

1760, France also lost Quebec and Montreal to England. In the Caribbean, England captured the French islands including Martinique, the neutral islands and Guadeloupe. Once Spain entered the conflict as France's ally, England claimed Havana and the Philippines. When the smoke cleared, England was the decisive victor. William Pitt for England and the Duke of Choiseul for France negotiated the Treaty of Paris in 1763. More American territory changed hands with this peace negotiation than by any international settlement before or since.

According to the treaty, the British conquests in the French West Indies were restored though England kept the neutral islands except St. Lucia, which was recognized as French. Cuba was returned to Spain. Britain kept Florida, which included the Florida parishes of present-day Louisiana. All of Canada and the eastern half of the Mississippi Valley was ceded to England, which should have included Louisiana. However, in the separate Franco-Spanish Treaty of Fontainebleau of 1762, France had secretly given Louisiana to Spain.

At the end of the Seven Years War, the balance of power in America was British. However, in the next decade Britain's 13 American Colonies would wage war against the mother country in the American Revolution, and the Americans would emerge victorious in their claim for independence.

LOUISIANA'S FLORIDA PARISHES

West Feliciana Parish along with East Feliciana, East Baton Rouge, Livingston, St. Helena, St. Tammany and Washington comprise the Florida Parishes of Louisiana. This territory within the top of the "toe" of present-day

Republic of West Florida flag

Louisiana is located between the Pearl and Mississippi rivers and above Lake Maurepas and Lake Pontchartrain. Though a distinct part of Louisiana today, this area was originally Spanish Florida and was referred to then and now as the Florida Parishes.

Following the Treaty of Paris, Louisiana's Florida Parishes came under British control. In 1764, British troops occupied the fort at Baton Rouge and established forts on Thompson's Creek in the Feliciana district. To solidify their control of the area, the British offered land grants to retired soldiers. Officers received from 3,000 to 5,000 acres. Privates received up to 300 acres. Recipients of the land grants and British loyalists during the American Revolution migrated to the Florida Parishes from the Atlantic seaboard. By 1766, a colony from North Carolina had made the long journey to settle between Baton Rouge and Natchez and a strong English component was introduced to the area.

1803 map showcasing the Florida Parishes

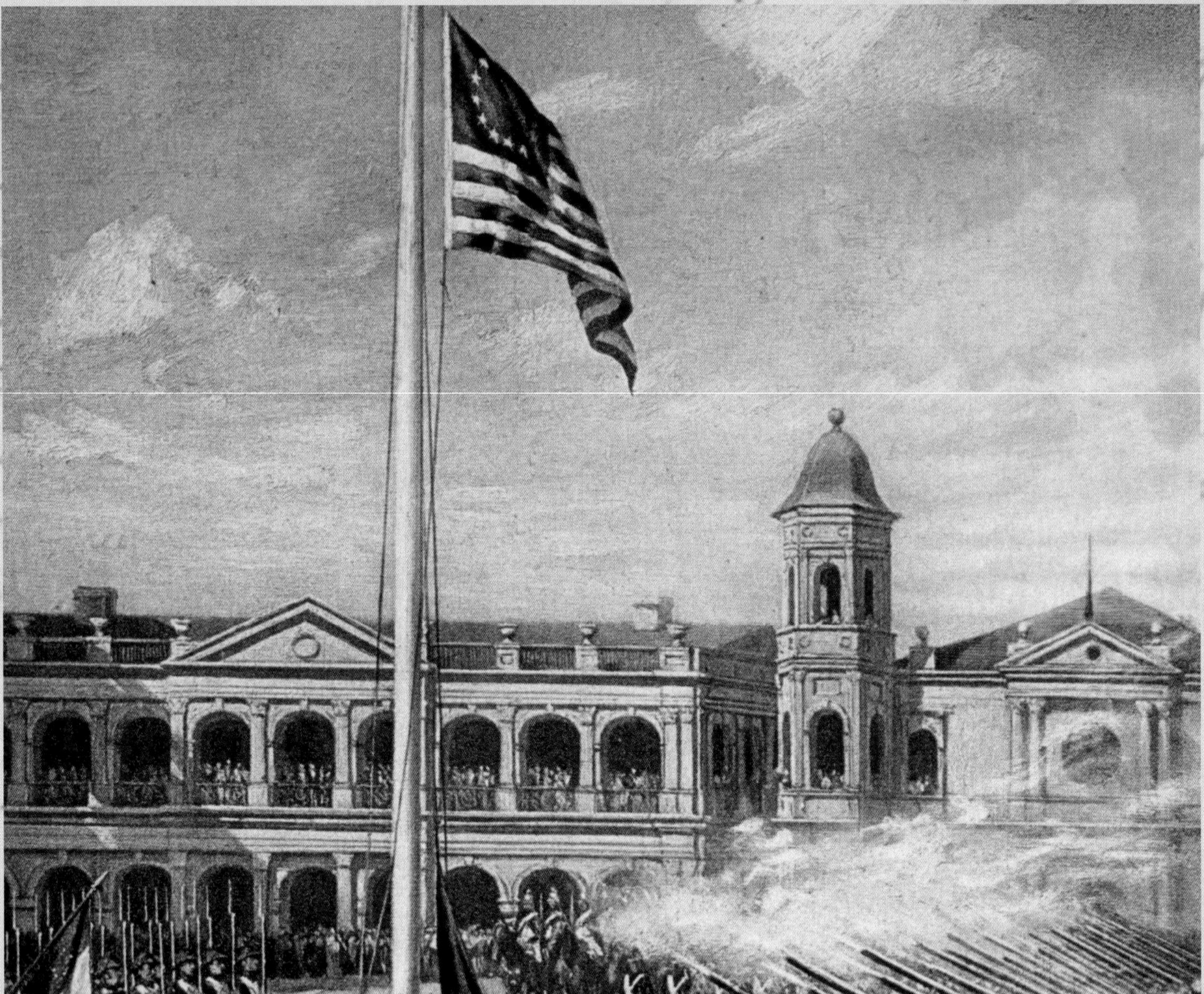

Transfer of Louisiana from France to the United States

Thomas Jefferson

William Charles Cole Claiborne, Louisiana's first American governor

Napoleon Bonaparte, French Emperor and military leader

French Prefect, Laussat

Grace Episcopal Church, St. Francisville

Purchase territory included the present-day states of Arkansas, Missouri, Iowa, Minnesota west of the Mississippi, North Dakota, South Dakota, Nebraska, Oklahoma, almost all of Kansas, the portions of Montana, Wyoming and Colorado east of the Rocky Mountains and Louisiana west of the Mississippi and New Orleans. However, the fate of the Florida Parishes was uncertain.

In 1804, West Florida residents attempted to overthrow Spanish control to stabilize the area. The Kemper Rebellion failed, because insurrectionists represented a pro-American faction, which was quelled by the pro-British, pro-French and pro-Spanish elements. Chaos prevailed and by autumn 1810 tensions exploded in the West Florida Rebellion. The American settlers, located primarily in the Felicianas, led a surprise raid capturing the fort at Baton Rouge and proclaiming the West Florida Territory independent. The Republic of West Florida lasted 74 days before its president, Fulwar Skipwith, allowed William Charles Cole Claiborne (Louisiana's first American governor) to take control of the territory for the United States. On October 27, 1810 President James Madison issued a proclamation declaring that West Florida was part of the Louisiana Purchase. Still, delays ensued in establishing an effective judicial system, and land disputes were further aggravated when American officials issued new land grants. In 1811, Congress prepared to admit the Orleans Territory as a state without including West Florida, so rebellion raged again. Though Louisiana was admitted

However, British control was short lived. In 1779, Bernardo de Gálvez, governor of the Orleans Territory, seized West Florida in support of the American revolutionaries. The British living in the area were allowed to stay and could keep their land as long as they swore loyalty to the Spanish crown and accepted Catholicism.

Gálvez thought it important to build barriers against the encroaching Americans. Small but significant settlements were scattered throughout Livingston and St. Tammany parishes. Immigrants from the Canary Islands (Los Isleños) located along the Amite River with their primary settlement being at Galveztown. German Catholic immigrants and the Acadians were also sent to the Florida Parishes. In 1785, more than 200 Acadians settled at Manchac in the area connecting Lake Maurepas and Lake Pontchartrain. That same year another group of Acadians located at Thompson's Creek in West Feliciana. By 1810, French-speaking communities flourished at Port Vincent and French Settlement in Livingston Parish. Other French-speaking people settled on the lakeshore in St. Tammany Parish.

Like the British, the Spanish offered large land grants in the area. Unfortunately, Spanish grants often conflicted with or overlapped British land grants causing tension between the pro-British and pro-Spanish factions.

The Spanish government in this region was weak and corrupt. Land disputes were unresolved, and district courts were not able to contend with the growing criminal element. Army deserters, Tories and desperadoes saw West Florida as a safe haven. They attacked wagons and travelers on the trails and highways. West Florida residents were

discontent and did not believe Spain could adequately police or promote the territory.

The matter was further complicated with the Louisiana Purchase of 1803. When France sold all 885,000 square miles of the Louisiana Territory to the United States for $15 million, the West Florida Parishes were only presumed to be included. (It is important to note that in a secret treaty in 1800, the Louisiana Territory was returned to France from Spain.) With interest payments the final price amounted to about four cents per acre. The Louisiana

Oakley Plantation, St. Francisville

Flooded Bayou Sara

to the Union on April 12, 1812, it was not until August 4, almost four months later, that West Florida from the Mississippi to the Pearl River was included as part of the new state.

WEST FELICIANA

West Feliciana is one of Louisiana's most beautiful and fertile parishes. The Tunica Hills bound the area on the north, the Mississippi River flanks the parish on the west and chalk cliffs make up the southern and eastern border. Many describe the parish as a veritable Eden and the "garden of Louisiana" with botanists and naturalists searching the perfumed woodlands from the earliest days. Virburnum, magnolia fuscata, purple magnolia, sweet olive, azaleas, jasmine, blue periwinkles, crocus, narcissus, hyacinths, jonquils, lilies and iris are only a few examples of Feliciana garden vegetation. Because West Feliciana lies within the apex of the great Mississippi Valley migratory flyway, it serves as a nesting or temporary feeding ground for a variety of birds. With the woodland offering a vast array of berries, fruits and grass seed plus an abundant water supply, it is no wonder that birds literally flock to the area. Thrashers, orioles, martins, field larks, cardinals, hawks, owls, herons and woodcocks are only a few of the birds that artist John James Audubon captured on canvas. Audubon, who decided to paint all of the birds in America, lived for a short while in West Feliciana during the 1820s where he painted no fewer than 80 of his famous folios. He and his wife, Lucy, lived at Oakley Plantation where she tutored the plantation owner's daughter to earn money for publication of Audubon's *The Birds of America*.

Native Americans made this area home long before white men penetrated the forest. The Houmas Indians lived in the area before many were massacred and others driven south by the Tunica in the early 1700s. Henri de Tonti, the "Iron Hand," was the first known white man to visit Feliciana. An Italian mercenary, Tonti was descending the Mississippi River in search of La Salle.

The French were the first Europeans to settle in what is now St. Francisville establishing a fort named St. Reine. Before the fort was abandoned in 1733 a small settlement grew called the "Village of St. Francis" in honor of St. Francis of Assisi, the founder of the Franciscan order. When Galvez captured the area for Spain in 1779, the whole region was named "Feliciana," meaning "happy land," in honor of Galvez's wife. Around 1780 the Spanish Capuchins built a monastery on the ridge. About 1785 the monastery burned and the Capuchins departed. St. Francisville was chartered under the Spanish colonial rule prior to 1808. Down the hill from St. Francisville where Bayou Sara emptied into the Mississippi River, a batture developed, which would become the largest river port between New Orleans and Natchez.

Immigrants of English descent dominated the Felicianas with large numbers of Scotch-Irish settlers calling the place home. Following the American Revolution, many settlers from Georgia, the Tidewater region of Virginia and the Carolinas moved to the Florida Parishes. Many of these were Tories fleeing persecution in American-controlled areas. Many settlers arrived during the first decade of the 1800s, because of the isolation and the volume of cheap land available.

Because tobacco and indigo farming were marginally successful in the West Florida Parishes, cotton farming was introduced in the early 1800s. The Siamese black seed cotton variety was particularly adaptable and prosperity flourished seemingly overnight. During the same period, slave rebellions in Saint Domingue deprived European manufacturers of one of their primary sources of cotton, so prices skyrocketed causing an economic boom for West Florida planters. By the 1830s, Louisiana and Mississippi surpassed Georgia and South Carolina in cotton production. The larger farms averaged between 50 and 200 cotton bales annually, making West Feliciana one of the wealthiest areas in the South.

The large cotton and sugarcane plantations coupled with an intelligent, cultured and hospitable aristocracy made West Feliciana one of the few examples of the traditional Old South. Rosedown, Ellerslie, Greenwood, Highland, The Cottage and Waverly plantations are a few examples of the lingering Old South in West Feliciana.

Bayou Sara railroad depot

ENGLISH SETTLEMENT: THE BARROW AND TURNBULL FAMILIES

Wealth, tradition and English influence in West Feliciana Parish was perhaps best exemplified by the Turnbull-Barrow family, one of the most socially prominent of the era.

In 1797, the widow Olivia Ruffin Barrow left Halifax County, N.C. for Tennessee. After two years, she and five of her seven children plus their slaves left for Nueva Feliciana to make enormous profits raising cotton. According to family legend 30 covered wagons moved the family, slaves, gold and prized household possessions. After Spanish authorities granted permission to enter the

territory, they acquired their land and settled by early 1801.

One of the first Anglo-Saxon families to settle in the South, the Barrows came from England during American colonial days, settling first in Virginia and later in the Carolinas. The family left a legacy of leadership in the West Feliciana

community. The Barrow grandchildren became known for their elaborate homes and beautiful gardens. In fact, Greenwood, Afton Villa, Ellerslie and Rosedown were among the outstanding country houses in America.

In 1828 Martha Hilliard Barrow married Daniel Turnbull uniting two socially prominent pioneer families of West

Rosedown Plantation

Feliciana Parish. Martha's father was William Barrow III, one of the widow Olivia's sons, and her mother was Pheraby Hilliard, the daughter of a wealthy planter from Northampton County, N.C. Martha's father built Locust Grove, known later as Highland, the first Federal-style house in West Feliciana. Martha and her siblings were educated at home until they were old enough to attend finishing schools and universities. Two of Martha's brothers attended Princeton, while she attended Madam Legoin's Institute in Philadelphia, acquiring knowledge in clothing style, manners and tastes. Martha's father instilled in his children family values, loyalty and respect for the land.

Daniel Turnbull, Martha's husband, was educated at Northern institutions. His father came to America in the last quarter of the 1700s from Dumfriesshire, Scotland. After successful business ventures in Alabama, he settled in West Feliciana on a Spanish land grant in 1783.

Following Martha and Daniel's magnificent society wedding, they traveled to Europe for the Grand Tour. In England, the Grand Tour was the final step in the education of a lady or gentleman. Martha was inspired by Versailles in France and the gardens of Italy. As she saw avenues of trees, statuary and ornamental gardens, she envisioned the garden she would create. In fact, Martha spent almost 60 years perfecting her gardens, importing trees, shrubs and flowers and carefully recording the garden work in her diary. While traveling, the couple saw a romantic play entitled *Rosedown*, which became the name of their future home.

Construction began on Rosedown in November 1834. By May 1835 the lavish home was completed. Most of the cypress and cedar used in construction came from the Rosedown property and was processed at the plantation sawmill. Slaves molded and fluted the 18 veranda and gallery columns. The home's total cost was $13,109. 20.

A housewarming party celebrated completion of the new home. In her diary, Martha recorded the foods needed to serve her 30 guests. There were six chickens for chicken salad, two turkeys, two ducks, one ham, one tongue, roast mutton, two roast chickens and one pig. Numerous cakes were created using 12 dozen eggs. Two ornamental pound cakes were served each weighing 12 pounds. There was a 10-pound fruitcake, six pounds of mixed cakes and lady

Daniel Turnbull

fingers. Six eggs were used for salad. Also needed were 16 pints of cream, jelly, blancmange, 50 spoonfuls of coffee, four decanters of wine, four decanters of Brandy, eight bottles of Champagne and four pounds of candy fruit. A jar of grapes, 24 bananas, two hogsheads of ice and six pineapples were obtained. The party cost $224 including $60 for the musicians.

Though beef, hogs, chickens, ducks and geese were raised and crops of corn and vegetables grown, plantation self-sufficiency was not the goal. Growing cotton was much more lucrative than saving a few pennies by raising food crops, which could be purchased. In 1835, Rosedown Plantation produced 170,624 pounds of cotton, or 426 400-pound bales, which sold between 13 cents and 18 ½ cents per pound. The cotton was shipped from New Orleans to

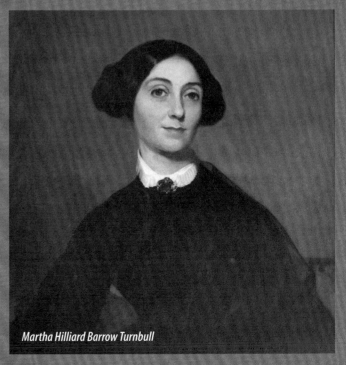

Martha Hilliard Barrow Turnbull

Cotton factor's grading room, probably New Orleans, ca. 1920

Generally, the Turnbull's summered in Saratoga returning in September or October to avoid the yellow fever epidemics that plagued Louisiana, particularly New Orleans. These sojourns lasted until the 1850s when the family began choosing Southern spas, because of Northern anti-slavery tensions.

molasses for their work while others demanded pay. In 1874, Martha filed a Civil War claim for property confiscated by the United States in 1863. Her claim included 300 hogsheads of sugar worth $60,000; 600 barrels of molasses worth $18,000; 200 mules worth $30,000; 100 horses worth $10,000; 700 cattle worth $14,000; 80 cane and other wagons worth $12,000; 300 hogs worth $3,000; 6,000 bushels of corn worth $6,000; 50 bales of cotton worth $18,000; 100 barrels of pork worth $4,000; 3,000 pounds of salted meat worth $6,000; and 20 sacks of coffee worth $2,000. Even after her death, Martha's daughter, Sarah, periodically re-filed the claim, though it remained unpaid.

Liverpool for Manchester Mills.

Besides Rosedown, Daniel owned Styopa, DeSoto and Inheritance plantations. He owned approximately 450 slaves, placing him among the wealthiest of the plantation aristocracy. In fact, in the 1850s West Feliciana Parish was home to 38 of the wealthiest plantation families in the South. While the majority of Daniel's slaves worked in the fields, others were household servants, gardeners, millers, blacksmiths, carpenters, drivers or foremen. Daniel built a barn, which was used as a slave dance hall. He also built a church and employed a Baptist minister to conduct service on Sunday mornings.

West Feliciana men hunted and fished. Martha's brother, W. H. Barrow, built a 75-foot steamboat with stables for 12 horses and six packs of dogs. The *Nimrod* was equipped with cabins, the best rifles, fowling pieces, fishing tackle, a bar and a Negro crew dressed in long tailcoats. Card playing, horse racing and gambling were favorite pastimes as well. In fact, horse racing, a sport of English origin, was recorded in St. Francisville as early as March 1831. Jockey clubs sprang up all along the Mississippi.

Music and reading were favorite indoor pastimes. Plantation owners and their families enjoyed serenading and often spent evenings traveling from plantation to plantation singing seasonal or period songs. Informal balls were celebrated in the spring and fall with musicians from New Orleans and Natchez. Carriage drives through the countryside were popular as well.

A typical Sunday breakfast at Rosedown Plantation in the late 1800s would have consisted of steak, rolls, hominy, Irish potato croquets and waffles. Sunday dinner would have been turkey, steak, rice, sweet potatoes, squash, tomatoes, potatoes, carrots, ice cream and chocolate cake.

For supper, broiled chickens, wafers, biscuits, cake, strawberry preserves and curd would have been served.

The War Between the States brought difficult days. Southern lifestyles died with the Confederacy. Former

Louisiana Derby, 1939

government leaders were stripped of power. Slaves became masters, and women living in luxury were reduced to poverty. Outsiders came to capitalize on the destruction.

Martha Turnbull bargained with her former slaves to care for her garden. Some accepted food such as coffee, sugar and

Tennis players in the Felicianas

THE BATTLE OF NEW ORLEANS

From 1793 to 1815, France and Great Britain were almost constantly at war, and America, unfortunately, was caught in the clash despite declarations of neutrality. Embargoes were placed on American goods. British ships searched American vessels and forced seamen into British service. Plus, the British instigated Indian uprisings against the Americans on the frontier.

Finally, on June 18, 1812 the United States Congress declared war on Great Britain. During the first two years there were few engagements. In fact, the war was fought more in the newspapers than on the battlefield, and peace negotiations began almost immediately. But when French Emperor and military leader Napoleon Bonaparte was defeated and sent into exile in 1814, Britain had more troops available for combat and the war front changed in America.

In August, the British captured Washington, D.C., burned the Capitol, the White House and other public buildings. Interestingly, the White House survived until the British officers had eaten President James Madison's meal and enjoyed his port wine. Only then was the house set ablaze. The British crossed the Potomac at Washington to capture Alexandria, Va. Battles continued to rage at Lake Champlain, Baltimore, Fort Erie and Mobile.

In October, the British Major General Sir Edward Michael Pakenham was commanded to lead the Gulf Coast campaign. Charged by recent victory in the Napoleonic Wars, Pakenham, his officers and troops were confident that New Orleans was an easy prize to seize. By obtaining New Orleans, Britain would control America's heartland including its major artery of commerce and trade.

U.S. Major General Andrew Jackson, known as "Old Hickory," was chosen to defend the American South. A traveling lawyer and Tennessee's first congressman, Jackson had been victorious in the Creek Indian uprising. He hated the British and was desperate to fight them. In fact, during the Revolutionary War Jackson refused to clean the boots of an officer who struck him on the head with his sword, leaving a permanent scar.

Jackson's arrival in New Orleans was eagerly anticipated on December 1. Since dawn the manor home of Bernard de Marigny on Esplanade was lit with hearth fires and candelabra. His Parisian chef had orchestrated a magnificent breakfast and the family silver was carefully placed on the damask tablecloths. In his journal de Marigny wrote, "The salon in my house was spacious, and no detail neglected so that the reception might be worthy of the guest."

But to de Marigny's disappointment and disdain, his guest never arrived. He continued in his journal, "My name was not unknown to him. He had very recently been the guest of my father-in-law, M. Morales (former Spanish Intendant at New Orleans), who made known to me the desire of the General to stay with me, and it would have been infinitely agreeable to receive him..." De Marigny was offended and resented the General's shun.

Twelve miles north on Bayou St. John, John Kilty Smith received the General. Smith, a wealthy, retired bachelor, invited an aristocratic Creole neighbor to supervise the preparation of a magnificent breakfast, though Jackson refused the banquet requesting a bowl of hominy instead. Jackson had lived on acorns when fighting the Indians and suffered from dysentery. After traveling 350 miles over 11 days surveying the wilderness to determine where the British might land, Jackson was tired, dirty and drenched from the rain. Smith wrote of Jackson, "A tall, gaunt man, very erect...with a countenance furrowed by care and anxiety. His dress was simple and nearly threadbare. A small leather cap protected his head, and a short blue Spanish cloak his body, whilst his high dragoon boots were long innocent of polish...His complexion was sallow and unhealthy; his hair iron grey, and his body thin and emaciated like that of one who had just recovered from a lingering sickness."

At 10 o'clock a welcoming committee comprised of Edward Livingston, Governor Claiborne, Mayor Nicholas Girod and Commodore Patterson escorted Jackson into the city where a cannon from Fort St. Charles thundered a welcome and invited the citizens into the streets. Jackson addressed the crowd. Livingston translated the comments into French for the New Orleans citizenry.

Major General Andrew Jackson

British Major General Sir Edward Michael Pakenham

was virtually unprepared. On December 14, the British captured the American gunboats on Lake Bourgne. Clearly outnumbered, the citizens panicked, and Jackson declared a state of martial law. On December 23, approximately 2,100 British troops arrived and moved to the Mississippi River about eight miles below New Orleans. They camped at Villeré Plantation. Historians speculate that had the British pressed on, they could have been victorious that day. However, they halted their troops allowing them to rest and eat their first hot meal in days. In the end, this seems to have been a costly meal for the British. That night Jackson and his troops attacked the British encampment. Though the battle was indecisive, the British advance was halted.

Christmas Day began starkly for the British troops. The officers joined for Christmas dinner, sharing their small stock of provisions. They ate in huts or barns without plates, knives and forks. They made light of their misfortune, while ignoring the volleys of ball and grapeshot from the USS Carolina. That afternoon spirits soared with the arrival of General Pakenham.

On December 27, the British artillery destroyed the USS Carolina. On December 28, Pakenham ordered a probing attack against Jackson's line. Meeting stiff resistance, the British fell back. On January 1, Pakenham ordered an artillery assault at daybreak, but withdrew by midday because of logistical problems. Finally, Pakenham chose January 8 as the decisive battle day.

Ultimately, Britain's attack plans were easier to create than execute. There were numerous delays and the complicated plan dependent on split-second timing and coordination went askew from the outset. Riverbanks caved, dams collapsed, troops departed late and ladders and fascines

The General stated that he came to New Orleans with a single purpose, to "drive their enemies into the sea, or perish in the effort." The citizens were elated and shouted, "Vive Jackson."

Jackson surveyed the area for vulnerability. He ordered improvements at Fort St. Philip 75 miles below New Orleans and at Fort Petites Coquilles on the Rigolets. He ordered fortifications at potential invasion points and ordered blockage of all canals and bayous, which would allow British access to New Orleans.

Jackson's band of warriors was a motley crew of volunteers including free men of color, Choctaw Indians, river and flat boat crewmen and New Orleans business and professional men. Reinforcements came from Kentucky, Tennessee and Mississippi. Much to Jackson's chagrin, he ultimately accepted the assistance of the deplorable pirate Jean Lafitte and his murderous, marauding banditti.

On December 13, the British troops arrived on Lake Bourgne. Jackson was still making battle plans and

Battle of New Orleans and death of Pakenham

were not placed properly. The day was cold and gray with low clouds and mist as thick as fog over the battlefield. Pakenham hoped the fog would assist his strategy, but a breeze blew, the fog lifted and the British troops were exposed 650 yards from the American lines. The British were caught in their own crossfire. Chaos and confusion reigned at the head of the British column. The troops reaching Line Jackson stopped in their tracks to be shot like fish in a barrel. Pakenham rode forward to rally the troops, but was mortally wounded in the attempt.

American fire crushed the British attack in less than 45 minutes leaving three British generals dead and two wounded. The carnage at Chalmette left 2,000 British soldiers and 13 Americans dead.

The threat to New Orleans was over. By January 18 most of the British had evacuated. Sadly for those killed in action, the War of 1812 had ended on Christmas Eve with the signing of the Treaty of Ghent in Belgium. Unfortunately, communication was slow and neither the British nor the Americans knew that peace had been restored.

Remarkably, the British troops were masters of the linear tactics developed by Frederick the Great and had proved themselves by defeating every army with which Napoleon had challenged them. Their skill was the product of more than 100 years of regimental tradition and success. Yet, Jackson's army defeated those who had defeated Napoleon's best. The Battle of New Orleans fought six miles below the city at Chalmette, marks the last conflict America waged against Great Britain. This victory assured continued possession of the Louisiana Territory, encouraged westward expansion, restored confidence in the American people and brought unity to a divided nation. Andrew Jackson was a national hero and was elected seventh president of the United States.

JACKSON'S "HELLISH BANDITI": FROM PIRATES TO PATRIOTS

Jean Lafitte and his brothers were French Creoles from San Domingo. Displaced when the British captured the island, they moved to New Orleans and found a perfect breeding ground for their malfeasance. Locating in Barataria, the district just below New Orleans, Jean Lafitte's suave, unscrupulous character made him the perfect liaison between the cunning pirates and the corruptible Creoles. He had a flourishing arms trade with Mexican revolutionaries, which proved extremely embarrassing to the U.S. government. He was also a slave trader who captured his victims from unarmed vessels crossing the Atlantic en route to American slave markets. Jean Lafitte and his brothers operated under the guise of a blacksmith shop in New Orleans, which flourished until the sale of the Louisiana Territory to the United States. This transaction

was a death knell to their criminal careers because law and order were now important components of government officials who were moving Louisiana toward statehood. With new enforceable laws in New Orleans, pirates would be brought to justice.

In November 1813, Louisiana Governor William C. C. Claiborne offered a $500 reward for Lafitte. Three days later Lafitte countered with a proclamation offering a $5,000 reward for the governor! The following January the pirates attacked a group of revenue officers, killing or wounding them all. In July, a Federal Grand Jury indicted the Lafitte brothers for piracy. A few days later Pierre Lafitte, Jean's brother, was captured, clapped in irons and jailed without bond.

Help arrived for the Baratarians in the form of two British officers, Captain Nicholas Lockyer and Major Nichols. Though Great Britain did not condone piracy, if Lafitte would assist them in defeating New Orleans by placing his ships under Royal navy orders, he and his captains would be given rank in the Royal navy. Though Lafitte never

Jean Lafitte

Lafitte's Blacksmith Shop Bar

seriously considered the offer, it gave him bargaining power. He asked for two weeks to consider the matter and immediately wrote Claiborne about the British offer while pledging his loyalty to the United States. The price for his loyalty was a free pardon for himself and his brothers. Claiborne encouraged Jackson to accept Lafitte's offer. General Villeré and Livingston, acting upon orders by the Louisiana legislature, urged Jackson to accept the offer as well, but Jackson refused.

When Jackson refused to accept the pirate's offer, Judge Dominick Hall, who had no desire to proceed with what would inevitably be an embarrassing case, proposed that the legislature stop the proceedings against the pirates, if they would fight for the United States against the British. (When U.S. Commodore Patterson had earlier destroyed Lafitte's headquarters, guns and ammunition were found, along with several chests of treasure and letters from prominent New Orleans citizens linking them unequivocally to piracy. Lafitte was not going to be prosecuted without taking a few well-known citizens with him.) The act was passed, the pirates released and a pass sent to Lafitte in hiding allowing him to come to the city without incident.

On December 18, Jackson's engineer officer, Arsene Lacarriere Latour, who unbeknownst to Jackson was a close friend of Lafitte and Livingston, convinced the General to meet with Lafitte. In his typically suave manner, Lafitte offered his men's service, then played his trump card. Because of his arms deals with the Mexicans, Lafitte had a secret location called "The Temple" with vast stocks of powder, ball and shot. Despite repeated requests, Jackson did not have adequate arms and ammunition for his troops. In spite of Jackson's personal disdain for the pirates, Lafitte's offer was accepted, and Jackson's men were properly armed.

Lafitte escorted Major Michael Reynolds to his secret store of ammunition. Three companies of Baratarians reinforced the forts guarding the city's main approaches. Two pirate gun crews participated in the battle. Lafitte's older brother, who called himself Dominique Youx, led one crew. Renato Beluche, Jean Lafitte's uncle, led the other. Though no one is sure where Lafitte was during the battle, he was certainly nowhere near the fighting.

FAREWELL TO JACKSON

On January 23 a day of thanksgiving was celebrated in New Orleans. A triumphal arch with six columns was built in the center of the Place d'Armes, present-day Jackson Square. Plauche's Battalion of Orleans Volunteers formed a double line from the Mississippi River to St. Louis Cathedral. Young ladies stood from the arch to the Cathedral representing each state and territory in the

Union. General Jackson and his staff marched from the arch, where he received victory laurels from children, to the Cathedral where Father Dubourg escorted him to a seat near the altar. After Mass, an honor guard escorted Jackson to his quarters.

But the city notorious for parties, had only just begun to celebrate the victory. Though the traditional Mardi Gras season was at hand, Mardi Gras celebrations were not permitted at this time, so citizens improvised with balls honoring George Washington. During 1815 the balls were modified to honor Andrew Jackson. Period newspapers are replete with invitations to and reports about balls throughout the city honoring Jackson for his splendid and heroic defense of the city.

On April 1, 1815 a splendid farewell dinner was given at Davis' long room by citizens and officers in Jackson's honor. At 4 o'clock in the afternoon approximately 200 gentlemen sat for an elegant dinner. Flags and battalion colors filled the room as did good humor, songs and numerous toasts.

That evening's dinner menu included hors d'oeuvres of buttered radishes, sausage and cold salmon with cornichons. The soup course featured oyster gumbo and a spring soup. Oven cooked ragout of red snapper was served as was fried trout. There were veal cutlets, filets of beef with mushrooms, roasted stuffed wild turkey and roasted duck. Asparagus, little green peas and potatoes accompanied the entrée and strawberry tarts, lemon tarts and hot bananas with coffee and Cognac concluded the meal. Of course, red and white wine appropriately accompanied each course.

In Jackson's farewell address to his army he stated,

"The expression of your General's thanks is feeble; but the gratitude of a country of freemen is yours-yours the

Jackson Square, New Orleans

applause of an admiring world."
Of course, the evening was filled with elegant farewell dinner toasts including the following.

"The worthy few-who fell in defense of Louisiana-their memory will ever be dear to Americans-their death was avenged by the blood of thousands of the enemy."

"The Mississippi Territory – her deeds of youth would deck a warrior's brow."

"The army of the U.S. – the boasted legions of Europe can no longer mock – comparisons have been made in the field, not on paper."

"Tennessee – may that day never arrive when Louisiana shall cease to feel towards this her sister state, more than the slow utterance of praise can publish."

"The fair sex-if the brave alone deserve the fair, who have greater claim than the defenders of Louisiana."

OUR LADY OF PROMPT SUCCOR

Many New Orleans citizens believed Our Lady of Prompt Succor was one of General Jackson's warriors. Devotion to the Blessed Virgin Mary, Our Lady of Prompt Succor, began in New Orleans when Mother Michel Gensoul arrived at the Ursuline convent in 1810, carrying with her a statue of Our Lady. Devotion spread rapidly among the nuns, students and visitors for answers to urgent prayers.

Apprehension swept through the convent and the city with the British invasion. On the night of January 7, women and elderly men gathered with the Ursulines in the convent chapel to pray to Our Lady of Prompt Succor to beseech Almighty God to protect the city and give strength and courage to the troops. Everyone prayed for an American victory. Mother Olivier de Vezin ordered that the statue of Our Lady of Prompt Succor be moved to the main altar during the all night vigil. During those anxious hours of incessant prayer, Mother de Vezin vowed in the community's name to offer a thanksgiving Mass annually, if God heard the prayers of Our Lady of Prompt Succor and gave victory to the Americans.

During Holy Mass on the morning of January 8 as Very Reverend Louis William Dubourg offered Communion, a battlefield messenger ran in shouting, "Victory is ours!" The Mass ended in thanksgiving with everyone chanting the "Te Deum," the jubilation hymn. Even Jackson declared that divine intervention achieved the victory. He visited the Ursulines to thank them for their prayers and requested that Father Dubourg hold a religious service of thanks to Almighty God.

To this day a Mass is offered in the Ursuline chapel on the anniversary of the victory with a statue of Our Lady of Prompt Succor prominently displayed on the altar.

Our Lady of Prompt Succor

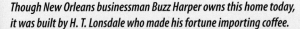
Though New Orleans businessman Buzz Harper owns this home today, it was built by H. T. Lonsdale who made his fortune importing coffee.

NEW ORLEANS' GARDEN DISTRICT

Few people from the United States lived in New Orleans during the colonial period, but following the 1803 Louisiana Purchase, Americans swarmed New Orleans to capitalize on Mississippi River commerce. Louisiana's cotton and sugar cash crops, the slave trade and national banks fueled the local economy.

When the crude new Americans arrived, there was an immediate culture clash with the well-established aristocratic Creoles. The overcrowded French Quarter forced the snubbed Americans to move upriver to create their own residential district. They settled in the city of Lafayette, now New Orleans' Garden District, which was annexed to the city of New Orleans in 1852. Successful entrepreneurs and the "nouveau riche" of that time built large, elegant mansions typifying architectural styles including Greek Revival, Italianate and Queen Anne Victorian. New Orleans' Garden District, once a large sugar plantation, is now home to many native New Orleanians and a favorite tourist attraction for visitors.

Italy

Banana wharf

POST CIVIL WAR LABOR WOES & IMMIGRANT RECRUITMENT

The Civil War slowed sugar cultivation in Louisiana, and when the battlefields cleared a more alarming problem arose. When the slaves were freed by the adoption of the 13th Amendment to the U.S. Constitution, the secure labor force the planters were accustomed to eroded like Mississippi River silt. Many planters were so disgusted with Negro emancipation and refusals to work according to pre-war conditions, they moved to Cuba and Brazil. Many planters simply abandoned their land. Those who continued their plantation operations were required under federal occupation terms to take a U.S. oath of allegiance.

In 1861, more than 1,200 plantations produced Louisiana's sugar crop. By 1864, only 175 operating plantations remained. Northern businessmen and merchants invested capital and labor into Louisiana's depressed sugar industry. After 1870 at least half of the planters were Northerners or were supported by Northern money. Few Louisiana

families maintained their plantations after the Civil War, and those who did were the exception not the rule.

The planters' free laborers now demanded work schedules and wages or they abandoned the cane fields completely and moved to industrial cities. White planters considered these former slaves an unpredictable, unreliable labor force, because often they moved from plantation to plantation for higher wages, pay advances or weekly rather than monthly wages. Negro labor groups who struck for higher wages during crucial crop periods such as planting and grinding seasons particularly irritated planters. Nevertheless, the loss of slave labor was detrimental to the region's prosperity and planters' profits. An alternate labor force was ultimately sought.

Initially, immigrant recruitment favored no particular nation or group. Chinese laborers came. Planters hoped they would force the Negro to be more industrious. The 1867 and 1869 newspapers supported the idea of Chinese workers, many of whom came by railroad from San Francisco. At first, the Chinese experiment proved

successful. Some Chinese contracted for five years at 50 cents a day and worked from sunrise to sunset, agreeing to obey all orders. One plantation contract with the Chinese in 1870 specified 26 days of labor for $14 monthly paid in gold, plus daily rations of two pounds of fresh meat, two pounds of rice and 1.3 ounces of tea. Unfortunately, the Chinese were also guilty of breaking contracts to work elsewhere for higher wages. Soon, the Chinese immigration effort ceased.

Next, immigration efforts turned to Scandinavian laborers from the Midwest, but these workers were in great demand, and Southern wages were not competitive. Even those convinced to travel to the South for employment were diverted en route by more attractive offers.

In 1871 and 1873, Spanish and Portuguese laborers were recruited to Lafourche Parish, but by 1880 the Spanish government issued a royal order in Madrid opposing the further recruitment of citizens to Louisiana.

Godchaux sugar refinery

Italian olive jars, Ardoyne Plantation

Finally, in 1873, the Louisiana Immigration and Homestead Association, along with other period groups such as the Iberia Immigration Society and a similar immigration society in Vermilion Parish, emerged to formally recruit foreign immigrants. These immigrants were not only a labor force for agriculture, public works, railroad construction, commerce and industry, but also a solution to "political troubles." At that time, many white Southerners believed that the great numbers of black Americans in the Mississippi Delta region might result in the loss of economic and political control by white Americans. Thus, there was a dual purpose in recruiting foreigners.

Since the late 1860s, many had observed the commercial ties between Louisiana and the Mediterranean, particularly south Italy and Sicilian ports. While Louisiana grew cereals, they grew fruits. Louisiana exported cotton, tobacco, rice and petroleum and imported fruits, olive oil, wines, sardines and art works. Italy had a surplus population, a climate similar to South Louisiana, and knowledge of fruit and wine production. Idle fields in Louisiana would be planted with grapes, olives, figs, oranges, lemons and other fruits and vegetables.

New Orleans' Italian population emerged even before the Civil War. Commercial citrus trade was established between Sicily and New Orleans. The Italians imported citrus fruit, unloaded the ships, sold the fruit throughout the city and distributed it to surrounding areas. New Orleans' location served Louisiana well as a distribution center for foreign goods to other parts of the United States.

The sugar planters recognized this link between the citrus trade routes and Italian immigration, and in 1881 the Louisiana Sugar Planters' Association approved an advertising propaganda campaign to recruit laborers from Italy. Some Italians already living in New Orleans worked on sugar plantations to the great satisfaction of their employers. In fact, planters were so satisfied that many paid for their immigrant laborers' passages. A Committee on Italian Immigration was appointed and began a regular passenger steam route between New Orleans and southern Italy with a fare of $40 per person. Information was distributed throughout Sicily and southern Italy about wages and job certainty. Instructions were included for getting to Louisiana. An average of three passenger steamships docked monthly in New Orleans where immigrants were met and cared for until they reached their final destination.

Planters' interest in the Italian workers increased as they learned that they were hardworking, money-saving people who were content with limited comforts. The Italians worked well with little or no supervision. They were thorough, neat, dependable, diligent, eager and adapted to all plantation tasks. What they lacked in physical strength as compared to the Negro laborers, they made up in volume of work achieved. Centuries of farming worn-out land made the Italians, in the planters' estimation, among the best farmers in the world. By 1902, Italian immigrants rapidly replaced Negro labor in the sugar fields.

Jules Godchaux who owned plantations in St. John, Jefferson, Orleans and Lafourche parishes valued Italian laborers as did many planters. In fact, many planters encouraged the permanent residency of the

Italians to guarantee a stable work force. Godchaux encouraged the Italian laborers on his Reserve Plantation to become tenants. The Italians raised cane, sold it to the Godchaux family sugar mill, saved their money, then purchased land with their savings. Eventually, they created a colony called "Virgin Mary" at the Bonne Carre Crevasse.

While the planters thought Italian immigration was a viable solution to their labor shortage, the peasants of southern Italy became convinced that migration to Louisiana was definitely for their greater good.

EMIGRATION FROM ITALY

The second half of the 19th century in Italy was intolerable for most. Relief came only through emigration. In 1860, Giuseppe Garibaldi liberated Sicily and placed it under the House of Savoy for protection. Hopes were high that reform was imminent. Land management, land distribution, an overburdened tax structure and loathsome working conditions were critical issues for Sicilians. When Camillo de Cavour retracted Garibaldi's proposal for an autonomous state, Sicilians' resentment and rage toward the new national government ignited.

Many government officials were Sicilians, but they worked for their personal gain and to the detriment of their people. Corrupt officials flourished and controlled Sicily politically. Sicilians lived in misery and desperation. By 1885, nothing had changed since unification. Because of the exorbitant national tax burden, many small landowners lost their land to bankruptcy. Even when church lands were confiscated and redistributed, the peasants reaped no benefit. Large estate owners purchased the land for cultivation. Discouragement reigned among peasant

The S. S. Manilla arrived in the New Orleans port between 1901 and 1905 with Sicilians from Genoa and Palermo.

and brown velvet jackets and pants, and footwear similar to English riding boots. The passengers were greeted with hugs and kisses from those who preceded them to America. Even the men kissed each other. Also on board this ship were 4,522 boxes of lemons, 21 boxes of figs, two barrels of olives, two hogsheads of olive oil and two kegs of preserved tomatoes.

Many new arrivals resided in New Orleans while most reported to work on plantations. The immigrants' arrival was eagerly anticipated by planters in the sugar parishes of Ascension, West Baton Rouge, Iberia, Iberville, Jefferson,

and working classes. There were few crops, no farming improvements, inadequate transportation, no network of roads and the mafia intimidated the fruit growers and controlled their water supply.

The grain, wine and fruit producers were most affected by the agricultural depression. Most Sicilians from the interior lacked money to migrate to America. During the 1890s, the Sicilians rebelled. They ransacked tax offices, burned land registers and opened prisons. The government stifled the uprisings, but the continued deplorable working and living conditions forced many Sicilians to move to America.

Most Italian immigrants of the 1890s were from central and north-central Sicily where unrest was the greatest. The Sicilians who came to work on the sugar plantations were laborers, farmers, domestic and personal service workers from Contessa Entellina, Ustica, Bisacquino, Termini Immerese, Poggioreale, Corleone, Cefalu, Palazzo Adriano, Trapani, Chiusa Sclafani, Trabia and Palermo.

From the late 19th century to World War I more than one and a half million Sicilians left their homeland. Some villages lost the majority of their male population. The Sicilians wrote their relatives about America and sent money so others could leave. Ultimately, Sicily suffered a labor shortage, which resulted in increased wages. Landowners were forced to seek field-workers while many sold land or granted more equitable leases. Laborers were even encouraged to grow tomatoes and artichokes in dormant fields.

Sicilian immigration to Louisiana declined after 1907 possibly because of the American depression that year,

higher wages in construction and industrial centers in the United States and the decline of the citrus fruit trade to New Orleans. Improvements in Sicily such as jobs and land reform kept many prospective immigrants at home as well.

THE IMMIGRANTS ARRIVE

Since New Orleans' founding in 1718, Italian immigrants were part of the populace. By 1850, New Orleans' Italian population numbered 915, which was larger than that of any city in the United States, even New York, which was home to just 833 Italians.

The greatest period of Sicilian migration to Louisiana occurred between 1889 and 1910. The Italians came on "protracted sojourns," which meant they were temporary U.S. residents for an indefinite time period. The daily papers carried headlines such as "Immigrants from Italy: Two Hundred and Ten Passengers from Palermo Arrive on the British Steamship Scindia." In this 1880 news account the writer described the six-week voyage including a crankshaft breaking, the stop for coal in Gibraltar and heavy gales experienced in the Gulf. The immigrants' green boxes and long, white canvas bags carrying all of their worldly possessions were piled on the wharf for inspection and for the apparent amusement of spectators. The only contraband discovered on board the Scindia were nuts and cheese, which were not confiscated. The men and women dressed in colorful handkerchiefs and neckerchiefs with both sexes wearing earrings. The men wore capes, black

St. Charles, St. Bernard, Plaquemines, St. James, St. John the Baptist, Lafourche, Assumption, Terrebonne and St. Mary.

In another article from The Times Democrat in 1889, 850 Sicilians arrived aboard the Triancria. The wharf swarmed with expectant relatives and new arrivals "talking meantime with their whole anatomy and rendering the scene one of animation and excitement." The ship from Palermo made the journey in 21 days with passengers crammed between decks, on lower decks, in the lower hold and on the main deck.

The *Letimbro* arrived from Palermo in October 1889 carrying 655 passengers. In October 1890 the *Entilla* arrived with 841 Italian immigrants. The ships continued to arrive carrying a much needed labor force to Louisiana's sugar fields.

Local news stories continued through the late 1890s. The accounts recorded passenger ship arrivals, travel conditions of the voyage, illnesses aboard, the inspection process and immigrants' future work places, which were either on the

The Liguria, one of the ships arriving monthly carrying Sicilians during the immigration wave between 1880 and 1910.

sugar plantations or for the Southern Pacific Railroad. An 1898 account from *The Daily Picayune* entitled "Another Batch of Surly Sicilians" recounted the exuberance with which the new immigrants arrived at the port of New Orleans to meet their relatives.

". . . there arose a chorus of excited yells, queries, exclamations, calls in high-pitched vernacular that was positively deafening. And the gyrations of arms, heads, and the bodily contortions which, strangely, seem to be indispensable with the exchange of greetings among

some of the Latin races, were enough to cause any sedate and practical onlooker to fear that a limb or two of the most vehement of the excited performers would suddenly be severed and fly off."

Before debarkation each immigrant was scrutinized to verify that no paupers, idiots, insane persons or anyone suffering from infectious or contagious diseases were aboard. One inspector commented that the Italian immigrants arriving in New Orleans were the "healthiest, cleanest and most self-supporting set of immigrants he had inspected at any port of the United States in many years." Most were young, sturdy and capable of hard work. The ship manifests recorded each passenger's name, age, sex, occupation, embarkation port and the number of bags each carried, which was usually only one.

The Sicilians arrived with little money and few possessions. Generally, they were illiterate peasants and laborers with one goal: to make money. They performed back-breaking labor for 18 hours a day. They cut cane, loaded wagons for the grinding shed, cut hay, chopped corn, dug ditches or labored as night watchmen for 50 cents a night. During the grinding and

George Fredrick Coniglio, Sr., arrived from Palermo, Sicily in the late 1800s.

harvesting season workers made a dollar a day. Planting and cultivating workers made 50 to 60 cents a day. Wages included lodging, cooking fuel and a small plot for a garden.

Most immigrants survived on meager incomes. They grew vegetable gardens and kept chickens, cows and goats for meat as well as milk. They made cheese. They collected grasses such as bull tongue, arrowroot and peppergrass for salads. Most Italian families had large, white brick plaster ovens in their yards for baking.

Because the Italians were great gardeners, their needs from the plantation store were minimal. Nevertheless, plantation stores stocked boxes of spaghetti, macaroni, cheese, olives and sardines. Often, the Italians made their own macaroni and dried it in the sun.

The Italians valued education, were proud of their heritage and were fiercely allegiant to the United States. They were faith-filled and family-oriented with a strong belief in community and an incredible work ethic. Most were laborers, factory workers or field hands. Many became entrepreneurs and small business owners in the food industry, especially the grocery business. In 1880, about seven percent of the retail grocers in New Orleans were Italians. In 1900, the number had grown to 19 percent and by 1920, 49 percent of the grocery stores in New Orleans were Italian owned. Many Italians worked as longshoremen, stevedores and draymen while others worked on the levee system.

Though their early years in Louisiana were difficult and their living conditions on the plantations less than desirable, their lives were still better than in Italy. Ultimately, because the Italians worked and lived like the Negroes, they lost their status as white men, and Southerners typically classed the Italians and the Negroes together.

The number of Italians in Louisiana's sugar region had grown from 431 in 1880 to nearly 4,000 by 1890. By 1900 the number had grown to 17,000 and by 1904 some 30,000 Italians lived in Louisiana. Even with these great numbers of immigrants, there were never enough Italian laborers to meet the demand. During the height of immigration, Italian immigrants comprised less than one third of the entire cane field work force.

Family of strawberry farmers near Hammond in Tangipahoa Parish around 1923. Front row, left to right: Mr. & Mrs. Maturana. Back row, left to right: Virginia Maturana Scalise, Laura Maturana, George Maturana and Jennie Maturana.

Soon, the Italians' frugal nature allowed them to save enough money to purchase their own land to the dismay and dissatisfaction of the planters. During the 1890s opportunities arose for the Italian immigrants to earn more money and to buy cheap farmland in nearby Tangipahoa Parish.

THE STRAWBERRY FARMERS

Tangipahoa Parish was created in March 1869 primarily as a product of the Illinois Central Railroad whose tracks ran through the parish center. During the mid-1850s, the railroad company tried to make the land along its tracks available for immigrants to settle and make productive.

The first Italian immigrants to live and own land in the parish, the George Narretto family, arrived in the mid-1830s from Genova, Italy. After working as a lumberjack, Narretto bought 80 acres in 1861 and began subsistence farming. By the late-1880s the first Sicilians moved into the parish. In 1888, J. B. Zobolio bought land in Hammond and Paul and Nunzia Tufaneo purchased land in Amite City. Many contend that berry farming began prior to the Civil War at Tickfaw, though others believe it began near Independence following Reconstruction. Robert L. Cloud, a national authority on strawberries and a Hammond resident, insisted that prior to the Civil War R. David Manard grew strawberries near Tickfaw and shipped them to the New Orleans market via train. The Civil War interrupted farming but the crop resumed during Reconstruction. By 1870, many American farmers as well as German and Spanish immigrant farmers were growing strawberries.

Though Tangipahoa leaders in the 1880s recruited immigrants from the Midwest to work the fields, the parish's fledgling strawberry industry needed pickers, and foreign laborers were the answer. In spring 1890 an Italian family from New Orleans arrived in Independence to pick the strawberry crop at the invitation of one of America's most prosperous strawberry farmers. In the fall another Italian family arrived to work the fields. Certainly, the "padroni" who assisted immigrants to find work, helped populate the area with Italian laborers. The Illinois Central Railroad, which provided rail transportation for seasonal workers from the North, New Orleans and the sugar parishes, was vital as well.

Italian immigrants were paid a daily wage or one cent per picked pint, averaging $1.50 - $1.75 daily. Many seasonal workers eventually bought strawberry farms and settled in the area. Louisiana's Bureau of Immigration worked to place families in the area by providing lists of available strawberry farms and land in Hammond, Natalbany and Independence. Recruitment efforts aside, life in Tangipahoa Parish was attractive to Italian immigrants. They escaped urban and plantation life and saved money to buy land. The immigrants spread the word about the opportunity in Tangipahoa Parish and soon Sicilians arrived from all parts of Louisiana, the North and their homeland.

By 1910, Sicilian immigrants in Independence cleared stumps, removed lumber, dug numerous ditches to drain the berry fields and worked collaboratively to create a three-mile drainage canal, work the American farmers would not attempt. Because of the land improvements, real estate valued at approximately $800,000 in 1900 rose to more than $4 million by 1911. Soon, the Italians earned the respect of the locals.

During the off-season the Sicilians worked in the lumber mills, at Gullet's Gin Manufacturing Company at Amite City or at one of the two canning or macaroni factories. They worked in box and veneer factories building crates and wooden boxes to pack and ship strawberries and other vegetables.

Strawberry field

THE ORIGINAL DIXIELAND JAZZ BAND

New Orleans is recognized internationally as the birthplace of jazz. Developed from a mixture of African and European traditions, jazz music spread rapidly across America in the late 1910s and early 1920s.

The Original Dixieland Jazz Band, the first group to bring national attention to jazz, the first group to popularize jazz in the United States and England and the first group to record jazz, was led by cornet player Dominic James (Nick) LaRocca, the son of an Italian immigrant. The band was comprised of four other New Orleans musicians including Larry Shields (clarinet), Tony Sbarbaro (drums), Harry Ragas (piano) and Eddie Edwards (trombone). Their Victor recording of "Livery Stable Blues" or "Barnyard Blues" sold a million copies. LaRocca composed "Tiger Rag One Step," Louisiana State University's famous fight song.

New Orleans' black musicians were noteworthy during this period as well. Certainly, LaRocca must have heard and been influenced by the Eagle Band, Oscar Celestin, cornetists Bunk Johnson, King Oliver, Freddie Keppard, Tig Chambers and Manuel Perez.

Dominic James "Nick" LaRocca composed Louisiana State University's famous fight song, Tiger Rag One Step.

Sicilians built the strawberry industry into the largest money-making business in the parish. When they first arrived, strawberries were a secondary crop to cotton. By the 1890s cotton farming was abandoned for the more profitable strawberry crops.

The Illinois Central Railroad helped farmers get their crops to market easier. The Southern Express Company and the Adams Express Company donated free plants to the farmers, and strawberry production soared. Farmers of Tangipahoa Parish-grown strawberries began shipping their cargo to Memphis, Chicago and other Northern cities.

During the late 1880s an average of two carloads of strawberries were shipped daily to New Orleans. By 1892, the average increased to six carloads. In 1901, Cloud introduced the "Klondike" plant, a strawberry variety that replaced all Louisiana plants and became the leading U.S. variety. The Klondike shipped better, which meant fewer losses and more profit to the strawberry industry. In 1904, Italians from Independence shipped about 275 carloads of strawberries valued between $500,000 - $700,000. By 1905, Independence was known as the "blue ribbon strawberry shipper of Louisiana" and the "Little Italy" of the South with nearly 180 Italian families living in the area. By the end of the decade, most store owners were Italian and business signs were written in Italian, not English. In 1913, the strawberry crop sold for more than $1,100,000.

Ice manufacturing companies and banks grew from the success of the strawberry industry as did canning factories such as Star Canning Factory and the Enterprise Canning Factory. The Italian Macaroni Manufacturing Company

---

was established in Independence with $6,500 from Italian strawberry farmers and businessmen.

ITALIAN BUSINESSMEN BUILD LOUISIANA'S FOOD EMPIRE

Sicilians worked hard to "make good" in America. Pushcart peddlers graduated to counter shops in their own businesses. Importers and exporters were born from truck farmers and produce dealers. By 1913, Italians dominated the businesses through which 73 million tons of produce were exported to Latin America.

Sicilian merchants imported wine and citrus including Sicilian lemons, Spanish oranges and Honduran bananas. As the Central American citrus business slowed, Italian businessmen wholesaled Louisiana-grown products such as tomatoes, onions, garlic and added products such as bell peppers, eggplant and zucchini. Many became restaurateurs as well.

The Italians established a network among themselves of food peddlers and small grocers. The Italians' presence was felt from New Orleans and Houma to Lafayette, Alexandria, Shreveport, Tallulah and Hammond. They dominated the Creole food empire including truck farms, labor supply, wholesale and grocery retail. They established specialty niches including bakeries, ice dealerships, restaurants, coffee shops, peanut vending, ice cream parlors, delicatessens, candy shops, fruit stands and fish markets. Undoubtedly, they influenced and expanded South Louisiana cuisine.

Cargo of bananas

business. Nicholas Cusimano came to New Orleans from Contessa, Sicily, in 1899. In 1931, he opened the Cusimano Brokerage Company, a wholesale dealership and brokerage firm for domestic and tropical vegetables and fruits. Business growth was tremendous and grew to include all of Latin America, Cuba and most major fruit and vegetable centers in the United States.

Another Italian success story was that of Joseph Vaccaro, born in Contessa Entellina, Sicily. He peddled fruit from a basket, which led to importing bananas from Central

The Roman Chewing Candy Wagon was founded by Sam Cortese. The wagon still rolls today.

While many Sicilians left their homeland following Italy's economic collapse, the first settlers were not peasants but merchants, shippers and craftsmen from Palermo. Joseph and Peter Torre were sons of Palermo's harbormaster and knew New Orleans meant opportunity. The brothers located in the city to import Mediterranean produce such as citrus fruit that could then be distributed throughout the Mississippi Valley. They established The Royal Mail

Line from Palermo, which was their own regular packet service. Eventually, Peter Torre focused on the tropical fruit business from the Caribbean, particularly Central America.

The Italians handled the majority of the fruit trade with Central and South America, which by 1920 was a $700 million

America with his brothers, Luca and Felix, and partners Salvador, Vincent and Carmelo Dantoni. He purchased a ship to import bananas for his firm, Vaccaro Brothers, which later became the Standard Fruit and Steamship Company.

In 1861, J. B. Solari founded a grocery store on the corner of Royal and Iberville streets that became one of New Orleans' favorite places. Solari's featured

Solari's, one of New Orleans' favorite grocery stores, was founded by J. B. Solari in 1861. Pictured here are diners at the lunch counter in the 1930s.

a large lunch counter, a delicatessen with gourmet delicacies, a candy kitchen, groceries and a liquor store. During the 1930s Solari's was a popular lunch venue for shoppers and ladies dressed in hats, gloves, jewelry and high-heeled shoes. Sadly, a parking garage replaced Solari's in 1961.

Still in existence is Angelo Brocato's Italian ice cream parlor and pastry shop and Sam Cortese's Roman Chewing Candy Wagon. The wagon still peddles candy along New Orleans' streets.

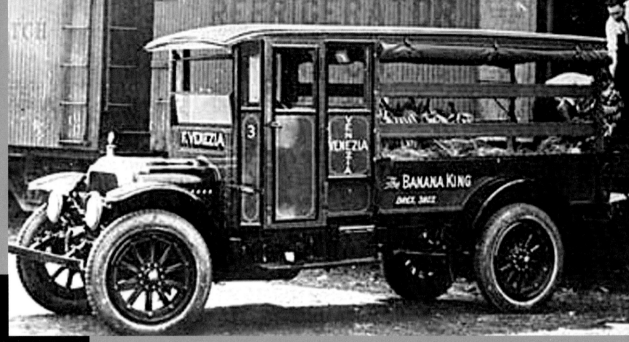

The Banana King business was owned by the Venezia family. Deliveries were made in their 1928 truck.

Scalise family grocery store in New Orleans. From left to right: Joseph Scalise, Virginia Scalise Rizzo, Peter Scalise and Victor Scalise.

Frank Prestia's Ice Cream Factory was located on South Scott Street, 1917.

Giuseppe Uddo, another Italian success story, arrived in New Orleans in 1908 and established an Italian food import business with his father who lived in Italy. The business prospered until World War I, when Italian food importation nearly stopped. To save his business Uddo purchased California-grown products and a Sicilian cheese made in Colorado. He became one of the largest distributors of Southern California vegetables and olive products. The entire Uddo family came in 1919, and

The Bagille Seafood Company sold rabbits as well as seafood.

Giuseppe's brother Frank joined the company now named Uddo Brothers and Company, Inc. Headquartered in New Orleans, branch offices were located in Los Angeles and Buena Park, Calif., and New York City. A merger occurred in 1926 between the Uddos and the Taormina Brothers, a local business specializing in canning tomato and other vegetable products under the Progresso label. The Sierra Heights Canning Plant of Arlington, Calif., was purchased and all three businesses became the corporate entity of Uddo-Taormina Company, which opened offices in New York, California, Texas and Mississippi. In 1936, Sure-Klean products bought out the Taormina interest, but the company name remained. Sure-Klean products included house cleaners, bleach, detergent, dish soap and disinfectants. In 1938, Frank sold his business interest to Giuseppe and established F. Uddo and Sons, which carried the Sure-Klean products. F. Uddo and Sons became the

Standard Fruit Company founders

Uddo Company after Frank's death. The Uddo-Taormina Company prospered until 1970 when the family sold the tomato and vegetable product business to a major Canadian food company.

Many Italians worked in banking, retail, wholesale and real estate. Another prosperous Italian businessman was Antonio Monteleone who arrived from Contessa, Sicily, in 1880. Within eight years of opening his cobbler's shop at 241 Royal Street, Monteleone bought the 14-room Commercial Hotel located across the street. Within five years he added 30 rooms and changed the hotel name to the Monteleone, the city's most innovative hotel, which is still in operation. In 1908, 200 rooms were added in a new 11-story building next to the original site. The luxurious rooms offered private baths and some had carpet. There was an ice plant on site and an engine room to provide steam heat and electricity. Following Monteleone's death,

his son Frank continued to make the Monteleone one of the finest and largest hotels in the South. In 1928, another 200 rooms were added with amenities such as closets, radios and ceiling fans. By 1930, the Monteleone was the first New Orleans hotel to provide an air-conditioned lobby.

Less than 100 years after their immigration, many Italian-Americans moved from the lower to the middle or even upper economic classes of society.

TRADITIONAL SICILIAN CUISINE

Conquering civilizations influenced the region and cuisine of Sicily, which in turn was enhanced by Sicilian ingenuity and imagination. The Greeks added black and green olives, honey, wine, salted ricotta cheese, fish and lamb grilled over charcoal to Italian cuisine.

During the Roman period, baked onions seasoned with oil and vinegar, stuffed cuttlefish, mashed broad beans and sausages including blood sausages were served at elaborate banquets. After the Roman Empire declined, Sicily fell victim to Northern invaders such as the Franks and the Goths, who left no discernable culinary influence. Later, the Byzantines imported Eastern spices still used today.

Under the Arabs, Sicily flourished and its cuisine became varied and sophisticated. The cultivation of sugarcane brought refined sugar, which was used as a main ingredient in dishes such as marzipan. Refined sugar became associated with ricotta and candied orange and lemon peels. It influenced the development of the famous cassata. Arabs introduced the cultivation of citrus fruits to Sicily. Mulberries, aniseed, sesame and spices such as cinnamon and saffron also date to the Arab period. Sorbets were made with essences from fruit, flowers and snow from Mount Etna. Ice cream made with jasmine oil can still be found in the Trapani area.

The Norman conquest brought salted cod and salted and smoked herring. Around 1282, the Kingdom of Sicily was established. After the discovery of the Americas, tomatoes were introduced to Sicilian cuisine, which complemented the eggplant, onions and sweet peppers of so many dishes. Wild fennel use was inherited from the Canary Islands. Other Sicilian ingredients included capers, oregano and Caciocavallo cheese. Fish and seafood were staples of the Sicilian diet.

Italian cuisine was the grand cuisine of Europe during the 1500s. In fact, it was a major influence on French cuisine, particularly when Catherine de' Medici, the daughter of Lorenzo de' Medici, married the future Henry II in 1533 and brought her cooks to France.

THE FATHER OF LOUISIANA'S RICE INDUSTRY

Angelo Socola was born in the Italian port town of San Remo on the Italian Riviera. He emigrated from Italy in 1849, when he was 18 years old. Soon after his arrival in New Orleans, he left for college in Kentucky to master the English language. After college, he returned to New Orleans, becoming a junior partner in A. Gandolfo and Co., an importer of Italian and Mexican products. By 1860 he owned the firm. It was then that he became interested in planting and milling rice.

In those days, Louisiana's average rice production annually was 30,000 sacks of an inferior product called "Creole Rice." Socola experimented with rice seeds and land rotation. Soon, he developed a superior rice strain that produced high yields. He also determined that rice fields should lay dormant every other year or be planted with a crop other than rice.

Because of Socola's research, more than a million sacks of rice were harvested annually. Rice crops previously confined to Plaquemines Parish spread throughout South Louisiana. Socola received international acclaim for his agricultural contributions, and his rice was exhibited in countries such as Germany, Belgium and Austria.

Socola introduced steam-powered rice mills and threshing mills. He owned Franklin and Farmers' Mill in Plaquemines Parish. He owned the St. John the Baptist Mill in St. John Parish and controlled the Empire Parish and Courthouse Mill in Plaquemines Parish. Socola Rice Mills, built in New Orleans in 1890, was the largest and best-equipped mill in America. Socola was also a distribution agent for rice threshers.

In addition to being the "Father of Louisiana's Rice Industry," Socola founded and directed the Louisiana People's Bank. He organized the Plaquemines Parish Canal Company, which built the canal connecting the Mississippi River and Barataria Bay, Grand Isle and western Louisiana. The canal was a major shipping lane for years.

Lorenzo Milano, Donaldsonville

The Sicilians who immigrated to Louisiana were fisherman and farmers of citrus fruits, wheat, garden vegetables, olives and grapes. They were destined to be truck farmers, because they grew vegetables in Sicily. Their wine called "mamertino" was that which drew praise from Julius Caesar and Martial, the Classical poet. The most famous Sicilian creations were sweets and pastries including cannoli and cassata. Cassata, a layer cake with filling delicately woven between the layers, was often served at weddings signifying the beginning of a new way of life. Candied almonds were thrown at weddings with cheers of, "May your life be fruitful and sweet."

The poverty-stricken Sicilians were gifted in making a little food go a long way. They ate sausage, bread and cheese and drank wine for lunch when they toiled in the fields, a tradition that continued in Louisiana. In Sicily, they baked bread in small, igloo-shaped ovens built near the fireplace in the kitchen. Similar outdoor ovens were constructed in Louisiana.

Central Grocery, New Orleans

THE BIRTH OF THE MUFFULETTA

Around 1900, a Sicilian baker in New Orleans baked and sold a variety of Sicilian breads including a round loaf called a "Muffuletta." Laborers, farmers and workers from the nearby farmers' market purchased the loaves daily for lunch along with meats, cheeses and olive salad obtained from a local grocer. Each item was eaten separately as was tradition.

One day Lupo Salvatore, a Sicilian immigrant and owner of Central Grocery on Decatur, negotiated with the baker to buy the Muffuletta bread that he then resold to hungry workers along with the meats, cheeses and olive salad. In 1906, Salvatore stuffed the ingredients into the bread, wrapped the sandwich in paper and the Muffuletta sandwich was born. The foods were easier to carry and became an immediate success for Central Grocery. A century later, the Muffuletta is still a popular lunch item.

Muffuletta sandwich

ST. JOSEPH'S DAY ALTARS

According to legend, a merciless drought in the Middle Ages killed Sicily's vegetation and dried the streams and wells leaving the people to die of hunger and thirst. Desperate for help, the poor people prayed to St. Joseph, the foster father of Jesus and the patron saint of Italy, for guidance and intercession. If their petition for rain was answered, they promised to honor him perpetually on his feast day, and every generation to come would do the same. At midnight on the day their prayers were offered it rained. By daylight, wells were filled and streams rushed with water. Fish teemed in the waters and the vegetation was lush and green.

Thereafter, St. Joseph was remembered annually with food altars in Sicily. Often, individuals promised altars to St. Joseph in answer to personal prayers and favors granted.

The tradition of St. Joseph's altars came to Louisiana via the immigrants from western Sicily in the late 1800s. Still today on March 19, St. Joseph's feast day, altars constructed in homes and churches throughout South Louisiana are overfilled with regional favorites.

St. Joseph's Day altar

Family tradition keeps altar building alive. Many are constructed in thanksgiving and gratitude for an answered prayer. Many faithful Catholics, and many non-Catholics, promise to build altars for prayers answered, especially cures received or the safe return of soldiers from battle. A promise to create a St. Joseph's altar is a commitment never broken. Those who can afford to build an altar must beg for foods and supplies from neighbors and businesses as a sacrifice. The time and money spent building altars by those who cannot afford the practice, is their sacrifice. Many individuals willingly donate time, food and money toward the construction of altars, because of their devotion to St. Joseph.

An altar is generally built a week before the feast day amidst a great deal of preparation and planning. The original altars had three tiers and a canopy. The table extending from the three tiers is often made into a cross. In the middle of the top row is a statue of St. Joseph or a picture of the holy family assuring that they are the center of attention. Three breads symbolic of the holy family are placed alongside their picture. Altars are usually adorned in blue and white colors to honor the Blessed Virgin Mary.

Food preparation begins weeks in advance. Traditionally, Sicilians grew the altar foods or purchased them fresh from the market. Because this is a Lenten celebration, there is no meat on the altar. Instead, there are fish, vegetables, fruit, breads, cakes and pastries.

Altar breads are made in various religious shapes. Palm leaves symbolize the Blessed Mother; the beard, crook and ladder signify St. Joseph; the cross represents Christ's passion and death. The inside of the Italian bread is dried, toasted with sugar and sprinkled atop spaghetti instead of Parmesan cheese. Many refer to this "mollicu" as St. Joseph's sawdust.

A large red fish, symbolic of Christ, is placed on the saint's table in Louisiana. Various vegetables are fried in egg batter and served hot or cold. Stuffed artichokes are another popular altar dish.

Pasta has its place on the altar with sauce of fennel, hard-boiled eggs and sugar. It is not unusual to need

In Louisiana, palm leaves on gateposts or woven into door wreaths signify an invitation to visit the altar. In Sicily, an olive branch is the designation.

Altar ceremonies generally begin at noon. Three people represent Jesus, Mary and Joseph. Originally, the poor were invited to come and eat from the altar as representatives of different saints. Today, the person hosting the altar invites special people to represent favored saints at the altar table.

The celebration begins with the holy family dressed in costumes and bread crowns parading around the house exterior and knocking at the door. The first time Joseph knocks and asks, "Do you have room for us?" The door is slammed in his face. They walk around the house again. Mary knocks and asks, "Can you provide us with shelter?" She is refused. After the third walk, Jesus knocks. Someone asks, "Who is there?" Jesus says, "Jesus, Mary and Joseph." The door opens and they are given food and shelter. Jesus blesses the altar with the sign of the cross using a parsley sprig dipped in holy water. As a sign of respect, the hands and feet of the holy family are washed with water or wine and kissed by those present. Then, special prayers are said and candles lit. Money donations are given as a gift to St. Joseph. Customarily, the holy family and saints eat a taste of all the altar foods. Once the holy family and saints have been served, guests may eat.

St. Joseph's bread, fava beans and visits to numerous altars are all considered lucky. During the year, altar crumbs and St. Joseph's bread are tossed into storms to prevent destruction. Fava beans prevent one from going broke. They are also a memento of the altar. During the legendary famine, Sicilians ate fava beans though this was animal food. It was also believed that visiting nine altars in succession made a wish come true.

Often, a procession honoring St. Joseph is held on the Sunday closest to the feast day. A statue of St. Joseph is carried through the parade and the rosary may be recited during the walk.

Everyone visiting an altar receives gifts of cookies, fava beans, St. Joseph's bread, prayer cards and sometimes, religious candles

This unique, centuries-old Sicilian custom of creating St. Joseph's Day altars is a tremendous showcase of Italian foods and a magnificent gesture of charity and faith.

110 pounds of spaghetti and 40 gallons of sauce for the hundreds of altar visitors.

Cookies include fig, seed, ginger, lemon, orange, cherry and chocolate. Pignolata are made as well as lamb-shaped cakes covered with shredded coconut.

Food is placed on the altar the night before the celebration. Then, lilies or other flowers, candles, wine and religious statues are added. Often, the Host, the Eucharistic bread that the priest consecrates during Mass, is displayed. The parish priest usually blesses the altar the night before the celebration.

Cuccidata cake

Creole

Laura Plantation

"Creole cooks are born as others, less favored, are born poets."
Charles Gayerre, Louisiana Historian

Laura Locoul Gore

DEFINING CREOLE

As early as 1520, the Spanish conquistadors invented the word "criollo." The French adopted the Spanish word and changed it to "Creole." Few words in American English are as misunderstood or as frequently misused.

The term "Creole" is believed to have derived from the Latin word "creare" meaning "to create." Originating in the Western Hemisphere, the term "Creole" was used about 1590 by Father de Acosta, a Spanish priest, to distinguish newborn West Indies children from everyone else.

New World intercultural relationships were inevitable, and their descendants were considered different. They were not Spanish, French, African or Native American, but a newly created people. Officials wrote the new term as "crioulo," "criollo" and "creole." Generally, the designation was not about race or color. For 18th century Louisianians, "Creole" meant "new born native to the soil" and signified "of local origin." Black and white children born in the colony were designated "Creole" to distinguish them from Louisiana's European and African settlers.

According to Charles Gayerre, a Louisiana historian, "The word was created by the Spanish to distinguish their children, the natives of their conquered colonial possessions, from the original inhabitants. To be Creole was considered an honor."

With time and changing cultural influences the term evolved and specifically applied to the new born of French or European parents living in the West Indies or more particularly, Louisiana.

Captain Bossu, a French officer, observed in 1750 that, "Creoles are children born in Louisiana of a French father and a French or European mother." More broadly, Guy Soniat Dufossat, author of the *Synopsis of the History of Louisiana*, stated, "Creoles are the children of Europeans born in the colony."

George Washington Cable, the celebrated Creole author, said, "The title did not first belong to the descendants of the Spanish, but of the French." Cable agreed that the term implied a certain excellence of origin and entitlement to social rank. He stated, "Creoles will not share their distinction and consider even the worthy Acadian as Creole only by courtesy." Furthermore, "There are no Italian or Sicilian Creoles, nor English, Scotch, Irish or Yankee Creoles, unless of parentage married into and themselves thoroughly converted into Creole society."

The first native French Creole was born in the Louisiana colony at Old Mobile in 1704. He was Jean-Francois Le Can, son of Jean Le Can and Magdelaine Robert.

In later years the definition of "Creole" was broadened even further to designate children of mixed blood. According to the Americans, "Creole" was anything associated with this mixture of peoples. Items such as tomatoes, ponies, furniture, architecture, music and cooking became "native to Louisiana" and signified better quality. By the late 1800s, Louisiana was affectionately called the "Creole State."

Today, Creole is defined as anyone born on Louisiana soil from the intermarriage of Europeans, Africans and Native Americans who contributed significantly to the culture and cuisine of Louisiana.

CREOLES: LOUISIANA'S "CREATED" ARISTOCRACY

In colonial Louisiana, Creoles sought power and prestige while enjoying a highly refined sense of social status. They were friendly and cordial with a captivating innocence. These law-abiding citizens had a quiet charm and a gay spirit that delighted in festivities. Generally,

Michel Bernard Cantrelle

Creoles were conservative and slow to change habits and customs. New Orleans Creole society included government officials, officers, local militia, wealthy planters and successful merchants.

For those who could afford it, living standards were high. The Creoles owned handsome homes with polished floors and wide, covered galleries. The rooms were filled with imported luxuries. For example, the household inventory of Bernard de Verges included cypress and walnut chairs, beds and wardrobes, horsehair mattresses, walnut

Cabonocey Plantation

consoles, carved tables, armchairs and rocking chairs upholstered in leather and scarlet velvet, mirrors, pictures, linens, down quilts, embroidered cloths, porcelain, silver and a sedan chair. Jean Baptiste Prevost, socially and financially distinct, owned an India table worth 120 livres. His collection included tapestries, backgammon boards, chairs, bedsteads, walnut daybeds, mirrors, silver candlesticks and a copper bathtub. Perhaps most impressive was his 3,000-volume library. His wardrobe comprised 30 trimmed and seven plain shirts, three-dozen

SAINT JACQUES DE CABAHANOCE

An organized ecclesiastical parish prior to 1757. The church was then in charge of Fr. Barnabé, a French Capuchin and Pastor of Saint Charles (Destrehan), on east bank of river. The registers were kept in French until 1786. The diocese came under Havana, Cuba, in 1771.

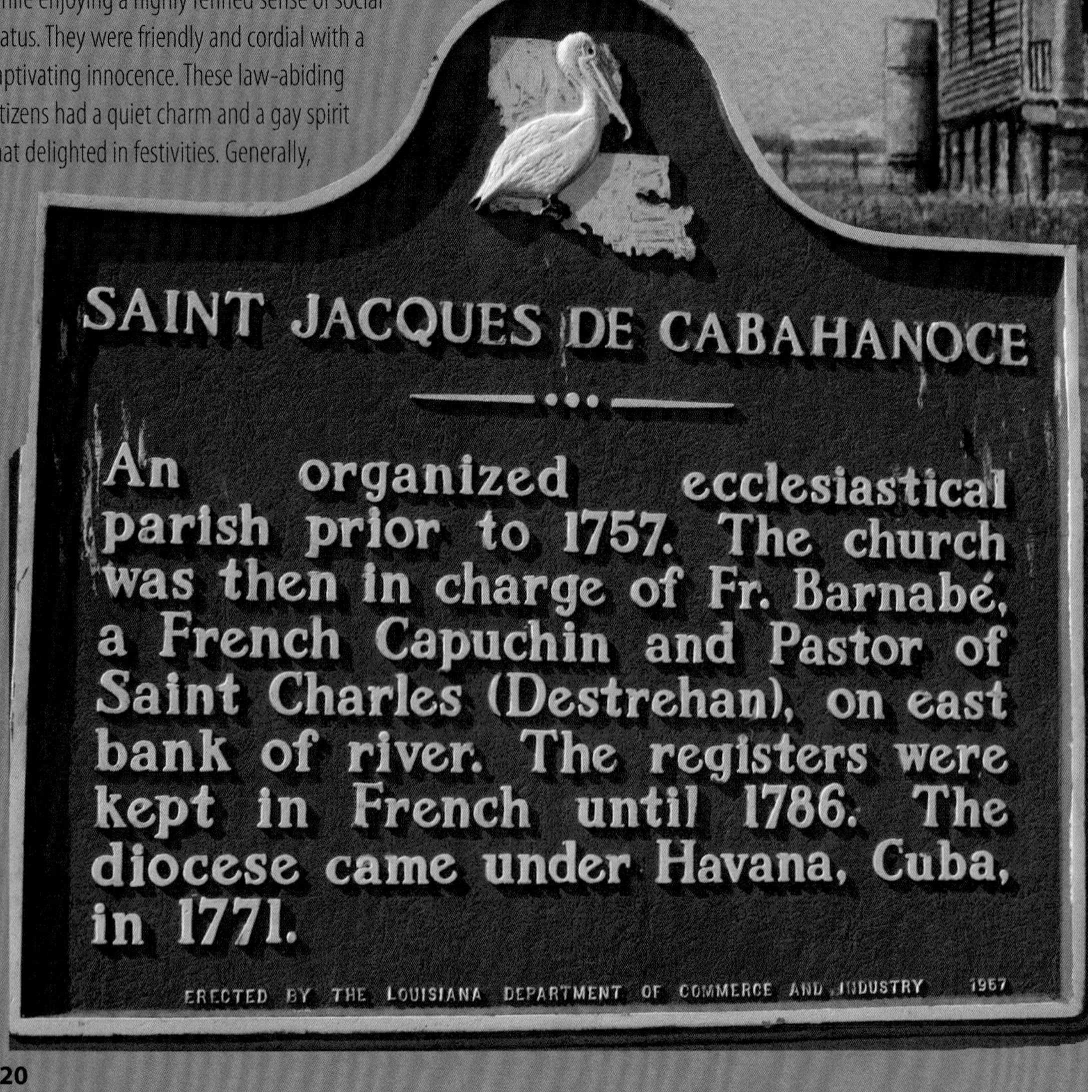

ERECTED BY THE LOUISIANA DEPARTMENT OF COMMERCE AND INDUSTRY 1967

handkerchiefs, suits of black velvet, crimson and blue taffeta and white silk and gold braided waistcoats.

The elaborate homes of the Creoles had detached kitchens containing cast iron kettles from which came a variety of dishes to adorn their tables. Many of these Creole delicacies included imports such as figs, liqueurs, anchovies, prunes, almonds and

Jacques Cantrelle, II

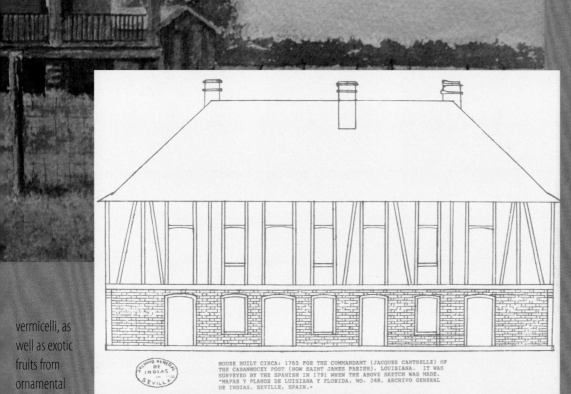

HOUSE BUILT CIRCA: 1765 FOR THE COMMANDANT (JACQUES CANTRELLE) OF THE CABANNOCEY POST (NOW SAINT JAMES PARISH), LOUISIANA. IT WAS SURVEYED BY THE SPANISH IN 1791 WHEN THE ABOVE SKETCH WAS MADE. "MAPAS Y PLANOS DE LUISIANA Y FLORIDA, NO. 248, ARCHIVO GENERAL DE INDIAS, SEVILLE, SPAIN."

vermicelli, as well as exotic fruits from ornamental gardens such as bananas, lemons, limes, ginger and pineapple. An army of servants attended this Creole aristocracy. Many believed this Creole society resembled France during the reign of Louis XV.

Occasionally, elaborate dinners were given such as one held by French Prefect, Laussat. Dancing and cards continued through the night with the last of the more than 300 invited guests leaving by 8 o'clock the next morning. Doors were removed; fire pots illuminated the outdoors;

and more than 220 wax candles lit the rooms. Supper was served at dozens of tables, and there was an all-night buffet.

Creole farmers or planters built fine homes along the Mississippi River and amassed large landholdings called plantations. Trying to duplicate the estates of their home country, plantation life was punctuated with great privilege. The initial crop was indigo from which a fine blue dye was produced. Ultimately, cotton and sugarcane were grown for the world market. Creole prosperity continued following the Louisiana Purchase in 1803, reaching its height in the 1830s during the reign of "King Sugar."

Creole homes, unlike the Greek Revival antebellum mansions of the early to mid-1800s, featured classic West Indies architecture. The homes were strong, simple and built to endure a warm, damp climate. Creole homes featured raised basements with living quarters above and a four-sided, hip roof with galleries. Existing examples between Baton Rouge and New Orleans include St. Joseph, Laura, Destrehan and L'Hermitage plantations. All were completed between 1780 and 1820.

Among the celebrated Creole royalty were Gabriel Valcour Aime of Le Petite Versailles Plantation in St. James Parish; his neighbor, Jacques Telesphore Roman of Bon Sejour (Oak Alley); and Jacques and Michel Cantrelle of Cabanocee

Victorin Zeringue, great-grandfather of Chef John Folse who purchased Cabanocey Plantation in the early 1900s

Jefferson College

Plantation. Notable Creoles of Ascension Parish included Michel Doradou Bringier of L'Hermitage and Augustin Dominique Tureaud of Union Plantation.

Leading Creole families along the Great River Road at the

Jefferson College baseball team, ca. 1890

Valcour Aime

end of the 18th century included Allain, Beauregard, Chauvin, Colomb, D'Arensbourg, de Boré, d'Estrehan, Fagot, Forstall, Fortier, Gayerre, Hebert, LeBeouf, Mandeville, Milhet, Pontalba, Roman, Trepagnier, Tureaud and Verret. Of military fame was the Creole West Point graduate General Pierre Gustave Tousant (P. G. T.) Beauregard.

For Creoles, family was everything, and they firmly believed in living life to the fullest. Their legacy was their attitude of "le joie de vivre" or "the joy of life." They laughed heartily, but always as decorum permitted. For a century and more, regardless of who ruled Louisiana, the Creole's interests, manners and philosophy stemmed from Paris, not New York or Washington. Creole hospitality was virtually limitless with guests treated as royalty. They were well acquainted with fine wines and superb cooking. Creole cuisine was inventive,

Gabriel Aime

refined and generously seasoned. Though French in origin, Creole cuisine masterfully combined other cultural influences including Native America, Spain, Germany, England, Africa and Italy. A sophisticated, aristocratic cuisine based on European techniques, Creole cooking used wine- or liquor-based sauces to enhance its subtle, delicate flavors.

While the Creoles were intelligent people, they lagged behind citizens of other countries culturally. Understandably, they were isolated from the cultural centers of the world and most of their energies were spent in gaining a livelihood. In 1831, Jefferson College was

General Pierre Gustave Tousant (P. G. T.) Beauregard

Jacques Telesphore Roman

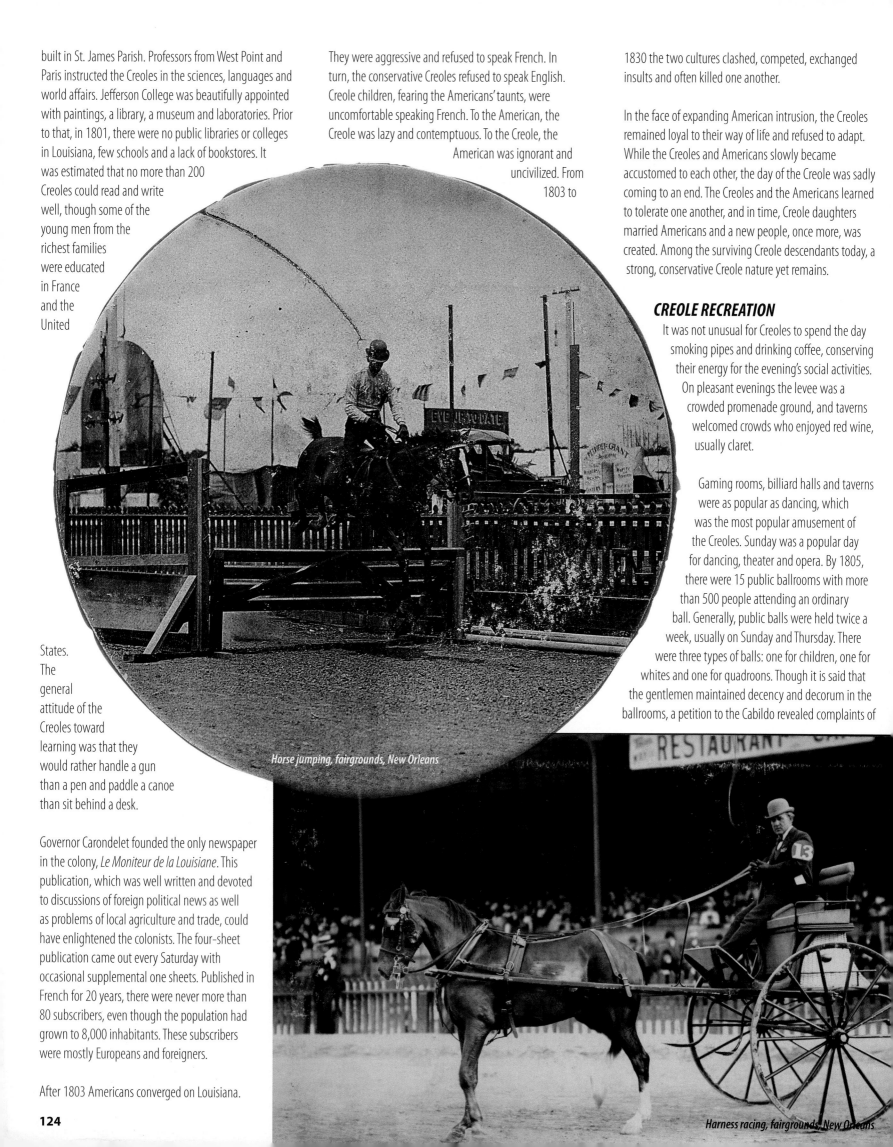

built in St. James Parish. Professors from West Point and Paris instructed the Creoles in the sciences, languages and world affairs. Jefferson College was beautifully appointed with paintings, a library, a museum and laboratories. Prior to that, in 1801, there were no public libraries or colleges in Louisiana, few schools and a lack of bookstores. It was estimated that no more than 200 Creoles could read and write well, though some of the young men from the richest families were educated in France and the United States. The general attitude of the Creoles toward learning was that they would rather handle a gun than a pen and paddle a canoe than sit behind a desk.

Governor Carondelet founded the only newspaper in the colony, *Le Moniteur de la Louisiane*. This publication, which was well written and devoted to discussions of foreign political news as well as problems of local agriculture and trade, could have enlightened the colonists. The four-sheet publication came out every Saturday with occasional supplemental one sheets. Published in French for 20 years, there were never more than 80 subscribers, even though the population had grown to 8,000 inhabitants. These subscribers were mostly Europeans and foreigners.

After 1803 Americans converged on Louisiana.

They were aggressive and refused to speak French. In turn, the conservative Creoles refused to speak English. Creole children, fearing the Americans' taunts, were uncomfortable speaking French. To the American, the Creole was lazy and contemptuous. To the Creole, the American was ignorant and uncivilized. From 1803 to 1830 the two cultures clashed, competed, exchanged insults and often killed one another.

In the face of expanding American intrusion, the Creoles remained loyal to their way of life and refused to adapt. While the Creoles and Americans slowly became accustomed to each other, the day of the Creole was sadly coming to an end. The Creoles and the Americans learned to tolerate one another, and in time, Creole daughters married Americans and a new people, once more, was created. Among the surviving Creole descendants today, a strong, conservative Creole nature yet remains.

CREOLE RECREATION

It was not unusual for Creoles to spend the day smoking pipes and drinking coffee, conserving their energy for the evening's social activities. On pleasant evenings the levee was a crowded promenade ground, and taverns welcomed crowds who enjoyed red wine, usually claret.

Gaming rooms, billiard halls and taverns were as popular as dancing, which was the most popular amusement of the Creoles. Sunday was a popular day for dancing, theater and opera. By 1805, there were 15 public ballrooms with more than 500 people attending an ordinary ball. Generally, public balls were held twice a week, usually on Sunday and Thursday. There were three types of balls: one for children, one for whites and one for quadroons. Though it is said that the gentlemen maintained decency and decorum in the ballrooms, a petition to the Cabildo revealed complaints of

Horse jumping, fairgrounds, New Orleans

Harness racing, fairgrounds, New Orleans

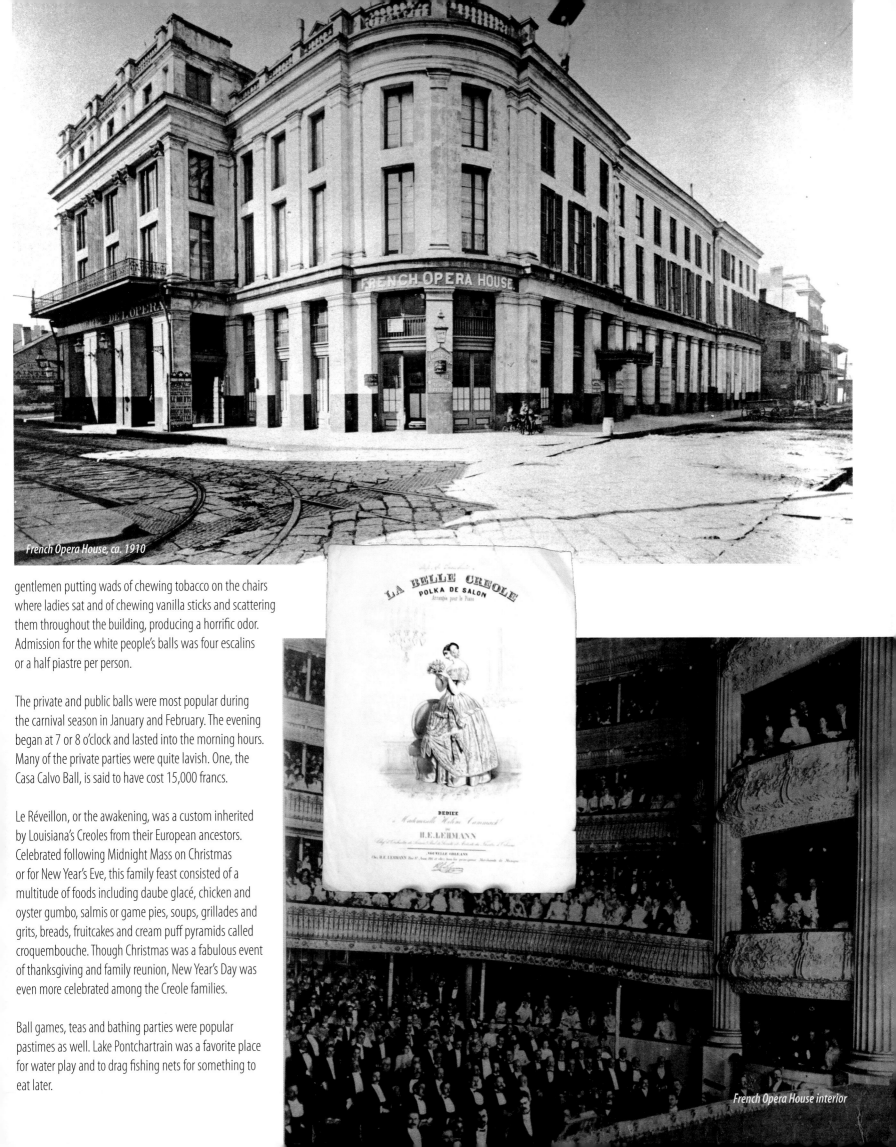

French Opera House, ca. 1910

gentlemen putting wads of chewing tobacco on the chairs where ladies sat and of chewing vanilla sticks and scattering them throughout the building, producing a horrific odor. Admission for the white people's balls was four escalins or a half piastre per person.

The private and public balls were most popular during the carnival season in January and February. The evening began at 7 or 8 o'clock and lasted into the morning hours. Many of the private parties were quite lavish. One, the Casa Calvo Ball, is said to have cost 15,000 francs.

Le Réveillon, or the awakening, was a custom inherited by Louisiana's Creoles from their European ancestors. Celebrated following Midnight Mass on Christmas or for New Year's Eve, this family feast consisted of a multitude of foods including daube glacé, chicken and oyster gumbo, salmis or game pies, soups, grillades and grits, breads, fruitcakes and cream puff pyramids called croquembouche. Though Christmas was a fabulous event of thanksgiving and family reunion, New Year's Day was even more celebrated among the Creole families.

Ball games, teas and bathing parties were popular pastimes as well. Lake Pontchartrain was a favorite place for water play and to drag fishing nets for something to eat later.

French Opera House interior

Roux, Stocks & Sauces

Madame Begue's restaurant kitchen, ca. 1907

Like their classical French and other regional ancestors, many Cajun and Creole recipes have at their heart a reliance on rich, hearty, aromatic stocks. While a stock may simply be a liquid enriched by simmering meat, seafood, wild game or vegetables, it is also the essential building block of all sauces, soups, marinades and braises. In fact, another term for stock, fond, is derived from the word "foundation." Add to that stock a golden roux and selected seasonings, and a sauce is born. In Louisiana the Old World principles used in creating stocks, sauces and roux have been adapted, and local ingredients substituted, to produce a taste and texture unique to this region.

When making a traditional stock, the ingredients are strained from the liquid and discarded once the flavors have been extracted. The Creoles held to this classical stock-making technique, but for the Cajuns, the idea of simply throwing out hearty, flavorful ingredients was appalling. Cajuns cooked anything they could hunt, trap or hook in a black iron pot and the natural stock remained as the gravy. Cajun stocks followed the basic principles of Creole and classic cooking, but the seasonings were retained and became part of the dish.

The thickening of a stock may be achieved by reduction or through the addition of eggs, vegetable purées, cream, foie gras, bread, starches or even blood. The roux, a perfect blending of equal parts fat and flour, has always been the primary thickening agent of classical cuisine, but in Louisiana the simple roux has been revolutionized and has become the cornerstone of Cajun and Creole cooking.

In classical cuisine there are three basic roux used to create various sauces and soups: the white roux, for béchamel; the blond roux, for béchamel or velouté; and the brown roux, for dark sauces. After arriving in Bayou Country, both the Europeans and the Cajuns adapted these classical roux to their regional interpretations and ingredients. Traditionally the Creoles created roux with butter as the base. The Cajuns, on the other hand, made their roux primarily with lard and later with oil. A dark brown roux, unique to the Cajuns, is created by cooking oil and flour over medium-high heat until the base becomes caramel colored. This dark brown roux has less thickening power than a lighter roux, but its richness and depth have made it the secret to creating traditional Cajun sauce piquants, gumbos and dark brown gravies. There is arguably no finer aroma in Cajun Country than onions, celery, bell peppers and garlic sautéing in a brown roux. Cajun children have been known to enjoy a snack of nothing more than a vegetable-infused roux on a slice of warm French bread.

Stock and roux are the crucial elements in creating a sauce, which is essentially a thickened, seasoned liquid used to enhance or complement the flavor and appearance of other foods. While some recipes call for hot stock to be added to cold roux and others just the reverse, many chefs insist they should never be combined at the same temperature. No matter the combination, a sauce should always be brought to a boil after the roux is added to create the perfect thickening effect.

Cajun and Creole sauces, as in many other regional cuisines, find their origins in the four primary types of sauces found in classical cuisine. These include béchamel, velouté, espagnole (demi-glace) and tomato sauce. However, in Cajun cooking the sauce is quite often created in the pot without the fuss and waste of classical or even Creole cooking. Few could argue that a sauce piquant created in a black iron pot in St. James Parish is not a worthy rival in flavor, texture and character to an espagnole sauce simmered all day by the finest French chef. Of course, the final crucial step in creating the perfect sauce, particularly in Louisiana, is the careful addition of seasonings.

Some of Louisiana's most popular sauces are simply traditional sauces with a twist. Two of the most notable are cocktail sauce and rémoulade. What is interesting is that both were originally used hot, and yet today are more often served cold. Louisiana cocktail sauce, commonly served as a cold, tomato-based dip for seafood, actually descended from a warm tomato sauce served with fish. Rémoulade, a spicy mayonnaise-based sauce used for seafood and salads is thought to be an evolution of ravigote sauce, a traditional sauce once served with meat and seafood. On old Creole tables ravigote was spiced with mustard, tarragon or cayenne and thickened with eggs, cream or flour. There were both hot and cold variations of this sauce. Eventually, chefs began to use mayonnaise to thicken the ravigote, which then became rémoulade. Although rémoulade may occasionally be used to top a hot fillet of fish, it is more commonly served cold.

What distinguishes Louisiana's cooking from that of the rest of the country is adaptation. Here even traditional elements found new manifestations. Derived from the classics and flavored by Cajun and Creole influences, these recipes and techniques for stocks, roux and sauces are quite literally the heart and soul of Louisiana cuisine.

STOCK TECHNIQUES

Although stocks may seem simple to prepare, it is important to remember that with a poor stock as its base, the final dish may be less than perfect. Some basic principles almost always apply. Always start with cold water as it naturally draws out the flavors from the bones or vegetables being used. Bring the

water to a boil slowly to aid natural clarification, and do not boil too vigorously or too long. What is essential to the process is a gentle simmering roll in the liquid. Impurities and fat can be skimmed from the surface as it simmers.

There are four major ingredients used in a stock: bones, mirepoix (aromatic vegetables), bouquet garni (spices and herbs) and liquid (water and wine). It is important to understand when and how to use each of these components.

BONES

Stock can be made from any type of bones. To create a white stock suitable for veal, fish, shellfish or chicken, select bones suitable for the stock desired. Wash the bones, then expose the marrow by breaking or cutting them into small, manageable pieces. To create a dark stock suitable for beef, veal, game or duck, brown bones well with a light coating of oil, being careful not to burn them. Browned bones will add rich color and flavor to the stock.

MIREPOIX

The classic mirepoix consists of onions, celery and carrots, but a variety of vegetables can be used to infuse aromatic flavor into a stock. Try using shallots, the white portion of scallions or leeks, garlic, mushrooms, tomatoes or whatever is available. However, never use bell peppers, cabbage, cauliflower or similar vegetables because they will overpower the stock and make it bitter. Vegetables should be cut smaller if the stock will be cooked for a short time and larger if it will be cooked for a long time. When used in a white stock, sauté the vegetables in butter beforehand. For a brown stock, add the mirepoix as the bones brown.

BOUQUET GARNI

Bouquet garni is a combination of black peppercorns, parsley, whole thyme, bay leaf and cloves tied up in a leek or cheesecloth. The bundle is placed in the liquid as it cooks. If the stock will cook more than an hour or two, add the bouquet garni during the last hour. Once the stock is completed, remove and dispose of the bouquet garni.

LIQUID

Cold water is essential to the process of extracting color, flavor, nutrients and gelatin from bones. The water should always be cold in order to draw out the essence of the ingredients. Red or white wine can be used to enhance the taste of a stock. Never add salt to the liquid. As the stock reduces, the salt will remain making it too salty. To produce a hearty, flavorful, clear stock, simmer the liquid slowly and skim off all impurities and fat that rise to the surface.

Roux

Troubleshooting a Roux

I have often been asked why a roux will seem to separate or "break" when stock or liquid is added. This can happen for one of three reasons: too much liquid is added at once; the temperature of the liquid contrasts too strongly with the roux; or the flour is not fresh.

First, as you will see when reading the roux recipes, normally one cup of roux will thicken 3 quarts of stock or water to a light gumbo consistency. If too much liquid is added at once, the roux may break. I recommend adding the liquid in one-quart intervals, stirring constantly, and allowing the roux to absorb the liquid totally prior to adding more. In fact, the mixture should simmer for 30 seconds prior to the next addition of liquid. This will guarantee that the proper amount of liquid is added to achieve the consistency you are looking for in the finished product, with no separation.

Secondly, if a cold liquid is added to a hot roux then the fat in the roux may coagulate in the liquid, and float to the surface, trapping browned flour particles in the mass as it rises. Don't panic. As the liquid comes to a boil, simply use a wire whisk to blend the mixture back into suspension.

Finally, a problem may occur if a bag of flour has been sitting around for six months or more or has not been properly sealed against excess humidity from the refrigerator or cupboard. In these situations, the flour may tend to lose its ability to absorb liquid when used for a roux. When the stock is added, the roux may break or clump. If it cannot be salvaged with the first two suggestions, discard and begin again. To avoid this problem, always be careful to make a roux with fresh or properly stored flour.

Should you wish to further thicken a stew or soup after the roux has been incorporated, you may add a little cornstarch dissolved in water or a few tablespoons of flour browned in hot oil. As always, be sure to stir constantly while adding either, to ensure proper distribution.

OIL-BASED ROUX

Comment:

Although conventional French roux is made with butter, Cajuns have traditionally used oil to make the roux they use in classic dishes like gumbo. The following recipes, which use 1 cup each of oil and flour, thicken the following:

- 6 cups stock to a thick brown sauce consistency
- 8 cups stock to a thick gumbo consistency
- 10 cups stock to a perfect Louisiana gumbo consistency
- 12 cups stock to a light gumbo consistency

The 4 Steps To Making Roux

ADD OIL

ADD FLOUR

BLEND WELL

COOK

LIGHT BROWN CAJUN ROUX

Ingredients:
1 cup oil
1 cup flour

Method:
In a cast iron pot or skillet, heat oil over medium-high heat to approximately 325°F. Slowly whisk in flour, stirring constantly for approximately 2 minutes or until roux is peanut butter in color. This roux is normally used in étouffée, fricassées and to thicken vegetable dishes such as corn macque choux or butter beans with ham.

DARK BROWN CAJUN ROUX

Ingredients:
1 cup oil
1 cup flour

Method:
In a cast iron pot or skillet, heat oil over medium-high heat to approximately 365°F. Slowly whisk in flour, stirring constantly for 3–5 minutes or until roux is light caramel in color. This roux should be almost twice as dark as the light brown roux but not as dark as chocolate. The final temperature should reach 385°F–395°F. You should remember that the darker the roux gets, the less thickening power it holds and the more bitter it will become. This roux is used most often in sauce piquants, crawfish bisques and game gumbos. However, it is perfectly normal to use the dark brown Cajun roux in any dish in Cajun cooking.

BUTTER ROUX: THE CLASSICAL AND CREOLE ROUX

Comment:

Butter roux was made in early New Orleans by the Creoles. They had access to volumes of butter from vendors in the marketplace. Cajuns traditionally used butter on hot French bread, and they considered it wasteful to use good butter in a roux.

The following recipes, which use 1 cup each of butter and flour, thicken the following:

- 6 cups stock to a thick white sauce consistency
- 8 cups stock to a concentrated soup consistency
- 10 cups stock to a thick soup consistency
- 12 cups stock to a perfect Louisiana gumbo consistency
- 14 cups stock to a light gumbo consistency

THE WHITE BUTTER ROUX

Ingredients:

1 cup butter
1 cup flour

Method:

In a heavy-bottomed sauté pan, melt butter over medium-high heat. Whisk in flour, stirring constantly until the flour and butter are well blended and bubbly. Do not brown. This roux can be used in béchamels, cream sauces and soups.

THE BLOND BUTTER ROUX

Ingredients:

1 cup butter
1 cup flour

Method:

In a heavy-bottomed sauté pan, melt butter over medium-high heat. Whisk in flour, stirring constantly until roux becomes pale gold. Continue whisking during the cooking process to prevent flour from scorching. Blond butter roux is best used to thicken étouffées or vegetables such as butter beans and petits pois.

THE BROWN BUTTER ROUX

Ingredients:

1 cup butter
1 cup flour

Method:

In a heavy-bottomed sauté pan, melt butter over medium-high heat. Whisk in flour, stirring constantly until roux becomes light brown. Continue whisking during the cooking process, as flour will tend to scorch when browning begins. Should black specks appear in the roux, discard and begin again. This roux is primarily used to thicken gravies and sauces.

OIL-LESS ROUX

Comment:

1 cup of oil-less roux thickens 6 cups of stock to a proper gumbo consistency

Ingredients:

2 cups flour

Method:

Preheat oven to 375°F. Spread flour evenly across the bottom of a 15-inch cast iron skillet. Bake, stirring occasionally, for approximately 1 hour. Make sure to stir well around the edges of the skillet so flour does not scorch. Cook flour until desired color is achieved, depending on use. The roux will become darker when liquid is added. When the roux is cooked, cool on a large cookie sheet, stirring occasionally. Store in a sealed jar for future use.

MICROWAVE ROUX

Comment:

Although many Cajun cooks would think it absurd, a roux can be made rather simply in your microwave. This recipe will create a perfect dark brown roux that can be used immediately or stored for later use. The finished product will thicken 3 quarts of liquid to a gumbo consistency.

Ingredients:

1 cup oil
1 cup flour

Method:

Combine oil and flour in a microwavable glass bowl. Whisk thoroughly until all lumps are removed. Microwave on high 6 minutes then remove and stir well. Return to microwave for 3 minutes then stir again. Continue to microwave in 3-minute increments, stirring after each, until mixture is the color of caramel. (In a 900-watt microwave, a perfect dark brown roux is achieved in 18 total minutes. Cooking times may differ depending on your microwave.) You may stir 1 cup diced onions, ½ cup diced celery, ¼ cup diced bell peppers and 1 tbsp minced garlic into the hot roux to help it cool. NOTE: Roux will become very hot during the cooking process. Use caution when stirring.

Stocks

CHICKEN STOCK

Prep Time: 1 Hour
Yields: 2 Quarts

Ingredients:

2 pounds chicken bones
2 pounds chicken necks, wings and gizzards
2 onions, chopped
2 carrots, peeled and sliced
6 cloves garlic
2 celery stalks, chopped
2 bay leaves
2 sprigs parsley
1 tsp dried thyme
12 whole black peppercorns
1 gallon cold water
2 cups dry white wine

Method:

Have a butcher select 2 pounds of chicken bones and 2 pounds of chicken necks, wings and gizzards. Place all ingredients in a 2-gallon stockpot. Bring to a rolling boil, reduce to simmer and cook 1 hour. During cooking process, skim off all impurities that rise to surface of stock. Strain through cheesecloth or a fine sieve and allow stock to rest for 30 minutes. Skim off all oil that rises to surface of stock. Return stock to a low boil and reduce to 2 quarts.

FISH OR SHELLFISH STOCK

Prep Time: 1 Hour
Yields: 2 Quarts

Ingredients:

2 pounds fish bones
  OR 1 pound each crab, shrimp and crawfish shells
2 onions, chopped
2 carrots, sliced
2 celery stalks, chopped
6 garlic cloves
4 sprigs parsley
2 bay leaves
1 tsp dried thyme
6 whole black peppercorns
1 lemon, sliced
1 gallon cold water
3 cups dry white wine

Method:

Ask your seafood supplier to reserve 2 pounds of white fish bones or 3 pounds of shellfish shells, depending upon stock desired. Combine all ingredients in a 2-gallon stockpot. Bring to a rolling boil, reduce to simmer and cook 45 minutes. During cooking process, skim off all impurities that rise to surface. Add water if necessary to retain volume. Strain stock through cheesecloth or a fine sieve. Return stock to simmer and reduce to 2 quarts.

BEEF, VEAL OR GAME STOCK

Prep Time: 6 Hours
Yields: 2 Quarts

Ingredients:

6 pounds marrow bones
3 large onions, unpeeled and quartered
3 carrots, peeled and sliced
3 celery stalks, peeled and chopped
3 heads garlic, cut in half to expose pods
2 bay leaves
4 sprigs parsley
15 whole black peppercorns
1 tsp whole thyme
2 gallons water
3 cups dry red wine

Method:

Preheat oven to 400°F. Have a butcher select 6 pounds of beef or veal marrow bones, depending on stock desired. If preparing game stock, save 6 pounds of game marrow bones from your next hunt. NOTE: Game bones may be frozen as they come available for up to 6 months before using. Place bones, onions, carrots, celery and garlic in roasting pan. Cook 30–45 minutes or until bones are golden brown. Place browned bones, cooked vegetables, bay leaves, parsley, peppercorns, thyme and water in a 3-gallon stockpot. Deglaze roasting pan with red wine and add to stockpot. Bring to a rolling boil, reduce to simmer and cook 6–8 hours, adding water if necessary to retain volume. During this process, skim off impurities that rise to surface of pot. Remove pot from heat and strain stock through cheesecloth or a fine sieve. Allow stock to rest 1 hour, then skim off all oil that rises to top. Return stock to a low boil and reduce to 2 quarts. Use as-is to make gravy or as a base for demi-glace.

Sauces

DEMI-GLACE

Prep Time: 1 Hour
Yields: 1 Quart

Comment:
Demi-glace is an essential sauce in classical cuisine. It is not only used as a sauce by itself, but is also an ingredient in many other classical sauces.

Ingredients:
2 quarts beef, veal or game stock (see recipe)
½ cup white butter roux (see recipe)
1 ounce tomato sauce

Method:
Equally divide stock into 2 heavy-bottomed saucepans and bring to a low boil. Using a wire whisk, add white butter roux into 1 saucepan, stirring constantly as mixture thickens. Blend tomato sauce into thickened mixture. This creates what is classically known as an espagnole sauce. If this sauce is not full-flavored, you may wish to add a mirepoix or bouquet garni. (See stock techniques.) Continue simmering while skimming off all impurities that rise to surface. As espagnole sauce reduces, replace volume with stock from second pot until all has been incorporated. Strain sauce through cheesecloth or a fine sieve. If desired, add an ounce of sherry or brandy to enhance flavor.

GLACE DE VIANDE

Prep Time: 1 Hour
Yields: 1 Cup

Comment:

This recipe uses beef or veal stock to make a meat glace or "Glace de Viande," produced by reducing a rich, clear beef or veal stock. Glaces may also be made from chicken (Glace de Volaille), duck (Glace de Canard), fish (Glace de Poisson) and game stocks (Glace de Gibier).

Ingredients:

1 quart beef or veal stock (see recipe)

Method:

In a heavy-bottomed saucepan, simmer stock over medium to medium-high heat. As stock reduces, you may transfer it from time to time to smaller pots, straining it each time through cheesecloth. Reduce stock until it is thick enough to "nappe" or coat the back of a spoon. This syrupy mixture becomes firm and rubbery upon refrigeration. Glace is used to coat meat, giving it sheen and additional flavor. It can also enhance soups, sauces or even beurre blanc. Meat glaces may be refrigerated for weeks at a time.

VELOUTÉ

Prep Time: 45 Minutes
Yields: 2 Quarts

Comment:

Velouté is the base for all great cream soups and flavored white sauces. It is the most practical of all mother sauces and is created with relative ease. In classical cuisine, it is defined as an ordinary white stock. However, in Creole cooking, roux is added to the white stock prior to calling it Velouté.

Ingredients:

2 quarts chicken or fish stock (see recipe)
½ cup white butter roux (see recipe)
salt and white pepper to taste

Method:

In a heavy-bottomed saucepan, bring stock to a low boil. Reduce to simmer then whisk roux into hot stock. Continue to whisk until mixture is smooth and slightly thickened. Season with salt and white pepper. Reduce heat to low and cook approximately 30 minutes, skimming off all impurities that rise to surface.

BÉCHAMEL SAUCE

Prep Time: 30 Minutes
Yields: 1 Quart

Comment:

This sauce is the primary ingredient for all creamed vegetable casseroles and au gratin dishes. For more flavor, add a small amount of chicken or fish stock.

Ingredients:

1 quart milk	2 small bay leaves
1 small onion, diced	½ cup white butter roux (see recipe)
3 whole cloves	salt and white pepper to taste
pinch of thyme	pinch of nutmeg
6 whole peppercorns	

Method:

In a heavy-bottomed saucepan, heat milk over medium-high heat. Add onions, cloves, thyme, peppercorns and bay leaves. Continue to scald milk with seasonings for approximately 20 minutes. Do not boil. Strain scalded milk through cheesecloth into another saucepan. Discard vegetables. Bring milk back to a low boil and add roux, stirring constantly with a wire whisk. Continue to whisk until mixture achieves a thickened sauce consistency. Be careful not to scorch sauce. When thickened, remove from heat and season with salt, pepper and nutmeg.

SAUCE ACADIAN

Prep Time: 1 Hour
Yields: 2 Quarts

Comment:

Technically speaking, this sauce is a Nantua, which is classically made by adding crawfish butter and paprika to a béchamel. In Louisiana, we have further enriched the recipe to create Sauce Acadian.

Ingredients:

2 pounds crawfish shells, heads included
2 cups chopped onions
1 cup chopped celery
1 cup chopped carrots
6 cloves garlic
2 bay leaves
1 tsp dried thyme
15 whole peppercorns
1 gallon cold water
2 cups dry white wine
½ cup tomato sauce
½ cup white butter roux (see recipe)
1 pint heavy whipping cream
½ ounce brandy
salt and white pepper to taste

Method:

In a 2-gallon stockpot over medium-high heat, combine crawfish shells and heads, onions, celery, carrots, garlic, bay leaves, thyme, peppercorns, water and wine. Bring mixture to a low boil, reduce heat to simmer and cook 30 minutes. During cooking process, skim off all impurities that rise to surface. When cooked, strain stock through cheesecloth or fine sieve. Discard shells and vegetables. Return hot stock to pot, bring to a low boil and reduce to approximately 2 quarts. Add tomato sauce and white roux, whisking constantly until roux is well blended and sauce is slightly thickened. Reduce heat to simmer and cook 15 minutes. Add heavy whipping cream and brandy. Season with salt and pepper. Strain sauce for a second time, adjust seasonings and allow to cool.

BÉARNAISE SAUCE

Prep Time: 15 Minutes
Yields: 1 Cup

Comment:

Béarnaise, a variation on hollandaise, is one of the classic sauces of French cuisine. This sauce is wonderful when served over Tournedos of Beef and is also excellent with fish or chicken.

Ingredients:

8 ounces unsalted butter
3 tbsps tarragon vinegar
½ cup white wine
1 tsp lemon juice
dash of Louisiana hot sauce
1 tbsp chopped tarragon
1 tsp sliced green onions
1 tsp chopped parsley
3 egg yolks
salt and cayenne pepper to taste

Method:

In a small sauté pan, melt butter over medium-high heat. Set aside and cool slightly. In a separate sauté pan, combine vinegar, white wine, lemon juice, hot sauce, tarragon, green onions and parsley. Bring to a slight boil, whisking constantly, and reduce to half volume. In a stainless steel bowl, whisk egg yolks into vinegar mixture until well blended. Place bowl over a double boiler and whisk constantly until egg mixture has doubled in volume and is smooth and creamy. Be careful not to overheat, as eggs will scramble. Remove bowl from saucepan and add melted butter in a slow steady stream, whisking constantly. If sauce becomes too thick, add a few drops of warm water. Season with salt, pepper and additional lemon juice if necessary. This sauce is best when served immediately. NOTE: To make a quick, easy blender béarnaise sauce, simply follow blender hollandaise method. (See recipe.) Substitute tarragon vinegar for red wine vinegar and stir in tarragon, green onions and parsley by hand after sauce is blended.

HOLLANDAISE SAUCE

Prep Time: 30 Minutes
Yields: 1 Cup

Comment:

Hollandaise Sauce is often used to add a light, citrus flavor to fish or vegetables. It is the best sauce to use when a delicious, yet subtle flavor is desired. Try adding other herbs and spices for a more creative finish.

Ingredients:

8 ounces unsalted butter
3 tbsps red wine vinegar
½ cup dry white wine
1 tsp lemon juice
dash of Louisiana hot sauce
3 egg yolks
salt and white pepper to taste

Method:

In a small saucepan, melt butter over medium-high heat. Remove from heat and keep warm (at about 150°F). In a separate sauté pan, add vinegar, wine, lemon juice and hot sauce. Place over medium heat and reduce to approximately half volume. Remove from heat and keep warm. In a stainless steel bowl, whisk egg yolks with vinegar mixture. Place over double boiler and whisk constantly until egg mixture has doubled in volume and becomes smooth and creamy. Do not allow mixture to overheat, as eggs will scramble. Remove from heat and add melted butter in a slow steady stream, whisking constantly. If sauce is too thick, add a few drops of warm water while whisking. Season with salt, white pepper and additional lemon juice if necessary. This sauce is best when served immediately. If allowed to cool, butter will harden; sauce cannot be reheated.

BLENDER HOLLANDAISE SAUCE

Prep Time: 15 Minutes
Yields: 1½ Cups

Comment:

The blender method for hollandaise sauce is a shortcut to creating the classical hollandaise. The same light, citrus flavor is created in this quick, simple process.

Ingredients:

8 ounces unsalted butter
3 egg yolks
2 tbsps red wine vinegar
1 tbsp dry white wine
1 tsp lemon juice
dash of Louisiana hot sauce
salt and white pepper to taste

Method:

Fill a blender with hot tap water and set aside for 5 minutes. Pour out water. In a small saucepot, melt butter, swirling constantly until it reaches 150°F. In blender, combine egg yolks, vinegar, wine, lemon juice, hot sauce, salt and white pepper. Blend mixture on high speed for 2 minutes. As mixture continues to blend, slowly pour in butter in a steady stream until all is added. Serve immediately. This sauce cannot be reheated as butter will melt and separate.

BORDELAISE SAUCE

Prep Time: 15 Minutes
Yields: 1 Cup

Comment:
In the city of New Orleans, Bordelaise Sauce has a completely different look and taste than that of classical cuisine. Bordelaise means "the sauce from Bordeaux." Originally, the sauce was made with Sauternes (a white dessert wine from Bordeaux), tarragon and garlic, and it was garnished with rounds of marrow. The Creoles of early New Orleans, making do with what was available, changed this sauce completely by substituting red Bordeaux wine and eliminating the marrow.

Ingredients:
¾ cup butter
3 tbsps olive oil
¼ cup minced garlic
1 tsp cracked black peppercorns
¼ cup sliced green onions
1 ounce red Bordeaux wine
1 tbsp minced pimientos
¼ cup chopped parsley
salt to taste
Louisiana hot sauce to taste

Method:
In a heavy-bottomed sauté pan, melt butter with olive oil over medium-high heat. Add garlic, peppercorns and green onions. Sauté 2–3 minutes or until vegetables are wilted. Be careful not to over-brown garlic, as it will become bitter. Deglaze with red wine and stir in pimientos and parsley. Season with salt and hot sauce. Remove from heat.

MARCHAND DE VIN

Prep Time: 30 Minutes
Yields: 2 Cups

Comment:

Marchand de Vin, or the wine merchant sauce, is probably the most famous of the New Orleans sauces. Though the original version used bone marrow, the ingredient has been removed in this Creole version.

Ingredients:

¼ cup butter
¼ cup minced ham
½ cup sliced green onions
¼ cup minced garlic
2 tbsps minced onions
½ cup dry red wine
1 cup demi-glace (see recipe)
salt and cracked black pepper to taste
cayenne pepper to taste

Method:

In a heavy-bottomed sauté pan, melt butter over medium-high heat. Sauté ham, green onions, garlic and onions 3–5 minutes or until vegetables are wilted. Deglaze with red wine and reduce to half volume. Add demi-glace and return mixture to a simmer. Season with salt and peppers. Continue to reduce until sauce is slightly thickened and all flavors are developed. This sauce is best served over sautéed or grilled meat or veal.

BROWN MEUNIÈRE SAUCE

Prep Time: 15 Minutes
Yields: 1 Cup

Comment:

Brown Meunière Sauce is the most popular sauce at Lafitte's Landing Restaurant. Its tart taste and rich flavor go well with both meat and fish. However, many exciting variations can be made using meunière as the base sauce.

Ingredients:

4 ounces demi-glace (see recipe)
2 ounces dry white wine
1 ounce lemon juice
½ pound unsalted butter, chilled
salt and cayenne pepper to taste

Method:

In a sauté pan, combine demi-glace, wine and lemon juice over medium-high heat. Whisk until all ingredients are well blended. Bring to a low boil and reduce to half volume. Swirling pan constantly, add a few pats of butter at a time until all is used. Pan must be swirling constantly or hot spots will develop and butter will break down. Season with salt and cayenne pepper. Keep warm. Since this is a basic butter sauce, it cannot be reheated as butter will separate.

LOUISIANA-STYLE HUNTER SAUCE

Prep Time: 30 Minutes
Yields: 2 Cups

Comment:

Hunter sauce, or sauce chasseur, is the most complex flavor that can be derived from a demi-glace. The sauce is similar to the Grand Veneur or Royal Hunt Sauce and is dependent on the concentration of wild game flavor in the stock. This sauce can be used with venison and roasted wild duck dishes.

Ingredients:

¼ cup butter
¼ cup diced Louisiana wild mushrooms
¼ cup sliced green onions
1 tbsp minced garlic
¼ cup diced ripe tomatoes
1 ounce dry red wine
1 ounce brandy
1 cup demi-glace of game (see recipe)
1 tbsp chopped parsley
salt and cracked black pepper to taste

Method:

In a heavy-bottomed saucepan, melt butter over medium-high heat. Add mushrooms, green onions, garlic and tomatoes. Sauté 3–5 minutes or until vegetables are wilted. Deglaze with red wine and brandy. Reduce heat to simmer and cook until sauce reduces to half volume. Stir in game demi-glace and parsley. Season with salt and pepper. Simmer 5 minutes or until sauce is slightly thickened and full-flavored.

OYSTERS ROCKEFELLER SAUCE

Prep Time: 1 Hour
Yields: 6 Servings

Comment:

This sauce is based on Oysters Rockefeller (see recipe), the most famous of all oyster dishes. The original recipe was developed by Jules Alciatore at Antoine's Restaurant in New Orleans in 1899. Named Rockefeller because of its incredibly rich flavor, the original dish included no spinach.

Ingredients:

1 dozen shucked oysters with liquid
¼ pound butter
¼ cup diced onions
¼ cup diced celery
½ cup sliced green onions
2 tbsps minced garlic
1 cup frozen spinach, thawed

1 tbsp flour
1 pint heavy whipping cream
½ ounce Pernod or Herbsaint
1 tsp sugar
1 tbsp Worcestershire sauce
1 tsp Louisiana hot sauce
salt and cracked black pepper to taste

Method:

In a 2-quart saucepan, melt butter over medium-high heat. Sauté onions, celery, green onions and garlic 3–5 minutes or until vegetables are wilted. Using a metal spoon, chop spinach into vegetable mixture. Cook until spinach is hot and mixed into seasonings. Blend flour into mixture, being sure to remove all lumps. Add whipping cream and oyster liquid, stirring constantly until sauce is thick and bubbly. Stir in Pernod, sugar, Worcestershire sauce and hot sauce until well blended. Season with salt and pepper. To ensure a sauce-like consistency, stir in additional cream or water. Continue to cook approximately 10 minutes. Stir in oysters and cook 5 minutes. Pour contents of saucepan into a blender and purée on high speed. Serve 2 ounces of this sauce with a trout, chicken or veal dish.

BEURRE BLANC

Prep Time: 15 Minutes
Yields: 1 Cup

Comment:

This sauce comes to us from the regional cuisine of Brittany. The city of Nantes, on the Loire River, is famed for serving this sauce with pike and Loire shad. Today in Louisiana, Beurre Blanc is usually served with chicken or fish.

Ingredients:

8 ounces unsalted butter, chipped
½ cup dry white wine
2 tbsps white vinegar
1 tsp lemon juice
1 tsp diced shallots
1 clove garlic, minced
1 tbsp sliced green onions
salt and white pepper to taste
1 tsp chopped parsley

Method:

In a heavy-bottomed sauté pan, combine wine, vinegar, lemon juice, shallots, garlic and green onions over medium-high heat. Stir constantly until liquid is reduced to approximately 2 tablespoons. At this point, it is commonly known as a gastrique. Reduce heat to low. Swirling pan constantly, add a few chips of butter at a time until all is used. Do not stir with a metal spoon or whisk as hot spots may develop and butter will separate. Remove from heat and season with salt and white pepper. Garnish with chopped parsley.

BEURRE CAJUN

Prep Time: 15 Minutes
Yields: 1 Cup

Comment:

This sauce is excellent when served over pan-sautéed or charbroiled fish.

Ingredients:

8 ounces unsalted butter, chipped
¼ cup crawfish tails with fat
½ cup dry white wine
1 tbsp lemon juice
1 clove garlic, minced
1 tbsp sliced green onions
¼ cup sliced andouille
dash of Louisiana hot sauce
salt and cayenne pepper to taste

Method:

In a sauté pan, combine crawfish tails, wine, lemon juice, garlic, green onions, andouille and hot sauce over medium-high heat. Sauté 3–5 minutes or until liquid is reduced to half volume. Swirling pan constantly, add a few chips of butter at a time until all is used. Do not stir with a metal spoon or wire whisk as hot spots will develop and butter will separate. Remove from heat and season with salt and cayenne pepper.

BEURRE CREOLE

Prep Time: 15 Minutes
Yields: 1 Cup

Comment:
This sauce is excellent over broiled or sautéed fish or grilled shrimp.

Ingredients:
8 ounces unsalted butter, chipped
½ cup dry white wine
2 tbsps lemon juice
2 thin lemon slices
¼ cup claw crabmeat
¼ cup diced tomatoes
1 clove garlic, minced
1 tbsp sliced green onions
8–10 whole peppercorns
1 whole bay leaf
3 whole basil leaves
1 tsp tomato sauce
Louisiana hot sauce to taste
salt and cayenne pepper to taste

Method:
In a sauté pan, combine wine, lemon juice, lemon slices, crabmeat, tomatoes, garlic, green onions, peppercorns, bay leaf and basil over medium-high heat. Sauté approximately 3 minutes or until juices are rendered. Blend in tomato sauce and continue to cook until juices have been reduced to approximately 2 tablespoons. Swirling pan constantly, add a few chips of butter at a time until all is used. Do not stir with a metal spoon or wire whisk as hot spots may develop and butter will separate. Season with hot sauce, salt and cayenne pepper. Strain prior to serving.

BEURRE CITRON

Prep Time: 15 Minutes
Yields: 1 Cup

Comment:
This citrusy sauce is excellent over broiled or poached fish.

Ingredients:
8 ounces unsalted butter, chipped
½ cup dry white wine
3 tbsps lemon juice
2 tbsps orange juice
1 tbsp lime juice
2 cloves garlic, minced
1 tbsp sliced green onions
Louisiana hot sauce to taste
salt and cayenne pepper to taste

Method:
In a sauté pan, combine wine, juices, garlic and green onions over medium-high heat. Bring to a low boil and sauté until liquid is reduced to approximately 3 tablespoons. Swirling pan constantly, add a few chips of butter at a time until all is used. Do not stir with a metal spoon or wire whisk as hot spots will develop and butter will separate. Season with hot sauce, salt and cayenne pepper.

BEURRE POIVRE VERT

Prep Time: 15 Minutes
Yields: 1 Cup

Comment:
Yet another variation on Beurre Blanc, this sauce is excellent when served with fish or veal.

Ingredients:
8 ounces unsalted butter, chipped
3 tbsps green peppercorn liquid
½ cup dry white wine
2 tbsps lemon juice
2 cloves garlic, minced
1 tbsp sliced green onions
2 tbsps green peppercorns
Louisiana hot sauce to taste
salt to taste

Method:
In a sauté pan, combine peppercorn liquid, wine, lemon juice, garlic and green onions over medium-high heat. Bring to a low boil and add green peppercorns. Continue to sauté until liquid is reduced to approximately 2 tablespoons. Swirling pan constantly, add a few chips of butter at a time until all is used. Do not stir with a metal spoon or wire whisk as hot spots will develop and butter will separate. Remove from heat and season with hot sauce and salt.

CRAWFISH BUTTER

Prep Time: 30 Minutes
Yields: 1½ Cups

Comment:

Crawfish Butter is ideal for adding that unique Cajun and Creole flavor to any classical butter sauce. Simply place a tablespoon of this compound butter into any beurre blanc-based sauce and miracles happen.

Ingredients:

¼ cup butter
½ cup chopped onions
¼ cup chopped celery
¼ cup chopped carrots
2 cloves garlic, minced
½ pound live crawfish
¼ cup brandy
½ pound unsalted butter, softened

Method:

In a heavy-bottomed sauté pan, melt butter over medium-high heat. Sauté onions, celery, carrots and garlic 3–5 minutes or until vegetables are wilted. Add crawfish. Cover pan and swirl approximately 2 minutes or until crawfish are pink. Simmer 3 minutes. Deglaze with brandy, being careful as brandy will ignite. Place all ingredients in a food processor with a metal blade and blend on high until well chopped. Remove and chill. Once chilled, blend crawfish mixture into softened, unsalted butter. Force mixture through a fine sieve to remove all foreign debris and shells. Place in a ceramic or plastic container, cover and chill.

RED RÉMOULADE SAUCE

Prep Time: 15 Minutes
Yields: 2 Cups

Comment:
This Creole-style rémoulade is thought to be the original Louisiana version. This sauce can be served over shrimp, lump crabmeat or salad.

Ingredients:
1 cup olive oil
¼ cup red wine vinegar
¾ cup Creole mustard
½ cup sliced green onions
¼ cup chopped parsley
¼ cup minced celery
1 tbsp minced garlic
1 tbsp paprika
salt to taste
Louisiana hot sauce to taste

Method:
In a large ceramic mixing bowl, combine olive oil, vinegar and Creole mustard. Whisk until well blended. Mix in green onions, parsley, celery and garlic. Add paprika for color. Continue mixing until well blended. Season with salt and hot sauce. Cover with plastic wrap, place in refrigerator and allow to sit overnight.

WHITE RÉMOULADE SAUCE

Prep Time: 30 Minutes
Yields: 6 Servings

Comment:
Many different versions of rémoulade sauce may be found in restaurants across South Louisiana. The rémoulades of New Orleans are normally Creole mustard-based and highly seasoned. However, this River Road version is made primarily with mayonnaise. White rémoulade sauce is wonderful when served over fish.

Ingredients:
1½ cups heavy-duty mayonnaise
¼ cup diced celery
½ cup sliced green onions
2 tbsps minced garlic
½ cup Creole mustard
¼ cup chopped parsley
½ cup ketchup
½ tbsp lemon juice
1 tbsp Worcestershire sauce
1 tsp Louisiana hot sauce
salt and cracked black pepper to taste

Method:
In a 2-quart mixing bowl, combine all ingredients and whisk well. Once blended, cover and place in refrigerator, preferably overnight. A minimum of 4 hours is required for flavor to develop. When ready, remove from refrigerator and adjust seasonings.

RAVIGOTE SAUCE

Prep Time: 15 Minutes
Yields: 1½ Cups

Comment:
Rémoulade, a spicy mayonnaise-based sauce used for seafood and salads in South Louisiana, is thought to be derived from this older Creole standard, which was made with eggs. Like rémoulade, ravigote sauce could be served either cold or warm and was a favorite accompaniment to seafood.

Ingredients:
6 green onions, sliced
3 cloves garlic, minced
1 dill pickle, minced
2 tbsps chopped parsley
1 tbsp chopped thyme
1 tbsp Creole mustard
2 tbsps red wine vinegar
¼ cup plus 2 tbsps olive oil
salt and cracked black pepper to taste
1 egg yolk

Method:
In a large mixing bowl, combine green onions, garlic, pickle, parsley and thyme. Stir in mustard. Add vinegar and olive oil, mixing well. Season with salt and pepper. Beat egg yolk into mixture to create a sauce consistency. Serve cold with cold meats or seafood. NOTE: For a warm ravigote sauce to serve with hot fish, simply heat gently in a double boiler with 140°F water. Stir constantly to prevent egg from scrambling.

LOUISIANA TARTAR SAUCE

Prep Time: 15 Minutes
Yields: 2 Cups

Comment:
Tartar sauce is usually served with all fried seafood dishes in South Louisiana. You may wish to try this sauce as a dip for catfish beignets or as a topping for a seafood terrine.

Ingredients:
1½ cups heavy-duty mayonnaise
2 tbsps lemon juice
¼ cup minced pimiento olives
¼ cup minced sweet pickles
1 tbsp sweet pickle juice
¼ cup chopped parsley
¼ cup chopped capers
1 tbsp sliced green onions
salt to taste
Louisiana hot sauce to taste

Method:
In a large ceramic bowl, whisk together mayonnaise and lemon juice. Blend in olives, pickles, pickle juice, parsley, capers and green onions. Season with salt and hot sauce. If you prefer a more tart taste, add a little lemon juice or white vinegar. If a sweeter taste is preferred, add more sweet pickle juice or a touch of sugar. Cover with plastic wrap and refrigerate overnight to allow flavors to develop.

LOUISIANA SEAFOOD COCKTAIL SAUCE

Prep Time: 15 Minutes
Yields: 2 Cups

Comment:
Found primarily in the city of New Orleans, cocktail sauce is always served with boiled seafood. There are many variations of cocktail sauce, but most are tomato ketchup based and spiced with a touch of horseradish.

Ingredients:
1 cup tomato sauce
¼ cup ketchup
2 tbsps red wine vinegar
3 tbsps Worcestershire sauce
1 tbsp horseradish
¼ cup minced bell peppers
¼ cup minced celery
1 tbsp minced garlic
salt to taste
Louisiana hot sauce to taste

Method:
In a large ceramic bowl, whisk together tomato sauce, ketchup, vinegar, Worcestershire and horseradish. Add bell peppers, celery and garlic. Season with salt and hot sauce. Continue to blend until seasonings are evenly mixed. If more sweetness or tartness is desired, adjust seasonings to taste. Cover and refrigerate overnight to allow flavors to develop.

CREOLE TOMATO SAUCE

Prep Time: 30 Minutes
Yields: 6–8 Servings

Comment:

Most people don't realize that tomatoes are a product of the Americas. The word "tomato" actually comes from the Aztec word "tomatl." However, many people believe tomatoes originated in Italy and somehow found their way to Bayou Country. The Creole tomato is a product of St. Bernard and Plaquemines parishes and is known for its sweet, sugary juice. This tomato was originally used in New Orleans to create the now famous Creole sauce.

Ingredients:

12 Creole tomatoes or 24 Roma tomatoes, peeled and seeded
¼ cup extra virgin olive oil
¼ cup vegetable oil
10 cloves garlic, sliced
1 cup chicken stock (see recipe)
12 large basil leaves, chopped
salt and black pepper to taste

Method:

In a stainless steel saucepot, heat oils over medium-high heat. Using a wooden spoon, stir in garlic and sauté approximately 3 minutes or until slices are pale yellow or very light brown around edges. Blend tomatoes into garlic mixture. Bring to a low simmer and slowly add chicken stock to retain moisture and create fresh sauce. Cook 5–7 minutes then add basil. Season with salt and pepper. Stir in additional stock as necessary to retain sauce-like consistency. Serve as a pasta topping or a base for fish and veal. NOTE: When serving over pasta, cook and drain pasta then toss with a small amount of olive oil. Blend 1–2 serving spoons of fresh sauce into pasta along with a generous sprinkle of Parmesan cheese. Once pasta is coated, place in center of a serving platter and top with more simmering sauce.

CLASSIC BOLOGNESE SAUCE

Prep Time: 2 Hours
Yields: 8–10 Servings

Comment:

This classic Italian meat sauce from Bologna traditionally uses at least two different kinds of meat. It can be served over pasta, used in lasagna or incorporated into other Italian dishes. You may use any brand of canned tomato you wish. However, Cento is excellent.

Ingredients:

1 pound ground pork
1 pound ground beef
¼ cup olive oil
½ pound minced pickled pork
2 cups diced onions
1 cup diced celery
2 tbsps minced garlic
1 cup diced carrots
2 cups beef stock
2 (28-ounce) cans diced plum tomatoes, not drained
6 tbsps tomato paste
2 bay leaves
sugar as needed
salt and pepper to taste
½ cup chopped parsley

Method:

In a heavy-bottomed pot, heat oil over medium-high heat. Stir in pickled pork and sauté 2–3 minutes to render fat. Add ground pork and ground beef. Cook until meat is well browned and slightly caramelized on bottom of pot. Meat should be separated and crumbly. NOTE: If you cook the meat in a longer, slower fashion, you will bring out the best flavor. Blend in onions, celery, garlic and carrots. Sauté 3–5 minutes. When vegetables are wilted, stir in stock, tomatoes and tomato paste. Bring sauce to a boil then reduce to simmer. Add bay leaves. Cover and simmer 1 hour, stirring occasionally. Additional stock may be needed to retain consistency; however, sauce should be thick. Sugar may be added to cut acid if necessary. Season with salt and pepper then add parsley. Cook 2–3 additional minutes.

SAUCE BASQUAISE

Prep Time: 1 Hour
Yields: 2 Quarts

Comment:

The Basque region in Western Europe is comprised of areas of both France and Spain. This Sauce Basquaise is usually considered a Spanish sauce. However, since the sauce came out of the Basque region, it also has heavy French influence and is evocative of the best country flavors.

Ingredients:

½ cup vegetable oil
2 cups diced onions
1 cup diced bell peppers
6 cloves garlic, sliced
½ cup minced shallots
4 cups diced tomatoes, peeled and seeded
2 pinches hot pepper flakes
½ tbsp flour
2 cups dry white wine
salt and black pepper to taste

Method:

Preheat oven to 350°F. In a large braising pan, heat oil over medium-high heat. Add onions, bell peppers, garlic and shallots. Sauté 3–5 minutes or until vegetables are wilted. Add tomatoes and pepper flakes. Cook on medium-high heat for 5–10 minutes. Whisk in flour, stirring to form a roux. (See roux recipes.) When well blended, stir in white wine. Reduce to low heat or place in oven until sauce thickens to a nice tomato purée consistency. Season with salt and pepper.

GUY DISALVO'S PREMIER MARINARA SAUCE

Prep Time: 30 Minutes
Yields: 1 Quart

Comment:

Guy DiSalvo, from Latrobe, Pa., is an exceptional Italian chef. His marinara is a great example of simplicity and seasoning done just right to create an amazingly tasty dish.

Ingredients:

24 Roma tomatoes, peeled and seeded
¼ cup extra virgin olive oil
¼ cup vegetable oil
10 cloves garlic, sliced
1 cup chicken stock (see recipe)
12 large basil leaves, chopped
salt and black pepper to taste

Method:

In a stainless steel saucepot, heat oils over medium-high heat. Sauté garlic slices in oil until very lightly browned around edges. Add tomatoes and blend well. Bring to a low simmer, stirring in chicken stock to retain moisture as needed. Cook 5–7 minutes then stir in basil. Season with salt and pepper. Continue to cook 5–10 minutes, adding stock as needed. Serve as a pasta topping or a base for fish and veal. Shrimp, crab or crawfish may be folded into finished sauce to create a seafood Creole. NOTE: When serving this sauce over pasta, cook and drain pasta then toss with a small amount of olive oil. Blend 1–2 serving spoons of fresh marinara into pasta along with a generous sprinkle of Parmesan cheese. Once pasta is coated, place in center of a serving platter and top with more simmering marinara.

Creole tomatoes simmer for Guy DiSalvo's Premier Marinara Sauce.

CHIVE POTATO SAUCE

Prep Time: 30 Minutes
Yields: 6 Servings

Comment:

The Germans of Louisiana used the humble potato to create many hearty dishes. Often, a creative twist was added to the vegetable to give it flair. Chive potato sauce, which is delicious under grilled fish, is a great example of one of these inventive potato recipes.

Ingredients:

2 tbsps sliced chives
1 large white potato, cut in ½-inch cubes
5 ounces hot chicken stock (see recipe)
salt and black pepper to taste

Method:

Boil potato in lightly-salted water until tender. Strain and place in food processor with half of stock. Purée completely then add remaining stock. Blend until smooth, but do not overmix. Fold in chives, salt and pepper. NOTE: This sauce must be made immediately before serving. If it sits, it will solidify.

SOUTHERN FRIED CHICKEN GRAVY

Prep Time: 10 Minutes
Yields: 1½ Cups

Comment:

This chicken gravy is wonderful with Port Hudson Fried Chicken. Cover your fried chicken with this gravy for a delicious Southern treat.

Ingredients:

¼ cup flour
2½ cups milk or water
⅛ tsp nutmeg
½ tsp salt
¼ tsp pepper

Method:

Prepare chicken according to Port Hudson Fried Chicken recipe. Pour off pan drippings from fried chicken, reserving ¼ cup drippings in skillet. Place skillet over medium heat. Whisk flour into drippings, stirring constantly until browned. Heat milk to help prevent lumping. Stir in milk gradually. Cook, stirring constantly for 3–5 minutes or until thickened and bubbly. Stir in nutmeg, salt and pepper. Serve immediately.

HONEY CREOLE MUSTARD GLAZE

Prep Time: 15 Minutes
Yields: ½ Cup

Comment:

Sweet and spicy glazes are used most often for coating wild game or baked hams during the holiday season. These unique flavors are good as dips for fried seafood and vegetables. Feel free to substitute any jam or jelly in this recipe.

Ingredients:

¼ cup honey
¼ cup orange marmalade
1 tbsp Zatarain's® Creole Mustard

Method:

In a stainless steel mixing bowl, whisk all ingredients until well blended. Set glaze aside and allow flavors to develop for 3–4 hours. Use glaze to baste cooked ham, duck or other game at 5-minute intervals for approximately 15 minutes.

HOT RED PEPPER SAUCE

Prep Time: 30 Minutes
Yields: 2 Quarts

Comment:
There are hundreds of hot sauces available in Louisiana. However, if you wish to make a fresh, homemade version, this recipe is one of the best. This sauce contains no vinegar or salt; therefore, it may be used as an accompaniment to any dish.

Ingredients:
6 pounds sweet red cherry peppers
3 pounds hot red jalapeño peppers

Method:
NOTE: It is always best to wear rubber gloves when working with hot peppers. Using a paring knife, remove stems from peppers and quarter. Retain seeds. In a large saucepot, place peppers and seeds with enough water to cover them by ¼-inch. Bring to a rolling boil, reduce to simmer and cook until peppers are tender, but still bright red. Do not brown. Remove tenderized peppers from liquid and run through a food mill or purée in a food processor.

SWEET RED PEPPER SAUCE

Ingredients:
9 pounds sweet red bell peppers

Method:
To create a sweet red pepper sauce, follow the method above substituting the cherry and jalapeño peppers with sweet red bell peppers.

PEACH BARBECUE SAUCE

Prep Time: 45 Minutes
Yields: 1½ Cups

Comment:
Ruston, La. is the home of peach orchards that produce a very sweet variety of the fruit. Although the Ruston fruit is slightly smaller than normal, the flavor is exceptional. Peach season for Louisiana growers usually lasts from May until August. If available, feel free to substitute the canned peaches in this recipe with fresh ones.

Ingredients:
2 (15-ounce) cans peaches, drained
1½ cups vinegar
1 cup oil
½ tsp crushed garlic
2 tbsps Dijon mustard
1 tsp ground cinnamon
3 tbsps lemon juice
1 tbsp Worcestershire sauce
¼ tsp ground ginger
½ tsp black pepper
¾ cup maple syrup
1 cup brown sugar
2 tbsps cornstarch

Method:
Purée peaches. Combine all ingredients, except cornstarch, in a large saucepan. Heat to a low boil, stirring occasionally. Continue to simmer 30 minutes, stirring frequently. Sauce may be thin at end of cooking time. If so, mix cornstarch with a little water and add this mixture to sauce. Peach sauce should be consistency of a commercial barbecue sauce.

SPICY, GARLICKY BARBECUE KETCHUP

Prep Time: 2 Hours
Yields: 4 Pints

Comment:
Ah, summertime in Louisiana! It's the time of year when you'll find fresh tomatoes ripening in the garden and barbecue pits smoking in the backyard. This interesting recipe takes the bounty from the garden and creates a unique sauce that's perfect with steaks, chicken or fish on the grill.

Ingredients:
10 pounds Creole tomatoes, peeled and chopped
3 cups diced onions
¼ cup minced garlic
1 tbsp crushed red pepper flakes
1 tbsp celery seed
1 tbsp dry mustard
2 tsps salt
1½ tsps mace
1 tsp ginger
1 tsp cinnamon
1 cup brown sugar
1 cup apple cider vinegar
½ cup Steen's® Pure Cane Syrup
⅓ cup lemon juice
1 tbsp Louisiana hot sauce
4 (1-pint) glass jars with lids

Method:
Place jars and lids in simmering water (180°F) until ready to use. In a large saucepot, combine tomatoes, onions, garlic, red pepper and celery seed. Bring mixture to a rolling boil then reduce to simmer. Cover and cook 30 minutes, stirring occasionally. Put tomato mixture through a sieve or a food mill and press out liquid and pulp. Discard seeds. Return tomato mixture to a large saucepot and cook uncovered until reduced to half volume. Add remaining ingredients and continue to cook over low heat, stirring frequently until mixture thickens to a ketchup consistency. When done, remove jars and lids from hot water and place on a towel. Carefully ladle hot ketchup into jars, leaving approximately ¼-inch headspace. Place lid on jar and screw down band firmly. Place jars in boiling water and process for approximately 20 minutes. Cool, label and store in a cool, dark place.

GINGER PLUM BARBECUE SAUCE

Prep Time: 30 Minutes
Yields: 1 Cup

Comment:
Any plum variety will do in this recipe as long as the fruit is super sweet. Try this barbecue sauce the next time you grill. It adds a wonderfully interesting flavor to any type of meat.

Ingredients:
6 plums, pitted
1 tbsp minced ginger
1 stalk fresh lemongrass, trimmed and chopped
1 hot chile, seeded
2 green onions, trimmed and chopped
1 clove garlic, minced
2 tbsps soy sauce
2 tbsps sweet soy sauce
2 tbsps honey
1 tbsp rice vinegar
2 tsps fresh lemon juice
½ cup water

Method:
Combine all ingredients in a heavy-bottomed saucepan and bring to a rolling boil over medium heat. Reduce heat to medium-low and cook uncovered 5 minutes or until plums are very soft. Transfer mixture to a blender and purée. Return to pan. Adjust seasonings to taste, adding more soy sauce, honey or lemon juice as necessary. The sauce should be sweet, sour and spicy. If too thick, add a little water. Transfer to a serving bowl and serve warm or at room temperature. Sauce can be refrigerated for up to 1 week.

CRÈME FRAÎCHE

Prep Time: 12 Hours
Yields: 1 Cup

Comment:

Crème Fraîche is similar to heavy buttermilk or sour cream. This unique cream often finishes demi-glace-based sauces, helping to smooth out the flavor while giving it a nice tangy bite.

Ingredients:

8 ounces heavy whipping cream
3 tsps buttermilk

Method:

In a ceramic bowl, combine cream and buttermilk. Cover with clean cloth and let sit at room temperature 8–12 hours. NOTE: Most cooks will combine cream with buttermilk and place mixture on a pantry shelf overnight. Place finished sauce in a covered container and store in refrigerator. Use this sauce the same as heavy whipping cream or sour cream.

PRALINE CRÈME ANGLAISE

Prep Time: 1 Hour
Yields: 3 Cups

Comment:

Because we love to make things our own, praline liqueur has been added to traditional crème anglaise giving the sauce a unique South Louisiana flavor.

Ingredients:

3 cups heavy whipping cream
1 cup sugar
pinch of nutmeg
1 tbsp vanilla
4 egg yolks, beaten
pinch of cinnamon
1 tbsp cornstarch
¼ cup praline or hazelnut liqueur

Method:

In a 3-quart cast iron saucepan, scald whipping cream over medium-high heat. In a separate mixing bowl, combine sugar, cinnamon, nutmeg, vanilla, egg yolks and cornstarch. Whisk until well mixed and creamy. Add liqueur and fold once or twice until blended. Ladle 1 cup of hot cream into mixing bowl, stirring constantly while pouring. Transfer contents of mixing bowl to pot of hot cream, whisking constantly. Cook 1–2 minutes and remove from heat. Should mixture become too thick, add a little cold whipping cream.

CRÈME ANGLAISE

Prep Time: 1 Hour
Yields: 3 Cups

Comment:

The classical French Crème Anglaise is a basic custard sauce of eggs, sugar and cream. In Louisiana, we add bourbon to make a whiskey sauce, the best accompaniment for bread pudding and custard. This versatile sauce can even be served with ice cream. Try adding different liqueurs for a unique flavor.

Ingredients:

2 cups heavy whipping cream
1 cup sugar
pinch of cinnamon
pinch of nutmeg
1 tbsp pure vanilla extract
4 egg yolks, beaten
1 tbsp cornstarch
¼ cup bourbon

Method:

In a heavy-bottomed saucepan, scald whipping cream over medium-high heat. In a separate mixing bowl, combine sugar, cinnamon, nutmeg, vanilla, egg yolks and cornstarch. Whisk until well mixed and creamy. Add bourbon and fold once or twice until blended. Ladle 1 cup of hot cream into mixing bowl, stirring constantly while pouring. Whisk contents of mixing bowl into pot of hot cream, stirring constantly. Cook 1–2 minutes and remove from heat. Should mixture become too thick, add a little cold whipping cream.

PECAN PRALINE SAUCE

Prep Time: 45 Minutes
Yields: 1½ Cups

Comment:
Normally, butter and brown sugar are cooked to the candy stage
and pecans are added at the end of the cooking process to produce
pralines. Here, we are using the same flavor and technique, but we
stop the cooking just in time to produce the perfect sauce topping
for cheesecake, ice cream or any other dessert.

Ingredients:
1 cup chopped pecans
¼ pound butter
1 cup brown sugar
¼ cup cane syrup
1 tbsp pure vanilla extract
cinnamon to taste
nutmeg to taste
1 cup praline liqueur

Method:
In a heavy-bottomed skillet, melt butter over medium-high heat.
Whisk in brown sugar and cane syrup, blending well into butter
mixture until melted. Add pecans, vanilla, cinnamon, nutmeg and
praline liqueur. Stir constantly as praline sauce will reduce quickly
and tend to scorch. Once liquid has reduced to a sauce consistency,
remove from heat and cool.

STRAWBERRY GLAZE

Prep Time: 30 Minutes
Yields: 1½ Pints

Comment:
Strawberry glaze is especially popular during the height of strawberry season. The delicious, fruity glaze can be used on barbecued or roasted game or as a topping for ice cream, waffles or pancakes. Make this recipe in large batches and save it for later use.

Ingredients:
1 pint strawberries, cleaned and pared
2 pints sugar
1 pint water

Method:
In a 3-quart cast iron saucepan, bring sugar and water to a boil. Sugar and water will form a simple syrup and mixture will thicken slightly. Add strawberries and simmer 15–20 minutes then strain.

BLUEBERRY SAUCE

Prep Time: 30 Minutes
Yields: 2¼ Cups

Comment:

A tablespoon of this mixture may be placed into natural drippings of duck, venison or lamb to enhance the sauce. It can also be served warm over ice cream or other desserts.

Ingredients:

2 cups fresh blueberries
⅔ cup sugar
2 tbsps cornstarch
pinch of nutmeg
pinch of cinnamon
1 cup water
2 tbsps lemon juice

Method:

In a small saucepot over medium heat, combine sugar, cornstarch, nutmeg and cinnamon. Gradually stir in water and cook until mixture boils and thickens. Fold in fresh blueberries and lemon juice. Cook 10–15 minutes or until sauce is rich and full-colored. Cool slightly.

CRANBERRY SYRUP

Prep Time: 30 Minutes
Yields: 3 Cups

Comment:

Cranberry syrup is an interesting alternative to everyday maple syrup. This sweet sauce can be served as a breakfast item during the holidays to add a special touch to your meal.

Ingredients:

1 (16-ounce) can whole cranberries
1¼ cups maple syrup

Method:

In a small saucepan, combine cranberries and syrup over medium heat. Bring mixture to a low boil and cook 5 minutes, stirring occasionally. Store cranberry syrup in a glass jar for later use or serve hot over waffles.

PURE VANILLA EXTRACT

Prep Time: 1–6 Months
Yields: 1 Pint

Comment:

When comparing vanilla extracts in the grocery store, you will find that they vary greatly in price. The cheaper brands are probably made from extract of tonka beans. This bean, a member of the pea family, has a high concentration of coumarin. Coumarin has a strong vanilla-type aroma, but no flavor. Pure vanilla extract, however, is made from expensive vanilla beans aged in bourbon, brandy or vodka, raising the cost of production. The high cost of these extracts is reasonable because, when created properly, the vanilla will last forever, aging like a fine wine.

Ingredients:

4 vanilla beans, split, scraped and chopped into 1-inch pieces
1 pint bourbon or vodka

Method:

Place vanilla beans and scrapings into bottle of liquor. Place cap on bottle and tighten. Allow to steep 1–6 months, depending on strength you wish to achieve, longer is better. Shake bottle occasionally to disperse ingredients. It will keep indefinitely. You can continue to add alcohol to bottle as extract is used. When extract has reached ideal flavor for cooking, you may strain beans from liquor using a coffee filter and return extract to bottle. There is no need to refrigerate.

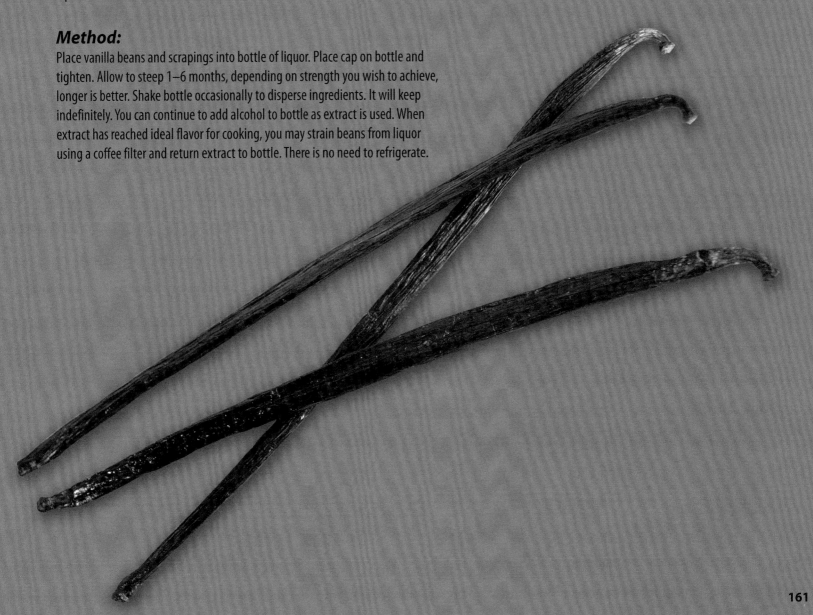

Breakfast & Brunch

Old-fashioned French dinner table, Begue's Restaurant

By now you've probably caught on to the idea that in South Louisiana we not only appreciate a good thing, we improve upon it. That's about the only way to express the new heights to which we have taken breakfast and brunch, particularly in New Orleans. While some consider breakfast something to be rushed through or skipped, we consider it, even in its simplest form, something to be relished. In fact, among the top "must do's" for visitors to New Orleans are breakfast at Brennan's, jazz brunch at Commander's Palace and coffee and beignets at Café Du Monde. The book *Breakfasts and Brunches for Every Occasion*, by Helen and Philip Brown, quotes a gentleman named Morton Shand as saying, "Breakfast, an essentially unsocial meal, is an appropriate time for disinheriting one's natural heirs." Perhaps it was because Louisiana's Napoleonic law did not allow a gentleman to disinherit his heirs that we took the opposite view and made breakfast and brunch a leisurely and delightful social occasion. Then again, it could just be that delicacies such as raised calas (rice cakes), pain perdu, eggs Sardou, eggs à la crème, grits and grillades, beignets and café au lait made it impossible to have such a dour outlook on either life or the first meal of the day.

Breakfast, while not revered by all, is a fairly universal habit. It is the first meal after a night's rest, literally the breaking of the fast, and it is necessary to revitalize the body and prepare it for the day. Most of us have little time for a lavish breakfast, but we do try to grab a little something to get us going. This is true almost everywhere. For centuries Chinese laborers have started the day with a bowl of gruel or noodles. Their counterparts in the Middle East might grab flat bread and cheese, while the Japanese prefer soup and tea. For many others, breakfast is simply tea or coffee and a roll or pastry, now known internationally as Continental breakfast. What many people don't realize about Continental breakfast is that on the Continent itself (meaning Europe) this light start was followed later by a second, more hearty "fork breakfast," which may well have been the predecessor to brunch.

The founders of New Orleans brunch: Madame Elizabeth Kettenring Dutrey Bégué with her husband, Hypolite Bégué

While Americans are now known for the wide variety of breakfast convenience foods that can be grabbed on the run, in the 19th century both America and England earned some notoriety for the expansive spreads laid out for the standard morning meal. Perhaps two of the most lavish examples of breakfasts and brunches in America can be found in Louisiana history—the planter's breakfast and the steamboat breakfast. History indicates that after stepping out early to make the plantation rounds before the heat became oppressive, the plantation owner would return to the main house

Early packaging from Foltz Tea & Coffee Co., New Orleans

cabins, the meal might start with a toddy of Tafia or persimmon beer followed by sweet potatoes, cracklin' bread, potatoes, fried salt pork and greens or a number of other simple but substantial foods designed to fortify the workers for a long, hard morning.

for a lavish breakfast. The meal began with Tafia, a rum drink, or a Mint Julep. After that, a typical breakfast might include a salad of mixed greens with oil and vinegar dressing, eggs scrambled with calf brains or crawfish, tripe fried in fritter batter, boudin blanc, beef grillades and grits, oysters in patty shells, beef pies, kidneys in wine, wild game, rice fried in egg batter, bacon strips, yam sausage, soft cheeses, cheese toast, stewed apples with cream, battercakes drowned in butter and honey, French bread, biscuits, corn pone, strawberry preserves, crab-apple jelly, muscadine jelly, molasses and of course, coffee. Since the distances between the plantations and New Orleans were substantial, there were often overnight guests to accommodate as well. It was a matter of social reputation to ensure that even unexpected guests were housed and fed lavishly. Sunday breakfasts following a Saturday soirée would be especially extravagant. In 1861, William Howard Russell said that while he was a guest at Houmas House his breakfast feast included "grilled fowl, prawns, eggs and ham, fish from New Orleans, potted salmon from England, preserved meats from France, claret, iced water, coffee and tea, varieties of hominy mush and African vegetable preparations." Even the field hands ate what many would consider a hearty breakfast by today's standards. Prepared before dawn in their tiny

The steamboats too, were famous for creating extravagant breakfasts for their somewhat captive audience. Sometimes the boats' customers were the planters who were accustomed to hearty breakfast fare and rich accommodations. Breakfast would include bacon, sausage, eggs, grits, lye hominy, jambalaya, rolls, milk, coffee and pancakes topped with Louisiana cane syrup. By the golden age of steamboat travel (1870–1900) the accommodations and meals on board rivaled the finest hotels, and of these meals, breakfast was the least extravagant. This is hard to imagine based on the description of the day's first meal aboard the *Thompson Dean*. The menu listed ham, breakfast bacon, calf's liver with onions and mackerel. Beefsteak was served plain, with onions, tomatoes and mushrooms, or with a variety of sauces including bordelaise and Creole. Also included were pork and mutton chops, fried calf's brains, fish, mush, codfish balls, plantains, hominy fritters and sausage balls. In addition there were grits, potatoes, hash, jambalaya, stewed kidney, tripe and stewed chicken. Waffles, muffins, buckwheat cakes, dipped toast, corn bread, hot rolls, buttered toast, graham rolls and white rolls served as side orders, while beverages included green tea, black tea, oolong tea, Java, Mocha, hot chocolate, milk and claret.

Those not so graced by wealth obviously consumed simpler fare for their morning meal. Even on the steamboats, poorer passengers would not be offered such a feast, but were instead expected to bring their own rations aboard. In Cajun Country, those who did not live on plantations might start their day with coush coush, a concoction made of cornmeal, or simply some French bread and Creole cream cheese. Also enjoyed were pain perdu, a hearty version of what we call French toast, calas or rice cakes, grits, grillades, biscuits and beignets. While not extravagant, when served with a dark rich cup of black coffee, it was a perfect start to the day. Actually, these simpler "country breakfasts" are closer to what might be enjoyed today on a daily basis, both in New Orleans and in outlying parishes.

Down to earth spots such as Mother's, Camellia Grill, and the Old Coffee Pot in New Orleans have attracted a devoted morning following for many years. For more sophisticated fare, breakfast or brunch at Commander's Palace, Arnaud's or Brennan's continues the tradition established by Madame Bégué in the 19th century, serving an extravagant "second breakfast" to vendors and customers in the French Market. At any of these establishments you will find breakfast items elevated to extraordinary heights, particularly the humble egg. Consider eggs Sardou, eggs Benedict, eggs Hussarde, eggs St. Charles and eggs Owen, not to mention exotic omelets showcasing local specialties like tasso, andouille and oysters. These restaurants also recreate the habit practiced on 19th century plantations and steamboats of enjoying cocktails with breakfast or brunch. These "breakfast beverages" are covered in more detail in the Beverages chapter, but consider ordering a Mimosa, Mint Julep, Mr. Funk, Brandy Milk Punch or Ramos Gin Fizz to make your meal complete.

Oh breakfast! Oh breakfast! The meal of my heart!
Bring porridge, bring sausage, bring fish for a start,
Bring kidneys, and mushrooms, and partridge's legs,
But let the foundation be bacon and eggs!
-A.P. Herbert, British author, humorist, Member of Parliament

While the origins of breakfast are quite logical, albeit difficult to date, brunch poses more of a puzzle. We know the name, a portmanteau or blending of the words "breakfast" and "lunch," was coined around 1895 in England. Evidence is offered in an excerpt from the British magazine *Punch* which claimed in an 1896 issue, "to be fashionable nowadays, we must brunch." However, no one accepts that the concept itself was a new one. In England, members of the upper class had long been in the habit of eating late breakfasts after the hunt

or, as early as 1800, holding "breakfast parties" at noon (what most of us would consider brunch). In 19th century New Orleans, Catholic churchgoers would abstain from food and drink after midnight on Saturday so that they might "break the fast" with their communion wafer at Sunday Mass. They emerged from church Sunday morning too late for breakfast and too early for lunch, but ravenous nonetheless. The origins of brunch in Louisiana are often traced to those Catholic cravings and the many vendors that catered to them, offering coffee, calas and other sundries on the streets outside of church. We must also credit the European tradition of the "second breakfast" for those who rose early to tend to fields or other work before dawn. This idea was also embraced in New Orleans' French Market, where coffee stalls were as common as those for fish and meat. By 10 or 11 in the morning, the quick, pre-dawn bite of bread and coffee or ale had worn off, and something more substantial was desired. First the coffee stalls and later the nearby restaurants began to serve food for vendors and customers who needed mid-morning nourishment. Madame Bégué's, which stood where Tujague's restaurant operates today near the French Market, was one of the earliest and most successful restaurants in New Orleans to offer this late morning option. Depending on the size of the earlier breakfast, this meal could consist of anything from a cup of tea or coffee and a pastry, to a hearty, multi-course affair which might properly be deemed brunch.

The idea of a mid-morning snack, known in England as "elevenses" because of the time at which it is enjoyed, is popular in other countries, too. In the Mediterranean this second breakfast is known as *merenda*, and in certain German-speaking regions it is called *zweite Fruhstück*. In Chile, per English custom, it is called *salas de onces*. In South Louisiana, this is also the perfect time of day to take a break with café au lait and beignets. These signature pastries of Café Du Monde are said to have been brought to New Orleans by the Ursuline nuns in 1727. While their French counterparts are filled with cream or fruit, these perfect puffs of fried dough topped with powdered sugar need no embellishment. When paired with café au lait, a sweetened mixture of equal parts dark coffee with chicory and steamed milk, beignets are paradise found.

If you can't manage breakfast at Brennan's or even a coffee break at Café Du Monde, don't despair, but don't settle for cold cereal or a microwaved muffin. Instead, try any one of these delicious recipes to start your day in style. Better yet, imagine yourself on a plantation porch or a Mississippi riverboat and try five or six! And don't forget the Champagne.

While many New Orleans restaurants now offer a breakfast and brunch menu that would make Madame Bégué proud, Owen Brennan was considered to be going out on a limb when he first promoted the concept of a three-hour, multi-course breakfast laced with Champagne and other spirits. Brennan reasoned that if Frances Parkinson Keye's 1948 book, *Dinner at Antoine's*, could spark a culinary trend, then so could the idea of "Breakfast at Brennan's." His business intuition once again proved correct. Beginning the day at Brennan's remains an institution today.

Brennan's Restaurant

Eggs are one of nature's perfect foods and may be served in a variety of ways. For this reason, eggs are considered the premier basic kitchen ingredient. They are unsurpassed as a breakfast dish and may be fried, scrambled, poached, boiled, baked or coddled. To add even more flavor to eggs, an omelet may be made with any number of ingredients. The following are a few of the most widely used preparation methods for this unique food.

FRIED EGGS

Place approximately ¼-inch vegetable oil in a non-stick skillet. Add 1 tablespoon butter and heat to 325°F. Crack 2 eggs in a bowl, 1 at a time, then place in hot oil. Season with salt and pepper. When white begins to solidify, use a large cooking spoon to baste yolk with hot oil until desired consistency is acheived. Using a spatula, remove eggs and serve hot.

SCRAMBLED EGGS

For a single order, beat 3 eggs lightly with a fork until yolks and whites are broken slightly but not over-mixed. Blend in ¼ cup milk or heavy whipping cream then season with salt and pepper. A tablespoon of fresh chopped parsley may be added for color. In a large skillet, melt 2 tablespoons butter over medium-high heat, but do not brown. Add eggs, reduce heat to medium and stir constantly until cooked to your liking. Perfect scrambled eggs should be firm but not dry. If desired, add bits of cooked bacon or seafood such as lump crabmeat or shrimp to butter prior to adding eggs.

POACHED EGGS

To obtain best looking poached eggs, use stainless steel poaching rings, which may be purchased at any gourmet food store. Poaching rings allow the egg white to be contained in a perfectly round shape during poaching process. If poaching rings are not available, simply crack eggs directly into water. Eggs should be poached 2 at a time, though a larger pan will allow for multiple eggs. Place a shallow skillet or baking pan onto burner. Distribute poaching rings evenly around pan and cover them with water. Bring to a rolling boil. Season water with salt and pepper and add 1 tablespoon vinegar. When water returns to a boil, turn off heat and crack 1 egg into each ring or directly into water. Let egg stand 12–15 minutes in water or longer for well done. Eggs may be poached well in advance and cooled for later use. To reheat, simply place poached egg into 200°F water for 1–1½ minutes.

OMELET

Break 3 eggs into a bowl and season with salt and pepper. Add ¼ cup heavy whipping cream and whisk eggs until fluffy and blended. Fully prepare any meat, seafood or vegetable fillings before frying eggs. Fully cook vegetables, such as broccoli or asparagus, before adding to omelet. Into a 6-inch non-stick skillet or omelet pan, melt 2 tablespoons butter over medium-high heat. Do not allow butter to brown. Pour beaten eggs into skillet. Using a fork, break surface of omelet in several places to allow uncooked egg to reach bottom of pan. Continue this process until omelet starts to solidify. Place any desired filling ingredients onto surface of omelet and top with cheese. Shake pan vigorously to release omelet from bottom. When omelet is loose, fold it in half onto a serving plate. Allow to rest 1–2 minutes to fully melt cheese and heat filler ingredients.

BOILED EGGS

To make a perfect soft-boiled egg, bring 4 inches of water to a rolling boil. Place eggs in boiling water 3½ minutes. Remove eggs and cool slightly under cold water prior to peeling. Peeled eggs may be reheated 1½ minutes in boiling water prior to serving. For hard-boiled eggs, follow the same procedure, but allow egg to boil 10 minutes. The shell is easy to remove if egg is soaked in ice water a few minutes.

CODDLED EGGS

An egg coddler, which is a porcelain dish with a metal lid, is required for this method. Fill a saucepan with enough water to reach bottom rim of coddler. Bring water to a rolling boil. Butter inside of each coddling cup. If desired, add ½ teaspoon heavy whipping cream to cups. Crack 1–2 eggs in each cup, depending on size. Season with salt and pepper. If desired, add any herbs and spices to eggs. Cover and place coddlers in boiling water. Reduce heat and allow to simmer 6–8 minutes. Carefully remove cups from hot water. Serve egg in coddling dish alongside toast or biscuits.

BAKED EGGS

Each custard cup will make 1 serving. Preheat oven to 350°F. Place 1 teaspoon melted butter into each custard cup. Break 2 eggs into each cup and season with salt, pepper and a dash of paprika. Top with ⅛ teaspoon butter and bake 12–15 minutes for medium or 20 minutes for well done.

Italian egg cups

BAKED EGGS WITH CRAWFISH AND MUSHROOMS IN HAM BASKETS

Prep Time: 1 Hour
Yields: 6 Servings

Comment:
This dish includes all ingredients necessary to create a complete meal. These baked eggs are simple to prepare and are a perfect "breakfast in bed" dish.

Ingredients:
12 eggs
½ pound crawfish tails
¾ pound diced mushrooms
12 slices sugar-cured ham
2 tbsps unsalted butter
¼ cup minced shallots
salt and cracked black pepper to taste
2 tbsps sour cream
1 tbsp finely chopped tarragon
fresh tarragon leaves for garnish

Method:
Preheat oven to 400°F. In a large heavy-bottomed skillet, melt butter over medium-high heat. Add mushrooms and shallots. Cook 8–10 minutes, stirring occasionally until liquid has evaporated. Add crawfish tails and cook 3 additional minutes. Season with salt and pepper. Remove from heat then stir in sour cream and chopped tarragon. In a lightly-greased muffin pan, place 1 slice of ham in each cup allowing ends to hang over edges. Divide mushroom and crawfish mixture evenly among cups. Crack 1 egg into each ham basket. Season eggs with salt and pepper. Place on middle oven rack and bake 15 minutes or until egg whites are cooked, but yolks are still runny. Remove and serve with Creole Home Fries. (See recipe.)

COLUMBUS BREAKING THE EGG.
Printed and Published by W. Davison Alnwick

STUFFED EGGS ITALIAN STYLE

Prep Time: 1 Hour
Yields: 24 Servings

Comment:
Italian cooking is famous for its pesto flavor. Normally thought of as a basil-based sauce, pesto may be made with parsley, sage or any other fresh herb. Pesto generally holds well in the refrigerator and can be used in a variety of dishes.

Ingredients:
12 eggs
4½ cups fresh basil, loosely packed
1 cup extra-virgin olive oil
½ cup pine nuts or pecans
5 cloves garlic
salt to taste
½ cup grated Parmesan cheese
½ cup mayonnaise
¼ cup minced celery
¼ cup minced red bell peppers
¼ cup minced sweet pickles
salt and cracked black pepper to taste
Louisiana hot sauce to taste

Method:
In a saucepan, cover eggs with 2 inches of water. Bring to a rolling boil and cook 10 minutes. Remove from heat, drain and plunge eggs in cold water until cool. Peel and set aside. In a food processor, purée basil, oil, pine nuts, garlic, salt and Parmesan. Adjust seasonings if necessary. Remove pesto from processor, place in bowl with lid and set aside. Slice eggs in half lengthwise. Place yolks in a mixing bowl and mash with a fork. Add mayonnaise, celery, bell peppers and pickles, blending well. Season with salt, pepper and hot sauce. Blend 2 tablespoons pesto into egg mixture. Fill egg whites with egg/pesto mixture, cover with plastic wrap and refrigerate. These eggs may be stuffed 1 day prior to use. Eggs will taste better as flavor develops. Refrigerate remaining pesto to use as a pasta sauce, spread or flavoring for grilled fish or chicken.

CREOLE TOMATO, BASIL AND TASSO OMELET

Prep Time: 20 Minutes
Yields: 1 Omelet

Comment:
Tasso, spicy Cajun ham, is cured, smoked and rubbed in spices. Tasso is often used as a flavoring for vegetables and soups, but it is also excellent as a breakfast item. If desired, substitute a high-quality, heavy-smoked ham and spice up the dish with a pinch of cayenne pepper.

Ingredients:
2 Creole tomato slices
1 tbsp chopped basil
2 tbsps diced tasso
3 eggs
2 tbsps unsalted butter
salt and black pepper to taste
Creole seasoning to taste
2 tbsps diced red bell peppers

Method:
In a 9-inch omelet pan, melt butter over medium-high heat. In a large mixing bowl, whisk eggs, salt, pepper and Creole seasoning. Set aside. In omelet pan, sauté tasso and bell peppers 1–2 minutes. Pour eggs into pan over tasso. Using a fork, distribute sautéed ingredients evenly into omelet. Shake pan to loosen eggs, taking care not to scorch eggs. When edges begin to curl and turn light brown, place tomatoes and basil across front half of omelet. When cooked to your liking, slide omelet halfway onto a serving plate and turn top half over tomatoes to form a half moon. Allow to sit 2–3 minutes prior to serving.

PRUDENT MALLARD OMELET

Prep Time: 15 Minutes
Yields: 1 Omelet

Comment:

Prudent Mallard was a French furniture maker who immigrated to New Orleans and became the premier furniture designer in the South. In the 1930s he started his own business on Royal Street. Prudent is credited with creating the half-tester bed, complete with a silk-lined half canopy and mosquito net. His furniture is found in many Southern plantations.

Ingredients:

2 eggs	½ tsp Creole seasoning
2 tbsps butter	¼ cup sliced green onions
3 oyster mushrooms, sliced	1 tbsp diced red bell peppers
2 tbsps milk	¼ cup shredded Cheddar cheese

Method:

In a 6-inch crêpe pan, melt 1 tablespoon butter over medium-high heat. Sauté mushrooms 2–3 minutes or until thoroughly heated and softened. Remove from pan and set aside. In a mixing bowl, combine eggs, milk and Creole seasoning. Using a fork, blend well without over mixing. In same pan, melt remaining butter over medium-high heat. Pour in egg mixture, reduce heat to medium and cover. When omelet starts to solidify, add sautéed mushrooms, green onions, bell peppers and cheese. Fold both sides of omelet toward center, cover pan and remove from heat. Allow omelet to sit 1 minute. Crumbled bacon or finely diced ham may be added if desired.

EGGS HUSSARDE

Prep Time: 30 Minutes
Yields: 6 Servings

Comment:

This dish can be enjoyed at breakfast or brunch. It is a signature dish created at Brennan's Restaurant in New Orleans. It is credited with putting "Breakfast at Brennan's" on the map.

Ingredients:

12 poached eggs (see recipe)	2 cups Marchand de Vin Sauce (see recipe)
2 tbsps butter	2 cups Hollandaise Sauce (see recipe)
12 slices Canadian bacon or ham	6 broiled tomato halves for garnish
12 Holland rusks or English muffin halves	

Method:

NOTE: To cook tomatoes, season each half with salt and pepper. Place under broiler 3–5 minutes or until cooked to your liking. In a large sauté pan over low heat, melt butter. Add Canadian bacon and cook until warm. Place 2 Holland rusks on each plate and top each with a slice of warm Canadian bacon. Spoon Marchand de Vin over meat then set a poached egg on each slice. Ladle Hollandaise over eggs. Garnish with tomatoes and serve.

SPINACH & LUMP CRABMEAT QUICHE

Prep Time: 1 Hour
Yields: 8 Servings

Comment:

Quiche is an egg-based dish that can be served for breakfast, lunch or dinner. Any ingredient imaginable can be added to a quiche. In South Louisiana, seafood is most often used.

Ingredients:

6 eggs, beaten
1 (10-ounce) package frozen spinach, thawed
½ pound jumbo lump crabmeat
¼ cup melted butter
½ cup minced onions
¼ cup minced red bell peppers
¼ cup minced yellow bell peppers
1 tbsp minced garlic
1 cup grated Swiss cheese
1 cup grated Colby cheese
3 tbsps flour
1 cup half-and-half
salt and black pepper to taste
⅛ tsp nutmeg
2 (9-inch) unbaked pie shells

Method:

Preheat oven to 350°F. In a heavy-bottomed sauté pan, melt butter over medium-high heat. Add onions, bell peppers and garlic. Sauté 3–5 minutes or until vegetables are wilted. Blend in spinach and cook 2 additional minutes. Remove pan from heat then add cheeses and flour, stirring until well blended. In a mixing bowl, combine eggs, half-and-half, salt, pepper and nutmeg. Add spinach mixture to eggs and blend well. Place pie shells in 2 (9-inch) pie pans. Distribute crabmeat evenly over bottom of shells. Top with spinach and egg mixture. Bake pies 45 minutes or until quiche is set and lightly browned.

EGGS DOMINIQUE YOUX

Prep Time: 1 Hour
Yields: 6 Servings

Comment:

Dominique Youx, the creator of Café Brûlot, is rumored to have been the brother of pirate Jean Lafitte. Youx was said to have been a great cook and many dishes, including this one, are attributed to the pirate.

Ingredients:

12 eggs
12 (2-inch) slices tasso ham
12 Creole tomato slices
1 loaf French bread
¼ pound butter
¼ cup sliced green onions
1 tbsp minced garlic
¼ cup diced red bell peppers
½ cup sliced mushrooms
¼ cup minced tasso
2 ounces port wine
3 cups veal stock (see recipe)
   OR beef consommé
salt and cracked black pepper to taste

Method:

Preheat oven to 300°F. Slice French bread into 12 (¾-inch) round croutons. Place croutons on a cookie sheet and set aside. In a heavy-bottomed sauté pan, melt half of butter over medium-high heat. Add green onions, garlic, bell peppers, mushrooms and minced tasso. Sauté 3–5 minutes or until vegetables are wilted. Pour in wine and reduce to half volume. Add veal stock, bring to a rolling boil and cook 10 minutes or until a sauce-like consistency is achieved. Season with salt and pepper. Set aside and keep warm. In a separate sauté pan, melt remaining butter over medium-high heat. Sauté sliced tasso 2–3 minutes to heat thoroughly. Remove and keep warm. Sauté tomato slices in same manner until heated thoroughly but not overcooked. Set aside and keep warm. In a home-style egg poacher, poach eggs to desired doneness. (See recipe.) Place French bread croutons in oven 3–5 minutes or until toasted. To serve, place 2 croutons in the center of a 10-inch plate. Top each crouton with 2 slices tasso and 1 tomato. Season tomato lightly with salt and pepper. Place a poached egg on top of each tomato and top with 1 tablespoon wine sauce.

EGGS À LA CRÈME

Prep Time: 30 Minutes
Yields: 6 Servings

Comment:

I've been served many exotic egg dishes in my travels including the thousand-year eggs of China. However, I can think of no better egg dish or one more beautifully presented than these Eggs à la Crème. This elegant dish was first created by Maugie Pastor of T'Frere's House in Lafayette, La. Eggs à la Crème and a cup of hot black Cajun Coffee is the perfect start to any day.

Ingredients:

12 eggs
¼ cup melted butter
⅛ cup minced onions
⅛ cup minced celery
⅛ cup minced red bell peppers
⅛ cup minced green bell peppers
½ tbsp flour
1 cup heavy whipping cream
salt and black pepper to taste
Creole seasoning to taste
1 tsp chopped thyme
2 tbsps chopped basil
1 tbsp minced garlic
2 tbsps chopped parsley
2 tbsps sliced green onions
¼ cup vegetable oil
1 cup crawfish tails
chopped parsley for garnish
dash of paprika for garnish

Method:

In a cast iron skillet, melt butter over medium-high heat. Add onions, celery and bell peppers. Sauté 3–5 minutes or until vegetables are wilted. Blend in flour then add ½ cup whipping cream. Stir until thickened white sauce is achieved. Season with salt, pepper and Creole seasoning. Remove from heat and set aside. In a large mixing bowl, combine eggs, thyme, basil, garlic, parsley, green onions, remaining whipping cream and prepared white sauce. Using a wire whisk, blend well to create a whipped egg mixture. Season with salt, pepper and Creole seasoning. In a large cast iron skillet, heat oil over medium-high heat. Add crawfish and sauté 2–3 minutes. Add whipped egg mixture. Using a spatula, stir eggs gently until scrambled but not dry and overcooked. Spoon eggs into a stemmed champagne goblet and garnish with chopped parsley and paprika. Serve with toast.

EGGS SARDOU

Prep Time: 30 Minutes
Yields: 4 Servings

Comment:

Eggs Sardou is a true New Orleans breakfast dish. It was created at Antoine's Restaurant for French playwright Victorien Sardou. We have included creamed spinach in this recipe, which makes it slightly different from the original still served at Antoine's.

Ingredients:

8 Poached Eggs (see recipe)
8 canned artichoke bottoms, drained
¼ cup butter
4 cups cleaned spinach leaves
½ cup chicken stock (see recipe)
½ cup minced ham
salt and pepper to taste
1 cup Hollandaise Sauce (see recipe)

Method:

Rinse artichoke bottoms well under cold water. Place in a saucepot and cover with 1-inch lightly-salted water. Blanch 5–10 minutes or until bottoms are fork tender but not overcooked. While artichokes are cooking, place butter in a cast iron skillet over medium-high heat. Add spinach and sauté until wilted. Add chicken stock, and with the edge of cooking spoon, chop spinach leaves until somewhat creamed. Add minced ham, and season with salt and pepper. When ready to serve, poach eggs. Divide spinach equally in bottom of 4 serving plates. Top with 2 drained artichoke bottoms. Place 1 poached egg in each artichoke, and top with a spoonful of Hollandaise Sauce.

LAYERED EGG CASSEROLE

Prep Time: 2 Hours
Yields: 10 Servings

Comment:
This dish is the ultimate omelet casserole. The combination of vegetables, meat and dairy all in one dish definitely feeds a crowd. For a smaller yield, cut recipe in half.

Ingredients:
18 eggs
3 (10-ounce) packages frozen chopped spinach
12 strips bacon, cooked and drained
1 cup cubed ham
¼ pound butter
½ cup minced onions
1 cup flour
4 cups milk
salt and black pepper to taste
Creole seasoning to taste
1 cup heavy whipping cream
½ cup canned fried onion rings, crushed
1 cup grated Monterey Jack cheese

Method:
Butter a 9" x 13" baking dish and set aside. Cook spinach according to package directions, drain completely and chop once more. In a large sauté pan, melt half of butter over medium-high heat. Pan-fry ham 3–4 minutes then remove and set aside. In same skillet, sauté onions 2–3 minutes or until wilted. Whisk in flour, a little at a time, until white roux is achieved. (See roux recipes.) Stir in milk, 1 cup at a time, bring to a low boil and continue stirring until smooth. Remove from heat then gently fold in chopped spinach. Season with salt, pepper and Creole seasoning. Keep warm. In a large sauté pan, melt remaining butter over medium-high heat. In a large mixing bowl, whisk eggs and whipping cream. Season lightly with salt and pepper. Pour mixture into sauté pan and soft scramble eggs until lightly set. Do not overcook. Spread half of eggs in bottom of baking dish. Top with half of ham, bacon and spinach mixture. Repeat layers. Top with onion rings and Monterey Jack cheese. This casserole must be covered and refrigerated overnight prior to baking and may be frozen for later use. When ready to cook, preheat oven to 275°F and bake uncovered 1 hour.

EGGS VICTORIA

Prep Time: 30 Minutes
Yields: 6 Servings

Comment:
Eggs Victoria is probably the most elegant breakfast dish in the South. Only in Louisiana would a cook consider placing jumbo lump crabmeat and crab fingers atop poached eggs at the breakfast table.

Ingredients:
12 poached eggs (see recipe)
12 Holland rusks or English muffin halves
1 pound jumbo lump crabmeat
¼ pound melted butter
½ cup minced onions
1 tbsp minced garlic
¼ cup diced red bell peppers
¼ cup sliced green onions
2 dozen peeled crab claws
1 cup Hollandaise Sauce (see recipe)
Creole seasoning for garnish

Method:
In a large sauté pan, melt butter over medium-high heat. Add onions, garlic, bell peppers and green onions. Sauté 3–5 minutes or until vegetables are wilted. Blend in lump crabmeat, being careful not to break lumps. Cook 2–3 minutes or until crab is heated thoroughly. Using a slotted spoon, push crabmeat mixture to one half of skillet and add crab fingers to other side to warm thoroughly in juices. Set aside and keep warm. To assemble, place 2 Holland rusks or English muffins in the center of a 10-inch plate, top each with a poached egg and an equal portion of crabmeat mixture. Top each egg with a tablespoon of Hollandaise and 2 crab claws. Sprinkle top of Hollandaise sauce with a pinch of Creole seasoning for color.

BEATEN BISCUITS WITH HAM

Prep Time: 1½ Hours
Yields: 12 Servings

Comment:

Beaten biscuits are actually more of a scone or shortbread. Once the dough is made, the biscuits are beaten with a broomstick or small rolling pin until blisters appear on the surface. This process gives the biscuits a unique texture and prevents them from rising too high during baking. Many old Cajuns say the biscuits need to be beaten 20 minutes for family and 30 minutes for company.

Ingredients:

1 cup flour
1 cup cake flour
1 tbsp sugar
½ tsp salt
¼ tsp baking powder
6 tbsps lard
   OR shortening
¼ cup minced ham
½ cup skim milk

Method:

Preheat oven to 325°F. In a food processor, combine flours, sugar, salt and baking powder. Pulse 5 seconds then add shortening and ham. Blend 10–15 seconds or until mixture resembles coarse crumbs. Add milk and process until dough ball forms. Enclose dough in plastic wrap and let rest 10 minutes. Place dough on an unfloured surface and beat with the smooth side of a meat mallet 15–20 minutes or until blistered. Fold dough over occasionally while beating. Dough will become less sticky and stronger during this process. Pinch off walnut-sized pieces of dough. On a baking sheet, arrange pieces closely, but not touching. Flatten biscuits slightly to evenly cook surface. Prick each biscuit twice with a fork. Bake 30–40 minutes or until tops begin to brown.

CAPTAIN JOHN'S CATHEAD BISCUITS

Prep Time: 30 Minutes
Yields: 8 Servings

Comment:

The creator of this recipe obviously thought that the uneven shapes of the biscuits resembled cats' heads. Try cathead biscuits plain with melted butter or fold crackling, cheese or herbs into the batter for a unique flavor.

Ingredients:

2 cups flour
1 tbsp baking powder
½ tsp baking soda
½ tsp salt
⅓ cup shortening
4 tsps butter
⅔ cup buttermilk

Method:

Preheat oven to 450°F. In a mixing bowl, sift flour, baking powder, baking soda and salt. Blend well. Using a pastry cutter, cut in shortening and butter until it resembles coarse cornmeal. Using a large cooking spoon, blend buttermilk into flour mixture until moistened. On a lightly-floured surface, knead dough until it comes together. Do not overwork dough as the less it is handled, the flakier the biscuits. Break dough into 8 equal portions and pat approximately ½-inch thick onto a baking sheet. Biscuits should be irregular in shape, but no more than ½-inch high and 1-inch apart. Bake 10–15 minutes or until golden brown. Remove from oven and brush with melted butter.

RAISED CALAS (RICE CAKES)

Prep Time: 30 Minutes
Yields: 4 Servings

Comment:

The Africans brought rice-growing techniques to America from Senegal. In addition, they created calas, or rice cakes, as a different type of breakfast food. To give the rice cakes a sweet touch, add powdered sugar and cane syrup.

Ingredients:

1 cup long grain white rice
1½ cups cold water
1 tsp salt
½ tsp butter
1 package dry yeast
½ cup warm water
3 large eggs, beaten
¼ cup sugar
¼ tsp freshly-grated nutmeg
½ tsp salt
1¼ cups flour
2 cups vegetable oil
powdered sugar

Method:

In a 2-quart cast iron saucepan, bring cold water, salt and butter to a rolling boil. Add rice then reduce heat to simmer. Cover and cook 30 minutes. Do not remove cover or stir rice during cooking process. When done, stir rice and place in a large mixing bowl. Using the back of a wooden spoon, mash rice and allow to cool. Dissolve yeast in warm water. Stir yeast into rice and beat thoroughly with a spoon approximately 2 minutes. Cover bowl with a towel and set in a warm place to rise overnight. Once raised, blend in eggs, sugar, nutmeg, salt and flour. Stir well and cover bowl. Set in a warm place to rise 30 additional minutes. In a 14-inch cast iron skillet, heat oil over medium-high heat. Drop heaping tablespoons of rice batter into hot oil. Deep fry 4–5 cakes at a time until golden brown on all sides. Remove and drain. Top each cake with powdered sugar. Serve hot.

UPSIDE-DOWN ORANGE BISCUITS

Prep Time: 1 Hour
Yields: 10–12 Servings

Comment:

The orange glaze under these homemade biscuits is so good that it can also be used to flavor can biscuits. This syrup can also be used as a topping over croissants or French toast.

Ingredients:

½ cup orange juice
1 tbsp grated orange zest
¾ cup sugar
¼ cup butter
2 cups flour
½ tsp salt
3 tsps baking powder
4 tbsps shortening
¾ cup milk
½ tsp cinnamon

Method:

Preheat oven to 375°F. Butter 2 (8-compartment) muffin tins. In a small saucepan, combine orange juice, zest, ½ cup sugar and butter. Whisk constantly over medium heat until sugar is dissolved. Distribute mixture evenly among muffin cups. In a large mixing bowl, sift together flour, salt and baking powder. Using a pastry cutter, blend in shortening. Add milk and stir until dough ball forms. Place dough on a lightly-floured surface and knead 15–20 seconds. Roll dough ¼-inch thick and sprinkle with remaining sugar and cinnamon. Roll dough jelly roll-style and cut into 1-inch slices. Lay biscuits in muffin tins over orange mixture. Bake 15–20 minutes. Serve hot.

BASIC BUTTERMILK BISCUITS

Prep Time: 30 Minutes
Yields: 10 Biscuits

Comment:
Most cathead or drop biscuits in the Old South were made with clabber or buttermilk. These acidic products reacted with baking powder or soda to create flaky, tender biscuits. Today, self-rising and soft winter wheat flours create the same effect. Nevertheless, most cooks still use buttermilk in their biscuits simply because it tastes so good!

Ingredients:
⅓ cup butter or margarine
2 cups self-rising flour
¾ cup buttermilk
butter or margarine, melted

Method:
Preheat oven to 425°F. Blend ⅓ cup butter into flour with a pastry cutter until mixture is crumbly. Add buttermilk, stirring until mixture is moistened. Turn dough onto a lightly-floured surface and knead 3–4 times. Roll dough ¾-inch thick, cut with a 2½-inch round cutter then place biscuits on a baking sheet. Bake 12–14 minutes. When done, brush immediately with melted butter.

Variations
Cornmeal-Jalapeño Biscuits:
Substitute 1 cup self-rising cornmeal for 1 cup self-rising flour. Add 1 cup (4 ounces) shredded Monterey Jack cheese with peppers or 1 cup shredded sharp Cheddar cheese and 1 unseeded, chopped jalapeño pepper. Bake as directed.

Beer-and-Cheese Biscuits:
Add 1 cup (4 ounces) shredded Swiss cheese and 1 teaspoon dried whole leaf or rubbed sage. Substitute ¾ cup beer for buttermilk. Bake as directed.

Country Ham Biscuits:
Reduce butter and buttermilk to ¼ cup each. Add 1 (8-ounce) carton sour cream and 1 cup finely chopped cooked country ham. Bake as directed.

YELLOW CORN BISCUITS

Prep Time: 1½ Hours
Yields: 14 (2½-inch) Biscuits

Comment:
These biscuits are a great complement to many entrées such as pork roast or game salmis. For a delectable dish, split biscuits and fill with our Fricassée of Rabbit. (See recipe.)

Ingredients:
3 ears corn, raw
6 tbsps heavy whipping cream
8 tbsps cold unsalted butter
1 cup coarsely-ground yellow cornmeal
2½ cups flour
1 tbsp plus 1 tsp non-alum baking powder
3 tbsps sugar
1 tsp salt
½ tsp cracked black pepper
1 egg
1½ cups plus 2 tbsps buttermilk

Method:
Cut raw kernels off corncobs. Scrape cobs over a bowl to release all of corn's "milk." Lightly chop kernels. In a heavy-bottomed saucepan, combine corn, corn "milk" and cream. Cook over medium heat 5 minutes or until cream is thick and reduced to a third. Set aside and let cool at room temperature. Process corn mixture lightly or mash it to break up kernels. Preheat oven to 400°F. Dice butter and chill in refrigerator. In a large mixing bowl, combine cornmeal, flour, baking powder, sugar, salt and pepper. Cut in butter with a pastry cutter or 2 forks until mixture resembles a coarse meal. This should be done quickly to prevent butter from getting warm. In a separate bowl, beat egg and buttermilk. Blend in corn then slowly add mixture into flour mixture, blending until dough comes together. Dough may be slightly wet, but can be handled easily with a light dusting of flour. Place dough on a floured board and round it out with your hands. Pat dough 1-inch thick. Cut biscuits with a 2½-inch cutter and place on baking sheet. Bake on top rack of oven 15–20 minutes or until golden brown. Remove from oven and brush tops of biscuits with melted butter.

CRACKLIN' BISCUITS

Prep Time: 30 Minutes
Yields: 8–10 Biscuits

Comment:

The Cajuns, always looking for variation in recipes, have added hog cracklings to biscuit dough to create a unique breakfast item. If cracklings are not available, substitute salted pork skins.

Ingredients:

4 cups flour	½ cup unsalted butter
2 tbsps baking powder	1½ cups buttermilk
1 tsp baking soda	¾ cup chopped hog cracklings
1½ tbsps sugar	¼ cup melted butter
1 tsp salt	

Method:

Preheat oven to 400°F. In a large mixing bowl, combine flour, baking powder, baking soda, sugar and salt. Blend well. Using a pastry cutter, blend in butter. Add buttermilk and cracklings. Continue to mix until dough is formed. Place dough on a lightly-floured board and knead lightly. Roll dough out approximately ¾-inch thick. Cut biscuits with a 3-inch round cutter. Place biscuits in a greased 12-inch cast iron skillet and drizzle with remaining melted butter. Bake 25 minutes or until golden brown.

BRUNCH OR AFTERNOON TEA CREAM BISCUITS

Prep Time: 30 Minutes
Yields: 10 Biscuits

Comment:

These sweet, golden brown biscuits are a perfect accompaniment to a brunch buffet or afternoon tea. Serve them with fresh fruit, lemon curd or your favorite homemade preserves.

Ingredients:

2 cups flour	½ tsp salt
1 tbsp double-acting baking powder	1¼ cups heavy whipping cream
3–4 tbsps sugar	whole milk, for brushing tops of biscuits

Method:

Preheat oven to 425°F. In a large mixing bowl, sift together flour, baking powder, sugar and salt. Slowly add cream, stirring until dough is just formed. Gather dough into a ball and turn onto a lightly-floured surface. Roll or pat out dough ½-inch thick. Cut out as many rounds as possible with a 2½-inch cutter. Transfer biscuits to an ungreased baking sheet. Gather scraps, re-roll dough and cut out more rounds until all is used. Brush tops of biscuits lightly with milk. Bake 15 minutes or until golden brown. Transfer biscuits to wire rack and let cool 5 minutes.

PORK AND YAM BREAKFAST SAUSAGE

Prep Time: 1 Hour
Yields: 25–30 (3-ounce) Patties

Comment:

Pork is often served with fruit or fruit-flavored sauces to help enhance the taste. Although technically vegetables, yams have a sweet flavor that makes them an equally suitable accompaniment to the meat. In this recipe, cubed yams are added to sausage prior to cooking to add flavor and visual appeal.

Ingredients:

5 pounds ground pork	2 tbsps salt
1 (16-ounce) can yams, drained	1½ tsps nutmeg
¼ cup chopped parsley	1 tbsp black pepper
2 tsps dried thyme	1 tbsp cayenne pepper
1½ tbsps rubbed sage	1½ tbsps granulated garlic
1 tsp ginger	1 cup ice water

Method:

NOTE: When making sausage of any type, it is always best to keep the meat chilled at 35–40°F. The ice water will help maintain cold temperature in meat and set fat in sausage. Slice yams and dice into ¼-inch cubes. Spread cubes on a cookie sheet and freeze for later use. In a large mixing bowl, combine pork and all herbs and seasonings. Add ice water. Using your hands, mix sausage well by turning and pushing meat 10–15 minutes to ensure proper blending. Gently fold in frozen yams, being careful not to break up so solid cubes are visible in finished product. Roll sausage into 3-inch patties or stuff into hog casing and tie off into 6-inch links. Cook patties the same as any other breakfast sausage or grill links over charcoal.

A Miller's Tale

Once you try home ground, slow-cooked yellow corn grits, "you'll have no more need for the unleaded variety," quips Papa Tom Bonnecaze, who sold me the antique grits mill now in use at my White Oak Plantation in Baton Rouge. The mill, which was manufactured in Wilkesboro, N.C. about a century ago, consists of two grooved granite stones and a series of screens. Yellow corn grits are created by grinding very dry, hard, germinated corn kernels between the granite stones. As smaller particles are formed they move through the series of grooves and out onto the screens. The finer cornmeal filters through leaving the grits on the larger screen. Commercially made grits are made from the de-germinated kernels from which the corn oil has been extracted. Home-milled yellow corn grits still have the corn oil in them and retain much more of the original corn flavor. However, the resulting grits must be refrigerated, because the corn oil will eventually make the yellow grits rancid.

To prepare yellow corn grits, boil 2 cups of water, one cup of milk and a teaspoon of salt. Once the liquid is at a full boil, add the grits in slowly. While boiling, stir with a wire whisk for 3 to 4 minutes. Reduce the heat to low, cover the pan and cook for 20 minutes. The biggest difference between yellow corn grits and commercial grits is the predominant corn flavor, said Bonnecaze.

The mill Bonnecaze sold to me was previously owned by a retired airplane engineer in Arkansas. If you ask Papa Tom why he sold me the mill, he'll probably tell you I beat him out of it. It's true. I just had to have it, but lest you worry that Papa Tom has been reduced to the unleaded variety of grits, he had already purchased a second mill. The North Carolina company that manufactured my mill is still in business today and provides spare parts.

CREOLE TOMATO GRITS

Prep Time: 45 Minutes
Yields: 6 Servings

Comment:
While basic boiled grits are perfect in their simplicity for breakfast, additional ingredients are often added to the grain at bigger meals. Here, ripe Creole tomatoes and cheese are used to give flair to plain grits.

Ingredients:
1 cup yellow stone-ground grits
2 large Creole tomatoes, chopped
½ cup bacon, chopped
¼ cup butter
¼ cup sliced garlic
3 cups water
½ cup heavy whipping cream
1 tsp salt
2 tbsps canned chopped green chiles
¼ cup shredded mild Cheddar cheese

Method:
In a heavy-bottomed saucepan, cook bacon until crisp. Reserve drippings in pan. Add tomatoes, butter and garlic. Sauté until garlic is tender. Mix in water, cream, salt and chiles then bring to a boil. Gradually stir in grits, blending well. Reduce heat to medium-low. Cover and cook 15–20 minutes, stirring occasionally until thickened. Remove from heat then blend in cheese until melted.

CHEESE GARLIC GRITS SOUFFLÉ

Prep Time: 1 Hour
Yields: 6 Servings

Comment:
Grits and garlic have an ancient affinity in the South. Cooks who wouldn't use garlic in any other form have been slipping a bit into cheese grits for years. Many cooks add a lot more garlic by roasting it first and often refer to it as their "secret ingredient." Cheese Grits Soufflé is usually served as a brunch or luncheon dish and has a character very much like a sharply flavored spoon bread.

Ingredients:
1 cup stone-ground grits
1½ cups shredded sharp Cheddar cheese
½ cup freshly-grated Parmesan cheese
1 garlic clove, crushed
2 cups water
2 cups milk
½ tsp salt
2 tbsps unsalted butter
½ tsp ground white pepper
dash of Worcestershire sauce
Louisiana hot sauce to taste
4 eggs, separated

Method:
Preheat oven to 350°F. In a large saucepan, heat water and milk over medium-high heat. Bring mixture to a rolling boil, then add salt. Slowly stir in grits and reduce heat to simmer. Continue to cook grits approximately 20 minutes, stirring often. Grits should be quite thick and creamy. Remove grits from heat and stir in cheeses, garlic, butter, pepper, Worcestershire and hot sauce. Allow to cool slightly. In a small mixing bowl, beat egg yolks lightly with a fork. Pour beaten yolks into grits and stir until well blended. In a separate mixing bowl, whisk egg whites until soft peaks form, then fold into grits. Butter a deep 2-quart baking dish. Pour batter into dish and bake approximately 30 minutes or until lightly browned and well-puffed.

BERRIES AND CREOLE CREAM CHEESE CRÊPES

Prep Time: 30 Minutes
Yields: 4 Servings

Comment:

Start your day off with a great mix of berries and Louisiana's own Creole cream cheese. We have wrapped fresh mixed berries and cool Creole cream cheese in warm, delicate crêpes for a breakfast beyond compare. Any seasonal berries such as strawberries, blackberries, blueberries or raspberries may be used for the crêpe filling.

Ingredients for Crêpes:

2 eggs
½ cup flour
1½ tsp sugar
½ tsp pure vanilla extract
1 tbsp Triple Sec
1 tbsp melted butter
¾ cup milk
salt to taste
¼ cup vegetable oil

Method:

In a large mixing bowl, whisk together eggs, flour, sugar, vanilla and Triple Sec until smooth. Blend in butter and milk until batter is smooth and has the consistency of heavy whipping cream. Season with salt. For best results, refrigerate batter at least 6 hours, preferably overnight. Place 2 (6-inch) crêpe pans over medium-high heat. Add 2 tablespoons of vegetable oil into first pan and swirl to coat bottom. Once hot, pour excess oil into second crêpe pan. Place approximately 2 ounces crêpe batter into first pan, tilting in a circular motion until it spreads evenly. Cook crêpe until outer edge browns and loosens from pan. Flip crêpe and cook 1 additional minute. Using a thin spatula, remove crêpe from pan then sprinkle with sugar. Continue process, using both pans and adding oil each time, until all crêpes are done. To store overnight or freeze, place plastic wrap between each crêpe to prevent sticking and place in a large plastic zipper bag prior to refrigerating or freezing.

Ingredients for Filling:

½ cup Bittersweet Plantation Dairy Creole Cream Cheese
2 cups fresh mixed berries
2 tbsps sugar
½ lemon

Method:

In a mixing bowl, combine berries, sugar and a squirt of lemon. Toss to combine. Spread 2 tablespoons Creole cream cheese over each cooked crêpe. Top with ¼ berry mixture. Fold each crêpe into quarters and serve with syrup or puréed mixed berries and sugar.

WILD BLACKBERRY CRÊPES

Prep Time: 1 Hour
Yields: 12 Crêpes

Comment:

Crêpes are very versatile. They can be eaten as a dessert or a breakfast item. Crêpes are even stuffed with seafood or meat for a fabulous lunch or dinner treat. Try these fresh blackberry crêpes at your next breakfast or brunch.

Ingredients for Crêpes:

4 eggs	2 tbsps melted butter
1 cup flour	1½ cups milk
1 tbsp sugar	salt to taste
1 tsp pure vanilla extract	½ cup vegetable oil
2 tbsps Grand Marnier liqueur	½ cup sugar

Method:

In a large mixing bowl, whisk eggs, flour, sugar, vanilla and liqueur until smooth. Add butter and milk. Continue to blend until batter reaches consistency of heavy whipping cream and all lumps are removed. Season with salt. It is best to make crêpe batter 6 hours prior to use and refrigerate, preferably overnight. Place 2 (6-inch) crêpe pans over medium-high heat. Add 2 tablespoons vegetable oil into one pan and swirl to coat to bottom of pan. Once hot, pour excess oil into second crêpe pan. Place 2 ounces of crêpe batter into first pan, tilting in a circular motion until batter spreads evenly. Cook until outer edge browns and loosens from pan. Flip and cook 1 additional minute. Using a spatula, remove crêpe from pan and sprinkle with remaining sugar. Continue process until all crêpes are cooked. If you wish to store crêpes overnight or freeze, place plastic wrap between each crêpe to prevent sticking. Store in a large plastic zipper bag.

Ingredients for Blackberry Filling:

3 cups wild blackberries	½ cup sugar
2 tbsps butter	⅛ tsp cinnamon
2 tbsps cornstarch	⅛ tsp nutmeg
1 cup water	1 cup whipped cream
½ cup white wine	mint leaves for garnish

Method:

In a sauté pan, melt butter over medium-high heat. Dissolve cornstarch in water until thoroughly blended. Pour cornstarch mixture, wine, and sugar into sauté pan. Bring mixture to a rolling boil, reduce to simmer then add 2 cups blackberries, cinnamon and nutmeg. Continue to cook 3 minutes or until sauce thickens. When ready to serve, divide an equal amount of fresh blackberries into center of 12 crêpes. Place 1 tablespoon cooked sauce over berries, and roll each crêpe into a cigar shape. Place 2 crêpes in the center of a serving plate and top with hot blackberry syrup and 1 tablespoon whipped cream. Garnish with fresh mint leaves.

CRÈME BRÛLÉE LOST BREAD

Prep Time: 1½ Hours
Yields: 6 Servings

Comment:

Crème Brûlée Lost Bread, one of the most interesting breakfast dishes, came about because of a need to use stale bread. There are numerous versions in and around New Orleans for this traditional dish, but no matter what the recipe, it should always be topped with powdered sugar and cane syrup.

Ingredients:

12 French bread croutons, cut 1-inch thick
½ cup melted butter
1 cup brown sugar, lightly packed
2 tbsps Louisiana cane syrup
5 eggs
1 cup milk
½ cup heavy whipping cream
⅛ tsp cinnamon
⅛ tsp nutmeg
1 tbsp pure vanilla extract
1 tbsp praline liqueur or Frangelico

Method:

French bread croutons should be cut out of a baguette-style loaf (2½–3 inches in diameter). In a cast iron skillet, combine butter, brown sugar and cane syrup over medium-high heat. Cook mixture, stirring constantly, until bubbly. When sugar has dissolved, pour syrup into bottom of a 13" x 9" x 2" baking dish. Allow to cool slightly then top with croutons. In a large mixing bowl, whisk eggs, milk, cream, cinnamon, nutmeg, vanilla and liqueur. Blend thoroughly then pour evenly over croutons. Using your fingertips, press bread down gently to allow custard to absorb into croutons. Be careful not to break bread. Cover dish with plastic wrap and chill overnight. Preheat oven to 350°F. Allow custard to sit out at room temperature approximately 1 hour. Bake uncovered 40 minutes or until bread is puffed with golden brown edges. Allow to cool 10 minutes prior to serving. When ready to serve, invert 2 croutons on the center of a 10-inch plate. Top with powdered sugar and drizzle with Louisiana cane syrup.

ORANGE PAIN PERDU

Prep Time: 30 Minutes
Yields: 6 Servings

Comment:

Pain Perdu, meaning "lost bread," is a French toast recipe. Much like Crème Brûlée Lost Bread, this dish is created with leftover, stale "lost" bread. Had it not been dipped in eggs and milk, then pan fried, the bread would have certainly been lost.

Ingredients:

1 (8-ounce) loaf French bread
3 eggs
1 cup sugar
1 cup whole milk
1 cup evaporated milk
½ cup fresh squeezed orange juice
1 tsp cinnamon
½ tsp nutmeg
1 tsp pure vanilla extract
⅓ cup butter
½ cup powdered sugar

Method:

Cut bread into 1-inch slices. In a large mixing bowl, whisk together eggs and sugar. Add whole milk, evaporated milk, orange juice, cinnamon, nutmeg and vanilla. Continue to whisk until well blended. In a 12-inch cast iron skillet, melt butter over medium-high heat. Dip bread into custard, a few slices at a time, then sauté until golden brown on both sides. Continue until all bread has been cooked. As bread is removed from skillet, top it with powdered sugar.

PAIN PERDU
COUNT PONTCHARTRAIN

Prep Time: 30 Minutes
Yields: 6 Servings

Comment:

When New Orleans was founded, French explorer Bienville named Lake Pontchartrain in honor of the French count in the court of Louis XV. Pain Perdu, or lost bread, is a simple breakfast dish made from stale French bread abundant in the Creole cupboard.

Ingredients:

2 (10-inch) loaves day-old
  French bread
3 eggs
¼ cup sugar
2 tbsps pure vanilla extract
1 tsp cinnamon
1 tsp nutmeg
1½ cups milk
¾ cup butter
2 cups water
½ cup dry white wine
½ cup sugar
2 tbsps cornstarch
2 cups raspberries
1 cup blackberries
1 cup blueberries
½ cup strawberries
whipped cream for garnish
powdered sugar for garnish

Method:

In a large mixing bowl, combine eggs, sugar, vanilla, cinnamon and nutmeg. Whisk until well blended. Slowly blend in milk. Cut French bread on a bias into ½-inch thick croutons, and discard ends of bread. Soak croutons in egg mixture 1–2 minutes. In a cast iron skillet, melt butter, ¼ cup at a time, over medium-high heat. Add more butter as needed. Sauté bread in butter 1–2 minutes on each side or until golden brown. Remove and keep warm. In a separate sauté pan, combine water, wine, sugar and cornstarch, whisking thoroughly. Bring mixture to a rolling boil, stirring constantly until reduced to half volume. This simple syrup should thicken due to cornstarch. Remove from heat then add fruit, tossing until well coated. Allow fruit to sit in syrup until warmed and sauce is colored from natural fruit juices. Place 2 pieces of lost bread in the center of a 10-inch serving plate and top with a tablespoon of fresh fruit syrup. Garnish with whipped cream and powdered sugar if desired.

Hot Beignets at Café Du Monde, New Orleans

STRAWBERRY FRITTERS

Prep Time: 30 Minutes
Yields: 24 Fritters

Comment:

There are thousands of fritter recipes throughout the South. Fritters range from savory to sweet, and from flat and dense to light and airy. This batter is sweet and light much like the famous New Orleans Beignets. Serve these fritters with powdered sugar and strawberry syrup for a sweet treat.

Ingredients for Fritters:

¾ cup diced strawberries
vegetable oil for frying
¾ cup sugar
3 eggs
1 tbsp butter, melted
¼ cup milk
4 tsps pure vanilla extract
⅛ tsp cinnamon
1¼ cups flour
1 tsp baking powder
⅛ tsp salt

Method:

In a home-style deep fryer, such as a FryDaddy, heat oil to 375°F. In a medium mixing bowl, combine strawberries, sugar, eggs, butter, milk, vanilla and cinnamon. Mix well. In a separate bowl, blend together flour, baking powder and salt. Slowly pour strawberry mixture into dry ingredients, whisking constantly. Blend just until ingredients are combined. Do not over mix. Using a 1-ounce cookie dough scoop, scoop up portions of batter and place in oil. Cook 3–5 minutes, flipping often, until golden brown.

Ingredients for Strawberry Syrup:

2 pints strawberries, stemmed and puréed
½ cup sugar
1 cup strawberry syrup

Method:

Mix all ingredients until sugar dissolves. Serve over strawberry fritters or ice cream.

NEW ORLEANS BEIGNETS

Prep Time: 1½ Hours
Yields: 10–12 Servings

Comment:

This classical fried "doughnut" of the Crescent City was made famous in restaurants such as Café Du Monde. It is believed that the Ursuline nuns brought beignets to New Orleans. This simple fried confection is always served dusted in powdered sugar and dipped in hot Café au Lait.

Ingredients:

1 package dry yeast
4 tbsps warm water
3½ cups plus 2 tbsps flour
1 tsp salt
¼ cup sugar
1¼ cups milk
3 eggs, beaten
¼ cup melted butter
vegetable oil for deep frying
powdered sugar for dusting

Method:

In a measuring cup, combine yeast and warm water. Using a teaspoon, stir to blend well then set aside. In a large mixing bowl, whisk flour, salt and sugar until well blended. With a wooden spoon, stir in blossomed yeast, milk, eggs and butter. Mix until dough is formed. Cover with a dish towel and set in a warm place to rise 1 hour. Heat vegetable oil to 350°F in a home-style deep fryer, such as a FryDaddy, according to manufacturer's directions. Turn dough onto a lightly-floured surface. Knead once or twice and roll out ⅜–½-inch thick. Cut dough into 3-inch squares and place on a lightly-floured pan. Cover and allow to rest 10 minutes. Deep fry beignets, 2–3 at a time, approximately 2 minutes on each side or until golden brown and puffed. Remove beignets from oil, drain and dust generously with powdered sugar. Beignets should be served 3 per person with a cup of steaming hot Café au Lait. (See recipe.)

LUMBERMAN'S APPLE PANCAKE

Prep Time: 1 Hour
Yields: 4 Servings

Comment:
Lake Charles, La., was the site of a lumber boom in the mid 1800s that attracted workers from Michigan. These lumbermen and carpenters, known as "Michigan Men," arrived to buoy the city's fledgling lumber industry. This recipe was named in honor of these men. Feel free to substitute any local fruit as a filling for this unique pancake.

Ingredients:
1 red apple, cored and diced
1 green apple, cored and diced
¼ cup butter
¼ cup brown sugar
1 tbsp lemon juice
¼ cup golden raisins
⅛ tsp cinnamon
⅛ tsp nutmeg
4 eggs
2 cups flour
¼ cup sugar
½ tsp salt
½ cup milk
1 tbsp pure vanilla extract
½ cup whipped cream
powdered sugar for garnish

Method:
Preheat oven to 375°F. Grease a 9-inch, non-stick ovenproof frying pan with approximately 1 tablespoon butter. Set aside. NOTE: It is imperative that a non-stick frying pan be used in this recipe. In a separate sauté pan, melt ¼ cup butter over medium-high heat. Add red and green apples and sauté 10–12 minutes or until tender but not overcooked. Stir in brown sugar, lemon juice, raisins, cinnamon and nutmeg until sugar is melted and apples are coated. Remove from heat and set aside. In a large mixing bowl, combine eggs, flour, sugar and salt. Add milk and whisk thoroughly to dissolve all lumps. Add vanilla and whisk 1 additional minute. Pour batter into greased frying pan and place on center rack of oven. Bake pancake 20–25 minutes or until golden brown around edges. During cooking process, pancake will rise approximately 2 inches out of pan in a soufflé-style. When pancake is done, remove from oven and fill with apple mixture. Slide pancake onto a large serving platter and fold top half over apple filling, creating a half-moon shape. Cut pancake into 4 equal slices and gently place on serving plates. Top with whipped cream and powdered sugar.

BUTTERMILK PANCAKES WITH ORANGE HONEY BUTTER

Prep Time: 30 Minutes
Yields: 12 Pancakes

Comment:
This simple pancake batter can be made and refrigerated overnight if necessary. The Orange Honey Butter is delicious on top of a stack of basic pancakes and can be quickly whipped up while cooking.

Ingredients for Orange Honey Butter:
½ cup softened butter
⅓ cup honey
2 tbsps orange juice concentrate

Method:
Whisk well and allow to sit at room temperature away from heat, until pancakes are cooked.

Ingredients for Buttermilk Pancakes:
1¾ cups flour
1 tsp baking powder
1 tsp baking soda
½ tsp salt
1½ cups buttermilk
3 eggs
4 tbsps vegetable oil
1 tbsp honey
powdered sugar for garnish

Method:
Place dry ingredients in a mixing bowl and whisk just until combined. Add buttermilk, eggs, 2 tablespoons oil and honey whisking just until batter is smooth. In a cast iron skillet or a non-stick electric griddle heat remaining 2 tablespoons oil over medium-high heat. Pour ¼ cup batter at a time onto hot griddle. When bubbles appear on top, turn and cook second side until golden brown. Remove and spread a small amount of Orange Honey Butter on top of each pancake. Stack 3 high with a dollop of butter on top. Serve with powdered sugar.

CREOLE COUNTRY CORNMEAL PECAN WAFFLES

Prep Time: 30 Minutes
Yields: 8 Waffles

Comment:

This interesting waffle recipe was created by two Creole women, Ms. Young and Ms. Murphy of New Orleans. These frugal women never let a single thing go to waste and often combined leftover fruit with syrups for waffle toppings. Their favorite flavor was a combination of canned cranberries with maple syrup.

Ingredients:

1½ cups yellow cornmeal
½ cup chopped pecans
2¼ cups flour
½ cup sugar
3 tbsps baking powder
2¼ tsps salt
¼ pound melted butter
6 eggs, beaten
3 cups milk
2 tbsps vegetable oil

Method:

Preheat waffle iron to medium heat according to manufacturer's directions. In a large mixing bowl, combine cornmeal, flour, sugar, baking powder and salt. Using a wooden spoon, blend well. Fold in pecans until thoroughly coated. In a separate bowl, combine butter, eggs and milk. Whisk well. Using a wooden spoon, stir liquid ingredients into dry ingredients until smooth. Continue to stir until all lumps have been removed. Place a small amount of vegetable oil or spray on preheated waffle iron. Ladle ¾ cup batter onto hot waffle iron and cook 3–3½ minutes. Once cooked, keep waffles warm until all are done. Serve with cranberry syrup or your favorite fruit-syrup mixture.

STRAWBERRY PANCAKE EN SURPRISE

Prep Time: 30 Minutes
Yields: 4–6 Servings

Comment:

Pancakes and crêpes can often become mundane when continuously presented in the same fashion time after time. Many people will add fruit or chocolate to make the dish more interesting. This recipe creates a large cake rather than individual ones. Try substituting local, seasonal fruit in the place of Louisiana strawberries.

Ingredients:

½ cup diced Louisiana strawberries
½ cup powdered sugar
2 tbsps butter
2 eggs
½ cup flour
¾ cup milk
⅛ tsp nutmeg
2 tbsps rum
juice of ½ lemon

Method:

Preheat oven to 400°F. Dust a 12-inch round platter with ¼ cup powdered sugar and set aside. In a 10-inch cast iron skillet, melt butter over medium-high heat. Sauté strawberries 2–3 minutes, stirring occasionally. In an electric mixer, beat eggs slightly. Blend in flour. Add milk and nutmeg continuing to blend until well-mixed. Batter may be a bit lumpy. When strawberries are tender, pour batter into skillet over strawberries. Place skillet in oven and bake 15–20 minutes or until pancake is golden brown. Remove from oven and score edges of cake with a paring knife so it will fall easily to platter. Flip pancake out onto sugared-platter and sprinkle with rum and lemon juice. Dust top of pancake with remaining ¼ cup powdered sugar and serve.

RIZ JAUNE

Prep Time: 30 Minutes
Yields: 6–8 Servings

Comment:

Riz Jaune, or yellow rice, is a favorite in most Cajun homes as a means of using leftover rice in a breakfast dish while still beginning the day with eggs. To make the dish interesting, bacon and ham are added for flavor. Often in South Louisiana, tasso or andouille are substituted to add a Cajun touch.

Ingredients:

3 cups cooked white rice
9 eggs
6 strips bacon
½ cup diced ham
½ cup sliced green onions
¼ cup chopped parsley
salt and black pepper to taste

Method:

In a large cast iron skillet, render bacon fat over medium-high heat. Do not burn fat in the process. When bacon is brown, set aside to cool then crush. Place ham in bacon fat and sauté 2–3 minutes. Crack in eggs, being careful not to break. Cook until egg whites are firm, but yolks are still sunny-side-up. Add rice, crushed bacon, green onions and parsley. Stir well, breaking egg yolks into rice to give it a bright yellow color. Season with salt and pepper. Serve as a breakfast entrée or a brunch side dish.

PERSIMMON JELLY

Prep Time: 1 Hour
Yields: 3 (½-pint) Jars

Comment:

It's unfortunate that many people think of persimmons as an astringent fruit, one not very pleasant to eat or cook. What a fallacy! The fruit is sugary sweet and syrupy once it ripens and becomes soft in mid to late October.

Ingredients:

3½–4 pounds persimmons
2 cups water
3 tbsps lemon juice
1 package powdered fruit pectin
½ cup honey

Method:

Sterilize 3 (½-pint) jars with lids. Wash persimmons and remove blossom end. Place in 6–8 quart stainless steel or enamel saucepan with water. Bring mixture to a rolling boil. Mash persimmons then reduce heat and simmer 10 minutes. Remove from heat. Pour contents into a strainer and press to remove pits and skin. Return approximately 3 cups pulp to pot. Stir in lemon juice and pectin. Bring mixture to a rolling boil. Stir in honey and let mixture return to a rolling boil. Boil 1–2 minutes, stirring constantly. Test by dropping 1 teaspoon mixture into water and check firmness. When jelly is firm enough, ladle into sterilized jars, leaving ¼-inch space at top. Seal jars then process 10 minutes in a boiling water bath.

FREEZER PERSIMMON JAM

Prep Time: 1 Hour
Yields: 4 Cups

Comment:
The name persimmon is a derivation of the Algonquin word for the fruit. The Algonquin Indians enjoyed ripe persimmons and were known to dry the fruit for later use.

Ingredients:
1½ pounds soft persimmons
3 cups sugar
1 (3-ounce) pouch liquid pectin
¼ cup lemon juice

Method:
Cut or pull off any persimmon stems and discard. If persimmons are firm enough, peel with a knife. For softer fruit, cut in half and scoop out pulp instead of peeling. Discard all seeds and skin. In a food processor, mash fruit, but do not purée. This should create approximately 1½ cups of fruit. In a mixing bowl, blend fruit and sugar. Let stand 10 minutes, stirring occasionally. In a separate bowl, mix pectin and lemon juice. Add to fruit and stir gently 3 minutes. NOTE: Do not stir vigorously as air bubbles may get trapped, making the jam cloudy. Fill ½-pint jars or freezer containers to ½-inch of rim. Cover and let stand 12–16 hours at room temperature. Unopened jars will last up to 6 months in the refrigerator. If opened, the jam will last 1 month. Freeze to store longer, but once thawed be sure to keep covered and chilled.

WATERMELON JAM

Prep Time: 45 Minutes
Yields: 4 Cups

Comment:
Almost every fruit grown in the South has been turned into a jam, jelly or marmalade. This rosy pink, sweet spread is a bit crunchy and is best served with breakfast items such as muffins, scones or French toast.

Ingredients:
1½ cups watermelon, chopped and seeded
3 cups sugar
¼ cup lemon juice
1 package (1.75 ounces) powdered fruit pectin
¾ cup water

Method:
Sterilize 2 (1-pint) jars with lids according to package directions. Set aside. In large bowl, stir together watermelon, sugar and lemon juice. Set aside 10 minutes, stirring occasionally. In small saucepan, blend pectin and water. Boil mixture over high heat 1 minute, stirring constantly. Pour pectin mixture into watermelon and stir 3 minutes or until sugar is dissolved. Quickly pour jam into sterilized jars and seal. Boil jars in water 12–15 minutes. Let stand at room temperature 24 hours to set. Opened jars may be stored in refrigerator up to 3 weeks.

VERY STRAWBERRY BUTTER

Prep Time: 20 Minutes
Yields: ½ Cup

Comment:
Instead of spreading butter and preserves on your toast in the morning, use this quick and easy strawberry butter. The smooth, fruity flavor is sure to please any strawberry lover.

Ingredients:
¼ pound unsalted butter
2½ tbsps strawberry preserves
¼ cup chopped strawberries

Method:
In a small mixing bowl, beat butter with a wooden spoon until it almost resembles the creamy texture of sour cream. Beat in preserves, 1 tablespoon at a time. Butter will acquire a curdled look. Mix in chopped strawberries. Place butter in a serving bowl and refrigerate 1–2 hours or until firm. Prior to use, remove butter from refrigerator, allow to reach room temperature then stir and serve.

WATERMELON RIND CHUTNEY

Prep Time: 1 Hour 15 Minutes
Yields: 3 Cups

Comment:
When eating watermelon, most people throw away the rind. After trying this chutney recipe, you will never again consider the rind as something inedible. Serve this chutney with game, pork or cheese.

Ingredients:
1 (8-pound) piece watermelon, flesh and rind
1½ cups cider vinegar
1½ cups water
2 cups sugar
¼ cup fresh ginger, minced and peeled
2 tbsps minced cayenne peppers
1½ tbsps minced garlic
1 tsp salt
½ tsp crushed black peppercorns

Method:
Remove watermelon flesh from rind. Scrape off and discard any remaining pink flesh. Cut rind crosswise into 2-inch wide strips. Using a sharp knife, remove green peel and discard. Cut white rind into ½-inch cubes. In a 4-quart saucepan, combine rind, vinegar, water, sugar, ginger, cayenne, garlic, salt and pepper. Bring to a boil and stir until sugar dissolves. Simmer 45–55 minutes or until rind is tender, translucent and liquid is syrupy. Jar according to approved canning methods. Place in refrigerator 1–2 days prior to use to allow flavors to develop if expecting to eat soon.

MAMERE'S FIG PRESERVES

Prep Time: 3 Hours
Yields: 2 Quarts

Comment:

No fruit, wild or store bought, has been preserved in Louisiana more often than figs. My grandmother was an expert at preserving figs, and I can't remember a day that a jar of her specialty wasn't sitting in the center of our kitchen table.

Ingredients:

1 gallon figs
12 cups sugar
1 quart water
4 lemon slices

Method:

Sort figs and remove any that are overripe or blemished. Wash figs well in cold, running water. Bring a pot of water to a boil, drop in figs, remove from heat and allow to stand 3 minutes. Quickly remove and drain. The hot water will help set color in fruit. In a 2-gallon, heavy-bottomed saucepot, combine sugar and water and bring to a rolling boil. Stir constantly until sugar is melted and syrup is formed. Add lemon slices then gently place figs into boiling liquid. Reduce heat to medium and cook figs 2½ hours or until transparent. During cooking process, shake pot gently. Stirring will mash fruit. Using a slotted spoon, scoop figs into hot, sterilized jar then top with syrup. Leave ¼-inch headspace in jar. Wipe syrup from rim then tightly cover and seal. Place jars in a hot water bath and simmer approximately 10 minutes. Remove, cool, label and store for later use. NOTE: Figs may be left overnight in syrup to plump prior to packing in jars. Should you decide to do this, fill jars with fruit and syrup, seal and place in a boiling water bath approximately 20 minutes.

HERBAL SPREADS

Prep Time: 10 Minutes
Yields: 1 Cup

Comment:

With Louisiana's semi-tropical climate, a wide variety of herbs can be found at all times. By incorporating these herbal flavors with butter and cream cheese, perfect spreads for breads, muffins or pancakes can be created.

Ingredients for Honey Orange Spread:

1 stick butter
4 ounces cream cheese
2 tbsps honey
2 tbsps chopped mint
zest of 1 large orange
½ cup orange juice

Ingredients for Garlic Chive Spread:

1 stick butter
4 ounces cream cheese
1 tbsp marjoram
2 tbsps garlic chives

Method:

In a large mixing bowl, combine all ingredients for desired spread. Mix until well blended. Store in an air-tight container in refrigerator for up to 1 month. Serve with hot French bread, toast or muffins.

"Ten Cents a Dozen"

While the exact origins of the appetizer and hors d'oeuvre are not clear, historical accounts describe an ancient Athenian meal where guests were offered assorted small plates of garlic, sea urchin, marinated fish and wine-soaked bread. These small dishes all "offered variety but did not satisfy the belly." Today, variations on the idea of serving small tasty bites before, or as the beginning portion of the meal exist in all parts of the world. French *amuse bouchee* literally "entertain the mouth," while Spanish *tapas* allow guests to drink and socialize. The "little bites," or *zakuski*, of Russia originally referred to the sweets that came after a meal but are now snacks usually accompanied by vodka that precede the meal. In the Mediterranean, *mezze*, from the Persian "taste or relish," are either simple snacks served with drinks or the first part of the main meal, much like the Italian *antipasto*, which literally means "before the pasta." Although the Swedish *smorgasbord* has come to be interpreted as a feast, it can also be an offering of a variety of dishes preceding the main meal. For the Chinese, *dim sum* consists of a wide variety of appetizer-sized portions served as a meal. In Louisiana, whatever you call them, no gathering is complete without good company, good conversation and a little something to nibble on.

The terms appetizer and hors d'oeuvre both refer to a small portion of a flavorful food served to whet the appetite. Although the terms are often

used interchangeably, they are not technically the same. Hors d'oeuvres (which taken literally means "outside the main work") are usually associated with receptions or cocktail parties and are served before the meal. On the other hand, appetizers are the first course of the sit-down portion of a meal. Whichever term you use, these miniature masterpieces are often the most anticipated part of any affair and can include delicacies such as shrimp, oysters and caviar.

Why is there a need for food before the main meal? Was it an excuse for socializing before getting down to the more formal structure of a sit-down dinner? Could it have been an effort to temper the effects of pre-dinner cocktails, or conversely, to encourage bar patrons to linger a little longer and order another round? Was it a way to demonstrate affluence and hospitality by tempting one's guests with a wide variety of foods? Was it merely intended to titillate the taste buds to ensure ultimate enjoyment of the pièce de résistance? Or was it perhaps a delaying tactic to keep early comers happy while the finishing touches were put on the main entrée? Whatever the original reason, appetizers in their many variations remain popular today alone, as a prelude to lunch or dinner, or as the first course in a multi-course meal.

Like so many aspects of Cajun and Creole cuisine, appetizers in Louisiana have evolved from the traditional crudités, canapés, antipasto and finger sandwiches of Europe into such tantalizing treats as shrimp Malarcher, catfish beignets, crabmeat au gratin, shrimp rémoulade and oysters Rockefeller. Some recipes are simply a new presentation of an old idea, others are a classical presentation of regional delicacies, and still others borrow from the classics while embracing new ideas and ingredients. In a region as blessed with the fruits of the sea (and bayou) as ours, it is particularly easy to create appetizers and hors d'oeuvres that are delightful and delicious. Sometimes an appetizer can be simply a smaller portion of a main entrée. For example, crawfish étouffée is often served in tiny pastry shells instead of as a large plateful over rice. Even the traditional South Louisiana social event of a shrimp or crawfish boil has been encapsulated into an appetizer form. Guests may share a few pounds of boiled shellfish with cocktail sauce and visit over a beer on the porch before heading inside for supper. In other cases, what would normally be considered an appetizer item, such as oysters Bienville, has grown in portion size to become a meal in itself. In addition, when hors d'oeuvres are passed around at a cocktail party, it is possible for guests to consume an entire meal's worth of food, making the original purpose of stimulating the appetite without satisfying it seemingly moot.

When creating appetizers, remember, no matter the type or method of presenting them, appetizers are always fun and appreciated. These tasty tidbits should be flavorful and attractive, taking only two bites to eat. Ingredients chosen for appetizers should complement rather than repeat ingredients in the main meal. Beyond these simple guidelines, appetizers and hors d'oeuvres are limited only by the imagination and creativity of the chef and the ingredients that are readily available.

LUMP CRABMEAT VIALA

Prep Time: 30 Minutes
Yields: 6 Servings

Comment:

Viala Plantation was the original home of Lafitte's Landing Restaurant. Built in 1797, Viala served as a base for the notorious pirate, Jean Lafitte. After a devastating fire in 1998, the plantation home was destroyed. However, the legacy of Jean Lafitte lives on in Lafitte's Landing Restaurant at Bittersweet Plantation.

Ingredients:

1 pound jumbo lump crabmeat
1½ cups mayonnaise
¼ cup sliced green onions
1 tbsp chopped parsley
1 tbsp chopped tarragon
1 tsp chopped dill
1 tbsp minced garlic
2 tbsps lemon juice
dash of hot sauce
dash of Worcestershire sauce
salt and cayenne pepper to taste
¼ cup minced red bell peppers

Method:

Gently pick through crabmeat, removing all shells and cartilage. Cover and place in the refrigerator. Place mayonnaise, green onions, parsley, tarragon, dill, garlic, lemon juice, hot sauce and Worcestershire in a food processor. Blend on high speed for 1 minute then season with salt and cayenne pepper. Continue to blend 1 minute longer. Place mixture in a serving bowl and stir in minced red bell peppers for color. Cover tightly with clear wrap and refrigerate overnight. The flavor of tarragon and dill will only develop after the sauce has been resting for 8 hours. Remove from refrigerator and adjust seasonings if necessary. Blend crabmeat carefully into the sauce. Serve on romaine lettuce leaves with garlic-flavored croutons.

FRENCH-FRIED CRAB CLAWS

Prep Time: 30 Minutes
Yields: 6 Servings

Comment:

Frying units, such as the FryDaddy, make deep-frying in your kitchen fast and easy. There are a number of lighter unsaturated vegetable oils on the market. Try using these oils to make deep-frying a little healthier.

Ingredients for Batter:

1 cup milk
½ cup water
2 eggs
3 tbsps Creole mustard
salt and cracked black pepper to taste

Method:

In a 1-quart mixing bowl, combine all batter ingredients. Using a wire whisk, stir until well blended. Set aside.

Ingredients for Breading:

2 cups yellow corn flour
2¼ tsps salt
1½ tsps granulated garlic
1½ tsps cracked black pepper
1½ tsps cayenne pepper
1½ tsps dried thyme

Method:

In a 1-quart mixing bowl, combine all breading ingredients. Set aside.
NOTE: Yellow corn flour can be found in most gourmet food stores. The flour may be packaged as a preseasoned seafood breading mix such as Zatarain's Fish-Fri. If unavailable in your area, plain flour or equal parts flour and yellow corn meal may be substituted.

Ingredients for Frying:

1 pound cleaned crab claws
1½ quarts vegetable oil

Method:

In a home-style fryer, preheat oil according to manufacturer's directions (or to 375°F). Place crab claws in batter mixture and allow to sit 10–15 minutes. Drain excess liquid from crab claws and place in breading mixture. Shake off excess breading and deep-fry a few dozen at a time until claws turn golden brown and float to top. Remove and drain on paper towels. Serve claws hot with Louisiana Seafood Cocktail Sauce or Louisiana Tartar Sauce. (See recipes.)

BAYOU LACOMBE CRAB BOULETTES

Prep Time: 30 Minutes
Yields: 20 Boulettes

Comment:
These fried crab boulettes are often served as an hors d'oeuvre. They are also the perfect addition to pasta sauce or étouffée.

Ingredients:
1 pound white crabmeat
½ cup vegetable oil
¼ cup minced onions
¼ cup minced celery
¼ cup minced red bell peppers
1 tbsp minced garlic
¼ cup sliced green onions
2 whole eggs
2 cups seasoned Italian bread crumbs
salt and black pepper to taste
Louisiana hot sauce to taste

Method:
Pick through the crabmeat to remove any shells. In a 1-gallon cast iron Dutch oven, heat oil to 350°F. In a large mixing bowl, combine vegetables and eggs. Using a wooden spoon, blend until thoroughly mixed then add crabmeat. Sprinkle in enough breadcrumbs to hold the mixture together, being careful not to make the dressing too dry. Season to taste using salt, pepper and hot sauce. Roll the boulettes into 1-inch balls, sprinkle with remaining bread crumbs and fry until golden brown.

MARINATED CRAB CLAWS

Prep Time: 1 Hour
Yields: 6 Servings

Comment:
These crab claws are a Cajun tradition, resulting, as so many recipes do, from the need to preserve food for future use. This process not only preserves the crabmeat for a short time, but also makes it a quite delicious appetizer.

Ingredients:
1 pound crab claws, peeled
½ cup olive oil
½ cup water
¼ cup red wine vinegar
1 tbsp lemon juice
¼ cup minced garlic
1 tsp horseradish
¼ cup sliced green onions
¼ cup chopped parsley
3 tbsps Worcestershire sauce
1 tbsp chopped thyme
1 tbsp chopped basil
salt and black pepper to taste
Louisiana hot sauce to taste

Method:
In a large glass mixing bowl, whisk together oil, water, vinegar, lemon juice, garlic, horseradish, green onions, parsley and Worcestershire sauce until well blended. Add thyme and basil then season to taste using salt, pepper and hot sauce. Fold crab claws into seasoning mixture making sure they are well coated. Cover bowl with plastic wrap and refrigerate overnight.

SPINACH, LUMP CRAB AND ARTICHOKE DIP

Prep Time: 30 Minutes
Yields: 10–12 Servings

Comment:
At your next cocktail party, try this combination of spinach, crabmeat and artichokes for a unique, tasty dip. This interesting recipe can be adjusted to make a soup by simply adding more cream. You may also try adding 2 cups of chopped spinach and replacing the crabmeat with oysters to create an oysters Rockefeller dip.

Ingredients:
1 cup cooked spinach, squeezed
1 pound jumbo lump crabmeat
2 (8½-ounce) cans artichoke hearts, drained
¼ pound butter
½ cup diced onions
¼ cup diced celery
¼ cup diced red bell peppers
¼ cup diced yellow bell peppers
2 tbsps minced garlic
½ cup flour
¼ tsp granulated garlic
¼ tsp nutmeg
2 cups chicken stock (see recipe)
1 pint heavy whipping cream
1 ounce dry white wine
salt and cayenne pepper to taste
¼ cup sliced green onions
¼ cup chopped parsley
2 cups grated Parmesan cheese
½ tsp chopped basil

Method:
Begin by rinsing artichoke hearts well under cold water to remove the brine. Place artichokes in a food processor, chop coarsely and set aside for later use. In a 2-quart heavy-bottomed sauté pan, melt butter over medium-high heat. Add onions, celery, bell peppers and minced garlic. Sauté 3–5 minutes or until vegetables are wilted. Stir in artichokes and cook 5 additional minutes. Whisk in flour and blend well to form a white roux. Do not brown. Season with granulated garlic and nutmeg. Add chicken stock and cream, one cup at a time, whisking constantly until a thick cream sauce is achieved. Reduce heat to simmer, add white wine and season to taste using salt and cayenne pepper. Simmer 15 minutes, stirring occasionally to keep from scorching. Additional cream or stock may be added if the mixture becomes too thick. Add spinach, green onions and parsley then fold in lump crabmeat. Cook 5 minutes then remove from heat. Fold in Parmesan cheese and basil and adjust seasonings if necessary. Place the mixture in a chafing dish and serve with garlic croutons or crackers.

LUMP CRABMEAT DIP

Prep Time: 1 Hour
Yields: 6 Servings

Comment:
This dish started out as a crab and cheese soup. By simply removing milk from the original recipe, this delicious crab appetizer was created. You can recreate the soup by adding 3 cups of either milk or chicken stock to the ingredients below.

Ingredients:
1 pound jumbo lump crabmeat
½ cup butter
1 cup diced onions
½ cup diced celery
¼ cup diced red bell peppers
¼ cup minced garlic
½ cup flour
3 cups heavy whipping cream
½ pound grated Swiss cheese
½ ounce sherry
salt and black pepper to taste
Louisiana hot sauce to taste

Method:
In a heavy-bottomed Dutch oven, melt butter over medium-high heat. Add onions, celery, bell peppers and garlic. Sauté 3–5 minutes or until vegetables are wilted. Whisk in flour and stir until white roux is achieved. Pour in cream, bring to a rolling boil and reduce to simmer. Add cheese and sherry. Continue to cook until cheese is melted. Fold in crabmeat and season to taste using salt, pepper and hot sauce.

CRAWFISH-STUFFED MUSHROOMS

Prep Time: 1 Hour
Yields: 6 Servings

Comment:
Most stuffed mushroom recipes call for crabmeat or sausage. This Cajun version of the appetizer uses crawfish for a delightful twist.

Ingredients:
36 large button mushrooms, stemmed
1 pound chopped crawfish tails
¼ cup butter
¼ cup minced onions
¼ cup minced celery
¼ cup minced red bell peppers
¼ cup minced garlic
⅛ cup diced tasso
2 tbsps flour
1 cup skim milk
¼ cup sliced green onions
1 tbsp chopped basil
1 tbsp chopped thyme
pinch of nutmeg
salt and black pepper to taste
Louisiana hot sauce to taste
1 cup plain bread crumbs
½ cup grated Parmesan cheese
paprika for color
6 ounces sherry

Method:
Preheat oven to 350°F. Rinse mushrooms under cold water to remove any grit or sand. In a heavy-bottomed sauté pan, melt butter over medium-high heat. Add onions, celery, bell peppers, garlic and tasso. Sauté 3–5 minutes or until vegetables are wilted. Using a wire whisk, blend flour into the vegetable mixture. Slowly pour in milk, stirring constantly. Bring to a low boil then add crawfish, green onions, basil, thyme and nutmeg. Blend well and season to taste using salt, pepper and hot sauce. Remove from heat and sprinkle in bread crumbs to absorb any remaining liquid. Once mixture has cooled slightly, over-fill each mushroom with the stuffing. Place mushrooms on a large baking sheet or in individual au gratin dishes. Top with Parmesan cheese and paprika for color. Pour sherry around the bottom of the mushrooms and bake, uncovered, for 15–20 minutes.

SPICY PLANTATION SEAFOOD DIP

Prep Time: 1 Hour
Yields: 12–20 Servings

Comment:

The abundance of shellfish in Louisiana's bayous provides the opportunity to combine many different varieties in one dish. Here, more than in any other part of the country, you will see the marriage of meats and vegetables to seafood in a wealth of dishes. In this recipe, it is acceptable to substitute any local seafood available. You may also use only 2 of the 3 shellfish in adjusted quantities if you prefer.

Ingredients:

½ pound cooked crawfish tails, chopped
½ pound cooked shrimp, chopped
½ pound jumbo lump crabmeat
¼ pound butter
¼ cup diced onions
¼ cup diced celery
¼ cup diced red bell peppers
¼ cup diced yellow bell peppers
¼ cup minced garlic
¼ cup diced tasso ham
¼ cup sliced green onions
¼ cup chopped parsley
1 tbsp chopped dill
1 (8-ounce) package cream cheese, softened
1 cup mayonnaise
Worcestershire sauce to taste
salt and cracked black pepper to taste
Louisiana hot sauce to taste
juice of one lemon

Method:

In a heavy-bottomed sauté pan, melt butter over medium-high heat. Add onions, celery, bell peppers, garlic and tasso. Sauté 3–5 minutes until vegetables are wilted. Stir in crawfish, shrimp, green onions and parsley. Continue to sauté for 3–5 minutes. Remove from heat and allow to cool. Transfer mixture to a large mixing bowl. Whisk in dill, cream cheese, mayonnaise and Worcestershire. Season to taste with salt, pepper, hot sauce and lemon juice. Gently fold in the crabmeat and adjust seasonings if necessary. Pour seafood dip into a decorative fish mold, if serving immediately, or chill for later use. Serve with a basket of assorted crackers.

SOUTH LOUISIANA SHRIMP RÉMOULADE

Prep Time: 30 Minutes
Yields: 6 Servings

Comment:

Rémoulade is a sauce of French origin that has been adopted in many New Orleans dishes. The sauce comes in many different varieties, the most common of which are red and white. This recipe gives instructions to prepare shrimp that are wonderful when paired with a rémoulade sauce. To make a true shrimp rémoulade, use either of the rémoulade sauce recipes found in Roux, Stocks & Sauces.

Ingredients:

3 dozen (21–25 count) shrimp, peeled and deveined
2 quarts cold water
1 onion, diced
½ cup diced celery
2 tbsps cracked black pepper
3 bay leaves
¼ cup lemon juice
1 sliced lemon
4 tbsps salt
rémoulade sauce (see recipe)

Method:

In a 4-quart stockpot over medium-high heat, place all ingredients except shrimp. Bring to a rolling boil then reduce heat and simmer for 15 minutes to allow flavors to develop. Bring liquid back to a rolling boil, stir in shrimp and cook 3–5 minutes. At this point, shrimp should be pink and curled. Once water returns to a boil, shrimp are perfectly done. Pour off boiling water and replace with cold tap water to stop the cooking process. Drain and place shrimp in a serving bowl, cover with clear wrap and refrigerate. (This may be done the night before.) When ready to serve, top with red or white rémoulade sauce.

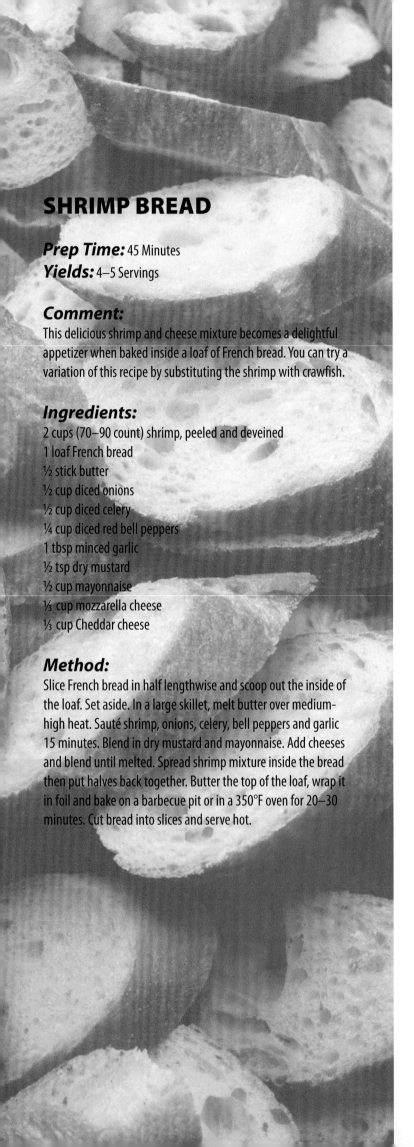

SHRIMP BREAD

Prep Time: 45 Minutes
Yields: 4–5 Servings

Comment:
This delicious shrimp and cheese mixture becomes a delightful appetizer when baked inside a loaf of French bread. You can try a variation of this recipe by substituting the shrimp with crawfish.

Ingredients:
2 cups (70–90 count) shrimp, peeled and deveined
1 loaf French bread
½ stick butter
½ cup diced onions
½ cup diced celery
¼ cup diced red bell peppers
1 tbsp minced garlic
½ tsp dry mustard
½ cup mayonnaise
⅓ cup mozzarella cheese
⅓ cup Cheddar cheese

Method:
Slice French bread in half lengthwise and scoop out the inside of the loaf. Set aside. In a large skillet, melt butter over medium-high heat. Sauté shrimp, onions, celery, bell peppers and garlic 15 minutes. Blend in dry mustard and mayonnaise. Add cheeses and blend until melted. Spread shrimp mixture inside the bread then put halves back together. Butter the top of the loaf, wrap it in foil and bake on a barbecue pit or in a 350°F oven for 20–30 minutes. Cut bread into slices and serve hot.

LEMON-GARLIC SHRIMP BRUSCHETTA

Prep Time: 2 Hours
Yields: 25 Hors d'oeuvres

Comment:
From the Italian bruscare meaning "to roast over coals," bruschetta is traditionally made by rubbing slices of toasted bread with garlic cloves then drizzling the bread with extra virgin olive oil. By adding Panzanella and marinated shrimp, we have created a more elegant hors d'oeuvre.

Ingredients for Bruschetta:
25 French bread slices, preferably baguette size
4 whole garlic cloves, halved as needed
6 tbsps extra virgin olive oil
salt and black pepper to taste

Method:
Preheat oven to 300°F. Rub French bread slices with garlic halves. Place bread on a large cookie sheet, drizzle with olive oil and season with salt and pepper. Bake for 5–10 minutes or until croutons are crisp and slightly golden brown.

Ingredients for Panzanella:
3 cups diced Creole tomatoes
¾ cup grated Parmesan cheese
6 cloves garlic, sliced
2 tbsps chopped basil
¼ cup red wine vinegar
1 tsp chopped thyme
¼ cup extra virgin olive oil
salt and black pepper to taste

Method:
In a large mixing bowl, combine tomatoes, cheese, garlic, basil, vinegar, thyme and olive oil. Season to taste with salt and pepper. Blend well, cover and refrigerate 1–2 hours.

Ingredients for Shrimp:
25 large shrimp, peeled and deveined
¼ cup lemon juice
3 tbsps minced garlic
½ cup white wine
1½ tbsps chopped oregano
salt and black pepper to taste
¼ cup olive oil

Method:
In a separate mixing bowl, combine all ingredients except olive oil and marinate at least 30 minutes. Heat olive oil in skillet then sauté shrimp 3–5 minutes or until slightly pink. Place croutons on a serving platter, top each with a heaping tablespoon of Panzanella and garnish with 1 shrimp.

SHRIMP MOUSSE

Prep Time: 45 Minutes
Yields: 20 Servings

Comment:

The addition of shrimp brings another level of flavor to this light fish terrine. For a beautiful holiday presentation, color 1 cup of mayonnaise with red food coloring and 1 cup with green. Using a pastry bag with a star tip, pipe colored mayonnaise around the base of the terrine and garnish with a fresh tomato rose.

Ingredients:

3 cups boiled shrimp, chopped
4 (5–8 ounce) catfish fillets, poached
1 cup heavy-duty mayonnaise
½ cup sour cream
1 tbsp minced garlic
¼ cup chopped parsley
¼ cup diced red bell peppers
¼ cup diced yellow bell peppers
1 tbsp lemon juice
½ ounce sherry
1 tbsp Worcestershire sauce
dash of Louisiana hot sauce
2 packages unflavored gelatin, dissolved
  in ¼ cup warm water
salt and cracked black pepper to taste

Method:

Coarsely chop poached catfish. In a 2-quart mixing bowl, blend together all ingredients. Season with salt and pepper if necessary. Pour mixture into a terrine mold, cover with plastic wrap and place in refrigerator overnight. When ready to serve, remove from mold and garnish with French bread or garlic croutons.

LOUISIANA SEAFOOD SAUSAGE

Prep Time: 45 Minutes
Yields: 80 Links

Comment:

You'll find hundreds of combinations and variations of sausage here in Cajun Country. Although this recipe contains primarily pork, shrimp is the dominant flavor.

Ingredients:

10 pounds ground pork
7 pounds ground shrimp
3 pounds whole shrimp
1 cup minced pimiento
1 cup finely chopped parsley
½ cup Old Bay® seasoning
4 cups minced onions
¾ cup minced garlic
⅓ cup dried thyme
3 cups sliced green onions
⅓ cup dried basil
2 cups ice water
60 feet (38 mm) hog casing

Method:

Place all ingredients, except ice water and hog casing, into a large mixing bowl. With such a large amount of mixture, it is best for two people to mix the ingredients using their hands. After blending 5–10 minutes, add the ice water and continue mixing 5 minutes longer. No salt or pepper is needed in this recipe because of the Old Bay seasoning which has the perfect amount of each for this volume of ingredients. Using commercial hog casing, stuff ingredients into 6-inch links of approximately 4 ounces each. NOTE: Hog casing can be purchased in bulk from any local meat market or butcher shop.

ZATARAIN'S
A New Orleans Tradition · Since 1889

CRAWFISH,
SHRIMP &
CRAB
BOIL

LOUISIANA
FISH FRY PRODUCTS
BRING THE TASTE OF LOUISIANA HOME

ZATARAIN'S
A New Orleans Tradition · Since 1889

DEFINING THE FLAVOR OF

REX
CAYENNE

Celery
Salt

ARAIN'S
Tradition · Since

ENTRATED
RIMP &
B BOIL

OZ. (236ml)

BOILED SHRIMP

Prep Time: 2 Hours
Yields: 12 Servings

Comment:
Boiling seafood in the backyard is a traditional Louisiana event. Boiling shrimp, crawfish or crabs gives families and friends a reason to get together for a day of food and fun. Enjoy the seafood and vegetables hot with pitchers of ice cold beer.

Ingredients:
20 pounds (35 count) head-on shrimp, washed
30 quarts cold water
6 medium onions, quartered
6 heads of garlic, slit in half exposing pods
6 lemons, quartered
1 cup cooking oil
4 pounds salt
½ pound cayenne pepper
4 (3-ounce) bags crab boil
24 medium red potatoes
12 ears of corn

Method:
In a 60-quart stockpot, bring water to a rolling boil. Add onions, garlic, lemons, oil, salt, pepper and crab boil. Allow ingredients to boil for 30 minutes in order to infuse flavor into the water. Put in red potatoes and cook 10–12 minutes. Add corn and cook 10 minutes, then stir in shrimp. When water returns to a boil, cook shrimp 7–10 minutes, turn off heat and allow to soak in water 12 additional minutes.

SHRIMP MALARCHER

Prep Time: 45 Minutes
Yields: 6 Servings

Comment:

This dish was named in honor of the famous Malarcher sugar planters of the Louisiana River Road. The sugar cane plantation was located west of New Orleans in Convent, Louisiana.

Ingredients:

3 dozen (21–25 count) shrimp, peeled and deveined
¼ pound butter
1 tbsp minced garlic
¼ cup sliced green onions
¼ cup sliced mushrooms
¼ cup diced red bell peppers
¼ cup diced yellow bell peppers
¼ cup diced green bell peppers
2 tbsps flour
1 ounce dry white wine
2½ cups hot shellfish or chicken stock (see recipe)
1 tsp lemon juice
1 tsp chopped parsley
salt and cracked black pepper to taste

Method:

In a heavy-bottomed sauté pan, melt butter over medium heat. Sauté garlic, green onions and mushrooms 2 minutes or until mushrooms are slightly wilted. Stir in all bell peppers and cook 1 additional minute. Add shrimp and stir-fry 2 minutes or until they begin to turn pink and curl. Whisk in flour and blend until a white roux is achieved. Deglaze with wine and add hot stock, whisking well into seasoning mixture. Add lemon juice and parsley then season to taste using salt and pepper. Cook until sauce is thickened and shrimp are perfectly done. Use additional chicken stock if the sauce becomes too thick. Serve in an au gratin dish or heated chafing dish with garlic croutons.

CAJUN CATFISH BEIGNETS

Prep Time: 45 Minutes
Yields: 50 Beignets

Comment:

Try this fun, different way to serve fried catfish. The bite-sized pieces are wonderful as an appetizer for a party or as a meal for kids. These tiny beignets of tender catfish may be served with tartar, rémoulade or cocktail sauce.

Ingredients for Batter:

5 (5–8 ounce) catfish fillets
½ cup milk
½ cup water
½ cup heavy-duty mayonnaise
1 egg
¼ cup Creole mustard
1 tsp granulated garlic
1 tbsp cracked black pepper
1 tsp salt

Method:

Cut catfish fillets into 1½-inch cubes and set aside. In a 1-quart mixing bowl, whisk together all remaining ingredients. Add catfish cubes and allow to sit at room temperature for 15 minutes.

Ingredients for Frying:

1½ quarts vegetable oil
3 cups yellow corn flour
1½ tsps salt
2 tsps granulated garlic
1½ tsps cracked black pepper
½ tsp cayenne pepper
½ tsp dried thyme

Method:

In a home-style deep fryer, such as a FryDaddy, preheat oil according to manufacturer's instructions (or to 375°F). In a 2-quart mixing bowl, combine all other ingredients. Mix well to ensure proper blending of spices. Remove catfish cubes from batter mixture and place in corn flour mixture. Coat catfish well on all sides and shake off excess breading. Deep-fry a few pieces at a time until catfish are golden brown or they float to the top. Place cooked pieces on a drain board or on paper towels.

TERRINE OF SMOKED CATFISH

Prep Time: 1 Hour
Yields: 20 Servings

Comment:

Catfish has always been considered the fish of choice by Southerners. An ample supply of farm-raised blue channel catfish allows for the creation of many interesting fish recipes. This premium finfish has made catfish terrine a Southern delicacy revered nationwide.

Ingredients for Smoking:

4 (5–8 ounce) catfish fillets
½ cup olive oil
¼ cup red wine vinegar
1 tsp dried thyme
1 tsp dried basil
1 tsp cracked black pepper
dash of Louisiana hot sauce

Method:

NOTE: You can presoak any wood chips, such as pecan or hickory, in root beer for a unique flavor. Preheat home-style smoking unit according to manufacturer's instructions. Blend together all ingredients and pour over catfish fillets. Allow to sit at room temperature for 30 minutes. Smoke fillets for approximately 35 minutes until flaky. Remove and allow to cool.

Ingredients for Terrine:

4 (5–8 ounce) smoked fillets (from above method)
1 cup heavy-duty mayonnaise
½ cup sour cream
1 tbsp minced garlic
¼ cup chopped parsley
¼ cup diced red bell peppers
¼ cup diced yellow bell peppers
1 tbsp lemon juice
½ ounce sherry
1 tbsp Worcestershire sauce
2 packages unflavored gelatin, dissolved in ¼ cup warm water
2 tbsps cracked black pepper
dash of Louisiana hot sauce
salt to taste

Method:

Coarsely chop smoked catfish. In a 2-quart mixing bowl, combine fish with all terrine ingredients, blending well. Adjust salt and pepper if necessary, pour mixture into a terrine mold, cover and place in refrigerator overnight. When ready to serve, remove from mold and garnish with French bread or garlic croutons.

OYSTER AND ANDOUILLE PASTRIES

Prep Time: 1 Hour
Yields: 6 Servings

Comment:

In this recipe, the traditional Cajun and Creole ingredients of oysters and andouille are added to a classic butter sauce and served over a French pastry. The incorporation of these different components is a great example of how Cajun and Creole cooking uses classical elements to create truly unique cuisine.

Ingredients:

2 dozen select oysters, reserve liquid
2 (8½" x 13") sheets puff pastry
1 egg, beaten
¼ cup butter
½ cup diced andouille sausage
2 tsps minced garlic
¼ cup sliced mushrooms
¼ cup sliced green onions
¼ cup diced tomatoes
¼ cup diced red bell peppers
2 ounces Champagne
1 cup heavy whipping cream
¼ pound cold, chipped butter
salt and cracked black pepper to taste

Method:

Preheat oven to 400°F. Place the 2 sheets of puff pastry on top of each other, then cut into 3-inch squares. Place pastry squares on a lightly buttered baking sheet. Brush top of each square with beaten egg to enhance color. Bake pastry 10–15 minutes, or until golden brown. Remove from oven and keep warm. In a heavy-bottomed saucepan, melt butter over medium-high heat. Sauté andouille, garlic, mushrooms, green onions, tomatoes and bell peppers 3–5 minutes or until vegetables are wilted. Add oysters and oyster liquid then deglaze with Champagne. Sauté 2 minutes or until edges of oysters begin to curl. Stir in heavy whipping cream, bring to a slight boil and reduce to half volume. Mixture should thicken to a sauce consistency. Swirling pan constantly, add a few chips of butter at a time until all is incorporated. Do not use a metal spoon or wire whisk as hot spots may develop and butter will separate. Season to taste using salt and pepper. Place each pastry square in the center of a 6-inch serving plate, remove top half of pastry and fill with equal parts of oysters and oyster butter sauce. Replace top half of pastry and serve.

OYSTER-STUFFED ARTICHOKE BOTTOMS

Prep Time: 1 Hour
Yields: 6 Servings

Comment:

One of the most famous soups in South Louisiana is Oyster and Artichoke Bisque. (See recipe.) The flavors of these two ingredients are often married in Louisiana cuisine. Here is just another example of the flavor of oysters and spinach used together to create a delicious appetizer. You may wish to try using crabmeat instead of oysters. Replace the cup of oysters with ½ pound of lump crabmeat.

Ingredients:

12 artichoke bottoms, fresh or canned
1 cup chopped oysters
¼ cup butter
½ cup minced onions
½ cup minced celery
¼ cup minced red bell peppers
1 tbsp diced garlic
3 cups cooked spinach
¼ cup tomato ketchup
salt and cracked pepper to taste
Louisiana hot sauce to taste
½ ounce Herbsaint or anise
½ cup seasoned Italian bread crumbs
¼ pound butter
1 ounce sherry
2 tbsps chopped parsley

Method:

Preheat oven to 350°F. If the artichoke bottoms are canned, soak in cold water for one hour to remove the brine and vinegar taste. In a heavy-bottomed skillet, melt ¼ cup butter over medium-high heat. Add onions, celery, bell peppers and garlic. Sauté 3–5 minutes or until vegetables are wilted. Finely chop the cooked spinach and add to the vegetables. Blend well and add oysters. Stir until all ingredients are well incorporated. Simmer 5 minutes then add ketchup, salt, pepper and hot sauce. Lower heat to simmer and cook 10–15 additional minutes. Blend Herbsaint into the oyster and spinach mixture and remove from heat. Sprinkle in bread crumbs and allow the mixture to cool slightly. Once cooled, stuff the center of each artichoke bottom with the oyster and spinach mixture. Place the artichokes in a large baking pan and top with an equal portion of melted butter and sherry. Sprinkle with parsley and bake uncovered for 15–20 minutes. Serve 2 artichokes with a spoon of sherry-butter sauce. You may wish to place one whole oyster on the bottom of the artichoke prior to stuffing.

OYSTER AND ARTICHOKE DIP

Prep Time: 1 Hour
Yields: 8 Servings

Comment:

This dip is a delightful blend of two Louisiana favorites: oysters and artichokes. Served hot, the dip is an excellent alternative to oysters Rockefeller or oysters Bienville. Try topping oysters on the half shell with the mixture before baking.

Ingredients:

1 pint fresh oysters, drained and chopped
1 (14-ounce) can artichoke hearts, drained and chopped
¼ cup butter
¼ cup diced onions
¼ cup diced celery
½ cup diced red bell peppers
½ cup diced yellow bell peppers
¼ cup minced garlic
1 tsp lemon juice
¼ tsp chopped tarragon
1 cup heavy whipping cream
¼ cup chopped parsley
salt and black pepper to taste
Louisiana hot sauce to taste
1 cup Italian bread crumbs
½ cup grated Parmesan cheese
paprika for color

Method:

Preheat oven to 350°F. In a large heavy-bottomed cast iron skillet, melt butter over medium-high heat. Add onions, celery, bell peppers and garlic. Sauté 3–5 minutes or until vegetables are wilted. Stir in lemon juice, tarragon, whipping cream and artichokes. Bring mixture to a rolling boil, reduce to simmer and cook 5 minutes. Fold in oysters and cook to render juices. Simmer 5 minutes then add parsley. Remove from heat and season to taste using salt, pepper and hot sauce. Sprinkle in bread crumbs and stir well to absorb liquid. Using the back of cooking spoon, smooth mixture well into skillet. Top with Parmesan cheese and paprika. Bake 15–20 minutes, until heated thoroughly and slightly brown. Serve in the cast iron skillet with French bread croutons.

POINT HOUMAS GRILLED OYSTERS

Prep Time: 1 Hour
Yields: 6 Servings

Comment:
Historically, oysters were often used as a main ingredient at many Louisiana plantations. An abundant supply of Gulf oysters was transported up the Mississippi River allowing easy access to plantation tables.

Ingredients:
36 fresh shucked oysters, reserve shells
¼ pound butter
¼ cup olive oil
¼ cup minced onions
¼ cup minced celery
¼ cup minced red bell peppers
1 tbsp minced garlic
¼ cup lemon juice
dash of Worcestershire sauce
pinch of thyme
pinch of basil
pinch of oregano
salt and cracked black pepper to taste
Louisiana hot sauce to taste
1 cup grated Parmesan cheese
½ cup chopped parsley

Method:
A backyard barbecue pit is best when preparing this dish. The grill seems to impart a unique flavor to the oysters. However, the recipe works fine in a conventional oven. Scrub the oyster shells well to remove all grit and sand and hold in cold, salted water. Place empty shells on the grill to heat thoroughly for 5 minutes. While shells are heating, melt butter in a cast iron skillet over medium-high heat. Add olive oil, onions, celery, bell peppers and garlic. Sauté 3–5 minutes or until vegetables are wilted. Stir in lemon juice, Worcestershire, thyme, basil and oregano. Season lightly with salt, pepper and hot sauce. Place raw oysters in the hot shells and top with 1 teaspoon of sauce and a sprinkle of cheese. Grill for 3–4 minutes or until oysters begin to curl. Garnish with chopped parsley and serve hot off the grill.

OYSTERS MARIE LAVEAU

Prep Time: 1 Hour
Yields: 6 Servings

Comment:
Marie Laveau was the voodoo queen of Bourbon Street. Legend has it that the pirate Jean Lafitte often met Marie at the Old Absinthe House late in the evening where they enjoyed oysters on the half shell while trading secrets of Barataria Bay.

Ingredients for Oysters:
3 dozen select oysters, reserve liquid
3 tbsps butter
1 tsp garlic
1 tsp chopped parsley
½ ounce Pernod or Herbsaint

Method:
In a heavy-bottomed sauté pan, melt butter over medium-high heat. Stir in garlic and parsley and sauté 2 minutes. Add oysters and cook until edges begin to curl, but do not overcook. Deglaze with Pernod and cook 1 minute. Remove oysters, reduce liquid to half volume and reserve for sauce.

Ingredients for Sauce:
¼ pound butter
½ cup diced onions
¼ cup diced celery
2 tbsps minced garlic
¼ cup sliced green onions
½ cup white crabmeat
    OR ½ cup chopped cooked shrimp
2½ tbsps flour
3 cups heavy whipping cream
1 ounce dry white wine
reserved cooked liquid from oysters
reserved oyster liquid
⅛ tsp nutmeg
¼ cup diced red bell peppers
¼ cup diced yellow bell peppers
salt and cracked black pepper to taste

Method:
Preheat oven to 375°F. In a 1-quart heavy-bottomed saucepan, melt butter over medium-high heat. Add onions, celery, garlic and green onions and sauté 3 minutes. Stirring constantly, add crabmeat or shrimp and sauté 1 minute. Whisk in flour until a white roux is achieved then whisk in cream and wine. Bring to a low boil, stirring constantly as mixture thickens. Pour in cooked liquid from oysters and reserved oyster liquid. Reduce heat to simmer and cook 10–15 minutes, adding hot water if the sauce becomes too thick. Add nutmeg and bell peppers then season to taste using salt and pepper. Place 6 oysters each in au gratin dishes, top with a generous serving of sauce and bake until bubbly. You may wish to sprinkle Parmesan cheese on top prior to baking. Serve with garlic croutons.

Oysters Rockefeller

OYSTERS ROCKEFELLER

Prep Time: 1 Hour
Yields: 6 Servings

Comment:
This famous Louisiana oyster appetizer was created by Jules Alciatore in 1899. Because of the incredibly rich flavor of Rockefeller sauce, it has been adapted for use as a topping in many other dishes.

Ingredients:
2 dozen shucked oysters, reserve
   liquid and shells
¼ pound butter
¼ cup diced onions
¼ cup diced celery
½ cup sliced green onions
2 tbsps minced garlic
2 (10-ounce) packages cooked frozen
   spinach, thawed
2 tbsps flour
1 cup heavy whipping cream
½ ounce Pernod or Herbsaint
½ cup tomato sauce
1 tsp sugar
2 tbsp Worcestershire sauce
1 tsp Louisiana hot sauce
salt and cracked black pepper to taste
4 cups of rock salt

Method:
Preheat oven to 450°F. In a 2-quart saucepan, melt butter over medium-high heat. Sauté onions, celery, green onions and garlic 3–5 minutes or until wilted. Using a metal spoon, chop cooked spinach into the vegetable mixture. Cook until spinach is hot and well incorporated into seasonings. Whisk in flour, being sure to remove all lumps. Blend in whipping cream and oyster liquid, stirring constantly until sauce is thick and bubbly. Stir in Pernod, tomato sauce, sugar, Worcestershire and hot sauce then season to taste using salt and pepper. Place rock salt on the bottom of an 11"x14" baking pan to ensure the oysters will not tip over while baking. Place one oyster on each shell and top with generous serving of sauce. Set oysters on the salted pan and bake 10–15 minutes or until hot and bubbly. Serve four oysters per person.

SMOKED OYSTER SPREAD

Prep Time: 30 Minutes
Yields: 3 Cups

Comment:
This oyster spread will be a success at any party. For the best results, prepare the dish one day ahead to allow the flavors to fully develop. Place a bowl of the spread in the center of a large platter and surround with garlic croutons for a beautiful presentation.

Ingredients:
1 (4-ounce) can smoked oysters, drained and chopped
1 (8-ounce) package cream cheese, softened
1½ cups mayonnaise
¼ cup chopped green olives
1 tsp minced garlic
¼ cup chopped parsley
1 tbsp lemon juice
salt to taste
Louisiana hot sauce to taste
chopped parsley for garnish
lemon wedge for garnish

Method:
In a large mixing bowl, combine cream cheese, mayonnaise, olives, garlic and parsley. Using a wire whisk, stir until all ingredients are well blended. Stir in chopped oysters and lemon juice then season to taste using salt and hot sauce. Place the spread in a small serving bowl and garnish with parsley and a wedge of lemon.

A salty raw oyster is placed in the glass over the horseradish and garlic mixture.

Top with as much V- 8 juice as you like.

Add ice cold vodka.

Season to taste using cracked black pepper.

OYSTER SHOOTERS

Prep Time: 1 Hour
Yields: 12 Servings

Comment:

Oyster Shooters is a recipe concocted by a bartender, after all, it contains most of the ingredients for a good Bloody Mary. (See recipe.) For an interesting variation, serve the chilled liquids with warm grilled or sautéed oysters.

Ingredients:

1 dozen raw oysters
6 ounces ice cold vodka
1 cup V-8® juice
1 tbsp minced jalapeño peppers
1 tbsp minced garlic
1 tsp horseradish
⅛ tsp cracked black pepper
juice of 1 lemon

Method:

Place vodka in freezer to chill thoroughly. In a mixing bowl, combine all ingredients except oysters and vodka. Mix thoroughly and refrigerate 1 hour. When ready to serve, place 1 raw oyster into each of 12 shot glasses. Top oyster with an equal amount of horseradish mixture. Pour in ½ ounce vodka. Serve 1 as a cocktail or 3 as an appetizer. If oysters are to be served warm, pour tomato mixture in a shot glass, grill or sauté oysters, add oysters to glasses then top with vodka. Serve immediately. If preparing in front of guests, you may wish to layer the flavors as illustrated in the photographs.

NOTE: Those with immune deficiencies should only eat oysters fully cooked.

April Reid enjoys an Oyster Shooter.

SAUTÉED CHICKEN LIVERS ORLEANS

Prep Time: 30 Minutes
Yields: 6 Servings

Comment:

Chickens could always be found on the farms in early Louisiana. The accessibility of the meat allowed many unique chicken dishes to emerge from Cajun kitchens. This recipe has been served in Louisiana homes since the early 1900s and is still a favorite in New Orleans today.

Ingredients:

2 dozen chicken livers
¼ pound butter
¼ cup diced onions
¼ cup diced celery
¼ cup sliced green onions
1 tbsp minced garlic
1 bay leaf
pinch of filé powder
pinch of dried thyme
pinch of basil
2 ounces brandy
1 cup veal demi-glace (see recipe)
salt and cracked black pepper to taste
2 tbsps chopped parsley

Method:

In a heavy-bottomed sauté pan, melt butter over medium-high heat. Sauté chicken livers 5 minutes or until brown on all sides. Add onions, celery, green onions, garlic, bay leaf, filé powder, thyme and basil. Continue to sauté 3–5 minutes or until vegetables are wilted. Deglaze pan with brandy and add demi-glace. Bring to a slight boil, reduce heat to simmer and cook 5 minutes. Season to taste using salt and pepper. Remove from heat and add parsley for color. Serve four pieces of liver covered with sauce in au gratin dish, over toast points or with pasta.

CHICKEN LIVER PÂTÉ

Prep Time: 1 Hour
Yields: 5 Cups

Comment:

This recipe is a great way to use chicken livers that may be leftover after cooking a chicken stew. Originally, the dish was prepared by boiling the livers in stock with vegetables and mashing them with butter.

Ingredients:

2 pounds fresh chicken livers
½ cup butter
¼ cup diced onions
¼ cup diced celery
1 tsp minced garlic
¼ cup sliced green onions
½ cup brandy
½ cup heavy whipping cream
salt and cracked black pepper to taste
pinch of allspice
pinch of ground thyme
Louisiana hot sauce to taste
1 cup melted butter

Method:

In a large sauté pan, melt butter over medium-high heat. Add onions, celery, garlic and green onions. Sauté 3–5 minutes or until vegetables are wilted. Stir in chicken livers. Continue to sauté for 15 minutes, stirring occasionally, until livers are thoroughly cooked. Remove pan from heat and carefully pour in brandy, as alcohol will ignite. Return to burner and allow alcohol to burn a few minutes. If using an electric stove, carefully use a kitchen match to ignite. Allow liquids to reduce to half volume. Spoon the mixture into a food processor and blend for 1 minute. Add cream, salt, pepper, allspice, thyme and hot sauce to the food processor. Continue to blend. Pour in melted butter, blending thoroughly. Spoon resulting pâté mixture into a lightly oiled 5-cup soufflé mold. Cover with clear wrap and chill in the refrigerator a minimum of 4 hours, preferably overnight. When ready to serve, unmold, place in the center of a large serving platter and surround with garlic croutons, crackers or toast points. You may wish to garnish the pâté with orange zest and fresh parsley.

BAKED SPARERIBS
PIERRE LAFITTE

Prep Time: 1½ Hours
Yields: 6–8 Servings

Comment:

Pierre Lafitte, brother of the pirate Jean Lafitte, was rumored to be quite a cook. He was excellent at making candies and jellies. This wonderful spareribs dish is said to be another of Pierre's culinary creations.

Ingredients:

2 pounds spareribs
¼ cup butter
¼ cup minced onions
1 tbsp minced garlic
1½ cups mayhaw or muscadine jelly
¼ cup Louisiana cane syrup
¼ cup soy sauce
pinch of ground ginger
salt and cracked black pepper to taste
Louisiana hot sauce to taste

Method:

Have your butcher cut spareribs into individual pieces then again across the center to form 2–3-inch pieces. Rinse ribs in cold water, drain well, place in a large bowl and season lightly with salt and pepper. Set aside. In a heavy-bottomed cast iron skillet, melt butter over medium-high heat. Add onions and garlic. Sauté 3–5 minutes or until vegetables are wilted. Whisk in jelly, cane syrup and soy sauce until well blended. Reduce heat to low then season to taste using ginger, salt, pepper and hot sauce. Remove sauce from heat and pour over the ribs. Blend well, cover and place into refrigerator 3–4 hours. Once ribs have marinated, preheat oven to 350°F. Pour the ribs onto an oiled 11″ x 14″ baking sheet with 1-inch lip, separate and cook uncovered for 1 hour.

FRIED BOUDIN BALLS

Prep Time: 30 Minutes
Yields: 4 Servings

Comment:

This traditional sausage is normally poached and served hot as a breakfast or luncheon item. Today, boudin is prepared in many ways including grilled on hot French bread as a sandwich. One very popular way to serve boudin is to deep fry a breaded, golf-ball-sized portion and serve it hot with a glass of cold beer.

Ingredients:

2 links boudin
2 cups oil
2 cups corn flour

salt and cracked black pepper to taste
pinch of thyme
pinch of basil

Method:

Preheat oil to 375°F. Season flour with salt, pepper, thyme and basil. Cut boudin into 2-inch slices and roll each piece into a ball. Dust each ball in flour, shaking off excess. Fry 3–5 minutes or until golden brown. Serve hot.

SPICY MEATBALLS

Prep Time: 1 Hour
Yields: 3 Dozen

Comment:

Most Cajuns love hot and spicy food. In the fall of the year, Tabasco, cayenne and jalapeño peppers can be seen growing in many bayou gardens. This recipe most likely evolved when a Cajun family threw slices of these hot peppers into a pot of meatballs being prepared for a holiday treat or a wedding.

Ingredients for Meatballs:

½ pound ground beef
½ pound ground pork
¼ cup minced onions
¼ cup minced celery
¼ cup minced red bell peppers
1 tbsp minced garlic
2 eggs
salt and cracked black pepper to taste
pinch of thyme
pinch of basil
Louisiana hot sauce to taste
¾ cup Italian bread crumbs

Method:

In a large mixing bowl, combine meats, onions, celery, bell peppers, garlic and eggs. Using your hands, blend all ingredients well. Season to taste using salt, pepper, thyme, basil and hot sauce. Continue to mix until seasonings are well blended. Mix in bread crumbs. Shape mixture into 1-inch meatballs.

Ingredients for Sauce:

¼ cup butter
½ cup ketchup
½ cup barbecue sauce
1 tbsp minced jalapeño, Tabasco or cayenne peppers
2 tbsps brown sugar
1 tbsp Louisiana cane syrup
1 tbsp red wine vinegar
1 tsp Creole mustard
dash of Worcestershire sauce
salt to taste
Louisiana hot sauce to taste
¼ cup chopped parsley

Method:

In a 14-inch sauté pan, melt butter over medium-high heat. Add meatballs and brown on all sides. Remove meatballs from pan and set aside. In the same pan, whisk together ketchup, barbecue sauce, jalapeños, brown sugar, cane syrup and vinegar. Add mustard, Worcestershire, salt and hot sauce. Continue to whisk until ingredients begin to simmer. Place cooked meatballs into sauce, reduce heat to simmer and cook 15–20 minutes. Sprinkle in fresh parsley. Transfer meatballs and sauce to a chafing dish and serve hot.

PEPPERED HAM SALAD

Prep Time: 30 Minutes
Yields: 6 Servings

Comment:
Jalapeños add just enough heat to this ham salad to entice your taste buds. The salad may be used as a filling for party sandwiches or as a topping for crisp lettuce.

Ingredients:
3 cups diced cooked ham
¼ cup minced celery
¼ cup minced yellow bell peppers
¼ cup minced black olives
2 tbsps minced pimientos
1 tbsp minced jalapeño peppers
2 cups mayonnaise
½ cup sliced green onions
1 tbsp Worcestershire sauce
salt and black pepper to taste
Louisiana hot sauce to taste

Method:
In a food processor, finely mince cooked ham. Place ham in a mixing bowl and, using a wooden spoon, blend in celery, bell peppers, olives, pimientos, jalapeños, mayonnaise and green onions. Stir in Worcestershire, salt, pepper and hot sauce. Refrigerate before serving.

GERTIE'S BREAD AND BUTTER PICKLES

Prep Time: 2 Hours
Yields: 4–5 Pints

Comment:
Nobody made better bread & butter pickles than Donaldsonville, La. native, Gertrude Connell. Gertie's husband, Joe, would grow cucumbers and pick them when they were about 3–4 inches long. Gertie would jar her pickles and onions and save the delicacy for Christmas gifts.

Ingredients:
4 pounds cucumbers, 3–4 inches long
2 large Bermuda onions, sliced
½ cup kosher salt
2½ cups granulated sugar
½ tsp celery seed
½ tsp mustard seed
½ tsp ground turmeric
3 cups cider vinegar
1 teaspoon crushed red pepper flakes

Method:
Using the slicing blade of a food processor, or a short paring knife, slice cucumbers as thin as possible. In a large ceramic bowl, layer cucumbers, onions and salt, cover with water and refrigerate overnight. Using a colander, drain the cucumbers and onions well and refrigerate until ready to use. In a 2-gallon saucepan, combine sugar, celery seed, mustard seed, turmeric, vinegar and pepper flakes. Bring mixture to a boil and stir occasionally until sugar is completely dissolved. When mixture has reached a rolling boil, add chilled cucumber mixture and stir to heat the contents evenly. When the mixture returns to a low boil, reduce heat, but keep hot. Using a slotted spoon, fill hot sterilized jars with cucumbers and onions to 1-inch from the top. Once all the jars are filled, cover with the boiling syrup almost to overflowing. Divide any remaining spices that have fallen to the bottom of the saucepot evenly among the jars. Seal jars tightly and label. Store pickles 60–90 days before using.

BACON AND ROASTED BELL PEPPER FINGER SANDWICHES

Prep Time: 30 Minutes
Yields: 80 Finger Sandwiches

Comment:
Roasted peppers and bacon create a creamy, smoky spread that produces delightful finger sandwiches for any occasion.

Ingredients:
4 pounds bacon
3–4 whole bell peppers
2 loaves sandwich bread
¼ cup minced celery
12 hard boiled eggs, chopped
16 ounces cream cheese
16 ounces mayonnaise
½ cup sliced green onions
salt and cracked black pepper to taste
Louisiana hot sauce to taste

Method:
To roast peppers, place whole peppers directly over the open flame or under the broiler of your stove, turning frequently. Broil on all sides until skin blisters and blackens. Remove peppers from flame and place into a brown paper bag for 10–15 minutes. Peel the blistered skin from the pepper under cold running water. Seed peeled peppers and slice or chop. Trim the crust off bread slices and set aside. In a cast iron skillet, fry bacon until crisp. Drain and crumble. In a large mixing bowl, combine bacon, bell peppers, celery, eggs, cream cheese, mayonnaise and green onions. Season to taste using salt, pepper and hot sauce. Spread mixture onto bread and cut into various shapes. Refrigerate before serving.

DAUBE GLACÉ

Prep Time: 2½ Hours
Yields: 12–15 Servings

Comment:

Daube glacé is a classic Creole hors d'oeuvre. Daube is traditionally beef braised with vegetables. This glacé is made with leftover cooked daube, which is seasoned and set with gelatin. Any combination of leftover meats can be used in this glacé, for example, chicken, turkey, ham, or pork. You can use any type of terrine mold. During the holidays, try using a festive shape to add a little flair to your table.

Ingredients:

1 (3-pound) cooked daube (see recipe)
2 quarts beef stock
reserved sauce from precooked daube
½ cup minced onions
½ cup minced celery
½ cup minced red bell peppers
¼ cup minced garlic
½ cup minced carrots
½ cup chopped parsley
salt and cayenne pepper to taste
3 envelopes unflavored gelatin, dissolved in ¾ cup warm water

Method:

In a cast iron Dutch oven, bring beef stock and sauce from cooked daube to a light boil. Cut cooked daube into 1-inch cubes. Combine daube, onions, celery, bell peppers and garlic with sauce. Reduce heat to simmer and allow to cook until meat becomes very tender and easily shreds apart. Strain all ingredients from liquid through a fine sieve and set aside. Return liquid to heat and reduce to 1½ quarts. Add carrots and parsley then season to taste using salt and cayenne pepper. Whisk dissolved gelatin into sauce. Remove from heat and allow to cool slightly. Break the meat into small pieces and place equal amounts into two terrine molds. Divide cooked vegetables from the original sauce between the two molds. Ladle stock over the meat, cover with plastic wrap and allow to set in the refrigerator. Daube glacé is best when allowed to sit for 24 hours for flavors to develop. When set, slice daube glacé and serve with garlic croutons.

HOG'S HEAD CHEESE

Prep Time: 3 Hours
Yields: 5 Loaves (10 servings per loaf)

Comment:

Many cooks today feel that hog's head cheese is a country rendition of the more classical daube glacé. Though similar in nature, hog's head cheese is actually the by-product of sausage making and has been around for hundreds of years.

Ingredients for Stock:

1 hog's head, halved
4 pounds Boston butt
4 pig's feet
3 large onions, quartered
4 stalks of celery, quartered
1 head of garlic, halved
2 bay leaves
1 tsp salt
1 tsp black pepper

Method:

Place all ingredients in a large stockpot. Cover ingredients with 6-inches of cold water. Bring to a rolling boil, reduce heat to simmer and cook 2½ hours or until meat is tender and falling from bones. Using a ladle, skim off the foam that rises to the top of the pot during the cooking process. Adjust seasonings with salt and pepper. When meat is tender, remove, strain and reserve poaching liquid. Bone meat and grind using the chili blade of your meat grinder. Set aside.

Ingredients for Cheese:

4 packages unflavored gelatin
cooked ground pork
reserved poaching liquid
2 cups minced onions
2 cups minced celery
2 cups minced red bell peppers
¼ cup minced garlic
salt and black pepper to taste
Louisiana hot sauce to taste
2 cups sliced green onions
1 cup chopped parsley

Method:

Once the poaching liquid has been strained and allowed to sit for 1–2 hours, oil will form on top. Using a ladle, carefully remove all oil from the surface of the liquid. Dissolve gelatin in 1 cup of cooled poaching liquid. Place the cooked ground pork, onions, celery, bell peppers and garlic in a large pot. Cover ingredients with reserved stock by ½-inch, bring to a rolling boil, reduce to simmer and allow to cook 25–30 minutes. While cooking, add stock to retain volume. Season to taste with salt, pepper and hot sauce. Remove from heat, stir in green onions, parsley and dissolved gelatin. Allow to cool slightly. Ladle the cheese into five 4"x 9" loaf pans, cover with clear wrap and refrigerate overnight.

VENISON AND LOUISIANA YAM SAUSAGE

Prep Time: 1 Hour
Yields: 70 Links

Comment:

Both the Germans and the Cajuns of Louisiana are famous for making and curing meat. There has been an ongoing debate between these groups over the actual origin of many of our popular sausages. This venison and yam sausage is great as an appetizer or a breakfast item.

Ingredients:

10 pounds ground venison
5 sweet potatoes
10 pounds ground pork
3 pounds ground pork fat
¼ cup butter
2 cups minced shallots
1 cup minced garlic
5 tsps chopped thyme
6 tbsps chopped sage
3 tbsps chopped tarragon
5 ounces salt
4 tbsps black pepper
3 cups ice water
35–40 feet sausage casing

Method:

Peel sweet potatoes and dice into ¼-inch cubes. Poach in lightly salted water until potatoes are al dente, but not overcooked. Chill potatoes immediately in ice water, drain well, spread on a large cookie sheet and freeze for later use. In a heavy-bottomed skillet, melt butter over medium-high heat. Add shallots and garlic. Sauté 3–5 minutes or until vegetables are wilted. Remove from heat and allow to cool. Place the ground venison, pork and fat into a large mixing bowl. Add sautéed seasonings, thyme, sage, tarragon, salt and pepper. Mix in ice water to retain moisture and to keep the fat congealed. NOTE: It is always a good idea to sauté a small piece of the sausage mixture to test seasonings before stuffing casing. Remove diced sweet potatoes from the freezer and fold into the meat mixture. Stuff the mixture into the sausage casing and tie off in 6-inch links.

MALLARD DUCK SAUSAGE

Prep Time: 1 Hour
Yields: 20 Links

Comment:

Although duck is the main ingredient in this dish, the sausage can be made using any type of wild game including rabbit, venison and alligator. When duck is not available, try one of these other, equally enjoyable variations. The sausage can also be made with Long Island or domestic duck meat.

Ingredients:

2½ pounds wild mallard duck, boned
2½ pounds pork
½ pound pork fat
½ pound bacon
¼ pound butter
2 cups diced onions
1 cup diced celery
½ cup sliced green onions
2 tbsps minced garlic
½ cup port
¼ cup cognac
1 tbsp dried thyme
1 tbsp cracked black pepper
½ cup chopped parsley
salt and cayenne pepper to taste
10–12 feet (35–38 mm) sausage casing

Method:

Grind duck, pork, pork fat and bacon using the fine cutting blade of a meat grinder. Once ground, place in a mixing bowl and remove all visible sinew and bone that may have passed through cutting blade. Set aside. In a heavy-bottomed sauté pan, melt butter over medium-high heat. Sauté onions, celery, green onions and garlic until wilted. Remove from heat and add port and cognac. Return to burner carefully, as cognac will ignite on an open flame. If using an electric range, carefully ignite using a kitchen match. Cognac will burn 2 minutes. Reduce liquid to half volume. Blend in thyme and black pepper. Remove from heat and cool to room temperature. Once cool, add sautéed vegetable mixture to ground meat and blend well. Mix in parsley for color. Season to taste using salt and cayenne pepper. To check for proper seasoning, form a small patty and sauté in hot oil for a few minutes. Taste and adjust seasonings if necessary. Stuff into casing using the sausage attachment of a meat grinder or take the mixture to your local butcher for stuffing. Poach links in simmering water for 5–10 minutes. Slice sausage into 1-inch pieces and serve with Creole mustard as an hors d'oeuvre or leave links whole and serve as an appetizer. You may wish to use a Beurre Cajun or Creole (see recipes) to accompany the dish.

SPINACH AND ANDOUILLE SOUFFLÉ

Prep Time: 1½ Hours
Yields: 6–8 Servings

Comment:
The word soufflé will often scare cooks. However, this is one soufflé recipe that can be accomplished by even the most inexperienced chef. Since spinach is available all year long, fresh or frozen, there is no excuse not to attempt this dish.

Ingredients:
3 pkgs frozen leaf spinach
1 cup minced andouille
¼ cup butter
¼ cup minced onions
¼ cup minced celery
¼ cup minced red bell peppers
1 tbsp minced garlic
salt and cracked black pepper to taste
pinch of nutmeg
1½ cups milk
3 eggs, beaten
1 cup bread crumbs
1 cup grated Swiss cheese

Method:
Preheat oven to 350°F. Butter a 6-cup soufflé mold, line the bottom with wax or parchment paper and set aside. Thaw spinach in refrigerator overnight. Using a colander, drain and squeeze out all excess liquid from spinach. Place spinach on a cutting board and, using a sharp French knife, chop until almost puréed. You may chop the spinach in a food processor, but be careful not to over-chop. In a large sauté pan, melt butter over medium-high heat. Add onions, celery, bell peppers and garlic. Sauté 3–5 minutes or until wilted. Stir in andouille and continue to cook 2–3 minutes. Blend spinach into the mixture, cover the pan and, stirring occasionally, cook 5–10 minutes or until done. Season to taste using salt, pepper and nutmeg. Remove from heat then slowly blend in milk and eggs, stirring constantly. Stir in bread crumbs and cheese. Once blended, pour soufflé mixture into buttered mold and place in baking pan with a 3-inch lip. Pour 1-inch of water into pan to form a bath around the mold. Bake 45 minutes to 1 hour or until a knife inserted into the soufflé comes out clean. NOTE: You may make the soufflé and freeze it uncooked. The frozen mixture will need to bake 1½ hours.

Smokehouse Row

PANZANELLA

Prep Time: 30 Minutes
Yields: 4 Servings

Comment:

This Old World delicacy was brought here from Italy. The simple dish combines ingredients that develop an indescribable flavor. Try Panzanella as an hors d'oeuvre or as a garnish for any Italian or Southwestern dish.

Ingredients:

3 cups diced Creole tomatoes
¾ cup grated Parmesan cheese
2 tbsps chopped basil
¼ cup red wine vinegar
1 tsp chopped thyme
½ cup extra virgin olive oil
salt and black pepper to taste
25 whole basil leaves
25 French bread croutons, toasted

Method:

In a large mixing bowl, combine all ingredients except whole basil leaves and croutons. Blend well, cover and refrigerate 1–2 hours. When ready to serve, place one whole basil leaf on top of a crouton and top with 1 heaping tablespoon of Panzanella.

MULTI-TASK YOUR MADELEINE

Perfect on its own, Spinach Madeleine can also be combined with a variety of exotic or even mundane ingredients to create new, delightful dishes. For example, you can spruce it up for the holidays simply by adding ¼ cup diced red bell peppers when you sauté the onions. Here is a sampling of the many dishes that can be made from this versatile casserole.

Spinach & Crabmeat Bisque: Add 1 pound jumbo lump crabmeat and 1 quart half-and-half (or more for desired consistency) then season with salt and pepper. Simmer approximately 15 minutes.

Crawfish Spinach Dip: Add 1 pound Louisiana crawfish tails when you add the cheese and serve warm with tortilla chips.

Oyster-Stuffed Artichokes Rockefeller: Add 1 tablespoon Herbsaint liqueur and ½ cup Italian bread crumbs when you add the spinach to the cheese mixture. Then, using canned artichoke bottoms, place 1 oyster in the center of each artichoke. Cover each oyster with a heaping teaspoon of Spinach Madeleine and bake at 350° F until bubbly.

Spinach Madeleine Cauliflower Casserole: In a 3-quart casserole dish place 1 large head of boiled cauliflower florets. Top with Spinach Madeleine and seasoned Italian bread crumbs. Bake at 350°F until top is golden brown.

SPINACH MADELEINE

Prep Time: 30 Minutes
Yields: 5–6 Servings

Comment:
This traditional Louisiana recipe has received acclaim around the world. The surprising kick of the jalapeños and the overall cheesy, velvety character of the dish make it quite distinctive.

Ingredients:
2 packages frozen, chopped spinach
4 tbsps butter
2 tbsps diced onions
2 tbsps flour
½ cup evaporated milk
½ cup reserved spinach liquor
1 tsp Worcestershire sauce
½ tsp black pepper
¾ tsp celery salt
¾ tsp garlic salt
6 ounces Monterey Jack cheese, sliced into ¼-inch cubes
1 tbsp minced jalapeños
salt and cayenne pepper to taste
buttered bread crumbs, (optional)

Method:
Cook spinach according to directions on package. Drain and reserve ½ cup of liquid. In a medium saucepan, melt butter over low heat. Add onions and sauté 3–5 minutes or until wilted. Whisk in flour, stirring until blended and smooth, but not brown. Slowly stir in evaporated milk, spinach liquor and Worcestershire sauce. Stirring constantly, cook mixture until smooth and thick. Add pepper, celery salt, garlic salt, cheese and jalapeños. Stir until cheese is melted then combine with cooked spinach. Season to taste with salt and cayenne pepper. The dish may be served immediately. However, the flavor is improved if you put the mixture into a casserole, top with buttered bread crumbs, cover and refrigerate overnight. Just before serving, reheat uncovered in a 350˚F oven until golden brown.

SPANISH OLIVE TAPENADE

Prep Time: 1 Hour
Yields: 1 Cup

Comment:

Spanish manzanilla olives are small, slightly sweet green olives available on most supermarket shelves. Spanish olive oil has a smooth, sweet flavor reminiscent of fruit and almonds that mellows the flavor of this tapenade. This appetizer is wonderful when spread on toasted croutons and served alongside almonds and dried cherries with a Fino sherry.

Ingredients:

1½ cups pitted Spanish manzanilla olives
1 clove garlic, minced
1 tsp capers, drained
¼ cup extra virgin Spanish olive oil
1 tsp lemon juice
2 tbsps chopped cilantro leaves
cracked black pepper to taste

Method:

In a food processor, combine olives, garlic and capers. Process until just smooth, scraping down the sides of the bowl if necessary. With the machine running, slowly drizzle in oil and lemon juice through the feed tube and process until well blended. Transfer mixture to a bowl and fold in cilantro and pepper. Let sit at room temperature for 1 hour to allow flavors to develop.

CAPONATA

Prep Time: 2 Hours
Yields: 15 Servings

Comment:
This classic Italian eggplant dish may be served as a salad or antipasto. This recipe makes a large amount of caponata. You may preserve the excess by packing it into hot, sterilized Mason jars and boiling for 15 minutes.

Ingredients:
8 medium eggplants, peeled and cubed
1 cup olive oil
3 cups diced onions
3 cups diced celery
1 cup diced red bell peppers
¼ cup minced garlic
2 cups tomato paste
2 cups tomato sauce
⅔ cup sugar
1½ cups red wine vinegar
1 (22-ounce) jar salad olives, diced
2 tsps oregano
salt and cayenne pepper to taste
Louisiana hot sauce to taste

Method:
Place eggplant in a large pot and cover with 1-inch of hot water. Bring to a rolling boil, reduce to simmer and cook 10–15 minutes. Drain and set aside. In a large heavy-bottomed sauté pan, heat oil over medium-high heat. Add onions, celery, bell peppers and garlic. Sauté 3–5 minutes or until vegetables are wilted. Blend in tomato paste, tomato sauce, sugar and vinegar. Simmer 10–15 minutes then stir in drained eggplant and olives. Season to taste using oregano, salt, cayenne pepper and hot sauce. Cook 30–45 minutes or until eggplant is extremely tender and full-flavored. You may wish to serve caponata as an appetizer with crackers or French bread croutons or as a vegetable.

CREOLE CAPONATA

Prep Time: 1 Hour
Yields: 6–8 Servings

Comment:

This traditional Italian eggplant dish has been redefined here as Creole with the addition of yellow squash and zucchini. Caponata is perfect for jarring or canning and can be refrigerated, eaten cold or served warm as a vegetable or side dish.

Ingredients:

½ cup extra virgin olive oil
⅓ cup corn oil
8 whole cloves garlic
1 medium white onion, thinly sliced
½ yellow bell pepper, sliced
½ red bell pepper, sliced
¼ cup diced jalapeño peppers
2 cups sliced yellow squash, skin-on
2 cups sliced zucchini, skin-on
2 cups diced eggplant, skin-on
2 cups peeled, diced tomatoes
¼ cup basil leaves
salt and black pepper to taste

Method:

In a large sauté pan, heat oils over medium-high heat. Add garlic, onions and bell peppers. Cook 2–3 minutes, stirring occasionally. Stir in peppers, squash, zucchini and eggplant. Stirring occasionally, cook 15 minutes or until ingredients are al dente. Add tomatoes and basil and continue to cook 5–7 minutes. Season to taste using salt and pepper.

ROASTED ONION AND EGGPLANT PÂTÉ

Prep Time: 1 Hour
Yields: 6 Servings

Comment:

This pâté is a rich, savory mixture that is wonderful when served as a dip or on croutons or crackers.

Ingredients:

1 large onion, quartered
1 medium eggplant
olive oil
1 cup cream cheese
1 clove garlic
pinch of chili powder
salt and black pepper to taste
lemon or lime juice to taste

Method:

Preheat oven to 425°F. Place onion quarters on a baking sheet with whole eggplant. Season lightly with salt and pepper then drizzle with olive oil. Roast for 45 minutes or until eggplant is blackened and the skin is wrinkled. Allow eggplant to cool then remove skin and cut off the end of the vegetable and discard. Place whole, peeled eggplant in a food processor with onion, cream cheese, garlic and chili powder and blend until completely smooth. Season pâté with salt, pepper and lemon or lime juice.

EGGPLANT BELLE ROSE

Prep Time: 1 Hour
Yields: 6 Servings

Comment:

This eggplant dish, a tradition on the Louisiana table, borrows from the classical French style to produce an unforgettable blend of seafood and vegetables.

Ingredients for Batter:

1 medium eggplant
½ cup vegetable oil
½ cup milk
¼ cup water
1 egg
salt and cayenne pepper to taste
1 cup flour

Method:

In a sauté pan, preheat oil to approximately 350°F. In a mixing bowl, whisk together milk, water and egg. Season to taste using salt and cayenne pepper. Cut six ¼-inch thick slices from the center of the eggplant. Place slices in egg mixture and set aside. Season 1 cup of flour to taste using salt and cayenne. Remove eggplant from egg wash, dip in flour and pan fry 3 minutes on each side or until golden brown and tender to the touch. Drain and keep warm.

Ingredients for Sauce:

¼ cup melted butter
¼ cup sliced green onions
1 tsp minced garlic
¼ cup chopped mushrooms
1 pound crawfish tails or lump crabmeat
½ ounce white wine
1 tsp lemon juice
salt and cayenne pepper to taste
12 ounces brown meunière sauce (see recipe)
6 ounces hollandaise sauce (see recipe)
2 tsps chopped parsley

Method:

In a sauté pan, melt butter over medium-high heat. Sauté green onions, garlic and mushrooms 2–3 minutes. Add crawfish tails or crabmeat, stir and cook 1 minute. Deglaze pan with white wine and lemon juice then season to taste using salt and cayenne pepper. Continue cooking until seafood is thoroughly hot. Place 2 ounces of meunière sauce in center of serving plate and top with one eggplant medallion. Distribute an equal amount of seafood on each fried eggplant slice and garnish with hollandaise sauce and chopped parsley.

RED BEAN DIP

Prep Time: 1½ Hours
Yields: 10–12 Servings

Comment:

This delicious home-style dip offers an abundance of flavor and may be served hot or cold with fresh vegetables, tortilla chips or French bread croutons.

Ingredients:

1 pound dried red kidney beans
¼ cup oil
1 cup diced onions
½ cup diced celery
½ cup diced bell peppers
2 tbsps minced garlic
1 cup sliced andouille
3 quarts chicken stock
¼ cup sliced green onions
¼ cup chopped parsley
salt and black pepper to taste
Louisiana hot sauce to taste

Method:

NOTE: To reduce the cooking time, soak beans overnight in cold water. In a 5-quart Dutch oven, heat oil over medium-high heat. Add onions, celery, bell peppers, garlic and andouille. Sauté 3–5 minutes or until vegetables are wilted. Put in red beans and cover by 2-inches with chicken stock. Bring to a rolling boil, reduce to simmer and cook until beans are tender and mash easily with a fork. Strain chicken stock from pot, reserving 2 cups for later use. Place strained ingredients in a food processor and blend in 15-second intervals until beans are thoroughly mashed. Fold in green onions and parsley then season to taste using salt, pepper and hot sauce. If beans are too dense or stiff, add enough chicken stock or water to reach dip consistency. Place the finished dip into a suitable mold or chafer. NOTE: Any remaining dip may be frozen.

FROG IN THE HOLE

Prep Time: 30 Minutes
Yields: 24 Appetizers

Comment:

It's a mystery where the name of this recipe originated, but most children in Bayou Country have eaten this dish on some occasion. Cooking an egg inside of a slice of toast creates a fun dish that most kids happily eat. Any type of egg can be used, but the quail eggs make a more elegant appetizer.

Ingredients:

2 dozen quail eggs
6 slices bread
½ cup melted butter
salt and black pepper to taste
1 cup hollandaise sauce (see recipe)

Method:

Preheat an electric non-stick 11" x 14" flat griddle according to manufacturer's directions. Trim the crust from the bread and cut each slice diagonally into four triangles. Using a ¾-inch pastry cutter, cut a hole into the center of each triangle. NOTE: You may wish to use a ½-inch thick French bread crouton in the place of sliced bread. Lightly brush each side of bread slice with melted butter. Place the triangles on hot griddle and crack a quail egg into hole in each slice. Cook 2–3 minutes on one side. Using a spatula, flip and cook until golden brown. The quail egg should be cooked to medium. Garnish the toast with hollandaise sauce. NOTE: Try topping with ½ teaspoon of caviar for an interesting hors d'oeuvre.

BARBECUED PECAN HALVES

Prep Time: 20 Minutes
Yields: 8–10 Servings

Comment:

In Louisiana, pecans are found in dishes ranging from rice dressings to desserts. This recipe gives these aromatic nuts an unusual twist that makes them a great hors d'oeuvre for your next cocktail party.

Ingredients:

4 cups pecan halves
2 tbsps butter
¼ cup Worcestershire sauce
1 tsp Louisiana cane syrup
1 tbsp barbecue sauce
Louisiana hot sauce to taste
salt to taste

Method:

Preheat oven to 325°F. In a cast iron skillet, melt butter over medium-high heat. Pour in Worcestershire sauce, cane syrup, barbecue sauce and hot sauce. Stir until ingredients are well blended. Gently stir in pecan halves until well coated with barbecue mixture. Spread pecans evenly on a large cookie sheet and bake for 15 minutes, stirring occasionally. Place the pecans on a paper towel to drain and sprinkle with salt. Cool thoroughly before serving.

PICKLED OKRA

Prep Time: 30 Minutes
Yields: 1 Pint

Comment:

Cajuns love to pickle vegetables. Historically, this process dates back to the days before refrigeration when the need to preserve food by various means was essential. Although okra is normally thought of as a main ingredient in gumbo, it is often served at cocktail parties as a cold pickled appetizer.

Ingredients:

2 pounds small okra

1 cup white vinegar

¼ cup water

2 tsps plain salt

1 tsp dill seed

1 tsp celery seed

2 cloves garlic

1 tsp mustard seed

1 hot green or red pepper, sliced

Method:

Wash okra and tightly pack lengthwise in a 1-pint sterilized jar. In a saucepan, bring vinegar, water and salt to a rolling boil. Sprinkle all dry seasonings in jar and cover with hot vinegar mixture. Seal and allow to pickle 2–3 weeks at room temperature. Serve cold.

St. Joseph steamboat

Beautiful soup, so rich and green,
Waiting in a hot tureen!
Who for such dainties would not stoop?
Soup of the evening, beautiful soup!
　　　　　　Lewis Carroll "The Mock Turtle's Song"

While the exact origins of soup are unknown, culinary historians are confident that soups in some form have been a nourishing part of just about every culture for more than 10,000 years. It is believed that soups were being created and consumed long before the innovations most associated with this food—the pot and spoon. Earliest records indicate that soup and porridge-type dishes were common among all ancient peoples, but it was not until

the Bronze Age that a pot could have been made to hold them. Ancient civilizations are therefore thought to have practiced two unique cooking methods for soup. In one method, meat was boiled in water using the skin of the animal itself as the "pot" staked over or near a fire. The water boiling inside this makeshift container would simultaneously cook the meat and prevent the skin from catching fire. In the second method, stones were heated in a fire then rolled or shoveled into a hole filled with water. As the superheated stones caused the water to boil, meat, vegetables and grain were added. In both cooking methods, it is assumed the liquid was consumed along with the meat as soon as ancient civilizations devised a way to scoop it out.

Often, these boiled dishes included some type of grain or cereal. When boiled, these ingredients would expand and thicken the liquid, a technique still used today. Thickening of early soups was also achieved with bread. The word soup itself is a derivation of the Germanic word "sop," which originally referred not to the soup itself, but to the bread over which the pottage, broth or other liquid was poured. Sops were commonly used before such luxuries as individual bowls and spoons were in general use. It was a complementary relationship; the bread added heartiness to the soup, and the soup both flavored and softened the bread (a necessity with many early breads). The liquid could be sipped directly from the bowl, which was often communal, and the solids would be scooped out by hand or speared with a knife. From the word "sop" came "sup" and "suppe" as well as other cultures' terms such as zuppa, sopa and shorpa. From this variety of words it is easy to gain insight into how important a role soup played. The word "sup" was another word for "eat," and "supper" denoted the meal itself. Eventually the French settled on "soupe" to describe a liquid meal, which could be anything from a thin broth to a hearty dish more closely resembling a stew. The word "soup" remains an extremely broad term encompassing many subcategories and modes of preparation, as well as an infinite array of ingredients from the extremely mundane to the incredibly exotic.

Like soup in general, the specific origins of Louisiana gumbo are unknown and its variations too numerous to mention. The arguments over how gumbo originated and what ingredients it should include can grow quite heated. The one fact nobody questions, is that gumbo draws its name from an African word for okra. In Angola, Africa, okra was called "ki ngombo." This was passed along as "quingombo," and then later became "gombo" or "gumbo." The small green pods were brought to this country by African slaves and are used both to flavor and thicken some versions of gumbo. The term has also come to mean a compilation of disparate things, much like the Louisiana culture itself. Some contend that gumbo descended from the French court bouillon, a seasoned liquid designed to give flavor to the fish and other seafood poached therein. However the idea of eating only the poached fish and throwing out the seasoned water with the herbs and vegetables goes so strongly against the vein of the Cajun lifestyle, that it is unlikely that the classic court bouillon inspired gumbo. In addition, Cajun and Creole cuisine includes several other dishes termed "courtbouillons" which were entrées of smothered or poached seafood, later thickened with a roux. This Louisiana version was also dissimilar to classic court bouillon, because the liquid and

vegetables stayed in the pot and became part of the final dish.

Many contend that the French bouillabaisse is a more likely predecessor to gumbo. Both time-honored oral history and reliable historical studies

support the premise that such an important dish in French cooking would have evolved into a central part of Cajun and Creole cuisine. It is hard to conceive that the Creole settlers would not have made a concerted effort to adapt their beloved bouillabaisse to their new homeland. As further reinforcement of the theory that they are close cousins, both gumbo and bouillabaisse offer a Lenten variety made with greens rather than meat and seafood. In Louisiana this soup is called gumbo des herbes (literally gumbo of grass), gumbo z'herbes or even gumbo vert, which simply means "green gumbo" and is also the term for smothered greens in France. The tradition of serving gumbo des herbes on "Maundy Thursday" of Holy Week is actually adapted from the German custom of making a soup from an odd number of greens or herbs for luck and good health. Of course, the gumbo further evolved with the addition of okra from Africa and the undeniable African influence in the Creole kitchen. In addition, the Choctaw Indians taught the Cajuns and Creoles how to grind sassafras leaves into gumbo filé used to flavor and thicken the soup. Among the many gumbo "experts" in South Louisiana, you will find some who swear that the dish must have both okra and filé, others that swear by one or the other and still others who use neither.

Indeed, gumbo is the most well-known soup of Louisiana, but there are others that have been adapted to Cajun and Creole culture and are quite notable themselves. Crawfish bisque, a unique adaptation of the French original, is a prime example. The classical bisque d'écrevisse was a puréed crawfish soup flavored with consommé and mirepoix and thickened with rice. The dish was then strained and finished with cream. When Cajuns and Creoles make crawfish bisque, nothing is strained out. The vegetables remain and a dark brown Cajun roux is added to give the dish flavor and depth unlike that of classical cuisine. Additionally, crawfish heads are cleaned and stuffed with ground crawfish meat to create a garnish, and the finished product is served over rice.

Like those in Louisiana, soups around the world reflect the customs and available foods of the time period. They are often classified by the types of ingredients used and the mode of preparation. For example, the term bisque generally refers to a puréed soup which, until the 1800s, would only have been made from game birds or poultry. More recent manifestations include a base of shellfish cooked with mirepoix and seasonings of cayenne and shellfish butter—an easy jump to the Cajun and Creole bisques. Originally thickened by rice or bread fried in butter, roux is more commonly used as the thickening agent today. However some soups, such as sopa de ajo, are still thickened with a paste made of fried bread croutons seasoned with paprika. This hot garlic soup is a tradition in Spain, Italy and Southern France so it seems a natural addition to Creole cuisine.

Unlike a bisque, a potage or vegetable soup is defined in The Art & Science of Culinary Preparation as a soup containing one or more vegetables diced, brunoise, julienne or chiffonade as well as the liquids they have flavored. Potages are usually made with seasonal vegetables, kitchen trimmings, meat leftovers or any other fresh ingredients chosen at the chef's whim. Both rich and poor consumed potage in versions of varying refinement. The term potage was originally used in both France and England to mean "what is in the pot." The term became pottage in England and eventually came to denote dishes more closely related to porridges and puddings. In France, however, the term still describes a vegetable and meat soup of varying ingredients.

Before embarking on a gumbo or other Louisiana soup recipe, there are some time-honored principles that you should know. First, be sure to familiarize yourself with the section on roux and keep in mind that vegetables added to the roux will slow the cooking process. The moisture from the vegetables helps prevent the roux from burning, while allowing it to continue to brown slightly. Because the roux is crucial and easy to burn, you should have your vegetables ready to add before beginning. The order in which the vegetables are added is also important. You will notice that in almost every recipe, the onions are first and most plentiful, the celery second and the bell peppers and garlic third. While the "trinity" of onions, celery and bell peppers is omnipresent in Cajun and Creole cookery, some reserve a special place for the garlic, which ranks only second in importance to the onion in many recipes.

If the importance of stocks has not yet been impressed on you, read that section carefully before starting on soups. While water will do as a substitute, it will not add the depth of flavor achieved by a superb stock. Fish stock may be used for seafood gumbos, but shellfish stock is superior in flavor. Game and chicken stocks may also be used in other soup and bisque recipes. The stock may be added to the roux once the vegetables have become translucent and slightly caramelized. As in sauces, there are varying opinions about the temperatures of stock and roux when combining. If you do add hot

Allen J. Ellender, a U.S. Senator from Terrebonne Parish, was famous for the Cajun and Creole recipes he took with him to Washington D.C., particularly his shrimp gumbo. Ellender, who served for 35 years, would invite fellow statesman to sample his food. Among his most distinguished guests were five U.S. presidents. It is said that President Lyndon B. Johnson once dropped by uninvited to sample Ellender's gumbo. He was drawn by the delicious aroma emanating from the third floor office of the Capitol.

liquids to hot roux, beware of the splatter. Constant stirring as the liquid is added will ensure a smooth result and will allow the vegetables to continue to cook.

At this point, parsley, green onions and seasoning spices may be added. Seafood should not be added until the gumbo has reached the correct consistency, and oysters, crabmeat and filé should be added immediately prior to serving. Sausage and andouille should be added after the vegetables and directly into the roux. Poultry should be browned in the oil prior to adding the flour for the roux.

In her 1850 book, *Homes of the New World*, Swedish novelist Fredrika Bremer referred to a New Orleans gumbo as "the crown of all the savory and remarkable soups in the world—a regular elixir of life of the substantial kind. He who has once eaten gumbo may look down disdainfully upon the most genuine turtle soup." Of course, it is certainly not recommended that you refrain from eating turtle soup, for which a delicious recipe is included here. It is assured, however, that one bite of rich roux-based gumbo, and you will cease to care where it came from and ask only where more can be found. Experiment with some of the other recipes here, and you may also come to understand how the biblical Esau could sell his birthright for a "mess of pottage"—a humble bowl of lentil soup.

DOC'S PRIMO CHILI

Prep Time: 3½ Hours
Yields: 15–20 Servings

Comment:

Most cooks say the secret to great chili is to cook it a long time to get the best possible flavor. What makes this chili unique is the substitution of chicken gizzards in the place of beef or pork. This ingredient gives the recipe a healthy twist because the gizzards are not only high in flavor, but also low in fat. In addition, this dish has a flavor unlike any other chili because of the apple pie spice and cocoa powder.

Ingredients:

6 pounds ground chicken gizzards
½ cup vegetable oil
3 large onions, diced
1 cup diced celery
1 cup diced bell peppers
¼ cup minced garlic
1 (28-ounce) can tomatoes
1 (28-ounce) can V-8 juice
3 ounces beef bouillon
3 tbsps liquid smoke
½ cup beer
3 tsps cumin
6 ounces chili powder
2 tsps paprika
2 tbsps apple spice
6 tbsps ground fennel seed
1 tsp cocoa powder
salt and black pepper to taste
Louisiana hot sauce to taste
3 jalapeño peppers, seeded and diced

Method:

In a 12-quart cast iron pot, heat oil over medium-high heat. Add ground gizzards and cook until golden brown, stirring occasionally. While meat is browning, place onions, celery, bell peppers and garlic into a food processor and chop finely. When meat is golden brown, add vegetables to the pot and sauté until wilted. Blend in tomatoes, V-8, beef bouillon, liquid smoke and beer. Bring to a rolling boil then reduce to simmer. Stir in cumin, chili powder, paprika, apple spice, fennel and cocoa. Season lightly with salt, pepper, hot sauce and jalapeños. Reduce heat to simmer and cook 4 hours, stirring often. The longer chili cooks, the better it will taste. NOTE: Add 1 can of cooked kidney beans 10 minutes prior to serving if desired.

VEGETABLE CHILI

Prep Time: 2 Hours
Yields: 10–12 Servings

Comment:

The Spanish introduced many wonderful flavors and cooking techniques to Louisiana. This vegetable chili with its green chile peppers and various beans is a great example of Spanish-influenced cooking.

Ingredients:

½ pound white navy beans
½ pound red kidney beans
1 cup diced zucchini
1 cup diced summer squash
½ cup chopped broccoli
¼ cup vegetable oil
1 cup diced onions
½ cup diced celery
¼ cup diced green bell peppers
¼ cup minced garlic
2 tsps chili powder
1 (4-ounce) can diced green chiles
1 (14-ounce) can peeled tomatoes, reserve juice
5 cups cold water
salt and cracked pepper to taste
Louisiana hot sauce to taste
sprig of fresh cilantro
¼ cup chopped parsley

Method:

Combine navy and kidney beans in a colander and rinse under cold water. Place the beans in a ceramic bowl, cover with cold water and keep in refrigerator overnight. This process will reduce the cooking time by a third. When ready to cook, rinse the beans in cold water. In a cast iron pot, heat oil over medium-high heat. Add onions, celery, bell peppers and garlic. Sauté 3–5 minutes or until vegetables are wilted. Stir in beans, chili powder, chiles, tomatoes and juice. Pour in water and bring to a rolling boil. Reduce heat to simmer and cook approximately 1½ hours or until beans are tender. Add zucchini, squash and broccoli. Season to taste using salt, pepper and hot sauce. Flavor with cilantro and parsley then allow to cook until squash is tender but not mushy. Serve with hot garlic bread or corn bread sticks.

CORN AND CRAB BISQUE

Prep Time: 1 Hour
Yields: 12 Servings

Comment:

Corn was growing wild in Louisiana when the Acadians arrived in 1755. The people quickly married the flavor of Louisiana seafood to the sweet corn creating delicious dishes such as this bisque.

Ingredients:

3 cups whole kernel corn
1 pound jumbo lump crabmeat
1 cup butter
1 cup diced onions
1 cup diced celery
½ cup diced red bell peppers
¼ cup minced garlic
1 cup flour
2½ quarts shellfish stock (see recipe)
1 pint heavy whipping cream
½ cup sliced green onions
½ cup chopped parsley
salt and white pepper to taste

Method:

In a 2-gallon stockpot, melt butter over medium-high heat. Add corn, onions, celery, bell peppers and garlic. Sauté 5–10 minutes or until vegetables are wilted. Whisk in flour until white roux is achieved, but do not brown. (See roux recipes.) Slowly add stock, one ladle at a time, stirring constantly. Bring to a low boil, reduce to simmer and cook 30 minutes. Add heavy whipping cream, green onions and parsley. Continue cooking 3 minutes. Gently fold in lump crabmeat, being careful not to break lumps. Season with salt and white pepper. NOTE: Try making a stock with corncobs. Reduce liquid to 1 quart and add it into this soup in place of half the shellfish stock.

ROASTED RED PEPPER AND CRAB SOUP

Prep Time: 1 Hour
Yields: 6 Servings

Comment:
Sweet bell peppers have been a tradition in Louisiana cooking since the 1800s. As colored varieties emerged, the peppers became an important ingredient, enhancing both the flavor and color of a dish.

Ingredients:
4 red bell peppers
1 pound claw crabmeat
¼ cup butter
1 cup diced onions
½ cup diced celery
¼ cup minced garlic
¼ cup flour
2 quarts chicken stock (see recipe)
6 ounces heavy whipping cream
salt and cayenne pepper to taste
Louisiana hot sauce to taste
2 tbsps chopped parsley

Method:
To roast peppers, place whole peppers directly over the open flame or under the broiler of your stove. Turn frequently until skin blisters and blackens on all sides. Remove and place into a brown paper bag, seal tightly and let steam 10–15 minutes. Peel the blistered skin from the pepper under cold running water. Seed peppers. Dice 3 peppers and reserve the last one for garnish. NOTE: Peppers may also be blackened on a cookie sheet in a 400°F oven. In a 12-quart cast iron Dutch oven, melt butter over medium-high heat. Add onions, celery, garlic and diced bell peppers. Sauté 3–5 minutes or until vegetables are wilted. Whisk in flour until blond roux is achieved. (See roux recipes.) Blend in chicken stock. Add cream, bring to a rolling boil and reduce heat to simmer. Allow mixture to cook 30 minutes or until thickened. Purée remaining pepper in a food processor. Remove and set aside for garnish. Fold crabmeat into soup, being careful not to break lumps. Season to taste with salt, pepper and hot sauce. Serve in a large soup bowl and garnish with fresh parsley and roasted red peppers.

SPINACH AND LUMP CRABMEAT BISQUE

Prep Time: 1 Hour
Yields: 10–12 Servings

Comment:
Often in Louisiana, unlikely ingredients are found in the pots of innovative Creoles. The abundance of domesticated meats and seafood and the variety of fresh vegetables in the state contribute to the creation of the unique and interesting recipes for which Louisiana is famous.

Ingredients:
3 cups chopped spinach
½ pound jumbo lump crabmeat
1 pound claw crabmeat
¼ pound butter
½ cup diced onions
½ cup diced celery
½ cup diced yellow bell peppers
¼ cup minced garlic
1 tsp chopped tarragon
¾ cup flour
2 quarts shellfish stock (see recipe)
1 pint heavy whipping cream
½ cup sliced green onions
¼ cup chopped parsley
½ cup minced red bell peppers
salt and black pepper to taste
Louisiana hot sauce to taste

Method:
Pick through crabmeat to remove all shells and cartilage. In a cast iron Dutch oven, melt butter over medium-high heat. Add onions, celery, yellow bell peppers and garlic. Sauté 3–5 minutes or until vegetables are wilted. Stir in tarragon and 2 cups of spinach. Sauté an additional 3 minutes. Place spinach mixture into a food processor and purée. Return purée to Dutch oven and whisk flour into mixture. Slowly add shellfish stock, one ladle at a time, until soup-like consistency is achieved. Fold in claw crabmeat. Bring to a rolling boil then reduce to simmer. Cook for 30 minutes, adding stock as needed. Add heavy whipping cream, green onions, parsley and red bell peppers. Season to taste using salt, pepper and hot sauce. Immediately before serving, bring mixture to a low boil and add remaining spinach. Cook 2 minutes. Remove from heat and gently fold in lump crabmeat. Adjust seasonings if necessary.

OYSTERS ROCKEFELLER SOUP

Prep Time: 1 Hour
Yields: 12 Servings

Comment:
It is such a great concept to create a soup from the premier oyster dish of New Orleans! This soup has become famous at Lafitte's Landing Restaurant and is requested on more occasions than all other soups combined.

Ingredients:
6 dozen freshly shucked oysters
1 quart oyster liquid
1 cup butter
1 cup diced onions
1 cup diced celery
½ cup diced bell peppers
¼ cup minced garlic
1 (10-ounce) package cooked
   frozen spinach, thawed
½ cup minced andouille sausage
1 cup flour
1½ quarts chicken stock
1 pint heavy whipping cream
½ cup sliced green onions
½ cup chopped parsley
salt and white pepper to taste
½ ounce Pernod or Herbsaint

Method:
In a 2-gallon stockpot, melt butter over medium-high heat. Add onions, celery, bell peppers and garlic. Sauté 3–5 minutes or until vegetables are wilted. Using a metal spoon, chop spinach into vegetable mixture then add andouille. Whisk in flour, stirring constantly until a white roux is achieved. (See roux recipes.) Add chicken stock and oyster liquid, one ladle at a time, stirring constantly until all is incorporated. Bring to a low boil, reduce to simmer and cook 30 minutes. Add heavy whipping cream, oysters, green onions and parsley. Continue to cook until edges of oysters begin to curl. Season to taste using salt and white pepper. Stir in Pernod or Herbsaint. Adjust seasonings if necessary. This soup may be garnished with diced yams. NOTE: It is absolutely necessary to use oyster liquid in this recipe. Give your seafood supplier ample time to reserve 1 quart.

LOUISIANA OYSTER SOUP

Prep Time: 1 Hour
Yields: 8 Servings

Comment:
Many Cajun and Creole fishermen prepared meals for their families while fishing on boats in the Gulf of Mexico. These meals would always contain seafood from the day's catch. This oyster soup was a favorite among the fishermen.

Ingredients:
1 quart fresh oysters, drained
3 tbsps olive oil
2 cups diced onions
1 cup diced celery
½ cup diced bell peppers
¼ cup minced garlic
1½ cups diced salt meat
1 (8-ounce) can tomato sauce
3 quarts water
1 cup chopped parsley
½ cup sliced green onions
2 tbsps Worcestershire sauce
½ pound spaghetti
salt and black pepper to taste
Louisiana hot sauce to taste

Method:
In a large cast iron Dutch oven, heat olive oil over medium-high heat. Add onions, celery, bell peppers, garlic and salt meat. Sauté 3–5 minutes or until vegetables are wilted. Continue to cook until salt meat is light brown, being careful not to scorch vegetables. Reduce heat to medium then mix in tomato sauce. Cook, stirring often, for 5–10 minutes or until tomato sauce thickens and turns slightly brown. Fold in oysters, cover and allow juices to render. Add water, parsley, green onions and Worcestershire. Bring to a rolling boil, reduce to simmer and allow to cook uncovered for 10–15 minutes. Add spaghetti and stir occasionally until tender. Season to taste with salt, pepper and hot sauce. This soup is best when served over saltine crackers.

SHE-CRAB SOUP

Prep Time: 1 Hour
Yields: 6 Servings

Comment:

It is easy to distinguish between a male crab and a female crab by looking at its underside. An easier and safer way to differentiate the two without getting pinched is to look at the color of the claws. Female crabs have red tips on their pinchers, which makes it look like their fingernails are painted.

Ingredients:

1 pound jumbo lump crabmeat
½ cup crab roe
¼ cup butter
½ cup minced onions
¼ cup minced celery
¼ cup minced red bell peppers
1 tbsp minced garlic
2 tbsps flour
3 cups milk
2 cups heavy whipping cream
½ tsp ground mace
1 tsp grated lemon peel
salt and black pepper to taste
¼ cup dry sherry
1 tsp paprika
2 tbsps chopped parsley

Method:

Pick through crabmeat to remove all shell and cartilage. Chop roe and set aside. In a Dutch oven, melt butter over medium-high heat. Add onions, celery, bell peppers and garlic. Sauté 3–5 minutes or until vegetables are wilted. Sprinkle in flour, blending well into vegetable mixture. Add milk and whipping cream. Season with mace, lemon peel, salt and pepper. Bring to a low boil, reduce to simmer and add half of crabmeat. Cook 10–15 minutes, stirring occasionally. Adjust salt and pepper if necessary. Add roe, remaining crabmeat, and sherry. Return to a low boil and heat crabmeat thoroughly. Garnish with a pinch of paprika and parsley. NOTE: If buying whole crabs, you will need 8 or 9 large females to get enough meat for 6 people.

OYSTER AND ARTICHOKE BISQUE

Prep Time: 1 Hour
Yields: 12 Servings

Comment:

Gulf oysters add rich flavor and depth to many Louisiana dishes. One of the most famous soups using this shellfish is the cream-based oyster stew of New Orleans. This bisque of oyster and artichokes was first shared with other Louisiana restaurants by Chef Warren Leruth of LeRuth's Restaurant in Gretna, La. It was the state's first Mobil Five-Star restaurant.

Ingredients:

6 dozen freshly shucked oysters
1 quart oyster liquid
8 artichoke bottoms, sliced and uncooked
1 cup butter
1 cup chopped onions
1 cup chopped celery
½ cup chopped bell peppers
¼ cup diced garlic
1 cup flour
1½ quarts chicken stock
1 pint heavy whipping cream
1 cup sliced green onions
1 cup chopped parsley
salt and white pepper to taste

Method:

In a 2-gallon stockpot, melt butter over medium-high heat. Add onions, celery, bell peppers, garlic and artichoke bottoms. Sauté 5–10 minutes or until vegetables are wilted and artichokes are tender. Place vegetable mixture into a food processor. Process on high speed approximately 1 minute or until mixture is puréed. Return to stockpot and bring back to a simmer. Whisk in flour, stirring constantly until white roux is achieved. (See roux recipes.) Add chicken stock and oyster liquid, one ladle at a time, stirring constantly. Bring to a low boil, reduce to simmer and cook 30 minutes. Stir in heavy whipping cream, oysters, green onions and parsley. Return to a boil, and cook until edges of oysters begin to curl. Season to taste using salt and white pepper. NOTE: It is absolutely necessary to use oyster liquid in this recipe. Give your seafood supplier ample time to reserve 1 quart.

BISQUE OF
LOUISIANA CRAWFISH

Prep Time: 1 Hour
Yields: 6–8 Servings

Comment:

The term "crawfish bisque" has two meanings in Louisiana. The early Cajuns created a bisque by stuffing the cleaned heads of crawfish with a spicy crawfish mixture and then simmering them in a rich roux-based stew. The Creoles, with their European influence, created a lighter bisque, simmering the crawfish tails in a shellfish stock and finishing with heavy whipping cream. This recipe is an example of the Creole-style bisque.

Ingredients:

2 pounds cooked crawfish tails
½ pound butter
2 cups minced onions
1 cup minced celery
1 cup minced red bell peppers
2 tbsps minced garlic
1 cup flour
¼ cup tomato sauce
2 quarts shellfish stock (see recipe)
1 tbsp chopped thyme
1 tbsp chopped tarragon
1 pint heavy whipping cream
salt and black pepper to taste
Creole seasoning to taste
sherry (optional)

Method:

In a heavy-bottomed stockpot, melt butter over medium-high heat. Add onions, celery, bell peppers and garlic. Sauté 3–5 minutes or until vegetables are wilted. Whisk in flour, stirring constantly until a white roux is achieved. (See roux recipes.) Stir in tomato sauce. Slowly add stock, one ladle at a time, stirring constantly until it reaches a soup-like consistency. Reserve any extra stock. Fold in 1 pound of crawfish tails. Bring to a rolling boil, reduce heat to simmer and cook for 20 minutes, stirring occasionally. Add thyme and tarragon. Season to taste with salt and pepper. Stir in heavy whipping cream and return mixture to a low simmer. Fold in remaining crawfish tails. Add reserved stock as necessary to maintain soup-like consistency. Finish with a touch of Creole seasoning. When ready to serve, ladle a generous portion of bisque into a soup bowl and garnish with a tablespoon of sherry, if desired.

VELOUTÉ OF BOILED CRAWFISH, CORN AND POTATOES

Prep Time: 1 Hour
Yields: 12 Servings

Comment:
The word "velouté" refers to the traditional velvety-smooth sauce the French people have made for centuries. Velouté perfectly describes this soup, which can be created with the leftovers following a crawfish boil. Use the discarded crawfish shells to make a delicious boiled crawfish stock.

Ingredients:
2 pounds boiled crawfish tails
1 cup whole kernel corn
6 cubed small potatoes
1 cup butter
1 cup diced onions
1 cup diced celery
½ cup diced red bell peppers
¼ cup minced garlic
1 cup flour
2½ quarts crawfish stock
1 pint heavy whipping cream
1 cup sliced green onions
1 cup chopped parsley
salt and white pepper to taste
Louisiana hot sauce to taste

Method:
In a heavy-bottomed stockpot, melt butter over medium-high heat. Add onions, celery, bell peppers and garlic. Sauté 3–5 minutes or until vegetables are wilted. Blend in corn and continue to cook 3–5 minutes. Whisk in flour, stirring constantly until a white roux is achieved. (See roux recipes.) Slowly add crawfish stock, one ladle at a time, stirring constantly until creamy. Reserve any extra stock. Bring soup to a low boil, then add half of crawfish and all potatoes. Cook until potatoes are tender, but not mushy. Add remaining crawfish, heavy whipping cream, green onions and parsley. Additional crawfish stock may be added, as needed, to adjust consistency of soup. Season to taste using salt, white pepper and hot sauce.

CREOLE BOUILLABAISSE

Prep Time: 1½ Hours
Yields: 12 Servings

Comment:
Bouillabaisse, the elaborate soup from the South of France, incorporates many different types of seafood into a single dish. This variation of the dish uses Louisiana ingredients alongside traditional French components such as white wine and fine herbs to create a Creole delicacy.

Ingredients:
4 (1½-pound) cleaned red snappers
2 pounds (31–35 count) head-on shrimp
2 pounds live crawfish
12 fresh cleaned crabs
1 cup olive oil
2 cups diced onions
2 cups diced celery
1 cup diced red bell peppers
4 whole tomatoes, diced
¾ cup tomato sauce
¼ cup minced garlic
4 whole bay leaves
2 medium carrots, diced
3 quarts shellfish stock (see recipe)
2 cups dry white wine
1 tsp dried thyme
1 tsp dried basil
1 cup sliced green onions
1 cup chopped parsley
salt and cayenne pepper to taste

Method:
Pour olive oil into a 2-gallon stockpot. In the pot, layer onions, celery, bell peppers, tomatoes, tomato sauce, garlic, bay leaves and carrots. On top of vegetables, layer whole snapper, shrimp, crawfish and crabs. Do not stir. Cover pot and steam over medium-high heat for 3–5 minutes. Add shellfish stock, white wine, thyme and basil. Bring to a low simmer, approximately 190°F, just below boiling point. Cook 30 minutes then remove from heat. Strain all seafood and vegetables. Discard vegetables and retain stock. Peel shrimp, crawfish and crabs, then bone fish. Bring stock back to a low boil. Add seafood, reduce to a simmer then stir in green onions and parsley. Season to taste using salt and cayenne pepper. Serve by placing a generous amount of seafood in center of a soup bowl and ladling on hot soup.

Cheryl Nicholas prepares ingredients for the Mirliton Soup.

MIRLITON SOUP

Prep Time: 1½ Hours
Yields: 6 Servings

Comment:

Mirlitons, commonly called chayote squash, are useful because they pick up the flavor of other ingredients in a dish. In this soup, the mirlitons not only absorb and enhance the taste of the shrimp, but also smooth out the texture of the finished product.

Ingredients:

12 mirlitons	¾ cup flour
2 pounds (70–90 count) shrimp, peeled and deveined	3 quarts chicken stock
	1 cup sliced mushrooms
½ cup butter	1 cup half-and-half
2 cups diced onions	½ cup chopped parsley
1 cup diced celery	salt and black pepper to taste
½ cup sliced green onions	Louisiana hot sauce to taste
¼ cup minced garlic	

Method:

Cut mirlitons in half lengthwise. Boil in lightly salted water until tender but not overcooked. Remove from heat and cool under tap water. Peel, remove seeds and dice into ¼-inch cubes. Reserve approximately 1 cup of cubes for garnish. Mash or purée remaining mirliton and set aside. In a cast iron Dutch oven, melt butter over medium-high heat. Add onions, celery, green onions and garlic. Sauté 3–5 minutes or until vegetables are wilted. Stir in mashed mirliton and half of shrimp. Continue to sauté 5–10 minutes or until mirliton is well blended and shrimp are pink and curled. Sprinkle in flour and mix well. Add chicken stock, one ladle at a time, stirring constantly until it reaches a soup consistency. Bring to a low boil, reduce to simmer and cook 20–30 minutes, stirring often. Add remaining shrimp and mushrooms, then blend in half-and-half and parsley. Cook an additional 5 minutes or until shrimp are done. Season to taste using salt, pepper and hot sauce. When serving, garnish each bowl with a tablespoon of diced mirlitons.

BISQUE OF THREE LETTUCES

Prep Time: 1 Hour
Yields: 12 Servings

Comment:

The combination of these three lettuce flavors is incredible. This soup was created quite by accident, but has been one of the best creations ever to come out of our kitchen.

Ingredients:

2 cups chopped romaine lettuce
2 cups chopped bibb lettuce
2 cups chopped red leaf lettuce
1 cup butter
1 cup diced onions
1 cup diced celery
½ cup diced bell peppers
¼ cup minced garlic
1 cup sliced mushrooms
½ cup diced andouille sausage
1 cup flour
2½ quarts chicken stock
2 ounces sherry
1 pint heavy whipping cream
1 cup sliced green onions
1 cup chopped parsley
salt and white pepper to taste

Method:

In a 2-gallon stock pot, melt butter over medium-high heat. Add lettuces, onions, celery, bell peppers, garlic, mushrooms and andouille. Sauté and stir constantly 5–10 minutes or until lettuces are wilted. Remove ingredients from stockpot and place in food processor with metal blade. Chop on high speed until vegetables are puréed. Return mixture to pot and bring to simmer. Whisk in flour, stirring constantly until white roux is achieved. (See roux recipes.) Do not brown. Add chicken stock, one ladle at a time, stirring constantly. Pour in sherry and heavy whipping cream. Stir in green onions and parsley. Cook an additional 10–15 minutes. Season to taste using salt and white pepper. If desired, garnish with julienne pieces of lettuce. NOTE: You may finish this soup by adding a pound of jumbo lump crabmeat.

BISQUE OF THREE SHELLFISH WITH SHOEPEG CORN

Prep Time: 1 Hour
Yields: 6 Servings

Comment:

Louisiana cooks have developed many fine seafood soups due to the abundance of shellfish on the Gulf Coast. With our semitropical climate, it makes perfect sense to combine these seafoods with vegetables to create an even more interesting dish.

Ingredients:

18 (21–25 count) peeled
   and deveined shrimp
1 pound jumbo lump crabmeat
18 shucked oysters, reserve liquid
1 (15-ounce) can shoepeg or cream-style corn
½ cup butter
1 cup diced onions
1 cup diced celery
½ cup diced red bell peppers
2 tbsps minced garlic
½ cup flour
3 cups shellfish stock (see recipe)
1 pint heavy whipping cream
1 tbsp chopped basil
1 tbsp chopped thyme
1 tsp chopped tarragon
salt and black pepper to taste
Creole seasoning to taste

Method:

In a heavy-bottomed saucepan, melt butter over medium-high heat. Stir in onions, celery, bell peppers and garlic. Sauté 3–5 minutes or until vegetables are wilted. Whisk in flour, stirring constantly until a white roux is achieved. (See roux recipes.) Blend in corn. Add shellfish stock, one ladle at a time, stirring constantly. Stir in whipping cream, basil, thyme and tarragon. Season lightly with salt, pepper and Creole seasoning. Fold in reserved oyster liquid and half of each type of seafood. Bring to a rolling boil, reduce to simmer and cook 10–12 minutes. Add remaining seafood, and cook 3–5 minutes or until shrimp are pink and curled. Adjust seasonings if necessary. When ready to serve, ladle a generous portion of soup with an equal amount of shellfish into each bowl.

T'Frere's Turtle Soup

T' FRERE'S TURTLE SOUP

Prep Time: 1 Hour
Yields: 6 Servings

Comment:

There's been much debate as to whether restaurants should feature turtle soup due to the endangered species issue surrounding sea turtles. However, in Louisiana, turtle soups such as this are made with snapper. This delicious meat arguably makes the best and most sought-after turtle soup in the world.

Ingredients:

2 pounds ground turtle meat
salt and cayenne pepper to taste
¾ cup vegetable oil
1 cup flour
2 cups diced onions
1 cup diced celery
1 cup diced green bell peppers
¼ cup minced garlic
2 (8-ounce) cans tomato sauce
2½ quarts beef stock (see recipe)
1 lemon, sliced
Louisiana hot sauce to taste
½ cup sliced green onions
¼ cup chopped parsley
¼ tsp nutmeg
3 boiled eggs, grated
6 ounces sherry

Method:

Season turtle well with salt and cayenne pepper. In a heavy-bottomed stockpot, heat ¼ cup vegetable oil over medium-high heat. Pan-fry turtle until water has evaporated from meat and turtle is caramelized and golden brown. Remove and drain on paper towels then set aside. In same pot, heat remaining vegetable oil over medium-high heat. Whisk in flour, stirring constantly until a dark brown roux is achieved. (See roux recipes.) Add onions, celery, bell peppers and garlic. Sauté 3–5 minutes or until vegetables are wilted. Stir in tomato sauce and cook 2–3 additional minutes. Slowly add beef stock, one ladle at a time, stirring constantly until it reaches a soup-like consistency. Return meat to pot, add lemon slices and season lightly using salt, cayenne pepper and hot sauce. Bring soup to a rolling boil, reduce to simmer and cook approximately 45 minutes or until turtle is fork-tender. Add green onions, parsley and nutmeg. Cook 2–3 minutes then adjust seasonings if necessary. When ready to serve, ladle a generous portion of soup into a serving bowl and garnish with grated eggs. Gently pour 1 ounce of sherry over each bowl of soup when served.

THE QUEEN'S SOUP

Prep Time: 1 Hour
Yields: 6 Servings

Comment:

This soup was created to honor the Queen of Mardi Gras at the extravagant carnival balls. It is obvious from this recipe that elegant foods were a major part of these functions. The soup was usually served in a large gilded tureen.

Ingredients:

4 boneless, skinless chicken breasts
1 gallon chicken stock (see recipe)
½ cup wild rice
½ cup converted white rice
½ cup butter
½ cup flour
½ cup diced carrots
½ cup diced yellow bell peppers
1 tbsp chopped thyme
1 tbsp chopped sage
¼ cup chopped chives
1 cup heavy whipping cream
salt and black pepper to taste

Method:

In a 3-gallon stockpot, heat chicken stock to a simmer. Poach chicken breasts in hot stock for 10–15 minutes or until thoroughly cooked. Remove, allow to cool, dice into ¼-inch cubes and set aside. Stir wild rice into the simmering stock and cook 30 minutes. Add white rice and cook 15 additional minutes or until rice is tender. Rice will act as a thickening agent. In a separate saucepan, melt butter over medium-high heat. Whisk in flour, stirring constantly until a white roux is achieved. (See roux recipes.) Add carrots, yellow bell peppers, thyme, sage and chives. Cook 3–5 minutes then add this roux mixture to stock, stirring constantly. Stir in heavy whipping cream and bring to a low boil. Season with salt and pepper. Mix in diced chicken and cook 2 additional minutes. Use additional stock or water to retain soup-like consistency. Adjust seasonings if necessary. Serve in warmed soup bowls over fresh garlic croutons.

CAJUN WHITE BEAN SOUP

Prep Time: 2 Hours
Yields: 12 Servings

Comment:
Red kidney beans can be used in the place of white beans. You can also make this soup by using leftover red or white beans from Monday's lunch.

Ingredients:
1 large package Great Northern beans
2 pieces heavy smoked ham hocks
1 cup julienned tasso
¾ cup oil
2 cups diced onions
2 cups diced celery
1 cup diced bell peppers
¼ cup minced garlic
2 cups diced tomatoes
water as needed
1 bay leaf
salt and cracked black pepper to taste

Method:
Presoak dried beans overnight in cold water. Drain and wash beans again before cooking. In a 2-gallon stockpot, heat oil over medium-high heat. Add onions, celery, bell peppers, garlic and tomatoes. Sauté 3–5 minutes or until vegetables are wilted. Add ham hocks and tasso. Continue to sauté for an additional 5 minutes. Stir beans into vegetable mixture and sauté 2 minutes. Pour in enough cold water to cover beans by 2 inches. Bring to a rolling boil, reduce to simmer and cook, stirring occasionally, for approximately 1 hour. Once beans begin to become tender, mash them against side of pot to create creaminess. Season with bay leaf, salt and pepper. Simmer approximately 1½ hours, continuing to stir and mash beans occasionally. Soup is ready when it has reached the creamy white consistency of cream of mushroom soup. Adjust seasonings if necessary.

WHITE BEAN, GARLIC AND ROSEMARY SOUP

Prep Time: 2 Hours
Yields: 10–12 Servings

Comment:
Cannellini, or white kidney beans, are a traditional Italian ingredient. The addition of garlic and rosemary to the beans creates a delicious, creamy, Italian-style soup.

Ingredients:
4 cups uncooked Cannellini beans
12 cloves garlic
1 sprig rosemary
¼ cup olive oil
1 cup diced onions
1 cup diced celery
½ cup diced red bell peppers
½ cup diced green bell peppers
1 cup julienned andouille sausage
3 quarts chicken stock (see recipe)
1 cup sliced green onions
½ cup chopped parsley
salt and cracked black pepper to taste
Louisiana hot sauce to taste

Method:
Soak beans in cold water overnight in refrigerator. This process will soften beans and reduce cooking time by about 30 minutes. Once soaked, rinse beans under cold running water in a colander and set aside. In a 2-gallon stockpot, heat olive oil over medium-high heat. Sauté garlic cloves until slightly browned. Using a slotted spoon, remove garlic and set aside. Stir in onions, celery, bell peppers and andouille. Sauté 3–5 minutes or until vegetables are wilted. Blend beans into vegetable mixture. Pour in chicken stock, bring to a rolling boil then reduce to simmer. Cook approximately 1 hour, stirring occasionally to keep beans from scorching. Add rosemary, cook for about 30 minutes then remove the sprig to avoid an overpowering flavor. Cook soup 1 hour. Using a cooking spoon, mash beans on inside of pot to cream and thicken soup. Mash browned garlic cloves with a fork and stir them into soup. Before serving, stir in green onions and parsley. Season to taste with salt, pepper and hot sauce. NOTE: Use precooked, canned beans to help cut cooking time.

RED BEAN AND SAUSAGE SOUP

Prep Time: 2½ Hours
Yields: 4 Servings

Comment:

Red beans and rice is Louisiana's Monday dish. Here, the traditional recipe has been made into a hearty soup that can be used as a starter or an entrée.

Ingredients:

2 cups dried red kidney beans
¼ pound smoked sausage, sliced
¼ cup diced tasso (optional)
9 cups chicken broth
½ cup diced onions
¼ cup diced celery
¼ cup diced bell peppers
¼ cup sliced green onions
2 tbsp chopped parsley
2 tbsp minced garlic
1 bay leaf
2 tsp cider vinegar
¼ tsp thyme
¼ tsp chili powder
¼ tsp freshly ground black pepper

Method:

Place all ingredients in a 1-gallon heavy-bottomed stockpot and bring to a boil. Reduce to a simmer, cover and cook 2 hours, stirring occasionally to prevent sticking. Cook until beans are very tender. Remove about ½ cup of beans from pot and purée in a food processor with 2 cups of liquid. (Or, you may mash the beans in the pot with the back of a cooking spoon.) Return puréed beans to soup to create a thicker consistency. NOTE: White or black beans can be substituted for red beans for an easy variation to this dish.

BRINGER'S NINE BEAN SOUP

Prep Time: 2 Hours
Yields: 6–8 Servings

Comment:

When the Spanish arrived in New Orleans in 1765, they brought new and interesting beans to the area. Kidney, pinto and black beans were the favorites of the Spanish. Black-eyed peas were later introduced by the Africans. In this soup, the mixture of beans from different cultures demonstrates the Creole practice of blending ingredients to create unique cuisine.

Ingredients:

¼ cup navy beans
¼ cup red kidney beans
¼ cup lima beans
½ cup cannellini beans
¼ cup pinto beans
½ cup black beans
¼ cup black-eyed peas
½ cup split peas
½ cup sliced green beans
¼ cup butter
1 cup diced onions
½ cup diced celery
¼ cup diced red bell peppers
¼ cup diced yellow bell peppers
¼ cup diced green bell peppers

1 tbsp minced garlic
1 ham hock
2 slices salt pork
1 (14-ounce) can diced tomatoes
1 gallon beef stock (see recipe)
3 bay leaves
1 tsp dried thyme
½ tsp dried oregano
½ tsp cayenne pepper
1 cup sliced andouille sausage, ¼-inch
     thick
1 cup diced ham
salt to taste
Louisiana hot sauce to taste

Method:

Rinse dried beans and peas twice, discarding any that are discolored or float to surface. Soak beans (except green beans) and peas in cold water a minimum of 4 hours, preferably overnight. NOTE: Soak black beans separately. This process will cut the cooking time by one-third. Discard soaking liquid, rinse beans and peas and set aside. In a large stockpot, melt butter over medium-high heat. Stir in onions, celery, bell peppers and garlic. Sauté 3–5 minutes or until vegetables are wilted. Add ham hock and pork. Continue to sauté 2–3 minutes. Stir in tomatoes, beef stock, beans (except green beans) and peas. Bring mixture to a rolling boil, reduce to simmer and season with bay leaves, thyme, oregano and cayenne pepper. Cover pot and simmer approximately 1½ hours, stirring occasionally. As beans become soft, mash a portion of them against side of pot with a cooking spoon. This will thicken soup and create a creamy consistency. Add more stock to retain volume during cooking process. Stir in green beans, sausage and ham. Simmer an additional 30 minutes and season with salt and hot sauce.

CARMEN'S BLACK BEAN SOUP

Prep Time: 3 Hours
Yields: 8 Servings

Comment:

Latin Americans introduced black beans to Cajun cuisine. This great bean soup is a variation on a recipe created many years ago by a wonderful Cuban cook, "Grandma Carmen."

Ingredients:

1 pound dried black beans
2 quarts chicken stock
½ cup peanut oil
1 cup diced onions
1 cup diced bell peppers
¼ cup minced garlic
1 bay leaf
1 tsp ground cumin
1 cup picante sauce
salt and black pepper to taste
Louisiana hot sauce to taste
4 tbsps lemon juice
2½ tbsps olive oil

Method:

Wash beans well and soak in cold water overnight in refrigerator. Drain and rinse well. In a cast iron Dutch oven, combine beans and chicken stock. Bring to a rolling boil, reduce to simmer and cook approximately 45 minutes. In a cast iron skillet, heat oil over medium-high heat. Stir in onions, bell peppers and garlic. Sauté 3–5 minutes or until vegetables are wilted. Add sautéed vegetables to soup along with bay leaf, cumin and picante sauce. Bring to a rolling boil, reduce to simmer, cover and cook 1½ hours, stirring occasionally. Additional stock may be needed to retain volume. Season to taste using salt, pepper and hot sauce. Immediately prior to serving, blend lemon juice and olive oil into soup.

BLACK-EYED PEA AND OKRA SOUP

Prep Time: 1½ Hours
Yields: 8–10 Servings

Comment:

In the plantation days, this dish was referred to as "good luck" soup. The name originated from the belief that eating black-eyed peas on New Year's Day will bring good luck throughout the year.

Ingredients:

1 pound dried black-eyed peas
1 (10-ounce) package cut okra
1 pound cubed ham
¼ cup butter
2 cups diced onions
1 cup diced celery
½ cup diced red bell peppers
¼ cup minced garlic
1 bay leaf
1 sprig of thyme
2½ quarts chicken stock
1 cup diced and seeded tomatoes
¼ cup sliced green onions
¼ cup chopped parsley
salt and cracked black pepper to taste
Louisiana hot sauce to taste

Method:

In a heavy-bottomed Dutch oven, melt butter over medium-high heat. Add onions, celery, bell peppers and garlic. Sauté 3–5 minutes or until vegetables are wilted. Stir in ham, bay leaf and thyme and cook an additional 3–5 minutes. Pour in chicken stock and black-eyed peas, bring to a rolling boil then reduce to simmer. Cover and cook approximately 1 hour, stirring occasionally. When peas are soft, mash them on side of pot with a cooking spoon to help thicken finished soup. Stir in okra, tomatoes, green onions and parsley. Season to taste with salt, pepper and hot sauce. Allow to cook 20–30 minutes longer or until soup is creamy. Serve with cornbread muffins.

Chickens on a farm

CREAM OF CHICKEN AND ARTICHOKE SOUP

Prep Time: 1 Hour
Yields: 10–12 Servings

Comment:

Many people are not aware that artichokes are grown in Louisiana. However, the vegetable is abundant in the state and has been used as an ingredient in Cajun and Creole dishes for many decades.

Ingredients:

1 whole young fryer
8 (canned) artichoke bottoms, sliced and uncooked
3½ quarts cold water
1 cup butter
1 cup diced onions
1 cup diced celery
½ cup diced red bell peppers
¼ cup minced garlic
1 cup flour
3 quarts reserved chicken stock (see below)
1 pint heavy whipping cream
1 cup sliced green onions
1 cup chopped parsley
1 tbsp thyme
1 tbsp basil
salt and white pepper to taste
Louisiana hot sauce to taste

Method:

In a 2-gallon stockpot, place fryer and water. If desired, add 1 quartered onion, 1 split head of garlic and 1 stalk of celery. Bring to a rolling boil and cook until chicken is tender and falling off bones. When done, remove chicken and strain stock through a fine chinois or cheesecloth. Reserve 3 quarts of stock. (Discard any vegetables used.) Bone chicken and set aside. In same pot, melt butter over medium-high heat. Add onions, celery, bell peppers, garlic and artichokes. Sauté 5–10 minutes or until vegetables are wilted and artichokes are tender. Whisk in flour, stirring constantly until white roux is achieved. (See roux recipes.) Slowly add reserved chicken stock, one ladle at a time, stirring constantly. Bring to a low boil, reduce to simmer and cook 30 minutes. Stir in chicken and cream. Return to simmer then add green onions, parsley, thyme and basil. Season to taste with salt, white pepper and hot sauce.

OXTAIL SOUP

Prep Time: 4 Hours
Yields: 4–6 Servings

Comment:

This classic English soup was popular in the late 19th century. Today, oxtails are readily available at any good butcher shop, and they are surprisingly cheap. The high fat content of the tailbone makes this a tasty and nourishing soup wonderful for a cold winter evening.

Ingredients:

1 (1½ pound) oxtail
¼ cup flour
2 ounces butter
1 onion, chopped
1 celery stalk, diced
4 carrots, chopped
10 peppercorns
¼ tsp thyme
¼ tsp tarragon
1 bay leaf
salt and pepper to taste
5 cups beef stock
5 cups water
1 cup sherry or port wine

Method:

Cut oxtail into 2-inch pieces and coat with flour. In a 2-gallon stockpot, melt butter over medium-high heat. Place oxtail in pot and brown 10–15 minutes, then add onions, celery and carrots. Sauté 2–3 minutes or until vegetables are wilted. Add peppercorns and herbs, then season with salt and pepper. Pour in stock and water, bring to a rolling boil and skim surface for impurities. Cover and boil 2 hours or until oxtail is tender. Remove from heat and strain vegetables and meat from liquid. Separate meat and vegetables. Remove meat from bones. Discard bones. Purée vegetables in a blender or food processor. Return meat and puréed vegetables to stock. Heat to just below boiling then add sherry or wine. Adjust seasonings to taste and serve.

CREAM OF CAULIFLOWER AND DUCK SOUP

Prep Time: 1½ Hours
Yields: 12 Servings

Comment:

This soup can be altered a variety of ways. You can substitute the duck with chicken or seafood for a different taste, or you can eliminate the meat entirely and use chicken stock to create a velvety cream of cauliflower soup.

Ingredients for Duck Stock:

1 (3–4 pound) Long Island duck
6 quarts cold water
2 cups diced onions
2 cups diced celery
2 cups diced carrots
1 bay leaf
1 tbsp black peppercorns
1 cup dry white wine

Method:

Preheat oven to 350°F. In a 2-gallon stockpot, combine all stock ingredients. Bring to a rolling boil, reduce to simmer and cook until duck is tender and falling apart. Strain, set duck aside, discard vegetables and reserve 3 quarts of stock for soup. Let sit 20 minutes and skim off any fat that rises to surface. Remove skin from duck. Bake skin 10–15 minutes or until crispy and brown. When done, cut into strips and set aside. Bone duck and dice meat into ¼-inch cubes.

Ingredients for Soup:

4 cups chopped cauliflower
reserved meat from duck
1 cup butter
2 cups diced onions
2 cups diced celery
1 cup diced bell peppers
¼ cup minced garlic
1 cup flour
2½ quarts reserved duck stock
1 ounce brandy
1 pint heavy whipping cream
1 cup sliced green onions
1 cup chopped parsley
salt and cracked black pepper to taste
reserved duck skin

Method:

In a 2-gallon stockpot, melt butter over medium-high heat. Mix in cauliflower, onions, celery, bell peppers and garlic. Sauté approximately 25 minutes, stirring constantly until cauliflower can be mashed against bottom of pot. Mash cauliflower and allow to brown slightly. Whisk in flour, stirring constantly until a white or light brown roux is achieved. (See roux recipes.) Add duck stock, one ladle at a time, stirring constantly. Stir in brandy and whipping cream, bring to a rolling boil and reduce to simmer. Cook approximately 30 minutes. Add duck meat, green onions and parsley. Season to taste using salt and pepper. When serving, garnish each bowl with a small amount of baked duck skin.

FRONT PORCH CARROT BISQUE

Prep Time: 1 Hour
Yields: 6 Servings

Comment:

This carrot soup is best when served in coffee cups either hot or cold. Enjoy it while swaying on a porch swing or sitting in a comfortable patio rocker.

Ingredients:

1 pound fresh carrots, peeled and sliced
2 medium-sized potatoes, peeled and sliced
7 cups chicken stock (see recipe)
1 cup diced onions
1 cup diced celery
½ cup diced red bell peppers
1 tbsp Worcestershire sauce
Creole seasoning to taste
salt and black pepper to taste
½ cup heavy whipping cream
⅛ tsp nutmeg
¼ cup chopped parsley

Method:

In a cast iron Dutch oven, combine carrots, potatoes, chicken stock, onions, celery, bell peppers and Worcestershire sauce. Bring mixture to a low boil then reduce to simmer. Cover and cook 15–20 minutes or until potatoes and carrots are tender. Season to taste using Creole seasoning, salt and pepper. Strain vegetables from soup and reserve stock. Place cooked vegetables into a blender or food processor. Add enough hot stock to cover vegetables by 1 inch. Do not overfill, because hot liquid will expand, and the steam will cause the top to pop up during blending. Pulse until soup is smooth and creamy. Return puréed soup to Dutch oven, and stir in remaining reserved liquid. Bring mixture to a low boil. Add heavy whipping cream, nutmeg and parsley. Adjust seasonings if necessary. It may be served hot or cold and can be garnished with fresh chives and sour cream.

BISQUE OF WILD MUSHROOM WITH FRENCH-FRIED OYSTER CROUTON

Prep Time: 1 Hour
Yields: 10–12 Servings

Comment:

It is best to use some variety of wild mushrooms to create this soup. However, you may substitute dried forestière mushroom packs, which can be found in most grocery stores. If necessary, fresh button mushrooms combined with any other varieties will certainly do.

Ingredients:

1 pound fresh mixed mushrooms, sliced
¼ pound butter
1 cup diced onions
½ cup diced celery
¼ cup diced bell peppers
2 tbsps minced garlic
6 tbsps flour
1 quart hot chicken stock
1 cup heavy whipping cream
1 tsp chopped thyme
1 tsp chopped sage
salt and black pepper to taste
1 ounce sherry
Deep-Fried Oysters (see recipe)

Method:

In a 1-gallon stockpot, melt butter over medium-high heat. Add mushrooms and sauté 5–7 minutes or until wilted. Add onions, celery, bell peppers and garlic. Sauté 10 additional minutes or until vegetables are slightly caramelized but not brown. Place cooked mushrooms and vegetables into a food processor. Process until mixture is puréed but not liquefied. There should be bits of mushroom still visible. Return purée to stockpot and whisk in flour, blending well. Add hot chicken stock, one ladle at a time. Stir in heavy whipping cream, thyme and sage. Season to taste with salt and pepper. Bring to a rolling boil, reduce to simmer and cook 30 minutes. Add sherry and stir well. Ladle soup into a bowl, and garnish with 2 fried oysters.

POTATO AND CABBAGE SOUP

Prep Time: 1 Hour
Yields: 4 Servings

Comment:
Originally, potato and cabbage soup was served on Mondays in Ireland. This dish was usually made from leftovers of the traditional Irish Sunday dinner of boiled bacon, cabbage and mashed potatoes.

Ingredients:
2 large boiling potatoes, peeled and diced
½ head green cabbage, shredded
4 tbsps butter
2 onions, peeled and diced
1 leek, washed and diced
1 bay leaf
¼ tsp nutmeg
1 cup milk
3 cups chicken stock
salt and freshly ground white pepper to taste
½ cup lightly whipped heavy cream
¼ cup chopped parsley

Method:
In a 1-quart heavy-bottomed saucepan, melt butter over medium-high heat. Add onions, leek and potatoes. Sauté 3–5 minutes or until soft. Stir in cabbage, bay leaf and nutmeg. Simmer 3–4 minutes. Pour in milk and chicken stock, bring to a rolling boil then reduce to simmer. Cook an additional 30 minutes. Remove bay leaf. Transfer soup to a food processor and purée until smooth. Season to taste with salt and white pepper. Serve in 10-inch soup bowls garnished with a teaspoon of cream and a pinch of parsley.

CALLALOO SOUP (CARIBBEAN GREENS)

Prep Time: 2½ Hours
Yields: 6–8 Servings

Comment:
Callaloo is a thick, kale-like leafy vegetable that grows in the Eastern Caribbean, where this soup is a favorite. The dish is thick and green, much like a creamy spinach soup.

Ingredients:
2 pounds fresh kale
½ pound callaloo or fresh spinach
12 okra pods
¼ pound salt pork, cut into thin strips
½ pound lean pork, cubed
2 onions, thinly sliced
1 hot pepper, seeded and sliced
1 tbsp chopped thyme
8 cups chicken stock
salt and black pepper to taste

Method:
Pull stems from kale and callaloo and discard. Wash leaves thoroughly to remove any sand or grit. Roughly chop greens. Slice okra into ½-inch circles. In a 7-quart cast iron Dutch oven, sauté salt pork and lean pork 7–10 minutes, stirring occasionally to render fat. Discard all but 2 tablespoons of fat. Add onions and continue to sauté 5 minutes or until meat is brown and onions are translucent. Stir in kale, callaloo, okra, hot pepper, thyme and chicken stock. Bring to a rolling boil and reduce to simmer. Cover and cook approximately 2 hours. Use additional chicken stock to retain volume. Season to taste using salt and pepper. Many Caribbean cooks remove salt pork before serving.

SPINACH AND SWEET POTATO SOUP

Prep Time: 1 Hour
Yields: 8–10 Servings

Comment:

Japanese chefs know a simple truth about cooking: if food looks good, it will certainly taste good. This basic principle is proven in the phenomenal visual appeal and flavor that vivid green spinach and bright orange sweet potatoes give this soup.

Ingredients:

4 cups spinach leaves
2 cups (¼-inch) diced sweet potatoes
1 cup julienned smoked sausage
½ cup butter
1 cup diced onions
½ cup diced celery
¼ cup diced red bell peppers
¼ cup minced garlic
1 cup flour
3 quarts chicken stock (see recipe)
1 quart heavy whipping cream
½ cup sliced chives
½ cup chopped parsley
salt and cracked black pepper to taste
Louisiana hot sauce to taste

Method:

Wash spinach leaves removing stems and chop into ¼-inch squares. Reserve ¼ cup of spinach for garnish. In a heavy-bottomed Dutch oven, melt butter over medium-high heat. Stir in smoked sausage, onions, celery, bell peppers and garlic. Sauté 3–5 minutes, stirring constantly. Whisk in flour, stirring until a blond roux is formed. (See roux recipes.) Add chicken stock, one ladle at a time, stirring constantly until soup consistency is achieved. Stir in sweet potatoes. Bring to a rolling boil, reduce to simmer and cook approximately 30 minutes. Use additional stock to retain proper consistency. Mix in heavy whipping cream, spinach, chives and parsley. Season to taste using salt, pepper and hot sauce. When potatoes are tender, serve in soup bowls and garnish with reserved spinach.

MAMERE'S OLD-FASHIONED VEGETABLE SOUP

Prep Time: 2½ Hours
Yields: 24 Servings

Comment:

Vegetables are canned or jarred during the spring months to ensure a good supply throughout winter. Often, when the weather is cold, Cajuns cook a huge pot of vegetable soup using canned provisions. Such a large quantity of soup is made so that some can be frozen for later use. Any of your favorite vegetables such as turnips, sweet potatoes or white beans may be added to the soup.

Ingredients:

3 pounds soup meat with marrow bone
¼ pound butter
2 cups coarsely chopped onions
2 cups coarsely chopped celery
1 cup coarsely chopped green bell peppers
¼ cup minced garlic
4 quarts beef stock (see recipe)
1 (12–15 ounce) can diced tomatoes
2 (12–15 ounce) cans tomato sauce
1 cup sliced carrots
1 (12–15 ounce) can whole kernel corn
1 (12–15 ounce) can lima beans
1 (12–15 ounce) can black-eyed peas
1 (12–15 ounce) can red kidney beans
1 small head cabbage, cubed
2 cups cubed red potatoes, skin-on
1 (8-ounce) package vermicelli
salt and cracked black pepper to taste

Method:

In a 2-gallon stockpot, melt butter over medium-high heat. Add soup meat and bones and cook 10–12 minutes or until golden brown on all sides. Add onions, celery, bell peppers and garlic. Sauté 3–5 minutes or until vegetables are wilted. Pour in beef stock, tomatoes and tomato sauce. Bring to a rolling boil, reduce to simmer and cook 2 hours or until meat is tender. Add beef stock or water during cooking process to retain soup-like consistency. NOTE: Do not drain canned vegetables. Blend in carrots, corn, lima beans, black-eyed peas, red beans, cabbage and all liquid from cans. Cook 12–15 minutes or until carrots are tender. Add potatoes and vermicelli and cook 12–15 minutes or until potatoes and pasta are tender. Season to taste with salt and pepper.

SPICY CREOLE GAZPACHO

Prep Time: 1 Hour
Yields: 8–10 Servings

Comment:

In the hot Louisiana climate, a chilled tomato soup such as this one is revered as a delicacy. Serve this gazpacho in a punch or coffee cup as an interesting appetizer before the guests are seated at the dinner table.

Ingredients for Croutons:

4 French bread slices, ¾-inch thick
¼ cup butter
¼ cup olive oil
1 tsp chopped oregano
1 tsp chopped basil
½ tsp chopped rosemary
1 tsp minced garlic
salt to taste

Method:

Preheat oven to 300°F. Cut French bread into ¾-inch cubes with crust on. In a heavy-bottomed cast iron skillet, heat butter and olive oil over medium-high heat. Stir in oregano, basil, rosemary and garlic. Sauté 1–2 minutes, being careful not to scorch garlic. Add French bread and sauté until croutons are thoroughly coated. Season lightly with salt. Remove croutons from skillet, spread evenly on a large cookie sheet, and bake for 30 minutes or until crisp. Set aside.

Ingredients for Soup:

6 (6-ounce) cans V-8 juice
2 cups tomato juice
3 tbsps white wine vinegar
juice of ½ lemon
1 cup seeded diced tomatoes
1 cup diced cucumbers
½ cup diced green bell peppers
½ cup diced yellow bell peppers
½ cup diced zucchini
½ cup diced summer squash
¼ cup diced onions
¼ cup minced garlic
salt and cracked black pepper to taste
Louisiana hot sauce to taste
¼ cup chopped cilantro or parsley

Method:

In a large mixing bowl, combine all ingredients except cilantro or parsley. Season to taste using salt, pepper and hot sauce. Stir in all but 1 tablespoon of cilantro or parsley. Cover soup tightly with plastic wrap and chill a minimum of 4–6 hours. To serve, pour gazpacho into chilled cups or bowls and top with croutons and a sprinkle of cilantro or parsley.

CREAM OF EGGPLANT SOUP

Prep Time: 1 Hour
Yields: 12 Servings

Comment:

Eggplant stuffed with crabmeat and ground pork is one of the most common vegetable dishes in Louisiana. Incorporating eggplant into a soup is a more recent, but equally popular, use of this vegetable. You might want to try adding a teaspoon of curry powder to intensify the flavor of this dish.

Ingredients:

2–3 medium eggplant, peeled and diced
1 cup butter
2 cups diced onions
2 cups diced celery
1 cup diced bell peppers
¼ cup minced garlic
¼ cup diced tomatoes
1 cup flour
2½ quarts chicken stock (see recipe)
1 pint heavy whipping cream
1 cup sliced green onions
1 cup chopped parsley
salt and white pepper to taste

Method:

In a 2-gallon stockpot, melt butter over medium-high heat. Stir in eggplant, onions, celery, bell peppers, garlic and tomatoes. Sauté 5–10 minutes or until vegetables are wilted. Whisk in flour, stirring constantly until white roux is achieved. (See roux recipes.) Add chicken stock, one ladle at a time, stirring constantly. Bring to a low boil and cook 30 minutes. Stir in cream, green onions and parsley. Cook 10 additional minutes. Season to taste with salt and white pepper. NOTE: To create an interesting twist in this recipe, add julienned andouille and fresh shellfish such as crab or shrimp.

FRENCH ONION SOUP

Prep Time: 1½ Hours
Yields: 6 Servings

Comment:
This classic soup was traditionally a hangover remedy sold in all-night cafés in Paris. It was thought that the rich beef broth flavored with sautéed onions and topped with a hearty crouton would revive revelers in the early hours of the morning following a night of indulgence.

Ingredients:
4 large onions, finely sliced
¼ cup butter
2 tbsps olive oil
2 tbsps minced garlic
½ cup Pinot Noir
4 cups beef broth
2 large bay leaves
salt and pepper to taste
6 thick slices of French bread
¾ cup grated Swiss cheese

Method:
Preheat oven on broiler setting. In a large cast iron Dutch oven, heat butter and oil together. Add onions and garlic. Cook over medium heat 30–45 minutes, stirring occasionally, until caramelized but not burned. To create a slightly thickened soup, sprinkle in 1½ tablespoons flour. Pour in Pinot Noir and swirl to deglaze pan. Stir in broth. Season with bay leaves, salt and pepper. Bring to a rolling boil, reduce to simmer, cover and cook 30 minutes. Remove bay leaves and adjust seasonings if necessary. Place 6 soup bowls on a cookie sheet and fill with soup to ¾ volume. Top with a slice of French bread and a layer of Swiss cheese. Place bowls under broiler until bread is toasted and cheese is melted. Serve immediately.

SOPA DE AJO (GARLIC SOUP)

Prep Time: 1 Hour
Yields: 6 Servings

Comment:
Hot garlic soup is a tradition not only in Spain, but also in Italy and Southern France. This simple soup is always made with eggs to add protein to the dish. In order to serve the egg perfectly poached, the soup should be eaten immediately after poaching.

Ingredients:
8 cloves of garlic, sliced
¼ cup extra virgin olive oil
12 (2-inch) French bread cubes
½ tsp paprika
½ cup tomato sauce
5 cups chicken stock (see recipe)
1 bay leaf
salt and black pepper to taste
6 whole eggs
¼ cup chopped parsley

Method:
In a large cast iron skillet, heat oil over medium-high heat. Add garlic and sauté 2–3 minutes or until lightly browned around edges. Remove garlic, mash and set aside. In same skillet, sauté bread cubes until golden brown on all sides. Sprinkle in paprika, remove bread, mash into a paste and combine with garlic. In a sauté pan, combine tomato sauce, chicken stock and bay leaf. Season to taste with salt and pepper. Bring to a rolling boil, reduce to simmer, whisk in bread paste and cook 15 minutes. Adjust seasonings if necessary. Turn off heat and crack eggs into soup, allowing them to poach for 5 minutes. Using a slotted spoon, remove poached eggs and place in 6 soup bowls. Top each egg with hot broth and sprinkle with parsley.

GRANDPA'S POTATO AND HAM SOUP

Prep Time: 45 Minutes
Yields: 6 Servings

Comment:

Historically, Cajuns cured their own ham in smokehouses. Even when there was little else to eat, the smokehouse would always have some trimmings left from a boucherie. Potatoes, found in abundance year round, were a hearty addition to any soup.

Ingredients:

3 cups diced red potatoes
2 cups diced lean ham
4 cups chicken stock
1 cup diced onions
1 cup diced celery
¼ cup minced garlic
1 tsp herbes de Provence
1½ cups milk
1 tbsp butter
¼ tsp Worcestershire sauce
½ tsp dill weed
1 thinly sliced green onion
salt and black pepper to taste
Louisiana hot sauce to taste

Method:

In a cast iron Dutch oven, heat stock over medium-high heat. Stir in potatoes, ham, onions, celery, garlic and herbes de Provence. Bring to a rolling boil then reduce heat to simmer. Cover and cook until vegetables are tender. Strain liquid and reserve. Separate ham, vegetables and potatoes. Using a potato masher or large spoon, mash potatoes until puréed. Place ham, vegetables and potatoes back into pot over medium-high heat. Add milk, butter, Worcestershire, dill and green onions. Stir in reserved poaching liquid, one ladle at a time. Reduce heat to simmer. Do not boil. Season to taste using salt, pepper and hot sauce. Simmer 10–15 minutes and serve.

ROASTED RED, YELLOW AND GREEN SWEET PEPPER SOUP

Prep Time: 1½ Hours
Yields: 10–12 Servings

Comment:

Roasting sweet peppers has been a tradition in Louisiana ever since the Italians first arrived to work in the cane fields and markets of the state. The roasted peppers, when served with basil and cracked pepper in a cream soup, make a tasty and beautiful dish.

Ingredients:

4 red bell peppers
4 yellow bell peppers
4 green bell peppers
1 cup butter
½ cup diced tasso ham
1 cup diced onions
1 cup diced celery
¼ cup minced garlic
1 cup seeded, diced tomatoes
1 cup flour
3 quarts chicken stock (see recipe)
1 cup heavy whipping cream
2 tbsps chopped basil
salt and white pepper to taste
Louisiana hot sauce to taste

Method:

To roast peppers, place whole peppers directly over open flame or under broiler. Turn frequently until skin blisters and blackens on all sides. Remove and place into a brown paper bag, seal tightly and let stand 10–15 minutes. Peel blistered skin from pepper under cold running water. Seed and dice peppers then set aside. In a 2-gallon stockpot, melt butter over medium-high heat. Add tasso, onions, celery and garlic. Sauté 3–5 minutes or until vegetables are wilted. Blend in tomatoes and half of roasted peppers. Whisk in flour, stirring constantly until a white roux is achieved. (See roux recipes.) Stir in chicken stock, one ladle at a time. Pour in cream, bring to a low boil and reduce to simmer. Cook 30 minutes. Add basil and remaining peppers. Season to taste using salt, pepper and hot sauce. NOTE: This soup, when reduced to half volume, makes a wonderful sauce for pasta, fish and chicken.

CABBAGE AND GROUND BEEF SOUP

Prep Time: 1½ Hours
Yields: 8 Servings

Comment:

This soup is a great example of one of the interesting ways the Germans of Louisiana incorporated cabbage into their cooking.

Ingredients:

1 small cabbage, cubed
1 pound ground beef
1 cup diced onions
1 cup diced celery
½ cup diced bell peppers
¼ cup minced garlic
1 (5½-ounce) can tomato juice
1 (10-ounce) can stewed tomatoes
1 (10-ounce) can Ro*tel® tomatoes
3 (20-ounce) cans red kidney beans
¼ cup white vinegar
¼ cup sugar
2 cups chicken or beef stock (see recipes)
salt and black pepper to taste
Louisiana hot sauce to taste

Method:

In a cast iron Dutch oven, brown ground beef over medium-high heat. Stir constantly to render fat while chopping to separate beef. Drain fat then blend in onions, celery, bell peppers and garlic. Cook 5 minutes. Add tomato juice, stewed tomatoes and Ro*tel® tomatoes. Bring to a rolling boil and reduce to simmer. Blend in beans, vinegar, sugar and cabbage. Pour in stock and continue cooking 30 minutes. Season to taste with salt, pepper and hot sauce.

LOUISIANA SEAFOOD GUMBO

Prep Time: 1 Hour
Yields: 12 Servings

Comment:

Seafood gumbo is the premier soup of Cajun Country, and it is known worldwide as the dish to seek out when visiting South Louisiana. Every Louisiana home has its own unique ingredients and methods for cooking gumbo.

Ingredients:

1 pound (35-count) shrimp, peeled and deveined
1 pound jumbo lump crabmeat
2 dozen shucked oysters, reserve liquid
1 pound claw crabmeat
1 cup chopped frozen okra
1 cup vegetable oil
1 cup flour
2 cups diced onions
1 cup diced celery
1 cup diced bell peppers
¼ cup minced garlic
½ pound sliced andouille sausage
3 quarts shellfish stock (see recipe)
2 cups sliced green onions
½ cup chopped parsley
salt and cayenne pepper to taste
Louisiana hot sauce to taste
cooked white rice

Method:

In a 7-quart cast iron Dutch oven, heat oil over medium-high heat. Whisk in flour, stirring constantly until brown roux is achieved. (See roux recipes.) Add onions, celery, bell peppers and garlic. Sauté 3–5 minutes or until vegetables are wilted. Blend in andouille and sauté an additional 3–5 minutes. Stir in claw crabmeat, ½ cup shrimp and okra. Slowly add hot shellfish stock, one ladle at a time, stirring constantly. Bring to a low boil, reduce to simmer and cook 30 minutes. If necessary, additional stock may be used to retain volume. Add green onions and parsley. Season to taste using salt, cayenne and hot sauce. Fold in shrimp, lump crabmeat, oysters and reserved oyster liquid. Return to a low boil and cook approximately 5 minutes. Adjust seasonings if necessary. Serve over cooked rice.

SHRIMP AND OKRA GUMBO BAYOU TECHE

Prep Time: 1 Hour
Yields: 6–8 Servings

Comment:

Bayou Teche winds its way through Acadiana bisecting many Cajun villages along the way. Regardless of what bayou bank they reside on, all the people of Cajun Country are great gumbo cooks. This gumbo, or one similar to it, can be found simmering in most Acadian homes.

Ingredients:

3 pounds (35-count) shrimp, peeled and deveined
1 (16-ounce) package cut frozen okra
2½ quarts shellfish stock (see recipe)
1 cup vegetable oil
1½ cups flour
2 cups diced onions
1 cup diced celery
1 cup diced green bell peppers
¼ cup minced garlic
2 bay leaves
2 tbsps chopped thyme
2 tbsps chopped basil
1 cup diced Creole tomatoes
salt and black pepper to taste
Creole seasoning to taste
1 cup sliced green onions
½ cup chopped parsley
Louisiana hot sauce to taste

Method:

If you have head-on shrimp or reserved shrimp shells, make a shellfish stock according to the recipe. Otherwise, use purchased clam juice or seafood bouillon cubes. Water may also be used as a stock substitute. In a cast iron Dutch oven, heat oil over medium-high heat. Whisk in flour, stirring constantly until a Cajun brown roux is achieved. (See roux recipes.) Stir in onions, celery, bell peppers and garlic. Sauté 3–5 minutes or until vegetables are wilted. Add stock, one ladle at a time, until soup-like consistency is achieved. Bring to a rolling boil, whisking constantly. Reduce heat to simmer then stir in bay leaves, thyme, basil, tomatoes and okra. Season lightly using salt, pepper and Creole seasoning. Simmer 30 minutes, stirring occasionally. Stir in half of shrimp and continue to cook for 15 minutes. Additional stock may be used to reach desired consistency. Add green onions and parsley. Adjust seasonings if necessary. Remove bay leaves and gently fold in remaining shrimp. Cook 3–5 minutes or until shrimp are pink and curled. Serve a generous portion in a soup bowl over steamed white rice with a dash of hot sauce. You may also wish to sprinkle ½ teaspoon of filé powder or ground sassafras leaves over gumbo before serving.

CHICKEN AND SAUSAGE GUMBO

Prep Time: 2 Hours
Yields: 8–10 Servings

Comment:

Chicken and sausage are the most popular gumbo ingredients in Louisiana. The ingredients were readily available since most Cajun families raised chickens and made a variety of sausages. Oysters were often added to this everyday dish for a special Sunday or holiday version.

Ingredients:

1 (5-pound) stewing hen
1 pound smoked sausage or andouille
1 cup oil
1½ cups flour
2 cups diced onions
2 cups diced celery
1 cup diced bell peppers
¼ cup minced garlic
3 quarts chicken stock
24 button mushrooms
2 cups sliced green onions
1 bay leaf
sprig of thyme
1 tbsp chopped basil
salt and cracked black pepper to taste
Louisiana hot sauce to taste
½ cup chopped parsley
cooked white rice

Method:

Using a sharp boning knife, cut hen into 8–10 serving pieces. Remove as much fat as possible. Cut smoked sausage or andouille into ½-inch slices and set aside. In a 2-gallon stockpot, heat oil over medium-high heat. Whisk in flour, stirring constantly until golden brown roux is achieved. (See roux recipes.) Stir in onions, celery, bell peppers and garlic. Sauté 3–5 minutes or until vegetables are wilted. Blend chicken and sausage into vegetable mixture, and sauté approximately 15 minutes. Add chicken stock, one ladle at a time, stirring constantly. Bring to a rolling boil, reduce to simmer and cook approximately 1 hour. Skim any fat or oil that rises to top of pot. Stir in mushrooms, green onions, bay leaf, thyme and basil. Season to taste using salt, pepper and hot sauce. Cook an additional 1–2 hours, if necessary, until chicken is tender and falling apart. Stir in parsley and adjust seasonings. Serve over hot white rice. NOTE: You may wish to boil chicken 1–2 hours before beginning gumbo. Reserve stock, bone chicken and use meat and stock in gumbo.

DEATH BY GUMBO

Prep Time: 2 Hours
Yields: 12 Servings

Comment:

This gumbo was created for Craig Claiborne of *The New York Times*. When he asked me to come to his home on Long Island to create a special dinner depicting the evolution of Cajun and Creole cuisine, I knew this unusual dish would be the perfect choice.

Ingredients for Quail:

12 boneless bobwhite quail
1½ cups cooked white rice
salt and cracked black pepper
1 tsp filé powder
2 tbsps chopped parsley
12 (⅛-inch) slices of andouille
12 oysters poached in their own liquid

Method:

NOTE: Although it is best to use boneless quail for this recipe, you may also use bone-in birds if boneless are not available. Season birds inside and out using salt and cracked black pepper. Season cooked white rice with salt, pepper, filé powder and chopped parsley. Stuff cavity of quail with 1 tablespoon rice, 1 slice andouille, 1 oyster and a second tablespoon of rice. Continue this process until all quails have been stuffed. Cover with plastic wrap and set aside.

Ingredients for Gumbo:

12 stuffed and seasoned
   bobwhite quail
1 cup vegetable oil
1½ cups flour
2 cups diced onions
2 cups diced celery
1 cup diced bell peppers
¼ cup minced garlic
1 cup sliced mushrooms
½ cup sliced tasso
3 quarts chicken stock (see recipe)
1 tsp thyme
salt and cracked black pepper
1 cup sliced green onions
1 cup chopped parsley

Method:

In a 2-gallon stockpot, heat oil over medium-high heat. Whisk in flour, stirring constantly until a light brown roux is achieved. (See roux recipes.) Add onions, celery, bell peppers and garlic. Sauté 3–5 minutes or until vegetables are wilted. Stir in mushrooms and tasso. Cook an additional 3 minutes then add chicken stock, one ladle at a time, stirring constantly. Stir in thyme, bring to a rolling boil, reduce to simmer and cook 30 minutes. Season to taste using salt and pepper. Place stuffed quail into gumbo and allow to simmer 30 minutes. When quail are tender and legs separate from body easily, remove birds to a platter and keep warm. Strain all seasonings from gumbo through a fine sieve and reserve gumbo liquid. Return stock to pot, add quail, green onions and parsley then bring to a low boil. When serving, place 1 quail in center of soup bowl and cover with gumbo liquid.

DUCK, ANDOUILLE AND OYSTER GUMBO

Prep Time: 2 Hours
Yields: 12 Servings

Comment:

Almost every species of wild game in Louisiana has been used in the creation of gumbo. Because most Cajun men were hunters, it is not surprising that the day's kill was used in the evening meal. Many of the hunters preferred mallard duck and smoked andouille gumbo.

Ingredients:

2 mallard ducks, cut into serving pieces
2 pounds sliced andouille
2 pints select oysters
1 cup vegetable oil
1½ cups flour
2 cups diced onions
1 cup diced celery
1 cup diced bell peppers
¼ cup minced garlic
3 quarts chicken stock (see recipe)
12 chicken livers
2 cups sliced green onions
1 cup chopped parsley
salt and black pepper to taste
Louisiana hot sauce to taste
cooked white rice

Method:

In a 2-gallon stock pot, heat oil over medium-high heat. Whisk in flour, stirring constantly until golden brown roux is achieved. (See roux recipes.) Stir in onions, celery, bell peppers and garlic. Sauté 3–5 minutes or until vegetables are wilted. Fold in duck and andouille. Sauté approximately 15 minutes. Add chicken stock, one ladle at a time, stirring constantly. Bring to a rolling boil, reduce to simmer and stir in chicken livers. Cook 1 hour, adding stock as needed until duck is tender. Add oysters then sprinkle in green onions and parsley. Season to taste with salt, pepper and hot sauce. Cook an additional 5 minutes and serve over steamed white rice.

"Cooking is just like religion. Rules don't no more make a cook than sermons make a saint."
Told to Leah Chase by old African-American cook

GUMBO DES HERBES

Prep Time: 3 Hours
Yields: 8–10 Servings

Comment:

Although there are many versions of this recipe, Leah Chase, owner of Dooky Chase Restaurant in New Orleans, has the best recipe in the world for this dish. Leah, the Queen of Creole Cooking, serves this famous gumbo on Holy Thursday at her restaurant on Orleans Avenue.

Ingredients:

1 bunch mustard greens
1 bunch collard greens
1 bunch turnip greens
1 bunch watercress
1 bunch beet tops
1 bunch carrot tops
½ head lettuce
½ head cabbage
1 bunch spinach
3 cups diced onions
1 cup diced celery
1 cup diced bell peppers
¼ cup minced garlic
2 gallons water
5 tbsps flour
1 pound smoked sausage
1 pound smoked ham
1 pound brisket or pork butt, cubed
1 pound beef stew meat
½ tsp thyme leaves
salt and cayenne pepper to taste
1 tbsp filé powder
cooked white rice (optional)

Method:

Clean all greens 2–3 times under cold, running water, making sure to remove bad leaves and to rinse away any soil or grit. Remove large center stem from leaves and discard. Chop greens coarsely. In a 12-quart pot bring greens, onions, celery, bell peppers, garlic and water to a rolling boil. Reduce to simmer, cover and cook 30 minutes. Strain greens and reserve liquid. Purée greens in a food processor. Pour greens into a mixing bowl, blend in flour and set aside. Slice all meats into 1-inch pieces and place in pot. Return reserved liquid to pot, bring to a boil, cover and cook 30–45 minutes. Strain, remove meat from liquid and reserve each separately. In empty pot, add puréed greens, meat and enough liquid to create a soup-like consistency. Season with thyme, salt and pepper. Bring to a low boil stirring occasionally to keep greens from sticking. Cook 45 minutes, adding stock or water to retain volume. Add filé powder, stir well and adjust salt and pepper if necessary. May be served over white rice or eaten alone.

RED BEANS AND RICE GUMBO

Prep Time: 1 Hour
Yields: 10–12 Servings

Comment:

In South Louisiana, we think of red beans as a "Monday" dish, and we always serve them over rice with a link of smoked sausage. This gumbo started out as a perfect way to make use of leftover red beans and rice, and since has become a fall delicacy.

Ingredients:

1 (16-ounce) can Blue Runner New Orleans Red Beans
1 (10–12-ounce) can red kidney beans in water
1 cup cooked long grain rice
¼ cup vegetable oil
¼ cup bacon fat
½ cup flour
1 cup diced onions
1 cup diced celery
½ cup diced bell peppers
¼ cup minced garlic
1 quart chicken stock or water (see recipe)
1 pound diced sugar-cured ham
½ pound sliced smoked sausage
½ cup sliced green onions
½ cup chopped parsley
salt and pepper to taste

Method:

In a 7-quart cast iron pot, heat oil and bacon fat over medium-high heat. Whisk in flour, stirring constantly until dark brown roux is achieved. (See roux recipes.) Stir in onions, celery and bell peppers. Sauté 3–5 minutes or until vegetables are wilted. Blend in garlic and sauté, stirring occasionally, for an additional 3 minutes. Add chicken stock, one ladle at a time, stirring constantly. Stir in ham and smoked sausage and cook 3–5 minutes. Blend Blue Runner beans into the stock. Bring to a rolling boil, reduce to simmer and cook 45 minutes. Use additional stock or water as necessary to maintain soup-like consistency. Stir in kidney beans, rice, green onions and parsley. Season to taste with salt and pepper. Return to a low boil and serve immediately.

LUSCIOUS LEMON SOUP

Prep Time: 1 Hour
Yields: 6–8 Servings

Comment:

Lemon soup is the perfect beginning or ending to any meal, especially during hot Louisiana summers. This soup is so wonderfully cooling, perhaps it should be called luscious lemon malt!

Ingredients:

3 tbsps freshly squeezed lemon juice
2 tbsps grated lemon peel
2 eggs
½ cup sugar
1 tbsp pure vanilla extract
1 quart buttermilk
1 cup vanilla ice cream
fresh mint leaves

Method:

In a large bowl, whisk together eggs, sugar and vanilla. Add lemon juice, lemon peel and buttermilk, continuing to whisk until well blended. Pour mixture into a 9-cup food processor. NOTE: If you do not have a large enough processor, blend the soup in 2 or 3 equal batches. Add ½ cup ice cream and blend mixture 1–2 minutes or until liquid has become frothy. Transfer soup into a large crystal pitcher, cover and chill for a minimum of 4 hours. Serve soup in champagne glasses and garnish with remaining ice cream, mint and zest, if desired. NOTE: When grating lemon peel, be careful to remove only the yellow outer layer and not the white skin underneath.

CHILLED WATERMELON SOUP

Prep Time: 30 Minutes
Yields: 4 Servings

Comment:
Watermelon, a gift from Africa, is a great summer joy in the South. Creating a cold, refreshing soup from this luscious fruit is a wonderful treat during the hot summer months.

Ingredients:
2 pounds diced seedless watermelon
1 mango, finely diced
½ ounce grated ginger
8 ounces peach, apricot or berry purée
2 kumquats, sliced
edible flowers for garnish

Method:
Place 1 pound of diced watermelon in a food processor and blend to liquefy. Set aside and refrigerate. Finely dice remaining watermelon, then place in a bowl with mango and grated ginger. Allow fruit to marinate 1 hour. When ready to serve, place an equal amount of fruit purée in 4 soup bowls with equal portions of marinated melon-mango mixture. Top with watermelon juice. Garnish rim of bowl with kumquat slices and edible flower petals.

GOLDEN GAZPACHO

Prep Time: 1½ Hours
Yields: 6 Servings

Comment:
Gazpacho originated in the Andalusia region of southern Spain. This refreshingly chilled soup is the perfect treat during the hot summers on the bayou.

Ingredients:
1 large cantaloupe, peeled, seeded and chopped
3 yellow peppers, seeded and chopped
1 cup plain yogurt
½ cup dry white wine
¼ cup sliced onion
1 tbsp chopped cilantro
1½ tbsps lime juice
salt to taste
6 sprigs cilantro

Method:
In a food processor, purée cantaloupe, peppers, yogurt, wine, onion and cilantro. Stir in lime juice and season with salt. Refrigerate until well chilled. When ready to serve, ladle soup into bowls and top each with a sprig of cilantro.

Ferris's Grocery, Donaldsonville, La.

Salads

The predecessors of today's salads have existed for centuries. The name originally derived from the Latin herba salata, which literally means "salted greens." The Romans were known to garnish raw and cooked vegetables with a concoction of oil, vinegar, herbs and seasonings. By the 17th and 18th centuries, various types of salad greens, meat and poultry were included in European salads. Today the term "salad" can be applied to a variety of dishes and presentations, from those filled with greens topped with light dressings to those consisting of meat or seafood in a mayonnaise-based dressing.

Salads may include any combination of leafy greens, raw or cooked vegetables, fruit, meat, seafood, cheese, rice or pasta. While the term may be applied to a plate of chopped iceberg with a dollop of commercially prepared dressing, you won't find that salad "recipe" here. In fact, a traditional Cajun salad might consist of very untraditional ingredients, what many of us might consider weeds. It was common in South Louisiana to peel the skin and spines from thistles or *chadron*, slice the stems like celery and eat them with vinegar and pepper. Also common in Cajun salads was purslane, an edible wild green popular in Europe since the Middle Ages. The habit of eating purslane probably came to Louisiana with French and German settlers. Although often used in ethnic foods, in most of the United States it is considered a pest. Another strange salad component, pokeweed, was commonly eaten in the Southern United States as poke salat or poke salad, but it is now shunned as a poisonous plant by many. The Native Americans apparently showed early colonists how to render this toxic weed safe to eat by boiling it twice and changing the water each time. Some Europeans took the plants home with them, and poke salat remains popular in Europe as well. In Louisiana, the very young, tender first shoots of the plants have long been plucked and eaten as uncooked greens. Although this practice is not recommended, you can be assured that prepared properly, poke salat is safe to eat. This green can

even be found commercially canned and sold in grocery stores.

Two more ingredients traditionally found in Cajun and Creole salads are watermelon and tomatoes. Louisiana's climate is perfectly suited for producing large, sweet, juicy watermelons. In New Orleans, vendors would create a bed of ice for their wares and set up tables on the "neutral ground" of the dual carriageways. Workers could enjoy a refreshing treat on the way home or purchase a melon to be enjoyed later on its own, sprinkled with salt or cubed over a bed of greens. Tomatoes fresh from the garden are also an ever-present guest at the summer table. Whether tossed with other ingredients or simply sliced and dressed with salt and pepper, or perhaps mayonnaise, tomatoes alone can be the making of the perfect salad.

The salad dressing most closely associated with Cajun and Creole cuisine is rémoulade. There are numerous variations of this creamy, spicy dressing, and most cooks swear theirs is the only true way. No Creole meal would be complete without a salad at its side, perhaps a tribute to the ancient belief that lettuce had magical soothing powers. The French style of topping a salad with oil, vinegar and seasonings is preferred by the Creoles. This oil and vinegar dressing is derived from the earliest salads created in Rome and France. A new twist on this tradition can be found in Cane Syrup Vinaigrette,

The gardeners at White Oak Plantation, Baton Rouge, La., pause for a lunch break.

which is enhanced with the sweet flavor of Louisiana sugarcane.

It is generally held that dressing a salad is not simply a matter of placing leaves and other ingredients in a salad bowl; it is a ritual in itself. An ancient proverb attributed to both the Spanish and the Romans states that a perfect salad requires "a miser for vinegar, a spendthrift for oil, a wise man for salt and a madcap to mix the ingredients together."

Whatever the ingredients may be, creating a wonderful salad can be a simple task. Remember to always use fresh ingredients and arrange them artfully to create a pleasing combination of textures

and colors. Most importantly, make sure the combination of ingredients creates a well-balanced flavor.

A salad can be an entrée, an appetizer, an accompaniment, a dessert or even a palate cleanser between courses. In Louisiana, the soil and climate produce the ultimate ingredients, including local delicacies such as Creole tomatoes and Ponchatoula strawberries. Our seemingly endless waterways provide an equally limitless supply of seafood and crawfish. Here, the creation of sensational salads is a simple science.

ORANGE-BASIL VINAIGRETTE

Prep Time: 5 Minutes
Yields: 6 Servings

Comment:
The sweet orange flavor infused with basil creates a refreshing dressing.
This vinaigrette is also wonderful as a sauce over grilled fish and is a perfect
topping for our Herb-Encrusted Salmon Salad. (See recipe.)

Ingredients:
1 tbsp orange zest
¼ cup orange juice
¼ cup minced basil
2 cloves minced garlic
½ tsp ground ginger
salt and black pepper to taste
½ cup extra virgin olive oil

CANE SYRUP VINAIGRETTE

Prep Time: 30 Minutes
Yields: 2½ Cups

Comment:

Many Louisianians love to add the flavor of cane syrup to dressings and sauces. Most people compare the flavor of cane syrup to molasses. However, the two syrups are very different. Molasses is a much stronger, darker syrup used in dishes such as gingerbread and spice cakes; whereas cane syrup is used as a topping for breakfast items.

Ingredients:

1 egg yolk
1 tbsp minced onions
1 tbsp minced garlic
1 tsp chopped basil
1 tsp chopped thyme
1 tsp cracked black pepper
1 tsp Creole mustard
¼ cup red wine vinegar
2 tbsps orange juice
2 tbsps Steen's Cane Syrup
1 cup vegetable oil
1 cup olive oil
salt and cracked black pepper to taste

Method:

Place egg yolk in a large mixing bowl and whisk 1 minute. Add onions, garlic, basil, thyme, pepper, mustard, vinegar, orange juice and cane syrup. Continue to whisk until all ingredients are blended. Pour in oils in a slow steady stream, whisking constantly. Season to taste with salt and pepper.

Method:

Combine all ingredients in a 1-pint mason jar. Tightly screw lid on jar. Shake vigorously to thoroughly mix ingredients. Adjust salt and pepper if necessary.

1800s sugar nipper for cutting sugar loaves

NICE AND SPICY COLESLAW

Prep Time: 2 Hours
Yields: 8–10 Servings

Comment:
This is an easy, delicious coleslaw recipe. To make the preparation even simpler, you can "cheat" and use this dressing with a pack of precut coleslaw vegetables from the supermarket.

Ingredients:
6 cups shredded cabbage
1 small onion, grated
1 carrot, peeled and grated
1 tbsp minced parsley
¼ cup vegetable oil
3 tbsps cider vinegar
¼ cup mayonnaise
1 tbsp sugar
¼ tsp dry mustard
⅛ tsp garlic powder
½ tsp celery seed
salt and cracked black pepper to taste

Method:
Toss cabbage, onions, carrots and parsley until well mixed then set aside. In a small bowl, combine all remaining ingredients. Mix well. Pour dressing over cabbage mixture and toss gently. Chill for at least 2 hours before serving.

SWEET AND SPICY COLESLAW

Prep Time: 1 Hour
Yields: 8–10 Servings

Comment:
This is the perfect recipe when looking for a spur of the moment side dish. It is excellent with fried fish or chicken, but I often use it as the perfect topping for a seafood po'boy.

Ingredients:
5 cups shredded green cabbage
1 cup thinly sliced purple onions
1 yellow bell pepper, thinly sliced
1 green bell pepper, thinly sliced
1 red bell pepper, thinly sliced
¼ cup white wine vinegar
3 tbsp olive oil
1 tbsp sugar
¾ tsp dry mustard
¾ tsp salt
½ tsp black pepper

Method:
NOTE: To shred cabbage, cut head in half, then into quarters; core and thinly slice crosswise. In a large ceramic bowl, toss shredded cabbage, onions and sweet peppers. In a small saucepan, bring vinegar, oil, sugar, mustard, salt and pepper to a rolling boil. Stir until sugar is dissolved. Pour hot dressing over cabbage mixture and toss to coat. Let cool at room temperature for 1 hour then serve. Slaw can be refrigerated in airtight container for up to 24 hours.

MARDI GRAS SLAW

Prep Time: 1 Hour
Yields: 8–10 Servings

Comment:
This festive fruit-filled coleslaw tastes unbelievable with dishes such as barbecued ribs or shredded pork. Do not let the slaw sit for too long before serving or the apples and avocados may darken. The lemon juice in the dressing will help to slow this process.

Ingredients for Dressing:
1 cup poppy-seed dressing
1 cup fresh lemon juice (or apple cider vinegar)
1 tsp salt
1 tsp cracked black pepper

Method:
Whisk poppy-seed dressing with lemon juice. Season with salt and pepper then cover and refrigerate for at least 1 hour and up to 6 hours.

Ingredients for Slaw:
1 large head purple or green cabbage
2 cups whole, seedless red and green grapes
2 avocados, pitted, peeled and sliced
2 tart apples, peeled and chopped
¾ cup pecans
5–6 green onions, sliced
2 tbsps chopped cilantro

Method:
Core and halve cabbage. Slice ½–¾-inch thick and chop. Toss cabbage, grapes, avocados, apples and pecans in a large bowl. Pour dressing over slaw. Add onions and cilantro and mix gently. Serve immediately or cover and refrigerate.

MARINATED SAUERKRAUT SALAD

Prep Time: 30 Minutes
Yields: 6–8 Servings

Comment:

Early German immigrants definitely left their mark on Creole cuisine. Cabbage and cauliflower are often seen in salads because of this German presence, but nothing exemplifies their cooking better than a sauerkraut salad.

Ingredients:

1 (16-ounce) jar sauerkraut	½ cup minced yellow bell peppers
½ cup white vinegar	1 tbsp minced garlic
¾ cup sugar	½ cup grated carrots
¼ cup vegetable oil	1 tsp caraway seeds
½ cup minced onions	1 tsp celery seeds
½ cup minced celery	salt and cracked black pepper to taste
½ cup minced red bell peppers	Louisiana hot sauce to taste

Method:

Thoroughly drain and rinse sauerkraut once or twice, then place in a large mixing bowl and set aside. In a heavy-bottomed skillet, heat vinegar over medium-high heat. Whisk in sugar and oil until well blended. Stir in onions, celery, bell peppers and garlic. Sauté 3–5 minutes or until vegetables are wilted. Remove from heat and blend in carrots. Allow carrots to wilt, then pour mixture over sauerkraut. Mix in caraway and celery seeds. Season to taste with salt, pepper and hot sauce. Blend well, cover and chill a minimum of 6–8 hours, preferably overnight. Serve as a salad over mixed greens or as a topping for sausage, ham or franks.

RÉMOULADE SLAW

Prep Time: 30 Minutes
Yields: 6 Servings

Comment:

Commonly served with shrimp or other seafood, Rémoulade Sauce can be found in any restaurant in South Louisiana. This rémoulade slaw is wonderful on The Peacemaker: Ultimate Oyster Po'boy. (See recipe.)

Ingredients for Rémoulade Sauce:

1½ cups heavy-duty mayonnaise
½ cup Creole mustard
1 tbsp Worcestershire sauce
1 tsp hot sauce
½ cup spicy ketchup
¼ cup minced red bell peppers
¼ cup minced yellow bell peppers
½ cup minced celery
2 tbsps minced garlic
¼ cup minced parsley
½ tbsp lemon juice
salt and cracked black pepper to taste

Ingredients for Slaw:

4 cups shredded iceberg lettuce
¾ cup shredded red cabbage
¾ cup Rémoulade Sauce

Method:

Combine rémoulade ingredients and blend well. Toss lettuce and cabbage with prepared sauce and serve.

SPINACH SALAD WITH SAUTÉED PEARS

Prep Time: 30 Minutes
Yields: 6 Servings

Comment:
Pears are often grown in backyards or home orchards in Louisiana. The abundance of the fruit lends to many interesting cooked pear recipes. This salad combines the sweet pear flavor with crisp, fresh spinach.

Ingredients:
6 cups torn, fresh spinach
2 pears, cored and diced
¼ cup lemon juice
¼ cup olive oil
4 slices bacon, chopped
1 cup sliced onions
½ cup sliced red bell peppers
½ cup sliced yellow bell peppers
½ cup white wine vinegar
½ cup red wine vinegar
2 tbsps sugar
1 tsp grated orange peel
1 tsp chopped thyme
½ tsp chopped basil
salt and cracked black pepper to taste
Louisiana hot sauce to taste

Method:
Wild cooking pears are recommended for this dish; however, you may substitute any available local variety. The pears will brown once diced. To prevent discoloration, place diced fruit and ¼ cup lemon juice into a bowl until ready to cook. In a large sauté pan, heat olive oil over medium-high heat. Add bacon, stirring until fat is rendered and bacon is crispy. Mix in onions and bell peppers. Sauté 3–5 minutes or until vegetables are wilted. Stir in diced pears and cook until al dente. It is important for pears to have a firm texture. Mix in vinegars, sugar and orange peel. Bring to a low boil then reduce to simmer. Season to taste with thyme, basil, salt, pepper and hot sauce. Place spinach in a large salad bowl and pour pear mixture over greens. Toss quickly and serve immediately.

GREEN BEAN AND VIDALIA ONION SALAD

Prep Time: 30 Minutes
Yields: 6 Servings

Comment:

The Georgia-grown Vidalia onion is known for its sweet, mild flavor. This onion has acquired a reputation as the world's sweetest onion. Vidalia onions complement the flavor of green beans superbly in this relatively simple recipe.

Ingredients:

2 (10-ounce) packages frozen cut green beans
½ cup sliced Vidalia onions
1 tbsp sugar
½ cup olive oil
3 tbsps white wine vinegar
¼ tsp dried mustard
¼ tsp salt
cayenne pepper to taste
4 slices cooked bacon, crumbled
1 cup shredded Swiss cheese.

Method:

Cook green beans according to package directions, drain and chill. Place onions in a small bowl and top with sugar. Cover and chill. In a pint jar, combine oil, vinegar, mustard, salt and cayenne pepper. Seal and shake vigorously. To serve, toss beans, onions, bacon and cheese in a large bowl. Shake salad dressing again and pour over salad. Toss well and serve.

ROASTED GARLIC, GREEN BEAN AND PASTA SALAD

Prep Time: 1 Hour
Yields: 6–8 Servings

Comment:

Garlic is the perfect vegetable seasoning for any dish. Roasted garlic and pasta enhance the common cold green bean salad for a unique flavor.

Ingredients:

4 elephant toe garlic cloves
1 pound fresh tiny green beans
1 cup cooked tiny seashell pasta
1 red bell pepper
1 yellow bell pepper
½ cup olive oil
3 tbsps balsamic vinegar
2 tbsps lime juice
2 tbsps chopped basil
2 tbsps toasted pecans
salt and cracked black pepper to taste
Louisiana hot sauce to taste

Method:

Preheat oven to 375°F. Place whole peppers directly over the open flame or under broiler of stove, turning frequently. Broil on all sides until skin blisters and blackens. Remove from flame and place into a brown paper bag for 10–15 minutes. Peel blistered skin from pepper under cold running water. Seed peeled peppers, julienne and set aside. In a 1-gallon stockpot, cook beans in lightly salted water until tender but still firm. Drain and cool under tap water to stop cooking process then set aside. In a heavy-bottomed sauté pan, heat ¼ cup olive oil over medium-high heat. Sauté garlic cloves 5–7 minutes or until golden brown on all sides. Do not scorch as garlic will become bitter. Cover skillet and place in oven 8–10 minutes or until garlic cloves are tender. Remove garlic, cool, chop and set aside. If olive oil is not scorched or over-browned, reserve and add to dressing mixture for added flavor. In a large mixing bowl, whisk together remaining olive oil, vinegar, lime juice and basil. In a separate bowl, place green beans, garlic, bell peppers, cooked pasta and toasted pecans. Season to taste with salt, pepper and hot sauce. Top with salad dressing and mix well to coat all ingredients. Serve in a large crystal salad bowl or place green bean mixture atop a variety of colorful mixed greens. NOTE: If desired, sauté garlic and roast peppers 1–2 days ahead of time.

MIXED GREENS WITH WARM PONCHATOULA STRAWBERRY VINAIGRETTE

Prep Time: 15 Minutes
Yields: 8–10 Servings

Comment:

No other strawberries can compare to the flavor of those grown in Louisiana. During the early spring, strawberry vinaigrette can be made to take advantage of the abundance of the fruit. This salad can be served before your meal or used as a bed for your favorite meat. Try serving this salad under Herb-Encrusted Lamb Lollipops. (See recipe.)

Ingredients:

2 (5-ounce) bags mixed salad greens or greens of choice
½ cup chopped Louisiana strawberries
¼ cup olive oil
1 tbsp minced onions
1 tbsp minced garlic
¼ cup red wine vinegar
1 tsp chopped basil
1 tsp chopped thyme
1 tsp cracked black pepper
2 tsps Creole mustard
4 tbsps orange-strawberry juice blend
2 tbsps Steen's Cane Syrup
1 cup vegetable oil
¾ cup olive oil
salt and cracked black pepper to taste

Method:

In a large skillet, heat ¼ cup olive oil over medium-high heat. Add onions and garlic and sauté for 2–3 minutes or until softened. Stir in strawberries and vinegar. Bring to a simmer. Blend in basil, thyme, pepper, mustard, juice and cane syrup. Whisk in vegetable oil and ¾ cup olive oil. Cook until warm. In a large mixing bowl, toss salad greens with warm dressing. Season to taste with salt and pepper.

SPINACH AND STRAWBERRY SALAD PONCHATOULA

Prep Time: 30 Minutes
Yields: 6 Servings

Comment:

Ponchatoula, La., is the strawberry capital of the world. It is surprising to the residents of this sleepy South Louisiana town that the rest of the world considers the strawberry to be only a dessert ingredient. Strawberries can be used in soups or sauces, over pork roast or lamb and even atop salads. Berries for this salad should be slightly overripe but not mushy.

Ingredients:

10 ounces fresh spinach leaves, cleaned and dried
1 pint ripe Louisiana strawberries, sliced
1 egg yolk
1 tbsp balsamic vinegar
4 tbsps strawberry wine
6 ounces vegetable oil
1 tbsp chopped thyme
1 tbsp chopped tarragon
salt and pepper to taste
1 tbsp extra virgin olive oil
1 (5-ounce) block Parmesan cheese

Method:

Rinse spinach leaves 2–3 times under cold running water to remove all sand and grit. Dry well and set aside. Using the large holes of a grater, hand-grate Parmesan cheese. Whisk together egg yolk, vinegar and wine in a stainless steel bowl. Whisking constantly, add vegetable oil in a steady stream. A smooth emulsified dressing will emerge. Stir in thyme and tarragon. Season to taste with salt and pepper. Continue whisking until ingredients are well blended. Refrigerate dressing in a glass until ready to use. Prior to serving, toss spinach with extra virgin olive oil and drizzle with desired amount of vinaigrette. Once leaves are evenly coated, but not wilted, add strawberries and cheese and toss once or twice. Serve in a large crystal salad bowl.

ROASTED BEET SALAD

Prep Time: 1½ Hours
Yields: 6 Servings

Comment:

In Louisiana, beets are used most often as a salad ingredient. Nothing is better than freshly boiled beets with a simple touch of oil, vinegar, salt and pepper. This salad is best when prepared one day ahead of time and allowed to chill.

Ingredients:

5 pounds medium beets with greens
½ cup extra virgin olive oil
¼ cup balsamic vinegar
1 tbsp minced garlic
¼ cup chopped chives
salt and cracked black pepper to taste
6 tbsps mayonnaise

Method:

Preheat oven to 350°F. Separate beets from tops and reserve greens. Wash beets and wrap tightly in an aluminum foil pouch. Bake 45 minutes or until tender when pierced with a fork. Remove, unwrap and allow to cool. While beets are cooling, bring 2 quarts of lightly salted water to a rolling boil. Rinse beet greens under cold tap water to remove any sand or grit. Remove large stem from center of greens then poach in boiling water. Cook until tender but not overcooked. Remove, drain and cut into fine strips. Place greens on salad plates and set aside. When beets are cool, peel away outer skin. Thinly slice and equally distribute over greens. In a mixing bowl, whisk together olive oil, vinegar, garlic and chives. Season to taste with salt and pepper. Pour dressing over salad and top with a dollop of mayonnaise.

STUFFED CREOLE
TOMATO SALAD

Prep Time: 30 Minutes
Yields: 6 Servings

Comment:
Luscious red Creole tomatoes provide the focal point for this showpiece salad.

Ingredients:
6 Creole tomatoes, chilled
½ cup diced cucumbers
½ cup diced celery
¼ cup diced onions
¼ cup diced bell peppers
½ tsp diced garlic
½ cup cottage cheese
¼ cup Parmesan cheese
2 boiled eggs, diced
½ tsp salt
black pepper to taste
2 tbsps Italian dressing
½ tsp chopped basil

Method:
In a large mixing bowl, combine all ingredients except tomatoes. Mix well, cover and refrigerate at least 2 hours. Cut ¾-inch off top of each tomato and reserve. Using a teaspoon, scoop out tomato seeds and pulp. Turn tomatoes upside down and allow to drain well on paper towels. Dice one cup of sliced tomato tops and mix in with chilled vegetables. When tomatoes are well drained, stuff each with an equal amount of vegetable mixture. Serve on multicolored lettuces as a salad or appetizer.

MARINATED CREOLE TOMATO AND
RED ONION SALAD

Prep Time: 30 Minutes
Yields: 6 Servings

Comment:
Creole is the marketing name given to all tomatoes grown in St. Bernard Parish. These tomatoes are the reddest, ripest and juiciest of the Louisiana varieties.

Ingredients:
5 Creole tomatoes, cubed
1 Bermuda onion, thinly sliced
¼ cup vegetable oil
¼ cup extra virgin olive oil
¼ cup red wine vinegar
1 tbsp Louisiana cane syrup
juice of 1 lemon
1 tsp chopped garlic
2 tbsps chopped basil
1 tsp fresh thyme leaves
1 tsp chopped oregano
1 tsp chopped tarragon
dash of hot sauce
1 tbsp Worcestershire sauce
salt and cracked black pepper to taste

Method:
Using a sharp paring knife, cut Creole tomatoes into 1-inch cubes, discarding stems. In a large mixing bowl, combine tomatoes and onions. In a separate mixing bowl, blend together all remaining ingredients. Pour dressing over tomato mixture and stir until coated. Cover with plastic wrap and marinate in refrigerator for 2 hours. When ready to serve, spoon marinated tomato mixture into center of a salad plate garnished with multicolored lettuces such as mesclun mix. Top with additional cracked black pepper. Garnish with bleu cheese crumbles or diced mozzarella cheese, if desired.

TOMATO SALAD

Prep Time: 30 Minutes
Yields: 4 Servings

Comment:

This colorful, zesty medley of tomatoes will enhance any meal. The fresh basil and oregano gives this salad a distinctly Mediterranean character.

Ingredients:

1 Creole tomato
1 orange tomato
1 yellow tomato
1 large Bermuda or red onion
1 tsp chopped basil
1 tsp chopped oregano
olive oil
Steen's Cane Vinegar
salt and black pepper to taste
Louisiana hot sauce to taste

Method:

Slice tomatoes ¼ -inch thick. Slice onions ⅛-inch thick and separate. On a 10-inch platter, arrange sliced tomatoes and top with onions. Sprinkle with fresh basil and oregano. Top with olive oil and vinegar. Season to taste using salt, pepper and hot sauce.

SLICED GREEN TOMATO AND ONION SALAD WITH ORANGE CANE SYRUP VINAIGRETTE

Prep Time: 1 Hour
Yields: 6 Servings

Comment:

In the South, green tomatoes are normally fried or pickled. However, this marinated salad is excellent. For added visual appeal, try adding a few layers of sliced red tomatoes.

Ingredients for Orange Cane Syrup Vinaigrette:

¼ cup cane syrup
½ cup vegetable oil
½ cup olive oil
⅓ cup red wine vinegar
2 tbsps orange juice
½ tsp ground allspice
1 tsp grated orange rind
½ tsp cracked black pepper
½ tsp salt
½ tsp dried mustard

Method:

Combine all ingredients in a quart jar, cover and shake vigorously. Chill thoroughly and shake well before serving. Use as a marinade over sliced tomatoes or as a dressing on salad greens or fresh fruit.

Ingredients for Salad:

6 sliced green tomatoes
2 thinly sliced Bermuda onions
¼ cup sliced green onions
¼ cup minced garlic
¼ cup minced red bell peppers
¼ cup minced yellow bell peppers

Method:

In a large mixing bowl, place alternating layers of tomatoes, Bermuda onions, green onions and garlic. Pour vinaigrette over tomatoes to coat. Cover with plastic wrap and refrigerate 2–3 hours. To serve, place tomatoes and Bermuda onions in a circular pattern around a crystal or glass serving platter. Pour remainder of dressing over tomatoes and garnish with red and yellow bell peppers.

SHOEPEG CORN SALAD

Prep Time: 1 Hour
Yields: 6 Servings

Comment:

Shoepeg corn has a small, white, peg-shaped kernel. This variety is sweeter than most yellow corn, but is not as sweet as some new hybrids. Shoepeg corn is available canned and frozen in some parts of the United States, especially in the South.

Ingredients:

3 (11-ounce) cans white shoepeg corn, drained
1 cup mayonnaise
¼ cup canola oil
2 tbsps red wine vinegar
1 tsp dried mustard
1 tsp sugar
salt and black pepper to taste
Louisiana hot sauce to taste
1 cup diced celery
½ cup diced red bell peppers
½ cup finely sliced green onions
2 tomatoes, diced

Method:

In a large mixing bowl, whisk together mayonnaise, oil, vinegar, mustard and sugar. Season to taste with salt, pepper and hot sauce. You may wish to slightly overseason with pepper to enhance corn. Stir in corn, celery, bell peppers and green onions until thoroughly coated. Carefully fold in tomatoes. Cover with plastic wrap and refrigerate a minimum of 6 hours. This salad may be added to fresh spinach or served alone.

MEDITERRANEAN ORZO SALAD

Prep Time: 1½ Hours
Yields: 6 Servings

Comment:

The literal Italian translation for "orzo" is "barley," but orzo pasta is rice-shaped pasta traditionally used in soups. This cold pasta salad combines orzo with marinated artichoke hearts, Feta cheese and mixed olives to create a great tasting dish straight from the Greek isles.

Ingredients:

1½ cups uncooked orzo pasta
2 (6-ounce) cans marinated artichoke hearts
1 pint cherry or grape tomatoes, halved
1 cucumber
¼ cup minced yellow bell peppers
1 red onion, halved and thinly sliced
1 cup crumbled Feta cheese
1 (2-ounce) can sliced black olives, drained
1 cup Italian olive salad, not drained
¼ cup chopped parsley
1 tsp chopped oregano
salt and cracked black pepper to taste

Method:

Bring a large pot of lightly salted water to a rolling boil. Add pasta and cook 8–10 minutes or until al dente. Peel cucumber, slice in half lengthwise, seed and slice each half. Drain orzo, run under cold water until completely cooled and place in a large bowl. Fold in artichoke hearts (with liquid), tomatoes, cucumbers, bell peppers, onions, Feta, olives, olive salad, parsley and oregano. Season to taste with salt and pepper. Chill at least 1 hour. Serve in a large chilled bowl.

STEAMED BROCCOLI WITH ORANGE GINGER PECAN DRESSING

Prep Time: 30 Minutes
Yields: 6 Servings

Comment:

Broccoli is a great "stand-by" vegetable because it is always ready to be cooked in a hundred different recipes at a moment's notice. Additionally, broccoli is available all year long so there can never be too many ways to prepare this delicacy.

Ingredients:

2 bunches broccoli
½ tsp salt
2 tbsps peanut oil
1 tbsp Louisiana cane syrup
1 tbsp soy sauce
1 tbsp grated orange zest
juice of 1 orange
1 tsp minced garlic
1 tbsp chopped ginger
salt and black pepper to taste
¼ cup chopped pecans

Method:

Separate broccoli florets from stalk using a paring knife and cut away thick woody bottom. You may peel stems if skin is a bit tough. Pour 3 inches of water into a 1-gallon pot, season with ½ teaspoon salt and bring to a rolling boil. Place broccoli in water and cook 5 minutes or until fork-tender. Do not overcook. While broccoli is boiling, combine oil, cane syrup and soy sauce in a blender or food processor. Add orange zest, orange juice, garlic and ginger. Process 2–3 times, scraping down sides as needed. Season to taste with salt and pepper. When ready to serve, remove broccoli from boiling liquid, place in a serving bowl and top with dressing and chopped pecans. Toss gently then season to taste with salt and pepper. Serve hot as a vegetable or cold as a salad.

PINEAPPLE-CARROT CONGEALED SALAD

Prep Time: 1 Hour
Yields: 6 Servings

Comment:

As unappetizing as it might sound to folks who are unaccustomed to the word, "congealed" is a common term in Louisiana. It is a molded salad of flavored gelatin with other ingredients added, like pieces of fruit or vegetables, nuts, cottage cheese or marshmallows. This is a common recipe among Cajun families. One caution: Children might not eat much of any other food if this salad is on the table.

Ingredients:

1 (20-ounce) can crushed pineapple
¾ cup grated carrots
1 (4-ounce) envelope lime gelatin
1¾ cups cold water
⅓ cup sugar
¼ cup lemon juice
¼ tsp salt
¾ cup chopped celery
2 tbsps mayonnaise
lettuce leaves for garnish

Method:

In a 2-quart saucepot, combine gelatin and water, stirring until dissolved. Add sugar, lemon juice and salt. Bring mixture to a rolling boil and reduce to simmer. Stir constantly 3–5 minutes or until gelatin is thoroughly dissolved and clear. Remove from heat. Blend in pineapple with juice, carrots and celery. Allow to cool to room temperature. Whisk in mayonnaise. Pour mixture into a decorative mold, cover with plastic wrap and refrigerate until firm. To serve, unmold congealed salad onto a platter garnished with colored lettuce.

CARROT SALAD BON SEJOUR

Prep Time: 1 Hour
Yields: 6 Servings

Comment:
This version of carrot salad originated in St. James Parish. This dish was commonly served at my home on Bon Sejour Lane near Oak Alley Plantation.

Ingredients:
12 large carrots, peeled
2 cups (150-200 count) shrimp, peeled and deveined
4 boiled eggs
1 cup mayonnaise
¼ cup yellow mustard
1 tbsp Creole mustard
3 tbsps salad oil
½ cup minced celery
¼ cup diced red bell peppers
1 tbsp minced garlic
½ cup sliced green onions
salt and cracked black pepper to taste
Louisiana hot sauce to taste

Method:
Cut carrots into ½-inch thick slices. When reaching larger end of carrot, you may cut the slice in half for more uniformity. In a 1-quart saucepot, bring lightly salted water to a low simmer. Poach shrimp 1–2 minutes or until pink and curled but not overcooked. Using a skimmer or slotted spoon, remove shrimp. Cool and set aside. In same water, poach carrots until al dente. Quickly chill under cold water to stop cooking process. Separate egg whites from yolks and dice whites into ¼-inch cubes. In a large mixing bowl, mash yolks with a fork. Mix in mayonnaise, mustards and oil. Stir in celery, bell peppers, garlic and onions. Season to taste with salt, pepper and hot sauce. Fold in cooled carrots, shrimp and egg whites. Adjust seasonings if necessary. Place in a crystal salad bowl and serve.

PICKLED CARROT SALAD

Prep Time: 1 Hour
Yields: 6 Servings

Comment:
Pickling vegetables is an age-old technique created to preserve food over a year. The pickled flavor allowed the vegetables to have multiple uses. Pickled vegetables can be found as an ingredient in salads or as a garnish in alcoholic beverages such as the Bloody Mary.

Ingredients:
10 sliced carrots
¼ cup oil
½ cup red wine vinegar
¼ cup sugar
1 tbsp dried mustard
1 tbsp Worcestershire sauce
1 can tomato soup
1½ cups julienned bell peppers
½ cup sliced Bermuda onions

Method:
Boil carrots in lightly salted water until tender but not overcooked. Cool under running tap water, drain and set aside. In a saucepot, combine oil, vinegar, sugar, mustard, Worcestershire and tomato soup. Stirring constantly, bring mixture to a rolling boil. In a large serving bowl, layer carrots, onions and bell peppers. Pour boiling soup mixture over carrots. Cool slightly and refrigerate a minimum of 12 hours prior to serving.

LAFITTE'S BLACK, WHITE AND RED BEAN SALAD

Prep Time: 2 Hours
Yields: 6 Servings

Comment:
This beautiful, eye-catching salad is sure to stir up much conversation at the dinner table. Try any of your own favorite dressings on the beans for a more personal touch.

Ingredients:
1 cup black beans
1 cup Great Northern white beans
1 cup red kidney beans
¼ cup chopped parsley
1 tbsp minced garlic
2 tbsps Creole mustard
2 tbsps sour cream
¼ cup white wine
½ cup salad oil
½ cup olive oil
salt and cracked black pepper to taste
Louisiana hot sauce to taste
1 small red onion, sliced
¼ cup diced yellow bell peppers
2 tomatoes, diced
3 large radishes, diced

Method:
Soak beans in individual containers overnight in refrigerator. Drain and rinse under cold water. Place beans in 3 separate saucepots and boil in lightly-salted water 45 minutes or until tender, but not mushy. Rinse beans under cold water to stop cooking process. Drain, transfer to a large bowl and set aside. In a mixing bowl, whisk together parsley, garlic, mustard and sour cream. Add wine and oils. Continue to whisk until well blended. Season with salt, pepper and hot sauce. When ready to serve, toss beans, onions, bell peppers, tomatoes and radishes in a mixing bowl with dressing. Allow to sit at room temperature 1 hour prior to serving. The marinated beans keep in refrigerator for up to 1 week.

CREOLE TOMATO AND WHITE BEAN SALAD

Prep Time: 1 Hour
Yields: 6 Servings

Comment:
Traditionally, white navy beans and red kidney beans are cooked every Monday in Cajun Country. Our love of beans helped inspire this dish, which was created in Bayou Teche.

Ingredients:
6 small Creole tomatoes
1 (19-ounce) can white navy beans
½ cup minced ham
½ cup minced Bermuda onions
½ cup minced celery
¼ cup minced red bell peppers
¼ cup chopped parsley
1 tsp minced garlic
1 tsp chopped thyme
½ cup extra virgin olive oil
2 tbsps red wine vinegar
salt and cracked pepper to taste
Louisiana hot sauce to taste

Method:
Drain and rinse beans well. In a large mixing bowl, blend together beans, ham, onions, celery, bell peppers, parsley, garlic and thyme. Mix in olive oil and vinegar. Season to taste with salt, pepper and hot sauce. Cover and refrigerate a minimum of 6 hours. Approximately 2 hours before serving, remove beans from refrigerator and allow to reach room temperature, stirring occasionally. When ready to serve, cut top off each tomato. Using a teaspoon, scoop out pulp, removing as many seeds as possible. Mince pulp and stir thoroughly into bean mixture. Adjust seasonings if necessary. Lightly season inside of tomatoes with salt and pepper. Carefully spoon salad mixture evenly into tomatoes. Serve on a nest of decorative lettuces.

MARINATED ZUCCHINI AND SUMMER SQUASH SALAD

Prep Time: 1 Hour
Yields: 6 Servings

Comment:

Romantics say that it's the simple things in life that are best. Well if that's so, then this straightforward zucchini and squash salad should set hearts aglow. To enhance presentation, place salad into a decorative serving bowl and garnish with edible flower petals such as pansies, dianthuses or marigolds.

Ingredients:

3 medium zucchini, shredded
3 medium summer squash, shredded
1 small Bermuda onion, thinly sliced
½ red bell pepper, julienned
½ yellow bell pepper, julienned
2 tbsps minced garlic
¼ cup sweet pickle relish
⅓ cup salad oil
⅓ cup red wine vinegar
1 tsp dried basil
1 tsp dried thyme
1 tsp salt
1 tsp cracked black pepper

Method:

In a large mixing bowl, combine squash, onions, bell peppers, garlic and relish. In a separate mixing bowl, combine oil, vinegar, basil, thyme, salt and pepper. Whisk until well blended. Pour marinade evenly over vegetables, cover and refrigerate overnight. Before serving, toss salad and drain excess liquid.

CHUNKY CHICKEN SALAD PLANTATION STYLE

Prep Time: 30 Minutes
Yields: 6 Servings

Comment:

This salad makes great use of leftover fried chicken. Try this dish at your next picnic or as a light lunch alternative. You may want to purchase fresh fried chicken to use in this recipe.

Ingredients:

3 fried chicken breasts, skin-on
¾ cup mayonnaise
¼ cup orange juice
¼ cup heavy whipping cream
salt and cracked black pepper to taste
Louisiana hot sauce to taste
½ cup sliced seedless green grapes
½ cup mandarin sections
½ cup chopped toasted pecans
½ cup finely diced celery
¼ cup chopped parsley
1 tbsp chopped thyme
1 tbsp chopped basil

Method:

Remove meat from breastbone, keeping skin intact to retain seasonings. Cut meat into ¾-inch cubes and set aside. In a large mixing bowl, blend together mayonnaise, orange juice and cream. Season to taste with salt, pepper and hot sauce. Stir in all remaining ingredients except chicken, and blend well. Gently fold cubed chicken into mixture. Once coated, adjust seasonings if necessary. Serve on fresh spinach or romaine lettuce.

MARINATED FRENCH MARKET SALAD

Prep Time: 1 Hour
Yields: 6–8 Servings

Comment:
Vegetable gardens are quite common in South Louisiana. The bayous supply water and a rich soil for crops. In early summer, varieties of vegetables unseen in other parts of the country are produced. Historically, this abundance of produce was made available to the city dwellers at the French Market in New Orleans. Residents could purchase a wide medley of items to include in their dinner salads.

Ingredients:
1 cup cooked sliced carrots
1 cup cooked whole kernel corn
1 cup cooked green beans
1 cup diced cucumber
2 cups diced tomatoes
1 cup diced red bell peppers
1 cup diced yellow bell peppers
½ cup sliced green onions
½ cup diced Bermuda onions
1 cup chopped celery
1½ cups olive oil
1½ cups salad oil
¾ cup red wine vinegar
1 cup Parmesan cheese
¼ cup chopped ruffled basil
¼ cup chopped thyme
salt and cracked black pepper to taste
Louisiana hot sauce to taste

Method:
In a large mixing bowl, combine all vegetables and toss. In a separate bowl, whisk together oils, vinegar, cheese, basil and thyme. Season to taste with salt, pepper and hot sauce. Pour dressing over vegetables and toss to coat all ingredients. Cover and chill at least 8 hours before serving. This salad keeps well in refrigerator for several days. NOTE: The hardest thing about making this colorful salad is chopping vegetables. You may wish to substitute high-quality canned vegetables, such as corn, carrots and green beans, when possible. You will lose the crunchy texture of fresh vegetables, but you will cut your preparation time considerably.

PECAN AMBROSIA

Prep Time: 30 Minutes
Yields: 12–14 Servings

Comment:
Flavored fruit salads have many variations throughout the country. Often they simply call for only one or, at the most, two main ingredients. In Louisiana, we tend to use all that is at hand to create an ambrosia unlike any other.

Ingredients:
1 (20-ounce) can sliced peaches
1 (20-ounce) can crushed pineapple
6 mandarin oranges, peeled and sectioned
1 diced red apple
1 diced green apple
1 (3½-ounce) can flaked coconut
½ cup sliced maraschino cherries
1 cup chopped pecans
1 cup sliced strawberries
1 (8-ounce) carton whipped topping

Method:
In a large mixing bowl, combine all ingredients except strawberries and whipped topping. Toss ingredients until thoroughly mixed. Cover with plastic wrap and place in refrigerator for a minimum of 4 hours, allowing ingredients to marinate. Immediately before serving, fold in sliced strawberries and whipped topping. Blend until fruit is coated. You may wish to serve a spoonful of ambrosia in a slice of butter lettuce and garnish with grated cheddar cheese for added appeal.

SPICY FRIED CHICKEN PASTA SALAD

Prep Time: 1 Hour
Yields: 10 Servings

Comment:
One of the greatest challenges faced when planning an outdoor patio party is determining the accompaniments to the main dish and whether they should be served hot or cold. One great characteristic of Cajun and Creole dishes is that most may be served either way. This pasta salad can be made with either leftover or fresh fried chicken.

Ingredients:
6 pieces cold, spicy fried chicken
6 cups cooked rotini pasta
6 boiled eggs, yolks separated
1 cup mayonnaise
1 tbsp Creole mustard
¼ cup minced onions
¼ cup minced celery
1 tsp minced garlic
¼ cup minced red bell peppers
¼ cup minced green bell peppers
¼ cup sliced green onions
½ cup sweet pickle relish
salt and black pepper to taste

Method:
Bone chicken and cut into cubes, making sure that skin is left intact. Set aside. In a large mixing bowl, mash egg yolks with a fork. Blend in mayonnaise and Creole mustard. Finely dice egg whites and add to mixture. Add all remaining ingredients except chicken and pasta and mix well. Fold in pasta then gently toss in chicken. Season with salt and pepper. Place on a large serving platter. You may wish to surround pasta with additional whole pieces of hot fried chicken. You may adjust the mayonnaise dressing with any seasonings typically used in potato salad.

COTTAGE CHEESE
AND FRUIT SOUFFLÉ

Prep Time: 1 Hour
Yields: 6 Servings

Comment:
This simple recipe is a mini-version of the fruit soufflé often served on holidays.

Ingredients:
¾ cup cottage cheese
1 cup crushed pineapple
1 apple, diced
1 cup water
1½ tbsps vinegar
¾ cup Coca-Cola®
½ cup shredded carrots
⅓ cup diced celery
½ cup mayonnaise
1 (4-ounce) package lemon gelatin

Method:
In a large saucepan, heat water, vinegar and coke over medium-high heat. Bring to a low boil, remove from heat and blend in gelatin. Once mixture is thoroughly dissolved, pour it into a large bowl and chill in refrigerator until firm around edges but still soft in center. Remove from refrigerator. Using a rotary mixer, whip gelatin, soufflé-style. Using a rubber spatula, fold cheese, pineapple, apple, carrots, celery and mayonnaise into whipped gelatin. Pour into a decorative mold and chill until firm. Serve as a light luncheon salad over multicolored lettuce or as a summer dessert.

LAYERED FRUIT
AND SHRIMP SALAD

Prep Time: 1 Hour
Yields: 10 Servings

Comment:
In Louisiana, it is understood that fruit is not just for dessert. With its wide range of colors and textures, nothing makes a more beautiful entrée salad than layers of fresh or canned fruit. Create an interesting and unique summer salad by combining colorful, healthy fruit with fresh shrimp or other seafood.

Ingredients:
2 cups watermelon balls
2 cups cantaloupe balls
2 cups honeydew balls
2 cups sliced peaches
2 cups sliced pears
2 cups quartered orange sections
2 cups sliced plums
1 cup fresh blueberries
1 cup fresh strawberries
1 cup cubed pineapple
2 dozen (21-25 count) boiled shrimp
2 cups crawfish tails
1 cup jumbo lump crabmeat
6 chopped apple mint leaves
6 chopped lemon balm leaves
1 cup orange juice
1 cup strawberry yogurt
½ cup chopped pecans

Method:
In a large glass serving bowl, layer fruit alternating strata of color. Once all fruit has been layered, line shrimp, crawfish and crabmeat in a decorative pattern around edge of bowl. In a separate bowl, whisk together apple mint, lemon balm, orange juice and yogurt. When ready to serve, sprinkle in pecans and pour yogurt dressing over salad. Toss mixture to blend dressing into fruit and serve immediately.

OLD MAID'S POTATO SALAD

Prep Time: 1 Hour
Yields: 6–8 Servings

Comment:
This simple hot potato salad gets its name from the ladies who invented the dish. Since "old maids," or unmarried women, sold their chicken eggs for money, they did not have any left to go into potato salad and other dishes. Instead, these imaginative women substituted vinegar, oil and garden vegetables to enhance this eggless dish.

Ingredients:
20 new potatoes, skin-on, cubed
¾ cup olive oil
½ cup sliced purple onions
¼ cup diced celery
¼ cup julienned red bell peppers
¼ cup julienned yellow bell peppers
¼ cup sliced green onions
1 tbsp minced garlic
¼ cup red wine vinegar
1 tsp chopped thyme
1 tsp chopped basil
salt and cracked black pepper to taste
Louisiana hot sauce to taste
¼ cup sweet pickle relish

Method:
Wash potatoes and boil in salted water for 20 minutes or until tender. Do not overcook. When potatoes are nearly done, heat olive oil in a cast iron skillet over medium-high heat. Add onions, celery, bell peppers, green onions and garlic. Sauté 3–5 minutes or until vegetables are wilted. Pour in vinegar, remove from heat and season with thyme, basil, salt, pepper and hot sauce. Drain boiled potatoes, place in a large mixing bowl and top with hot dressing. Add pickle relish and stir until evenly coated. Serve warm.

WARM NEW POTATO SALAD WITH BEER DRESSING

Prep Time: 1 Hour
Yields: 6 Servings

Comment:

No two ingredients are more German than potatoes and beer. Both of these staples were in great supply in and around St. James and St. John the Baptist parishes from the time the Germans arrived in the early 1700s. This dish is exceptional for a patio party or backyard barbecue.

Ingredients:

3 pounds new potatoes, skin-on
1 cup Heineken® beer
¼ cup olive oil
¼ cup sliced green onions
¼ cup chopped parsley
¼ cup Louisiana cane syrup
1 tbsp minced garlic
1 tbsp Creole mustard
½ tsp sugar
¼ cup salad oil
salt and cracked black pepper to taste
Louisiana hot sauce to taste
2 small Bermuda onions, sliced
¼ cup julienned green bell peppers
¼ cup julienned yellow bell peppers

Method:

In a 1-gallon stockpot, boil potatoes in lightly salted water 20 minutes or until tender. Do not overcook. When tender, drain, spread on cutting board and allow to cool slightly. In a sauté pan, heat olive oil over medium-high heat. Stir in green onions, parsley, beer, cane syrup and garlic. Bring to a low boil and cook for 2–3 minutes. Place hot ingredients in a blender or food processor. Add mustard and sugar and blend ingredients well. While blending, pour in salad oil. Remove from blender and season to taste using salt, pepper and hot sauce. When potatoes are cool enough to handle but still warm, slice ¼-inch thick. Place in a large mixing bowl and toss with onions, bell peppers and dressing. Serve immediately.

HOT GERMAN POTATO SALAD

Prep Time: 30 Minutes
Yields: 8–10 Servings

Comment:

The Germans arrived in Louisiana in 1722 and settled outside of New Orleans near present-day Hahnville. These farmers and dairymen were also excellent cooks. The early Germans gave us many of our most often used recipes such as this potato salad.

Ingredients:

20 new potatoes, skin-on
4 hard-boiled eggs, peeled and chopped
8 slices bacon, chopped
1 cup diced onions
2 tbsps Creole seasoning
¼ cup flour
1 cup chicken stock (see recipe)
¾ cup vinegar
½ cup sugar
½ cup sliced green onions

Method:

Place potatoes in a large pot of lightly salted water and bring to a boil. Boil 20 minutes or until tender. Drain and cool under cold running water. Slice potatoes ¼-inch thick and place in a large bowl. Mix in eggs and set aside. Sauté bacon in a 10-inch skillet over high heat 7 minutes or until browned. Remove bacon from skillet with a slotted spoon and set aside. Pour off all but 2 tablespoons of bacon fat and return skillet to high heat. Stir in onions and sauté 3–5 minutes, scraping bottom of skillet occasionally, until onions are golden. Sprinkle in Creole seasoning then whisk in flour. Slowly whisk in stock, vinegar and sugar. Cook 5–6 minutes or until mixture is thick, whisking frequently. Remove from heat. Fold dressing into potato and egg mixture. Add green onions and cooked bacon. Blend well.

TRADITIONAL POTATO SALAD

Prep Time: 30 Minutes
Yields: 4–6 Servings

Comment:
Made with leftover Easter eggs, this pastel yellow dish looks great on the table every Easter Sunday. Additionally, it serves as the perfect side dish for seafood soups and gumbos. Of course, potato salad is also ideal at outdoor cooking events such as barbecues.

Ingredients:
2 large white baking potatoes, peeled and 1-inch cubed
4 eggs
½ cup mayonnaise
1 tbsp yellow mustard
¼ cup minced celery
¼ cup sweet pickle relish
1 tbsp chopped lemon thyme
1 tbsp minced chives
salt and black pepper to taste

Method:
In a large saucepot over medium-high heat, cook potatoes in lightly salted water 12–15 minutes or until fork tender. Potatoes should be tender but not mushy or overcooked. While potatoes are cooking, boil eggs in a separate pot for 12–15 minutes. NOTE: If desired, cut prep time in half by boiling potatoes and eggs in the same pot. When potatoes are done, strain and slightly cool. Peel eggs, and in a large mixing bowl, separate whites from yolk. Using a paring knife, dice egg whites. In a smaller bowl, mash yolks with a fork and combine with egg whites. Blend in mayonnaise and mustard. With a large mixing spoon, fold in celery, pickle relish, thyme, chives and potatoes. Stir carefully, making sure to keep potatoes chunky. Season with salt and pepper and serve.

CELERY AND POTATO SALAD WITH LEMON MAYONNAISE

Prep Time: 1 Hour
Yields: 6 Servings

Comment:
The Germans who settled the River Road of Louisiana developed many variations of potato salad. Potatoes were one of the staple crops found in most bayou gardens. This celery-enhanced potato salad was created as a perfect side dish for seafood soups and stews.

Ingredients:
1½ cups diced celery
1 pound new potatoes, skin-on
1 tbsp grated lemon peel
¾ cup heavy-duty mayonnaise
½ cup minced onions
¼ cup minced red bell peppers
¼ cup sweet pickle relish
salt and black pepper to taste

Method:
Quarter potatoes and boil in lightly-salted water until tender but not falling apart. Drain and rinse under cold water. In a large mixing bowl, combine celery, lemon peel, mayonnaise, onions, bell peppers and relish. Using a wooden spoon, stir until ingredients are well blended. Drain potatoes thoroughly and add to mixture. Continue to blend, being careful not to break potatoes. Season with salt and pepper. Cover, refrigerate and allow potatoes to marinate in lemon dressing a minimum of 4 hours before serving.

FIESTA MACQUE CHOUX SALAD

Prep Time: 1 Hour
Yields: 6 Servings

Comment:

Macque Choux is an early Louisiana dish that borrows its name from the Creole word for corn, maque, and the French word for cabbage, choux. Although cabbage doesn't appear in the dish today, it is believed to have been in the original vegetable casserole. Today, macque choux is a baked corn and shrimp dish enjoyed by the Cajuns of River Road. This fiesta salad gives the 200-year-old mixture a Mexican twist.

Ingredients for Vinaigrette:

1¼ cups olive oil
½ cup white wine vinegar
¼ cup lime juice
¼ cup cilantro leaves
1 avocado, diced

Method:

Combine olive oil, vinegar, lime juice and cilantro in a food processor. Pulse for 1 minute. Add avocado and pulse again for 30-second intervals or until blended. Do not over-blend. Pour vinaigrette into a bowl and chill.

Ingredients for Salad:

2 dozen (16-20 count) shrimp, peeled and deveined
½ cup lime juice
¼ cup lemon juice
½ cup tequila
2 tbsps Triple Sec
1 tbsp chopped basil
1 tbsp chopped thyme
salt and cayenne pepper to taste
1–2 red bell peppers
1–2 yellow bell peppers
1 cup whole kernel corn
1 cup diced Creole tomatoes
½ cup diced zucchini
½ cup canned black beans, rinsed
½ cup diced Bermuda onions
1 tbsp minced jalapeños
¼ cup chopped cilantro
2 tbsps olive oil for sautéing

Method:

In a large mixing bowl, combine shrimp, lime juice, lemon juice, tequila, Triple Sec, basil and thyme. Season with salt and cayenne pepper. Toss and marinate shrimp in refrigerator for approximately 30 minutes. While shrimp are marinating, roast red and yellow bell peppers directly over the open flame or under the broiler of your stove, turning frequently. Broil on all sides until skin blisters and blackens. Remove and steam in a brown paper bag for 10–15 minutes. Peel blistered skin from pepper under cold running water. Seed and dice peppers. In a large bowl, toss peppers, corn, tomatoes, zucchini, black beans, onions, jalapeños and chopped cilantro. Set aside. Remove shrimp from marinade. Discard marinade. In a heavy-bottomed sauté pan, heat olive oil over medium-high heat. Sauté shrimp 2–3 minutes or until pink and curled. Remove from pan. Toss shrimp and roasted pepper salad with ½ cup of avocado vinaigrette. Garnish the rim of a large margarita glass by dipping it in lime juice and minced cilantro. Fill glass with salad. Garnish with lime slice. Serve with tortilla chips.

SHRIMP SALAD LIPARI

Prep Time: 1 Hour
Yields: 6 Servings

Comment:

This spicy shrimp salad was created by Luke Lipari of Berwick, La. His Italian and French heritage influenced his cuisine.

Ingredients:

3 pounds (50-60 count)
   shrimp, peeled and deveined
1 onion, quartered
1 lemon, sliced
1 bay leaf
2 heads of garlic
½ tsp salt
Louisiana hot sauce to taste

1½ cups mayonnaise
1 cup ketchup
2 tbsps horseradish
1 head lettuce
2 tomatoes, diced
1 cup diced celery
½ cup diced onions

Method:

In a 5-quart saucepan, combine onion, lemon, bay leaf, garlic, salt and hot sauce in 2 quarts of water. Bring to a rolling boil and cook 15 minutes to develop flavors. Add shrimp. When water returns to a boil, cook 2–3 minutes or until shrimp are pink and curled. Do not overcook. Chill under cold tap water. Remove shrimp and set aside. Discard vegetables. In a large mixing bowl, combine mayonnaise, ketchup and horseradish. Season with hot sauce and whisk well. Fold in shrimp, coat with sauce and refrigerate. When ready to serve, wash lettuce and tear into bite-size salad pieces. Drain and place in a large salad bowl along with tomatoes, celery, onion and shrimp mixture. Using a wooden spoon, blend well. Serve on 6 individual salad plates. NOTE: Boil the shrimp in crab boil if desired.

SEAFOOD COLESLAW WITH WILD ONION VINAIGRETTE

Prep Time: 30 Minutes
Yields: 6–8 Servings

Comment:

This recipe is indicative of the creative nature of the Cajuns and Creoles. Try substituting local seafood in place of those listed in the ingredients. Although originally made with wild spring onions from Bayou Country, this recipe uses farm-raised green onions.

Ingredients for Coleslaw:

1 head red cabbage, shredded
1 head green cabbage, shredded
½ cup shredded carrots
¼ cup diced red bell peppers
¼ cup diced green bell peppers
½ pound boiled shrimp
¼ pound crabmeat
¼ pound crab claws
salt and cracked black pepper to taste
dash of Louisiana hot sauce

Method:

Combine all ingredients in a large mixing bowl. Chill.

Ingredients for Vinaigrette:

1 egg yolk
½ cup red wine
¼ cup Creole mustard
¼ cup sliced green onions
¼ cup lemon juice
¼ cup orange juice
1 cup olive oil
1 cup vegetable oil

Method:

In a large mixing bowl, whisk together egg yolk, red wine, mustard, green onions, and lemon and orange juices. Pour in olive oil slowly in a steady stream while whisking constantly. Repeat process with vegetable oil. Drizzle vinaigrette over coleslaw and allow to sit 1 hour prior to serving.

LUMP CRAB AND ROASTED PEPPER SALAD

Prep Time: 1 Hour
Yields: 6–8 Servings

Comment:

With the Germans and English both cultivating vegetables in the River Parishes, a wide variety of sweet peppers were available. Bell pepper soups, stuffed bell peppers and finally roasted pepper salads began to emerge from these gardens. It wasn't long before seafood was added for more interesting flavors.

Ingredients:

1 pound jumbo lump crabmeat
2 large green bell peppers
2 large red bell peppers
2 large yellow bell peppers
½ cup olive oil
juice of ½ lemon
juice of ½ lime
2 tbsps balsamic vinegar
2 tbsps chopped parsley
1 tbsp chopped oregano
1 tbsp chopped purple basil
1 tsp chopped thyme
1 tsp chopped tarragon
¼ cup sliced green onions
¼ cup chopped parsley
¼ cup grated Parmesan cheese
salt and cracked black pepper to taste
Louisiana hot sauce to taste

Method:

To roast peppers, place whole peppers directly over the open flame or under the broiler of stove. Turn frequently until skin blisters and blackens on all sides. Remove and place in a brown paper bag, seal tightly and let steam 10–15 minutes. Peel blistered skin from peppers under cold running water. Seed and julienne each pepper into 6 equal strips. Place in a large plastic bowl and set aside. In a smaller bowl, whisk together oil, juices, vinegar, parsley, oregano, basil, thyme and tarragon. Mix in green onions, parsley and Parmesan cheese. Season to taste with salt, pepper and hot sauce. Sprinkle crabmeat over peppers and add dressing. Toss 2–3 times to coat peppers and crabmeat well. Cover and refrigerate 4–6 hours before serving.

CRABMEAT IN ARTICHOKE PIROGUES

Prep Time: 1½ Hours
Yields: 6 Servings

Comment:

During the 1600s, French chef LaVarenne introduced soup as an important starter course and roux as a thickening agent. Those innovations alone should have made him famous, but LaVarenne gave us many more important culinary techniques. As chef to Marquis d'Uxelles, he introduced the duxelles stuffing from mushrooms; lemon juice and vinegars as simple sauces; and the globe artichoke as a main item on the dinner table.

Ingredients:

½ pound jumbo lump crabmeat
6 large artichokes
1 lemon, sliced
¼ cup olive oil
1 tbsp chopped garlic
salt and cracked black pepper to taste
½ cup mayonnaise
¼ cup sour cream
1 tsp Creole mustard
1 tbsp lemon juice
1 tsp grated lemon peel
1 tsp chopped tarragon
1 tsp chopped thyme
1 tsp chopped basil
Louisiana hot sauce to taste
6 lemon slices
parsley for garnish
paprika for garnish

Method:

Trim pointed ends from artichoke leaves and rinse under cold water. In a large stockpot, place artichokes, sliced lemon, olive oil, garlic and enough water to cover ingredients. Season with salt and pepper. Bring to a rolling boil, reduce to simmer and cook 30–45 minutes. The large outer leaves along bottom of artichoke should pull away easily when done. Remove, drain and allow artichokes to cool. In a large mixing bowl, whisk together mayonnaise, sour cream and mustard. Add lemon juice, lemon peel, tarragon, thyme and basil. Continue to whisk until blended. Season with salt, pepper and hot sauce. Fold in crabmeat gently. Using a sharp knife, cut artichokes in half lengthwise and scrape out tender center leaves with a teaspoon. Leave bottom intact. Season center with salt and pepper. Stuff artichoke with crabmeat dressing, top with lemon slice. Garnish with parsley and paprika. Serve as a lunch or dinner entrée salad.

MARDI GRAS CRAWFISH SALAD

Prep Time: 30 Minutes
Yields: 6 Servings

Comment:
Though Mardi Gras, or Fat Tuesday, is celebrated the day before Ash Wednesday, dishes named for the holiday are served all year long. This particular salad can be made with or without seafood. You may wish to substitute smoked chicken or cottage cheese in its place.

Ingredients:
2 cups cooked crawfish tails
1 head red leaf lettuce
1 (10-ounce) package fresh spinach leaves
½ cup crumbled cooked bacon
½ cup diced Bermuda onions
2 cups mandarin orange sections, canned
1 cup sliced mushrooms
¾ cup salad oil
½ cup cider vinegar
¼ cup sugar
¼ cup orange juice
1 tsp dried mustard
1 tbsp chopped sage
1 tbsp chopped basil
salt and black pepper to taste

Method:
Wash lettuce and spinach leaves well under cold water. Remove large stems and tear into 1-inch pieces. Drain and place in a large mixing bowl. Add crawfish, bacon, onions, oranges and mushrooms. Toss well to blend ingredients. Allow to sit for 30 minutes. In a separate bowl, whisk together oil, vinegar, sugar and juice. Stir in mustard, sage and basil. Season with salt and pepper. Pour dressing over salad mixture. Toss to coat all ingredients well. Serve equal portions in 6 cold salad plates. NOTE: You may wish to drain juice from orange sections and reserve for use in place of orange juice.

CRAWFISH PASTA SALAD

Prep Time: 15 Minutes
Yields: 4–5 Servings

Comment:
This Italian-influenced Louisiana recipe is right at home on the holiday table or at a tailgate party.

Ingredients for Dressing:
1 cup vegetable oil
5 tbsp red wine vinegar
4 tbsp sour cream
1½ tsp salt
2 tbsp minced garlic
½ tsp dry mustard
2 tbsp sugar
cracked black pepper to taste
2 tsp chopped parsley

Method:
Whisk together all dressing ingredients and set aside. This may be done ahead of time.

Ingredients for Salad:
1 pound peeled crawfish tails
1 pound small shell pasta, cooked
½ cup thinly sliced green onions
½ cup minced celery
½ cup minced red bell peppers
½ cup minced yellow bell peppers
chopped dill weed to taste

Method:
In a mixing bowl, combine crawfish tails, pasta, green onions, celery and bell peppers. Season with dill weed. Pour dressing over crawfish mixture and serve.

GRILLED FISH SALAD

Prep Time: 2 Hours
Yields: 6 Servings

Comment:
Grilled fish salads were often presented at Louisiana plantation events. Most of these homes were located on rivers and bayous, so seafood was plentiful and had to be used.

Ingredients for Grilling:
2 pounds white fish fillets (preferably striped bass, flounder or catfish)
½ cup vegetable oil
1 tbsp chopped dill
1 tsp ground sassafras (filé powder)
pinch of thyme
1 tbsp lemon juice
salt and black pepper to taste
Louisiana hot sauce to taste

Ingredients for Salad:
1½ cups mayonnaise
½ cup sour cream
½ cup minced onions
¼ cup minced celery
¼ cup minced red bell peppers
¼ cup minced yellow bell peppers
1 tsp chopped dill
1 tsp chopped basil
1 tsp chopped tarragon
juice of ½ lemon
salt and black pepper to taste
Louisiana hot sauce to taste
1 tbsp Worcestershire sauce

Method:
Preheat barbecue grill according to manufacturer's directions. You may wish to presoak some pecan wood chips to give the fish added flavor. In a large mixing bowl, combine fillets, oil, dill, sassafras, thyme and lemon juice. Season with salt, pepper and hot sauce. Pierce fish with fork and allow it to marinate in seasoning ingredients 30 minutes before grilling. If fish is very delicate, line grill with aluminum foil to keep it from falling through during cooking. Place soaked wood chips on coals and grill fish, covered, for 12–15 minutes or until done. Remove fish, place on cookie sheet and chill in refrigerator.

Method:
Once chilled, cube fish and dice gelatin that has collected in pan. Place fish in a large mixing bowl. Add mayonnaise, sour cream, onions, celery, bell peppers, dill, basil, tarragon and lemon juice. Using a large spoon, blend ingredients well. Season with salt, pepper, hot sauce and Worcestershire. Form fish into a decorative loaf or spoon into a fish mold. Chill a minimum of 2–3 hours allowing flavors to develop. Serve on a mixture of multicolored lettuces or with croutons or toast points as an appetizer. If desired, garnish with diced gelatin.

HOT CRAWFISH SPINACH SALAD

Prep Time: 30 Minutes
Yields: 4 Servings

Comment:
Spinach is normally topped with hot bacon dressing. To add their own Bayou Country flair, Cajuns have substituted a hot dressing flavored with crawfish.

Ingredients:
6 ounces crawfish tails
1 (12-ounce) bunch fresh spinach
½ cup vegetable oil
1 cup diced onions
½ cup diced celery
½ cup diced yellow bell peppers
¼ cup minced garlic
¼ cup Creole mustard
¼ cup Steen's Cane Syrup Vinegar
1 tbsp Steen's Cane Syrup
salt and black pepper to taste
Louisiana hot sauce to taste
½ cup diced tomatoes
½ lemon, sliced
½ cup sliced mushrooms

Method:
In a 10-inch cast iron skillet, heat oil over medium-high heat. Add onions, celery, bell pepper and garlic. Sauté 3–5 minutes or until vegetables are wilted. Whisk in mustard, vinegar and cane syrup. Season with salt, pepper and hot sauce. Fold in crawfish and cook until thoroughly heated. Break spinach into bite-sized pieces and place in center of a ceramic bowl. Pour crawfish dressing over spinach and toss to coat well. Garnish with tomatoes, lemons and mushrooms.

HERB-ENCRUSTED SALMON SALAD

Prep Time: 1 Hour
Yields: 6 Servings

Comment:
Salmon is delicious with chilled salad greens and tomatoes. This fish is the perfect ingredient for a Louisiana summer salad. Top it with a light vinaigrette and serve with fresh-squeezed lemonade or iced tea.

Ingredients:
6 (5–8 ounce) salmon fillets
¼ cup fresh herbs (tarragon, thyme, basil, chervil), mixed and chopped
mixed baby salad greens
pear and currant tomatoes
½ cup vegetable oil
salt and cracked black pepper to taste
1½ cups rice flour
1 tbsp chopped chives

Method:
Preheat oven to 275°F. In a 10-inch heavy-bottomed sauté pan, heat oil over medium-high heat. Season fillets with salt and pepper, then coat evenly with herb mixture. Coat with rice flour and shake off excess. Sauté 2 fillets at a time, 3–5 minutes on each side or until golden brown and crispy. Place cooked fish on a large cookie sheet in oven to keep warm. Wash salad greens and tomatoes and dry well. Divide greens and tomatoes into 6 bowls. Slice each salmon fillet into about 4 (1-inch) cubes and place on top of greens. Garnish with chives. Serve with Orange-Basil Vinaigrette or Cane Syrup Vinaigrette. (See recipes.)

SEAFOOD JAMBALAYA
RICE SALAD

Prep Time: 30 Minutes
Yields: 6 Servings

Comment:

Traditional jambalaya of New Orleans is a warm, tomato-based dish, flavored with a combination of sausages, ham and chicken. This is an unusual but memorable cold seafood variation on the classic recipe.

Ingredients:

2 cups cooked rice
1 cup mayonnaise
½ cup Creole mustard
1 cup diced tomatoes
1 cup diced Bermuda onions
1 tbsp chopped thyme
1 tbsp chopped basil
salt and black pepper to taste
Louisiana hot sauce to taste
1 cup crawfish tails
1 cup jumbo lump crabmeat
1 cup (60-90 count) boiled shrimp
½ cup diced ham
½ cup sliced smoked sausage
½ cup sliced green onions
¼ cup chopped parsley

Method:

Place rice in a large mixing bowl. Blend in mayonnaise, mustard, tomatoes and onions. Season to taste with thyme, basil, salt, pepper and hot sauce. Mix in seafood, ham and sausage. Blend thoroughly then stir in green onions and parsley. Refrigerate 2 hours. Serve on lettuce leaves.

SEAFOOD PASTA SALAD

Prep Time: 30 Minutes
Yields: 10–12 Servings

Comment:

This blend of fresh seafood, canned seafood and pasta is a great Louisiana picnic recipe for a weekend outing. Keep on ice for an easy, chilled salad that everyone will love.

Ingredients:

1 (6-ounce) can pink salmon, drained
1 (6-ounce) can tuna, drained
1 (3.75-ounce) can sardines in hot sauce, chopped (optional)
1 pound crawfish tails, drained
1 pound penne pasta, cooked
4 boiled eggs
1¼ cup mayonnaise
2 tbsps yellow mustard
2 tbsps minced celery
2 tbsps sweet pickle relish
2 tbsps minced red bell peppers
2 tbsps minced yellow bell peppers
¼ cup sliced green onions
2 tbsps chopped parsley
1 tbsp chopped thyme
¼ cup extra virgin olive oil
salt and black pepper to taste
2 tbsps Creole seasoning or to taste

Method:

In a large mixing bowl, finely chop eggs with a pastry cutter or potato masher. Blend in mayonnaise, mustard, celery, relish, bell peppers, green onions, parsley and thyme. Fold in pasta, salmon, tuna, sardines, and crawfish very gently being careful not to break up fish. Pour in olive oil and toss to blend. Season with salt, pepper and Creole seasoning. Serve in a large chilled bowl. If serving this outdoors or on a buffet table, place bowl in a larger bowl of ice to keep cold. Always keep covered.

Vegetables

New Orleans French Market

While Louisiana's unparalleled cuisine may find its roots in her diverse culture, tribute must also be paid to her fertile soil and subtropical climate. These features guarantee a limitless supply of fresh vegetables and herbs that both comprise and inspire many Cajun and Creole recipes. Whether natural to the region or imported, almost any plant can thrive here. The reliance on fresh vegetables is evident at our state's ubiquitous roadside stands offering fresh greens, Creole tomatoes, eggplant, sweet potatoes and okra. Even family grocery stores and large grocery chains are sure to make precious room on their shelves for seasonal, local produce.

Our devotion to, or rather, obsession with vegetables is apparent in that here, they are not only served as side dishes, but also as appetizers, entrées and desserts. Consider the eggplant, which is an appetizer when served in single slices with a seafood sauce as in Eggplant Belle Rose. When the vegetable is breaded and fried, it is a side dish. As the main ingredient in a casserole enhanced with ground beef and shrimp, it is an entrée. Eggplant can even make an unusual dessert when whisked into beignet batter. In the same way, white pattypan squash is used in soups and dressings and can be stuffed to serve as the main dish. Yet in Louisiana we are compelled to make a sweet pudding out of the squash as well.

Why are we not content to let vegetables serve the simple and often solitary roles common in most cuisines? Neither the Cajuns nor Creoles took the natural abundance of their new homeland for granted. In addition to adapting traditional recipes to include the vegetables that grow here, these cooks found new, unusual and delicious ways to use them. The simple stuffed pepper found on so many American tables cannot compare to Louisiana's mirliton stuffed with ground pork and crabmeat or our eggplant stuffed with river shrimp. Even basic vegetables such as peas have been transformed by adding roux and andouille for a Cajun flair.

Vegetables are necessary to add flavor, color and texture to so many Cajun and Creole recipes that almost every household once had a vegetable garden close by. In addition to vegetables, those gardens housed the parsley, mint, chicory, garlic and shallots used to season most dishes. These kitchen gardens or "potagers" could range from a simple plot outside the kitchen door of a Cajun cabin to a more elaborate, ornamental garden of vegetables, herbs and fruit trees on the grounds of a grand plantation home. The tradition of the potager in its various forms was brought to Louisiana by settlers from Europe. For centuries, European peasants, lords, monks and nuns depended on these gardens for sustenance and medicinal herbs. They were sometimes enclosed and used to cultivate new species, provide privacy and protection from a hostile environment or, in the monks' example, worldly distractions. Later, potagers were also used to demonstrate horticultural expertise and featured elaborate designs and exotic plants. The kitchen garden in all of these forms could be found in early Louisiana history.

Even if kitchen gardens are not quite as common today, Louisiana's mild winters and three growing seasons ensure that at almost any time of year, locally grown produce is readily available. Peppers, onions, beans, root vegetables, eggplant, okra, squash and tomatoes can all be found growing

here. While all cultures recognize the nutritional and culinary value of vegetables, to Cajun and Creole cuisine, they are absolutely essential. Almost every major recipe calls for, at the very least, onions, celery and bell peppers. This combination is deemed the "trinity" in Louisiana, because like the Holy Trinity, it is omnipresent. Vegetables have also been used in many cultures as a means to stretch small amounts of meat to feed a family. It is no wonder that the Cajuns, in particular, embrace them so wholeheartedly and refuse to throw them out even when merely used to flavor poaching water.

In fact, in this culture, vegetables are more than a side dish, they are a tradition. A Monday without red beans and rice is a rarity, Thanksgiving without baked cushaw is a sacrilege, and summer without Creole tomato sandwiches is a crime. The humble red bean is so revered it has been immortalized as jewelry by Louisiana designer Mignon Faget, and New Orleans restaurants are not rated with stars but with beans. The Creole tomato, among other fruit and vegetables, has its own festival.

It is of note that some of the "vegetables" in this chapter are technically classified as fruits or legumes, but they have been included here because they primarily serve vegetable roles.

Collards
$1.00 bunch

Fresh Broccoli
75¢ each

STUFFED ARTICHOKES

Prep Time: 2 Hours
Yields: 6 Servings

Comment:

At one time, stuffed artichokes were the Italians' best-kept secret. There are many flavor variations to this dish, especially those using fresh herbs such as basil, rosemary and oregano. This recipe, however, is a very simple rendition that is packed with flavor.

Ingredients:

6 whole artichokes
3 cups freshly grated Romano cheese
2 tbsps minced garlic
6 cups Italian bread crumbs
salt and cracked black pepper to taste
3 cups olive oil

Method:

In a large mixing bowl, blend cheese, garlic and bread crumbs. Season with salt and pepper. Clean artichokes by clipping tips of leaves with sharp scissors. Cut large stems from bottom so artichokes will sit flat. Rinse artichokes well and press firmly down to spread open leaves. Scrape inside center of artichoke down to bottom, removing all purple leaves and pulp with a tablespoon. Place one artichoke at a time into a bowl with mixed seasonings. To stuff, fill center then each leaf from top down, pushing as much into leaves as possible. Continue until all 6 artichokes have been stuffed with equal amounts of breading. Place stuffed artichokes in a large roasting pan with lid. Pour 1 inch of water in bottom. Slowly drizzle ½ cup olive oil over each artichoke to coat well. Cover, bring water to a boil then reduce to simmer. Allow artichokes to steam 1–1½ hours. Add water to pot occasionally so that artichokes do not stick and scorch. Test for tenderness by tasting one leaf removed from center. Serve one whole artichoke as an entrée or split in half and serve as an appetizer. NOTE: It is always best to grate fresh Romano cheese for this recipe. The pre-grated variety looses a lot of flavor on the shelf, so it is best to avoid it.

BAKED ARTICHOKES

Prep Time: 1 Hour
Yields: 6 Servings

Comment:

Catherine de Medici introduced the artichoke to France in the 1500s when she moved from Italy to wed King Henry II. The artichoke has been popular in both cultures ever since, so it stands to reason that its popularity would have come to Louisiana with settlers from those nations.

Ingredients:

3 (8½-ounce) cans artichoke hearts
½ cup reserved artichoke juice
½ cup olive oil
½ cup melted butter
¼ cup chopped black olives
¼ cup chopped pimiento olives
1 tbsp minced garlic
1 tbsp olive juice
1½ cups Italian bread crumbs
½ cup mozzarella cheese

Method:

Preheat oven to 350°F. Drain artichoke hearts and reserve ½ cup of liquid. Cut artichoke hearts into quarters. In a heavy-bottomed sauté pan, heat olive oil and butter over medium-high heat. Add artichokes and sauté 3–5 minutes. Stir in olives and garlic. Sauté until heated thoroughly then stir in olive juice and reserved artichoke liquid. Pour contents of skillet into a 2-quart casserole dish and fold in 1 cup of bread crumbs, blending well. Top casserole with cheese and enough bread crumbs to absorb excess liquid. Do not to allow mixture to become too dry. Bake uncovered for 30 minutes.

CAJUN ROUX PEAS

Prep Time: 30–45 Minutes
Yields: 6 Servings

Comment:

Peas are a mainstay across the southern United States. However, the vegetable is enjoyed in a very different manner in Cajun Country. Peas are flavored with a mixture of fresh seasonings and smoked meat and cooked in a light roux.

Ingredients:

2 pounds fresh peas, shelled
½ pound smoked sausage, diced
½ cup vegetable oil
½ cup diced onions
½ cup diced celery
½ cup diced red bell peppers
¼ cup minced garlic

1½ tbsps flour
3 cups chicken stock
salt and black pepper to taste
½ cup sliced green onions
Louisiana hot sauce to taste
¼ cup chopped parsley

Method:

Rinse shelled peas once or twice in cold water to remove any debris. Drain and set aside. In a cast iron Dutch oven, heat oil over medium-high heat. Add smoked sausage and sauté 3–5 minutes. Stir in onions, celery, bell peppers and garlic. Sauté 3–5 additional minutes, stirring occasionally. Sprinkle in flour and blend well. Mix in fresh peas and stock. Season lightly with salt and pepper. Bring to a rolling boil then reduce to simmer. Cook until peas are tender and a slightly thickened gravy has formed. Depending on age of peas, additional stock may be necessary to retain volume during cooking. Once peas are tender, season with salt, pepper and hot sauce. Garnish with parsley.

ENGLISH PEAS WITH PEARL ONIONS AND ANDOUILLE

Prep Time: 45 Minutes
Yields: 6–8 Servings

Comment:

In early writings about life in Louisiana, many references were made to English pea casseroles. The heavy German influence in the area led to the addition of smoked andouille sausage in traditional pea dishes.

Ingredients:

2 (17-ounce) cans tiny English peas
12 pearl onions, peeled
½ cup julienned andouille
3 tbsps butter
¼ cup minced celery
¼ cup minced red bell peppers
1 tbsp minced garlic
2 tbsps flour
1 cup water
salt and cracked black pepper to taste
sprig of fresh thyme
pinch of nutmeg

Method:

Drain peas and reserve 1 cup of liquid for later use. In a 2-quart saucepan, melt butter over medium-high heat. Sauté celery, bell peppers and garlic 3–5 minutes or until wilted. Mix in andouille and sauté 2–3 minutes to give vegetables a smoked flavor. Stir in pearl onions, sprinkle in flour and blend well. Pour in liquid from peas and 1 cup of water. Bring to a rolling boil then reduce to simmer. Stir in peas and season with salt and pepper. Add thyme and nutmeg. Allow peas to cook approximately 15 minutes or until full-flavored.

BACON-WRAPPED GREEN BEANS

Prep Time: 1½ Hours
Yields: 6 Servings

Comment:

This is an old Cajun dish from Bayou Lafourche. The green beans are wrapped in bacon to add a wonderfully smoky flavor to the dish. The bundles of beans and bacon create a beautiful presentation perfect for a vegetable side dish or even an appetizer.

Ingredients:

1 pound bacon
2 pounds frozen green beans
¼ cup margarine
½ cup diced onions
¼ cup diced red bell peppers
¼ cup diced yellow bell peppers
1 (8-ounce) can tomato sauce
1 tsp mustard
1 tbsp Worcestershire sauce
1 tsp brown sugar
1 tbsp white sugar
salt and cayenne pepper to taste

Method:

Preheat oven to 400°F. In a large sauté pan, precook bacon, a few slices at a time, to get rid of some fat. Do not cook until crispy. Drain on paper towels and set aside. Discard bacon fat. In same skillet, melt margarine over medium-high heat. Sauté onions and bell peppers 3–5 minutes or until wilted. Stir in tomato sauce, mustard and Worcestershire sauce. Bring to a rolling boil, reduce to simmer and add sugars. Simmer approximately 15 minutes, stirring occasionally. If tomato sauce becomes too thick, thin with a small amount of water. Season with salt and cayenne pepper. Roll 3 green beans in 1 strip of bacon and secure with a toothpick. Line rolled green beans in a 9" x 13" casserole dish. When all beans are wrapped, pour tomato sauce over rolls and adjust seasonings if necessary. Bake 35–45 minutes or until bacon is crisp.

SNAP BEANS WITH NEW POTATOES

Prep Time: 1 Hour
Yields: 6 Servings

Comment:

Green beans, also called snap beans, and new potatoes are probably the most frequently eaten vegetable-starch combination in the homes of Cajun Country. This recipe will cause the snap beans to be overcooked by most standards. However, this has been the Cajuns' preferred method of cooking these beans.

Ingredients:

1 pound fresh snap beans
10 peeled new potatoes
½ cup shortening or bacon drippings
½ cup diced onions
½ cup diced celery
½ cup diced red bell peppers
¼ cup minced garlic
½ pound smoked ham, diced
2 cups chicken stock
½ cup sliced green onions
salt and cracked black pepper to taste
Louisiana hot sauce to taste

Method:

In a 4-quart stockpot, melt shortening or bacon drippings over medium-high heat. Sauté onions, celery, bell peppers, garlic and smoked ham 3–5 minutes or until vegetables are wilted. Add beans and potatoes and stir-fry 3 minutes. Pour in chicken stock, cover pot and reduce heat to simmer. Stir in green onions. Cook approximately 30 minutes or until potatoes are tender. Once tender, season with salt, pepper and hot sauce. Serve as a vegetable or, as the Cajuns do, over steamed white rice as a side dish.

CAJUN BLACK-EYED PEAS

Prep Time: 1½ Hours
Yields: 6 Servings

Comment:

Black-eyed peas, or congree, is a gift to America from the Africans. Today black-eyed peas are not only found on tables throughout America on New Year's Day, but also are used year-round in recipes ranging from soups to appetizers and entrées.

Ingredients:

1 pound dried black-eyed peas
1 pound heavy smoked pork sausage
½ pound smoked ham, cubed
½ cup shortening or bacon drippings
1 cup diced onions
1 cup diced celery
1 cup diced bell peppers
¼ cup minced garlic
1 tsp dried basil
1 bay leaf
salt and cracked black pepper to taste
1 cup sliced green onions
½ cup chopped parsley

Method:

Soak peas in cold water overnight. This will cut cooking time by a third. Drain peas and rinse in cold tap water. In a 1-gallon stockpot, melt shortening or bacon drippings over medium-high heat. Sauté onions, celery, bell peppers, garlic, basil, sausage and ham 10–15 minutes, or until vegetables are wilted. Add peas, bay leaf and enough cold water to cover by 2 inches. Bring to a low boil and cook 30 minutes, stirring occasionally. Reduce heat to simmer and continue to cook 45 minutes or until peas are tender. Stir occasionally to keep peas from sticking to bottom of pot. Once tender, mash about a third of peas on side of pot with a metal cooking spoon to create a creamy texture. Season with salt and pepper. Stir in green onions and parsley and continue to cook until peas are creamy.

BUTTER BEANS WITH HAM

Prep Time: 2 Hours
Yields: 6 Servings

Comment:

Better known as butter beans in Louisiana, lima beans are often cooked casserole-style with different smoked meats. In this recipe, however, the beans are cooked slowly to create a creamy, flavorful dish.

Ingredients:

1 pound fresh butter beans
½ pound smoked ham, cubed
2 smoked ham hocks
½ cup shortening or bacon drippings
1 cup diced onions
1 cup diced celery
1 cup diced red bell peppers
¼ cup minced garlic
1 cup sliced green onions
½ cup chopped parsley
salt and cracked black pepper to taste

Method:

Rinse beans and remove any that are hard or discolored. The beans will cook faster if they are soaked in cold water overnight in the refrigerator. When ready to cook, rinse beans once again in cold water. In a 2-quart saucepot, melt shortening over medium-high heat. Sauté onions, celery, bell peppers, garlic and smoked ham 5 minutes or until vegetables are wilted. Add ham hocks and cook 5 additional minutes. Add beans and cover with cold water by 2 inches. Stir in green onions. Bring to a rolling boil, then reduce to simmer and allow to cook for 90 minutes. Stir occasionally to prevent vegetables from scorching. After 45 minutes of cooking, use a metal spoon to mash a quarter of the beans against pot to create a creaming effect. Season with salt and pepper, and garnish with parsley. Beans should be tender and of a butter consistency when ready to serve. Butter beans may be served on top of cooked white rice or as a side vegetable.

Westlake laundry

LOUISIANA WHITE OR RED BEANS WITH HAM AND SAUSAGE

Prep Time: 1½ Hours
Yields: 8–10 Servings

Comment:

Beans with ham and sausage have been cooking in the pots of South Louisiana for 300 years, especially on Monday, which was traditionally "wash day." The beans could slowly cook while the women got their washing done. People of all walks of life and in every area, from the bayous to New Orleans, found beans to be the basis of a delicious and satisfying meal. You may freeze any leftover beans for later use.

Ingredients:

1 pound dried red kidney or
   great Northern beans
½ cup shortening or bacon drippings
1 cup diced onions
1 cup diced celery
½ cup diced bell peppers
¼ cup minced garlic
2 cups sliced green onions
2 cups diced smoked ham
6 (3-inch) links smoked sausage
½ cup chopped parsley
salt and Louisiana hot sauce to taste

Method:

Soak beans overnight in cold water. This will help soften outer shell and shorten cooking time. Drain beans and rinse in cold water. In a 4-quart stockpot, melt shortening or bacon drippings over medium-high heat. Sauté onions, celery, bell peppers, garlic, 1 cup green onions and ham for 5–10 minutes or until vegetables are wilted. Stir in sausage and beans. Cook 2–3 minutes, then pour in enough cold water to cover beans by 2 inches. Bring to a rolling boil and allow to cook 30 minutes, stirring occasionally to avoid scorching. Reduce heat to simmer, and cook 1 hour or until beans are tender. Stir occasionally, as beans will settle to bottom of pot as they cook. Stir in chopped parsley and remaining green onions. Season with salt and hot sauce. Using a metal spoon, mash approximately a third of the beans against side of pot to create a creaming effect. Once beans are tender and creamy, they are ready to be served. For maximum flavor, this dish should be cooked 1 day before serving.

CALABRIAN WHITE BEANS WITH SMOKED HAM AND SAUSAGE

Prep Time: 2 Hours
Yields: 6–8 Servings

Comment:

Unlike Tuscan beans, Calabrian white beans are further flavored with a variety of smoked pork products making them quite similar to Cajun-style white beans.

Ingredients:

2 pounds cannellini or great
   Northern beans
½ pound smoked ham, diced
3 links Italian sausage
1 gallon chicken stock
1 pound salt meat, diced
1 tbsp olive oil
4 cloves garlic, minced
1 tbsp chopped oregano
¼ cup sliced green onions
salt and black pepper to taste

Method:

Preheat oven to 375°F. In a heavy-bottomed stockpot, boil beans, stock, ham and salt meat until beans are tender but still slightly chewy and unbroken. Do not overcook. Strain liquid from cooked beans and reserve. Add Italian sausage, olive oil, garlic, oregano and green onions to beans. Season slightly with salt and pepper. Ladle in just enough of reserved liquid to bring level up to beans in pot without covering them. Cover tightly with aluminum foil and bake 45 minutes. When beans are extremely tender, strain and serve as a vegetable or starter course.

QUICK AND SMOKY CAJUN BAKED BEANS

Prep Time: 45 Minutes
Yields: 6–8 Servings

Comment:
Not everyone has time to make baked beans from scratch. This recipe begins with canned great Northern beans, but the smoke of the grill and the sweet flavor of brown sugar and cane syrup will make the dish taste homemade.

Ingredients:
2 (15-ounce) cans great Northern beans
2 (15-ounce) cans pinto beans
¼ cup butter
½ pound bacon, cubed
1 cup diced sugar-cured ham
2 cups diced onions
1 cup diced red bell peppers
¼ cup minced garlic
1 tbsp grated fresh ginger
½ cup firmly packed brown sugar
½ cup Louisiana cane syrup
½ cup barbecue sauce
¼ cup ketchup
2 tbsps Worcestershire sauce
1 tbsp dry mustard
1 tbsp prepared mustard
1 tbsp cider vinegar
¼ cup chopped parsley
¼ cup sliced green onions
salt and cracked black pepper to taste

Method:
Light grill according to manufacturer's directions. Prepare 2 or 3 pieces of your favorite smoke wood to add to pit once bean pot has been placed over coals. In a cast iron pot, melt butter over medium-high heat. Add bacon and stir occasionally until fat is rendered and bacon is crispy. Stir ham, onions and bell peppers into bacon fat. Cook 5–7 minutes or until vegetables are wilted. One at a time, blend in all remaining ingredients except beans, stirring well after each addition. Once blended, mix in beans and bring to a simmer. Place pot on barbecue grill for 30–45 minutes, stirring occasionally until beans have picked up a nice smoky flavor. This dish may also be prepared in your oven by baking at 350°F for approximately 30 minutes.

BRAISED RED CABBAGE IN APPLE CIDER

Prep Time: 1 Hour
Yields: 6 Servings

Comment:
Braising red cabbage with fresh fruit is very common in the German communities of Louisiana. Though often thought of as a holiday dish, this vegetable is a delicious accompaniment to any wild game entrée.

Ingredients:
3 pounds shredded red cabbage
1 cup apple cider
¼ cup butter
½ cup diced onions
¼ cup diced celery
1 tsp diced garlic
2 cups julienned red apples
½ cup chicken stock (see recipe)
1 tbsp sugar
2 bay leaves
salt and cracked black pepper to taste

Method:
In a cast iron pot, melt butter over medium-high heat. Sauté onions, celery and garlic 3–5 minutes or until vegetables are wilted. Stir in shredded cabbage and cook 30 minutes, stirring occasionally until cabbage begins to wilt. Blend in cider, apples, chicken stock and sugar. Add bay leaves and continue cooking, uncovered, 15–20 minutes. Season with salt and pepper. Remove bay leaves and serve with lamb, beef or game.

BROCCOLI WITH DIJON VINAIGRETTE

Prep Time: 30 Minutes
Yields: 6–8 Servings

Comment:

As with the artichoke, we have Catherine de Medici to thank for introducing this vegetable to France from Italy. Since then, the popularity of broccoli has spread all over the world. This broccoli dish can be served as a salad or a vegetable.

Ingredients:

2 pounds fresh broccoli spears
1 tbsp Dijon mustard
4 tsps olive oil
¼ cup sliced green onions
¼ tsp dried tarragon
½ tsp dry mustard
1 tbsp minced garlic
2 tbsps red wine vinegar
4 tbsps water
salt and cracked black pepper to taste

Method:

Cut broccoli into serving-size pieces, place in a 5-quart saucepan and cover with 2 inches of water. Bring to a rolling boil and cook 4–5 minutes. Do not overcook. Drain broccoli, place in a serving bowl and keep warm. In a small sauté pan, heat olive oil over medium-high heat. Add green onions, tarragon, mustard and garlic. Using a wooden spoon, blend all ingredients and sauté 2–3 minutes. Remove from heat, add vinegar, water and Dijon mustard. Season with salt and pepper. Drizzle hot vinaigrette over steamed broccoli and serve immediately.

BROCCOLI AND CAULIFLOWER CASSEROLE

Prep Time: 1 Hour
Yields: 6 Servings

Comment:

Broccoli and cauliflower were commonly found on the Creole tables of New Orleans. However, the Cajuns did not actually use these vegetables until the late 1950s when they became available in the stores and markets around the bayous.

Ingredients:

1 head broccoli
1 head cauliflower
½ cup butter
¼ cup diced onions
¼ cup diced celery
¼ cup diced red bell peppers
¼ cup minced garlic
¼ cup diced tasso
½ cup sliced mushrooms
½ cup flour
3 cups heavy whipping cream
salt and white pepper to taste
pinch of nutmeg
½ cup grated Parmesan cheese
½ cup Italian bread crumbs

Method:

Preheat oven to 375°F. Cut broccoli and cauliflower into florets and boil in lightly salted water until tender but still firm. Do not overcook. Remove, cool under tap water and set aside. In a 1-quart saucepan, melt butter over medium-high heat. Sauté onions, celery, bell peppers, garlic, tasso and mushrooms 5–10 minutes or until vegetables are wilted. Whisk in flour, stirring constantly until white roux is achieved. (See roux recipes.) Do not brown. Pour in cream, whisking constantly to form white cream sauce. Do not scorch. Season with salt, white pepper and nutmeg. Place cooked broccoli and cauliflower in a baking dish and top with cream sauce. Sprinkle generously with Parmesan cheese and bread crumbs. Bake on center oven rack until casserole is bubbly and slightly brown on top. If desired, use grated Cheddar cheese in place of Parmesan for a milder taste.

VOODOO GREENS

Prep Time: 1 Hour
Yields: 8–10 Servings

Comment:

Voodoo is a religion brought to Louisiana by slaves which blends Roman Catholic, African theological and magical elements. Just as a voodoo sorceress can wield mysterious power over her intended prey with a supernatural potion, this dish can hold you under its spell with a vast array of herbs, greens, sausages and meats. Partake of voodoo greens if you dare!

Ingredients:

1 bunch mustard greens
1 bunch collard greens
1 bunch turnips
1 bunch watercress
1 bunch beet tops
1 bunch carrot tops
1 bunch spinach
3 cups diced onions
¼ cup minced garlic
3 quarts chicken stock or water
1 pound smoked sausage, sliced
1 pound smoked ham, diced
1 pound hot sausage, sliced
½ pound smoked ham hocks
1 tsp thyme leaves
1 tbsp filé powder
salt and cayenne pepper to taste
Louisiana hot sauce to taste

Method:

Rinse greens 2–3 times under cold running water to remove all soil and grit. Pick out bad leaves, remove large center stem and chop greens coarsely. In a 12-quart pot, combine greens, onions, garlic, stock and meats. Bring mixture to a rolling boil, reduce to simmer and cook 1–1½ hours, stirring occasionally. Remove ham hocks from pot and cut away skin. Remove meat from bone, chop coarsely and return to pot. Add thyme and filé powder, then season with salt, cayenne and hot sauce. Continue to cook until vegetables are extremely tender. Serve as a vegetable side dish or stuffing for chicken and fish.

CHOUCROUTE GARNI

Prep Time: 3 Hours
Yields: 8 Servings

Comment:

Sauerkraut is one of the most underrated dishes in the South. Most southerners are reminded of the sour, bitter kraut they were served during their elementary school days, rather than the richly-garnished sauerkraut of Alsace Lorraine, France. Olga Hirsch brought this recipe from that region when she moved to Donaldsonville in the 1940s. It is a classic and well worth the effort!

Ingredients:

2 (32-ounce) jars Vlassic® sauerkraut
½ pound bacon, cubed
3 links heavy smoked sausage, sliced
1 ham steak, bone-in and cubed
3 pieces smoked pork hocks
6 links Polish sausage
2 cups diced onions
¼ cup minced garlic
1½ tbsps flour
1 quart chicken stock
1 (12-ounce) bottle beer
1 cup dry white wine
6 juniper berries
salt and black pepper to taste
2 small bay leaves
8 small potatoes, halved

Method:

The secret to great sauerkraut is removing the sour brine from cabbage. Prior to cooking, rinse product under cold running water 2–3 times and drain well. In a cast iron pot, sauté bacon over medium-high heat until fat is rendered. Do not brown. Add smoked sausage and cook 2–3 minutes longer. Add onions and garlic and sauté 3–5 minutes. Stir in flour then add chicken stock, beer, wine and juniper berries. Bring to a rolling boil, then season with salt and pepper. Blend in sauerkraut. Return to a rolling boil. Reduce heat to simmer. Add ham and bone, pork hocks and Polish sausage. Season with bay leaves. Cover and simmer 1½ hours, stirring occasionally. Stir in potatoes and continue to cook 15–20 minutes or until tender. Serve sauerkraut with equal portions of meat.

HOMEMADE SAUERKRAUT

Prep Time: 4–5 Weeks
Yields: 4 Quarts

Comment:

Although sauerkraut is German for "sour cabbage," it is not truly German. More than 2,000 years ago, the Chinese workers building the Great Wall of China ate it on a regular basis. It eventually made its way to Europe and became a favorite dish of the Germans.

Ingredients:

8 heads cabbage, shredded
¾ cup sea salt
dried juniper berries

Method:

Layer shredded cabbage and salt in a 5-gallon crock, beginning with a 2-inch layer of cabbage. Sprinkle 1 tablespoon sea salt over each layer, squeezing cabbage down each time. Place a heavy-duty trash bag inside another heavy-duty trash bag, and set double bag on top of layered cabbage, open side up. Pour approximately 2 gallons water into the bag to act as a weight on top of cabbage. Make sure bag fits tightly around inner edge of crock to act as an airtight seal over cabbage. Place crock in a cool place 4 weeks for mild kraut or 5 weeks for sour. NOTE: As cabbage begins to ferment, liquid will exude from shredded cabbage. Crock should be placed in a container to catch any overflow. After 4–5 weeks, remove plastic bags and skim any mold or scum that may have formed on top sauerkraut. Pack sauerkraut into pint or quart jars until ¾ full, then fill with fermented liquid from crock. Add 2–3 dried juniper berries. Seal jars with approved canning lids and process in boiling water 15–20 minutes to ensure a good seal.

Antique German cabbage shredder

Shredding cabbage into crocks

Salting the cabbage

SMOTHERED CABBAGE AND ANDOUILLE

Prep Time: 1 Hour
Yields: 6 Servings

Comment:
This dish can be found on the New Year's Day table of most homes in South Louisiana. Many people believe eating cabbage on this day will ensure financial security in the upcoming year.

Ingredients:
1 large head of cabbage
½ pound andouille sausage, sliced
½ cup bacon drippings
1 cup diced onions
1 cup diced celery
½ cup diced bell peppers
¼ cup minced garlic
1 cup sliced green onions
1½ cups chicken stock
salt and cracked black pepper to taste

Method:
Quarter cabbage and discard the center heart and large exterior leaves. Chop quarters into 2–3 pieces and separate leaves. In a 4-quart saucepan, melt bacon drippings over medium heat. Sauté andouille, onions, celery, bell peppers, garlic and green onions for 5 minutes or until vegetables are wilted. Stir in cabbage and sauté until leaves are wilted. Add chicken stock, then reduce heat to simmer. Cover pot and allow to cook 45 minutes, stirring occasionally. Season with salt and pepper. Continue cooking until cabbage is smothered. NOTE: This dish will be overcooked by most standards. However, this is the method preferred by both Cajuns and Creoles.

CREOLE TOMATO BASIL PIE

Prep Time: 45 Minutes
Yields: 6–8 Servings

Comment:

This pie with a heavy Italian influence first appeared in Natchitoches, the oldest city in Louisiana. The dish, though Creole in origin has been given a Cajun spin with the addition of crawfish tails and andouille.

Ingredients:

5–6 medium Creole tomatoes
½ cup torn basil leaves
1 cup grated Monterey Jack cheese
1 (9-inch) pre-baked pie shell
½ cup olive oil
½ cup julienned andouille sausage
1 cup crawfish tails
½ cup Cheddar cheese
½ cup Parmesan cheese
salt and cracked black pepper to taste
1 small Bermuda onion, sliced
1 cup Italian bread crumbs

Method:

Preheat oven to 350°F. Cut tomatoes into ¼-inch slices. Drain approximately 1 hour on paper towels to remove excess liquid; otherwise pie will be soggy. Create 2–3 layers in pie shell. Start with a layer of Monterey Jack topped with sliced tomatoes. Paint tomatoes with olive oil. Sprinkle with basil, andouille, crawfish, Cheddar and Parmesan. Season with salt and pepper. Add 2–3 slices Bermuda onion. Repeat layers until pie is filled. Once top layer has been added, sprinkle generously with bread crumbs and Parmesan. Top with Monterey Jack and basil. Bake 15–20 minutes or until cheese is melted and bread crumbs are well browned. Allow pie to cool slightly before serving. If desired, place finished pie in refrigerator and serve cold or freeze for later use.

SMOTHERED OKRA AND TOMATOES

Prep Time: 1½ Hours
Yields: 6–8 Servings

Comment:

Okra, or gombo, was brought to Louisiana by the Africans in the early 1700s. The vegetable was quickly adapted for use in many dishes, especially gumbo. Smothered okra and tomatoes can be eaten alone or made into a side dish by adding lump crabmeat or shrimp. Many Louisianians make large batches of this dish to freeze for later use in gumbo.

Ingredients:

2 quarts sliced fresh okra
3 cups diced tomatoes
¼ cup vegetable oil
1 cup diced onions
1 cup diced celery
½ cup diced bell peppers
¼ cup minced garlic
½ cup hot water
salt and cracked black pepper to taste
Louisiana hot sauce to taste

Method:

NOTE: It is important to select only young and tender okra for smothering. As the season progresses, okra hardens and is no longer prime for smothering. In a 4-quart saucepan, heat oil over medium-high heat. Sauté okra, onions, celery, bell peppers and garlic approximately 30 minutes. Stir constantly until okra stops "stringing." Stir in tomatoes and hot water, bring to a low boil and cook approximately 1 hour, stirring occasionally. Season with salt, pepper and a dash of hot sauce.

HOLIDAY CARROT SOUFFLÉ

Prep Time: 1 Hour
Yields: 8 Servings

Comment:
This wonderful recipe was created by Piccadilly Cafeteria in Baton Rouge, La. Over the years, this carrot dish has become one of the most sought after recipes in the South. Although this soufflé may be prepared year-round, it is exceptional on the holiday table.

Ingredients:
2 pounds carrots, chopped
½ cup melted butter
1 cup sugar
3 tbsps flour
1 tsp baking powder
1 tbsp pure vanilla extract
pinch of nutmeg
pinch of cinnamon
3 eggs, beaten
1 tbsp powdered sugar for dusting

Method:
Preheat oven to 350°F. Bring a large pot of lightly-salted water to a boil. Add carrots and cook 15 minutes or until tender. Drain carrots, place in a large mixing bowl and mash. Whisk in melted butter, sugar, flour, baking powder, vanilla, nutmeg, cinnamon and eggs until well blended. Transfer mixture to a 2-quart casserole dish and sprinkle with powdered sugar. Bake 30 minutes. Serve as a side dish to any main course or use as a filling for pies, tarts or turnovers.

HONEY MINT GLAZED CARROTS

Prep Time: 30 Minutes
Yields: 6–8 Servings

Comment:
Carrots may be commonplace at the dinner table, but the contrast of sweet honey and crisp mint transforms this everyday vegetable into a sumptuous side dish.

Ingredients:
3 cups diagonally sliced carrots
3 tbsps honey
3 tbsps chopped mint
3 tbsps butter
3 slices cooked bacon, crumbled
pinch of cinnamon
pinch of nutmeg
½ ounce brandy
sprig of mint (optional)

Method:
In a 1-quart saucepan, poach carrots in lightly-salted water 6–8 minutes or until tender. Remove from heat, strain, reserve ½ cup of poaching liquid and set aside. Cool carrots under cold running water. In a heavy-bottomed sauté pan, melt butter over medium-high heat. Blend in honey. If mixture becomes too thick, add 2 or more tablespoons of poaching liquid. Stir in bacon, cinnamon and nutmeg. Once blended, remove from heat and pour in brandy. NOTE: When pouring brandy into a hot pan, remove it from any open flame, as it may flare up for 10–15 seconds before extinguishing itself. Stir well, then add mint and carrots. Toss gently until glazed. Continue to cook until thoroughly heated. Place in a serving bowl and garnish with a sprig of fresh mint if desired.

CREAMED RADISHES

Prep Time: 1 Hour
Yields: 6–8 Servings

Comment:
This seemingly odd dish was enjoyed by people in the early 1800s. Making creamed radishes probably dates back to the arrival of the English at Jamestown. The vegetable is a unique accompaniment to any entrée and is especially good when served with game.

Ingredients:
4 cups sliced, unpeeled radishes
2 tbsps butter
¼ cup minced onions
¼ cup minced celery
1 tsp minced garlic
¼ cup chopped parsley
2 tbsps flour
½ cup heavy whipping cream
salt and cracked black pepper to taste

Method:
In a 2-quart saucepan, poach radishes in lightly-salted water until tender, but not overcooked. Strain and reserve 1 cup of liquid. Cool radishes under cold running water then set aside. In a sauté pan, melt butter over medium-high heat. Sauté onions, celery, garlic and parsley 3–5 minutes or until wilted. Blend in flour. Add cream and reserved poaching liquid to create a pink-colored cream sauce. Season with salt and pepper. Fold radishes into sauce and cook 10 minutes. Place in a serving dish.

TURNIP CASSEROLE

Prep Time: 1 Hour
Yields: 6 Servings

Comment:
As a young boy, turnips were my least favorite vegetable. Mom would cook them in every fashion imaginable, and still I failed to be persuaded. Today, I have come to love turnips and this is one of my favorite recipes.

Ingredients:
8–10 medium-sized turnips, peeled
¼ pound butter
1 cup diced onions
½ cup diced celery
½ cup diced red bell peppers
¼ cup minced garlic
¼ cup sliced green onions
1½ cups diced ham
½ cup cooked, crumbled bacon
¼ cup chopped parsley
½ cup Italian bread crumbs
salt and cracked black pepper to taste
1 cup grated Cheddar cheese

Method:
Preheat oven to 375°F. Cube turnips and boil in lightly-salted water until tender. Do not overcook. Once tender, remove and cool under tap water. In a heavy-bottomed, 10-inch sauté pan, melt butter over medium-high heat. Sauté onions, celery, bell peppers, garlic, green onions, ham and bacon 5–10 minutes or until vegetables are wilted. Add cubed turnips and sauté slowly until turnips are reheated. Fold in parsley and sprinkle with bread crumbs. Season with salt and pepper. Place turnip mixture in a baking dish and top with grated Cheddar cheese. Cover and bake on center rack until cheese is melted and casserole is bubbly.

CAJUN RATATOUILLE

Prep Time: 1½ Hours
Yields: 6–8 Servings

Comment:
Ratatouille is the most famous vegetable casserole in Italy and the South of France. It is often made with a combination of vegetables and other local seasonings. Here in Bayou Country, we add smoked sausage to give the dish a Cajun twist.

Ingredients:
1 cup diced eggplant
1 cup diced zucchini
1 cup diced yellow squash
1 cup diced tomatoes
½ cup sliced black olives
½ cup olive oil
1 pound sliced smoked sausage
1 cup diced onions
1 cup diced celery
¼ cup diced red bell peppers
¼ cup diced yellow bell peppers
¼ cup minced garlic
2 cups tomato sauce
¼ cup chopped thyme
¼ cup chopped basil
¼ cup fresh oregano
salt and cracked black pepper to taste
Louisiana hot sauce to taste

Method:
Preheat oven to 375°F. In a 14-inch cast iron skillet, heat olive oil over medium-high heat. Sauté smoked sausage until golden brown. Remove and set aside. Sauté onions, celery, bell peppers and garlic 3–5 minutes or until vegetables are wilted. Blend in eggplant, zucchini, squash, tomatoes, olives and sausage. Sauté 30 minutes, stirring occasionally to prevent scorching. Once eggplant mixture is wilted, stir in tomato sauce, thyme, basil and oregano. Season with salt, pepper and hot sauce. Continue to cook 10–15 minutes. Remove from heat, and spoon ratatouille into an ovenproof baking dish. Bake uncovered 30 minutes. Serve as a vegetable casserole or as a stuffing for chicken and game birds.

OLD-FASHIONED POTATO STEW

Prep Time: 1 Hour
Yields: 6 Servings

Comment:
Potato stew cooked with shrimp became a pleasant substitution for red beans and rice on Monday washdays in Louisiana. Both dishes could be cooked in the black iron pot next to the wash kettle, making lunch a little easier to prepare.

Ingredients:
4 large potatoes, peeled and cubed
2 cups (150–200 count) shrimp, peeled and deveined
½ cup vegetable oil
½ cup flour
1 cup diced onions
1 cup diced celery
½ cup diced bell peppers
¼ cup minced garlic
4 cups chicken stock (see recipe)
½ cup sliced green onions
½ cup chopped parsley
salt and cracked black pepper to taste

Method:
In a 2-quart saucepot, heat oil over medium-high heat. Whisk in flour, stirring constantly until a light brown roux is achieved. (See roux recipes.) Stir in onions, celery, bell peppers and garlic. Sauté 5–10 minutes or until vegetables are wilted. Add potatoes and continue to sauté 3–5 minutes. Pour in chicken stock, one ladle at a time. Bring to a low boil, stir in green onions then reduce to simmer. Cook 20–30 minutes or until potatoes are tender. Once tender, stir in shrimp and parsley. Season with salt and pepper. Continue cooking until shrimp are pink and curled, but not overcooked. This dish makes a wonderful breakfast hash when combined with leftover roast beef or turkey. NOTE: For an interesting flavor twist, add ¼ -inch slices of heavy smoked sausage when chicken stock is added.

OLD-FASHIONED SMOTHERED POTATOES

Prep Time: 30 Minutes
Yields: 6 Servings

Comment:
In Louisiana, the term "smother" refers to cooking vegetables, such as potatoes or cabbage, until they are completely reduced and very tender. Smothered potatoes are excellent when served with eggs and sausage as a breakfast accompaniment, but can be cooked alone to create a great side dish for any meal.

Ingredients:
6 medium red potatoes, peeled and sliced ¼-inch thick
½ cup vegetable oil
salt and cracked black pepper to taste
garlic powder to taste
1 tbsp minced garlic
¼ cup sliced green onions
½ tsp chopped parsley (optional)

Method:
In a cast iron skillet, heat oil over medium-high heat. Season potatoes with salt, pepper and garlic powder. Add potatoes and cook uncovered for 10 minutes, stirring occasionally. Stir in garlic and green onions. Continue to cook, stirring often, until potatoes are tender and resemble home fries. Further flavor may be added by using ½ teaspoon of chopped parsley.

HERB-ROASTED NEW POTATOES

Prep Time: 1 Hour
Yields: 6 Servings

Comment:

There are as many potato varieties available to the cook today as there are methods to prepare them. The tiny, new red potato is the best variety for simple roasting or as an accompaniment to roasted meats. These potatoes can be seasoned well ahead of time and baked when ready. Serve this dish as a side to roasted meats such as Cornish hen.

Ingredients:

2 pounds new potatoes, quartered
½ cup diced onions
½ cup diced red bell peppers
½ cup diced yellow bell peppers
2 tbsps minced garlic
2 tbsps chopped rosemary
2 tbsps chopped thyme
¼ cup olive oil
¼ cup melted butter
2 tbsps red wine vinegar
salt and black pepper to taste
2 tsps Creole seasoning

Method:

Place potatoes in a large plastic zipper bag. Add onions, bell peppers, garlic and herbs to bag. Pour in olive oil, butter and vinegar. Season to taste with salt, pepper and Creole seasoning. Seal bag and shake vigorously to completely coat potatoes. Place bag in refrigerator until ready to bake. Preheat oven to 400°F. Pour contents of bag onto a large baking sheet and roast 45–60 minutes or until potatoes are tender and golden brown, stirring occasionally.

WHIPPED POTATO CLOUDS

Prep Time: 1 Hour
Yields: 6 Servings

Comment:

In the South, a giant bowl of mashed potatoes is always served with crispy, southern-fried chicken. The secret to good mashed potatoes is to leave a few lumps so that everyone at the table knows they are made from scratch.

Ingredients:

6 large russet potatoes
12 cloves garlic, minced
8 tbsps butter
1 cup heavy whipping cream

salt and white pepper to taste
pinch of nutmeg
2 pats of butter
¼ cup chopped parsley

Method:

Peel potatoes and remove any discolored spots or "eyes." Cut each potato in half lengthwise and each half into equal thirds. In a 1-gallon stockpot, place enough water to cover potatoes by 3 inches. Salt water liberally, being careful not to over-salt. Bring water to a rolling boil, then add potatoes and garlic. Return to a full boil, reduce heat to medium and boil 15–20 minutes or until tip of a knife can easily pass through potato. Do not overboil. When cooked, drain in a colander and toss to remove all cooking liquid. In a heavy-bottomed sauté pan, melt 8 tablespoons butter over medium-high heat. Add cream, salt, white pepper and nutmeg. Bring to a low simmer, stirring occasionally. Place drained potatoes in a large mixing bowl and mash major pieces with a fork or potato masher, leaving some lumps. Blend cream mixture into potatoes and adjust seasonings to taste. Serve in a warmed bowl and top with butter and parsley.

LATKES

Prep Time: 1 Hour
Yields: 8 Servings

Comment:
Latkes are pan-fried potato pancakes made from seasoned grated potatoes. These potato cakes are traditionally eaten on Hanukkah, the Jewish festival of lights. Many fried foods are eaten on this holiday because oil is a reminder of the miraculous oil that burned eight days, giving origin to the celebration. Potato pancakes is a favorite dish of the Germans of Louisiana.

Ingredients:
4 cups white baking potatoes, peeled and grated
1 large onion, chopped
1½ tsps salt
2 tbsps flour
black pepper to taste
2 eggs
¼ cup vegetable oil

Method:
Squeeze liquid from grated potatoes. Combine potatoes, onions, salt, flour and pepper. Lightly beat eggs then stir into mixture. In a skillet, heat oil over medium-high heat. Form the mixture into medium-sized patties. Brown on one side, turn and brown lightly on the other. Repeat until all potatoes are cooked. Serve with applesauce, cottage cheese, yogurt, sour cream or Creole cream cheese.

CREOLE HOME FRIES

Prep Time: 30 Minutes
Yields: 6 Servings

Comment:
These home fries are simple to make and are guaranteed to be tender because of the poaching process. The Creole seasoning gives the potatoes that magic taste of New Orleans.

Ingredients:
4 russet potatoes, peeled and diced ½-inch
3 tbsps vegetable oil
½ cup minced onions
1 tbsp minced garlic
salt and black pepper to taste
cayenne pepper to taste
Creole seasoning to taste
¼ cup sliced green onions

Method:
Preheat oven to 375°F. Place potatoes in a medium saucepan and cover with cold water by 2 inches. Lightly season water with salt. Bring to a rolling boil, then reduce heat and simmer 6 minutes or until tender. Drain, cool and set aside. In a large cast iron skillet, heat oil over medium-high heat. Sauté onions and garlic 3–5 minutes or until wilted. Add poached potatoes then season with salt, cayenne, black pepper and Creole seasoning. Gently fold in green onions, being careful not to mash potatoes. Place skillet in oven and bake 15–20 minutes or until tips of potatoes turn golden brown. Remove and serve warm.

Chef Jeremy Langlois in the kitchen at White Oak Plantation, Baton Rouge, La.

DOUBLE-FRIED FRENCH FRIES

Prep Time: 1 Hour
Yields: 6 Servings

Comment:

Sometime in the 1700s, an unsung culinary genius decided to try dropping a potato into hot fat. After that moment, the fried potato took the world by storm. Both the Belgians and the French take credit for this development. Thomas Jefferson reportedly featured "potatoes served in the French manner" at Monticello in 1802. As simple as they are delicious, French fries can be one of the toughest dishes to cook.

Ingredients:

2 pounds baking potatoes
peanut or other vegetable oil for frying
salt to taste

Method:

Fill a deep fryer or heavy saucepan halfway with oil. Preheat to 325°F. Peel potatoes. Using a knife or a French fry cutter, slice into uniform sticks. Place cut potatoes in a bowl of ice water to release starch and to keep from turning brown. Place fries on paper towels and allow to dry thoroughly. Fry potatoes in batches so pan isn't crowded and oil temperature does not plummet. Cook each batch 3 minutes or until potatoes are soft but not browned. Remove potatoes with a long-handled metal strainer and drain on brown paper bags. This step may be completed 2 to 3 hours in advance. When ready for the final frying, increase oil temperature to 375°F. Fry all potatoes, one batch at a time, for 4 more minutes or until golden and crispy. Drain on fresh brown paper bags then place in a serving bowl lined with paper towels. Salt and serve immediately.

MAMERE'S FAVORITE CANDIED YAMS

Prep Time: 2 Hours
Yields: 6–8 Servings

Comment:

No one made yams better than Mamere Folse. Her recipe uses seasonal fruit to enhance the flavor of the yams and to give the dish a special touch. Mamere's favorite version included a combination of red and green apples, spiced raisins and yams.

Ingredients:

2 (24-ounce) cans Bruce's® cut yams	4 tbsps butter
1 cup golden raisins	1 cup brown sugar
1 red apple	1 tsp cinnamon
1 green apple	1 tsp nutmeg
1½ tbsps cornstarch	1 tbsp grated orange zest

Method:

Preheat oven to 350°F. Drain yams and reserve juice of 1½ cans. Layer yams in a 9" x 13" ceramic baking dish and top with raisins. Using a paring knife, cut apples into ¼-inch cubes. Do not peel. Submerge apples in water to retain their color. Dissolve cornstarch in 1 cup of yam syrup and set aside. In a cast iron skillet, melt butter over medium-high heat. Add remaining yam syrup, cornstarch mixture, brown sugar, cinnamon, nutmeg and orange peel. Bring to a rolling boil and stir constantly until mixture resembles thickened syrup. Lower heat, stir in diced apples and cook approximately 5 minutes. Ladle apple syrup over yams in baking dish until juice reaches top of yams. Cover and bake 1½ hours.

SIMPLE AND DELICIOUS HOLIDAY YAMS

Prep Time: 2 Hours
Yields: 6–8 Servings

Comment:

Most holiday yam recipes contain numerous spices and a marshmallow topping. This recipe may seem much more boring, but even with fewer ingredients, these yams are magnificent.

Ingredients:

8 yams
¼ pound butter
1 cup sugar
1 tbsp pure vanilla extract

Method:

Yams should all be about the same size so they cook uniformly. Smaller yams are best for this recipe. Peel yams. In a large stainless steel pot, cover yams and butter with 1 inch of water. Bring to a rolling boil, then reduce to simmer and cover. Cook 30 minutes or until yams are fork tender. Drain all but ¼-inch of water. Add sugar and vanilla. Simmer until a simple syrup is achieved and yams have absorbed most of liquid. Do not overcook yams, as they will fall apart prior to serving. Serve 1 yam with a serving of syrup to each guest.

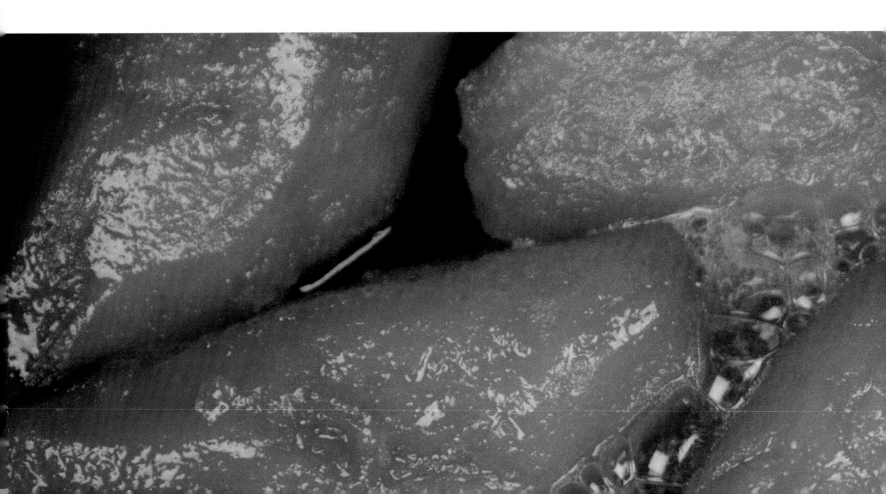

YA-YA STUFFED YAMS

Prep Time: 2 Hours
Yields: 8 Servings

Comment:

Although it has several definitions, one meaning of the Creole term "ya-ya" is "a little of this and a little of that," which certainly applies to this creation. The use of coconut and allspice is very Caribbean, while the apple and raisins add a distinctly American note to this fun and tasty dish.

Ingredients:

4 yams
2 eggs
1 stick butter
½ cup shredded coconut
½ cup chopped pecans
1 cup raisins
1 apple, peeled, cored and chopped coarsely
3 tbsps brown sugar
2 tsps allspice
2 tbsps Louisiana cane syrup
¼ cup shredded coconut for garnish
¼ cup chopped pecans for garnish

Method:

Preheat oven to 350°F. Bake yams until fork tender. Do not over bake. Scoop out inside, leaving a thin shell. In a mixing bowl, combine yam meat and all ingredients except garnishes. When blended, spoon mixture into yam shells and mound slightly. Top with reserved coconut and pecans. Bake 30 minutes. After baking, let stand 4–5 minutes before serving.

PAN-FRIED CANDIED SWEET POTATOES

Prep Time: 1 Hour
Yields: 6 Servings

Comment:

In plantation days, the planters would arrive from the fields at about 10 a.m. to enjoy what we would today call brunch. This "Planter's Breakfast" would have certainly included pan-fried sweet potatoes.

Ingredients:

3 sweet potatoes, peeled
¼ cup butter
¼ cup brown sugar
2 tbsps Louisiana cane syrup
pinch of cinnamon
pinch of nutmeg
¼ cup chopped pecans

Method:

Boil sweet potatoes in lightly-sweetened water until tender but not mushy and falling apart. Remove, cool and reserve ½ cup of poaching liquid. In a heavy-bottomed skillet, melt butter over medium-high heat. Whisk in brown sugar, cane syrup, cinnamon and nutmeg until sugar dissolves. Pour in reserved poaching liquid as needed to retain a liquid state. Slice sweet potatoes into ½-inch circles, and sauté 2–3 minutes in brown sugar glaze. When thoroughly heated, move to a serving platter and top with chopped pecans.

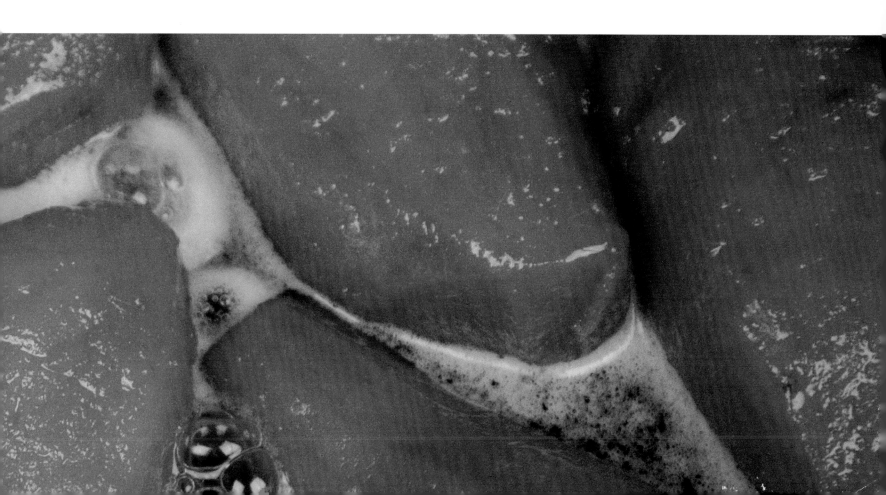

BOILED CORN

Prep Time: 10 Minutes
Yields: 6 Servings

Comment:
Conventional wisdom in Louisiana says that sweet corn should never be boiled. If corn was tender and sweet enough to boil, it should either be eaten raw off the cob or warmed just long enough in hot water to melt butter. However, boiling corn a few minutes with sugar and cream brings out the vegetable's full sweetness.

Ingredients:
6 ears of corn, shucked and cleaned
2 quarts water
2 cups heavy whipping cream
½ cup sugar
1 stick butter
salt and black pepper to taste

Method:
In a large pot, combine water, cream, sugar and ½ stick of butter. Bring to a rolling boil, add corn to pot and cook 3–5 minutes. Using a pair of tongs or a slotted spoon, remove corn to a stainless steel bowl. Season lightly with salt and pepper. Add remaining butter and toss bowl gently to coat corn. Butter will melt as it comes in contact with corn. Serve hot. NOTE: Poaching liquid from boiled corn makes the perfect stock for a corn and shrimp soup. This stock may be frozen for 6 months.

CORN MACQUE CHOUX

Prep Time: 1 Hour
Yields: 8 Servings

Comment:

Although macque choux is normally thought of as a corn soup, the River Road Cajuns cooked a similar vegetable flavored with freshwater shrimp from the Mississippi River. Macque choux is widely known as a Cajun dish of corn and tomatoes.

Ingredients:

8 ears fresh corn
½ cup bacon drippings
1 cup diced onions
½ cup diced celery
½ cup diced green bell peppers
½ cup diced red bell peppers
¼ cup minced garlic
¼ cup minced andouille
2 cups chopped tomatoes
2 tbsps tomato sauce
2 cups (150–200 count) shrimp, peeled and deveined
1 cup sliced green onions
salt and black pepper to taste

Method:

Select tender, well-developed ears of corn and shuck. Using a sharp knife, cut lengthwise through kernels to remove them from cob. Scrape each cob again to remove all "milk" (juice remaining on cob) and additional pulp from corn. The richness of this dish will depend on how much milk and pulp can be scraped from cobs. In a 3-quart cast iron Dutch oven, melt bacon drippings over medium-high heat. Sauté corn, onions, celery, bell peppers, garlic and andouille 15–20 minutes or until vegetables are wilted and corn is tender. Stir in tomatoes, tomato sauce and shrimp. Cook 15–20 minutes or until juice from tomatoes and shrimp is rendered into dish. Add green onions, then season with salt and pepper. Continue to cook 15 minutes or until full flavor of corn and shrimp develop. Serve as a vegetable or add stock to create a soup.

CORN AND HAM PUDDING

Prep Time: 1 Hour
Yields: 4 Servings

Comment:

Combining vegetables and smoked meats has always been a common cooking technique in Louisiana. However, combining these flavors with cream and eggs to create a soufflé or casserole is new to Bayou Country.

Ingredients:

7 cups whole kernel corn
1 cup diced ham
¼ cup butter
1 cup diced onions
½ cup diced celery
¼ cup diced yellow bell peppers
¼ cup diced red bell peppers
¼ cup minced garlic
3 eggs, beaten
1 cup milk
salt and cracked black pepper to taste
pinch of thyme
pinch of basil
¼ cup sliced green onions

Method:

Preheat oven to 375°F. In a 10-inch sauté pan, melt butter over medium-high heat. Sauté ham, onions, celery, bell peppers and garlic 3–5 minutes or until vegetables are wilted. In a large mixing bowl, combine eggs, milk and corn. Season with salt, pepper, thyme and basil. Place sautéed ham and vegetables into baking dish. Add corn mixture and stir well. Sprinkle in green onions. Place baking dish in 2-inch deep pan filled with approximately 1 inch water. Bake in water bath 30 minutes.

STUFFED EGGPLANT
IN ITALIAN GRAVY

Prep Time: 3 Hours
Yields: 8 Servings

Comment:

Tomato sauce or "salsa di pomodoro" is more often called "Italian gravy" by the Italians of Louisiana. This sauce is used in many great recipes, including this delectable eggplant dish.

Ingredients for Eggplant:

4 large eggplant
2 gallons ice water
1 (8-ounce) block mozzarella cheese, grated
1 pound ground beef
1 cup diced onions
½ cup diced celery
½ cup diced bell peppers
¼ cup chopped parsley
1 tbsp Worcestershire sauce
¼ cup evaporated milk
2 eggs beaten
¾ cup Italian bread crumbs
salt and black pepper to taste
½ cup olive oil

Ingredients for Gravy:

¼ cup olive oil
2 cups diced onions
1 cup diced celery
½ cup diced bell peppers
¼ cup minced garlic
reserved minced eggplant
2 (16-ounce) cans whole tomatoes
4 (8-ounce) cans tomato sauce
2 (6-ounce) cans tomato paste
3 cups water
1 tbsp dried basil
1 tbsp dried oregano
2 tsps sugar
salt and black pepper to taste
cooked pasta (optional)
¾ cup grated Romano cheese
¾ cup grated Parmesan cheese

Method:

Peel eggplant and cut in half lengthwise. Lay each half face up. Using a long sharp knife, remove 2 (1-inch wide, 1-inch deep) wedges from each half to provide space for stuffing. Mince removed wedges and reserve for sauce. Soak eggplant in ice water for 15–20 minutes. Remove, drain and completely dry. Divide mozzarella into 8 equal portions and sprinkle it inside slits of each eggplant. Cover eggplant and set aside. In a large mixing bowl, combine beef, onions, celery, bell peppers and parsley. Mix ingredients well. Using your hands, blend in Worcestershire, milk, eggs and bread crumbs to form stuffing. Season with salt and pepper. Stuff a generous amount of ground meat mixture into each slit. Any leftover stuffing may be formed into meatballs and added to gravy. In an oval cast iron Dutch oven, heat olive oil over medium-high heat. Gently roll each eggplant over and over in hot olive oil until meat is well seared. Once all have been seared, drain and keep warm.

Method:

Using the same Dutch oven as eggplant, heat olive oil. Sauté onions, celery, bell peppers, garlic and reserved minced eggplant 5–10 minutes or until vegetables are wilted. Crush whole tomatoes through your fingers as they are added to sauce. Blend in tomato sauce, paste and water. Season with basil, oregano, sugar, salt and pepper. Simmer 1 hour. Add stuffed eggplant, baste well and cook 1–1½ hours or until eggplant is extremely fork tender. When done, serve eggplant over a side dish of pasta and garnish with grated Romano and Parmesan cheeses.

ITALIAN FRIED EGGPLANT

Prep Time: 1 Hour
Yields: 4 Servings

Comment:

Once again we can see the strong Italian influence of cooking in Louisiana in this classic, simple recipe for fried eggplant. Serve this dish as a vegetarian entrée or as a side dish with meat or poultry.

Ingredients:

1 large (2-pound) eggplant, peeled and
    sliced into ¼-inch slices
salt and black pepper to taste
2 cups Italian bread crumbs
½ cup freshly grated Parmesan cheese
1 cup milk
2 eggs
2 cups flour
vegetable oil for frying

Method:

Sprinkle both sides of eggplant slices with salt and pepper. In a bowl, thoroughly mix bread crumbs and cheese then spread on a plate. In a separate bowl, combine milk and eggs, blending well. Spread flour on a plate. Dredge both sides of eggplant in flour, shaking off excess. Coat slices with egg mixture then dredge both sides of eggplant in bread crumbs, shaking off excess. Heat ¼-inch vegetable oil in a heavy-bottomed 12-inch skillet over medium-high heat until approximately 350°F. Fry 2–3 slices at a time for approximately 2 minutes or until golden brown. Turn and fry 2 minutes on other side. Drain on paper towels and serve immediately.

STUFFED EGGPLANT WITH RIVER SHRIMP

Prep Time: 1½ Hours
Yields: 6 Servings

Comment:

This dish is commonly eaten as an entrée, although smaller portions can be served as a side dish. You can substitute shrimp with ½ pound of crabmeat for a different flavor.

Ingredients:

5 eggplant
4 cups river shrimp tails
¼ pound butter
1 cup diced onions
½ cup diced celery
½ cup diced red bell peppers
¼ cup minced garlic
½ cup diced tomatoes
½ pound ground pork
½ pound ground beef
1 cup chicken stock
salt and cracked black pepper to taste
1½ cups Italian bread crumbs
¾ cup grated Parmesan cheese

Method:

Preheat oven to 375°F. Split 3 eggplant lengthwise and boil in lightly-salted water until tender. Remove and cool under tap water. Using a metal spoon, scrape meat from inside of halved eggplant, being careful not to tear shell. Save shells to be stuffed later. Peel and cube remaining 2 eggplant. Add uncooked cubes to scraped eggplant meat and set aside. In a 4-quart saucepot, melt butter over medium-high heat. Sauté onions, celery, bell peppers, garlic and tomatoes 10–15 minutes or until vegetables are wilted. Stir in pork and beef. Slowly cook until golden brown and each grain of meat is separated. Add small amounts of chicken stock if meat becomes too dry. Add eggplant and cook an additional 30 minutes. Remove from heat and season with salt and pepper. Gently fold in river shrimp and sprinkle bread crumbs into mixture to absorb most liquid. Using a metal cooking spoon, stuff shells with cooked eggplant mixture, dividing equally between 6 shells. Sprinkle additional bread crumbs and Parmesan cheese on top of stuffed eggplant. Place on baking pan, and bake until bread crumbs and cheese are golden brown.

EGGPLANT CASSEROLE

Prep Time: 1½ Hours
Yields: 6 Servings

Comment:
Typical of most vegetables served in South Louisiana, the eggplant is often prepared casserole-style. By combining meat, seafood and vegetables, the Cajuns and Creoles are able to create much heartier dishes for their tables.

Ingredients:
4 medium eggplant, peeled and cubed
½ pound ground beef
½ pound (150–200 count) shrimp, peeled and deveined
¼ pound butter
1 cup diced onions
1 cup diced celery
½ cup diced bell peppers
¼ cup minced garlic
1 cup chicken stock (see recipe)
salt and cracked black pepper to taste
2 cups Italian bread crumbs

Method:
Preheat oven to 375°F. Boil eggplant in lightly-salted water until tender and almost mushy. Drain and set aside. In a 4-quart saucepot, melt butter over medium-high heat. Sauté onions, celery, bell peppers and garlic 3–5 minutes or until vegetables are wilted. Add ground beef and slowly cook 25–30 minutes or until golden brown and each grain of meat is totally separated. If meat has become too dry during cooking, slowly add a little chicken stock. Stir in cooked eggplant and shrimp. Cook approximately 30 minutes or until vegetables, meat and eggplant are well blended. Season with salt and pepper. Remove from heat and sprinkle in 1 cup of bread crumbs to absorb liquid. Place eggplant mixture in a baking dish and top with remaining bread crumbs. Bake 20–30 minutes or until golden brown.

EGGPLANT PARMESAN

Prep Time: 1 Hour
Yields: 6–8 Servings

Comment:
Eggplant is one of the truly underrated culinary joys. The simple elegance of fresh vegetables and herbs crowned with grated Parmesan then baked must be tasted to be understood.

Ingredients:
2 large eggplant
1 cup fresh grated Parmesan cheese
¾ cup extra virgin olive oil
2 cups seasoned flour
1 cup diced onions
¼ cup minced garlic
¼ cup diced jalapeños
3 cups diced tomatoes
½ cup chopped basil
salt and black pepper to taste

Method:
Preheat oven to 375°F. Cut eggplant into 12–14 slices, ½-inch thick. In a large sauté pan, heat ¼ cup olive oil over medium-high heat. Dredge eggplant in seasoned flour, shaking off excess. Sauté 4–5 slices at a time until golden brown on both sides. Remove, drain and set aside. Continue to fry eggplant, adding extra olive oil as needed. In a separate sauté pan, heat ¼ cup olive oil over medium-high heat. Sauté onions, garlic and jalapeños 2–3 minutes. Stir in tomatoes and basil. Cook 15 minutes or until a fresh tomato sauce is achieved. Do not overcook. Season with salt and pepper. Place eggplant in a 9" x 13" baking dish and spoon an even amount of tomato sauce over each slice. Sprinkle generously with Parmesan cheese and bake until cheese is completely melted.

WHITE SQUASH WITH SHRIMP

Prep Time: 1 Hour
Yields: 6 Servings

Comment:

The white squash is similar to the pattypan squash found throughout America. It is grown in abundance here in the bayous and is normally the only squash seen on tables in South Louisiana.

Ingredients:

5 medium white squash
1 cup (150–200 count) shrimp, peeled and deveined
¼ pound butter
1 cup diced onions
1 cup diced celery
½ cup diced red bell peppers
¼ cup minced garlic
¼ cup sliced green onions
salt and cracked black pepper to taste
¼ cup chopped parsley
1 cup Italian bread crumbs

Method:

Preheat oven to 375°F. Peel squash, remove all seeds from center then dice. Boil in lightly-salted water 15–20 minutes or until tender. Remove and cool under tap water, then set aside. In a 10-inch heavy-bottomed sauté pan, melt butter over medium-high heat. Add onions, celery, bell peppers, garlic, green onions and shrimp. Sauté 5–10 minutes or until vegetables are wilted and shrimp are pink. Stir squash into vegetables and cook approximately 15 minutes longer. Remove from heat and season with salt and pepper. Add parsley and mix in bread crumbs to absorb excess liquid. Place cooked squash in baking dish and top with remaining bread crumbs. Bake until golden brown. NOTE: Mixture may be stuffed into hollowed-out squash halves and baked for a unique presentation.

GIANT MUSHROOMS STUFFED WITH CRAWFISH AND TASSO CARDINAL

Prep Time: 1 Hour
Yields: 6 Servings

Comment:

These stuffed mushrooms are smothered in a rich sauce flavored with crawfish and tasso, the smoky, spiced meat of the Cajuns. This sauce may also be served over chicken, fish or pasta.

Ingredients:

24 large mushroom caps, stems removed
1 pound crawfish tails, cooked
½ cup tasso ham, diced
¼ cup butter
½ cup minced onions
¼ cup minced celery
¼ cup minced red bell peppers
¼ cup minced garlic
¼ cup diced tomatoes
5 tbsps flour
1 ounce sherry
¼ cup tomato sauce
2 cups crawfish stock
2 cups heavy whipping cream
¼ cup sliced green onions
salt and black pepper to taste
Creole seasoning to taste
Louisiana hot sauce to taste

Method:

Preheat oven to 375°F. Brush any dirt or grit from mushroom caps. Place 4 mushrooms in 6 au gratin-style baking dishes. In a heavy-bottomed sauté pan, melt butter over medium-high heat. Sauté tasso, onions, celery, bell peppers and garlic 3–5 minutes or until vegetables are wilted. Stir in half of crawfish tails and all tomatoes, blending well. Sauté 2–3 additional minutes. Whisk in flour to create a white roux. (See roux recipes.) Pour in sherry and tomato sauce. Stir in stock and cream until a creamy sauce is achieved. Add green onions and simmer for 5–10 minutes, adding liquid as needed to retain consistency. Add remaining crawfish and season with salt, pepper, Creole seasoning and hot sauce. Cook 3 minutes, then distribute sauce evenly over mushrooms. Bake 15–20 minutes or until sauce is bubbly and mushrooms are al dente.

CRABMEAT AND SHRIMP STUFFED SUMMER SQUASH

Prep Time: 45 Minutes
Yields: 6 Servings

Comment:
Once again, we take a traditional vegetable of Bayou Country and give it a different twist by stuffing it with shellfish. Try using local vegetables in this recipe.

Ingredients:
3 medium yellow summer squash
½ pound lump crabmeat
½ pound small shrimp
¼ pound butter
1 cup minced zucchini
¼ cup minced onions
¼ cup minced celery
1 tbsp minced garlic
¼ cup minced red bell peppers
1 tsp lemon juice
salt and cayenne pepper to taste
1 cup Italian bread crumbs

Method:
Preheat oven to 375°F. Slice yellow squash lengthwise into 2 equal halves. Remove neck from squash, place halves in pot of boiling water. Cook 8–10 minutes or until skin is tender. Finely dice neck of squash and set aside. Remove squash from water and allow to cool. In a heavy-bottomed sauté pan, melt butter over medium-high heat. Sauté diced yellow squash, zucchini, onions, celery, garlic and bell peppers 3–5 minutes or until vegetables are wilted. Gently fold in lump crabmeat and shrimp. Pour in lemon juice and cook 1 minute. Remove from heat and season with salt and cayenne pepper. Mix in bread crumbs, a little at a time, until mixture is held together but not too dry. Using a metal spoon, scoop seed section from center of squash and discard. Divide stuffing equally into 6 portions then stuff into squash halves. Place on a baking pan, sprinkle with additional bread crumbs and bake 10–15 minutes or until squash is golden brown.

CRABMEAT AND SHRIMP STUFFED MIRLITON

Prep Time: 1½ Hours
Yields: 6 Servings

Comment:
Mirliton, which originated in Mexico, is known by many Americans as "chayote squash" or "vegetable pear" and by the French as "christophene." The vegetable was brought to Bayou Country by the Canary Islanders, called "Los Isleños," who relocated to Louisiana when Spain took ownership of New Orleans from France. This South Louisiana delicacy is wonderful when stuffed with shrimp and crabmeat.

Ingredients:
6 mirlitons, sliced lengthwise
1 pound jumbo lump crabmeat
1 pound (70–90 count) shrimp, peeled and deveined
¼ pound butter
1 cup diced onions
1 cup diced celery
½ cup diced red bell peppers
¼ cup minced garlic
1 tbsp chopped basil
salt and black pepper to taste
Louisiana hot sauce to taste
¼ cup chopped parsley
2 cups Italian bread crumbs
12 pats butter

Method:
Preheat oven to 375°F. Boil sliced mirlitons in lightly-salted water 30–40 minutes or until meat is tender enough to scoop from shells. Once tender, remove from water and cool. Using a teaspoon, remove seeds and gently scoop all meat out of shell, being careful not to tear shell. Discard excess liquid accumulated while scooping meat. Reserve meat and save shells for stuffing. In a 12-inch cast iron skillet, melt butter over medium-high heat. Sauté onions, celery, bell peppers, garlic and basil 3–5 minutes or until vegetables are wilted. Blend in shrimp and cook 2–3 minutes or until pink and curled. Mix in reserved meat from mirlitons and chop large pieces while cooking. Cook 15–20 minutes, stirring until flavors develop. After most of liquid has evaporated, remove from heat and season with salt, pepper, hot sauce and parsley. Fold in crabmeat, being careful to not break lumps. Sprinkle in approximately 1½ cups of bread crumbs to absorb any excess liquid and to hold stuffing intact. Divide mixture into 12 equal portions and stuff into hollowed-out shells. Place stuffed mirlitons on baking pan and sprinkle with remaining bread crumbs. Top each mirliton with 1 pat of butter. Bake 30 minutes or until golden brown. Serve 1 mirliton half as a vegetable or 2 halves as an entrée.

JUIRDMON: CUSHAW PUMPKIN PIE FILLING

Prep Time: 1 Hour
Yields: 3½ Pounds

Comment:

Most of the old Cajun and Creole cooks referred to the meat of the cushaw, a green and white, striped crookneck pumpkin, simmered in sugar and spices, as Juirdmon. This filling could be placed into a pie shell or made into turnovers. Children sometimes simply ate it from a cereal bowl, hot from the pot.

Ingredients:

1 (3-pound) cushaw	½ tsp allspice
2 cups sugar	½ tsp nutmeg
¾ pound butter	½ tsp ground ginger
½ cup Steen's cane syrup	½ tsp cinnamon
1 teaspoon pumpkin pie spice	2 tbsps pure vanilla extract

Method:

Select a cushaw with a main section approximately the size of a soccer ball. Using a large French knife, chop cushaw into 2-inch squares. Using a paring knife, scrape or cut away seeds and stringy matter from each square. Place cushaw squares in a large pot and cover with 2 inches of hot water. Add 1 cup of sugar and bring to a rolling boil. Boil pumpkin approximately 30 minutes or until pulp is extremely tender, but not mushy. Remove from heat then strain and chill under cold water. Once pumpkin is cool to touch, scrape meat into a large mixing bowl and discard shell. Using a pastry cutter, mash pumpkin. In a heavy-bottomed saucepan, melt butter over medium-high heat. Stir in mashed pumpkin, remaining sugar and cane syrup until well blended. Stir in remaining spices and vanilla. Bring to a low simmer and cook 15–20 minutes to blend flavors thoroughly. The pumpkin will be slightly dry, so it will be necessary to stir occasionally. Juirdmon is done when pumpkin is tender and creamy. Use as a pie filling or eat as a sweet vegetable side dish.

BAKED CUSHAW SQUARES

Prep Time: 1½ Hours
Yields: 6–8 Squares

Comment:

Cushaw, a striped crookneck pumpkin, is commonplace along the highways of Louisiana. Although this pumpkin is normally peeled, boiled and cooked casserole-style with brown sugar for the holiday table, this simple recipe is good all year long.

Ingredients:

1 medium cushaw
5 cups sugar
½ pound butter
¼ cup cane syrup
1 cup brown sugar
1 tsp allspice
pinch of cinnamon
pinch of nutmeg
candy corn for decoration (optional)

Method:

Preheat oven to 400°F. In a stockpot, whisk sugar into 1 gallon of water until dissolved. Bring water to a rolling boil. Using a very sharp butcher knife, cut cushaw in half and remove seeds and stringy pulp. Cut each half into 3-inch squares. Add cushaw to boiling water and cook until tender but not mushy. Once tender, place them on a large cookie sheet and set aside. In a heavy-bottomed saucepan, melt butter over medium-high heat. Stir in syrup, brown sugar and spices. Bring mixture to a low boil, stirring constantly until bubbly syrup is achieved. Do not scorch. Top each cushaw piece with syrup, then bake until thoroughly heated. Decorate with candy corn for a festive touch. Scoop the sweetened meat from shell before eating.

ONION CAKE

Prep Time: 2 Hours 15 Minutes
Yields: 1 (9-inch) Pie

Comment:

The Germans of Alsace-Lorraine and those from the Rhineland enjoyed the onion cake as a side dish to meat and seafood as well as a starter course. The cake may be made in the fashion of a pie or tart or, if served as an appetizer, may be presented in the style of a pizza.

Ingredients for Crust:

¼ pound cold, chipped butter
1⅓ cups flour
1 tbsp sugar
¼ cup ice water

Method:

Place butter, flour and sugar in a food processor and pulse 1 minute or until a coarse meal texture is achieved. Slowly add ice water, a little at a time, until dough forms into a ball. Remove and place on a lightly-floured surface. Roll dough to ⅛-inch thickness. Firmly press into an ungreased 9-inch pie pan. Place crusts in refrigerator and chill 30 minutes.

Ingredients for Batter:

4 small Vidalia onions, diced
3 strips bacon
4 ounces grated Swiss cheese
1 tsp chopped chives
½ cup Bittersweet Plantation Dairy Creole Cream Cheese
⅛ tsp caraway seeds
1 egg
1 egg yolk
1½ tsps salt
½ tsp black pepper

Method:

Preheat oven to 350°F. In a heavy-bottomed sauté pan, brown bacon over medium-high heat. Turn occasionally, being careful not to scorch fat. Cook until bacon is crispy then remove and let cool. Chop bacon and set aside. In same pan, sauté onions in bacon fat over medium-high heat for 20–30 minutes or until wilted and lightly browned around edges. Do not caramelize. Remove from heat, scrape contents into a large metal bowl and allow to cool slightly. Stir in bacon, cheese, chives, cream cheese, caraway seeds, egg and egg yolk, mixing until well blended. Season with salt and pepper. Pour onion batter into prepared pie crust and bake 1 hour or until a toothpick inserted into center of pie comes out clean.

COUSH COUSH

Prep Time: 30 Minutes
Yields: 6 Servings

Comment:

The name "coush coush" comes from "couscous," a North African dish of steamed semolina. Coush coush is a very old Cajun cornmeal recipe that was most often used as a hot cereal. The people of every Cajun cabin had their own method of preparation for this dish and had a different tradition for serving it. Many years ago, on the coldest winter nights, this dish would be cooked in a cast iron pot in the fireplace. It's hard to imagine that a dish so simply prepared could taste so good.

Ingredients:

2½ cups white or yellow cornmeal
¾ tsp salt
1¼ tsps baking powder
1¾ cups milk
¾ cup vegetable oil

Method:

In a large mixing bowl, combine cornmeal, salt, baking powder and milk. Blend well. In a cast iron skillet, heat oil over medium-high heat. When oil is hot, pour in cornmeal mixture and cook approximately 5 minutes, allowing a crust to form over edges. Once crust has set, stir, lower heat and cook 15 minutes. Allow another crust to develop, but stir occasionally to break crust as it forms. Serve with milk as a cereal or topped with cane syrup.

HOMEMADE SEMOLINA PASTA

Prep Time: 1 Hour
Yields: 1½ Pounds Fresh Pasta

Comment:
Pasta is one of the world's greatest foods. It is delicious, healthy and low in fat. You can make pasta in any imaginable shape and serve it with almost any food. Invest in a small pasta machine for your kitchen, and make your own fresh pasta.

Ingredients:
2 cups semolina flour
2 cups flour
2 eggs, well beaten
1 tbsp extra virgin olive oil
½ tsp salt
1½ cups cold water

Method:
Mix 2 flours together and make a mound on top of a clean surface. Make a well in center of mound. In a large bowl, beat eggs and mix in olive oil, salt and 1 cup cold water. Pour egg mixture into flour well. With your hands, mix flours and liquids together and knead until you have a ball of dough. Use up to ½ cup of water to moisten dough, as necessary. Work dough by rolling it away from you on counter while simultaneously tearing it in half. Pull it back together while rolling it back toward you, always keeping some pressure on dough with balls of hands. Keep rolling and tearing for 5 minutes, until mixture is uniform and smooth. Dust with flour occasionally to prevent dough from sticking. Make dough into shape of a bread loaf and dust with white flour. Cover with a dry cloth and allow pasta dough ball to rest for 5 minutes. Cut off a piece of dough about the size of your fist and flatten it into a disk. Dust it lightly with flour. Dough is now ready to be shaped using pasta machine.

Antique dies for pasta making

WHITE RICE

Prep Time: 30 Minutes
Yields: 3 Cups

Comment:

In Cajun and Creole cooking, rice is second in importance only to the roux. Rice can be found at every meal. Most often, rice is served with famous Cajun dishes such as gumbo, étouffée, sauce piquant, crawfish bisque and, of course, red beans.

Ingredients:

1 cup long grain rice
1½ cups water
1 tsp salt
1 tbsp butter

Method:

Wash rice a minimum of 2 times in cold running water. This process will remove excess dust and starch from grains. Drain well. In a heavy-bottomed saucepan, combine all ingredients. Place pan over medium-high heat and bring to a rolling boil. Reduce temperature to simmer, cover and cook 30 minutes. While cooking, do not remove the cover or attempt to stir rice. One cup of raw rice will yield 2½–3 cups cooked rice. Use ½ cup of cooked rice per serving.

FETTUCCINE ALFREDO

Prep Time: 20 Minutes
Yields: 4 Servings

Comment:

Italian cooking is very simple and usually very fast. It uses fewer ingredients for each dish than any other cuisine. This recipe is a prime example of that fact.

Ingredients:

12 ounces fettuccine, cooked
¼ cup unsalted butter
1 tbsp minced garlic
2 cups heavy whipping cream
1 cup chicken broth
2 egg yolks
½ cup freshly-grated Parmesan cheese
¼ cup chopped chives or parsley
salt and cracked black pepper to taste

Method:

In a large sauté pan, melt butter over medium-high heat. Sauté garlic 1–2 minutes. Stir in cream and chicken broth. Bring to a rolling boil, reduce to simmer and cook until cream is slightly thickened. Remove from heat and quickly whisk egg yolks into center of cream. Whisk constantly to keep eggs from scrambling. Fold cooked pasta into mixture. Follow with cheese and chives or parsley, continuing to blend. Season with salt and pepper. Serve immediately or pasta will become pasty.

Always Ready for Rice

Rice, a staple for about 5,000 years, is grown in Louisiana and, while it is said that a Cajun will eat anything, he is most proud to eat what is homegrown.

Since the Civil War, Louisiana has been a major rice producer. Our copious rainfall, flat topography and hot climate make this state perfect for rice growing even though it is not native to the region. In fact, while rice is now cultivated on every continent except Antarctica, all of America's rice originally came from abroad. Rice was among the many new plants and vegetables brought by the Spanish, French and English to their New World colonies. The first recorded cultivation of rice in America took place in the Carolinas in the late 1600s. Legend has it that in 1685, the Carolina colonists helped make repairs to a storm-battered ship from Madagascar. To thank them for their kindness, the captain gave the colonists some "golden seede rice" which, once planted, soon became a thriving crop. By 1726, nearly 4,500 metric tons of "Carolina Gold Rice" were being shipped out of Charleston alone. Some accounts indicate that during the American Revolution the British almost crushed the American rice industry. During their occupation of Charleston, the British apparently shipped the entire year's rice crop to England without leaving any seed to plant for the following year. In these accounts, Thomas Jefferson is credited with saving the American rice industry by illegally smuggling seed out of Italy during a diplomatic mission.

After the Civil War, the destruction of croplands, the dissolution of the slave labor force and the devastation of hurricanes eventually took their toll on the East Coast rice plantations. Louisiana and Texas soon became the prime areas for rice growing for they not only offered the perfect climate, but also had firmer ground that made mechanization possible. The Cajuns had long planted rice in marshy areas unfit for other crops, simply by tossing the rice seed into the water. Whatever grew out of this crude technique was called Providence Rice and was used for the farmer's own subsistence. German farmers who came to Louisiana from the Midwest were the first to grow rice for profit by applying the skills they had acquired farming wheat. As with other agricultural ventures in Louisiana, the Africans also proved invaluable not just for labor, but also because of their experience growing similar crops in West Africa.

The Louisiana rice industry received several major boosts with the creation of canals for more controlled irrigation, the development of varieties better suited to our soil and climate, and the arrival of the railroad. Additionally, in the 1800s it was discovered that the mechanization used in wheat farming in the Midwest could be used for rice cultivation and harvesting. These changes revolutionized the rice industry and paved the way for Louisiana to be one of the top producers in the country. Some of the original rice companies, such as Riviana, founded by Frank Godchaux, and Crystal Rice Plantation, founded by Sol Wright, are still in business today. The Konriko Rice Mill, built by P. A. Conrad in 1912, is the nation's oldest, continuously operating mill and is located near New Iberia, La.

Seafood

Ladies with redfish

J ust as early cave paintings depict hunting scenes, ancient elaborate illustrations of fish and fishing implements indicate that seafood was enjoyed by even the earliest civilizations. The fact that ancient communities soon discovered how to smoke and salt seafood so it could be preserved and carried far inland demonstrates the importance of this food source all over the world. It was popular in the markets and on the tables of the ancient Greeks and Romans, and it could also be found in the cuisines of Asia and Europe. It was the food of peasants, but also an integral part of royal feasts, a fact highlighted in most culinary histories by Vatel's plight. Vatel, a steward for the Prince de Condé, was so distressed when the seafood he ordered for a feast honoring Louis XIV did not arrive, he took his own life.

No South Louisianian will ever find himself in Vatel's shoes, provided he doesn't stray far from home. Not only is Louisiana a coastal state with easy access to the fish-laden Gulf of Mexico on its southern border, but the state is 16 percent water, with miles of streams, rivers, and bayous from which to draw sustenance. In fact, the state's east and west boundaries are defined by the Mississippi and Sabine rivers. On any given day, Louisiana natives may feast on crawfish, catfish, bass, oysters, shrimp, pompano, red snapper, redfish, lemon fish, scallops, speckled trout, mackerel, swordfish or crabs and still not exhaust their choices. The Acadians even consider one of the region's game birds, the poule d'eau, as seafood. Because this type of duck fed exclusively on fish, it was not considered meat. This opinion was even respected by the Catholic priests who allowed consumption of the poule d'eau on Fridays during Lent. However, seafood is not taken lightly here, it is almost a religion in itself. You might hear someone say they would die for a soft-shell crab po'boy, but there is no need to imitate poor Vatel.

Seafood has always been plentiful in Louisiana, providing a staple for the Native Americans long before the members of the other six nations arrived. According to Eating in America, tribes in coastal regions of the United States regularly ate sea turtle or green turtle, cod, lemon sole, flounder, catfish, crawfish, crabs and shrimp. At one time turtles were so plentiful on the Gulf Coast and so important a food source to the native tribes, they were called the "Buffalo of the Caribbean." The colonists were also fond of turtle meat, but their affections remained truer over time to the oyster. Oysters were so abundant and cheap that by the 1800s it was hard to find a city on the coast without an oyster house. Recipes from that period often included oysters, sometimes calling for 100 or more in a single dish. They were commonly served raw, cooked, in soups or combined with bread, rice or meat in stuffings. Many of the early American recipes for oysters were similar to ones popular in Europe as far back as the Middle Ages. Of course, the exposure to new ingredients and the seemingly endless supply of oysters soon prompted new recipes, particularly in areas where the shellfish seemed to thrive. In his book, The Bayous of Louisiana, Harnett Kane points out that oysters tend to grow best in water that is neither fresh, nor salt, thus Louisiana's coastal combination of the two (brackish water) provides particularly fertile "soil" for this crop. Oysters remain so popular and plentiful in Louisiana that many restaurants offer a weekly 25-cent oyster night, a price unheard of in most of the country.

In Louisiana, catching and cooking seafood holds almost as much importance as consuming it—a prime example is the state's love affair with crawfish. When one considers that Louisiana's combined annual yield of commercially harvested and freshwater farmed crawfish ranges from 75 million to 105 million pounds, it is truly amazing how little of the catch ever leaves the state. The total economic impact exceeds $120 million annually, and more than 7,000 people depend directly or indirectly on the crawfish industry. Crawfish, like shrimp and crab, hold such a special place in the hearts of Louisianians that there is a festival dedicated to them. Even when no festival date is marked on the calendar, the people here create a celebration out of the simple act of boiling crawfish. This ritual is anticipated for months before the crawfish season starts, and predictions abound as to what effect the current rainfall and temperatures will have on the developing crop. Once the crawfish are in season, generally from January until June, crawfish boils are planned for every occasion from weddings to anniversaries and birthdays to graduations. A crawfish boil can also be just another excuse to get together, eat good food, drink beer and catch up with friends and neighbors. That said, there has never been a crawfish boil where the size of the crawfish, the spice level of the boil, the ease or difficulty of peeling or the preference for particular accompaniments (such as corn, potatoes, mushrooms, garlic, artichokes), are not up for discussion. While true Louisianians will claim to be able to spot a foreigner by how slow they peel and whether or not they suck the heads, many a novice has caught on pretty quickly. And should you think South Louisianians ever settle for the status quo, a new delicacy, the soft-shell crawfish, has gained popularity in recent years. Harvested during one of the crawfish's quarterly molting periods, the soft-shell variety continues to inspire new and delicious recipes.

While some of the varieties of fish and seafood may have been somewhat unfamiliar to the early settlers in Louisiana, there was little challenge in adapting recipes to suit. In fact, the freshness and availability of seafood here soon pushed it to the forefront of Cajun and Creole cuisine, where it became a significant part of Louisiana's reputation worldwide. Many credit blackened redfish as the single recipe that started the Cajun food craze. National demand for the dish actually led to overfishing and a commercial ban on redfish (red drum). Luckily, there are enough varieties of fish available in Louisiana waters to keep both sportsmen and chefs more than happy. Being a Southern state, Louisiana is also known for its catfish. The recipes created here,

such as catfish in oyster andouille butter and catfish Boulettes, were probably instrumental in helping this humble bottom-dweller to improve its reputation and gain acceptance at the finest restaurants. We must also credit the development and success of aquaculture methods that now provide a steady supply of good quality catfish without the muddy taste associated with the wild variety. An average of about 65 million pounds of farm-raised catfish are produced each year in Louisiana.

Shrimp have become so vital to Louisiana's economy and cuisine that every year the shrimp fleet receives a holy blessing as recounted here in an excerpt from *The Bayous of Louisiana*.

> "Deus, qui dividiens aquas ab arida..." God who had separated sea from land, was being asked once again to grant favor to those who follow the water. Two thousand years earlier, the first Christians sought by ceremonial to invoke safety and good fortune for the ships that they sent across the Mediterranean. Centuries later, off the Normandy and Brittany coasts, French peasant-fisherman knelt while their priests intoned the same words. In coastal Louisiana, with rites that have changed little through the years, the Church of Rome was bestowing its blessing on the shrimp fleet.

Since 1937, shrimp have been honored in their own festival, of which the blessing of the fleet is a part. In more recent years shrimp have shared the spotlight with another key provider of jobs and capital in South Louisiana. Since 1967, the annual celebration in Morgan City has been dubbed the Shrimp & Petroleum Festival. While it may not sound very appetizing, the festival emphasizes the unique way in which these two seemingly different industries work hand-in-hand culturally and environmentally in this area. The festival honors those who have worked tirelessly through rain and shine to provide the area's economic lifeblood for over half a century. While shrimp may be common fare around the world, Cajun and Creole cuisine has not failed to claim shrimp as its own, as you will discover when making Cajun Drunken Shrimp, Shrimp and Okra Pie, or Jumbo Shrimp in Creole Mustard Cream. A uniquely New Orleans take on Barbecued Shrimp, created at Manale's Restaurant (now Pascal's Manale), demands that you abandon decorum and soak up the spicy sauce with bits of bread. Louisiana's German settlers caught on quickly, and were combining beer and herbs to steam shrimp more than a century ago.

Crabs are also a fundamental part of Louisiana's seafood repertoire. The blue crab finds its way into dips, gumbos, au gratins, boils and more. Most revered in Louisiana, and perhaps elsewhere, is the soft-shell crab. As Kane puts it, the crab at this stage is "at his most delicious, his most defenseless, and, for the consumer, his most expensive." The high price reflects the careful timing and precise process of catching the crab just after it molts its hard shell and before it grows another. One taste of this soft-shell delicacy either fried or broiled, and few care about the price.

Whether boiled, broiled, steamed, baked, fried or stewed, Louisiana's cuisine is a true celebration of the bounty of the

bayous, streams, lakes and bays. In *Something Old, Something New*, Kay Walker Mabile was quoted as saying, "Food done here in the Louisiana bayou country, comes close to being a state religion—as much ceremony as sustenance—and it's generally a special occasion." It should be no surprise that she was talking about seafood.

DEEP-FRIED SHRIMP, OYSTERS OR CATFISH

Prep Time: 30 Minutes
Yields: 6 Servings

Comment:
Deep-frying seafoods is still quite common in the South. High quality vegetable or peanut oil should be used. Corn flour is a double-ground yellow cornmeal that can be found in the gourmet section of most food stores, possibly sold as a prepackaged fish fry.

Ingredients for Batter:
1 egg
1 cup milk
1 cup water
4 tbsps yellow mustard
salt and cracked black pepper to taste

Method:
In a 1-quart mixing bowl, blend all ingredients. Set aside.

Ingredients for Frying:
3 pounds seafood
vegetable oil
4 cups yellow corn flour or cornmeal
granulated garlic to taste
salt and cracked black pepper to taste
cayenne pepper to taste

Method:
Using a home-style deep fryer such as a FryDaddy, heat oil according to manufacturer's directions. In a large mixing bowl, blend corn flour, garlic, salt and peppers. Dip seafood in egg batter and then in seasoned corn flour. Fry a few pieces at a time until golden brown and beginning to float. Continue until all seafood is done. NOTE: Fried shrimp are best when served hot with cocktail or tartar sauce or when placed on a po'boy.

ICE WATER MARINATED SEAFOOD

Prep Time: 1 Hour
Yields: 6 Servings

Comment:

Many trappers in South Louisiana found it inconvenient to batter seafood in milk and eggs because these ingredients were not available. Instead, they created this unique and interesting method of marinating fish, shrimp and oysters prior to deep-frying.

Ingredients:

48 tiny catfish fillets,
   OR 48 (21–25 count) shrimp, peeled and deveined,
   OR 48 fresh oysters
salt and cracked black pepper to taste
Louisiana hot sauce to taste
granulated garlic to taste
1 gallon ice cubes
1–2 quarts water
vegetable oil
6 cups yellow cornmeal

Method:

Place seafood in a large ceramic bowl and season generously with salt, pepper, hot sauce and garlic. It is important to over season because most flavor washes off in ice water. Cover with ice cubes and 1–2 quarts water, depending on size of bowl. Allow to sit 1 hour. While seafood is marinating, heat oil in a Dutch oven or FryDaddy to 365°F. In a large bowl or brown paper bag, place cornmeal and season with salt, pepper and granulated garlic. Remove seafood from ice water and shake well to remove excess liquid. Coat pieces in seasoned cornmeal. Fry seafood in small batches until golden and floating to surface. Serve with Louisiana Seafood Cocktail Sauce or Louisiana Tartar Sauce. (See recipes.)

CLASSIC DEEP-FRIED SHRIMP OR OYSTER PO'BOY

Prep Time: 30 Minutes
Yields: 6 Servings

Comment:

Whether stuffed with ham, shrimp, oysters, roast beef or catfish, the po'boy is a staple of the New Orleans diet. This sandwich was named "poor boy" because of the inexpensive ingredients that were originally used as fillings. Today you can find great po'boys in delis, restaurants and even convenience stores throughout the Crescent City.

Ingredients:

3 dozen (70–90 count) shrimp
   OR 3 dozen shucked oysters
6 (10-inch) po'boy loaves
vegetable oil
1 egg, beaten
1 cup milk
1 cup water
2 tbsps Creole mustard
1 tbsp mustard
salt and cracked black pepper to taste
3 cups yellow corn flour
2 tbsps granulated garlic
6 tbsps Louisiana Tartar Sauce (see recipe)
6 tbsps ketchup
18 thin slices tomato
2 cups shredded lettuce

Method:

Preheat oven to 375°F. Using a home-style deep fryer such as a FryDaddy, heat oil according to manufacturer's directions. Slice po'boy bread lengthwise and place on a large cookie sheet, crust down. Set aside. In a mixing bowl, combine egg, milk, water, mustards, salt and pepper. In a separate mixing bowl, combine corn flour, garlic, salt and pepper. Set aside. When ready to prepare po'boys, place bread in oven and turn off heat to allow bread to become crispy and warm. Dip shrimp or oysters, 6 at a time, in egg batter and then corn flour mixture. Fry pieces in 2–3 batches, 3 minutes or until seafood floats. Remove, drain and keep warm. Continue until all seafood is done. While shrimp and oysters are cooking, remove bread from oven, and top one side with tartar sauce and second side with ketchup. Place 3 slices of tomato on bottom half and sprinkle with shredded lettuce. Place 6 shrimp, oysters or a combination of both over lettuce, and top with other po'boy half. Secure with toothpicks and slice in half. Serve hot. NOTE: To spice up this dish, sprinkle a dash of hot sauce on each po'boy.

Rienzi Plantation, a gift to the Chef John Folse Culinary Institute at Nicholls State University, Thibodaux, La., from the Levert Land Company

Paella cooking

PAELLA VALENCIANA

Prep Time: 1½ Hours
Yields: 8 Servings

Comment:

Paella is considered the national dish of Spain. The dish was first created in the city of Valencia. Although there are many variations of paella and much debate over which is the original, Paella Valenciana is definitely the most famous.

Ingredients:

2 dozen black mussels

2 dozen (21–25 count) shrimp, head-on

1 fryer chicken

1 small rabbit

10 cups chicken stock or water

1 tbsp saffron threads

½ cup olive oil

1 pound chorizo
    OR 1 pound pork sausage

2 cups diced onions

1 cup diced celery

1 cup diced red bell peppers

¼ cup sliced garlic

2 cups diced tomatoes

3 cups arborio rice

salt and black pepper to taste

1 cup sweet peas

16 snow peas

Method:

Place saffron in 1 cup of stock and set aside. In a 14-inch paella pan or cast iron skillet, heat oil over medium-high heat. Cut both chicken and rabbit into 8–10 pieces each, cutting breast of chicken and back legs of rabbit in half. Season meat with salt and pepper, add to pan and cook until golden brown. Remove from pan and set aside. NOTE: If using pork sausage, add 1 teaspoon paprika when frying. In same pan, cook chorizo or sausage until medium-well. Remove and set aside with rabbit and chicken. Sauté onions, celery, bell peppers and garlic 3–5 minutes or until vegetables are wilted. Add tomatoes and sauté 2 minutes. Stir-fry rice into vegetables 3–5 minutes. Pour in all stock and saffron then season with salt and pepper. Return meats to pan, bring to simmer and stir constantly until rice absorbs all liquid. Distribute meats evenly around dish and top with sweet peas, mussels, shrimp and snow peas. Cover pan tightly with foil and place on low heat or bake at 350°F for 30–40 minutes. Serve immediately.

CIOPPINO

Prep Time: 1 Hour
Yields: 2 Servings

Comment:

Cioppino is an Italian stew made primarily of fish, shellfish and tomatoes. Italian immigrants would throw only a small portion of the day's catch into the pot, but the resulting stew would feed the entire community. Feel free to substitute other types of shellfish to ensure the freshest quality.

Ingredients:

4 clams in shells, washed
4 mussels in shells, washed and debearded
4 medium shrimp
4 medium–large oysters
4 scallops
4 calamari, cleaned and sliced
1 (2-ounce) trout fillet, sliced
2 cans Italian plum tomatoes with juice
1 tbsp extra virgin olive oil
1 tbsp chopped onions
1 tsp chopped garlic
¼ tsp crushed red pepper
½ cup dry white wine
1 tsp salt
½ cup fish stock (see recipe)
salt and white pepper to taste
1 tsp chopped basil
1 tsp chopped oregano
1 tsp chopped Italian parsley
Louisiana hot sauce to taste
¼ tsp Worcestershire sauce
2 portions cooked linguine

Method:

In a saucepan over medium-high heat, heat olive oil until very hot. Sauté onions and garlic until light brown. Add clams, mussels, red pepper and wine. Cover and steam shellfish until they open. (The mussels will open first.) Remove shellfish from pan and place in 1 quart warm water with 1 teaspoon salt. Wash sand out and remove any beards from mussels. While shellfish are soaking, add fish stock and tomatoes to pan and bring to a boil. Add shrimp, oysters, scallops and calamari. Cook over medium-low heat. When pan returns to a boil, season with salt, white pepper, basil, oregano, parsley, hot sauce and Worcestershire. Cook 3 minutes then add trout, clams and mussels. Cook for another 3 minutes, until trout begins to flake. To serve, place clams and mussels around edge of a large platter. Place linguine in center and pour rest of pan contents onto plate.

CASSEROLE OF SEAFOOD AND POTATO FLORENTINE

Prep Time: 1 Hour
Yields: 10 Servings

Comment:

Casseroles were made famous in the 1950s when women started entering the workforce. Leftover meats and vegetables were combined to make quick, one-dish meals that could feed a large family. Seafood, potatoes and spinach are blended with a rich cream sauce to make the perfect Lenten dinner.

Ingredients:

1 pound catfish, cubed
½ pound shrimp (70–90 count), peeled and deveined
1 pound crawfish tails, drained
3 medium potatoes, peeled and boiled until fork tender
Creole seasoning to taste
Louisiana hot sauce to taste
salt and black pepper to taste
¼ cup olive oil
¾ cup diced onions
½ cup diced celery
¼ cup diced red bell peppers
1 tbsp minced garlic
1 bag baby spinach leaves, rinsed and stems removed
1 cup heavy whipping cream
1 cup fresh grated Parmesan cheese
1 cup Italian bread crumbs

Method:

Preheat oven to 350°F. In a mixing bowl, combine fish, shrimp and crawfish. Season lightly with Creole seasoning and hot sauce then mix well. Spray a 2½-quart casserole dish with cooking spray. Thinly slice cooked potatoes and layer in bottom of casserole dish. Sprinkle with salt and pepper. In a medium skillet, heat olive oil over medium heat. Sauté onions, celery, bell peppers and garlic 2–3 minutes or until tender. Add spinach and toss 1–2 minutes or until wilted. Season with salt and pepper. Cover potatoes with spinach mixture. Gently pour cream over spinach. Sprinkle with half of Parmesan cheese and half of bread crumbs. Spread seafood evenly on top. In a small bowl, combine remaining cheese and bread crumbs, and sprinkle evenly on top of casserole. Bake 50–60 minutes or until golden brown and center of dish reaches 160°F. Allow casserole to sit 15 minutes so that sauce is absorbed completely.

SEAFOOD SAUCE PIQUANT ST. JAMES

Prep Time: 1½ Hours
Yields: 10 Servings

Comment:

Seafood sauce piquant is a great example of the combination of different influences in Creole cooking. The sauce piquant, meaning hot or spicy, gets its flavor from the hot Spanish peppers that came to Louisiana from South America. The French brown roux adds color and enhances flavor in the dish. Five to six pounds of turtle or other domestic meat may be substituted for the seafood.

Ingredients:

6 fresh fish fillets, cubed
1 pound crawfish tails
1 pound claw crabmeat
3 pounds (50–60 count) shrimp
1½ cups vegetable oil
1½ cups flour
3 cups diced onions
2 cups diced celery
1 cup diced bell peppers
½ cup minced garlic
1 (8-ounce) can tomato sauce
2 (10-ounce) cans Ro*tel® tomatoes
1 gallon hot fish or shellfish stock (see recipe) or water
2 cups sliced green onions
1 cup chopped parsley
salt and black pepper to taste
Louisiana hot sauce to taste

Method:

In a 12-quart Dutch oven, heat oil over medium-high heat. Whisk in flour, stirring constantly until a dark brown roux is achieved. (See roux recipes.) Add onions, celery and bell peppers. Cook 3–5 minutes or until vegetables are wilted. Stir in garlic and tomato sauce. Cook 5 minutes, stirring occasionally then add tomatoes. Pour in hot stock, 1 cup at a time, until a stew-like consistency is achieved. Do not use all of stock. Bring to a rolling boil then reduce to simmer and add ¼ of each seafood. Cook 30–40 minutes, adding stock as necessary to maintain consistency. Season with salt, pepper and hot sauce. Add remaining seafood, green onions and parsley. Bring to a boil, stirring occasionally. Reduce to simmer and cook 3–5 minutes or until seafood is well done but not overcooked. Stew should be consistency of a heavy whipping cream. Adjust seasonings if necessary. Serve over steamed white rice.

SHRIMP AND REDFISH COURTBOUILLON

Prep Time: 1½ Hours
Yields: 6 Servings

Comment:

Although court bouillon is best known as a flavorful poaching liquid for fish and shellfish, in Louisiana it has evolved into a sumptuous roux-based fish stew. At one time, redfish was the only ingredient used in the courtbouillons of Cajun Country. Redfish should always be the first choice, but any firm-fleshed fish may be substituted.

Ingredients:

1 pound (21–25 count) shrimp, peeled and deveined
3 (8-ounce) redfish fillets
¾ cup vegetable oil
¾ cup flour
2 cups diced onions
1 cup diced celery
½ cup diced red bell peppers
¼ cup minced garlic
1 (12-ounce) can diced tomatoes
1½ quarts fish stock (see recipe)
¾ cup dry red wine
2½ tbsps lemon juice
3 bay leaves
1 tbsp chopped thyme
1 tbsp chopped basil
¼ tsp dried marjoram
⅛ tsp allspice
salt and black pepper to taste
Louisiana hot sauce to taste
1 cup sliced green onions
½ cup chopped parsley
6 lemon slices

Method:

Cut each fillet into 3 equal slices and set aside. In a cast iron Dutch oven, heat oil over medium-high heat. Whisk in flour, stirring constantly until dark brown roux is achieved. (See roux recipes.) Add onions, celery, bell peppers and garlic. Sauté 3–5 minutes or until vegetables are wilted. Stir in tomatoes with juice. Pour in fish stock, 1 ladle at a time, until a sauce-like consistency is achieved. Add red wine, lemon juice, bay leaves, thyme, basil, marjoram and allspice. Bring to a rolling boil, reduce to simmer and cook 45 minutes, stirring occasionally. Additional stock may be needed to retain sauce-like consistency. Sauce should be slightly thick. When seafood is added, liquid will be rendered and thin the sauce. Blend in shrimp and fish then bring to a low boil, and cook 3–5 minutes or until firm but not falling apart. Season with salt, pepper and hot sauce. Add green onions and parsley then adjust seasonings if necessary. Serve over steamed white rice and garnish with lemon slices.

MAMERE'S RIVER SHRIMP AND POTATO STEW

Prep Time: 30 Minutes
Yields: 4 Servings

Comment:

As common as red beans and rice, potato stew became a pleasant substitution on Mondays in Louisiana. Both dishes could be cooked in the black iron pot next to the wash kettle, making lunch a little easier on washdays. During spring, river shrimp were often added to create a magnificent shrimp and potato soup.

Ingredients:

1½ pounds river shrimp, peeled and deveined

6 potatoes, cubed	¼ cup minced garlic
¾ cup vegetable oil	1½ quarts shellfish stock (see recipe)
¾ cup flour	¼ cup sliced green onions
2 cups diced onions	1 tbsp chopped parsley
1 cup diced celery	salt and black pepper to taste
1 cup diced bell peppers	granulated garlic to taste

Method:

In a large cast iron Dutch oven, heat oil over medium-high heat. Whisk in flour, stirring constantly until a dark brown roux is achieved. (See roux recipes.) Add onions, celery, bell peppers and garlic. Sauté until golden brown, stirring constantly. Pour in stock, 1 ladle at a time, until a sauce-like consistency is achieved. Add potatoes and cook 15 minutes or until fork tender. Do not overcook. Fold in shrimp, green onions and parsley. Season with salt, pepper and granulated garlic. Cook 5–10 additional minutes or until shrimp are pink and curled.

DRIED SHRIMP STEW

Prep Time: 1 Hour 45 Minutes
Yields: 6 Servings

Comment:

Prior to the days of refrigeration, drying shrimp in the sun was considered the best way to preserve them. This technique was perfected by the Native Americans in Louisiana. Today, dried shrimp are packaged in small cellophane bags and sold in the grocery stores of Bayou Country. The distinctive flavor of the shrimp is appreciated in dishes ranging from spaghetti to stews.

Ingredients:

1 cup dried shrimp	¼ cup minced garlic
5 medium potatoes	2 quarts water
1 cup vegetable oil	8 boiled eggs
1 cup flour	1 cup sliced green onions
2 cups diced onions	½ cup chopped parsley
½ cup diced celery	salt and cayenne pepper to taste
1 cup diced bell peppers	

Method:

Soak shrimp in 1 cup water for 30 minutes then discard water. Peel and dice potatoes into 1-inch cubes. Set aside. In a large Dutch oven, heat oil over medium-high heat. Sprinkle in flour, whisking constantly until dark brown roux is achieved. (See roux recipes.) Add onions, celery, bell peppers and garlic. Sauté 3–5 minutes or until vegetables are wilted. Whisk in water until smooth. Add shrimp and cook 30 minutes. Fold in potatoes, cook 15 minutes then add eggs, green onions and parsley. Cook 10 minutes. Season with salt and cayenne pepper.

Louisiana shrimper readies the nets

BLACK-EYED PEA BATTERED SHRIMP

Prep Time: 30 Minutes
Yields: 6 Servings

Comment:

Shrimp are deep-fried every day in Louisiana, but the batters used to coat and flavor them are as varied as the cooks preparing the seafood. This recipe was created by Robert Harrington, dean of the Chef John Folse Culinary Institute at Nicholls State University.

Ingredients:

36 (16–20 count) shrimp, head-on
¾ cup black-eyed peas, cooked
¼ cup diced onions
1 tbsp minced garlic
⅛ tsp ginger
Creole seasoning to taste
salt and black pepper to taste
2 eggs
2 ounces vegetable oil
1¼ cups beer
2 cups flour
Louisiana hot sauce to taste
1 quart vegetable oil

Method:

Peel shells from tail of shrimp, being careful not to remove head. Devein shrimp. In a food processor, combine peas, onions, garlic, ginger, Creole seasoning, salt and pepper. Blend on high speed 2–3 minutes or until peas are coarsely chopped. Add eggs, 2 ounces oil and beer. Blend 1–2 minutes or until peas are puréed. Add flour and blend 1–2 minutes. Pour black-eyed pea batter into a ceramic bowl. In a home-style deep fryer such as a FryDaddy, heat oil according to manufacturer's directions. If a deep fryer is not available, place 3 inches of oil in a large pot and heat to 350°F. Dip shrimp tail portion only into batter and allow all excess to drain. Gently place shrimp into deep fryer and allow to cook until golden brown and partially floating.

SHRIMP AND OKRA PIE

Prep Time: 1½ Hours
Yields: 6 Servings

Comment:

In the South, okra is prepared in many different ways. The vegetable can be found boiled, pickled, fried or smothered, and of course used in gumbos. This pie is a unique okra recipe.

Ingredients:

2 pounds (90–110 count) shrimp, peeled and deveined
3 pounds fresh okra, sliced ¼-inch thick
1 pie shell
1 cup diced onions
⅓ cup diced bell peppers
2 tbsps minced garlic
¼ cup vegetable oil
1 tbsp white vinegar
⅓ cup sliced green onions
¾ cup Italian bread crumbs
salt and black pepper to taste
Louisiana hot sauce to taste

Method:

Preheat oven to 375°F. In a 12-quart Dutch oven, bake okra, onions, bell peppers and garlic in oil 30–45 minutes, stirring occasionally. Once sautéed and browned, add vinegar and blend well. Continue to bake 10–15 minutes, stirring frequently. Remove pan from oven and place over medium-high heat. Stirring constantly, add green onions and shrimp. Cook 3–5 minutes or until shrimp are pink and curled. Place pie shell in oven and bake until golden brown. While pie shell bakes, sprinkle ½ cup bread crumbs into shrimp mixture then season with salt, pepper and hot sauce. Remove pie shell from oven and fill with okra mixture. Top with remaining bread crumbs. Bake 5–7 minutes or until light brown.

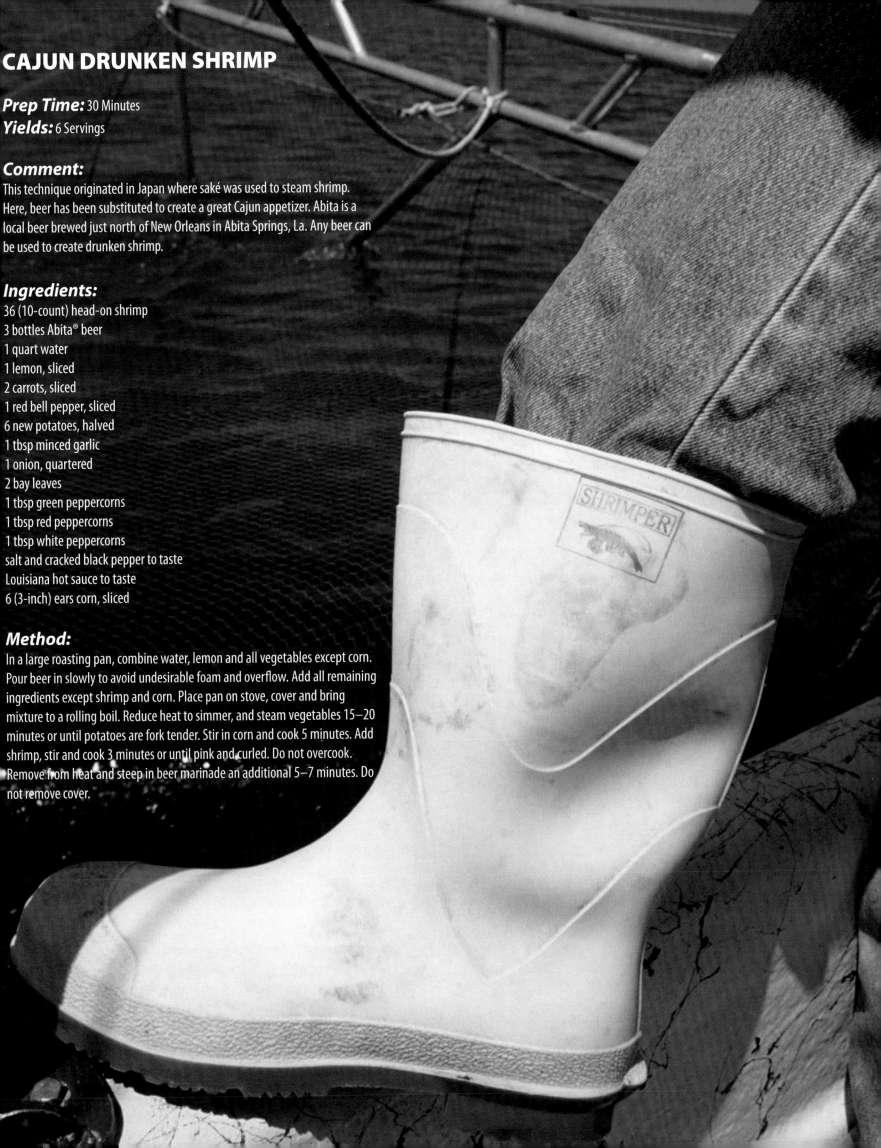

CAJUN DRUNKEN SHRIMP

Prep Time: 30 Minutes
Yields: 6 Servings

Comment:
This technique originated in Japan where saké was used to steam shrimp. Here, beer has been substituted to create a great Cajun appetizer. Abita is a local beer brewed just north of New Orleans in Abita Springs, La. Any beer can be used to create drunken shrimp.

Ingredients:
36 (10-count) head-on shrimp
3 bottles Abita® beer
1 quart water
1 lemon, sliced
2 carrots, sliced
1 red bell pepper, sliced
6 new potatoes, halved
1 tbsp minced garlic
1 onion, quartered
2 bay leaves
1 tbsp green peppercorns
1 tbsp red peppercorns
1 tbsp white peppercorns
salt and cracked black pepper to taste
Louisiana hot sauce to taste
6 (3-inch) ears corn, sliced

Method:
In a large roasting pan, combine water, lemon and all vegetables except corn. Pour beer in slowly to avoid undesirable foam and overflow. Add all remaining ingredients except shrimp and corn. Place pan on stove, cover and bring mixture to a rolling boil. Reduce heat to simmer, and steam vegetables 15–20 minutes or until potatoes are fork tender. Stir in corn and cook 5 minutes. Add shrimp, stir and cook 3 minutes or until pink and curled. Do not overcook. Remove from heat and steep in beer marinade an additional 5–7 minutes. Do not remove cover.

SHRIMP AND POTATO PANCAKES

Prep Time: 1½ Hours
Yields: 20 (4-inch) Pancakes

Comment:

The Germans are famous for their pancakes and dumplings. Potatoes, a major cash crop of the Germans, became one of their favorite ingredients and was used in many different dishes. Here, their love of pancakes and seafood are combined with the beloved potato for a perfect breakfast or side dish. Try this recipe topped with a poached or fried egg.

Ingredients:

½ pound (70–90 count) shrimp, peeled and deveined
6 (medium–large) Idaho potatoes, peeled and halved
1 cup minced onions
½ cup minced garlic
¼ cup sliced green onions
¼ cup chopped parsley
salt and black pepper to taste
3 eggs, beaten
¼ cup vegetable oil

Method:

Boil potatoes in lightly-salted water 20 minutes or until fork tender. Drain and refrigerate a minimum of 2 hours, preferably overnight. Mash potatoes with a fork. Coarsely chop shrimp and squeeze off excess liquid. In a large mixing bowl, combine shrimp, potatoes, onions, garlic, green onions and parsley. Season with salt and pepper then fold in eggs and blend well. Form mixture into 4-inch pancakes, approximately ½-inch thick. In a 12-inch cast iron skillet, heat oil over medium heat. Cook 2–3 pancakes at a time 5–7 minutes, turning occasionally. Serve as a breakfast pancake or as an accompaniment to any meat or seafood dish.

SHRIMP AND GRITS

Prep Time: 45 Minutes
Yields: 6 Servings

Comment:

Grits are a staple on the South Louisiana breakfast table. Often, this traditional breakfast dish is combined with other ingredients to create something truly unique that can be enjoyed for breakfast, brunch or dinner.

Ingredients for Shrimp:

2 dozen (21–25 count) shrimp, peeled and deveined
½ cup butter
¼ cup minced red bell peppers
¼ cup minced yellow bell peppers
¼ cup minced green bell peppers
½ cup minced red onions
½ cup minced celery
1 tbsp minced garlic
½ cup minced andouille sausage
¼ cup flour
4 cups shrimp stock
½ cup heavy whipping cream
¼ cup sliced green onions
salt and black pepper to taste

Method:

In a large skillet, melt butter over medium-high heat. Add all vegetables and andouille. Sauté 3–5 minutes, stirring occasionally. Sprinkle in flour, stirring constantly 3–5 minutes or until slightly golden. Slowly add shrimp stock, 1 cup at a time, stirring until a sauce-like consistency is achieved. Additional stock may be added if necessary. Blend in cream, bring to a low boil then add green onions and shrimp. Cook 3–5 minutes or until shrimp curl and turn pink. Season with salt and pepper.

Ingredients for Grits:

1½ cups stone-ground grits
3½ cups whole milk
3¼ cups water
1½ tbsps salt
½ tsp white pepper
4 tbsps butter
½ pound shredded Gouda cheese, not smoked

Method:

In a 1-gallon stockpot, combine milk, water, salt, white pepper and butter. Bring to a low boil over medium-high heat. Add grits and stir well. Reduce heat to medium-low and cover. Cook 12–14 minutes, stirring occasionally until thickened. Remove from heat and blend in cheese. Adjust seasonings if necessary. Top each portion of grits with 4 large shrimp and a generous serving of sauce.

Chef Jon Tarver selects the finest shrimp for his recipe.

JUMBO SHRIMP IN CREOLE MUSTARD CREAM

Prep Time: 30 Minutes
Yields: 6 Servings

Comment:

The Germans were the first to create a grainy, stone-ground mustard in Bayou Country. Since then, Creole mustard has been used to season hundreds of dishes and is enjoyed on sandwiches, in dressings and on fried seafood.

Ingredients:

3 dozen (12–15 count) shrimp, head-on
2 tbsps Creole mustard
¼ pound butter, sliced
¼ cup chopped chives
½ cup sliced green onions
¼ cup diced red bell peppers
1 tsp dried tarragon
½ cup dry sherry
2 tbsps flour
1 cup heavy whipping cream
1 cup shellfish stock (see recipe)
salt and black pepper to taste
1 pound cooked pasta

Method:

Peel shell from tail of each shrimp, being careful to keep head intact. Using a sharp paring knife, devein and rinse under cold water. Set aside. In a large sauté pan, melt half of butter over medium-high heat. Be careful not to brown or burn butter. Sauté shrimp 1–2 minutes or until pink and curled, a few at a time. Remove from pan and keep warm. Add chives, green onions, bell peppers and tarragon. Sauté 2–3 minutes or until vegetables are wilted. Deglaze pan with sherry, and cook until all but 1 tablespoon of liquid has evaporated. Sprinkle in flour and blend well. Whisk in Creole mustard, whipping cream and shellfish stock until sauce thickens. Additional stock or water may be used if sauce becomes too thick. Season with salt and pepper. Bring sauce to a low boil and whisk in remaining butter, a few pats at a time. Add shrimp and cook until heated through. On a 10-inch plate, place 6 shrimp over favorite cooked pasta, such as penne or fettuccine. Top with a generous serving of mustard cream sauce.

SHRIMP CREOLE

Prep Time: 1 Hour
Yields: 6 Servings

Comment:

Shrimp Creole is a signature New Orleans dish. Just as red beans became a traditional Monday dinner, this dish is often seen on South Louisiana tables on Friday. The flavor of this dish is enhanced by the use of a rich shrimp and shellfish stock.

Ingredients:

3 pounds (21–25 count) shrimp, peeled and deveined
¾ cup vegetable oil
¾ cup flour
1 cup diced onions
1 cup diced celery
1 cup diced bell peppers
2 tbsps minced garlic
2 cups tomato sauce
1 cup diced tomatoes
1½ quarts shellfish stock (see recipe)
1 cup chopped green onions
½ cup chopped parsley
salt and cracked black pepper to taste
Louisiana hot sauce to taste

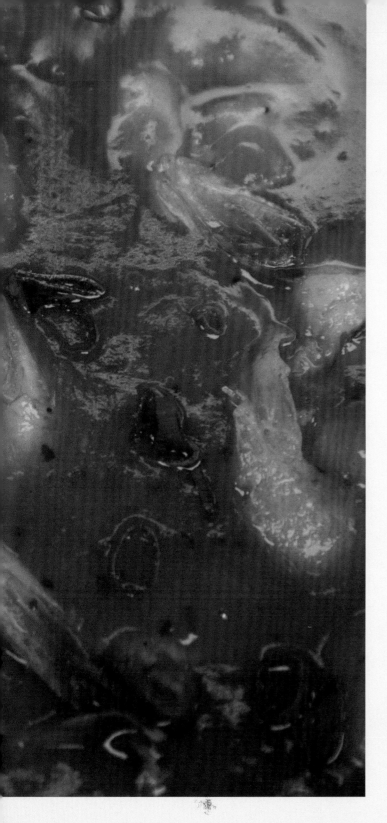

SHRIMP SCAMPI

Prep Time: 45 Minutes
Yields: 4 Servings

Comment:
Although scampi is a term used in parts of the world to describe a species of shrimp, in America it is used to describe an Italian dish. This simple recipe is magnificent when served over pasta, alongside rice pilaf or atop chicken and fish.

Ingredients:
1½ pounds (20–25 count) shrimp, peeled and deveined
½ cup flour
salt and cracked black pepper to taste
¼ tsp cayenne pepper
½ cup olive oil
6 cloves garlic, sliced
¼ cup chopped shallots
2 tbsps fresh basil
2 tbsps fresh oregano
½ cup sliced mushrooms
¼ cup minced parsley
½ cup dry white wine

Method:
In a mixing bowl, blend flour, salt and peppers. Dust shrimp lightly in seasoned flour and set aside. In a large sauté pan, heat oil over medium-high heat. Add garlic and sauté 1–2 minutes or until edges turn golden. Blend in shrimp, shallots, basil and oregano. Using a slotted spoon, turn shrimp occasionally until pink and curled. Add mushrooms and parsley then deglaze with white wine. Season with salt and peppers. Serve shrimp over pilaf or any seasoned rice.

Method:
In a 2-gallon heavy-bottomed saucepan, heat oil over medium-high heat. Whisk in flour, stirring constanlty until light brown roux is achieved. (See roux recipes.) Add onions, celery, bell peppers and garlic. Sauté 3–5 minutes or until vegetables are wilted. Blend in tomato sauce and diced tomatoes. Slowly add shellfish stock, stirring constantly until a sauce-like consistency is achieved. Cook approximately 15 minutes, stirring occasionally. More stock may be added if mixture becomes too thick. Add shrimp, green onions and parsley then cook 5 minutes. Season with salt and pepper. Serve over steamed white rice with a dash of hot sauce.

TUSCAN SHRIMP PASTA

Prep Time: 45 Minutes
Yields: 6 Servings

Comment:

Tuscany is without a doubt one of the regions of Italy best known for its cuisine. This wonderful shrimp dish is of Tuscan origin and may be served over a multitude of pastas.

Ingredients:

3 dozen (21–25 count) shrimp, peeled and deveined
2 pounds pasta, cooked al dente
¼ pound butter
1 tbsp sliced garlic
¼ cup sliced green onions
¼ cup sliced mushrooms
¼ cup julienned red bell peppers
¼ cup julienned yellow bell peppers
¼ cup julienned green bell peppers
½ cup diced Creole tomatoes
¼ cup sliced black olives
2 tbsps flour
1 ounce dry white wine
2½ cups hot shellfish or chicken stock (see recipes)
1 tsp lemon juice
1 tsp parsley
salt and black pepper to taste

Method:

In a heavy-bottomed sauté pan, melt butter over medium-high heat. Sauté garlic, green onions and mushrooms 2 minutes or until mushrooms are slightly wilted. Stir in bell peppers, tomatoes and olives, and cook 1 minute. Stir-fry shrimp into vegetables 2 minutes or until shrimp turn pink and curl. Whisk in flour, stirring constantly until white roux is achieved. (See roux recipes.) Flour will absorb most liquid in pan and act as a thickening agent for sauce. Deglaze with white wine then whisk in hot stock. Add lemon juice and parsley. Season with salt and pepper. Cook until sauce is thickened and shrimp are perfectly cooked, but not overdone. Additional stock may be added if sauce becomes too thick. Serve over favorite pasta.

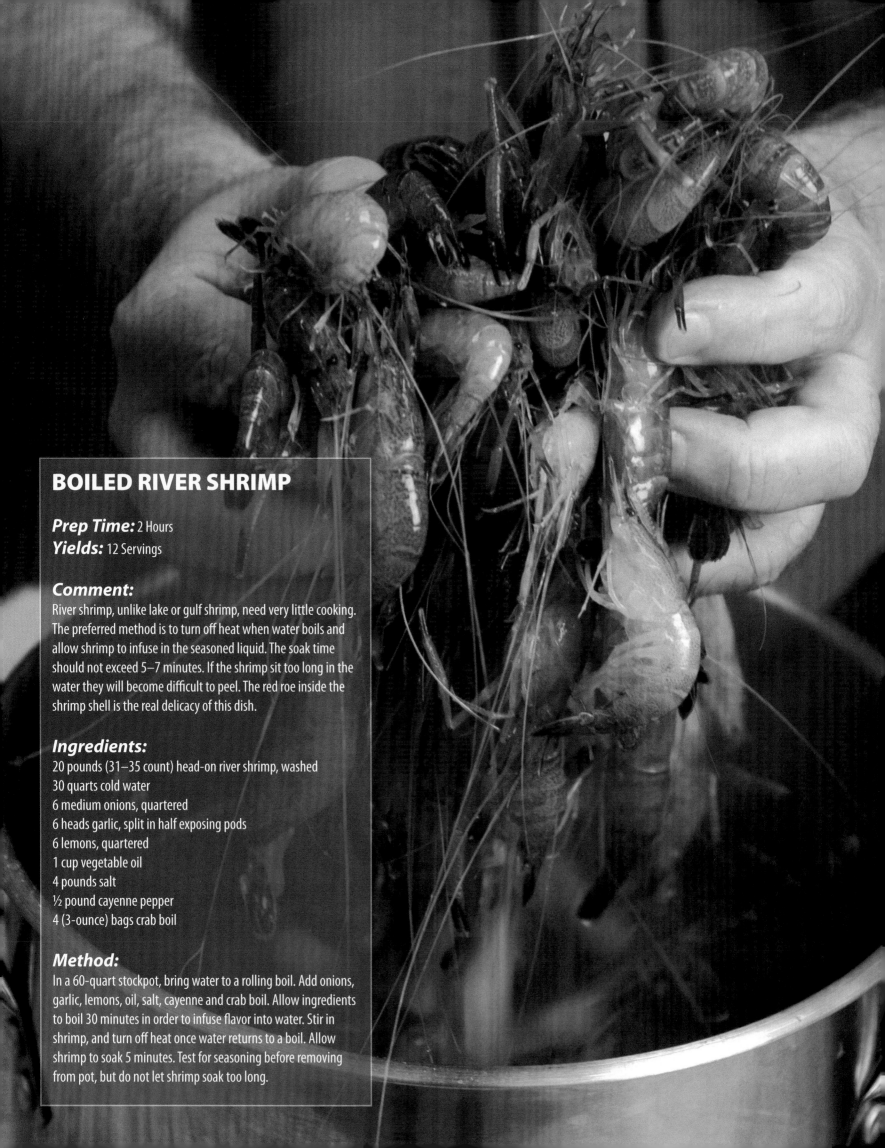

BOILED RIVER SHRIMP

Prep Time: 2 Hours
Yields: 12 Servings

Comment:
River shrimp, unlike lake or gulf shrimp, need very little cooking. The preferred method is to turn off heat when water boils and allow shrimp to infuse in the seasoned liquid. The soak time should not exceed 5–7 minutes. If the shrimp sit too long in the water they will become difficult to peel. The red roe inside the shrimp shell is the real delicacy of this dish.

Ingredients:
20 pounds (31–35 count) head-on river shrimp, washed
30 quarts cold water
6 medium onions, quartered
6 heads garlic, split in half exposing pods
6 lemons, quartered
1 cup vegetable oil
4 pounds salt
½ pound cayenne pepper
4 (3-ounce) bags crab boil

Method:
In a 60-quart stockpot, bring water to a rolling boil. Add onions, garlic, lemons, oil, salt, cayenne and crab boil. Allow ingredients to boil 30 minutes in order to infuse flavor into water. Stir in shrimp, and turn off heat once water returns to a boil. Allow shrimp to soak 5 minutes. Test for seasoning before removing from pot, but do not let shrimp soak too long.

RIVER SHRIMP REVERIE

Long before I ever heard the terms "white" or "brown" Gulf shrimp, we were catching and cooking that exotic variety of shellfish called river shrimp. These freshwater shrimp from the Mississippi River usually appeared in great numbers in early spring and were enjoyed until the beginning of summer. In the lakes and the Gulf, shrimp are harvested in large nets pulled behind shrimp boats. River shrimp, however, are caught in rectangular, wooden boxes made from Louisiana cypress, with wire funnels that act as doors on all four sides. The box is baited with cottonseed cake, a dense, dry cottonseed meal pressed into ¾-inch thick slabs. If one could not afford this form of bait, fish heads or even chicken pieces such as necks or wings could be substituted. A hinged door on the top of the box allowed easy access for loading bait or harvesting the catch. The boxes were hauled into the river by young boys who would anchor them to stakes driven into the river silt or attach them to the limb of a willow tree reaching out into the river current. I remember well wading out into the chin-deep water and feeling the sensation of literally thousands of river shrimp picking at my legs, indicating, sight unseen, that the shrimp box would be overfilled. The cypress boxes were untied from their stakes and dragged onto the riverbank where the shrimp were emptied into No. 3 tubs. Fresh bait was placed in the boxes, which were then returned to their moorings until the next morning. River shrimp were eaten boiled or used as the perfect stuffing for mirliton or eggplant. One of my all-time favorite river shrimp dishes is Mamere's River Shrimp and Potato Stew.

Today, although the practice of shrimping in the Mississippi River is almost extinct because of heavy barge and oceangoing vessel traffic, there are still those that keep the tradition alive. These diehards, mostly in Ascension and St. James parishes, keep us few remaining river shrimp aficionados amply supplied.

Bribe or Reward?

Once boiled, the red roe or caviar of the river shrimp is considered a sweet delicacy by the Cajuns and Creoles. Children were enticed to help with the task of peeling the shrimp knowing that the reward for a job well done was a plate of the rich red roe.

STUFFED CRABS

Prep Time: 1 Hour
Yields: 8 Servings

Comment:

Many Louisianians will make this stuffing with picked crabmeat from leftover boiled crabs instead of with lump crabmeat. However, the previously seasoned crabmeat may affect the finished flavor. It is important to spread the crabmeat over a cookie sheet and pick all remaining cartilage and shells from the meat. When using lump crabmeat, handle it gently to avoid breaking the lumps into smaller pieces.

Ingredients:

2 pounds jumbo lump crabmeat
½ pound butter
½ cup diced onions
½ cup diced celery
½ cup diced red bell peppers
¼ cup diced garlic
1 tsp chopped thyme
1 tsp chopped basil
¼ cup chopped parsley
¼ cup sliced green onions
2 eggs, beaten
salt and black pepper to taste
Louisiana hot sauce to taste
2 cups Italian bread crumbs
8–10 cleaned crab shells

Method:

Preheat oven to 350°F. In a large cast iron skillet, melt butter over medium-high heat. Add onions, celery, bell peppers and garlic. Sauté 3–5 minutes or until vegetables are wilted. Stir in thyme, basil, parsley and green onions. Sauté 3–5 minutes longer. Remove skillet from heat and pour contents into a large mixing bowl. Carefully fold in lump crabmeat. Blend in eggs then season with salt, pepper and hot sauce. Sprinkle in enough bread crumbs to hold mixture together without drying out stuffing. Divide mixture into 8–10 servings and fill each crab shell. If shells are not available, use au gratin dishes or ramekins. Place stuffed crabs on a cookie sheet and top with bread crumbs. Bake 15–20 minutes or until crabs are thoroughly heated and golden brown.

CRAB CAKES REX

Prep Time: 30 Minutes
Yields: 8 Servings

Comment:

The crab cakes of Bayou Country are usually dense in texture due to the abundance of bread crumbs in the recipe. For a more appetizing texture, this recipe has fewer bread crumbs and more crabmeat.

Ingredients:

1 pound lump crabmeat
3 tbsps butter
½ cup diced onions
½ cup diced celery
½ cup diced red bell peppers
¼ cup minced garlic
1 cup Italian bread crumbs
¼ cup thinly sliced green onions
¼ cup mayonnaise
1 egg
2 tbsps minced parsley
2 tsps Worcestershire sauce
2 tsps lemon juice
2 tbsps Old Bay® seasoning
1 tsp Creole mustard
salt and cracked black pepper to taste
Louisiana hot sauce to taste
½ cup Italian bread crumbs
¼ cup vegetable oil

Method:

Pick through crabmeat to remove any shell or cartilage. In a sauté pan, melt butter over medium-high heat. Add onions, celery, bell peppers and garlic. Sauté 3–5 minutes or until vegetables are wilted. Remove and cool slightly. In a large mixing bowl, combine sautéed vegetables and all remaining ingredients except crabmeat, ½ cup bread crumbs and oil. Use hands to gently fold in crabmeat, continually checking for shell or cartilage. Adjust seasonings if necessary. Gently form crab mixture into 1" x 2½" patties, dust lightly with bread crumbs then place on a cookie sheet. Chill in refrigerator at least 1 hour. In a sauté pan, heat vegetable oil over medium-high heat. Sauté crab cakes 2–3 minutes on each side, turning each cake over gently to avoid breaking. Place crab cake in center of dinner plate and top with White or Red Rémoulade Sauce. (See recipes.) If serving as a brunch dish, top each crab cake with a Poached Egg and Hollandaise Sauce. (See recipes.)

Brunch-style Crab Cakes Rex

LUMP CRABMEAT AU GRATIN

Prep Time: 45 Minutes
Yields: 6 Servings

Comment:
Au gratin refers to the crusty topping of bread crumbs or cheese on top of a baked or broiled dish. The most famous of all au gratins in Louisiana is the Jumbo Lump Crabmeat au Gratin. Try adding shrimp or crawfish to the recipe to further enhance the dish.

Ingredients:
2 pounds jumbo lump crabmeat
¼ pound butter
¼ cup diced onions
¼ cup diced celery
¼ cup diced green bell peppers
¼ cup diced red bell peppers
¼ cup diced yellow bell peppers
¼ cup sliced green onions
1 tbsp minced garlic
3 tbsps flour
3½ cups heavy whipping cream, hot
1 ounce dry white wine
1 tsp lemon juice
dash Louisiana hot sauce
½ cup grated Cheddar cheese
salt and cracked black pepper to taste
¼ cup chopped parsley

Method:
Preheat oven to 375°F. In a 2-quart, heavy-bottomed saucepan, melt butter over medium-high heat. Add onions, celery, bell peppers, green onions and garlic. Sauté 3–5 minutes or until vegetables are wilted. Be careful not to brown vegetables. Sprinkle in flour and blend well to form a white roux. (See roux recipes.) Whisk in cream and bring to a low boil, stirring constantly to prevent scorching. Cream should thicken quickly to a white sauce consistency. Reduce heat to simmer. Add wine, lemon juice and hot sauce. Sprinkle in half of cheese and stir constantly until melted. Season with salt and pepper. Add parsley and cook 5–7 minutes, stirring constantly. Sauce will thicken immediately. Thin with water or milk if necessary. Place equal portions of crabmeat in bottom of 6 au gratin dishes, top with sauce and sprinkle with remaining cheese. Bake 10 minutes or until cheese is bubbly.

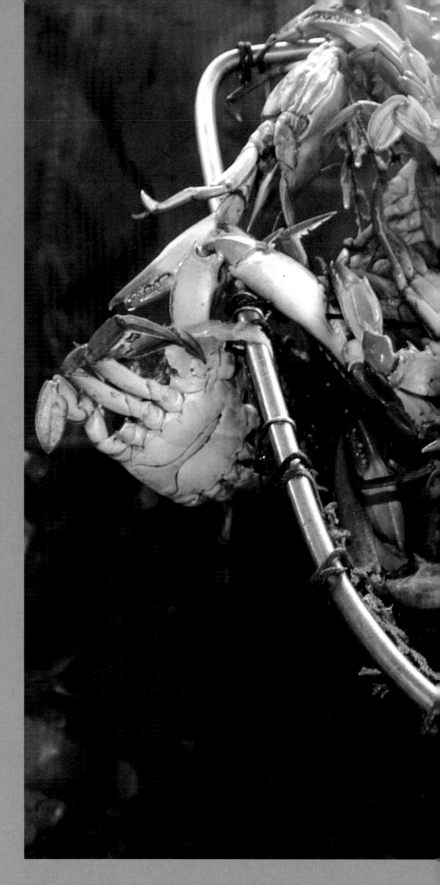

LAKE DES ALLEMANDS CRAB STEW

Prep Time: 1 Hour
Yields: 6 Servings

Comment:
Have your seafood supplier clean the crabs well and cut in half, keeping the large claws intact. As with most crab recipes, leftover crabs and meat from a boil can be used in this stew.

Ingredients:

1½ pounds lump crabmeat

1 dozen small crabs, cleaned and halved

1 (6-ounce) can tomato paste

¼ pound melted butter

2 (8-ounce) cans tomato sauce

2 cups hot water

2 cups diced onions

1 cup diced celery

½ cup diced bell peppers

1 tbsp minced garlic

1 tbsp Worcestershire sauce

2 tbsps sugar

1 bay leaf

salt and black pepper to taste

Louisiana hot sauce to taste

Method:

Rinse halved crabs well and set aside. Spread lump crabmeat on a cookie sheet, and remove all remaining cartilage and shells. In a heavy-bottomed Dutch oven, brown tomato paste over medium-high heat. Blend in melted butter, tomato sauce and water. Cook 5–10 minutes or until mixture is simmering. Add onions, celery, bell peppers and garlic. Simmer 10 additional minutes and add Worcestershire, sugar and bay leaf. Add shelled crabs to sauce and simmer approximately 1 hour. Additional water may be added if mixture becomes too thick. Season with salt, pepper and hot sauce. When flavor is fully developed, gently fold in lump crabmeat. Adjust seasonings if necessary and cook 5 minutes. Serve over rice or pasta. Eat shelled crabs and claws exactly as you would boiled crabs.

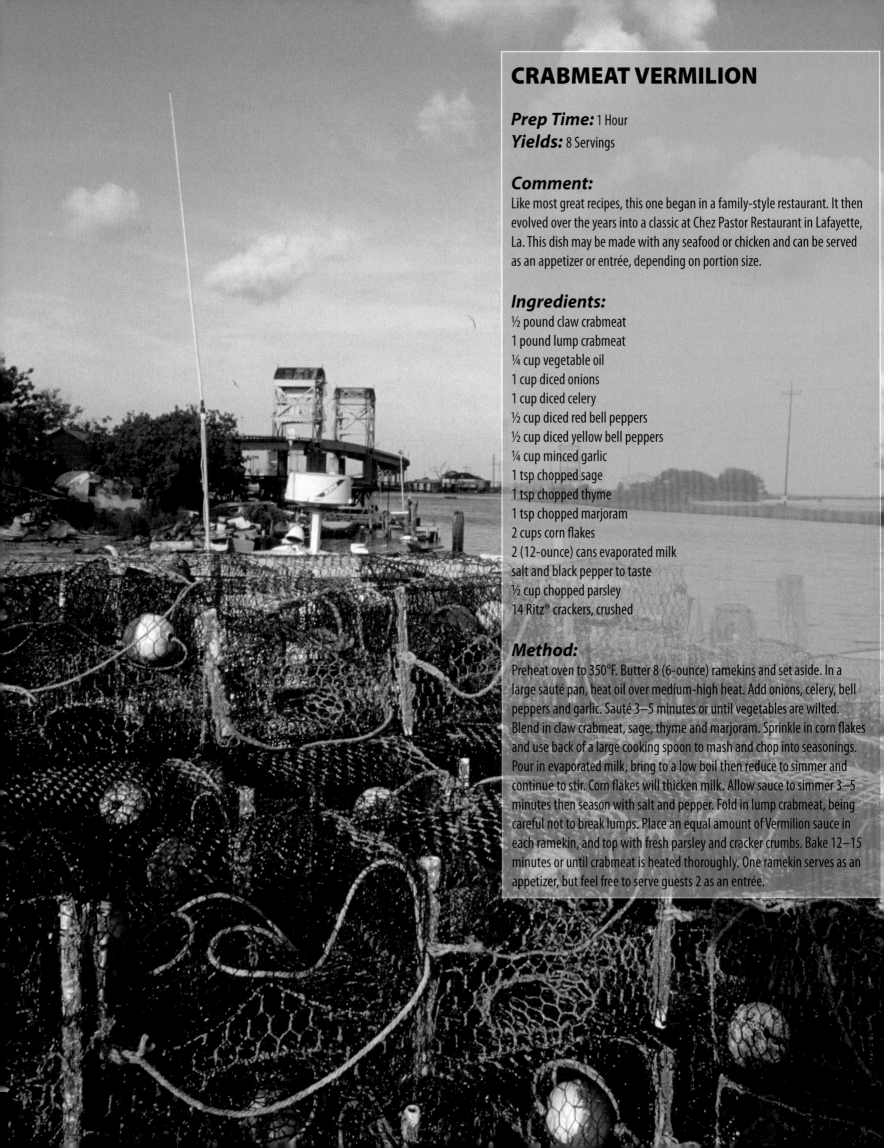

CRABMEAT VERMILION

Prep Time: 1 Hour
Yields: 8 Servings

Comment:

Like most great recipes, this one began in a family-style restaurant. It then evolved over the years into a classic at Chez Pastor Restaurant in Lafayette, La. This dish may be made with any seafood or chicken and can be served as an appetizer or entrée, depending on portion size.

Ingredients:

½ pound claw crabmeat
1 pound lump crabmeat
¼ cup vegetable oil
1 cup diced onions
1 cup diced celery
½ cup diced red bell peppers
½ cup diced yellow bell peppers
¼ cup minced garlic
1 tsp chopped sage
1 tsp chopped thyme
1 tsp chopped marjoram
2 cups corn flakes
2 (12-ounce) cans evaporated milk
salt and black pepper to taste
½ cup chopped parsley
14 Ritz® crackers, crushed

Method:

Preheat oven to 350°F. Butter 8 (6-ounce) ramekins and set aside. In a large sauté pan, heat oil over medium-high heat. Add onions, celery, bell peppers and garlic. Sauté 3–5 minutes or until vegetables are wilted. Blend in claw crabmeat, sage, thyme and marjoram. Sprinkle in corn flakes and use back of a large cooking spoon to mash and chop into seasonings. Pour in evaporated milk, bring to a low boil then reduce to simmer and continue to stir. Corn flakes will thicken milk. Allow sauce to simmer 3–5 minutes then season with salt and pepper. Fold in lump crabmeat, being careful not to break lumps. Place an equal amount of Vermilion sauce in each ramekin, and top with fresh parsley and cracker crumbs. Bake 12–15 minutes or until crabmeat is heated thoroughly. One ramekin serves as an appetizer, but feel free to serve guests 2 as an entrée.

FRIED SOFT-SHELL CRABS

Prep Time: 30 Minutes
Yields: 6 Servings

Comment:

As crabs grow, they must molt and lose their old shells to make room for new, larger ones. Once the old shell has been shed, the new covering is soft for only a couple of hours. Soft-shell crabs have become somewhat of a delicacy in Louisiana and are eaten in many ways, but frying them is definitely the most popular method of preparation.

Ingredients for Batter:

1 cup milk	3 tbsps Creole mustard
½ cup water	salt and cracked black pepper to taste
2 eggs	

Method:

In a 1-quart mixing bowl, whisk together all ingredients until well blended. Set aside.

Ingredients for Breading:

2 cups yellow corn flour	1½ tsps cracked black pepper
2¼ tsps salt	1½ tsps cayenne pepper
1½ tsps granulated garlic	1½ tsps thyme

Method:

In a 1-quart mixing bowl, combine all breading ingredients. Set aside.

Ingredients for Frying:

6 soft-shell crabs
1½ quarts vegetable oil

Method:

In a home-style deep fryer, preheat oil according to manufacturer's directions or to 375°F. Place soft-shell crabs in batter and allow to marinate 10–15 minutes. Drain excess liquid from crabs and coat well in breading mixture, shaking off excess. Fry 1 at a time until crab turns golden brown and floats to top of frying unit. Remove and drain on paper towels. Serve hot, topped with Louisiana-Style Crawfish Étouffée. (See recipe.)

HOW TO CLEAN SOFT-SHELL CRABS:

If cleaning them yourself, use the following method. Lift pointed end of top shell away from main body. Scrape off lungs or white spongy substance located at each end of crab. Using a sharp paring knife or scissors, cut away eyes and mouth located in front-center of crab. The "apron" or small loose shell that comes to a point in center of under shell may also be removed. Once completed, wash crab thoroughly in cold water.

BROILED SOFT-SHELL CRABS

Prep Time: 1 Hour
Yields: 6 Servings

Comment:

The crab will shed its hard shell at different times during the year. During this brief period, the soft-shelled delicacy is widely sought after. Whether broiled, deep-fried or pan-sautéed, soft-shell crab is a masterpiece in Cajun cooking.

Ingredients:

12 soft-shell crabs
egg wash (1 egg, ½ cup milk, ½ cup water—beaten)
2 cups flour
1 pound melted butter
salt and cayenne pepper to taste
granulated garlic to taste
Creole seasoning to taste

Method:

Preheat oven to broil setting. Dredge crabs in egg wash and then in flour, shaking off all excess. On a large baking sheet with a 1-inch lip, place crabs shell side up. Drench each crab with melted butter. Season with salt, cayenne pepper, granulated garlic and Creole seasoning. Place crabs under broiler and cook 5–7 minutes. Turn crabs and cook an additional 5–7 minutes, basting occasionally. Serve with lemon and parsley butter or tartar sauce. This dish may also be eaten po'boy style.

OVEN-BAKED GARLIC CRABS

Prep Time: 1 Hour
Yields: 4–6 Servings

Comment:

This crab recipe calls for many cloves of garlic. Once the garlic has been sautéed in butter sauce and baked with crabs, it becomes quite sweet. The garlic can then be spread on French bread along with butter dipped from the baking pan.

Ingredients:

1 dozen crabs, cleaned
1 pound melted butter
1 cup olive oil
40 cloves garlic
¼ cup diced onions
¼ cup diced celery
¼ cup diced red bell peppers
¼ cup sliced green onions
¼ cup chopped parsley
2 bay leaves
Worcestershire sauce to taste
Louisiana hot sauce to taste
salt and cracked black pepper to taste
French bread for dipping

Method:

Preheat oven to 400°F. In a large sauté pan, melt butter over medium-high heat. Pour in olive oil to prevent butter from burning. Add garlic, onions, celery, bell peppers, green onions, parsley and bay leaves. Stir constantly to prevent garlic from scorching. Garlic that is over-browned will taste bitter. Season with Worcestershire, hot sauce, salt and pepper. Place crabs in a large casserole dish with a 1 or 2-inch lip and cover with garlic butter mixture. Bake 15–20 minutes, remove and serve warm with hot French bread.

FRIED POPCORN CRAWFISH

Prep Time: 30 Minutes
Yields: 4 Servings

Comment:
Fried crawfish are perfect atop a seafood platter of fried fish, shrimp and oysters or when served as a bite-sized appetizer.

Ingredients:
1 pound crawfish tails, cleaned
1 quart vegetable oil
2 tbsps thyme
2 tbsps basil
salt and black pepper to taste
Louisiana hot sauce to taste
1 egg
1 cup milk
1 cup water
1 cup seasoned corn flour

Method:
Preheat oil in a home-style deep fryer according to manufacturer's directions or to 350°F. Season crawfish with thyme, basil, salt, pepper and hot sauce. In a mixing bowl, combine egg, milk and water. Season with salt and pepper. Dip crawfish in batter then coat in breading. Deep-fry in small batches until golden brown. Serve with a dipping sauce such as Rémoulade or Louisiana Seafood Cocktail Sauce. (See recipes.) Popcorn crawfish also add flavor to create a wonderful salad.

CRAWFISH PIE

Prep Time: 1 Hour
Yields: 6 Servings

Comment:
Crawfish pie is a mainstay in Louisiana cooking. For a flavorful twist, use leftover boiled crawfish tails that are extra spicy.

Ingredients:
1 pound crawfish tails, chopped
½ cup melted butter
1 cup diced onions
1 cup diced celery
1 cup diced red bell peppers
¼ cup minced garlic
1 cup heavy whipping cream
½ cup Italian bread crumbs
1 egg, beaten
½ cup sliced green onions
½ cup chopped parsley
salt and black pepper to taste
Louisiana hot sauce to taste
2 (9-inch) deep-dish pie shells

Method:
Preheat oven to 450°F. Press 1 unbaked pie shell into a pie pan and set aside. In a cast iron skillet, melt butter over medium-high heat. Add onions, celery, bell peppers and garlic. Sauté 3–5 minutes or until vegetables are wilted. Blend in crawfish and sauté 3–5 minutes. Stir in cream, simmer 10 minutes then remove from heat. Blend bread crumbs and egg into crawfish. Add green onions and parsley then season with salt, pepper and hot sauce. Place mixture in pie shell and cover with second crust. With a knife, make 4 (1-inch) slits in top for ventilation. Place pie on a cookie sheet and bake 10 minutes. Reduce heat to 350°F, and bake 20 minutes or until crust is golden brown. Serve hot.

CRAWFISH AND ASPARAGUS RISOTTO

Prep Time: 1½ Hours
Yields: 4 Servings

Comment:

Risotto is a dish of short-grain rice cooked in butter or oil with stock and various seasoning vegetables such as onions and bell peppers. The arborio rice used in this recipe is very tender and creamy. This recipe is enhanced by the addition of asparagus and crawfish.

Ingredients:

1 pound crawfish tails
1 bunch asparagus spears
2 cups arborio rice
6 tbsps extra virgin olive oil
¼ cup minced shallots
½ cup dry white wine
1 tsp minced garlic
6 cups chicken stock (see recipe)
kosher salt to taste
2 tbsps unsalted butter
½ cup chopped flat-leaf parsley
fresh Parmigiano-Reggiano cheese, grated
salt and cracked black pepper to taste

Method:

Trim 1-inch off cut ends of asparagus. Bring a large pot of salted water to a boil, and cook asparagus spears 2–3 minutes or until crisp-tender. Drain and chop into ½-inch pieces then set aside. Reserve asparagus tips to use as garnish. In a medium saucepan, heat oil over medium-high heat. Add shallots and sauté 3 minutes or until translucent. Stir in rice and cook until opaque. Blend in wine, garlic, ½ cup stock and kosher salt. Stir until stock is absorbed. Continue adding stock in ½ cup increments, stirring until all has been absorbed, about 15 minutes. Add crawfish, asparagus, butter and parsley. Blend well. Season with Parmigiano-Reggiano, salt and pepper. Remove from heat and serve in shallow soup bowls, leveling mound on each plate with a wooden spoon. Garnish with blanched asparagus tips and shaved Parmigiano-Reggiano.

CRAWFISH-STUFFED PASTA SHELLS

Prep Time: 30 Minutes
Yields: 6 Servings

Comment:

Here is another example of the innovative Creoles using a seafood stuffing to create an interesting entrée. Normally this was done in either chicken or in turbans of trout. In this recipe, the crawfish is stuffed into Italian pasta shells and baked. This dish is wonderful when topped with Sauce Acadian. (See recipe.)

Ingredients:

2 pounds crawfish tails, chopped
1 box jumbo pasta shells
¼ pound butter
1 cup minced onions
½ cup minced green bell peppers
½ cup minced red bell peppers
6 tsps minced garlic
4 tbsps Worcestershire sauce
2 tbsps Louisiana hot sauce
salt to taste
Creole seasoning to taste
2 eggs, beaten
½ cup grated Parmesan cheese
1 cup Italian bread crumbs

Method:

Preheat oven to 350°F. Boil pasta according to package directions until al dente. Set aside. In a medium saucepan, melt butter over medium-high heat. Add onions and bell peppers. Sauté 1–2 minutes or until wilted. Stir in garlic and crawfish tails and heat thoroughly. Blend in Worcestershire, hot sauce, salt and Creole seasoning. Remove from heat and allow to cool. Add eggs to crawfish mixture. Fold in Parmesan cheese and bread crumbs. Stuff each pasta shell with an equal amount of crawfish stuffing. Place shells in a 9" x 13" baking pan. Cover with your favorite pasta sauce or alfredo. If desired, create a sauce by blending 2 cans cream of shrimp soup with ½ cup white wine. Bake 15–20 minutes or until stuffing is completely heated.

LOUISIANA-STYLE CRAWFISH ÉTOUFFÉE

Prep Time: 1 Hour
Yields: 6 Servings

Comment:

The French word, étouffée means to stew, smother or braise. This technique is found in dishes using shrimp, crab, crawfish, meat or game. Though more Creole in origin, étouffées are found throughout Louisiana.

Ingredients:

2 pounds crawfish tails, cleaned
¼ pound butter
1 cup diced onions
½ cup diced celery
½ cup diced green bell peppers
½ cup diced red bell peppers
½ cup diced tomatoes
2 tbsps minced garlic
2 bay leaves
½ cup tomato sauce
1 cup flour
2 quarts shellfish stock (see recipe) or water
1 ounce sherry
1 cup sliced green onions
½ cup chopped parsley
salt and cayenne pepper to taste
2 cups steamed white rice
Louisiana hot sauce to taste

Method:

In a 2-gallon stockpot, melt butter over medium-high heat. Add onions, celery, bell peppers, tomatoes, garlic and bay leaves. Sauté 3–5 minutes or until vegetables are wilted. Blend crawfish tails and tomato sauce into mixture. Whisk in flour, stirring constantly until a white roux is achieved. (See roux recipes.) Slowly add shellfish stock or water until a sauce-like consistency is achieved. Add more stock as necessary to retain consistency. Bring to a rolling boil then reduce to simmer and cook 30 minutes, stirring occasionally. Add sherry, green onions and parsley. Cook 5 minutes then season with salt and cayenne pepper. Serve over steamed white rice with a few dashes of hot sauce.

CRAWFISH BISQUE

Prep Time: 2 Hours
Yields: 6 Servings

Comment:

Crawfish bisque is a tradition in Louisiana. This dish is often made toward the end of crawfish season in May or June. Usually, an immense pot of bisque is made to feed an entire family and have enough left over for everyone to freeze a portion to enjoy later.

Ingredients for Stuffing:

2 pounds crawfish tails, cleaned	2 tbsps minced garlic
60 cleaned crawfish heads	½ cup chopped parsley
1½ cups minced onions	3 eggs, beaten
1 cup minced celery	2 cups Italian bread crumbs
½ cup minced bell peppers	salt and black pepper to taste

Method:

Ask your seafood supplier to clean 60 crawfish heads. The shells may be frozen for an extended period of time. If desired, soak heads overnight in cold soda water prior to using them. Preheat oven to 350°F. In a food processor, grind crawfish tails, onions, celery, bell peppers, garlic and parsley. Transfer ingredients to a mixing bowl then blend in eggs. Add bread crumbs, a little at a time, using just enough to hold mixture together. Season with salt and pepper. Stuff equal amounts into crawfish heads. Bake 20 minutes or until lightly browned. Remove and set aside.

Ingredients for Sauce:

1 pound crawfish tails, cleaned	2 tbsps minced garlic
1 cup vegetable oil	¼ cup tomato sauce
1 cup flour	3 quarts shellfish stock (see recipe)
1½ cups diced onions	1 cup sliced green onions
1 cup diced celery	½ cup chopped parsley
½ cup diced bell peppers	salt and black pepper to taste

Method:

In a heavy-bottomed Dutch oven, heat oil over medium-high heat. Whisk in flour, stirring constantly until dark brown roux is achieved. (See roux recipes.) Add onions, celery, bell peppers and garlic. Sauté 3–5 minutes or until vegetables are wilted. Blend in crawfish tails and tomato sauce. Slowly add shellfish stock until a sauce-like consistency is achieved. Additional stock may be needed during cooking process. Bring to a rolling boil then reduce to simmer. Gently stir stuffed crawfish heads into mixture. Simmer 45 minutes, stirring occasionally to prevent crawfish from settling to bottom of pot and scorching. Add green onions and parsley then season with salt and pepper. Serve in a 10-ounce soup bowl over steamed white rice.

MR. ROYLEY'S CRAWFISH STEW

Prep Time: 1 Hour
Yields: 10 Servings

Comment:

Like gumbo and jambalaya, crawfish stew is synonymous with Cajun cooking. This is a perfect recipe to prepare on a cool night at the camp. There is much time for relaxing and entertaining company as the stew slowly simmers.

Ingredients:

5 pounds crawfish tails
1 cup crawfish fat (optional)
2 cups crawfish claws (optional)
¼ cup vegetable oil
salt and black pepper to taste
1½ cups vegetable oil
1½ cups flour
2 cups diced onions
1 cup diced bell peppers
¼ cup minced garlic
1 cup tomato sauce
3 quarts water
2 bay leaves
Louisiana hot sauce to taste
1 cup sliced green onions
1 cup chopped parsley

Method:

In a 12-inch cast iron skillet, heat ¼ cup vegetable oil over medium-high heat. Drain crawfish tails in a colander, reserving fat and natural juices. Sauté tails 5–10 minutes or until curled and heated thoroughly but not overcooked. Season with salt and pepper then set aside. In a heavy-bottomed Dutch oven, heat remaining oil over medium-high heat. Whisk in flour, stirring constantly until dark brown roux is achieved. (See roux recipes.) Add onions, bell peppers and garlic. Sauté 3–5 minutes or until vegetables are well caramelized. Stir occasionally to prevent vegetables from scorching. Pour in tomato sauce and cook 3 minutes. Slowly add water, 1 quart at a time, until thick stew consistency is achieved. Add crawfish fat, reserved drippings and bay leaves. Season liquid lightly with salt and pepper. Bring stock to a rolling boil then reduce to simmer and add sautéed crawfish, including pan drippings. Simmer stew approximately 45 minutes, stirring occasionally. Do not boil. Additional water may be needed during cooking process to retain volume and consistency. Once stew is full-flavored, adjust seasonings with salt, pepper and hot sauce. Add green onions, parsley and optional crawfish claws. Cook 15–20 minutes or until desired richness is achieved. Adjust seasonings if necessary. Serve over steamed white rice.

FIRE-ROASTED OYSTERS

Prep Time: 1 Hour
Yields: 6 Servings

Comment:

Oysters in the shell can be cooked successfully on the grill. Heat from the grill steams the oysters and pops the shell open, while poaching the meat inside. Try serving this dish as an appetizer prior to grilling steaks or ribs.

Ingredients:

3 dozen oysters, in shells
2 cups rock salt
½ pound salted butter
2 tbsps minced garlic
2 tbsps minced shallots
2 tbsps chopped parsley
1 tbsp dried basil
1 tbsp dried tarragon
1 tsp dried thyme
1 tbsp Louisiana hot sauce
2 tbsps Worcestershire sauce
juice of 1 lemon
salt and black pepper to taste

Method:

Wash oysters under clean, running water to remove any sand or mud. Place oysters in a bucket and cover by 1 inch with clear water. Add rock salt and allow oysters to sit 1 hour. Make a sauce by melting butter over medium-high heat. Add all remaining ingredients. Remove from heat and set aside to allow flavor to develop. Heat grill according to manufacturer's directions. Place prepared sauce on edge of grill to keep warm. Do not boil. Place oysters on grill, 8–10 at a time, and close lid. In 2–3 minutes, oysters should begin to pop open. Using a grill glove, remove oysters and open outer shell with an oyster knife. Top with ¼ teaspoon sauce and serve hot. NOTE: For a patio party, have 6 oyster knives along with 6 heavy-duty gloves or kitchen towels. This will allow guests to hold hot oysters as they are removed from grill. Oysters should be eaten directly from shell while steaming hot.

OYSTERS DUNBAR

Prep Time: 1 Hour
Yields: 6 Servings

Comment:

This dish was named after the great restaurateur, Corinne Dunbar. She had one of the few potluck restaurants. This simply meant that what was in the pot was being served that evening—no options. This dish was a mainstay at her restaurant and later became sought after on other New Orleans restaurant menus.

Ingredients:

3 dozen oysters
1 cup reserved oyster liquid
12 oyster shells
2 cups artichoke hearts
¼ pound butter
½ cup diced onions
¼ cup diced celery
¼ cup diced red bell peppers
¼ cup diced yellow bell peppers
¼ cup minced garlic
¼ cup flour

2 cups heavy whipping cream
1 tsp Worcestershire sauce
1 tsp Creole seasoning
¼ cup sliced green onions
1 tbsp chopped basil
1 tsp chopped thyme
¼ tsp nutmeg
salt and black pepper to taste
Louisiana hot sauce to taste
3 cups Italian bread crumbs

Method:

Preheat oven to 375°F. Wash oyster shells once or twice with hot soapy water then rinse under cold running water to remove soap. Keep shells in cold water until ready to use. Chop 2 dozen oysters and all artichoke hearts into bite-sized pieces then set aside. In a cast iron Dutch oven, melt butter over medium-high heat. Add onions, celery, bell peppers and garlic. Sauté 3–5 minutes or until vegetables are wilted. Blend in chopped oysters and artichoke hearts, and sauté 5–7 minutes. Whisk in flour and stir constantly to create a white roux. (See roux recipes.) Add heavy whipping cream and reserved oyster liquid, stirring constantly until a slightly-thickened sauce is achieved. Add Worcestershire, Creole seasoning, green onions, basil, thyme and nutmeg. Season lightly with salt, pepper and hot sauce. Cook 7–10 minutes, then remove from heat. Stir in 2 cups bread crumbs until mixture resembles a stuffing. Place 1 whole oyster in center of each oyster shell and top with equal portions of stuffing. Place shells on a cookie sheet and sprinkle with remaining bread crumbs. Bake 30 minutes or until stuffing is heated thoroughly. It is important for oysters to be hot and fully cooked. Serve 4 as an entrée.

THE PEACEMAKER: ULTIMATE OYSTER PO'BOY

Prep Time: 30 Minutes
Yields: 6 Servings

Comment:

This unique po'boy combines delicious deep-fried oysters with crusty French bread and rémoulade slaw. Many Louisianians feel that the oyster po'boy, or "Peacemaker" as it is called in New Orleans, is the best way to enjoy fried oysters.

Ingredients:

4 dozen fresh oysters
6 (10-inch) po'boy loaves
vegetable oil for deep frying

Ingredients for Egg Wash:

1 egg, beaten
1 cup milk
1 cup water
2 tbsps Creole mustard
1 tbsp yellow mustard
salt and cracked black pepper to taste

Ingredients for Breading:

1½ cups yellow cornmeal
1½ cups yellow corn flour
2 tbsps granulated garlic
salt and cracked black pepper to taste

Ingredients for Dressing:

3 cups Rémoulade Slaw (see recipe)
18 thin slices of tomato
spicy ketchup

Method:

Preheat oven to 375°F. Using a home-style deep fryer such as a FryDaddy, heat oil according to manufacturer's directions. Slice po'boy bread lengthwise, place on a large cookie sheet then set aside. In a mixing bowl, combine egg wash ingredients. In a separate mixing bowl, combine breading ingredients. Set aside. When ready to prepare po'boys, create Rémoulade Slaw and set aside. (See recipe.) Place bread in oven and turn off heat to allow bread to become crispy and warm. Dip 6 oysters at a time in egg wash then in breading mixture. Fry oysters at 365°F for 3 minutes per batch or until they begin to float. Remove, drain and keep warm. Continue until all oysters are fried. While oysters are cooking, remove po'boy bread from oven. Place Rémoulade Slaw and tomato slices on bottom side of bread and spicy ketchup on top side. Place 6 oysters over slaw and top with other po'boy half. Secure with toothpicks, slice in half and serve hot.

DEVILED OYSTERS

Prep Time: 30 Minutes
Yields: 6 Servings

Comment:
This dish can be served as a stuffing or casserole for brunch or a light lunch.

Ingredients:
2 pints select oysters in liquid
1 cup melted butter
1 cup minced onions
1 cup minced celery
½ cup minced red bell peppers
½ cup sliced green onions
1 tbsp minced garlic
1 cup heavy whipping cream

2 boiled eggs, diced
½ cup chopped parsley
1 tbsp Worcestershire sauce
1 tbsp Louisiana hot sauce
2½ cups Italian bread crumbs
salt and black pepper to taste
granulated garlic to taste

Method:
Preheat oven to 350°F. In a 2-quart saucepot, melt butter over medium-high heat. Add onions, celery, bell peppers, green onions and garlic. Sauté 2–3 minutes or until vegetables are wilted. Stir in heavy whipping cream, bring to a low boil then reduce to simmer. Add oysters and oyster liquid. Cook until oysters are slightly curled. Remove from heat and blend in egg, parsley, Worcestershire and hot sauce. Sprinkle in bread crumbs, 1 cup at a time, until mixture is moist but held together. Season with salt, pepper and granulated garlic. Place in a greased 9" x 13" baking dish, and bake approximately 30 minutes or until golden brown.

OYSTERS BIENVILLE

Prep Time: 30 Minutes
Yields: 6 Servings

Comment:
Sometimes called the "Father of Louisiana," Jean-Baptiste Le Moyne, Sieur de Bienville, was chosen to command the expedition for Louis XIV to found a colony in Louisiana. Responsible for founding the settlement of New Orleans, Bienville became an early governor of Louisiana. This succulent dish named in his honor was created at Antoine's by Chef Auguste Michel. However, it gained notoriety at Arnaud's Restaurant after Arnaud Cazenave tasted Michel's concoction and began serving it.

Ingredients:
3 dozen oysters in liquid
1 stick butter
½ cup minced onions
¼ cup minced celery
1 red bell pepper, minced
1 bunch green onions, sliced
¼ cup minced garlic
4 tbsps flour
½ cup Chardonnay
1 cup heavy whipping cream
2 cups oyster liquid
salt and black pepper to taste
½ cup grated Parmesan cheese
½ cup Italian bread crumbs

Method:
Preheat oven to 375°F. Poach oysters in their liquid 1 minute, until edges begin to curl. Strain oysters out of liquid and set aside. Add enough water to poaching liquid to bring it to 2 cups then set aside. Melt butter in a saucepan over medium-high heat. Add onions, celery, bell peppers, green onions and garlic. Sauté 3–5 minutes or until vegetables are wilted. Add flour and cook 2 minutes. Deglaze with Chardonnay then whisk in whipping cream and oyster liquid. Season with salt and pepper. Simmer a few minutes until sauce thickens. Fold in cheese then remove from heat. Sprinkle in bread crumbs. Let cool. Arrange oysters in individual ovenproof dishes (6 per dish) and cover with Bienville sauce. Bake 15 minutes or until sauce begins to brown on top. NOTE: This sauce can be served over an oyster in the half shell then baked.

CAJUN OYSTER STEW IN PATTY SHELLS

Prep Time: 1 Hour
Yields: 6 Servings

Comment:
Many recipes claim to be the original oyster stew of New Orleans, but the brown oyster stew is likely to be the original. Cream or milk used in many oyster stews today were not found in New Orleans recipes in the early 1700s. Additionally, oysters were not considered edible until the Native Americans in Bayou Country introduced the Cajuns to the delicacy. With the addition of the dark brown roux of the Cajuns, the brown oyster stew was born.

Ingredients:
24 select oysters
6 patty shells
¾ cup vegetable oil
1 cup flour
1 cup diced onions
½ cup diced celery
½ cup diced bell peppers
1 tbsp minced garlic
2 quarts oyster liquid
¾ cup sliced green onions
½ cup chopped parsley
salt and cracked black pepper to taste

Method:
Check with your seafood supplier in advance to have 2 quarts of oyster liquid reserved. If oyster liquid is not available, purchase 1 extra pint of oysters and purée in a blender with 1½ quarts cold water. Bake patty shells according to package directions then set aside. In a heavy-bottomed saucepot, heat oil over medium-high heat. Whisk in flour, stirring constantly until a dark brown roux is achieved. (See roux recipes.) Add onions, celery, bell peppers and garlic. Cook 3–5 minutes or until vegetables are wilted. Slowly add oyster liquid and whisk until well blended. Remember that once fresh oysters are added, natural juices will thin out stew. Simmer 20–30 minutes stirring occasionally, then add oysters. Cook until edges of oysters are curled, but not overcooked. Garnish with green onions and parsley then season with salt and pepper. Ladle a generous serving of oyster stew into center of patty shell. Serve as an appetizer or entrée.

One of many oyster bars in the French Quarter

NATHANIEL BURTON'S STUFFED FLOUNDER

Prep Time: 1 Hour
Yields: 6 Servings

Comment:

Master Chef Nathaniel Burton, co-author of *Creole Feast*, was born in McComb, Miss., in 1914. Starting as a busboy at the Hotel New Orleans, he worked at many fine places including Hotel Pontchartrain. He shared his experience with cooks at the Culinary Institute of America at Hyde Park and Cornell University Hotel School.

Ingredients:

6 (1-pound) flounder, boned
salt and black pepper to taste
¼ cup melted butter
1 cup minced onions
1 cup minced celery
½ cup minced red bell peppers
½ cup minced green bell peppers
¼ cup minced garlic
1 cup white wine
1 cup heavy whipping cream
1 pound lump crabmeat
Italian bread crumbs
¼ cup grated Parmesan cheese
1 cup water

Method:

Preheat oven to 375°F. Have your seafood supplier thoroughly clean, scale and remove heads from 6 flounder. Using a sharp paring knife, cut a slit down center of dark side of flounder from head to tail. Following rib bone, cut a pocket down each side of fish. Season flounder well, inside and out, with salt and pepper. In a large sauté pan, melt butter over medium-high heat. Add onions, celery, bell peppers and garlic. Sauté 2–3 minutes or until vegetables are wilted. Deglaze with ½ cup wine and reduce to half volume. Pour in cream, bring to a rolling boil then reduce to simmer. Blend in crabmeat. Season with salt and pepper. Sprinkle in bread crumbs, 1 cup at a time, until stuffing consistency is achieved. Try to use minimal amount of bread crumbs to hold mixture together. Remove from heat and fold in Parmesan cheese. Adjust seasonings if necessary. Place flounder on a large cookie sheet and divide stuffing equally among fish. Stuff each slit generously. If desired, add a slice of lemon and a dash of paprika on top of stuffing in each pocket. Add remaining wine and water to bottom of cookie sheet and bake 25 minutes or until stuffing is heated throughout. Serve immediately.

HERB-BAKED LARGE MOUTH BASS

Prep Time: 1 Hour
Yields: 6 Servings

Comment:

The Spanish influence around Toledo Bend Lake gave origin to this tomato-based fish stew. The Spanish settled Sabine Parish prior to the Louisiana Purchase, and many of their great fish dishes became a major part of our Louisiana cuisine. Keeping the fish whole and stuffing it with fresh herbs prior to baking makes this dish a perfect centerpiece on any table. Feel free to use bass or any other available Gulf species.

Ingredients for Fish:

1 (3–4 pound) large mouth bass
salt and cracked black pepper to taste
Louisiana hot sauce to taste
1 cup chopped thyme
1 cup chopped basil
1 cup chopped dill
4 bay leaves
4 lemon slices
8 slices red onion

Method:

Preheat oven to 375°F. Remove gills and eyes of fish and thoroughly clean cavity. It is best to cook fish with head on. Season inside cavity with salt, pepper and hot sauce. Stuff fish with equal parts thyme, basil, dill, bay leaves and lemon slices. Using a sharp knife, cut 3 diagonal slits across top fillet of fish. This will assist in flavoring as well as presentation. Place red onions on bottom of a large baking pan. Top with fish and season with salt, pepper and hot sauce. Set aside.

Ingredients for Sauce:

¼ cup olive oil	1 tbsp chopped basil
1 cup diced onions	1 tbsp chopped thyme
1 cup diced celery	2 bay leaves
½ cup diced bell peppers	salt and black pepper to taste
¼ cup minced garlic	Louisiana hot sauce to taste
1 cup diced tomatoes	4 lemon slices for garnish
2 cups tomato juice	¼ cup sliced green onions
2 (8-ounce) cans tomato sauce	¼ cup chopped parsley

Method:

In a cast iron Dutch oven, heat oil over medium-high heat. Add onions, celery, bell peppers and garlic. Sauté 3–5 minutes or until vegetables are wilted. Add tomatoes, tomato juice and sauce. Bring to a rolling boil then reduce to simmer and cook 10–15 minutes. Add basil, thyme and bay leaves. Season with salt and pepper. Remove from heat and pour hot sauce over stuffed fish. Garnish with lemon slices, green onions and parsley. Cover pan with foil and bake approximately 30 minutes. To serve, transfer fish to a large platter, top with sauce and garnish with fresh herbs.

STUFFED FLOUNDER FILLETS WITH CHIVE CREAM SAUCE

Prep Time: 1 Hour
Yields: 6 Servings

Comment:

Flounder are plentiful in the Gulf of Mexico and are often found on menus of seafood restaurants in South Louisiana. The most popular method of preparing flounder is to stuff it with another seafood. This wonderful crab-stuffed fish is topped with a delicious chive sauce for an enhanced flavor.

Ingredients for Stuffed Flounder:

6 (5–7 ounce) flounder fillets, skin off	1 egg
1 pound jumbo lump crabmeat, cartilage removed	¾ cup bread crumbs
¼ cup olive oil	salt and black pepper to taste
½ cup minced onions	1 cup water
¼ cup minced celery	2 ounces dry white wine
¼ cup minced red bell peppers	½ tsp fresh lemon juice
1 tsp minced garlic	Creole seasoning to taste
½ cup sliced green onions	granulated garlic to taste
2 tsps chopped parsley	paprika for color
¼ tsp thyme	6 thin slices lemon
¼ tsp basil	

Method:

Preheat oven to 350°F. In a 9-inch skillet, heat oil over medium heat. Add onions, celery, bell peppers, garlic, green onions, parsley, thyme and basil. Sauté 2–3 minutes, stirring occasionally until vegetables are wilted. Remove from heat, place in a mixing bowl and reserve skillet. Add egg, crabmeat and enough bread crumbs to hold mixture together. Season lightly with salt and pepper. Divide stuffing into 6 equal portions and shape into balls. Wrap a flounder fillet around each ball. Secure with a toothpick, or tie with string to hold fillet in place while cooking. Place stuffed fillets on a baking dish with a 1-inch lip. Pour in water, wine and lemon juice. Sprinkle outside of fish with Creole seasoning, granulated garlic, salt, pepper and paprika. Place a thin slice of lemon on top of each fish and bake 20–30 minutes or until fillets are cooked and lemons are lightly browned on surface. A cooking thermometer inserted into stuffing should read 140°F. When fish is browned well and cooked through, carefully transfer to warm plates and reserve cooking liquid.

Ingredients for Chive Cream Sauce:

¼ cup chopped chives
3 tbsps butter
1 tbsp minced garlic
1½ cups heavy whipping cream
salt and cracked black pepper to taste

Method:

Remove ½ cup cooking liquid from baking dish with fish. Set aside. In reserved skillet, melt 3 tablespoons butter over medium-high heat. Blend in garlic, and sauté 2–3 minutes. Add chives, cream and reserved cooking liquid. Bring to a rolling boil and reduce to ½ cup. Season with salt and pepper. Place 1 fillet in center of each plate, and top with an equal portion of chive sauce.

TOMATO AND BASIL FLOUNDER

Prep Time: 30 Minutes
Yields: 4 Servings

Comment:
No herb complements tomato better than basil. The two come together perfectly as a sauce for this sautéed flounder. Although basil works best, you may wish to try other herbs such as tarragon or chives to create a unique dish.

Ingredients:
6 Roma tomatoes, diced
2–3 leaves fresh basil
4 (4-ounce) flounder fillets
olive oil
salt and cracked black pepper to taste
granulated garlic to taste
seasoned flour for dusting
½ cup julienned onions
3 cloves garlic, sliced
1 red bell pepper, julienned
1 green bell pepper, julienned
2 tbsps fresh oregano
12 asparagus stalks
water or chicken stock (optional)
chopped parsley for garnish
4 sprigs fresh basil for garnish

Method:
Coat a large sauté pan with olive oil and heat over medium-high heat. Rinse fish in cold water then season with salt, pepper and granulated garlic. Lightly dust fillets in seasoned flour. Lower heat to medium and sauté fish. When done, remove fillets and keep warm. In same pan, sauté onions and garlic until onions are translucent. Add bell peppers, cook 2 minutes then add tomatoes, oregano and basil. Season with salt and pepper. Cook 10 minutes then add asparagus. A small amount of water or chicken stock may be needed to retain moisture. Cook 5 minutes and serve. Place fillet on plate and top with vegetable mixture, chopped parsley and a sprig of fresh basil.

CASPIANA FRIED CATFISH

Prep Time: 30 Minutes
Yields: 6 Servings

Comment:

Fried catfish is a staple of the Cajun diet. Although wonderful served alone or with tartar sauce, the fish is often used as a base for many dishes. Fried catfish can be found under a simmering étouffée, alongside grilled shrimp or even layered with onions, as done here.

Ingredients:

12 (3–5 ounce) whole catfish fillets
vegetable oil for deep-frying
1 cup yellow mustard
¼ cup Worcestershire sauce
1 tbsp dried thyme
1 tbsp dried basil
salt and cracked black pepper to taste
granulated garlic to taste
Louisiana hot sauce to taste
3 cups yellow corn flour
2 small Bermuda onions, thinly sliced
1 cup sliced green onions
½ cup red wine vinegar

Method:

In a home-style deep fryer such as a FryDaddy, heat oil according to manufacturer's directions. If using a Dutch oven, heat oil to 375°F. In a large mixing bowl, combine mustard and Worcestershire sauce. Whisk in thyme, basil, salt, pepper, granulated garlic and hot sauce until well blended. Add fillets and toss in marinade to coat. Allow to sit at room temperature 15 minutes. Place corn flour in a large paper bag and season with salt, pepper and granulated garlic. Remember not to overseason, since fish has been seasoned in marinade. Place fillets in corn flour. Seal bag tightly and shake vigorously until fish are well coated. Fry 2–3 fillets at a time until golden brown and floating at top of oil. Remove and drain. Stack fish on a large serving platter, and top each layer with Bermuda onions, green onions and a sprinkle of vinegar. This will create a steaming effect, and a hint of flavor will permeate fish.

CATFISH BOULETTES

Prep Time: 1½ Hours
Yields: 8–10 Servings

Comment:

Boulettes are normally thought of as ball-shaped portions of ground meat or seafood. Although they are most often cooked in a stew or gravy, for ease of preparation, they are sometimes cooked patty style and served in a sandwich or as a side dish.

Ingredients:

6 (8-ounce) catfish fillets
1 pound new potatoes, peeled and diced
½ cup minced onions
½ cup minced celery
¼ cup minced garlic
¼ cup sliced green onions
2 eggs
salt and black pepper to taste
cayenne pepper to taste
½ cup vegetable oil
1 cup seasoned flour

Method:

In a 1-gallon saucepot, place 4 inches of lightly-salted water. Bring to a rolling boil and reduce to low simmer. Add catfish and poach until fork tender but not falling apart. Drain and reserve liquid. Return poaching liquid to a low boil, add potatoes and cook 12–15 minutes or until tender enough to mash. Combine fish, potatoes, onions, celery, garlic, green onions and eggs. Season with salt and peppers. Form mixture into hamburger-sized patties. In a 10-inch skillet, heat half of oil over medium-high heat. Dust patties in flour. Fry 2–3 patties at a time, turning occasionally, 7–10 minutes or until golden brown. Drain well and serve warm. NOTE: If desired, form the mixture into meatballs and cook in a brown or tomato gravy.

CATFISH IN OYSTER ANDOUILLE BUTTER

Prep Time: 1 Hour
Yields: 6 Servings

Comment:

Andouille adds a delicate smoked flavor to this interesting cream sauce. If desired, substitute shrimp, crabs or crawfish in place of oysters.

Ingredients:

6 (5–8 ounce) catfish fillets
24 fresh shucked oysters
¼ cup julienned andouille sausage
¾ cup vegetable oil
1 cup egg wash (1 egg, ½ cup water, ½ cup milk)
salt and white pepper to taste
granulated garlic to taste
½ cup flour
1 tsp garlic
½ cup sliced mushrooms
1 ounce dry white wine
1½ cups heavy whipping cream
½ cup sliced green onions
4 tbsps cold, chipped butter

Method:

Preheat oven to 275°F. In a 10-inch heavy-bottomed sauté pan, heat oil over medium-high heat. Blend egg wash to ensure that egg, milk and water are mixed. Season flour with salt, pepper and granulated garlic. Dip catfish fillets into egg wash and then into flour, coating evenly on all sides. Sauté 3 fillets at a time for 3–5 minutes on each side or until golden brown. Once cooked, place on a cookie sheet in oven to keep warm. In same pan, sauté andouille and garlic 2–3 minutes, scraping bottom of pan to incorporate drippings. Add oysters and sauté until edges are curly. Stir in mushrooms, wine and cream. Bring to a rolling boil then reduce to simmer. Blend in green onions and reduce cream to ½ cup. Sauce should be extremely thick. Do not scorch. Swirling pan constantly, add butter, a few chips at a time, until melted into sauce. Remove pan from heat at 1-minute intervals while swirling to keep butter from separating. (See Beurre Blanc recipe.) Remove from heat and serve immediately. Place 2–3 ounces oyster butter in center of a serving plate and top with catfish fillet. Garnish each serving with 4 cooked oysters.

BAKED CATFISH CREOLE

Prep Time: 1½ Hours
Yields: 6 Servings

Comment:

This Creole sauce is simply made by using prepared tomato sauce. However, it is enhanced with a little spice from the Ro*tel® tomatoes. This sauce is also wonderful when added to a few pounds of fresh shrimp for the ultimate shrimp Creole.

Ingredients for Creole Sauce:

½ cup olive oil
1 cup diced onions
1 cup diced celery
½ cup diced bell peppers
¼ cup minced garlic
2 bay leaves
2 (8-ounce) cans tomato sauce
1 (10-ounce) can Ro*tel® Diced Tomatoes and Green Chilies
½ tsp sugar
pinch dried thyme
pinch dried basil
1 cup sliced green onions
½ cup chopped parsley
salt and cracked black pepper to taste

Method:

In a 2-quart heavy-bottomed saucepan, heat oil over medium-high heat. Sauté onions, celery, bell peppers, garlic and bay leaves 3–5 minutes or until wilted. Add tomato sauce and tomatoes. Bring to a low boil then reduce to simmer and cook 30 minutes, stirring occasionally. Stir in sugar, thyme, basil, green onions and parsley. Cook 10 minutes then season with salt and pepper. Remove from heat and set aside.

Ingredients for Fish:

4 (5–8 ounce) catfish fillets
1 cup (90–110 count) shrimp, peeled and deveined
reserved Creole Sauce
4 cups steamed white rice
¼ cup chopped parsley for garnish

Method:

Preheat oven to 375°F. Place catfish in an ovenproof casserole dish large enough to hold 4 fillets. Sprinkle shrimp evenly on top of fillets. Spoon Creole Sauce generously over fish and shrimp until well covered. Cover dish, place in oven and cook 30 minutes or until fish is done. Place an equal amount of warm rice in center of each serving plate and top with Baked Catfish Creole. Garnish with chopped parsley. This dish may also be served over pasta.

PAN SAUTÉED FILLET OF TROUT NIÇOISE

Prep Time: 1 Hour
Yields: 4 Servings

Comment:
Although this recipe has a Mediterranean origin, it is similar to many Creole dishes. Ripe Creole tomatoes, black olives and capers give this fish a Louisiana flavor. Any Gulf fish can be substituted for trout.

Ingredients:
4 (6-ounce) trout fillets
¼ cup extra virgin olive oil
4 cloves garlic, thinly sliced
1 cup diced Creole tomatoes, seeded and peeled
2 tbsps chopped basil
¼ cup niçoise olives
2 tbsps capers with juice
1 cup dry white wine or chicken stock
salt and black pepper to taste
½ cup seasoned flour
¼ cup olive oil
4 sprigs basil for garnish

Method:
NOTE: It is always best to prepare sauce prior to sautéing fish. Sauce and fish will be cooked at approximately the same time. In a heavy-bottomed sauté pan, heat extra virgin olive oil over medium-high heat. Add garlic and sauté until edges are slightly browned. Stir in tomatoes, basil and olives. Roast on high heat 5 minutes. Sprinkle in capers and wine, bring to a rolling boil then reduce to simmer. Cook 10–12 minutes, stirring occasionally. Add water if necessary to retain a sauce-like consistency. Season to taste with salt and pepper. While sauce is reducing, place a skillet over medium-high heat. Dust fillets in seasoned flour and set aside. Pour olive oil into skillet, and as it begins to smoke slightly, add fish, skin side down. Cook 2–3 minutes on each side or until crispy and golden brown. Do not overcook. Sauce should be reduced by this point. It is done when flavors are well combined and there is a slight presence of liquid. Adjust seasonings if necessary. To serve, place a generous serving of tomato sauce in center of a 12-inch serving plate, top with fish fillet and garnish with a sprig of basil.

PAN SAUTÉED TROUT IN CRABMEAT GARLIC BEURRE BLANC

Prep Time: 15 Minutes
Yields: 6 Servings

Comment:
Compound butter sauces are part of the way of life in South Louisiana. Though similar in method, each beurre sauce has its own ingredient that makes it unique. This classic beurre blanc is flavored Louisiana-style with lump crabmeat and andouille.

Ingredients for Sautéing:
6 (6-ounce) speckled trout fillets
½ cup vegetable oil
2 cups flour
salt and black pepper to taste
egg wash (1 egg, ½ cup milk, ½ cup water)

Method:
In a heavy-bottomed sauté pan, heat oil over medium-high heat. Season flour with salt and pepper. Dip trout fillets in egg wash then in flour. Sauté 3–5 minutes on each side or until golden brown. Remove and keep warm.

Ingredients for Sauce:
1 pound jumbo lump crabmeat
2 tbsps minced garlic
¼ cup melted butter
¼ cup julienned andouille
¼ cup sliced green onions
¼ cup sliced mushrooms
¼ cup dry white wine
½ cup heavy whipping cream
¾ pound chipped butter
salt and white pepper to taste

Method:
In a 10-inch heavy-bottomed sauté pan, melt butter over medium-high heat. Add andouille, garlic, green onions and mushrooms. Sauté 3–5 minutes or until vegetables are wilted. Deglaze with wine and reduce to half volume. Stir in heavy whipping cream, bring to a low boil and reduce to half volume. Blend in crabmeat. Swirling pan constantly, add a few chips of butter at a time until all is incorporated. Do not stir with a metal spoon or whisk as hot spots may develop and butter will separate. Remove from heat and season with salt and white pepper. To serve, place a generous serving of garlic beurre blanc in center of 10-inch plate. Top with sautéed trout and a small portion of crabmeat.

TROUT A LA MEUNIÈRE

Prep Time: 15 Minutes
Yields: 6 Servings

Comment:

The term meunière means "of the miller's wife." In classical cooking, meunière refers to a simple brown butter sauce thickened with flour drippings, from food such as fish, flavored with a squeeze of lemon. In Creole Country, the sauce has been elevated to a rich emulsified butter sauce flavored with veal stock, wine and lemon juice. (See Brown Meunière Sauce recipe.)

Ingredients:

6 (7-ounce) trout fillets
½ cup vegetable oil
2 cups rice flour
1 cup egg wash (1 egg, ½ cup milk, ½ cup water)
salt and black pepper to taste
1 pound butter
juice of 1 lemon
1 tbsp minced parsley

Method:

In a heavy-bottomed sauté pan, heat oil over medium-high heat. Separately season flour and trout with salt and pepper. Dip trout in egg wash then in flour. Sauté 3–5 minutes on each side or until golden brown. Remove and keep warm. In same skillet, melt butter over medium-high heat until it browns around edges of pan. Squeeze in lemon juice, and add minced parsley. Serve over sautéed trout.

COUSHATTA GARFISH STEW

Prep Time: 1½ Hours
Yields: 6–8 Servings

Comment:

The tribal symbol of the Coushatta Indians is the garfish. This fish not only symbolizes sustenance and nourishment, but it also plays an important part in tribal customs. The bones are used for jewelry and costuming, while the hide is used for shoes and clothing. This prehistoric fish also symbolizes strength and survival.

Ingredients for Garfish Patties:

4 cups poached garfish meat
½ cup diced onions
½ cup diced celery
¼ cup diced red bell peppers
¼ cup diced yellow bell peppers
1 tbsp minced garlic
2 eggs
¼ cup sliced green onions
1 cup Italian bread crumbs
½ cup melted butter

Method:

Preheat oven to 375°F. In a large mixing bowl, combine all ingredients except bread crumbs and butter. Using your hands, mix until well blended. Remove ½ cup mixture for use in stew. Slowly add bread crumbs. Form mixture into 12 (2½-inch) patties. Place on a cookie sheet, drizzle with butter and bake 15–20 minutes. Remove and set aside.

Ingredients for Stew:

1 cup vegetable oil
1 cup flour
1 cup diced onions
1 cup diced celery
¼ cup diced red bell peppers
¼ cup diced yellow bell peppers
¼ cup minced garlic
½ cup reserved fish mixture
½ cup tomato sauce
2 quarts shellfish stock (see recipe)
1 cup sliced green onions
1 cup chopped parsley
pinch of thyme
pinch of basil
2 bay leaves
Worcestershire sauce to taste
salt and cracked black pepper to taste
Louisiana hot sauce to taste

Method:

In a large Dutch oven, heat oil over medium-high heat. Whisk in flour, stirring constantly until light brown roux is achieved. (See roux recipes.) Add onions, celery, bell peppers and garlic. Sauté 3–5 minutes or until vegetables are wilted. Blend in reserved fish and tomato sauce. Slowly add stock until a heavy cream-like consistency is achieved. Bring mixture to a rolling boil, reduce to simmer and cook 30 minutes. Stir in green onions, parsley, thyme, basil and bay leaves. Add garfish patties and stir gently, being careful not to break. After a few minutes of cooking, patties will become firm. Season with Worcestershire, salt, pepper and hot sauce. If mixture becomes too thick, add more stock. Serve over steamed white rice or pasta.

TROUT REX

Prep Time: 1 Hour
Yields: 6 Servings

Comment:

This is a great trout recipe to serve at Carnival for either dinner or brunch. Notice that the vegetable accompaniments are purple, green and yellow: the colors of Mardi Gras.

Ingredients:

6 (5–8 ounce) trout fillets
½ cup vegetable oil
salt and cracked black pepper to taste
1½ cups seasoned flour
¼ cup butter
1 tbsp minced garlic
2 tbsps sliced shallots
¼ cup sliced green onions

½ pound jumbo lump crabmeat
2 cups julienned zucchini skins
2 cups julienned yellow squash skins
1 cup chicken stock (see recipe)
1 tsp chopped thyme
1 tbsp chopped basil
2 cups julienned purple cabbage

Method:

Preheat oven to 300°F. In a 10-inch heavy-bottomed sauté pan, heat oil over medium-high heat. Season trout with salt and pepper. Coat fish lightly with seasoned flour and shake off excess. Sauté 2 fillets at a time, 3–5 minutes on each side or until golden brown. When done, remove and place in oven to keep warm. In same sauté pan, melt butter over medium-high heat. Sauté garlic, shallots and green onions 2–3 minutes or until wilted. Add crabmeat, zucchini and squash. Sauté 3–5 minutes or until vegetables are wilted. Add ½ cup chicken stock then season with thyme, basil, salt and pepper. Bring mixture to a high simmer, and cook until vegetables are al dente. Add purple cabbage just prior to serving, and cook 3–5 minutes or until wilted. This last-minute addition will prevent discoloration caused by purple coloring of cabbage. When ready to serve, place equal portions of Mardi Gras medley in center of 6 serving plates, and top with trout fillet. If desired, garnish with additional crabmeat and a spoon of Hollandaise Sauce. (See recipe.)

BLACKENED REDFISH

Prep Time: 30 Minutes
Yields: 6–8 Servings

Comment:

Rumor has it that an African-American cook at the famed Commander's Palace in New Orleans cooked this dish for his lunch on a flat-top range in the restaurant. Chef Paul Prudhomme, executive chef of Commander's at the time, improved upon the recipe and made it world famous. It became so famous in fact that redfish was put on the endangered species list.

Ingredients:

8 (8–10 ounce) redfish fillets
2 sticks melted butter
2 tbsps paprika
1 tbsp granulated garlic
½ tsp dried thyme
½ tsp oregano
1 tbsp salt
1 tsp black pepper
1 tsp cayenne pepper
1 stick melted butter for garnish

Method:

NOTE: I recommend cooking this dish outside on a propane burner due to the large amount of smoke created during cooking. Preheat oven to 250°F. Heat a large cast iron skillet over high heat at least 7–10 minutes or until almost white hot. Skillet cannot be too hot for this dish. In a flat bowl, place 2 sticks melted butter. Dip fillets in butter, 2–3 at a time, coating each side well. Lay butter-coated fillets on a large platter. In a mixing bowl, thoroughly combine all seasonings. Sprinkle both sides of each fillet generously with seasoning mixture. Pat seasonings gently into fish. Place fish into hot skillet, 2 pieces at a time, being careful as butter may ignite momentarily. Cook uncovered 2 minutes or until underside looks charred. Turn fish over and pour 1 tablespoon butter on each fillet. Cook 2 minutes more. Remove fish to a large cookie sheet and place in oven to keep warm. Repeat process with remaining fillets. To serve, place 1 fillet in the center of a serving plate and top with 1 tablespoon melted butter.

FRENCH-FRIED FROG LEGS

Prep Time: 1 Hour
Yields: 6 Servings

Comment:
Although the frog leg is a rare seafood delicacy, it is quite common in South Louisiana. Frog legs can be prepared many different ways, but definitely try them beer-battered and deep-fried.

Ingredients:
2 dozen frog legs
1 quart buttermilk
1 egg
3 tbsps Creole mustard
1 (10-ounce) beer
salt and cracked black pepper to taste
granulated garlic to taste
Worcestershire sauce to taste
Louisiana hot sauce to taste
4 cups seasoned yellow corn flour
2 cups vegetable oil

Method:
In a home-style deep fryer such as a FryDaddy, preheat oil to 375°F. Place frog legs in a mixing bowl, top with buttermilk and allow to sit 1 hour at room temperature. In a separate bowl, whisk together egg, mustard and beer. Season lightly with salt, pepper, garlic, Worcestershire and hot sauce. Place corn flour in a paper bag. Remove frog legs from buttermilk, coat in beer batter then place in bag. Seal tightly and shake vigorously to coat. Fry until golden brown. Serve with Louisiana Tartar Sauce or Louisiana Seafood Cocktail Sauce. (See recipes.)

FROG LEGS PROVENÇAL

Prep Time: 30 Minutes
Yields: 6 Servings

Comment:
Provençal refers to the style of cooking from the South of France bordering the region of Provence on the Mediterranean Sea. Tomatoes smothered in garlic and olive oil along with herbs de Provence set the tone for this style of cooking.

Ingredients:
1 dozen frog legs
¼ pound melted butter
2 tbsps extra virgin olive oil
1 cup seasoned white flour
½ cup minced Bermuda onions
¼ cup sliced garlic
1 cup diced Creole tomatoes
1 ounce dry white wine
1 cup chicken stock (see recipe)
¼ cup sliced green onions
salt and black pepper to taste
Louisiana hot sauce to taste

Method:
In a 10-inch sauté pan, heat butter and olive oil over medium-high heat. Coat frog legs in seasoned flour and shake off excess. When butter is hot, sauté frog legs 2–3 minutes on each side. Add onions and garlic. Sauté 3–5 minutes or until vegetables are wilted. Stir in tomatoes and cook 2–3 additional minutes. Deglaze with wine then add chicken stock. Bring to a rolling boil then reduce to simmer and cook 5–7 minutes or until frog legs are tender. Sauce should be slightly thickened. Add green onions, and season with salt, pepper and hot sauce. Additional stock may be added to maintain consistency.

CRABMEAT-STUFFED FROG LEGS

Prep Time: 1 Hour
Yields: 6 Servings

Comment:

Removing bones from frog legs is quite easy. Using a sharp paring knife, gently scrape the thigh meat, pushing it down, away from bone toward the knee. Be careful not to tear the meat. This will become the pocket to hold the stuffing. Once you reach the knee joint, cut the thighbone from the knee and discard. Now you can begin preparing this masterpiece.

Ingredients for Stuffing:

18 frog legs, cleaned and boned
1 pound claw crabmeat
¼ cup diced onions
¼ cup diced celery
¼ cup diced red bell peppers
¼ cup diced yellow bell peppers
¼ cup minced garlic
1 cup mayonnaise
½ cup Creole mustard
1 tbsp thyme
1 tbsp basil
salt and black pepper to taste
½ cup Italian bread crumbs

Method:

In a large mixing bowl, combine crabmeat, onions, celery, bell peppers, garlic, mayonnaise and mustard. Stir well then season with thyme, basil, salt and pepper. Sprinkle in bread crumbs and mix until well blended. Stuff frog legs completely until all are done. Secure opening with a toothpick. Set aside.

Ingredients for Frog Legs:

18 stuffed frog legs (see above)
1 cup vegetable oil
salt and black pepper to taste
Louisiana hot sauce to taste
1 cup diced onions
1 cup diced celery
1 cup diced green bell peppers
¼ cup minced garlic
1 cup diced tomatoes
½ cup sliced black olives
1 cup tomato sauce
2 cups chicken stock (see recipe)
½ cup sliced green onions
¼ cup chopped parsley

Method:

In a 14-inch cast iron skillet, heat oil over medium-high heat. Add stuffed frog legs and season with salt, pepper and hot sauce. Fry until golden brown on all sides. Sauté onions, celery, bell peppers and garlic with frog legs 3–5 minutes or until vegetables are wilted. Stir in tomatoes, olives and tomato sauce. Mix well then pour in chicken stock. Bring to a rolling boil then reduce to simmer and cook 20–30 minutes. Prior to serving, add green onions, parsley and hot sauce. Serve over pasta.

Jay Folse frogging in the Louisiana swamp

FROG LEGS DEMI-BORDELAISE

Prep Time: 20 Minutes
Yields: 4 Servings

Comment:

In French, the word "demi" means half. However, in this recipe it simply refers to a lighter version of New Orleans' most famous Bordeaux sauce. The white Bordeaux wine gives the sauce a less pronounced flavor than that of a red wine sauce but makes it the perfect accompaniment for these frogs.

Ingredients:

1 dozen frog legs
¼ pound butter
salt and cracked black pepper to taste
dash of Louisiana hot sauce
½ cup minced red onions
¼ cup minced garlic
¼ cup sliced green onions
¼ cup chopped parsley
¼ cup minced red bell peppers
2 tbsps flour
1 cup white Bordeaux wine
1 cup chicken stock (see recipe)
juice of 1 lemon

Method:

In a 12-inch heavy-bottomed skillet, melt butter over medium-high heat. Season frog legs with salt, pepper and hot sauce. Sauté frog legs, turning occasionally, until seared on all sides. Add red onions, garlic, green onions, parsley and bell peppers. Sauté 3–5 minutes or until vegetables are wilted. Sprinkle in flour and stir well into vegetable mixture. Deglaze with wine, and slowly add chicken stock and lemon juice. Bring sauce to a low boil then reduce to simmer and season with salt and pepper. Cook 10–12 minutes or until frog legs are tender and fully cooked.

TURTLE SAUCE PIQUANT

Prep Time: 2½ Hours
Yields: 6 Servings

Comment:

Many dishes in South Louisiana cooking with a hot flavor are called "piquant." However, only a rich brown roux-based dish colored with tomato and just the right hint of spice is a true Louisiana sauce piquant.

Ingredients for Stock:

4 pounds snapping turtle, cleaned and defatted
1 large onion, quartered
1 carrot, sliced
2 bay leaves
4 cloves garlic, smashed
½ tsp black pepper

Method:

In a 1-gallon heavy-bottomed stockpot, place all ingredients and enough lightly-salted water to cover by 2 inches. Bring mixture to a rolling boil then reduce to simmer and skim off surface impurities. Cook 1 hour or until turtle is tender. Strain, reserve 3 quarts stock, discard vegetables and set turtle meat aside.

Ingredients for Sauce Piquant:

1 cup vegetable oil
1 cup flour
1 cup diced onions
1 cup diced celery
1 cup diced bell peppers
2 tbsps minced garlic
1 (8-ounce) can tomato sauce
1 cup diced tomatoes
1 tbsp diced jalapeños
2 bay leaves
½ tsp thyme
½ tsp basil
salt and black pepper to taste
1 cup sliced green onions
1 cup chopped parsley

Method:

In a 1-gallon heavy-bottomed saucepot, heat oil over medium-high heat. Whisk in flour, stirring constantly until dark brown roux is achieved. (See roux recipes.) Add onions, celery, bell peppers and garlic. Sauté 3–5 minutes or until vegetables are wilted. Blend in tomato sauce, diced tomatoes and jalapeños. Add bay leaves, thyme and basil. Slowly add reserved turtle stock, stirring constantly. Bring to a low boil then reduce to simmer and cook 30 minutes. Gently stir in turtle meat and continue to cook 30–45 minutes. Season with salt and pepper. Additional stock may be added to retain volume. Stir in green onions and parsley. Adjust seasonings if necessary. Serve over steamed white rice or pasta.

Poultry

Chickens on a farm

Defined as any domestic bird used as food, the term poultry is generally used for chicken and turkey, but can embrace former game birds like duck, goose and quail that are now also farm-raised. People have been raising fowl for food for thousands of years, so it is no surprise that they are also popular in Cajun and Creole pots.

Chicken is extremely versatile, lending itself to just about any type of preparation and variety of seasoning. Some of the most popular chicken recipes in South Louisiana can be directly attributed to Spanish, Italian, French and African influences. Chicken sauce piquant was influenced by the Spanish, baked garlic chicken was created by the Italians and sold in New Orleans' French Market, chicken in Burgundy wine is a variation on the French coq au vin, and chicken and andouille gumbo has African roots. You can also find chicken paired with oysters, eggplant, Creole tomatoes, yams, okra and eggplant. For generations, chicken has been a regular at Cajun and Creole Sunday dinners, whether French roasted or in a gumbo or stew. Part of the weekend ritual in South Louisiana was selecting, killing and plucking Sunday's main course. Chickens are low cost and low maintenance. Most homesteads would have a few around even when times were tough. Even a stringy old bird can be made into a meal when it stops laying eggs. Some Louisianians also believed that keeping a "frizzly" old chicken around the house was good luck.

Chicken is a favorite ingredient in one of Louisiana's signature dishes, gumbo. An old custom during rural Mardi Gras celebrations was for masked revelers to go house to house begging for chickens and other ingredients for the gumbo pot. Called the Courir de Mardi Gras, this ancient and raucous tradition can be traced back to medieval times and was a part of the pre-Lenten festivities in most French parts of Louisiana in the 19th century. The Courir de Mardi Gras has made a comeback in recent years and can be witnessed in Mamou, Eunice and a handful of other rural communities.

Both wild and domesticated turkeys predated the arrival of the Cajuns and Creoles in Louisiana. Yet it is only in recent times that the bird associated with Christmas and other feast days in Europe found a place in local celebrations. Although wild turkey can be found in the woods of South Louisiana, the ones that grace modern tables are more likely descended from a domestic variety the Spaniards took back to their country from Central America in the 1500s. Because it was Turkish merchants that brought them from Spain to England, the exotic birds acquired the name "turkie-cock" which was later shortened to "turkey." The

Whatever the name, the American turkey gained immediate popularity in Europe and eventually made its way back to the New World with European settlers. Despite this rather complicated path to their tables, leave it to the Cajuns to take old ideas and make them their own. Cajun deep-fried turkey, as bizarre as it may sound, is gaining national popularity because of the quick cooking time, wonderful seasonings and delicious, moist meat.

The term "turkey" was also once applied to the guinea fowl, a domesticated bird of African origin, which was reintroduced to Europe around the same time as the American turkey's arrival. Guinea fowl could be found serving a dual role as both food and watchdog (because of their

Turks themselves called the birds "hindi" implying an East Indian rather than West Indian origin. This misconception was shared by the French, Germans and Italians.

distinctive cry) on Louisiana plantations. Their tendencies to elude capture and to roost in trees meant they could also provide some sport and be shot like game when one was needed for the pot. Of course, it may just have been the conceit of the wealthy plantation owners that demanded the presence of the "Hen of the Pharaohs" on their estates. Recreating another noble privilege, many plantation owners also raised doves and pigeons on their properties.

Louisiana's love of poultry is evident in one particularly unusual recipe, which combines three different birds. Turducken is made by stuffing a whole turkey with a whole duck, which is in turn, stuffed with a whole chicken, all with the bones removed. This roasted delicacy has been resurrected by Hebert's Specialty Meats in Maurice, La. The story goes that bored Louisiana hunters created the dish as an alternative to the traditional preparations for the birds they shot. While turducken is gaining popularity as a holiday dish, the idea is not new. Medieval banquets featured similar creations as *piece montif*. These edible centerpieces often featured swans and geese stuffed with a succession of smaller birds such as chicken, pheasant or quail.

Whatever your choice of bird, included here are a variety of recipes that guarantee a moist, juicy and delicious result every time. The key to cooking poultry is that it must be well done without being overcooked. Provided here are many new definitions for "well done" with some of the best ways to prepare chicken and turkey you will ever encounter. In honor of their former status as game birds, recipes for all other fowl have been included in the Game chapter.

OVEN-FRIED CHICKEN

Prep Time: 1 Hour
Yields: 6–8 Servings

Comment:

Deep-fried chicken is delicious, but if you want a healthier version of crispy chicken, try this oven-fried method. By baking the chicken at a high temperature, the meat will reach an almost-fried crispness without the oil.

Ingredients:

6 chicken drumsticks
4 bone-in chicken breast halves, skinned
1 quart water
1 tsp salt
½ cup nonfat buttermilk
3 cups cornflake crumbs
2–3 tsps Creole seasoning
2 tsps Italian seasoning
½ tsp garlic powder
½ tsp cracked black pepper
½ tsp cracked red pepper (optional)
vegetable cooking spray

Method:

Combine water and salt in a large bowl, then add chicken pieces. Cover and refrigerate a minimum of 8 hours. Preheat oven to 400°F. Drain chicken. Rinse with cold water and pat dry. Place chicken in a shallow dish. Pour buttermilk over chicken, turning pieces to coat. In a heavy-duty, gallon-size plastic zipper bag, combine cornflake crumbs and all seasonings and spices. Place 2 pieces of chicken in bag and seal. Shake to coat completely. Remove chicken and repeat process with remaining pieces. Place coated chicken, bone side down, in a 15" x10" x1" jellyroll pan coated with cooking spray. Spray chicken with cooking spray. Place pan on lowest rack in oven. Bake 45 minutes without turning.

SPICY HONEY DRUMETTES

Prep Time: 40 Minutes
Yields: 28 Pieces

Comment:

It's amazing how many successful restaurant chains have opened across America serving only chicken drumettes. The chicken is usually marinated then fried or broiled and topped with sauces ranging from spicy to savory. In Cajun Country, we have elevated this simple ingredient to new heights in dishes such as jambalaya, gumbo and even this spicy baked method.

Ingredients:

3 pounds chicken drumettes
1 cup honey
2 tbsps Worcestershire sauce
2 tbsps soy sauce
1 tsp red pepper flakes
salt to taste

Method:

Preheat oven to 400°F. Rinse drumettes and pat dry. Arrange chicken in a single layer on a baking sheet. Bake 10 minutes. In a small bowl, blend together remaining ingredients. Spoon half of honey mixture over drumettes, then bake 10 additional minutes. Using tongs, turn each drumette over. Spoon remaining honey mixture over chicken, and continue to bake 10 minutes. Let cool slightly before serving.

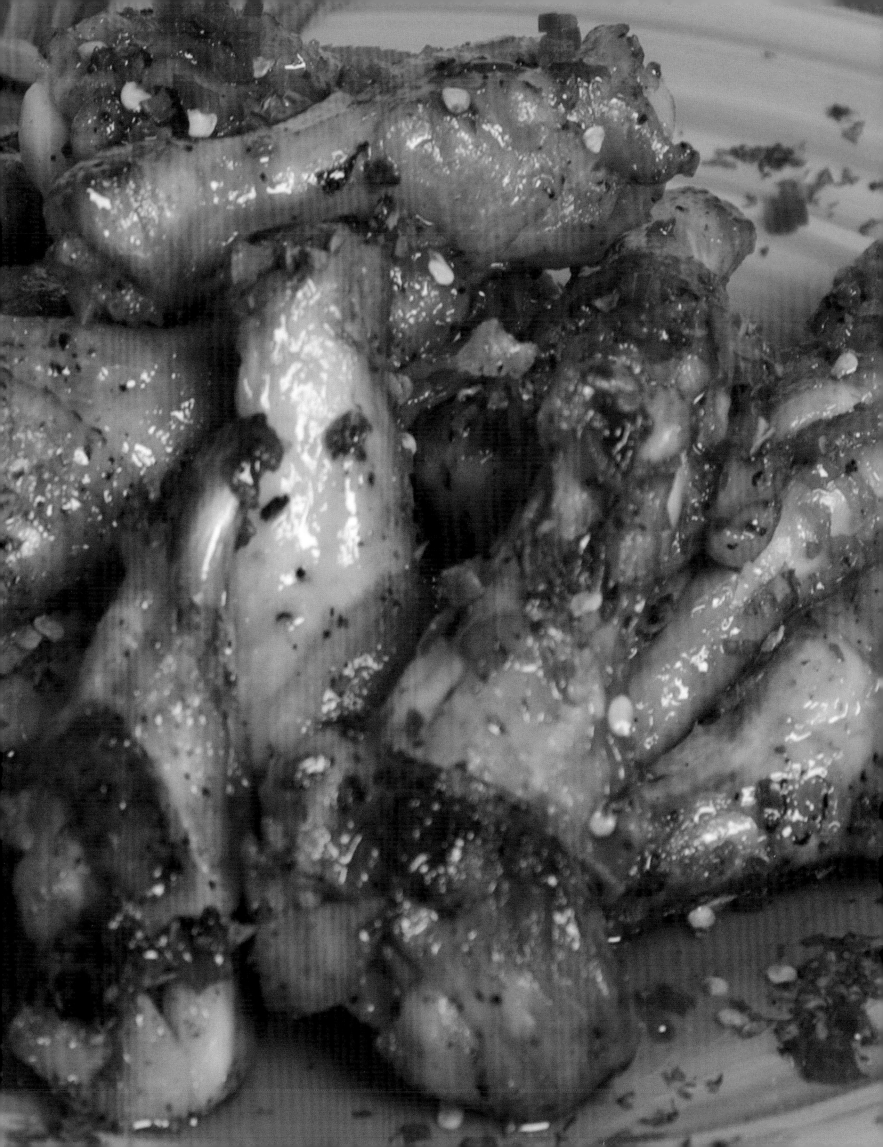

Wiley Rowe, caretaker of White Oak Plantation in Baton Rouge, reveals
a Chef John Folse secret: this southern-fried chicken is the best recipe in the book.

PORT HUDSON'S SOUTHERN-FRIED CHICKEN

Prep Time: 1 Hour
Yields: 4 Servings

Comment:
Port Hudson is a small town on the edge of St. Francisville, La., where one of the longest and bloodiest battles of the Civil War ensued. Today, a national cemetery lies on the battle site.

Ingredients:
1 (2–2½-pound) fryer chicken, cut into serving pieces
3 quarts water
salt and black pepper to taste
1 cup flour
2 cups vegetable oil
¼ cup bacon drippings

Method:
In a large mixing bowl, combine water and salt. Place chicken pieces in water, cover and refrigerate 8 hours. NOTE: You may substitute 2 cups buttermilk in place of salt water to soak chicken. Drain chicken, rinse with cold water and pat dry. Heat vegetable oil and bacon drippings to 360°F in a cast iron skillet or chicken fryer. Season chicken and flour separately with salt and pepper. In a gallon-size plastic zipper bag, place seasoned flour and 2 pieces of chicken. Seal bag and shake to coat each piece of chicken completely. Remove chicken, and repeat process with remaining pieces. Fry chicken, a few pieces at a time, skin side down. Once chicken is added, temperature will drop to 300°F–325°F; this is the ideal temperature for frying. Cover and cook chicken 6 minutes, then uncover and cook 9 minutes. Turn chicken pieces, cover and cook 6 minutes. Uncover and cook 5–9 minutes. For even browning, turn chicken pieces during last 3 minutes of cooking. Drain chicken on a paper towel-lined plate over a large bowl of hot water.

SMOTHERED CHICKEN AND MACQUE CHOUX CASSEROLE

Prep Time: 1½ Hours
Yields: 6 Servings

Comment:
This recipe incorporates two of Bayou Country's greatest dishes, Baked Chicken and Corn Macque Choux. This recipe was often cooked for Sunday lunch in many homes along River Road.

Ingredients:
1 (3-pound) fryer chicken, cut into serving pieces
4 ears fresh corn
1 cup shoepeg corn
1 cup whole kernel corn
½ cup bacon drippings
1 cup diced onions
½ cup diced celery
½ cup diced green bell peppers
½ cup diced red bell peppers
¼ cup minced garlic
¼ cup diced andouille
2 cups coarsely chopped tomatoes
2 tbsps tomato sauce
1 quart chicken stock
2 cups (150–200 count) shrimp, peeled and deveined
1 cup sliced green onions
salt and black pepper to taste
Louisiana hot sauce to taste

Method:
Preheat oven to 375°F. Select tender, well-developed ears of corn and shuck. Using a sharp knife, cut lengthwise through kernels to remove them from cob. Scrape each cob again to remove all "milk" (juice remaining on cob) and additional pulp from corn. The richness of this dish will depend on how much milk and pulp can be scraped from cobs. In a 7-quart cast iron Dutch oven, melt bacon drippings over medium-high heat. Sauté chicken in oil until golden brown on each side. Add corn, onions, celery, bell peppers, garlic and andouille. Sauté 3–5 minutes or until vegetables are wilted. Stir in tomatoes, tomato sauce, stock and shrimp. Continue cooking 15–20 minutes or until juices from tomatoes and shrimp are rendered. Add green onions, then season with salt and pepper. Cover Dutch oven and bake 1 hour or until chicken is tender and flavors of corn and shrimp have developed.

CASSEROLE OF BAKED CHICKEN AND OYSTERS

Prep Time: 1½ Hours
Yields: 6 Servings

Comment:

Oyster dishes are found everywhere in Bayou Country. From the delicate oyster soups to our hearty roux-based Oyster Stew in Patty Shells (See recipe.), many wonderful creations use oysters as a main ingredient. Here, Gulf oysters are combined with a young chicken to create a masterpiece.

Ingredients:

1 (3-pound) fryer chicken
2 pints oysters in liquid
salt and cracked black pepper to taste
Louisiana hot sauce to taste
½ cup vegetable oil
½ cup diced onions
½ cup diced celery
¼ cup diced red bell peppers
1 tbsp minced garlic
½ cup flour
1 quart chicken stock (see recipe)
1 cup heavy whipping cream
pinch of thyme
pinch of basil
1 cup grated Parmesan cheese
¼ cup chopped parsley
paprika for garnish

Method:

Preheat oven to 350°F. Drain oysters and reserve liquid. Cut chicken into 8 serving pieces. Season with salt, pepper and hot sauce. In a 10-inch sauté pan, heat oil over medium-high heat. Brown chicken lightly on all sides. Remove and place in an ovenproof baking dish. In the same pan, sauté onions, celery, bell peppers and garlic 3–5 minutes or until vegetables are wilted. Whisk in flour, stirring until blond roux is achieved. (See roux recipes.) Add reserved oyster liquid and stock, 1 ladle at a time. Blend ingredients until sauce-like consistency is achieved. Stir in cream and half of oysters. Bring to a rolling boil then reduce to simmer. Season with thyme, basil, salt, pepper and hot sauce. Place remaining oysters over chicken in casserole dish. Pour in oyster sauce then top with cheese. Garnish with parsley and paprika. Bake covered 30–45 minutes or until chicken is tender. Remove cover and allow to brown slightly.

OODLES OF NOODLES CASSEROLE

Prep Time: 45 Minutes
Yields: 8 Servings

Comment:

This casserole makes good use of leftover fried chicken by combining it with another homemade favorite, macaroni and cheese.

Ingredients:

½ cup diced spicy fried chicken, boned
1 (8-ounce) package elbow macaroni, cooked
¼ cup butter
1 cup thinly sliced smoked sausage
1 cup diced onions
1 cup diced celery
½ cup diced red bell peppers
1 tbsp flour
½ tsp paprika
½ tsp yellow mustard
1½ cups milk
1 (11.5-ounce) package Bittersweet Plantation Dairy Creole Cream Cheese
1½ cups shredded Cheddar cheese
salt and black pepper to taste
¾ cup bread crumbs
½ cup grated Parmesan cheese
nonstick cooking spray

Method:

Preheat oven to 350°F. In a saucepan, melt butter over medium-high heat. Add sausage and brown slightly, being careful not to burn butter. Add onions, celery and bell peppers. Sauté 3–5 minutes or until vegetables are wilted. Sprinkle in flour and blend to create white roux. (See roux recipes.) Stir in paprika, mustard and milk. Bring to a low boil, stirring occasionally. Blend in cream cheese and Cheddar. Stir for 5 minutes or until cheese is melted. Fold in fried chicken pieces then season with salt and pepper. Remove from heat and set aside. Combine bread crumbs and Parmesan cheese in a bowl and set aside. Coat a 9"x13" casserole dish with cooking spray. Place cooked macaroni in dish and blend in cheese sauce. Top with bread crumb mixture. Bake uncovered 20 minutes or until lightly browned.

CHICKEN AND BROCCOLI CASSEROLE

Prep Time: 1½ Hours
Serves: 6 Servings

Comment:
In 1835, Martha Turnbull noted in her journal that chickens, turkeys and ducks were served at Rosedown Plantation's grand opening, in St. Francisville, La. This English plantation featured a fabulous vegetable garden and certainly would have had a dish such as this one on their menu.

Ingredients:
3 whole chicken breasts
3 cups cooked broccoli florets
1 carrot, cubed
1 onion, cubed
2 cloves garlic
¼ cup butter
½ cup diced onions
¼ cup diced celery
¼ cup diced red bell peppers
1 tbsp minced garlic
½ cup flour
1 cup milk
½ tsp grated lemon zest
pinch of nutmeg
salt and cracked black pepper to taste
Louisiana hot sauce to taste
1 cup sour cream
½ cup grated Parmesan cheese
paprika for garnish

Method:
Preheat oven to 350°F. Place chicken, carrots, onions and garlic cloves in a stockpot over medium-high heat. Cover chicken with 1 inch of lightly-salted water. Bring to a rolling boil, then reduce to simmer and cook 20 minutes or until chicken is tender. Remove chicken, cool and reserve 1 cup of stock. Bone chicken, cube meat and set aside. In a heavy-bottomed Dutch oven, melt butter over medium-high heat. Add onions, celery, bell peppers and garlic. Sauté 3–5 minutes or until vegetables are wilted. Whisk in flour, stirring constantly until blond roux is achieved. (See roux recipes.) Pour in milk and 1 quart reserved chicken stock. Continue to stir until well blended, adding more stock if necessary. Add lemon zest and nutmeg. Season with salt, pepper and hot sauce. Remove from heat and allow to cool slightly. Fold in sour cream and adjust seasonings if necessary. In a 2-quart casserole dish, place chicken then top with broccoli and sauce. Sprinkle casserole with Parmesan cheese and paprika. Bake uncovered 25–30 minutes or until cheese is golden brown. Top with additional paprika if desired.

CASSEROLE OF CHICKEN AND EGGPLANT

Prep Time: 1½ Hours
Yields: 6 Servings

Comment:
The Italians arrived in South Louisiana in the late 1800s seeking work on the sugar plantations. They not only proved to be skilled laborers, but they brought wonderful cooking techniques to Bayou Country. This casserole was created near Opelousas, La.

Ingredients:
6 boneless, skinless chicken breasts
1 medium eggplant
2 eggs, beaten
1 cup Italian bread crumbs
½ cup olive oil
1 cup diced onions
½ cup diced celery
½ cup diced bell peppers
2 tbsps minced garlic
½ cup sliced green olives
2 (16-ounce) cans stewed tomatoes
1 tsp sugar
1 tsp sweet marjoram
1 tsp chopped thyme
1 tbsp chopped basil
1 tsp chopped oregano
salt and cracked black pepper to taste
½ cup sliced green onions
¼ cup chopped parsley
¼ cup grated Parmesan cheese
1 cup shredded mozzarella cheese

Method:
Preheat oven to 375°F. Slice eggplant into 6 medallions of equal thickness then set aside. Pound chicken lightly then season with salt and pepper. Dip chicken in egg and coat with bread crumbs. Place on a baking sheet, cover and refrigerate 10–15 minutes. In a heavy-bottomed Dutch oven, heat oil over medium-high heat. Sauté breasts 3–5 minutes on each side. Remove and place in ovenproof casserole dish. In the same pot, sauté eggplant until golden brown on both sides. Remove from oil and allow to drain. Place 1 slice of eggplant on top of each chicken breast. Sauté onions, celery, bell peppers, garlic and olives in Dutch oven 3–5 minutes or until vegetables are wilted. Add tomatoes, sugar, marjoram, thyme, basil and oregano. Blend ingredients well, bring to a rolling boil then reduce to simmer. Season with salt and pepper. Allow sauce to cook 30 minutes. Add green onions and parsley. Adjust seasonings if necessary. Spoon sauce over chicken breasts and top evenly with cheeses. Bake 15–20 minutes or until mozzarella melts and sauce is bubbly. This dish may be served over hot pasta.

ARROZ CON POLLO
(Chicken with Rice)

Prep Time: 1½ Hours
Yields: 8–10 Servings

Comment:
Arroz con Pollo originated in Spain and is a favorite throughout Latin America. This dish is one of the forefathers of chicken jambalaya, but the addition of saffron makes it unique.

Ingredients:
2 small fryers, cut up
2 cups uncooked rice
½ cup olive oil
1 pound lean pork, cubed
2 cups diced onions
1 cup diced celery
1 cup diced bell peppers
¼ cup minced garlic
1 cup diced tomatoes
1 (8-ounce) can tomato sauce
1 tsp lemon juice
1 bay leaf
1 tbsp saffron, bloomed in ¼ cup hot water
¼ cup dry white wine
5 cups chicken stock
salt and black pepper to taste
½ cup chopped parsley

Method:
Note: Place saffron in a bowl and microwave 30 seconds before blooming. Preheat oven to 350°F. In a large cast iron Dutch oven, heat oil over medium-high heat. Add chicken and sauté until golden brown. Remove from pot. Sauté pork in the same manner then set aside. In the same pot, combine onions, celery, bell peppers and garlic. Sauté 3–5 minutes or until vegetables are wilted. Blend in tomatoes, tomato sauce, lemon juice, bay leaf, saffron in water, white wine and chicken stock. Add rice and pork, stir well and season with salt and pepper. Top with chicken and parsley. Stir once, cover and cook 1 hour, checking at 30-minute intervals. Do not stir while cooking.

CHICKEN PAELLA

Prep Time: 1 Hour
Yields: 6 Servings

Comment:

Paella significantly influenced Louisiana cooking. Not only was the dish the forefather of jambalaya, but it was also a hearty meal that kept many Cajun and Creole families alive during hard times.

Ingredients:

1 (3-pound) fryer chicken
½ cup olive oil
½ cup diced onions
½ cup diced celery
½ cup diced red bell peppers
¼ cup minced garlic
½ cup sliced green onions
½ cup sliced mushrooms
½ cup diced ham
½ pound andouille, sliced
1 cup cooked black-eyed peas
1 cup diced tomatoes
3 cups long grain rice
4 cups chicken stock (see recipe)
1 tsp dried thyme
1 tsp dried basil
salt and cracked black pepper to taste
Louisiana hot sauce to taste

Method:

Cut chicken into serving pieces and season with salt, black pepper and hot sauce. In a 4-quart Dutch oven, heat olive oil over medium-high heat. Sauté chicken, a few pieces at a time, until browned on all sides. Remove and keep warm. In same oil, sauté onions, celery, bell peppers, garlic, green onions, mushrooms, ham, andouille, black-eyed peas and tomatoes 3–5 minutes or until vegetables are wilted. Add rice and stir-fry into vegetables 3 minutes. Stir in chicken stock, thyme and basil. Season with salt, pepper and hot sauce. Bring to a low boil and cook 3 minutes, stirring occasionally. Blend in chicken, then reduce heat to low and cover pot. Cook 30–45 minutes, stirring at 15-minute intervals.

CHICKEN AND SAUSAGE JAMBALAYA

Prep Time: 2 Hours
Yields: 15–20 Servings

Comment:

In the early 1700s, Spanish settlers in New Orleans brought their famous paella. Since the traditional Spanish ingredients for paella were not found in South Louisiana, the recipe was adapted to indigenous ingredients. Oysters and crawfish replaced clams and mussels, and fresh pork or andouille took the place of cured ham. The new dish was influenced by many different cultures, including the Africans who contributed their rice, or yaya, to jambalaya. The French later named the dish Jambon à la Yaya, meaning ham with rice.

Ingredients:

3 pounds cubed chicken
2 pounds smoked sausage, sliced
¼ cup shortening or bacon drippings
2 cups diced onions
2 cups diced celery
1 cup diced bell peppers
½ cup minced garlic
8 cups beef or chicken stock
2 cups sliced mushrooms
1 cup sliced green onions
½ cup chopped parsley
salt and cayenne pepper to taste
Louisiana hot sauce to taste
5 cups uncooked long-grain rice

Method:

In a 7-quart cast iron Dutch oven, heat shortening or bacon drippings over medium-high heat. Sauté cubed chicken 30 minutes or until dark brown on all sides and beginning to stick to bottom of pot. This process is important because jambalaya's brown color is derived from the color of the meat. Add smoked sausage and stir fry 10–15 minutes. Tilt pot to one side and ladle out all oil, except 1 large cooking spoonful. Add onions, celery, bell peppers and garlic. Continue cooking until all vegetables are well caramelized, being careful not to scorch them. Pour in stock, bring to a rolling boil then reduce heat to simmer. Cook 15 minutes to allow flavors to develop. Stir in mushrooms, green onions and parsley. Season with salt, cayenne pepper and hot sauce. If desired, slightly over-season dish since rice has not yet been added. Add rice, reduce heat to low, cover and cook 30–45 minutes. Stir every 15 minutes. Do not uncover except to stir.

CREOLE-STYLE CHICKEN

Prep Time: 1 Hour
Yields: 6 Servings

Comment:
This recipe is similar in flavor to the sauce piquant. The difference, however, is that almost every culture of early New Orleans added their own flavor to this dish.

Ingredients:
1 (5-pound) stewing hen
½ cup vegetable oil
½ cup flour
2 cups diced onions
1 cup diced celery
½ cup diced bell peppers
¼ cup minced garlic
1 dozen button mushrooms
2 cups diced tomatoes
1 tbsp minced jalapeños
½ cup tomato paste
1 tsp crushed oregano
½ tsp dried thyme
pinch of marjoram
½ tsp basil
1 cup dry red wine
4 cups chicken stock (see recipe)
salt and cracked black pepper to taste
Louisiana hot sauce to taste

Method:
Cut hen into serving size pieces. Larger pieces such as breasts may be cut into 2 pieces. In a 2-gallon Dutch oven, heat oil over medium-high heat. Whisk in flour, stirring constantly until golden brown roux is achieved. (See roux recipes.) Add onions, celery, bell peppers, garlic, mushrooms, tomatoes and jalapeños. Sauté 5–10 minutes or until vegetables are wilted. Blend in chicken and continue cooking 3 minutes. Add tomato paste, oregano, thyme, marjoram and basil. Blend well. Slowly stir in wine and chicken stock. Bring to low boil then reduce to simmer. Cook 1 hour, stirring occasionally. Add small amounts of chicken stock if mixture becomes too thick. Season with salt, pepper and hot sauce. Continue cooking until chicken is tender. Serve over white rice or as a side dish with jambalaya.

CHICKEN BAYOU LAFOURCHE WITH ANDOUILLE TARRAGON CREAM

Prep Time: 1 Hour
Yields: 6 Servings

Comment:
Bayou Lafourche flows from the Mississippi River in Donaldsonville, La., to the Gulf of Mexico. Over the past 200 years, many of the Creole cultures have settled this area. These families have developed many interesting cooking methods not only for seafood, but also for poultry and beef. This recipe combines crawfish, a staple of the bayou, with chicken and traditional Cajun andouille.

Ingredients for Chicken:
6 boneless chicken breasts
salt and cracked black pepper to taste
½ pound chopped crawfish tails
¼ cup diced onions
¼ cup diced celery
¼ cup diced red bell peppers
1 tsp minced garlic
¼ cup sliced green onions
¼ cup chopped parsley
½ tsp Pernod or Herbsaint
1 tbsp sherry
½ cup Béchamel Sauce (see recipe)
½ cup Italian bread crumbs
1 cup seasoned flour
½ cup vegetable oil

Method:
Preheat oven to 375°F. Pound chicken breasts lightly to flatten then season with salt and pepper. In a 1-quart mixing bowl, combine all remaining ingredients except flour and oil. Blend well and adjust seasonings if necessary. Place an equal amount of stuffing in center of each breast, roll into a turban shape and secure with toothpicks. Dust lightly in flour and set aside. In a 10-inch sauté pan, heat oil over medium-high heat. Add chicken and sauté until brown on all sides. Remove chicken from pan, place in a baking dish and bake 20–30 minutes. Drain off all but 1 tablespoon of oil from skillet. When chicken is done, remove excess fat from dish and keep meat warm.

Ingredients for Andouille Tarragon Cream:
¼ cup andouille
1 tbsp chopped tarragon
¼ cup melted butter
1 tbsp sliced shallots
1 tbsp minced garlic
1 tsp flour
1 ounce white wine
1½ cups heavy whipping cream
salt and black pepper to taste

Method:
In reserved skillet, heat butter over medium-high heat. Add shallots, garlic and andouille. Sauté 3–5 minutes or until vegetables are wilted. Blend in flour, then add tarragon and deglaze with white wine. Stir in heavy whipping cream and reduce to half volume. Season with salt and pepper. Pour finished sauce over chicken in baking pan.

CHICKEN AND DUMPLINGS RANDOLPH

Prep Time: 2 Hours
Yields: 6–8 Servings

Comment:

Chicken and dumplings is one of those great old-fashioned Southern dishes that is often taken for granted. People don't eat this food as much as they used to. Perhaps it's time to resurrect this dish to its prominent place on the Sunday dinner table.

Ingredients for Chicken:

2 (3-pound) broiler chickens	4 carrots, sliced
2 medium onions, cubed	2 bay leaves
2 celery stalks, quartered	2 sprigs of thyme
1 bell pepper, quartered	15–20 black peppercorns
1 head of garlic, halved	

Method:

Cut each chicken into 8 serving pieces. In a large stockpot, place chicken, onions, celery, bell peppers, garlic, carrots, bay leaves, thyme and peppercorns. Cover chicken with lightly-salted water by 2 inches. Bring to a rolling boil, reduce to simmer and cook 1 hour or until chicken is tender. Remove chicken from stock and allow to cool. Bone and tear meat into irregular serving pieces. Set aside. Return bones to stock and cook an additional 30 minutes. Strain and reserve 3 quarts of stock.

Ingredients for Dumplings:

2 cups flour	½ cup diced carrots
1½ tsps baking powder	½ cup sliced celery
3 tbsps shortening	¼ cup sliced green onions
¾ cup buttermilk	¼ cup chopped parsley for garnish
salt and cracked black pepper to taste	

Method:

In a separate mixing bowl, combine flour, baking powder and shortening. Fold shortening into flour until mixture resembles coarse meal. Add buttermilk and stir with a folk until ingredients are moist. Season with salt and pepper. Turn dough out onto a lightly-floured surface and knead gently 4–5 times. Cover with a dry cloth and set aside. Return chicken stock to a low boil. Add chicken, carrots, celery, green onions and parsley. While vegetables are poaching, roll dough ¼-inch thick. Slice or pinch dough into 1-inch squares. Drop dumplings into boiling broth and stir gently after each addition. Reduce heat to low and cook 8–10 minutes or until dumplings are tender. Season broth to taste. Serve in large soup bowls with chicken, vegetables and dumplings. Garnish with chopped parsley.

CHICKEN SAUCE PIQUANT

Prep Time: 1½ Hours
Yields: 6 Servings

Comment:

The sauce piquants were brought to Louisiana by the Spanish in 1690. It was the innovative Cajuns, however, who made "sauce piquant" a household name. Today, any wild game or domestic meat may be found in this signature Cajun dish.

Ingredients:

1 (5-pound) stewing hen
½ cup vegetable oil
½ cup flour
1 cup diced onions
1 cup diced celery
½ cup diced bell peppers
¼ cup diced garlic
2 bay leaves
½ tsp basil
½ tsp thyme
1 cup diced tomatoes
½ cup tomato sauce
2 tbsps diced jalapeños
6 cups chicken stock (see recipe)
1 cup sliced mushrooms
1 cup sliced green onions
½ cup chopped parsley
salt and cracked black pepper to taste

Method:

Cut stewing hen into serving pieces. Larger cuts, such as breasts may be cut in half. In a 2-gallon saucepot, heat oil over medium-high heat. Whisk in flour, stirring constantly until light brown roux is achieved. (See roux recipes.) Add onions, celery, bell peppers, garlic, bay leaves, basil and thyme. Sauté 5–10 minutes or until vegetables are wilted. Stir in tomatoes, tomato sauce and jalapeños. Cook 3–5 minutes then add hen pieces. Pour in chicken stock, one ladle at a time, stirring constantly. Bring to a rolling boil, reduce to simmer and cook 45 minutes. Add mushrooms, green onions and parsley. Season with salt and pepper. Continue cooking 30 minutes, stirring occasionally until meat is tender and sauce thickens. Serve over rice or pasta.

CHICKEN AND OKRA STEW

Prep Time: 1 Hour
Yields: 6 Servings

Comment:

Okra was one of the newfound delicacies which offered cooks variety and versatility in the kitchens of New Orleans in the late 1700s. Not only was okra a main ingredient in the gumbo pots of Louisiana, but it was also added to many other soups and stews. No okra dish was better known than the chicken and okra stew of Bayou Country.

Ingredients:

1 whole chicken, cut in pieces
1 cup sliced okra
1 cup vegetable oil
1 cup flour
1 cup diced onions
1 cup diced celery
½ cup diced green bell peppers
¼ cup diced yellow bell peppers
¼ cup diced red bell peppers
¼ cup minced garlic
½ cup diced tomatoes
½ cup tomato sauce
1 cup sliced smoked sausage
pinch of thyme
pinch of basil
2 quarts chicken stock (see recipe)
½ cup sliced green onions
¼ cup chopped parsley
1 bay leaf
salt and cracked black pepper to taste
Louisiana hot sauce to taste

Method:

In a cast iron pot, heat oil over medium-high heat. Whisk in flour, stirring constantly until golden brown roux is achieved. (See roux recipes.) Sauté onions, celery, bell peppers, garlic and tomatoes in roux 3–5 minutes or until vegetables are wilted. Blend in chicken then add tomato sauce, sausage, thyme and basil. Continue to cook 3–5 minutes. Slowly pour in chicken stock and stir well. Use enough stock to achieve a stew-like consistency. Add green onions, parsley and bay leaf. Season with salt, pepper and hot sauce. Cook 10–15 minutes. Add okra and continue to cook until chicken is tender. Chicken stock may be added to maintain consistency. Serve over steamed rice.

SWEET AND SPICY CHICKEN ÉTOUFFÉE

Prep Time: 1½ Hours
Yields: 6 Servings

Comment:

In many cultures, sweet and spicy go hand-in-hand like sweet and sour. In South Louisiana, where sugar and cayenne pepper are found as the main ingredients in so many recipes, it is obvious how this dish evolved.

Ingredients:

1 (3-pound) fryer, cut into 8 serving pieces
¼ cup Worcestershire sauce
4 tsps salt
3 tsps cayenne pepper
¼ tsp black pepper
1 tbsp granulated garlic
¾ cup flour
½ cup vegetable oil
3 cups sliced Bermuda onions
1 cup diced celery
1 cup sliced red bell peppers
1 cup sliced yellow bell peppers
2 cups chicken stock (see recipe)
¼ cup brown sugar

Method:

In a mixing bowl, combine chicken with Worcestershire, salt, cayenne, black pepper and garlic. Marinate chicken in seasonings 1 hour at room temperature. NOTE: It is acceptable to leave chicken at room temperature, but it must be cooked immediately following marinating. Place chicken on a large cookie sheet and reserve marinating liquid. Dust meat with flour and set aside. In a cast iron Dutch oven, heat oil on medium-high. Carefully brown chicken without scorching. Remove and set aside. Sauté onions, celery and bell peppers in Dutch oven 2–3 minutes or until vegetables are wilted. Add chicken stock, reserved marinade and brown sugar. Bring to a rolling boil then return chicken to pot. Reduce heat to simmer, cover and cook 45 minutes or until chicken is tender. Adjust seasonings if necessary. Serve over steamed white rice.

MAMA'S CHICKEN FRICASSÉE

Prep Time: 1½ Hours
Yields: 6 Servings

Comment:

The best fricassée is made like Mama's, in an old cast iron pot. Mama would always fry her chicken first, and many times she had to fry extra because the kids would eat it before it got to the stew. In Louisiana it is traditional to finish a fricassée with sour cream.

Ingredients:

1 (3-pound) fryer chicken
1½ cups flour
1 cup vegetable oil
2 cups diced onions
1 cup diced celery
½ cup diced bell peppers
1 tbsp minced garlic
1½ quarts chicken stock (see recipe)
1 cup sliced mushrooms
1 cup sliced green onions
¼ cup chopped parsley
1 cup sour cream
salt and black pepper to taste
Louisiana hot sauce to taste

Method:

Rinse chicken under cold running water then cut it into 8 serving pieces. Drain chicken in colander. Season meat with salt, pepper and hot sauce. In a large Dutch oven, heat ½ cup vegetable oil over medium-high heat. Dust chicken in 1 cup of flour, shaking off excess. Once oil is hot, fry pieces, a few at a time, until golden brown on all sides. Caution: Heat may need to be adjusted to avoid scorching flour and oil. Remove chicken and set aside. Retain pan drippings for roux. If necessary, add oil to pan to reach ½ cup of drippings. Whisk in remaining flour, stirring until a golden brown roux is achieved. (See roux recipes.) Sauté onions, celery, bell peppers and garlic in roux 3–5 minutes or until vegetables are wilted. Add chicken stock, a little at a time, until stew-like consistency is achieved. Return fried chicken to pot and add mushrooms. Bring to a rolling boil, reduce heat to simmer and cook 45 minutes or until chicken is tender. Blend in green onions, parsley and sour cream. Season with salt, pepper and hot sauce. Additional stock may be needed to retain consistency. Serve over steamed white rice or noodles.

FRICASSÉE OF CHICKEN AND SMOKED SAUSAGE

Prep Time: 1½ Hours
Yields: 6 Servings

Comment:
Next to Southern Fried Chicken, the fricassée or "stewed chicken" is the most popular dish in the kitchens of New Orleans. The traditional fricassée was always prepared on Sunday. In order to make the dish special for guests, a mélange of vegetables and seasoning meats were added.

Ingredients:
1 (3-pound) fryer chicken
1 pound smoked sausage, sliced
salt and black pepper to taste
¾ cup vegetable oil
1 cup flour
1 cup diced onions
½ cup diced celery
½ cup diced red bell peppers
¼ cup minced garlic
6 cups chicken stock (see recipe)
1 cup sliced carrots (½-inch thick)
½ cup sliced celery (¼-inch thick)
1 cup cubed potatoes (¾-inch cubes)
Louisiana hot sauce to taste
½ cup sliced green onions
¼ cup chopped parsley

Method:
Cut fryer into 8 serving pieces and season well with salt and pepper. In a large cast iron Dutch oven, heat oil over medium-high heat. Whisk in flour, stirring constantly until dark brown roux is achieved. (See roux recipes.) Add onions, diced celery, bell peppers and garlic. Sauté 3–5 minutes or until vegetables are wilted. Dissolve roux by adding chicken stock and stirring constantly. Blend in chicken pieces and sausage. Bring to a rolling boil, then reduce to simmer and cook 30 minutes. Add carrots, sliced celery and potatoes. Season with salt, pepper and hot sauce. Continue to cook until chicken is tender, adding stock if needed. Add green onions and parsley, and cook 5 minutes. Serve over steamed white rice.

RATATOUILLE STUFFED CHICKEN

Prep Time: 1 Hour
Yields: 6 Servings

Comment:
The use of multiple vegetables in casseroles and stuffing was prevalent throughout the English, Spanish and German sections of north Louisiana. Large gardens guaranteed an ample supply of the necessary ingredients. This vegetable stuffing was often used in the kitchens of Creole Louisiana.

Ingredients:
6 large boneless chicken breasts, skin-on
¼ cup butter
¼ cup diced onions
¼ cup diced celery
2 tbsps diced red bell peppers
2 tbsps diced yellow bell peppers
1 tsp minced garlic
¼ cup diced tomatoes
¼ cup chopped black olives
½ cup diced yellow squash
½ cup diced zucchini
1 cup diced eggplant
pinch of thyme
pinch of basil
salt and black pepper to taste
Louisiana hot sauce to taste
1 cup Italian bread crumbs
1 cup flour
¼ cup olive oil

Method:
Preheat oven to 375°F. Using a paring knife, cut a pocket lengthwise through center of breast. In a large sauté pan, melt butter over medium-high heat. Add onions, celery, bell peppers and garlic. Sauté 3–5 minutes or until vegetables are wilted. Stir in tomatoes, black olives, squash, zucchini and eggplant. Continue to sauté until vegetables are cooked but not mushy. Season with thyme, basil, salt, pepper and hot sauce. Sprinkle in bread crumbs and stir. Remove from heat. Once mixture cools, divide it into 6 equal portions. Season chicken with salt and pepper, then stuff ratatouille into pocket of each piece. Secure opening with toothpick then dust lightly in flour. In a heavy-bottomed sauté pan, heat oil over medium-high heat. Sauté 3 chicken breasts at a time 3–5 minutes or until golden brown on each side. Remove chicken and bake 15 minutes or until cooked. Serve over Creole Tomato Sauce. (See recipe.)

JOLLOF RICE OF NIGERIA

Prep Time: 1½ Hours
Yields: 4 Servings

Comment:
This dish is common throughout West Africa and can be made with chicken, beef, goat or pork. Jollof rice can be compared to a cross between red jambalaya and chicken Creole.

Ingredients:
1 (2–3 pound) fryer chicken, cut into 8 pieces
1 cup uncooked rice
2 tbsps vegetable oil
salt and black pepper to taste
cayenne pepper to taste
2 onions, sliced
2 cups chicken stock (see recipe)
1 (28-ounce) can diced plum tomatoes, drained
1 tbsp tomato paste
1 tsp salt
½ tsp pepper
¼ tsp dried thyme
8 ounces fresh green beans, cut in 1-inch pieces
2 cups frozen black-eyed peas

Method:
In a large cast iron Dutch oven, heat vegetable oil over medium-high heat. Season chicken with salt, cayenne and black pepper. Brown chicken 10–15 minutes. Add onions, and sauté 10–15 minutes or until slightly browned. Stir in stock, tomatoes, tomato paste, salt, pepper and thyme. Bring to a rolling boil then reduce to simmer. Cover and cook 30 minutes, stirring as needed. Add rice, green beans and black-eyed peas. Continue cooking 20 minutes or until rice is completely cooked and chicken is done.

CHICKEN AND ARTICHOKE HEARTS

Prep Time: 1½ Hours
Yields: 6 Servings

Comment:
Artichokes were first introduced to the gardens of New Orleans for their visual appeal. Nothing is more dynamic than a beautiful artichoke flower, except the vegetable itself when presented in a delicious recipe such as this one.

Ingredients:
6 skinless chicken breasts
2 cans artichoke hearts, drained
¼ cup olive oil
salt and black pepper to taste
¼ cup vegetable oil
¼ cup flour
1 cup diced onions
2 tbsps minced garlic
1 cup sliced green onions
4 cups chicken stock (see recipe)
1 (8-ounce) can green peas
½ cup chopped parsley

Method:
In a cast iron Dutch oven, heat olive oil over medium-high heat. Season chicken with salt and pepper. Sauté meat until golden brown on both sides, remove and set aside. Discard olive oil and add vegetable oil. Whisk in flour, stirring constantly until golden brown roux is achieved. (See roux recipes.) Add onions, garlic and green onions. Sauté 3–5 minutes or until vegetables are wilted. Blend in chicken stock. Bring to a rolling boil then reduce to simmer. Add chicken, artichokes and peas. Cover and cook 45 minutes. Season with salt and pepper. Top with parsley. Serve over steamed white rice or pasta.

COQ AU VIN

Prep Time: 2½ Hours
Yields: 6–8 Servings

Comment:

This classic French braised chicken dish is normally made with an older rooster or a large baking hen, which allows for longer cooking time. Long braising ensures that the flavors of the meat, vegetables, spices and wine will fully infuse. This dish can be made with white or red wine, however, red is preferred. For best results I always braise Coq Au Vin in the oven rather than on the stovetop.

Ingredients:

6 large leg quarters or whole baking hen
salt and black pepper to taste
granulated garlic to taste
¾ cup flour
¼ cup vegetable oil
½ pound bacon, chopped
¼ cup cognac
2 cups diced onions
1 cup diced celery
1 cup diced carrots
12 garlic cloves, halved

12 pearl onions, peeled
3 cups Burgundy wine
3 cups beef stock (see recipe)
   OR beef bouillon
1 tbsp tomato paste
18 button mushrooms
1 bay leaf
1 cup demi-glace (optional)
2 tbsps chopped
   bittersweet chocolate
1 cup fresh or frozen early peas

Method:

Preheat oven to 400°F. If using a whole baking hen, cut into 6–8 serving pieces. Season with salt, pepper and granulated garlic. Season flour lightly with salt, pepper and granulated garlic. Dust chicken in flour, shaking off excess. In a large Dutch oven or roasting pan, heat vegetable oil over medium-high heat. Sauté bacon, stirring constantly until bacon fat is rendered, taking care not to burn oil. Using a slotted spoon, remove bacon. In same pan, cook 3–4 pieces of chicken at a time 3–5 minutes on each side or until golden brown, turning occasionally. Remove chicken from pan and set aside. Once chicken is browned, deglaze with cognac taking care because it may ignite when it hits pan. Add onions, celery, carrots and garlic. Sauté 3–5 minutes or until vegetables are wilted. Add pearl onions and cook an additional 2–3 minutes. Add wine and beef stock, blending well into vegetable mixture. Whisk tomato paste into simmering liquid. Return chicken pieces to pan. Add stock if necessary to cover chicken by ¼ inch. Add mushrooms and bay leaf. Bring to a rolling boil, cover and place in oven for 1½ hours. Check for tenderness, because age and size of bird will determine cooking time. Chicken should be fork tender, but not falling apart. When done, gently remove chicken pieces from braising liquid and place on a sheet pan. Return braising liquid and vegetables to stovetop and bring to a low boil over medium-high heat. If necessary, thicken sauce with 1–2 tablespoons dark brown roux. (See roux recipes.) When sauce is thickened, adjust seasonings using salt, pepper and granulated garlic. Add demi-glace. Blend in chocolate and peas. Simmer 10–12 minutes or until peas are tender. Return chicken to braising liquid and reheat. When ready to serve, place a portion of chicken in center of a soup bowl and top with sauce and braised vegetables.

CACCIATORE CREOLE

Prep Time: 1 Hour
Yields: 6 Servings

Comment:

Cacciatore is a braised chicken dish that usually takes hours to create. In the city of New Orleans, the Italians created this recipe in order to speed up the process while retaining the great flavor.

Ingredients:

6 boneless chicken breasts
salt and cracked black pepper to taste
1 cup flour
¼ cup olive oil
1 cup diced onions
1 cup diced celery
½ cup diced bell peppers
2 tbsps minced garlic
2 cups sliced mushrooms
2 (16-ounce) cans stewed tomatoes
½ cup white wine
2 bay leaves
1 tsp sweet marjoram
1 tsp chopped thyme
1 tbsp chopped basil
1 tsp chopped oregano
½ cup sliced green onions
¼ cup chopped parsley
6 cups cooked spaghetti

Method:

For best results, boil spaghetti in chicken stock when making cacciatore. Season chicken lightly with salt and pepper. Dust with flour and shake off excess. In a heavy-bottomed Dutch oven, heat oil over medium-high heat. Sauté chicken until golden brown on both sides. Remove and keep warm. Sauté onions, celery, bell peppers, garlic and mushrooms in Dutch oven 3–5 minutes or until vegetables are wilted. Blend in tomatoes, wine, bay leaves, marjoram, thyme, basil and oregano. Season with salt and pepper. Allow sauce to simmer 30 minutes. Add chicken breasts and cook 10 minutes. Stir in green onions and parsley. Adjust seasonings if necessary. Serve over hot spaghetti.

PECAN-PESTO CHICKEN

Prep Time: 1 Hour
Yields: 6 Servings

Comment:

Pesto is usually made with chopped garden herbs, such as basil, blended with pine nuts and olive oil. In South Louisiana, pecans have been substituted for pine nuts to give this pesto Southern flair. Pesto is ideal as a pasta coating or pizza topping and can also be eaten on garlic bread.

Ingredients:

6 boneless chicken breasts, skin-on
⅓ cup pecans
½ cup freshly-grated Parmesan cheese
1 tbsp minced garlic
⅔ cup loosely-packed basil leaves
½ cup extra virgin olive oil
salt and black pepper to taste
¼ cup vegetable oil
½ cup flour
¼ cup diced shallots
½ cup sliced oyster mushrooms
1 tsp minced garlic
1½ tbsps flour
½ cup dry white wine
1 cup chicken stock (see recipe)
1 cup heavy whipping cream

Method:

Preheat oven to 200°F. In a food processor, combine pecans, Parmesan cheese, 1 tablespoon minced garlic and basil leaves. Pulse 1–2 minutes or until mixture is well chopped and blended. With processor running, add olive oil in a slow, steady stream until mixture resembles paste. Do not over-process or basil will darken and appear unappetizing. Season with salt and pepper. Set aside. NOTE: If stored in a glass jar and refrigerated, pesto will be good for about 2 weeks. Store in freezer if a longer holding time is desired. In a sauté pan, heat vegetable oil over medium-high heat. Rinse chicken under cold water and pat dry. Season meat with salt and pepper then coat lightly in flour. Sauté chicken, skin-side down, 3–5 minutes. Turn and continue to sauté an additional 3–5 minutes. Remove from pan and place on cookie sheet in warm oven. In same pan, sauté shallots, mushrooms and remaining garlic 2–3 minutes or until vegetables are wilted. Sprinkle in 1 tablespoon flour and blend well. Whisk in white wine and chicken stock. Bring sauce to a low boil then reduce to simmer. Add 2 level tablespoons of prepared pecan-pesto sauce to pan along with heavy whipping cream. Whisk until blended. Season with salt and pepper. When ready to serve, place a small amount of sauce on bottom of 10-inch plate and top with chicken, skin-side up. Place additional sauce over edges of chicken as garnish. A bouquet of fresh basil leaves may be placed in the center for color. Serve alongside cooked pasta.

CHICKEN AND CREOLE TOMATO POMODORI

Prep Time: 1 Hour
Yields: 6 Servings

Comment:
While Italian tomato sauces are traditionally made with Roma tomatoes, here in South Louisiana the Creole tomato is a delicious alternative. The vine-ripened tomato is wonderful in this sauce. If Creole tomatoes aren't available, it is probably best to use canned tomatoes.

Ingredients:
4 boneless chicken breasts
2½ cups diced Creole tomatoes
3 tbsps poultry seasoning
salt and black pepper to taste
Louisiana hot sauce to taste
½ cup extra virgin olive oil
½ cup grated Parmesan cheese
1 cup diced onions
¼ cup minced garlic
1 cup dry white wine
2 bay leaves
pinch of oregano
pinch of rosemary
pinch of basil
pinch of thyme

Method:
Slice chicken breasts into ½-inch strips and season with poultry seasoning, salt, pepper and hot sauce. In a cast iron skillet, heat ¼ cup olive oil over medium-high heat. Sauté chicken until golden brown, remove and sprinkle with Parmesan cheese. Set aside and keep warm. Pour remaining olive oil into skillet. Add onions and garlic. Sauté 3–5 minutes or until vegetables are wilted. Blend in tomatoes and sauté until tender. Add wine, bay leaves, oregano, rosemary, basil and thyme. Bring to a rolling boil, reduce to simmer and cook 10 minutes. Gently stir in chicken. Cover and cook 10 minutes. Season with salt and pepper. This dish is excellent when served over rice, pasta or with toasted garlic bread.

CHICKEN PARMESAN

Prep Time: 1½ Hours
Yields: 6 Servings

Comment:
The Italians arrived at the port of New Orleans in the late 1800s. These Sicilian people brought with them a love of family, a passion for food and a work ethic second to none. Many of Louisiana's most famous dishes can be attributed to the Italian kitchen.

Ingredients:
6 boneless chicken breasts
¼ cup olive oil
2 cups diced onions
¼ cup minced garlic
1 (16-ounce) can chopped tomatoes
1 (6-ounce) can tomato paste
2 cups hot water
½ tsp oregano
1 tsp dried basil
1 tsp sugar
salt and black pepper to taste
4 eggs
2 tbsps water
½ cup olive oil
2 cups Italian bread crumbs
½ cup grated Parmesan cheese
6 slices mozzarella cheese

Method:
Preheat oven to 400°F. In a cast iron skillet, heat ¼ cup olive oil over medium-high heat. Add onions and garlic. Sauté 3–5 minutes or until vegetables are wilted. Blend tomatoes and paste into onion mixture, stirring constantly. Simmer 20 minutes. Add hot water, oregano, basil and sugar. Season with salt and pepper, then simmer 20 additional minutes. Remove and keep warm. Using a meat mallet, lightly flatten chicken. Season with salt and pepper. In a small mixing bowl, whip eggs and 2 tablespoons water. In a large skillet, heat ½ cup olive oil over medium-high heat. Dip chicken breasts in egg mixture and then in bread crumbs. Sauté 3–5 minutes on each side until golden brown. Remove chicken and keep warm. Pour tomato sauce into bottom of an 11"x 7" baking dish. Place sautéed chicken breasts in sauce, and top each with Parmesan cheese and 1 slice of mozzarella. Bake 15–20 minutes or until cheese is melted and chicken is heated. This dish is excellent served over angel hair pasta or spaghetti.

BAKED CHICKEN AND SPAGHETTI

Prep Time: 1 Hour 45 Minutes
Yields: 6 Servings

Comment:

It would be interesting if someone were able to identify the number of dishes created in Cajun and Creole cuisine featuring chicken. Of course, this would be an impossible task. However, we do know that each of the seven Creole nations, as well as the Cajuns, featured chicken recipes in their repertoire that are too numerous to count.

Ingredients:

1 (3-pound) fryer chicken
2 cups diced onions
2 cups diced celery
1 bay leaf
salt and cayenne pepper to taste
¼ pound butter
2 tbsps flour
1 (14-ounce) can crushed tomatoes
1 cup sliced mushrooms
3 cups reserved chicken stock
1 (12-ounce) package spaghetti
1 cup grated Cheddar cheese

Method:

Preheat oven to 350°F. Cut fryer into 8 serving pieces. Place chicken in a large pot with enough water to cover by 2 inches. Add 1 cup onions, 1 cup celery and bay leaf. Season water with salt and cayenne pepper. Bring to a rolling boil, reduce to simmer and cook 45 minutes or until chicken is tender. Strain and reserve chicken stock. Cool and bone chicken. In a cast iron Dutch oven, melt butter over medium-high heat. Whisk in flour and stir until white roux is achieved. (See roux recipes.) Add remaining onions and celery. Sauté 3–5 minutes or until vegetables are wilted. Stir in tomatoes, mushrooms and reserved chicken stock. Bring to a rolling boil, then reduce to simmer and cook 5–10 minutes. Prepare spaghetti according to package directions. Drain and set aside. In an ovenproof casserole dish, layer spaghetti, chicken, sauce and cheese. Continue layering until all ingredients are used. Add a few spoonfuls of chicken stock and bake 20–30 minutes. Additional stock may be added if sauce becomes too thick.

CHICKEN PICCATA

Prep Time: 20 Minutes
Yields: 4 Servings

Comment:

This is one of Louisiana's favorite home-style Italian dishes. Although it is most often made with veal, it can be made with chicken or fish fillets.

Ingredients:

4 boneless chicken breasts
1 cup flour
½ cup vegetable oil
1 tbsp minced garlic
½ cup dry white wine
1 cup chicken broth or chicken stock
3 tbsps fresh lemon juice
2 tbsps capers, drained
4 lemon slices, thinly cut
4 tbsps unsalted butter
¼ cup chopped parsley
salt and black pepper to taste

Method:

Slice each chicken breast in half. Place slices between sheets of plastic wrap, and pound to an even thickness. Season chicken with salt and pepper. Dust lightly in flour and shake off excess. In a large sauté pan, heat oil over medium-high heat. Sauté breast cutlets, a few at a time, 2–3 minutes on each side. Remove meat from pan and pour off all but 2 tablespoons of oil. Add garlic and sauté 1 minute. Deglaze with wine. Bring to a rolling boil and reduce to half volume. Add stock, lemon juice, capers and lemon slices. Return chicken to pan and simmer 1–2 minutes or until heated thoroughly. Add butter and parsley, constantly swirling pan until a butter sauce is achieved. Remove from heat and serve over rice or pasta.

CHICKEN AND ANDOUILLE PASTA

Prep Time: 30 Minutes
Yields: 6 Servings

Comment:

This dish truly reflects the many cultures that contributed to the cuisine of South Louisiana. Chicken came with the Spanish and Germans in the late 1600s, andouille with the French in the mid 1700s and pasta with the Italians in the 1800s.

Ingredients:

5 boneless chicken breasts
1 cup diced andouille
¾ cup flour
½ cup olive oil
¼ cup diced onions
¼ cup diced celery
¼ cup diced yellow bell peppers
½ cup diced tomatoes
½ cup sliced mushrooms
¼ cup minced garlic
pinch of dried thyme
pinch of dried basil
1 ounce dry white wine
4 cups heavy whipping cream
salt and cayenne pepper to taste
¼ cup chopped parsley
3 cups cooked rotini pasta

Method:

Cut chicken breasts into 1-inch cubes, then season with salt and pepper. Dust lightly with flour and set aside. In a 10-inch heavy-bottomed saucepan, heat oil over medium-high heat. Sauté chicken until lightly browned on all sides. Add andouille, onions, celery, bell peppers, tomatoes, mushrooms and garlic. Sauté 3–5 minutes or until vegetables are wilted. Stir in thyme and basil then deglaze with white wine. Add heavy whipping cream and bring to a low boil, stirring occasionally. Allow cream to reduce and thicken to half volume. Season with salt and pepper. Add parsley and cooked pasta, blending well. Serve immediately.

CHICKEN PIE

Prep Time: 2 Hours
Yields: 8 Servings

Comment:

Entrée-type pies were prevalent in many cultures. Just as the English had shepherd's pies, the Cajuns had meat pies. This cooking technique enabled the plantation kitchen to make use of leftovers to create hearty, flavorful dishes.

Ingredients for Stock:

2 (3-pound) broiler chickens
1 large onion, quartered
2 celery stalks, chopped
6 cloves of garlic
1 bay leaf
sprig of thyme
10 black peppercorns

Method:

Preheat oven to 400°F. Cut chicken into quarters and place in a 2-gallon stockpot over medium-high heat. Add onions, celery, garlic, bay leaf, thyme and peppercorns. Cover chicken by 1 inch with lightly-salted water. Bring to a rolling boil, then reduce to simmer and cook 45 minutes or until chicken is tender. Remove chicken, bone and set meat aside. Return bones to pot. Simmer stock 15 minutes, strain and reserve 6 cups. Cube chicken and set aside.

Ingredients for Pie:

¾ cup butter
1 cup diced onions
1 cup diced celery
½ cup diced red bell peppers
¼ cup minced garlic
¾ cup flour
1½ quarts reserved stock
1 tbsp chopped thyme
1 tbsp chopped basil
1 tsp chopped sage
½ cup diced carrots
1 cup frozen peas
salt and cracked black pepper to taste
Louisiana hot sauce to taste
4 (9-inch) prepared pie crusts

Method:

In a heavy-bottomed Dutch oven, melt butter over medium-high heat. Add onions, celery, bell peppers and garlic. Sauté 3–5 minutes or until vegetables are wilted. Whisk in flour, stirring constantly until blond roux is achieved. (See roux recipes.) Slowly add stock, one ladle at a time. Blend in thyme, basil, sage, carrots and peas. Season with salt, pepper and hot sauce. Allow sauce to simmer 30 minutes. Remove and cool slightly. Fold chicken into sauce. Place pie crusts in 2 (9-inch) pie pans. Bake 5–10 minutes or until light brown. Fill baked crusts with chicken mixture. Cover each pie with remaining crust, seal edges and pierce with fork to vent steam. Bake 20 minutes or until golden brown. Any remaining chicken and gravy can be heated and served in a casserole dish.

Glenda Daigle feeds her chickens, Paincourtville, La.

CREOLE CHICKEN AND BISCUITS

Prep Time: 1½ Hours
Yields: 6 Servings

Comment:
In Cajun Country, leftover biscuits or French bread were often used as the starch in a meal. Here, traditional chicken fricassée is placed in homemade biscuits rather than over rice to create a new dish.

Ingredients for Stock:
1 (3-pound) fryer chicken, halved
2 carrots, sliced
1 onion, quartered
2 stalks celery, chopped
6 cloves garlic, mashed

Method:
Place halved chicken in a stockpot along with carrots, onions, celery and garlic. Add 2½ quarts cold water. Bring to a low boil then reduce to simmer. Cook 30–40 minutes or until chicken is tender but not falling apart. Strain and reserve 2 quarts of stock. Cool chicken, remove skin and bone. Chill stock and remove any fat that rises to the surface. Save stock and meat for later use.

Ingredients for Fricassée:
½ cup vegetable oil
½ cup flour
1½ cups diced onions
1 cup diced celery
½ cup diced red bell peppers
½ cup diced yellow bell peppers
¼ cup minced garlic
1 can Ro*tel tomatoes, drained
1 tsp chopped basil
1 tsp chopped thyme
2 quarts chicken stock (see above recipe)
1 bay leaf
1 cup sliced mushrooms
1 cup sliced green onions
salt and black pepper to taste
½ cup chopped parsley for garnish
6 Basic Buttermilk Biscuits (see recipe)

Method:
Preheat oven to 350°F. In a Dutch oven, heat oil over medium-high heat. Whisk in flour, stirring constantly until dark brown roux is achieved. (See roux recipes.) Sauté onions, celery, bell peppers and garlic in roux 3–5 minutes or until vegetables are wilted. Stir in Ro*tel tomatoes, basil and thyme. Add hot chicken stock, 1 cup at a time, until stew is slightly thick. Blend in bay leaf, mushrooms and half of green onions. Bring to a rolling boil, then reduce to simmer and cook 30 minutes. Place biscuits in oven to heat. Add chicken to Dutch oven. Season with salt and pepper. Stock or water may be added to retain stew-like consistency. Add remaining green onions, parsley and adjust seasonings if necessary. When hot, remove biscuits from oven and split in half. Place bottom half in the center of a 10-inch plate and top with a generous portion of chicken fricassée. Top with remaining biscuit half. Garnish with parsley.

FRENCH-ROASTED CHICKEN SANDWICH

Prep Time: 1½ Hours
Yields: 4 Servings

Comment:
This wonderful sandwich can be made from any type of oven-roasted or store-bought chicken. This method can also make a great after-holiday turkey sandwich. Substitute leftover turkey meat (both dark and white) in the place of chicken.

Ingredients:
1 (4-pound) roasted chicken, reserve pan drippings
  OR 1 deli-style rotisserie chicken
8 (½-inch thick) slices Italian or French bread
2 cups shredded lettuce
1 tomato, sliced
1 red onion, thinly sliced

Ingredients for Dressing:
¾ cup heavy-duty mayonnaise
¼ cup Creole mustard
¼ cup hot & spicy ketchup
1 tsp capers (drained)
½ tsp Louisiana hot sauce
1 tsp Worcestershire sauce
1 tsp lemon juice
2 tbsps minced red bell peppers
2 tbsps minced yellow bell peppers
¼ cup minced celery
1 tbsp finely minced garlic
2 tbsps minced parsley
salt and cracked black pepper to taste

Method:
Remove dark meat from chicken and finely chop. Slice breast meat against grain, cover with plastic wrap and set aside. Combine all dressing ingredients in a mixing bowl and blend well. Season with salt and pepper. In a separate bowl, combine dark meat with enough dressing mixture to coat. Cover and set aside. Remaining dressing can be refrigerated and used as a sandwich spread or seafood cocktail mix. Brush one side of each bread slice with reserved pan drippings. Grill or broil bread 1 minute. Divide dark meat chicken salad among 4 slices of grilled bread. Top with breast meat, lettuce, tomato and onion. Top with a second slice of grilled bread and cut in half.

BOUDIN-STUFFED FRENCH-ROASTED CHICKEN

Prep Time: 2 Hours
Yields: 6 Servings

Comment:
In Cajun Country, the combination of unlikely ingredients is commonplace. Stuffing a chicken, turkey or wild duck with boudin, the premier sausage of this region, gives a special Louisiana touch to a traditional French dish.

Ingredients:
2 pounds Boudin Blanc (see recipe)
2 (3-pound) broiler chickens
¼ pound butter
¼ cup chopped basil
¼ cup chopped thyme
¼ cup chopped sage
1 tbsp chopped tarragon
2 tbsps minced garlic
salt and cracked black pepper to taste
8 sage leaves
dash of Louisiana hot sauce

Method:
NOTE: If you do not wish to make the Boudin Blanc, buy white boudin from a butcher shop. Preheat oven to 375°F. Soften butter to room temperature and place in a large mixing bowl. Add basil, thyme, chopped sage, tarragon and garlic. Whisk until blended. Season inside cavity of chickens generously with salt and pepper. Remove casing from boudin and form into a ball. Divide boudin in half and place an equal amount in cavity of each chicken. Rub herbed butter over chicken, and gently lift skin of breasts and place a generous amount of butter under skin. Place 2 sage leaves under skin on each side of breasts. Season generously with salt and pepper. Add a dash of hot sauce. Tie legs together to keep them in place during cooking process. Place birds on a large baking sheet with a 1-inch lip. Roast uncovered 1–1½ hours, basting occasionally with drippings. Remove, place on a serving platter and let rest 15–20 minutes prior to carving. Garnish with whole fresh herbs.

CHICKEN BONNE FEMME

Prep Time: 2 Hours
Yields: 6–8 Servings

Comment:

This chicken and potato dish originated in the French Quarter during the mid-1900s. Though many variations exist today, this is the original.

Ingredients:

6 chicken quarters
  OR 2 (1½-pound) fryer chickens
4 large baking potatoes
salt and black pepper to taste
granulated garlic to taste
Louisiana hot sauce to taste
½ cup vegetable oil
juice of 1 lemon
½ pound sliced bacon
¼ cup vegetable oil
2 cups diced onions
1 (8-ounce) can sliced mushrooms, drained
¼ cup chopped parsley

Method:

Preheat oven to 350°F. Cut chicken into 8 quarters, rinse and drain. Peel potatoes and slice ¼-inch thick. Place potatoes in a bowl of ice water and set aside. Place chicken in a 3-inch deep baking pan. Season meat with salt, pepper, granulated garlic and hot sauce. Lay chicken skin-side down and brush with vegetable oil and lemon juice. Place 2 strips of bacon over each quarter and bake 30 minutes or until chicken is golden brown and bacon is crispy. Move bacon strips from time to time to ensure chicken browns evenly. Remove bacon and set aside. Turn chicken skin-side up, and brush with oil and lemon juice. Cover with additional strips of fresh bacon and continue to bake 20 minutes or until golden brown. Remove from oven, and remove chicken from pan. In a large bowl, combine potatoes, oil, onions and mushrooms. Season with salt, pepper and granulated garlic. Place potato mixture in bottom of baking pan and blend into drippings. Return chicken to pan, skin side up. Crumble bacon and sprinkle over chicken. Bake 15–20 minutes or until potatoes are tender and chicken is done. Place on a large serving platter and garnish with parsley.

BAKED GARLIC CHICKEN

Prep Time: 1–1½ Hours
Yields: 6 Servings

Comment:

One of the largest settlements in the city of New Orleans is Little Italy. The Italians operated the produce and truck farming industries in Louisiana. Often, garlic chicken was sold at the market by these farmers.

Ingredients:

2 young baking hens
salt and cracked black pepper to taste
16 cloves garlic
½ pound butter
1 small onion, quartered
1 celery stalk, halved
2 small carrots

Method:

Preheat oven to 350°F. Season hens inside and out with salt and pepper. Over-season inside of cavity since only a small amount of these spices will affect hen's flavor. Inside each cavity, place 4 cloves of garlic, ⅛-pound of butter and half of onions, celery and carrots. Place hens in a deep roasting pan. Rub each breast with remaining butter, garlic, onions, celery and carrots in bottom of roasting pan. Cover and bake 1 hour, basting occasionally. Once hens are tender, remove cover and allow to brown 15 minutes.

CHICKEN AND YAMS POINT HOUMAS

Prep Time: 1–1½ Hours
Yields: 6 Servings

Comment:

Point Houmas was the home camp of the Houmas Indians and is located 10 miles east of Donaldsonville, La. While Native Americans used yams as a full-course entrée, Cajuns and Creoles created many innovative dishes by making them the main ingredient in other recipes.

Ingredients:

1 (3-pound) fryer chicken
4 large yams
salt and cracked black pepper to taste
1 sweet Vidalia onion, sliced
¼ cup pecan halves
½ pound melted butter
¼ cup Creole mustard
½ cup Louisiana cane syrup
1 cup chicken stock
1 cup orange juice

Method:

Preheat oven to 375°F. Cut fryer into serving pieces, season with salt and pepper and set aside. Peel yams and slice into ¼-inch slices. Rinse under cold water and arrange yams and onions across bottom of a 4-quart baking dish. Season vegetables lightly with salt and pepper. Place chicken pieces on top of yams and sprinkle with pecan halves. In a small sauté pan, heat butter over medium-high heat. Add mustard, cane syrup, chicken stock and orange juice. Bring to a light boil then season with pepper. Generously spoon sauce over chicken and potatoes. Cover baking dish and bake 1 hour. Remove cover and bake 15 minutes or until chicken is brown and tender. NOTE: For faster cooking times, slightly parboil yams and use a smaller bird such as a Cornish hen.

OVEN-BARBECUED CHICKEN

Prep Time: 1–1½ Hours
Yields: 6–8 Servings

Comment:
If prepared properly, no one will know this "barbecue" was prepared in the oven. This technique was created by an old chef who loved barbecue, but whose health did not permit him to cook outdoors. This recipe allowed him to enjoy barbecued chicken anytime.

Ingredients:
2 (2½-pound) fryer chickens
½ cup melted butter
½ cup Worcestershire sauce
¼ cup Louisiana hot sauce
2 tbsps liquid smoke
salt and cracked black pepper to taste
granulated garlic to taste
1½ tbsps chili powder
1½ tbsps ground cumin
¾ cup brown sugar
1 cup water
1–1½ cups barbecue sauce

Method:
Preheat oven to 350°F. Cut chicken into serving pieces, rinse under cold water and set aside. Mix together all liquid ingredients. Coat chicken well with liquid mixture. Season chicken with salt, pepper and granulated garlic. Place it in a large baking pan with a 1-inch lip. Sprinkle chili powder and cumin on all sides of chicken. Turn chicken skin-side up and space evenly in pan. Rub an equal amount of brown sugar on each piece. Pour water into bottom of pan. Cover pan with foil then place on center rack of oven. Bake 45 minutes. Uncover and bake 10–15 minutes, basting with barbecue sauce until golden brown.

BRICKS AND MORTAR CHICKEN

Prep Time: 1½ Hours
Yields: 2–4 Servings

Comment:

The success of this recipe depends on the chicken having the proper amount of weight pressing the meat onto the hot skillet. Anything from an antique clothes iron to a smaller skillet filled with a jar of stones can be used for this process. To simplify the task, use a clay brick wrapped in foil.

Ingredients:

1 (3-pound) fryer chicken
2 sprigs rosemary, minced
½ tsp dried thyme
½ tsp dried basil
3 cloves garlic, minced
1 tsp kosher salt
1 tsp black pepper
½ tsp paprika
¼ cup extra virgin olive oil
juice of 1 lemon
½ cup vegetable oil
2 bricks wrapped in heavy foil

Method:

Using a sharp boning knife, split chicken lengthwise into 2 halves. Remove backbone, breastbone and first 2 joints from each wing. Rinse chicken well and pat dry. Place skin-side down on a large cookie sheet. In a small mixing bowl, combine rosemary, thyme, basil, garlic, salt, pepper, paprika, olive oil and lemon juice. Mix well. Spoon half of mixture over chicken, rubbing well into meat. Turn chicken and repeat process on other side, making sure to rub seasoning above and under skin. Cover chicken with plastic wrap and refrigerate a minimum of 4 hours, preferably overnight. Remove chicken from refrigerator and let sit 1 hour at room temperature. In a cast iron skillet, heat vegetable oil over medium-high heat. Place chicken in skillet, skin-side down. Immediately place 2 foil-covered bricks on top of chicken, pressing down to flatten. Let cook undisturbed for 15 minutes or until skin is crispy. Remove bricks, turn chicken and replace bricks. Continue cooking 12–15 minutes or until thigh meat is cooked. Depending on portion size, this recipe serves 4 quarters or 2 halves.

CHICKEN OREGANO

Prep Time: 2 Hours 15 Minutes
Yields: 4–6 Servings

Comment:

This delicacy is from Mosca's Italian restaurant on the West Bank of New Orleans. Mosca's made Italian food famous in that area and created many meat and seafood dishes using the technique from this recipe.

Ingredients:

1 large fryer chicken
4 tbsps chopped oregano
12 small garlic cloves
salt and black pepper to taste
Louisiana hot sauce to taste
granulated garlic to taste
paprika for color
¼ cup butter
¼ cup olive oil
1 cup chicken stock (optional)

Method:

Preheat oven to 350°F. Using a sharp boning knife, cut chicken into 8 serving pieces. If breasts are large, cut them in half, creating 2 additional serving pieces. In a large mixing bowl, season chicken generously with salt, pepper, hot sauce, granulated garlic and paprika. Allow chicken to sit at room temperature 1 hour prior to cooking. In a large cast iron skillet, heat butter and oil over medium-high heat. Sauté chicken until golden brown on both sides. Blend in garlic cloves and oregano. Cook 3–5 minutes then remove from heat. Cover with foil, place in oven and bake 45 minutes–1 hour. Remove foil and bake until browned.

CHICKEN IN BURGUNDY WINE

Prep Time: 1–1½ Hours
Yields: 6 Servings

Comment:

A classic Creole dish of the city of New Orleans, this recipe undoubtedly has its roots in French Coq au Vin. The introduction of fresh vegetables and the trinity of Cajun seasonings makes this a true Louisiana dish.

Ingredients:

1 (3-pound) fryer chicken
¾ cup bacon drippings
salt and cracked black pepper to taste
1 cup flour
2 cups diced onions
1 cup diced celery
1 cup diced bell peppers
¼ cup minced garlic
2 cups sliced carrots
1 cup diced new potatoes
2 cups small button mushrooms
1 cup diced tomatoes
1 bay leaf
½ tsp dried thyme
½ tsp dried basil
3 cups Burgundy wine

Method:

Preheat oven to 375°F. In a heavy-bottomed Dutch oven, melt bacon drippings over medium-high heat. Season chicken well with salt and pepper, and dust lightly with flour. Sauté chicken pieces, a few at a time until golden brown. Remove and keep warm. Place all remaining ingredients, except wine, in Dutch oven. Stir-fry 5–10 minutes or until vegetables are wilted. Return chicken to Dutch oven and place on top of sautéed vegetables. Add wine and season with salt and pepper. Cover and bake 45 minutes, stirring occasionally. Add a small amount of chicken stock if ingredients become too dry during cooking. Chicken and sauce may be served with white rice or on fettuccine.

SMOTHERED CHICKEN

Prep Time: 2 Hours
Yields: 6 Servings

Comment:
Here is another of the traditional South Louisiana chicken dishes. Unlike the more complex chicken stew, this dish is quicker to make and is cooked more often.

Ingredients:
1 (3-pound) fryer chicken
salt and cracked black pepper to taste
½ cup flour
¾ cup vegetable oil
½ cup diced onions
½ cup diced celery
¼ cup diced bell peppers
1 tbsp minced garlic
2 cups chicken stock (see recipe)
½ cup sliced green onions
½ cup chopped parsley

Method:
Cut fryer into serving pieces and season well with salt and pepper. Lightly coat chicken in flour then set aside. In a 1-gallon Dutch oven, heat oil over medium-high heat. Sauté chicken, a few pieces at a time until golden brown on all sides. Remove and set aside. Using same oil, sauté onions, celery, bell peppers and garlic 3–5 minutes or until vegetables are wilted. Place chicken on top of sautéed vegetables in Dutch oven. Add 1 cup of chicken stock and reduce heat to simmer. Cover and cook chicken 45 minutes. Stir occasionally, adding chicken stock if necessary. Season with salt and pepper. Add green onions and parsley. Continue to cook 45 minutes or until chicken is tender. Serve over jambalaya or as an entrée.

SMOTHERED CHICKEN WITH BUTTER BEANS

Prep Time: 1–1½ Hours
Yields: 6 Servings

Comment:
My grandfather grew beans of every variety in his garden on Cabanocey Plantation. We all anticipated getting some of his fresh butter beans. I vividly remember the eight Folse children circling a large washtub to shell the fresh limas. These beans went into everything from shrimp dishes to casseroles, including this favorite.

Ingredients:
1 (3-pound) fryer chicken
4 cups fresh butter beans
¼ cup oil
¼ cup flour
1 cup diced onions
1 cup diced red bell peppers
¼ cup minced garlic
3 cups chicken stock (see recipe)
salt and black pepper to taste
½ cup sliced green onions

Method:
Cut fryer into 8 serving pieces. Rinse, drain and set aside. In a cast iron Dutch oven, heat oil over medium-high heat. Whisk in flour until light brown roux is achieved. (See roux recipes.) Add onions, bell peppers and garlic. Sauté 3–5 minutes or until vegetables are wilted. Blend in chicken and cook 5–10 minutes or until well seared. Pour in chicken stock and blend well. Additional stock or water may be necessary to achieve a stew-like consistency. Add butter beans and season with salt and pepper. Bring to a rolling boil, then reduce to simmer and cook 30–45 minutes. Add green onions and adjust seasonings if necessary. Serve over steamed white rice.

CHRISTMAS CAPON

Prep Time: 3½ Hours
Yields: 6–8 Servings

Comment:

Capon is a castrated rooster that has been cooked in many dishes since the time of the Greeks and Romans. This bird is known for its oversized meaty breast and tender, super-moist texture. The French community in Louisiana often serves capon for Christmas dinner.

Ingredients:

1 (4–6-pound) capon with giblets
salt and black pepper to taste
½ cup softened butter
4 tbsps chopped basil
2 tbsps chopped thyme
4 tbsps chopped tarragon
1 tbsp chopped rosemary
3 tbsps minced garlic
4 basil leaves

2 medium onions, quartered
2 celery stalks, chopped
2 red apples, diced
2 green apples, diced
1 tbsp flour
½ cup white wine
2 cups chicken stock
granulated garlic to taste

Method:

If frozen, thaw bird in refrigerator for 2 days. Preheat oven to 375°F. Rinse bird under cold running water. Place capon in center of roasting pan or Dutch oven and season generously with salt and pepper, inside and out. In a small bowl, blend softened butter, chopped herbs and garlic. Rub herb paste under breast skin and distribute evenly over outer skin and inside cavity. Remaining paste should be placed in pan around base of bird. Place 2 basil leaves under skin of each breast. Surround capon with giblets, vegetables and apples. Cover tightly with foil or lid of Dutch oven and roast 1½ hours. Uncover, reduce oven temperature to 350°F and cook until golden brown on all sides. Do not overcook or meat will dry out. Capon is done when internal temperature reaches 175°F. Remove bird from roasting pan, cover with a foil "tent" and allow to rest, keeping warm. Keep all giblets and seasonings in pan. Pour all but 2 tablespoons of drippings into a bowl and let sit. Stir flour into pan, place over high heat and deglaze with wine. Add stock, stirring constantly, to create a sauce naturale. Skim all fat from surface of reserved drippings. Add skimmed drippings to sauce. Season with salt, pepper and granulated garlic. Serve sauce with sliced capon.

SMOTHERED TURKEY NECKS IN ONION GRAVY

Prep Time: 2½ Hours
Yields: 6–8 Servings

Comment:
Stews and gumbos made with turkey necks are often served at large family gatherings in Louisiana. Many of our Creole cultures take credit for this dish, but it was probably created by the African Americans who knew how to make masterful dishes out of lesser-used ingredients.

Ingredients:
8 turkey necks
salt and black pepper to taste
Louisiana hot sauce to taste
½ cup bacon drippings
2 cups sliced onions
1 cup diced celery
1 cup diced red bell peppers
¼ cup minced garlic
¼ cup flour
2 tbsps Worcestershire sauce
1½ quarts beef or chicken stock (see recipes)
1 cup sliced green onions
¼ cup chopped parsley

Method:
Necks are usually sold already cut into 6-inch sections. If packaged whole, cut necks in half for easier handling. Season meat well with salt, pepper and hot sauce. Preheat oven to 400°F. In a large Dutch oven, heat bacon drippings over medium-high heat. Brown necks, cooking larger ends first. Cook each batch until necks are golden brown on all sides. Regulate heat to prevent bacon fat from burning. Remove necks and keep warm. In same Dutch oven, sauté onions, celery, bell peppers and garlic 3–5 minutes or until vegetables are wilted. Blend in flour to help thicken finished sauce. Add Worcestershire sauce and 1 quart of stock. Blend well and bring to a rolling boil. Reduce heat to simmer then add turkey. Make sure stock covers necks half way. Add more stock if necessary. Return mixture to a rolling boil then top with green onions and parsley. Cover, place in oven and bake 2 hours. Check for tenderness at 1½ hours. Continue baking until meat is tender enough to fall from bones. Serve over steamed white rice or alongside whipped potatoes.

TURKEY HASH IN PUFF PASTRY

Prep Time: 45 Minutes
Yields: 5–6 Servings

Comment:
The turkey and ham can be taken from leftovers remaining from Thanksgiving Day dinner. However, in most supermarket deli cases, these items may be found at any time. Feel free to substitute chicken or any other fowl in place of turkey.

Ingredients:
3 cups diced turkey
3 cups diced ham
¾ cup vegetable oil
¾ cup flour
2 cups diced onions
1 cup diced celery
½ cup diced red bell peppers
½ cup diced green bell peppers
1 tbsp minced garlic
2 quarts chicken stock (see recipe)
2 tbsps chopped basil
1 tbsp chopped thyme
2 cups diced potatoes
1 cup diced carrots
1 cup sliced green onions
¼ cup chopped parsley
salt and black pepper to taste

Method:
In a cast iron pot, heat oil over medium-high heat. Whisk in flour, stirring constantly until light brown roux is achieved. (See roux recipes.) Sauté onions, celery, bell peppers and garlic in roux 3–5 minutes or until vegetables are wilted. Blend in meats and mix well. Add hot stock, 1 ladle at a time, to reach a stew-like consistency. Stir in basil and thyme. Bring to a rolling boil, reduce to simmer and cook 15 minutes. Add potatoes, carrots, green onions and parsley. Return to simmer and season with salt and pepper. Cook until potatoes are tender. Add more stock if necessary to retain stew-like consistency.

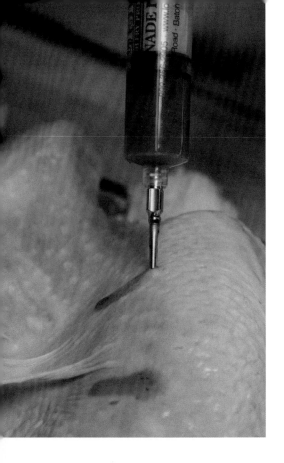

DEEP-FRIED TURKEY

Prep Time: 1½ Hours
Yields: 8–10 Servings

Comment:
Most hardware stores in Louisiana carry a special pot for deep-frying turkeys. This pot not only enables you to use less oil, approximately 3 gallons, but also includes an apparatus specially designed to lift the turkey out of the pot. Numerous companies in Louisiana, such as Cajun Injector, make prepared marinades and even the injector itself for seasoning turkeys. Injecting the bird immediately prior to frying creates the same level of flavor as preparing it the night before.

Ingredients:
1 (16-pound) turkey	salt and black pepper to taste
3 gallons peanut oil	cayenne pepper to taste
8 ounces Italian dressing	onion powder to taste
Louisiana hot sauce to taste	garlic powder to taste
Worcestershire sauce to taste	celery salt to taste

Method:
Outdoors, in a turkey frying pot over a propane burner, preheat oil to 350°F. Use a candy thermometer to verify temperature. In a blender or food processor, combine all seasoning ingredients with Italian dressing and ½ cup water. Blend 2–3 minutes to liquefy dried seasonings. Inject seasoning 2–3 times into each breast and upper thigh. Using handles included in frying set, slowly submerge turkey, 2–3 inches at a time. Maintain a frying temperature of 335–350°F. Cook 3 minutes per pound or until internal temperature of breast reaches 150–155°F, approximately 50 minutes for 16 pounds. Remove turkey from oil, cover or wrap in foil and allow to rest 30 minutes prior to slicing. When oil has cooled, strain through a cheesecloth. Oil may be bottled and refrigerated for later use and can be reused 3–4 times.

ROASTED TURKEY

Prep Time: 4 Hours
Yields: 10–12 Servings

Comment:
When planning a dinner, remember that one pound of uncooked turkey will feed one person. Allow bird to defrost in the refrigerator for approximately two days prior to roasting.

Ingredients:
1 (15-pound) turkey	4 cups diced onions
salt and cracked black pepper to taste	2 cups diced celery
granulated garlic to taste	2 cups diced carrots
¼ pound butter, softened	3 oranges, quartered
2 tbsps minced garlic	8 whole cloves garlic
6 basil leaves	paprika for color

Method:
Preheat oven to 350°F. Remove giblets from neck cavity. If a wire retainer is holding legs in place, remove it prior to seasoning bird. Rinse turkey well, inside and out, with cold water. Place in a roasting pan and season generously, inside and out, with salt, pepper and granulated garlic. Extra seasoning should be placed inside cavity. Blend butter and garlic, and rub mixture under breast skin. Place 3 basil leaves under skin on each side of breast. Stuff half of onions, celery, carrots, oranges and garlic inside bird and place remaining half in baking pan. Squeeze juice of 2 orange quarters over turkey breast. Rub paprika evenly on breasts and legs. Tie legs in place with butcher's twine, then cover roasting pan tightly with foil. Bake approximately 3½ hours then remove foil and check meat. Turkey is done when legs pull away easily and internal temperature reaches 170°F. Remove cover and allow turkey to brown 30 minutes. It is best to allow bird to rest 30–45 minutes prior to carving. Serve turkey with natural drippings, or strain drippings and thicken with a light roux. A turkey usually requires a cooking time of 12–15 minutes per pound.

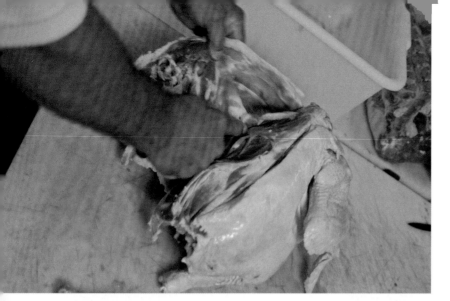

Step 1: Bone turkey beginning at backbone.

Step 2: Continue until carcass can be removed intact, without piercing breast skin. Lay meat flat on board and season to taste.

Step 4: Proceed to bone duck following the above procedures. Season well.

Step 5: Birds are ready for stuffing procedure.

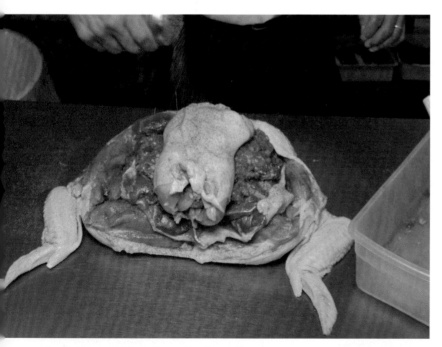

Step 7: Season each layer thoroughly after stuffing.

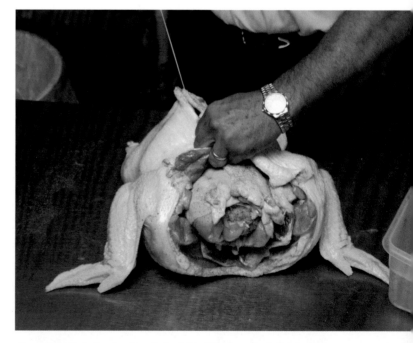

Step 8: Sew the turkey closed on the backside. This places the turkey back into its natural form.

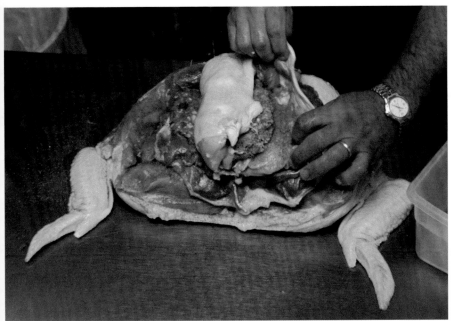

Step 3: Proceed to bone chicken in same fashion as turkey. Lay flat and season thoroughly.

TURDUCKEN

Comment:

Turducken is a Louisiana dish that combines three types of poultry. A whole turkey is stuffed with a whole duck which is stuffed with a whole chicken. The bones are removed from all of the birds, and various stuffings are used to separate the layers of meat. Preparing a turducken on your own is quite a task, so it is recommended that you purchase an uncooked one from a specialty shop and roast it at home. In Louisiana, you can find turducken at Hebert's Specialty Meats in Maurice (337) 893-5062 or at Chris' Specialty Meats in Baton Rouge (225) 755-1783.

Method:

Normally, turducken are sold frozen. It will take 4–5 days to defrost in a refrigerator or 6–9 hours in cold tap water. Your meat supply shop should provide detailed instructions on how to prepare the bird. After defrosting, remove any packaging. Preheat oven to 375°F. Place turducken in a large covered roasting pan. Cook 15–18 minutes per pound. A 10-pound bird will take about 3 hours. Uncover and brown 1 additional hour. NOTE: It is also recommended to turn turducken breast-side down to brown. However, be extremely careful, as bird is very heavy and difficult to handle. Turducken is done when internal temperature reaches 165°F. Allow to cool at room temperature 30 minutes prior to carving. The meat will be quite delicate so take care when removing from pan. It is best to first slice in half then slice each side perpendicular to original cut. A gravy can be made with natural drippings. Turducken may be made a day in advance and refrigerated. Reheat in a 250°F oven 1½ hours.

Step 6: Place stuffing over turkey and continue with duck and chicken. Each bird should be stuffed prior to final seasoning and sewing.

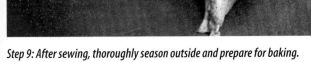

Step 9: After sewing, thoroughly season outside and prepare for baking.

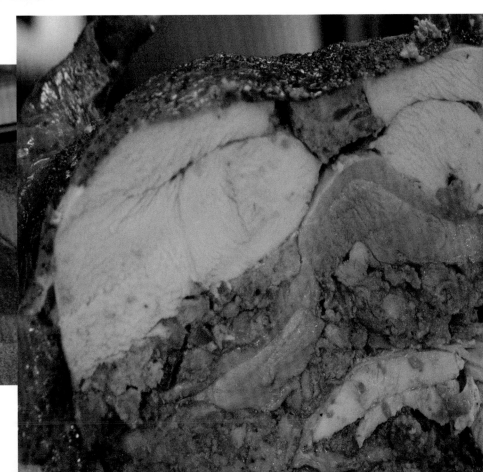

Meat

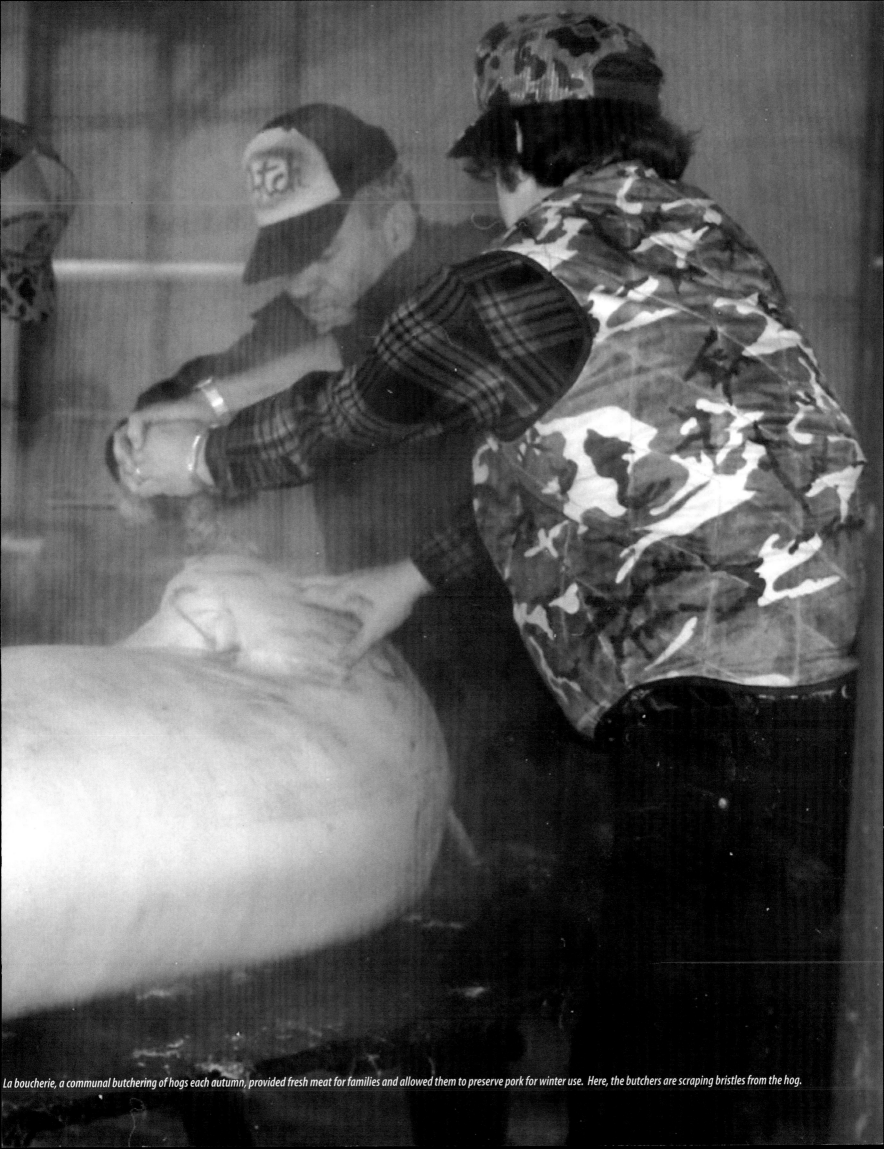

La boucherie, a communal butchering of hogs each autumn, provided fresh meat for families and allowed them to preserve pork for winter use. Here, the butchers are scraping bristles from the hog.

While modern Cajun and Creole cuisine has now made a place for veal and lamb, the original recipes were focused on beef, pork and smoked meat. Until the German settlers established their vacheries (French for cattle farm), beef was scarce, and the cuisine reflected it. Cajun and Creole cooks created dishes that stretched small amounts of meat to feed their families and added seasonings and vegetables to disguise poor quality cuts. In their frugality, South Louisianians even incorporated trimmings and organ meat with brown roux and wild mushrooms to make a hearty dish known as "debris." Smoked meats were relied upon, because smoking was one of the few methods of preservation available.

If it weren't for the early German settlements, beef probably would not have found as much prominence in the Cajun and Creole diet. But Antoine Folse and others like him used the land near Lake Des Allemands, granted to them by the Spanish government, to establish vacheries. The Germans also shared their own knowledge of butchering and charcuterie (sausage-making) with their neighbors and influenced some of the products associated with the Cajun la boucherie.

Pork was not only more plentiful and popular in Creole and Cajun kitchens but was also central to the Cajun tradition of a community butchering or la boucherie. The communal butchering of hogs (and sometimes cows) was born of necessity and developed into the main social event throughout the fall and winter. It was extremely difficult for one family to do all of the work and make use of all of the meat from the slaughter of a hog without waste or spoilage. To aid in the tremendous task of butchering and processing a pig or cow, the extended Cajun family would gather with other friends and family as well as expert butchers. This was known as la boucherie de compagnie. The lack of refrigeration and the value of each animal made it essential that the process was efficient, fair and that nothing was wasted. With la boucherie each family was guaranteed a steady supply of fresh meat no matter whose hog was being slaughtered. The spirit of cooperation and the inevitable feast afterward soon turned the occasion into a social event, complete with a fais do do, or party, in the evening spiced with music and dancing.

Weeks prior to the special day, the hogs designated for butchering were sectioned off and put on a straight diet of corn. Weighing as much as 800 pounds, anywhere from three to six could be killed on one day. With as many as 20 families working hand in hand, it was not unusual to have 150 men, women and children involved in the preparations and work. In later years, the gathering would include several African-American families who shared in the

Several 800-pound hogs might be killed in one day during the boucherie.

division of the meat because of their butchering expertise.

The evening before the event, the men and boys gathered to plan and set up for the following day. The boys collected firewood, and the men set up the huge, well-oiled and seasoned black iron pots on bricks so a fire could be laid underneath. The pots were filled with water, which would later be boiled for scalding the bristles from the hog and sterilizing the meat. While the boys hurried about they listened to the stories, jokes and cooking tips the men shared over handfuls of salted "graton" or cracklings from a previous boucherie. While the boys considered it fun, they were also unwittingly absorbing these tales and traditions to pass on to the next generation. Once the preparations were complete, both men and boys retired early in order to rise before dawn to light the fires and kill the hogs.

In the morning the hogs were slaughtered. The jugular vein was cut, and the women collected the blood in washtubs. Vinegar and salt were added to prevent coagulation, and the tubs were covered with sheets. This "sang de porc" (pig's blood) would be used later in the preparation of boudin rouge, a Cajun delicacy. Made with cooked pork and rice, this Cajun blood sausage is descended from a similar sausage still prepared in France. While one team of women washed and chopped the onions, celery, bell peppers, garlic, green onions and parsley for the many dishes that would arise from the day's work, others cleaned the hogs. Boiling water from the black iron pots was poured over the pigs and the skin scraped clean of bristles. The hogs were then hauled over tree branches with the help of mules. They were slit from jaw to tail so the women could gather the entrails. The intestines were separated from the "hook-up," which consisted of the kidneys, liver, heart, lungs and tongue. The intestines would be cleaned by hand, thoroughly washed inside and out, scraped until clear and soaked in baking soda and cold water. They would later serve an important role as the casings for andouille, boudin and saucisse. The "hook-up" was slowly simmered in a rich brown gravy and seasoned with onions, celery, bell peppers and green onions, to create a soul-satisfying dish called "debris," which fed the workers throughout the day. The evening meal would consist of grillades, which were thin slices of meat trimmed from the neck and backbone, cooked down with vegetables and mushrooms, then served over grits and pork and andouille jambalaya. Small round meat patties or platines were seasoned, wrapped in caul fat and fried. They were served on top of jambalaya or white beans and rice.

Boiling water is poured over the slaughtered hog to make removing the bristles an easier task.

Central to the spirit of la boucherie was that nothing was wasted. Fresh pork was cut into roasts, chops and ribs; tasso and andouille were smoked; and hams were cured in a sugar brine and then smoked. The head and feet of the hog were simmered with lean trimmings, vegetables and seasonings for hours. The tender meat was removed from the pot, finely diced and put in molds. The liquid was reduced, seasoned and then poured over the meat and cooled until jelled. The resulting hogs head cheese is still a delicacy today. The skin of the hog was also used. A one-inch layer of fat and skin was removed from the pig, cut in squares and placed in No. 25 pots with a few cups of cold water. As the water boiled, the lard was rendered from the fat, and the gratons or crackling would brown in the lard. Once golden brown, the cracklings were squeezed of excess grease and drained. When salted they became a delicious traditional snack. The lard was reserved in five-gallon tin cans for future baking and cooking. The reserved and cleaned intestines would be stuffed using boudinieres or four-inch cow horns to make sausages, boudin and andouille. A string of boudins and sausages would often be placed in the five-gallon cans of hot lard. Once the lard cooled, the boudin would be fully cooked and preserved.

Once the work was done, knives and pots were traded for fiddles, squeeze boxes (Cajun accordians), scrub boards and triangles, and the fais do do or party could begin. While the term fais do do has come to refer to any Cajun party, it is believed that the name originally came about at the boucherie when, before the dancing began, the mothers would tell their children to "faire do do" or "go to sleep." After an evening of French songs and dancing, the families retired with the bounty of la boucherie and stories to share at the next one.

On the day of la boucherie and on any other when the meat supply was more plentiful than needed, smoking was a necessary part of Cajun and Creole culture. There was no refrigeration, and Louisiana's mild winters, though welcome, offered little help for food preservation. As is true of so much of this region's cuisine, the Cajuns and Creoles turned necessity into delicacy. Smoked tasso and andouille sausage are now highly prized ingredients in many recipes, but at the time were just a product of the need to preserve the fruits of the boucherie. In addition to making sausage and ham, smoking was also used to preserve other meats and game, so they would be available for later use. The results were so delicious the tradition continued long beyond the need.

Butchers portion the pork.

Making cracklin'

Although today there are not so many Cajun butchers and refrigeration has rendered community sharing of meat unnecessary, there are still boucheries. Special events such as Memorial Day, Labor Day or even tailgating parties can be reason enough to recreate a traditional boucherie very much like the old days. The resulting gratons, andouille, grillades, jambalaya and hogs head cheese are still just as delicious. Even if you are unsuccessful in finding a boucherie to attend, all of the ingredients are available, and the recipes are right here.

Our own family boucherie would have sorely missed the skills of the brothers Shank and Pelank and their good friend Grippy. These three African-American men and their families not only provided some of the finest butchering expertise in St. James Parish, but they truly symbolized the camaraderie of the boucherie. They worked hard but always had time for fun and pranks. They brought music and laughter to the day's labors and were an essential part of the team. At the end of the day, they took home their share of the fruits of the boucherie.

PECAN RICE DRESSING

Prep Time: 1 Hour
Yields: 8–10 Servings

Comment:

Pecan rice dressing is found on most holiday tables in South Louisiana. It incorporates the best ingredients of Bayou Country including seafood, meat and nuts. This recipe has been a tradition for more than 150 years.

Ingredients:

½ cup chopped pecans
6 cups steamed white rice
6 chicken livers
1 pound ground beef
1 pound ground pork
¼ pound butter
1 cup diced onions
1 cup diced celery
1 cup diced green bell peppers
¼ cup diced red bell peppers
2 tbsps minced garlic
1 pint select oysters in liquid
½ cup sliced green onions
½ cup chopped parsley
salt and cracked black pepper to taste

Method:

In a small sauté pan, poach chicken livers in lightly-salted water. Allow to cool, chop and reserve poaching liquid. In a large, heavy-bottomed sauté pan, melt butter over medium-high heat. Sauté ground beef and pork 30 minutes or until golden brown and grains of meat are totally separated. Stir in chopped chicken livers, onions, celery, bell peppers and garlic. Continue to sauté 30 minutes or until vegetables are cooked. If necessary, add reserved poaching liquid to moisten mixture. Stir in oysters and oyster liquid. As oysters cook, chop them into meat mixture with edge of cooking spoon until they are almost cooked away. Season with salt and pepper. Stir in rice. Garnish with green onions, parsley and pecans. Adjust seasonings if necessary. Serve as a rice casserole or use as a stuffing for turkey or duck.

CREOLE DIRTY RICE

Prep Time: 2 Hours
Yields: 6–8 Servings

Comment:

This Creole dish is much better known in New Orleans than in the bayous. The name dirty rice was given to the dish because of the dark color that results from the addition of liver and giblets.

Ingredients:

6 cups steamed white rice
½ pound chicken giblets
½ pound chicken livers
½ cup butter
1 cup diced onions
1 cup diced celery
1 cup diced bell peppers
2 tbsps minced garlic
1 cup chicken stock (see recipe)
½ cup sliced green onions
½ cup chopped parsley
salt and cracked black pepper to taste

Method:

In a small saucepot, poach giblets in lightly-salted water 45 minutes or until tender. Remove and cool, reserving poaching liquid. Chop giblets into tiny pieces and remove all tough membrane. Set aside. In a large heavy-bottomed sauté pan, melt butter over medium-high heat. Sauté livers 15–20 minutes or until golden brown on all sides. Remove livers from pan, and place on a chopping board to cool. In same pan, sauté onions, celery, bell peppers and garlic 3–5 minutes or until wilted. Coarsely chop livers. Return livers and giblets to pan. Pour in chicken stock and a small amount of poaching liquid. Bring to a low boil and cook until volume of liquid is reduced to approximately ¼ cup. Fold in rice and garnish with green onions and parsley. Season with salt and pepper.

SHOEPEG CORN BREAD STUFFING

Prep Time: 2–2½ Hours
Yields: 6 Servings

Comment:
Most often in South Louisiana, meat and oyster dressings are found as accompaniments on the holiday table. Bread or corn bread stuffings are definitely a Southern tradition, but are seldom seen in Bayou Country. As an added flavor enhancer, add 1 pint of shucked oysters with liquid to the pot during the final cooking phase.

Ingredients:
1 cup yellow cornmeal
1 (11-ounce) can shoepeg corn
½ cup flour
2 tsps baking powder
1 tsp salt
2 tbsps sugar
1 egg
5 tbsps melted butter
¾ cup milk
4 chicken leg quarters
½ cup diced onions
½ cup diced celery
½ cup diced red bell peppers
1 tbsp minced garlic
¼ tsp rubbed sage
⅛ tsp dried basil leaves
⅛ tsp dried thyme
¼ cup minced pimientos
¼ cup sliced green onions
¼ cup chopped parsley
1 pint oysters with liquid (optional)
salt and black pepper to taste

Method:
Preheat oven to 375°F. In a mixing bowl, combine cornmeal, flour, baking powder, salt and sugar. In a separate bowl, whisk egg, 2 tablespoons melted butter and milk. Add egg mixture to cornmeal and blend well. Pour corn bread batter into a well-greased 9-inch cake pan and bake 15–20 minutes. Remove and cool. Separate chicken legs from thighs. In a 2-quart stockpot, combine chicken, onions, celery, bell peppers and garlic. Cover with 6 cups of cold water, bring to a rolling boil, then reduce to simmer. Cook 30–40 minutes or until chicken is tender and falling from bones. Remove chicken and allow to cool. Retain stock and seasoning. Bone and finely chop cooled chicken. Return meat to pot with stock and seasonings. Stir in shoepeg corn, sage, basil, thyme, butter, pimientos, green onions and parsley. Bring to a rolling boil, reduce to simmer and cook 15 minutes. If desired, add oysters and liquid. Cook 2 minutes longer. Strain stock and reserve 3 cups. Crumble corn bread into a large mixing bowl. Season reserved stock with salt and pepper. Add chicken and seasonings to crumbled corn bread along with 2½ cups of seasoned stock. Stir until well-blended. Stuffing should be very moist, but not watery. If desired, use unbaked stuffing to stuff roasts, such as Crown Roast of Pork. (See recipe.) To serve as a side, pour mixture back into cake pan and drizzle with 3–4 tablespoons of stock. Bake uncovered 20–30 minutes or until it begins to brown lightly around edges. Stuffing may be made the evening before cooking, but should be baked immediately prior to serving. Do not overcook as it will tend to dry out.

Ingredients for Sweet Farre Dressing

SWEET FARRE DRESSING

Prep Time: 3–3½ Hours
Yields: 8–10 Servings

Comment:

Farre is a meat dressing brought to Louisiana by the Germans. In many Cajun and German communities of the River Road west of New Orleans, farre was often seen as a sandwich spread at weddings, parties and funerals. This is one of our many variations, which includes sweet potatoes and is undoubtedly from the German Coast of Louisiana.

Ingredients:

12 cups shredded sweet potatoes
1½ pounds ground beef
1½ pounds ground pork
½ pound chicken livers
1 quart chicken stock (see recipe)
2 cups diced onions
1 cup diced celery

½ cup diced green bell peppers
¼ cup diced red bell peppers
2 tbsps minced garlic
1 cup sliced green onions
½ cup chopped parsley
salt and black pepper to taste
Louisiana hot sauce to taste

Method:

In a cast iron skillet, sauté ground beef and pork over medium-high heat. Cook 30 minutes, chopping occasionally until meat is golden brown and grains are separated. This process is extremely important, as the slow browning method will increase flavor in the finished dish. While meat is browning, poach livers in chicken stock for approximately 20 minutes. Drain livers and reserve stock for later use. Once meat is browned, add livers, onions, celery, bell peppers, garlic and sweet potatoes. Sauté 12–15 minutes or until vegetables are wilted. Using side of cooking spoon, chop livers into meat mixture. Reduce heat to simmer, and add stock as necessary to retain moisture. Simmer 2 hours, stirring occasionally until meat is extremely tender and sweet potatoes have disappeared. Continue to add stock as needed. Stir in green onions and parsley. Season with salt, pepper and hot sauce. The final consistency should be soft and tender. This dish can be mixed with an equal amount of cooked white rice and used as a stuffing or dressing.

RUTH FERTEL'S PLAQUEMINES PARISH OYSTER DRESSING

Prep Time: 1½ Hours
Yields: 15–20 Servings

Comment:

Oyster dressing is a classic dish that is served on virtually every Thanksgiving table in Plaquemines Parish. This magnificent recipe is from the famous founder of Ruth's Chris Steak House, Ruth Fertel.

Ingredients:

1 gallon oysters with liquid	¼ cup minced garlic
¼ pound butter	12 chicken bouillon cubes
1 pound smoked sausage, minced	salt and black pepper to taste
1 pound hot pork sausage, minced	red pepper flakes to taste
3 cups diced onions	3 (30-inch) loaves stale French bread
2 cups diced celery	1 dozen eggs, beaten
2 cups diced green bell peppers	1 pound melted butter
1 cup diced red bell peppers	

Method:

Pour oysters with liquid into a large pan and examine carefully, removing any partial shells. Heat oysters until edges curl. Drain, reserve liquid and set aside. When oysters are cool to touch, chop coarsely and set aside. In a large Dutch oven, melt ¼ pound butter over medium-high heat. Sauté sausages until fat is rendered. Add onions, celery, bell peppers and garlic. Sauté 3–5 minutes or until vegetables are wilted. Stir in chopped oysters, oyster liquid and bouillon cubes. Bring to a rolling boil, reduce to simmer and cook 5 minutes. Season with salt, pepper and red pepper flakes. Preheat oven to 350°F. Chop bread into 1-inch cubes. Stir bread into oyster mixture, 2 cups at a time, until enough bread has been added to absorb liquid but mixture is still moist. Remove from heat and blend in eggs and remaining melted butter. Pour into a large baking pan, cover with foil and bake 1 hour. Remove foil and brown 15 minutes.

FRIED OYSTER DRESSING

Prep Time: 2½ Hours
Yields: 10–12 Servings

Comment:

While it is unusual to include a fried seafood item in a dressing, Louisianians have been known to try anything to enhance flavors in their cooking. This dish contains fried oysters as well as many of the classic items found in Creole cooking, including chicken giblets and livers.

Ingredients:

2 dozen select oysters	1 tsp chopped basil
1 pint chicken livers	salt and black pepper to taste
1 cup giblets (from fowl)	Louisiana hot sauce to taste
¼ cup vegetable oil	1 cup vegetable oil
2 cups diced onions	1 cup cornmeal
2 cups diced celery	4 cups cooked rice
1 cup diced bell peppers	1 egg, beaten
¼ cup minced garlic	½ cup sliced green onions
1 bay leaf	¼ cup chopped parsley
1 tsp chopped thyme	

Method:

NOTE: If desired, 1 cup of ground pork may be substituted for giblets. Place giblets in a saucepot and cover by 2 inches with lightly-salted water. Bring to a rolling boil then reduce to simmer. Cover and cook 1 hour or until fork tender. Add water if necessary. Remove cooked giblets, chop and set aside. In same liquid, poach livers 3–5 minutes. Strain, retaining stock. Chop livers and set aside. In a 10-inch sauté pan, heat ¼ cup vegetable oil over medium-high heat. Sauté livers and giblets 3–5 minutes. Add poaching liquid if mixture becomes too dry during sautéing. Stir in onions, celery, bell peppers and garlic. Continue to sauté, stirring occasionally, 10–15 minutes or until vegetables are wilted. Pour in 1 cup retained stock then add bay leaf. Cook 10–15 minutes. Meat should be moist but not runny. Stir in thyme, basil, salt, pepper and hot sauce. Add more stock if necessary. While mixture is simmering, heat 1 cup of vegetable oil in a 10-inch cast iron skillet over medium-high heat. Dredge oysters in cornmeal and fry, a few at a time, until golden brown. Drain on paper towels and keep warm. Stir rice, beaten egg, green onions and parsley into giblet mixture, stirring quickly to coat rice with all seasonings. Gently fold in fried oysters and adjust seasonings if necessary. Serve as a side dish to any roasted fowl or as a stuffing for turkeys or ducks.

HOG CRACKLING

Prep Time: 2 Hours
Yields: 70–80 (1-pound) Bags

Comment:

This recipe comes from Poche's in Breaux Bridge, La. Crackling (more commonly called "cracklins") is pork rind, fried until crisp. Anyone raised in rural Louisiana can probably remember the taste of "cracklins fresh out of the grease." For you dieters, crackling is one of the tastiest, most satisfying zero-carb snacks of all time!

Ingredients:

1 quart hog lard or water
10 pounds skin-on hog fat cut into 1-inch cubes
salt to taste

Method:

In a 10-quart cast iron pot, place hog lard or water over medium-high heat. Add pork fat and stir occasionally to begin rendering fat. Continue stirring often to prevent sticking. As fat renders, crackling will begin to float and brown. When this occurs, lower heat slightly so as not to burn. Cook until crackling begins to pop occasionally and crack slightly. The fatty portion of cracklings should be well rendered, and skin should be tender and bubbly in appearance. Remove with a slotted spoon and drain on paper towels. While still hot, salt to taste. Crackling is better served fresh but can keep well for a short time in a tightly sealed container. After lard (or grease) left over from cooking is cooled, strain and pour it into jars to save for baking or biscuit making. NOTE: For a spicy alternative, toss cooked crackling in 1 cup vinegar and season with salt and cayenne pepper.

BOUDIN BLANC

Prep Time: 3 Hours
Yields: 125 Links

Comment:

Boudin Blanc, the Cajun pork and rice sausage, is without a doubt the best-known sausage in South Louisiana. The use of rice and extra spice make Louisiana boudin much different from those of France. Boudin is a delicious by-product of the boucherie, and it is well worth the extra effort. Serve boudin cold as a Cajun canapé, or hot as a breakfast item.

Ingredients:

10 pounds Boston butt, cubed
2 pounds pork liver
1 pound green onions
1 pound parsley
8 ounces salt
6 tbsps cayenne pepper
4 tbsps black pepper
6 pounds cooked white rice
½ gallon cold water
1 cup chopped pimientos
75 feet sausage casing

Method:

Using a home-style meat grinder, alternately grind meat, liver, green onions and parsley. Season ground ingredients with salt and peppers. Place mixture into a large mixing bowl then add cooked white rice, water and pimientos. Using both hands, blend until all is incorporated. NOTE: It is always a good idea to cook a small piece of sausage mixture to test seasonings before stuffing casing. Using a sausage stuffer, fill casing and twist into 6-inch links. Place boudin links into a home-style steamer, cover and cook 45 minutes or until sausage is firm.

WHITE BOUDIN CHICOT

Prep Time: 3 Hours
Yields: 40–50 (6-inch) Links

Comment:

This recipe was first discovered at Landry's Meat Market near Chicot State Park outside of Opelousas, La. Although Landry's is now closed, their wonderful boudin is still touted by many to be the best in the state.

Ingredients:

10 pounds fresh picnic shoulder, cubed 1-inch
1½ pounds pork liver
4 large onions, peeled and halved
3 cups medium grain rice, raw
3 bunches green onions, tops only, sliced
3 cups reserved stock
salt and black pepper to taste
25 feet (28–30mm) hog casing

Method:

In a large stockpot, place pork shoulder and cover with 6 inches cold water. Bring to a rolling boil then reduce to high simmer. Cook 1½ hours. While meat boils, cook White Rice. (See recipe.) Add pork liver to stockpot then return to a boil and cook 30 minutes. Remove meat and liver from stock and set aside. In same liquid, cook onions 20 minutes at high simmer. Remove onions, set aside and reserve 3 cups stock. Using a fine grinder plate, grind pork, liver and onions. Place ground meat and onions in a large mixing bowl. Blend in cooked rice and green onions. Pour in hot stock to achieve desired consistency. Season with salt and pepper. Stuff mixture into hog casing, twisting at 6-inch intervals. Serve for breakfast, as an entreé, or enjoy as a po'boy on French bread.

PLATINES

Prep Time: 1 Hour
Yields: 15 Patties

Comment:

Platines are highly-seasoned pork sausages that are formed into round, burger-like patties prior to cooking. Unlike most sausage, platines are wrapped in caul fat rather than stuffed into sausage casings. Caul fat is a very thin, veil-like web fat that may be purchased from any butcher shop or specialty sausage market. This recipe will use enough caul fat to wrap 3 pounds of pork patty sausage.

Ingredients:

3 pounds ground pork butt
1 cup diced onions
½ cup diced celery
½ cup diced red bell peppers
2 tbsps minced garlic
½ cup thinly sliced green onions
¼ cup chopped parsley
1 tbsp paprika for color
salt and black pepper to taste
½ cup ice water
caul fat (optional)

Method:

Blend together meat, vegetables and paprika. When thoroughly mixed, season with salt and pepper. Blend in ice water to keep fat congealed and to add moisture. Cook a small piece of mixture and taste for flavor. Adjust seasonings if necessary. Divide mixture into equal 4-ounce portions. Form mixture into patties ¾-inch thick and 3 inches in diameter. If desired, wrap each patty with caul fat to hold meat in shape during cooking. Platines may be fried or grilled as a breakfast sausage. They are also wonderful when simmered in a rich, brown gravy or tomato sauce and served over rice or grits.

Boudin Blanc

CAJUN DEBRIS

Prep Time: 3 Hours
Yields: 6–8 Servings

Comment:

Debris is a pork stew made with various cuts of leftover meats, but mostly containing the organ meats of the pig. This dish was served to the butchers on the day of the boucherie over rice or yellow stone-ground grits. This dish was normally cooked by the women as they were preparing the entrails of the pig for other dishes. Small portions were taken and added to this dish, making a handy luncheon entrée. The original recipe called for lungs and arteries, but here they have been eliminated to make the dish more palatable for modern tastes.

Ingredients:

2 pounds cubed pork butt
½ pork heart, cubed
½ pound pork liver
1 pork kidney, cubed
1 cup vegetable oil
1 cup flour
2 cups diced onions
1 cup diced celery
1 cup diced bell peppers
¼ cup sliced garlic
1 gallon beef stock (see recipe)
   OR water
⅛ tsp dried thyme
½ tsp dried basil
1 cup sliced green onions
½ cup chopped parsley
salt and black pepper to taste
granulated garlic to taste

Method:

In a heavy-bottomed Dutch oven, heat oil over medium-high heat. Brown pork pieces well on all sides then remove from pot. Whisk in flour, stirring constantly until a brown roux is achieved. (See roux recipes.) Add onions, celery, bell peppers and garlic. Sauté 3–5 minutes. Return meats to pot and blend well. Pour in stock, 1 ladle at a time, creating a fairly thin stew. Stew must be thin or it will scorch during the long braising time. Bring to a rolling boil then reduce to simmer. Cook 2½–3 hours, stirring occasionally. While cooking, stock will slowly evaporate and stew should cook down to a thickened consistency as meat becomes tender. Additional stock or water may be added as necessary to tenderize the meat. Add green onions and parsley. Season with salt, pepper and granulated garlic.

SMOKED SAUSAGE

Prep Time: 1 Hour
Yields: 12–15 (6-inch) Links

Comment:

This same basic sausage recipe can be used for platines or smoked sausage. The difference is that this recipe calls for pork fat and is stuffed into sausage casing.

Ingredients:

3 pounds ground pork butt	½ cup thinly sliced green onions
1 pound pork fat	¼ cup chopped parsley
1 cup diced onions	1 tbsp paprika for color
½ cup diced celery	salt and black pepper to taste
½ cup diced red bell peppers	½ cup ice water
2 tbsps minced garlic	10 feet sausage casing (32–35mm) for stuffing

Method:

Blend together meat, fat, vegetables and paprika. When thoroughly mixed, add salt and pepper. Pour in ice water to keep fat congealed and to add moisture. Cook a small piece of mixed sausage and taste for flavor. Adjust seasonings if necessary. Stuff mixture into casing and twist into 6-inch links. Smoke sausages in a home-style smoker with pecan wood flavoring until internal temperature reaches 160°F. Sausages keep 3–4 days in refrigerator or up to 6 months frozen. NOTE: 32–35mm natural hog casings may be purchased from any butcher shop or specialty sausage market.

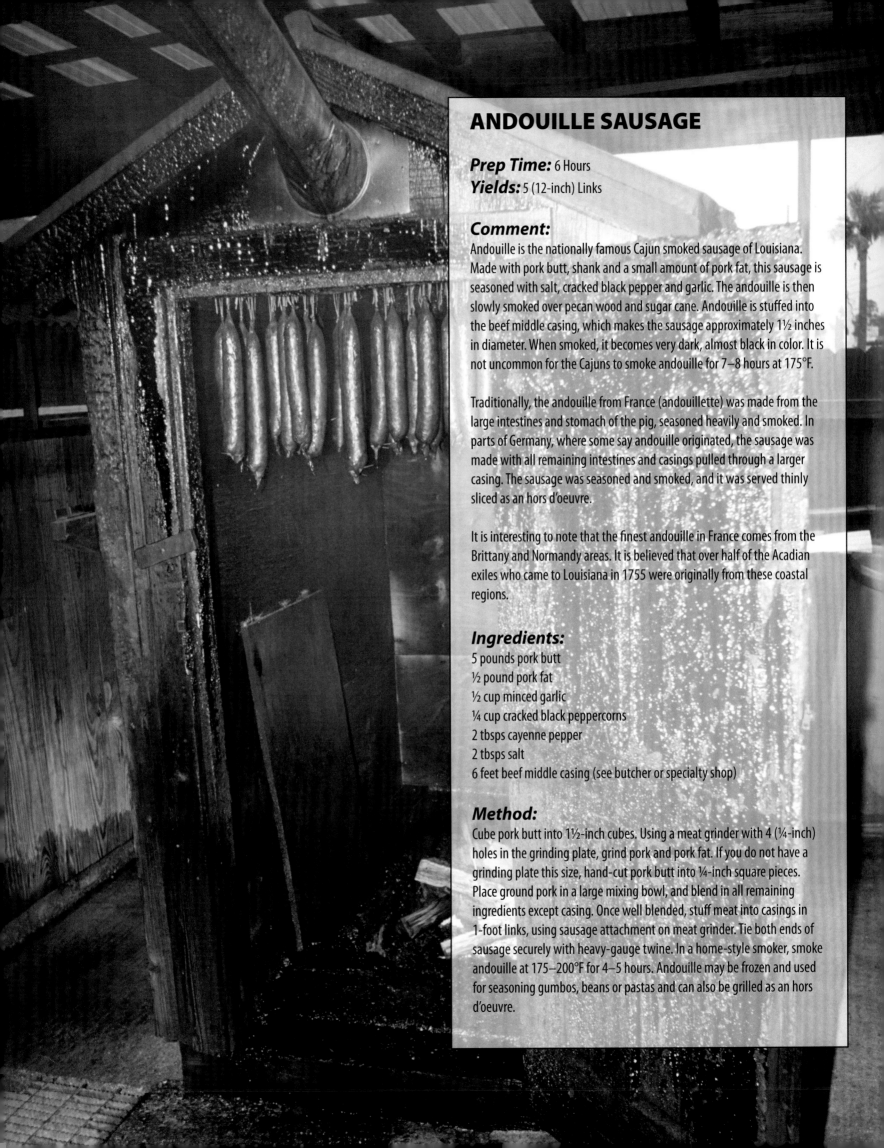

ANDOUILLE SAUSAGE

Prep Time: 6 Hours
Yields: 5 (12-inch) Links

Comment:

Andouille is the nationally famous Cajun smoked sausage of Louisiana. Made with pork butt, shank and a small amount of pork fat, this sausage is seasoned with salt, cracked black pepper and garlic. The andouille is then slowly smoked over pecan wood and sugar cane. Andouille is stuffed into the beef middle casing, which makes the sausage approximately 1½ inches in diameter. When smoked, it becomes very dark, almost black in color. It is not uncommon for the Cajuns to smoke andouille for 7–8 hours at 175°F.

Traditionally, the andouille from France (andouillette) was made from the large intestines and stomach of the pig, seasoned heavily and smoked. In parts of Germany, where some say andouille originated, the sausage was made with all remaining intestines and casings pulled through a larger casing. The sausage was seasoned and smoked, and it was served thinly sliced as an hors d'oeuvre.

It is interesting to note that the finest andouille in France comes from the Brittany and Normandy areas. It is believed that over half of the Acadian exiles who came to Louisiana in 1755 were originally from these coastal regions.

Ingredients:

5 pounds pork butt
½ pound pork fat
½ cup minced garlic
¼ cup cracked black peppercorns
2 tbsps cayenne pepper
2 tbsps salt
6 feet beef middle casing (see butcher or specialty shop)

Method:

Cube pork butt into 1½-inch cubes. Using a meat grinder with 4 (¼-inch) holes in the grinding plate, grind pork and pork fat. If you do not have a grinding plate this size, hand-cut pork butt into ¼-inch square pieces. Place ground pork in a large mixing bowl, and blend in all remaining ingredients except casing. Once well blended, stuff meat into casings in 1-foot links, using sausage attachment on meat grinder. Tie both ends of sausage securely with heavy-gauge twine. In a home-style smoker, smoke andouille at 175–200°F for 4–5 hours. Andouille may be frozen and used for seasoning gumbos, beans or pastas and can also be grilled as an hors d'oeuvre.

CHAURICE SAUSAGE

Prep Time: 1 Hour
Yields: 9 (12-inch) Links

Comment:
Chaurice is a spicy pork sausage used extensively in Creole cooking. One of the few sausages seasoned with fresh vegetables, chaurice is seen time and time again in different presentations on the Creole table. The sausage is related to the Spanish chorizo which is commonly used in paella, the forefather of our own jambalaya. Chorizo is also used to flavor garbanzo beans. Today in South Louisiana, chaurice is seen most often as a pan-fried side dish for white or red beans.

Ingredients:
4 pounds pork butt
2 pounds pork fat
2 cups minced onions
1 cup minced celery
½ cup minced garlic
2 cups minced green onions
½ cup finely chopped parsley
1 tbsp dry thyme
¼ cup cracked black pepper
2 tbsps cayenne pepper
3 tbsps salt
½ cup ice water
12 feet pork casing

Method:
Cut pork butt into 1½-inch pieces. Using a meat grinder with a coarse chopping plate, grind pork and pork fat. In a large mixing bowl, combine pork and all remaining ingredients except water and casing. Blend well to ensure that all seasonings are evenly distributed. Mix in ice water to keep fat congealed and to add moisture. Use sausage attachment on your meat grinder to stuff into casings, twisting at 1-foot intervals. Tie off sausage at each end using a heavy gauge twine. Sausage may be frozen for later use. To cook, place chaurice in a heavy-bottomed sauté pan with approximately ¼ cup cold water. Bring to a low simmer and cover. Cook 30 minutes, adding water if necessary. Uncover pan and raise temperature to medium-high. Continue cooking 15 minutes or until sausage is brown on all sides.

JOSEPH IONADI'S SWEET ITALIAN SAUSAGE

Prep Time: 2 Hours
Yields: 160 (6-inch) Links

Comment:
Joseph Ionadi was born in Calabria, Italy and moved to Toronto, Canada in 1958. Today, he owns Donnalia Fruit Market on Jane Street in Toronto. This sausage, created by Ionadi, is representative of the Italian variety of sausage often enjoyed in Louisiana Creole cuisine.

Ingredients:
50 pounds ground pork butt
6 cups sweet red pepper sauce (see recipe)
2 ounces red peppers, dried and crushed
2½ ounces cracked black pepper
9½ ounces salt
1 ounce fennel seed
90 feet (38mm) hog casing

Method:
Grind pork butt through a ⅜-inch die to achieve perfect-sized grind. Blend pork and all remaining ingredients. Stuff mixture into 38mm hog casing. Grill or pan sauté finished sausage with smothered onions and peppers.

DUO OF SAUSAGES SMOTHERED IN APPLES

Prep Time: 1 Hour
Yields: 6 Servings

Comment:

Early settlers found wild apple trees growing in Louisiana and often made wine with the fruit or included it in recipes. This sausage, created in central Louisiana, is flavored with apples and cider.

Ingredients:

1 pound fresh pork sausage
1 pound fresh beef sausage
1 cup diced red apples
1 cup diced green apples
1 cup apple cider
¼ cup vegetable oil
1 cup diced onion
½ cup diced celery
½ cup diced red bell peppers
1 tbsp minced garlic
1 cup chicken stock
½ cup sliced green onions
salt and black pepper to taste

Method:

Preheat oven to 375°F. Using a toothpick or fork, prick sausage skin once or twice at 3-inch intervals. In a 12-inch cast iron skillet, heat oil over medium-high heat. Cook sausages until golden brown on all sides. Remove and set aside. In the same skillet, sauté onions, celery, bell peppers and garlic 3–5 minutes or until vegetables are wilted. Pour in apple cider and chicken stock, then bring to a low boil. Return sausages to pan and top with apples and green onions. Season with salt and pepper. Cover skillet with a tight-fitting lid or foil. Bake 45 minutes. To serve, place sausage links in center of a round platter and surround with apples.

THE BAYOU TWO STEP

Prep Time: 1 Hour
Yields: 8 Servings

Comment:

Sausages have always been a very important part of Cajun and Creole cooking. Sausage makes use of the trimmings and pieces left over from butchering animals. In addition, tougher cuts of meat are excellent when ground for sausage. With the ample supply of wild game, seafood and pork in Cajun Country, a combination of meats are often used to make sausage. Frequently, two different sausages are cooked together for added appeal and flavor. This Bayou Two Step is served at hunting camp dinners using Italian sausage in the skillet until deer sausage is made.

Ingredients:

1½ pounds fresh seasoned pork sausage
1½ pounds Italian sausage
¼ cup vegetable oil
2 cups sliced Bermuda onions
½ cup diced celery
1 red bell pepper, sliced
1 yellow bell pepper, sliced
1 green bell pepper, sliced
¼ cup minced garlic
1 cup sliced green onions
1 (15-ounce) can diced tomatoes, drained
1 tsp basil
1 tsp thyme
1 cup beef bouillon
salt and black pepper to taste
Louisiana hot sauce to taste
¼ cup chopped parsley

Method:

Preheat oven to 375°F. Leaving sausage in its original length, place two sausages side-by-side and coil into a circle, jelly-roll fashion. Finished product should be a complete spiral with alternating lengths of Italian and pork sausage, from center to outside. Using a small paring knife or toothpick, pierce sausage casings at 1-inch intervals. Carefully place spiral sausage in a 14-inch cast iron skillet. Pour in vegetable oil and place skillet over medium-high heat. Cook until sausage is well-browned on bottom. Using a large spatula, flip sausage spiral over to brown other side. Remove from skillet and hold on a large platter. Drain all but ¼ cup of oil from skillet. Sauté onions, celery, bell peppers and garlic 3–5 minutes or until vegetables are wilted. Stir in green onions, tomatoes, basil and thyme. Return sausage to skillet, placing it directly on top of vegetables. Pour in bouillon and bring to a rolling boil. Cover pan and place in oven. Season with salt, pepper and hot sauce. Bake 30–45 minutes or until sausage is cooked. When done, garnish with chopped parsley and adjust seasonings if necessary. Cut spirals into 6-inch links and serve over steamed white rice.

SMOKED TASSO

Prep Time: 2½ Hours
Yields: 3 Pounds

Comment:

Tasso is a dried product that is seasoned with cayenne pepper, garlic and salt then heavily smoked. The word tasso is believed to have come from the Spanish word "tasajo" which is dried, cured beef. Although this delicacy is often thinly sliced and eaten alone, it is primarily used as a pungent seasoning for vegetables, gumbos and soups. Today in South Louisiana, tasso has become a popular seasoning for new and creative dishes. It has also gained wide acclaim as an hors d'oeuvre served with dipping sauces or fruit glazes.

Ingredients:

4 pounds pork butt
½ cup Worcestershire sauce
1 tbsp Louisiana hot sauce
¼ cup cayenne pepper
¼ cup cracked black pepper
¼ cup salt
½ cup granulated garlic

Method:

Cut pork butt into ½-inch strips. Place on a baking pan and season with Worcestershire and hot sauce. Blend liquids and meat. Add all remaining ingredients and mix well to ensure that each piece of meat is coated. Cover with plastic wrap and refrigerate overnight. Using a home-style smoker, smoke tasso at 175–200°F for 2½ hours. Once cooked, tasso may be frozen or used to season gumbos, vegetables or beans. NOTE: If desired, smoke tasso over briquettes flavored with pecan wood and sugar cane strips.

CROWN ROAST OF PORK WITH SHOEPEG CORN BREAD STUFFING

Prep Time: 3 Hours
Yields: 10 Servings

Comment:

The crown roast, or bone-in pork loin roast, has always been the choice in Creole kitchens as the table centerpiece during the holiday season. It may be stuffed with everything from meat and fruit to rice and vegetables.

Ingredients for Roast:

1 (9–11 pound) crown roast of pork, rib ends frenched
Shoepeg Corn Bread Stuffing (see recipe)
¼ cup minced garlic
¼ cup sliced green onions
1 tbsp salt
1½ tbsps black pepper
granulated garlic to taste
salt and black pepper to taste
¼ cup chopped basil
¼ cup chopped thyme
¼ cup chopped sage
1 cup diced onions
1 cup diced carrots
1 cup diced celery
1 cup diced apples

Method:

Preheat oven to 350°F. NOTE: If you are not familiar with crown roast, have your butcher "french" or clean end of rib bones of any meat or sinew. Ask butcher for a quick demonstration in tying roast into crown shape. In a small mixing bowl, combine garlic, green onions, salt and black pepper. Using a paring knife, make 8–10 (¾-inch) slits into loin and season generously with mixture. Season roast inside and out with granulated garlic, salt, pepper and remaining herbs. Tie roast into crown shape and place on a large sheet of foil. Place in a baking pan with a 2-inch lip. Fill center of roast with shoepeg corn stuffing, placing any excess into corners of roasting pan. Surround outside of roast with onions, carrots, celery and apples. Fold foil up side of crown roast and over rib ends to cover loosely during cooking process. Bone should be protected well to keep from burning or turning overly brown while baking. Place in middle of oven and cook 2 hours. Open foil and brown roast 45 minutes or until meat thermometer reaches 155–160°F. A sauce may be made from drippings by allowing pan to sit for 1 hour and skimming excess fat. Thicken drippings slightly with 1 tablespoon cornstarch.

SOUL PORK ROAST

Prep Time: 2½ Hours
Yields: 6 Servings

Comment:
The word "soul" is used to describe the music and the cooking style created in the slave quarters and cotton fields of the South. Lesser cuts of meat, trimmings and leftover vegetables were often thrown into a black iron pot in a slave cabin to create a dish that far surpassed an entrée in the "main house." It takes a lot of soul to create something out of nothing.

Ingredients for Stuffing:
1 (5-pound) Boston butt roast
¼ cup minced garlic
¼ cup sliced green onions
1 tsp thyme
1 tsp basil
2 jalapeño or cayenne peppers, diced
4 tbsps salt
4 tbsps cracked black pepper
Louisiana hot sauce to taste

Method:
In a small mixing bowl, combine garlic, green onions, thyme, basil, peppers, salt and pepper. Using a paring knife, pierce approximately 10 (1-inch) holes in roast and season each pocket with an equal amount of mixture. Season outside of roast completely with salt, pepper and hot sauce.

Ingredients for Roasting:
¼ cup vegetable oil
2 cups diced onions
1 cup diced celery
1 cup diced bell peppers
6 garlic cloves, chopped
6 carrots, sliced 1-inch
1 quart beef or chicken stock
1 cup sliced green onions
½ cup chopped parsley
Louisiana hot sauce to taste

Method:
In a heavy-bottomed Dutch oven, heat oil over medium-high heat. Place roast in pot and sear 3–5 minutes on all sides. Surround roast with onions, celery, bell peppers, garlic and carrots. Pour in stock, bring to a rolling boil and reduce to simmer. Cover and place in oven. Cook 2–2½ hours or until roast is tender. Add green onions, parsley and a dash of hot sauce. Remove roast and place on a serving platter. Allow to rest 15 minutes before slicing. Serve over steamed white rice with a generous portion of pan drippings and a slice of corn bread.

STRAWBERRY-GLAZED PORK LOIN

Prep Time: 2 Hours
Yields: 6–8 Servings

Comment:
Ponchatoula, La. is the undisputed strawberry capital of the world. Since pork is so widely used in South Louisiana cooking, it is easy to understand how strawberries found their way into the pork dishes of this area. In most places, apple sauce is used as a fresh fruit flavoring with pork loin, but here strawberries are the ideal substitute.

Ingredients:
1 cup diced strawberries
½ cup strawberry syrup
24 fresh, large strawberries
1 (3–5 pound) pork loin
2 tbsps minced onions
1 tbsp minced celery
2 tbsps thinly sliced green onions
2 slices diced bacon
salt and cracked black pepper to taste
¼ cup melted butter
1 cup diced onions
½ cup diced celery
½ cup diced red bell peppers
2 cups beef stock
1 sprig rosemary
Louisiana hot sauce to taste

Method:
Preheat oven to 375°F. In a large mixing bowl, combine diced strawberries, minced onions, celery, green onions, bacon, salt and pepper. Cut 1-inch long slits in pork loin and stuff with seasoning mixture. Drizzle strawberry syrup and melted butter over top of pork loin. Season with salt and pepper. Place loin in a large Dutch oven or roasting pan and surround with whole strawberries, remaining onions, celery, bell peppers and beef stock. Season with rosemary and hot sauce. Cover roasting pan and bake 1–1½ hours. Slice roast and surround with strawberry sauce.

SMOKED SAUSAGE-STUFFED LOIN OF PORK

Prep Time: 1½ Hours
Yields: 8 Servings

Comment:
Often in Louisiana, a combination of meat and seafood is used to create a flavorful dish. This stuffed pork loin is a delicious way to blend only the best flavors.

Ingredients:
1 pound center-cut pork loin, cleaned and boned
1 pound smoked sausage
salt and cracked black pepper to taste
1 tsp basil
1 tsp thyme
¼ cup minced garlic
¼ cup cane syrup
10 pearl onions
1 red onion, sliced
6 diced yams
dash of Louisiana hot sauce
¼ cup vegetable oil

Method:
Preheat oven to 375°F. Using a metal sharpening steel or knife, pierce a hole through loin from end to end. Using your hands, push whole sausage through hole. Place loin in a large roasting pan and season with salt, pepper, basil, thyme and garlic. Glaze loin with cane syrup and garnish with onions and yams. Season with salt, pepper and hot sauce. Drizzle oil over meat, cover with foil and bake 1 hour. Slice and serve.

ROASTED LOIN OF PORK WITH NATURAL JUICES

Prep Time: 1 Hour
Yields: 6 Servings

Comment:
Pork is the most flavorful of all meats, but often a little tricky to cook. The loin is especially challenging because it tends to be dry. Ample seasoning and quick pan-searing before roasting is the key to a successful pork loin entrée.

Ingredients:
1 (2½-pound) boned pork loin
1 tbsp vegetable oil
1 tbsp crushed rosemary
1 tbsp minced garlic
1 tbsp rubbed sage
salt and black pepper to taste
¼ cup olive oil
1 tbsp butter
2 tbsps flour
2 cups chicken stock (see recipe)

Method:
Preheat oven to 400°F. Place pork loin in a large baking pan and top with vegetable oil. Rub oil over entire loin. Season with rosemary, garlic, sage, salt and pepper. In a large cast iron Dutch oven or skillet, heat olive oil over medium-high heat. Brown pork loin well on all sides, turning occasionally. Return loin to baking pan. Place on center shelf of oven and cook uncovered for 45 minutes–1 hour or until internal temperature reaches 150°F. Remove from oven, place loin on a platter and keep warm. Pour off all but 1 tablespoon of drippings from roasting pan. Add butter to reserved pan drippings. When butter has melted, whisk in flour to create a white roux. Blend in chicken stock. Place pan over medium-high heat and bring mixture to a low boil, whisking until juices thicken to a sauce consistency. Adjust seasonings if necessary. Strain sauce through a fine sieve into a gravy boat and serve with sliced loin.

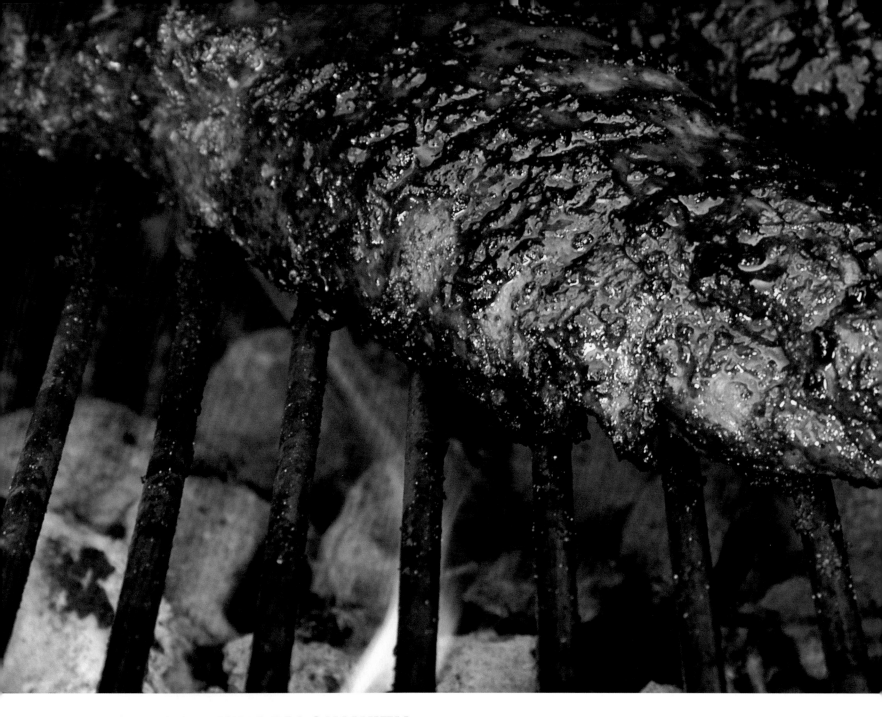

GRILLED PORK TENDERLOIN WITH BLACKBERRY BARBECUE SAUCE

Prep Time: 1½ Hours
Yields: 8 Servings

Comment:

Grilling is a great way to infuse smoky flavor into pork tenderloin. For best results, build a coal bed on one side of the grill. Place tenderloin away from hot coals, so it will receive medium-high heat. Do not overcook. Use a meat thermometer to monitor internal temperature of roast.

Ingredients:

1 (2–3 pound) pork tenderloin
1 tbsp granulated garlic
2 tbsps ground black pepper
1 tbsp salt
1 tbsp mustard powder
1 tbsp chili powder

1 tbsp ground cumin
1 tbsp packed brown sugar
2 tbsps ground paprika
½ tsp dried oregano
Blackberry Barbecue Sauce
  (see recipe next page)

Method:

In a small mixing bowl, combine all seasonings. Sprinkle tenderloin with mixture and rub in spices. Let rubbed meat sit at least 1 hour in refrigerator. Light grill. Cook tenderloin, turning once halfway through cooking process. Remove when internal temperature reaches 128°F for rare to 150°F for well done. When pork is almost done, brush with barbecue sauce.

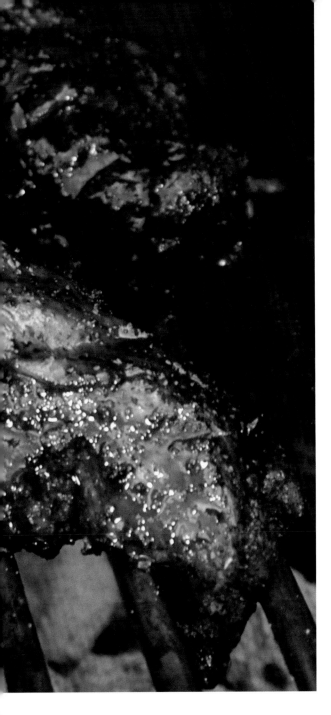

PEPPER-LACED PORK ROAST

Prep Time: 4 Hours
Yields: 6 Servings

Comment:
Highly seasoned, peppery pork roasts are a hallmark of Louisiana cuisine. This excellent recipe uses fresh cayenne and jalapeño peppers to give the roast that extra kick.

Ingredients:
1 (5–6 pound) boneless Boston butt
¼ cup sliced cayenne peppers
¼ cup sliced jalapeño peppers
6 cloves garlic, minced
2 cups sliced green onions
⅛ tsp dried thyme
⅛ tsp dried basil
1 tsp salt
⅛ tsp black pepper

salt and black pepper to taste
Louisiana hot sauce to taste
¼ cup vegetable oil
2 cups diced onions
¼ cup diced celery
¼ cup diced bell peppers
¼ cup parsley
1 cup beef stock (see recipe)

Method:
Preheat oven to 375°F. In a small mixing bowl, combine garlic, green onions, thyme, basil, salt and pepper. Pierce holes through roast and fill each cavity with mixture. Next, stuff peppers into holes, leaving approximately 2 inches of peppers exposed. Season roast with salt, pepper and hot sauce. In a 12-quart cast iron Dutch oven, heat oil over medium-high heat. Sear roast in hot oil on all sides. Place onions, celery, bell peppers, parsley and beef stock in Dutch oven. Cover and bake 3½ hours or until tender. Add water if necessary during cooking. Reserve broth for serving.

"The man that eats no pepper is weak; pepper is the staff of life."
Yoruba Proverb

BLACKBERRY BARBECUE SAUCE

Prep Time: 10 Minutes
Yields: 8 Servings

Comment:
This interesting barbecue sauce is a natural accompaniment to pork tenderloins, chops or ribs. The blackberries and cane syrup add a slightly sweet, yet subtle flavor to pork.

Ingredients:
½ cup blackberry preserves
1½ cups ketchup
⅛ cup packed brown sugar
2 tbsps Louisiana cane syrup

⅛ tsp cayenne pepper
¼ tsp mustard powder
2 tbsps red wine vinegar
½ cup fresh blackberries

Method:
In a mixing bowl, combine all ingredients. Mix well. Brush sauce over grilled pork tenderloin, pork chops or ribs when they are almost cooked.

ROOT BEER GLAZED HAM

Prep Time: 3 Hours
Yields: 6 Servings

Comment:

This is a wonderful recipe to create your own special holiday ham. It is quite simple to accomplish, but you will receive rave reviews with this dish. Try adding a few of your own secret spices.

Ingredients for Boiling Ham:

1 (5–10 pound) smoked ham
6 bottles high-quality root beer
1 red apple, sliced
1 green apple, sliced
1 cup red seedless grapes
½ orange, sliced
½ tsp ground cloves
cracked black pepper to taste
1 tsp filé (ground sassafras)

Method:

Place ham in a cast iron pot or Dutch oven. Surround ham with apples, grapes, oranges and ground cloves. Pour in root beer and dust with pepper and filé. Bring to a rolling boil and reduce to simmer. Boil approximately 1 hour. Turn ham and continue boiling until root beer is reduced to a thick syrup. Remove ham and set aside. Continue to reduce syrup until it is consistency of molasses, being careful not to scorch. Remove syrup and place in a mixing bowl. Allow to cool and reserve for later.

Ingredients for Root Beer-Mustard Sauce:

½ cup root beer syrup (reserved)
1 cup Creole mustard
½ cup brown sugar
¼ cup pineapple juice
¼ cup cracked black pepper
pinch of cinnamon
pinch of nutmeg
pinch of allspice
6 cloves
6 pineapple slices

Method:

Preheat oven to 350°F. In a mixing bowl, combine all ingredients and whisk well. Place ham in center of a Dutch oven and coat completely with root beer mixture. Bake uncovered 1 hour. NOTE: If you wish to decorate ham, cut slits ⅛-inch deep diagonally across ham. Continue in same pattern from opposite side until even diamonds appear from cuts. Stud with cloves. Using toothpicks, secure pineapple slices to top of ham before baking.

BITTERSWEET PLANTATION SUGAR-CURED SMOKEHOUSE HAM

Prep Time: 3 Days
Yields: 1 (12–15 pound) Ham

Comment:

Most butcher supply companies will sell a brown sugar cure for hams. I prefer to use Art's Brown Sugar Cure, which can be purchased from Targil Seasoning & Butcher Supply in Opelousas, La. You can contact them at (337) 942-6276.

Ingredients:

1 (12–15 pound) shank-on fresh ham
1 (1½-pound bag) Art's Brown Sugar Cure
3 gallons cold water
1 cup brown sugar
1½ cups Louisiana cane syrup
¼ cup cracked black pepper

Method:

In a 5-gallon pot or plastic pail, blend brown sugar cure, water, ½ cup brown sugar and ¾ cup cane syrup. Whisk together thoroughly. Using a large meat syringe, inject ham on each side (in 6–10 places) with cure mixture. Ham must be injected with an amount of cure equivalent to 10 percent of ham's weight. Place ham in remaining cure (brine) and allow to marinate 36 hours. Preheat smokehouse or home-style smoker to 120°F. When ready to cook, remove ham from brine and pat dry. Make a rub using remaining sugar, syrup and pepper. Coat ham thoroughly with rub then place in a cheesecloth or "ham sock." NOTE: Cheesecloth suitable for smoking a ham can be purchased at any butcher supply company. Place ham in preheated smokehouse. With drafts open, cook 12 hours. Increase temperature to 140°F, and add pecan wood or hickory chips. With drafts half open, cook 8 hours. Close drafts completely and increase temperature to 165°F. Add smoke wood and cook until internal temperature of ham reaches 152°F. Remove and cool at room temperature 6–8 hours prior to refrigeration. Serve hot or chilled. Ham may be frozen for later use.

GUARANTEED TO BE TENDER BABY BACK RIBS

Prep Time: 3 Hours
Yields: 8 Servings

Comment:

Most grilling experts will prepare barbecued ribs using the long and slow method, cooking them over indirect heat 3–4 hours. However, this slow method requires constant attention, whereas my "guaranteed to be tender" recipe allows more free time for the cook.

Ingredients:

4 (2–2¼ pound) slabs baby back ribs
1 onion, quartered
1 celery stick, chopped
5 cloves garlic
½ tsp red pepper flakes
salt to taste

Method:

Using a sharp knife, cut each slab of ribs into 2 equal parts creating 8 portions. Place ribs in a large Dutch oven with onions, celery, garlic, pepper flakes and salt. Cover with water by 1 inch and bring to a rolling boil. Reduce to simmer and cook 1½–2 hours. Ribs should be fork tender, but not falling apart. Remove ribs, place on a large cookie sheet and allow to drain and dry thoroughly, approximately 30 minutes. While ribs are draining, heat barbecue pit according to manufacturer's directions. If desired, use a few pieces of smoked wood for enhanced flavor. When coals have subsided to medium heat, place ribs on pit, bone-side down. Turn every 2–3 minutes to achieve a golden brown color. Once ribs are brown, glaze with oriental barbecue sauce on each side.

Ingredients for Oriental Barbecue Sauce:

½ cup ketchup
½ cup soy sauce
½ cup hoisin sauce
½ cup oyster sauce
½ cup honey
½ cup brown sugar
½ cup Steen's cane syrup
½ cup cream sherry
2 tbsps grated and peeled ginger
2 tbsps black bean garlic sauce
6 garlic cloves, minced
½ tsp Chinese five-spice powder

Method:

Combine all ingredients in a medium sauce pot and bring to a simmer. Blend well. Sauce may be used immediately or placed in a ceramic bowl, covered and refrigerated for up to 1 week. NOTE: Black bean garlic sauce is available at your local Asian market or in the Asian foods section of many supermarkets.

FINGER-LICKING HONEY RIBS

Prep Time: 2 Hours
Yields: 4 Servings

Comment:

Despite the fact that they are baked and not grilled, these ribs are luscious and tender, with a succulent, spicy honey-based sauce.

Ingredients:

2 (2-pound) slabs baby back ribs
½ cup honey
1 cup chili sauce
½ cup minced onions
¼ cup minced garlic
2 tbsps dry red wine
1 tbsp Worcestershire sauce
1 tbsp soy sauce
1 tsp liquid smoke
1 tsp Dijon-style mustard
salt and black pepper to taste

Method:

Preheat oven to 375°F. Using a sharp paring knife, trim excess silver skin from ribs. In a small sauce pot, combine all ingredients except ribs, salt and pepper. Bring to a boil over medium heat, stirring constantly. Reduce heat and simmer 5 minutes then remove and set aside. While sauce is cooking, season ribs with salt and pepper. Place ribs in a large baking pan or cookie sheet with 1-inch lip. Cover tightly with foil and bake 45 minutes. Uncover and bake 1 hour, brushing with sauce every 15 minutes until fully cooked and tender. When done, rib bone should be exposed approximately ¾ inch at end. Cut ribs into portions and serve with remaining sauce.

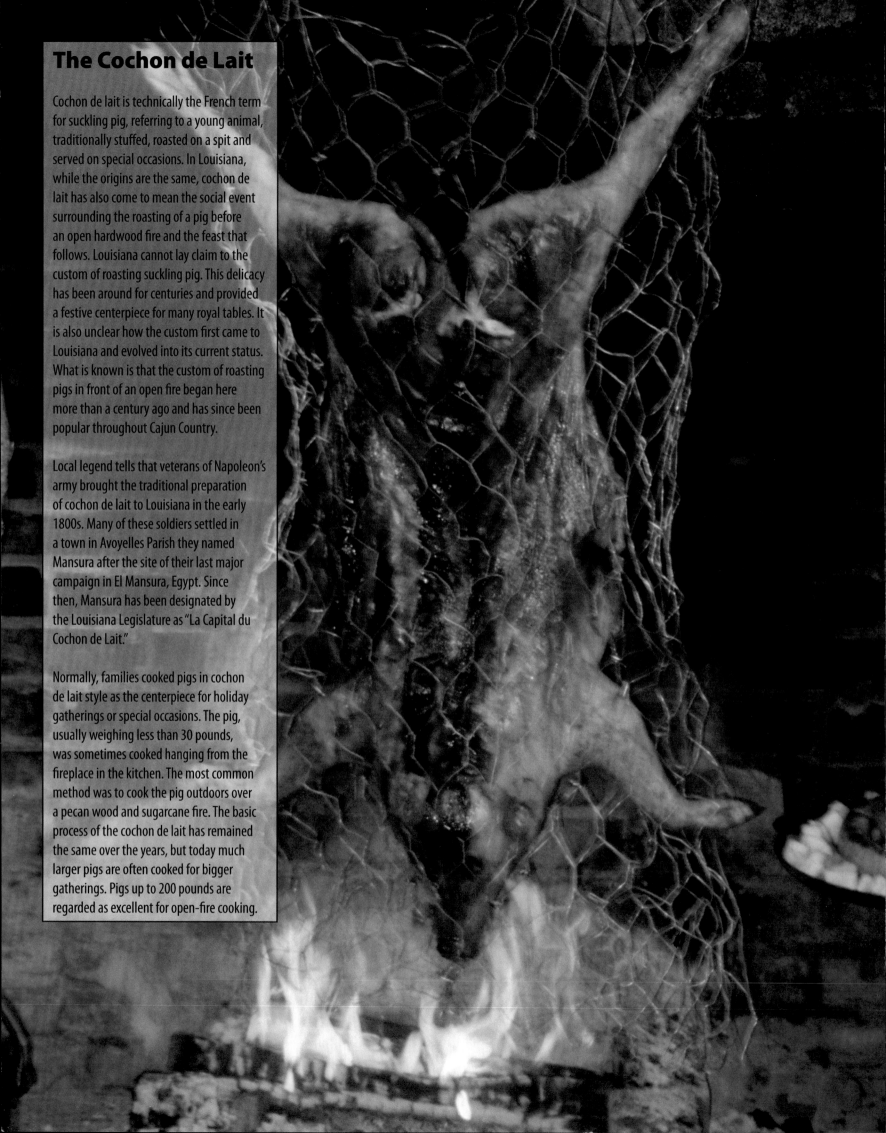

The Cochon de Lait

Cochon de lait is technically the French term for suckling pig, referring to a young animal, traditionally stuffed, roasted on a spit and served on special occasions. In Louisiana, while the origins are the same, cochon de lait has also come to mean the social event surrounding the roasting of a pig before an open hardwood fire and the feast that follows. Louisiana cannot lay claim to the custom of roasting suckling pig. This delicacy has been around for centuries and provided a festive centerpiece for many royal tables. It is also unclear how the custom first came to Louisiana and evolved into its current status. What is known is that the custom of roasting pigs in front of an open fire began here more than a century ago and has since been popular throughout Cajun Country.

Local legend tells that veterans of Napoleon's army brought the traditional preparation of cochon de lait to Louisiana in the early 1800s. Many of these soldiers settled in a town in Avoyelles Parish they named Mansura after the site of their last major campaign in El Mansura, Egypt. Since then, Mansura has been designated by the Louisiana Legislature as "La Capital du Cochon de Lait."

Normally, families cooked pigs in cochon de lait style as the centerpiece for holiday gatherings or special occasions. The pig, usually weighing less than 30 pounds, was sometimes cooked hanging from the fireplace in the kitchen. The most common method was to cook the pig outdoors over a pecan wood and sugarcane fire. The basic process of the cochon de lait has remained the same over the years, but today much larger pigs are often cooked for bigger gatherings. Pigs up to 200 pounds are regarded as excellent for open-fire cooking.

COCHON DE LAIT

Comment:

The cochon de lait is a Louisiana tradition and one of the main social events of the Cajuns and Creoles. Remember that each pig is different and will require varying seasoning amounts and cooking times. Any measurements given here are approximate and will work best on a 50-pound pig.

Ingredients:

1 pig
salt and cracked black pepper to taste
granulated garlic to taste
4 cups melted butter
   OR vegetable oil
2 bottles beer
1 cup Louisiana hot sauce
½ cup granulated garlic

Method:

Season pig well inside and out with salt, pepper and granulated garlic. Combine butter, beer, hot sauce and ½ cup granulated garlic. Use more or less of each ingredient depending on size of pig. Inject front and rear hams and tenderloin with this infused liquid. Using a meat saw, cut through backbone at neck and tail. Lay pig open flat. Wrap pig in wire mesh and secure it with wire to hold in proper form during long cooking process. Hang this wire basket from chains or hooks 4 feet in front of a hardwood fire made preferably with oak or pecan wood. Remember, hot coals and radiant heat will cook the pig, not fire. The fire simply creates coals used for cooking. Begin by placing pig hams down and bone side in. After first hour of cooking, flip pig front shoulders down and bone in. After every hour, flip pig to ensure even cooking. You may wish to baste with your favorite marinade or more injection liquid while cooking. Estimate 1 hour of cooking time for every 10 pounds, but keep in mind that not all pigs will cook at same rate. If fire is maintained, it will cook a 50-pound pig in 6 hours.

In order to meet the demand for fire-roasted pigs at White Oak Plantation in Baton Rouge, a "cochon de lait factory" was installed. The open-pit ovens enable chefs to cook 18 (30-pound) pigs at one time.

OVEN-STYLE COCHON DE LAIT

Prep Time: 3–5 Hours
Yields: 10 Servings

Comment:

Although cochon de lait is traditionally prepared outdoors before an open fire, the same delicious results can be achieved in the home. By using a small suckling pig and your home oven, you can cook a wonderfully flavorful cochon de lait for your family.

Ingredients:

1 pig	3 heads garlic, halved
salt and cracked black	1 bunch celery
pepper to taste	6 apples, halved
granulated garlic to taste	2 cups red wine
thyme to taste	1 quart demi-glace (see recipe)
basil to taste	1 dozen roasted potatoes
sage to taste	1 dozen roasted carrots
Pecan Rice Dressing	2–3 bunches parsley for garnish
(see recipe)	tomatoes for garnish
4 large onions, quartered	orange slices for garnish

Method:

Select a suckling pig that is 5–6 weeks old and weighing 15–20 pounds. Have your butcher clean pig thoroughly, removing all entrails, tongue, eyes, etc. Season pig inside and out with salt, pepper, granulated garlic, thyme, basil and sage. Due to thickness of skin, only a portion of this seasoning will affect taste. Preheat oven to 350°F. Stuff pig with Pecan Rice Dressing, but do not overstuff, as dressing will expand slightly during cooking. Using (4-inch) skewers, truss belly cavity and tie securely with butcher's twine. Turn pig over and place front feet under its head and back feet under its belly. Secure with skewers. Using the point of a paring knife, make ⅛-inch deep slits at 2-inch intervals along each side of backbone. Make 1 incision from back of neck to top of tail along back. These cuts will allow fat to escape and baste pig during cooking. Place a large carrot or a small block of wood in pig's mouth to keep it open during cooking to permit garnishing later. Place pig, feet down in a roasting pan and brush lightly with butter. Wrap ears, nose and tail in foil to prevent burning. Place raw vegetables and apples in bottom of pan then cover tightly with foil. Place in oven and cook 12–15 minutes per pound. Baste every hour with natural drippings. When internal temperature reaches 150°F, uncover and allow to brown completely. Remove pig, reserve all pan juices and discard vegetables. On stovetop, bring pan drippings to a boil then deglaze with red wine and demi-glace. Scrape bottom of pan well to incorporate all drippings. Reduce to 4 cups then season with salt and pepper. Serve in a gravy boat. Place cochon de lait on a large silver tray or serving platter, and garnish with roasted potatoes and carrots. For additional color, you may wish to add a few bunches whole parsley, tomatoes and orange slices. If desired, place a cherry tomato in each eye and an apple in mouth. To carve, remove rear ham and front legs first. Slice all meat from these pieces. Insert carving knife in slit along backbone, remove loins and slice accordingly.

PORK, CHICKEN AND ANDOUILLE JAMBALAYA

Prep Time: 1½ Hours
Yields: 6 Servings

Comment:

In the early 1700s, Spanish settlers in New Orleans brought their famous paella. Since the traditional Spanish ingredients for paella were not found in South Louisiana, the recipe was adapted to indigenous ingredients. Oysters and crawfish replaced clams and mussels and andouille took the place of ham. The new dish was influenced by many different cultures, including the Africans, who named the dish Jambon a la yaya. Yaya is the African word for rice. Today, jambalaya is the best-known rice dish in America.

Ingredients:

1 pound cubed pork butt
1 pound cubed chicken
1 pound sliced andouille
¼ cup vegetable oil
2 cups diced onions
2 cups diced celery
1 cup diced bell peppers
¼ cup minced garlic
7 cups chicken stock
2 cups sliced mushrooms
1 cup sliced green onions
½ cup chopped parsley
salt and black pepper to taste
Louisiana hot sauce to taste
4 cups uncooked long grain rice

Method:

In a 2-gallon cast iron Dutch oven, heat oil over medium-high heat. Sauté pork 30 minutes or until dark brown on all sides and beginning to stick to bottom of pot. This process is very important as the brown color of jambalaya is derived from the meat. Stir in chicken and andouille. Reduce heat to medium and stir-fry 10–15 minutes. Tilt pot to one side and ladle out all oil, except for one large cooking spoonful. Add onions, celery, bell peppers and garlic. Continue cooking until all vegetables are well caramelized, being careful not to scorch them. Pour in stock, bring to a rolling boil then reduce heat to simmer. Cook 15 minutes to allow flavors to develop. Stir in mushrooms, green onions and parsley. Season with salt, pepper and hot sauce. If desired, slightly over-season dish since rice has not yet been added. Add rice and bring to a rolling boil. Reduce heat to very low, cover and cook 30 minutes. Stir every 15 minutes. Do not uncover except to stir. When cooked, stir and let steam 10 minutes.

SMOKED SAUSAGE AND CREOLE TOMATO JAMBALAYA

Prep Time: 1 Hour
Yields: 6 Servings

Comment:

The original jambalaya of New Orleans was tomato-based and flavored with a combination of sausages, ham and chicken. Often, the dish was "thrown together" at a moment's notice when unexpected friends dropped by and a quick entrée was needed. In such a case, sometimes smoked sausage and tomatoes were the only ingredients needed for a great spur-of-the-moment lunch.

Ingredients:

2 pounds smoked sausage, sliced
2 (8-ounce) cans tomato sauce
1 cup diced tomatoes
¼ cup vegetable oil
1 cup diced onions
1 cup diced celery
½ cup diced red bell peppers
1 tbsp minced garlic
3 cups chicken stock or water
3 cups long grain rice
salt and cracked black pepper to taste
Louisiana hot sauce to taste
½ cup sliced green onions
¼ cup chopped parsley

Method:

In a Dutch oven, heat oil over medium-high heat. Sauté onions, celery, bell peppers and garlic 3–5 minutes or until vegetables are wilted. Mix in smoked sausage and cook 5 minutes. Blend in tomato sauce, diced tomatoes and chicken stock. Bring to a rolling boil, and stir in rice. Return to a boil, then reduce heat to low. Season with salt, pepper and hot sauce. Cover pot and cook 20 minutes. Do not stir or remove lid. Remove cover, add green onions and parsley. Stir mixture once to ensure that rice is not sticking and scorching. Cover and cook 10–15 minutes longer. Remove from heat and allow to steam 15 minutes before serving.

ROSEMARY-STUFFED LEG OF PORK

Prep Time: 3 Hours
Yields: 6–8 Servings

Comment:

The fresh pork ham has been a tradition on the New Year's Day table for generations in Louisiana. Normally, the ham is stuffed with fresh seasonings and spices prior to roasting. Various fruits and glazes should also be considered when baking this centerpiece.

Ingredients:

1 (5–7 pound) fresh pork ham
½ cup chopped rosemary
¼ cup chopped thyme
¼ cup chopped basil
¼ cup chopped sage
½ cup sliced green onions
½ cup chopped parsley
½ cup minced garlic
salt and cracked black pepper to taste
½ cup melted butter
3 apples, quartered
1 large onion, quartered
10 garlic cloves
Louisiana hot sauce to taste

Method:

Preheat oven to 375°F. NOTE: Have your butcher remove heavy skin covering outer portion of leg. You may wish to remove lower portion of shank to ensure that roast will fit in a home oven. Using a sharp paring knife, cut approximately 15–20 (1-inch) slits throughout roast. In a small mixing bowl, combine rosemary, thyme, basil, sage, green onions, parsley and minced garlic. Season mixture generously with salt and pepper. Blend all ingredients and stuff a generous portion of seasoning mixture into slits. Place roast in a large baking pan and drizzle with melted butter. Coat roast with remaining seasoning mixture. Surround with apples, onions and garlic. Sprinkle entire roast with additional salt, pepper and hot sauce. Cover and bake 2½ hours or until golden brown and internal temperature reaches 165°F. Remove cover and allow roast to brown evenly. Allow to sit 30 minutes before slicing.

CREOLE PORK AND RICE CASSEROLE

Prep Time: 1½ Hours
Yields: 6 Servings

Comment:
This is a wonderfully flavored, one-pot dish that will satisfy everyone at your table. If you prefer, substitute chicken or beef in place of pork.

Ingredients:
6 (½-inch thick) center-cut pork chops
1 cup uncooked converted rice
½ cup olive oil
salt and black pepper to taste
Louisiana hot sauce to taste
1 cup diced onions
½ cup diced celery
½ cup diced green bell peppers
½ cup diced yellow bell peppers
½ cup minced garlic
1 (8-ounce) can tomato sauce
1½ cup beef stock or consommé
1 bay leaf
1 tsp chopped basil
½ cup sliced green onions
¼ cup chopped parsley

Method:
Preheat oven to 375°F. In a large cast iron skillet, heat oil over medium-high heat. Season chops well with salt, pepper and hot sauce. Brown chops on both sides, allowing them to caramelize in bottom of skillet. Once chops are golden brown, remove and keep warm. In same skillet, sauté onions, celery, bell peppers and garlic 3–5 minutes or until vegetables are wilted. Pour in tomato sauce and stock. Bring to a low boil, then reduce to simmer. Add bay leaf and basil. Season with salt and pepper. Slightly over-season since rice will absorb flavor. Stir in rice and blend well. Add green onions and parsley. Bring to a rolling boil. Boil 3–5 minutes, then reduce to low. Layer pork chops over rice. Bring to a rolling boil. Remove from heat. Cover pot tightly and bake 45 minutes. Do not stir.

MOMMA LINK'S BRAISED CHOPS

Prep Time: 4 Hours
Yields: 4 Servings

Comment:
Poppa and Momma Link worked in St. James Parish for most of their lives. Poppa was known for his knowledge in the art of butchering, and Momma was well known for her cooking. When the cold months of winter rolled around, Poppa Link's skills were in great demand. This recipe for braised, skin-on chops is one of Momma Link's favorites.

Ingredients:
4 thick-cut, skin-on pork chops
2 tbsps salt
2 tbsps cracked black pepper
½ pound bacon, chopped
1 cup diced onions
½ cup diced celery
¼ cup diced bell peppers
¼ cup sliced garlic
1 (8-ounce) can tomato sauce
5 cups beef stock
1 sprig rosemary
2 onions, quartered
3 carrots, cut into 2-inch pieces
8 new potatoes

Method:
Preheat oven to 375°F. Season chops well with salt and pepper. In a cast iron Dutch oven, sauté bacon until fat is rendered and bacon is crisp. Place chops in bacon fat and brown well on both sides. Stir in diced onions, celery, bell peppers and garlic. Sauté 3–5 minutes or until vegetables are wilted. Blend in tomato sauce. Add beef stock and rosemary. Bring to a rolling boil, then reduce heat to simmer. Cover Dutch oven and allow chops to simmer 1½ hours. Add quartered onions, carrots and potatoes. Replace cover and continue to simmer 1½–2 hours or until chops are fork tender. To serve, place chops along with a portion of onions, carrots and potatoes on a plate. Garnish with a sprig of rosemary.

POPPA LINK'S POT OF PORK

Prep Time: 5 Hours
Yields: 4 Servings

Comment:

Poppa Link was known for his butchering skills. Just as Momma Link had her favorite recipe for skin-on pork chops, so too did Poppa. He preferred a more soup-like consistency in this dish and enhanced it with red wine.

Ingredients:

4 thick-cut pork chops, skin-on	¼ cup tomato sauce
½ pound bacon	2 cups diced carrots
2 tbsps salt	1 cup dry red wine
2 tbsps cracked black pepper	5 cups beef stock
½ cup bacon drippings or vegetable oil	1 sprig rosemary
2 cups diced onions	4 onions, quartered
2 cups diced celery	1 tbsp butter
1 cup diced bell peppers	6 carrots, halved
¼ cup minced garlic	8 new potatoes

Method:

Preheat oven to 400°F. Cut 2 strips of bacon into ¼-inch strips (about 1½ inches long). Combine salt and pepper with garlic. Using a sharp paring knife, cut 6–8 (1-inch deep) slits into pork chops. Roll bacon strips and place 1 roll in each slit along with some salt, pepper and garlic mixture. Continue until all slits have been stuffed. Season chops well on all sides using salt and cracked black pepper. In a cast iron Dutch oven, heat bacon drippings over medium-high heat. Brown chops well on all sides. When golden brown, add onions, celery, bell peppers and garlic. Sauté 3–5 minutes or until vegetables are wilted. Blend in tomato sauce, carrots and red wine. Pour in beef stock and add rosemary. Bring to a rolling boil, then reduce heat to simmer. Cover Dutch oven and allow chops to simmer 3½ hours. Top onion quarters with butter, wrap in foil and bake 1 hour. When chops are tender, remove from stock. Strain stock and discard vegetables. Return stock and chops to pot. Add carrots and potatoes. Bring to a boil and cook until vegetables are tender. To serve, place a portion of baked onions, potatoes and carrots with chops in a soup bowl. Top with stock and eat as a soup.

CORN BREAD
STUFFED PORK CHOPS

Prep Time: 2 Hours
Yields: 6 Servings

Comment:

In the 1800s, pork was preferred to other meats because of its availability and versatility. Crown roast was the most sought after dish but was too much for a small family. Instead, many people simply stuffed the center-cut chops with a variety of local fillings to create a delicious pork meal.

Ingredients:

6 (1-inch) center-cut pork chops	1 cup (150–200 count) shrimp
3 cups crumbled corn bread	¼ cup sliced green onions
salt and cracked black pepper to taste	¼ cup chopped parsley
Louisiana hot sauce to taste	1 tbsp chopped sage
½ cup butter	1 tbsp chopped thyme
1 cup diced onions	1 tbsp chopped basil
½ cup diced celery	1 quart hot chicken stock (see recipe)
¼ cup diced red bell peppers	4 cups Sauce Acadian (see recipe)
¼ cup diced garlic	

Method:

Preheat oven to 375°F. Have your butcher split chops down center to form a pocket for stuffing. Season chops inside and out with salt, pepper and hot sauce. Set aside. In a cast iron skillet, melt butter over medium-high heat. Sauté onions, celery, bell peppers and garlic 3–5 minutes or until vegetables are wilted. Stir in shrimp, green onions, parsley, sage, thyme and basil. Blend well and cook 10 minutes or until shrimp are pink. Sprinkle in corn bread. Add chicken stock, 1 ladle at a time, to keep stuffing moist and prevent it from sticking. Season with salt, pepper and hot sauce. Once stuffing is full-flavored, remove from heat and allow to cool. Stuff equal amounts of corn bread mixture into center of chops. Place chops in an ovenproof casserole dish and top with Sauce Acadian, or substitute 2 cans of cream of shrimp soup. Bake covered 1½ hours or until chops are tender.

MEDALLIONS OF PORK IN FIG GLAZE

Prep Time: 1 Hour
Yields: 6 Servings

Comment:
In the evolution process, it is quite natural that Cajuns continue to combine ingredients at hand to create interesting dishes. In this dish, sautéed pork medallions are flavored with Louisiana figs for a unique flavor.

Ingredients:
12 medallions of pork
¼ cup vegetable oil
salt and cayenne pepper to taste
1 cup flour
½ cup sliced green onions
½ cup sliced mushrooms
1 tbsp minced garlic
1 ounce port wine
½ cup fig preserves
2 cups demi-glace (see recipe)
1 tbsp chopped parsley

Method:
In a 10-inch sauté pan, heat oil over medium-high heat. Season pork with salt and cayenne pepper. Dust lightly in flour, and sauté until medium-rare and brown on both sides. Stir in green onions, mushrooms and garlic. Sauté 1–2 minutes or until vegetables are wilted. Deglaze with port wine. Stir in fig preserves and demi-glace. Continue cooking until sauce is slightly thickened and meat is cooked to your liking. Sprinkle in parsley and season with salt and cayenne pepper. Serve 2 medallions per person with a generous portion of fig demi-glace.

OUACHITA STUFFED PEPPERS

Prep Time: 1½ Hours
Yields: 6 Servings

Comment:
The Indians of Louisiana were instrumental in helping to develop the cuisines of the Cajuns and Creoles. Corn, squash, beans and cornmeal were part of the Natives' daily repertoire. These ingredients quickly found their way into the black iron pots. One of the most prominent tribes in Louisiana is the Ouachita tribe, from which this dish gets its name. In this recipe, Native American ingredients are combined with pork and beef to create a delicious entrée.

Ingredients:
2 each red, green and yellow bell peppers
2 pounds ground pork
2 pounds ground beef
¼ cup butter
1 cup diced onions
1 cup diced celery
¼ cup diced red bell peppers
¼ cup diced yellow bell peppers
¼ cup minced garlic
1 cup beef stock (see recipe)
½ cup sliced green onions
¼ cup chopped parsley
1 cup whole kernel corn
2 cups crushed corn bread
salt and cracked black pepper to taste
Louisiana hot sauce to taste
4 cups prepared tomato sauce

Method:
Preheat oven to 375°F. In a large cast iron skillet, melt butter over medium-high heat. Sauté pork and beef 30 minutes or until golden brown. Drain off all but 2 tablespoons of oil. Stir in diced onions, celery, bell peppers and garlic. Sauté 3–5 minutes or until vegetables are wilted. Add beef stock as necessary to keep mixture moist. Mix in green onions, parsley and corn. Sprinkle in crushed corn bread and blend well. Season with salt, pepper and hot sauce. Remove tops from bell peppers and clean all pulp from inside. Stuff with meat dressing, place in a large casserole dish and surround with a prepared tomato sauce. Bake 30 minutes or until peppers are tender.

PAN-FRIED PORK CHOPS
AND WILD PEARS

Prep Time: 2 Hours
Yields: 4–6 Servings

Comment:
Combining Louisiana cooking pears with meat was common in early Cajun homes. The pears are grown in abundance in the area, and they are often used for canning.

Ingredients:
6 thin pork chops
salt and cracked black pepper to taste
2 tsps granulated garlic
¼ cup vegetable oil
4 slices apple wood smoked bacon, chopped
1 cup minced onions
½ cup minced celery
2 cups peeled, cored and diced cooking pears
1 tbsp Louisiana cane syrup
2 cups chicken stock (see recipe)
½ cup sliced green onions
¼ cup finely chopped parsley

Method:
Season chops well using salt, pepper and granulated garlic. Set aside. In a heavy-bottomed Dutch oven over medium-high heat, add vegetable oil and bacon. Cook until bacon becomes transparent. Add chops and sauté until golden brown on all sides. Once browned, remove and keep warm. In same oil, sauté onions, celery and pears 5 minutes or until vegetables are wilted. Add cane syrup and chicken stock. Bring to a rolling boil. Add green onions and chops. Cover Dutch oven and allow chops to cook 1–1½ hours. Season with salt and cracked black pepper. Add parsley and continue cooking until pork chops are completely tender.

MUFFULETTA

Prep Time: 1 Hour
Yields: 4 Servings

Comment:

The Muffuletta is an Italian sandwich created in the late 1800s. The sandwich originated when Italian merchants working in the markets of New Orleans placed a mixture of broken green and black olives, found on the bottom of olive barrels, on loaves of round Italian bread known as "muffs." Over this mixture, they layered slices of ham, salami and Provolone cheese. The most famous of all Muffuletta sandwiches are found at the historic Central Grocery on Decatur Street in New Orleans.

Ingredients for Olive Salad:

¼ cup black olives	1 small can artichoke hearts
¼ cup green olives	1 tsp celery seed
¼ cup pimientos	1 tsp dried oregano
¼ cup capers	1 tbsp chopped garlic
¼ cup cocktail onions	½ cup olive oil
¼ cup coarsely chopped celery	2 tbsps red wine vinegar

Method:

In a food processor, combine all above ingredients and chop coarsely. Scrape into a bowl and set aside.

Ingredients for Sandwich:

1 loaf round Italian bread	¼ pound Mortadella (Italian bologna), thinly sliced
2 tbsps olive oil	
¼ pound ham, thinly sliced	3 slices mozzarella cheese
¼ pound Genoa salami, thinly sliced	1 cup prepared olive salad (see above)
¼ pound Provolone cheese, thinly sliced	

Method:

Split bread lengthwise and drizzle olive oil on each side. Arrange layers of meats and cheeses, then add olive salad. Cover with top layer of bread, cut and serve.

CAJUN STUFFED CHAUDIN (PONCE)

Prep Time: 3 Hours
Yields: 6 Servings

Comment:

Is it chaudin or is it ponce? Our research has revealed the mystery and although most areas of Louisiana refer to chaudin and ponce interchangeably, chaudin often refers to the pork stomach in the raw form. Once the chaudin has been stuffed, smoked or roasted it is called ponce. This mouth-watering dish creates its own natural sauce and is served with steaming white rice. Whether is it called chaudin or ponce, without chaudin there would be no ponce!

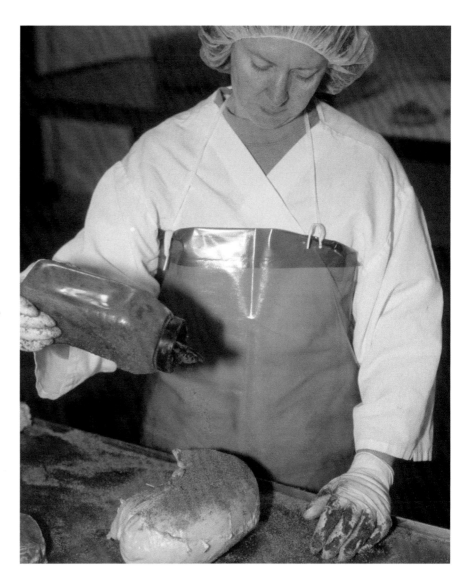

Ingredients for Stuffing:

1 medium chaudin (pork stomach)
2 quarts cold water
4 tbsps club soda
½ cup vinegar
½ cup butter
1 cup diced onions
½ cup diced celery
¼ cup diced red bell peppers
¼ cup minced garlic
½ cup sliced mushrooms
½ cup ground andouille sausage
½ pound ground beef
3 pounds ground pork
1 cup Italian bread crumbs
2 eggs
½ cup sliced green onions
½ cup chopped parsley
salt and cracked black pepper to taste

Method:

Have your butcher clean one chaudin properly for you. Place chaudin in a large bowl filled with water, soda and vinegar. Soak for 1 hour. In a heavy-bottomed sauté pan, heat butter over medium-high heat. Sauté onions, celery, red bell peppers, garlic, mushrooms and andouille 3–5 minutes or until vegetables are wilted. Add ground beef and pork. Continue to cook 45 minutes or until meat is well-browned and separated. Stir in bread crumbs, eggs, green onions and parsley. Cook an additional 3 minutes and season with salt and pepper. Remove from heat and set aside. Remove chaudin from soda water and rinse under tap 2 or 3 times. Using a large metal spoon, stuff chaudin with ground meat dressing until completely full. Secure open ends with toothpicks and heavy gauge twine.

Ingredients for Ponce:

½ cup vegetable oil
2 small onions, sliced
1 cup diced celery
½ cup diced bell peppers
¼ cup minced garlic
½ cup diced carrots
2 cups sliced mushrooms
3 cups chicken stock
salt and cayenne pepper to taste

Method:

In a heavy-bottomed Dutch oven, heat oil over medium-high heat. Sauté onions, celery, bell peppers, garlic, carrots and mushrooms 2 minutes or until vegetables are wilted. Place ponce in Dutch oven and brown well on all sides. Pour in chicken stock, bring to a low boil and reduce heat to simmer. Cover Dutch oven and allow ponce to cook approximately 1 hour, turning occasionally. Season with salt and cayenne pepper. Once cooked, cut into ½-inch slices and serve with natural sauce.

TOURNEDOS OF
BEEF MARCHAND DE VIN

Prep Time: 30 Minutes
Yields: 2 Servings

Comment:

Filet mignon is the most tender cut of meat. The tournedos are 3-ounce medallions cut from the center of the filet. Marchand de vin, "the wine merchant's sauce," is a well-known New Orleans meat sauce traditionally served with filet.

Ingredients:

4 (3-ounce) medallions of filet mignon
¼ cup butter
salt and black pepper to taste
¼ cup unseasoned flour
¼ cup diced shallots
1 tbsp minced garlic

¼ cup sliced green onions
½ cup sliced mushrooms
½ cup Burgundy wine
3 cups beef consommé
　OR　2 cups prepared brown gravy or sauce

Method:

In a heavy-bottomed sauté pan, melt butter over medium-high heat. Season medallions lightly with salt and pepper. Dust in flour and shake off all excess. Sauté filets in butter until golden brown on both sides, but do not burn butter. Move medallions to one side of skillet, then add shallots, garlic, green onions and mushrooms. Sauté 2–3 minutes or until vegetables are wilted. Pour in Burgundy to deglaze pan and reduce to ¼ cup. Stir in beef consommé, bring to a rolling boil and reduce to approximately 1 cup, turning beef occasionally. Season with salt and pepper. For a varied flavor, use Louisiana fruit such as fig preserves or kumquats to finish the dish.

FILET OF BEEF VIALA

Prep Time: 30 Minutes
Yields: 6 Servings

Comment:

The old Viala Plantation, named for a prominent Louisiana family, was reputed to have been the home of the famous pirate, Jean Lafitte from 1799–1804. In 1979, Chef John Folse opened his Lafitte's Landing Restaurant in this historic plantation.

Ingredients:

6 (8-ounce) filets mignons
½ pound lump crabmeat
½ cup bacon drippings or vegetable oil
salt and cracked black pepper to taste
½ cup minced onions
½ cup minced celery
1 tbsp minced garlic
¼ cup sliced mushrooms
¼ cup thinly sliced green onions
2 ounces Marsala wine
3 cups beef demi-glace (see recipe)
¼ cup chopped parsley
¼ pound butter
¼ cup diced red bell peppers
1 ounce white wine

Method:

Preheat oven to 350°F. In a 10-inch heavy-bottomed saucepan, heat bacon drippings over medium-high heat. Season filets with salt and pepper. Sauté beef until golden brown on all sides. Remove from pan, place on a baking sheet and set aside. In same pan, sauté onions, celery, garlic, mushrooms and green onions 2–3 minutes or until vegetables are wilted. Deglaze with Marsala and allow to reduce to a syrup consistency. While wine is reducing, place filets in oven 10–15 minutes or until internal temperature reaches 130° for medium. Once wine is reduced, stir in demi-glace and parsley. Season with salt and pepper. Remove from heat and keep warm. In a 9-inch sauté pan, melt butter over medium-high heat. Sauté red bell peppers and lump crabmeat 2–3 minutes or until crabmeat is hot. Do not overcook. Pour in white wine, bring to a low boil and season with salt and pepper. Remove filets from oven when done to your liking. Top with generous serving of Viala demi-glace sauce and sautéed lump crabmeat.

BLACK-AND-BLUE SUGAR STEAK

Prep Time: 3 Hours
Yields: 4 Servings

Comment:

Among Pittsburgh steelworkers, the term "black-and-blue" is used to describe a steak that has been charred on the outside but remains rare on the inside. Here in Louisiana, brown sugar or cane syrup is used to create a sweet meat marinade.

Ingredients:

1 (2½-pound) porterhouse steak
¼ cup Steen's Cane Syrup
¼ cup fresh squeezed orange juice
3 tbsps Worcestershire sauce
2 tsps dried basil leaves
2 tsps dried tarragon leaves
1 tsp dried thyme leaves
2 tsps granulated garlic
1 tbsp olive oil
1 tsp black pepper
1 tsp Louisiana hot sauce
salt to taste

Method:

Whisk together syrup and all other ingredients to create a marinade. Pour marinade into a glass jar and allow flavors to develop overnight. Pour marinade over porterhouse and turn 2 or 3 times to coat evenly. Allow steak to sit at room temperature 1–2 hours, turning occasionally. Heat grill according to manufacturer's directions. Grill steak on high heat, turning occasionally, until inside temperature reaches 125°F and outside is browned and slightly charred around edges. If you prefer your steak medium or well done, cook on a lower heat, turning occasionally, until cooked to your preference.

PEPPER-MARINATED GRILLED FLANK STEAK

Prep Time: 4½ Hours
Yields: 6–8 Servings

Comment:
This steak can be sliced and served in many different ways. For a unique dish, try using tortillas to create a fajita wrap.

Ingredients:
1 (2-pound) flank steak, trimmed
¼ cup vegetable oil
¼ cup balsamic vinegar
1 tbsp Louisiana hot sauce
1 tbsp Louisiana cane syrup
¼ cup minced garlic
½ tsp red pepper flakes
¼ tsp cracked black pepper
2 tbsps chopped thyme
2 tbsps chopped basil
⅛ tsp ground cloves
2 tbsps firmly packed brown sugar
salt to taste
Creole seasoning to taste

Method:
Place steak in a large baking pan. Using a sharp paring knife, cut ¼-inch slits at 1-inch intervals across top of flank. Pour oil, vinegar, hot sauce and cane syrup over meat. Using tips of your fingers, rub liquid generously around steak. In a small mixing bowl, combine garlic, peppers, thyme, basil, cloves and sugar. Rub herb mixture over steak. Season with salt and Creole seasoning. Cover pan and allow meat to sit at room temperature a minimum of 4 hours. Meanwhile, heat a home-style grill according to manufacturer's directions. If desired, soak pecan wood chips in root beer and toss them onto pit for added flavor. When ready to cook, place steak directly over hottest part of coals and cook 5 minutes on each side for medium-rare or 8–10 minutes on each side for medium. When done, place flank steak on a wooden cutting board and thinly slice on a 45° angle prior to serving.

BRAISED ROUND STEAK AND GRAVY

Prep Time: 2 Hours
Yields: 6 Servings

Comment:
On Sunday in Louisiana, you will find succulent round steak smothered in gravy on many dinner tables. Traditionally, this dish is served with steamed white rice and a side of roux peas. This mouth-watering recipe was created in St. James Parish.

Ingredients:
1 (2-pound) round steak, bone-in
salt and cracked black pepper to taste
¼ cup vegetable oil
2 cups diced onions
½ cup diced celery
¼ cup diced bell peppers
¼ cup minced garlic
3 cups water
¼ cup sliced green onions
¼ cup chopped parsley

Method:
Cut steak into serving pieces 2–3 inches wide, and season lightly with salt and pepper. In a 12-inch cast iron skillet, heat oil over medium-high heat. Oil should be very hot to caramelize meat on bottom of skillet. When oil reaches 375°F, place steak in skillet and brown well on all sides. When meat is done, remove it from skillet and keep warm. Sauté onions, celery, bell peppers and garlic 3–5 minutes or until vegetables are wilted and caramelized residue has dissolved in bottom of pan. Pour in water. Return meat to skillet, bring liquid to a rolling boil, then reduce heat to simmer. Cover and cook approximately 1½ hours or until meat is tender. If necessary, use additional water to keep meat moist. When meat is tender, add green onions and parsley. Adjust seasonings if necessary. Cook an additional 3–5 minutes.

BROCIOLONI

Prep Time: 1½ Hours
Yields: 6 Servings

Comment:

The Italians moved upriver from New Orleans in the late 1800s to work on sugar plantations. Many of these Italian families later opened grocery stores, vegetable stands and meat markets. The Italian cooking was an important influence on shaping the cuisine of America.

Ingredients for Seasoning:

2 large round steaks
salt and cracked black pepper to taste
½ cup diced onions
½ cup diced celery
¼ cup minced garlic
¼ cup sliced green onions
½ cup sliced pimiento olives
½ cup grated Parmesan cheese
¼ cup grated Romano cheese
¼ cup pine nuts
¼ cup golden raisins
½ cup Italian bread crumbs

Method:

Place 1 round steak between 2 large sheets of wax paper and gently pound with a meat mallet to flatten and tenderize meat. Repeat with second steak. Place steaks on a large work surface and overlap them by 2–3 inches to form a large rectangle. The 2 pieces combined should be approximately 1 foot wide. Season meat generously with salt and pepper. Spread all ingredients evenly over steaks. Roll meat in jellyroll fashion and secure with butcher's twine or toothpicks to keep intact during cooking process.

Ingredients for Cooking:

¼ cup extra virgin olive oil
1 cup diced onions
1 cup diced celery
1 cup diced bell peppers
¼ cup minced garlic
1 cup sliced carrots
1 pound Italian sausage, cut into 2-inch pieces
1 (35-ounce) can Italian plum tomatoes, chopped
1 cup dry red wine
1 (8-ounce) can tomato sauce
1 quart chicken stock (see recipe)
Louisiana hot sauce to taste

Method:

In a large heavy-bottomed Dutch oven, heat olive oil over medium-high heat. Brown steak well on all sides, turning occasionally. Add onions, celery, bell peppers, garlic, carrots, sausage, tomatoes, red wine, tomato sauce and 2 cups chicken stock. Bring mixture to a rolling boil, then reduce to simmer. Cover and cook 1–1½ hours. Chicken stock may be added as needed to retain volume. Once meat is tender, season sauce with salt, pepper and hot sauce. If sauce is watery, remove meat to a serving platter and reduce sauce over medium-high heat until proper consistency is achieved. When ready to serve, slice brocioloni into 6 portions and top with tomato sauce.

The digester: 18th century pressure cooker

GRILLADES AND GRAVY SPANISH STYLE

Prep Time: 2 Hours
Yields: 6 Servings

Comment:

Grillades were first created by butchers in early Louisiana as they prepared a freshly killed pig. Settlers from Spain heavily influenced this popular version of grillades. The olives, olive oil and fresh herbs give this recipe a distinctly Mediterranean character.

Ingredients:

1 (2-pound) round steak
salt and black pepper to taste
¼ cup olive oil
1 cup diced onions
½ cup diced celery
½ cup diced bell peppers
¼ cup minced garlic
2 tbsps flour
1 (8-ounce) can tomato sauce
1 (14.5-ounce) can diced tomatoes
  in juice
½ cup sliced black olives
3 cups beef stock (see recipe)
2 tbsps chopped basil
1 tsp chopped thyme
Louisiana hot sauce to taste
½ cup sliced green onions
¼ cup chopped parsley

Method:

Cut round steak into 3-inch squares and pound lightly. Season with salt and pepper. In a cast iron skillet, heat olive oil over medium-high heat. Brown round steak on all sides. Remove and keep warm. Add a tablespoon of olive oil to skillet if necessary. Sauté onions, celery, bell peppers and garlic 3–5 minutes or until vegetables are wilted. Blend in flour until smooth. Stir in tomato sauce, diced tomatoes and black olives. Pour in stock and blend well. Add basil, thyme, salt, pepper and hot sauce. Return round steak to skillet and bring mixture to a rolling boil. Reduce to simmer, cover and cook 1–1½ hours or until meat is fork tender. Use additional stock or water during cooking process if necessary. Once tender, add green onions and parsley. Adjust seasonings if necessary. Serve over hot, buttered grits.

GRILLADES

Prep Time: 1 Hour
Yields: 6 Servings

Comment:

The origin of grillades has been the subject of many arguments in Bayou Country. It is believed that the dish originated when the country butchers preparing the boucherie sliced thin pieces of fresh pork and pan-fried these with sliced onions. The cooking probably took place in black iron pots over the boucherie fires. The grillades were then eaten over grits or rice throughout the day. Today, grillades and grits are a tradition on many Sunday brunch menus. Most recipes call for veal round pounded lightly and smothered in its natural juices.

Ingredients:

2 medium round steaks
salt and cracked black pepper to taste
1 cup flour
¼ cup shortening or bacon drippings
1 cup minced onions
1 cup minced celery
½ cup minced bell peppers
1 cup diced tomatoes
1 cup thinly sliced green onions
¼ cup minced garlic
3 cups beef stock
1 cup sliced mushrooms
¼ cup chopped parsley

Method:

Cut round steak into 3-inch squares. Season with salt and cracked black pepper. Dust pieces generously with flour and set aside. In a heavy-bottomed Dutch oven, heat shortening over medium-high heat. Sauté meat until brown on all sides. Add onions, celery, bell peppers, tomatoes, green onions and garlic. Sauté 3–5 minutes or until vegetables are wilted. Pour in beef stock, bring to a low boil then reduce to simmer. Cover Dutch oven and allow grillades to cook slowly for approximately 45 minutes. Stir occasionally to keep seasonings from scorching. Once tender, add mushrooms and parsley. Adjust seasonings if necessary and cook 10 minutes. Serve over grits as a breakfast item or over rice as an entrée.

ROAST TENDERLOIN
OF BEEF IN CANE SYRUP

Prep Time: 3 Hours
Yields: 6 Servings

Comment:
This recipe is another example of the use of cane syrup as a marinade. Here, the syrup is used both as a tenderizer and as a flavoring.

Ingredients:
1 trimmed beef tenderloin
½ cup port wine
¼ cup cane syrup
1 tbsp dried thyme
1 tbsp dried basil
1 tbsp dried tarragon
2 tbsps minced garlic
½ cup cracked black pepper
1 tbsp salt

Method:
Preheat oven to 400°F. Place tenderloin into a baking pan with a 1-inch lip. Cover with port wine, rubbing well into meat. Allow excess wine to remain in bottom of baking pan. Pour on cane syrup and rub well. Season meat completely with remaining ingredients. Allow to sit at room temperature 1 hour. Place baking pan in center of oven and cook uncovered approximately 25 minutes for medium-rare. A meat thermometer may be used for accuracy. This dish may be served hot or cold. For a variation, grill or smoke meat on an outdoor pit and top cooked tenderloin with Marchand De Vin Sauce. (See recipe.)

SAUERBRATEN,
LOUISIANA STYLE

Prep Time: 2 Hours
Yields: 6–8 Servings

Comment:
Sauerbraten or sweet-and-sour roast beef is normally made with a beef top or rump roast. When the Germans settled Louisiana, they altered the recipe slightly by using cubed beef rather than whole roast. Today, sauerbraten made with cubed pork is served in Louisiana's bayou region as well.

Ingredients:
5 pounds beef rump roast, cubed
2½ cups water
1½ cups red wine vinegar
1 tbsp brown sugar
1 tbsp salt
¼ tsp ground ginger
10 whole cloves
6 bay leaves
6 whole peppercorns
1 purple onion, sliced
2 lemon slices
¼ cup vegetable oil
1 cup diced onions
1 cup diced celery
1 cup sliced carrots
1 tbsp minced garlic
¼ cup sliced green onions
beef or chicken stock (optional)
1 cup broken ginger snap cookies
¼ cup raisins
salt and cracked black pepper to taste
hot buttered noodles
½ cup chopped parsley

Method:
In a crock pot or large bowl, combine water, vinegar, sugar, salt, ginger, cloves, bay leaves, peppercorns, sliced onions and lemons. Stir well, then mix in cubed beef. Coat meat well with marinade and refrigerate overnight, turning occasionally. In a large heavy-bottomed Dutch oven, heat oil over medium-high heat. Remove meat from marinade and reserve. Place roast into Dutch oven and brown well. Sauté onions, celery, carrots, garlic and green onions with meat 3–5 minutes or until vegetables are wilted. Pour in reserved marinade, bring to a rolling boil, cover and reduce heat to simmer. Allow meat to cook approximately 2 hours, checking occasionally for tenderness. If necessary, use additional beef or chicken stock to flavor sauce. Using a slotted spatula, remove meat from liquid and set aside. Stir in ginger snaps and raisins and cook until sauce is thickened. Season with salt and pepper. Return meat to pot and blend well into mixture. Serve over hot noodles and garnish with parsley.

A DUO OF POT ROASTS

Prep Time: 3 Hours
Yields: 8 Servings

Comment:
In all large families, it is often difficult to please everyone at the dinner table. Since some people love pork roast and others crave beef, cook both in the same pot. The mingled flavors create a magnificent dish everyone can enjoy.

Ingredients:
1 (4-pound) beef rump roast
1 (4-pound) Boston butt
½ cup minced garlic
½ cup sliced green onions
black pepper to taste
¼ cup salt
1 cup seasoned flour
½ cup vegetable oil
3 cups diced onions
1 cup diced celery
½ cup diced bell peppers
4 cups beef bouillon

Method:
In a large mixing bowl, combine garlic, green onions, pepper and ⅛ cup salt. Using a paring knife, cut 8–10 (1-inch) slits in both roasts. Divide seasoning mixture and stuff into slits. Season outside of each roast with remaining salt and pepper. Dust in seasoned flour. In a large Dutch oven, heat oil over medium-high heat. Brown roasts evenly on all sides. Once browned, remove roasts to a holding platter. In same Dutch oven, sauté onions, celery and bell peppers 3–5 minutes or until vegetables are wilted. Return roasts to Dutch oven and pour in beef bouillon. Bring to a rolling boil, then reduce to simmer. Cover and cook 2–3 hours or until roasts are fork tender. Remove meat and reduce sauce until slightly thickened. Slice roasts and top with thickened sauce. This dish is excellent when accompanied by a fresh lettuce and tomato salad and baked sweet potatoes. Leftover roast makes a perfect French bread sandwich.

VENTRESS ISLAND RUMP ROAST

Prep Time: 4 Hours
Yields: 8 Servings

Comment:
This recipe hails from Ventress, La., also known as the "Island Side" of False River. This rump roast is a favorite for Sunday family dinners in Ventress.

Ingredients:
1 (4-pound) boneless rump roast
4 large potatoes
8 carrots
1 large onion, minced
¼ cup diced red bell peppers
¼ cup diced yellow bell peppers
¼ cup diced green bell peppers
¼ cup minced garlic
1 medium jalapeño, diced
salt and black pepper to taste
¼ cup Worcestershire sauce
¼ cup liquid smoke
¼ cup peanut oil
½ cup seasoned flour
2 cups beef consommé
1 cup sliced mushrooms

Method:
Preheat oven to 350°F. Peel potatoes and cut into 1-inch cubes. Peel carrots and slice 1-inch thick. Set aside. In a large mixing bowl, combine onions, bell peppers, garlic, jalapeños, salt and pepper. Blend well and set aside. In a separate bowl, combine Worcestershire and liquid smoke. Using a paring knife, cut 10–12 (2-inch) slits around rump roast. Stuff each slit with equal parts of vegetable mixture. Add ¼ teaspoon of Worcestershire mixture to each slit. Apply remainder of Worcestershire to outside of roast. Season with salt and pepper. It is best to allow roast to sit overnight or a minimum of 1 hour prior to cooking. In a large Dutch oven, heat oil over medium-high heat. Dust roast in seasoned flour to coat well. Brown roast on all sides to enhance flavor and color. Drain off excess oil and pour in consommé. Bring to a rolling boil, then remove from heat. Cover, place in oven and bake approximately 2 hours. Remove lid and add potatoes, carrots and mushrooms. Cover and cook 1–1½ hours, basting occasionally, until tender. Slice roast and arrange meat and vegetables on a serving platter. Top with natural juices and serve over steamed white rice.

VEAL DAUBE

Prep Time: 5 Hours
Yields: 8 Servings

Comment:

Daube is commonly found on tables in South Louisiana at Christmas. This cut of meat is normally tougher than others, but the slow cooking process helps to tenderize it.

Ingredients:

2 (1½-pound) veal eye-of-the-round roasts
½ pound bacon
¼ cup diced garlic
2 tbsps salt
2 tbsps cracked black pepper
salt and cracked black pepper to taste
½ cup bacon drippings or vegetable oil
2 cups diced onions
2 cups diced celery
1 cup diced bell peppers
¼ cup minced garlic
¼ cup tomato sauce
2 cups diced carrots
1 cup dry red wine
5 cups beef stock (see recipe)
1 sprig rosemary
4 onions, quartered
4 tbsps butter
6 carrots, halved
8 new potatoes

Method:

Preheat oven to 400°F. Cut 2 strips of bacon into ¼-inch strips about 1½ inches long. Combine garlic, salt and pepper. Using a paring knife, cut 6–8 (1-inch deep) slits into veal roasts. Roll bacon strips and place 1 in each slit along with a portion of garlic seasoning mixture. Season roasts with additional salt and pepper. In cast iron Dutch oven, heat bacon drippings over medium-high heat. Brown roasts on all sides. When golden brown, add diced onions, celery, bell peppers and garlic. Sauté 3–5 minutes or until vegetables are wilted. Blend tomato sauce, diced carrots and red wine into vegetable mixture. Add beef stock and rosemary. Bring to a rolling boil and reduce heat to simmer. Cover Dutch oven and allow roasts to simmer 3½ hours. Salt and pepper quartered onions, and wrap along with 4 tablespoons of butter in foil. Bake 1 hour. When roasts are tender, remove from stock and strain. Discard vegetables and return stock to pot. Return roasts to pot, add carrots and potatoes, bring to a boil and cook until vegetables are tender. Serve by placing a portion of onions, potatoes and carrots with roast in a soup bowl. Top with stock. It is always best to cook daube a day in advance and reheat.

DAUBE

Prep Time: 3 Hours
Yields: 6–8 Servings

Comment:

Although a less tender, inexpensive cut of beef, daube is commonly found on the tables in South Louisiana. Slow cooking the roast with vegetable seasonings makes this dish a full-flavored entrée.

Ingredients:

1 (5-pound) beef shoulder roast
¼ pound salt pork fat
¼ cup salt
¼ cup cracked black pepper
¼ cup minced garlic
½ cup bacon drippings or vegetable oil
2 cups diced onions
2 cups diced celery
1 cup diced bell peppers
¼ cup minced garlic
¼ cup tomato sauce
2 cups diced carrots
1 cup dry red wine
1 quart beef stock (see recipe)
salt and cracked black pepper to taste

Method:

Cut salt pork fat into ¼-inch strips about 2 inches long. Using a sharp paring knife, cut 6–8 (1-inch) slits into shoulder roast. Combine salt and pepper, and stuff slits with generous amounts of garlic, salt, pepper and pork fat. Season roast well on all sides with salt and cracked black pepper. In a cast iron Dutch oven, heat bacon drippings over medium-high heat. Brown roast on all sides. When golden brown, add onions, celery, bell peppers and garlic. Sauté 3–5 minutes or until vegetables are wilted. Blend in tomato sauce, carrots and red wine. Pour in beef stock, bring to a rolling boil then reduce to simmer. Cover Dutch oven and allow roast to simmer 2½ hours. Season with salt and cracked black pepper. Cook until roast is tender. Slice and serve with natural sauce.

PRIME RIB OF BEEF

Prep Time: 2½ Hours
Yields: 12–14 Servings

Comment:
This classic prime-rib preparation is as popular in Louisiana as it is in the rest of the nation. It is truly the foremost example of a food simply prepared, yet wonderfully delicious.

Ingredients:
1 (18–22-pound) prime rib roast, oven-ready
salt and black pepper to taste
granulated garlic to taste
4 medium onions, quartered
½ bunch celery, sliced
6 cloves of garlic
1 pound carrots, sliced
2 cups red wine
1 quart beef stock

Method:
Preheat oven to 400°F. Place roast in large roasting pan with 2-inch sides. Season with salt, pepper and granulated garlic by cutting 1-inch slits in roast and stuffing ¼ teaspoon of each seasoning into slits. Surround with vegetables and cover pan tightly with foil. Place in oven and reduce temperature to 350°F. Cook approximately 1½ hours before checking temperature. An internal temperature of 130°F at center of meat is medium-rare, 145°F is medium and 155°F is medium-well. Remove roast from oven and set aside on large serving platter. Allow drippings in roasting pan to rest 30 minutes, then slowly tilt pan to remove grease rising to surface of natural drippings. Return pan to stove on medium-high heat. Once vegetables begin to sizzle, pour in red wine to deglaze pan. Allow wine to reduce to half volume. Pour in beef stock and continue to boil until flavors have blended. Strain sauce and discard vegetables. Serve sauce alongside roast.

BRAISED BEEF SHORT RIBS

Prep Time: 2½ Hours
Yields: 8 Servings

Comment:
Braising is a process of cooking food in a little water over a long period of time. This method is used on tougher cuts of meat to guarantee tenderness and to impart a vegetable-infused flavor.

Ingredients:
6 pounds beef short ribs
8 slices bacon, chopped
2 large onions, quartered
3 stalks celery, quartered
3 carrots, sliced
8 cloves garlic, smashed
6 cups beef stock, bouillon or water
1 cup dry red wine
3 sprigs fresh thyme
6 leaves fresh basil
salt and pepper to taste

VEAL BIRDS WITH OYSTER STUFFING

Prep Time: 1 Hour
Yields: 6 Servings

Comment:

Because the Cajuns and Creoles preferred to raise their calves to full maturity, veal was seldom seen in South Louisiana. However, things have changed and today veal is used in a variety of dishes.

Ingredients for Stuffing:

1 pound bulk pork sausage
1 pint fresh shucked oysters
¼ pound butter
½ cup diced onions
½ cup diced celery
½ cup diced red bell peppers
2 tbsp minced garlic
¼ cup sliced green onions
1 egg, beaten
½ cup Italian bread crumbs
salt and cracked black pepper to taste

Method:

In a 10-inch sauté pan, melt butter over medium-high heat. Add sausage and chop in pan. Cook until golden brown. Stir in oysters, onions, celery, bell peppers, garlic and green onions. Sauté until vegetables are wilted. Remove from heat, then add egg and blend well. Sprinkle in bread crumbs, a little at a time, blending until consistency is tightened but not dry. Season with salt and pepper. Set aside.

Ingredients for Veal Birds:

6 (6-ounce) veal cutlets
1 cup flour
salt and white pepper to taste
½ cup vegetable oil
½ cup dry white wine
2 cups demi-glace (see recipe)
1 cup heavy whipping cream

Method:

NOTE: Have your butcher tenderize veal cutlets by pounding gently or running through a meat tenderizer. Preheat oven to 350°F. Place cutlets on a large baking sheet with a 1-inch lip. Place an equal amount of stuffing in center of each cutlet, roll into a turban shape and secure with toothpicks. Dredge each roll in flour, and lightly season with salt and white pepper. In a 10-inch heavy-bottomed sauté pan, heat oil over medium-high heat. Sauté veal until lightly browned. Remove veal, place in baking pan and bake 15–20 minutes for medium rare. While meat is baking, discard excess oil from sauté pan, but reserve pan drippings. Deglaze pan with white wine and add demi-glace. Bring to a rolling boil and reduce by half. Add heavy whipping cream. Reduce to simmer. Season with salt and white pepper. Remove veal from baking pan and place in sauté pan with sauce. Simmer veal 3–5 minutes. Serve each veal bird with cream sauce.

Method:

Preheat oven to 375°F. Season short ribs with salt and pepper. In a 10-quart Dutch oven, brown bacon over medium-high heat to render fat. Do not burn. Remove crisp bacon and set aside. Brown short ribs in bacon fat, 4 at a time, taking care not to burn bacon fat. Once all ribs are brown, remove from pan. Add onions, celery, carrots and garlic to pan. Sauté 2–3 minutes to tenderize vegetables. Pour in stock and red wine. Bring to a rolling boil, then reduce to simmer. Add cooked bacon, browned short-ribs, thyme and basil. Season stock with additional salt and pepper if necessary. Return mixture to a rolling boil, cover and place in preheated oven and cook 1½ hours. When ribs are fork-tender, remove from stock and set aside. Reduce stock by half. When ready to serve, strain stock, return ribs to pot along with sauce and reheat in oven. Ribs may be prepared up to 3 days in advance and remain in stock until ready to serve.

BREAST OF VEAL WITH POTATO SPINACH STUFFING

Prep Time: 4½ Hours
Yields: 12 Servings

Comment:

Simple braised dishes such as this one are enhanced by the creativity of the cook. With the addition of rustic potatoes and spinach, this breast of veal is transformed into a wonderful entrée centerpiece.

Ingredients for Stuffing:

3¾ pounds russet potatoes, peeled and cut into 1-inch cubes
¼ cup vegetable oil
4 cups diced onions
1 pound ground veal
6 ounces chopped fresh spinach leaves (about 6 cups packed)
½ cup matzo meal
salt and black pepper to taste
2 large eggs, beaten

Method:

In a large pot, boil potatoes in salted water 20 minutes or until tender. Drain and return potatoes to pot to mash. In a large heavy-bottomed skillet, heat oil over high heat. Add onions and sauté 10 minutes or until beginning to brown. Stir in ground veal. Sauté 5 minutes or until no longer pink while breaking up meat with back of spoon. Add spinach and sauté 2 minutes or until wilted. Add veal mixture to potatoes and blend well. Mix in matzo meal. Season stuffing with salt and pepper, then blend in eggs. NOTE: Stuffing can be prepared 1 day ahead. Cover and refrigerate until ready to use.

Ingredients for Veal:

1 (11½-pound) whole breast of veal with pocket for stuffing
4 shallots, chopped
2 celery stalks, chopped
1 carrot, chopped
1 tbsp tomato paste
salt and black pepper to taste

Method:

Ask your butcher to cut a large pocket in veal to hold stuffing. For a veal breast this size, use a deep roasting pan at least 18" x 12". Preheat oven to 375°F. Season veal pocket with salt and pepper. Spread 5 cups of stuffing in pocket. Close pocket with small metal skewers or toothpicks. Sprinkle outside of veal with salt and pepper. Place in large roasting pan, bone side down. Sprinkle shallots, celery and carrots around veal. Pour in tomato paste. Cover pan with heavy-duty foil. Spoon remaining stuffing into an greased baking dish. Cover dish with foil; chill. Roast veal 3 hours then uncover. Place covered dish of stuffing in oven and cook until hot. Continue to roast veal 45 minutes or until top is well browned and meat is tender. Transfer veal to large platter. Let stand 15 minutes. Pour pan juices into large measuring cup and remove fat. Purée pan juices and vegetables in food processor until almost smooth. Season with salt and pepper. Transfer gravy to dish. Slice veal and serve with gravy and extra stuffing.

FRICASSÉE OF VEAL
AND HAM WITH ARTICHOKES

Prep Time: 1 Hour
Yields: 6 Servings

Comment:

Veal is found in many Creole recipes. In fact, veal grillades are more popular than the original pork version. This dish is an excellent example of how Creole cuisine is influenced by many cultures. The Germans who settled the Crescent City added ham, and the Italian immigrants gave the artichokes.

Ingredients:

3 pounds boneless veal stew meat, cubed
1 pound diced ham
12 artichoke bottoms
¾ cup vegetable oil
¾ cup flour
1 cup diced onions
½ cup diced celery
½ cup diced red bell peppers
½ cup diced yellow bell peppers
2 tbsps minced garlic
1½ quarts beef stock (see recipe)
½ pound sliced mushrooms
2 tbsps chopped thyme
1 tbsp chopped basil
½ cup Marsala wine
salt and black pepper to taste
¼ cup butter
¼ cup chopped parsley

Method:

In a large cast iron Dutch oven, heat oil over medium-high heat. Whisk in flour, stirring until dark brown roux is achieved. (See roux recipes.) Add onions, celery, bell peppers and garlic. Sauté 3–5 minutes or until vegetables are wilted. Blend in veal and diced ham, and cook an additional 2–3 minutes. Pour in beef stock, 1 cup at a time, until stew-like consistency is achieved. Bring mixture to a rolling boil, reduce to simmer, cover and cook 30 minutes. Add mushrooms, thyme, basil and wine. Cook an additional 30 minutes or until veal is tender. If necessary, add stock to retain consistency. Season with salt and pepper. It is best to cook this dish 1 day prior to serving and refrigerate overnight to enhance flavors. When ready to serve, bring veal fricassée to a simmer. Rinse artichoke bottoms in cold running water. In a sauté pan, melt butter over medium-high heat. Add artichoke bottoms and sauté until warm. Place 2 artichoke bottoms on a 10-inch serving plate and top with a ladle of fricassée. Garnish each dish with parsley. Try serving steamed artichokes with this dish. The artichoke leaves are an excellent decoration to the plate, and fricassée makes a wonderful dipping sauce.

GRILLED VEAL CHOP
WITH CHANTERELLE SAUCE

Prep Time: 30 Minutes
Yields: 2 Servings

Comment:

A reporter once asked, "What is the best steak at Ruth's Chris Steak House?" Owner Ruth Fertel replied, "The sirloin, but my favorite cut of meat here is the veal chop!"

Ingredients:

4 veal chops
2 ounces Chanterelle mushrooms
¼ cup sliced shallots
1 tbsp thyme leaves
3 tbsps butter
¼ cup white wine
1 cup brown veal stock
salt and black pepper to taste
½ cup heavy whipping cream

Method:

Carefully wash mushrooms in cold water and allow them to soak 3 hours. Remove and dry thoroughly. Leave mushrooms whole if they are small, but slice them if they are large. In a small sauté pan, melt butter over medium-high heat. Add shallots and thyme leaves. Sauté 2–3 minutes. Add mushrooms and cook an additional 2–3 minutes. Deglaze with white wine, add veal stock and reduce to half volume. Season with salt and pepper. Add cream and continue to cook until sauce is thick enough to coat back of a spoon. Heat grill according to manufacturer's directions until coals are white hot. You may add a handful of your favorite smoked wood for extra flavor. Season chops with salt and pepper. Cook 3–5 minutes on each side for medium rare. Grill longer if desired. Serve with a generous portion of chanterelle sauce.

SCALLOPS OF VEAL WITH TASSO AND WILD MUSHROOM ESSENCE

Prep Time: 1 Hour
Yields: 6 Servings

Comment:

Wild mushrooms are plentiful in the Feliciana parishes of Louisiana. Varieties such as wild oyster, golden trumpet and chanterelle can be found growing in Feliciana. Tasso, a spicy ham from Bayou Country, and wild mushrooms are the perfect complement to veal.

Ingredients:

6 (3-ounce) veal loin slices, pounded ⅛-inch thick
½ cup julienned tasso or ham
2 cups sliced chanterelles
black pepper to taste
1 tbsp Creole seasoning
½ cup seasoned flour
¼ cup olive oil
¾ cup Marsala wine
¾ cup veal stock (see recipe)
6 slices mozzarella cheese

Method:

Preheat oven to 375°F. Season veal with pepper and Creole seasoning. Dust lightly in flour and set aside. In a 12-inch sauté pan, heat olive oil over medium-high heat. Sauté veal 1–2 minutes on each side. Remove and place in a baking pan. Add mushrooms and tasso to sauté pan drippings and stir-fry 2 minutes. Deglaze vegetables with wine and veal stock. Bring to a rolling boil and reduce liquid to half volume. Flour left in sauté pan from veal should thicken sauce perfectly. Adjust seasonings if necessary. Remove sauce from heat and keep warm. Place 1 slice of mozzarella on each loin. Bake 5–10 minutes to heat veal and melt cheese. Place 1 portion of veal in center of serving plate and top with tasso and wild mushroom essence.

SWEETBREADS IN LEMON CAPER CREAM

Prep Time: 1 Hour
Yields: 6 Servings

Comment:

Sweetbreads are the thymus glands found in young suckling animals and are considered a delicacy when prepared from young calves. Sweetbreads have always been a delicacy in Creole homes, and New Orleans chefs have prepared them for generations.

Ingredients:

1 pound veal sweetbreads
1 carrot, diced
1 small onion, diced
1 celery stalk, sliced
2 garlic cloves, mashed
12 peppercorns
1 bay leaf
1 cup dry white wine
1 quart water
salt and black pepper to taste

Method:

Have your butcher select 3 whole pieces, approximately 1 pound, of fresh sweetbreads. In a 1-gallon stockpot, combine carrots, onions, celery, garlic cloves, peppercorns, bay leaf, wine and water. Bring liquid to a rolling boil, then reduce to simmer. Cover and cook 30 minutes. Add whole sweetbreads and cook 3–5 minutes, turning once or twice until firm to touch. Do not overcook. Remove sweetbreads and cool. NOTE: You may poach sweetbreads 1 day prior to use. Strain and reserve 1 cup of poaching liquid. Once sweetbreads are cool, use your fingers to remove veil-type membrane covering them. Using a sharp boning knife, slice meat ½-inch thick. Smaller pieces that break away can also be used. Season sweetbreads with salt and pepper. Dust with flour. In a cast iron skillet, melt butter over medium-high heat. Be careful not to brown. Add sweetbreads and sauté a few at a time until light brown and crispy. Remove and keep hot. In same skillet, sauté shallots and garlic 3–5 minutes or until wilted. Add lemon juice and capers, then deglaze with wine. Pour in cream and ¼ cup of poaching liquid. Reduce sauce over medium-high heat for 7–10 minutes or until liquid coats the back of a spoon. Be careful to prevent cream from boiling over. Season with salt and pepper. Add chopped chives and lemon zest. Place sweetbreads in the center of a 10-inch serving plate and surround with a generous portion of lemon caper cream. If you hold sauce prior to serving, you may need to thin it with additional poaching liquid.

Sweetbreads in Lemon Caper Cream

WIENER SCHNITZEL

Prep Time: 30 Minutes
Yields: 6 Servings

Comment:

This recipe is from Chef Gunter Preuss of Broussard's Restaurant in New Orleans. Chef Preuss is famous for serving Weiner Schnitzel during October in honor of the German Oktoberfest celebration. Each year, the community of South Louisiana enjoys this traditional holiday dish.

Ingredients:

6 (4-ounce) slices of veal top round
salt and white pepper to taste
2 tbsps lemon juice
1 cup flour
3 eggs, beaten
1 cup bread crumbs
4 tbsps margarine

Method:

Pound veal slices until thin. Season with salt and white pepper. Sprinkle lightly with lemon juice. Dredge seasoned veal rounds in flour, dip in egg wash then dredge in bread crumbs. In a cast iron skillet, heat margarine over medium-high heat. Add veal rounds and sauté on both sides until golden brown. Arrange on warm dinner plates and serve.

BRAISED OSSO BUCO

Prep Time: 1 Hour
Yields: 6 Servings

Comment:

Osso buco or "long bone" is the shank portion of the leg in beef, veal and lamb. This bone is surrounded by a large portion of meat that is perfect for slow braising. Though inexpensive, when cooked properly, osso buco becomes a very elegant meal.

Ingredients:

12 (1-inch thick) osso buco
1 cup seasoned flour
½ cup olive oil
2 cups diced onions
1 cup diced celery
½ cup diced bell peppers
¼ cup minced garlic
1 tbsp chopped thyme
1 tbsp chopped basil
1 tbsp oregano
½ cup red wine
1 (28-ounce) can plum tomatoes, drained
2 cups beef stock (see recipe)
1 cup sliced mushrooms
1 cup pearl onions
salt and cracked black pepper to taste
Louisiana hot sauce to taste
4 cups cooked angel hair pasta

Method:

Preheat oven to 375°F. In a heavy-bottomed Dutch oven, heat oil over medium-high heat. Dust shanks in seasoned flour, shaking off excess. Place meat in pan and brown on both sides. Remove and set aside. Add onions, celery, bell peppers, garlic, thyme, basil and oregano. Sauté 3–5 minutes or until vegetables are wilted. Deglaze with red wine, then add tomatoes and beef stock. Bring to a rolling boil and reduce to simmer. Stir in mushrooms and pearl onions. Season with salt, pepper and hot sauce. Return shanks to sauce, cover and bake 45 minutes or until tender. Serve over angel hair pasta.

BOILED BRISKET
WITH VEGETABLES

Prep Time: 3 Hours
Yields: 8 Servings

Comment:
This simple, yet tasty boiled meat and vegetable dish can be attributed to the English. Boiled brisket is similar to corned beef that is found on most St. Patrick's Day tables. The major difference between the dishes is the elimination of the cabbage and the addition of various fall vegetables. This boiled brisket is a perfect cold weather dish and is also excellent as a sandwich on rye with a bit of English mustard.

Ingredients:
1 (5-pound) corned beef, trimmed
1 tsp ground allspice
1 tsp dried thyme
2 tbsps black peppercorns
3 bay leaves, crushed
3 whole cloves
6 cloves garlic
1 large onion, quartered
2 stalks celery, sliced
3 carrots, peeled and sliced
8 new potatoes
2 yams, 1-inch cubed
16 baby carrots, peeled
4 turnips, peeled and quartered

Method:
Place brisket in large Dutch oven with enough water to cover by 3 inches. If a seasoning pack was included with brisket, add to water. Add allspice, thyme, peppercorns, bay leaves, cloves, garlic, onion, celery and sliced carrots. Bring to a rolling boil. Reduce to a low boil and cook 2½–3 hours or until brisket is tender at thickest part. Meat is fully cooked when fibers begin to loosen and a fork can be easily inserted. Brisket must be tender for this dish. Remove brisket from pot and place it on a large baking pan. Strain poaching liquid and discard seasonings. Return liquid to Dutch oven. Add potatoes, yams, baby carrots and turnips. Bring stock to a boil, then reduce to simmer and cook 20 minutes or until vegetables are fork-tender and have absorbed flavors. When ready to serve, slice brisket into ¼-inch pieces across grain. Transfer sliced meat to a large serving platter and surround with freshly poached vegetables and a generous serving of hot poaching liquid.

HOMEMADE
CORNED BEEF BRISKET

Prep Time: 3 Hours
Yields: 8 Servings

Comment:
There is no dish better suited for dining in front of the fire than corned beef brisket. Most people eat this dish on St. Patrick's Day, but try it with friends around the open hearth on any cold day.

Ingredients:
1 (5-pound) beef brisket, trimmed
½ cup kosher salt
1 tbsp ground allspice
1 tbsp dried thyme
¾ tbsp paprika
2 tbsps black peppercorns
3 bay leaves, crushed
1 pound peeled, sliced carrots
1 pound peeled, quartered turnips
2 pounds halved new potatoes
1 small cabbage

Method:
Place brisket in a large pan. Using a skewer or meat fork, pierce meat 25–30 times on each side. Rub each side of brisket evenly with salt. Rub meat with allspice then thyme and paprika. Place brisket in a 2-gallon plastic zipper bag. Add peppercorns and bay leaves to bag, then squeeze to remove excess air. Place bag on a baking sheet. On top of bag, place a second pan weighted with 2 bricks or similar objects. Refrigerate brisket a minimum of 7 days, turning once each day. Remove brisket from bag and drain thoroughly. In a 2-gallon stock pot, place brisket and cover by 1-inch with cold water. Bring to a low boil, skimming impurities that rise to the surface. Cover pot and boil 2½ hours or until meat is tender at thickest part. Meat is fully cooked when muscle fibers begin to loosen, and a fork can be inserted easily. When ready to cook, preheat oven to 200°F. Remove brisket from pot and allow poaching liquid to simmer. Place brisket in a large baking pan with 1–2 cups of cooking liquid. Cover pan with foil and place in oven to keep warm. Add carrots, turnips and potatoes to poaching liquid and continue to simmer 10–12 minutes. Cut cabbage into 6 wedges, core and add to pot. Continue to simmer until cabbage is fork tender. When ready to serve, remove brisket from oven and slice across grain into ¼-inch pieces. Transfer sliced meat to large serving platter and surround with poached vegetables and a serving of cooking liquid.

ST. FRANCISVILLE CORNED BEEF HASH

Prep Time: 1 Hour
Yields: 6 Servings

Comment:
The English were extremely fond of corned beef. The process of curing beef in pickling spice with brown sugar and saltpeter, prior to boiling or baking, was quite common in English households. When the English came to settle the "Rolling Felicianas" of Louisiana, they brought their methods of preparing corned beef with them.

Ingredients:
4 cups cooked corned beef
1 large white potato
½ cup butter
½ cup diced onions
½ cup diced celery
¼ cup diced red bell peppers
¼ cup minced garlic
¼ cup sliced green onions
1 tsp chopped thyme
salt and cracked black pepper to taste
Louisiana hot sauce to taste
6 poached eggs

Method:
Using a paring knife, cut potato into ¼-inch cubes. Poach in lightly-salted water until tender but not overcooked. Drain, cool and set aside. In a large sauté pan, melt butter over medium-high heat. Add onions, celery, bell peppers, garlic, green onions and thyme. Sauté 3–5 minutes or until vegetables are wilted. Blend in corned beef and potatoes. Season with salt, pepper and hot sauce. Sauté an additional 2–3 minutes. Using the bottom of a cooking spoon, mash contents of skillet into a large patty. Reduce heat to low, cover and cook 10 minutes or until corned beef has browned slightly. Uncover and turn hash with large spatula. Cook 5 minutes or until browned. Divide hash into 6 equal servings and top with poached eggs.

ROLLED VEGETABLE AND POTATO MEATLOAF

Prep Time: 2 Hours
Yields: 12 Servings

Comment:
The Creole settlement of Natchitoches, La. is famous worldwide for its meat pies. Slow braised meat flavored with vegetables and herbs and made into a loaf or pie is traditional in many cultures. However, in this old Louisiana settlement cooking meatloaf or pie is more than a tradition—it is a way of life.

Ingredients:
2 pounds ground chuck
1 pound lean ground pork
½ cup diced onions
¼ cup diced celery
¼ cup diced red bell peppers
2 tbsps minced garlic
¼ cup sliced green onions
¼ cup chopped parsley
3 eggs
⅓ cup heavy whipping cream
salt and cracked black pepper to taste
Louisiana hot sauce to taste
½ cup Italian bread crumbs
¼ cup chopped basil
½ cup diced white potatoes
½ cup cooked whole kernel corn
½ cup crawfish tails, shrimp or crabmeat (optional)
4 cups tomato sauce or Creole Tomato Sauce (see recipe)

Method:
Preheat oven to 350°F. In a large mixing bowl, combine ground chuck, pork, onions, celery, bell peppers, garlic, green onions and parsley. Using your hands, mix ingredients until well blended. Add eggs, whipping cream, salt, pepper, hot sauce and bread crumbs. Continue to blend. On a large sheet of wax paper, press ground meat mixture into a 12" x 10" rectangle of even thickness (approximately ¼-inch). Beginning ½-inch from edge of meat, top evenly with basil, potatoes, corn and desired seafood. Using the tips of your fingers, gently press ingredients into meat. Using wax paper, roll meat from the 10" side like a jelly roll until it is sealed. Place in a large casserole dish, top with tomato sauce and sprinkle with a pinch of salt and pepper. Bake uncovered 1–1½ hours or until internal temperature reaches 160°F.

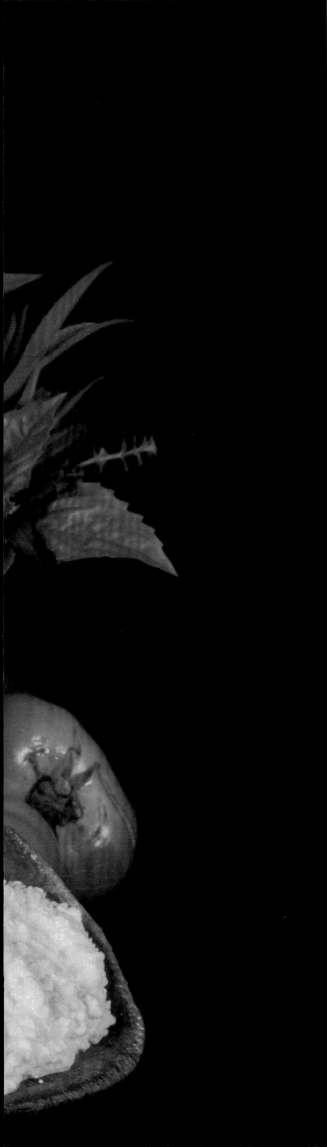

MAMA FRESINA'S LASAGNA

Prep Time: 1½ Hours
Yields: 6–8 Servings

Comment:

Phyllis Fresina, affectionately referred to as "Mama," and her husband Buster create the finest pasta in Baton Rouge, La. At their store, Phyllis, Buster and their sons use an antique pasta maker to produce wonderful, fresh pastas. This delectable family recipe is from the kitchen of Mama Fresina.

Ingredients:

2 pounds ground beef
1 (8-ounce) package lasagna noodles
¼ cup olive oil
2 cups diced onions
¼ cup minced garlic
1 tsp oregano
2 tsps parsley
2 tsps sweet basil
½ tsp garlic salt
1 tsp salt
1 tsp black pepper
3 (8-ounce) cans tomato sauce
2 (6-ounce) cans tomato paste
1 cup sliced mushrooms
1 cup cottage cheese
1 cup Ricotta cheese
2 cups frozen spinach (drained)
2 cups shredded mozzarella cheese

Method:

Preheat oven to 350°F. In lightly-salted water, boil lasagna noodles according to package directions. Drain and toss with a little olive oil to prevent sticking together. Set aside. In a cast iron Dutch oven, brown ground meat over medium-high heat. Chop and cook beef 20–30 minutes or until it browns and grains separate. Add onions and garlic. Sauté 3–5 minutes or until vegetables are wilted. Drain excess fat. Season with oregano, parsley, basil, garlic salt, salt and pepper. Blend in tomato sauce and paste, then bring to a low simmer. Add mushrooms and cook 15–20 minutes, stirring occasionally. Remove from heat and adjust seasonings if necessary. Fold in cottage cheese, Ricotta and spinach. Once blended, place a layer of sauce in the bottom of 9" x 13" baking dish. Add a layer of noodles then top with sauce and shredded mozzarella. Repeat 3 times, leaving approximately ½-inch at the top of dish for overflow. Sprinkle evenly with mozzarella. Bake uncovered 30 minutes.

Antique cottage cheese pail and scoop

Late 18th century commercial wooden meat grinder

TENDER AND JUICY
SPAGHETTI AND MEATBALLS

Prep Time: 2 Hours
Yields: 8–10 Servings

Comment:
Nothing is worse than sitting at the table ready to enjoy a plate of spaghetti and meatballs only to discover the meatballs are tough and dry. This recipe will teach you the secret to making juicy, tender meatballs, a skill that can only be learned in Italy.

Ingredients for Meatballs:
1 pound ground chuck
1 pound ground pork
6 eggs
1 cup minced onions
1 cup minced celery
¼ cup minced garlic
¼ cup chopped basil
1¾ cup Italian bread crumbs
½ cup grated Parmesan cheese
2 tbsps salt
2 tbsps black pepper

Method:
In a large mixing bowl, combine beef and pork. Using your hands, blend meat well. Add eggs, onions, celery, garlic, basil, bread crumbs and cheese. Continue to blend, then season with salt and pepper. Fry a small patty of meat mixture in a sprinkle of extra virgin olive oil to test seasoning. Adjust seasonings if necessary. Roll meatballs to desired size. Meatballs should be slightly larger than a golf ball. Place on a cookie sheet, cover and refrigerate. This recipe will make approximately 20 meatballs.

Ingredients for Sauce:
4 (35-ounce) cans Italian plum tomatoes with juice
½ cup extra virgin olive oil
2 cups diced onions
1 cup diced celery
¼ cup minced garlic
¼ cup chopped basil
salt and pepper to taste
cooked spaghetti

Method:
Drain tomatoes through a sieve and retain juice. Chop tomatoes into ¼-inch pieces, return to juice and set aside. In a 3-gallon saucepot, heat oil over medium-high heat. Add onions, celery and garlic. Sauté 3–5 minutes or until vegetables are wilted. Stir in tomatoes with juice and chopped basil. Bring to a low boil, reduce to simmer and cook 30 minutes, stirring occasionally. Gently drop raw meatballs into sauce. Return sauce to a simmer. Do not stir for first 10 minutes of simmering, or meatballs will break. When stirring, use a wooden spoon and move the meatballs gently. Simmer 1 hour, adding water or chicken stock if sauce becomes too thick. Season with salt and pepper. Place cooked spaghetti in a large serving bowl, top with 6–8 ounces of sauce and toss well to coat. Pour spaghetti in center of a large serving platter, and arrange meatballs on top of pasta. Top with additional sauce and Parmesan cheese.

THE GREAT AMERICAN HAMBURGER

Prep Time: 1½ Hours
Yields: 6 Servings

Comment:

A great hamburger starts with a flavorful cut of meat with 15–20 percent fat, such as sirloin, chuck or round. The meat should be ground twice; first through the coarse plate of a grinder, then through the fine plate. The fewer ingredients added to the meat, the better; allow garnishes to add flavor. Remember to handle meat as little as possible so the burger maintains its juiciness and flavor.

Ingredients for Burgers:

2¼ pounds ground round, chuck or sirloin
2 tbsps melted unsalted butter or olive oil
salt and cracked black pepper to taste
6 hamburger buns
6 slices (½-inch thick) Vidalia onion or other sweet onion (optional)

Ingredients for Toppings:

iceberg lettuce
sliced tomatoes
sliced dill or sweet pickles
cooked bacon, 2 strips per burger
ketchup
mustard
mayonnaise

Method:

Preheat grill to high. Divide meat into 6 equal portions. Lightly wet your hands with cold water, and then form each portion of meat into a round patty, 4 inches wide and of even thickness. When ready to cook, oil the grill grate. Brush one side of patties and onion slices lightly with melted butter. Season with salt and pepper. Arrange burgers and onion slices butter side down on hot grate. Grill 4 minutes or until nicely browned. Brush top of patties and onions lightly with melted butter and season with salt and pepper. Turn with a spatula and continue grilling 4 more minutes for medium or until cooked to your preference. Brush insides of buns with remaining melted butter. Place buns cut side down on grill for last 2 minutes. Set out toppings. Place burgers and onion slices on buns, garnish and serve.

Antique cast iron meat grinder

NATCHITOCHES MEAT PIES

Prep Time: 2 Hours
Yields: 4 Servings

Comment:

Natchitoches, La. is the oldest town in the Louisiana Purchase. It is home to the oldest and largest Creole settlement outside of New Orleans. Meat pies, a Christmas Eve tradition, were probably brought to Louisiana by the Cajuns upon their exile from Nova Scotia in 1755.

Ingredients:

½ pound ground beef
½ pound ground pork
½ cup vegetable oil
½ cup diced onions
½ cup diced celery
¼ cup diced green bell peppers
¼ cup diced red bell peppers
1 tbsp minced garlic
2 cups beef stock (see recipe)
2 (9-inch) pie shells
1 egg
½ cup water
salt and cracked black pepper to taste

Method:

Preheat oven to 400°F. In a heavy-bottomed sauté pan, heat oil over medium-high heat. Sauté beef and pork until golden brown. Stir until all juices have evaporated. Add onions, celery, bell peppers and garlic. Sauté 3–5 minutes or until vegetables are wilted. Allow meat and vegetables to cook 1 hour. Add beef stock as necessary to prevent sticking. Season with salt and pepper. Remove from heat and allow to cool. Cut pie crusts in half. Spoon a generous portion of meat mixture onto each piece of dough. Brush egg wash around edge of shell, fold over and press edges with a fork, similar to the preparation of an apple turnover. Place on a greased cookie sheet or pan. Make small slits in dough to vent steam. Brush egg wash over each pie and bake 30 minutes. Pies may also be deep fried.

BEEF BOURGUIGNONNE

Prep Time: 2 Hours
Yields: 6 Servings

Comment:

This recipe is typical of the country French techniques recreated in early New Orleans. In this dish, Burgundy wine is used for both flavoring and tenderizing the meat.

Ingredients:

2 ½–3 pounds cubed beef chuck
⅓ cup flour
¼ cup vegetable oil
4 slices of bacon
2 cups diced onions
½ cup grated carrots
¼ cup minced garlic
1 cup sliced mushrooms
3 cups Burgundy wine
4 cups beef broth
1 tbsp tomato paste
½ tsp dried thyme
1½ cups sliced green onions
¼ cup chopped parsley
salt and black pepper to taste

Method:

In a large mixing bowl, season meat with salt and pepper. Coat well with flour. In a cast iron Dutch oven, heat oil over medium-high heat. Sauté sliced bacon until golden brown. Remove, crush and keep warm. Add meat in 3 separate batches. Brown meat on all sides and allow it to caramelize in bottom of pot. Remove and keep warm. Sauté onions, carrots and garlic in pot 3–5 minutes or until vegetables are wilted. Blend in mushrooms, Burgundy, broth and tomato paste. Scrape bottom of pot to release caramelized flavor. Return meat to Dutch oven. Add bacon and thyme. Cover and simmer 1½ hours or until meat is tender. Add green onions and parsley, then adjust seasonings if necessary. Serve over hot pasta.

BAYOULAND BEEF STEW WITH VEGETABLES

Prep Time: 2 Hours
Yields: 6 Servings

Comment:

Cajun cuisine is best identified by its use of one-pot cooking. In this recipe, the meat, vegetables and starch are slowly simmered together to create yet another hearty, Cajun delicacy.

Ingredients:

3 pounds beef chuck, cubed
salt and black pepper to taste
Louisiana hot sauce to taste
⅓ cup flour
¼ cup vegetable oil
1 cup diced onions
1 cup diced celery
½ cup celery leaves
¼ cup minced garlic
1 bay leaf
2 tbsps Worcestershire sauce
1 quart hot water or beef stock (see recipe)
1 pound sliced carrots
2 pounds quartered new potatoes
1 pound sliced mushrooms
1 cup sliced green onions
½ cup chopped parsley

Method:

Place beef in a large mixing bowl and season with salt, pepper and hot sauce. Sprinkle in flour to coat meat well. In a cast iron Dutch oven, heat oil over medium-high heat. Add meat and brown on all sides. Once meat is golden brown and caramelized on bottom of pot, remove and keep warm. Stir in onions, celery, celery leaves and garlic. Sauté 3–5 minutes or until vegetables are wilted. Return meat to pot and blend well. Add bay leaf and Worcestershire sauce. Pour in hot water or stock, scraping bottom of pot to remove any drippings. Blend in carrots and potatoes. Bring to a rolling boil then reduce to simmer. Cover and cook 1–1½ hours or until meat is tender. Add mushrooms, green onions and parsley. Adjust seasonings if necessary. Cook 5–10 minutes longer. Serve over steamed white rice.

SAUCE PIQUANT OBERLIN

Prep Time: 1 Hour
Yields: 8 Servings

Comment:
This recipe goes back generations. The dish changed often depending on what ingredients were available. Because it can always be altered, this sauce piquant will never get boring. Originally, this recipe was slow-cooked over a wooden fire in a cast iron pot, creating a perfectly flavored stew.

Ingredients:
3 pounds lean stew meat, cubed
salt and cayenne pepper to taste
1 pound smoked tasso, cubed
½ cup water
2 cups chopped Bermuda onions
1 cup diced celery
1 cup diced bell peppers
¼ cup minced garlic
2 (10-ounce) cans Ro*tel® tomatoes
1 (4-ounce) can sliced mushrooms
½ cup sliced green onions

Method:
Season stew meat with salt and cayenne pepper. In a large Dutch oven, bring water to a low simmer. Add stew meat and tasso, stirring constantly to render fat. After meat has browned evenly, add onions, celery, bell peppers and garlic. Sauté 3–5 minutes or until vegetables are wilted. Add tomatoes and mushrooms without draining. Bring to a rolling boil, then reduce to simmer and cook 1 hour or until meat is tender. Add green onions and adjust seasonings if necessary. Serve finished dish over white rice. NOTE: For an interesting variation, add 1 cup of beer during simmering.

STEAK AND OYSTER PIE

Prep Time: 1½ Hours
Yields: 2 (9-inch) Pies

Comment:
It may seem unconventional to combine meat and seafood as often as Louisianians do in their cooking. However, methods such as this one where available meat and seasonal seafood are combined have become a hallmark of Cajun cooking.

Ingredients:
1 pound cubed beef stew meat
1 pint oysters in liquid
2 tbsps butter
½ cup diced onions
½ cup diced celery
1 tbsp minced garlic
2 tbsps flour
1 quart beef broth
3 red potatoes, diced
6 button mushrooms, sliced
1 tbsp parsley
salt and black pepper to taste
4 (9-inch) pie crusts
egg wash (1 egg and 2 tbsps water, beaten)

Method:
Preheat oven to 350°F. In a cast iron Dutch oven, melt butter over medium-high heat. Season beef with salt and pepper and sear until brown on all sides. Remove and set aside. Sauté onions, celery and garlic in Dutch oven 5 minutes or until vegetables are wilted. Whisk in flour, stirring until roux is achieved. (See roux recipes.) Add broth and meat, bring to a rolling boil then reduce heat. Simmer 20 minutes or until beef is tender. Stir in potatoes and mushrooms. Cook an additional 10 minutes. Add oysters and parsley, then adjust seasonings with salt and pepper. Spoon mixture into 2 pie crusts. Brush edges of crusts with egg wash. Cover pies with a second crust. Crimp edges and trim excess dough. Using a paring knife, cut 3–4 decorative holes in top of pie to vent steam. Brush top of pie with egg wash. Place pies on a large baking sheet. Bake 35 minutes or until golden brown. Serve while hot and bubbly.

SAUTÉED LIVER AND ONIONS

Prep Time: 1 Hour
Yields: 6 Servings

Comment:
Although today many people dislike the flavor of liver, this item was in high demand during the plantation days. Because there was only one liver to each cow, customers had to stand in line for this delicacy.

Ingredients:
2 pounds calf liver, sliced
8 ounces bacon
2 large onions, thinly sliced
1 cup seasoned flour
salt and cracked black pepper to taste
¼ cup chicken stock (see recipe)

Method:
In a cast iron skillet, cook bacon over medium-high heat until crispy. Remove, chop and set aside. Season liver with salt and pepper then dust in flour and shake off excess. In same skillet, sauté liver 10 minutes or until golden brown on each side. Set aside and keep warm. Add onions to skillet and cook 20 minutes, stirring until onions are wilted and caramelized. When done, push onions to one side of skillet then add bacon and liver. Pour in chicken stock. Bring to a rolling boil, and cook 5 minutes. To serve, place liver in the center of plate and top with caramelized onions and bacon.

BRAISED BEEF HEART WITH SAVORY OYSTER STUFFING

Prep Time: 3 Hours
Yields: 6–8 Servings

Comment:
Although organ meats are plentiful in butcher shops throughout Louisiana, they have somehow fallen into the category of "lesser-used" cuts. This beef heart recipe offers a wonderful and creative presentation, which hopefully will encourage the cook to use this fabulous meat item.

Ingredients:
1 (3½-pound) beef heart
1 cup chopped oysters
¼ cup butter
1 cup diced onions
½ cup diced celery
1 tbsp chopped garlic
¼ tsp rubbed sage
¼ tsp thyme leaves
1½ cups Italian bread crumbs
salt and black pepper to taste
Louisiana hot sauce to taste
¼ cup vegetable oil
4 cups Beef Stock or consommé (see recipe)
¼ cup water
4 large skewers
4 (10-inch) pieces butcher's twine

Method:
Preheat oven to 350°F. Cut heart lengthwise and wash thoroughly inside and out. In a large cast iron skillet, melt butter over medium-high heat. Add onions, celery and garlic. Sauté 3–5 minutes or until vegetables are wilted. Blend in oysters, sage and thyme. Cook 5 minutes or until oyster juice has been rendered. Sprinkle in bread crumbs to absorb liquid and to create a savory stuffing. Season with salt, pepper and hot sauce. Cool stuffing slightly, then place a generous layer on one half of heart. Cover with second half. Skewer heart on both sides, top and bottom. Using twine, tie 2 sides tightly around skewers to hold in place. Season well with salt, pepper and hot sauce. In a cast iron Dutch oven, heat oil over medium-high heat. Sauté stuffed heart well on all sides until golden brown. Add beef stock and water. Bring to a rolling boil, cover and place pot in oven. Bake 3 hours or until meat is tender. When done, remove skewers, slice and serve with a generous portion of stuffing.

CHARBROILED LEG OF LAMB

Prep Time: 2 Hours
Yields: 6–8 Servings

Comment:

Fresh leg of pork is often considered the meat of choice over an open fire. In Louisiana, exotic meats such as game or lamb are often substituted. In this recipe, the leg is boned and marinated prior to grilling.

Ingredients for Grilling:

1 (5-pound) leg of lamb, boned and butterflied
1 cup olive oil
⅔ cup lemon juice
¼ cup minced garlic
4 fresh bay leaves

2 tbsps rubbed sage
2 tbsps chopped rosemary
2 tbsps thyme
salt and black pepper to taste
Creole seasoning to taste

Method:

Have your butcher bone lamb and remove all visible fat. Place lamb in a large baking pan and top with olive oil, lemon juice, garlic, bay leaves and herbs. Rub seasoning mixture thoroughly over lamb. Cover and refrigerate overnight. When ready to prepare, drain and reserve marinade. Preheat outdoor grill according to manufacturer's directions. When pit is ready, season lamb inside and out with salt, pepper and Creole seasoning. Meat is best when cooked on a rotisserie, however, if that is not available, it may be cooked flat on the grill. If cooking flat, be sure to turn occasionally and coat with marinade. Cook lamb approximately 45 minutes, brushing occasionally with marinade. When internal temperature reaches 130°F, remove and allow to rest 20 minutes prior to slicing.

LEG OF LAMB

Prep Time: 3 Hours
Yields: 8–10 Servings

Comment:

Lamb was eaten most often by the English who settled north of St. Francisville, La. in the Felicianas. This meat, normally prepared in the spring, has become an Easter tradition throughout Cajun Country. A young spring lamb is the perfect size for this dish.

Ingredients:

1 (8-pound) leg of lamb, bone in
½ cup olive oil
⅓ cup lemon juice
salt and black pepper to taste
½ cup minced garlic
2 tbsps rubbed sage
2 tbsps chopped rosemary
2 tbsps fresh thyme leaves
4 fresh bay leaves
8–10 sprigs fresh rosemary
½ cup dry red wine
Creole seasoning to taste

Method:

Have your butcher trim most of the fat from leg. Preheat oven to 350°F. Place lamb in a large baking pan and rub with olive oil and lemon juice. Using a paring knife, make 8–10 (1-inch) slits on top of lamb. Stuff generously with salt, pepper, ¼ cup garlic and sage. Season outside of roast with salt, pepper, Creole seasoning, chopped rosemary, thyme leaves and remaining garlic. Insert sprigs of rosemary into each of the seasoned slits, then place 4 bay leaves in bottom of roasting pan. Place lamb in pan and roast 11–13 minutes per pound or until internal temperature reaches 150°F for medium. Remove lamb from pan and allow to rest 30 minutes prior to slicing. Place baking pan on stove top over medium heat. Remove fat from pan, but retain drippings. Deglaze with red wine, scraping all particles from bottom of pan. Reduce liquid by half. Strain sauce through a fine sieve and serve alongside lamb.

Ingredients for Sauce:

2 cups lamb stock (see recipe)
½ cup dry red wine
2 tbsps sliced green onions
1 tsp rubbed sage
1 tsp chopped rosemary
1 tsp thyme
2 tbsps butter
salt and black pepper to taste
Creole seasoning to taste
sprig of rosemary

Method:

Place stock, red wine, green onions and herbs in a saucepot over medium-high heat. Bring sauce to a rolling boil and reduce liquid to approximately ¾ cup. Slice lamb and shingle it on a large serving platter. Immediately prior to serving, whisk butter into stock. Season with salt, pepper and Creole seasoning. Ladle sauce over lamb, and garnish with a large sprig of fresh rosemary.

Mrs. Margaret K. Shaffer, owner of Ardoyne Plantation, and Chef John Folse share favorite lamb recipes.

HERB-ENCRUSTED LAMB LOLLIPOPS

Prep Time: 30 Minutes
Yields: 4 Servings

Comment:

In this dish, the lamb has been seasoned with herbs to enhance the flavor of the meat. For a fun presentation, french the lamb chops and scrape the meat off the bone. Eat it with your hands like a lollipop.

Ingredients:

1 rack of lamb, frenched
salt and black pepper to taste
granulated garlic to taste
¼ cup fresh herbs (tarragon, thyme, basil), mixed and chopped
1½ cups rice flour
¼ cup vegetable oil

Method:

Cut rack of lamb into chops. Season with salt, pepper and granulated garlic. Pat herbs onto both sides of each chop then dredge in flour. In a medium skillet, heat oil over medium-high heat. Sauté each chop 5 minutes per side until browned. This dish is wonderfully complemented by a salad such as Mixed Greens with Warm Strawberry Vinaigrette. (See recipe.)

CRAWFISH-STUFFED RACK OF LAMB

Prep Time: 1 Hour
Yields: 6 Servings

Comment:

By stuffing the lamb rack with Louisiana seafood, we give this earthy flavored meat a new dimension. This dish has won gold medals in culinary competitions and will certainly be a winner on your table.

Ingredients for Stuffing:

6 (4-bone) lamb racks
2 cups cooked crawfish
¼ cup diced onions
¼ cup sliced green onions
1 tsp diced garlic
1 tbsp diced red bell peppers
½ cup béchamel sauce (see recipe)
½ cup Italian bread crumbs
salt and cayenne pepper to taste

Ingredients for Cooking:

¼ cup melted butter
2 tbsps dried thyme
2 tbsps dried basil
1 tbsp dried tarragon
1 tbsp crushed rosemary
2 tbsps minced garlic
salt and cracked black pepper to taste
1 cup dry red wine
3 cups demi-glace

Method:

Have your butcher select 6 choice lamb racks and trim each. In a 1-quart mixing bowl, combine crawfish and all seasonings. Blend until mixed evenly. Stuffing should be moist but stiff enough to stand on its own. Using a 6-inch paring knife, cut a ¾-inch slit in center of each lamb rack. Do not cut completely through meat. Pocket should be large enough to hold a generous portion of stuffing. Lightly season inside of pocket with salt and cayenne pepper. Stuff each rack with an equal amount of seafood stuffing. Set aside.

Method:

Preheat oven to 400°F. Place stuffed lamb racks, bone side up, on a large baking pan with a 1-inch lip. Moisten lamb with melted butter and season generously with thyme, basil, tarragon, rosemary, garlic, salt and pepper. Bake approximately 25 minutes for medium rare. Remove from oven and deglaze baking pan with wine. Scrape bottom. Pour ingredients into a 10-inch sauté pan and add demi-glace. Bring to a boil and reduce until slightly thickened. Using a sharp knife, slice lamb racks into 4 chops each and top with a generous portion of demi-glace.

SPICY LAMB STEW ON RIGATONI PASTA

Prep Time: 2 Hours
Yields: 6–8 Servings

Comment:
In the mid 1800s nearly one-fifth of the population of New Orleans was Irish. Althouth Irish immigrants were not centrally located, a section of the city became known as the Irish Channel. Today, the Irish Channel is a reminder of the influence of these early immigrants. This recipe is a modified version of a traditional Irish stew. It honors the patron saint of Ireland, St. Patrick, and is often served on his holiday.

Ingredients:
1 pound boneless lamb shoulder, cubed ¾-inch
¼ cup extra virgin olive oil
¼ pound chopped bacon
1½ cups diced onions
¾ cup diced red bell peppers
¼ cup minced garlic
¾ cup dry red wine
1 (28-ounce) can diced tomatoes
1 cup chicken stock (see recipe) or broth
1 cup diced carrots
1 bay leaf
½ tsp crushed red pepper
2 tbsps chopped basil
salt and black pepper to taste
¼ cup sliced green onions
¼ cup chopped parsley
1 pound rigatoni pasta, cooked
Parmesan or Romano cheese for garnish

Method:
In a 5-quart cast iron Dutch oven, heat olive oil over medium-high heat. Cook bacon and stir until fat is rendered. Add lamb, stirring occasionally for 15 minutes or until meat is browned. Stir in onions, bell peppers and garlic. Cook over medium heat 5–10 minutes or until softened, stirring occasionally. Deglaze pan with red wine and simmer until evaporated, scraping up any browned bits from bottom of pan. Add tomatoes, stock, carrots, bay leaf, red pepper and basil. Bring to a rolling boil and reduce to simmer. Cover and cook 1–1½ hours or until lamb is tender, stirring occasionally. Use additional stock if necessary to retain consistency. Season with salt and pepper. Blend in green onions and parsley. Discard the bay leaf. Serve stew over cooked rigatoni. Garnish with Parmesan or Romano cheese.

SHEPHERD'S PIE

Prep Time: 1 Hour
Yields: 6 Servings

Comment:
Shepherd's Pie is an example of the resourcefulness of the English. Here, left over meats and vegetables are used to create a wonderful new meal.

Ingredients:
3 cups cooked lamb, chopped
2 large cloves garlic, peeled
1 medium onion, quartered
1 tsp chopped rosemary
¼ pound butter
2 tbsps flour
¾ cup beef broth
salt and cracked black pepper to taste
4 medium potatoes, cooked and mashed

Method:
Preheat oven to 325°F. In a mixing bowl, combine lamb, garlic, onion and rosemary. Grind ingredients twice in a meat grinder or chop finely in a food processor. In a skillet, melt butter over medium heat. Stir in flour and cook until smooth and blended. Slowly pour in beef broth. Cook 5 minutes or until thickened. Add lamb mixture to skillet and stir to blend well. Season with salt and pepper. Spoon mixture into a 1½-quart casserole or deep pie dish. Spread mashed potatoes evenly on top of lamb mixture. Make crisscross designs on top with a fork. Bake 45–50 minutes or until meat is bubbling hot and potatoes are browned.

Cabanocey barnyard in the snow, early 1950s

Wild Game

Hunter's paradise

For hundreds of thousands of years, game has provided sustenance to people all over the world. Beyond providing food, hunting was the inspiration for the first artwork, tools and weapons. Hunting may even have been at the root of the earliest religion because hunters often gave thanks to the spirits of the animals they killed or kept some part of them as protective totems. Even now, when few cultures rely on game as their only means of food, hunting remains a passion steeped in ritual. In many cultures however, particularly in Europe, hunting was a privilege reserved for the aristocracy. Penalties for poaching were incredibly severe. According to *History of Food*, by Maguelonne Toussaint-Samat, William the Conqueror would blind a man for poaching a wild boar, and a peasant desperate enough to illegally catch a hare during Charlemagne's reign could be fined the price of 60 cows.

One can only imagine the wonder of the first settlers to the New World when they found wild game in such abundance and yet available to anyone. Game soon became not just the means for survival, but also the main sustenance for early Americans. It remained an important source of meat during and beyond the Civil War, when the majority of Americans still lived a rural lifestyle, and the ravages of war had taken their toll on livestock. Some have even attributed America's meaty diet to this early dependence on a seemingly endless supply of game.

Nowhere was the abundance of game more notable than in Louisiana, where even today the state is considered a "Sportsman's Paradise." Early settlers to Louisiana could find black bear, white-tailed deer, rabbits, raccoons, muskrats, squirrels, opossum and even wild boar descended from the pigs first brought to Florida by Hernando de Soto. Like the settlers on the East Coast, the Cajuns relied on the Native Americans to teach them to hunt some of the species they found here. Most notably, the Choctaw and Chickasaw tribes introduced the Cajuns to the black bear, which was not only a primary food source at the time, but also provided a valuable source of cooking fat in the absence of butter or lard. Early Creole cookbooks contain recipes for the proper preparation of bear meat.

Feathered game was also plentiful in the form of wild turkey, bobwhite quail, snipe, woodcock, geese, mallards, pintails, teal and more. In *Eating in America*, authors Waverley Root and Richard de Rochemont state, "When it comes to feathered game, Louisiana has perhaps the most favored situation of any state in the Union." The early Cajun and Creole settlers likely agreed. The marshes and woods of Louisiana were home to a wide variety of native species, and the state was and remains the winter home or resting spot for many migratory ducks and geese. The Acadians had stumbled on the wintering site of the very birds they so anxiously awaited the return of each spring in Nova Scotia. As evidence of their joy at this discovery, the Acadians erected the Church of Saint Jacques de Cabahanoce in 1757. If there was any doubt as to the reason for this dedication, cabanocey is the Indian word for "clearing where mallard ducks roost."

While the Creoles may not have been as actively involved in hunting for survival, game still played a prominent role in their meal selection. When they didn't participate in the hunt itself, game could be purchased from Native American or Cajun hunters. According to James Trager's *The Food Chronology*, game birds shot by commercial hunters for market were the mainstay of most Americans' diet in the early 19th century. Accustomed to preparing game in their native Spain and France, ingredients like

Nonc Paul's hunting camp, Cabanocey Plantation, St. James, La.

duck, quail, deer and rabbit were familiar to the Creoles, who prepared chevreuil a la chasseur (hunter-style venison), salmis des canards (a Creole duck stew made with wine), sauvage a la Creole (stewed wild ducks) and lapin en matelote (rabbit cooked in roux, tomatoes, spices and claret). Recipes for mallard, teal and canvasback were common at any plantation home along the Mississippi. Other less familiar types of game like muskrat, opossum and squirrel probably were more common in Cajun pots because the Cajuns were famous for creating recipes for just about anything. The Cajuns and Creoles were certainly faring better than their cousins in France who, during the same period, subsisted largely on bread. This bread could cost as much as 60 percent of their earnings. The obvious delight of the Cajuns and Creoles at the abundance and variety of food in Louisiana is reflected in their recipes.

Game is technically a term used for animals hunted for sport or food. While their availability once depended on the season or the skill of the hunter, many "game" animals, such as duck, quail, pheasant, deer or rabbit, are now farm raised for food but still retain the classification. Certain types of game are best hung before cooking to allow the meat to mature. Modern tastes generally require a much less "aged" product than in previous centuries, but for certain animals who are exerting themselves when killed, it is necessary to allow the glycogen stored in the muscles to be converted to lactic acid to tenderize the flesh. Marinades of wine, spirits and aromatic herbs also serve to tenderize the meat and to disguise the stronger flavors.

Because game was so plentiful in America, little was done to ensure continued supply. Overzealous hunting and increasing urbanization led to the extinction of several species common to early settlers, like the passenger pigeon, which once numbered in the billions, the Eskimo curlew, the Labrador duck and the heath hen. As farming made domestic meat more available, and railroads and refrigeration made it more accessible, the importance of game in America's cuisine diminished. In Louisiana, however, the love affair continues. Hunting remains almost a religion in South Louisiana, and the recipes for preparing game still remain a source of pride and competition. While some recipes may originally have been devised for game birds, their more readily available domestic cousins make fine substitutes.

While wild ducks are still plentiful during hunting season, domestic ducks are available year-round so are often used as a substitute. The raising of domestic ducks in the United States can be traced back to just a few pairs of Pekin ducks brought from China via ship. Although the popularity of duck farming gradually spread across the states, the best domestic ducks are still said to come from the original point of entry, Long Island, N. Y. It is said that in 1873, at the request of a merchant named McGrath, a sea captain named James Palmer brought a dozen of the white mallards from the imperial aviaries in Beijing. Only nine survived the trip to Long Island. Palmer was said to have delivered five to McGrath's family, who, not realizing their importance, ate them. Palmer kept the remaining four for himself and bred them. Long Island ducks are now produced in greater numbers than any other variety in the world and are said to have descended from Palmer's original four.

UNCLE PAUL'S WOODCOCK

Prep Time: 1–1½ Hours
Yields: 6 Servings

Comment:

Paul Zeringue was my great uncle on my mother's side of the family. Uncle Paul's hunting camp was located on the bayou crossing the rear of Cabanocey Plantation in St. James Parish. Paul was known throughout the family as the best cook of all, and many of us apprenticed at his apron strings. I thank God for that opportunity.

Ingredients:

6 woodcocks, cleaned
salt and black pepper to taste
cayenne pepper to taste
5 tbsps flour
¼ pound butter
¼ cup vegetable oil
1 cup diced onions
1 cup diced celery
½ cup diced bell peppers
¼ cup minced garlic
1 tsp chopped tarragon
1 tbsp chopped basil
½ cup sliced green onions
1 cup diced carrots
2 cups sliced mushrooms
1 cup dry white wine
3 cups chicken stock (see recipe)
2 bay leaves
2 red apples, cored and diced

Method:

Preheat oven to 350°F. Season woodcocks inside and out with salt and peppers then dust with flour. In a 12-quart cast iron Dutch oven, heat butter and vegetable oil over medium-high heat. Place woodcocks in oil and cook, turning occasionally, until well browned. Add onions, celery, bell peppers and garlic. Sauté 3–5 minutes or until vegetables are wilted. Stir in tarragon, basil, green onions, carrots, mushrooms, wine and stock. Bring to a rolling boil. Add bay leaves and apples. Cover and place in oven 45 minutes or until woodcocks are tender. Remove cover and brown 5–10 minutes. If woodcocks become dry during cooking process, add more chicken stock. Serve over steamed white rice.

SQUAB WITH THYME AND ROASTED GARLIC

Prep Time: 1 Hour
Yields: 6 Servings

Comment:

There is a saying in New Orleans that "more is better." Often this is not the case in cooking. When squab is sautéed with roasted garlic, not much else is needed in the pot. With only a bit of thyme and a touch of red wine, this simple dish becomes a delicacy.

Ingredients:

6 young squabs
salt and cracked black pepper to taste
Louisiana hot sauce to taste
24 garlic cloves
6 sprigs thyme
1 cup seasoned flour
½ cup butter
½ cup dry red wine
2 cups game stock (see recipe)

Method:

Rinse squabs under cold running water. Season inside and out with salt, pepper and hot sauce. In a cast iron skillet, melt butter over medium-high heat. Sauté garlic until slightly browned on all sides, being careful not to scorch. Remove garlic and keep warm. Lightly dust squabs with seasoned flour, shaking off excess. In same skillet, sauté birds until golden brown on all sides. Pour off all but 2 tablespoons of butter, return pan to stove and deglaze with red wine. Add thyme and garlic, and reduce wine to half volume. Pour in game stock, cover and cook 30–45 minutes or until squabs are tender. Season with salt and pepper. Remove and keep warm. Reduce stock to a sauce consistency. Serve squabs with a generous portion of sauce and roasted garlic.

POT-ROASTED SQUAB WITH KUMQUATS

Prep Time: 1 Hour
Yields: 6 Servings

Comment:

Squabs are young pigeons that are only 25–30 days old and have not yet learned to fly. The dark meat of a squab is very moist and tender. The Native Americans found squab to be a delicacy, and most tribes had it as a part of their diet.

Ingredients:

6 squabs, cleaned
salt and cracked black pepper to taste
1 cup whole kumquats
¼ cup vegetable oil
½ cup seasoned flour
1 cup diced onions
½ cup diced celery
½ cup diced bell peppers
2 tbsps minced garlic
2 ounces plum or fruit wine
1 quart chicken stock (see recipe)
1 tsp chopped thyme
1 tsp chopped basil
pinch of file' powder
Louisiana hot sauce to taste
4 cups cooked wild or popcorn rice

Method:

In a large Dutch oven, heat oil over medium-high heat. Season squabs inside and out with salt and pepper. Stuff cavity of each squab with onions, celery, bell peppers and 1 kumquat. Save remaining vegetables and kumquats. Dust birds with flour and brown on all sides. Add remaining onions, celery, bell peppers and garlic. Sauté 3–5 minutes or until vegetables are wilted. Deglaze with plum wine then add stock. Blend thyme, basil, filé powder and remaining kumquats into mixture. Season with salt, pepper and hot sauce. Cover and cook squabs until tender. Check occasionally. Do not overcook or squabs will fall apart. Remove birds and keep warm. Reduce cooking liquid to consistency of a thickened sauce. Adjust seasonings if necessary. Place a generous portion of popcorn or wild rice in center of plate and top with squab and kumquat sauce.

WILD DOVE IN MADEIRA WINE

Prep Time: 1½ Hours
Yields: 6 Servings

Comment:

Though Louisiana is the dove capital of the South, many Louisiana hunters today are traveling south of the border to Mexico for their annual hunts. Breast of dove has become a main ingredient in many recipes and can be found wrapped in bacon on a grill or simmering in a gumbo pot.

Ingredients:

18 doves, cleaned
1 cup butter
2 cups flour
1 cup diced onions
1 cup diced celery
1 cup diced bell peppers
2 tbsps minced garlic
2 cups sliced mushrooms
2 tbsps flour
6 purple plums, quartered
3 cups Madeira wine
1 quart chicken stock (see recipe)
salt and cracked black pepper to taste

Method:

Wash birds inside and out, and remove any visible shot. In a large Dutch oven, melt butter over medium-high heat. Dust doves with flour and brown well on all sides. Remove and set aside. In same pot, sauté onions, celery, bell peppers, garlic and mushrooms 3–5 minutes or until vegetables are wilted. Sprinkle in 2 tablespoons of flour and blend well. Stir in plums, wine and stock. Bring to a rolling boil then reduce to simmer. Return birds to sauce. Season lightly with salt and pepper. Cover and cook 1–1½ hours. Add more stock if mixture becomes too thick. To serve, place 3 doves on each plate with a generous amount of sauce.

Braised Doves Evangeline

SHERRIED DOVES

Prep Time: 3 Hours
Yields: 6–8 Servings

Comment:
Often when special guests arrived by steamboat to visit family in Plantation Country, the hunters in the family would harvest a "mess" of doves or quail for breakfast. Nothing made a more elegant breakfast or brunch than fresh game birds simmered in sherry sauce over toast, grits or rice.

Ingredients:

20 doves, cleaned	1 can Ro*tel® tomatoes
2 cups Italian salad dressing	½ cup sherry
½ cup vegetable oil	1 tsp chopped thyme
½ cup flour	1 tsp chopped sweet basil
1 cup diced onions	2 cups sliced mushrooms
1 cup diced celery	1–1½ tbsps salt
½ cup diced bell peppers	1 tsp cayenne pepper
¼ cup minced garlic	½ cup sliced green onions
1 quart chicken stock (see recipe)	¼ cup chopped parsley

Method:
Rinse doves well under cold running water and remove any visible shot. Place doves in a large bowl with Italian dressing and marinate in refrigerator overnight. Remove from marinade and drain. In a 12-quart cast iron Dutch oven, heat oil over medium-high heat. Whisk in flour, stirring constantly until dark brown roux is achieved. (See roux recipes.) Add onions, celery, bell peppers and garlic. Sauté 3–5 minutes or until vegetables are wilted. Stir in stock, tomatoes, sherry, thyme and basil. Bring to a rolling boil then reduce to simmer and add mushrooms. Season doves with salt and cayenne pepper. Place birds breast side up in simmering stock. Cover and cook 2½ hours or until doves are tender. Add green onions and parsley. Serve over wild or saffron rice.

BRAISED DOVES EVANGELINE

Prep Time: 1½ Hours
Yields: 6 Servings

Comment:
In Bayou Country, dove season meant not only good sport shooting but also wonderful game birds for the table. My grandmother made the best dove and andouille sausage gumbo. Often when special folks came to visit for breakfast, she would sauté dove breasts in butter, flame them in sherry and serve them over French bread croutons. However, the dish I remember most is the braised dove served alongside wild rice or rice dressing.

Ingredients:
3 dozen cleaned dove breasts, bone-in
salt and cayenne pepper to taste
1 cup seasoned flour
½ cup vegetable oil
2 tbsps butter
1 cup diced onions
½ cup diced celery
½ cup diced green bell peppers
¼ cup minced garlic
2 quarts chicken stock (see recipe)
2 tbsps chopped thyme
2 tbsps chopped basil
Louisiana hot sauce to taste
½ cup sliced green onions
¼ cup chopped parsley

Method:
Wash doves inside and out and remove any visible shot. Drain then season well with salt and cayenne pepper. Dust doves with seasoned flour, shaking off excess. In a large cast iron skillet, heat oil and butter over medium-high heat. Brown a few doves at a time until all are done. Remove and set aside. Pour off all but ½ cup of oil. Add onions, celery, bell peppers and garlic. Sauté 3–5 minutes or until vegetables are wilted. Reduce heat. Continue to cook 10–12 minutes or until well caramelized, stirring occasionally. Do not scorch. Return doves to skillet. Add stock, thyme and basil. Season with salt, cayenne and hot sauce. Bring liquid to a rolling boil then reduce to simmer. Cover and cook 45 minutes or until doves are tender but not falling apart. Sprinkle in green onions and parsley prior to serving. Serve braised doves over a wild rice blend or Sweet Farre Dressing. (See recipe.)

DOVE AND WILD RICE CASSEROLE

Prep Time: 1–1½ Hours
Yields: 6 Servings

Comment:
Dove hunting is considered a great sport in Louisiana's St. James Parish. However, the small bones that break off from the legs, thighs and backs during the cooking process make the birds less desirable to eat. To solve the problem and have fewer bones in the dish, cut away the wings, legs and backs and only cook with the breasts of the doves.

Ingredients:
18 dove breasts, cleaned
½ cup vegetable oil
salt and black pepper to taste
cayenne pepper to taste
granulated garlic to taste
1 cup diced onions
1 cup diced celery
1 cup diced red bell peppers
¼ cup minced garlic
1 cup canned tomatoes, diced
1 cup sliced mushrooms
1 tbsp chopped basil
1 tbsp chopped thyme
5 cups chicken stock (see recipe)
3 cups Uncle Ben's® wild rice mix
1 cup sliced green onions
¼ cup chopped parsley

Method:
Clean dove breasts by removing legs, wings and backbones. Rinse birds under cold running water. Season breasts well with salt, peppers and granulated garlic. In a 12-quart cast iron Dutch oven, heat vegetable oil over medium-high heat. Brown dove breasts well on all sides. When golden brown, remove and keep warm. In same pot, sauté onions, celery, bell peppers and garlic 3–5 minutes or until vegetables are wilted. Add tomatoes, mushrooms, basil and thyme. Sauté 2 minutes then add stock and stir well. Place dove breasts into pot. Bring to a rolling boil then reduce to low simmer. Add rice, green onions and parsley. Reduce temperature to low, cover and cook 30 minutes. Do not stir during cooking process so that doves do not break apart. Keep heat on lowest setting to prevent rice from scorching. Remove from heat and stir gently once. Allow to steam 15 minutes prior to serving.

OYSTER-STUFFED QUAIL

Prep Time: 1 Hour
Yields: 6 Servings

Comment:
This is a gold medal dish of Lafitte's Landing Restaurant. It was served at the opening dinner of Lafitte's Landing East in Moscow on May 15, 1988.

Ingredients:
12 quail, boned
2 pints select oysters
½ cup minced onions
½ cup minced celery
1 tbsp minced garlic
¼ cup minced red bell peppers
¼ cup béchamel sauce (see recipe)
1 cup Italian bread crumbs
salt and cracked black pepper to taste
½ cup melted butter
½ cup dry red wine
2 cups demi-glace (see recipe)
½ cup heavy whipping cream

Method:
Have a butcher remove bones from 12 quail breasts. Bones may remain in legs and wings. Preheat oven to 450°F. Coarsely chop oysters. In a large mixing bowl, blend together oysters, onions, celery, garlic, bell peppers and béchamel sauce. Slowly stir in bread crumbs until stuffing is moist but held together. Season with salt and pepper. Stuff each quail with an equal amount of oyster stuffing then secure legs with a toothpick. Place birds in a 10-inch ovenproof skillet or baking dish. Drizzle quail with melted butter then season with salt and pepper. Place in oven and cook 30 minutes or until golden brown. Remove quail and set aside. Deglaze baking dish with wine. Add demi-glace and cream. Bring to a low boil then reduce to simmer and cook until sauce is slightly thickened. Place 2 quail in center of a serving plate, remove toothpicks from legs and top with a generous serving of sauce.

GRILLED QUAIL

Prep Time: 1 Hour
Yields: 6 Servings

Comment:

This is a simple yet elegant way to serve quail. Grilled quail can be served as an appetizer, salad, entrée or an hors d'oeuvre.

Ingredients:

12 quail, split at backbone
½ cup dry red wine
¼ cup red wine vinegar
¾ cup Louisiana cane syrup
2 tbsps minced garlic
1 tbsp dried thyme
1 tbsp dried basil
1 tbsp dried tarragon
salt and cracked black pepper to taste

Method:

NOTE: For a unique flavor, soak a few pecan wood chips in water and add to grill just before cooking. Preheat outdoor charbroiler or barbecue grill according to manufacturer's instructions. In a mixing bowl, combine all ingredients except quail. Quail should be split across backbone and completely flattened. Place birds on a large baking pan and coat well with seasoning mixture. Allow to sit at room temperature 1 hour. Position quail, bone side down, on hot grill. Cook 3–5 minutes, basting with marinade. Turn quail, meat side down, being careful not to burn should fire become too hot. Cook 2–3 minutes and continue turning until birds are done. Try serving grilled quail hot with sweet mustard. This dish is also excellent served cold.

CANE SYRUP GLAZED CORNISH HENS

Prep Time: 1½ Hours
Yields: 6 Servings

Comment:

In the late 1700s, sugar was first crystallized on a Louisiana plantation. Prior to that time, honey and syrup were used as sweeteners and glazes while cooking.

Ingredients:

6 Cornish hens
salt and cracked black pepper to taste
Louisiana hot sauce to taste
3 small onions, quartered
3 celery stalks, quartered
12 cloves garlic
½ cup Louisiana cane syrup
¼ cup orange juice
¼ cup butter
¼ cup chopped thyme
¼ cup chopped sage
2 oranges, sectioned
paprika for color
½ cup white wine
2 cups chicken stock (see recipe)

Method:

Preheat oven to 375°F. Wash hens well. Season inside cavity with salt, pepper and hot sauce then stuff each with onions, celery and garlic. Reserve extra vegetables. Place birds breast side up in a roasting pan and season skin with salt, pepper and hot sauce. In a mixing bowl, combine syrup, orange juice, butter, thyme and sage. Brush hens lightly with glaze. Sprinkle birds with paprika to ensure even browning. Surround hens with remaining vegetables and orange sections. Cover tightly and roast 45 minutes. Uncover and allow to brown evenly. Baste once or twice with cane syrup mixture during browning process. Remove hen and deglaze baking pan with wine. Add stock and reduce to sauce consistency over medium-high heat. Reduce to about 1 cup.

CREOLE MUSTARD-GLAZED CORNISH HENS

Prep Time: 1 Hour
Yields: 6 Servings

Comment:

The great thing about this type of dish is that many variations and flavors can be achieved if the cook gets creative. This recipe can also be made with boneless breasts of chicken on the grill. The hens could also be substituted with a large roasting capon.

Ingredients:

6 (2-pound) Cornish hens
¼ cup lemon juice
¼ cup melted butter
3 tbsps chopped basil
3 tbsps chopped thyme
3 tbsps chopped tarragon
4 tbsps minced garlic
salt and black pepper to taste
Creole seasoning to taste
4 tbsps Creole mustard
1½ tbsps honey

Method:

Preheat oven to 400°F. Rinse hens inside and out under cold running water. Drain well and place birds on a large roasting pan with 1-inch lip. Rub lemon juice and melted butter over chicken and under breast skin. In a large mixing bowl, combine basil, thyme, tarragon and garlic. Place a small amount of herb mixture under breast skin. Rub remaining herbs inside and out of each hen then season generously with salt, pepper and Creole seasoning. Roast chicken uncovered 30–40 minutes or until golden brown and completely cooked. In a small bowl, combine mustard and honey. Using a pastry brush, coat breasts and legs with honey glaze. Bake 5–10 additional minutes or until glaze is golden brown.

BAKED GAME HENS VACHERIE

Prep Time: 45 Minutes
Yields: 6 Servings

Comment:
The Germans were among the first to settle South Louisiana. Their original settlement was west of New Orleans, in present day St. Charles Parish. This wonderful baked hen dish was one of the Germans' many contributions to Louisiana cuisine.

Ingredients:
6 Cornish game hens
salt and cracked black pepper to taste
3 tbsps minced garlic
4 tsps green peppercorns
6 tsps Worcestershire sauce
3 tsps Louisiana hot sauce
½ pound melted butter
2 tsps dried thyme
2 tsps dried basil
paprika for color
1 ounce dry white wine
¼ cup chopped parsley

Method:
Preheat oven to 350°F. Split hens in half and remove backbone and wing tips. Season bird well, inside and out with salt, pepper and garlic. Using a sharp paring knife, cut small pockets in breasts and thighs of each hen. Insert green peppercorns in each pocket then place hens skin side up on baking sheet. In a mixing bowl, combine Worcestershire, hot sauce, butter, thyme, basil and paprika. Coat outside of hen well with seasoning mixture. Add salt and pepper if necessary. Pour white wine and any excess seasonings in bottom of baking pan. Bake 30 minutes, basting occasionally with drippings. Hens are done when legs separate easily from thighs. Remove from oven, place hens on serving platter and keep warm. Add chopped parsley to pan drippings, blend well into sauce and pour over hens.

BLUEBERRY CORN BREAD STUFFED GAME HENS

Prep Time: 1½ Hours
Yields: 6 Servings

Comment:
Cornish game hens make an elegant dish for a dinner party or special celebration. Normally, a whole hen can be served to each person, making for a wonderful presentation. Serve this dish with a dark green vegetable such as asparagus or broccoli and a loaf of warm French bread.

Ingredients:
6 Rock Cornish game hens
2 cups fresh blueberries
4 cups cooked corn bread, crumbled
1 cup orange juice
salt and black pepper to taste
granulated garlic to taste
Louisiana hot sauce to taste
¼ pound butter
½ pound bulk pork sausage
2 cups diced onions
¼ cup diced celery
¼ cup diced red bell peppers
¼ cup diced garlic
½ cup diced apples
¼ cup chopped parsley
¼ cup sliced green onions
1 tsp chopped sage
½ tsp chopped thyme
½ tsp chopped rosemary
3 cups chicken stock (see recipe)
½ cup chopped pecans
1 cup dry sherry
½ cup melted butter

Method:
NOTE: Fresh pork sausage removed from casing may be substituted for bulk sausage. Preheat oven to 350°F. Rinse hens under cold running water. Drain well. Place birds in a large cast iron Dutch oven and sprinkle with orange juice. Season hens inside and out with salt, pepper, granulated garlic and hot sauce. In a cast iron skillet, melt ¼ pound butter over medium-high heat. Add sausage and cook until brown. Stir in onions, celery, bell peppers and garlic. Sauté 3–5 minutes or until vegetables are wilted. Blend in apples. When apples are slightly cooked, pour contents of skillet into large mixing bowl. Using a wooden spoon, carefully fold in blueberries, corn bread, parsley, green onions, sage, thyme and rosemary. Pour in enough stock to moisten corn bread and hold stuffing together, approximately 2 cups. Add pecans then season with salt and pepper. Fill hens with equal amounts of stuffing, placing any excess in corners of roasting pan. Top hens with sherry and melted butter. Bake uncovered 1 hour, basting frequently. When golden brown, remove from oven and serve with natural pan drippings.

LOUISIANA MALLARDS IN MANDARIN GLAZE

Prep Time: 3 Hours
Yields: 6 Servings

Comment:
Citrus fruits are often used to enhance the taste of wild game, especially duck. This recipe calls for mandarins, but feel free to substitute kumquats, oranges or tangerines to achieve the same results.

Ingredients:
3 (1-pound) mallard ducks
6 mandarins, peeled and sectioned
salt, cayenne and black pepper to taste
Louisiana hot sauce to taste
3 cups diced onions
2 cups diced celery
2 cups diced bell peppers
2 cups diced carrots
½ cup minced garlic
1 cup flour
½ cup vegetable oil
¼ cup orange juice concentrate
1½ quarts chicken stock (see recipe)
12 strips bacon

Method:
Preheat oven to 375°F. Clean ducks well and remove all visible shot. Place ducks in a large ceramic mixing bowl and season inside and out, with salt, peppers and hot sauce. In a mixing bowl, combine onions, celery, bell peppers, carrots and garlic. Use half of vegetable seasonings to stuff cavities of ducks. Dust birds lightly with flour. In a 12-quart cast iron Dutch oven, heat oil over medium-high heat. Brown ducks in oil, turning occasionally. Surround browned ducks with remaining onions, celery, bell peppers, carrots and garlic. Add mandarins, orange juice and chicken stock. Bring mixture to a rolling boil then remove from heat and top breast side of each duck with 4 strips of bacon. Cover pot and roast 2½ hours, checking occasionally. Ducks are done when legs pull apart easily from body. Remove cover and bake until ducks brown. Serve with natural drippings, or strain all vegetables from stock and thicken with a light brown roux.

SMOKED DUCK HAM

Prep Time: 2 Hours
Yields: 6 Servings

Comment:

Mallard ducks are prevalent in the marshy regions of Louisiana, and they are the most abundant ducks in the Mississippi Valley. These ducks like fresh water, although they rarely dip beneath the surface except to avoid danger.

Ingredients:

4 mallard duck breasts
2 tsps salt
1 tbsp brown sugar
1 tsp black pepper
1 tbsp minced garlic
1 tbsp chopped thyme
1 tbsp chopped basil
1 tbsp chopped tarragon
½ cup dry red wine
¼ cup Louisiana cane syrup or maple syrup
2 tbsps vegetable oil
2 bottles root beer

Method:

NOTE: For added flavor, soak wood chips in water and add to coals just before cooking. In a large mixing bowl, combine duck breasts with all ingredients except root beer. Massage seasonings into meat. Place duck and all ingredients into a plastic zipper bag. Refrigerate meat in marinade 1 day prior to smoking. Turn bag often while marinating. Heat a home-style smoker according to manufacturer's directions. Fill smoker's water pan with root beer and 1 quart water. Remove ducks from marinade and place on top of smoker. Pour remaining marinade into water pan. Smoke breasts 1 hour or until internal temperature reaches 155°F. Cut each breast into 6–8 slices and serve as an entrée or with your favorite dipping sauce.

ROASTED CANE RIVER MALLARDS

Prep Time: 2 Hours
Yields: 6 Servings

Comment:

Early settlers hunted mallard ducks along the Cane River, which runs through the Creole town of Natchitoches, La. These ducks can be prepared a variety of ways, but roasting delivers an enticing flavor. A variety of fresh fruit may be substituted in the place of apples.

Ingredients:

3 mallard ducks, cleaned
1 tbsp chopped thyme
1 tbsp chopped basil
1 tbsp chopped sage
salt and black pepper to taste
Louisiana hot sauce to taste
3 medium onions, quartered
2 stalks celery, cubed
2 tbsps minced garlic
2 red apples, cubed
2 green apples, cubed
1 cup cubed andouille sausage
¼ cup vegetable oil
2 red apples, quartered
2 green apples, quartered
1 quart chicken stock
¼ cup melted butter
4 tbsps mayhaw or fruit jelly

Method:

Preheat oven to 450°F. Season ducks well, inside and out, with thyme, basil, sage, salt, pepper and hot sauce. Stuff cavities of ducks with onions, celery, garlic, cubed apples and sausage. In a large Dutch oven, heat oil over medium-high heat. Brown ducks well on all sides then remove from heat and surround with remaining red and green apples and chicken stock. Drizzle butter over ducks and use a pastry brush to coat breasts with jelly. Cover with foil and roast 1½ hours. Check for tenderness, remove foil and allow breasts to brown evenly. Remove ducks and keep warm. Reduce stock to a sauce consistency over medium-high heat then strain and degrease. On a 10-inch plate, serve half of duck topped with a generous serving of sauce.

John Stassi bags his limit.

POT-ROASTED WOOD DUCK IN FIG GLAZE

Prep Time: 3 Hours
Yields: 6 Servings

Comment:
Figs are in an over-abundant supply in Louisiana during the month of July. Remove a "mess" of ducks from your freezer during this month to put this recipe to the test.

Ingredients:
3 wood ducks, cleaned
2 cups fresh figs
salt and black pepper to taste
½ pound bacon, chopped
2 cups diced onions
1 cup diced celery
¼ cup minced garlic
3 sprigs fresh thyme
1 sprig fresh sage
1 quart chicken stock (see recipe)
1 cup sliced green onions
½ cup chopped parsley

Method:
Preheat oven to 350°F. Rinse ducks well to fully clean. Season ducks inside and out with salt and pepper. In a large cast iron Dutch oven, cook bacon over medium-high heat. When bacon is crisp, remove and set aside. Place ducks in hot bacon drippings and slowly sear on all sides until golden brown. Remove ducks and set aside. In same pot, sauté onions, celery and garlic 3–5 minutes or until vegetables are wilted. Return ducks to pot, breast side up. Add figs, bacon, thyme, sage and stock. Bring mixture to a rolling boil then reduce to simmer and cover. Place pot in oven and allow ducks to roast 2½ hours or until tender. Remove from oven and transfer ducks to a warming plate. Return pot to stove and bring sauce to a low simmer over medium-high heat. Add green onions and parsley. Reduce sauce slightly to intensify flavor. Adjust seasonings if necessary. Strain sauce through a fine sieve and allow to rest 5–10 minutes. Using a spoon or ladle, skim any fat that rises to surface. To serve, cut ducks in half and top with a generous portion of fig glaze. Serve with Pecan Rice Dressing. (See recipe.)

CAJUN FRIED DUCK BREAST

Prep Time: 2½ Hours
Yields: 4 Servings

Comment:
Fried duck breast is normally reserved for smaller, more tender birds such as wood or teal. If you wish to pan-fry larger breasts such as mallard, it is best to pound them with a meat mallet or use your favorite tenderizer prior to cooking.

Ingredients:
2 duck breasts
1½ cups milk
2 eggs, beaten
1 tsp salt
½ tsp black pepper
⅛ tsp cayenne pepper
1 cup cracker crumbs
shortening, lard preferred

Method:
Tenderize breasts slightly with meat mallet then cut each into 3 equal pieces. Soak meat in milk 2 hours. Remove duck from milk and dip in beaten eggs. Season with salt, cayenne and black pepper. Dredge each breast piece in finely crumbled crackers. In a large skillet, heat approximately 1 inch of shortening over medium heat. Fry each piece in lard 10–15 minutes on each side until cooked to your preference.

BAKED LONG ISLAND DUCK

Prep Time: 2½ Hours
Yields: 6 Servings

Comment:
Long Island ducks were brought to New York from Beijing, China in 1873. These birds are very plump and succulent, and are often mistaken for geese. Each great-tasting duck will feed three people.

Ingredients:
2 Long Island ducklings
salt and cracked black pepper to taste
granulated garlic to taste
paprika for color
2 medium onions, halved
2 medium carrots, halved
2 stalks celery, halved

Method:
Preheat oven to 475°F. Rinse ducks inside and out under cold water. Remove necks, livers and gizzards from cavity. Place birds in a roasting pan with a 2-inch lip. Season ducks inside and out with dry seasonings. Over-season inside of ducks, as only a small amount of seasoning will affect taste. Stuff cavity of each duck with half of fresh vegetables. Place birds in roasting pan, breast side up and surround with necks, livers, gizzards and remaining vegetables. Do not put water or butter in pan. Cover pan tightly with aluminum foil and bake 1½ hours. Remove foil and bake uncovered 30 minutes. Steam created in a tightly covered pan creates a condition that not only tenderizes ducks, but also ensures that fat is cooked away from under skin. When done, legs of duck will separate easily from body, meat will be tender and skin will be crisp.

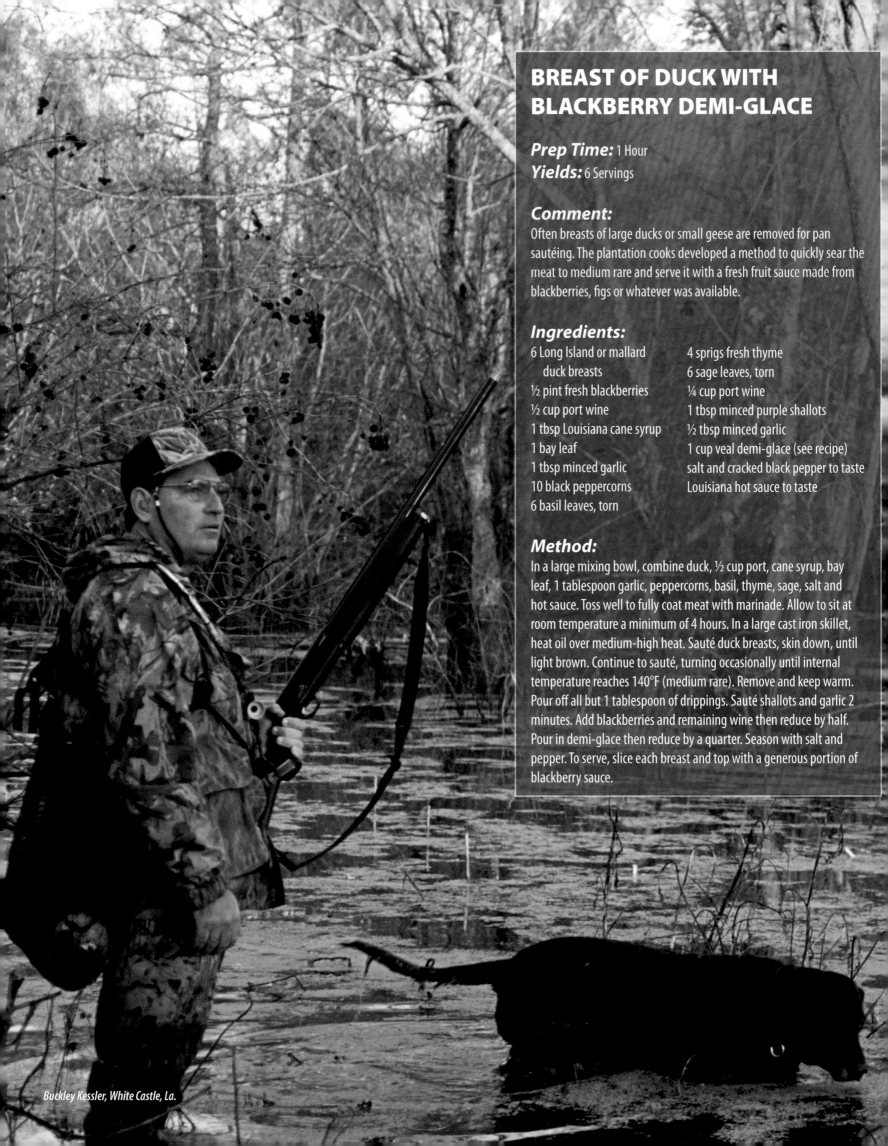

BREAST OF DUCK WITH BLACKBERRY DEMI-GLACE

Prep Time: 1 Hour
Yields: 6 Servings

Comment:

Often breasts of large ducks or small geese are removed for pan sautéing. The plantation cooks developed a method to quickly sear the meat to medium rare and serve it with a fresh fruit sauce made from blackberries, figs or whatever was available.

Ingredients:

6 Long Island or mallard
   duck breasts
½ pint fresh blackberries
½ cup port wine
1 tbsp Louisiana cane syrup
1 bay leaf
1 tbsp minced garlic
10 black peppercorns
6 basil leaves, torn

4 sprigs fresh thyme
6 sage leaves, torn
¼ cup port wine
1 tbsp minced purple shallots
½ tbsp minced garlic
1 cup veal demi-glace (see recipe)
salt and cracked black pepper to taste
Louisiana hot sauce to taste

Method:

In a large mixing bowl, combine duck, ½ cup port, cane syrup, bay leaf, 1 tablespoon garlic, peppercorns, basil, thyme, sage, salt and hot sauce. Toss well to fully coat meat with marinade. Allow to sit at room temperature a minimum of 4 hours. In a large cast iron skillet, heat oil over medium-high heat. Sauté duck breasts, skin down, until light brown. Continue to sauté, turning occasionally until internal temperature reaches 140°F (medium rare). Remove and keep warm. Pour off all but 1 tablespoon of drippings. Sauté shallots and garlic 2 minutes. Add blackberries and remaining wine then reduce by half. Pour in demi-glace then reduce by a quarter. Season with salt and pepper. To serve, slice each breast and top with a generous portion of blackberry sauce.

Buckley Kessler, White Castle, La.

CASSOULET

Prep Time: 3 Hours
Yields: 6–8 Servings

Comment:

Cassoulet is a baked dish of white beans and any combination of meats and seasonings. Just as each Louisiana home has its own version of gumbo, each region of France has its own recipe for cassoulet. This cassoulet is made with duck, although any game or domestic meat may be substituted. The dish is especially good with venison.

Ingredients:

2 pounds duck
4 cups great northern beans
5 quarts beef or chicken stock (see recipes)
½ pound pork salt meat, cubed
½ pound pork butt, cubed
1 pound smoked sausage
1 pound bacon, cubed
2 cups diced onions
½ cup diced celery
¼ cup minced garlic
½ cup puréed tomatoes
3 cups dry white wine
½ tsp thyme
2 bay leaves
salt and black pepper to taste

Method:

Preheat oven to 375°F. In a large saucepot, bring beans, stock and salt meat to a rolling boil. Reduce to simmer and cook 45 minutes or until beans are al dente. Do not overcook. When done, drain and reserve stock. While beans are boiling, place duck, pork butt and sausage in a stockpot. Cover meat by 2 inches with water. Bring to a rolling boil and cook 45 minutes or until meat is tender. Strain meat and combine stock with bean stock. In a heavy-bottomed saucepot, cook bacon over medium-high heat until light brown and fat is rendered. Add onions, celery and garlic. Sauté 3–5 minutes or until vegetables are wilted. Stir in tomatoes and wine then reduce to half volume. Place beans and poached meat in a large ceramic or glass baking dish. Cover with vegetable mixture and stir well. Ladle in enough combined stock to cover beans by ½ inch. Add thyme and bay leaves. Season with salt and pepper. Cover and bake 30–45 minutes or until most water has been absorbed into cassoulet.

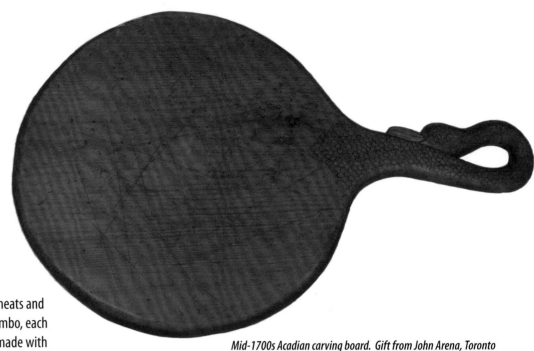

Mid-1700s Acadian carving board. Gift from John Arena, Toronto

ROASTED GOOSE

Prep Time: 3 Hours
Yields: 6 Servings

Comment:

South Louisiana is a haven for game birds, which may be one of the reasons that the state is known as Sportsman's Paradise. Canadian and speckled bellied geese are found by the thousands in the marshlands. This dish calls for a domestic goose, but feel free to use any wild species.

Ingredients:

1 (8–10 pound) goose	paprika for color
salt and cracked black pepper to taste	2 cups sliced mushrooms
granulated garlic to taste	2 cups red seedless grapes
4 cups diced onions	2 red apples, diced
2 cups diced celery	2 green apples, diced
2 cups diced carrots	¼ cup chopped basil
10 cloves garlic	¼ cup chopped thyme

Method:

Preheat oven to 375°F. Clean goose well inside and out. Remove giblets and place in roasting pan. Season bird inside and out with salt, pepper and granulated garlic. Place a generous amount of onions, celery, carrots and garlic inside cavity. Sprinkle outside of goose with a small amount of paprika for even color. Place goose in a heavy roasting pan or Dutch oven. Add mushrooms, grapes, apples, basil, thyme and remaining vegetable seasonings to pan. Cover tightly with lid or foil. Bake 2½ hours and check tenderness. Goose is cooked when legs pull away easily from body. Once tender, remove cover and allow to brown. Roasted goose may be served with natural drippings, or juices may be strained and thickened with a light roux.

POT-ROASTED TEAL HOPPING JOHN

Prep Time: 2 Hours
Yields: 6 Servings

Comment:
If you wish to use mallard or some other duck in this recipe, take special care to ensure that the meat is tender prior to removing it from the stock.

Ingredients for Stock:
6 teal ducks
1 onion, quartered
1 stalk celery
1 head garlic
thyme to taste
basil to taste
Worcestershire sauce to taste
salt and black pepper to taste
Louisiana hot sauce to taste

Method:
Bone teals and remove breasts. Set breasts aside. In a 2-gallon stock pot, place remaining teal pieces, all stock ingredients and water to cover by 2-inches. Bring mixture to a rolling boil, reduce to simmer and cook 1 hour. Remove from heat, strain and reserve 1 quart of liquid. Remove meat from carcass then discard vegetables and bones.

Ingredients for Roasted Duck:
reserved teal meat and breasts
1 cup black-eyed peas
2 tsps chopped thyme
1 tbsp chopped basil
salt and black pepper to taste
Louisiana hot sauce to taste
1 cup vegetable oil
¼ cup butter
1 cup diced onions
1 cup diced celery
1 cup diced bell peppers
¼ cup minced garlic
½ cup diced tasso
1 ear corn, sliced
1 cup tomato sauce
2 cups rice
1 cup chopped pecans
½ cup sliced green onions
¼ cup chopped parsley

Method:
Season teal breasts with thyme, basil, salt, pepper and hot sauce. In a 10-inch cast iron skillet, heat oil over medium-high heat. Place duck breasts in oil skin side down, and sear until light brown. Remove, drain and set aside. In a 3-quart Dutch oven, melt butter over medium-high heat. Add onions, celery, bell peppers and garlic. Sauté 3–5 minutes or until vegetables are wilted. Add black-eyed peas, tasso and corn. Continue to sauté 10 minutes. Pour in 3 cups reserved stock. (You will need 1½ cups stock per 1 cup rice.) Blend in tomato sauce. Season with salt, pepper, hot sauce, thyme and basil. Bring mixture to a rolling boil then reduce to simmer. Cook 10 minutes then stir in breasts and boned duck meat, rice and pecans. Cover, reduce heat to simmer and cook 30 minutes. Do not remove lid or stir rice during cooking process. Garnish with green onions and parsley. Serve hot with French bread.

Pot-Roasted Teal Hopping John

POT-ROASTED TEAL DUCKS

Prep Time: 3 Hours
Yields: 6 Servings

Comment:
Of all the game birds found throughout the world, teal ducks stand out as the most tender and flavorful. Often, wood ducks are substituted in this recipe because of their small size.

Ingredients:

6 teal ducks
½ cup minced garlic
½ cup minced green onions
salt, cayenne and black pepper to taste
2 bottles Pinot Noir
½ cup vegetable oil
2 cups diced onions

1 cup diced celery
1 cup diced bell peppers
¼ cup minced garlic
1 tbsp basil
1 tsp thyme
Louisiana hot sauce to taste

Method:

Clean ducks inside and out, removing all pinfeathers from wings and backs. Drain well then place ducks breast side down on a cutting board. Using a paring knife, cut 2 slits in each breast following breast bone on backside. In a small mixing bowl, blend together ½ cup garlic, green onions, salt and peppers. Stuff an equal portion of seasonings into slits of each breast. Season ducks inside and out with remaining mixture. Place ducks in a deep bowl and top with Pinot Noir. Cover and refrigerate 24 hours. In a heavy-bottomed Dutch oven, heat oil over medium-high heat. Drain ducks, reserving marinade, then season birds with salt, pepper and hot sauce. Place ducks in hot oil and turn often until golden brown on all sides. Remove and keep warm. In same oil, sauté onions, celery, bell peppers and garlic 3–5 minutes or until vegetables are wilted. Return ducks to pot and add reserved marinade. Bring to a rolling boil then reduce to simmer. Cover and cook 1½–2 hours or until ducks are tender. A small amount of chicken stock may be added while ducks cook to retain volume and increase flavor. Serve over Creole Dirty Rice. (See recipe.)

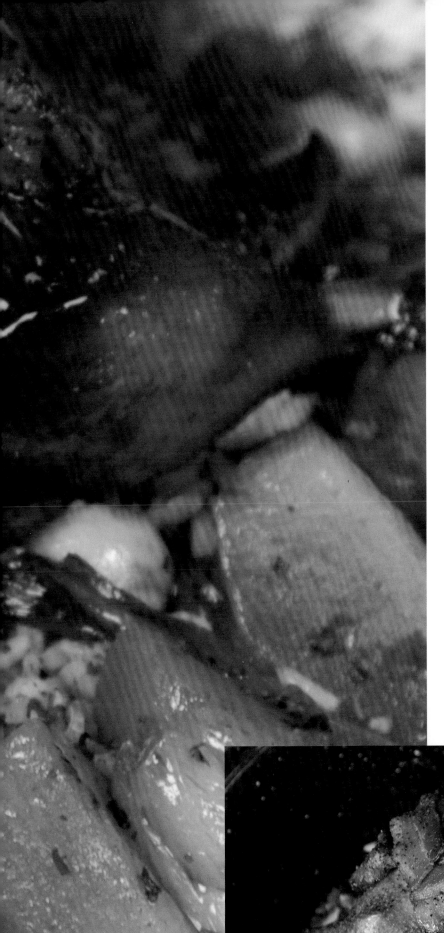

POT-ROASTED GOOSE FALSE RIVER

Prep Time: 4 Hours
Yields: 6 Servings

Comment:

False River is an oxbow lake in New Roads, La. This "river" is a haven for sportsmen hunting geese, ducks and more. This speckled belly goose recipe was created in hunting camps surrounding False River. There is enough meat on a goose to serve six hungry hunters or an entire family.

Ingredients:

1 large speckled-belly goose, cleaned	¼ cup diced garlic
Creole seasoning to taste	1 cup sliced green onions
salt and cayenne pepper to taste	1 quart chicken stock (see recipe)
¼ cup vegetable oil	1 cup Merlot
2 cups diced onions	4 slices bacon
1 cup diced celery	2 cups diced turnips

Method:

Rinse goose well using cold water. Season bird inside and out with Creole seasoning, salt and cayenne pepper. In a cast iron Dutch oven, heat oil over medium-high heat. Sear goose well on all sides, turning as needed for even browning. Remove bird and set aside. In same oil, sauté onions, celery, garlic and green onions 3–5 minutes or until vegetables are wilted. Return goose to Dutch oven and add chicken stock and Merlot. Arrange bacon in a crisscross pattern over goose's breast. Bring stock to a rolling boil then reduce to simmer. Cover and cook goose 2–3 hours or until tender. Depending on age and size of goose, cooking could take up to 4 hours. Add turnips and cook 30 additional minutes. When ready to serve, place goose on a large serving platter surrounded by turnips, vegetable seasonings and a small amount of stock. Goose may also be served over Sweet Farre Dressing or Creole Dirty Rice. (See recipes.)

SQUIRREL JAMBALAYA

Prep Time: 1½ Hours
Yields: 4 Servings

Comment:

Squirrel hunting is probably most difficult for young hunters because in order to hunt squirrels you have to sit very quietly under a tree for hours at a time. Although the task is arduous, the reward is a "skirt" of the animals hanging from your belt on the walk home.

Ingredients:

5 squirrels, cleaned
Creole seasoning to taste
Louisiana hot sauce to taste
Worcestershire sauce to taste
salt and cayenne pepper to taste
¼ cup white vinegar
¼ cup vegetable oil
2 cups diced onions
½ cup diced celery
¼ cup minced garlic
5 cups water or chicken stock
3 cups long grain rice
½ cup sliced green onions
½ cup chopped parsley

Method:

Cut each squirrel into 8–10 serving pieces and rinse thoroughly under cold running water. Drain then place in a large mixing bowl and season with Creole seasoning, hot sauce, Worcestershire, salt, cayenne and vinegar. Blend meat and seasonings well. In a 3-gallon cast iron pot, heat oil over medium-high heat. Cook squirrel 5–10 minutes or until golden brown on all sides, and beginning to caramelize on bottom of pot. Add onions, celery and garlic. Sauté 3–5 minutes or until vegetables are wilted. Pour in water, bring to a rolling boil then reduce to simmer. Cover and allow to simmer 30 minutes or until tender. Stir in rice, green onions and parsley. Adjust seasonings if necessary. Rice will absorb all flavoring, so make sure that there is enough salt and cayenne pepper for finished dish. Reduce heat to simmer, cover and cook 30 minutes. Do not uncover or stir while cooking.

SMOTHERED SQUIRREL IN PAN GRAVY

Prep Time: 2 Hours
Yields: 6 Servings

Comment:

Food obtained through fishing and hunting provides most of the meals in Cajun Country. To enhance the meat or fish, fresh home-garden vegetables are used. This squirrel dish can be made with any other small game such as rabbit or nutria.

Ingredients:

3 medium squirrels, quartered
salt and black pepper to taste
cayenne pepper to taste
Louisiana hot sauce to taste
1 cup flour
½ cup vegetable oil
2 cups diced onions
1 cup diced bell peppers
¼ cup chopped garlic
3 cups water or chicken stock
1 cup sliced green onions

Method:

Rinse squirrel well under cold running water. In a large bowl, season squirrel with salt, peppers and hot sauce. Dust squirrel with flour and shake off excess. In a large cast iron skillet, heat oil over medium-high heat. Cook squirrel in oil, turning often to brown evenly on all sides. When browned, remove and keep warm. In same skillet, sauté onions, bell peppers and garlic 3–5 minutes or until vegetables are wilted. Return squirrel to skillet and slowly add water or stock. Bring to a rolling boil then reduce to simmer. Cover and cook 1–1½ hours or until squirrel is tender. Continue to add water as necessary to simmer squirrels and develop gravy. When meat is tender, add green onions and serve over steamed white rice.

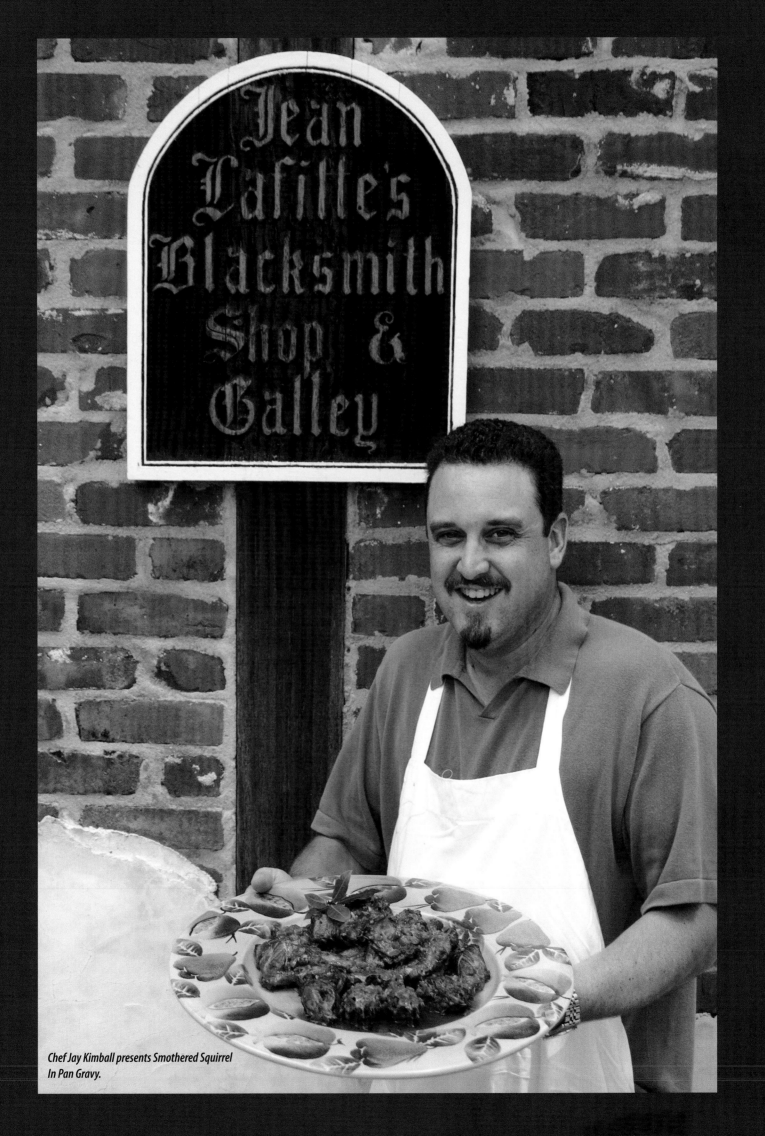

Chef Jay Kimball presents Smothered Squirrel
In Pan Gravy.

FRICASSÉE OF RABBIT

Prep Time: 2 Hours
Yields: 6 Servings

Comment:

The fricassée is probably the most popular method of cooking rabbit in South Louisiana. Slowly cooked in the black iron pot, this simple dish offers up the best tasting rabbit in Bayou Country. When served over our Yellow Corn Biscuits, this fricassée is truly a delight.

Ingredients for Stock:

2 young rabbits
1 onion, diced
1 cup diced celery
4 cloves garlic
1 carrot, sliced

Method:

Cut rabbit into 8 serving size pieces. In a stockpot, place rabbit and cover with 2 inches of water. Add onions, celery, garlic and carrots. Bring to a rolling boil then reduce to simmer. Cook 1 hour or until rabbit is tender. Bone meat and reserve stock.

Ingredients for Fricassée:

¾ cup vegetable oil
1 cup flour
2 cups diced onions
1 cup diced celery
1 cup diced bell peppers
2 tbsps minced garlic
1 cup diced tomatoes
2 cups sliced oyster mushrooms
1½ quarts reserved stock
1 tsp chopped thyme
1 tsp chopped basil
salt and cracked black pepper to taste

Method:

In a 1-gallon cast iron pot, heat oil over medium-high heat. Whisk in flour, stirring constantly to create a brown roux. (See roux recipes.) Add onions, celery, bell peppers, garlic and tomatoes. Sauté 3–5 minutes or until vegetables are wilted. Stir in rabbit then add mushrooms, reserved stock, thyme and basil. Season with salt and pepper. Bring to a low boil then reduce heat to simmer. Cover pot and allow to braise 1 hour. Additional stock or water may be added to retain a stew-like consistency. Adjust seasonings if necessary. Serve over Yellow Corn Biscuits. (See recipe.)

RABBIT AND OYSTER MUSHROOM SAUCE PIQUANT

Prep Time: 1½ Hours
Yields: 6 Servings

Comment:

Sauce piquant or "spicy" sauce was made even more flavorful in Creole kitchens with the addition of hot peppers from the Spanish. Hot jalapeño or habañero peppers definitely give this dish a kick!

Ingredients:

1 large rabbit
1 cup sliced oyster mushrooms
¾ cup vegetable oil
¾ cup flour
1 cup diced onions
1 cup diced celery
½ cup diced red bell peppers
¼ cup minced garlic
1 (8-ounce) can tomato sauce
1 cup diced tomatoes
2 whole bay leaves
½ tsp fresh thyme
½ tsp fresh basil
¼ cup chopped jalapeños
3 quarts beef stock (see recipe)
1 cup sliced green onions
1 cup chopped parsley
salt and cayenne pepper to taste
Louisiana hot sauce to taste

Method:

Cut rabbit into 8 serving pieces. In a 2-gallon cast iron saucepot, heat oil over medium-high heat. Whisk in flour stirring constantly until dark brown roux is achieved. (See roux recipes.) Add rabbit and cook 10–15 minutes. Sauté onions, celery, bell peppers, garlic and mushrooms in roux 3–5 minutes or until vegetables are wilted. Blend in tomatoes and tomato sauce. Add bay leaves, thyme, basil and jalapeños. Slowly stir in stock. Bring to a low boil then reduce to simmer and cook 45 minutes. Additional stock may be added to retain volume. Stir in green onions and parsley. Cook 15 minutes then season with salt, cayenne pepper and hot sauce. Adjust seasonings if necessary. Serve over steamed white rice or pasta.

SALMIS OF RABBIT

Prep Time: 2½ Hours
Yields: 6 Servings

Comment:

Salmis is traditionally a stew made from leftover game birds, but this creative entrée is made with rabbit. The stew is placed in a pie shell and baked in the same fashion as Natchitoches Meat Pies. (See recipe.) These pies may be made with any combination of wild or domestic game.

Ingredients for Stock:

2 large wild rabbits
2 large onions, quartered
2 carrots, sliced
1 stalk celery, chopped
1 head garlic, split
1 tbsp peppercorns
1 bay leaf
salt to taste

Method:

Cut each rabbit into 8 pieces. In a large stockpot, place meat, onions, carrots, celery, garlic, peppercorns, bay leaf and salt. Cover ingredients by 2–3 inches with cold water. Bring to a rolling boil then reduce to simmer. Cook until rabbit is tender and falling from bones. It is important to skim impurities from surface of stock during cooking process. Once rabbit is tender, remove from stock and allow to cool. Strain 1 quart of rabbit stock and set aside. When rabbit cools, bone meat and discard bones.

Ingredients for Salmis:

¼ pound butter
¼ cup flour
1 cup diced onions
1 cup diced celery
½ cup diced red bell peppers
¼ cup minced garlic
1 quart reserved rabbit stock (see above)
1 ounce Burgundy wine
1 tbsp chopped thyme
1 tsp chopped basil
½ tsp rubbed sage
salt and cracked black pepper to taste
¾ cup sliced green onions
½ cup chopped parsley
2 (9-inch) prepared pie crusts

Method:

Preheat oven to 375°F. In a large cast iron skillet, melt butter over medium-high heat. Whisk in flour, stirring constantly to form a light brown roux. (See roux recipes.) Add onions, celery, bell peppers and garlic. Sauté 3–5 minutes or until vegetables are wilted. Slowly add stock until stew-like consistency is achieved. Blend in wine, thyme, basil and sage. Season with salt and pepper. Break rabbit into small pieces and place in simmering sauce. Cook 1 hour, adding stock if necessary. Majority of sauce should be absorbed by rabbit toward end of cooking process. Add green onions and parsley then adjust seasonings if necessary. Pour contents onto a large baking pan and allow to cool to room temperature. Press 1 pie shell into bottom of a pie pan. Spoon cooled rabbit into pie. Cover with second pie crust. Crimp edges of crust together and cut away excess. Using a paring knife, pierce pie 3–4 times to allow steam to escape. Bake 30 minutes or until golden brown. Allow to cool slightly prior to serving.

SAUTÉED RABBIT TENDERLOIN IN BRANDY CREAM

Prep Time: 30 Minutes
Yields: 6 Servings

Comment:

The tenderloin of domestic rabbit is perfect for this dish. Wild rabbits have a much smaller tenderloin, but it is still quite flavorful.

Ingredients:

12 rabbit tenderloins
½ cup butter
½ cup flour
1 tbsp minced garlic
¼ cup sliced green onions
¼ cup sliced mushrooms
½ tsp dried thyme
½ tsp dried basil
¼ cup brandy
1 cup demi-glace (see recipe)
½ cup heavy whipping cream
salt and cracked black pepper to taste

Method:

In a 10-inch heavy-bottomed sauté pan, melt butter over medium-high heat. Dredge rabbit tenderloins in flour then sauté in butter until golden brown on all sides. Add garlic, green onions, mushrooms, thyme and basil. Sauté 2 minutes or until vegetables are wilted. Remove sauté pan from heat and add brandy. When pan is returned to heat, brandy may ignite. Reduce wine to half volume then add demi-glace and whipping cream. Bring to a low boil and cook until sauce is slightly thickened. Season with salt and pepper. Serve 2 tenderloins in center of a dinner plate and top with brandy cream sauce.

CAJUN-STUFFED LEG OF RABBIT

Prep Time: 2 Hours
Yields: 6 Servings

Comment:
The stuffed leg of rabbit has been a gold medal winner in culinary competitions throughout Louisiana. This dish is a fixture on the menu at Lafitte's Landing, and it has been the entrée for many gourmet dinners served worldwide.

Ingredients:
6 hind legs of rabbit, boned
1 pound lump crabmeat
¼ cup diced onions
¼ cup diced celery
¼ cup diced red bell peppers
2 tbsps minced garlic
2 tbsps sliced green onions
½ cup béchamel sauce (see recipe)
½ cup Italian bread crumbs
salt and cayenne pepper to taste
½ cup melted butter
½ cup Louisiana cane syrup
1 tbsp dried thyme
1 tbsp dried basil
1 tbsp dried tarragon
1 tbsp cracked black pepper
½ cup dry red wine
2 cups demi-glace (see recipe)

Method:
Ask butcher to bone 6 hind legs of rabbit to knee joint. This process will create a pocket perfect for stuffing. In a large mixing bowl, combine lump crabmeat, onions, celery, bell peppers, garlic, green onions and béchamel. Blend well. Slowly add bread crumbs then season with salt and cayenne pepper. Place an equal amount of crabmeat stuffing inside pocket of each leg. Place legs on a large baking sheet. In a mixing bowl, combine butter, cane syrup, thyme, basil, tarragon and pepper. Drizzle legs with syrup mixture then let sit at room temperature for 1 hour. Preheat oven to 450°F. Bake rabbit legs 25–30 minutes or until golden brown and stuffing is cooked. Remove legs from baking pan and deglaze with red wine. Scrape all drippings into a 9-inch sauté pan and add demi-glace. Bring to a low boil, reduce to simmer and cook until sauce is slightly thickened. Slice rabbit leg into 3 equal pieces. Place in center of serving plate, and spoon a generous amount of sauce next to rabbit.

SMOTHERED NUTRIA

Prep Time: 45 Minutes
Yields: 6 Servings

Comment:

Nutria are prevalent in the bayous and swamps surrounding New Orleans. In fact these rodents are so numerous they are destroying coastal wetlands vital to Louisiana's fishing and conservation. There has been a push by the state to get people to help solve the nutria problem in the best way Louisianians know how, by using it as an ingredient in various dishes.

Ingredients:

1 large nutria, cut into serving pieces
2 tbsps vegetable oil
granulated garlic to taste
Creole seasoning to taste
2 cups diced onions
1 cup diced green bell peppers
1 tbsp flour
salt and black pepper to taste
3¾ cups chicken stock or (see recipe) broth

Method:

In a 5-quart heavy-bottomed pot, heat oil over high heat. Sprinkle meat with garlic and Creole seasoning. Add nutria to pot and cook 10 minutes, stirring until brown on all sides. Add onions, bell peppers and flour. Cook 10 minutes, stirring constantly. Season with salt and pepper then add stock. Cook 15 minutes, stirring occasionally and scraping bottom of pot to remove pan drippings. Serve over steamed white rice, pasta or Whipped Potato Clouds. (See recipe.)

STUFFED NUTRIA HINDQUARTERS

Prep Time: 2½ Hours
Yields: 15 Servings

Comment:

Nutria were brought to Louisiana from South America in the mid 1900s. Since that time, the state has become a permanent home to the water-loving animals. Nutria meat, similar to domesticated rabbit, is lean, low in cholesterol and high in protein. When cooked with Louisiana crawfish tails, nutria is sure to become a new favorite.

Ingredients:

15 nutria hindquarters
3 tbsps butter
½ pound ground pork
4 cups diced onions
½ cup diced green bell peppers
½ cup diced red bell peppers
salt and cayenne pepper to taste
Creole seasoning to taste
1 cup chicken stock (see recipe) or water
1 (10¾-ounce) can cream of mushroom soup
2 cups fresh Louisiana crawfish tails, chopped
2 cups Italian bread crumbs

Method:

Preheat oven to 350°F. In a 5-quart pot, melt butter over medium-high heat. Add pork, onions and bell peppers. Cook 10 minutes, stirring occasionally. Season with salt, cayenne and Creole seasoning. Cook 5 minutes. Slowly stir in stock and cook 10 minutes. Reduce heat to medium. Add cream of mushroom and cook 7 minutes. Add crawfish and cook 5 minutes. Remove from heat, add bread crumbs and stir until mixture is moist but held together. Remove large leg bone from each hindquarter then pound out legs with a meat tenderizer. Sprinkle salt, cayenne and Creole seasoning evenly on both sides. Lay leg flat, place stuffing mixture inside, roll and tie with cooking string. Place stuffed legs in greased baking pan. Bake covered 1½ hours or until tender. Uncover and bake 10 minutes or until brown. NOTE: May be braised in onion gravy similar to Braised Round Steak and Gravy or Grillades. (See recipes.)

BARBECUED RACCOON

Prep Time: 2 Hours
Yields: 8–10 Servings

Comment:
Although raccoon may seem somewhat unconventional, this meat may be found in many rural roadside markets throughout South Louisiana. Coon was served often on Cabanocey Plantation. Smoked coon and andouille gumbo was a favorite of the hunters.

Ingredients:
1 large raccoon, cut into serving pieces
1 cup dry red wine
½ cup Louisiana cane syrup
2 onions, sliced
½ cup minced garlic
3 bay leaves
2 tbsps fresh thyme leaves
1 tbsp chopped basil
1 tbsp paprika
1 tbsp cumin
1 tbsp chili powder
1 tbsp cayenne pepper
salt and black pepper to taste
granulated garlic to taste
2 cups barbecue sauce

Method:
In a mixing bowl, combine all ingredients except salt, pepper, granulated garlic and barbecue sauce. Place raccoon pieces in a large pan. Pour marinade over meat. Using your hands, massage seasonings into meat. Cover pan with plastic wrap and refrigerate overnight. Remove meat from pan and pat dry. Season raccoon with salt, pepper and granulated garlic. Heat grill according to manufacturer's directions. Place coals on half of pit, leaving other half as a cool zone. Place seasoned meat over hot coals and cook 1 hour, turning occasionally to prevent burning. After 1 hour, move meat to cool side of pit. Add a small amount of your favorite wood chips to hot coals allowing meat to smoke gently until done to your liking. When meat is fork tender, return to hot side and baste generously with barbecue sauce. NOTE: This dish may be cooked in an oven at 350°F. Adjust method by adding 1 tbsp of liquid smoke to marinade and cooking 1–1½ hours or until tender.

ROAST OF WILD BOAR

Prep Time: 2½ Hours
Yields: 6–8 Servings

Comment:
Wild boar are plentiful in the swamps of Louisiana, and the hunting season provides a great supply of meat. Since the meat tends to be a bit oily, proper cooking methods are imperative to success with this game.

Ingredients:
1 (2-pound) loin of wild boar
6 cloves garlic, thinly sliced
½ cup sliced green onions
salt and black pepper to taste
granulated garlic to taste
4 ounces olive oil
1 cup diced onions
1 cup diced celery
1 cup diced bell peppers
¼ cup minced garlic
2 tbsps tomato paste
6 ounces red wine
1 quart pork or beef stock (see recipe)
5 ounces sliced pancetta

Method:
Preheat oven to 325°F. In a mixing bowl, combine garlic slices, green onions, salt, pepper and granulated garlic. Make incisions in meat and stuff with garlic/green onion mixture. In a roasting pan, heat oil over medium-high heat. Brown boar on all sides. Remove meat from pan. In same oil, sauté onions, celery, bell peppers and minced garlic until wilted. Mix in tomato paste then deglaze with wine. Cook until wine is reduced by half. Add 2 cups of stock, return meat to pan and cover with pancetta. Cover pan then place in oven and bake 2 hours or until meat is fork tender. Remove roast from pan and add remaining stock. Bring to a simmer then remove from heat. Chop pan drippings in a blender or food processor. Allow roast to rest under a foil tent 30 minutes. Slice roast and serve with a generous portion of sauce.

ROAST OF VENISON
WITH CAJUN SAUSAGE

Prep Time: 2 Hours
Yields: 6–8 Servings

Comment:

Venison is a delicious meat, but it tends to be dry. To retain moisture, slow roast or combine with other fatty meats such as bacon or sausage. Here, sausage is used to keep the meat juicy and to add flavor. In Louisiana, sausage is enhanced with garlic, green onions and herbs such as thyme and basil. If seasoned Cajun sausage is unavailable, use fresh pork sausage and add the above spices.

Ingredients:

1 (5-pound) leg of venison, boned
1½ pounds fresh seasoned sausage
salt and cracked black pepper to taste
Louisiana hot sauce to taste
¼ cup vegetable oil
1 cup diced onions
1 cup diced celery
1 cup diced bell peppers
¼ cup minced garlic
4 apples, cubed
1 cup sliced green onions
¼ cup chopped parsley
2 cups chicken stock (see recipe)

Method:

Preheat oven to 375°F. Fill cavity of venison roast with sausage. Truss or tie cavity shut if desired. Season roast with salt, pepper and hot sauce. In a large Dutch oven, heat oil over medium-high heat. Brown roast well on all sides. Add onions, celery, bell peppers and garlic. Sauté 3–5 minutes or until vegetables are wilted. Remove from heat then add apples, green onions and parsley. Pour in chicken stock and adjust seasonings if necessary. Cover and bake 1½–2 hours or until tender. Remove and allow to rest 30 minutes prior to slicing. If desired, reduce drippings to a sauce consistency before serving.

ROASTED LEG OF
VENISON BAYOU BLUE

Prep Time: 2½ Hours
Yields: 6–8 Servings

Comment:

Bayou Blue is a small body of water that runs through the Coushatta Indian reservation. Venison was a primary ingredient in the Native American diet. The Coushattas created this venison dish that uses pine nuts from long needle pine trees.

Ingredients:

1 (3–5 pound) venison leg roast
pinch of thyme
pinch of basil
salt and cracked black pepper to taste
Louisiana hot sauce to taste
¼ cup vegetable oil
3 cups oyster or button mushrooms
2 cups sliced Bermuda onions
10 cloves garlic
4 sweet potatoes, cubed
2 cups muscadines or red grapes
1 cup pine nuts
2 quarts beef stock (see recipe)

Method:

Preheat oven to 400°F. Season roast with thyme, basil, salt, pepper and hot sauce. In a large Dutch oven, heat oil over medium-high heat. Brown venison well on all sides. Surround roast with mushrooms, onions, garlic, sweet potatoes, muscadines and pine nuts. Pour in stock, 1 cup at a time, then bring to a rolling boil. Remove from heat, cover and bake 1½–2 hours or until roast is tender. Remove roast from pot and keep warm. Return pot to stove and reduce cooking liquid to sauce consistency. If preferable, thicken with a light brown roux. (See roux recipes.) Adjust seasonings if necessary. To serve, slice roast and top with sauce.

A friend helps Buckley Kessler skin a deer.

VENISON OSSO BUCO

Prep Time: 3 Hours
Yields: 6 Servings

Comment:

The Italians brought the famous veal osso buco to Louisiana from Milan. In Bayou Country, venison shank was substituted for the traditional veal and this wonderful dish was created.

Ingredients:

16 (1½-pound) venison shanks
¼ pound butter
2 cups diced onions
½ cup diced celery
¼ cup minced garlic
1 cup diced carrots
salt and black pepper to taste
Louisiana hot sauce to taste
¾ cup flour
½ cup olive oil
1 cup dry red wine
3 cups chicken stock (see recipe)
1 tsp basil
1 tsp thyme
1 (14.5-ounce) can whole tomatoes, drained
3 bay leaves
½ cup chopped parsley
1 tbsp grated lemon zest
1 tbsp minced garlic
¼ cup chopped parsley for garnish

Method:

Preheat oven to 350°F. In a heavy-bottomed sauté pan, melt butter over medium-high heat. Add onions, celery, garlic and carrots. Sauté 3–5 minutes or until vegetables are wilted. Remove from heat and set aside. Season venison shanks generously with salt, pepper and hot sauce. In order to keep meat from falling apart during cooking, tie each shank across center with a piece of butcher's twine. Coat venison well in flour, shaking off excess. In a 14-inch cast iron skillet, heat olive oil over medium-high heat. Brown shanks, a few at a time, until golden brown on all sides. Place browned shanks side by side in a large casserole dish. Spoon sautéed vegetables over meat. Pour off all but 1 tablespoon of oil from skillet. Add red wine and bring mixture to a rolling boil. Reduce wine to approximately ½ cup while scraping all drippings from skillet. Blend in chicken stock, basil, thyme, tomatoes, bay leaves and parsley. Bring to a low boil, chopping tomatoes into mixture. Once boiling, pour ingredients over shanks in casserole dish. Cover and bake 1½–2 hours, basting occasionally. Test for tenderness by piercing meat with tip of a sharp knife or serving fork. When meat is tender, arrange venison shanks decoratively on a heated platter and spoon vegetable sauce from casserole dish over meat. In a mixing bowl, combine lemon zest, garlic and parsley. Sprinkle mixture over venison as a garnish. Osso buco should be served over pasta, risotto or jambalaya.

VENISON ROAST

Prep Time: 3 Hours
Yields: 6–8 Servings

Comment:

Feel free to use any large cut of venison in this recipe. However, the back leg is most often used in this dish. It is important to cook the roast long enough to guarantee tenderness.

Ingredients:

1 (3–5 pound) venison leg roast
20 cloves garlic, thinly sliced
½ cup sliced green onions
6 bacon strips, cubed ¼-inch
salt and black pepper to taste
granulated garlic to taste
1 cup Worcestershire sauce
4 cloves garlic, mashed
2 tbsps chopped thyme
2 tbsps chopped basil
2 tbsps chopped tarragon
3 bay leaves
¼ cup hot sauce
¼ cup vegetable oil
2 cups diced onions
½ cup diced celery
¼ cup diced red bell peppers
¼ cup minced garlic
1 cup dry red wine
6 cups beef stock (see recipe)
2 cups sliced mushrooms
4 red potatoes, quartered
6 carrots, sliced

Method:

Preheat oven to 375°F. In a mixing bowl, combine sliced garlic, green onions, bacon, salt, pepper and granulated garlic. Blend well. Using a paring knife, cut approximately 15 (1-inch) slits into roast for stuffing. Press an equal amount of bacon mixture into each slit. Place stuffed roast into a gallon-sized plastic zipper bag and pour in Worcestershire, mashed garlic, thyme, basil, tarragon, bay leaves, hot sauce, salt, pepper and granulated garlic. Marinate in refrigerator overnight, turning bag occasionally. In a 3-gallon cast iron Dutch oven, heat oil over medium-high heat. Remove roast from bag and discard marinade. Season meat with salt, pepper, granulated garlic and hot sauce then brown well in oil on all sides. Remove roast from pot. In same oil, sauté onions, celery, bell peppers and garlic 3–5 minutes or until vegetables are wilted. Return roast to pot and add red wine, beef stock and mushrooms. Cover and bake 2½ hours, checking every 30 minutes and adding stock if necessary. When fork tender, add potatoes and carrots. Cover and cook until vegetables are tender. Remove roast, potatoes and carrots from pot, cover with foil tent and allow to sit 30 minutes. Retain 4 cups of stock, including vegetables. Slice meat into serving pieces. When ready to serve, place sliced roast, potatoes and carrots in reserved stock. Heat thoroughly on stove or in oven.

VENISON TENDERLOIN CARENCRO

Prep Time: 3 Hours
Yields: 6 Servings

Comment:

Carencro, La. is a small Cajun village located directly between Opelousas, the yam capital of the world, and Lafayette, the heart of Acadiana. In Carencro, venison tenderloin prepared in this manner is often served to important guests.

Ingredients:

6 (6-ounce) venison tenderloin steaks
2 tbsps chopped thyme
2 tbsps chopped basil
1 tbsp chopped tarragon
2 tbsps minced garlic
1 cup dry red wine
¼ cup vegetable oil
salt and cracked black pepper to taste
1 tbsp flour
3 cups game or veal stock (see recipe)

Method:

In a small mixing bowl, combine herbs and garlic. Place venison steaks in a large baking pan and coat with red wine. Rub herb and garlic mixture into steaks. Set aside and marinate 2 hours at room temperature. Reserve marinade for later use. NOTE: Steaks must be cooked immediately upon completion of marinating because they will spoil if refrigerated prior to cooking. Preheat oven to 350°F. In a cast iron skillet, heat oil over medium-high heat. Season steaks with salt and pepper. Sauté steaks, a few at a time, until golden brown on all sides. Return steaks to skillet and place in oven until internal temperature reaches 130°F for medium. Remove and keep warm. Pour off all but 1 tablespoon of drippings from skillet. Place skillet over medium-high heat. Whisk in flour stirring constantly until light brown roux is achieved. (See roux recipes.) Pour in reserved marinade and stock. Bring mixture to a rolling boil, stirring constantly until thickened and reduced to sauce-like consistency. Season with salt and pepper. Place an equal portion of game sauce in center of a 10-inch dinner plate and top with a venison steak. If desired, garnish with a mixture of fall vegetables such as melon-balled yams, carrots, beets or potatoes.

RACK OF VENISON WITH MUSCADINE GLAZE

Prep Time: 2 Hours
Yields: 6–8 Servings

Comment:

Muscadines are a variety of grapes that grow well in Louisiana. This fruit is perfect for making jams, jellies and wines. Muscadines can also be cooked down with any game dish to create a sweet, fruity sauce.

Ingredients:

6 (4-bone) racks of venison
½ cup melted butter
¼ cup dried thyme
¼ cup dried basil
¼ cup dried rosemary
2 tbsps dried tarragon
3 tbsps minced garlic
salt and black pepper to taste
¼ cup vegetable oil
1 cup fresh Muscadines or red grapes
1 quart beef stock or consommé

Method:

Preheat oven to 400°F. In a large baking pan, spread venison racks evenly. Top each rack with an equal amount of butter then rub to coat evenly. In a mixing bowl, combine herbs, garlic, salt and pepper. Rub herb mixture into meat. Allow to sit at room temperature for 1 hour. In a heavy-bottomed cast iron skillet, heat vegetable oil over medium-high heat. Brown 1–2 racks at a time, until golden brown on all sides then return to baking pan. In same skillet, bring Muscadines and stock to a low boil. Cook until volume has reduced by half and consistency is slightly thickened. While sauce is simmering, bake venison 15 minutes for medium-rare or 20 minutes for medium. Strain thickened sauce to remove Muscadine pulp, keep warm. Slice 3–4 venison chops on each plate and top with an equal portion of Muscadine glaze.

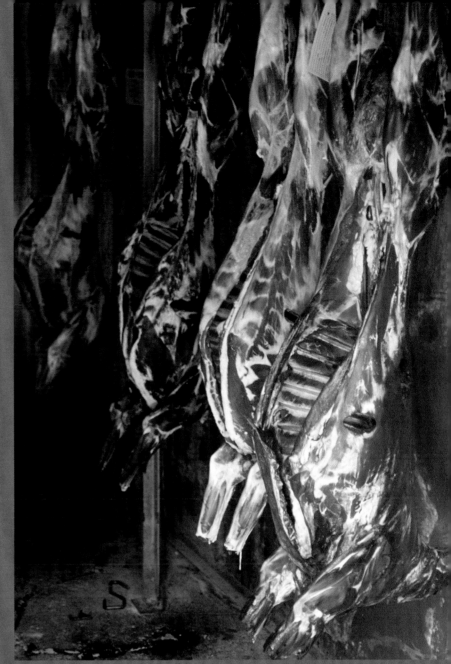

VENISON PIE

Prep Time: 2½ Hours
Yields: 6–8 Servings

Comment:

Louisiana is truly "Sportsman's Paradise." From ducks and doves to rabbits and deer, hunters across the state can find whatever game they desire. These men and women have become masters at creating new ways to prepare wild meats. This dish is similar to our world famous salmis.

Ingredients:

1½ pounds lean venison, cubed
2 tbsps bacon fat
salt and cayenne pepper to taste
2 cups diced onions
¼ cup diced garlic
2 cups diced tomatoes
1 tsp chopped thyme
3 cups chicken or beef stock (see recipe)
4 carrots, diced
¼ cup diced celery
2 cups tiny English peas
1 cup flour
¾ cup yellow cornmeal
2 tsps sugar
1 tbsp baking powder
½ tsp salt
¾ cup milk
3 tbsps vegetable oil
1 egg, beaten

Method:

Preheat oven to 425°F. In a 12-inch cast iron skillet, heat bacon fat over medium-high heat. Season meat thoroughly with salt and cayenne pepper. Brown venison in bacon fat. Add onions and garlic. Sauté 3–5 minutes or until vegetables are wilted. Blend in tomatoes, thyme and stock. Bring to a rolling boil, reduce to simmer, cover and cook 1–1½ hours or until venison is tender. Stir carrots, celery and peas into sauce and cook 5–10 minutes. In a large mixing bowl, combine flour, cornmeal, sugar, baking powder and salt. Blend well. Add milk, oil and egg. Mix thoroughly then spoon over venison stew. Place in oven and bake 25–30 minutes or until topping has cooked thoroughly and browned evenly. Topping should resemble that of a homemade cobbler.

VENISON JERKY

Prep Time: 9 Hours
Yields: 1 Pound

Comment:
Smoking or dry-curing game meat was a way of preserving the ample harvest. As certain dishes made their way from the hunting camps to the home, variations of flavors were created by different cultures. In this recipe an Asian influence is seen in the addition of teriyaki and soy sauces.

Ingredients:
2 pounds lean venison, sliced thin (against grain)
½ cup liquid smoke
¼ cup soy sauce
½ cup Worcestershire sauce
¼ cup Louisiana hot sauce
2 tbsps Louisiana cane syrup
1½ tsps meat tenderizer
1½ tsps salt
2 tbsps brown sugar
¼ cup teriyaki sauce (optional)
2 tbsps Creole seasoning
2 tbsps granulated garlic

Method:
Whisk together all ingredients except for meat. Blend in meat then marinate 24 hours in refrigerator. After marinating process, place in a dehydrator 9 hours or until properly dehydrated.

HOTH PONI

Prep Time: 2½ Hours
Yields: 10 Servings

Comment:
What we call vegetable soup, the Native Americans of Louisiana called Hoth Poni. The ingredients of this dish must have been surprising to the early colonists. In Europe, corn was considered animal feed, and tomatoes were thought to be poisonous. Many people believe this dish is the predecessor of succotash; nevertheless, it is revered in many Louisiana homes today.

Ingredients:
2 pounds venison meat, cubed
1½ gallons beef stock (see recipe)
salt and cracked black pepper to taste
2 cups whole kernel corn
2 cups lima beans
1 cup sliced tomatoes
2 carrots, peeled and sliced
1 bay leaf
1 tbsp basil
1 tsp chopped thyme

Method:
In a 2-gallon Dutch oven, place venison and enough beef stock to cover by 2 inches. Season lightly with salt and pepper. Bring mixture to a rolling boil, reduce heat to simmer and cook 1½ hours or until tender. Add all remaining ingredients and continue to cook 30 minutes longer or until flavor has developed. Additional beef stock may be needed to retain volume. Adjust seasonings if necessary. Serve Hoth Poni in a soup bowl with Maw Maw Coniglio's Fry Bread. (See recipe.)

VENISON SAUSAGE

Prep Time: 1 Hour
Yields: 25 (6-inch) Links

Comment:
Combining equal amounts of pork with game meat creates a juicy sausage. This recipe incorporates the trinity of Louisiana flavors along with typical sausage spices to create a magnificent sausage.

Ingredients:
2 pounds ground venison
2 pounds ground pork
½ pound pork fat
¼ cup diced onions
¼ cup diced celery
¼ cup diced red bell peppers
¼ cup minced garlic
½ cup sliced green onions
¼ cup chopped parsley
salt and black pepper to taste
1 tbsp ground sage
1 tbsp caraway seeds
15 feet pork sausage casing

Method:
In a large mixing bowl, combine meats, pork fat, onions, celery, bell peppers, garlic, green onions and parsley. Using your hands, blend ingredients. Season with salt, pepper, sage and caraway seeds. Continue to blend seasonings into meat mixture. Force meat through a meat grinder to stuff into casing. Tie off sausages at 6-inch intervals. This sausage may be smoked, pan-fried or poached.

ALLIGATOR SAUCE PIQUANT

Prep Time: 2½ Hours
Yields: 6 Servings

Comment:
This recipe proves the point that in Cajun Country anything can go into a sauce piquant pot. In this spicy sauce, it is recommended that you use alligator tail meat due to its texture and light to white color.

Ingredients:
1½ pounds alligator, cut into 1-inch cubes
1 cup vegetable oil
1 cup flour
2 cups diced onions
2 cups diced celery
1 cup diced bell peppers
¼ cup minced garlic
2 (10-ounce) cans Ro*tel® tomatoes
2 quarts water
salt and cracked black pepper to taste
Louisiana hot sauce to taste

Method:
In a heavy-bottomed pot, heat oil over medium-high heat. Whisk in flour, stirring constantly until dark brown roux is achieved. (See roux recipes.) Add alligator and sauté 10 minutes or until well browned. Stir in onions, celery, bell peppers and garlic. Sauté 3–5 minutes or until vegetables are wilted. Pour in tomatoes and water. Blend well then season with salt, pepper and hot sauce. Bring mixture to a rolling boil then reduce heat to medium. Cook 2 hours or until meat is tender. Add water to retain volume if necessary.

FRIED ALLIGATOR TAIL

Prep Time: 1 Hour
Yields: 6–8 Servings

Comment:
Cajun "popcorn" made its way to appetizer and bar menus throughout Bayou Country in the early 1980s. However, this popcorn is not exploded corn kernels; instead, it is deep-fried crawfish tails, lump crabmeat, small shrimp or even diced alligator.

Ingredients for Marinade:
1 onion, sliced
1 cup salad oil
1 cup red wine vinegar
3 cups water

Method:
In a mixing bowl, combing all ingredients and let sit at room temperature for 1 hour. Add alligator and marinate 24 hours in refrigerator.

Ingredients for Alligator Tail:
3 pounds alligator tail, cut into ¾-inch cubes
2 eggs, beaten
2 cups milk
1 cup water
salt and cayenne pepper to taste
3 cups seasoned corn flour
vegetable oil for frying

Method:
Using a home-style deep fryer such as a FryDaddy, heat oil according to manufacturer's directions. In a mixing bowl, blend eggs, milk and water. Season with salt and cayenne pepper. Remove alligator from marinade, drain well and dip into egg batter. Coat pieces in seasoned corn flour then fry until golden brown. Serve hot with cocktail or tartar sauce.

SCALOPPINE OF ALLIGATOR

Prep Time: 30 Minutes
Yields: 6 Servings

Comment:
Scaloppine refers to small, thin slices of meat that are pounded flat. The medallions are then dredged in flour, sautéed and served in a wine sauce. Traditionally, scaloppine uses veal or pork, but in this Cajun version, alligator is used. Tenderloin of alligator or the top portion of the tail meat works best in this recipe.

Ingredients:
12 (3-ounce) medallions of alligator
¼ cup chopped basil
1 tbsp chopped thyme
¼ cup chopped parsley
salt and cracked black pepper to taste
Louisiana hot sauce to taste
egg wash (1 egg, ½ cup water, ½ cup milk, blended)
2 cups seasoned flour
½ cup butter
½ cup thinly sliced pickled okra
½ cup diced red bell peppers
1 tbsp minced garlic
1 cup white wine

Method:
Pound medallions between 2 sheets of wax paper until ¼-inch thick. In a large mixing bowl, combine basil, thyme and parsley. Season medallions with salt, pepper and hot sauce. Dip in egg wash then coat with flour and press into herb mixture. In a 10-inch sauté pan, melt butter over medium-high heat. Pan sauté alligator until golden brown on both sides. Add okra, bell peppers and garlic. Sauté 3–5 minutes or until vegetables are wilted. Deglaze with wine and reduce to sauce consistency. To serve, place 2 medallions over angel hair pasta and top with sauce.

Desserts

OLD TOWN PRALIN
721 ROYAL ST

With sugar playing such an integral role in Louisiana's history and economy, you might expect Louisianians to get more excited about desserts than they do. Make no mistake, desserts are as important an ending to the perfect meal as anywhere else. They are a great source of pride to those who create them, but here the simple and the traditional reign supreme. Variations on bread pudding, rice pudding, pies and cobblers were perhaps created in Cajun and Creole kitchens as comforting reminders of the Old Country, for their originals are still consumed in Germany, France, England, Spain and Italy. Cajun and Creole desserts also reflect the astounding variety of fruits and other ingredients either natural or long-acclimatized to this territory: apples, figs, plums, quince, persimmons, peaches, pears, strawberries, blueberries, blackberries, pecans, yams and clover honey. In addition, because New Orleans has long been a major port, the Creoles had early access to even more exotic ingredients such as bananas and coconuts, which quickly found permanent homes in their dessert repertoire. In fact, bananas and coconuts already figured prominently when Lafcadio Hearn published his *Creole Cookbook* in 1885, as did sponge cakes, trifles, blancmanges (a sweet, jellied dessert made from milk and corn flour), custards and bread puddings. The French and English influence on Creole dessert trays is immediately obvious because of the similarities to traditional European choices. We must also give special credit to the Germans, who not only brought their recipes to share, but were largely responsible for making milk, butter and eggs widely available in South Louisiana. Before this, when milk and butter were not so easy to come by, you might be surprised to learn that Cajun and Creole cooks used the same solution as the ancient Romans to create delicious desserts…cream cheese. The Louisiana version, Creole cream cheese, was born of necessity, but soon became a treasured ingredient. Absent for a few decades, Creole cream cheese regained popularity in the 21st century thanks to the Chef John Folse Bittersweet Plantation Dairy. In turn, this humble, but delicious cream cheese has inspired a variety of cheesecakes, ice creams and other desserts.

It is generally accepted that pralines and other French delicacies made their way to the New World with those who cooked for the Creole settlers, and strangely enough, also with the missionary nuns, who were renowned for their pastry skills in France. Legend has it that the Ursuline nuns, lacking the traditional hazelnuts and almonds they would have used in France, substituted local pecans. These New World pralines were soon as much a hit here as the originals had been in France. Earlier accounts claim that the praline of France was named for the Duke of Choiseul-Praslin in whose kitchen a happy accident (the details of which vary) yielded the delicious sweet. Now the delicious sugary flavor of pralines, whether chocolate or traditional, is used to enhance cheesecakes, ice cream, fudge, crêpes and more.

New Orleans is home to many signature desserts such as bananas Foster and bread pudding, but one of the most famous, the King cake, has been a part of Mardi Gras celebrations for decades. King cake season officially begins on Twelfth Night, the 12th day after Christmas. Within these brightly colored ring-shaped confections is hidden a small plastic baby, representing either the new year or the baby Jesus who was visited by the Magi or three kings on that day. In earlier years the baby was porcelain and before that, a bean or other trinket was hidden in the cake. Current tradition dictates that whoever gets the baby in his or her slice must purchase the next King cake or give the next Mardi Gras party. On Twelfth Night, whoever finds the baby in the King cake is crowned the king of the revelries. While New Orleans claims Gateau de Roi or King cake as its own, Twelfth Night cake traditions can be traced back to the Roman tradition of choosing the "king" of Saturnalian revels by baking a bean into a cake. The practice of eating a cake with a bean can also be found in Italy, England, Portugal and France, all many years before Mardi Gras was celebrated in New Orleans. In France the gallette des rois (cake of kings) is sliced into as many slices as there are guests, plus one for God. According to *The History of Food*, these French cakes were once octagonal and known as gorenflot, named for the monk who made them for the French Court in the 16th century.

The Portuguese make a ring-shaped cake like ours, called a bolo-Rei, the English use a fruitcake and the Italians a simple focaccio, but all are consumed on Twelfth Night and all include a bean or trinket, which denotes either who will be king or good luck. Of course, few dispute the fact that New Orleans has put its own special twist on both Mardi Gras and King cake. For starters, Louisianians don't limit consumption of King cake to Twelfth Night alone. This pre-Lenten indulgence is made with many variations of fillings and toppings. It is consumed by Louisiana revelers (and shipped around the world) until Ash Wednesday.

Another dessert-favorite, which Louisiana cannot call its own, but has taken to new limits, is ice cream. Legend has it that Marco Polo brought the recipe for sherbet from Persia to Italy and that the Italians were the first to introduce ice cream to England and France. Some say ices and ice creams came to France with Catherine de Medici of Florence when she married the French Dauphin, Henri of Valois in 1533. Ices of different flavors were prepared for each day of the wedding celebration and offered the French nobility their first taste of this predecessor to ice cream. In 1675 a Sicilian pastry chef opened the first ice cream parlor in Paris. The Parisians fell in love so completely that there were reportedly 200 establishments selling ice cream there by 1680.

The Italians were probably also the first to bring ice cream to America commercially. We know that both George Washington and Thomas Jefferson were fond of this frozen treat, which they encountered in France. As early as 1790, our first president ran up a bill of $200 for a summer's worth of ice cream purchased from an ice cream merchant. Both Washington and Jefferson also owned ice cream makers and served the cold treat at parties. Details on Washington's "cream machine for making ice," purchased in Philadelphia in 1784, are slim, but we know Thomas Jefferson brought his sorbetière from France and that it used ice and salt in an exterior chamber to freeze the ice cream in the interior chamber. As early as 1808 the Exchange Coffeehouse in New Orleans advertised in the *Louisiana Courier* it would serve ice cream daily between noon and 9 p.m.—a luxury no doubt made possible by the increasing availability of ice shipped from cooler states. By the 1850s, ice cream was so popular in America that Ralph Waldo Emerson quipped, "We dare not trust our wit for making our house pleasant to our friends, and so we buy ice cream." Owen Edward Brennan, founder of Brennan's restaurant, also recognized the power of ice cream. Before he became a famous restaurateur, Brennan owned a drugstore that sold ice cream. Noticing some domestic workingwomen suffering in the Louisiana heat one day, he sent one of his workers with ice cream "compliments of Brennan's." The women's employers, hearing the story and impressed by his generosity, soon became customers. Seeing what a great business move his act of kindness turned out to be, he continued the tradition, sending ice cream out as a welcome for newcomers to the city. While ice cream may now be considered an all-American treat, you will find several ice cream recipes with a Louisiana influence.

Obviously, one essential ingredient in most dessert recipes is sugar. More than a culinary treasure, sugar was also an essential part of Louisiana's economy as early as the 1700s. Efforts to cultivate sugarcane here had been made since 1725, but it was Etienne de Boré who finally succeeded. With the help of experts from Saint Domingue (Haiti), he was able not just to grow sugarcane on his plantation near present-day Audubon Park, but also to crystallize sugar on a commercial scale. De Boré was so revered for this achievement that he was later made mayor of New Orleans. The original black iron sugar kettle used by de Boré still holds a place of honor in front of Louisiana State University's Audubon Sugar Institute. While de Boré's achievement is often noted in historical accounts of the Louisiana sugar industry, many fail to credit Norbert Rillieux for inventing a safer, less labor intensive method for refining sugar.

Patented in 1846, the Rillieux apparatus consisted of an evaporating pan that enclosed a series of condensing coils in vacuum chambers. In addition to reducing labor, the device conserved fuel and produced a superior refined product. Although the device was widely used on sugar plantations in Louisiana, Mexico and the Caribbean, and was the forerunner of techniques still used today, Rillieux initially did not receive the recognition he deserved because he was the son of a French planter and a slave mother.

Because refined sugar was initially very expensive, the cheaper byproducts of the refining process such as cane syrup and molasses were commonly used as sweetening ingredients in many households, particularly by the Cajuns. Cane syrup still remains popular as a sweetener and as an ingredient for both traditional and innovative recipes today. For a while Louisiana was one of the world's most prominent sources of sugar, but the ravages of the Civil War and the emancipation of the African-Americans who provided the plantations with labor dealt the industry a blow from which it never fully recovered. Many sugar plantations switched to rice cultivation and those that remain have had to defend against hurricanes, competition from the sugar beet industry and the impact of international trade agreements. Despite these challenges, sugar remains one of Louisiana's leading industries. Each September the sugarcane crop receives a formal blessing as part of the Sugarcane Festival in New Iberia, La.

Cheap sugar, refrigeration, availability of exotic ingredients and pre-packaged desserts may have made it much easier for modern cooks to be creative, but they have not dampened the drive that pushes the more adventurous to try new combinations of ingredients and achieve new levels of delight. They have also failed to replace the standard, traditional desserts that still complete the perfect Cajun or Creole meal today. Just try some of these recipes and you will soon discover why.

MARDI GRAS KING CAKE

Prep Time: 2½ Hours
Yields: 10 Servings

Comment:

The King cake is the traditional dessert of the Carnival season and was originally served on the Feast of the Epiphany. To make the dessert fun and unique, a bean was pressed into the dough prior to cooking. Whoever got the slice containing the bean had to host a party for all guests in attendance. Today, the bean has been replaced with a plastic baby to signify the New Year.

Ingredients for Dough:

½ ounce instant yeast
1½ cups warm water
½ cup sugar
5 cups flour
½ cup dry milk powder
2 tsps salt
2 eggs, beaten
1 cup melted butter

Antique King cake charms

Method:

In a measuring cup, combine yeast and ½ cup of water. Set aside. In a large mixing bowl, sift together all dry ingredients. Using a dough hook on an electric mixer, blend ingredients 2–3 minutes on low speed. In a separate mixing bowl, combine eggs, ¾ cup butter and remaining water. Slowly pour liquids and blossomed yeast into mixing bowl with flour, gradually increasing speed. Mix 8–10 minutes or until dough separates from bowl. An additional ½ cup of flour may be sprinkled into bowl if dough is too wet. Brush a large stainless bowl with melted butter until coated then place dough inside. Brush dough with remaining butter and cover tightly with plastic wrap. Allow dough to proof in a warm place 1 hour or until double in size.

Ingredients for Glaze:

2 pounds powdered sugar
1 pinch salt
1 tbsp almond extract
¾ cup water
3 tbsps cinnamon

Method:

In an electric mixer, combine sugar and salt. Mix on low speed while slowly pouring in almond extract and water. Add cinnamon and continue to blend until glaze is smooth. Set aside.

Ingredients for Assembly:

¼ cup melted butter
½ cup sugar
1 tbsp cinnamon
egg wash (½ cup milk, 2 eggs beaten)
purple, green and gold sugars

Method:

Preheat oven to 350°F. After dough has proofed, roll out onto a well-floured surface into an 18" x 12" rectangle. In a small bowl, combine sugar and cinnamon. Brush top of dough with melted butter, then sprinkle with sugar and cinnamon mixture. Cut cake vertically into 3 even sections. Pinch together end of each strip. Starting from the joined end, form into a basic 3-strand braid. Shape braid into a circle and pinch together to hold form. Brush entire cake with egg wash and proof in a warm place until it doubles in size. Bake 20–25 minutes or until golden brown. Drizzle glaze over entire cake and sprinkle with purple, green and gold sugars. These sugars are available at pastry and cake decorating outlets.

OLD-FASHIONED LEMON POUND CAKE WITH LEMON CURD

Prep Time: 1½ Hours
Yields: 6–8 Servings

Comment:

This simple lemon pound cake is the perfect dessert for any spring menu. It is often served as a special treat on Easter Sunday. The cake is topped with a spoonful of lemon curd and can be garnished with fresh blueberries.

Ingredients for Lemon Curd:

½ cup fresh squeezed lemon juice
½ cup sugar
6 tbsps unsalted butter, cut ½-inch thick
1 tbsp grated lemon zest
3 large eggs, beaten

Method:

In a double boiler over simmering water, combine all ingredients. Cook, whisking frequently, 12–15 minutes or until a custard forms and bubbles appear at surface. Remove from heat and strain through a sieve into a ceramic bowl. Cover with plastic wrap and chill.

Ingredients for Pound Cake:

½ pound unsalted butter, melted
1¼ cups sugar
2 tbsps grated lemon zest
juice of 2 lemons
4 large eggs
1½ tsps pure vanilla extract
1½ cups cake flour
1 tsp baking powder
½ tsp salt

Method:

Preheat oven to 350°F. Grease a 9"x 5" loaf pan with 1 tablespoon of melted butter, then dust with 1 tablespoon of cake flour and tap out excess. In a food processor, combine sugar and lemon zest. Pulse 4–5 times in 1 second intervals. With machine off, add lemon juice, eggs and vanilla. Process approximately 5 seconds. With machine on, add melted butter through feed tube in a steady stream. This should take no more than 20–25 seconds. Do not over mix. Transfer mixture to a large bowl. In a separate bowl, combine flour, baking powder and salt. Sift mixed flour into egg mixture, gently whisking until just combined. Pour batter into loaf pan and bake 15 minutes. Reduce oven temperature to 325°F and bake 45–55 minutes or until deep golden brown. Rotate pan halfway through baking time. Cake is done when a toothpick inserted in center of cake comes out clean. Remove cake from oven and cool 10 minutes.

Ingredients for Glaze:

½ cup sugar
¼ cup lemon juice

Method:

In a saucepan, bring sugar and lemon juice to a low simmer, whisking until dissolved. Turn cake onto a wire rack. Using a toothpick, poke 15–20 holes in top of cake then brush with lemon glaze. Slice cake and serve with a generous tablespoon of lemon curd and fresh blueberries. Any remaining cake may be wrapped tightly in plastic wrap and stored at room temperature for up to 5 days.

GÂTEAU DE FIGUE (FIG CAKE)

Prep Time: 3 Hours
Yields: 8–10 Servings

Comment:

In the summer months, figs are plentiful in South Louisiana. Many households gather and preserve this fruit for later use. Fig preserves are used as a breakfast topping or even as an ingredient in desserts such as this cake.

Ingredients:

1 cup fig preserves
¾ cup butter
1¼ cup sugar
3 eggs
2½ cups flour
1 tsp baking powder
1 tsp baking soda
1 tsp nutmeg
1 tsp cinnamon
1 tsp ginger
1 cup buttermilk
1 tsp pure vanilla extract
1 cup chopped pecans

Method:

Preheat oven to 350°F. Grease and flour a Bundt pan and set aside. In a large mixing bowl, cream butter and sugar. Add eggs, 1 at a time, blending after each addition. In a separate bowl, combine flour, baking powder, baking soda and spices. A little at a time, add dry ingredients to sugar mixture, alternating with buttermilk. Stir constantly to mix all ingredients into batter. Fold in preserves, vanilla and pecans. Stir well then pour into greased pan. Bake 1 hour or until cake tester comes out clean. Let cool and remove from pan. Serve with ice cream or a dollop of whipped cream.

RED VELVET CAKE

Prep Time: 1 Hour
Yields: 10 Servings

Comment:

Although the exact origin of red velvet cake is unknown, there is a legend that the recipe was unknowingly bought by a woman from the Waldorf Astoria Hotel in New York City. Whatever its beginnings, this cake has become a favorite throughout the country and is especially loved by Southerners.

Ingredients for Cake:

½ cup shortening
1½ cups sugar
2 eggs
2 cups flour
1 tbsp cocoa
½ tsp salt
1 cup buttermilk
2 ounces red food coloring
1 tsp baking soda
1 tbsp vinegar

Method:

Preheat oven to 350°F. In a large mixing bowl, blend shortening and sugar with an electric mixer until smooth and creamy. Whisk in eggs and beat until fluffy. Sift together flour, cocoa and salt, then add to mixture. Fold in buttermilk, food coloring, baking soda and vinegar. Mix well then pour batter into 2 (9-inch) or 3 (8-inch) pans. Bake 30–35 minutes.

Ingredients for Icing:

1 cup milk
¼ cup flour
1 cup sugar
2 sticks butter
1 tsp pure vanilla extract

Method:

In a large saucepan, heat milk, flour and sugar over low heat until pudding consistency is achieved. Set aside. When cooled, add butter and vanilla and beat until fluffy. Spread icing evenly over 1 layer of cake and place another layer on top. Coat second layer thoroughly and repeat with third layer. Cover entire cake with icing.

OLD-TIME COCONUT CAKE

Prep Time: 1 Hour
Yields: 8 Servings

Comment:

In early Louisiana, coconut was a novelty used mostly in dessert making. Prior to World War II, most wedding cakes in Cajun Country were made with coconut. Today, many South Louisiana families have their own unique recipe for this cake.

Ingredients for Cake:

1 cup butter	1 tsp salt
2 cups sugar	1⅓ cups milk
3 cups cake flour, sifted	2 tsps pure vanilla extract
4 tsps baking powder	6 egg whites, beaten

Method:

Preheat oven to 350°F. Butter and flour 3 (9-inch) cake pans and set aside. In a large mixing bowl, cream butter and sugar. In a separate bowl, combine flour, baking powder and salt. Slowly add to butter mixture, blending thoroughly. Should mixture become too stiff, add a little milk. Add remaining milk and vanilla then fold in egg whites. Blend batter thoroughly and distribute evenly among 3 pans. Bake 35 minutes or until a toothpick inserted in center of cake comes out clean. Remove from oven and cool.

Ingredients for Filling:

1 (3½-ounce) can coconut	1 cup milk
2 cups sugar	½ stick butter
2 tbsps flour	

Method:

In a large saucepan, combine coconut, sugar and flour. Blend well. Slowly stir in milk then add butter. Bring to a low boil and cook 10–15 minutes, stirring occasionally until filling thickens. Remove and set aside to cool.

Ingredients for Icing:

1½ cups sugar	1 tbsp corn syrup
3 egg whites	1 tbsp pure vanilla extract
5 tbsps water	¼ tsp cream of tartar

Method:

In a double boiler, combine all ingredients and blend well. Cook 7 minutes, whisking constantly until mixture is smooth and creamy. Remove and set aside. When cakes are cool, remove from pans and spread coconut filling between layers. Cover top and sides of cake with icing. If desired, garnish with fresh coconut.

MOIST AND YUMMY YAM CAKE

Prep Time: 1 Hour
Yields: 8–10 Servings

Comment:

Everybody loves a super-moist layer cake. This recipe makes the world's best yam layer cake, and it is a perfect batter for muffins or bread. If desired, add raisins or fruit for an interesting twist.

Ingredients:

1½ cups Bruce's® mashed yams
1½ cups vegetable oil
3 cups sugar
4 eggs
2 cups flour
3 tsps baking powder
3 tsps baking soda
1 tsp salt
2 tsps cinnamon
1 cup chopped pecans
2 tbsps pure vanilla extract
1 (20-ounce) can crushed pineapple
2½ tbsps cornstarch
8 ounces cream cheese
½ stick butter
1 pound powdered sugar

Method:

Preheat oven to 350°F. Oil and flour 3 (9-inch) cake pans. Set aside. In a large mixing bowl, cream oil and 2 cups sugar until well blended. Add eggs, 1 at a time, whisking after each addition. In a separate bowl, combine flour, baking powder, baking soda, salt and cinnamon. Slowly add dry mixture to eggs, blending well. Fold in yams, pecans and 1 tablespoon vanilla. Once blended, pour batter evenly into cake pans. Bake 40 minutes or until toothpick inserted in center comes out clean. While cake is baking, make filling by combining pineapple, cornstarch and 1 cup sugar. Bring to a low boil over medium-high heat, stirring constantly for 5 minutes. Once mixture thickens, remove from heat and let cool. In a separate bowl, combine cream cheese, butter, powdered sugar and 1 tablespoon vanilla. Blend on low speed until icing is fluffy and smooth then set aside. When cakes are done, remove from oven, cool then remove from pans. Spread pineapple filling between layers. Coat with cream cheese icing and serve.

GERMAN CHOCOLATE CAKE

Prep Time: 1 Hour
Yields: 6–8 Servings

Comment:

Although German Chocolate Cake became a much sought after recipe after a Dallas newspaper printed it in 1957, the chocolate that made it so desirable, Baker's German's Sweet Chocolate, was developed in 1952. The sweet chocolate baking bar, close in character to milk chocolate, was developed for Baker's Chocolate Co. by Sam German. However, in most recipes the apostrophe and the "s" have been dropped, fueling the assumption that it's German. The Germans of Louisiana however were extremely fond of chocolate desserts, many bringing their love of the ingredient from Bavaria, Switzerland and Austria.

Ingredients for Cake:

2 cups sugar
1 cup shortening
4 egg yolks
½ cup water
4 ounces German sweet chocolate
2½ cups flour
1 tsp baking soda
1¼ cups buttermilk
1 tbsp pure vanilla extract
pinch of salt
4 egg whites, beaten to peaks

Method:

Preheat oven to 350°F. In a large mixing bowl, cream sugar and shortening until fluffy. Add egg yolks, 1 at a time, blending well after each addition. Bring water to a low boil then add chocolate and stir until melted. Blend chocolate into sugar/shortening mixture. Stir in flour, soda and buttermilk then add vanilla and salt. Fold in stiffly beaten egg whites and blend well. Pour into 3 greased (9-inch) cake pans and bake 30–45 minutes or until done. Allow pans to cool completely before removing cakes.

Ingredients for Icing:

1½ cups sugar
1½ cups evaporated milk
¾ cup butter
4 egg yolks, beaten
2 cups coconut flakes
1 cup chopped pecans
2 tsps pure vanilla extract

Method:

Over a double boiler, combine sugar, milk, butter and egg yolks. Using a whisk, stir while cooking over low heat until thick. Remove from heat then add coconut, pecans and vanilla. Remove cooled cakes from baking pans. Spread icing between layers then stack and ice cake with remaining mixture.

BOUCHE NOIRE

Prep Time: 1½ Hours
Yields: 8–10 Servings

Comment:

This recipe is only for the chocolate addicts! The name, meaning "black mouth," comes from the effect of eating a cake made with 12 ounces of chocolate. Undecorated layer cakes such as this were often served in early Creole homes with a topping of fresh fruit and unsweetened whipped cream.

Ingredients:

12 ounces bittersweet chocolate
1½ cups sugar
½ cup bourbon
1 cup butter chips, softened
6 eggs (at room temperature)
1½ tbsps flour
2 cups sliced Louisiana strawberries (optional)
1 cup unsweetened whipped cream (optional)
julienned mint leaves for garnish

Method:

Preheat oven to 375°F. Butter a 9-inch springform pan, then place a buttered parchment sheet in bottom of pan. Cover outside of springform pan with foil to keep water from entering while cooking. Place cake pan into a large roasting pan with 1-inch sides. Set aside. Chop chocolate into ¼-inch pieces and place in a large stainless steel mixing bowl. In a saucepan, bring 1 inch of water to a simmer. Place bowl of chocolate on top of saucepan and stir occasionally as chocolate melts. In a separate saucepan, combine 1 cup sugar and bourbon. Bring mixture to a low boil, stirring occasionally. When sugar is fully dissolved, pour hot mixture over chocolate and stir until completely melted. Remove bowl from saucepan and place on a flat surface. Add butter, a few chips at a time, allowing them to melt completely before adding more. In a separate stainless steel mixing bowl, whisk eggs, flour and remaining sugar on high speed 5 minutes or until thick and pale yellow. Using a rubber spatula, fold egg mixture into melted chocolate and blend. Pour batter into springform pan and smooth top with spatula. Fill roasting pan with hot tap water until it reaches halfway up side of springform pan. Bake cake 1 hour. Top of cake should have a thin dried crust when cooked. Remove cake from oven and allow to cool 1 hour at room temperature. Cover pan with plastic wrap and refrigerate at least 4 hours. When ready to serve, carefully remove sides of springform pan. Place a cake plate or cardboard cake circle on top of cake and invert to remove bottom of pan and parchment paper. This cake is extremely rich and truffle-like. Cut portions into 1½-inch slices and top with fresh strawberries and unsweetened whipped cream. Garnish with julienned mint leaves.

PUMPKIN STREUSEL COFFEECAKE

Prep Time: 2 Hours
Yields: 16 Servings

Comment:

This cake is perfect with coffee on a crisp fall morning or as an afternoon snack with hot cider.

Ingredients for Streusel:

½ cup brown sugar
1 tsp cinnamon
½ cup chopped pecans
¼ tsp allspice
2 tsps butter

Method:

In a small mixing bowl, combine all ingredients. Blend with a fork until crumbly. Set aside.

Ingredients for Cake:

3 cups flour
2 tsps baking soda
1 tbsp cinnamon
1 tsp salt
1 cup butter, softened
2 cups sugar
4 eggs
1 cup canned pumpkin
1 cup sour cream
2 tsps pure vanilla extract

Method:

Preheat oven to 350°F. Grease and flour a 12-cup Bundt pan. In a medium mixing bowl, combine flour, baking soda, cinnamon and salt. In a large bowl, using an electric hand mixer, cream butter and sugar. Add eggs and blend well. Stir in pumpkin, sour cream and vanilla. Gradually add flour mixture, blending on low speed. Spread half of batter in pan. Evenly sprinkle in prepared streusel then top with remaining batter. Bake 55–60 minutes or until toothpick inserted in cake comes out clean. Cool in pan on wire rack for 30 minutes. Invert on wire rack, and remove pan to allow cake to cool completely. Sprinkle with powdered sugar.

CARROT CAKE

Prep Time: 1 Hour
Yields: 8 Servings

Comment:

Carrots are a very versatile vegetable. They are cooked in many different ways, served as vegetable side dishes or entrees. Carrots are also used in desserts because of their high sugar content. Carrot cake is especially popular in the springtime when carrots are plentiful. This is a super-moist version of the traditional Easter recipe.

Ingredients for Cake:

3 cups grated carrots
2 cups sugar
1½ cups vegetable oil
4 eggs
2 cups flour
3 tsps baking powder
3 tsps baking soda
1 tsp salt
2 tsps cinnamon
1 tbsp pure vanilla extract
1 cup chopped pecans

Method:

Preheat oven to 350°F. Grease and flour 4 (9-inch) cake pans. Set aside. In a large mixing bowl, cream sugar and oil until well blended. Add eggs, 1 at a time, whisking after each addition. In a separate bowl, combine flour, baking powder, baking soda, salt and cinnamon. Add dry ingredients to eggs, a little at a time, blending well. Fold in carrots, vanilla and pecans. Once blended, pour batter evenly into pans. Bake 30–40 minutes or until cake tester comes out clean. Remove and let cool.

Ingredients for Filling:

1 (20-ounce) can crushed pineapple
1 cup sugar
2½ tbsps cornstarch

Method:

In a medium saucepot, combine pineapple, sugar and cornstarch. Bring to a low boil over medium-high heat, stirring constantly 5 minutes or until thickened. Remove from heat and allow to cool. Remove cakes from baking pans and spread pineapple filling between layers.

Ingredients for Icing:

3½ cups powdered sugar
8 ounces cream cheese
½ cup butter, softened
1¼ tsps pure vanilla extract

Method:

In a medium bowl, combine all ingredients and beat until smooth. Cover cake with cream cheese icing and serve.

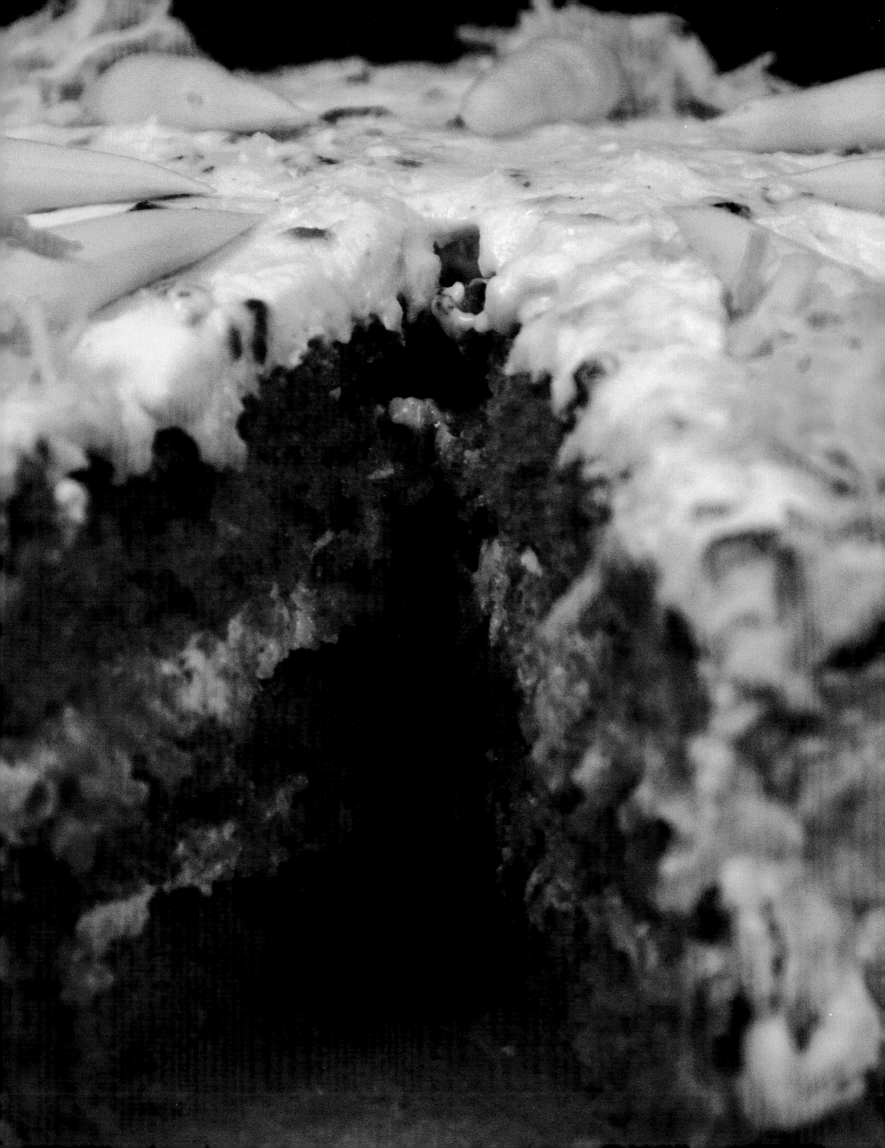

SICILIAN CANNOLI CAKE

Prep Time: 7 Hours
Yields: 8–10 Servings

Comment:

When I first tasted this Cannoli cake at an Italian wedding in Louisiana, little did I know I would later experience it in the place of its origin, Palermo, Sicily. I learned, when eating at Ristorante Cutino in Palermo, that Cassata Alla Siciliana is considered the national cake of Sicily.

Ingredients for Cake:

¼ cup milk	1 cup flour
3 tbsps butter	1 tsp baking powder
8 eggs	½ tsp salt
2 cups plus 2 tbsps sugar	1 tbsp pure vanilla extract

Method:

Preheat oven to 350°F. In a small saucepan, heat milk and butter. When hot, set aside. Using an electric mixer fitted with a wire whisk, combine eggs and sugar. Whisk on medium-high speed 8–10 minutes or until pale yellow and tripled in volume. While mixer is running, slowly add heated milk. In a large mixing bowl, sift flour, baking powder and salt. Sprinkle flour mixture into eggs and continue to whisk to remove lumps. Add vanilla. Spray a large cookie sheet with cooking spray or line with parchment paper. Sprinkle 1 tablespoon of sugar over surface. Pour cake batter into pan and bake 25 minutes or until cake springs back when touched. Cool 5 minutes. Use a long, thin knife to loosen edges of cake then flip it onto a wire rack or flat work surface.

Ingredients for Filling:

2½ cups whole milk Ricotta cheese	¼ cup chopped candied orange peel
1 cup powdered sugar	¼ cup chopped candied green and red cherries
1 tbsp pure vanilla extract	
3 tbsps rum	¼ cup chopped pistachios
¼ heavy cream, whipped stiff	¼ cup Grand Marnier
¼ cup chopped candied lemon peel	1½ cups sweetened whipped cream

Method:

In a mixing bowl, combine Ricotta, powdered sugar, vanilla and rum. Using wooden spoon, cream ingredients until smooth and well blended. Fold in cream and all but 1 tablespoon each candied fruit and pistachios. Set aside. Divide sheet cake into 4 equal pieces and trim each to snugly fit into a 10-inch loaf pan. Brush top of each piece with an equal amount of Grand Marnier. Line bottom of loaf pan with parchment paper, place 1 piece of cake in bottom of pan and spread with ⅓ of cheese and fruit filling. Continue layering cake and filling, ending with cake. Cover with plastic wrap and refrigerate 3 hours. Remove cake from refrigerator and turn onto a wire rack with a sheet pan underneath. Ice top and sides of cake with sweetened whipped cream and return to refrigerator at least 1 hour.

Ingredients for Icing:

3 cups chopped semisweet chocolate
½ cup prepared coffee, cold
½ pound cold butter, cubed

Method:

While cake is chilling, melt chocolate and coffee in a heavy-bottomed saucepan over medium-high heat, whisking constantly. Remove from heat and whisk in butter until well blended. Cool mixture until it is almost thick enough to spread, but still able to be poured. Carefully pour chocolate icing over entire cake. Return to refrigerator and chill 2 hours, until icing is set. Remove cake from refrigerator. Use a long, thin spatula to carefully lift it off of rack and onto a serving platter. Sprinkle top of cake with remaining fruit and nuts. Slice and serve. NOTE: White chocolate may be used for icing. If you prefer this method, almond extract should be used in place of vanilla, Frangelico liqueur in place of the Grand Marnier and almonds in place of pistachios.

RUSSIAN APRICOT SPONGE CAKE

Prep Time: 24 Hours
Yields: 8–10 Servings

Comment:

This is a traditional Russian dessert known as Biskvitnyi Abrikosovyi Tort. Filled with apricot jam and iced with a rich lemon butter cream, this cake is a wonderful teatime treat or afternoon snack. It is especially enjoyed in the summer. The chocolate-dipped, rum-soaked apricots make the cake a beautiful piece of edible art.

Ingredients for Syrup:

4 tbsps sugar
6 tbsps water
½ cup rum
¼ tsp rum extract
16 dried apricots

Method:

Bring sugar and water to a rolling boil then reduce to simmer and cover 1½ minutes. Let cool then stir in rum and rum extract. Add dried apricots and allow to soak 24 hours. Drain, reserving syrup, and set apricots to dry on a plate in refrigerator 2 hours or until surface is dry. Turn fruit once or twice during drying process.

Ingredients for Sponge Cake:

7 eggs, separated
1 cup sugar
1 cup flour
1 ounce melted butter

Method:

Place egg yolks in 1 mixing bowl and egg whites in another. Add half of sugar to each bowl. Beat both until peaked. When stiff, fold whites into yolk mixture. Gradually add flour, mixing with a wooden spoon or spatula. Mix in butter. Pour mixture into a 10-inch greased cake pan. Bake 20 minutes or until spongy and golden. Remove from oven and allow to cool completely. Once cooled, slice cake in half horizontally into 2 even layers. Set aside.

Ingredients for Lemon Butter Cream:

3½ cups sugar
1 cup water
12 egg yolks
2 pounds unsalted butter, softened
3–5 tbsps lemon juice

Method:

In a medium saucepan, bring sugar and water to a boil until temperature reaches 240°F. Beat egg yolks with an electric mixer until light and fluffy. With mixer at half speed, carefully pour hot sugar into yolks. Whisk until mixture is cool. Add softened butter in small batches, blending well after each addition. When butter is mixed, add lemon juice to taste.

Ingredients for Assembly:

2 ounces unsweetened chocolate
¾ cup jarred apricot jam
24 toasted whole almonds

Method:

Melt chocolate according to manufacturer's directions. Dip end of each soaked apricot into chocolate. Let fruit cool on edge of plate until chocolate hardens. Place 1 layer of sponge cake on cake stand or serving platter. Brush layer with an ample serving of rum syrup. Spread apricot jam evenly over layer. Brush second layer with rum syrup then position it evenly on top of first layer. Whisk prepared lemon butter cream gently to ensure that it is soft and fluffy. Reserve about ½ cup of cream for decoration. Using a spatula, ice top and sides of cake evenly with remaining butter cream. Place reserved cream into a pastry bag fitted with a ¼-inch star tip. Pipe a border around top and bottom of cake. Arrange chocolate-dipped apricots evenly around top of cake. Add toasted almonds in a decorative pattern around bottom edge. Refrigerate cake 1½ hours or until butter cream hardens. It will keep in refrigerator for up to 24 hours, but it tastes best fresh.

TARTE Á LA BOUIE

Prep Time: 1 Hour
Yields: 8 Servings

Comment:
Because eggs and milk were so plentiful in Bayou Country, custard-based desserts were quite common. Tarte á la Bouie is one of the oldest desserts from this area.

Ingredients for Custard:
2 cups milk
1 cup half-and-half cream
1 egg
½ cup sugar

4 tbsps cornstarch
1 tbsp pure vanilla extract
½ cup butter

Method:
Preheat oven to 350°F. In a heavy-bottomed stainless steel pot, combine milk and cream. Scald mixture over low heat, approximately 200°F, until skin forms on surface but milk does not boil. In a large mixing bowl, combine egg, sugar and cornstarch. Whisk gently until dissolved. Add approximately 1 cup hot milk to egg mixture while beating constantly to temper eggs. Pour egg mixture into remaining milk, whisking constantly, until thickened to texture of a very heavy cream. Blend in vanilla and butter. Cook until thick custard is achieved. Remove from heat and cool thoroughly before pouring into uncooked pie crust.

Ingredients for Crust:
2 eggs
1 cup sugar
¼ pound butter

1 tsp pure vanilla extract
2½ tsps baking powder
2 cups flour

Method:
In a food processor fitted with a metal blade, combine eggs, sugar, butter and vanilla. Blend 1–2 minutes. Add baking powder and flour. Blend until flour is absorbed and a dough ball forms. Remove dough and refrigerate 1 hour. Roll dough into a large circle, approximately ⅛-inch thick then place in pie pan. Allow excess dough to hang off sides of pan. Pour cooled custard into pie shell and fold pie dough over to center of pie in an uneven fashion. Do not seal crust on top. Allow filling to show in center. Bake 30–45 minutes or until crust is golden brown.

PURPLE PLUM TORTE

Prep Time: 1½ Hours
Yields: 1 (9-inch) Torte

Comment:
Gaston and Olga Hirsch arrived in the United States shortly after World War II. They settled in Donaldsonville, La., 45 miles west of New Orleans. The Hirsch's were both trained in the restaurant and hotel business. Gaston's family owned "La Marne," a grand hotel in Saverne, France, and Olga's family owned "La Forestiere," a family restaurant in the town of Veymerange, Lorraine. Her specialties were pâtés, terrines and Tortes.

Ingredients for Crust:

1⅓ cups flour
¼ pound chipped cold butter
1 tbsp sugar
¼ cup ice water

Method:

In a food processor equipped with a metal blade, combine flour, butter and sugar. Pulse 1 minute or until mixture reaches texture of coarse meal. Slowly pour in water until dough forms into a ball. Remove and place on a floured surface. Roll dough into a circle approximately ⅛-inch thick. Firmly press into a 9-inch pie or torte pan and set aside.

Ingredients for Filling:

12 ripe purple plums
2 tbsps sugar
¼ cup heavy whipping cream
2 eggs
½ cup sugar

¼ cup pure vanilla extract
pinch of cinnamon
pinch of nutmeg
¼ cup powdered sugar

Method:

Preheat oven to 375°F. Using a sharp paring knife, cut plums into ¼-inch slices and discard seeds. Arrange slices neatly around dough until all have been used. Place pie on bottom oven rack and bake approximately 20 minutes to render juices from fruit. While pie is baking, combine cream, eggs, sugar, vanilla, cinnamon and nutmeg in a mixing bowl. Whisk until well blended. When pie crust is done, remove from oven and pour cream mixture evenly over baked plums. Return to oven and cook 20 minutes or until custard is set. Remove from oven and dust generously with powdered sugar. This Torte may also be made with red or green apples.

TURTLE CHEESECAKE DES AMIS

Prep Time: 2 Hours
Yields: 6–8 Servings

Comment:

In this cheesecake, the "turtle" mixture of pecan and caramel is not only used as a topping for the cake, but also is baked between the crust and filling. Almonds or walnuts can be substituted, but Louisianians prefer pecans.

Ingredients:

15 Oreo® cookies
6 tbsps melted butter
1 (14-ounce) bag caramel candy
1 (5-ounce) can evaporated milk
2 cups chopped pecans
1½ pounds cream cheese, softened
½ cup sour cream
4 large eggs
½ cup sugar
2 tbsps pure vanilla extract
½ cup semisweet chocolate chips

Method:

Preheat oven to 350°F. Spray a 9-inch springform pan with cooking spray and set aside. In a food processor, chop cookies to fine crumbs then toss with melted butter. Using your fingertips, press cookie crumbs evenly into pan to form crust then set aside. In a ceramic bowl, combine caramel and evaporated milk. Place mixture in microwave and cook on high at 2-minute intervals, stirring until smooth and creamy. Remove and allow caramel topping to cool 10 minutes or until slightly thickened. Pour half of caramel mixture over cookie crust and garnish with half of chopped pecans. In a large mixing bowl, blend cream cheese and sour cream with an electric mixer. Add eggs and sugar, continuing to blend until smooth. Stir in vanilla then pour batter into pan. Bake cake 45–60 minutes or until toothpick inserted into center comes out clean. Remove and allow cake to cool 30 minutes. Top cake with chocolate chips, remaining caramel and pecans. Let cake set in refrigerator overnight.

MANDARIN ORANGE CHEESECAKE

Prep Time: 1½ Hours
Yields: 8–10 Servings

Comment:

If you are old enough to have experienced the dreamsicle or young enough to have enjoyed an orange push-up, you will love the flavor of this cheesecake. The vivid orange color of the cake makes for an exciting presentation.

Ingredients for Crust:

1½ cups graham cracker crumbs
4 tbsps melted butter
¼ cup sugar

Method:

Combine graham cracker crumbs and sugar. Drizzle melted butter into mixture and blend well. Using your fingertips, press graham cracker mixture into a 10-inch round springform pan. Refrigerate 15 minutes or until crust is firm.

Ingredients for Cheesecake:

1 cup chopped mandarins with juice
1½ pounds cream cheese, softened
¼ cup heavy whipping cream
4 medium eggs
1 cup sugar
¼ tsp orange "hard-candy" flavoring OR orange or mandarin flavoring
¼ tsp orange No. 6 food coloring
1 tsp pure vanilla extract
½ cup chopped pecans

Method:

Preheat oven to 300°F. In a large mixing bowl, blend cream cheese and heavy whipping cream with a hand mixer until smooth. Add eggs, 1 at a time, whisking completely between each addition. Slowly whisk in sugar. Fold in mandarins and juice, orange flavoring, vanilla and food coloring, blending well after each addition. Stir in chopped pecans. Pour batter into refrigerated crust. Rotate pan until mixture flattens. Bake 1 hour or until firm to touch. NOTE: Cake may be topped with a sour cream icing made by combining 1 pound sour cream, 4 tablespoons sugar and ½ teaspoon vanilla. Blend together until creamy. Add to top of slightly-cooled cheesecake and place in a 400°F oven for 5 minutes.

SKILLET PEACH COBBLER WITH BLUEBERRIES

Prep Time: 1 Hour
Yields: 8 Servings

Comment:
In the mid-1800s, many visitors wrote about their experiences at the plantation homes of Louisiana. One such visitor commented on the wonderful Mint Juleps served before breakfast and the fabulous peach cobbler that ended every meal.

Ingredients:
1 (29-ounce) can sliced peaches, reserve syrup
½ cup fresh blueberries
1 tsp cornstarch
¼ pound butter
1 cup self-rising flour
½ cup sugar
1 cup milk
1 tsp baking powder
¼ tsp nutmeg

Method:
Preheat oven to 350°F. In a mixing bowl, whisk approximately ¼ cup peach syrup with cornstarch until well blended. Set aside. In a 10-inch cast iron skillet, melt butter over medium heat. When melted, remove from heat and allow to cool slightly. In a large mixing bowl, combine flour and sugar. Slowly pour in milk, whisking constantly. Add baking powder and continue to whisk until well blended. Batter will appear slightly lumpy. Pour batter into skillet over melted butter. Sprinkle blueberries over batter. In a mixing bowl, combine dissolved cornstarch, remaining peach syrup, peaches and nutmeg. Pour peach mixture over batter and blueberries. Bake in skillet on bottom rack of oven 50–60 minutes or until golden brown. Allow to cool slightly before serving.

PRALINE AU BENNE

Prep Time: 1 Hour
Yields: 12–15 Pieces

Comment:
Benne, or sesame seeds, can be purchased in either black or white. Although this recipe uses white seeds, feel free to sprinkle in a tablespoon of black for effect. Often when pecans were not available or were out of season, sesame seeds were substituted during praline making.

Ingredients:
4 cups sesame seeds
¾ stick butter or margarine
pinch of salt
4 cups sugar
1 cup milk
1 tbsp light corn syrup

Method:
In a heavy-bottomed skillet, roast sesame seeds over medium-high heat, stirring constantly until light brown. Pour onto a cookie sheet to cool. In a heavy-bottomed stainless steel pot, cook butter, salt, sugar, milk and syrup to soft-ball stage (234–240°F). Test by dropping ¼ teaspoon of syrup into cold water and quickly rolling it between your thumb and forefinger. Soft-ball stage is reached if mixture is soft, pliable and holds shape. Quickly stir in seeds. Remove from heat and continue to stir vigorously with a wooden spoon until candy holds its shape. Do not allow to cool. Pour mixture into a well-greased cake pan and allow to cool at room temperature. Once cooled, break into pieces.

CAJUN PRALINES

Prep Time: 30 Minutes
Yields: 50 Pralines

Comment:
The Ursuline nuns brought knowledge of great pastry making to Louisiana when they arrived in the 1700s. Their most important contribution was the gift of praline candy to the city of New Orleans. Although this sugar candy was originally made with hazelnuts, Bayou Country recipes used pecans because of regional abundance. If desired, pecans may be roasted before being added to the pralines. To roast, bake pecans on a sheet pan at 275°F for 20–25 minutes or until slightly browned.

Ingredients:
1½ cups sugar
¾ cup light brown sugar, packed
½ cup milk
1 tsp pure vanilla extract
¾ stick butter
1½ cups pecans

Method:
Combine all ingredients and stir constantly until mixture reaches soft-ball stage (234–240°F). Remove from heat and stir until thickened. Praline mixture should become creamy and cloudy, and pecans should stay in suspension. Drop spoonfuls onto buttered wax paper, foil or parchment paper. NOTE: When using wax paper, be sure to buffer with newspaper underneath as hot wax will transfer to whatever is beneath.

Mountain of brown sugar, CoraTexas, White Castle, La.

PRALINE PECAN FUDGE

Prep Time: 30 Minutes
Yields: 20 Pieces

Comment:

Chocolate, peanut butter and divinity are typical flavors of fudge created in homes of Bayou Country. The addition of roasted pecans and praline liqueur adds an interesting twist.

Ingredients:

½ ounce praline liqueur
1 cup chopped pecans
¼ pound butter
1½ cups sugar
5 ounces evaporated milk
1 (12-ounce) package semisweet chocolate morsels
1 tbsp pure vanilla extract
1 (7-ounce) jar marshmallow cream

CHALMETTE SUGAR COOKIES

Prep Time: 1 Hour
Yields: 12–14 Cookies

Comment:
Chalmette Plantation was the actual site of the famed Battle of New Orleans during the War of 1812. The battle was a victory for America. Unfortunately, at the time the battle was fought, the Treaty of Ghent had already been signed, meaning the war was over.

Ingredients:
1 cup butter, softened
1½ cups powdered sugar
1 egg
1 tsp pure vanilla extract
½ tsp almond extract
2½ cups flour
1 tsp baking soda
1 tsp cream of tartar
½ cup brown sugar

Method:
In a large mixing bowl, whisk together butter and powdered sugar until well blended. Stir in egg, vanilla and almond. In a separate bowl, combine flour, soda and tartar. Blend flour into butter mixture. Form dough into a ball, cover and chill a minimum of 2 hours. Preheat oven to 375°F. Place dough on a floured surface and roll ¼-inch thick. Cut into desired shapes and sizes then sprinkle with brown sugar. Place on a lightly-greased cookie sheet, and bake 7–8 minutes or until edges of cookies are light brown. If desired, top cookies with colored icing.

Method:
Line a 9-inch glass baking dish with foil then set aside. In a 2-quart heavy-bottomed pot, melt butter over medium-high heat. Blend in sugar and milk. Bring to a rolling boil then reduce heat to simmer and cook approximately 5 minutes, stirring constantly. Be careful not to scorch butter, as mixture will caramelize. Remove from heat. Stirring constantly with a large cooking spoon, add chocolate, vanilla, marshmallow cream, praline liqueur and pecans. Mixture should be creamy and slightly thickened. Pour into foil-lined baking dish and allow to cool. Cut fudge into 1-inch squares and serve.

Icing German Christmas Cookies

PLATZCHENS (GERMAN SUGAR COOKIES)

Prep Time: 1 Hour
Yields: 40 Cookies

Comment:
Platzchens were a mainstay in German homes of Louisiana and were often served to visiting family and friends. These tender and crisp cookies make a great snack with coffee or milk.

Ingredients:

1 cup butter	4 cups flour
2¼ cups sugar	3 tsps baking powder
2 tbsps heavy whipping cream	½ tsp salt
2 eggs	½ cup flour
1 tbsp pure vanilla extract	¾ cup sugar

Method:
Preheat oven to 350°F. In a large mixing bowl, cream butter and 2¼ cups of sugar with an electric mixer. Add cream and eggs, one at a time, blending well after each addition. Blend in vanilla. Sift 4 cups of flour, baking powder and salt into mixture. Mix until dough is well blended. Remove dough ball, knead once or twice then divide into 4 equal portions. On a flat working surface, sprinkle ½ cup flour and ½ cup sugar. Separately roll each section of dough very thin, about ¼-inch thick. (Thinner is better for a crispier cookie). Sprinkle top of rolled pastry with remaining sugar. Cut cookies with a cookie cutter. Use a spatula to place each cookie on a lightly-greased cookie sheet. Bake 10 minutes. Remove and let cool on pan. Store in an air-tight container.

GERMAN CHRISTMAS COOKIES

Prep Time: 30 Minutes
Yields: 12–14 Cookies

Comment:
Germans have long been famous for their gingerbreads and spice cakes. These cookies, sometimes called Lebkuchen, are used as a sweet holiday treat and as decorations. German Christmas trees are made special by hanging cookies cut into various holiday shapes between branches.

Ingredients for Cookies:

½ cup honey	½ tsp baking soda
½ cup molasses	1 tsp cinnamon
¾ cup brown sugar	1 tsp cloves
1 egg	1 tsp allspice
1 tbsp lemon juice	1 tsp nutmeg
1 tsp grated lemon zest	½ cup citron
2¾ cup flour	¾ cup chopped nuts

Method:
In a small heavy-bottomed saucepot, bring honey and molasses to a low boil over medium-high heat while whisking constantly. Remove from heat and allow to cool slightly. Pour into an electric mixer. Blend in sugar, lemon juice and zest on medium speed until sugar dissolves. Blend in egg. In a mixing bowl, sift together flour, baking soda and spices. Add flour to running mixer then stir in citron and nuts. Once well mixed, place dough in refrigerator overnight. Preheat oven to 400°F. Divide dough into 4 pieces. One piece at a time, remove from refrigerator and roll ¼-inch thick. Cut into rectangles (1½ " x 2½") or cut into shapes using cookie cutters. Place on a greased cookie sheet, 1 inch apart, and bake 10–12 minutes.

Ingredients for Icing:

1 cup sugar	¼ cup powdered sugar
½ cup water	food coloring, optional

Method:
In a small saucepot, bring sugar and water to a boil until it reaches thread stage (230°F). Remove from heat then stir in powdered sugar. Coat top of cookies with hot icing. Return pot to heat and add a little water if mixture becomes too thick. For decorative cookies, add a few drops of food coloring to the hot icing and blend well.

PETIT GÂTEAUX (CHRISTMAS TEA COOKIES)

Prep Time: 1 Hour
Yields: 30 (3-inch) Cookies

Comment:

Florence Gravois, grandmother of 31, would make these cookies every Christmas Eve. Each grandchild was supposed to leave his or her share out with a glass of milk for Santa Claus. The children often ate the cookies long before Santa saw them!

Ingredients:

1½ cups sugar
¼ pound butter
3 eggs

2 tbsps pure vanilla extract
4 cups flour
4 tsps baking powder

Method:

In a large mixing bowl, cream sugar and butter with an electric mixer. Add eggs, 1 at a time, beating well after each addition. Blend in 2 tablespoons vanilla. Gradually beat in flour and baking powder until well blended. Roll dough into a large ball, cover and refrigerate overnight. When ready to bake, preheat oven to 350°F. Flour a large work surface and roll dough ¼-inch thick. Using cookie cutters, cut into decorative shapes and place on an ungreased cookie sheet. Bake 5–10 minutes or until cookies are lightly browned.

Ingredients for Icing:

¼ pound butter
6 ounces powdered sugar
1 tsp pure vanilla extract

¼ cup milk
food coloring (optional)

Method:

Melt butter in a heavy-bottomed saucepan over medium-high heat. Add powdered sugar and vanilla. Remove from heat and pour in milk until consistency is that of soft peanut butter. Blend in your favorite food coloring as desired. Once cookies are cool, spread with icing and allow to dry.

CAJUN GINGER COOKIES

Prep Time: 1 Hour
Yields: 45 Cookies

Comment:
Ginger root grew throughout the swamps of Louisiana and was often used by early cultures to flavor desserts. Although not commonly grown here today, most grocery stores supply fresh ginger root.

Ingredients:

1 tsp ginger	1 egg
10 tbsps margarine	2 cups flour
1 cup sugar	2 tsps baking soda
¼ cup molasses	1 tsp cinnamon

Method:
Preheat oven to 350°F. In a large mixing bowl, cream margarine and ¾ cup sugar. Using a hand mixer, blend at medium speed until light and fluffy. Blend in molasses and egg. In a separate bowl, combine ginger, flour, soda and cinnamon. Add dry ingredients to creamed mixture, stirring constantly until well blended. Due to molasses and sugar, this dough will be extremely sticky. Divide dough into 2 equal portions, cover with plastic wrap and freeze 1 hour. Coat a large cookie sheet with nonstick cooking spray. Tear dough into approximately 45 (1-inch) balls. Sprinkle remaining sugar on a work surface, and roll balls in sugar. Place pieces 2 inches apart on cookie sheet. Bake approximately 15 minutes. Cool on a wire rack.

PERFECT LEMON BARS

Prep Time: 1 Hour
Yields: 24 Bars

Comment:
It is hard to find a really good lemon bar recipe. Some have too much crust and not enough filling, while others lack lemon flavor. This recipe achieves a delicious lemon flavor by using lemon zest and fresh lemon juice.

Ingredients for Crust:
1¾ cup flour
⅔ cup powdered sugar
¼ cup cornstarch
¾ tsp salt
12 tbsps unsalted butter, room temperature

Method:
Preheat oven to 350°F. Lightly grease a 13" x 9" baking dish and line with parchment or wax paper allowing edges to come over sides. In a food processor, combine flour, powdered sugar, cornstarch and salt. Pulse until mixed. Cut butter into 1-inch thick pieces then add to mixture and blend 8–10 seconds. Continue to pulse until mixture resembles coarse meal. Sprinkle crust into lined pan. Press firmly into an even layer along bottom of pan. Crust should slightly go up sides of pan to hold in filling. Refrigerate approximately 30 minutes. Bake 20 minutes or until golden brown. After crust is finished baking, reduce oven temperature to 325°F.

Ingredients for Filling:
4 large eggs, beaten lightly
1⅓ cups sugar
3 tbsps flour
½ cup fresh squeezed lemon juice, strained
2 tsps grated lemon zest
⅓ cup milk
⅛ tsp salt
powdered sugar for garnish

Method:
In a medium mixing bowl, whisk together eggs, sugar and flour. Stir in juice, zest, milk and salt. Blend well. When crust is done, blend filling mixture again. Pour filling into warm crust and bake 20 minutes or until firm to touch. Transfer pan to wire rack. Cool 1 hour or until near room temperature. To cut, lift out of pan using sides of parchment or wax paper. Fold paper off sides of dessert then cut into bars, wiping knife between each cut. Sprinkle bars with powdered sugar to garnish.

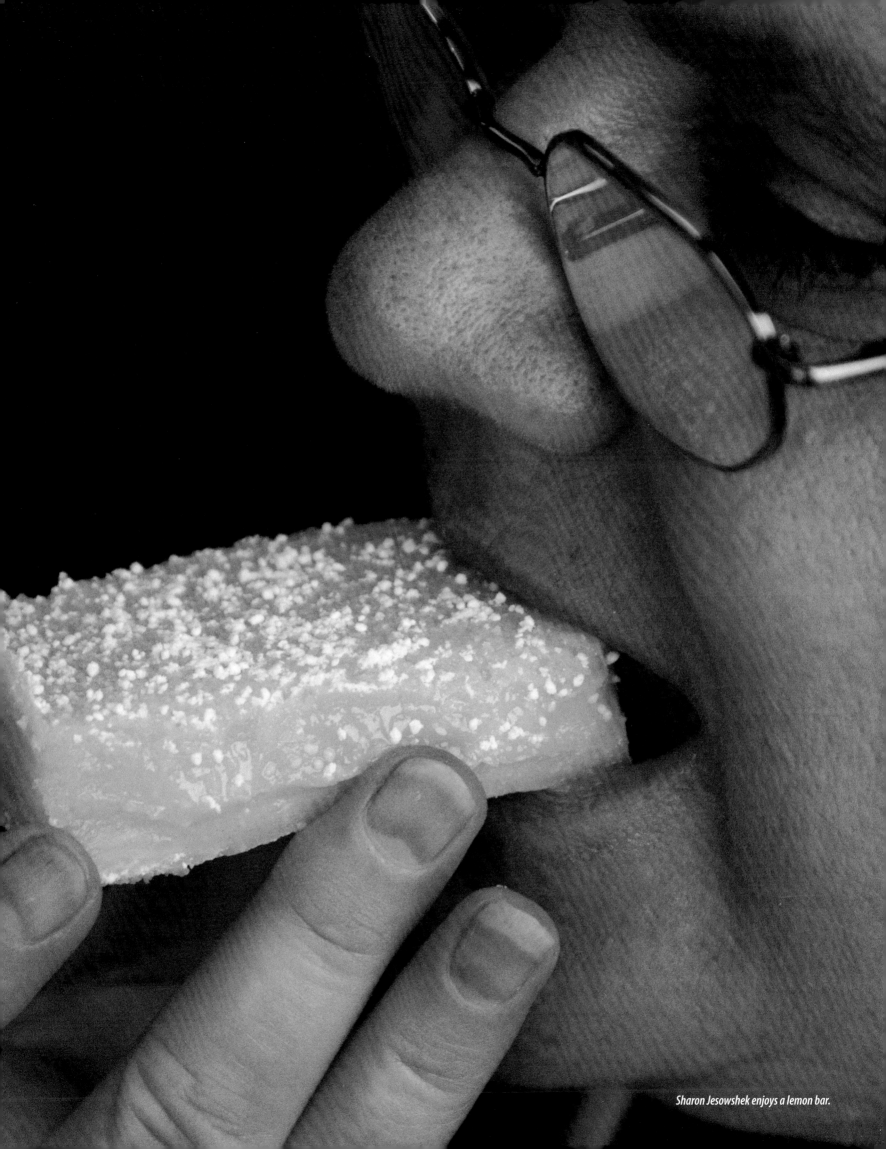

Sharon Jesowshek enjoys a lemon bar.

ANISE COOKIES

Prep Time: 1 Hour
Yields: 42 Cookies

Comment:
These cookies are challenging to make, but they have such a light texture that it is worth trying. The cookies are similar to meringues, but they have the unique essence of freshly crushed anise seeds.

Ingredients:
1 tsp pure anise extract
6 eggs
3 cups sugar
4½ cups flour

Method:
Preheat oven to 350°F. Butter 2 (9" x 13") cookie sheets and set aside. In an electric mixer, combine eggs and sugar. Mix on high speed 30 minutes. This mixing time is essential. Reduce speed to low and add flour, 1 tablespoon at a time, until all is used. Add anise extract and blend 1 minute. Using a rubber spatula, scrape down sides of bowl to ensure that flour is well mixed. Drop cookie batter onto greased pans in teaspoon-sized portions. Bake 15–20 minutes or until cookies are light brown on outer edges and have a cream-colored center. Cookies will become hard if baked too long. Store in an airtight container to retain freshness.

ITALIAN BISCOTTI

Prep Time: 1 Hour
Yields: 60–72 Slices

Comment:
A great Italian chef, Guy DiSalvo, first taught me how to make biscotti. This Italian cookie is most often eaten in Louisiana with a cup of hot cappuccino, espresso or dark roast Community® Coffee.

Ingredients:
6 eggs
1¼ cups sugar
zest of 1 orange
1 tsp pure vanilla extract
1¼ cups vegetable oil
2 cups flour
2 tbsps baking powder
2 pounds toasted pecans

Method:
Preheat oven to 350°F. In a small mixing bowl, combine eggs, sugar, orange zest and vanilla. Using a hand mixer, blend on medium speed 10–12 minutes. Slowly add vegetable oil while continuing to blend. In a separate bowl, combine flour and baking powder. Slowly add flour mixture to egg mixture, a little at a time, blending constantly. Blend on low speed 2 minutes. Do not overmix. Using a wooden spoon, knead mixture until all lumps are removed. Using a rubber spatula, slowly fold in pecans. Coat 6 standard loaf pans with nonstick cooking spray. Divide dough evenly among pans so each has approximately 1 inch of batter. Bake approximately 15 minutes. Remove from oven and let set in pans 5 minutes. Remove from pans and place biscotti on a cooling rack 5 minutes. Slice each loaf into 10–12 (1-inch) slices. Arrange biscotti on a cookie sheet and place in oven 5–6 minutes or until lightly toasted.

SANDRA SCALISE JUNEAU'S CUCCIDATA ITALIAN FIG COOKIES

Prep Time: 2 Hours
Yields: 24 Cookies

Comment:

Each year, Sandra Scalise Juneau prepares well in advance for St. Joseph's Day. Her elaborately designed cuccidata cakes are used to decorate altars in honor of the patron saint of Sicily. This recipe will make about 2 dozen fig cookies. However, by modifying the dough and assembly process, fig cakes can be made instead. Traditionally, 10 pounds of figs or more are prepared at one time, so making cuccidata becomes a community project. Because of the elaborate process of grinding figs and rolling dough, family and friends are often invited to help with the preparation.

Cuccidata cake

Ingredients for Fig Filling:

2 pounds dried Greek figs
1 tbsp cinnamon
4 tbsps honey
2 tbsps orange zest
⅛ tsp black pepper

Method:

Remove stems from figs. Rinse thoroughly in warm water to soften. Drain off any excess water. Season figs with cinnamon, mixing thoroughly. Coat with honey then blend in orange zest and black pepper. Using an electric meat grinder, finely grind fig mixture. Do not use a food processor. Blend ground ingredients well. Divide mixture in half, wrap each section with plastic wrap then seal in plastic zipper bags. This mixture will keep in refrigerator for several weeks, or it may be frozen up to 6 months.

Ingredients for Dough:

5 cups flour
¾ cup white vegetable shortening
¾ cup sugar
1–2 cups warm water

Method:

NOTE: This amount of dough will make cookies or small cakes. For a larger cake, use 1 cup shortening, 1 cup sugar and additional water if necessary. In a food processor, blend flour and shortening to a cornmeal texture. Set aside. Dissolve sugar in warm (tepid, not boiling) water. Slowly add sugar water to flour mixture, blending until dough forms a ball. If dough is too dry, gradually add more water as needed until moist. Cover, set aside and allow dough to rest 10 minutes. Separate dough into workable sized balls (for large cakes, about 6 inches across, for individual cookies, about 3 inches across). Knead each ball into smooth texture and return to bowl. Cover again, then allow dough to rest several minutes.

Ingredients for Assembly:

prepared fig filling
prepared dough balls

Method:

Preheat oven to 250°F. Roll a small piece of dough (2-inch ball) into thickness of pie pastry. Cut into 4" x 12" strips. Shape fig filling into ½-inch wide rolls. Fill center of dough with fig mixture. Fold sides of pastry over figs, overlapping dough slightly. Turn over, seam side down, and pat lightly to flatten. Cut on an angle into 1-inch long bars. Cut slits in sides and on top to allow filling to cook through. Bake 20–30 minutes. Cookies should be slightly browned on bottom only. Allow to cool before icing cookies. NOTE: Large cakes can be made in any desired shape.

Ingredients for Icing:

1 tbsp milk
2 drops almond extract
2 cups powdered sugar
colored nonpareils (sugar sprinkles)

Method:

Combine milk and almond extract then gradually blend in sugar, mixing to a smooth paste. Icing should be texture of heavy cream. Thoroughly cool cookies before icing. Working over a small bowl, spoon icing onto each cookie, allowing excess to drip into bowl. Allow each cookie to dry slightly then sprinkle with nonpareils. Be sure cookies are completely dry before packaging.

SUMMER AFTERNOON BROWNIES

Prep Time: 1 Hour
Yields: 24 Brownies

Comment:
This simple brownie is enhanced with the addition of instant coffee. In South Louisiana, the unofficial state coffee, Community, would be used. This brownie is best served with a scoop of homemade white chocolate or vanilla ice cream.

Ingredients:
12 ounces semisweet chocolate
12 tbsps unsalted butter
1½ cups sugar
1 cup flour
¼ cup cocoa, sifted
2 tsps baking powder
¼ tsp salt
4 large eggs, room temperature
2 tbsps instant Community® Coffee
1 tbsp pure vanilla extract
½ cup chopped pecans (optional)

Method:
Preheat oven to 350°F. Spray bottom and sides of 9" x 13" baking pan with nonstick cooking spray. Line pan with parchment paper and spray again. Break chocolate into small pieces and slice butter into tablespoons. In a double boiler, melt chocolate, butter and sugar over simmering water. Remove from heat and cool to room temperature. In a separate bowl, whisk flour, cocoa, baking powder and salt. In a separate mixing bowl, beat eggs, coffee and vanilla until foamy. Whisk egg mixture into cooled chocolate then fold in dry ingredients in small increments. Blend well then add pecans. Spread batter evenly in pan. Bake 22–25 minutes or until a toothpick inserted in center is barely moist. Remove from oven and cool completely in pan. Run a knife around edge of pan to loosen brownies. Place a rack on top of pan and flip over. Peel off paper. Invert again onto cutting surface. Trim edges and cut brownies into 2-inch squares.

POACHED BRANDIED PEARS

Prep Time: 1½ Hours
Yields: 6 Servings

Comment:

There are many pears on the market that are perfect for poaching, such as Bartletts, Boscs and Kiefers. In Bayou Country, pears are usually sliced, cooked and jarred for later use as a dessert topping or pie filling. However, preparing pears by poaching them should not be taken for granted.

Ingredients:

6 firm pears
2 cups water
2 cups red wine
3½ cups sugar
1 tbsp pure vanilla extract
¼ cup lemon juice
pinch of cinnamon
pinch of nutmeg
1 ounce brandy
1 tbsp cornstarch
6 mint leaves
1 cup fresh whipped cream

Method:

Peel pears then score them using a channeling tool or paring knife. NOTE: Submerge pears in a bowl of water with 1–2 tablespoons of lemon juice to keep them from turning brown. In a heavy-bottomed stockpot, combine 2 cups water, wine and sugar. Bring to a rolling boil, stirring constantly until sugar is dissolved. Add vanilla, lemon juice, cinnamon and nutmeg. Reduce heat just below simmer and add pears. Place a clean dishcloth or small plate over pears to keep them submerged in liquid for even poaching. Cook 30–45 minutes or until pears are tender, but not mushy. Remove from heat. Allow pears to rest in poaching liquid, preferably overnight, so color and flavor of liquid will be absorbed. When ready to serve, place 1½ cups of poaching liquid in a sauté pan. Add brandy and bring to a rolling boil. Dissolve cornstarch in ¼ cup cold poaching liquid. Stir in dissolved cornstarch to thicken. Remove from heat and allow to cool. To serve, place cooled brandy sauce on a 10-inch plate. Top with a chilled pear, chopped mint leaves and a dollop of whipped cream.

LOUISIANA COOKING PEAR PRESERVES

Prep Time: 1 Hour
Yields: 2–3 Pints

Comment:

There are numerous pear varieties available for cooking. In Bayou Country the Kiefer pear, which is similar in texture to a raw potato, is harvested around Labor Day. The pear is wonderful as a topping for pancakes, waffles or ice cream. It is also versatile enough to be used for a flavoring in barbecue sauces or game dishes.

Ingredients:

6 large cooking pears, peeled and cored
1–2 tbsps lemon juice
2 cups sugar

Method:

NOTE: Remember that pears oxidize quickly. When peeling and slicing, make sure to keep them submerged in water with lemon juice. Peel and core pears. Slice ½-inch thick or dice into ¾-inch cubes. Keep submerged in water until ready to use. Drain and place pears in a large bowl. Top with sugar then cover with plastic wrap and refrigerate overnight. In a heavy-bottomed saucepot, place pears and remaining juices from bowl. Bring to a rolling boil over medium-high heat then reduce to low and simmer 1 hour or until pears are fork tender but not falling apart. Jar according to jar manufacturer's directions or freeze in a suitable container.

BANANAS FOSTER

Prep Time: 30 Minutes
Yields: 6 Servings

Comment:

As a major port city, New Orleans has always had an ample supply of fresh bananas shipped in from Latin America. In 1951, Owen Brennan of Brennan's Restaurant asked Chef Paul Blangé to create a recipe using this fruit and bananas Foster was born. The dessert was named for Owen's good friend and fellow member of the New Orleans Crime Commission, Richard Foster. Today, almost 20 tons of bananas are flamed each year at Brennan's in the preparation of this now world-famous dessert.

Ingredients:

4 bananas
¼ pound butter
1 cup brown sugar
½ tsp cinnamon
¼ cup banana liqueur
¼ cup dark rum

Method:

Cut bananas in half lengthwise then dice into 1-inch cubes. In a heavy-bottomed sauté pan, melt butter over medium-high heat. Stir in sugar and cinnamon. Whisk until sugar dissolves and sauce is bubbly. Blend in bananas and banana liqueur. Sauté until softened. Remove pan from flame. Add rum then carefully return pot to heat because rum will ignite. Stir constantly. When flames subside, remove from heat and serve as a topping over vanilla ice cream or cheesecake.

SAUTÉED APPLES CALVADOS

Prep Time: 30 Minutes
Yields: 6 Servings

Comment:

Calvados, apple brandy, and Kirsch, which is cherry brandy, are used to create the sauce for these apples. This dish can be served as a topping for ice cream or in au gratin dishes topped with puff pastry.

Ingredients:

¼ cup Calvados
4 Fuji apples
1 tbsp lemon juice
¼ cup butter
½ cup brown sugar
¼ cup apple cider
1 ounce Kirsch
⅛ tsp cinnamon
pinch of cloves
pinch of ginger
pinch of nutmeg

Method:

Preheat oven to 350°F. Peel apples, core and cut into ⅛-inch slices. Submerge in water with lemon juice to keep apples from turning brown. In a 10-inch skillet, melt butter over medium-high heat. Drain apples then add to skillet and sauté 3–5 minutes. Stir in all remaining ingredients. Continue to simmer until sugar is dissolved and apples are fork tender but not falling apart. Remove from heat and allow to cool slightly. Distribute an equal amount of apples among 6 au gratin dishes. Any heat-resistant serving dish may be used if au gratin dishes are not available. Prior to serving, place in oven 5–10 minutes or until sauce is bubbly.

CANDIED FRUIT

Prep Time: 30 Minutes
Yields: 1 Cup

Comment:

Glazed fruit must be made only with fresh fruit. To ensure success, prepare this dish in dry weather, and eat it the day it is made. This dish is perfect to serve at holiday gatherings using lemon, lime and orange peel for a colorful presentation.

Ingredients:

1 cup sliced mixed fruit
1 cup sugar
¾ cup water
¼ tsp cream of tartar

Method:

In a heavy-bottomed saucepan, combine sugar, water and cream of tartar over medium-high heat. Bring to a rolling boil, cover and cook without stirring 3 minutes. This process will allow steam to wash down any sugar crystals that may have formed. Uncover, lower heat to simmer and cook to hard cracked stage (300–310°F). Remove pan from heat and place over very hot water. NOTE: Fruit must be at room temperature. If possible, dry on paper towels 4–6 hours prior to dipping. Dip fruit into mixture, a few pieces at a time. Quickly remove pieces with a toothpick or fork. Place on a wire rack until coating hardens. Should syrup begin to solidify, reheat over hot water and repeat dipping process. For best results, glaze fruit in small batches. Serve immediately. Fruit will not keep more than a day.

Sugar kettles, Rural Life Museum, Baton Rouge, La.

MERINGUES WITH SLICED STRAWBERRIES AND CHOCOLATE SAUCE

Prep Time: 3 Hours
Yields: 12 Servings

Comment:

For centuries cooks have created interesting desserts to make use of leftover egg whites. Île Flottante (see recipe) is one such dessert where meringue is used as a centerpiece to create a beautiful presentation. This recipe allows the cook to make meringue shells well in advance of dinner parties.

Ingredients for Meringues:

5 large egg whites
pinch of coarse salt
1¼ cups sugar

Method:

Place racks in first and third positions of oven then preheat to 250°F. Line 2 large baking sheets with parchment paper. Draw 6 (3½-inch) circles on each piece of parchment paper to use as a guide when making meringue shells. Using an electric mixer, beat egg whites and salt in large bowl until soft peaks form. Gradually add sugar, beating until stiff. Spoon approximately ⅓ cup whisked egg whites into center of each circle. Using the back of a cooking spoon, spread meringue evenly within circle and depress center to form a well. Bake meringues 1 hour 15 minutes or until crisp and almost dry. Turn off oven and leave door closed. Let meringues dry in oven 1 hour then remove and lift from parchment. NOTE: Meringues can be made 1 week ahead. Once cooked, wrap airtight and freeze for later use.

Ingredients for Topping:

12 ounces semisweet chocolate, chopped
3 pounds whole strawberries
6 tbsps cold water
3 tbsps sugar

Method:

Melt chocolate in a double boiler over 1 inch of water. Bring to a low simmer, stirring constantly until chocolate is melted and smooth. Dip 12 strawberries into chocolate, allowing a small portion of stem to remain uncoated. Remove and place berries on foil-lined plate then refrigerate until chocolate sets. Whisk cold water into remaining chocolate to create a sauce. Keep warm. Hull and slice remaining strawberries, then sprinkle with sugar. To serve, place a meringue in center of a 10-inch plate. Top with sliced berries, drizzle with chocolate and garnish with a whole dipped strawberry.

CREOLE COUNTRY VANILLA ICE CREAM

Prep Time: 1 Hour
Yields: 1 Quart

Comment:
Country ice cream derives its name from the country fresh milk, cream and eggs that were originally used to create it. Each version of this ice cream differs in its proportion of milk to cream and in the number of eggs added to achieve the desired texture and richness. This is an ultra-rich version.

Ingredients:
1½ cups milk
1½ cups heavy whipping cream
1½ tsps pure vanilla extract
2 eggs
½ cup sugar

Method:
In a saucepot, combine milk, cream and vanilla. Heat to 190°F, but do not boil. In a stainless steel mixing bowl, whisk together eggs and sugar. Slowly pour milk into eggs and sugar, whisking constantly. Pour mixture back into saucepot over medium heat. Stir constantly until mixture returns to 190°F. Do not boil because it will cause eggs to scramble. Pour mixture through a fine sieve and refrigerate overnight. When fully chilled, place contents in a home-style ice cream freezer and follow manufacturer's directions. NOTE: If you wish to lighten texture, separate egg yolks from whites. Whisk each separately with half of sugar. Fold egg white mixture into cream immediately before freezing. When adding fresh fruit to this recipe, remove milk and add ½ cup heavy whipping cream and 2 cups puréed fresh fruit.

WHITE CHOCOLATE STRAWBERRY ICE CREAM

Prep Time: 1 Hour
Yields: 1 Quart

Comment:
All great ice cream recipes begin with a basic vanilla custard such as this one. The addition of liqueurs, chocolate, herbs or fresh fruit convert this simple dessert into a magnificent creation. This version features fresh Louisiana strawberries for a cool summer treat.

Ingredients:
4 ounces white chocolate squares
¾ cup chopped strawberries
1½ cups milk
1½ cups heavy whipping cream
1 tbsp pure vanilla extract
¼ tsp nutmeg
2 eggs
½ cup sugar
sliced strawberries for garnish (optional)
strawberry syrup for garnish (optional)

Method:
Place white chocolate in a stainless steel bowl over a double boiler of 120°F water until chocolate is melted. Stir occasionally to maintain a liquid state. In a saucepot over medium heat, combine milk, cream, vanilla and nutmeg. Bring to 190°F or a very low simmer. Do not boil. In a stainless steel mixing bowl, whisk together eggs and sugar until blended. Slowly pour hot milk into eggs and sugar while whisking constantly. Continue whisking and pour melted chocolate into custard until blended. Pour mixture back into saucepot over medium-high heat, stirring constantly until 190°F. Do not boil because eggs will scramble. Pour mixture through a fine sieve and refrigerate, preferably overnight. When fully chilled, place contents in a home-style ice cream freezer and follow manufacturer's directions. When custard is half frozen, add chopped strawberries and continue to churn. NOTE: If you wish to lighten texture, separate egg yolks from whites. Whisk each separately with half of sugar. Fold egg white mixture into custard immediately before freezing. Garnish with sliced berries and strawberry syrup.

CANDIED YAM AND WHITE CHOCOLATE ICE CREAM

Prep Time: 1 Hour
Yields: 2 Quarts

Comment:
The idea for this recipe came from a German couple who farmed sweet potatoes for a living. After enjoying cold, mashed candied yams from the fridge, the idea to make it into an ice cream came naturally.

Ingredients:
1 (16-ounce) can Bruce's® Candied Yams
12 ounces white chocolate
1½ cups sugar
1½ cups water
8 egg yolks
½ tsp nutmeg
½ tsp cinnamon
1 tbsp pure vanilla extract
3 cups heavy whipping cream

Method:
Mash yams in their syrup until puréed then chill in refrigerator. Place white chocolate in a double boiler over 120°F water. Stir occasionally until chocolate is melted. In a 1-quart saucepan, combine sugar and water. Stir well and bring to soft-ball stage (234–240°F). In an electric mixer, blend eggs on low speed until slightly whipped. Once sugar has reached soft-ball stage, slowly pour it into eggs, blending on medium speed 5 minutes or until thick. Take special care because sugar will be extremely hot. Pour in melted chocolate then add nutmeg, cinnamon and vanilla, continuing to blend. Reduce speed to low and pour in cream. Remove beaters and use a rubber spatula to fold in puréed yams. Place entire mixture in refrigerator and chill, preferably overnight. Freeze in a home-style ice cream freezer according to manufacturer's directions.

Mistretta Candy Factory, Donaldsonville, La.

CHOCOLATE AND
CLOVER HONEY ICE CREAM

Prep Time: 1 Hour
Yields: 4 Quarts

Comment:

Liquor and liqueurs are often used to flavor ice creams and sorbets. In the South, sour mash whiskeys provide Southern flavor, which adds the perfect finish to chocolate ice cream.

Ingredients:

1 (5⅓ -ounce) package semi-sweet chocolate, chopped
½ cup honey
⅔ cup Jack Daniels® whiskey
1⅔ cups unsweetened cocoa powder
1¼ cups sugar
1 quart heavy whipping cream
1 quart half-and-half
12 large eggs, room temperature

Method:

In a heavy-bottomed saucepan, sift together cocoa powder and sugar. Whisk in cream and half-and-half until blended. Stir in chocolate and honey. Cook over medium-high heat, approximately 190°F, until chocolate is melted. Do not boil. Remove saucepan from heat and set aside. In a large mixing bowl, whisk eggs until frothy. Add half of chocolate mixture to eggs, whisking constantly to prevent eggs from scrambling. Reverse process by blending egg mixture into remaining chocolate, continuing to stir. Return pan to medium-high heat and cook 3–4 minutes, do not boil or eggs will scramble. Pour mixture into a glass bowl. Place this bowl inside a larger bowl of ice or cold water to help chill mixture. In a small saucepan, cook whiskey over medium-high heat until liquor ignites. NOTE: Take care as flame will flare up and extinguish itself quickly. Stir whiskey into chocolate mixture and allow to cool. NOTE: It is best to prepare this mixture 1 day prior to churning. When ready to churn, place chocolate custard into a home-style ice cream machine and freeze according to manufacturer's directions.

PRALINE AND PEACH ICE CREAM

Prep Time: 1½ Hours
Yields: 2–3 Quarts

Comment:

Peaches are plentiful in early summer and are often eaten on ice cream. By combining the traditional Louisiana dessert, pralines, with fresh Ruston peaches, an ice cream flavor like no other is created.

Ingredients:

3 cups fresh peaches
3 cups milk
1½ cups sugar
2 tbsps lemon juice
½ cup praline liqueur or Frangelico

3 eggs
3 cups heavy whipping cream
pinch of cinnamon
pinch of nutmeg

Method:

In a food processor, combine peaches, 1 cup milk, 1 cup sugar, lemon juice and liqueur. Blend until puréed. In a large mixing bowl, combine peach mixture, 2 cups milk, ½ cup sugar, eggs and whipping cream. Whisk until smooth. Add cinnamon and nutmeg. Place mixture in a 4-quart home-style ice cream freezer and follow manufacturer's directions. For best results, place frozen ice cream in home freezer 2–3 hours before serving.

LOUISIANA FIG ICE CREAM

Prep Time: 1½ Hours
Yields: 1 Quart

Comment:

Figs are plentiful in late summer. It is not uncommon to find fig preserves topping a bowl of vanilla ice cream. The fruit topping inspired the use of fig preserves as an ingredient in ice cream.

Ingredients:

1 cup mashed fig preserves
1½ cups milk
1½ cups heavy whipping cream

1½ tsps pure vanilla extract
2 eggs
½ cup sugar

Method:

In a heavy-bottomed saucepan, combine milk, cream and vanilla. Bring mixture to 190°F, whisking occasionally. Do not boil. In a separate bowl, whisk together eggs and sugar until blended. NOTE: Because fig preserves are naturally sweet, you may wish to reduce sugar to ¼ cup. Slowly pour milk into egg mixture, whisking constantly. Return mixture to saucepan at 190°F. Do not boil because eggs will scramble. Remove from heat and pour through a fine sieve. Refrigerate, preferably overnight. Whisk in fig preserves just prior to churning. Place contents in a home-style ice cream freezer and follow manufacturer's directions. NOTE: If a lighter ice cream texture is desired, separate egg yolks and whites. Whisk egg whites and fold into mixture immediately prior to freezing.

ÎLE FLOTTANTE
(FLOATING ISLAND)

Prep Time: 1 Hour
Yields: 6–8 Servings

Comment:

One of the original desserts of early Louisiana, "île flottante", arrived with the French in the late 1600s. Sweetened egg whites are poached and spooned over a thick custard creating the floating effect. The white eggs atop the custard gives the dish its other name, "oeufs à la neige" or snow eggs.

Ingredients:

6 cups heavy whipping cream	pinch of nutmeg
8 eggs, separated	2 tbsps cornstarch
1½ cups sugar	3 tbsps pure vanilla extract
pinch of cinnamon	½ cup sugar

Method:

In a 2-quart saucepot, heat cream over medium-high heat. In a large mixing bowl, combine egg yolks, 1½ cups sugar, cinnamon, nutmeg, cornstarch and vanilla. Bring cream to a low boil then ladle 1 cup of hot cream into egg mixture, stirring constantly while pouring. Reverse process by pouring egg mixture slowly into pot of hot cream. Stir constantly because eggs will scramble. Reduce heat to simmer and cook, stirring constantly, until a slightly-thick custard forms. Pour into a serving bowl and allow to cool. In a large mixing bowl, beat egg whites until stiff peaks form. Add sugar and continue beating 1–2 minutes. Poach spoonfuls of these floating isles in hot water over low heat, approximately 2 minutes on each side. Remove poached egg whites from hot water and place on top of custard. Serve 2 floating isles in a soup bowl of custard.

CHOCOLATE JAVA MOUSSE

Prep Time: 1 Hour
Yields: 6 Servings

Comment:

South Louisianians love drinking coffee with anything, at any time of day. Not only do we drink it with our desserts, we add the flavor to many of our sweets. This simple mousse recipe is quite elegant and incorporates the finest from the sweet cart, while borrowing a pinch of instant coffee from the cupboard.

Ingredients:

8 ounces semisweet chocolate
1 tbsp instant coffee granules
2 egg yolks
1 tsp Cointreau or brandy
8 ounces heavy whipping cream
2 tbsps orange zest
¼ cup finely grated white or dark chocolate
6 coffee beans (optional)
6 mint leaves (optional)

Method:

Chop chocolate into ¼-inch pieces. In a stainless steel bowl, combine chocolate and coffee. Place over a double boiler containing 1 inch of water and bring to a low simmer. Do not boil. Do not allow bottom of bowl to touch hot water. Stir chocolate gently with a wooden spoon until melted and smooth. Remove from heat then stir in egg yolks and Cointreau. Mixture will quickly thicken to a heavy mousse consistency. Set aside. In a large ceramic bowl, whisk cream until stiff peaks form. Blend 3 tablespoons whipped cream into chocolate mixture to help "loosen" heavy mousse. Using a rubber spatula, gently fold chocolate into bowl of whipped cream. Blend only until a marbling effect is created. Do not overblend. Cover bowl with plastic wrap and chill 1 hour, preferably overnight. When ready to serve, place an equal amount of mousse in 6 chilled wine glasses or decorative coffee cups. Top with orange zest, grated chocolate and a coffee bean. Garnish with fresh mint leaves.

FELICIANA SUMMER PUDDING

Prep Time: 1 Hour
Yields: 6 Servings

Comment:

English fare became commonplace in St. Francisville, La. The English began building their plantation empires in these hills, the "Rolling Felicianas." Summer pudding was a spring and early summer staple found on most English tables during the plantation period.

Ingredients:

4 pints strawberries, stemmed and quartered
2 pints blueberries
2 pints blackberries
1½ cups Champagne
1 cup water
2 cups sugar
2 tbsps lemon juice
pinch of salt
1 tbsp honey
3–4 tsps grenadine
3 (10-inch) loaves French bread

Method:

If French bread or baguettes are not available, substitute sliced bread with crust removed. In a 4-quart saucepan, combine Champagne, water and sugar over medium-high heat. Bring to a low simmer, whisking constantly until sugar dissolves. Add berries and cook 10–12 minutes or until fruit is softened and juice has been extracted into Champagne mixture. Add lemon juice and salt. Check for sweetness of juice and adjust with additional sugar if necessary. Set aside and cool slightly. Place 6 (6-ounce) ramekins on a cookie sheet and spoon 2–3 tablespoons of berry mixture into each. Slice French bread into ½-inch rounds, tearing if necessary to fit evenly into ramekins. Press 1 slice of bread gently into each ramekin. Top with more fruit and continue layering fruit and bread until each dish is filled. Be sure to press bread gently after each layer to absorb juice. Spoon all remaining juice into cups until nearly overflowing. Cover each ramekin in plastic wrap and top with a can or other weight then place in refrigerator overnight. When ready to serve, place a generous amount of Crème Anglaise in bottom of a 10-inch plate and unmold pudding in the center. (See recipe.)

CRÈME CARAMEL CUSTARD

Prep Time: 2½ Hours
Yields: 6 Servings

Comment:
Crème Caramel, a basic egg custard with a layer of caramel, is traditionally a French dessert. However, recipes for a similar custard can be found in many different countries. The Spanish call the dessert flan. To make the dessert unique to Louisiana, pecans are added as a garnish.

Ingredients:
1 cup sugar
1 tbsp water
4 eggs, beaten
¼ tsp salt
1 cup milk
1½ cups heavy whipping cream
2 tbsps pure vanilla extract
¼ tsp nutmeg
¼ tsp cinnamon
¼ cup chopped pecans (optional)

Method:
Preheat oven to 300°F. Butter 6 (5-ounce) custard cups and place them on a baking pan with a 2-inch lip. Fill pan with water approximately ½-inch from top of lip. Set aside. In a cast iron skillet, combine ½ cup sugar and water. Melt sugar over low heat 6 minutes or until edges are slightly brown, creating caramel. Do not stir or whisk during this process. Keep heat low enough to brown sugar evenly without burning it. Carefully pour an equal amount of hot caramel into each custard cup. In a large mixing bowl, whisk eggs, remaining sugar and salt until eggs are thick and lemon-colored. Stir in milk, cream and vanilla. Continue to whisk while adding nutmeg and cinnamon. Strain custard into each cup and allow foam to settle prior to baking. Bake custards 2 hours or until solid. Remove from oven and allow to cool overnight. When ready to serve, unmold custards and garnish with pecans.

RIZ AU LAIT

Prep Time: 1 Hour
Yields: 8 Servings

Comment:
Rice custard, like flan or bread pudding, is considered a premier Creole dessert. Many custard-based desserts evolved out of Cajun and Creole kitchens due to the availability of eggs and milk from the surrounding German settlements. By adding rice, this custard becomes an elegant finish for a Creole dinner.

Ingredients:
1 cup long grain rice
1½ cups water
1 tbsp butter
1 tsp sugar
4 eggs
¾ cup sugar
2 cups milk
1 tbsp grated orange zest
⅛ tsp nutmeg
1 tbsp pure vanilla extract

Method:
In a 1-quart saucepot, bring rice, water, butter and 1 teaspoon sugar to a rolling boil. Reduce to lowest heat, cover and simmer 30 minutes or until rice is fully cooked. Do not uncover. Remove from heat and allow to cool slightly. In a small mixing bowl, whisk together eggs and ¾ cup sugar until creamy and pale yellow then set aside. Combine rice mixture with milk and bring to a low boil. Add zest, nutmeg and vanilla, stirring constantly. Slowly add egg mixture to boiling milk and cook 1 minute. Remove from heat and pour into a large fluted custard bowl. You may garnish with additional nutmeg and orange zest. Cover and refrigerate until chilled. NOTE: To serve as a baked custard, spoon mixture into 8 custard cups. Place cups into a pan of water and bake at 350°F for 20 minutes. Custard may be served hot or cold.

LOUISIANA FRUIT TRIFLE

Prep Time: 1 Hour
Yields: 10–12 Servings

Comment:

Fruit trifle, the layered fruit and custard dessert, was brought to Louisiana by the English many years ago. The abundance of fresh berries and other seasonal fruit made the creation of this dish simple in Bayou Country. Feel free to use any variety of fresh fruit.

Ingredients for Custard:

2 cups half-and-half
4 egg yolks
½ cup sugar
1 tbsp pure vanilla extract
pinch of cinnamon
pinch of nutmeg
¾ tbsp cornstarch
1 tbsp water

Method:

In a saucepan, bring half-and-half to a low boil over medium-high heat. In a mixing bowl, whisk eggs, sugar, vanilla, cinnamon and nutmeg. In a measuring cup, dissolve cornstarch in water then set aside. When half-and-half begins to boil, remove from heat. Pour 1 cup of hot cream into egg mixture, whisking constantly. Pour egg and cream mixture back into pot, continuing to stir. Return saucepan to heat, pour in cornstarch and stir until custard begins to thicken. Remove from heat and continue to stir 3–5 minutes. Set aside.

Ingredients for Trifle:

1 angel food cake
¼ cup praline liqueur
1 cup sliced strawberries
1 cup blueberries
1 cup sliced bananas
1 cup blackberries or raspberries
2 cups prepared custard sauce (see above)
1 cup whipped cream
fresh mint for garnish
cinnamon for garnish

Method:

Cut angel food cake into 1-inch squares. Place squares in large mixing bowl and sprinkle with liqueur. In a large footed trifle dish, layer cake, fruit and custard sauce until all is used. Top with whipped cream and garnish with a sprig of fresh mint and a sprinkle of cinnamon.

WATERMELON PUDDING

Prep Time: 3 Hours 45 Minutes
Yields: 6 Servings

Comment:

Watermelon pudding is a perfect dessert for those long, summer days when the watermelon are so plentiful. Enjoy this with friends after the next barbecue.

Ingredients:

6 cups chopped watermelon, seeded
¼ cup and 1 tbsp cornstarch
½ cup sugar
1 tsp anise seeds
2 tsps fresh lemon juice
⅓ cup heavy whipping cream
1 tsp sugar
chopped pecans for garnish
chocolate shavings for garnish

Method:

In a blender, purée watermelon until smooth. Pour through a sieve into a 2-quart saucepan. Discard any remaining solids. In a mixing bowl, combine ¼ cup puréed watermelon and cornstarch. Stir until smooth. Boil remaining watermelon purée with ½ cup sugar and anise until sugar dissolves. Whisk cornstarch mixture into boiling watermelon juice then reduce heat and simmer 3 minutes, whisking occasionally. Blend in lemon juice. Pour pudding mixture through a sieve into a 1-quart serving dish. Chill uncovered 30 minutes. Cover and chill 3 hours or until set. NOTE: If desired, pudding can be chilled 1 day. Prior to serving, beat cream with 1 teaspoon sugar in an electric mixer until stiff peaks form. Top pudding with whipped cream and garnish with chopped pecans and chocolate shavings.

MIXED BERRIES IN BAY LEAF CUSTARD

Prep Time: 1½ Hours
Yields: 6 Servings

Comment:

The fresh berries that are plentiful during late spring and summer make this dessert a delectable treat. Any combination of berries can be used in this custard. For an elegant presentation, serve the dessert in a martini glass.

Ingredients:

5 egg yolks
½ cup sugar
2 cups heavy whipping cream
1 tsp pure vanilla extract
pinch of nutmeg
2–3 fresh bay leaves
6 cups mixed fresh berries (strawberries, raspberries, blueberries, blackberries or mulberries)
6 bay leaves for garnish

Method:

In a mixing bowl, whisk egg yolks and sugar 3 minutes or until thick and pale. Transfer mixture to a 3-quart heavy saucepan. Stir in cream, vanilla, nutmeg and bay leaves. Cook over medium-low heat 8–10 minutes, stirring constantly with a wooden spoon. Do not boil. Custard is done when mixture coats back of spoon and registers 175°F. Remove from heat and cool 1 hour or until custard reaches room temperature, stirring frequently. Discard bay leaves and serve custard over berries in a martini glass. Garnish each with a fresh bay leaf.

RUM RAISIN RICE PUDDING

Prep Time: 30 Minutes
Yields: 6 Servings

Comment:
Rice pudding is second only to bread pudding in Louisiana. While some special occasion versions add a splash of brandy to the recipe, this variation nods to the Creoles by including raisins and a bit of rum.

Ingredients:
2½ cups long grain rice
½ cup dark rum
½ cup golden raisins
6 cups whole milk
2 cups half-and-half
1 tsp pure vanilla extract
¼ tsp salt
⅛ tsp cinnamon
4 egg yolks
2½ cups sugar

Method:
Rinse rice until water is clear. In a saucepot, bring raisins and rum to a boil. If rum flares up, remove from heat and allow it to burn out naturally. Remove pot from heat and allow raisins to steep in remaining rum. In a large heavy-bottomed pot, combine rice, milk, 1 cup half-and-half, vanilla, salt and cinnamon. Heat to simmer, but do not boil. Cover and cook until tender, stirring occasionally. In a separate mixing bowl, whisk egg yolks, sugar and remaining half-and-half until well blended. Slowly add ¼ of hot rice mixture, a little at a time, carefully whisking so eggs do not scramble. Pour mixture back into pot and heat it gently until pudding begins to thicken. Do not boil or stir excessively as custard will break and pudding will become dense. Place pudding into a serving bowl and sprinkle with rum raisins. Serve immediately. If a cold pudding is desired, cover bowl with plastic wrap, pressing it directly on the surface so a skin does not form. Refrigerate until ready to use.

BREAD AND BUTTER PUDDING

Prep Time: 1½ Hours
Yields: 6 Servings

Comment:
No doubt this recipe was invented to use up the endless slices of bread and butter left over from every Victorian tea table. However, don't let an oversupply of bread be your only excuse for making this dessert. For an interesting variation, use slices of brown bread and spread them with marmalade as well as butter. Serve with cream.

Ingredients:
3 cups milk
zest of 1 lemon
2 tbsps sugar
4 slices white bread
½ cup raisins
3 eggs
1 tbsp brandy
¼ tsp grated nutmeg
1 tbsp dark brown sugar

Method:
Preheat oven to 325°F. In a small saucepan, heat milk, lemon zest and sugar. When mixture reaches a simmer, remove from heat. Set aside and allow milk to infuse zest at least 10 minutes. Butter a 1½-pint pie dish. Remove crusts from bread then spread each slice with butter and cut in half. Layer bread in pie dish, sprinkling raisins between layers. In a mixing bowl, beat eggs then add brandy. Blend egg mixture into milk. Pour entire mixture over bread and allow to soak 30 minutes. Sprinkle nutmeg and brown sugar on pudding. Bake 45 minutes or until top is golden.

WHITE CHOCOLATE
BREAD PUDDING

Prep Time: 2 Hours
Yields: 6–8 Servings

Comment:

Bread pudding is considered the "apple pie" of South Louisiana. Because of our heavy French influence, crusty French bread is abundant. Our German population gave us a good supply of milk and eggs. The combination of these cultures and their ingredients gave us one of our premier desserts.

Ingredients:

9 ounces white chocolate
3 (10-inch) loaves French bread
4 eggs
6 egg yolks
4 cups heavy whipping cream
1 cup milk
1 cup sugar

Method:

Slice French bread into ½-inch thick round croutons and set aside. In a large mixing bowl, whisk together eggs and egg yolks. Set aside. In a large saucepan, combine cream, milk and sugar. Bring mixture to a low simmer then add white chocolate. Whisk until chocolate is completely melted. Remove pot from heat, and quickly stir in whisked eggs. Blend thoroughly to keep eggs from scrambling. In a 9" x 13" baking dish, place bread slices in 2–3 layers. Pour half of cream mixture over bread. Press bread gently allowing cream mixture to be absorbed evenly into bread. Once most of mixture has been soaked up, pour remaining cream over bread and press gently. Cover dish with foil and let soak a minimum of 5 hours prior to baking. Preheat oven to 300°F. Bake covered approximately 1 hour. Remove foil and bake 45 additional minutes or until top is golden brown. This bread pudding is best chilled in refrigerator overnight then cut into squares and heated in individual portions in microwave. If desired, create a white chocolate sauce for topping bread pudding by combining 8 ounces melted white chocolate and 3 ounces heavy whipping cream. This may be done in a double boiler or microwave.

MOTHER'S CREAM PUFFS

Prep Time: 1 Hour
Yields: 6 Servings

Comment:

Although I was too young to remember the flavor and flakiness of Mother's homemade cream puffs, throughout the years I've been reminded of their superior quality by older relatives. Because Mom died when I was seven, I never had an opportunity to create one of my great Mother's Day dishes for her. I hope this cream puff recipe from our family archives will do justice to what she would have served.

Ingredients for Puff Pastry:

½ cup water
½ cup butter
½ cup flour
¼ tsp salt
2 eggs

Method:

Heat oven to 400°F. Grease cookie sheet. In a medium saucepan, bring water and butter to a rolling boil over medium heat. Stir in flour and salt. Cook, stirring vigorously, until mixture leaves sides of pan in a smooth ball. Remove from heat. Add eggs, 1 at a time, whisking constantly after each addition until smooth and glossy. Spoon 6 mounds of dough (about ¼ cup each) 3 inches apart onto greased cookie sheet. Bake 30–40 minutes or until golden brown. Remove from oven and prick puffs with sharp knife to allow steam to vent. Remove from cookie sheet, split in half and extract any filaments of soft dough.

Ingredients for Vanilla Pastry Cream:

2 eggs
¼ cup sugar
1 tbsp plus 2 tsps cornstarch
⅛ tsp nutmeg
1 cup milk
1 tbsp pure vanilla extract
2 tbsps cold butter

Method:

In a stainless steel mixing bowl, whisk eggs and sugar. Whisk in cornstarch and nutmeg until well blended. In a heavy-bottomed saucepot, combine milk and vanilla over medium-high heat until steam rises, but it is just short of boiling. Remove from heat, whisking constantly. Slowly pour into egg mixture. Stir constantly to prevent eggs from scrambling. Return mixture to pot over medium heat, stirring until stiff. As it begins to thicken, whisk vigorously to keep mixture from scorching and eggs from scrambling. Once thickened to custard consistency, remove from heat and stir in butter. Place hot custard in a ceramic bowl, cover with plastic wrap and let cool. It is important to cover custard so that it does not form a skin layer. Once cool, pipe vanilla cream into pastry puffs and serve.

OREILLES DE COCHON

Prep Time: 1 Hour
Yields: 8–10 Servings

Comment:
This old Cajun recipe gets its name from the shape the dough takes in the cooking process. The "pig's ear" is shaped by twisting the flattened dough with a fork as it hits the hot oil. This dessert is found mainly in the bayou region of Louisiana.

Ingredients:
¼ pound butter
½ tsp salt
1 tsp baking powder
3 eggs
2½ cups flour
1 quart peanut oil
½ cup brown sugar
½ cup Louisiana cane syrup
1 cup chopped pecans

Method:
In a large mixing bowl, combine butter, salt, baking powder and eggs. Using a metal spoon, cream ingredients together. Slowly sprinkle in flour, 1 cup at a time, blending well until dough ball forms. Remove from bowl, place on a well-floured surface and knead 5–10 minutes. Using a dough cutter, divide into 12 equal pieces. Roll each piece into a ⅛-inch thick circle. In a 12-inch sauté pan, heat oil over medium-high heat. Use a candy thermometer to maintain a 375°F temperature. Drop pig's ears into oil, 1 at a time. Using a long handled fork, twist pastry at top center to give it curled shape of pig's ear. Continue to fry on each side until golden brown and floating. Remove and drain on paper towels. To make sugar topping, combine sugar, syrup and pecans in a heavy-bottomed saucepan. Bring to a light boil and continue cooking until mixture reaches soft-ball stage (234–240°F). Once cooked, drizzle pecan sugar on top of pig's ears until coated.

Sewing sugar sacks at Colonial Sugar Refinery, Gramercy, La.

PRALINE CRÊPES

Prep Time: 1 Hour
Yields: 10 Crêpes

Comment:
This evolution of the Louisiana praline came about during the opening of our Lafitte's Landing in Fukuoka, Japan in 1986. The dessert was created especially for that event, but has since been used for many high-profile affairs.

Ingredients for Pastry Cream:
2 cups heavy whipping cream
½ cup sugar
6 egg yolks
½ cup flour
½ tsp salt
2 ounces praline liqueur
1½ tbsps pure vanilla extract
1 tbsp softened butter

Method:
In a heavy-bottomed saucepan, bring cream to a low boil then reduce heat to simmer. In a large mixing bowl, blend sugar, egg yolks, flour and salt. Whisk until creamy and smooth. Whisking constantly, pour 1 cup of hot cream into mixture. Once blended, pour contents of mixing bowl into saucepan, stirring constantly. Add praline liqueur and vanilla. Remove from heat and allow to cool. Once cool, fold in butter. Cover with plastic wrap and refrigerate.

Ingredients for Crêpes:
2 eggs
½ cup flour
½ tsp sugar
½ tsp pure vanilla extract
1 tbsp praline liqueur
1 tbsp melted butter
¾ cup milk
pinch of salt
¼ cup vegetable oil
¼ cup sugar
¾ cup chopped pecans

Method:
In a large mixing bowl, whisk eggs and flour until creamy. Add sugar, vanilla, praline liqueur, butter and milk. Continue to whisk until well blended and consistency of heavy whipping cream is achieved. Season with a pinch of salt. Heat an 8-inch crêpe pan over medium-high heat. Add 1 tablespoon oil, swirling to coat pan. Pour excess oil from crêpe pan back into original container. Place approximately 2 ounces of crêpe batter into hot pan, tilting in a circular motion until batter spreads evenly. Cook crêpe until outer edges begin to brown and loosen from pan. Flip crêpe and cook 1 additional minute. Using a thin spatula, lift crêpe from pan and sprinkle with sugar. Add one tablespoon oil to pan and repeat process, continuing until all crêpes are done. Place 1 tablespoon pastry cream in center of crêpe and top with chopped pecans. Heat in oven or serve cold. Crêpes may also be served on Crème Anglaise. (See recipe.)

CRÊPES ESTELLE

Prep Time: 1 Hour
Yields: 20 Crêpes

Comment:

Impressionist artist, Edgar Degas, resided with his uncle, Michel Munson, in New Orleans during the late 1800s. Munson's daughter Estelle was the subject of at least one Degas painting and obviously the namesake for this delectable crêpe dish.

Ingredients for Crêpes:

4 eggs
1 cup flour
1 tbsp sugar
1 tsp pure vanilla extract
2 tbsps Triple Sec

2 tbsps melted butter
1½ cups milk
pinch of salt
½ cup vegetable oil
½ cup sugar

Method:

In a large mixing bowl, whisk eggs, flour, sugar, vanilla and Triple Sec until smooth. Add butter and milk. Continue to blend until batter is smooth and a consistency of heavy whipping cream is achieved. Season with salt. NOTE: It is best to make crêpe batter prior to use and refrigerate 6–12 hours. Place 2 (6-inch) crêpe pans over medium-high heat. Add 2 tablespoons vegetable oil into a pan and swirl until bottom of pan is coated and oil is hot. Pour excess oil into second crêpe pan and heat. Place approximately 2 ounces of crêpe batter into first pan, tilting in a circular motion until batter spreads evenly. Cook crêpe until outer edges brown and loosen from pan. Flip and cook 1 additional minute. Using a thin spatula, remove crêpe from pan and sprinkle with sugar. Continue cooking process, using both pans, until all batter is used. If you wish to store overnight or freeze, place plastic wrap between each crêpe to prevent sticking and place in a large plastic zipper bag.

Ingredients for Sauce:

¼ pound butter
1 tbsp sugar
zest of 1 satsuma
juice of 2 satsumas

1 tsp grenadine or cherry juice
3 tbsps Cointreau or Triple Sec
3 tbsps Kirsch liquor
satsuma slices for garnish

Method:

Juice satsumas by peeling and pressing segments through a fine sieve. This can also be done by chopping fruit in a food processor then pushing them through a sieve, discarding pulp. In a cast iron skillet, melt butter over medium-high heat. Add sugar and satsuma zest, stirring until sugar is melted. Stirring constantly, add satsuma juice, grenadine and Cointreau. Remove skillet from heat and add Kirsch. Take caution when returning skillet to heat as alcohol may ignite for a couple seconds. Fold each crêpe in half, then in half again to create a triangle. Gently simmer crêpes, 1–2 at a time, in hot sauce and serve immediately. Place 2 crêpes on a 10-inch serving plate and garnish with a few sections of fresh satsuma.

APPLE PIE FOR 4th July

Blue Ribbon

Pies

Fresh Peach $13
Fresh Blueberry
Blueberry-Peach $4
Blackberry
Apple
Cushaw
Sweet Potato TARTS
Pumpkin $14 TARTS-$5
$15 TARTS 5

CLASSIC AMERICAN PIE CRUST

Prep Time: 2 Hours
Yields: 2 (9-inch) Pies

Comment:

In order to make a perfect pie, you must start with the perfect crust. This pie crust is ideal for any pie whether apple, strawberry or even pecan. The dough will keep in the freezer for 3 months and yields enough dough for 1 (9-inch) double-crust pie.

Ingredients:

2½ cups flour
1 tbsp sugar
½ tsp salt
6 tbsps cold water
¼ pound cold unsalted butter, cut in ½-inch pieces
¼ cup cold vegetable shortening, cut in ½-inch pieces
2 tsps fresh lemon juice

Method:

Preheat oven to 425°F. In a food processor, briefly blend flour, sugar and salt. Add butter and shortening. Blend 30 seconds or until coarse crumbs form. Blend in lemon juice and water until moist crumbs form. Gently shape into 2 equal circles 4–5 inches in diameter. Cover in plastic wrap and refrigerate at least 1 hour, preferably overnight. Place 1 circle of dough between 2 large pieces of lightly-floured parchment. Roll until ⅛-inch thick and 14 inches in diameter. Remove top sheet of parchment. Gently roll dough around pin and position pin over pie pan. Ease dough into pan gently, but firmly press it against sides and bottom. Do not pull or stretch dough. With scissors, trim edge of dough allowing it to hang over outer edge of pan. Tuck this dough under to rest on top of rim, and pinch-crimp edges. Repeat with second dough circle. Freeze crust for at least 30 minutes. Line frozen crust with large piece of foil, fill with pie weights and bake 12 minutes. Remove foil and weights. Continue baking approximately 8 minutes or until shell is gold.

CLASSIC APPLE PIE

Prep Time: 1 Hour
Yields: 8 Servings

Comment:

Ever since that first apple orchard was planted on Beacon Hill, overlooking Boston Harbor, apples have been the chief ingredient in America's premier dessert. After all, nothing is more American than apple pie.

Ingredients:

6 Golden Delicious apples, peeled, cored and thinly sliced
2 (9-inch) prepared pie crusts
¼ cup sugar
2 tbsps flour
1 tsp pure vanilla extract
½ tsp cinnamon
¼ tsp ginger
⅛ tsp mace
2 tbsps butter or margarine
heavy whipping cream or whole milk, for brushing crust

Method:

Heat oven to 425°F. Line a 9-inch pie pan with 1 prepared crust. In a large bowl, combine apples, sugar, flour, vanilla, cinnamon, ginger and mace. Pour apple mixture into pie crust then dot with butter. Cover apple filling with remaining pie crust. Pinch together edges of bottom and top crust to seal. Brush top crust with whipping cream or milk and cut several slits to vent steam. Place in oven and bake 20 minutes. Reduce oven heat to 375°F and bake 30–35 minutes or until apples are tender.

FRESH BLACKBERRY PIE

Prep Time: 2 Hours
Yields: 6–8 Servings

Comment:

Blackberries have been a part of the culinary repertoire of Bayou Country for centuries. Fresh blackberries are abundant in Louisiana and can be found growing wild in many areas of the state. The berry is of course used in every type of dish from jams and jellies to cobblers and pies and even in barbecue sauces.

Ingredients for Filling:

5½ cups fresh blackberries
1 cup sugar
¼ cup flour
2 tbsps fresh lemon juice

Method:

Combine all ingredients and toss gently to combine. Set aside.

Ingredients for Crust:

2 cups flour
1 tsp salt
⅔ cup shortening
¼ cup ice water
1 tsp sugar
whipped cream (optional)

Method:

Preheat oven to 425°F. In a food processor, combine flour, salt and shortening. Pulse once or twice to blend well. Add 2–3 tablespoons water, pulsing until mixture resembles coarse cornmeal. Remove dough onto a floured surface, knead once or twice and separate in half. Flatten each half into a round disc and cover in plastic wrap. Refrigerate at least 1 hour. Dough may be made 1 day in advance. Remove from refrigerator and allow to sit at room temperature 30 minutes or until slightly softened. Using a floured rolling pin and work surface, roll out 1 disc to approximately 12 inches in diameter. Transfer into a 9-inch pie pan, cutting excess dough from around pan. Roll out remaining disc into a 10–12 inch circle. Pour berry filling into pie and top with second crust. Press edges together in a decorative manner to seal. Using a sharp paring knife, cut several slits in top of crust to vent steam. Sprinkle with a teaspoon of sugar. Place pie on shelf in lower third of oven and bake 15 minutes. Reduce temperature to 350°F, and continue to bake 45 minutes or until crust is golden brown. Serve warm with whipped cream.

PONCHATOULA STRAWBERRY AND LEMON PIE

Prep Time: 1 Hour
Yields: 8 Servings

Comment:

When spring rolls around, the refreshing flavor of lemon pie fills the mouths of many people in South Louisiana. However, the tart lemon flavor can be enhanced with the addition of fresh strawberries or blueberries.

Ingredients:

½ cup diced Louisiana strawberries
3 pints Louisiana strawberries, sliced
3 tbsps fresh lemon juice
1 tbsp grated lemon zest
½ cup cornstarch
1¼ cups water
1¾ cups sugar
4 egg yolks, beaten
2 tbsps butter
1 (9-inch) baked pie shell
1 package whipped cream

Method:

In a saucepan, dissolve cornstarch in water, whisking until smooth. Add lemon juice, diced strawberries, sugar and egg yolks. Over medium heat, cook mixture 5 minutes, stirring until sauce has thickened and resembles pie filling. Remove saucepan from heat then add lemon zest and butter, stirring constantly. Pour pie filling into pre-baked shell. Set aside to cool. Once cooled, top pie with a generous amount of whipped cream and swirl it in a decorative fashion. Beginning in the center, shingle sliced strawberries in a circular fashion until top of whipped cream is covered totally with berries. If there are any sliced berries remaining, place in a bowl and sprinkle with 2 tablespoons sugar. Stir and refrigerate along with pie for a minimum of 4 hours. When ready to serve, slice pie and top each slice with a teaspoon of sugared berries.

MAMERE'S COUNTRY-STYLE LEMON PIE

Prep Time: 1 Hour
Yields: 8 Servings

Comment:
Mamere Zeringue was my grandmother on Mom's side of the family. She was not only a fabulous cook, but would have been considered a top pastry chef in her day. Although most country-style lemon pies are made with a similar recipe, this one has a bit less lemon juice so it's not quite as citrusy as a tart lemon pie. If a tart flavor is desired, add 2 tablespoons of fresh lemon juice to the recipe.

Ingredients:
3 tbsps fresh lemon juice
1 tbsp grated lemon zest
½ cup cornstarch
1¼ cups water
4 eggs, separated
2 cups sugar
2 tbsps butter
1 tsp cream of tartar
1 (9-inch) baked pie shell

Method:
Preheat oven to 375°F. In a saucepan, dissolve cornstarch in water over medium-high heat, whisking until smooth. In a small bowl, whisk egg yolks until beaten. Add yolks, lemon juice and 1¾ cups sugar into cornstarch. Stir mixture until sauce has thickened and resembles pie filling. Remove saucepan from heat, and stir in lemon zest and butter. Pour pie filling into pie shell. Set aside to cool slightly. In an electric mixer, whisk egg whites and cream of tartar on high speed until soft peaks form. Add remaining ¼ cup sugar and continue to whisk until sugar is dissolved and stiff peaks form. NOTE: It is important to whisk meringue until there are no visible signs of sugar, otherwise the meringue will weep after sitting for a few hours. Using a tablespoon, drop dollops of meringue on top of pie beginning at outer edge of pie and working toward the center. Continue this process until pie is completely covered. If meringue is allowed to adhere to pie crust, it will not shrink during baking. Place pie on center rack of oven and bake 10 minutes or until peaks are lightly browned. Remove from oven, allow to cool and refrigerate until ready to serve. This pie is best when refrigerated overnight.

Celeste figs prior to ripening

FIG AND PECAN PIE

Prep Time: 1 Hour
Yields: 6–8 Servings

Comment:

Figs were the most plentiful fruit available to the early Cajuns and Creoles. During the late summer, figs were canned in almost every household in Bayou Country. In addition, pecan trees can be found in backyards across the state. This delicious pie combines these two staples of Louisiana cuisine.

Ingredients:

½ cup chopped fig preserves
1 cup chopped pecans
½ cup sugar
1 tbsp cornstarch
1 cup light corn syrup
¼ cup Louisiana cane syrup

1 tbsp pure vanilla extract
3 eggs, beaten
pinch of cinnamon
pinch of nutmeg
1 (9-inch) uncooked pie shell

Method:

Preheat oven to 325°F. In a large mixing bowl, combine sugar and cornstarch. Whisk in syrups, vanilla and eggs until blended. Blend in preserves and pecans. Season with cinnamon and nutmeg. Pour ingredients into pie shell and bake on center rack 45 minutes.

FELICIANA SWEET POTATO PIE

Prep Time: 2 Hours
Yields: 6–8 Servings

Comment:

The Beauregard yam is one of the sweetest yams in Louisiana. This unique variety was originally produced at Louisiana State University in the late 1980s. The small Beauregard sweet potatoes are the best kind to use in this pie. The potato is normally 1½ inches in diameter and 4–6 inches in length. If only the larger sweet potato varieties are available, use 3–4 of that type instead of 6. Use only fresh sweet potatoes in this recipe for best results.

Ingredients:

6 Beauregard sweet potatoes,
   peeled and cubed ¼-inch
juice of ½ lemon
½ pound butter
1 cup sugar
1 tbsp pure vanilla extract

1½ tbsps flour
⅛ tsp allspice
⅛ tsp nutmeg
3 ounces cream cheese
1 cup flour

Method:

Preheat oven to 350°F. Place potatoes in a 4-quart stockpot with lightly-salted water. The water should almost cover potatoes, but not completely. Bring to a rolling boil over medium-high heat, and cook 15–20 minutes or until potatoes are tender and about 90 percent of water has been absorbed. Remove from heat and allow to cool slightly. Discard any remaining liquid. Using a fork, mash potatoes and transfer to a large mixing bowl. Blend in lemon juice and ¼ pound of butter. Add sugar, vanilla, 1½ tablespoons flour, allspice and nutmeg, blending well. Set aside. In a separate bowl, blend cream cheese and remaining butter. Sprinkle in 1 cup flour and mix thoroughly. Place dough on a floured board and knead 3–4 times. Roll pie crust ⅛-inch thick. Place crust in a 9-inch pie pan and fill with sweet potato mixture. Bake approximately 1 hour. Refrigerate overnight prior to serving.

PEACH CUSTARD PIE

Prep Time: 1½ Hours
Yields: 6–8 Servings

Comment:

This recipe is a favorite among the residents of Ruston, La. Over the years, Ruston has become known as the peach capital of Louisiana. The filling in this pie is typical of French and English custards.

Ingredients for Pie Crust:

1⅓ cups flour
¼ pound cold butter, chipped
1 tbsp sugar
¼ cup ice water

Method:

In a food processor equipped with a metal blade, combine flour, butter and sugar. Pulse 1 minute or until texture of mixture resembles coarse meal. Continuing to pulse, slowly add a little water at a time, until dough forms into a ball. Remove and place on a floured surface. Roll dough ⅛-inch thick. Firmly press into a 9-inch pie or tart pan. Set aside.

Ingredients for Filling:

6–8 medium peaches
¼ cup heavy whipping cream
2 eggs
½ cup sugar
¼ cup pure vanilla extract
pinch of cinnamon
pinch of nutmeg
¼ cup powdered sugar

Method:

Preheat oven to 375°F. Using a sharp paring knife, cut peaches into ¼-inch slices and discard seeds. Arrange slices neatly around dough until all have been used. Place pie on bottom oven rack, and bake approximately 20 minutes to render juices from fruit. While pie is baking, combine all remaining ingredients, except powdered sugar, in a mixing bowl. Whisk until well blended. Remove pie from oven and pour egg mixture evenly over baked peaches. Return pie to oven, and bake 20 minutes or until custard is set. Remove from oven, and dust generously with powdered sugar. This pie may be duplicated using red or green apples.

FUNERAL PIE

Prep Time: 1 Hour
Yields: 8 Servings

Comment:

As its name suggests, this pie was often served after a funeral. The dessert, also known as raisin pie, is still eaten after funerals among the Amish in America.

Ingredients:

2 cups raisins	½ tsp allspice
2 cups water	¼ tsp salt
½ cup brown sugar	1 tbsp cider vinegar
½ cup sugar	2 tbsps butter
3 tbsps cornstarch	1 tbsp grated orange zest
½ tsp cinnamon	2 (9-inch) prepared pie crusts

Method:

Preheat oven to 400°F. Press 1 (9-inch) pie crust firmly into pie pan. In a heavy-bottomed Dutch oven, heat raisins and ⅔ cup of water over medium-high heat. Simmer 5 minutes. In a separate bowl, combine sugars, cornstarch, cinnamon, allspice and salt. Whisk in remaining water, blend well then add mixture to simmering raisins. Stir constantly until mixture bubbles. Add vinegar, butter and zest. Continue to cook until butter melts. Remove and allow mixture to cool until lukewarm. Pour filling into unbaked pie shell. Top with second pie crust and crimp edges in a decorative fashion. Cut 2–3 slits in top of crust to vent steam. Bake 25–30 minutes or until crust is golden brown and pie is bubbling. Cool completely before slicing.

SUGARED BOURBON PECANS

Prep Time: 30 Minutes
Yields: 2 Cups

Comment:

This sweet treat can be served as a party food or on top of your favorite cake or ice cream.

Ingredients:

2 cups pecans, halved
1 cup white sugar
¼ tsp nutmeg
¼ tsp cinnamon
¼ cup bourbon

Method:

In a heavy-bottomed saucepot, combine sugar and spices over medium-high heat. Add bourbon. Stir mixture constantly until it reaches soft-ball stage (234–240°F). Fold in pecan halves and mix thoroughly. Spoon out on parchment paper and allow to cool.

PUMPKIN EGGNOG PIE

Prep Time: 50 Minutes
Yields: 6–8 Servings

Comment:

Most people think of eggnog as simply a Christmastime drink. However, the beverage can be used in recipes like this to add flavor and richness. This is a classic example of how eggnog can spice up an old holiday favorite like pumpkin pie.

Ingredients:

1 cup mashed pumpkin, canned
1 cup eggnog
½ cup brown sugar, firmly packed
½ cup sugar
½ tsp salt
½ tsp cinnamon
½ tsp ginger
½ tsp nutmeg
3 eggs
1 tbsp cornstarch
1 (9-inch) unbaked pie shell

Method:

Preheat oven to 350°F. In large mixing bowl, combine all ingredients. Blend well. Pour mixture into unbaked pie shell. Bake 45 minutes or until knife inserted in center of pie comes out clean. Let cool at least 2 hours before serving.

CHOCOLATE CHESS PIE

Prep Time: 3 Hours
Yields: 8 Servings

Comment:

This dessert was developed in the 1700s because of the volume of butter, eggs and molasses available on the plantations. Today variations of chess pie include ingredients such as buttermilk, raisins, nuts and even chocolate. Some believe the name of the pie is a corruption of the word cheese because of the filling's resemblance to English curd pie. Others say chess pie is derived from the chest or pie safe that these desserts were often stored in.

Ingredients for Pie Crust:

6 tbsps cold butter
1¼ cups flour
2 tbsps shortening
¼ tsp salt
3 tbsps ice water

Method:

Preheat oven to 425°F. In a large mixing bowl, combine butter, flour, shortening and salt. Using your fingertips or a pastry cutter, blend until flour resembles coarse meal. Drizzle ice water evenly over mixture and blend until dough is formed. Gently squeeze dough to make sure texture holds together without crumbling. Additional water may be added if necessary. Turn dough onto a floured work surface and knead 8–9 times. Cover dough with plastic wrap and refrigerate 1 hour. Remove and roll out approximately ⅛-inch thick and form into a 9-inch pie pan. Line pie crust with foil and pour in a cup of raw rice or beans for weight. Place pie on center rack of oven and bake 15 minutes. Remove foil and rice. Bake 5 additional minutes or until golden brown. Remove and set aside to cool.

Ingredients for Filling:

3 ounces bittersweet chocolate, chopped
6 tbsps unsalted butter
1⅓ cups sugar
2 tbsps flour
4 eggs
3 tbsps heavy whipping cream
2 tbsps rum
1 tbsp pure vanilla extract

Method:

Reduce oven temperature to 325°F. In a large mixing bowl, combine chocolate and butter. Place bowl over a double boiler with simmering water, making sure bottom of bowl does not touch water. Whisk occasionally until chocolate and butter are melted and smooth. Remove bowl and allow chocolate to cool slightly. In a separate mixing bowl, combine sugar and flour. Whisk in eggs. Pour in chocolate then add cream, rum and vanilla. Whisk thoroughly then pour mixture into cooked pie crust. Place on center rack of oven. Bake 40 minutes or until pie is set. Cool completely and refrigerate overnight.

BOURBON PECAN PIE

Prep Time: 1 Hour
Yields: 8–10 Servings

Comment:

The abundance of pecans has made this pie a staple on the Southern table. There are innumerable recipes for pecan pie across the South. Here we have substituted the traditional ingredients of white sugar and light corn syrup with brown sugar and cane syrup to give the pie a little extra Louisiana flair.

Ingredients:

1 cup chopped pecans
¼ pound butter
3 eggs
1 cup brown sugar
¾ cup Louisiana cane syrup
¼ cup honey
2 tbsps pure vanilla extract
pinch of nutmeg
pinch of cinnamon
1 ounce bourbon
1 (9-inch) uncooked pie shell

Method:

Preheat oven to 425°F. In a sauté pan, melt butter over medium-high heat until slightly browned around edges, creating a nutty flavor. Cool butter slightly and pour into a mixing bowl. One ingredient at a time, add eggs, brown sugar, cane syrup, honey and vanilla, blending well after each addition. Add all remaining ingredients except pecans. Whisk until completely smooth. Gently fold in pecans. Pour mixture into pie shell. Bake 10 minutes then reduce temperature to 385°F. Bake 35 additional minutes. Remove and allow to cool thoroughly before slicing. It is best to make the pie 1 day prior to serving and refrigerate it overnight to ensure a solid set.

HOLIDAY CHOCOLATE PECAN PIE

Prep Time: 1 Hour
Yields: 6–8 Servings

Comment:

This recipe makes an extra-special pecan pie perfect for holiday gatherings. Chocolate has been added to enrich the basic pecan pie, creating a seasonal masterpiece.

Ingredients:

½ cup chocolate morsels
1 cup chopped pecans
½ cup sugar
1 tbsp cornstarch
1 cup light corn syrup
¼ cup Louisiana cane syrup
1 tbsp pure vanilla extract
3 eggs, beaten
pinch of cinnamon
pinch of nutmeg
1 (9-inch) uncooked pie shell

Method:

Preheat oven to 425°F. In a large mixing bowl, combine sugar and cornstarch. Add syrups, vanilla and eggs. Whisk thoroughly. Blend in pecans and chocolate. Season with a pinch of cinnamon and nutmeg. Pour mixture into pie shell and bake 10 minutes on center rack of oven. Reduce temperature to 375°F and bake 35 minutes. Remove and allow to cool to room temperature, preferably overnight.

BANANAS FOSTER CREAM PIE

Prep Time: 1 Hour
Yields: 12 Servings

Comment:

Almost every Louisiana restaurant has some form of the famous bananas Foster dessert on its menu. This dessert features sweet, tender bananas with vanilla pastry cream spiked with a shot of dark rum and a chocolate cookie crust.

Ingredients for Crust:

2½ cups Oreo® cookie crumbs
¼ cup sugar
1 tsp cinnamon
5 tbsps melted butter

Method:

Grease a 10-inch springform pan. In a medium bowl, combine cookie crumbs, sugar and cinnamon. Mix well then stir in melted butter. Press mixture into bottom and 2½ inches up sides of prepared pan. Refrigerate until chilled.

Ingredients for Filling:

¼ cup unsalted butter
¾ cup brown sugar, firmly packed
1 tsp cinnamon
1 tsp ginger
½ tsp allspice
4 bananas, peeled and sliced

Method:

In a large sauté pan over high heat, cook butter and brown sugar 2 minutes or until bubbling. Add cinnamon, ginger, allspice and bananas. Sauté 3 minutes or until tender. Spoon bananas evenly over bottom of refrigerated crust. Set aside.

Ingredients for Pastry Cream:

3 cups half-and-half
1 vanilla bean, split lengthwise
8 egg yolks
½ cup sugar
¼ cup dark rum
3 tbsps cornstarch
mint leaves for garnish (optional)

Method:

In a saucepan over medium-high heat, boil half-and-half and vanilla bean. Reduce heat to medium, remove and discard bean. In a medium bowl, whisk egg yolks, sugar, rum and cornstarch. Add approximately 1 cup of half-and-half mixture, whisking well. Pour egg mixture into remaining half-and-half over medium heat, stirring frequently 3–5 minutes or until thick. Pour cream over roasted bananas in crust, and refrigerate 2–3 hours or until well chilled. To serve, carefully remove outer ring of pan, cut pie into slices, and top each with whipped cream and several mint leaves.

CREAMY COCONUT CREAM PIE

Prep Time: 2 Hours
Yields: 6 Servings

Comment:

This no-bake coconut cream pie is simple to make, but tastes like it took all day! If you wish to crack and grate a fresh coconut, 2 cups of the freshly grated product may be substituted for the canned product in the recipe.

Ingredients:

2 (3½-ounce) cans coconut
¾ cup sugar
3 tbsps cornstarch
⅛ tsp salt
3 egg yolks
2 cups milk
1 tbsp pure vanilla extract
⅛ tsp almond extract
1 (9-inch) pre-baked pie shell
1 cup chilled whipped cream
2 tbsps powdered sugar

Method:

In a large mixing bowl, combine sugar, cornstarch and salt. Blend thoroughly. Whisk in yolks until creamy. In a 1-quart saucepan, heat milk over medium-high heat. When milk begins to slightly boil, remove from heat. Use a 4-ounce ladle to gradually add hot milk to egg mixture while whisking constantly. Transfer mixture to saucepan over low heat, stirring constantly 3–4 minutes or until thick and shiny. Remove from heat. Blend in vanilla and almond extracts then fold in 1 can coconut flakes. Pour mixture back into mixing bowl. Cover and chill 1 hour. While cream filling is cooling, place whipping cream and powdered sugar in a mixing bowl. Using an electric mixer, beat until cream is stiff and firm. Cover and refrigerate. Pour cold coconut filling into baked pie shell. Top with whipped cream and sprinkle remaining coconut on top. Refrigerate 1 hour before serving.

PORT HUDSON BUTTERMILK PIE

Prep Time: 1½ Hours
Yields: 8–10 Servings

Comment:

Buttermilk was once a by-product of the churning of milk or cream to make butter. Today, this sour-flavored milk is used as a main ingredient in salad dressings, soups and desserts.

Ingredients:

½ cup buttermilk
¾ cup sugar
¼ cup flour
½ cup melted butter
3 eggs
2 tbsps lemon juice
1 tbsp pure vanilla extract
pinch of salt
pinch of cinnamon
pinch of nutmeg
1 (9-inch) unbaked pie shell

Method:

Preheat oven to 350°F. In a large mixing bowl, combine buttermilk, sugar, flour and butter. Whisk until all lumps are removed and batter is completely smooth. Whisk in eggs, lemon juice and vanilla. Season with salt, cinnamon and nutmeg. When blended, pour batter into pie shell and bake 1 hour or until light brown and a light crust has formed on top. Allow to cool prior to serving.

CAJUN SWEET DOUGH PIES WITH SPICED PEAR FILLING

Prep Time: 1 Hour 45 Minutes
Yields: 24 Servings

Comment:

In Cajun and Creole households, these pies are extremely popular. Here, a spiced pear filling is used, but feel free to be creative and use 8 cups of any precooked pie filling. Be sure to have filling prepared before making dough.

Ingredients for Filling:

16 cups pears, peeled, cored and ½ inch diced
⅓ cup butter
2 cups sugar
½ cup lemon juice
1 tbsp cinnamon
¼ tsp nutmeg
¼ tsp ginger
2 cups water
½ cup cornstarch

Method:

In a large saucepot, melt butter over medium-high heat. Add pears, sugar, lemon juice, cinnamon, nutmeg, ginger and 1 cup water. Simmer 25–30 minutes or until pears are softened. In a mixing bowl, combine remaining water and cornstarch, mixing until starch is dissolved. Stir cornstarch into simmering pear mixture, and cook 2–4 minutes or until thickened. Place pear mixture into a large mixing bowl. Place entire mixing bowl into a pan of ice water or into refrigerator and allow to cool completely before filling pies.

Ingredients for Pies:

¼ pound margarine	10 cups flour
1 cup shortening	4 tsp baking powder
3 cups sugar	1 tsp salt
3 eggs	4 cups flour (for kneading)
1½ cups milk	1 egg, beaten
2 tsps pure vanilla extract	8 cups Spiced Pear Filling

Method:

Preheat oven to 375°F. In an extra large mixing bowl, cream margarine and shortening with an electric mixer. Slowly add sugar while beating until mixture is light and fluffy. Add eggs, 1 at a time, beating well after each addition. Blend in milk and vanilla. Using a dough hook, blend in 2 cups flour at a time until all has been incorporated. Add baking powder and salt. Continue to blend until dough ball forms. Knead dough on a large floured surface. If dough is too soft, sprinkle in additional flour. Dough should be easy to handle and should not stick to fingers. Break dough into 24 equal baseball-sized portions. On the work surface, pat each portion into a flat circle. Using a rolling pin, roll into an 8-inch circle. Place 2 tablespoons of spiced pear filling onto one side of circle. Using a pastry brush, paint edge of circle with beaten egg and fold over into a half-moon shape. Pinch edges together or crimp with a fork. Pierce 1–2 steam holes into top of pie. Repeat until all ingredients are used. Bake on a cookie sheet for approximately 30 minutes.

CHOCOLATE SOUP WITH CARAMELIZED BANANAS

Prep Time: 45 Minutes
Yields: 6 Servings

Comment:

Chocolate soup was originally created at Le Cirque 2000 in New York City by talented pastry chef Jacques Torres. The dish can be enhanced with fresh fruit, pound cake or angel food cake. To make a special holiday treat, cut pound cake with shaped cookie cutters and place in bottom of each bowl. Heart shaped cake under chocolate soup topped with strawberries is perfect for Valentine's Day.

Ingredients:

6 ounces semisweet or bittersweet chocolate
4 cups half-and-half
½ cup sugar
4 egg yolks, room temperature
⅓ cup crème de cacao
3 tbsps Frangelico

Method:

In a medium saucepan, cook chocolate, half-and-half and sugar over medium-low heat, stirring frequently until chocolate melts and sugar dissolves. In a stainless steel mixing bowl, whisk egg yolks. Add 1 cup of melted chocolate and whisk. Slowly pour egg mixture into pot of chocolate, stirring frequently. Remove from heat and stir in liqueurs. If desired, pour mixture into a container, tightly cover and refrigerate until chilled, at least 2 hours or as long as 5 days. Chilled mixture may be warmed in a double boiler while whisking constantly.

Ingredients for Caramelized Bananas:

4 large bananas, peeled and diced
¼ cup dark rum
½ cup sugar
1 tbsp unsalted butter
6 pound cake slices, diced
½ cup heavy whipping cream, lightly whipped

Method:

In a medium-sized mixing bowl, toss bananas and rum to coat well. Set aside 20 minutes at room temperature. In a cast iron skillet, melt sugar over medium-high heat until golden brown. Do not burn. Remove from heat and immediately add butter, stirring until smooth. Add bananas and rum. Return skillet to medium-high heat. Take caution as rum may ignite. Continue to cook until almost all liquid has evaporated and bananas are soft but not mushy. Remove from heat and pour onto a plate. Cover with plastic wrap and let cool approximately 20 minutes. To serve, place pound cake cubes in 6 soup bowls. Ladle an equal amount of warm chocolate soup into each bowl, garnish with a portion of bananas and a dollop of whipped cream.

JELLY ROLL

Prep Time: 45 Minutes
Yields: 6–8 Servings

Comment:

My mother made the best jelly rolls. I remember those Saturday afternoons when she would whip up the batter as we scraped the blackberry jelly from the jars. After completing the jelly rolls, mother would trim the ends square prior to slicing. These trimmings were our reward for hard work.

Ingredients:

1 cup blackberry jelly
3 eggs
1 cup sugar
¼ cup cold water
1 tbsp pure vanilla extract
¾ cup flour
2 tsps baking powder
pinch of salt
¼ cup powdered sugar

Method:

NOTE: This recipe must be cooked in a 15" x 10" cookie sheet. It is best cooked on middle oven rack. Preheat oven to 300°F. Line a cookie sheet with lightly-greased parchment paper, and grease sides of pan. In a large mixing bowl, cream eggs and sugar 3–5 minutes, whisking until smooth, fluffy and pale yellow. Whisk in water and vanilla. Blend in flour, baking powder and salt. Pour mixture onto cookie sheet and spread out evenly. Bake 10–15 minutes or until cake batter is totally set and light brown on edges. Do not overcook. When done, remove and allow to cool slightly. Place a large dishtowel on counter and cover with parchment paper. Sprinkle powdered sugar evenly over paper. After cake has cooled 5–6 minutes, turn out onto sugared paper. Beginning at 10-inch end, roll cake, jelly roll style using the towel and parchment. Allow to sit 10 minutes. Unroll, spread evenly with jelly and roll again, this time using only the parchment paper. Allow to set until cool then slice into ¼-inch pieces, sprinkle with powdered sugar and serve.

The Model Bakery, Donaldsonville, La.

Bread. Walk into any kitchen where a fresh-baked loaf scents the air and you are its slave. No appetite is necessary to crave this staff of life. More than a mere food, bread is the stuff of religion and rebellion, princes and paupers, old worlds and new. Its origins date back to the first grains harvested by man, and yet it is still being perfected today in home kitchens and artisan bakeries. While many ancient civilizations were able to master flatbread, the Egyptians are credited with making the first raised, oven-baked bread as early as 2600 B.C. because they had ready access to wheat. Most of the early grains being used by man required toasting before threshing. The toasting process rendered the proteins immune to the effects of yeast, so leavened bread was not a possibility until the advent of wheat. Until then, grains were ground into a paste for flatbread or cooked into a kind of mush that provided nourishment, but bore little resemblance to the breads we eat today. Leavening was achieved by incorporating a fermented piece of dough from the previous day into the new dough. Later, the Greeks and Romans used yeasts drawn from the process of making wine or ale. Despite the advances made in leavening agents, some bread connoisseurs maintain that a sourdough starter is still the secret to truly great bread.

Bread has been essential to life for so many centuries. It has acquired great symbolic significance in most religions, particularly Christianity and Judaism. It has also become an important part of many rituals and occasions such as Easter, Christmas, Twelfth Night, weddings, saints' days, harvest holidays and more. The designs of the loaves, particularly in Europe, are also imbued with symbolism, representing fertility, birth, death and the seasons. In Louisiana, St. Joseph's Day altars feature bread ornately shaped, decorated and baked into crosses, wreaths, St. Joseph's staff, tools and crustaceans. The tradition is an ancient one brought to America by Sicilian immigrants. St. Joseph's altar bread is highly symbolic and once blessed, is considered sacred and powerful. It is said that a tiny piece cast into the wind and a prayer to St. Joseph can calm a storm, while a morsel kept in the house can protect a family from hunger. Bread has long been the subject of superstition in other cultures as well. An old Creole belief is that a loaf of bread upside down on the table is evidence that the devil is around. It was also once considered acceptable to beat one's wife if her bread didn't rise because it was evidence of infidelity.

By the Middle Ages bread had become so vital it was found at every meal and was for some the primary source of nourishment. Land was cleared by the monks for additional wheat fields to support the large and accomplished bakeries in the monasteries. Whiter bread was made of finer flour and was therefore considered to be of better quality. While the finer flour was reserved for the lordly tables, the peasants subsisted on "black" loaves made from coarser grinds and mixed grains. Bread's primary role at aristocratic tables was as a plate or tranchoir for the meat. After the meal, the gravy and fat-soaked slabs of bread were given to the poor. The villagers brought their grain to the lord's mill to be ground and their bread to the communal oven to be baked, both of which were taxed in kind by the lord. In feudal societies, bread was so essential to life that the Old English word for lord or landholder was "hlaford" or "loaf keeper." The lady of the house was known as "hlafdige" or "kneader of loaves."

Perhaps because of its importance to subsistence, bread tends to have fallen under strict regulation in many cultures including colonial New Orleans. Because the price of bread was generally set based on weight, bakers could be prosecuted for selling underweight loaves. In the Middle Ages, guilty bakers were forced to ride through town on a pillory or cart with the underweight loaves around their necks. In New Orleans, the offending loaves were simply tossed in the Mississippi River. There were also taxes on bread and flour in Louisiana that were enforced by Spanish Governor Don Francisco Luis Hector, Baron de Carondelet to help pay for lighting and night watchmen in the streets. In later years, flour was also subject to inspection and like the underweight loaves, was tossed in the river if found unfit.

Louisiana tends to trace its bread back to France, and the bakers of Paris trace their roots back to the 12th century when, according to *The History of Bread,* those engaged in sifting purchased their rights from the king and formed a guild. The word bolengier, meaning "he who shapes the dough into a ball," eventually lent the name to the hundreds of boulangeries or bakeshops in Paris. The Italians are actually credited with popularizing white bread throughout Europe and for sharing the milling and leavening secrets gleaned from ancient Greece and Rome. Italian bakers used both a finer grade of flour and brewer's yeast for leavening. Several Italian bakers were brought to France in the 1530s by Catherine de Medici of Italy when she married Prince Henry, the second son of King Frances I. In turn, the Viennese must be credited for creating what many consider a French classic, the croissant. Introduced to France by Marie Antoinette in 1770, the croissant was actually created by Viennese bakers commemorating the siege of Vienna by the Turks in 1683. Because the bakers were the ones that sounded the alarm, they were granted the privilege of making hörnchen, symbolic of the crescent moon on the Turkish flag.

New Orleans' first recorded commercial baker was a Frenchman called Lemesle who did business under the name Bellegarde. Lemesle opened his commercial bakery in New Orleans in 1722, but had served as a baker in Mobile, Ala., for two decades prior to that. Over the next 50 years the number of French bakers and bakeries continued to steadily increase. By 1820, New Orleans was home to almost 60 bakers. That number had increased to 150 by the end of the 19th century. Louisiana's bread industry remained dominated by the French until the 1830s and the arrival of the Germans. Interestingly, even though the number of German bakers eventually outnumbered the French, they too specialized in French items.

Due to the variety of influences or perhaps, as some have suggested, because of the water, New Orleans French bread is a creature apart from that of Paris. The bread features a golden, crisp crust, which is never tough; a light, lacy interior; and a slightly tangy taste. True to its French roots, New Orleans remains a city devoted to its bread. *The New Orleans Cookbook* states that in the Crescent City one can judge the success of a meal by the amount of French bread crumbs on the table linens and floor. In fact, according to Buddy Stall, "New Orleans consumes more French bread than any other city in the world, including Paris." And while at one time there were more than 400 bakeries in New Orleans, almost all of the genuine French bread made in the city is now baked by a handful of bakeries, none of them French. In many circles, it is actually New Orleans' German bakers that are credited with perfecting the city's French bread, and it is German and Italian bakeries that are famous for their French bread today.

The idea of putting meat and bread together for a meal on the go seems too elementary to credit one person with the invention of the sandwich. However, John Montague, Earl of Sandwich, is the one for whom the creation is named. Because he was unwilling either to leave his card game or his overburdened desk, he supposedly called for a piece of cold meat between two slices of bread. That is exactly what distinguishes a mere sandwich from the specialty ones created in New Orleans. We contend that if Montague had been offered a Peacemaker, po'boy or Muffuletta, he would have laid down his cards or his pen to eat. These are the sandwiches that have made casual dining in New Orleans famous, and unlike many tourist attractions, they remain near and dear to the locals' hearts, too. The Peacemaker may even have saved

a few lives or at the very least a few marriages. In reality just a fried oyster po'boy or oyster loaf, the Peacemaker was colorfully named for its powers to placate an irate wife. Many a husband brought the Peacemaker home after a night on the town with his friends and co-workers in hopes of getting out of the doghouse. It sounds deceptively simple—succulent oysters breaded and fried, then nestled into a bed of perfect French bread enhanced only by a little mayonnaise or butter, lettuce and tomato—but its powers are miraculous. While the Peacemaker may be New Orleans' most famous po'boy, others will testify to the delights of the fried shrimp, catfish, roast beef, debris or hot sausage po'boy. While the ingredients are important and must be of excellent quality to attract such devotees, any Louisianian can tell you that the true measure of a po'boy is the bread. It must be New Orleans French bread with a crisp crust and delicate interior. It must also impart flavor to the sandwich rather than simply serve as a bland vehicle. Without these qualities, it may be a sandwich, sub, hoagie, grinder or hero, but it is not a po'boy. So what are the origins of the Big Easy's strangely named specialty? Accounts vary of course, but two legends prevail. The first is that the term "poor boy" was coined at the French Market coffee stall run by Madame Bégué in 1896 where African-American youths with no money would beg for sandwiches "for a poor boy." Madame Bégué served her sandwiches on lengths of French bread like today's po'boys. Bennie and Clovis Martin, former employees of New Orleans' streetcar company also claim to have originated the sandwich. During the streetcar strike of 1929, the two offered free food to any "poor boy" or union member who came to their French Market coffee stand and restaurant. Apparently sandwiches served on French bread were on the menu and the name stuck.

As for the Muffuletta sandwich, the name may be Italian, but this delicacy is all New Orleans. In fact, if you have traveled to the city and left without trying one, another trip is in order. While you can now find the Muffuletta at sandwich shops across Louisiana, they are not all created equal. The secret lies in the bread, a 10-inch round Italian loaf, and the olive salad. The exact recipes for the salad are jealously guarded, but generally include a combination of green and black olives, pickled Italian vegetables, pimientos, olive oil, garlic, parsley and oregano. The sandwich also includes a generous helping of Genoa salami, Cappicola ham and Provolone cheese. Most famous for their Muffulettas are Central Grocery, where the sandwich was first created in the early 20th century, and Progress Grocery, once located nearby.

But man does not live by French and Italian bread alone. In fact, when the colonists first came to America they tried planting the grains familiar to them, especially wheat, but it was several years before the yield was sufficient to support them. Although corn was available and grew easily, the colonists initially rejected it strenuously, considering it only fit for livestock. Eventually they learned from the Native Americans to appreciate the merits of corn for making puddings and breads. By the time wheat became more plentiful and affordable, corn had found a permanent place in American kitchens. Corn pone, corn pudding and of course, corn bread are still popular in "old-fashioned" cooking, particularly in the South. Commercially baked bread was available to those who lived in the city, but those out in the country had a more difficult time. Ovens were few, flour was scarce, and in Louisiana the heat was excessive, so traditional bread baking was not a priority. Instead, the Cajuns and Creoles made corn pudding, sweet potato pudding, corn bread, biscuits or rice cakes called calas.

By the 19th century, American cookbooks included an astonishing number of recipes for breads, rolls, biscuits and pastries, despite the fact that most cooks were still limited to open fireplaces and perhaps a cast iron Dutch oven. During the Civil War crude, outdoor ovens would be built to bake the daily bread for the soldiers as they moved from

place to place. In fact, in the 1800s a Folse family relative baked bread for his Confederate comrades while they were stationed near Vacherie, La. While it might not have been available to Folse in the field, bakers did receive a big help just prior to the Civil War with the advent of a leavening agent called saleratus—later named baking soda. The soda, when mixed with an acid like cream of tartar, provided a rising effect for breads and cakes. By 1856, baking powder, which pre-combined the soda and acid, was available. Commercial yeast was not available until 1868. As the authors of *Eating In America* point out, it is no wonder that in this country, as in many civilizations before, bread making was one of the first things that homemakers were more than happy to hand over to commercial providers. The industrialization and commercialization of the 20th century and two world wars also had the effect of drawing women out of the kitchen and into the workplace, leaving little time for breadmaking. According to authors Root and de Rochemont, 95 percent of the flour sold in the United States in 1900 was purchased for home baking, but by 1970, that number had fallen to 15 percent.

While many have willingly given up baking the family's daily bread as far too time consuming, quickbreads, muffins, biscuits and pancakes still remain firmly in the realm of home baking. Most of these breads do not require yeast and are therefore more adaptable to our busy lifestyles. There is even a wide variety of pre-mixed products that can make the most inexperienced baker feel accomplished. Without a doubt, there is a satisfaction and joy to turning out one's own bread. The recipes that follow are tried and true and guarantee delicious, aromatic results each time. Impress your family, amaze your friends and become a boulangier.

Clifton "Kippy" Hymel, Sr.

Bread From Heaven

I grew up down the River Road from a wonderful little bakery in St. James run by the Hymel family. My many fond memories of the St. James Bakery, were recently enhanced for me by an account written by Nathan Folse, the great-grandson of bakery co-founder George Hymel. The bakery was opened by Valsin Hymel, who had learned the business working at another bakery owned by his uncle and godfather, Louis Hymel. With backing from Louis, Valsin and his son George started off by renting an existing bakery and opened for business as V. Hymel and Son Bakery in 1908. The store became a mainstay in the St. James community for 65 years. In 1918 the father and son team built their own shop. By then George had married Marie Guidry and the couple raised their 12 children in the main house in front of the bakery.

In the bakery's early days the bread was delivered house-to-house by horse and buggy. Later, delivery trucks took over, delivering bread between the communities of Welcome and Saint Philip and from north to south Vacherie. Preparations for the next day's bread deliveries began the morning before.

French bread, raisin bread, buns, pan bread, Pullman bread (a rectangular loaf cooked in a lidded pan), ginger cake, brioche and more were baked in a brick hearth oven which was initially fired by wood and later by natural gas. As they grew, George's children all had jobs sweeping up flour, wrapping bread, greasing pans and carrying firewood. The older boys helped with deliveries and even made a little extra money delivering items such as *The Times-Picayune* newspaper with the morning's bread.

World War II was a trying time for the bakery. Four of the Hymel boys were drafted and wartime restrictions on sugar, tires and gasoline took their toll. The bakery survived, but in 1945 Valsin Hymel died. George changed the bakery's name to St. James Bakery, the name I grew up knowing. George retired in 1963, but died just two years later. His brother Jules, who had worked at the bakery since 1921, retired in 1969, leaving Marie and her son Ivy as sole proprietors. Unfortunately, the bakery closed in 1973 and the building burned in 1976. All that remained were the brick walls of the oven and my childhood memories of delicious bread from St. James Bakery.

SWEET AND AIRY CORN BREAD

Prep Time: 30 Minutes
Yields: 9 Servings

Comment:
The best corn bread recipes in the South create a light and fluffy bread that can even be used as a dessert.

Ingredients:
1 cup cornmeal
1 cup flour
1½ tbsps baking powder
½ cup sugar

1 tsp salt
1½ cups milk
2 eggs, beaten
¼ cup melted butter

Method:
Preheat oven to 450°F. In a large mixing bowl, sift together cornmeal, flour, baking powder, sugar and salt. Whisk in milk, eggs and butter, blending until lumps are removed. Lightly grease an 8-inch square baking pan with cooking spray or butter. Pour batter into greased pan and bake 20–25 minutes. NOTE: For an interesting twist, add ½ cup fresh kernel corn and 1 tablespoon chopped jalapeños.

SOUTHERN-STYLE CORN BREAD

Prep Time: 45 Minutes
Yields: 8 Servings

Comment:

Southern corn bread is thin, crusty and decidedly savory. Though some styles of Southern corn bread are dry and crumbly, this is a dense, moist, tender version. The secret of this recipe is to mix the cornmeal mush to the right texture. Corn bread is best prepared in a preheated cast iron skillet. However, a 9-inch round or square pan will produce the same results. To cook in 9-inch pan, double recipe, grease pan lightly and bake 25 minutes.

Ingredients:

4 tsps bacon drippings
   OR 1 tbsp melted butter
   and 1 tsp vegetable oil
1 cup stone-ground yellow cornmeal
1 cup flour
2 tbsps sugar

½ tsp salt
2 tbsps baking powder
1 tbsp baking soda
½ cup rapidly boiling water
1 cup buttermilk
1 large egg, beaten lightly

Method:

Adjust oven rack to lower middle position and heat to 450°F. Set an 8-inch cast iron skillet with bacon drippings in oven. In a mixing bowl, combine ⅔ cup cornmeal, flour, sugar, salt, baking powder and baking soda. Set aside. In a separate bowl, place remaining ⅓ cup cornmeal and pour in boiling water. Stir to create a stiff mush. Gradually whisk in buttermilk, breaking up lumps until smooth. Whisk in egg. When oven is preheated and skillet very hot, stir dry cornmeal mixture into mush until just moistened. Carefully remove skillet from oven. Stir hot bacon drippings into batter. Quickly pour batter into heated skillet. Bake 20 minutes or until golden brown. Remove from oven and immediately turn corn bread onto wire rack. Cool 5 minutes then serve immediately.

SPICY CORN BREAD SKILLET CAKE

Prep Time: 1 Hour
Yields: 6 Servings

Comment:

There are many recipes in the South that have evolved from corn bread batters. After the Civil War, food was scarce, so people were unable to cook extravagant dishes. Therefore, simple dishes emerged with added twists to "fancy 'em up." This skillet cake is a variation of corn bread that is interesting and versatile.

Ingredients:

1 cup yellow cornmeal
½ cup flour
1 tbsp sugar
½ tsp salt
⅛ tsp cayenne pepper
2 tsps baking soda
½ cup milk
1 egg, beaten
1 tbsp melted butter
½ cup cream corn
1 jalapeño, diced
½ cup minced onions
¼ cup sliced green onions
½ cup crushed bacon
2 tbsps bacon drippings

Method:

Preheat oven to 350°F. Lightly grease a 10-inch cast iron skillet and set aside. In a large mixing bowl, whisk together cornmeal, flour, sugar, salt, cayenne pepper, baking soda, milk and egg. Add butter, corn, jalapeños, onions and green onions. Whisk until completely smooth. Thoroughly blend in bacon and bacon drippings. Pour batter into greased skillet and bake 20–25 minutes or until golden brown. Serve with flavored butter or cream cheese.

CREOLE CORN BREAD

Prep Time: 45 Minutes
Yields: 8 Servings

Comment:

Ever since the Native Americans introduced corn to Americans, corn bread has been a staple on the Southern table. The Creoles adapted this simple bread, using different ingredients and flavorings such as jalapeños to create new recipes.

Ingredients:

1 cup cornmeal
1 can cream corn
1 pound ground meat
1 tsp salt
1 tsp baking soda
1 cup milk
1 egg
1 onion, diced
1½ cups grated cheese
2 jalapeño peppers, seeded and minced

Method:

Preheat oven to 375°F. In a medium saucepan, brown meat over medium-high heat. In a separate bowl, combine cornmeal, corn, salt, baking soda, milk and egg. Blend well. Pour half of cornmeal mixture into a cast iron skillet. Layer ground meat, onions, cheese and jalapeños on top of corn batter. Pour remaining cornmeal over layers. Place in oven and bake 45 minutes or until golden brown.

PERSIMMON NUT BREAD

Prep Time: 1½ Hours
Yields: 1 Loaf

Comment:

Persimmons are no different from any other fruit. Before their peak of ripeness, they can be bitter and astringent. However, once ripe and soft to the touch, this fruit explodes with a sweet, sugary flavor. Persimmons are perfect for jams, jellies and breads.

Ingredients:

1½ cups mashed persimmons
1 cup chopped pecans
2 cups flour
1½ tsps baking powder
½ tsp baking soda
2 eggs

5 tbsps butter
¼ cup buttermilk
1 tsp lemon juice
½ cup sugar
¼ tsp salt

Method:

Preheat oven to 350°F. Grease and flour a standard loaf pan. In a large mixing bowl, sift together flour, baking powder and baking soda. Set aside. In an electric mixer, food processor or blender, combine persimmons, eggs, butter, buttermilk, lemon juice, sugar and salt. Blend until smooth. Slowly add flour mixture, continuing to mix. Fold in nuts. Pour batter into pan and bake 1 hour 25 minutes or until toothpick inserted in bread comes out clean.

YAM BREAD

Prep Time: 1½ Hours
Yields: 3 Loaves

Comment:

Yam bread is quite similar to breakfast breads such as banana nut or zucchini. These types of breads are especially delicious when eaten slightly warm with a pat of butter.

Ingredients:

2½ cups sugar	1 tsp cinnamon
1 cup vegetable oil	1 tsp nutmeg
4 eggs	⅔ cup water
2½ cups sifted flour	2 cups cooked sweet potatoes, mashed
2 tsps baking soda	1 cup chopped pecans
½ tsp salt	

Method:

Grease 3 (9" x 5") loaf pans. Preheat oven to 350°F. In a large mixing bowl, whisk together sugar and oil. Add eggs, 1 at a time, whisking after each addition. In a separate mixing bowl, combine dry ingredients. Add egg mixture, a little at a time, alternating with water. Fold in sweet potatoes and chopped nuts. Pour batter into 3 pans and bake 1 hour or until toothpick inserted in center comes out clean.

SOUTHERN PUMPKIN AND PECAN BREAD

Prep Time: 1 Hour 15 Minutes
Yields: 2 Loaves

Comment:

Pumpkin is a unique vegetable that can fit into any recipe ranging from soups to desserts because of its flavor and texture. This pumpkin and pecan bread recipe is perfect for Southern dinners.

Ingredients:

2 cups canned pumpkin	1 tsp nutmeg
1 cup corn oil	1 tsp cinnamon
4 eggs, beaten	2 tsps baking soda
⅔ cup water	3 cups sugar
3⅓ cups sifted flour	½ cup golden raisins
1½ tsps salt	½ cup chopped pecans

Method:

Preheat oven to 350°F. Grease and flour 2 loaf pans. In a large mixing bowl, combine pumpkin, oil, eggs and water. Whisk thoroughly. Sprinkle in flour until well blended. Add salt, nutmeg, cinnamon, baking soda and sugar, stirring gently. Fold in raisins and pecans. Pour mixture into loaf pans and bake 1 hour.

SWEET POTATO PUMPKIN BREAD

Prep Time: 1½ Hours
Yields: 1 Loaf

Comment:

Both sweet potatoes and pumpkins are indigenous to South Louisiana and are most often cooked in desserts or sweetened casseroles. Here, the two are combined to create a quick and easy bread that is sure to please.

Ingredients:

¾ cup sweet potatoes, cubed
¾ cup pumpkin, cubed
3 cups sugar
4 eggs
½ cup oil
2 tbsps cinnamon
2 tbsps nutmeg
3½ cups flour
1 tsp salt
2 tsps baking soda
½ cup water
¾ cup raisins
1 cup pecans
pecan halves for garnish

Method:

NOTE: This recipe may be simplified by using 8-ounce cans of cooked sweet potatoes and pumpkin in place of fresh vegetables. Preheat oven to 350°F. In a saucepot, parboil sweet potatoes and pumpkin cubes until tender. Drain, mash and set aside. In a large mixing bowl, blend sugar and eggs with a hand mixer until creamy. Add oil, sweet potatoes and pumpkin. Mix on high speed until creamy. Reduce speed to low while adding dry ingredients alternately with water. Beat until well blended. Stir in raisins and pecans. Pour batter into a standard loaf pan. Bake 1 hour or until golden brown. Garnish with pecan halves or for an added touch, glaze with Louisiana cane syrup.

BANANA ZUCCHINI BREAD

Prep Time: 1½ Hours
Yields: 2 Loaves

Comment:

There are many recipes in regional cookbooks that combine fruit and vegetables. Most often, this combination is found in bread and muffin recipes. This unique banana bread is excellent for breakfast. The batter can also be used to make muffins.

Ingredients:

2 cups mashed bananas
2 cups grated zucchini
3 eggs, beaten

2 cups sugar
1 cup vegetable oil
1 tsp pure vanilla extract

3½ cups self-rising flour
1 tsp cinnamon
1 cup chopped pecans

Method:

Preheat oven to 350°F. Grease 2 standard loaf pans and set aside. In a large mixing bowl, whisk together eggs, sugar, oil and vanilla. Blend in zucchini. Slowly add flour, stirring until well blended. Gently fold in bananas, cinnamon and pecans. Spoon batter into loaf pan and bake 45 minutes or until toothpick inserted in center comes out clean. Cool in pans for 5 minutes then remove to a wire rack. For best taste, serve warm.

BLUEBERRY-ORANGE-PECAN QUICK BREAD

Prep Time: 1 Hour 15 Minutes
Yields: 1 Loaf

Comments:

Not all breads take the whole day to make. With quick recipes such as this one, bread can be served piping hot in a little over an hour. Unlike most quick breads, fruit-and-nut loaves taste better if they are wrapped in foil and allowed to sit for a day or two before slicing. To keep the berries from sinking to the bottom of the batter, sprinkle them with flour then shake off the excess in a colander before folding them in.

Ingredients:

1 cup fresh or frozen blueberries
½ cup squeezed orange juice
2 tsps grated orange zest
½ cup chopped pecans
2 cups flour
2 tsps baking powder
½ tsp salt
¼ tsp baking soda
¼ tsp nutmeg
½ cup sugar
2 eggs, lightly beaten
¼ cup milk
⅓ cup butter, melted and cooled

Method:

Preheat oven to 350°F. Lightly grease and flour a standard loaf pan. In large mixing bowl, sift together flour, baking powder, salt, baking soda, nutmeg and sugar. Stir in pecans. In a separate bowl, beat eggs, milk, orange juice and zest. Blend in butter. Pour liquids into dry ingredients, stirring until barely moist. Gently fold in blueberries. Pour batter into loaf pan. Bake 1 hour or until crust is golden brown and toothpick inserted in center comes out clean. Let cool in pan 10 minutes then turn out onto a wire rack to cool.

BANANA WALNUT BREAD IN A JAR

Prep Time: 1 Hour
Yields: 8 (1-pint) Jars

Comment:
Cooks are always looking for perfect homemade gifts to give during the holidays or when visiting friends and family. Jar cakes are perfect for such occasions because many can be made and stored in the pantry for future use.

Ingredients:
2 cups mashed bananas
⅔ cup chopped walnuts
⅔ cup shortening
2 ⅔ cups sugar
4 eggs
3⅓ cups flour
½ tsp baking powder
2 tsps baking soda
1½ tsps salt
1 tsp cinnamon
1 tsp ground cloves
⅔ cup water

Method:
Preheat oven to 325°F. In a large mixing bowl, cream together shortening and sugar. Beat in eggs and bananas. In a separate bowl, sift together flour, baking powder, baking soda, salt, cinnamon and cloves. Add dry mixture to bananas. Fold in nuts and water, blending well. Grease 8 widemouthed pint jars. Using a large-mouth funnel, fill jars halfway with batter. Wipe any excess batter off of rim. Do not put lids on jars for baking. Place jars on a large baking sheet, place in oven and bake approximately 45 minutes. Sterilize lids and rings in boiling water. When bread is done, quickly remove 1 jar at a time from oven and clean its sealing edge with a dry towel to remove any residue or oil. Immediately apply and firmly tighten a 2-piece widemouthed canning lid. Lid will form a vacuum seal as jar cools. Jars of cooled bread may be stored on pantry shelves with other canned foods or in the freezer. Bread is safe to eat as long as jars remain vacuum sealed and free of mold growth.

BASIC QUICK BREAD

Prep Time: 1 Hour 15 Minutes
Yields: 1 Loaf

Comment:

A quick bread uses baking powder and baking soda instead of yeast to help it to rise. The bread does not require kneading or rising time before baking. Quick bread recipes range from savory to sweet and can have any number of fruit, vegetable and nut ingredients.

Ingredients:

2 cups flour
½ tsp baking powder
½ tsp baking soda
½ tsp salt
½ cup butter, softened
¾ cup sugar
2 eggs
1 cup buttermilk

Method:

Preheat oven to 350°F. Grease and flour a standard loaf pan. In large bowl, combine flour, baking powder, baking soda and salt. In a separate mixing bowl, beat butter and sugar with an electric mixer on high speed 3 minutes or until light and fluffy. Blend in eggs then add buttermilk. Mix in dry ingredients on low speed until blended. Spoon batter into loaf pan. Bake 1 hour or until toothpick inserted in center comes out clean. Let cool in pan 5 minutes. Remove from pan and cool 1 hour on a wire rack before slicing.

HERBAL BEER BREAD

Prep Time: 1 Hour
Yields: 1 Loaf

Comment:

This recipe produces a dense loaf with a textured, crunchy crust. The bread is excellent for snacks and perfect as an accompaniment for hearty dishes like gumbo, stew or pasta.

Ingredients:

3 cups self-rising flour
3 tbsps sugar
1 tbsp dried herbs or 2 tbsps fresh herb blend
12 ounces beer, room temperature
3 tbsps butter or margarine

Method:

Preheat oven to 350°F. Generously grease a standard loaf pan then set aside. In a 2-quart bowl, combine flour, sugar and herbs. Stir to mix thoroughly. Gently fold in beer just until mixture is evenly moistened, do not over mix. Pour batter into pan and dot with remaining butter. Bake 45–50 minutes or until crust is lightly browned. Remove from oven, cut into thick slices and serve immediately. Enjoy this bread with a cheese spread or Herbal Spreads. (See recipes.)

BEER, SUN-DRIED TOMATO AND OLIVE QUICK BREAD

Prep Time: 50 Minutes
Yields: 1 Loaf

Comment:

Although quick breads are made without yeast, this loaf has a yeast-like flavor from the addition of beer. Try toasting slices of this bread and using it to make your favorite sandwich.

Ingredients:

1 (12-ounce) bottle of beer (not dark)
½ cup chopped sun-dried tomatoes packed in oil
⅓ cup chopped pimiento-stuffed olives
3½ cups flour
1 tsp salt
½ tsp baking soda
1 tsp double-acting baking powder
1 large egg, lightly beaten

Method:

Preheat oven to 350°F. Grease and flour a standard loaf pan. In a large bowl, whisk together flour, salt, baking soda and baking powder. Whisk in egg. Drain tomatoes, reserving 1 teaspoon oil. Add beer, tomatoes with reserved oil and olives. Stir mixture until just combined. Pour batter into pan and bake on middle rack of oven 40 minutes or until a toothpick inserted in center comes out clean. Turn bread out onto a wire rack and allow to cool.

ROLLIN' FELICIANA BRAN MUFFINS

Prep Time: 1 Hour
Yields: 48 Muffins

Comment:
The Feliciana Parishes of Louisiana are quite different from other areas of the state because of their rolling hills. Settlers often compared the area to the English countryside. This bran muffin recipe originated in the Feliciana Parishes.

Ingredients:
1 (20-ounce) box raisin bran cereal
4 cups sugar
5 cups flour
1½ tbsps baking soda
2 tsps salt
1 tbsp cinnamon
1 tsp nutmeg
4 eggs, beaten
1 quart buttermilk
1 cup vegetable oil
1 cup raisins

Method:
Preheat oven to 400°F. In a large mixing bowl, combine all dry ingredients. Using a large spoon, blend well. Add eggs, buttermilk and oil. Continue to blend while using the back of a cooking spoon to break cereal into smaller pieces. Fold in raisins then set aside.

Ingredients for Filling:
2 (8-ounce) packages cream cheese
⅔ cup sugar
4 tbsps flour
2 tbsps pure vanilla extract

Method:
Allow cream cheese to soften at room temperature. In a large mixing bowl, combine cream cheese with sugar and flour. Blend well then stir in vanilla. NOTE: This filling may be refrigerated for up to 2 weeks prior to use. Grease muffin tin and dust with flour. Place 1-ounce ladle of raisin bran batter into each muffin compartment. Top with 1 teaspoon of cream cheese filling. Top cream cheese with another 1-ounce ladle of batter. Bake 20–25 minutes or until golden brown.

STRAWBERRY PECAN MUFFINS

Prep Time: 30 Minutes
Yields: 12 Muffins

Comment:
In many ways muffins are like biscuits, but they are usually made with a looser, sweeter dough. To keep muffins moist and tender, keep mixing to an absolute minimum, stirring only in 10–20 second intervals.

Ingredients:
¾ cup chopped strawberries
¼ cup chopped pecans
2 cups flour
2 tsps baking powder
½ tsp salt
2 tbsps sugar
pinch of cinnamon
pinch of nutmeg
1 cup milk
1 egg, beaten
3 tbsps vegetable oil

Method:
It is always best to sift dry ingredients to give muffins a lighter texture, but it is not mandatory. Preheat oven to 425°F. In a large mixing bowl, sift together flour, baking powder, salt, sugar, cinnamon and nutmeg. In a separate bowl, whisk together milk, egg and oil. NOTE: If desired, sauté strawberries in 3 tablespoons oil to render liquid prior to adding to milk mixture. This will ensure muffins are not watery or soggy, especially if berries are overripe. Fold strawberries and pecans into milk mixture. Pour liquid ingredients into flour mixture, stirring gently with a fork until moist. DO NOT beat this batter. Once blended, fill greased muffin cups ⅔ full. Bake on center oven rack 20–25 minutes or until toothpick inserted in center comes out clean.

CORN BREAD MUFFINS

Prep Time: 1 Hour
Yields: 16 Muffins

Comment:

Corn bread can be made in skillets, stick pans or muffin tins. However, it is hard to make a good corn bread without cast iron cookware. The pan should always be heated to about 400°F in the oven before the batter is added. Older South Louisianians suggest adding crackling or bacon and whole kernels of corn to enhance the flavor. Corn bread has been referred to as skillet bread, hush puppies, spoon bread and corn sticks. Whatever you call it and however you cook it, it is still good ol' Southern corn bread.

Ingredients:

1¼ cups yellow cornmeal
¼ cup whole kernel corn
¾ cup flour
2½ tsps double-acting baking powder
2 tbsps sugar
1 tsp salt
1 egg
3 tbsps melted butter
1 cup milk

Method:

Preheat oven to 425°F. Grease 2 (8-cup) muffin pans and set aside. In a large mixing bowl, combine flour, baking powder, sugar and salt. Mix well then add cornmeal. Blend in egg, butter and milk. Fold corn into batter. Pour batter into muffin tins and bake 20–25 minutes or until golden brown.

ORANGE MARMALADE MUFFINS

Prep Time: 1 Hour
Yields: 8 Muffins

Comment:

These simple muffins have a delicious fruity flavor perfect for breakfast. If desired, substitute any fruit marmalade or preserve.

Ingredients:

½ cup orange marmalade
2 cups flour
½ cup sugar
1 tbsp baking powder
1 large egg
1 cup plain yogurt or buttermilk
¼ cup melted butter
1 tsp pure vanilla extract
¾ cup chopped pecans

Method:

Preheat oven to 375°F. Grease 8 muffin cups or line with baking cups. In a large mixing bowl, whisk together flour, sugar and baking powder. In a separate bowl, combine egg, yogurt or buttermilk, butter, vanilla and pecans. Whisk until smooth. Pour egg mixture into flour and fold 2–3 times until moistened. Do not over mix. Spoon 1 heaping tablespoon of batter into each muffin tin. Using the back of a teaspoon, press a small dimple into batter. Place 1 teaspoon of marmalade into the dimple of each muffin and top with 2 additional tablespoons batter. Bake 25–30 minutes or until muffins are golden brown. Allow muffins to cool 5 minutes prior to removing from oven. Cool 5 minutes at room temperature then serve warm with softened butter.

ZUCCHINI MUFFINS

Prep Time: 1 Hour
Yields: 36 Muffins or 2 Small Loaves

Comment:

The Italians brought many different vegetable breads to Louisiana that have since been transformed to muffins, cakes and bread puddings. These breads are not only a great way to get your daily vegetable requirements, but they are also an interesting alternative to ordinary breakfast muffins.

Ingredients:

3 cups shredded zucchini
3 eggs, beaten
1 cup applesauce
2 cups sugar
1 tbsp pure vanilla extract
3 cups flour
1 tsp baking soda
½ tsp baking powder
1 tbsp cinnamon
¼ tsp salt
½ cup chopped pecans

Method:

Preheat oven to 325°F. Grease a muffin pan or 2 square loaf pans. In a large mixing bowl, combine eggs, applesauce, sugar and vanilla. Whisk until well blended. Using a cooking spoon, blend in flour. Add baking soda, baking powder, cinnamon and salt. Mix well. Fold in pecans and zucchini until well blended. Pour batter equally into muffin or loaf pans, and bake 20 minutes for muffins and 40 minutes for loaves.

NEW ORLEANS FRENCH BREAD

Prep Time: 3 Hours
Yields: 2 Loaves

Comment:
New Orleans French bread is the only bread you should use to make an authentic po'boy. This loaf differs somewhat from a French baguette in that the interior is not as dense.

Ingredients:
1 tsp yeast
¾ cup and 2 tbsps water (90°F)
6 tbsps bread flour
1¼ cups and 2 tbsps high gluten flour
¾ tsp vital wheat gluten
1¼ tsps pure cane syrup or brown sugar
½ tsp salt
½ tsp shortening

Method:
Dissolve yeast in 90°F water. Set aside. In an electric mixer, combine bread flour, gluten flour, wheat gluten, cane syrup and salt. Add dissolved yeast and mix 3 minutes. Use a dough hook attachment on medium-low speed, or mix by hand until dough develops a smooth and elastic texture. Add shortening and blend 3 minutes in mixer or 4–6 minutes by hand. Cover bowl with plastic wrap and let rest 20 minutes. Scrape dough onto lightly-floured surface and press out into a 12-inch wide rectangle. Fold in 3-fold fashion, bringing right side into middle and then folding left side on top of right. Lay dough back in bowl to rest 45 minutes. Scrape dough onto a lightly-floured surface, cut in half and roll each half into an oblong shape, cover and let rest 15–20 minutes. Pat down each piece and roll into shape of a loaf. Place on a perforated pan or a sheet pan. Cover bread with a larger pan. Set in a warm area and allow to rise until 2–3 times original size. Preheat oven to 450°F. Score top of loaf with 3 slits and brush bread lightly with water. Bake 10–12 minutes. When done, bread should be a light, pale brown color. Remove and allow to cool. Bread will soften in about 15–20 minutes. Let cool then wrap in plastic wrap. If available, brown paper is preferred. To reheat, unwrap and place in a 400°F oven for about 6–8 minutes or until crisp.

Chef David Harris bakes French bread at the Rural Life Museum, Baton Rouge, La.

HOT CROSS BUNS

Prep Time: 3 Hours
Yields: 18 Buns

Comment:

Traditionally, hot cross buns are served during the Lenten season especially in England. The symbol on the bread represents the cross of Christ. The now Christian custom probably originated from pagan rituals in which these types of breads were used in honor of goddesses.

Ingredients for Bread:

¾ cup warm water
1 tbsp active dry yeast
⅓ cup sugar
1 cup warm milk
8 tbsps unsalted butter, melted
1 tsp salt
3 large eggs
4–5 cups unbleached flour
1 cup dried currants
½ cup diced dried apricots
½ tsp ground mace
½ tsp pure vanilla extract

Method:

Twenty minutes before baking, place a rack in middle of oven and preheat to 375°F. In a small mixing bowl, combine ¾ cup warm water, yeast and a pinch of sugar. Stir until dissolved then let stand 10 minutes or until foamy. In a large mixing bowl, whisk together remaining sugar, milk, butter, salt, eggs and 1 cup flour until moistened. Using a wooden spoon, beat vigorously 1 minute. Add yeast mixture, dried fruits, mace, vanilla and 1 cup flour. Beat 1 minute or until well blended. Add remaining flour, ½ cup at a time, until a soft dough forms. Turn dough onto a lightly-floured surface and knead 3 minutes or until soft, smooth and springy. Dust dough with flour, 1 tablespoon at a time, as needed to prevent sticking. Blend in any fruit that falls out during kneading. Place dough in a deep, greased bowl, turn once to coat top then cover with plastic wrap. Let rise at room temperature 1 hour or until doubled in size. Gently deflate dough then turn out onto a floured work surface. Grease two baking sheets or line them with baking parchment. Divide dough into 2 equal portions. Roll each portion into a 10-inch log and cut into 9 equal portions. Form each portion into a round bun. Place each bun 1½ inches apart on baking sheets. Let rise, uncovered, 30 minutes or until doubled. With a sharp knife, cut a cross no more than ½-inch deep in each bun. Bake each sheet separately, 15–20 minutes or until buns are browned and sound hollow when tapped.

Christy Lill enjoys Hot Cross Buns.

HOLIDAY BREAD

Prep Time: 4 Hours
Yields: 2 Loaves

Comment:
This soft-centered bread is often served hot out of the oven on holidays as a special treat. This family recipe from Lake Charles, La., gives a simple technique that creates a masterful loaf.

Ingredients:
2 packages quick-acting yeast
1 tsp sugar
½ cup warm water
6 cups bread flour
1½ tsps baking powder
2 tbsps shortening
2 tbsps sugar
1 tsp salt
1½ cups warm water
¼ cup melted butter

Method:
Dissolve yeast and 1 teaspoon sugar in ½ cup warm water. Set aside to blossom approximately 10 minutes. Grease 2 loaf pans and set aside. In a large mixing bowl, combine flour, baking powder and shortening. Using a pastry cutter, mix shortening into flour. Add 2 tablespoons sugar, salt, 1½ cups warm water and blossomed yeast mixture. Blend well until a dough ball forms. On a lightly-floured surface, knead dough 5–8 minutes. Place in a lightly-greased bowl and cover with a dry cloth. Set in a warm place to rise approximately 1 hour. Once doubled in size, punch dough down, cover and allow it to rise 1 additional hour. Punch down dough again then divide in half. Form each half into a loaf and place in pans. Cover each pan and allow dough to double in size again. Preheat oven to 375°F. Bake bread 1 hour or until golden brown. Remove from oven and brush each loaf with melted butter. When ready to serve, slice and top with additional butter or honey.

Ingredients for Sugar Glaze:
¼ cup sugar
½ cup water

Method:
Combine sugar and water in a heavy saucepan. Boil uncovered 5 minutes. When buns are done, remove to a cooling rack and brush immediately with glaze. Let cool.

Ingredients for Lemon Icing:
1 cup sifted powdered sugar
1 tsp fresh lemon juice
1 tsp grated lemon zest
1½ tbsps milk

Method:
In a mixing bowl, combine all ingredients and whisk until smooth. When glaze is dry, place icing in a pastry bag fitted with a small, plain tip. Pipe a cross over top of each bun, following imprint of incision. Let stand 20 minutes or until set.

HUSH PUPPIES

Prep Time: 30 Minutes
Yields: 15–20 Hush Puppies

Comment:

Nobody really knows where the name "hush puppies" came from, but legend has it that an old Creole cook invented the term. As the cook was frying a batch of catfish, she was whipping up a batch of corn fritters that she called "croquettes de mais." Her hungry hunting dogs began to howl in the pen next door. The cook tossed a few pieces of croquettes to the dogs and yelled, "hush puppies!" The name has been associated with the bread ever since.

Ingredients:

1¼ cup yellow cornmeal
2 cups flour
3 tsps baking powder
1 tsp sugar
salt and cracked black pepper to taste
1 small onion, diced

1 egg, beaten
2 cups milk
2 cups whole kernel corn
¼ cup sliced green onions
vegetable oil for deep frying

Method:

In a home-style deep fryer, such as a FryDaddy, heat oil according to manufacturer's directions. In a large mixing bowl, combine cornmeal, flour, baking powder, sugar, salt and pepper. Mix until well blended. Add onions, egg, milk, corn and green onions. Mix until batter is smooth and free of lumps. Using a soup spoon or a small ice cream scoop, drop 1 portion of batter into oil to test. Hush puppy is done when it floats and is golden brown. Adjust seasonings and cooking time if necessary. Continue to fry until all are done.

SARAH'S HOT WATER BREAD

Prep Time: 30 Minutes
Yields: 10–12 Sticks

Comment:
Sarah Albriton is an authority on Louisiana and soul cooking. She owns Sarah's Kitchen in Ruston, La., where the sign outside proudly states, "The home of no box, no can cooking." In addition, Sarah represents Louisiana nationwide and has received accolades for her African-American cuisine. This simple, dense, sweet water corn bread was served to patrons who attended an evening with Sarah at the Smithsonian Institute in Washington, D.C.

Ingredients:
4 cups boiling water
2 cups white cornmeal
salt to taste
vegetable oil for frying
Louisiana cane syrup (optional)

Method:
In a large skillet, heat ½ inch oil over medium-high heat to approximately 350°F. In a large mixing bowl, combine boiling water, cornmeal and salt. Blend well until no lumps remain. Coat hands lightly with a layer of cooking oil and roll golf ball sized portions of batter into cigar-shaped pones. Fry bread in small batches 2–3 minutes or until golden brown on each side. Serve hot with cane syrup.

MAW MAW CONIGLIO'S FRY BREAD

Prep Time: 30 Minutes
Yields: 2 Dozen

Comment:
The Native Americans originally created fry breads with corn flour. It is believed that they began deep frying breads upon the arrival of the Europeans, who brought ironware and wheat flour to America. Fry breads are hearty breakfast breads that taste great and are inexpensive to make.

Ingredients:
2 cups self-rising flour
¼ cup flour
1 cup milk
1 cup vegetable oil

Method:
In a large mixing bowl, combine flours and milk. Turn dough onto a lightly-floured surface and knead until easy to handle. Pat dough into a flat pie shape, approximately ¼-inch thick. In a frying pan, heat oil. Cut dough in half, then cut it into 3" x 1" strips. Cut 1–2 long slits in each strip to help bread cook thoroughly. Fry strips in hot oil. The dough will fry quickly, so be careful to remove them as soon as they turn brown. NOTE: Fry breads taste best when dipped into a hot cup of Community® Coffee.

STUFFED OREILLE DE COCHON

Prep Time: 1 Hour
Yields: 4 Triangles

Comment:
The translation for this dish is literally "pig's ear." This peculiar name came about because of the appearance of the finished product. Originally, Oreille de Cochon was a fried triangle of dough that would curl during cooking. These pastries were served with cane syrup or powdered sugar as a dessert.

Ingredients:
2 cups biscuit mix
1¼ cups pancake mix
1 cup milk
12 ounces white boudin (see Boudin Blanc recipe)
vegetable oil for frying
powdered sugar (optional)
Louisiana cane syrup (optional)

Method:
In a home-style deep fryer, such as a FryDaddy, preheat oil according to manufacturer's directions to 375°F. In a large mixing bowl, blend together biscuit and pancake mix. Add milk and stir until dough ball forms. Turn dough onto a floured work surface and knead 8–10 times, dusting with additional flour if too sticky. Divide dough into 4 equal portions and roll each section into a rectangle shape approximately ¼-inch thick. Using a knife, trim each rectangle into a 6" x 9" triangle. Place 3 ounces of boudin along 6-inch side and roll dough in crescent roll fashion, pinching ends to seal in boudin. Fry triangles 3 minutes on each side or until golden brown and floating. Serve with powdered sugar and cane syrup.

D airy

NEW ORLEANS MILK MAID. NEW ORLEANS. LA.

New Orleans milk maid

For most of us, it has been many years since we awoke to the early morning clatter and clink of the milkman leaving bottles of milk at the front door, yet it remains a favorite bit of American nostalgia. Just the idea of cool, fresh milk with rich, golden cream on top waiting each morning with the newspaper is enough to evoke memories of the "good old days." It is hard to find such romance in the cardboard and plastic cartons lugged from the supermarket each week. Today's milk, while good, just doesn't seem to taste the same. For that matter, nor do the pre-packaged cheese, butter or eggs. It is a simple truth that high temperature pasteurization, homogenization, mass-production and preservatives, while making dairy products more available, affordable and hygienic have robbed us of some of the flavor. Additionally, in this age of mergers and monopolies, the small, local producer has had to struggle to compete. The good news is that there are a growing number of small, family-owned dairies and artisanal cheesemakers dedicated to recreating those tastes from the past, and the market for those products is developing rapidly. Take, for example, the ever-growing popularity of farmers' markets in urban areas and stores like Whole Foods Market and Wild Oats that cater to our cravings for artisanal, farmstead and organic products. After embracing convenience and low cost for so long in our industrialized lives, there seems to be a yearning for the way things were done centuries ago.

Actually, the history of humans drinking milk and making cheese can be traced back not hundreds, but thousands of years. It makes sense that the earliest civilizations dabbling in domesticating animals would recognize the nutritive power of milk and make use of it. Cave paintings in the Sahara, dating back as far as 5000 years B.C., depict the milking of herd animals and what appears to be cheesemaking. While it is difficult to prove, most accounts of ancient cheese history presume that at some point a nomadic traveler carried his milk in a pouch made from an animal's stomach. During his journey the motion of his horse, the heat and traces of rennet in the pouch inadvertently created a type of cheese. Upon arriving at his destination, the traveler found not milk, but curds and whey, both of which provided refreshment and nutrition. The idea apparently caught on because Egyptian and Sumerian records between 3500 and 3000 B.C. document the use of products made from curdled milk. Of course, by its very nature milk was hard to keep, so the creation of cheese was a natural way to combat spoilage. The happy result was a delicious product that retained milk's nutrition but could be enjoyed later. Cheese made from goat's and sheep's milk was an important commodity in ancient Greece and Rome and was used for trade. Both Homer (around 1184 B.C.) and Aristotle (around 385 B.C.) mentioned these cheeses in their writings. The Roman cheese trade expanded throughout Europe and grew substantial enough that by 300 A.D., maximum prices were fixed by the emperor for a variety of different cheeses, including some of the precursors to Feta and Parmesan. After the collapse of the Roman Empire, cheesemaking continued, and new cheeses developed based on terrain, taste and types of milk available. In the Middle Ages, European monks perfected the art of cheesemaking, while home-style cheese and butter were made by individuals who had access to milk. As a testament to the importance and popularity of cheese, *The Oxford Companion to Food* notes that the first printed cookbook was published in 1475 and the first dedicated to cheese alone, *Summa Lacticiniorum*, followed just two years later. The earliest recorded mention of Cheddar cheese was in 1500 A.D., Parmesan in 1579 and Stilton in 1785.

North America had no dairy history until the Spaniards brought cows, probably Iberian Longhorns, to Florida around the year 1550. Additional cows, as well as much more easily transportable goats, arrived with English colonists in the 1600s. Initially these limited numbers of cows would serve small colonies and then individual homesteads or farms, providing sustenance only for their owners and neighbors. Commercial dairying in the United States did not really take off until the 19th century, when records document the import of Ayrshires from Scotland in the 1820s, Holsteins from Holland in the 1850s, Guernseys and Jerseys from Great Britain in the 1840s and 50s, and Brown Swiss from Switzerland in the 1860s. Cheesemaking too, was primarily practiced in homes and on farms until the first American cheese factory was built in Oneida, N.Y., in 1851, but the concept of commercially made cheese soon caught on. By 1880 there were almost 4,000 dairy factories nationwide, and yet the demand for cheese continued to grow. Legend has it that the term "big cheese" evolved out of the 19th century habit of honoring queens and presidents with giant wheels of cheese. Thomas Jefferson was presented with a 1,235-pound specimen by supporters in Cheshire, Mass., in 1802, and Queen Victoria received a 1,250-pound cheese as part of her wedding celebrations. Presidents Martin Van Buren and Andrew Jackson also received similarly cheesy tributes.

Louisiana is not exactly thought of as a dairy state, and milk and eggs were scarce outside of New Orleans until the influx of German settlers in the 18th century. Nevertheless, there were several commercial dairies operating in Louisiana by the late 19th century. Because refrigeration and transportation were an issue, dairies both in the cities and in outlying parishes were generally limited to small, local markets. In the early 1900s, however,

Charles Adolph Kent Sr., for whom the town of Kentwood, La., is named, added a creamery to his existing ice works and bottling plant in Tangipahoa Parish. One of the first creameries in the South, it dramatically expanded the market for local dairy farmers. Kent shipped whole milk to New Orleans, produced condensed milk and supplied milk to ice cream manufacturers throughout the South. The venture was hugely successful but over-expansion, high costs and the Depression forced Kent Dairy Products into bankruptcy in 1929. Despite that blow, parts of Tangipahoa Parish and neighboring Washington Parish remain an important region for the Louisiana dairy industry. Closer to New Orleans, Godchaux's Belle Pointe Dairy in Reserve advertised in the 1940s that its cows were treated to daily showers and frequented "resting barns." Gold Seal Dairy, opened by Salvador "Sam" Centanni in the 1920s, operated in New Orleans until 1986 and was famous for its Creole cream cheese. Gold Seal also supplied dairy products to ships in port and Café Du Monde. Another early New Orleans dairy, Cloverland, had an active marketing campaign in the 1940s touting the benefits of milk, the cleanliness of their bottling plant and their delivery system—a mule-drawn milk cart.

In St. James Parish alone, there were at least eight small dairies serving the local population in the 1930s and 40s. According to P.J. Amato whose father ran one of them, most of the herds were Jersey or Guernsey because they provided creamy milk rich in butterfat. In those days, the quality of the milk was judged by how much cream rose to the top of the bottle. These small dairies usually milked by hand and did their own bottling and delivery. Few had equipment to pasteurize the milk and nobody homogenized. Probably the largest of these local St. James dairies was started by the Poche family in Paulina in the 1920s. Robert Poche, who helped his father Tom on the farm until 1951, was one of 13 siblings who all pitched in. In addition to home deliveries, they bottled milk in half-pint glass bottles for school lunches and made Creole cream cheese

Gold Seal Dairy played an important part in another New Orleans tradition. Sam Centanni's wife, Myra, collected and displayed a vast array of Christmas decorations at their home until her death in 1967. Her displays inspired Al Copeland (founder of Popeyes Chicken) to create his own dramatic and often controversial light displays. Many years later, with Sam's permission, Myra Centanni's decorations were the foundation of the spectacular annual Christmas exhibits at City Park.

in quart jars, which sold for 50 cents. By 1936 the Poche's were able to expand their herd to 80 cows and install electric milking machines. Around this same period of time, several residents of Vacherie (named for the early German cattle farms in this part of Louisiana) recall climbing the stairs to the back porch of Laura Plantation to buy their milk from the Waguespack sisters, one of whom managed the plantation's dairy. According to Norman Marmillion, to whom these experiences were recounted, there was a fair amount of ritual involved with the sisters' milk sales and buyers were never allowed onto the porch. Dairying was obviously not new to Laura Plantation, based on this description of life in the 1870s in the memoirs of Laura Locoul Gore, for whom the plantation was named:

"Every evening huge pails of milk were brought in and poured into large yellow bowls and allowed to clabber. The next morning the cream was skimmed off to make butter. It had been the custom since slavery to give the Negroes the surplus milk and clabber every morning. A stream of Negro children came with their tin pans from the quarters for the clabber." –from *Memories of the Old Plantation Home and Creole Family Album*, Laura Locoul Gore, with commentary by Norman and Sand Marmillion.

As in most of rural America, outside of the city limits,

milk would have been obtained from one's own or a neighbor's cows. Any butter or cheesemaking would also take place on a home basis and would normally be carried out by the women of the household. Very simple farm cheeses made from clabber or soured milk were common and may have been the predecessor to one well-kept Louisiana secret—Creole cream cheese. This farmer-style, acid-set cheese has been made in South Louisiana for about as long as milk has been available. Slightly tarter and creamier than the mass-produced variety, this cream cheese is made with a blend of skim milk, buttermilk and half-and-half cream. Believed to be inspired by recipes from the Brittany and Burgundy regions of France, Creole cream cheese was very much a part of life here and for a time was made by most of the area's commercial dairies. This single curd cheese could be eaten alone, with French bread, served sweet with sugar and strawberries, or used as an ingredient in other dishes such as cheesecake or ice cream. Even Laura Locoul Gore's memoirs of plantation life in the 19th century included a reference to fig preserves and cream cheese served in a heart-shaped mold and topped with thick, yellow cream. Economic pressures on the dairies meant that this delicacy all but died out in the 1980s, but Creole cream cheese has seen a rebirth through the efforts of the Chef John Folse Bittersweet Plantation Dairy. In turn, its success has prompted the development of a whole line of artisanal cheeses at Bittersweet Plantation Dairy, each a tribute to Cajun and Creole culture.

While in some regions of the world certain

Milk cow at Laura Plantation

cultures use the milk of horses, camels and water buffalo, most with a dairying background have focused on the milk drawn from cows, goats and sheep. The milk from each type of animal has a distinctive flavor, which is further influenced by the breed itself, the region and what the animal eats. Climate, season and even whether or not the milk is pasteurized also contribute to the final flavor of both the milk and cheese. Interestingly, in those parts of the world where dairy animals such as cows, sheep and goats were uncommon, there appears to be a pronounced genetic inability to digest milk among the adult population, more commonly known as lactose intolerance. In the United States, cow's milk cheese is the most common, although a return to traditional goat's milk cheeses began in the 1970s and is still gaining popularity. Sheep's milk cheeses still remain relatively rare in the United States primarily because of the scarcity of dairy sheep in this country, but some artisanal cheesemakers are quickly changing this, too. There are a few farmers in Louisiana raising dairy goats although both goats and sheep pose special challenges in our state. Sheep find the heat oppressive, and both goats and sheep have hoof problems because of the damp climate.

Most early dairy cow herds in North America included Jerseys, Guernseys and Brown Swiss, but when high butterfat content was no longer a selling point, the majority of farmers in Louisiana switched to Holsteins for their higher volume production. However, Jeff Addison, a local Jersey dairy farmer from whom Bittersweet Plantation Dairy buys milk for cheese and ice cream, says that many farmers are starting to realize that pound for pound, the output from a Jersey cow can exceed that of a Holstein. Jerseys also adapt better to the hot, humid climate because they are smaller and their light color doesn't absorb the heat like a Holstein's primarily black coat. They also eat less, have a better temperament and produce higher quality milk rich in butterfat. According to Addison, many farmers, if they can afford it, are switching back to Jerseys, Guernseys or Brown Swiss, or at the very least incorporating them into their herds or creating hybrids.

Despite the vast array of cheeses that have been made over the centuries, the basic principles of cheesemaking have not changed. Milk is coagulated through the natural souring process or with bacteria. Then an enzyme such as rennet (which originally came from a calf's stomach, but can also be artificially made) is added to coagulate the milk, which separates into curds and whey. For most cheeses, the whey is drawn off, the curds are cut, compressed, cooked or molded, and cheese is made. Some cheeses like cottage cheese and many goat cheeses are eaten fresh. Others are allowed to age and may receive further treatments such as brining, washing of the rind or inoculations of bacteria to achieve the desired flavor and consistency.

In the United States, milk products offered for commercial sale must be pasteurized or aged for 60 days in order for potentially harmful bacteria to die. While this is an important regulation that significantly improved the safety and the shelf life of the nation's milk supply, cheesemakers argue that it is an unnecessary precaution where their product is concerned. Pasteurization also alters both the taste and the type of cheese that can be made. Despite the controversy, pasteurization continues to be favored by the Food and Drug Administration. Homogenization is another matter. While most milk sold in the United States is homogenized, meaning the fat globules, which would normally form the cream, have been reduced in size and blended into the liquid, it is not a requirement for sale. Some dairies have begun offering non-homogenized milk for sale in limited markets, and the response has been phenomenal. In non-homogenized milk, the cream will separate naturally because the fat globules are lighter than water and rise to the top. In the past, cream was left to rise naturally, ripening slightly in the process and thus acquiring more flavor than today's cream. The longer it was left, the thicker the cream. These days cream is usually separated from the milk with a centrifuge and is then immediately pasteurized to prevent spoilage. The deliberate addition of bacteria to milk also creates a variety of other dairy products including sour cream, buttermilk, butter, crème fraîche, yogurt and cheese. The United States is now the largest cheese producer in the world even though for many years it did not offer quite the variety of other countries such as France. That began to change as Americans traveled overseas and developed a taste for more unusual cheeses. Once back at home, they sought these cheeses from their local suppliers. Now, small artisanal cheesemakers are rising to the occasion. In the early days of the 21st century the United States featured more than 200 artisanal and farmstead cheesemakers and about 600 artisanal cheeses. By 2003, per capita cheese consumption, which includes processed cheese products, had reached a record high in the United States. All signs point to continued growth in this sector as well as to positive changes in federal pasteurization policies.

Milk and cheese lend themselves naturally to cooking. They not only add flavor and texture, they also provide nutrition through the proteins, vitamins and minerals naturally present in dairy products. They are also the foundation of delicious creations such as cheesecake, ice cream and creamy soups and sauces. While Louisiana may not be known for its dairy history, its dairy recipes should be enough to convince you otherwise.

CREOLE CREAM CHEESE

Prep Time: 4 Hours
Yields: 10–12 Cups

Comment:
Creole cream cheese is a farmer-style cheese similar to a combination of cottage cheese and sour cream. Although originally a product of France, many New Orleans dairies such as Gold Seal and Borden's supplied the city with the product for many years. Today, Bittersweet Plantation Dairy produces the cheese. This homemade recipe is excellent.

Ingredients:
2 gallons skim milk
½ quart buttermilk
½ rennet tablet (available at cheese specialty stores)
half-and-half (optional)

Method:
In a stainless steel pot, combine skim milk, buttermilk and rennet, stirring constantly. Carefully monitor temperature with a thermometer until milk reaches 80°F. Continuing to stir, hold milk at 80°F for 5 minutes. Remove from heat, cover tightly and let sit 3 hours. Drain off whey (liquid remaining after curds are formed) and discard. Pack solids (curds) in 8-ounce portions. Top each portion with equal parts half-and-half, if desired. Chill and serve with sugar or fruit. Creole cream cheese is excellent in ice creams and pastries.

CREOLE CREAM CHEESE ICE CREAM

Prep Time: 2 Hours
Yields: 1 Quart

Comment:

Creole cream cheese was popular in early Louisiana. Chef John Folse's Bittersweet Plantation Dairy began manufacturing and distributing Creole cream cheese in 2002. The product may be found at many grocery stores across the state.

Ingredients:

1 (11.5-ounce) package	1½ cups heavy whipping cream
Creole Cream Cheese	2 tbsps pure vanilla extract
1½ cups sugar	⅛ tsp nutmeg
3 eggs	⅛ tsp cinnamon
1½ cups half-and-half	

Method:

In a large mixing bowl, whisk together sugar and eggs until fluffy and pale yellow. In a saucepot, combine half-and-half and cream. Simmer, but do not boil. Remove from heat. Slowly blend hot milk into egg mixture, 1 ladle at a time, stirring constantly to prevent eggs from scrambling. Continuing to blend, add vanilla, nutmeg and cinnamon. Strain mixture through a fine sieve and chill overnight or a minimum of 4 hours. When ready to use, thoroughly blend Creole cream cheese into custard mixture and whisk until all lumps are removed. Pour mixture into a home-style ice cream maker and freeze according to manufacturer's directions. Temper ice cream in freezer 2 hours prior to serving.

STRAWBERRY CREOLE CREAM CHEESE ICE CREAM

Prep Time: 2 Hours
Yields: 1 Quart

Comment:

Creole cream cheese is a dairy item unique to Louisiana. The product can be used in place of sour cream in many different recipes and is especially tasty when used to make ice cream.

Ingredients:

1 (11.5-ounce) package Bittersweet Plantation	1½ cups heavy whipping cream
Dairy Creole Cream Cheese	
¾ cup diced fresh strawberries	2 tbsps pure vanilla extract
1½ cups sugar	⅛ tsp nutmeg
3 eggs	⅛ tsp cinnamon
1½ cups half-and-half	

Method:

In a large mixing bowl, whisk together sugar and eggs until fluffy and pale yellow. In a saucepot, combine half-and-half and cream. Simmer, but do not boil. Remove from heat. Slowly blend hot milk into egg mixture, 1 ladle at a time, stirring constantly to prevent eggs from scrambling. Continuing to blend, add vanilla, nutmeg and cinnamon. Strain mixture through a fine sieve and chill overnight or a minimum of 4 hours. When ready to use, thoroughly blend Creole cream cheese and strawberries into custard mixture and whisk until all lumps are removed. Pour mixture into a home-style ice cream maker and freeze according to manufacturer's directions. Temper ice cream in freezer 2 hours prior to serving.

LEMON CREOLE CREAM CHEESE PANNA COTTA WITH PONCHATOULA STRAWBERRY SAUCE

Prep Time: 50 Minutes
Yields: 6 Servings

Comment:
The original panna cotta came from the Italians. This "egg-less" custard is a refreshing dessert for warm spring days. The custard is especially good when topped with fresh strawberry sauce and a sprig of mint.

Ingredients for Panna Cotta:
5 tbsps fresh lemon juice
2 tbsps grated lemon zest
1 (11.5-ounce) package Bittersweet Plantation Dairy Creole Cream Cheese
1 cup whole milk
1 cup heavy whipping cream
½ vanilla bean, split lengthwise
3½ tsps unflavored gelatin
½ cup sugar

Method:
Lightly grease 6 (1-cup) ramekins or custard cups. In a small, heavy-bottomed saucepan, mix milk and cream. Scrape seeds from vanilla bean then add scrapings and bean to pot. Bring to simmer then remove from heat. Cover and allow to steep 30 minutes. Remove vanilla bean. In a small bowl, combine lemon juice and gelatin, stirring until dissolved. Let stand 10 minutes or until gelatin softens. Return saucepan to low heat and stir in gelatin and sugar for 2 minutes or until just dissolved. Remove from heat. Whisk in Creole cream cheese and zest. Divide custard evenly among ramekins. Cover and chill 6 hours or until set, preferably overnight.

Ingredients for Ponchatoula Strawberry Sauce:
3 cups Louisiana strawberries, stemmed and sliced
2 tbsps dark brown sugar
3 tbsps strawberry wine
whole Louisiana strawberries for garnish
mint leaves for garnish

Method:
In a blender, combine sliced strawberries, brown sugar and wine. Mix until smooth. Add more brown sugar if necessary to achieve desired sweetness. To serve panna cotta, run a small knife around each ramekin. One at a time, place bottoms of ramekins in a small bowl of hot water for 45 seconds. Invert each panna cotta onto a plate or shallow bowl and surround with strawberry sauce. Garnish with whole strawberries and a sprig of mint.

CREOLE CREAM CHEESE CHEESECAKE

Prep Time: 2 Hours
Yields: 8–10 Servings

Comment:
In August 2002, Chef John Folse's Bittersweet Plantation Dairy resurrected the art of making Creole cream cheese. This unique regional product ceased production in Louisiana in the 1980s. The slight tart taste of this Creole specialty lends just the right flavor to this traditional cheesecake recipe.

Ingredients for Crust:
1½ cups graham cracker crumbs
¼ cup sugar
4 tbsps melted butter

Method:
Combine graham cracker crumbs and sugar. Drizzle melted butter into mixture until moistened. Using your fingertips, press graham cracker mixture into bottom of a 10-inch round springform pan. Place pan in refrigerator 30 minutes or until crust is firm to touch.

Ingredients for Cheesecake:
2 (11.5-ounce) packages Bittersweet Plantation Dairy Creole Cream Cheese
3 (8-ounce) packages cream cheese, room temperature
3 eggs
1½ cups sugar
1 pinch nutmeg
2 tbsps pure vanilla extract
1 tbsp lemon juice
2 tbsps lemon zest

Antique implements for Creole Cream Cheese making

Method:

Preheat oven to 350°F. In an electric mixer, blend Creole cream cheese, softened cream cheese, sugar, nutmeg, vanilla, lemon juice and zest on medium-high speed until all lumps are removed. Turn mixer speed down to lowest setting then add eggs, 1 at a time, whipping completely between each addition. Do not over whip. Remove crust from refrigerator and fill with batter. Rotate pan until batter flattens out. Place cake on middle rack of oven and bake 1 hour. Cake should be slightly browned around edges and may appear to be a little undercooked in center. Remove from oven and allow cake to rest 15–20 minutes. Turn oven temperature up to 400°F. While cooling, it is natural for cake to develop a crack or two in the center. These imperfections will be filled with sour cream topping.

Ingredients for Topping:

16 ounces sour cream
½ cup sugar
2 tbsps pure vanilla extract

Method:

In a mixing bowl, blend sour cream, sugar and vanilla. Whisk thoroughly until sour cream is ready to pour. Pour evenly over top of cake and place in oven 5–7 minutes. Remove and allow to cool. Cover cooled cake with plastic wrap. Refrigerate 5–6 hours, preferably overnight.

CREOLE CREAM CHEESE STRAWBERRY SHORTCAKE

Prep Time: 1 Hour
Yields: 10 Servings

Comment:
During strawberry season in Louisiana, trucks selling the sweet berries line the roads. Here, the fresh produce is combined with our Creole cream cheese to create the most famous and most loved strawberry dish.

Ingredients for Strawberries:
1 quart strawberries, sliced lengthwise
½ cup sugar, or to taste
1 ounce strawberry wine

Method:
Preheat oven to 425°F. In a medium mixing bowl, combine strawberries, sugar and wine. Mash with a potato masher or fork just until strawberries release their juices. Be careful not to mash to a pulp.

Ingredients for Whipped Cream:
1 (11.5-ounce) package Bittersweet Plantation Dairy Creole Cream Cheese
2 cups heavy whipping cream
½ tsp nutmeg
½ tsp cinnamon
¾ cup sugar

Method:
In an electric mixer, combine Creole cream cheese, cream, nutmeg and cinnamon. Whisk on medium-high speed until mixture starts to slightly thicken. Slowly add sugar and beat until very soft peaks form. Be careful to avoid creating a stiff whipped cream. Set aside.

Ingredients for Cream Biscuits:
2 cups flour
1 tbsp double-acting baking powder
3 tbsps sugar, or to taste
½ tsp salt
1½ cups heavy whipping cream
whole milk (for brushing tops of biscuits)

Method:
In a large mixing bowl, sift together flour, baking powder, sugar and salt. Slowly add cream and stir mixture until it just forms a dough. Gather dough into a ball and turn onto a lightly-floured surface. Roll or pat dough ½-inch thick. Using a 2½-inch cutter, cut out as many rounds as possible and transfer them to an ungreased baking sheet. NOTE: A 4-inch or 1-inch cutter may be substituted. Gather scraps, roll dough and cut out more rounds until all dough has been used. Brush tops of biscuits lightly with milk. Bake 15 minutes or until golden brown. Transfer biscuits to a rack and let cool 5 minutes. Split biscuits horizontally with a fork, arrange bottom halves on plates, and spoon strawberry mixture over them. Top strawberry mixture with whipped cream and arrange biscuit tops on cream. Serve remaining cream separately.

Hannah and Luke Addison lead the cows to the milk barn.

CREOLE CREAM CHEESE TIRAMISU

Prep Time: 1 Hour
Yields: 10–12 Servings

Comment:

Tiramisu is a classic Italian dessert recreated in restaurants worldwide. Tiramisu translated means "pick me up" which refers to the little jolt one gets from the chocolate, coffee and Marsala wine.

Ingredients:

1 (11.5-ounce) package Bittersweet Plantation Dairy Creole Cream Cheese
6 egg yolks
1½ cups sugar
¼ cup Marsala wine
2½ cups heavy whipping cream
¼ cup sugar
3 dozen lady fingers (see note)
1 cup instant espresso or dark roast coffee, prepared
2 ounces brandy
2 tbsps unsweetened cocoa powder
chocolate curls for garnish

Method:

NOTE: I recommend the soft, 3-inch ladyfingers produced by Specialty Bakers Inc., 1-800-755-9890. However, feel free to choose ladyfingers that are available at your local grocer or Italian specialty food shop. In a mixing bowl, whisk egg yolks, 1½ cups sugar and Marsala until thick and ribbony. Place bowl on top of a double boiler with 1 inch boiling water. Reduce heat to low and cook egg mixture 8–10 minutes, stirring constantly. Remove from heat and refrigerate 30 minutes. In a separate bowl, combine cream and ¼ cup sugar. Using an electric mixer, beat until stiff peaks form. Remove 1½ cups of cream from bowl and refrigerate. This chilled cream will be the dessert topping. Remove egg mixture from refrigerator and gently fold in Creole cream cheese. Using a rubber spatula, gently fold in remaining whipped cream. Place in refrigerator. Line bottom and sides of a 3-quart crystal bowl or trifle dish with ladyfingers. In a small bowl, combine espresso and brandy. Using a pastry brush, coat ladyfingers well with brandy mixture. Cover with a generous layer of egg/cream cheese mixture. Sprinkle in a small amount of cocoa powder and continue layering ladyfingers, custard and cocoa until all is used. Top dessert with chilled whipped cream. Garnish with chocolate curls and a sprinkle of cocoa powder. Refrigerate a minimum of 4 hours, preferably overnight.

CREOLE CREAM CHEESE CANNOLI

Prep Time: 2 Hours
Yields: 60 Servings

Comment:

Coming from Bayou Country, I was more a fan of pralines than cannoli, that is until I ate cannoli made by Bert Cutino of Monterey, Calif. The recipe came from Burt's mother-in-law. The filling is light and airy with just the right hint of sugar. We have taken this traditional recipe and given it a Creole twist by adding Bittersweet Plantation Dairy Creole Cream Cheese.

Ingredients for Filling:

2 pounds Ricotta cheese
4 (11.5-ounce) packages Bittersweet
   Plantation Dairy Creole Cream Cheese
2 tsps pure vanilla extract
1½ cups powdered sugar
½ tsp nutmeg
¼ cup milk
1 cup semi-sweet chocolate chips
½ cup glazed fruit (optional)

Method:

Place Ricotta and Creole cream cheese together in a strainer lined with cheesecloth. Allow to drain in refrigerator overnight. The next day, divide cheese mixture into 3 parts. Place 1 portion of cheese into a mixer and blend in vanilla, powdered sugar and nutmeg. With the mixer running, add remaining 2 portions of cheese, 1 at a time. If mixture gets too thick at any point, add a little milk. When adding third portion, pour in any remaining milk and add chocolate chips. Blend gently so as not to break chocolate. Taste for sweetness and add more sugar if necessary. If desired, add glazed fruit at this point. Cover and set aside for later use.

Ingredients for Shells:

6 cups sifted flour
¼ pound softened butter
2 tbsps shortening
2 tbsps sugar
3 eggs
1 cup Marsala wine
¼ cup red wine vinegar
30 maraschino cherries, halved
powdered sugar for garnish

Method:

Have your local hardware store cut a 1-inch dowel pin into 6-inch links. Prior to using, place dowel pins in your home-style fryer to heat thoroughly and coat with oil. Remove and drain. In a large mixing bowl, combine flour, butter, shortening and sugar. Blend eggs into mixture. Add wine and vinegar and continue to blend until dough ball is formed. Place dough on a lightly-floured surface and knead to a silky finish. Let rest a minimum of 2 hours. Preheat a home-style deep fryer to 350°F according to manufacturer's directions. Cut dough into manageable portions and roll ⅛-inch thick. Using a round pastry cutter, cut dough into 4-inch circles. Wrap each circle around a dowel and seal seam with water or egg wash (1 egg, 1 tablespoon water, beaten). Fry until browned and beginning to blister. Remove from oil and slide shells off dowel pins, allowing them to cool. Fill a pastry bag with Ricotta filling. Pipe filling into each shell then place a cherry half on each end. Sprinkle with powdered sugar and serve.

CREOLE COUNTRY AMBROSIA WITH TWIN CHOCOLATE SHAVINGS

Prep Time: 30 Minutes
Yields: 10 Servings

Comment:

According to Greek mythology, ambrosia was the food of the gods on Mount Olympus. The word ambrosia means "immortality." This dessert, which includes Creole cream cheese and chocolate shavings, is definitely fit for the gods.

Ingredients:

2 (11.5-ounce) packages Bittersweet Plantation Dairy Creole Cream Cheese
4 cups heavy whipping cream
1½ tsps nutmeg
1½ tsps cinnamon
1½ cups sugar
2 (8-ounce) cans fruit cocktail, drained
1 cup chopped pecans
2½ cups seedless green grapes
2 cups shredded coconut
2 (11-ounce) cans mandarin oranges, drained
2½ cups miniature marshmallows
1 (10-ounce) jar maraschino cherries, drained
2 (8-ounce) cans pineapple chunks, drained
1 cup white chocolate baking squares, shaved
1 cup milk chocolate baking squares, shaved
mint leaves for garnish
maraschino cherries for garnish

Method:

NOTE: It is important to drain fruit very well so that no excess moisture is in the finished dessert. In an electric mixer, combine Creole cream cheese, whipping cream, nutmeg and cinnamon. Whisk on medium-high speed until mixture starts to thicken. Slowly add sugar and beat until stiff peaks form. Set aside. NOTE: When adding a layer of whipped cream, use a generous amount. In a glass trifle bowl, layer ingredients in the following order: fruit cocktail, whipped cream, pecans, whipped cream, grapes, coconut, oranges, marshmallows, cherries, whipped cream and pineapple. Top with remaining whipped cream and sprinkle with white and milk chocolate shavings. Garnish with mint and maraschino cherries. This recipe can be created in individual servings by layering ingredients in same manner in parfait or pilsner glasses.

Ceramic French Cream Bowl

CREOLE CREAM CHEESE PECAN POUND CAKE

Prep Time: 2 Hours
Yields: 12 Servings

Comment:

Creole cream cheese can be used in the place of sour cream in any of your favorite recipes. It is perfect for creating a moist, delicious pound cake.

Ingredients:

1 cup Bittersweet Plantation Dairy Creole Cream Cheese
¼ cup chopped pecans
3 cups cake flour
½ tsp salt
¼ tsp baking soda
1 cup unsalted butter
3 cups sugar
6 eggs
1 tsp pure vanilla extract
⅓ cup flour
½ cup packed brown sugar
1 tsp cinnamon
2 tbsps melted butter

Method:

Preheat oven to 300°F. Grease and flour a 10-inch Bundt or tube pan. Sprinkle pecans on bottom of pan and set aside. In a medium bowl, sift together cake flour, salt and baking soda. Set aside. In a large bowl, cream unsalted butter and sugar until light and fluffy. Beat in eggs, 1 at a time. Stir in vanilla. Add flour mixture alternately with Creole cream cheese. Pour half of batter over pecans in prepared pan. In a small mixing bowl, combine flour, brown sugar and cinnamon. Cut in melted butter until mixture resembles coarse meal. Sprinkle mixture over batter in Bundt pan. Pour second half of batter on top of cinnamon and sugar mixture. Bake 75–90 minutes or until a toothpick inserted in center of cake comes out clean. Let cool in pan 20 minutes then turn onto a wire rack and cool completely.

SPINACH-HERB CREOLE CREAM CHEESE QUICHE

Prep Time: 1½ Hours
Yields: 12 Servings

Comment:
The seemingly strange array of ingredients in this cake is surprisingly delicious. This savory cheesecake is perfect for a wine and cheese party.

Ingredients:
4 cups shredded fresh spinach, loosely-packed
1 tbsp chopped dill
1 (11.5-ounce) package of Bittersweet Plantation Dairy Creole Cream Cheese
3 (8-ounce) packages cream cheese, softened
2 large Creole tomatoes, sliced
¾ tsp salt
¾ tsp cracked black pepper
1¼ cups pine nuts or pecans, toasted
1¼ cups Italian bread crumbs
10 tbsps butter, melted
1 (8-ounce) package Feta cheese, crumbled
3 large eggs
2 cloves garlic, pressed
2 tbsps flour

Method:
Preheat oven to 350°F. Sprinkle tomato slices with ¼ teaspoon salt and ½ teaspoon pepper. Drain on paper towels approximately 30 minutes. Grind pine nuts or pecans in a food processor. In a small bowl, combine nuts, bread crumbs and melted butter. Press into bottom of a 9-inch springform pan. Bake 10 minutes then cool in pan on wire rack. In an electric mixer, blend Creole cream cheese and cream cheese on medium speed. Blend in Feta and eggs. Add spinach, dill, garlic, flour, and remaining salt and pepper. Continue to blend until mixed. Pour spinach mixture into prepared crust. Lower oven temperature to 325°F and bake 20 minutes. Top with tomato slices then bake an additional 40 minutes or until set. Turn off heat and leave cheesecake in oven 20 minutes. Cool on a wire rack 10 minutes. Gently run knife along edge of cheesecake and carefully remove sides of pan. Cool 10 more minutes. Serve warm or cold.

BAKED CHILI CHEESE SPREAD

Prep Time: 1½ Hours
Yields: 24 Servings

Comment:
Green chiles and chili powder give this cheese spread a Spanish flair. This dish is the perfect food for an informal party or a big football game gathering.

Ingredients:
1 tbsp chili powder
2 tbsps yellow cornmeal
2 cups shredded Cheddar cheese
2 (11.5-ounce) packages Bittersweet Plantation Dairy Creole Cream Cheese
3 (8-ounce) packages cream cheese, softened
3 large eggs
2 tsps garlic powder
1½ tsps cumin
2 (4-ounce) cans diced green chiles
1 cup sliced green onions
1 (16-ounce) jar salsa

Method:
Preheat oven to 325°F. Grease a 9-inch springform pan. In a small bowl, combine chili powder and cornmeal. Sprinkle on sides and bottom of prepared pan. In a large mixing bowl, beat Creole cream cheese, cream cheese, eggs, garlic powder and cumin until smooth. Stir in chiles and ½ cup green onions. Pour half of batter into pan. Spread 1 cup of salsa over batter, and sprinkle with 1½ cups Cheddar cheese. Spread remaining batter on top of cheese. Bake 1 hour or until edges are set but center still moves slightly. Remove side of springform pan and cool completely on wire rack. When cooled, spread remaining salsa on top then sprinkle with remaining cheese and green onions. Serve with tortilla chips.

JALAPEÑO CHEESE AND SAUSAGE DIP

Prep Time: 45 Minutes
Yields: 15–20 Servings

Comment:

The Spanish originally brought peppers to North America after developing a taste for them during their contact with the Mayans and Incas. Many varieties of peppers thrived in Mexico and eventually came through Texas into Plantation Country.

Ingredients:

2 pounds diced Velveeta® cheese
1 (12-ounce) can jalapeños, chopped
1 pound diced andouille sausage
¼ cup butter
1 cup diced onions
¼ cup diced celery
¼ cup diced red bell peppers
2 tbsps minced garlic
1 (11.5-ounce) package Bittersweet Plantation Dairy Creole Cream Cheese
3 cups mayonnaise
salt and cracked black pepper to taste
Louisiana hot sauce to taste
¼ cup chopped parsley

Method:

Allow cheese to sit at room temperature for 30 minutes. Remove seeds from jalapeño peppers and rinse under cold running water. In a heavy-bottomed sauté pan, melt butter over medium-high heat. Add andouille, onions, celery, bell peppers and garlic. Sauté 3–5 minutes or until vegetables are wilted. Stir in jalapeños and sauté 2–3 minutes. Remove from heat and allow to cool. Pour ingredients from sauté pan into a food processor and blend until smooth. Place blended ingredients into a large mixing bowl and add Velveeta®, Creole cream cheese and mayonnaise. Whisk until mixture is consistency of a dipping sauce. Season with salt, pepper and hot sauce then sprinkle in parsley. Pour ingredients into a decorative serving bowl and heat in microwave. Place in center of a large serving platter surrounded by garlic croutons, toast points or tortilla chips. This dip may also be served cold and will hold well in the refrigerator for a couple of days.

JUMBO SHRIMP SALAD WITH CREOLE CREAM CHEESE DRESSING

Prep Time: 30 Minutes
Yields: 6–8 Servings

Comment:

There are many classic shrimp dishes using savory flavors, but shrimp are rarely used in recipes with a sweet and fruity finish. This dish, similar to ambrosia, combines shrimp with fruit for a unique flavor and presentation.

Ingredients:

2 dozen (21–25-count) shrimp, peeled and deveined
1 (11.5-ounce) package Bittersweet Plantation Dairy Creole Cream Cheese
2 quarts water
salt and black pepper to taste
2 cups heavy whipping cream
¾ tsp nutmeg
¾ tsp cinnamon
¾ cup sugar
2 (8-ounce) cans fruit cocktail, drained
1 cup chopped pecans
2½ cups seedless green grapes
2 cups shredded coconut
2 (11-ounce) cans mandarin oranges, drained
1 (10-ounce) jar maraschino cherries, drained
2 (8-ounce) cans pineapple chunks, drained
maraschino cherries for garnish

Method:

NOTE: It is important to drain fruit well so no excess moisture is in finished dessert. Pour water into large pot, and season with salt and pepper. Bring to a boil then add shrimp. Boil 2–3 minutes or until pink and curled. Do not overcook. Drain and set aside. In an electric mixer, combine Creole cream cheese, whipping cream, nutmeg and cinnamon. Blend on medium-high speed until mixture starts to thicken. Slowly add sugar, beating until stiff peaks form. Set aside. NOTE: When adding a layer of whipped cream, use a generous amount. In a glass trifle bowl, layer ingredients in the following order: fruit cocktail, whipped cream, pecans, whipped cream, grapes, coconut, oranges, whipped cream, 16 shrimp, cherries, whipped cream and pineapple. Top with remaining whipped cream. Garnish with maraschino cherries. Garnish bowl by curling 8 jumbo shrimp over edges. This recipe can be created in individual servings by layering ingredients in parfait or pilsner glasses.

THREE-LAYER CREOLE CREAM CHEESE LOAF

Prep Time: 30 Minutes
Yields: 18 Servings

Comment:

This spread is sure to be a hit at any social gathering. The creamy texture of Creole cream cheese and the delicious blend of seasonings creates a wonderful party spread. Serve this unique cheese with garlic croutons or on slices of New Orleans French Bread. (See recipe.)

Ingredients:

1 (11.5-ounce) package Bittersweet Plantation Dairy Creole Cream Cheese
3 (8-ounce) packages cream cheese, softened
3 tbsps chopped green olives with pimientos
2 tsps olive juice
¼ cup mayonnaise
1 cup shredded Cheddar cheese
1 (2-ounce) jar diced pimientos, drained
1 tsp grated onion
½ cup butter
2 garlic cloves, minced
1 tsp Italian seasoning
parsley for garnish

Method:

Line a 8" x 4" loaf pan with plastic wrap. Separate Creole cream cheese into 3 equal portions. In an electric mixer, blend 1 portion of Creole cream cheese with 1 package cream cheese until creamy. Stir in olives and olive juice. Spread mixture into pan. In mixer, blend second portion of Creole cream cheese with 1 package cream cheese until smooth. Blend in Cheddar, pimientos and onion. Spread mixture over first layer in pan. Beat remaining cheeses with butter until creamy. Season with garlic and Italian seasoning. Blend thoroughly. Spread in pan over second layer. Cover and refrigerate a minimum of 3 hours or until firm. Flip onto platter, remove plastic wrap and garnish with parsley.

Cheesemaker Dimcho Dimov samples milk before beginning another vat of Creole Cream Cheese

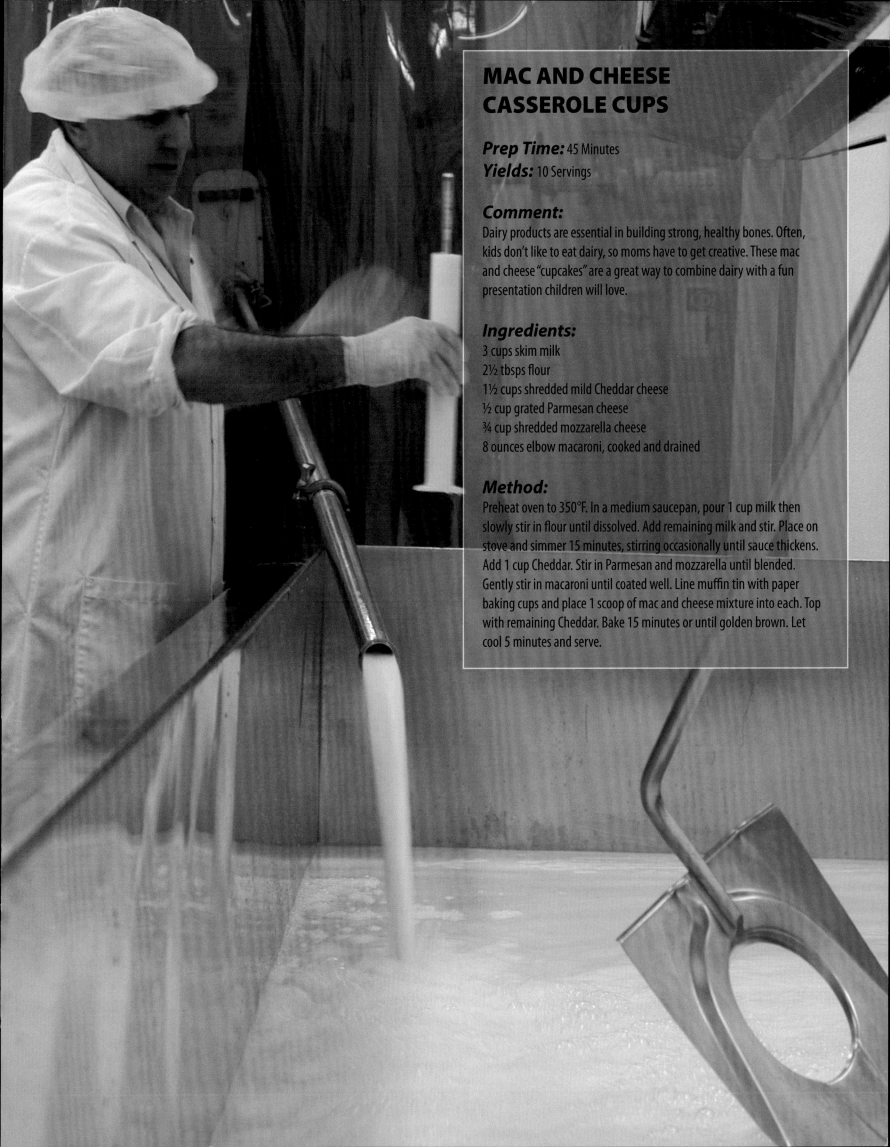

MAC AND CHEESE CASSEROLE CUPS

Prep Time: 45 Minutes
Yields: 10 Servings

Comment:
Dairy products are essential in building strong, healthy bones. Often, kids don't like to eat dairy, so moms have to get creative. These mac and cheese "cupcakes" are a great way to combine dairy with a fun presentation children will love.

Ingredients:
3 cups skim milk
2½ tbsps flour
1½ cups shredded mild Cheddar cheese
½ cup grated Parmesan cheese
¾ cup shredded mozzarella cheese
8 ounces elbow macaroni, cooked and drained

Method:
Preheat oven to 350°F. In a medium saucepan, pour 1 cup milk then slowly stir in flour until dissolved. Add remaining milk and stir. Place on stove and simmer 15 minutes, stirring occasionally until sauce thickens. Add 1 cup Cheddar. Stir in Parmesan and mozzarella until blended. Gently stir in macaroni until coated well. Line muffin tin with paper baking cups and place 1 scoop of mac and cheese mixture into each. Top with remaining Cheddar. Bake 15 minutes or until golden brown. Let cool 5 minutes and serve.

SPEAR ELEGANCE

Prep Time: 1 Hour
Yields: 1½ Cups

Comment:

This wonderful appetizer combines asparagus spears with a creamy
lemon-tarragon dipping sauce. It makes a very elegant presentation
when served in separate crystal glasses.

Ingredients:

48 asparagus spears, tough bottoms removed
1 (11.5-ounce) package Bittersweet Plantation
    Dairy Creole Cream Cheese
¼ cup mayonnaise
2 tbsps ketchup
3 tbsps minced red onions
2 tbsps lemon juice
4 tsps capers, drained and chopped
2 tsps dried tarragon
½ tsp onion powder
½ tsp sugar
¼ tsp pepper

FILLET OF CATFISH WITH APPLE-ANDOUILLE VINAIGRETTE

Prep Time: 1 Hour
Yields: 6 Servings

Comment:
This Cajun twist on the mainstream spinach salad highlights local ingredients. Sautéed catfish fillets and andouille sausage make this dish as unique as South Louisiana.

Ingredients:
6 (5-ounce) catfish fillets
1 cup apple cider vinegar
8 ounces julienned andouille sausage
2½ tbsps Creole mustard
⅓ cup honey
1 cup olive oil
2 tsps apple cider vinegar
salt and black pepper to taste
2 large eggs, beaten
1 cup milk
   OR water
3 cups white rice flour
1 tbsp granulated garlic
2 (6-ounce) packages baby spinach leaves
1 (4-ounce) wheel Bittersweet Plantation Dairy Fleur-de-Lis Fromage Triple Cream, cubed

Method:
In a medium skillet, sauté andouille over medium-high heat 10 minutes or until brown. Add 1 cup apple cider vinegar, Creole mustard and honey. Reduce liquid to a third. Whisk in ⅔ cup oil and remaining apple cider vinegar. Season with salt and pepper. Keep dressing warm. In a small shallow bowl, whisk together eggs and milk. In a separate shallow bowl, combine rice flour, garlic, salt and pepper. Season catfish with salt and pepper. Dip fillets into egg wash then dredge in rice flour. In a heavy-bottomed skillet, heat remaining oil over medium-high heat. Add fillets and cook approximately 3 minutes on each side or until edges are brown but center of fish is opaque. Place spinach in a large salad bowl. Toss with enough dressing to coat spinach leaves. Divide salad among 6 plates. Place a catfish fillet over each plate of salad. Sprinkle with cheese cubes, drizzle with additional dressing and serve.

Method:
In a 1-gallon stockpot, bring 2½ quarts of lightly-salted water to a boil. Blanch asparagus in boiling water 3–5 minutes or until slightly tender. Drain and immediately drop asparagus into a bowl of ice water to stop cooking process. In a mixing bowl, combine Creole cream cheese, mayonnaise, ketchup, onions, lemon juice, capers, tarragon, onion powder, sugar and pepper. Blend well and refrigerate until chilled. Serve asparagus in crystal glasses or on a platter with a bowl of dipping sauce.

BAKED FLEUR-DE-LIS EN CROÛTE

Prep Time: 1 Hour
Yields: 10–12 Servings

Comment:
Baking cheese in a pastry crust has been a holiday tradition in Europe for centuries. Start a new tradition in your family by serving this dish on Christmas Eve.

Ingredients:
1 (8-ounce) wheel Bittersweet Plantation Dairy Fleur-de-Lis Fromage Triple Cream
1 sheet frozen puff pastry or pie crust
egg wash (1 egg and 1 tbsp water, beaten)

Method:
NOTE: Frozen puff pastry may be purchased at most supermarkets. You may substitute a homemade or frozen pie crust if pastry is unavailable. Preheat oven to 375°F. Thaw pastry. On a lightly-floured surface, roll out pastry to a 12-inch circle. Place entire cheese wheel upside down in center of circle. Brush pastry edges with egg. Totally wrap cheese in dough. Seal thoroughly and remove excess dough. Place seam side down on a baking sheet. If desired, use a paring knife or pastry cutter to create decorative pieces of dough to garnish crust prior to baking. Decorative cut-outs such as leaves, birds or flowers are most often used. Brush with egg wash and bake 25 minutes. Cool 30 minutes prior to serving.

Fleur-de-Lis Triple Cream Cheese ages in the cave

LOUISIANA OYSTER AND FLEUR-DE-LIS BISQUE

Prep Time: 1 Hour
Yields: 10–12 Servings

Comment:

Other than New Orleans oyster soup, the famous oyster and Brie soup stands out as one of the most sought after bisque recipes. In South Louisiana, we have taken the liberty to incorporate Fleur-de-Lis fromage triple cream from Bittersweet Plantation Dairy to create a soup that is sure to rival either recipe.

Ingredients:

1 quart oysters in liquid
1 (8-ounce) wheel Bittersweet Plantation Dairy Fleur-de-Lis Fromage Triple Cream
¼ pound butter
1 cup minced onions
1 cup minced celery
1 tbsp minced garlic
¾ cup flour
1 quart chicken stock (see recipe)
1 quart heavy whipping cream
¼ cup minced green bell peppers
¼ cup minced red bell peppers
salt and black pepper to taste
¼ cup chopped parsley for garnish
¼ cup sliced green onions for garnish

Method:

Drain oysters and reserve liquid. In a heavy-bottomed saucepan, melt butter over medium-high heat. Sauté onions, celery and garlic 3–5 minutes or until vegetables are wilted. Blend in flour. Whisk in oyster liquid and chicken stock. Slowly add cream until all is blended. Bring to a rolling boil then reduce to simmer and cook 10 minutes, stirring occasionally. Cut wheel of Fleur-de-Lis into 8 pieces. Add cheese (including rind) to soup, stirring constantly until melted. Cook 5 additional minutes. Strain soup to remove seasonings and any remaining rind. Return soup to pot then add oysters and bell peppers. Season with salt and pepper. Garnish with parsley and green onions. Once oysters are curled and puffy but not overcooked, the soup is ready to be served.

RUSTIC CHICKEN AND FLEUR-DE-LIS TART

Prep Time: 1 Hour
Yields: 8 Servings

Comment:
This recipe is perfect for the cook who is tired of preparing the same old chicken dishes. Combine leftover chicken with red potatoes and chunky vegetables for a unique twist on the traditional pot pie. The addition of Bittersweet Plantation Dairy Fleur-de-Lis Fromage Triple Cream gives this rustic tart an elegant touch.

Ingredients for Pastry Crust:
1¼ cups flour
7 tbsps unsalted butter, chilled and sliced
¼ tsp salt
¼ tsp black pepper
4 tbsps ice water

Method:
Preheat oven to 350°F. In a food processor, combine flour, butter, salt and pepper. Pulse 10 seconds then add ice water. Continue to pulse 5–6 times until dough comes together. Place dough on a lightly-floured surface and work it into a ball. Cover with plastic wrap and refrigerate 30 minutes.

Ingredients for Filling:
1½ cups pulled or chopped chicken
1 (8-ounce) wheel Bittersweet Plantation Dairy Fleur-de-Lis Fromage Triple Cream
1 (4-ounce) wheel Bittersweet Plantation Dairy Fleur-de-Lis Fromage Triple Cream
¼ pound butter
8 pearl onions, peeled and halved
1 cup (½-inch) sliced celery
1 tsp minced garlic
½ cup julienned bell peppers
¾ cup bias cut baby carrots
4 tbsps flour
3 cups turkey or chicken stock
1½ cups cubed red potatoes, skin on
½ cup milk
¼ tsp salt
¼ tsp black pepper
1 tsp chopped oregano
1 tbsp chopped parsley
1 egg, beaten

Method:
In a large skillet, melt butter over medium-high heat. Add onions, celery, garlic, bell peppers and carrots. Sauté 5 minutes, stirring occasionally. Blend in flour, but do not brown. Stir in stock until roux dissolves. Bring to a low boil then reduce to simmer and cook 5 minutes. Add potatoes and cook 3–5 minutes. Add milk, salt, pepper, oregano and parsley. Cook, stirring occasionally, until mixture thickens to a heavy sauce consistency. Remove and discard rind from 8-ounce wheel of cheese. Remove skillet from heat then blend in 1 cup chicken and 8-ounce wheel of cheese. Allow mixture to cool 30 minutes. Remove dough from refrigerator and let sit at room temperature 15 minutes. Roll dough into a 15-inch circle, 1-inch thick. Carefully place dough on a ceramic pizza stone or cookie sheet lined with parchment paper. Spoon filling onto center of dough, leaving a 1½-inch space around edge. Fold 1½-inch edge over filling. Place remaining chicken on top of filling. Brush crust with egg and bake 20–30 minutes or until golden. Cut 4-ounce wheel of cheese into 8 equal portions. Place 1 piece of cheese on crust of each slice of warm tart and serve.

Bittersweet Plantation Dairy Gabriel and Evangeline goat cheeses

GOAT CHEESE AND PESTO MOLD

Prep Time: 20 Minutes
Yields: 6–8 Servings

Comment:

In 2004, Bittersweet Plantation Dairy began producing two goat cheeses, Evangeline and Gabriel. Both are soft-rind cheeses, but Gabriel is covered in a fine layer of vegetable ash. Try this interesting party spread with Bittersweet's exceptional goat cheese.

Ingredients:

4 (4-ounce) wheels Bittersweet Plantation Dairy Evangeline Goat Cheese
1 (11.5-ounce) package Bittersweet Plantation Dairy Creole Cream Cheese
4 cloves garlic, chopped
¼ cup chopped red bell peppers
¼ cup chopped yellow bell peppers
salt and black pepper to taste
Creole seasoning to taste
¾ cup prepared pesto sauce
basil for garnish
pecans for garnish

La Mancha, Saanen, Nubien and Alpine goats at Cindy McDonald's dairy in Jackson, La.

Method:

In a food processor, combine all ingredients except pesto and garnishes. Blend until smooth and well mixed. Line a ½–1 quart glass bowl or decorative mold with plastic wrap. Be sure to leave some excess wrap hanging over sides. Spread half of blended cheese mixture into mold. Top with pesto sauce then pour in remaining cheese. Cover and refrigerate a minimum of 8 hours. Flip onto a serving platter and remove plastic wrap. Serve on croutons of New Orleans French Bread. (See recipe.)

Evangeline, the namesake of our goat cheese at her home in Nova Scotia

Beverages

Woman making coffee

In Louisiana we are known both for our love of eating and our love of drinking. Each reputation is honestly earned, but lest you get the wrong idea, our love of beverages goes beyond Mardi Gras revels in New Orleans. In Louisiana, drinking, like eating, is an integral part of our social gatherings. A crawfish boil or turkey fry must feature beer, a brunch without champagne or a Sazerac is a shame, and starting the morning without coffee is an impossibility. Many attribute our "need" to drink to the same cultures that defined our food choices. Consider if you will the fact that the Germans, English, French, Spanish and Italians all had a lengthy history with alcoholic beverages before arriving here. Consider also that Louisiana's excessive heat and humidity required creativity and determination to keep the settlers' collective thirst quenched. Also, prior to the advent of refrigeration and sanitary codes, alcohol was a much safer alternative to water and milk, which was often contaminated. If you did have to boil water to make it safe to drink, you might as well have made coffee with it.

Let's start at the very beginning—of the day that is. Although 19th century plantation owners were known to start their day with Tafia, ale or perhaps a Mint Julep, most Louisianians begin theirs with coffee. Not just any coffee, but a thick, dark, black brew. It is perhaps the most ubiquitous drink consumed in Louisiana and while it has its variations, it's an obsession both in New Orleans and in Cajun Country. But we're not alone. From its unlikely beginnings as a stimulating treat for African goats, coffee has taken the world by storm, inspiring colonization, castigation, economic conquests and catastrophes. Coffee's earliest legend stems from the 9th century when an African goatherd observed that his charges became considerably more frisky after eating the berries of a certain bush. He tried the berries himself with similar effects. By 1000 A.D. coffee had migrated across the Red Sea and the Arabs were brewing the beans into the beverage we now know and love. Coffee's popularity traveled across the world with the spread of Islam, but the Arabs shrewdly created a monopoly by heating the beans to render them infertile prior to export. Legend has it, however, that in the 1600s an Indian pilgrim smuggled fertile beans out of Mecca and the monopoly was broken. Venetian merchants brought coffee home from Middle Eastern markets in 1615 and by the middle of the following century all of Western Europe was enjoying this natural stimulant. The Dutch, too, realized there was lucrative trade in coffee and started growing it in their colonies, but they also adopted the slightly naïve habit of presenting the trees as gifts to dignitaries such as France's Louis XIV. A kidnapped descendant of that tree was taken to Martinique to begin a thriving coffee industry. Current coffee giant, Brazil, broke into the business when a Portuguese envoy, ostensibly settling a border dispute in the Guianas, charmed some seedlings from a French official's wife and sneaked them back to Brazil. And the rest, as they say, is history.

Coffee came to the New World with the colonists, but might never have gained the popularity it did if it wasn't for the tea tax, which prompted not only the incident in Boston Harbor but also a boycott on tea. Coffee soon became America's hot beverage of choice. This fact is evident in Louisiana, where for almost three centuries now, coffee has been a mainstay. New Orleans is famous for its rich, strong dark-roasted coffee, which is a blend of several varieties of coffee beans mixed with roasted, ground chicory root. Chicory was first added to coffee to stretch short supplies during World Wars I and II. New Orleanians remained attached to the flavor even when rationing ceased. This strong black coffee has been enjoyed in French market coffee stalls and restaurants for years. Sometimes equal parts of dark coffee are mixed with hot steamed milk to create Café au Lait, the preferred partner of New Orleans Beignets (a French doughnut). In New Orleans, coffee is taken to yet another dimension at certain fine restaurants where it is spiked with spices, citrus peel, brandy and liqueur, flamed tableside, and then ladled into tall, narrow brûlot cups. Café Brûlot was created by Jules Alciatore for his patrons at Antoine's. He designed special cups and a suspended copper bowl to blend and flame the drink. In Cajun areas, the coffee is even stronger than the traditional New Orleans blend and usually lacks the chicory, but the devotion is just as intense.

> *"The newcomer, taking his first sip of Louisiana coffee, catches his breath and looks hard into the container. Black, dripped, strength incarnate, it stains the cup. If he stays in the southern part of the state, he will eventually be complaining when he gets anything else; a lesser mixture is an insult."*- Harnett Kane, The Bayous of Louisiana

Kane also reported that during World War II Cajun factory workers had to get special dispensations to take flasks or even pots of coffee with them to work, as they could not bear to give up the habit of drinking the thick black brew throughout the day.

Despite this devotion to coffee, many of Louisiana's traditional beverages found favor because of their ability to cool and refresh. On the plantations drinks were served almost slushy over chipped ice not only as a natural way to battle the blazing heat and dampening humidity, but also as evidence to visitors that no expense was being spared (ice being a luxury). Generally, ice was shipped down the Mississippi River on flatboats from cooler Northern states and stored in insulated icehouses in New Orleans or other ports along the river. The alcohol added to the Mint Julep or Planter's Punch was merely a pleasant bonus, although some visitors might have wondered how any work got done when observing the frequency with which these glasses were refilled. The Creoles also recreated the French and Italian custom of freezing fruit beverages as granits. Liqueurs and other beverages were served au frappée by simply filling a glass with crushed ice, pouring the beverage over it and serving it almost freezing. The Mint Julep and the Hurricane (a slushy and intoxicating fruit punch served at Pat O'Brien's

in New Orleans) are two delicious examples of this practice.

Common to a Creole dinner, luncheon or elegant supper was the coup de milieu, or middle course, adapted from the Creoles' French and Spanish heritage. This course consisted of an iced sherbet or punch containing fruit juices and liqueurs. These "fancy punches" were brought to the table in the middle of the feast, just prior to the arrival of the roasts. It should be noted that this course was always served chilled, though the alcohol prevented total freezing. Serving eau sucre, or sweet water, was also a Creole tradition observed at the end of every hearty meal. The drink was passed around the table to promote easy digestion and to prevent insomnia. Sweet water was also common as a summer beverage served to evening visitors, at evening receptions and during summer reunions. Principal sweet water drinks included orangeade, orgeat, lemonade and the Claret cup. Eau sucre parties were famous in old New Orleans, because they allowed poor young women to entertain as lavishly as the wealthier ladies. In fact, there was an unwritten law that anything beyond a glass of eau sucre to end a meal was simply unnecessary. Even Creole babies drank a small glass of the sweet beverage at bedtime to aid digestion and to ensure pleasant dreams.

As you might have gathered, much of Louisiana's beverage history came with the settlers from the six nations and was adapted to fit the lifestyles, conditions and ingredients available in their new homeland. They also learned from the seventh nation, the Native Americans, how to use many of the wild plants and trees that grew here to concoct medicinal and soothing teas such as Sassafras Tea. The French, Spanish and Italians, of course, brought their love of wine, but because grapes did not always fare so well here, they adapted their skills to what was available. Just about everyone knew how to gather what was in season, mulberries, mayhaws, blackberries, black cherries or muscadine grapes,

Making Café au Lait

and turn them into refreshing and delicious sweet wines, ratafias, cordials and bounces. The Germans brought their knowledge of beer and, less than a century after their arrival in Louisiana, there were already ten breweries in the New Orleans area. The English brought ciders, ales and rye whiskey. However, whiskey made from corn (bourbon) proved cheaper and easier to make in the New World. Homemade brews were not limited to wine, but also included ciders, jacks or brandies and cordials. Early Louisianians also recreated recipes for Ratafia, a 15th century beverage found in the regions of Spain, France and Italy bordering the Mediterranean. Ratafia is made from wine, brandy or distilled alcohol fortified with oranges or other fruits, herbs and spices. The Creoles prepared this delightful aperitif by infusing good French brandy with fruit juices or the actual fruits, nuts and odorous flowers. Sometimes aromatic substances were added to impart extra flavor to the liqueur. Ratafias were bottled in pints, sealed, labeled and left for six months. If allowed to sit for 12 months, a far finer cordial or sirop was produced. The Creoles were famous for the cordials or liqueurs that they made yearly and it is said that their anisette and homemade wines were better than any manufactured by the famous French distilleries.

Of course, Louisianians were not content with the status quo. New taste sensations were created out of the old. One of the most popular drinks for which New Orleans gained early notoriety was absinthe. Absinthe is a potent spirit flavored with anise and other herbs, the most notable of which was wormwood (artemsia absinthium). Known as the Green Fairy, this cloudy, bright green drink was developed in 18th century Switzerland by a French doctor, Pierre Ordinaire, for medicinal purposes. Wormwood had been used medicinally by the ancient Egyptians, Greeks and Romans but was extremely bitter. Ordinaire's concoction was far more palatable and soon became popular among artists, writers and musicians. In addition to a powerful alcoholic kick, some claimed the drink had other intoxicating effects, which although attributed to wormwood, were more likely due to the combination of ingredients rather than to one in particular. The drink was traditionally served in a glass over which a slotted absinthe spoon was suspended. Cold water was dripped over a cube of sugar in the spoon. As the sugar and water dripped into the absinthe it would turn cloudy, an effect known as louche. Eventually, in the wake of a wine shortage, absinthe became a popular working man's drink in Europe, but New Orleans was the only American city where it gained a devoted following. The drink was ultimately banned in both Europe and the United States following a sensational crime in 1905 involving a French laborer who murdered his pregnant wife and children after a prolonged drinking binge which included, among many other spirits, absinthe. The drink was also supposedly guilty of causing dementia and tremors, but scholars suggest this was more likely a result of less discriminating customers consuming knockoffs with toxic ingredients added to produce the desired green color.

However unjustly, absinthe is still banned in America. Therefore, if you are offered an Absinthe Suissesse or Absinthe Frappé in New Orleans, it is made with a wormwood-free, anise-flavored substitute or pastis, such as Pernod or Herbsaint, which were developed to fill the ousted green fairy's shoes. Many absinthe drinks were created at Cayetano Ferrer's Absinthe Room in the early 1870s. The Old Absinthe House still stands on Bourbon Street in the French Quarter today. Absinthe also played a role in another New Orleans classic, the Sazerac, which mixes absinthe or a suitable substitute with rye whiskey, simple syrup and Peychaud's bitters. Both the bitters and the drink were created by Antoine Amedee Peychaud, a wealthy French plantation owner who sought refuge in New Orleans following the uprising of natives in Santo Domingo in 1793. He opened a small shop and developed a tonic called "bitters" to cure stomach disorders. Peychaud is also credited by many accounts as being the father of the "cocktail," a mispronunciation of the coquetier, or egg cup in which he served his concotion of bitters and cognac. Soon his "cocktail" was being served in many New Orleans' coffee houses, but became particularly popular at the Sazerac Coffeehouse on Exchange Alley, named for a particular brand of cognac served there, Sazerac-du-Forge et Fils. The drink too, eventually adopted the name Sazerac, but didn't become a classic until an inspired bartender came up with the idea of first coating the glass with absinthe. Later the cognac was generally replaced with rye whiskey and the absinthe with Herbsaint.

Other famous New Orleans cocktails include Antoine's Smile, Pat O'Brian's Hurricane and of course the Ramos Gin Fizz. Ramos arrived in New Orleans in 1888 and purchased the Imperial Cabinet Saloon where he first served his rendition of an existing gin cocktail. The secret of his drink lies in the orange flower water and egg whites. The drink was so popular that he had to move his business to a larger location on Gravier Street. During Mardi Gras 1915, 35 boys were employed just to shake the fizzes, yet even with so many hands, they could not keep up. Not only was the drink popular among Mardi Gras revelers, but it also was a favorite of Louisiana's infamous governor, Huey Long. When he traveled to New York's Roosevelt Hotel, the bartender from the New Orleans Roosevelt accompanied him to ensure that his gin fizzes were prepared just as he liked them.

Many of New Orleans' famous cocktails are perhaps most revered during a leisurely mid-morning brunch. A Sazerac, Mimosa, Ramos Gin Fizz or Mint Julep are all at home here. Other popular brunch libations include Bloody Marys, a Brennan's Mr. Funk or a Brandy Milk Punch, descended from European syllabubs made with wine and cream. The milk punch is also a popular hangover cure, which perhaps positioned it as a perfect Sunday Brunch treat after an overindulgent Saturday night.

There's nothing Louisiana loves more than a party, and there's no doubt we have the beverages for them. Granted most Cajun and Creole holiday or feast day drinks have Old World roots, but that doesn't prevent Louisianians from claiming them as their very own. For example, at one time the French made a spiced wine called Vin de l'Eveque or "Bishop's Wine." When the wine was made with Claret, it became Vin de Cardinale or "Cardinal's Wine." These wines were served during feasts. The frozen punches common at modern day Cajun and Creole celebrations are reminiscent of this old French custom of serving spiced wines. The Creoles adapted oranges to their punch recipes, baking them so they could better extract the juices. They also steeped the oranges in wine and added a touch of Cochineal for a more brilliant cardinal color in their Ponche a la Cardinale. Pim Pom Punch is a makeshift punch made from berries and strawberry soda and traditionally served at Cajun weddings. Planter's Punch, with its combination of citrus juices, might be more reminiscent of the West Indian plantations than the Louisiana ones, but the lifestyle represented is the same. On festive occasions, the Creoles also serve eggnog, an ancient drink with variations in most European countries—although the habit of using rum rather than wine is an American one. The name is thought to come from the habit of serving these egg-based drinks in a carved wooden cup called a noggin. Eggnog was generally served cold at New Year's parties, but hot at Christmas and New Year's reveillons.

The recipes here provide just a taste of some of Louisiana's favorite beverages. While it is possible to recreate some of New Orleans' most famous cocktails, a visit to the city to experience them at their very best is recommended. Some of these libations can even be enjoyed at the very location where they were first created or made famous. However, for the many fruit wines, cordials, ratafias and punches, there is nowhere to find a finer version than the ones you can create yourself. Cheers! Salud! Prost! Santé! Saluté!

CHERRY BOUNCE

Prep Time: 6 Months
Yields: 3 Gallons

Comment:

This family recipe was originally created by Lucie "Cie" Greaud Guttner. Her son-in-law, Gary Anderson adapted the method slightly, but the flavor is still wonderful. Louisiana native black cherries, which ripen in May and June, are perfect for this wine.

Ingredients:

1 gallon black cherries
16 cups sugar
2 gallons whiskey

Method:

Rinse cherries well under running water. Remove and discard as many stems as possible. In a large crock, combine cherries and sugar. Add whiskey. NOTE: Gary recommends using J.W. Dant Bourbon; however, any bourbon will work. Cover crock with cheesecloth and let stand in a cool, dark place approximately 6 months. Cover should allow gas to escape but should not allow whiskey to evaporate. After 6 months, carefully strain wine. Taste for quality and serve, or bottle for later use. Cherry bounce is traditionally served for Thanksgiving.

BLACKBERRY BOUNCE

Prep Time: 7½ Months
Yields: 4 Gallons

Comment:

This recipe came from Herman Ledet, who is married to my Godmother, Anna Mae Zeringue-Ledet. I've been told his Blackberry Bounce is the best in Louisiana's St. James Parish.

Ingredients:

15 pounds blackberries
12½ pounds sugar
3 lemons
1 package yeast
9–10 cups brandy

Method:

In a large stockpot, combine 3 gallons of water and blackberries. Bring to a rolling boil then remove from heat and cool. Strain fruit from water and return water to stockpot. Squeeze blackberries through a cheesecloth. Add juice from blackberries to pot. Bring to a low simmer and dissolve sugar into hot liquid, stirring constantly. Do not boil. Using a whisk, stir constantly to ensure that sugar is dissolved. Squeeze juice from 3 lemons and strain into pot. Remove from heat and allow to cool to 90°F. Add 1 package of yeast. NOTE: Yeast will be killed if water temperature is higher than 90°F. In a 5-gallon water bottle, place 1 gallon of cold tap water. Add 3-gallon juice mixture to water bottle. Shake vigorously to blend well. Place a rubber or cork stopper with manometer attached in neck of bottle. Fill manometer with water according to package directions. NOTE: A manometer is available at your local wine or beer specialty store. Let stand in a cool, dark place for 6 weeks. Before bottling, pour ½ cup brandy into each fifth-sized bottle. This amount will fill about 17 bottles. Siphon blackberry wine into bottles with brandy, cap and store in a cool place for approximately 6 months.

HOMEMADE BLACKBERRY WINE

Prep Time: 6 Weeks
Yields: 4½ Gallons

Comment:
Due to the natural yeast found on the outer skin of wild fruit, such as blackberries, mayhaws and muscadines, sweet wine may be made simply by adding sugar and water to the fruit. The sugar not only sweetens the wine, but it also allows for yeast growth and fermentation.

Ingredients:
2 gallons fresh fruit (blackberries or muscadines)
10 pounds sugar
4½ gallons lukewarm water (100°F)

Method:
Rinse a 10-gallon crock or 2 (5-gallon) plastic water bottles and turn upside down to drain. NOTE: If using 2 bottles, divide all ingredients in half. In container(s), dissolve sugar in 100°F water. Lightly mash fruit then add it to sweetened water. Cover crock with cheesecloth and secure tightly with butcher's twine. If using a water bottle, place air-lock devices, such as manometers, in the mouths of each bottle. Place in a cool, dark room and allow to ferment 6 weeks. At the same time each week, stir crock or shake bottles vigorously to agitate and blend ingredients. When done, strain wine through cheesecloth 2—3 times. Wine is ready to drink. Bottle excess wine and store.

MUSCADINE OR WILD BERRY WINE

Prep Time: 7½ Months
Yields: 4 Gallons

Comment:
Although this recipe is usually made with wild fruits of the bayous such as blackberries, cherries, persimmons, loquats or muscadines, any seasonal fresh fruit will work. Wine should be allowed to ferment 6 weeks. After bottling, wine should sit 6 months prior to serving.

Ingredients:
1½ gallons muscadines or other fruit
10 pounds sugar
2 gallons hot tap water
2 gallons cold tap water

Method:
In a 2-gallon stockpot, mix sugar with hot water. Bring to a low simmer over medium heat, whisking constantly to dissolve sugar. Remove from heat; add cold water then set aside to cool. Over a large container, slightly mash fruit retaining all juice and pulp. Only mash to break skin and release juice. Do not crush completely. Place fruit with all juice and pulp into a 5-gallon crock or water bottle. Cover with sugar water and shake or stir to blend. If using a water bottle, use a rubber or cork stopper with a manometer attached. NOTE: A manometer may be purchased from any wine or beer specialty store. Place 1 inch of water into manometer to prevent air from reaching contents. Set aside in a cool, dark place 6 weeks. Vigorously shake or stir wine once a week. After 6 weeks, remove stopper and siphon liquid into a second 5-gallon bottle through a cheesecloth-lined funnel. Allow wine to sit undisturbed 2—3 hours. Siphon wine into approximately 17 fifth-sized bottles. During filling process, be careful to keep siphon tube 1 inch off bottom so resting sediment does not enter bottles. Place a screw cap or cork on bottles and store in refrigerator or cool, dark place 6 months.

BLOOD ORANGE AND ROSEMARY DAIQUIRI

Prep Time: 30 Minutes
Yields: 10 Cups

Comment:

Blood oranges can be found in most upscale grocery stores during the late fall to early spring. The blood-red juice from this fruit is perfect as a base for holiday punch. For an extra festive touch, garnish with green herbs such as rosemary. You will need about 15 large oranges to get the appropriate amount of juice.

Ingredients:

6 cups blood orange juice, freshly squeezed
3 cups water
1¼ cups sugar
2 large rosemary sprigs
2 tsps chopped rosemary
½ cup sugar for garnish
10 small rosemary sprigs for garnish (optional)

Method:

In 2 ice cube trays, pour 2½ cups of blood orange juice and freeze. Cover and chill remaining juice. In a saucepan, combine water, 1¼ cups sugar and 2 rosemary sprigs, whisking constantly. Bring to a rolling boil, reduce heat to simmer and cook 10 minutes to form a simple syrup. Remove from heat and discard rosemary. Pour into a storage container and chill. When ready to serve, place frozen juice cubes, remaining orange juice, syrup and chopped rosemary in a blender or food processor (2 batches may be necessary). Chop 10–15 seconds or until slushy. Press rim of 10 Champagne glasses in remaining sugar. Fill with punch and garnish with fresh rosemary sprigs.

WARM CHRISTMAS CIDER

Prep Time: 40 Minutes
Yields: 15–20 Servings

Comment:

The weather in the winter months in South Louisiana can be hard to predict. However, it seems that the two or three weeks before Christmas are almost always very cold. Here is an elegant and warming cider to serve on those chilly nights. This red punch with fresh green rosemary sprigs is perfect for a big holiday celebration.

Ingredients:

4½ cups cranberry juice
1½ cups orange juice
3 cups apple cider
2 tbsps dark brown sugar, firmly packed
1 tsp chopped rosemary
3 tbsps grenadine
3 cinnamon sticks
¾ tsp whole cloves
1 orange, thinly sliced
½ cup fresh cranberries
3 sprigs fresh rosemary, rinsed

Method:

In a large pot, combine juices, cider, sugar, chopped rosemary, grenadine, cinnamon, cloves and orange slices. Bring to a boil then reduce heat and simmer 15–20 minutes. Remove from heat. Add cranberries and rosemary sprigs. Pour into a decorative punch bowl and serve immediately. You may also keep cider warm by serving it from a crockpot set on low.

RATAFIA

Prep Time: 7½ Months
Yields: 10–12 (Fifth-sized) Bottles

Comment:
Originally a French beverage, Ratafia was embraced by the Creoles. Often various aromatic substances are added to the cordial to add delightful flavors. Any fruit including grapes, berries, apples, pears or oranges may be used in this wine.

Ingredients:
10 pounds grapes, berries or fruit
2 gallons inexpensive brandy
3 quarts water
7 pounds sugar

Method:
If using berries or grapes, place fruit in a large ceramic crock and smash gently to expose pulp and juice. It is not necessary to crush. Add brandy, cover with cheesecloth and allow to ferment 6 weeks in a cool, dark place. After 6 weeks, bring water to a simmer, add sugar and cook until dissolved. Cool liquid to room temperature then blend well with fruit/liquor mixture. Strain Ratafia once or twice through a double layer of cheesecloth to remove pulp. Be sure all foreign materials are removed. Pour into 10–12 (fifth-sized) bottles. Store in a dark, cool area 6 months prior to drinking. Ratafia may be consumed straight up, on the rocks or blended with crushed ice and club soda.

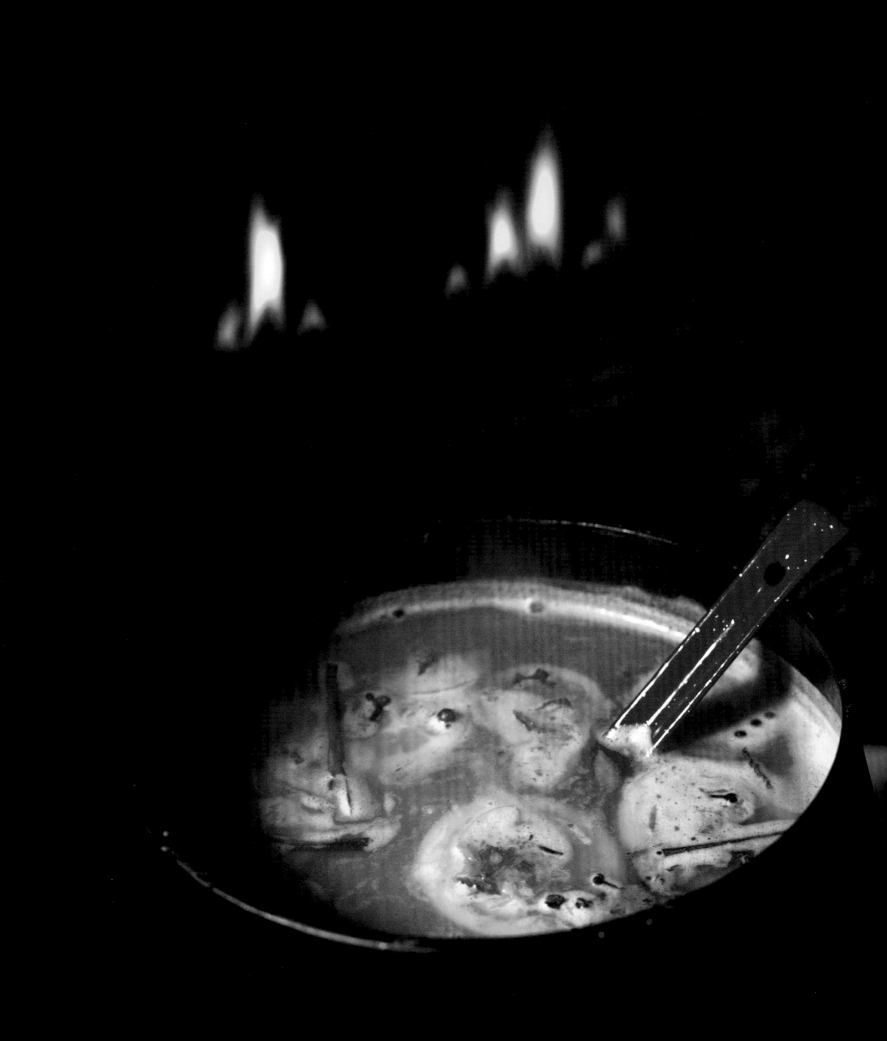

MULLED CIDER
WITH AROMATIC SPICES

Prep Time: 1 Hour
Yields: 20 (6-ounce) Servings

Comment:

Well, there's no doubt that apple cider was one of the warm drinks cherished by Michigan lumbermen. After leaving their northern homes, these settlers introduced the drink to Bayou Country. It wasn't long before interesting variations began to appear in the area of Lake Charles, La.

Ingredients:

4 quarts apple cider
1 cup orange juice
½ cup sugar
1 tsp allspice
½ tsp mace

1 tsp coriander seed
2 tbsps whole cloves
4 cinnamon sticks
2 tbsps grated orange zest
¼ tsp salt

Method:

In a large ceramic saucepan, combine apple cider and orange juice over medium-high heat. Blend well then add sugar, stirring until dissolved. Whisk in allspice, mace, coriander, cloves, cinnamon, orange zest and salt. Bring mixture to a rolling boil then reduce to simmer. Cover and cook 30 minutes. Strain cider and serve hot. For an interesting variation, chill cider and serve as a festive cold punch.

HOT CIDER PUNCH

Prep Time: 20 Minutes
Yields: 15 Servings

Comment:

This delicious punch has a festive presentation and is easy to make. The oranges studded with cloves add to the appearance and flavor of the drink.

Ingredients:

6 cups apple juice
4 tbsps fresh lemon juice
3 cups unsweetened pineapple juice
3 whole cinnamon sticks
½ cup honey
1 tsp nutmeg
2 oranges studded with 10 whole cloves

Method:

Preheat oven to 350°F. In a saucepot, bring juices and cinnamon sticks to a boil. Reduce to simmer, cover and cook 5 minutes. Uncover, add honey and nutmeg and continue to simmer 5 minutes. Place studded oranges on a baking pan with ¼-inch water in bottom. Bake 3–4 minutes to render orange oil to surface of rind. Place warm oranges into cider and serve hot.

MULLED WINE

Prep Time: 20 Minutes
Yields: 8–10 Servings

Comment:

Mulled wine is a heated beverage containing several different spices. Originally, the beverage was called Ypocras or Hipocris, after Hippocrates. Mulled wine was thought to be an elixir that would keep one healthy. Today, the drink is usually served for holiday gatherings.

Ingredients:

4 cups water
1½ cups sugar
1 lemon peel
1 orange peel
2 cinnamon sticks
½ ounce sliced ginger
15 whole cloves
1 pinch nutmeg
1 bottle red wine
1 cup brandy

Method:

In a 1-gallon saucepot, combine all ingredients except wine and brandy. Bring to a boil then reduce to simmer. Cook 10–15 minutes. Add wine and brandy. Simmer over low heat 2–3 minutes. Do not boil. Serve warm.

John Seago of Pontchartrain Vineyards and Winery, Bush, La.

PIM POM PUNCH

Prep Time: 30 Minutes
Yields: 10 Servings

Comment:
This recipe comes from E.J. Ourso, a business mogul born and raised in Donaldsonville, La. Growing up in a country home in Donaldsonville, E.J.'s family had to improvise to enjoy some of the simple pleasures in life. Running down to the grocery store and purchasing a large bottle of strawberry soda was a great substitution for a fancy punch recipe in Bayou Country.

Ingredients:
1 cup fresh blackberries
4 large strawberries, diced
3 (2-liter) bottles strawberry soda
4 multi-colored pansies

Method:
Place an equal amount of blackberries and strawberries in bottom of 4 coffee cups. Fill each coffee cup with strawberry soda, 1 inch from top. Place 1 pansy in each cup. Place in freezer overnight or until soda is solid. NOTE: This berry mixture may also be frozen in ice cube trays. Chill remaining strawberry soda in refrigerator. When ready to serve, pour chilled soda into a punch bowl. Remove frozen coffee cups from freezer and unmold. A little tap water may be needed to loosen molds. Add frozen soda to punch bowl. Serve in punch cups.

Donaldsonville Ice Co.

BLUE MAX PUNCH

Prep Time: 10 Minutes
Yields: 4 Drinks

Comment:
This recipe comes from the Wooden Boat Festival of Madisonville, La. The festival celebrates antique, classic and contemporary watercraft. Blue Max Punch is often enjoyed on the decks of boats as they line the shore of the Tchefuncte River during the festival.

Ingredients:
4 cups ginger ale
2 cups orange or pineapple juice
2 cups Champagne
1 cup blue curaçao
crushed ice

Method:
In a large punch bowl, combine all ingredients until blended. Pour over crushed ice in Champagne glasses.

PLANTER'S PUNCH

Prep Time: 10 Minutes
Yields: 2 Drinks

Comment:
This drink was undoubtedly named in jest of the Southern planters who loved having a drink or two while trying to conceal the contents of the glass. This rum "punch" was consumed daily and was often found on the breakfast table.

Ingredients:
3 ounces light rum
1 ounce grapefruit juice
1 ounce orange juice
1 ounce grenadine
1 ounce dark rum
2 orange slices for garnish
2 cherries for garnish

Method:
Into a cocktail shaker, pour light rum, juices and grenadine. Shake vigorously 1 minute. Fill 2 (12-ounce) wine glasses with ice cubes and pour mixture over ice. Float dark rum on top of drink and garnish with orange slice and cherry.

MINT JULEP

Prep Time: 10 Minutes
Yields: 1 Drink

Comment:

This Southern cooler was extremely popular during the plantation era. It has been said that the early planters would only drink Mint Juleps from silver tumblers. Mint gives the drink an extremely refreshing aroma, which makes it perfect on hot afternoons.

Ingredients:

6 mint leaves
2 tsps powdered sugar
1 ounce bourbon
1 ounce Southern Comfort
1 ounce simple syrup
1 cup crushed ice
1 sprig fresh mint

Method:

In bottom of a 9-ounce old-fashioned glass, place mint leaves and powdered sugar. Using a muddler, crush mint leaves into sugar. Add bourbon, Southern Comfort, simple syrup and crushed ice. Stir until well blended and frost has formed on outside of glass. Garnish with mint and serve with a straw.

HURRICANE

Prep Time: 5 Minutes
Yields: 1 Drink

Comment:

Everyone who visits New Orleans eventually goes to Pat O'Brien's for one of his famous Hurricanes. The drink, with its fruit punch taste, has packed a wallop on many unsuspecting parties. To my knowledge, this is the original recipe and not quite the same as the one served at Pat O'Brien's today.

Ingredients:

1 ounce lemon juice
4 ounces dark rum
4 ounces red passion fruit cocktail mix
crushed ice
orange slice for garnish
cherry for garnish

Method:

Pour lemon juice, rum and cocktail mix into a cocktail shaker. Shake vigorously 1–2 minutes. Pack crushed ice into a 10-ounce highball glass. Pour drink mixture over crushed ice. Garnish with an orange slice and cherry.

BREAKFAST CHEER

Prep Time: 30 Minutes
Yields: 6 Drinks

Comment:

In the South, it's considered good manners to serve a breakfast cocktail prior to the first meal of the day. This custom originated in the plantation days when a Mimosa or Mint Julep was part of a visitor's wake up call. This combination of fruit and Champagne is definitely a "kick-start" for the day.

Ingredients:

1 (15-ounce) can Bartlett pears
1 quart fresh squeezed orange juice
½ bottle Champagne
chopped Bartlett pears for garnish

Method:

Place 6 Pilsner glasses in freezer 1 day prior to serving this drink. In a blender or food processor, purée pears. Pour puréed mixture into a small pitcher then add orange juice and blend well. Place pitcher in refrigerator until ready to serve. Prior to breakfast, fill Pilsner glasses ¾ full with orange juice mixture. Top with Champagne. Garnish each glass with finely chopped pears.

GOOD MORNING MIMOSAS

Prep Time: 5 Minutes
Yields: 2 Drinks

Comment:

In New Orleans, it is customary to start off brunch with an alcoholic beverage. Mimosas are arguably the best known brunch drink. The orange juice makes this cocktail perfect for morning enjoyment.

Ingredients:

4 ounces orange juice
2 tbsps orange liqueur
12 ounces Champagne

Method:

Chill 2 Champagne glasses. Combine 2 ounces orange juice and 1 tablespoon liqueur in each glass. Fill with Champagne and serve.

Breakfast Cheer

MR. FUNK OF NEW ORLEANS

Prep Time: 5 Minutes
Yields: 1 Drink

Comment:

Herman Funk was the cellar master at Brennan's Restaurant in New Orleans for many years. The restaurant created this drink in his memory.

Ingredients:

3 ounces Champagne
2½ ounces cranberry juice
½ ounce peach Schnapps
1 whole strawberry

Method:

In a stemmed glass, pour Champagne then add cranberry juice and Schnapps. Garnish with a strawberry and serve.

*Recipe from *Breakfast at Brennans and Dinner, Too*
Copyright 1994, Brennan's Inc.

BRANDY MILK PUNCH

Prep Time: 10 Minutes
Yields: 1 Drink

Comment:

Brandy Milk Punch is a popular brunch drink served in South Louisiana. It is traditionally believed that a little warm milk punch will cure the ills of a bad hangover.

Ingredients

1½ ounces brandy
¾ cup heavy whipping cream
1 tbsp light crème de cacao
2 tsps powdered sugar
½ cup crushed ice
dash of nutmeg for garnish

Method:

In a cocktail shaker, combine all ingredients except nutmeg. Shake briefly then strain into a 9-ounce old-fashioned glass. Garnish with nutmeg and serve.

ABSINTHE FRAPPÉ

Prep Time: 10 Minutes
Yields: 1 Drink

Comment:

In the 1870s, bartender Cayetano Ferrer created this beverage at "Aleix's Coffee House" in the French Quarter. The coffee house was later renamed "The Absinthe Room" and a New Orleans legend was born. Although absinthe was eventually outlawed and the recipe had to be changed, the drink still remained popular.

Ingredients:

1 cup crushed ice
1 ounce Herbsaint or Pernod
1 ounce anisette
club soda

Method:

Fill a 9-ounce highball glass with crushed ice. Add Herbsaint and anisette. Stir in club soda, a little at a time, until glass is full. Continue to stir until frost forms on outside of glass. If desired, add a teaspoon of simple syrup or powdered sugar to sweeten drink. NOTE: All absinthe substitutes are flavored with anise. Because the flavor of this spice is quite pronounced, the drink should only be served to those who enjoy that taste.

RAMOS GIN FIZZ

Prep Time: 10 Minutes
Yields: 1 Drink

Comment:

This famous drink was named after Henry Ramos of the Imperial Cabinet Saloon in New Orleans. Although the drink existed before his time, he brought it to its highest level of popularity.

Ingredients:

1½ ounces gin
1 egg white
1 ounce heavy whipping cream
1½ tbsps powdered sugar
juice of 1 lemon
4 drops orange flower water
2 ounces club soda
½ cup crushed ice
1–2 drops pure vanilla extract (optional)

Method:

In a cocktail shaker, combine all ingredients except vanilla. Shake vigorously 3–5 minutes. Drink should be fairly thick at this point. If desired, add vanilla and give mixture another quick shake. Strain into a 9-ounce cocktail glass and serve immediately.

SAZERAC

Prep Time: 10 Minutes
Yields: 1 Drink

Comment:

The Sazerac cocktail was originally created by Antoine Peychaud in the 1830s. John Schiller named the beverage after the famous Sazerac-de-Forge et Fils Cognac served in his New Orleans coffee house. The business was sold to Thomas Handy in 1870, and the recipe was changed to the one we know today. Sazerac is often called "America's first cocktail."

Ingredients:

½ cup crushed ice
1 tsp sugar
1 dash Peychaud Bitters
1 dash Angostura Bitters
1½ ounces rye whiskey
1 dash Herbsaint
1 lemon peel twist

Method:

Pack a 3½-ounce old-fashioned glass with crushed ice. In a second glass, mix sugar, Peychaud and Angostura. Blend well then add whiskey. Continue to blend until sugar is dissolved. Place a few ice cubes into drink and stir until liquid is chilled. Discard ice from first glass. Add a dash of Herbsaint to chilled glass and swirl until coated. Pour out all excess Herbsaint. Pour mixed drink into chilled glass, garnish with lemon peel and serve.

CAJUN CURE FOR HANGOVERS

Prep Time: 30 Minutes
Yields: 2–4 Servings

Comment:

This concoction of high-vitamin vegetables will replenish your body after a long night of drinking and celebrating. For those who can handle a little alcohol, below is an alcoholic version of this tasty cocktail.

Ingredients:

2 (16-ounce) cans diced or crushed tomatoes
1 (8-ounce) V8® juice
1 green bell pepper, chopped
1 red bell pepper, chopped
1 small red onion, chopped
1 cucumber, peeled, seeded and chopped
1 tsp minced garlic
¾ tsp salt
3 tbsps red wine vinegar
1 tbsp extra virgin olive oil
1 can beef broth
salt and black pepper to taste
Louisiana hot sauce to taste
4 celery sticks for garnish
4 lime wedges for garnish

Method:

In a blender, purée tomatoes, V8®, bell peppers, onions, cucumbers, garlic, salt, vinegar and oil. Thin soup to drinking consistency by adding beef broth and additional V8® if necessary. Season with salt, pepper and hot sauce. Chill and serve in highball glasses. Garnish with celery stick and lime wedge.

LAFITTE'S SUNRISE:

For those who don't have a hangover, here is a vodka-laced version of this tasty cocktail. Separate prepared cocktail into servings and add 1 ounce high-quality vodka to each. Blend well in a martini shaker and serve in a highball glass garnished with spicy grilled jumbo shrimp.

BAYOU BLOODY MARY

Prep Time: 15 Minutes
Yields: 1 Drink

Comment:

While working in Harry's New York Bar in Paris, Pete Petoit developed this legend of a drink. It is said to be named for Mary Tudor, who massacred many Protestants in England. This hearty beverage is often thought to be a hangover cure.

Ingredients:

3 ounces water
1½ ounces vodka
½ cup tomato juice
½ tsp Worcestershire sauce
¼ tsp ground celery seed
½ tsp lemon juice
¼ tsp Louisiana hot sauce
2 tbsps beef bouillon or broth
pickled green beans for garnish

Method:

In an old-fashioned glass, combine all ingredients except beans. Mix well, garnish with green beans and serve.

SPIKED EGGNOG CABANOCEY

Prep Time: 1 Hour
Yields: 12–15 Servings

Comment:
Eggnog is found on every table in Cajun Country during Christmas season. Many believe that the "nog" in eggnog comes from the word "noggin," a small wooden mug in which the drink was served.

Ingredients:
2 eggs, separated
2 quarts heavy whipping cream
1 pound powdered sugar
2 tbsps pure vanilla extract
1 cup dark rum
1 cup bourbon
¼ tsp allspice
pinch of cloves
freshly-grated nutmeg for garnish

Method:
In a heavy-bottomed saucepot, heat heavy whipping cream to 190°F. Do not boil or allow cream to form a skin on top. Place egg yolks in an electric mixer and beat 2–3 minutes or until light and fluffy. Slowly add powdered sugar, beating constantly until mixture has a ribbon-like texture. Thoroughly blend in vanilla, rum and bourbon. Pour in approximately 1 quart of hot cream while blending slowly to temper yolks. Slowly pour egg mixture into pot of cream, whisking constantly. Allow to stand covered for approximately 1 hour to blend flavors. Add allspice and cloves. Refrigerate mixture a minimum of 3 hours. When ready to serve, whisk egg whites until stiff but not dry. Using a rubber spatula, fold whites into eggnog mixture. Pour into a serving bowl and sprinkle with nutmeg.

CREOLE KAHLÚA

Prep Time: 20 Minutes
Yields: 1 Quart

Comment:
This liqueur makes a great gift for adult coffee lovers. Although the drink may be served as is, for an interesting dessert, serve Creole Kahlúa over vanilla ice cream.

Ingredients:
1½ cups water
2½ cups sugar
2½ cups vodka
5 tbsps instant coffee
1 tbsp pure vanilla extract

Method:
In a saucepan, combine water and sugar over low heat until sugar is melted. Remove from heat then stir in vodka. Add coffee, stir until dissolved then add vanilla. Funnel into a decorative bottle and seal.

CAFÉ BRÛLOT

Prep Time: 15 Minutes
Yields: 6–8 Servings

Comment:

Café Brûlot is often served in New Orleans. In French, Brûlot means burned. The recipe for this famous blending of dark roasted Creole coffee with brandy and vermouth is attributed to Dominique Youx, top lieutenant to the pirate Jean Lafitte. If prepared at the table, Café Brûlot can be a magnificent ending to an elegant meal.

Ingredients:

2 cups Café Noir (see recipe)
1 lemon
1 orange
6 whole cloves
2 small cinnamon sticks
1½ ounces Triple Sec
1½ ounces brandy

Method:

A brûlot bowl, a mainstay in New Orleans households, is any silver or copper bowl that can be heated from below. Over brûlot bowl, peel lemon in one continuous motion so that peel is a long spiral. Any juice from lemon should fall directly into bowl. Peel orange in same fashion. Insert cloves into orange and lemon peels at 1-inch intervals then add to bowl. Add cinnamon, Triple Sec and brandy. Place a Sterno or candle under bowl and bring liquid to a simmer, stirring constantly. Carefully ignite simmering liquid with a long-handled lighter. NOTE: A ribbon of golden blue flame may be achieved by ladling liquors into air above bowl. Using a large, double-tined fork, lift orange and lemon peels out of liquid and hold in flame. This process will render more citrus flavor into coffee. Return peels to liquid and swirl bowl. When liquid has reduced to half volume or flame is extinguished, pour in hot coffee. If there is still a flame, stir until it dies out. Squeeze a small amount of orange and lemon juice into bowl to naturally sweeten coffee. Ladle hot brûlot into warm demi-tasse cups.

CREOLE CAFÉ NOIR

Prep Time: 15 Minutes
Yields: 6–8 Servings

Comment:

No coffee compares to that made in South Louisiana. No sumptuous Creole feast would be complete without a cup of traditional Café Noir, a blend of dark-roasted coffee and chicory. This beverage is still recognized for its therapeutic values. Many old Cajuns and Creoles have credited Café Noir for their longevity.

Ingredients:

5 tbsps ground dark roast coffee and chicory (Community Coffee New Orleans Blend®)
5 cups cold water

Method:

In the top of a French drip coffee pot, place coffee and chicory. In a 1-quart sauce pot, bring water to a rolling boil. Drip hot water, a few tablespoons at a time, through coffee until all is used. To keep coffee warm, place pot in a frying pan filled with water over low heat. Coffee may be refrigerated in a glass jar and heated whenever needed. This coffee is usually served black and only in demi-tasse cups.

CAJUN COFFEE

Prep Time: 1 Hour
Yields: 4–6 Servings

Comment:

This recipe makes a very strong black coffee that is enjoyed in the bayou region. Traditionally, the coffee is served in a demi-tasse with one heaping spoon of sugar.

Ingredients:

8 tbsps ground dark roast coffee
4½ cups cold water

Method:

In the top of a French drip coffee pot, place 8 tablespoons of dark roast coffee. In a 1-quart sauce pot, bring water to a rolling boil. Drip boiling water through coffee, 2–3 tablespoons at a time, until all water has been used. To keep coffee warm, place pot in a frying pan filled with water over low heat. The longer coffee sits, the stronger it will become.

CAFÉ AU LAIT

Prep Time: ½ Hour
Yields: 4–6 Servings

Comment:
Café au Lait is a tradition in South Louisiana. Many Louisianians won't drink their coffee any other way. The drink is normally served at breakfast with a heaping platter of beignets.

Ingredients:
2 cups brewed Cajun Coffee (see recipe)
4 cups heavy whipping cream
6 tbsps sugar

Method:
In a small saucepot, scald cream over medium-high heat. Do not boil. Add hot Cajun Coffee, blend well into cream then sweeten with sugar. Remember, it will be a little sweeter than regular coffee.

SASSAFRAS TEA

Prep Time: 1½ Hours
Yields: 2 Gallons

Comment:

The sassafras tree of Louisiana served multiple purposes in the kitchens of the Bayou State. The leaves were dried and ground into filé powder, a thyme-like spice, and sprinkled over gumbo and stews. The sassafras root was used in smoking and grilling, but it is best known for producing this beverage, the predecessor to America's root beer. In recent decades, studies have shown that the safrole in the sassafras root is a carcinogenic agent. Since this discovery, the tea has fallen out of favor, however many Cajuns still appreciate the flavor. It is recommended that you do your own research on the topic and fully understand the risks before trying this tea.

Ingredients:

1 sassafras root or 2 cups sassafras chips
2 gallons water
2 cups sugar
juice of 1 lemon
orange slices for garnish
mint leaves for garnish

Method:

Wash and strip bark from sassafras root. Using a sharp knife, chip away 2 cups of pulp. Place 2 gallons of water in a stockpot then add pulp chips. Bring to a rolling boil then reduce to simmer and cook approximately 1 hour. Strain tea into a large pitcher. Add sugar and lemon juice. Reserve root chips for future use. Chips may be used 4–6 times in tea then can be used for smoking or flavoring in a barbecue pit. Allow tea to cool then pour in a glass over ice. Garnish with lemon slices and mint leaves.

MINT LEMONADE

Prep Time: 12 Hours
Yields: 1 Gallon

Comment:
This wonderful, intense beverage was created by Robert Whitehurst. His method of extracting essential oils from mint is unique. This recipe requires a gallon jar with a tight-fitting lid.

Ingredients:
1 cup fresh mint	2 cups sugar
juice of 4 lemons	2 cups water
1 lemon peel, thinly sliced	1 gallon water

Method:
In a saucepan, bring sugar and 2 cups water to a boil. Stir constantly until sugar dissolves, creating a simple syrup. Allow syrup to cool to room temperature. Fill gallon jar with hot tap water (190°F). Allow jar to become very hot to touch then discard water. Immediately put mint into jar and screw lid on tightly. Refrigerate, allowing jar to cool completely. A partial vacuum seal will be created when jar cools, extracting all flavorful oils from mint. Remove lid from jar then add lemon juice, lemon peel and syrup. Shake vigorously then fill to top with water. Replace lid and allow to mature overnight.

Festivals

Rice Festival, Crowley, La.

In Louisiana we don't need a reason to celebrate, but give us one and the good times are sure to roll. Louisiana is home to more than 400 annual festivals celebrating everything from a local delicacy to a favorite saint, a good harvest to a particular heritage. Louisiana's natural abundance of fruit, vegetables, seafood and game is cause enough for at least one major festival a month. Many of these festivals had small, casual beginnings as church fundraisers, morale boosters or simple ceremonies and have grown into tremendous parties spanning several days. Central to any Louisiana festival is of course, food. Many of them, like the Gumbo Festival, Jambalaya Festival, Cochon de Lait Festival or Strawberry Festival were inspired by food. Even the festivals that are not food-related are, without fail, venues for great eats. Whether it is traditional fair food like hotdogs, fry bread and popcorn, or more exotic selections like alligator on a stick, duck and andouille gumbo or frog legs, nobody goes hungry at a Louisiana festival. Of course beer, wine and Daiquiris figure prominently, even at many of our church fairs.

Second only to the food at a Louisiana festival is the music. Many feature Cajun and Creole music, but others also highlight jazz, rock and roll or the music of a particular culture. Traditional Native American, African, French, German, Spanish or Italian music can all be heard. Whether it is rhythm and blues at the Black Heritage Festival or swamp pop at the Shrimp & Petroleum Festival, our festivals are truly treats for the ear. Most festivals also feature any combination of kids' activities, carnival rides and competitions, parades and prizes, religious ceremonies and historic exhibits.

Here we have selected just a taste of some of Louisiana's most notable festivals as well as some favorite recipes drawn from each. Descriptions of many more festivals as well as many more mouthwatering recipes can be found in *Louisiana Sampler*, a book dedicated to Louisiana's fairs and festivals, published by Chef John Folse & Company. Even then, there are many, many more festivals to be enjoyed firsthand whatever time of year you choose to visit Louisiana. As you plan your vacation, you can contact the Louisiana Office of Tourism at (800) 677-4082 to find out which of the more than 400 festivals you can include in your visit. You can also find more information at www.crt.state.la.us/crt/tourism/tourism.htm.

Rice Farming

Black Heritage Festival
Lake Charles, La.

This annual celebration of Louisiana's African-American heritage features educational, cultural and entertaining activities for all ages. Music is a highlight of this festival where some of the area's best-known artists treat the crowd to the sounds of gospel, jazz, blues and zydeco. The festival, which is held each March, also features historical and educational exhibits, a marketplace, a kid's zone and talent and fashion shows. The first Black Heritage Festival was held at the Lake Charles Civic Center in 1987 and continues to grow. This three-day event offers the perfect opportunity to immerse yourself in the culture that contributed so much to Louisiana's food, music and art.

BLACK-EYED PEAS WITH SALT MEAT AND HAM HOCK

Prep Time: 2 Hours
Yields: 8 Servings

Comment:

Black-eyed peas, a gift from the Africans, are treasured by all Southern cooks. The pea began as only a Southern tradition, but it soon found its way across America to become a favorite vegetable on the New Year's Day table.

Ingredients:

1 pound black-eyed peas
½ pound salt meat
1 smoked ham hock
½ cup shortening or bacon drippings
1 cup diced onions
1 cup diced celery
1 cup diced red bell peppers
¼ cup minced garlic
1 cup sliced green onions
½ cup chopped parsley
salt and black pepper to taste
Louisiana hot sauce to taste

Method:

Rinse beans and remove any that are hard or discolored. Beans will cook faster if soaked in water overnight in refrigerator. When ready to cook, rinse beans once again in cold water. In a 2-quart saucepot, melt shortening or bacon drippings over medium-high heat. Add onions, celery, bell peppers and garlic. Sauté 3–5 minutes or until vegetables are wilted. Stir in salt meat and ham hock. Cook 5 additional minutes. Add black-eyed peas and enough cold water to cover ingredients by 2 inches. Bring mixture to a rolling boil then reduce to simmer and cook 30 minutes. Stir occasionally to keep vegetables from scorching. Continue to cook 1–1½ hours or until peas are tender, stirring occasionally. Add green onions and parsley. Season to taste with salt, pepper and hot sauce.

SMOTHERED SEVEN STEAKS

Prep Time: 3½ Hours
Yields: 6 Servings

Comment:

The seven steak is so named due to the shape of the bone associated with the cut of meat. The steak is normally pan-fried and served with a light onion gravy. Seven steaks are often associated with the breakfast dish, grillades.

Ingredients:

4 pounds seven steaks or round steaks
4 tbsps vegetable oil
1 cup diced onions

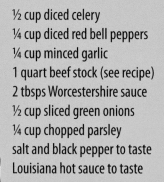

½ cup diced celery
¼ cup diced red bell peppers
¼ cup minced garlic
1 quart beef stock (see recipe)
2 tbsps Worcestershire sauce
½ cup sliced green onions
¼ cup chopped parsley
salt and black pepper to taste
Louisiana hot sauce to taste

Method:

In a 12-inch cast iron skillet, heat oil over medium-high heat. Add steaks and sear until golden brown. Remove meat from pan and keep warm. In same skillet, sauté onions, celery, bell peppers and garlic 3–5 minutes or until wilted. Return steaks to skillet and add stock and Worcestershire. Bring mixture to a rolling boil then reduce to simmer. Cover and cook 2½ hours. Add green onions and parsley then season with salt, pepper and hot sauce. Serve over rice or mashed potatoes. NOTE: This dish is also excellent when baked 2–2½ hours at 375°F.

Los Isleños Festival
St. Bernard, La.

One of Louisiana's most unique festivals is the Los Isleños Festival held each November by the descendants of Canary Islanders who settled in Louisiana between 1778 and 1783. Four settlements of these people were strategically placed around New Orleans to help Spain defend against British attack. The two-day festival features Canary Island dancers, music by Spanish artists, boat building, historical demonstrations, and authentic foods of the Isleños. While the thousands of descendants of the original Isleños are now spread throughout the New Orleans area, there is still a strong sense of tradition and community among them. The Isleños Center is dedicated to preserving and highlighting that culture year-round.

Caldo in antique blue porcelain s

CALDO

Prep Time: 2 Hours
Yields: 8 Servings

Comment:
Caldo, possibly a derivative of the word cauldron, means both broth and warm or hot. The Canary Islanders brought this famous vegetable and meat soup to Louisiana. Many think it is the corn and cabbage in this recipe that eventually gave the name macque choux to our famous corn and tomato dish.

Ingredients:
1 pound white beans
1 pound diced ham
1 pound pickled meat
½ cup vegetable oil
2 cups diced onions
1 cup diced celery
1 cup diced bell peppers
¼ cup minced garlic
2 (8-ounce) cans tomato sauce
1 gallon cold water
1 (15-ounce) can string beans
1 (15-ounce) can mustard greens
1 (15-ounce) can spinach
1 (15-ounce) can corn
1 (15-ounce) can peas
1 (15-ounce) can sweet potatoes
1 (15-ounce) can yellow squash
1 (15-ounce) can new potatoes
2 ears corn
1½ heads shredded cabbage
salt and black pepper to taste
Louisiana hot sauce to taste

Method:
In a 12-quart Dutch oven, heat oil over medium-high heat. Add ham and pickled meat. Sauté until golden brown. Stir in onions, celery, bell peppers and garlic. Sauté 3–5 minutes or until vegetables are wilted. Add white beans, tomato sauce and water. Bring mixture to a rolling boil and continue to cook 1 hour or until beans are tender. Blend in all canned vegetables along with cabbage and fresh corn. Continue to cook on medium heat approximately 30 minutes. Season with salt, pepper and hot sauce. Water may be added to retain consistency during cooking. Serve as a soup over steamed white rice.

MIRLITON PIE

Prep Time: 1 Hour 45 Minutes
Yields: 8 Servings

Comment:
The chayote squash, or vegetable pear, is called a mirliton in South Louisiana. The Los Isleños, or Canary Islanders, brought mirliton to the area in the 1700s. Today, it is the premier vegetable of the Cajuns and Creoles and is found in many entrées and side dishes.

Ingredients:
6–8 mirliton
1 cup sugar
3 eggs, well beaten
1 cup biscuit mix
½ cup milk
¼ cup melted butter
1 tbsp pure vanilla extract
⅛ tsp nutmeg
⅛ tsp cinnamon
1 (9-inch) unbaked pie shell

Method:
Preheat oven to 350°F. Slice mirliton lengthwise. Place in a large pot and cover by 2 inches of lightly-salted cold water. Bring to a rolling boil and cook 45 minutes or until extremely tender. Drain and allow to cool. Using a tablespoon, remove seeds and gently scoop meat from outer shell. Drain meat in a colander and discard shell. Measure 2 full cups of mirliton and set aside. In a large mixing bowl, whisk together sugar and eggs. Sprinkle in biscuit mix alternately with milk and melted butter. Blend well then add vanilla, nutmeg and cinnamon. Fold in mashed mirliton. Pour mixture into a prepared pie shell and bake 45–50 minutes or until done. This dish is similar to bread pudding and can be eaten as a dessert or vegetable.

Strawberry Festival
Ponchatoula, La.

Since 1972, Ponchatoula, the "Strawberry Capital of the World," has hosted a festival each April celebrating one of Louisiana's most important agricultural products. While most people associate April with spring showers, here in South Louisiana, it is the month where we are often granted a couple of weeks of near perfect weather. This weather is ideal for adding the final blush to Louisiana's strawberry crop in the area surrounding Ponchatoula, where most of them are grown. Almost 250,000 people visit this quaint little town for strawberry shortcake, strawberry bread, strawberry jam, strawberry Daiquiris and just about any other preparation imaginable for these sweet, red treasures.

The festival is also the perfect place to buy a flat or two to bring home. During the two-day festival you can catch a parade, ride the ferris wheel, visit festival booths, hear great music or even shop for antiques.

STRAWBERRY DAIQUIRI

Prep Time: 30 Minutes
Yields: 6 Drinks

Comment:

The number of fruits associated with coolers or Daiquiris in Bayou Country is too numerous to mention. The crushed ice Daiquiris of New Orleans started to take on a different look as the bartenders in the French Quarter began to use their imagination in blending various fruits into the alcohol mixture.

Ingredients:

2 pints fresh strawberries
    OR 1 (12-ounce) package frozen strawberries
10 cups crushed ice
1 cup light rum
2 tbsps lime juice
2 tbsps sugar
¼ cup strawberry liqueur
mint for garnish

Method:

In a blender, combine all ingredients. Blend at 10–15 second intervals until thoroughly mixed. Pour frappé into chilled cocktail or Champagne glasses. Before serving, garnish with fresh strawberries and mint.

PEPPER-SEARED LAMB CHOPS WITH STRAWBERRY GLACE

Prep Time: 45 Minutes
Yields: 6 Servings

Comment:

Every English garden in the Feliciana parishes of Louisiana grew strawberries during spring. The combination of lamb chops, rack or even roast with these sweet spring berries makes perfect sense in the Louisiana kitchen.

Ingredients:

12 lamb chops, ½-inch thick
¼ cup ground pink peppercorns
¼ cup ground black peppercorns
1 ounce strawberry wine
1 tbsp strawberry jam
¼ cup sliced strawberries
2 cups demi-glace (see recipe)
    OR beef gravy
½ cup vegetable oil
1 cup seasoned flour
½ cup sliced green onions
1 tbsp minced garlic
1 cup sliced oyster mushrooms
1 tsp chopped thyme
salt and cracked black pepper to taste

Method:

Place lamb chops on a large platter and evenly coat both sides with crushed peppercorns. Set aside. In a heavy-bottomed sauté pan, heat oil over medium-high heat. Dust chops in flour and shake off excess. Sauté until golden brown on both sides then remove, set aside and keep warm. In same pan, sauté green onions, garlic, mushrooms and thyme 3–5 minutes or until wilted. Remove pan from burner and add wine. NOTE: Be careful as alcohol will ignite and burn a few minutes. Add strawberry jam, sliced berries and demi-glace. Season with salt and pepper. Swirl skillet above burner until jam and demi-glace are blended. Bring to a rolling boil and reduce sauce until slightly thickened. Return chops to pan. Heat 2–3 minutes and serve with sauce.

Breaux Bridge Crawfish Festival

Breaux Bridge, La.

This festival celebrates the symbol most often associated with the Cajun people, the crawfish. Hundreds of thousands of people visit the small town of Breaux Bridge each May to taste a delicacy that may not be unique to Louisiana, but has certainly been mastered here. In fact, in 1959 Breaux Bridge celebrated its centennial and was dubbed "Crawfish Capital of the World" by the Louisiana Legislature. While spicy, boiled crawfish are the prime attraction, festival goers can also enjoy crawfish étouffée, crawfish jambalaya, crawfish pies, crawfish bisque, fried crawfish, crawfish-stuffed vegetables, and more. Here you can not only listen to great Cajun and zydeco music, but you can also learn to play it at the Cajun music workshops. The festival features crawfish races, a crawfish eating contest, a crawfish étouffée cooking contest and a Cajun dance contest. The fun never ends in "La Capitole Mondiale des Ecrivisseres," especially in May.

BOILED CRAWFISH

Prep Time: 2 Hours
Yields: 12 Servings

Comment:
The crawfish boil is the premier social event in the springtime in Louisiana. Friends and family gather for an afternoon under the shade of an oak tree to enjoy a delicacy unparalleled in the South.

Ingredients:

50 pounds cleaned crawfish
30 quarts cold water
12 medium onions, quartered
6 heads garlic, split in half, exposing pods
4 whole artichokes
2 pounds smoked sausage, sliced
12 lemons, quartered
1 quart vegetable oil
4 pounds salt
¼ pound cayenne pepper
4 (3-ounce) bags crab boil
3 (12-ounce) bottles beer
24 medium red potatoes
12 ears of corn

Method:
Live crawfish may be purchased already washed from your seafood supplier. However, a second rinsing in cold water would not hurt. Purging crawfish, that is, washing them in cold salted water, has been found to be useless. In a 60-quart stockpot, bring water to a rolling boil. Add onions, garlic, artichokes, sausage, lemons, oil, salt, pepper, crab boil and beer. Boil 30 minutes to ensure good flavor in liquid. Add red potatoes and cook 8–10 minutes then add corn. Boil 3–5 minutes. Place crawfish in water. Once water returns to a boil, cook crawfish 5–7 minutes. Turn off heat and allow crawfish to sit in hot water approximately 30 minutes. Test crawfish at 10-minute intervals during soaking until flavor is to your liking. Crawfish should be served hot with potatoes, corn and pitchers of ice cold beer.

FRIED SOFT-SHELL CRAWFISH

Prep Time: 30 Minutes
Yields: 6 Servings

Comment:
Like crabs, crawfish shed their shells in order to grow. During the period in which the shell is soft and thin, these Cajun delicacies can be enjoyed fried or sautéed.

Ingredients for Batter:
1 cup milk
½ cup water
1 egg
3 tbsps Creole mustard
salt and cracked black pepper to taste

Method:
In a 1-quart mixing bowl, combine all ingredients. Whisk until well blended. Set aside.

Ingredients for Breading:
2 cups seasoned corn flour
1½ tsps cracked black pepper
2¼ tsps salt
1½ tsps cayenne pepper
1½ tsps granulated garlic
1½ tsps dried thyme

Method:
In a 1-quart mixing bowl, combine all ingredients. Set aside.

Ingredients for Frying:
1 pound soft-shell crawfish
1½ quarts vegetable oil

Method:
In a home-style deep fryer such as a FryDaddy, preheat oil according to manufacturer's directions or to 375°F. Place soft-shell crawfish in batter mixture and allow to sit 10–15 minutes. Drain excess liquid from crawfish and coat well in breading. Shake off excess and fry crawfish, a few at a time, until golden brown and floating to top of fryer. Remove and drain on paper towels. Serve hot with Louisiana Cocktail or Tartar Sauce. (See recipes.)

Cochon de Lait Festival
Mansura, La.

Named by former soldiers of Napoleon who noted that this part of Louisiana reminded them of El Mansura, Egypt, this little town is steeped in French tradition. In 1960, the townspeople resurrected one such tradition, the cochon de lait, to celebrate the town's centennial. The idea caught on and the gathering turned into an annual festival, held on Mother's Day weekend. Translated literally, cochon de lait means "suckling pig," but generally larger young hogs are used for this outdoor culinary treat. The pigs, 20-30 pounds apiece, are lined up in rows over a very hot, open, hickory fire. Turned constantly for six to eight hours, the cochon de lait turns golden and crispy on the outside and remains tender and juicy on the inside. Even those who are a little squeamish at the sight of pigs being roasted whole generally succumb to the incredible aroma and taste of the finished product. The festival took a hiatus in the late 1970s and early 1980s but in 1987 returned in full force with all the trimmings you would expect from a Louisiana festival.

HOG'S HEAD CHEESE WITHOUT THE HEAD

Prep Time: 3 Hours
Yields: 3 Loaves

Comment:
For those among us who are looking for ways to cut back some of the fat in our cooking while enjoying the traditional flavors of Cajun Country, this recipe is perfect. Instead of pork fat, gelatin is used to hold the cheese together.

Ingredients:
6 pounds pork shoulder	1½ tsps cayenne pepper
6 pig's feet	1½ tsps salt
3 packages unflavored gelatin	½ tsp black pepper
10 cups water	1 cup chopped parsley
2 onions, quartered	1 cup minced carrots
3 cups sliced green onions	1 cup minced red bell peppers
2 bay leaves	

Method:
Prepare gelatin according to package directions using 2 cups of water. Set aside. Cut pork shoulder into 1-inch cubes and place in a large stockpot along with pig's feet and 8 cups water. Add onions, 1½ cups green onions, bay leaves, cayenne, salt and pepper. Bring to a rolling boil, reduce to simmer and cook 2 hours or until meat falls from bone. Remove meat from liquid and strain solids from stock. Reserve liquid and discard vegetables. Once meat is cooled, remove and discard bones. Grind or finely chop meat. Return liquid to stockpot and bring to a rolling boil. Add gelatin, ground meat, remaining green onions, parsley, carrots and bell peppers. Cook 10 minutes, remove from heat and allow to cool slightly. Ladle mixture into 2 or 3 standard loaf pans and allow to cool. Refrigerate overnight and serve with crackers or croutons.

Cooking on the Cochon de Lait pits at White Oak Plantation, Baton Rouge

SMOTHERED PORK WITH TURNIPS

Prep Time: 1 Hour
Yields: 6 Servings

Comment:
During winter, boucheries are performed along River Road in South Louisiana. Fortunately, winter is also turnip season. Pork and turnips has become a common dish on the Cajun table.

Ingredients:
2½ pounds cubed pork
4 turnips, peeled and diced
½ cup vegetable oil
½ cup flour
1 cup diced onions
1 cup diced celery
½ cup diced bell peppers
¼ cup minced garlic
4 cups beef or chicken stock (see recipe)
1 cup sliced green onions
½ cup chopped parsley
salt and cracked black pepper to taste

Method:
In a heavy-bottomed Dutch oven, heat oil over medium-high heat. Whisk in flour, stirring constantly until light brown roux is achieved. (See roux recipes.) Stir-fry pork into roux. Add onions, celery, bell peppers and garlic. Continue cooking 3–5 minutes or until vegetables are wilted. Blend in turnips. Pour in beef stock, a little at a time, stirring constantly. Bring to a low boil them reduce to simmer and cook 45 minutes. Add green onions and parsley. Season with salt and cracked black pepper. Continue to cook until pork is tender.

Creole Tomato Festival
New Orleans

One of the classic rites of summer in New Orleans, the Creole Tomato Festival, celebrates this homegrown treasure on the near-hallowed grounds of the French Market. Truly good enough to eat right off the vine, the Creole Tomato is also the star of many South Louisiana recipes. It is bigger, sweeter, juicier and meatier than most varieties and lends itself well to being stuffed, fried, sliced in a sandwich and so much more. It is so good in fact, it deserves a festival complete with street performers, jazz bands, celebrity chefs and great food. The best part is there are always plenty of tomatoes left over to take home, even with an average of 50,000 visitors to the festival each June. Of course, once you are at the French Market, there is a whole tantalizing world to explore just beyond its boundaries.

TOMATO BISQUE

Prep Time: 1½ Hours
Yields: 6–8 Servings

Comment:

The Creole tomato is more about a region than about a variety. Although a Creole tomato was developed by Louisiana State University, more often the term refers to those tomatoes grown in St. Bernard Parish. The soil there produces a super-sweet, juicy product sought after by many Louisiana cooks.

Ingredients:

6 medium Creole tomatoes
2 medium Creole tomatoes, seeded and coarsely chopped
1 cup tomato sauce
½ cup olive oil
2 cups diced onions
1 cup diced celery
½ cup diced bell peppers
¼ cup minced garlic
1 cup diced carrots
1 cup flour
1 cup dry white wine
3 quarts beef stock (see recipe)
1 tbsp chopped basil
1 tbsp chopped thyme
1 tbsp chopped oregano
1 cup heavy whipping cream
1½ tsps salt
⅛ tsp white pepper
Louisiana hot sauce to taste
8 leaves fresh basil, cut into strips for garnish

Method:

Cut 6 whole tomatoes in half, remove cores and squeeze out seeds. In a 5-quart cast iron Dutch oven, heat oil over medium-low heat. Add onions, celery, bell peppers, garlic and carrots. Sauté 3–5 minutes or until vegetables are wilted. Sprinkle in flour and whisk until a light brown roux is achieved. (See roux recipes.) Blend in halved tomatoes, tomato sauce and wine. Pour in beef stock, a little at a time, until a soup-like consistency is achieved. Bring to a low boil then reduce to simmer. Stir in basil, thyme and oregano. Cook 30 minutes, adding stock as necessary to retain volume. Fold in cream then season with salt, pepper and hot sauce. In a food processor or blender, purée bisque in small batches until smooth. When ready to serve, garnish with chopped tomatoes and fresh basil.

FRIED GREEN TOMATOES

Prep Time: 30 Minutes
Yields: 6 Servings

Comment:

Many people think that frying green tomatoes began in the Old South as a way of enjoying this spring vegetable prior to its red, ripened stage. Eventually, creative cooks began to top these crispy-fried tomatoes with various seafood sauces, creating frequently demanded delicacies.

Ingredients:

3 green tomatoes
1½ cups vegetable oil
1 cup flour
salt and black pepper to taste
1 tbsp chopped basil
1 cup Italian bread crumbs
1 cup milk
1 egg
1 cup water
Louisiana hot sauce to taste

Method:

In a 10-inch cast iron skillet, heat oil to 350°F. Slice tomatoes ½-inch thick and drain on a paper towel. Season flour with salt and pepper. In a small bowl, mix basil and bread crumbs. In a shallow bowl, whisk together milk, egg and water then season with salt, pepper and hot sauce. Dredge tomato slices first in flour, next in egg wash and finally in bread crumbs. Pan fry slices, a few at a time, until golden brown on both sides. Remove and drain well. Top with Red or White Rémoulade or Louisiana Tartar Sauce and serve as an appetizer or salad. (See recipes.)

Louisiana Catfish Festival
Des Allemands, La.

While Breaux Bridge can claim to be "Crawfish Capital of the World," the little town of Des Allemands has been declared "Catfish Capital of the Universe." Here the catfish is deemed almost sacred, perhaps because the Catfish Festival was founded by a priest in 1975 as a fundraiser to repair the leaky roof on St. Gertrude Church. Father Mac's idea was truly blessed, because not only was the roof repaired, but also the festival garnered national recognition for the town's catfish industry. While the festival only spans one weekend in July, tens of thousands of pounds of catfish are fried each year to feed the visitors. You can try your hand at cooking them yourself in the catfish cooking contest or enter the catfish eating contest. While catfish are their pride and joy, the people of Des Allemands also offer seafood gumbo, soft-shell crab and other Louisiana specialties at the festival. Live music and fun and games complement a perfect weekend.

SEAFOOD-STUFFED TURBAN OF CATFISH

Prep Time: 1 Hour
Yields: 6 Servings

Comment:
Whether farm raised or fresh caught, catfish are a favorite among Louisianians. Although the favorite method of preparation for the fish is fried, this recipe creates a more elegant dish. The interesting style of catfish wrapped around stuffing creates a beautiful plate presentation. This dish can be recreated with any thin-cut fillet of fish such as trout.

Ingredients:
6 (5–7 ounce) catfish fillets
2 pounds white or claw crabmeat
¼ cup chopped parsley
¾ cup butter
1 cup diced onions
1 cup diced celery
1 cup diced green bell peppers
1 cup diced red bell peppers
¼ cup minced garlic
salt and cracked black pepper to taste
2 cups Italian bread crumbs
¾ cup melted butter
¾ cup water
¾ cup white wine
1 tbsp paprika
Louisiana hot sauce to taste

Method:
Preheat oven to 375°F. In a heavy-bottomed sauté pan, melt ¾ cup butter over medium-high heat. Add onions, celery, bell peppers and garlic. Sauté 3–5 minutes or until vegetables are wilted. Blend in crabmeat and cook until juices are rendered. Season with salt and pepper. Remove from heat and sprinkle in bread crumbs, a little at a time, until desired consistency is achieved. Stuffing should not be too dry. Stir in parsley and blend well. Adjust seasonings if necessary. Place an equal amount of stuffing in the center of each fillet, roll into a turban shape and secure with toothpicks. Place fish in baking pan then add water and wine. Drizzle turbans with melted butter then sprinkle with paprika, salt, pepper and hot sauce. Bake 20 minutes or until stuffing reaches 160°F.

NICE AND SPICY CATFISH PO'BOY

Prep Time: 2½ Hours
Yields: 6 Servings

Comment:

The Blue Channel catfish of Louisiana is not only a favorite of the Cajuns and Creoles, but it is also revered as the best fish in the South. Catfish can be deep-fried in fillets or whole with skin and head on. In this recipe, the catfish is served po'boy-style on French bread and topped with coleslaw.

Ingredients for Slaw:

4 cups shredded cabbage
1 small onion, grated
1 carrot, peeled and grated
1 tbsp minced parsley
¼ cup vegetable oil
3 tbsps cider vinegar

¼ cup mayonnaise
1 tbsp sugar
¼ tsp dry mustard
⅛ tsp granulated garlic
½ tsp celery seed
cayenne pepper to taste

Method:

Toss cabbage, onions, carrots and parsley until well mixed. In a small bowl, combine oil, vinegar, mayonnaise, sugar and seasonings. Stir well. Pour dressing over cabbage mixture and toss gently. Refrigerate 2 hours while frying catfish.

Ingredients for Catfish:

6 (6–8 ounce) catfish fillets
1 cup milk
1 egg
½ cup water
3 tbsps Creole mustard
juice of 1 lemon
Louisiana hot sauce to taste
seasoned corn flour
6 (6-inch) po'boy loaves
1 red onion, thinly sliced

Method:

Preheat oven to 375°F. Submerge fish in a bowl of ice water 30 minutes prior to frying. This process will help to firm fish and keep it moist during cooking. In a large Dutch oven or FryDaddy, place enough oil to cover fish by 1–2 inches. Preheat oil to 365°F. In a mixing bowl, whisk together milk, egg, water, mustard, lemon juice and hot sauce. Remove fish from ice water and place in Creole mustard batter then in corn flour. Fry until golden brown and beginning to float to surface. Do not overcook. Fish are best when crisp on outside but tender and juicy inside. Drain on paper towels. Slice po'boy loaves in half and place on a cookie sheet. Toast lightly in oven. When bread is lightly browned, place 1 catfish fillet on ½ of toasted loaf. Top with sliced red onions and a generous portion of coleslaw. Top with remaining half of po'boy loaf and press firmly.

Louisiana Shrimp & Petroleum Festival
Morgan City, La.

The Shrimp & Petroleum Festival is one of Louisiana's best known and most strangely named festivals. It is also one of the oldest, although in its youth it was known only as the Shrimp Festival. Originally founded to highlight the area's thriving shrimp industry, in 1967 the festival changed its name to acknowledge the impact the oil industry had also made. Every Labor Day weekend this five-day festival begins with the "Blessing of the Fleet" where decorated shrimp and oilfield boats receive their annual splash of holy water to ensure their safety and prosperity. After this initial solemnity, a rollicking party begins with non-stop "Music in the Park" from the best Cajun, swamp rock, zydeco, country, and rhythm and blues artists around. The festival also features the Cajun Culinary Classic, fireworks, a parade, a rodeo, a fishing tournament, arts and crafts, antiques and fantastic food. There is even a Children's Village for the kids. This one is not to be missed.

Shrimp boat decorated for the Blessing of the Fleet

SHRIMP VIALA

Prep Time: 20 Minutes
Yields: 6 Servings

Comment:
This unique shrimp presentation was created at Lafitte's Landing Restaurant for use during the height of shrimp season. The dish was named in honor of J. P. Viala, builder of Viala Plantation, the original home of the restaurant.

Ingredients:
36 (21–25 count) shrimp, peeled and deveined
¼ cup olive oil
4 cloves garlic, sliced
¼ cup sliced green onions
¼ cup sliced mushrooms
¼ cup diced red bell peppers
¼ cup diced yellow bell peppers
¼ cup diced green bell peppers
½ cup diced Creole tomatoes
2½ tbsps flour
1 ounce dry white wine
2½ cups hot shellfish or chicken stock (see recipe)
1 tsp lemon juice
1 tsp parsley
salt and cracked black pepper to taste

Method:
In a heavy-bottomed sauté pan, heat oil over medium-high heat. Sauté garlic, green onions and mushrooms 2 minutes or until wilted. Stir in bell peppers and tomatoes. Cook 1 minute. Stir-fry shrimp into vegetables 2 minutes or until pink and curled. Sprinkle in flour and blend well to create a white roux. (See roux recipes.) Flour will absorb most liquids in pan and act as a thickening agent. Deglaze with wine. Whisk in 2 cups stock. Add lemon juice and parsley. Season with salt and pepper. Cook 2–3 minutes or until sauce is thickened and shrimp are done, but not overcooked. Additional stock may be added if sauce becomes too thick. This dish may be served with garlic croutons in an au gratin dish or heated chafing dish.

BARBECUED SHRIMP TANGIPAHOA

Prep Time: 30 Minutes
Yields: 6 Servings

Comment:
Barbecued shrimp first made its debut at Pascal's Manale Restaurant on Napoleon Avenue in New Orleans. The original owner of the restaurant served this wonderful garlic and herb shrimp to his friends who would visit the restaurant each week to partake in a poker game.

Ingredients:
36 (16–20 count) shrimp, head-on
½ pound butter
¼ cup olive oil
¼ cup minced garlic
¼ cup minced purple shallots
½ cup sliced green onions
3 tbsps chopped basil
3 tbsps chopped oregano
3 tbsps chopped rosemary
2 tbsps chopped thyme
½ cup Worcestershire sauce
1 cup beer
salt and cracked black pepper to taste
Creole seasoning to taste
Louisiana hot sauce to taste

Method:
Preheat oven to 350°F. In a 13" x 9" baking dish with a 2-inch lip, spread shrimp out evenly. In a 1-quart saucepot, heat butter and oil over medium-high heat. Add garlic, shallots, green onions, basil, oregano, rosemary and thyme. Sauté 3–5 minutes to flavor butter with herb mixture. Blend in Worcestershire and beer. Pour hot mixture over shrimp. Season with salt, pepper, Creole seasoning and hot sauce. Overseason because shells will prevent meat from absorbing most flavors. Place in oven and stir shrimp once during cooking. Cook 15 minutes or until shrimp are pink and curled. Do not overcook, as shrimp will become hard to peel. Place 6 shrimp in each of 6 soup bowls and top with equal portions of herbed-butter sauce. Serve with New Orleans French Bread. (See recipe.)

Rayne, La.

It's not easy being green…unless you are at the famous Frog Festival where all things "froggy" reign supreme. Frogs are always popular in the "Frog Capital of the World," but during the festival each September, the town goes "frog-wild." There are frog racing and jumping contests, a Frog Festival Queen competition, the Frog Parade and, yes frog lovers cover your ears, frog cooking and eating contests. Arts and crafts honor the frog in every way imaginable from paintings and posters to jewelry and home décor. While in Rayne be sure to check out the Boulevard of Banners, the frog murals and the nation's only cemetery that faces both north and south. There's plenty in Rayne to keep you hopping.

OSSO BUCO OF FROG LEGS

Prep Time: 1½ Hours
Yields: 6 Servings

Comment:
Osso Buco translated in Italian means "bone with a hole." Generally, the term refers to the shank portion of veal, lamb or pork. The meat surrounding this marrow-filled bone is perfect for long, slow braising in rich sauces. When the very large frog legs of South Louisiana are too tough and stringy for deep-frying, the braising method, or osso buco style, is perfect.

Ingredients:
6 frog legs, cleaned
½ cup olive oil
½ cup flour
1 tbsp chopped thyme
1 tbsp chopped basil
salt and black pepper to taste
Louisiana hot sauce to taste
½ cup diced carrots
½ cup diced potatoes
½ cup diced zucchini
½ cup diced squash

Method:
In a 10-inch cast iron skillet, heat olive oil over medium-high heat. Season flour with thyme, basil, salt, pepper and hot sauce. Dredge frog legs in flour and shake off excess. Place in skillet and sear until lightly browned on each side. Do not overcook. Add all vegetables and sauté 3–5 minutes or until wilted. Pour in beef stock, 1 ladle at a time, until well blended. Stir in red wine. Season with salt, pepper, Worcestershire and hot sauce. Cover pot and cook 30 minutes or until tender. Add green onions and parsley. Serve with pasta or rice.

FROG LEG FETTUCCINE

Prep Time: 1 Hour
Yields: 6 Servings

Comment:
People in South Louisiana love combining seafood with pasta. Like oysters, frog legs are said to be one of the edible aphrodisiacs. Keep this recipe in mind next time you are thinking about what to cook for that special someone.

Ingredients:
12 frog legs
1 package fettuccine noodles
1½ cups milk
salt and black pepper to taste
½ cup butter
1 cup diced onions
½ cup diced celery
½ cup diced bell peppers
¼ cup minced garlic
2 tbsps flour
¼ cup minced pimientos
2 cups half-and-half
1 cup chicken stock (see recipe)
1 tbsp minced jalapeño peppers
¼ cup sliced green onions
¼ cup chopped parsley
Louisiana hot sauce to taste
½ pound Velveeta® cheese, sliced ½-inch thick
¼ cup Parmesan cheese

Method:
Wash legs in ice water and soak in milk 1 hour in refrigerator. Pat dry with paper towels then season with salt and pepper. Preheat oven to 350°F. In a 10-inch cast iron skillet, melt butter over medium-high heat. Add onions, celery, bell peppers and garlic. Sauté 3–5 minutes or until vegetables are wilted. Blend in flour. Stirring constantly, add pimientos, half-and-half, stock and jalapeños. Bring to a rolling boil then add frog legs, green onions and parsley. Season with salt, pepper and hot sauce. Cover and cook on low heat approximately 20 minutes, stirring occasionally. Additional cream may be added if necessary. In a 4-quart stockpot, cook fettuccine according to package directions. Drain and place in a 3-quart casserole dish. Blend cheeses into sauce until melted. Pour cooked sauce over fettuccine and blend until coated. Bake 15–20 minutes or until bubbly.

Yambilee Festival
Opelousas, La.

Some of the first French visitors to Louisiana settled in Opelousas where they found the Native Americans already dining on sweet potatoes or yams. A settlement was founded there in 1720 and still thrives today, as does the sweet potato. A festival celebrating and promoting the sweet potato was dreamed up over a cup of coffee by J.W. "Bill" Low and Felix Dezauche and came to fruition in 1946. Since then many Yambilee Queens have been crowned and many a sweet potato has been eaten on the festival grounds. The versatile sweet potato is put to the test in contests featuring fresh, canned and cooked sweet potatoes. A more unusual contest highlights yam-i-mals, sweet potatoes that, when harvested, resemble an animal of some sort. There is also an auction, a parade, an arts and crafts show and a garden show. Of course, no festival would be complete without live music and great food. Sweet potatoes are truly taken to new heights at the Yambilee Festival each October.

STUFFED EASTER HAM

Prep Time: 1 Hour
Yields: 6–8 Servings

Comment:
Other than wild game, smoked ham is the most common meat used as a centerpiece on the holiday table in South Louisiana. Many families have a "secret" glaze or stuffing that they use to set their masterpiece apart.

Ingredients for Cajun Glaze:
1 cup Louisiana cane syrup
1 cup Creole mustard
½ cup brown sugar
1 tbsp cracked black pepper
½ tsp cinnamon
½ tsp cloves
½ tsp nutmeg
½ tsp filé powder

Method:
In a stainless steel mixing bowl, combine all ingredients. Blend well then set aside.

Ingredients for Ham:
1 (6–7 pound) boneless ham
2 yams, peeled
2 Bartlett pears, peeled
¼ cup butter
½ cup diced onions
½ cup diced celery
¼ cup diced green bell peppers
¼ cup diced red bell peppers
¼ cup minced garlic
¼ cup raisins
¼ cup fig preserves
½ cup chopped pecans
pinch of cinnamon
pinch of nutmeg
pinch of filé powder (optional)
salt and cracked black pepper to taste
6 Bartlett pear halves for garnish

Method:
Preheat oven to 350°F. Poach yams and pears in hot water until tender but not overcooked. Drain and chop into 1-inch cubes then set aside. In a heavy-bottomed sauté pan, melt butter over medium-high heat. Add onions, celery, bell peppers and garlic. Sauté 3–5 minutes or until vegetables are wilted. Fold in yams, pears, raisins, preserves and pecans. Sauté until mixture is well blended and resembles a chutney or stuffing. Season with cinnamon, nutmeg, filé, salt and pepper. Remove and allow to cool. Slice ham horizontally across middle. Spread a ¾-inch layer of stuffing on bottom half of ham. Top with upper section and secure in place with skewers. Garnish top of ham with pear halves. Brush ham and pears with Cajun Glaze. Bake 30-40 minutes and serve.

CANDIED YAM FLAN

Prep Time: 2 Hours
Yields: 8 Servings

Comment:
The English had their custards and the French their flans, but it was the Africans that gave these two cultures the sweet potato to further flavor the egg and milk desserts. The Louisiana yam adds both a fabulous flavor and color to this custard-like dish.

Ingredients:
1 cup Bruce's® candied yams, reserve syrup
1½ cups milk
1 cup heavy whipping cream
4 eggs
4 egg yolks
½ cup sugar
¼ tsp cinnamon
¼ tsp nutmeg
1 tbsp pure vanilla extract
1 tbsp praline liqueur

Method:
Preheat oven to 350°F. In a food processor, combine yams, syrup, milk, cream, eggs and egg yolks. Blend until yams are puréed. Pour ingredients into a mixing bowl. Gently whisk in sugar, cinnamon, nutmeg, vanilla and liqueur. Blend until sugar is dissolved and spices are mixed. Pour mixture into 8 ramekins or 1 large flan mold. Place cups or mold into a baking pan with 1-inch lip. Pour approximately ½ inch water into pan. Place pan on center rack of oven. Bake 45 minutes–1 hour for ramekins or 1½ hours for flan mold. Insert a tester into custard to ensure that it has set properly. Custard is best when chilled overnight.

Gumbo Festival
Bridge City, La.

Like so many other Louisiana festivals, Bridge City's annual Gumbo Festival began as a simple church fund-raiser, this one for Holy Guardian Angels Church in the 1970s. Obviously, a festival designed around a dish so central to Cajun and Creole cuisine would be a success. Every October, thousands of gallons of both seafood and chicken and sausage gumbo are prepared. New recipes and old are tested annually in the Gumbo Cooking Contest and the title of champion is highly coveted. Festival-goers are treated not only to gumbo, but also jambalaya, red beans and rice and other traditional fare. Live music and dancing are the prime entertainment and a 5K run over the bridge in the "Gumbo Capital of the World" can help assuage any guilt over eating too much.

Lionel Key grinds sassafras leaves to make filé powder.

SHRIMP, CRAB AND OKRA GUMBO

Prep Time: 1 Hour
Yields: 12 Servings

Comment:

This recipe is yet another take on the famed soup of the Cajuns. Creative variations of the dish are prominent at the Gumbo Cooking Contest at the Gumbo Festival in Bridge City, La.

Ingredients:

2 pounds (35-count) shrimp, peeled and deveined
1 pound jumbo lump crabmeat
2 pounds fresh okra
½ cup vegetable oil
1 cup diced onions
1 cup diced celery
½ cup diced bell peppers
2 tbsps minced garlic
1 cup vegetable oil
1 cup flour
1 cup diced tomatoes
1 (8-ounce) can tomato sauce
3 quarts hot shellfish stock (see recipe)
1 cup sliced green onions
½ cup chopped parsley
salt and cracked black pepper to taste
Louisiana hot sauce to taste
filé powder for garnish

Method:

In a large cast iron skillet, heat ½ cup oil over medium-high heat. Add okra, onions, celery, bell peppers and garlic. Stirring constantly, slowly sauté vegetables until okra is well cooked and slightly browned. Be careful okra does not stick and scorch. Remove from heat and set aside. In a heavy-bottomed Dutch oven, heat 1 cup oil over medium-high heat. Whisk in flour, stirring constantly until a dark brown roux is achieved. (See roux recipes.) Stir in tomatoes and tomato sauce. Pour off excess oil from okra mixture then add sautéed vegetables to roux. Blend well. Slowly add shellfish stock, 1 ladle at a time, until all is used. Bring to a rolling boil then reduce to simmer. More stock may be needed to retain a soup-like consistency. Add green onions and parsley. Season with salt, pepper and hot sauce. Cook 15 minutes. Add shrimp and cook 10–15 minutes longer. Fold in crabmeat and cook 1 minute. Adjust seasonings if necessary. Serve over steamed white rice. Garnish with a dash of filé powder prior to serving.

JALAPEÑO CORN BREAD

Prep Time: 45 Minutes
Yields: 1 Loaf

Comment:

A little Spanish flair is added to traditional Southern corn bread to create a fantastic flavor. This jalapeño bread is often served as a less-traditional accompaniment to gumbo.

Ingredients:

1 (4-ounce) can jalapeño peppers, drained and chopped
1½ cups yellow cornmeal
1 tbsp sugar
1 tbsp baking powder
1 tsp salt
1 cup milk
2 large eggs
1 (8.75-ounce) can cream-style corn
¼ cup shortening
1½ cups grated sharp Cheddar cheese

Method:

Preheat oven to 425°F. Grease a standard loaf pan. Sift together cornmeal, sugar, baking powder and salt then set aside. In a medium mixing bowl, combine milk, eggs, corn and shortening. Using an electric mixer, blend well. Add dry ingredients. Stir in peppers and cheese until well blended. Pour batter into loaf pan and bake 35 minutes or until golden brown.

Plantations

San Francisco Plantation

One of Louisiana's unique claims to fame is the abundance of beautifully preserved and restored reminders of the state's early history. Louisiana's rich agricultural heritage is marked by the many plantation homes that still dot the landscape, particularly along the banks of the Mississippi. A large number of Louisiana's plantations grew from land grants awarded while the territory was under Spanish rule. The only stipulation for receiving these large tracts of land was to build a home and plant a crop within a year. Louisiana planters took these stipulations to heart. Capitalizing on Louisiana's ideal growing climate, they entered first into tobacco and indigo farming and then into the more lucrative cotton and sugar trades. Because these plantations predated highways and railroads, most were placed along Louisiana's primary mode of transportation, the Mississippi River. The plantations were self-sufficient in many respects, providing their own food, clothing and labor. The grand homes were often constructed from lumber and bricks cut and fired on the estate grounds. Not only were thousands of acres of crops planted, maintained and harvested, but the end result was also processed on site. Many plantations had their own sugarhouses, dairies, chicken yards and of course, vegetable gardens. Some plantations literally housed and fed thousands of laborers on a daily basis.

In the heyday of the plantation era, just three or four successful harvests could make a millionaire. Prior to the Civil War there were more millionaires along the river between Natchez, Miss. and New Orleans than in the rest of the country put together. The design of these homes reflected the planters' success, with columned facades, double galleries, grand ballrooms, and pigeonnaires and garçonnieres flanking the main houses. The large homes were designed to not only accommodate the large families of those days, but also to be ready to house overnight guests. When entertaining, no expense would be spared, and the lavish meals and furnishings, often imported from Europe, were a constant reminder of the planters' status.

Perhaps one of the most lavish plantations belonged to Valcour Aime. Built in the late 18th century on the west bank of the Mississippi in present-day Vacherie, the house and gardens were so spectacular the plantation became known as Le Petit Versailles—a reference to the French palace and gardens of King Louis XIV. Beyond the bridges, streams and fountains that graced the landscape, the plantation was extremely productive. Aime made a fortune growing sugar, corn, rice, tobacco, pumpkins, potatoes and more. In addition he owned a large variety of livestock. The plantation also housed its own sugar mill, hospital, church and school. Le Petit Versailles was so self-sufficient that Valcour Aime once bet a friend $10,000 that he could provide him a multi-course meal with every ingredient coming from his plantation. The meal included turtle, shrimp, snipes, duck, vegetables, salads, fruit, wine and liqueurs. Aime's friend claimed to have won the bet when he was offered cigars and coffee. He insisted that these could not have come from the plantation grounds. After dinner, Aime took his friend for a ride and showed him coffee plants in a conservatory, tobacco in the field and the rooms where the dried leaves were being rolled into cigars. Valcour Aime had discovered that almost every epicurean delight could be found or cultivated in Louisiana and used it to his advantage.

Of course, almost all plantations were dependent on one "commodity," slave labor. Often isolated, these huge working farms could not have survived if they were dependent on the locals to work for them. Although most of Louisiana's early residents lived less lavishly than the planters, they were equally self-sufficient and did not need to work for another man. Cajuns in particular while happy to hunt, fish, trap and harvest moss to sell to plantation owners, had far too much pride to work directly for them. The slaves were not given that option. They were truly the lifeblood of the plantations, not only providing field labor, but also house help, cooking, nursing,

2101. OLD PLANTATION NEGROES.

for lack of somewhere else to go, others required a piece of land to sharecrop in exchange for their work or moved away entirely. Some plantations managed to stay in operation, but at a much higher cost. Many plantations were sold to Northern interests, the acreage divided, or the houses abandoned to nature. Often descendents of the original owners could no longer afford to maintain the financial albatross such a legacy represented, especially once the Great Depression hit.

In recent decades, some of these homes have been restored to their former glory due to a renewed interest in Louisiana's history and heritage, as well as the curiosity and dedication of private investors and historic foundations. Many are open to the public as very tangible reminders of an important part of Louisiana's history. Granted, the memories are not all fond. In fact, some are quite horrific, but the plantation era represents a tremendous part of the background of Louisiana's food, economy, traditions and the interaction of the many cultures that made the state what it is today.

sugar processing, gardening, animal handling and much more. Although they were trained to recreate the dishes many planters knew from their foreign birthplaces, many slaves brought their traditions and techniques to bear on both the crops that were grown and the food that was prepared. In that way, the Africans had a tremendous influence on the development of Louisiana cuisine.

Louisiana's lavish plantation lifestyle faltered during the Civil War and ultimately failed during reconstruction. Many plantations were occupied, ransacked and destroyed during the hostilities. Once New Orleans fell to the Union, the riverboats that brought the plantations' goods to market and also brought supplies to the planters, no longer ran. The most devastating blow to the plantation lifestyle was the emancipation of the slaves, which made it impossible to maintain a sufficient workforce. While some former slaves remained on the plantations

Here we feature just 12 of Louisiana's most notable plantation homes as well as recipes either drawn from the plantation collections or somehow tied to those locations. Additional information and recipes from these and many other plantations can be found in *Plantation Celebrations*,

D. L. Kernion with Nursemaid Marguerite, 1850

published by Chef John Folse & Company, or by calling the Louisiana Office of Tourism at (800) 677-4082. You can also visit their website at www. crt.state.la.us/crt/tourism/tourism.htm.

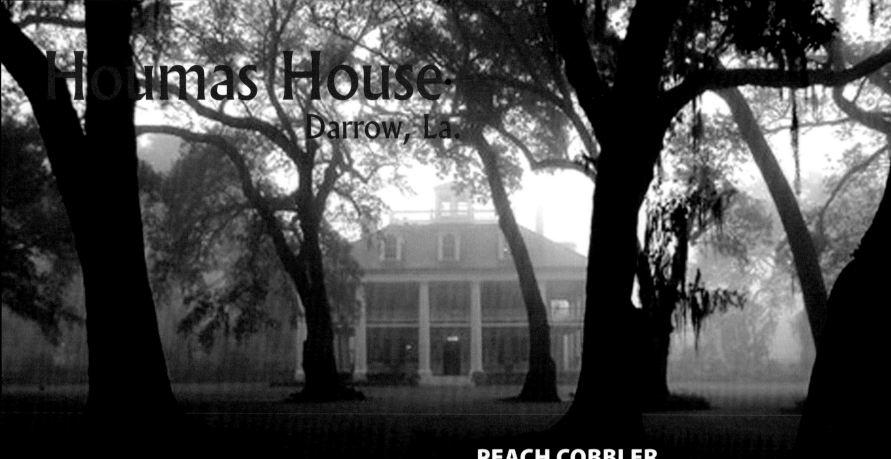

Houmas House
Darrow, La.

Houmas House stands on land once owned by the Houmas Indians along the Mississippi River. The original house built on the property reflects the colonial French and Spanish influences of the late 18th century. The house and land were eventually purchased by General Wade Hampton of South Carolina. In 1840, Hampton's daughter and her husband, John Smith Preston, built a new Greek Revival-style mansion directly in front of the original house. Both are still standing. A distinguishing feature of the mansion is the glass windowed belvedere, common on Carolina homes on the Eastern seaboard, but unusual in South Louisiana. Visitors to Houmas House, arriving by boat, would be greeted by "The Gentlemen," two parallel rows of stately live oak trees stretching from the river to the house. Those trees, hardy enough to withstand the ravages of time and the construction of a road and levee along the Mississippi, still grace the beautiful grounds of this antebellum home and are the subject of one of the house's ghost stories. In 1858, John Burnside purchased the property and almost doubled the plantation's size to 20,000 acres. He was one of the nation's largest sugar producers. The house has since undergone renovations at the hands of Dr. George Crozat and more recently, Kevin Kelly, to restore it to its former splendor.

PEACH COBBLER

Prep Time: 1½ Hours
Yields: 8 Servings

Comment:
In the 1800s, Houmas House Plantation was famous for ending meals with peach cobbler. This recipe is a rendition of the dish served during those plantation dinners.

Ingredients for Filling:
6 cups sliced fresh peaches
1½ cups sugar
¼ cup water
3 tbsps flour
¼ cup sugar

pinch of salt
pinch of cinnamon
pinch of nutmeg
pinch of allspice

Method:
Preheat oven to 400°F. In a heavy-bottomed saucepan, combine peaches, sugar and water. Bring to a rolling boil then reduce to simmer. Cook until fruit is softened. In a measuring cup, blend flour, sugar, salt, cinnamon, nutmeg and allspice. Pour seasoned flour into peach mixture, stirring constantly until thickened. Remove from heat and pour into a 9-inch cast iron skillet or cobbler pan. Allow to cool slightly.

Ingredients for Topping:
1 cup flour
½ cup sugar
2 tsps baking powder

¾ cup milk
½ tsp salt

Method:
In a mixing bowl, combine all ingredients except salt. Whisk until well blended. Season with salt. Pour batter in an irregular pattern over center of cobbler. Bake 45 minutes or until golden brown. If desired, garnish cobbler with fresh sliced peaches, powdered sugar and a sprig of mint.

Kent House
Alexandria, La.

Kent House is the oldest known structure standing in central Louisiana. Completed in 1800, it was built by Frenchman Pierre Baillio II on land received through a Spanish land grant in 1794. When purchased by Robert Hynson in 1842, the house was named for his previous home in Kent County, Md. Typical of Louisiana colonial construction, the walls of the house are made with wood beams and bousillage, a mixture of mud, Spanish moss and animal hair. The separate kitchen building is not original to Kent House but was brought from Augusta Plantation near Bunkie, La., to replace the one destroyed by a tornado. The main house survived the Civil War and was spared demolition in the 1960s. It is now home to museum-quality antiques and historically accurate grounds, gardens and outbuildings.

SMOTHERED PORK SAUSAGE IN APPLE CIDER

Prep Time: 1 Hour
Yields: 6 Servings

Comment:
Apple trees could be found in many Louisiana plantation gardens. The fruit was quickly put to use by all the cultures that settled the area. This apple-flavored sausage is a favorite dish of the Germans.

Ingredients:
2 pounds fresh pork sausage
½ cup chicken stock (see recipe)
1 cup diced onions
½ cup diced celery
½ cup diced red bell peppers
1 tbsp minced garlic
1 cup diced apples
1 cup apple cider
½ cup sliced green onions
¼ cup chopped parsley
salt and cracked black pepper to taste
Louisiana hot sauce to taste

Method:
Preheat oven to 375°F. In a cast iron skillet, place sausage and prick with a fork. Add stock. Cover skillet and cook over medium-high heat, turning sausage occasionally until fat is rendered. Once browned, remove sausage and pour all but ¼ cup drippings from skillet. Add onions, celery, bell peppers, garlic and apples. Sauté 3–5 minutes or until vegetables are wilted. Return sausage to skillet and add cider, green onions and parsley. Season with salt, pepper and hot sauce. Cover, place in oven and bake 30–45 minutes.

Longue Vue House
and Gardens
New Orleans

CORNED BEEF AND CABBAGE

Prep Time: 3 Hours
Yields: 6 Servings

Comment:

In the past, corned beef and cabbage was considered a winter dish. However, today many people eat this slowly simmered delicacy any time of year.

Ingredients:

1 (5–6 pound) corned beef
1 (3-pound) cabbage
3 large onions, quartered
12 carrots, peeled and halved
3 stalks celery, halved
6 whole cloves
12 black peppercorns
2 bay leaves
Louisiana hot sauce to taste
12 new potatoes
12 cloves garlic
salt and cracked black pepper to taste
chopped parsley for garnish

Method:

In a large stockpot, combine corned beef, onions, half of carrots, celery, cloves, peppercorns and bay leaves. Season with hot sauce then cover contents with 4 inches of lightly-salted water. Bring to a rolling boil then reduce to simmer. Cook 2½ hours or until beef is tender. Remove and keep warm. Strain broth, return it to stockpot and discard vegetables. Add potatoes, remaining carrots and garlic. Season with salt and pepper. Bring to a rolling boil then reduce to simmer and cook 10 minutes. Slice cabbage into 6 equal wedges, add to stock and cook 20–30 minutes or until vegetables are done. To serve, arrange beef on a warm serving platter and surround with cabbage and vegetables. Ladle hot broth over beef and vegetables. Garnish with chopped parsley. If desired, serve a sauceboat of horseradish cream alongside this dish.

Compared to most of the homes featured in this section, Longue Vue's history is relatively short, but that doesn't take away from the grandeur and importance of this home and gardens. Built as a getaway for philanthropists Edith and Edgar Stern, this "grand city estate" is a tribute both to a bygone way of life and to the generosity of its wealthy owners. The house is a Greek Revival Mansion built in the late 1930s. It is furnished and decorated with fine English and French antiques and rich Oriental carpeting. Eight acres of intricately designed gardens are a tribute to some of the most famous gardens in the world. They feature 23 fountains, some of which pre-date settlement of the United States. Edgar was a well-known cotton broker and Edith an heir to the Sears fortune, but they were also responsible for funding Dillard University, Flint Goodridge Teaching Hospital, Newcomb College Nursery School and many other institutions. The home, at which the Sterns entertained both John and Robert Kennedy, Pablo Casals, Jack Benny and many others, remains as it was when they lived there, complete with the original furnishings and collections of art, needlework, costumes, china and creamware.

Loyd Hall
Cheneyville, La.

While Loyd Hall has been a working plantation since 1800, the house itself fell into disrepair and was overgrown to such an extent that when the current owners, Frank and Virginia Fitzgerald bought the property in 1948, they were unaware a home was there. Only during an aerial survey of their purchase did they discover an overgrown shell of a house. Loyd Hall was built by William Loyd who, legend has it, was a disinherited son of the wealthy Lloyd's of London, sent to the colonies to start a new life under an altered name. The Loyds did not manage to stay out of trouble. During the Civil War, Union troops discovered that then owner, James Loyd, was trading secrets to the South and hung him as a spy. Local legend claims that his ghost is one of those that frequent Loyd Hall. The house was eventually claimed by the English syndicate in payment of debts owed, and there were no Loyd heirs to buy it back. After several owners, the house fell into disrepair and was abandoned. Now restored to its former glory, the Georgian-style house once again presides over a working plantation.

CORN AND SHRIMP SOUP

Prep Time: 1 Hour
Yields: 12–16 Servings

Comment:
There are many shrimp dishes in Louisiana, but one of the most famous is Creole-style sweet corn and shrimp soup. Although this recipe calls for canned corn, many Louisianians agree that the secret to a perfect soup is to use fresh corn. After scraping off kernels, boil cobs with shrimp shells, onions, celery, garlic and cayenne pepper to create a richly flavored stock.

Ingredients:
1 pound (70–90 count) shrimp, peeled and deveined
½ cup dried shrimp
5 (15-ounce) cans whole kernel corn
5 (15-ounce) cans cream-style corn
1 stick butter
2 cups diced onions
1 cup diced celery
1 cup diced bell peppers
¼ cup minced garlic
2 (15-ounce) cans stewed tomatoes
1 (10-ounce) can Ro*tel® tomatoes
2 (5-ounce) cans V-8® juice
salt and black pepper to taste
granulated garlic to taste

Method:
In a large saucepot, melt butter over medium-high heat. Add onions, celery, bell peppers and garlic. Sauté 3–5 minutes or until onions are transparent. Stir in raw shrimp and sauté until just pink. Blend in dried shrimp and all canned ingredients. Season with salt, pepper and granulated garlic. Bring to a boil then reduce to simmer and cook approximately 45 minutes. Add water if needed during cooking process. Adjust seasonings to taste.

Magnolia Mound
Baton Rouge, La.

BEET MARMALADE

Prep Time: 1 Hour
Yields: 6 Servings

Comment:
Since beets are both a winter and summer crop in Louisiana, many recipes for the vegetable have been created. This unconventional beet recipe is not only spectacular in flavor, but also makes for a beautiful presentation.

Ingredients:
8 medium beets, julienned
1½ tbsps sugar
1½ tbsps honey
½ tsp salt
1½ tbsps cornstarch, dissolved in water
salt and cracked black pepper to taste
pinch of ginger
¼ cup red wine vinegar

Method:
In a 1-quart stockpot, place beets and cover with water by 1 inch. Bring to a rolling boil then reduce to simmer. Cook, testing frequently until beets are tender. Do not overcook as beets will fall apart. Strain and reserve 1½ cups of boiling liquid. Cool beets under cold running water then set aside. In a heavy-bottomed sauté pan, combine reserved stock, sugar, honey, salt and dissolved cornstarch. Bring to a rolling boil then reduce to simmer and allow to thicken to a light syrup consistency. Season with salt, pepper and ginger. Add vinegar. Fold in beets. Continue cooking 15–20 minutes or until beets resemble marmalade or preserves. Adjust sugar if necessary.

In addition to being one of the oldest structures in Louisiana, Magnolia Mound is unusual in its design. Built in 1791 by James Hillen as the center of a 1,000-acre tobacco and indigo plantation, the home was constructed of bousillage and wood and is an excellent example of Louisiana Colonial/French Creole style. The home was purchased soon after by John Joyce, an Irishman. When Joyce drowned in Mobile, Ala., in 1798, his widow married Armand Duplantier, a Frenchman who had served under the Marquis de Lafayette. Duplantier was prominent in Louisiana society and the plantation soon became important in the cotton industry. The house is sometimes referred to as the Prince Murat House because a nephew of Napoleon I, Prince Charles Louis Napoleon Achille Murat, once stayed there as a guest of the Duplantiers. When Baton Rouge fell to federal troops in 1862, the Union army occupied the home. The house went through several ownerships and some remodeling until it was expropriated by the City of Baton Rouge in 1966 because of its historical significance. The house and several outbuildings are now operated as a museum by the East Baton Rouge Parish Recreation and Parks Commission.

THELMA PARKER'S SHRIMP PIE

Prep Time: 1½ Hours
Yields: 6 Servings

Comment:

Thelma Parker, long-time cook at Madewood Plantation, is famous for her Shrimp Pie. Her original recipe calls for canned shrimp soup, but this variation of her dish is a more traditional method.

Ingredients:

2 pounds (70–90 count) shrimp, peeled
¼ pound butter
1 cup diced onions
1 cup diced celery
½ cup diced green bell peppers
½ cup diced red bell peppers
2 tbsps minced garlic
½ cup diced tomatoes
2 bay leaves
½ cup tomato sauce
1 cup flour
1½ quarts shellfish stock (see recipe)
Worcestershire sauce to taste
1 cup sliced green onions
½ cup chopped parsley
salt and cracked black pepper to taste
Louisiana hot sauce to taste
3 (9-inch) prepared pie shells
1 egg
½ cup milk
½ cup water

Method:

Preheat oven to 350°F. If pie shells are frozen, allow them thaw at room temperature. Otherwise, leave in refrigerator until ready to use. In a 1-gallon stockpot, melt butter over medium-high heat. Add onions, celery, bell peppers, garlic, tomatoes and bay leaves. Sauté 3–5 minutes or until vegetables are wilted. Blend in shrimp and tomato sauce. Whisk in flour, stirring constantly until blond roux is achieved. (See roux recipes.) Slowly add stock, a little at a time, until sauce consistency is achieved. Bring to a low boil then reduce to simmer. Cook 30 minutes, stirring occasionally. Add Worcestershire, green onions and parsley. Cook 5 minutes then season with salt, pepper and hot sauce. Remove from heat and allow to cool thoroughly. Cut each pie shell in half. Place a generous portion of shrimp filling in center of each half. In a small mixing bowl, whisk together egg, milk and water. Paint edges of dough with egg wash. Fold dough over filling in a triangle shape. Use a fork to seal edges of pie. Pierce 2–3 holes in top of pies to allow steam to escape. Coat top of pies with egg wash then place on a baking sheet. Bake 20–25 minutes or until golden brown. Shrimp pies may be made in advance and frozen. To reheat, place frozen pies in oven at 375°F for 1 hour.

Madewood
Napoleonville, La.

Madewood was built in 1846 by Col. Thomas Pugh, a sugar planter, supposedly in an effort to show up the elegant mansion built by his nephew next door. While the mansion may have succeeded, Pugh did not live to see it finished. The wood for the house was cut and prepared on the property for four years before construction began, causing laborers to comment that they were "making wood," thus giving the plantation its name. This Greek Revival mansion is one of the largest plantation homes in Louisiana. Though spared during the Civil War, it eventually fell into disrepair. The Marshall family purchased the house in 1964, renovated it and furnished it with antiques imported from England.

The Myrtles
St. Francisville, La.

If you are into ghost stories, you've probably already heard of the "most haunted house in America." Named for the many crape myrtle trees on the property, the Myrtles was built on a 650-acre land grant awarded to General David Bradford. There are many theories surrounding why this plantation houses so many restless spirits, but the prevailing one is that Bradford cleared a Native American burial ground to build his home in 1797. It seems that those who lose their lives at the Myrtles are destined to stay forever and many have. Among the ghosts that haunt the house are two little girls, their mother and the slave, Chloe, who poisoned the three by putting oleander in a birthday cake and was then hung for her crime. There is also a surly caretaker who turns people away at the gate, a fatally shot gentleman who never quite reaches the top of the stairs and several more. In their eagerness to spot ghosts, many guests fail to notice the Myrtles exquisiteness. Elaborate ceiling medallions, friezes and fretwork decorate the home, and extravagant features like closets, glass doorknobs filled with mercury, marble mantelpieces and ornate wrought iron banisters abound.

OVEN-ROASTED GUINEA HEN

Prep Time: 2 Hours
Yields: 6–8 Servings

Comment:
The guinea hen, which originated in Africa, has dark flesh that is often compared to pheasant meat. This tender, delicate, full-flavored bird is perfect for a special occasion.

Ingredients:

2 (2½-pound) guinea hens	6 new potatoes
1 orange, halved	3 sliced carrots
2 onions, quartered	6 tiny beets, unpeeled
2 stalks celery, sliced	½ cup melted butter
2 carrots, sliced	½ cup Madeira wine
10 cloves garlic	salt and black pepper to taste
6 sprigs thyme	granulated garlic to taste
8 sage leaves	Louisiana hot sauce to taste

Method:
Preheat oven to 375°F. Wash birds well inside and out. Squeeze 1 orange half in cavity of each bird. Season cavity generously with salt, pepper, granulated garlic and hot sauce. Stuff hens with onions, celery, carrots, garlic and thyme. Place in a roasting pan, breast side up. Season outside of hens with salt, pepper, granulated garlic and hot sauce. Place 2 sage leaves under skin of each breast. Spread potatoes, carrots and beets in bottom of pan. Top hens with melted butter and wine. Cover tightly and roast 1 hour. Remove cover and allow to brown approximately 30 minutes. Let rest 30 minutes before carving. Prior to serving, peel beets. Place carved hens in center of a serving platter and surround with beets. Serve with hot pan drippings and Pecan Rice Dressing. (See recipe.)

SMOTHERED RABBIT WITH MUSHROOMS

Prep Time: 2 Hours
Yields: 6 Servings

Comment:

The swampland of South Louisiana is the perfect environment for wild rabbit. The ample underbrush provides protection and vast quantities of food and water are always available. The swamps around Nottoway Plantation provided a large supply of this game for the dinning room table during plantation days.

Ingredients:

2 young rabbits, cleaned
2 cups sliced mushrooms
salt and cracked black pepper to taste
Louisiana hot sauce to taste
2 cups seasoned flour
½ cup vegetable oil
1 cup diced onions
1 cup diced celery
½ cup diced red bell peppers
¼ cup minced garlic
½ cup diced tomatoes
2 bay leaves
3 cups game or chicken stock (see recipe)
½ cup sliced green onions
½ cup chopped parsley

Method:

Cut each rabbit into 8 serving pieces. Season meat well with salt, pepper and hot sauce. Dust each piece in flour and shake off excess. In a large Dutch oven, heat oil over medium-high heat. Brown rabbit on both sides, a few pieces at a time. Remove and set aside. In same pot, sauté onions, celery, bell peppers and garlic 3–5 minutes or until wilted. Add tomatoes, mushrooms, bay leaves and chicken stock. Bring mixture to a low boil then reduce to simmer and add rabbit. Cover and braise rabbit 1–1½ hours or until tender. Add green onions and parsley. Adjust seasonings if necessary. Serve over white or wild rice.

Nottoway
White Castle, La.

This magnificent Italianate home is so imposing it was dubbed "the white castle" by those who traveled the river. The house eventually lent its name to the nearby town of White Castle. John Hampton Randolph, father of 11, took 10 years to build the house, which was completed in 1859. It stood out not only because it differed from the Greek Revival and raised Creole cottage styles in the area, but also because of its size. Boasting 65 rooms and 53,000 square feet, this mansion towered over most, and unlike other plantations, after the construction of the levee, can still offer river views. Another unusual feature of this home is that it was built with indoor plumbing and also had a built-in acetylene gas plant to supply the gas lamps installed in each room. Six of Randolph's eight daughters were married in Nottoway's famous White Ballroom, which remains a favorite setting for weddings.

Oak Alley
Vacherie, La.

One of the most striking things about Oak Alley is, well, the oak alley—a twin row of gigantic live oak trees that have spanned the centuries. Planted by a very early settler to Louisiana some time in the late 1600s or early 1700s, the trees have flourished and survived a great deal of history. Some say the tree alley was planted by a trapper who wanted his residence to be easily identified from the river. The trees were surely a prime attraction when, many years later in 1836, Jacques Roman built his home at the end of the alley and dubbed it Bon Sejour, meaning "good rest." The trees asserted their prior claim however, and the name did not stick. The plantation has always been referred to as Oak Alley. The Greek Revival-style mansion is surrounded on all sides by Doric columns. Whether an intentional tribute or not, the columns number the same as the oaks, 28. Like many plantation owners, Roman's fortune did not survive the Civil War, and the family moved out in 1866. The Andrew Stewart family bought the property and restored it in 1925. It is now run by a non-profit foundation.

PLANTATION FRIED CHICKEN WITH GARLIC AND HERBS

Prep Time: 1 Hour
Yields: 4–6 Servings

Comment:
Every culture has its version of "sticky" fried chicken. In this recipe, chicken is pan-fried until golden brown and extremely tender. My grandmother was a master at this pan-frying technique, and this is her version.

Ingredients:
1 large fryer chicken
salt and cracked black pepper to taste
granulated garlic to taste
Louisiana hot sauce to taste
paprika for color
¼ cup butter
¼ cup olive oil
12 small cloves garlic
1 sprig rosemary

Method:
Using a boning knife, cut chicken into 8 serving pieces. If breasts are large, leave a portion of that meat attached to each wing. This will provide two additional serving pieces. In a large mixing bowl, season chicken generously with salt, pepper, granulated garlic, hot sauce and paprika. Marinate approximately 1 hour prior to frying. In a large cast iron skillet, heat butter and oil over medium-high heat. Sauté chicken until golden brown on both sides. Add garlic and rosemary then reduce heat to simmer. Cover and cook 30 minutes, turning occasionally. Chicken will release its own juices in pan to create a natural sauce. NOTE: If desired, create a gravy from pan drippings. Remove chicken from skillet, add 1 cup chicken stock, bring to a rolling boil and reduce to half volume. Season to taste.

POACHED SEAFOOD IN TOMATO ESSENCE

Prep Time: 1 Hour
Yields: 8–10 Servings

Comment:

Poached dishes, such as bouillabaisse, were always popular because of the wonderful, fresh flavor of the seafood. Today, we appreciate the method because it creates lighter, healthier dinners. Traditionally, these seafood stews were served with a New Orleans-style Rouille Sauce. (See recipe below.)

Ingredients for Poaching:

2 dozen (21–25 count) shrimp, peeled and deveined
1 pound cooked crawfish tails
12 fresh oysters
1 pound jumbo lump crabmeat
6 (6–8 ounce) trout or flounder fillets
½ cup olive oil
1 cup diced onions
1 cup diced celery
½ cup diced yellow bell peppers
¼ cup minced garlic
1 cup diced fresh tomatoes
2 quarts shellfish stock (see recipe)
1 cup dry vermouth
2 (8-ounce) cans V-8® juice
1 bay leaf
2 sprigs fresh dill
2 sprigs fresh thyme
2 tbsps chopped basil
salt and cracked black pepper to taste
Louisiana hot sauce to taste
½ cup sliced green onions
¼ cup chopped parsley

Method:

In a 2-gallon stockpot, heat oil over medium-high heat. Add onions, celery, bell peppers, garlic and tomatoes. Sauté 3–5 minutes or until vegetables are wilted. Add stock, vermouth and V-8®. Bring to a rolling boil then reduce to simmer. Blend in bay leaf, dill, thyme and basil. Cook approximately 30 minutes. Use additional stock or water to retain volume. Season with salt, pepper and hot sauce. Gently stir in shrimp, crawfish, oysters and crabmeat. Add green onions and parsley. Fold in fish and poach 3–5 minutes or until done to your liking. Adjust seasonings if necessary. Serve a generous portion of seafood in a soup bowl and top with poaching liquid.

Ingredients for Rouille Sauce:

1 bell pepper, roasted
1 small cayenne pepper, seeded
3 cloves garlic
1 egg yolk
salt and black pepper to taste
Louisiana hot sauce to taste
1 tbsp fresh lemon juice
1 tsp thyme
1 tsp basil
¾ cup extra virgin olive oil

Method:

In a food processor, purée bell pepper and cayenne pepper. Add all remaining ingredients except oil, and purée until smooth. Slowly drizzle in oil and blend. This mayonnaise-style sauce should be spread on hot French bread or croutons and dipped into poaching liquid.

San Francisco
Garyville, La.

San Francisco is easily the most colorful of the plantation homes along the river. The original builder, Edmund Marmillion, combined a variety of styles to create a truly unique, eye-catching piece of architecture. Built in 1856, this "steamboat-style" home was jokingly dubbed Sans Fruscins when Marmillion's son, Antoine Valsin, joked that the redecoration undertaken by his wife, Louise, left him sans fruscins or "without a penny." The name stuck until a later owner, Achille Bougere, perhaps disliking the implication, modified the name to San Francisco. The home is elaborately decorated both inside and out, with a use of vibrant color unusual to the times. Velvet drapes, ornate chandeliers, European wallpaper, vast murals and faux woodwork make it easy to imagine how the house got its original name. San Francisco was also equipped with running water supplied by enormous cisterns on either side of the house, a rare feature in houses of this era. A $2 million restoration was completed in 1977, with painstaking attention paid to recreating the original colors selected by Antoine and Louise.

Rosedown
St. Francisville, La.

Unlike many of the homes down the Mississippi, Rosedown was not a sugar plantation, but a cotton plantation. The house was built by Daniel and Martha Turnbull in 1835 and named for a play they attended on their honeymoon. The Turnbulls purchased the finest European furniture for their new home or had it crafted especially for them. Many wonderful pieces remain, but the most famous furniture at Rosedown is no longer there. These pieces were originally built to furnish Henry Clay's bedroom at the White House. When his bid for the presidency failed, the Turnbulls not only bought the furniture but also added two wings to Rosedown to accommodate it. Rosedown is also famous for its formal gardens, which are models of the European ones visited by the Turnbulls on their honeymoon. The gardens grew to encompass almost 28 acres. Prior to the Civil War the plantation was one of the most prosperous in the region. However, in 1861 Daniel Turnbull died and while the family remained on the plantation during the Civil War, the slave workforce was released and the plantation was looted by federal troops. Martha and her daughter Sarah lived in relative poverty there, surviving by leasing the land to sharecroppers and farming what they could. Four of Sarah's daughters never married and held onto the plantation until, in desperation, they opened the house to tourists in the 1930s. When the last daughter died in 1955, the house, free of mortgages, finally passed from the original family's hands. Luckily, Rosedown was purchased by Milton and Catherine Underwood who lovingly and painstakingly restored the house, gardens and remaining acres of the plantation to their original grandeur. The plantation is now owned by the State of Louisiana.

SUPER-MOIST FRUITCAKE

Prep Time: 3½ Hours
Yields: 6 (4-pound) Cakes

Comment:

The fruitcake may have originated in ancient Egypt or the Roman Empire. The confection was, and still is, widely loved in England where it was originally called plum cake and was served at weddings and other celebrations. Exactly how the fruitcake made it to Louisiana is hard to determine. Nevertheless, fruitcake is commonplace on the Christmas table in Bayou Country.

Ingredients:

2 pounds candied dried fruit mix
¾ cup raisins
¾ cup golden raisins
1 pound dates
1 cup whiskey
1½ cups port wine
½ pound butter
½ pound sugar
5 large eggs
2 tsps baking soda
1 tsp nutmeg
1 tsp cinnamon
2 ounces pure vanilla extract
4 (11.5-ounce) jars fig preserves
1½ cups brewed coffee
5 cups flour
1 pound chopped pecans
1 (20-ounce) can crushed pineapple in juice
1 cup red cherries in juice
1 cup green cherries in juice
30 red cherry halves for decorating
30 green cherry halves for decorating
30 pecan halves for decorating

Method:

Preheat oven to 350°F. In a large mixing bowl, combine candied dried fruit mix, raisins, dates, whiskey and wine. Blend well and allow to marinate at room temperature approximately 30 minutes. Grease and flour 6 standard loaf pans. Line bottom of pans with parchment paper to prevent sticking. Set aside. In an electric mixer, cream butter and sugar. Add eggs, 1 at a time, continuing to blend. Fold in baking soda, nutmeg, cinnamon, vanilla and fig preserves. Continue to blend on medium speed until well mixed. Pour in coffee then add flour, 1 cup at a time, blending until mixture is smooth. Pour contents into mixing bowl with marinating fruit. Fold in pecans, pineapple and whole cherries. Using a rubber spatula, blend until ingredients are evenly distributed. Pour mixture into greased pans and bake 35 minutes. Open oven, carefully slide shelf out and decorate top of each cake with 5 red and green cherry halves and 5 pecan halves. Slide cakes back into oven. Reduce temperature to 250°F and bake approximately 2½ hours. Cakes are done when toothpick inserted in center comes out clean. Cool cakes approximately 30 minutes then remove from pans, cover with wax paper and wrap well in foil. These cakes may be frozen or stored in an airtight tin for later use. NOTE: You may wish to leave cake in baking pan after it has cooled and marinate with a teaspoon of your favorite brandy or cognac each week for 1 month prior to eating. During this period, tightly wrap cake pan and refrigerate.

Shadows-on-the-Teche
New Iberia, La.

Situated on the banks of Bayou Teche, this home remained in the hands of the same family from 1834 until 1958. The most notable feature about this plantation is not architectural but archival. The members of the Weeks family were prolific letter writers, diary keepers and record keepers. In the attic of the home were 17,000 letters, photographs, receipts and records, providing an extremely detailed description of daily life on the plantation as well as the family's trials and tribulations. The house, built by David Weeks for his wife Mary and their children, was completed in 1834. Weeks died that same year in New Haven, Conn., from a prolonged illness and never lived in the home. Mary, with the help of her brothers, took over management of the plantation as well as the task of raising her children. In 1841 she married Judge John Moore but kept her estate separate from his. The two prospered until the Civil War, during which Union troops used the Shadows as their headquarters in New Iberia. Mary Moore became gravely ill and died a prisoner in her own home. After the war, the home gradually fell into disrepair, but in 1920, Weeks Hall, the builder's great grandson, returned from his studies in Paris and took up residence at the Shadows. He restored the house and entertained many prominent artists, writers and musicians there. When he died, he bequeathed the home to the National Trust for Historic Preservation.

ORANGE CANE SYRUP PECAN PIE

Prep Time: 1 Hour 15 Minutes
Yields: 8 Servings

Comment:
Though there are hundreds of variations of pecan pie throughout the South, this citrus-flavored version is a little lighter and less sweet, but still delicious.

Ingredients:
¼ cup fresh squeezed orange juice
1 tbsp grated orange zest
¾ cup chopped pecans
5 eggs
½ cup sugar
1 tbsp Louisiana cane syrup
1 cup light corn syrup
1 tbsp flour
1 (9-inch) unbaked pie shell
16 pecan halves

Method:
Preheat oven to 350°F. In a large mixing bowl, whisk together eggs and sugar. Do not over beat. Blend in syrups. Pour in orange juice and zest then sprinkle in flour. Blend until well mixed. Fold in chopped pecans. Place pie shell into a 9-inch pie pan. Pour mixture into shell. Arrange pecan halves in a circular pattern on outer edge of pie. Place pie on a cookie sheet and cover with parchment paper. Bake approximately 1 hour. It is best to cool pie overnight.

Holiday & Special Occasion Menus

King Rex's banquet

Every day we receive calls from across the nation requesting Louisiana holiday and other special occasion menus. Traditionally, Louisiana holidays are represented in our homes by dishes dictated by the season or cultural tradition. Feel free to use these menus or create your own from these suggestions. We have reverently described a little about All Saints' Day, given you a sensational taste of Mardi Gras and included traditional holiday fare as well.

New Year's Day

Appetizer
Terrine of Smoked Catfish (page 217)

Crawfish-Stuffed Mushrooms (page 210)

Soup
Duck, Andouille and Oyster Gumbo (page 280)

Salad
Roasted Beet Salad (page 299)

Seafood Jambalaya Rice Salad (page 327)

Vegetable
Cajun Black-Eyed Peas (page 337)

Smothered Cabbage and Andouille (page 344)

Seafood
Shrimp and Redfish Courtbouillon (page 382)

Black-Eyed Pea Battered Shrimp (page 384)

Poultry
Baked Long Island Duck (page 559)

Meat
Rosemary-Stuffed Leg of Pork (page 501)

Fried Oyster Dressing (page 481)

Pecan Rice Dressing (page 476)

Dessert
Mandarin Orange Cheesecake (page 603)

Sautéed Apples Calvados (page 617)

Mardi Gras

Mardi Gras, or Fat Tuesday, is the traditional day for fun and feasting prior to the start of Lenten fasting on Ash Wednesday. Mardi Gras was brought to Louisiana from Paris where it had been celebrated since the Middle Ages. The first Mardi Gras celebrated in Louisiana was in 1699 when Iberville and his men, mooring their ship for the night, realized that Mardi Gras was being celebrated back home in France. The spot was dubbed "Point de Mardi Gras." It was not until the 1700s and the founding of New Orleans that Mardi Gras balls were celebrated. These began on Twelfth Night with the selection of a king and continued through Mardi Gras Day. The revelry and parades associated with New Orleans Mardi Gras today did not begin until the 1820s. The parades began simply as processions of masqueraders on foot or horseback and were marked by violence. In 1857, the Mistick Krewe of Comus was formed and the first themed parade with floats and costumed revelers was presented. Comus set the stage for the future of New Orleans Mardi Gras and inspired the formation of other krewes with their own kings, queens and balls. Now the days between Twelfth Night and Ash Wednesday are filled with dozens of parades and balls in New Orleans and outlying areas.

Courir de Mardi Gras

Soup
Chicken and Sausage Gumbo (page 279)

Salad
Mardi Gras Crawfish Salad (page 323)

Traditional Potato Salad (page 318)

Vegetable
White or Red Beans with Ham and Sausage (page 338)

White Rice (page 371)

Dessert
Praline Pecan Fudge (page 606)

Rum Raisin Rice Pudding (page 628)

The Courir de Mardi Gras, literally the "running of the Mardi Gras," is still celebrated in rural South Louisiana, but is a far cry from what most people associate with Mardi Gras and Carnival. While the principle is the same, a last day of mischief and revelry before Lent, pageantry and balls are replaced by parody and pranksters. Once a part of pre-Lenten festivities in most French parts of Louisiana in the 19th century, the Courir de Mardi Gras has ancient roots dating back to medieval rites of passage. During the festivities, a band of revelers don strange disguises and elaborate masks while taking to their horses. Riding wildly through the countryside, they go from farm to farm and beg for chickens or other ingredients for the communal pot of gumbo. They often sing loudly or play pranks until the farmer or homeowner produces something for the pot, usually a live chicken that must be caught. While each band includes an unmasked capitaine to keep the peace, the celebration is still a raucous one. The tradition was all but forgotten in many parts of Louisiana, but in the mid-20th century it began to make a comeback both in an effort to preserve the Cajun culture and as an alternative to the huge crowds of tourists that descend on New Orleans. Mamou, Eunice, Church Point and a handful of other rural communities feature a Courir de Mardi Gras in the week or so prior to Lent. Always featured is a surplus of chicken and sausage gumbo, music and fun.

Easter

Soup
Cream of Chicken and Artichoke Soup (page 266)

Salad
Steamed Broccoli with
Orange Ginger Pecan Dressing (page 305)

Pineapple-Carrot Congealed Salad (page 305)

Vegetable
Butter Beans with Ham (page 337)

White Squash with Shrimp (page 365)

Seafood
Crawfish Bisque (page 408)

Poultry
Coq au Vin (page 449)

Meat
Pecan Rice Dressing (page 476)

Prime Rib of Beef (page 518)

Daube (page 516)

Dessert
Carrot Cake (page 596)

Mamere's Country-Style Lemon Pie (page 637)

Mother's Day

Appetizer

Oyster and Artichoke Dip (page 219)

Soup

Velouté of Boiled Crawfish, Corn and Potatoes (page 257)

Salad

Mixed Greens with Warm Ponchatoula Strawberry Vinaigrette (page 298)

Marinated Creole Tomato and Red Onion Salad (page 301)

Vegetable

Cajun Roux Peas (page 334)

Bacon-Wrapped Green Beans (page 335)

Honey Mint Glazed Carrots (page 347)

Seafood

Shrimp Creole (page 388)

Mr. Royley's Crawfish Stew (page 409)

Poultry

Baked Garlic Chicken (page 458)

Meat

Creole Dirty Rice (page 477)

Crown Roast of Pork with Shoepeg Corn Bread Stuffing (page 508)

Dessert

Mother's Cream Puffs (page 631)

Purple Plum Torte (page 600)

Fourth of July

Appetizer

Panzanella (page 234)

Roasted Onion and Eggplant Paté (page 239)

Shrimp Bread (page 212)

Soup

Chilled Watermelon Soup (page 285)

Salad

Pickled Carrot Salad (page 306)

Spicy Fried Chicken Pasta Salad (page 312)

Vegetable

Smothered Okra and Tomatoes (page 345)

Pan-fried Candied Sweet Potatoes (page 357)

Boiled Corn (page 358)

Seafood

Oven-Baked Garlic Crabs (page 400)

Cajun Drunken Shrimp (page 385)

Poultry

Oven-Barbecued Chicken (page 459)

Meat

"Guaranteed to be Tender" Baby Back Ribs (page 497)

Pork, Chicken and Andouille Jambalaya (page 500)

Dessert

Skillet Peach Cobbler with Blueberries (page 604)

Perfect Lemon Bars (page 610)

White Chocolate Strawberry Ice Cream (page 620)

All Saints' Day

The people of Louisiana can make a party out of just about anything, even death. Stories abound of "professional" funeral goers who attended every wake and funeral they could find because they could eat so heartily. The jazz funeral adds music and ritual gaiety to what normally would be the most solemn of processions. It should come as no surprise that at the traditional visitation of graves on November 1, All Saints' Day, the atmosphere is somewhat festive. The preparations for All Saints' Day can begin weeks ahead of time, for there is grass to be cut, plots to be weeded, fences to be whitewashed, tombs to be painted, decorations to be refreshed. Troops of women and children work to ensure the dead appear at their finest on this special day. While this practice still continues all over Louisiana, in 19th and early 20th centuries, New Orleans' All Saints' Day was a major social event. It was important that each family's gravesites were not outdone by their neighbors'. An untended or poorly decorated grave was a mark against a family that could be gossiped about the entire year. Family and friends gathered to bring flowers and to reminisce about those that had gone before them. Vendors sold candy, cold drinks, ice cream, pralines, gumbos and pies. The party atmosphere could make one forget the normally solemn setting for these activities. Some families even brought picnic lunches and spent the entire day among the tombs. As with any family gathering, large groups of people needed to be fed, so feasts of holiday proportions were often created.

Appetizer

Lemon-Garlic Shrimp Bruschetta (page 212)

Hog's Head Cheese (page 231)

Peppered Ham Salad (page 228)

Soup

Red Bean and Sausage Soup (page 263)

Salad

Rémoulade Slaw (page 295)

Old Maid's Potato Salad (page 316)

Vegetable

Smothered Okra and Tomatoes (page 345)

Mamere's Favorite Candied Yams (page 356)

Seafood

Ice Water Marinated Seafood (page 378)

Baked Catfish Creole (page 419)

Poultry

Sweet and Spicy Chicken Étouffée (page 445)

Meat

Pepper-Laced Pork Roast (page 495)

Game

Braised Doves Evangeline (page 549)

Venison Sausage (page 581)

Dessert

Funeral Pie (page 640)

Anise Cookies (page 612)

Thanksgiving

Appetizer

Mallard Duck Sausage (page 232)

Oyster and Andouille Pastries (page 218)

Soup

Spinach and Sweet Potato Soup (page 271)

Salad

Stuffed Creole Tomato Salad (page 301)

Pecan Ambrosia (page 311)

Vegetable

Broccoli and Cauliflower Casserole (page 341)

Simple and Delicious Holiday Yams (page 356)

Crabmeat and Shrimp Stuffed Mirliton (page 366)

Seafood

Cioppino (page 380)

Herb-Baked Large Mouth Bass (page 416)

Poultry

Roasted Turkey (page 467)

Deep-Fried Turkey (page 467)

Meat

Sweet Farre Dressing (page 480)

Charbroiled Leg of Lamb (page 536)

Game

Roasted Goose (page 561)

Dessert

Carrot Cake (page 596)

Pumpkin Eggnog Pie (page 640)

Le Réveillon

Le Réveillon, or "the awakening," is the morning feast following midnight Mass on Christmas Eve or New Year's Eve. It is an age-old custom inherited by Louisiana Creoles from their European ancestors. For Catholics, Le Réveillon was the ultimate feast for breaking the traditional Christmas Eve fast. It was a time of family reunions and thanksgiving, but it was also a time for eating a vast variety of rich holiday foods including Daube, Salmis of Rabbit, Sweetbreads and Chicken and Sausage Gumbo. Lavish desserts would follow accompanied by Eggnog, Cherry Bounce and Brandy Milk Punch. The celebration would traditionally last until the early hours of the morning. Around 3 a.m., the women and children might retire to bed, but the men would often stay up smoking cigars and sipping cordials until dawn. In rural South Louisiana, Le Réveillon was celebrated by many families into the 1960s. Family members would gather to walk to midnight Mass together by the light of the huge bonfires on the Mississippi River levee. A hearty breakfast always followed. A second, more elaborate Réveillon was often celebrated on New Year's Eve. For many years, the more lavish versions of Le Réveillon had all but died out in New Orleans and the rural areas, but many New Orleans restaurants have recently resurrected Réveillon menus for the holidays. Still celebrated in Europe, Le Réveillon is certainly a family tradition worth revisiting.

Christmas

With all the descriptions of holiday gaiety in Louisiana, it is easy to forget that the hard work of making a living could not always stop for Christmas and New Year's Day. On sugar plantations, Christmas fell right in the middle of the harvest and grinding season. Christmas festivities, particularly for the slaves that worked on the plantations, would often have to wait until grinding was complete. In the bayous of Louisiana, the holidays fell in the middle of the prime hunting and trapping season. For the trappers whose livelihood depended on winter furs, Christmas had to wait. The deferred celebration became known as "Trapper's Christmas" and was traditionally celebrated on February 25, particularly in the Bayou Dularge area of Louisiana.

Brunch

Lagniappe

agniappe derives from New World Spanish la ñapa, which means, "the gift." The word came into the Creole language where it acquired a French spelling. It is still used in Louisiana to denote a little bonus that a friendly shopkeeper might add to a purchase.

This section of *The Encyclopedia of Cajun & Creole Cuisine* is our lagniappe to you. It is dedicated to those who came before us in the food and restaurant industry as well as noteworthy restaurateurs and entrepreneurs at the beginning of the 21st century. In no way is this meant to be a complete list of Louisiana's outstanding culinarians, restaurateurs and manufacturers, just a little something to whet your appetite for Louisiana culture and cuisine.

In Louisiana we pride ourselves on our heritage, but we also look to the future for greatness. Among the graduates from the Chef John Folse Culinary Institute at Nicholls State University will be the next batch of culinary icons.

Inaugural Class, Chef John Folse Culinary Institute at Nicholls State University-Spring 1996

Bottom Row: Stephanie Pasqua, Darby Plaisance, Lisa Carline, Dr. Jerald Chesser, Dr. Donald Ayo, Chef John Folse, Brian Berry, Olive Dumez, Patrick Besson
Middle Row: Randall Boyd, Nicholas Oliver, Deborah Bergeron, Lynda Oncale, Louisa Landwher, Cherie Whipple, Kenneth Champagne, William Swanigan
Top Row: Brandon Pitre, Constancio Izaguirre, Gregory Hammer, Scott Henry, Thomas Guthrie, David Oufnac, Christina Biakey, Patricia Sills, Sidney Ordoyne

Abita Brewing Company

The Abita Brewing Company was founded in 1986 just 30 miles north of New Orleans in Abita Springs, La. It is the oldest craft brewery in the Southeast, and it produces five

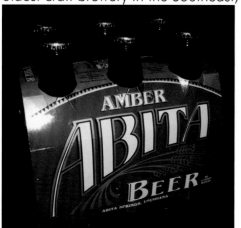

seasonal beer brews along with its five prime brews. The beer from Abita contains no preservatives, additives or stabilizers, which results in brews that have a shorter shelf life than most. In the first year, 1,500 barrels of beer were produced. Today, Abita puts out a staggering 40,000 barrels of its various brews and 3,000 barrels of root beer each day. In April 1994, the company moved into a larger facility to keep up with demand. The original site is now host to the Abita Brew Pub—a full-service restaurant and tasting bar.

Acme Oyster House

Acme Oyster House opened in 1910 in the three-story Acme Saloon building on Royal Street. After a fire in 1924, the

restaurant moved to its current location, an early 19th century townhouse on Iberville Street. Since then, Acme has become a mainstay in New Orleans and has opened two more local restaurants and one in Florida. Acme is known for quality food due to the private oyster beds from which the restaurant harvests its supply. The original French Quarter oyster house has been featured on the Food Network and PBS. In addition, the restaurant consistently wins awards from *New Orleans Magazine*, *Where Magazine* and *Gambit Weekly* for its seafood. After more than 90 years in the restaurant business, Acme Oyster House continues to serve up some of the best oysters in South Louisiana.

Amato's Winery

Amato's Winery in Independence, La., is one of a handful of wineries in Louisiana that is devoted to recreating the traditional sweet, fruit wines common to the region. Henry Amato is a second-generation Italian-American winemaker.

He founded Amato's Winery in 1993 with wines he created from his homegrown strawberries and his grandfather's recipes. He also makes a blueberry wine that is particularly popular in Japan and an orange wine that recreates the wines made for thousands of years in his ancestors' region of Italy.

Antoine's Restaurant

Frenchman Antoine Alciatore opened a small boarding house on Rue St. Louis in April of 1840. The profitable boarding house was transformed into a restaurant shortly

after Alciatore's marriage to Julie Freyss. The restaurant was relocated a few times, but ultimately ended up back on Rue St. Louis. After Alciatore's death, his son Jules took over the restaurant. Prior to that time, Jules had spent six years learning the business from his mother and four years cooking abroad in France and England. Jules was responsible for much of the success and fame of the restaurant. He was credited with creating oysters Rockefeller—a mainstay in most New Orleans restaurants. When Jules died in 1934, the restaurant was passed down to his son Roy. Two of the restaurant's 15 dining rooms were added by Roy Alciatore—the 1840 Room, a tribute to the restaurant's founding, and the Rex Room which honors the kings of Mardi Gras. Since then, many generations of Alciatores have run Antoine's, and the restaurant continues to be owned by family members today.

Arnaud's Restaurant

Leon Bertrand Arnaud Cazenave came to America with the intention of studying medicine. However, shortly after his arrival, the colorful Frenchman opened a small café on New Orleans' Bourbon Street. Then, in 1918, he opened Arnaud's Restaurant. Locals affectionately called him Count Arnaud. Along with his chefs, Count Arnaud created signature dishes such as shrimp Arnaud and oysters Bienville. His philosophy was that it is necessary for people to be able to relax and enjoy their meals. It was the Count's charm and creative flair that kept the Crescent

City's elite coming back to Arnaud's. Before his death in 1948, Arnaud Cazenave declared that his scandalous daughter Germaine Cazenave Wells was to be his successor. Because of her bad reputation, many believed the restaurant would fail under her care. Instead, Germaine helped the business gain worldwide exposure and prominence by being named one of the world's top five restaurants. In 1978, she agreed to lease Arnaud's to an Armenian man by the name of Archie Casbarian. Casbarian was an experienced manager and one of the nation's best hoteliers. With his expertise, Arnaud's was restored to its original splendor, and today many people enjoy the magnificence of fine dining at the French Creole restaurant.

Aunt Sally's Original Creole Pralines

More than 2.5 million pralines are produced each year by Aunt Sally's Original Creole Pralines. Pierre and Diane

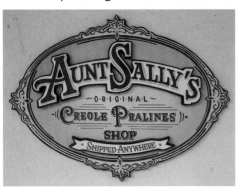

Bagur founded the company on Royal Street in their hometown of New Orleans during the early 1930s. The couple developed their own version of New Orleans' signature candy and made them by hand in a copper pot on a gas stove. The pralines were sold throughout the French Quarter by a traveling vendor. Today, Aunt Sally's is owned by fourth-generation family members and is located at the corner of Jackson Square on Decatur Street.

Barq's

Many people mistakenly presume that Barq's root beer originated in New Orleans. While Barq's does have many ties to the Big Easy, the root beer was actually formulated in nearby Biloxi, Miss. Barq's founder, Edward Charles Edmond Barq, was born in New Orleans but spent most of his youth

in France. After returning to New Orleans, he and his brother Gaston founded the Barq's Brothers Bottling Company in 1890. However, it was in Biloxi that Edward Barq created and bottled his first root beer. Even then the product was different from most root beers, with less head and more "bite" than the traditional. One of the first franchises was opened and run in New Orleans by Jesse Robinson, who had been raised by Edward Barq, and by 1950 there were approximately 200 across the country. Advertising was limited and understated, simply proclaiming, "Drink Barq's. It's Good." In 1976, the Barq's family sold the business to John Koerner and John Oudt, who relocated the headquarters to New Orleans. Much more aggressive and somewhat off-color marketing soon propelled Barq's into the position of No. 2 root beer in the nation. In the 1990s, Coca-Cola purchased the company and moved the headquarters down the coast to Mobile, Ala. While the company can market and bottle Barq's wherever they want, the syrup must still be bought from Jesse Robinson in New Orleans.

Baumer Foods

When Alvin and Mildred Baumer founded Baumer foods in 1923 they knew they had a hot product, they just didn't know how hot. Their first and signature product was Crystal

Hot Sauce, made from ground, aged cayenne peppers grown in their own fields. Currently, their plant on Tchoupitoulas Street in New Orleans churns out about 3 million gallons of hot sauce each year. Crystal Hot Sauce can be found in 75 countries around the world, and their sauces and peppers are ubiquitous on restaurant tables throughout the United States. Baumer Foods has also expanded its offerings to include Extra Hot Hot Sauce, steak, soy, Worcestershire, barbecue and teriyaki sauces, yellow, brown and specialty mustards, peppers in vinegar and various jams and jellies. Baumer Foods is still run by the Baumer family who continues to personally inspect the fields to ensure the cayenne peppers are at their very best prior to harvest.

Madame Bégué

Madame Elizabeth Kettenring Dutrey Bégué emigrated from Bavaria, Germany, to New Orleans in 1853. She is credited with popularizing brunch throughout the city. In 1863, she and her husband, Louis Dutrey, opened Coffee House in the French

Market. They served 3–4 hour long "second breakfasts" to area butchers each day at 11 a.m. Madame Bégué did all the cooking, and her husband handled the business. Three

years after Louis' death, she married local butcher Hypolite Bégué who was working for her as a bartender. The name of the restaurant was then changed to Bégué's. Although Madame Bégué was a German chef, she honed her skills in French cuisine. During the Cotton Centennial Exposition in 1884, the restaurant became distinguished among diners. Following the deaths of Madame Bégué and her husband Hypolite, the restaurant closed and was sold. The ground floor of the building is now home to Tujague's Restaurant.

John Besh

John Besh cooks Creole cuisine like only a native can. Born on the bayou, Besh grew up like many South Louisiana boys, hunting, fishing and ultimately cooking. Formal education

at the Culinary Institute of America and demanding apprenticeships in Europe allowed Besh to take his dishes to a higher level. Besh worked at many award-winning restaurants both in America and abroad before becoming executive chef of the much-acclaimed Restaurant August on Tchoupitoulas Street in New Orleans. In 2003, Besh launched The Besh Steakhouse at Harrah's where he is currently the executive chef. He has also received many personal accolades and is generally regarded as one of the newest stars on the American culinary scene. Besh is known for his innovative approach to classic Creole and French cuisine.

Paul Blangé

Paul Blangé was a Dutch chef credited with inventing many of the signature dishes at Brennan's Restaurant, including chicken pontalba, eggs Hussarde and bananas Foster.

According to legend, in 1951 Owen Brennan asked Blangé, to create a dish featuring bananas. Chef Blangé rose to the challenge and concocted the classic bananas Foster made with butter, sugar and liqueur. It was named for Richard Foster, a friend of Brennan and regular patron of the restaurant. Bananas Foster remains the most popular dish at the restaurant. Each year, Brennan's utilizes over 35,000 pounds of bananas for the world-renowned dessert. It is said that Blangé was so devoted to the restaurant that when he died he was buried with a Brennan's menu on his chest and that his ghost still watches over the restaurant's kitchen.

Blue Runner Foods

In 1918, Pierre Chauvin began canning figs and blackberries under the name Union Canning Factory. He realized the business potential for canning, and in 1946 he teamed up

with C.A. Englade to form Gonzales Products Company. Together they built a facility to house their operations in Gonzales, La. In 1950, Chauvin began canning white navy beans and then red beans. Gonzales Products Company became Blue Runner Foods, Inc., in 1993 when Richard Thomas purchased and took over the company. The cannery currently produces eleven different canned goods under its Blue Runner label—with Creole Cream Style Red Kidney Beans as their most famous product.

Bon Ton Cafe

Bon Ton Cafe was established in the coffee district of Magazine Street in the early 1900s. The original owner,

Albert Martin, was a master drink mixer. He created the Bon Ton Rum Ramsey, the ingredients for which remain a secret. However, Martin and the owners that followed experienced little success with the business until a man from the bayous of South Louisiana emerged. In 1953, Alvin Pierce bought the cafe, and his wife Alzina cooked breakfast and lunch. The

Pierces won over the business crowd in New Orleans with their traditional Cajun food and local charm. In 1964 they answered the demand from locals to remain open for dinner. Wayne Pierce, Alvin's nephew, began working at Bon Ton in 1966. Ownership was eventually passed to Wayne and his wife Debbie in 1979. The restaurant's current home is the historic Natchez Building. Bon Ton Cafe is still one of the best places to go for home-style Cajun cooking.

Brennan's Restaurant

In July 1946, Owen Edward Brennan showed his stubbornness by opening Owen Brennan's French and Creole Restaurant in order to prove to a local restaurateur

that an Irishman could run a successful French restaurant. The restaurant surpassed all expectations. The business was opened across from Brennan's property, The Old Absinthe House. A dispute over his lease caused the restaurant to move from Bourbon Street to its current location. Although Brennan died at 45 before the new location opened, the restaurant continued to succeed under his sister Ella. After Ella expanded the family business to include six Brennan's restaurants across the country, Owen Brennan's wife, Maude, and his three sons, Pip, Jimmy and Ted, assumed complete ownership of the original restaurant on Royal Street. Owen Edward Brennan's legacy lives on in the New Orleans tradition of a three-hour "Breakfast at Brennan's" and in some of the restaurant's signature dishes such as eggs Hussarde and bananas Foster.

Bruce Foods

One of America's largest privately-owned food manufacturers was founded in New Iberia, La. In 1928, Bruce Foods began providing Americans with Cajun and Tex-Mex food products.

J.S. "Si" Brown

Bruce Foods manufactures the original Louisiana Hot Sauce, Bruce's Yams and Casa Fiesta Mexican food items. The company has also acquired Cajun Injector marinades. Today, Bruce Foods produces more than 550 different food products. These goods are distributed throughout America and in more than 100

countries. Under nine major brands, Bruce Foods employs roughly 1,200 people in four plants in the United States and an affiliated facility in the Netherlands.

Nathaniel Burton

Nathaniel Burton was born in McComb, Miss., in 1914, but it was in New Orleans that he made his mark. Most noted as a chef at the Pontchartrain Hotel, Burton's biggest impact came from his 1978 book, *Creole Feast*. The book, which he co-authored with Rudy Lombard, paid tribute and gave a voice to the African-American chefs of New Orleans. Burton and the chefs in his book were all masters at their trade and truly fed the city. Unfortunately, they were part of an era that seldom recognized the talents of African-Americans.

Café Du Monde

Unless it is Christmas Day or there is a hurricane about to hit, you can get a hot cup of coffee and a fresh stack of hot beignets at Café Du Monde anytime, day or night.

The Original Café Du Monde Coffee Stand was established in 1862 in the New Orleans French Market. The current menu consists of dark roasted coffee with chicory, beignets, milk and fresh squeezed orange juice. The coffee is served black or au lait, meaning it is half hot milk. Beignets are square, French-style doughnuts, lavishly covered with powdered sugar. In 1988, Café Du Monde's menu expanded to include soft drinks and iced coffee. A visit to Café Du Monde is a must for tourists, but it is also a favorite coffee break spot for many who work in the city. Since it is open 24 hours a day, the restaurant provides a perfect oasis at which to recover from the overindulgence of the surrounding French Quarter.

Cajun Power Sauce

Chef Carroll "Caro" Thomas was a diligent student of Cajun heritage prior to creating his Cajun Power sauces. He studied food preparations and traditions from as far back as the mid-1800s and up until the 1950s. He put his knowledge to work in his restaurant, developing unique gourmet flavors based on these traditions. Now Caro shares his abilities through Cajun Power products, which are manufactured in Abbeville, La. Cajun Power Sauce Manufacturing has been crafting quality sauces and products using only Cajun ingredients since the late 1970s. The company understands that Cajun food is not about making everything hot and spicy—it is about using a blend of seasonings and spices to add flavor to life.

Camellia Grill

For breakfast, lunch or even late-night munchies, the Camellia Grill is a "must-do" in New Orleans. An old-time diner with a Greek Revival façade, the Camellia Grill is a

favorite hangout for students, locals and tourists alike. One visit and you'll understand why there's often a line snaking out the door and why it is definitely worth the wait. Once inside, patrons are seated on a round stool bolted to the floor, one of many facing the curving "double-U" countertop. The grill serves the ultimate comfort foods—thick, juicy burgers with grilled onions, sinfully delicious pies and freshly prepared freezes. However, the food is only part of the appeal. The waiters are truly artists at their trade, working flawlessly behind the counter with a joke, a flourish and always a smile. Some have literally worked at the Camellia for decades, clad all in white with bowties to boot. While the turnover is quick, you are never rushed, which is important considering the size of the portions. Camellia Grill is a nostalgic visit to a time when service was important and fat grams were not.

Caribbean Room at the Pontchartrain Hotel

The New Orleans Pontchartrain Hotel was built in 1927 by the Aschaffenburgs. Still in operation today, the 12-story hotel features magnificent theme suites, vaulted ceilings and sparkling crystal chandeliers. While a dramatic place to stay, the Pontchartrain is

most famous for its former restaurant, the Caribbean Room, which featured Creole and French cuisine. Signature dishes included crabmeat Remick and mile-high pie. While the rose-hued Caribbean Room is now used for group functions, the Pontchartrain has also been home to a favorite watering hole and meeting place for more than half a century, the Bayou Bar. Scores of celebrities considered the Pontchartrain their home when visiting New Orleans, so much so that some of the rooms are named for them, including Richard Burton, Mary Martin, Helen Hayes and Carol Channing.

Casa de Sue Winery

Casa de Sue Winery and Vineyards was founded in 1992, and it was the first licensed winery in Louisiana. It is a small family-owned winery specializing in fine muscadine and blueberry wines. Located in the rolling hills of East Feliciana Parish, the winery offers visitors delicious Louisiana wines, beautiful artwork and rustic antiques. In fact, each bottle of Casa de Sue wine has a label featuring artwork somehow related to Louisiana and its culture. Casa de Sue wines are available throughout Louisiana at grocery stores and wine retailers.

Casamento's Restaurant

If décor was everything, Casamento's, an unusual little shotgun restaurant on Magazine Street, probably wouldn't have amounted to much. Nevertheless, a commitment to cleanliness and to providing the best oysters in town has

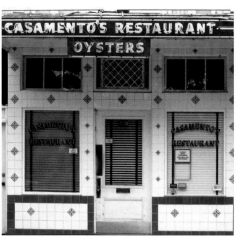

kept Casamento's in business since 1919. The establishment is so committed to quality that it closes during the hottest months of the summer. While oysters may be safe to eat all year round, the waters around Louisiana are so warm then, they are not at their best and therefore not

acceptable at Casamento's. The restaurant was opened by Joe Casamento, an immigrant from Ustica, Italy. He chose to put tile on every possible surface, both inside and out, in order to keep his restaurant as clean as possible. The effect is a little unusual, but Casamento's is always spotless and always crowded. The restaurant is long and narrow with just a few tables available at which to relish the cold, salty oysters, the famous oyster loaves on their signature pan bread, the ultimate soft-shell crab, the crispy fried trout or the steaming Italian spaghetti and meatballs. Despite the limited menu, there is something for everyone at Casamento's. Signed T-shirts around the restaurant attest to the fact that even the celebrities make a pilgrimage to Casamento's when in New Orleans.

Central Grocery

While the interior of Central Grocery in New Orleans may appear to be stuck in the 1950s, the history of this little

Italian store dates back even further. Opened by a Sicilian named Lupo Salvatore in 1906, the grocery featured Italian and Mediterranean specialties like olives, cheese and olive oils. Those delicacies and many more are still available, but Central Grocery is best known as the birthplace of the Muffuletta sandwich—

a round Italian loaf packed with mortadella ham, Genoa salami, Provolone cheese and olive salad. Tourists and locals make trips to Central Grocery to stand in line for their "muff" and a Barq's root beer.

Leah Chase of Dooky Chase Restaurant

Dooky Chase Restaurant in New Orleans is Creole cooking at its best. The restaurant was opened in 1941 by Edgar

"Dooky" Chase Sr., and his wife Emily Tenette. It quickly became a meeting place for the black community. Later, Edgar's son, "Dooky" Jr., got into the business along with his wife, Leah. Leah became the cook at Dooky Chase, and she prepared the Creole fare that made the restaurant famous.

Serving everything from red beans to fried chicken and an amazing gumbo des herbes, Dooky Chase has some of the best Creole food in the city.

On the outside, Dooky Chase looks like any other rustic building in New Orleans, but inside guests are treated to fine table linens, artwork and atmosphere. The restaurant almost looks like a museum. Perhaps this is because Leah Chase believes in giving her patrons something more than just wonderful food. Because of the jazz heritage of New Orleans, many of the paintings depict music scenes. Perhaps some of the restaurant's famous guests such as Duke Ellington, Lena Horne or Ray Charles helped influence the selection of artwork. At Dooky Chase, the customer is important, and Leah has even been known to write personal letters to guests who purchase a cookbook.

Chester's Cypress Inn

Chester's Cypress Inn in Donner, La., was opened in 1939 by Chester Boudreaux as a dance hall, but it served as a family grocery store before that. The grocery store and dance hall both served food. That practice eventually blossomed into the restaurant that operates today. Legend has it that a friend of Chester's, a state trooper, taught him how to make fried chicken. This recipe, as well as two others that Chester adapted for friends, soon earned Chester's a reputation for excellent fried chicken. Chester's is still owned by Boudreaux family members. It remains famous for fried chicken and also frog legs, onion rings and chicken livers.

Willy Coln

Willy Coln of Cologne, Germany, began his culinary studies by apprenticing in Germany and Switzerland. Coln then

traveled the world as a cook aboard a Holland America cruise ship. His travels took him to Asia, the South Seas, throughout Europe and finally New Orleans. "Once I saw the French Quarter, the bohemian atmosphere of the 1960s, I knew I would stay," said Coln.

After a long career with Sonesta hotels, he opened Willy Coln's Chalet restaurant. During his 13 years there, he was named Louisiana Chef of the Year by the Louisiana Chefs Association. Coln has cooked for many notable people including Audrey Hepburn, Richard Nixon, General Haig and heads of state. He became widely known for his slow-roasted veal shank and his black forest cake (his secret is lots of Kirsch).

Coln's respect for Louisiana cuisine centers on the global heritage of its people. "For years everybody came from all over the world and left their culture, cooks and recipes until we have something unique," said Coln. His distinctive cuisine crosses international boundaries and inspires newer chefs to work up to his consistently high standards.

Christian's Restaurant

Christian's Restaurant was opened in 1973 on Veterans Boulevard by partners Christian Ansel, a member of the Galatoire family, and Hank Bergeron. In 1977, they moved the restaurant into an old church in Mid-City New Orleans. The Lutheran church built in 1914 provides a charming atmosphere. It has beautiful stained glass windows and cathedral ceilings. The restaurant bar was previously the "crying room." Christian's serves lunch and dinner, specializing in a blend of classic French and New Orleans Creole cuisine. Christian's signature dishes include cold smoked soft-shell crab, veal Christian, filet mignon Farci "Bayou La Loutre" and oysters Roland.

Commander's Palace Restaurant

The Garden District of New Orleans has been home to Commander's Palace since the 1880s. Emile Commander's restaurant was synonymous with fine dining and was frequented by the distinguished neighborhood families. With Prohibition came change. Commander's Palace was under new management. It became a place where riverboat captains entertained prostitutes upstairs. In the 1940s, Frank and Elinor Moran bought the restaurant and returned it to its original grandeur. Commander's Palace is housed in an old Victorian mansion, and it is famous for its lush gardens and patio. The Morans are credited with adding the patio and greenery, but it was the 1969 purchase by the Brennan family that made Commander's Palace the eye-catching landmark that it is today. In a controversial move, the Brennan's decided to update the dark and dreary mansion by painting the exterior a bright turquoise—a tip from New Orleans designer Charles Gresham. Soon the dark reds of the interior were replaced with bright pastels and other rooms were designed and decorated to match. Overshadowing Commander's interesting décor is its exquisite food. Some of the world's best chefs, including Paul

Prudhomme, Emeril Lagasse and the late Jamie Shannon, have worked in the restaurant's kitchen. Ella Brennan and her family still own Commander's Palace, and the restaurant continues to win awards year after year. Commander's has been voted Zagat Survey's "Most Popular Restaurant in New Orleans" for 17 consecutive years.

Community Coffee Company

Since 1919, Community Coffee has prospered by selling their famous red bag variety of coffee. More than 85 years ago, Henry Norman "Cap" Saurage started brewing coffee in his Baton Rouge country store. Saurage named his coffee Community because of the constant support of friends and customers. Today, Community Coffee is the largest family-owned retail coffee brand in the United States with sales exceeding $100 million annually. The corporate headquarters are still located in Baton Rouge, while the roasting facility is on the banks of the Mississippi River in Port Allen, La. Community Coffee is distributed to grocery stores, offices, restaurants and hotels throughout the Southeast. The brand has inspired a New Orleans themed shop, CC's Gourmet Coffee House. The coffee shops are mostly located in Louisiana, and they serve more than 20 varieties of coffee as well as signature drinks and blends.

Al Copeland

Like so many of New Orleans' best-known entrepreneurs, Al Copeland started humbly with a job in a grocery store. From there he learned the donut business and the art of franchising from his brother Gil. This knowledge, combined with keen observations of what makes businesses succeed and fail, is the secret of Copeland's success. In 1972, Copeland opened Popeyes Fried Chicken in Arabi, a New Orleans suburb. He took a southern classic and added Louisiana seasonings to create a unique product. By 1976, Popeyes was franchising. In 1989, there were 800 Popeyes stores in the United States and abroad. Even though Copeland lost ownership of Popeyes, he retained the rights to the recipes and seasonings. Copeland's Famous New Orleans Restaurant and Bar, a full-service restaurant, opened in 1983. The Louisiana-influenced casual dining concept caught on and by 2001, there were 40 restaurants in 15 states. Copeland's latest restaurant success has been Copeland's Cheesecake Bistro. An award-winning salesman and restaurateur, Copeland is also a big supporter of food service education and charitable organizations. Like any good businessman, he is always on the lookout for the next big idea.

Corinne Dunbar's Restaurant

Located in an 1840s townhouse on St. Charles Avenue in New Orleans, Corinne Dunbar's was a gracious classic in a city awash with famous restaurants. Dunbar opened the restaurant in her home with her personal cook, Leona Victor, as her partner. The fine furnishings and delicious food served on Dunbar's china made dinners at this restaurant unique and memorable. The restaurant was identified only by a brass plaque announcing "Corinne Dunbar." Guests were greeted by a butler who escorted them first to a parlor and then to the dining room. Corinne Dunbar offered a set dinner consisting of several courses. Some of the restaurant's dishes, such as oysters Dunbar, are still famous today. Many say the restaurant's run ended when it was sold and moved to another location, but the business did not technically close until the second owner retired.

The Court of Two Sisters

The aristocratic Creoles, Emma and Bertha Camors are the two sisters for which The Court of Two Sisters was named. The building the restaurant is in was once home to the

sisters. In 1886 they opened the Shop of the Two Sisters on the ground floor. Their shop was made famous for outfitting the wealthy with formal gowns, carnival costumes and other Parisian imports. While catering to the material desires of shoppers, the sisters served tea and cakes in the courtyard to their best customers. During their lives, nothing could

separate the Camors sisters. They died within two months of each other in 1924. The property passed through five different owners, and during the transitions, the home of the Camors sisters was transformed into a restaurant. The building was restored to its former elegance when it was acquired by Joe Fein Jr., in the 1960s. The Court of Two Sisters features the largest courtyard in the French Quarter and serves a jazz brunch every day from 9 a.m. until 3 p.m. Diners can choose from more than 80 dishes while enjoying the sounds of a live jazz trio.

Crescent City Farmers Market

The Crescent City Farmers Market was founded in 1995 by Richard McCarthy of Loyola University and civic leaders

John Abajian and Sharon Litwin. It provides a meeting place for farmers and a model for new businesses. Since its inception, additional markets have opened throughout New

Orleans to cater to the growing number of vendors and patrons. More than 1,500 shoppers visit the four markets each week. The Farmers Market is run by a nonprofit organization, the Economics Institute, whose mission is to create ecologically sound economic development.

Dixie Brewing Company

Founded in 1907 by Valentine Merz, Dixie Brewing Company is one of just 12 remaining regional breweries in America

and the only privately held, family-owned regional brewery in the South. Dixie hit major obstacles during Prohibition and in the 1960s and '70s when most regional breweries were forced out of business by larger beer companies. Dixie was purchased by Joe and Kendra Bruno in 1985. The hard times Dixie had seen almost shut it down. However, the company recovered and has

made a comeback based on original brews like Dixie Blackened Voodoo Lager. Dixie also brews Crimson Voodoo

Ale and a dessert beer called White Moose. The traditional slow-brewed, hands-on method is maintained in each step of the unique brewing process. The Dixie Brewing Company is a tradition and a visible landmark on the streets of New Orleans.

Don's Seafood and Steak House

Since 1934, Don's Seafood and Steak House has been a favorite spot for succulent seafood and juicy steaks. Don's

is located in Lafayette, La. The area is famous for its wonderful food. Restaurant specialties include crawfish bisque, seafood gumbo and trout Landry.

Don's is a casual, family-style restaurant serving great food, heavily influenced by its Cajun surroundings.

Elmer Candy Corporation

Miller Candy Company was opened by 24-year-old German immigrant Christopher Henry Miller in 1853. Miller had worked in a pastry shop since his arrival in New Orleans at

age 16. After his death in 1902, Miller's sons and son-in-law, Augustus Elmer, took over the business. Elmer's sons joined the company in 1914, and the

name was changed to Elmer Candy Company. In 1963, the business was purchased by Roy Nelson, who because of lack of space, moved the candy manufacturing plant to Ponchatoula, La. Due to competition, Elmer's streamlined its candy production by only making products for Valentine's Day, Easter and Christmas. Today, the Nelson family still oversees the operations of the country's second-largest heart box chocolate manufacturer.

Feliciana Cellars

Feliciana Cellars is one of just a handful of wineries in Louisiana. In 1992, Rupert Thompson and Leroy Harvey convinced the Legislature to reduce the state licensing fee for wineries from $2,500 to $50 a year. They were also instrumental in the passage of the Native Wine Law, which allowed wineries to operate in the state. In 1994 they opened their winery along with Jim Hendrickson in Jackson, La. Like many Louisiana wineries, Feliciana Cellars makes

most of its wine from muscadine grapes, which grow well in the state's climate. Two other grape varieties, Blanc du Bois and Norton Cynthiana, are also grown there and are used in some of Feliciana Cellars' wines. Today, Feliciana Cellars produces 10 different types of wine. They produce more than 4,000 cases of wine annually, more than any other winery in Louisiana.

Ruth Fertel of Ruth's Chris Steak House

Ruth's Chris Steak House, the largest prime-aged steak house in the world, was started out of necessity. In 1965,

Ruth Fertel, a divorced mother of two, mortgaged her house for $22,000 in order to buy Chris Steak House in hopes that she would be able to earn enough money to send her sons to college. Her gamble paid off, and after only six months she was making twice as much as she did at her previous job with Tulane School of Medicine. Because of

an agreement with the original owner, Fertel continued to use the name of the steak house until a fire destroyed its original 60-seat building. She relocated the eatery and added 100 seats in the process. She opened a second restaurant in New Orleans. In the late '70s, the first Ruth's Chris Steak House franchise was granted to a Baton Rouge businessman. Today there are more than 80 locations worldwide. She taught herself to butcher when she first purchased the restaurant and eventually designed a specialized broiler for cooking the steaks. Fabulous steaks and fine service keep people coming back to Ruth's Chris Steak House.

Chef John Folse & Company

Chef John Folse & Company is actually many companies in one. The cornerstone property, Lafitte's Landing Restaurant, was internationally famous and led to the creation of several other Chef John Folse & Company enterprises.

When the original restaurant burned, a new restaurant and a bed and breakfast were created at Bittersweet Plantation in Donaldsonville, La. In addition, White Oak Plantation in Baton Rouge houses exceptional catering and event facilities in an antebellum setting. Chef John Folse & Company Manufacturing creates traditional Louisiana dishes and sauces for foodservice distributors, retail locations and restaurant chains across the country. The Bittersweet Plantation Dairy produces an ever-increasing line of artisanal cheeses, some of which have won top awards in both national and international competitions. The pastry division, Exceptional Endings, creates sumptuous pastries and desserts for Chef John Folse events as well as CC's Gourmet Coffee Houses. Chef John Folse & Company Publishing has not only published all of Chef John Folse's cookbooks, but has also published books by outside authors. In addition, Chef John Folse's radio show, *Stirrin' It Up*, and television show, *A Taste of Louisiana*, are aired across the country.

Chef Folse has received numerous national and international accolades including "Louisiana Restaurateur of the Year," the American Culinary Federation's "National Chef of the Year," the Research Chefs Association's "Pioneer in Culinology" award and an "Award of Excellence" for Lafitte's Landing Restaurant from Distinguished Restaurants of North America (DiRōNA).

Chef John Folse Culinary Institute

The Chef John Folse Culinary Institute is an academic college of Nicholls State University. Located in Thibodaux, La., the school is nestled in the heart of Cajun and Creole Country, 50 miles southwest of New Orleans and 65 miles southeast of Baton Rouge. Like its namesake, the Culinary Institute is dedicated to the preservation of

Louisiana's rich culinary heritage while fostering Louisiana's role as a culinary leader. At Nicholls State University, Louisiana's culture and cuisine provide a focal point for the study of classical culinary arts.

The institute accepted its inaugural academic class in January 1996 and was the first public university to award the Bachelor of Science in Culinary Arts. A two-year Associate of Science degree is also available. Faculty credentials, experience and a commitment to academic excellence ensure a new crop of culinary icons in Louisiana and beyond.

Goffredo Fraccaro

Goffredo Fraccaro has been an innovator and pioneer in Italian food for several decades. Born in Genoa, Italy, in

1923, Fraccaro worked at restaurants since childhood. Fraccaro moved to Baton Rouge, La., in 1961 to take the position of executive chef at The Village. There he built a solid reputation for both himself and the restaurant. In 1970, Fraccaro opened his own restaurant, La Riviera in Metairie and began introducing Louisiana to the delights of calamari, white veal, osso buco and white sauces. He made such an impact on the culinary arts, the Italian Government bestowed upon him the honor of Knight of the Republic. Fraccaro was also the first Italian chef to win a Gold Medal in the Crab Meat Olympics in San Francisco. His winning creation, agnolotti Pontchartrain or crabmeat ravioli, became La Riviera's signature dish. In addition to his new creations, Fraccaro is renowned for his superb renditions of the classics like piccata, marsala and spaghetti and meatballs. Although he no longer owns La Riviera, Fraccaro remains a presence there, sharing his secrets and successes with the next generation.

Galatoire's Restaurant

Jean Galatoire set sail from France in the 1880s, and he lived in Alabama and Illinois before settling in Louisiana. He opened a café on Dauphine Street in New Orleans and was eager to learn about Creole cooking and the restaurant business. Galatoire became good friends with Victor Bero,

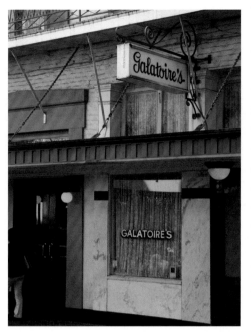

who owned Victor's Restaurant on Bourbon Street. The two became inseparable, and Bero agreed to sell his restaurant to Galatoire. In 1905, Galatoire's Restaurant opened, and Jean Galatoire worked tirelessly to attract the city's elite. The restaurant remains family-owned and continues to serve fine French Creole cuisine. Reservations are not accepted in the main dining room, so a line of people are often waiting outside on Bourbon Street. In 1999, the restaurant underwent a $3 million renovation that added a second-floor dining room that accepts reservations.

Gambino's Bakery

A New Orleans tradition for more than half a century,

Gambino's operates several neighborhood bakeries known for their cakes, cookies and confections. Gambino's is particularly famous for its Doberge and red velvet cake as well as their vast selection of King cake flavors. The bakeries, which are located in New Orleans, Baton Rouge, Lafayette, Kenner, Gretna and Metairie, ship King cake packages worldwide throughout the year.

Haydel's Bakery

Haydel's Bakery was originally opened in New Orleans as a

small, 24-hour window service shop. The bakery has now been family-owned and operated for more than three generations. Known for their fresh-baked pastries and cakes, but treasured for their Mardi Gras King cakes, Haydel's boasts unparalleled quality and service. They are particularly busy at Mardi Gras when, in addition to providing for their local customers, they ship King cakes all around the world.

Lafcadio Hearn

Patrick Lafcadio Hearn was born in 1850 on the island of Leucadia. He came to the United States at age 19 looking

for work. After a few years, he settled in Cincinnati where he worked for fellow countryman and printer Henry Watkins learning typesetting and proofreading. Watkins encouraged Hearn to submit writings to Cincinnati newspapers, and his journalistic career was born. In 1877, Hearn headed to New Orleans on an assignment to cover Louisiana politics. There, he was offered an assistant editor's job with the *New Orleans Item*. Hearn soon came to love the food of the city and became an authority on Creole cuisine and culture. He opened The Five-Cents Restaurant, "the cheapest eating-house in the South." The restaurant was renamed the Hard Times in 1879. Hearn published several books including *Gumbo Zherbes: A Little Dictionary of Creole Proverbs*, *The Creole Cookbook*, *Creole Sketches* and *La Cuisine Creole*, which is still one of the best-known authoritative works on Louisiana cooking. In 1890, Hearn left New Orleans to explore the wonders of Japanese culture and never returned to the city.

Hubig's Pies

For more than 100 years, the aroma of freshly baked and fried pies has floated over the Faubourg Marigny section of New Orleans. The end results of those tantalizing aromas, Hubig's Pies, have found a place on store shelves and in the "impulse buy" section next to cash registers all over the city and beyond. The famous Hubig's Pies actually originated in Dallas with Simon Hubig, but it was the New

Orleans franchise under Henry Barrett and later Otto Ramsey that truly thrived. As for the pies, they are quite addictive and come in a rainbow of flavors including apple, lemon, blueberry, cherry, peach and coconut. The bakery churns out approximately 20,000 pies a day. This family business strives to buy only local, seasonal ingredients for their pies, making them a treasured and much craved New Orleans institution.

Jack Sabin's Restaurant

In some families, the restaurant business seems to be in the blood. The Distefano's are one such family. Joe Distefano learned his trade helping out at his parents' restaurant, The Village, which was an icon in Baton Rouge. In 1968, Distefano purchased an existing steak and seafood restaurant called Jack Sabin's from its ailing owner. Not wanting to compete with The Village's Italian fare, he focused on turning Jack Sabin's into Baton Rouge's steak and seafood icon. True to the Distefano tradition, his restaurant soon became a favorite gathering spot for the city's elite. Jack Sabin's was known for its great seafood dishes such as snapper Suzanne stuffed with Alaskan crab and garnished with jumbo shrimp and lemon butter sauce. People also went there for the steaks and the oysters. Eventually a larger restaurant was built, but when the bottom fell out of Louisiana's oil business in the 1980s, Jack Sabin's had to close. In 1987 Distefano tried again with a new grill called Jack's, but Baton Rouge's economy had not yet recovered. Joe Distefano died in 2003, just two years after his mother, known to The Village's patrons as Miss Fannie. The Distefano legacy lives on however with Joe's son, Joey Distefano, a local chef who opened a restaurant named The Village in 2004.

Stanley Jackson

Growing up in New Orleans, Stanley Jackson was one of 10 children, so he started cooking out of necessity. Quite often, he would use his siblings to test his new experimental dishes. To fine-tune his skills, Jackson attended Chicago's John R. Thompson School of Culinary Arts. After school, Jackson returned to New Orleans and worked for several years at the restaurant in the D.H. Holmes department store. There, his skills caught the eye of Chef Paul Prudhomme who convinced Jackson to join him at Commander's Palace. When Prudhomme set out on his own and opened K-Paul's, Stanley Jackson was by his side as his executive chef.

Jacques-Imo's Cafe

As the child of a French mother and Italian father, it was no wonder that Chef Jacques Leonardi fell in love with

New Orleans food. In fact, while still commissioned in the Coast Guard, Leonardi secretly took a night job as a prep cook in the kitchen of Paul Prudhomme's K-Paul's Louisiana Kitchen. With $8,000 in his pocket, Leonardi soon left K-Paul's to try his hand at "Real N'awlins Food."

Stepping away from the tourist driven French Quarter, he opened Jacques-Imo's Café in 1996 in an old shotgun house in the Garden District. Jacques-Imo's menu features Creole-Soul cuisine that captures the spirit and spice of New Orleans. Its innovative approach to classic recipes has been Jacques-Imo's most admired contribution to the highly competitive and prestigious world of New Orleans' cuisine. In addition to bringing back to life the old classics like chicken pontalba with béarnaise sauce, the café offers a new take on old standards. For example, they serve deep-fried roast beef po'boys and gourmet fried chicken, which is prepared by New Orleans' soul food legend Austin Leslie of Chez Heléne restaurant. It has been Leonardi's creations like the delicious shrimp & alligator sausage cheesecake (featured on the Food Network) and grilled mahi mahi with a sweet pistachio reduction that bring huge crowds to this cozy and funky restaurant.

Jax Brewery

Many New Orleanians fondly remember Jax beer and the Jackson Brewing Company. The early history of Jax is somewhat vague, but it is known that the company was founded in 1890 by six men, one of whom, David Jackson, was the first president. Most people think that the company drew its name from the fact that the brewery building faced Jackson Square. Indeed, the figure of Andrew Jackson on

a horse, the centerpiece of Jackson Square, adorned the beer's label. The beer was a mellow brew, self-proclaimed as being "bright, clear and light," which would be popular features today, but not in turn-of-the-century New Orleans. For most of its history, the Jackson Brewing Company was owned and run by various members of the Fabacher family. In 1970 the brewery was bought by a Chicago company, Meister Brau, Inc. The brewery was closed four years later because Jax beer could not compete with national brands. The building was renovated and transformed into a French Quarter shopping center geared toward tourists. The formula and label for Jax beer was purchased by Pearl Brewing Company of San Antonio, but the beer is seldom bottled these days.

Anne Kearney

A graduate of the Greater Cincinnati Culinary Art Academy, Chef Anne Kearney came to New Orleans to work under

Chef John Neal at the acclaimed Bistro at the Maison deVille Hotel. When Neal left to open Peristyle in 1991, Kearney became his sous chef. With Neal's help, Kearney mastered classic French cooking techniques and perfected her own palate. In 1992 she left Peristyle for a three-year tenure with then-budding superstar Chef Emeril Lagasse. After a stint on the Emeril's Restaurant cook line, Kearney conducted research and formulated recipes for Lagasse's *Essence of Emeril* television show. She also developed and tasted recipes for his *Louisiana: Real and Rustic* cookbook. Although she was advancing her restaurant knowledge, Kearney longed to return to the kitchen. When Neal died in 1995, Kearney purchased his restaurant and immediately made the menu her own while keeping his legacies intact. Peristyle offers classically styled Provençal fare of the highest standard. Anne Kearney received the prestigious "Southeast Regional Best Chef" award from James Beard Foundation in 2002. Kearney's motto is "Food of Love."

Kentwood Springs

Kentwood Springs water is drawn from a deep, natural artesian spring discovered in 1963. The area is surrounded by a pristine pine forest with very little development, so it is the perfect place to find sparkling clean water. The water is further protected from impurities by a layer of impenetrable bedrock. Kentwood Springs water is naturally filtered through layers of sandstone while still underground. The water is also put through three purification stages prior to bottling. The Kentwood, La., water is then distributed to homes, offices and retail outlets throughout the South. Kentwood Springs water is so exceptional it has received the International Bottled Water Association's Excellence in Manufacturing award on numerous occasions. The water is bottled by DS Waters of America in Atlanta.

Chris Kerageorgiou of La Provence

Constantin Kerageorgiou, more commonly known as Chef Chris, is the chef and proprietor of La Provence restaurant in

Lacombe, La. His remarkable talents for hospitality have made him internationally recognized. Kerageorgiou was born in Port Saint Louis, Provence, France. After World War II, he found work cooking on ships. In 1947 on a trip to America with the Merchant Marine, he decided to take his chances in San Francisco. Eventually he made his way from California to New Orleans and continued his long tutelage as a baker, cook, waiter and maître d' at some of the city's finest establishments. Ultimately, Kerageorgiou's goal was to open a fine French restaurant. On Sept. 26, 1972, his dream was realized as La Provence held its grand opening. Since then, he has trained dozens of cooks, many of them successful in their own right. He continues his love affair with creative cuisine that pays homage to his Mediterranean roots.

Kleinpeter Farms Dairy

The Kleinpeter family came from Switzerland in 1774 and settled in what is now East Baton Rouge Parish. In 1913 Grandpa "Sib" and Leon Kleinpeter Sr., started a small

dairy business by rounding up and milking "woods" cows and shipping the cream to New Orleans. That year they purchased their first guernsey cows from Wisconsin, selecting them for their gentle disposition and premium milk, rich in vitamins and minerals. For several years, the company ceased milking its own herd and only operated as a processor. However, Kleinpeter has since returned to the dairy farming aspect of the business, operating a state-of-the-art milking facility in St. Helena Parish as well as a processing and packaging plant in Baton Rouge. The plant processes 160,000 gallons of milk each week and produces whipping cream, cottage cheese and fluid milk products. Kleinpeter Farms Dairy is one of the last family-owned, independent milk processors in the country.

Emeril Lagasse

As a boy in Fall River, Mass., Emeril Lagasse helped his mother Hilda at the kitchen stove. No one knew then that

he would become one of the most famous chefs in America. After culinary school at Johnson & Wales University, Emeril moved to New Orleans at the request of the Brennan family. There, he became executive chef at Commander's Palace. In March 1990, Lagasse opened his first restaurant in New Orleans, Emeril's. The success of Emeril's led to the opening of various restaurants in Louisiana and beyond, including Emeril's Delmonico and NOLA in New Orleans.

Emeril is well-known across the nation for his exciting cooking shows on the Television Food Network and his weekly appearances on *Good Morning America*. The popularity of his first program, *Essence of Emeril*, led to the production of *Emeril Live*, which won an award for best informational show in 1997. Over the years, Emeril has received numerous awards, including the James Beard Award for "Best Southeast Regional Chef." He has also written many cookbooks. In 2002, he created the Emeril Lagasse Foundation for children.

Langenstein's Supermarket

In 1922 Michael Langenstein and his two sons, George and Richard, started a small corner grocery store in uptown

New Orleans. Little did they know that their establishment, informally known as Langenstein's, would become a New Orleans icon. Today there are two locations that offer a complete line of homemade New Orleans cooked specialties such as crawfish étouffée, crawfish bisque, seafood gumbo, grillades and red beans and rice. These delicacies are created from family recipes that have been passed down through four generations. Langenstein's has also built a reputation for stocking gourmet items, unique New Orleans products and fine imported ingredients.

Lasyone's Meat Pie Kitchen and Restaurant

A *New York Times* article proclaimed that the best reason to visit Natchitoches, La., was its meat pies and many people

agree. Lasyone's Meat Pie Kitchen and Restaurant has been selling the pastry stuffed with 80 percent ground beef and 20 percent ground pork for nearly 40 years. Although meat pies were famous during the Civil War, they were sparse when James Lasyone ran his butcher shop during the 1960s. After spending more than a year perfecting his recipe, Lasyone began selling the fried pastries out of his butcher shop window. In 1967, Lasyone opened his restaurant in the first floor of a Masonic Lodge that was built in 1859. By the late '70s, he had acquired the whole building for his meat pie kitchen. The Lasyone family still owns and operates the restaurant, which offers a full menu of Cajun and Creole cuisine. Up to 1,000 meat pies are made by hand each day at Lasyone's.

G.H. Leidenheimer Baking Company

Better known as Leidenheimer's by its patrons, the G.H. Leidenheimer Baking Company was founded by German

immigrant George Leidenheimer in 1905. Leidenheimer was baking bread in New Orleans as early as the 1890s. He started out baking the heavy, brown breads of his native country. Ironically, it was through his perfection of New Orleans-style French bread that he found fame. Leidenheimer's markets its bread under its own ZIP brand as well as the Sunrise name. Leidenheimer's is still owned and operated by George's descendants and is a large supplier of bread for restaurants and po'boy shops.

Le Jeune's Bakery

Located on Main Street in the small town of Jeanerette, La., Le Jeune's Bakery has been sweetening the air with the aroma of fresh baked bread for more than 120 years. The bakery was opened in 1885 by Oscar Le Jeune. The

bread is baked fresh daily at what was originally named The Old Reliable Bakery. For many years, Le Jeune's bread was delivered by horse and buggy. Le Jeune's is still known for its French bread, but the bakery's real "bread and butter" comes from its traditional gingerbread.

Warren Leruth of LeRuth's Restaurant

New Orleans native Warren Leruth opened LeRuth's Restaurant in 1966, but it was his work in research and

development that made him famous throughout the world. Leruth learned the basics of cooking from his mother, but he spent years fine-tuning his skills by working with other chefs. He cooked and baked for numerous New Orleans establishments including Solari's and Galatoire's. As a member of the National Guard, Leruth was called to duty during the Korean War to serve as General Bruce C. Clark's personal chef. Additionally, he cooked for numerous presidents and religious leaders. After the war, LeRuth's Restaurant was opened in Gretna, La. Leruth made dining at his restaurant a personal experience

by baking his own bread and making his own salad dressings and ice cream. In 1982, Leruth retired from the restaurant business, leaving LeRuth's to his sons. He then started LeRuth Extract Co. to develop and market products containing vanilla. During his career, Leruth tested and developed a number of products including Seven Seas salad dressings and Chelsey's Frozen Custard. Even after his retirement, he continued to work on product development with companies such as Outback Steakhouse, Boston Chicken and Burger King. The restaurant has since closed, and Leruth passed away in late 2001, but his legacy lives on.

Austin Leslie

Austin Leslie began his cooking career at Portia's Restaurant on South Rampart Street in New Orleans. In the 1950s

he did a brief stint at D.H. Holmes Restaurant before serving two years in the armed forces. He later worked at his Aunt Helen's restaurant. At that time, his aunt moved her neighborhood eatery and renamed it Chez Heléne. Leslie took over the kitchen and transformed the neighborhood spot into an international sensation. Chez Heléne offered a unique combination of haute cuisine and soul food. The restaurant became so well known that it inspired a CBS sitcom

in the 1980s called *Frank's Place*. Leslie's reputation as a master of soul cooking and a wizard at fried chicken did not end at Chez Heléne. Though the restaurant closed in 1995, Austin Leslie became a consultant to Jacques Leonardi of Jacques-Imo's in 1996. Leslie helped Leonardi combine old tastes with new approaches and was instrumental in Jacques-Imo's early success.

Louisiana Caviar Company

The most famous caviar is Russian, harvested from sturgeon

in the Caspian Sea. In the early 20th century, caviar harvested from American sturgeon was also plentiful and popular, but the sturgeon was over-fished into near extinction. The choupique, which is found in the bayous of Louisiana, is a relative of the sturgeon, but it is bony and not particularly palatable. In the 1980s, John Burke began harvesting roe from choupique to make his Cajun Caviar. In 1989, Burke renamed the product Choupique Royale and went into serious caviar production in New Orleans as the Louisiana Caviar Company. His clients have included some of the finest restaurants overseas and here in South Louisiana, including Lafitte's Landing. Many say this truly American caviar rivals its much more expensive Eastern European competitors.

Mandina's Restaurant

Mandina's began as a neighborhood grocery store. Its owner, a Sicilian immigrant from Salaporati named Sebastian

Mandina, lived above the store with his sons Anthony and Frank. From this little grocery on the corner of Canal and Cortes streets gradually emerged Mandina's Restaurant. The traditional eatery offers a casual atmosphere, home cooking and reasonable prices. When Sebastian died in 1932, his sons took over the restaurant. The brothers left to serve their country during World War II and Anthony's wife, Hilda, was left in charge. Upon their return, Anthony ran the kitchen and Frank tended the bar. Mandina's has become famous in New Orleans for its draft beer, fragrant seafood dishes and spaghetti and meatballs, but its real pull is the allure of an old-time neighborhood restaurant.

Maylie's Restaurant

Maylie's Restaurant is another of New Orleans' loved establishments that has since been closed. Opened in 1876, the restaurant was originally named La Maison

Maylie et Esparbe after its founders, Bernard Maylie and Hypolite Esparbe. Like many restaurants of the period, Maylie's specialized in table d'hôte, meaning the menu consisted of several courses selected by the chef, not the diner. But, there were seldom any complaints. After Maylie and Esparbe's deaths, their widows, along with Bernard's sons, ran the business.

Bernard Maylie's grandson, William L. Maylie, bought the restaurant in 1946. Many of Maylie's recipes were developed as early as the 1870s and were published in a cookbook by Eugenie Maylie in 1939.

Middendorf's Seafood Restaurant

Middendorf's Seafood Restaurant was founded by World War I veteran Louis Herman Middendorf in 1934. Middendorf, son of a German immigrant, and his wife Josie

lived in Houston until the Crash of 1929, when the scarcity of work forced them to move in with Josie's mother in Manchac, La. They learned to fish and crab for a living until Louis' World War I bonus of $500 allowed them to open their small café in Ponchatoula, La. Hard work and a commitment to using only the freshest ingredients soon made Middendorf's a success. After World War II, Louis and Josie retired, and their son Richard and his wife Helen took over the restaurant. In 1980 Louis' granddaughter Susie and her husband Joey Lamonte took the restaurant into the third generation of family ownership and continued the commitment to tried and true recipes and fresh ingredients. Middendorf's signature dishes include thin fried catfish, shrimp and crab gumbo, soft-shell crab and boiled crab and shrimp.

"Diamond Jim" Moran

Former boxer, "Diamond Jim" Moran, was a friend and confidant to Governor Huey P. Long, the "Kingfish." Moran was known as "Diamond Jim" because of the diamond-encrusted vests and jewelry he sported. He also owned a restaurant that bore his name. Periodically, Moran's restaurant would feature a "Diamond Meatball Night," during which a lucky guest might find a diamond hidden in his or her meatball. The idea was said to have been inspired by his mother who lost the diamond from her engagement ring while making meatballs one day. Moran's restaurant was on Rue Iberville in the French Quarter of New Orleans.

Mosca's

Opened in 1946, Mosca's is further proof that good things come in small packages. This two-room restaurant is located on Hwy 90 outside of New Orleans. Its non-central location might have been an obstacle if not for the indisputable quality of the food. Mosca's food could be classified as

Creole-Italian. The restaurant features Louisiana-influenced classical Italian dishes. Mosca's serves food family style, meaning large portions on a platter from which the guests at the table help themselves. One dining room opens to the kitchen, enhancing the "family dinner in your grandmother's kitchen" atmosphere. Garlic and olive oil are prominent in Mosca's cooking. Two signature dishes, shrimp Mosca and oysters Mosca have definitely earned the right to bear the owner's name, but all of the food is exceptional.

Mother's Restaurant

There's a reason even the locals are willing to stand in line for lunch at this greasy spoon in the New Orleans Central Business District—it's just that good.

Mother's is best known for its po'boys dressed with shredded cabbage instead of lettuce. The restaurant offers other hearty breakfast and lunchtime fare as well, including étouffée, jambalaya and the ubiquitous red beans and rice. Their signature dish is the Ferdie, a po'boy stuffed with baked ham and roast beef debris (small pieces of meat and gravy from a roast). This sandwich may require a handful of napkins and probably some antacids, but it's worth it. The restaurant is small, crowded and decorated with Unites States Marine Corps memorabilia. The service is efficient and no-nonsense, but what Mother's lacks in ambience, is more than made up for by the food.

P&J Oyster Company

John Popich began cultivating and harvesting oysters in 1876. He distributed his product to restaurants in the New Orleans area. Around the turn of the century, Joseph Jurisich joined the business and focused on distribution, while Popich concentrated on oyster farming. The two formed Popich and

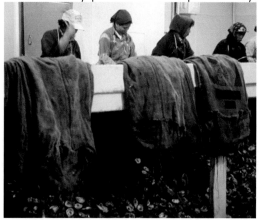

Jurisich, the largest oyster shucking business in the South. In 1921 they purchased the present oyster shucking house on the corner of Toulouse and North Rampart in New Orleans and hired a salesman, Alfred Sunseri. P&J's began shipping barrels of oysters via railroad throughout North America. United Fruit Company offered Alfred a national management position in Baltimore in the 1930s. After six months, Alfred came home to become the third full partner at P&J Oyster Company. Alfred's only son, Sal Sunseri, eventually took over the business and became the sole owner by the late 1970s. Today, Sal's children Alfred, Sal Jr. and Merri run the family oyster company.

The Palace Café

The Palace Café has been open since 1927 and is still operated by members of the Doucas family. The popular

diner offers down-home cooking. The cuisine is definitely local and primarily Cajun, with hearty and affordable lunch specials. The Palace also serves a variety of seafood dishes, including grilled catfish with crawfish étouffée and stuffed eggplant with crabmeat dressing and crawfish sauce. However, the fried chicken salad is hard to beat. The Palace Café is located on West Landry Street in Opelousas, La.

Pascal's Manale Restaurant

Founded in 1913 by Frank Manale, this family-run Italian-Creole restaurant is located in uptown New Orleans. Its original name was simply Manale's. When Frank died in the 1940s, his nephew Pascal took over. Pascal's daughter,

Frances Redosta Difelice and son-in-law, Steve, took over after him. At some point the name was changed to Pascal's Manale, but the reputation earned by Manale's remained

intact. The restaurant is most famous for its barbecued shrimp, which come in a wonderful, spicy sauce you can't help but sop up with bread. Pascal's Manale has also long been known for its cold and salty fresh-shucked oysters and its steaks.

Alex Patout

Alex Patout should be noted as one of the pioneers of the Cajun cooking movement. Born in New Iberia, La., Patout

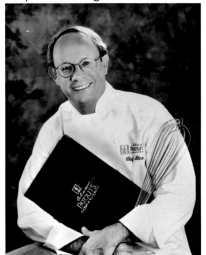

came from a family who left the sugarcane industry to open a restaurant in 1918. When the blackened redfish craze swept the country, Patout set out to prove that there was much more to Cajun cooking. Patout opened a restaurant in New Iberia and was the first Louisiana chef to open a Cajun restaurant outside of the state, in Los

Angeles. When he moved to New Orleans, Patout became enamored with Creole cuisine and realized it merged nicely with what he knew. He operates two restaurants in Louisiana, both bearing his name—one in the French Quarter and the other in Mandeville. In 2000 his New Orleans location was simultaneously named "Best Creole Restaurant" and "Best Cajun Restaurant" by two separate publications.

Pontchartrain Vineyards

After a series of experimental vineyards dating back to 1978, John V. Seago founded Pontchartrain Vineyards in St. Tammany Parish in 1991. This was the first vineyard and winery in Louisiana to produce wine from traditional bunch grapes since before Prohibition. Today, Pontchartrain Vineyards continues its mission of providing Louisiana with

distinctive regional wine, produced exclusively from bunch wine grapes. Two of their classic wines are made from grapes grown at Estate Vineyards located in the hills just north of Covington. Le Trolley, an aromatic, dry white wine is produced from the Blanc Du Bois grape. Rouge Militaire, a medium-bodied red wine, is produced from the Cynthiana/Norton grape.

Popeyes Chicken & Biscuits

Founded in New Orleans in the 1970s by Al Copeland, Popeyes Chicken & Biscuits now operates under parent

company AFC Enterprises. Since the early '90s Popeyes has experienced significant expansion including the opening of a state-of-the-art research facility and a system support center for franchisees. Popeyes Chicken & Biscuits now has more than 1,000 outlets across the country. They have consistently won awards for "Best Fried Chicken" in major cities such as Dallas, Atlanta and New Orleans. In addition to an ever-increasing product line featuring traditional Cajun and New Orleans spices, Popeyes is further emphasizing its New Orleans roots with a new "heritage" look for its restaurants.

Prejean's Restaurant

When in Lafayette, La., do as the Cajuns do and eat at Prejean's on Highway 167. Go for dinner and you'll hear live Cajun music. Opened in 1980 by Bob Guilbeau, Prejean's

quickly became a favorite spot of both locals and tourists. The restaurant specializes in seafood, steak and wild game prepared with a Cajun flair. "Big Al," a 14-foot alligator captured in Grand Chenier swamp, sits in the middle of the dining room to guard the culinary medals won by Prejean's staff.

Gunter Preuss of Broussard's Restaurant

Broussard's opened in 1920 when local chef Joseph Broussard married Rosalie Borrello and moved into her family mansion on Conti Street. The restaurant was on the first floor, and they lived upstairs. Today the couple behind the restaurant is Gunter and Evelyn Preuss. After working in various major U.S. cities, Preuss moved to New Orleans to become executive chef at the Fairmont Hotel. Later, he founded one of New Orlean's finest restaurants, the Versailles Restaurant. In 1989 Preuss was chosen to be one of the chefs to host papal dining festivities while Pope John Paul II was in town. Preuss and Broussard's have received many honors, and he was even featured on PBS's *Great Chefs of New Orleans*.

Paul Prudhomme

Chef Paul Prudhomme of Opelousas, La., has been spicing things up in kitchens across the globe since he was seven years old. After years helping his mother cook, Prudhomme decided to dedicate his life to cooking for others. In July 1979, Prudhomme and his wife, K. Hinrichs, opened K-Paul's Louisiana Kitchen in the French Quarter. The restaurant is revered for its blackened redfish, blackened steak and filé gumbo. Prudhomme always created his special seasonings, which those who dined in his restaurant often wanted for their pantries. This led to the creation of Magic Seasoning Blends. Through his career, Prudhomme has earned numerous accolades including becoming the first American-born chef to receive the Merité Agricole of the French Republic.

Reily Foods Company

You might be hard-pressed to decide which of Reily Foods' products is most essential in your pantry. Reily manufactures several long-time New Orleans traditions such as CDM

Coffee, Luzianne Tea, Abita Springs Water and Blue Plate Mayonnaise. Blue Plate was purchased by Reily Foods in 1974. Prior to that it was a division of Wesson-Snowdrift Oil and was at one time manufactured in a warehouse in Gretna, La. Reily Foods was founded in 1902 by a Monroe grocer, William Reily, and remains in his family's hands. The company has acquired and successfully marketed regional brands in Louisiana and even nationally.

Michael Roussel

Chef Michael Roussel's name has become almost synonymous with Brennan's Restaurant where he has been

executive chef for many years. Roussel started work at Brennan's in 1956 as a busboy. He moved up through the positions of waiter, headwaiter and maître d', but his culinary education was interrupted by a tour of duty with the U.S. Army. Upon his return, Roussel was chosen by executive chef Paul Blangé as his first apprentice. Under Blangé, Roussel became a master of his trade. In 1975, Michael Roussel was named executive chef of Brennan's. He has definitely left a mark on the restaurant—almost all of Brennan's signature dishes were created by either Roussel or Blangé.

Savoie's Sausage and Food Products

Since 1949, Savoie's has been producing "Real Cajun" food and specialties. The food products are created in their Cajun

Kitchen located along Bayou Little Teche in rural St. Landry Parish. The operation began as Savoie's Grocery, a small country store on Highway 742. Founders Eula and Tom Savoie made

their home in an attachment on the back of the store. When the value of the hogs they raised plummeted in 1955, the Savoie's decided to have a boucherie. They began making andouille, boudin, smoked sausage and other goods to sell in the store. The same goods are made today from the original recipes, but Savoie's has relocated to a larger facility along the bank of the bayou.

Sazerac Bar at the Fairmont Hotel

The Fairmont Hotel was built in 1893 in what is now the business district of New Orleans. Located near the French

Quarter, the Fairmont is one of the oldest grand hotels in the country. Famous in its own right, the Fairmont is also known for the historic Sazerac Bar, whose signature drinks include the Ramos Gin Fizz and of course,

the Sazerac. Although the hotel offers complete modern amenities, you can still get a taste of the opulent Creole lifestyle. Prior to the 1960s, this hotel was known as the Roosevelt and was famous for its restaurant, The Blue Room.

Solari's

Once a fixture on Royal Street, Solari's food emporium is

no more. However, the store is still fondly remembered by New Orleanians who browsed the aisles for an impressive array of delicacies from all over the world or met friends and fellow shoppers for lunch.

Founded in 1861 by J.B. Solari, the grocery store featured a lunch counter, gourmet delicatessen, liquor store and candy kitchen. When Solari's closed in the mid-1960s, the building was demolished to make way for what is now Mr. B's Bistro and a parking garage.

Susan Spicer of Bayona

Susan Spicer began her classical French training in 1979 as an apprentice to Chef Daniel Bonnot at the Louis XVI Restaurant in New Orleans. In 1982, she spent four months working at a French hotel then returned to New Orleans as chef de cuisine of Savoir Faire. After working in a few other New Orleans restaurants, she formed a partnership with Regina Keever. The two opened Bayona Restaurant in a 200-year-old, French Quarter Creole cottage that had previously housed two other restaurants. With three intimate dining rooms, a private "wine room" for small parties and a beautiful courtyard with seating for 30, Bayona offers a warm, romantic ambiance.

C.S. Steen Syrup Mill

C.S. Steen opened his mule-driven syrup mill in 1910 in a desperate effort to salvage a frozen sugarcane crop. Five generations later, the mill in Abbeville, La., still uses the

Charley Steen

same equipment and recipe to transform the juice extracted from freshly harvested sugarcane into dark, rich, 100 percent cane syrup. Immediately recognizable by the bright yellow can, Steen's is an essential ingredient in many traditional Louisiana recipes and is delicious drizzled over pancakes or biscuits.

Tabasco

The salt dome island of Avery Island, La., has been home to the world-famous Tabasco Sauce since 1868. After returning to Louisiana from self-imposed exile due to the Civil War, Edmund McIlhenny obtained hot pepper seeds from a traveler from Central America. After planting the seeds on the island, McIlhenny experimented with the product until he developed the concoction he liked. He began producing his own pepper sauce, and by 1870, the sauce was being sold

throughout the United States and England. In that same year, McIlhenny received a patent for his peppery red sauce. Tabasco is now distributed in more than 105 countries. The descendants of Edmund McIlhenny continue to oversee production at McIlhenny Company, making sure that everything meets their high standards. Each pepper is handpicked once it turns the correct shade of red, and everything from pepper plants to finished sauce is inspected by the family. Daily tours of Avery Island and the Tabasco factory are available.

Tony Chachere's Creole Foods

Tony Chachere's Creole Foods began in 1972 as a

retirement hobby for South Louisiana chef Tony Chachere. Born in 1905 in Opelousas, Tony's parents were descendants of French Creoles. A pharmacist by trade, Chachere developed over 150 new products including Mamou Cough Syrup and Bon Soir Bug Spray. At age 65, he retired and began focusing on his true love, cooking. In 1972, Chachere published the *Cajun Country Cookbook*, highlighting his seafood and wild game recipes. The book also featured popular recipes for gumbo, jambalaya, étouffée and his favorite seasoning blend, Creole Seasoning. The response to this recipe was so phenomenal that Chachere decided to manufacture his Creole Seasoning and thus his Creole Foods company was born. Tony Chachere's Creole Seasoning has been an essential item in Louisiana kitchens ever since. Tony Chachere died in 1995, just one week after being the first inductee into the Louisiana Chef's Hall of Fame, but his company continues to produce seasonings, rice mixes, sauces and various cooking ingredients.

Tujague's Restaurant

Tujague's, the second-oldest restaurant in New Orleans, has survived years of war, depression, fire and plague. Guillaume and Marie Abadie Tujague came to America from Bordeaux, France, in 1852. By 1886, Guillaume opened Tujague's Restaurant near the riverfront to serve breakfast and lunch to area workers. Before his death in 1912, Guillaume sold Tujague's to Philibert Guichet. In 1914, Guichet joined forces with Jean-Dominic Castet to buy a new location, the former

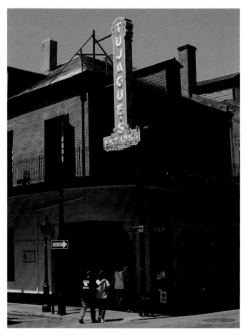

home of Madame Bégué's. Castet's wife Clemence ruled the kitchen and dining room of Tujague's with an iron fist until her death in 1969. In 1982, a new owner, Steven Latter, restored the restaurant, remodeling it to reflect its history. The saloon was furnished with a bar that was brought to America from France in 1856. Latter covered the walls with news clippings, photographs and memorabilia. He also brought back the specialty dishes Tujague's was once famous for serving—shrimp rémoulade, beef brisket with horseradish and the original cap bread. Tujague's prides itself on being unpretentious and uniquely New Orleans.

Uglesich Restaurant and Bar

Things are kept relatively simple at Uglesich Restaurant and Bar on Baronne Street in New Orleans. Owner Anthony

"Tony" Uglesich makes sure his customers get the freshest, highest-quality food every day. Uglesich is only open on weekdays from 10 a.m. until 4 p.m. for lunch. Anyone planning to devour oysters, gumbo or a seafood po'boy should plan to arrive early because the restaurant only has 10 tables, and they fill up quickly. It is regarded as one of the least-kept lunchtime secrets, and locals can be seen waiting in long lines daily. This no-frills lunch hangout has been in the same location since 1924. Although the building may be in need of remodeling, the restaurant's family atmosphere and customer loyalty has made it a New Orleans mainstay.

The Village

For many years, if you were looking to make a deal in Louisiana and needed a legislator or prominent businessman to help it along, The Village on Airline Highway in Baton Rouge was

the spot to go. Opened in 1947 by Vince and Stephanie Distefano, the restaurant originally had just eight tables and four waiters. Stephanie, better known as "Miss Fannie," did most of the cooking along with her sister-in-law and one other assistant. The restaurant featured both Northern and Southern Italian cooking and soon became a hit. Eventually the restaurant grew to seat 200 people and had a staff of 35. While patrons flocked there to eat Miss Fannie's beef manicotti and veal piccata, they also came to talk politics, do business and spot celebrities. Joey Distefano, Fannie's grandson and a chef in his own right, treasures her extensive collection of letters from celebrities, legislators, governors and more. He said that people regularly made the drive from New Orleans just to eat at The Village. When Vince died in 1964, Fannie ran the restaurant on her own. While she eventually hired some help, Miss Fannie kept the restaurant going strong until 1991 when she closed its doors for the last time. In 2004 Joey Distefano opened his own restaurant in Baton Rouge and named it The Village.

Justin Wilson

Justin Wilson delighted television viewers for years with his bright red suspenders, big smile and thick Cajun accent.

Born in Roseland, La., in April 1914, Wilson learned to cook from his mother. He was well known for his humor and often entertained residents along the bayous with his Cajun stories and jokes. His stories were recorded and the books sold millions. Wilson's entertainment abilities evolved to include songs and television shows. Working without a script before a live audience, Wilson recorded shows with PBS that gained nationwide attention. From his culinary abilities he wrote seven best-selling cookbooks. As Wilson would say, you'll love them, "I gar-on-tee!"

Yellow Bowl Restaurant

During the days of Prohibition there was still a good deal of

contraband alcohol available if you knew where to look. In those days, a bowl in front of a building was a code used to signify that alcohol was available in that establishment. The

Yellow Bowl Restaurant on Highway 182, near Jeanerette, La., got its name from the large yellow bowl that has been in front of the restaurant since those "drier" days. Now the Yellow Bowl is better known for its crawfish étouffée, Cajun gumbo and perfectly fried, grease-free crawfish and shrimp. Once a humble bus stop café, the Yellow Bowl is now one of the many little treasures to be found when traveling outside of the city.

Zapp's Potato Chip Company

Known as the Little Chippery in Gramercy, La., Zapp's Potato Chips was founded by Ron Zappe. Despite the small size of

the facility, Zapp's chips can be found across the country and are regularly shipped to homesick Louisianians abroad. Zapp's chips are slow cooked in peanut oil for a superior crunch. If that isn't enough, they also come in a variety of unique flavors that pay tribute to Southern tastes. There's Cajun Crawtator, Cajun Dill, Hotter'n Hot Jalapeño, Mesquite BBQ and many more. Zappe even sells chips packaged in the signature purple and gold tiger stripes of Louisiana State University and drives a fire truck painted to match in local parades.

Zatarain's

The nation's leading manufacturer of New Orleans-style food products was started by Emile A. Zatarain Sr. In 1889, Zatarain obtained his company's first trademark and began

selling root beer. Although they started with condiments and extracts, the company now makes more than 200 food products.

Zatarain's produces such items as rice and pasta dinner mixes, breadings, stuffings, seasonings, spices and seafood-oriented products. The company began as the Pa-Poose Products Company on Valmont Street, and it later operated under several variations of the name Zatarain. The business was sold and moved from New Orleans to Gretna in 1963. The company was formally named Zatarain's in 1967.

Zuppardo's Economical Supermarket

Zuppardo's Supermarket is the oldest self-service supermarket in the New Orleans area. Family owned and operated for over five generations, Zuppardo's prides itself on providing superior products and memorable service. The Zuppardo family began selling fruits and vegetables from

a cart in 1929. The tradition of making farm fresh produce available to its customers continues today. Meat and produce are inspected daily to assure quality.

While the store has changed with the times, its owners and employees still offer that old-fashioned dedication to service by special-ordering items, hand-cutting meat and carrying groceries to customers' cars. It's no wonder Zuppardo's remains a New Orleans area institution.

LOUISIANA SPECIALTY PRODUCTS

When cooking the cuisine of South Louisiana, numerous specialty products are used. Most of these unique items are grown or manufactured here in our state. At Chef John Folse & Company, we are able to make these unique items available to you anywhere in the country. Also, if you are interested in speaking engagements or cooking demonstrations by Chef John Folse, contact him at:

Chef John Folse & Company
2517 S. Philippe Ave.
Gonzales, LA 70737
(225) 644-6000
(225) 644-1295 fax

For more information about Chef John Folse & Company products or Louisiana specialty products visit the company Web site.

www.jfolse.com

We look forward to assisting you and hope to see you in Louisiana real soon.

Acknowledgements

A project of this magnitude, which compiles Louisiana's culinary and cultural history into an encyclopedia, would not be feasible without a multitude of contributors: writers, editors, photographers, curators, researchers, historians, librarians, food stylists and support staff. Special thanks must be given to all who worked diligently to ensure and inspire the success and accuracy of this publication. Like the early explorers, religious, aristocrats, pioneers and peasants who settled Louisiana's vast swamps and bayous, we, too, hope to leave a lasting legacy to our great state through this literature.

Simple thanks will never express the sincere gratitude to those who "defend and protect" Louisiana's archives and historic collections: the staff of the Louisiana State Museum especially former Director James Sefcik; Kathryn Page, curator of maps and manuscripts; and Tom Lanham, assistant registrar. To the staff of the Williams Research Center at The Historic New Orleans Collection especially Priscilla Lawrence, museum director; John Magill, head of research services; Sally Spier Stassi, reference associate; and Pamela Arceneaux, reference librarian. To the staffs and research associates of Hill Memorial Library and Middleton Library at Louisiana State University, especially Margie Orr. To the staff and research associates of Howard-Tilton Memorial Library and Special Collections at Tulane University; Susan Tucker and the staff at the Vorhoff Library at Newcomb College Center for Research on Women, Tulane University; the staffs of East Baton Rouge and Ascension parish public libraries; and Yvette Dornier at the St. James Tourist Commission. Special thanks also to the library staff at Nicholls State University and George Kaslow, instructor at the Chef John Folse Culinary Institute.

To the historians consulted especially Glenn Falgoust whose knowledge of Louisiana history and years of research were invaluable; Roger Busbice; Christopher G. Pena; Fred Logan; Jan Longone; Richard E. Scott; and Andrew Capone, president of the Fort Butler Foundation.

Thanks also to those who gave special permission to use historical photographs and images from collections including Dr. Florence M. Jumonville, Chair, Louisiana and Special Collections Department, Earl K. Long Library, University of New Orleans; Pat Threatt, McNeese State University; Randy DeSoto and the staff of St. John the Baptist Parish Library; Sonny Carter and Mary Linn Wernet at the Cammie G. Henry Research Center, Northwestern State University; Janet Colson, Creole Heritage Center, Northwestern State University; Shugana Campbell and the Amistad Research Center; Joseph Maselli and the American-Italian Museum, New Orleans; Dave Morgan, Museum of Mobile; Sandra Scalise Juneau; artist Claude Picard; Wayne Kerr and Guy LeBlanc of Parks Canada; Donna Doucet of the Société Promotion Grand-Pré; Steve Kleinpeter, Southern Photographic Images, Featuring the Fonville Winans Collection, www.spiart.com; James and Meriget Turner, Fonville Winans Collection; artist Robert Dafford and the Acadian Memorial in St. Martinville, La.; Josie Thavis, the German Heritage Museum in Robert's Cove, La.; Gloria Maurin and the German-Acadian Coast Historical & Geneological Society in Destrehan, La.; artist Wanda Kendrick Ballard, Pam and Ernie Lowe and the Minden-Germantown Festival Commission, Inc.; Helen Williams, Anne Stirling Weller and the West Feliciana Historical Society; Norman Marmillion and Laura Plantation; Joan and Thomas Gandy; Alice Garbeaux and Kent House in Alexandria, La.; Dennis LaBatt and Poverty Point; and Jon Gibson. Thanks for special assistance to Angela Falgoust, executive director of the Ascension Parish Tourist Commission; Melrose Plantation in Natchitoches, La.; Curator Polly Luttrull and Horticulturist Trish Aleshire from Rosedown Plantation, St. Francisville; and the Louisiana Office of Tourism.

To the staff and former staffs of Chef John Folse & Company especially Dawn Delhommer, Sharon Jesowshek, Jay Kimball, David Harris, John Tarver, Jeremy Langlois, Michael Schultz, James Morgan, Natalie Aprill and Beth Morrison.

To the students of the Chef John Folse Culinary Institute especially Randy Boyd, Robert Baucum and Greg Hamer, Jr. (Native American culture); Mark Bordelon, Marsha Serigny, Shane Von Hoven and David S. Oufnac (Spanish culture); Ron Davis, Jr., William Swanigan, Kenneth Champagne and Kevin S. Foil (German culture); Damian Mouton, Minh Le and Patrick Besson (African culture); Brenda Bell and LyndaRose Steen Oncale (English culture); Lee Percle, Stephanie Pasqua and Deborah Bergeron (Italian culture). Special and particular thanks to Rhonda Hammond and Cyn Guidry for assisting in the compilation of the volumes of recipes reviewed for this publication.

Special thanks to Beth Courtney and the staff of Louisiana Public Broadcasting; Miss Margaret M. Shaffer and Mrs. Margaret K. Shaffer, Ardoyne Plantation; Cliff Fenton, campus photo journalist, Nicholls State University; Zeb Mayhew, Oak Alley Plantation; Sal Sunseri and Merri Sunseri-Schneider, P&J Oyster Company; the Hermann-Grima House; LSU Rural Life Museum; Magnolia Mound Plantation; the Archdiocese of New Orleans; the Ursuline Convent; Georgie Manuel; Antoine and Florence Gravois; Therese Gravois Oubre; Royley Folse, Sr.; Amy Laurent; Joey Distefano; Bill Hyland on behalf of the Los Isleños Festival; Stella Miller on behalf of the Black Heritage Festival; Nicky Bordelon on behalf of the Cochon de Lait Festival; the Bridge City Gumbo Festival; the Rayne Chamber of Commerce; the Shrimp and Petroleum Festival Association; August Bradford; Jerry Folse; Gerard Arthur Becnel and Buzz Harper. Special thanks to Whole Foods Market, New Orleans, who generously allowed us to photograph in their store.

Despite the many listed here, it is certain we have neglected to mention a few selfless souls who gave their assistance and advice at some stage of this process. If we failed to acknowledge you, it is only because of the tremendous scope of this project and not because your help was not appreciated. Please accept our most sincere apologies for any omission.

Photography Credits

#145-334, Loading Moss on the River, Frank B. Moore Collection, Courtesy of the University of New Orleans

NATIVE AMERICA

Page 2: "La Salle taking Possession of Louisiana and the River ca. 1860 Bocquin color." The Historic New Orleans Collection, accession no. 1970.1.

Page 4: 1992.001.003, 1720 Colonial Louisiana, Mississippi River, Indian Tribes, Courtesy of the Louisiana State Museum.

Page 5: Louisiana Office of State Parks, Jon Gibson. (Poverty Point)

Page 5: Louisiana Office of State Parks. Artist unknown. (atlatl)

Page 5: Louisiana Office of State Parks. Photo by Steven Carricut. (cooking stones)

Page 6: 1992.19.2, 1753 Louisiana location of numerous Indian tribes, Courtesy of the Louisiana State Museum.

Page 7: "Chasse generale de Chevreuil." The Historic New Orleans Collection, accession no. 1980.205.23 PC 10-1-B.

Page 8: "Nature Morte: Hare and Birds." The Historic New Orleans Collection, accession no. 1997.130.26.

Page 8: "Pichou and Boeuf Sauvage." The Historic New Orleans Collection, accession no. 1980.205.22 PC 10-1-B.

Page 9: "Barbue, Poisson Arme & Spatule." The Historic New Orleans Collection, accession no. 1980.205.29 PC 10-1-B.

Page 10: "Page du Pratz-Indian Funeral." The Historic New Orleans Collection, accession no. 1980.205.36 PC 10-1-B.

Page 12: "Sassafras." The Historic New Orleans Collection, accession no. 1980.205.10 PC 10-1-B.

Page 13: "Indian Women Weaving Cane Baskets" 1923. Frank L. Moore photographer. American Missionary Association Addendum, Amistad Research Center at Tulane University.

Page 13: "Prospectus for the settling of Louisiana by Pierre Le Moyne, sieur d'Iberville." The Historic New Orleans Collection, accession no. 99-110-L.

Page 15: Louisiana Office of State Parks. Photo by Steven Carricut. (Arrowhead)

Page 16: "Indian Gumbo Sellers." The Historic New Orleans Collection, accession no. 1950. 56.

FRANCE

Page 19: "La Salle at the Mouth of the Mississippi." The Historic New Orleans Collection, accession no. 1974.25.10.15 PC 10-1-A.

Page 20: "Louis XIV Portrait." The Historic New Orleans Collection, accession no. 1991.34.4.

Page 21: "Marquette and Joliet Discover the Mississippi." The Historic New Orleans Collection, accession no. 1986.96.4 PC 10-2-A.

Page 22: "La Salle Portrait." The Historic New Orleans Collection, accession no. 1991.34.2.

Page 22: "La Salle Claims Mississippi for France (color)." The Historic New Orleans Collection, accession no. 1979.36 P.C. 10-2-A.

Page 22: "The Murder of La Salle." The Historic New Orleans Collection, accession no. 1980.200 PC 10-2-A.

Page 23: "Iberville Portrait." The Historic New Orleans Collection, accession no. 1991.34.3.

Page 23: "Dancing Calumet." The Historic New Orleans Collection, accession no. 1980.205.1 PC 10-1-B.

Page 24: "Philippe II, duc d'Orléans Portrait." The Historic New Orleans Collection, accession no. 1991.34.6.

Page 25: "Duke Orleans feeding coins to John Law (12)." The Historic New Orleans Collection, accession no. 60-63.

Page 26: "Portrait of Jean Baptiste Le Moyne, sieur de Bienville." The Historic New Orleans Collection, accession no. 1990.49.

Page 27: 1979.74 1718 Mother Map, Courtesy of the Louisiana State Museum.

Page 28: "Sou." The Historic New Orleans Collection, accession no. 1978.137.

Page 29: "Henry de Tonty, 1650-1704" by Nicholas Maes (1632-1695). Courtesy: The Museum of Mobile.

Page 30: 1997.078.082, 1719 Homanno, Io.-mapmaker, Courtesy of the Louisiana State Museum.

Page 30: #1981.132.040, Urusline Convent, Frances B. Johnston Collection, Courtesy of the Louisiana State Museum.

Page 31: "Filles a la Cassette." The Historic New Orleans Collection, accession no. 77-132-RL p. 167.

Page 32: Coureurs de bois. Artist unknown.

Page 32: Jackson Square at Dusk, New Orleans. Louisiana Office of Tourism.

Page 33: 1980.014.003, 1755, Jacques Nicolas Bellin, Courtesy of the Louisiana State Museum.

CAJUN
Page 34: "The Harvest" (or "Early Acadia") by Claude T. Picard, D.H.C.; Parks Canada.

Page 36: "Reading the Deportation Order" by Claude T. Picard, D.H.C.; Parks Canada.

Page 37: "Embarkation" (or "Ships Take Acadians Into Exile") by Claude T. Picard, D.H.C.; Parks Canada.

Page 38: "Burning and Lay Waste" (or "Settlements Are Burned") by

Claude T. Picard, D.H.C.; Parks Canada.

Page 39: "Country Estate," 1938 by Fonville Winans. James and Meriget Turner, Fonville Winans Collection. Steve Kleinpeter, Southern Photographic Images, Featuring the Fonville Winans Collection, www.spiart.com.

Page 39: "The Arrival of the Acadians in Louisiana" by Robert Dafford. ©City of St. Martinville, Louisiana. Funded by individual donations and memorials and by the National Endowment for the Arts, the Louisiana State Arts Council, and the Louisiana Division of the Arts, the Office of Cultural Development in the Department of Culture, Recreation and Tourism, and the Acadiana Arts Council.

Page 40: "Tony Kristicevich, 1939" by Fonville Winans. James and Meriget Turner, Fonville Winans Collection. Steve Kleinpeter, Southern Photographic Images, Featuring the Fonville Winans Collection, www.spiart.com.

Page 40: "Tonging," Grand Isle, 1938 by Fonville Winans. James and Meriget Turner, Fonville Winans Collection. Steve Kleinpeter, Southern Photographic Images, Featuring the Fonville Winans Collection, www.spiart.com.

Page 40: Order of the Good Time. Artist unknown.

Page 41: No. 3494, Augustine Woman Pounding Rice, 1892. Photograph Collection, Archives and Special Collections Department, Frazar Memorial Library, McNeese State University.

Page 42: Pelts on Cabin Wall. Artist unknown.

Page 43: Evangeline at memorial church in Grand-Pré, Nova Scotia. François Gaudet. Société Promotion Grand-Pré.

SPAIN
Page 44: "de Soto Discovers the Mississippi." The Historic New Orleans Collection, accession no. 1982.247 PD 10.

Page 46: 1987.1.9, 1525, Courtesy of the Louisiana State Museum.

Page 46: "de Soto's Burial – colored litho." The Historic New Orleans Collection, accession no. 1974.25.10.164 PD 10.

Page 47: 1987.1.10, 1550, Courtesy of the Louisiana State Museum.

Page 48: "Don Antonio De Ulloa Portrait." The Historic New Orleans Collection, accession no. 1991.34.12.

Page 48: "O'Reilly Portrait." The Historic New Orleans Collection, accession no. 1991.34.14.

Page 49: "Galvez Portrait." The Historic New Orleans Collection, accession no. 1991.34.15.

Page 49: "Miro Portrait." The Historic New Orleans Collection, accession no. 1991.34.16.

Page 49: "Carondelet Portrait." The Historic New Orleans Collection, accession no. 1991.34.18.

Page 51: No. 2960, Old Spanish Trail. Photo by Murray, Isaac. Photograph Collection, Archives and Special Collections Department, Frazar Memorial Library, McNeese State University.

Page 52: Cabildo. New Orleans. Louisiana Office of Tourism.

Page 54: Dining. New Orleans. Louisiana Office of Tourism.

Page 54: Paella. Cliff Fenton, campus photo journalist, Nicholls State University.

Page 55: P-98, 3.2, Cotton Levee & Canal St. (1880), Courtesy of the University of New Orleans.

AFRICA
Page 56: "Cooking Shrimps." The Historic New Orleans Collection, accession no. 1974.25.23.39.

Page 58: "Return of the Captured Africans." The Historic New Orleans Collection, accession no. 1977.296.87.

Page 58: 1982.114.14, 1840, Courtesy of the Louisiana State Museum.

Page 59: "Sale of Estates, Pictures and Slaves in the Rotunda." The Historic New Orleans Collection, accession no. 1974.25.23.4.

Page 60: "By Hewlett and Raspiller on Saturday, 14th April, inst." The Historic New Orleans Collection, accession no. 73-701-L.

Page 61: "Woman with Pie." The Historic New Orleans Collection, accession no. 1974.25.23.82.

Page 61: #145-527, Brother Jones, Frank B. Moore Collection, Courtesy of the University of New Orleans.

Page 62: "Old South-Relics of Slavery." The Historic New Orleans Collection, accession no. 1974.25.23.37.

Page 62: #1981.132.235, Laborer's Cottage at Columbia Plantation, Frances B. Johnston Collection, Courtesy of the Louisiana State Museum.

Page 63: No. 128, Rite In It. Photo by Sturdevant, E. K. Photograph Collection, Archives and Special Collections Department, Frazar Memorial Library, McNeese State University.

Page 64: "Man Cooking Meat." The Historic New Orleans Collection, accession no. 1974.25.23.92.

Page 65: #00612, Portrait of Etienne Bore, R. Bohunek, c. 1910, Courtesy of the Louisiana State Museum.

Page 67: P-262, 2.1, Sisters of the Holy Family Convent/School, 717 Orleans St., ca. 1940s, "Orleans Theater Quadroon Ball," Courtesy of the University of New Orleans.

Page 70: "P. B. S. Pinchback." The Historic New Orleans Collection, accession no. 1974.25.27.353.

Page 70: Norbert Rillieux, Cabildo, New Orleans.

Page 71: Marie Thereze Carmelite Anty Metoyer. Pat Henry, Jr. Collection, Cammie G. Henry Research Center, Watson Memorial Library, Northwestern State University of Louisiana.

Page 71: #11537, Marie Laveau, copy after Catlin, Frank Schnieder, c. 1915, Courtesy of the Louisiana State Museum.

Page 72: "Voodoo Dance." The Historic New Orleans Collection, accession no. 1974.25.23.127.

Page 72: "Le Pere Antoine de Sedella." The Historic New Orleans Collection, accession no. 1982.43.

Page 73: Mary Ferchaud. Courtesy of Jerry Folse.

Page 74: The Donaldsonville Cannoneers. Courtesy of August Bradford.

Page 74: Abraham Lincoln. Liquid Library.

Page 75: P-36, 3.1, Black Civil War soldier identified in accompanying copy of National Archives letter August 4, 1942 as Jules Dickerson alias Jules Dixon. He was a corporal in Company B, 80th United States Colored Volunteer Infantry. Mr. Jules Edward, a Dickerson descendant, stated that the subject was originally from St. James Parish, La. Courtesy of the University of New Orleans.

GERMANY
Page 76: "Law's Propaganda Poster." The Historic New Orleans Collection, accession no. 1952.3.

Page 78: "John Law (2)." The Historic New Orleans Collection, accession no. 60-63.

Page 79: "Law's Advertisement of Louisiana to the Germans." The Historic New Orleans Collection, accession no. 83-382.

Page 80: A-17, Perique Tobacco Field in Paulina, SJA, in 1920s. Courtesy of the German-Acadian Coast Historical & Genealogical Society; St. John the Baptist Parish Library; St. James Historical Society, and the Louisiana Endowment for the Humanities.

Page 81: Fabacher Family. Back row, left to right: Lawrence

Fabacher, Anthony Fabacher, Louis Fabacher, Barbara Fabacher, John Fabacher, Peter Fabacher and Albert Fabacher. Front row, left to right: Franz Joseph Fabacher, Jr., Madeline Frey Fabacher, Madeline Fabacher, Jr., Jacob Fabacher, Aloysius Fabacher and Joseph Fabacher, Sr. Courtesy of Charles Bahlinger.

Page 81: Fabacher family restaurant menu. Courtesy of Charles Bahlinger.

Page 81: "Philip Werlein Southern Music House." The Historic New Orleans Collection, accession no. 1949.1.26."

Page 81: "The Search" by Wanda Kendrick Ballard. A special commemorative print in celebration of Minden's Sesquicentennial sponsored by the Minden-Germantown Festival Commission, Inc. Courtesy of the Minden-Germantown Festival Commission, Inc.

Page 82: DD-2, Charles Francois Cambre in the Crevasse in front of his bakery shop, 1902-03. Courtesy of the German-Acadian Coast Historical & Genealogical Society; St. John the Baptist Parish Library; St. James Historical Society, and the Louisiana Endowment for the Humanities.

Page 83: Choucroute Garni. Cliff Fenton, campus photo journalist, Nicholls State University.

Page 84: Madam Elizabeth Kettenring Dutrey Begue with her husband, Hypolite Begue. Courtesy of Louisiana State Museum.

Page 85: DDD-12, Stella Guedry and friends on an outing in Norco. They were teachers from New Orleans and were using Joseph Lovetro's "vegetable truck." 1920. Courtesy of the German-Acadian Coast Historical & Genealogical Society; St. John the Baptist Parish Library; St. James Historical Society, and the Louisiana Endowment for the Humanities.

Page 86: X-6, Packing Carrots in the 1930s at the A. Montz Ice Plant, LaPlace, La., SJB. Left to right: Mrs. Denis Madere, Mrs. Hilda Webre Triche, Beatrice Webre, Willie Webre and C. F. Woodley, vegetable inspector. Courtesy of the German-Acadian Coast Historical & Genealogical Society; St. John the Baptist Parish Library; St. James Historical Society, and the Louisiana Endowment for the Humanities.

Page 86: X-4, Turnip Washing. 1936, LaPlace, La., SJB. Workers were paid 10 cents/hour and sometimes worked 17 hours a day at peak season. Courtesy of the German-Acadian Coast Historical & Genealogical Society; St. John the Baptist Parish Library; St. James Historical Society, and the Louisiana Endowment for the Humanities.

Page 86: X-1, A. Montz & Co., LaPlace, SJB, ca. 1930. Mr. C. F. Woodley, the vegetable inspector, inspected for grade and size. Courtesy of the German-Acadian Coast Historical & Genealogical Society; St. John the Baptist Parish Library; St. James Historical Society, and the Louisiana Endowment for the Humanities.

Page 87: YYY-34, Boucherie. As soon as the first cold spell of autumn hit the river parishes, residents knew that "boucherie" time was imminent. Courtesy of the German-Acadian Coast Historical & Genealogical Society; St. John the Baptist Parish Library; St. James Historical Society, and the Louisiana Endowment for the Humanities.

Page 87: U-13, Boucherie, ca. 1930s, at home of Charles Troxler in Taft, La., SCH. Boucherie was a yearly occasion usually taking place during the first cold weather. Courtesy of the German-Acadian Coast Historical & Genealogical Society; St. John the Baptist Parish Library; St. James Historical Society, and the Louisiana Endowment for the Humanities.

Page 87: Frey Brothers Truck. Courtesy of August Bradford.

ENGLAND

Page 88: Back Row Left to Right: George Shotwell, Isabell Bowman, Sarah Bowman, Sarah Turnbull Bowman (Daniel and Martha's daughter), James Bowman (Sarah's husband); Front Row Left to Right: Nina Bowman, Martha Bowman Fort and her infant son, William Fort III, Martha Turnbull and Corrie Bowman. Courtesy of Rosedown Plantation.

Page 91: "1803 Map." The Historic New Orleans Collection, accession no. 1984.3.

Page 92: "Transfer of Louisiana from France to U.S." The Historic New Orleans Collection, accession no. 1991.34.25.

Page 92: Proces-Verbal (Louisiana Purchase Document). The Historic New Orleans Collection, accession no. Mss. 125, 75-217-L.

Page 93: "Thomas Jefferson Portrait." The Historic New Orleans Collection, accession no. 1991.34.22.

Page 93: "Claiborne Portrait." The Historic New Orleans Collection, accession no. 1991.34.26.

Page 93: "Napoleon Portrait." The Historic New Orleans Collection, accession no. 1991.34.19.

Page 93: "Laussat Portrait." The Historic New Orleans Collection, accession no. 1991.34.21.

Page 93: Proces-Verbal (Louisiana Purchase Document). The Historic New Orleans Collection, accession no. Mss. 125, 75-217-L.

Page 94: Grace Episcopal Church. Courtesy of the West Feliciana Historical Society.

Page 94: Oakley Plantation. Courtesy of the West Feliciana Historical Society.

Page 95: Photo of Bayou Sara. Courtesy of Dr. Gandy and the West Feliciana Historical Society.

Page 95: Photo of Bayou Sara. Courtesy of Dr. Gandy and the West Feliciana Historical Society.

Page 97: Daniel Turnbull. Courtesy of Rosedown Plantation.

Page 97: Martha Hilliard Barrow Turnbull. Courtesy of Rosedown Plantation.

Page 98: P-263, 3.1, Cotton Factor's Grading Room, probably New Orleans, ca. 1920, Courtesy of the University of New Orleans.

Page 98: "Louisiana Derby," 1939 by Fonville Winans. James and Meriget Turner, Fonville Winans Collection. Steve Kleinpeter, Southern Photographic Images, Featuring the Fonville Winans Collection, www.spiart.com.

Page 98: Tennis players in the Felicianas. Courtesy of the West Feliciana Historical Society.

Page 99: "Major General Andrew Jackson." The Historic New Orleans Collection, accession no. 1979.112.

Page 100: "Sir Edward Pakenham Portrait." The Historic New Orleans Collection, accession no. 1991.34.30.

Page 100: "Battle of New Orleans and Death of Major General Pakenham." The Historic New Orleans Collection, accession no. 1949.16i,ii.

Page 101: "Jean Lafitte" drawing by C. M. Luria. Courtesy of The Historic New Orleans Collection.

Page 101: Lafitte's Blacksmith Shop. Courtesy of the Louisiana Office of Tourism.

Page 102: Jackson Square, New Orleans. Courtesy of the Louisiana Office of Tourism.

ITALY

Page 104: #145-312, Banana Wharf, Frank B. Moore Collection, Courtesy of the University of New Orleans.

Page 106: 981.132.257, Godchaux Sugar Refinery, Frances B. Johnston Collection, Courtesy of the Louisiana State Museum.

Page 107: Map of Italy. Artist unknown.

Page 108: The S. S. Manilla arrived in the New Orleans port between 1901 and 1905 with Sicilians from Genoa and Palermo. Courtesy of the American-Italian Museum, New Orleans.

Page 108: The Liguria, one of the ships arriving monthly carrying Sicilians during the immigration wave between 1880 and 1910. Courtesy of the American-Italian Museum, New Orleans.

Page 109: George Fredrick Coniglio, Sr. Courtesy of Bernice Coniglio York.

Page 110: Family of strawberry farmers near Hammond, La., in Tangipahoa Parish around 1923. Front row, left to right: Mr. & Mrs. Maturana. Back row, left to right: Virginia Maturana Scalise, Laura Maturana, George Maturana and Jennie Maturana. Courtesy of Sandra Scalise Juneau.

Page 110: #08482.165, Strawberries, John N. Teunisson Collection, Courtesy of the Louisiana State Museum.

Page 111: Dominic James "Nick" LaRocca composed Louisiana State University's famous fight song, Tiger Rag One Step. Courtesy of the American-Italian Museum, New Orleans.

Page 111: #145-311, Cargo of Bananas, Frank B. Moore Collection, Courtesy of the University of New Orleans.

Page 112: The Roman Chewing Candy Wagon was founded by Sam Cortese. The wagon still rolls today. Courtesy of the American-Italian Museum, New Orleans.

Page 112: Scalise family grocery store in New Orleans. From left to right: Joseph Scalise, Virginia Scalise Rizzo, Peter Scalise and Victor Scalise. Courtesy of Sandra Scalise Juneau.

Page 112: Solari's, one of New Orleans' favorite grocery stores, was founded by J. B. Solari in 1861. Pictured here are diners at the lunch counter in the 1930s. Courtesy of the American-Italian Museum, New Orleans.

Page 113: The Banana King business was owned by the Venezia family. Deliveries were made in their 1928 truck. Courtesy of the American-Italian Museum, New Orleans.

Page 113: Frank Prestia's Ice Cream Factory was located on South Scott Street, 1917. Courtesy of the American-Italian Museum, New Orleans.

Page 113: The Bagille Seafood Company sold rabbits as well as seafood. Pictured is Joseph Cefalu. Courtesy of the American-Italian Museum, New Orleans.

Page 114: Standard Fruit Company Founders. Courtesy of the American-Italian Museum, New Orleans.

Page 114: Angelo Socola, Father of the Louisiana Rice Industry. Courtesy of the American-Italian Museum, New Orleans.

Page 115: Lorenzo Milano, Donaldsonville, La. Courtesy of Eric Weill.

CREOLE

Page 119: Laura Locoul Gore. Courtesy of Laura Plantation.

Page 120: Michel Bernard Cantrelle. Courtesy of Fred Logan.

Page 120: "Cabanocey Plantation" by Kenneth Crawford.

Page 121: Jacques Cantrelle, II. Courtesy of Fred Logan.

Page 121: Sketch of Cabanocey Plantation. Courtesy of Fred Logan.

Page 122: #1981.132.284, Jefferson College, Frances B. Johnston Collection, Courtesy of the Louisiana State Museum.

Page 122: NN-20, Jefferson College Baseball Team, ca. 1890. Courtesy of the German-Acadian Coast Historical & Genealogical Society; St. John the Baptist Parish Library; St. James Historical Society, and the Louisiana Endowment for the Humanities.

Page 123: Valcour Aime. Courtesy of St. James Catholic Church.

Page 123: Gabriel Aime. Courtesy of St. James Catholic Church.

Page 123: "PGT Beauregard Portrait." The Historic New Orleans Collection, accession no. 1991.34.41.

Page 123: Jacques Telesphore Roman. Courtesy of Oak Alley Plantation.

Page 124: #08482.177.37, Horse Jumping, Fairgrounds, John N. Teunisson Collection, Courtesy of the Louisiana State Museum.

Page 124: #08482.177.51, Harness Racing, Fairgrounds, John N. Teunisson Collection, Courtesy of the Louisiana State Museum.

Page 125: P-205, 3.3, French Opera House ca. 1910, Courtesy of the University of New Orleans.

Page 125: La Belle Creole. Courtesy of Rosedown Plantation.

Page 125: #T0405.1990.3, French Opera House, John N. Teunisson Collection, Courtesy of the Louisiana State Museum.

ROUX, STOCKS AND SAUCES
Page 126: "ca. 1907 Madame Begue's Restaurant Kitchen." The Historic New Orleans Collection, accession no. 1981.261.32.

BREAKFAST & BRUNCH
Page 162: #145-342, Old Fashioned French Dinner Table, Begue's Restaurant, Frank B. Moore Collection, Courtesy of the University of New Orleans.

Page 164: Madam Elizabeth Kettenring Dutrey Begue with her husband, Hypolite Begue. Courtesy of Louisiana State Museum.

Page 171: "Columbus Breaking an Egg." The Historic New Orleans Collection, accession no. 1974.25.10.1 PC-10-1-A.

APPETIZERS AND HORS D'OUEVRES
Page 202: "Ten Cents a Dozen," 1939 by Fonville Winans. James and Meriget Turner, Fonville Winans Collection. Steve Kleinpeter, Southern Photographic Images, Featuring the Fonville Winans Collection, www.spiart.com.

SOUPS
Page 244: St. Joseph Steamboat. Courtesy of Thomas H. and Joan Gandy.

Page 266: #145-428, Chickens on a Farm, Frank B. Moore Collection, Courtesy of the University of New Orleans.

SALADS
Page 286: Ferris grocery store, Donaldsonville, La. Courtesy of August Bradford.

VEGETABLES
Page 328: #145-340, French Market Interior, Frank B. Moore Collection, Courtesy of the University of New Orleans.

Page 338: No. 1397, Westlake Laundry. Photo by Sturdevant, E. K. Photograph Collection, Archives and Special Collections Department, Frazar Memorial Library, McNeese State University.

SEAFOOD
Page 372: "Ladies with Redfish," 1940 by Fonville Winans. James and Meriget Turner, Fonville Winans Collection. Steve Kleinpeter, Southern Photographic Images, Featuring the Fonville Winans Collection, www.spiart.com.

Page 378: #1981.132.350, Rienzi Plantation House, Frances B. Johnston Collection, Courtesy of the Louisiana State Museum.

POULTRY
Page 430: #145-428, Chickens on a Farm, Frank B. Moore Collection, Courtesy of the University of New Orleans.

MEAT
Pages 470-475: Folse brothers and butchers at la boucherie. Photos by José Garcia.

Page 496 and 500: Kleinpeter Photography, Baton Rouge, La.

WILD GAME
Page 542: From the Maude Reid Scrapbook 1 (MR1-203), Hunter's Paradise. Photograph Collection, Archives and Special Collections Department, Frazar Memorial Library, McNeese State University.

Page 550: "Rice Festival float, Crowley, ca. 1940" by Fonville Winans. James and Meriget Turner, Fonville Winans Collection. Steve Kleinpeter, Southern Photographic Images, Featuring the Fonville Winans Collection, www.spiart.com.

DESSERTS
Page 584: "Making a Living," 1934 by Fonville Winans. James and Meriget Turner, Fonville Winans Collection. Steve Kleinpeter, Southern Photographic Images, Featuring the Fonville Winans Collection, www.spiart.com.

Page 620: Candy factory, Donaldsonville, La. Courtesy of August Bradford.

Page 632: XXX-2, 3, 4, Sewing sacks in Colonial Sugars in Gramercy, SJA. Courtesy of the German-Acadian Coast Historical & Genealogical Society; St. John the Baptist Parish Library; St. James Historical Society, and the Louisiana Endowment for the Humanities.

BREADS
Page 646: The Model Bakery. Donaldsonville, La. Courtesy of August Bradford.

Page 651: St. James Bakery Delivery Truck. Courtesy of Amy Laurent.

DAIRY
Page 672: PPP-117, Milk Maid, Courtesy of the University of New Orleans.

Page 676: Laura Plantation with Dairy Cow. Courtesy of Laura Plantation.

Page 697: Evangeline in Nova Scotia. Artist unknown.

BEVERAGES
Page 698: "Woman Making Coffee." The Historic New Orleans Collection, accession no. 1974.25.23.90.

Page 701: Man making café au lait. Courtesy of Robert Hennessey.

Page 705: Louisiana native black cherries. By Nettie Amedee.

Page 712: Ice house, Donaldsonville, La. Courtesy of August Bradford.

FESTIVALS
Page 726: "Rice Festival, Crowley" by Fonville Winans. James and Meriget Turner, Fonville Winans Collection. Steve Kleinpeter, Southern Photographic Images, Featuring the Fonville Winans Collection, www.spiart.com.

Page 727: No. 73, Rice Farming. Photograph Collection, Archives and Special Collections Department, Frazar Memorial Library, McNeese State University.

PLANTATIONS
Page 750: #1981.132.384, San Francisco Plantation, Frances B. Johnston Collection, Courtesy of the Louisiana State Museum.

Page 753: "Old Plantation Negroes." The Historic New Orleans Collection, accession no. 1974.25.23.63.

Page 753: #08516, D.L. Kernion with Nursemaid Marguerite, 1850 (photographer unknown), Courtesy of the Louisiana State Museum.

Page 763: Nottoway Plantation. Courtesy of the Louisiana Office of Tourism.

Page 764: Oak Alley Plantation. Courtesy of the Louisiana Office of Tourism.

Page 765: San Francisco Plantation. Courtesy of the Louisiana Office of Tourism.

Page 766: Rosedown Plantation. Courtesy of La. Office of Tourism.

MENUS
Page 770: #09216.1, King Rex's Banquet, John N. Teunisson Collection, Courtesy of the Louisiana State Museum.

Page 778: #145-382, Vaccaro Brothers Tomb, Decorated, Frank B. Moore Collection, Courtesy of the University of New Orleans.

Page 782: Christmas at Magnolia Mound, Will O'Halloran, O'Halloran's Designer Portraits, Baton Rouge, La.

LAGNIAPPE
Page 784: "Jiggin' Boys" by Fonville Winans. James and Meriget Turner, Fonville Winans Collection. Steve Kleinpeter, Southern Photographic Images, Featuring the Fonville Winans Collection, www.spiart.com.

Page 785: First class at the Chef John Folse Culinary Institute, Nicholls State University, Thibodaux, La. Photo by José Garcia.

Page 788: Madam Elizabeth Kettenring Dutrey Begue with her husband, Hypolite Begue. Courtesy of Louisiana State Museum.

Page 801: Maylie's Restaurant. Courtesy of Vorhoff Library at Newcomb College Center for Research on Women, Tulane University.

Page 804: Solari's, one of New Orleans' favorite grocery stores, was founded by J. B. Solari in 1861. Pictured here are diners at the lunch counter in the 1930s. Courtesy of the American-Italian Museum, New Orleans.

BACK COVER
#145-47, Pie Man, Frank B. Moore Collection, Courtesy of the University of New Orleans.

BOOK ENDSHEETS
The Historic New Orleans Collection, accession no. 1976.148.1 and 1978.148.2.

The Historic New Orleans Collection is located within a complex of historic French Quarter buildings. The oldest, constructed in the late 18th century, is one of the few structures to escape the disastrous fire of 1794. Today, The Collection serves the public as an accredited history museum, house museum and research center.

THE COLLECTION
THE HISTORIC NEW ORLEANS COLLECTION

533 Royal Street • 70130-2179 • www.hnoc.org • (504) 523-4662

Still Life with Cheese, Bottle of Wine and Mice. The Historic New Orleans Collection, accession no. 1997.130.27.

Bibliography

NATIVE AMERICANS

Bossu, Jean-Bernard. <u>Travels in the Interior of North America, 1751-1762</u>. Translated and edited by Seymour Feiler. Norman: University of Oklahoma Press, 1962.

Capone, Andrew. "La Pierre Folle de Vacherie: The Mad Stone of Vacherie." <u>Jambalaya</u>, Vol. 2, Issue 7, 28.

Chambers, Henry E. <u>Mississippi Valley Beginnings: An Outline of the Early History of the Earlier West</u>. New York and London: G. P. Putnam's Sons, 1922.

Dickinson, Samuel Dorris, ed. <u>New Travels in North America by Jean-Bernard Bossu, 1770-1771</u>. Natchitoches: Northwestern State University Press, 1982.

Gibson, Jon L. <u>Poverty Point: A Culture of the Lower Mississippi Valley</u>. Baton Rouge: Department of Culture, Recreation and Tourism, 1983.

Kniffen, Fred B. <u>The Indians of Louisiana</u>. Baton Rouge: Bureau of Educational Materials, Statistics and Research, College of Education, Louisiana State University and Agricultural and Mechanical College, 1945.

Kniffen, Fred B., Hiram F. Gregory, and George A. Stokes. <u>The Historic Indian Tribes of Louisiana: From 1542 to the Present</u>. Baton Rouge and London: Louisiana State University Press, 1987.

Le Maire, Francois. <u>Letters of Father Francois le Maire: A Missionary Priest in Louisiana Describing the Country and the Habits of the Indians, 1714-1717</u>. Survey of Federal Archives in Louisiana, 1937-1938.

McWilliams, Richebourg Gaillard, ed. <u>Fleur de Lys and Calumet: Being the Pénicaut Narrative of French Adventure in Louisiana</u>. Tuscaloosa and London: The University of Alabama Press, 1953.

McWilliams, Richebourg Gaillard, ed. <u>Iberville's Gulf Journals</u>. Tuscaloos and London: The University of Alabama Press, 1981.

Read, William A. <u>Louisiana Place Names of Indian Origin</u>. Baton Rouge: The University, 1927.

Survey of Federal Archives in Louisiana. <u>A Miscellany of Louisiana Historical Records</u>. New Orleans: Survey of Federal Archives in Louisiana, 1938.

http://www.500nations.com/Louisiana_Casinos.asp

http://www.indianaffairs.com/statemap.htm

http://www.indiangaming.org/info/pr/regulation.shtml

http://www.topcasinooffers.com/louisiana_casinos.html

FRENCH

Conrad, Glenn R., ed. <u>The Louisiana Purchase Bicentennial Series in Louisiana History</u>. Vol. 1, <u>The French Experience in Louisiana</u>. Lafayette: Center for Louisiana Studies University of Southwestern Louisiana, 1995.

Dart, Henry P., ed. "Allotment of Building Sites in New Orleans (1722)." <u>The Louisiana Historical Quarterly</u> 7 (January-October 1924): 564-566.

Falgoust, Glenn. "Celebrating Louisiana's Tri-Centennial: 500 Years in the Making." <u>Sauce Piquante</u>, Vol. 1, Issue 11, 8.

Hachard, Marie Madeleine. <u>The Letters of Marie Madeleine Hachard 1727-28</u>. Translated by Myldred Masson Costa. New Orleans: Laborde Printing Company, 1974.

Hamilton, Peter J. <u>Colonial Mobile</u>. University, Alabama: The University of Alabama Press, 1976.

Hamilton, Peter J. <u>The Private Life of Jean Baptiste Le Moyne, Sieur De Bienville</u>. Mobile: For the Bienville Monument Fund, 1909.

Higginbotham, Jay. <u>Old Mobile: Fort Louis de La Louisiane, 1702-1711</u>. Tuscaloosa and London: The University of Alabama Press, 1977.

Higginbotham, Jay, ed. <u>The Journal of Sauvole: Historical Journal of the Establishment of the French in Louisiana by M. de Sauvole</u>. Mobile: Colonial Books, 1969.

King, Grace. <u>Jean Baptiste Le Moyne Sieur De Bienville</u>. New York: Dodd, Mead and Company, 1892.

Rowland, Dunbar, ed. <u>General Correspondence of Louisiana: 1678-1763</u>. New Orleans: Polyanthos, 1976.

Rowland, Dunbar, ed. and A. G. Sanders, ed. <u>Mississippi Provincial Archives 1729-1740: French Dominion</u>. Publication of the Mississippi State Department of Archives and History, vol. 1. Jackson, Mississippi: Press of the Mississippi Department of Archives and History, 1927.

Rowland, Dunbar, ed. and Albert Godfrey Sanders, ed. <u>Mississippi</u>

Provincial Archives 1701-1729: French Dominion. Publication of the Mississippi State Department of Archives and History, vol. 2. Jackson, Mississippi: Press of the Mississippi Department of Archives and History, 1929.

Rowland, Dunbar, ed. and Albert Godfrey Sanders, ed. Mississippi Provincial Archives 1704-1743: French Dominion. Publication of the Mississippi State Department of Archives and History, vol. 3. Jackson, Mississippi: Press of the Mississippi Department of Archives and History, 1932.

Rowland, Dunbar, ed. and A. G. Sanders, ed. Mississippi Provincial Archives: French Dominion, 1729-1748. Vol. 4. Revised and edited by Patricia Kay Galloway. Baton Rouge and London: Louisiana State University Press, 1984.

Rowland, Dunbar, ed. and A. G. Sanders, ed. Mississippi Provincial Archives: French Dominion, 1749-1763. Vol. 5. Revised and edited by Patricia Kay Galloway. Baton Rouge and London: Louisiana State University Press, 1984.

Stall, Gaspar J. "Buddy." Proud, Peculiar New Orleans: The Inside Story. Baton Rouge: Claitor's Publishing Division, 1984.

http://lsm.crt.state.la.us/cabildo/cab3.htm

http://www.bruce.ruiz.net/PanamaHistory/americo_vespucci.htm

http://www.ci.baton-rouge.la.ua/History/historyBR.htm

http://www.datasync.com/~davidg59/biloxi1.html

http://www.enlou.com/time/timelineindex.htm

http://www.famousamericans.net/charlesetiennedenivelles

http://www.geocities.com/~colony/pelican.html

http://www.seniors-place.com/barbaramiles/barbhistory1.html

ACADIANS
Bluysen, Judith. Cajun: A Culinary Tour of Louisiana. New York: Rizzoli, 2002.

Brasseaux, Carl A. The Founding of New Acadia: The Beginnings of Acadian Life in Louisiana, 1765-1803. Baton Rouge and London: Louisiana State University Press, 1987.

Dormon, James H. The People Called Cajuns: An Introduction to an Ethnohistory. Lafayette, La.: The Center for Louisiana Studies University of Southwestern Louisiana, 1983.

Falgoust, Glenn. "L'Ascension: La Deuxieme Côte Des L'Acadiens." Sauce Piquante, May 1999, 14.

Feibleman, Peter S. and the editors of TIME-LIFE BOOKS. American Cooking: Creole and Acadian. New York: Time-Life Books, 1971.

Folse, John D. The Evolution of Cajun & Creole Cuisine. Gonzales, La.: Chef John Folse & Company Publishing, 2000.

Lambert, Marjie. Cajun Cooking: Succulent Recipes from Louisiana. New York: Crescent Books, 1991.

Leblanc, Dudley J. The True Story of the Acadians. Les Presses de la République de la Nouvelle-France, Ltd., 1998.

Minister of the Environment, Minister of Supply and Services, Canada. The Deportation of the Acadians. Canada: Minister of the Environment, Minister of Supply and Services, Canada, 1986.

Nightingale, Marie. Out of Old Nova Scotia Kitchens. New York: Charles Scribner's Sons, 1971.

Nova Scotia Department of Fisheries. Nova Scotia Seafood Cookery. Province of Nova Scotia: Nova Scotia Department of Fisheries, 1982.

Rushton, William Faulkner. The Cajuns: From Acadia to Louisiana. New York: Farrar Straus Giroux, 1979.

SPANISH
Casas, Penelope. "The Canary Islands." Gourmet, October 1995, 121.

Caughey, John Walton. Bernardo de Galvez in Louisiana 1776-1783. Gretna: Pelican Publishing Company, 1991.

De Pedro, José Montero. The Spanish in New Orleans and Louisiana. Translated by Richard E. Chandler. Gretna: Pelican Publishing Company, 2000.

Din, Gilbert C., ed. The Louisiana Purchase Bicentennial Series in Louisiana History. Vol. 2, The Spanish Presence in Louisiana, 1763 - 1803. Lafayette: Center for Louisiana Studies University of Southwestern Louisiana, 1996.

Funk & Wagnalls Standard Reference Encyclopedia, 1969 ed. Vol. 8. "De Soto."

Holmes, Jack David Lazarus. A Guide to Spanish Louisiana, 1762-1806. New Orleans: A. F. Laborde, 1970.

Krousel, Hilda S. Don Antonio De Ulloa: First Spanish Governor to Louisiana. Baton Rouge: VAAPR, INC.

Moore, John Preston. Revolt in Louisiana: The Spanish Occupation, 1766-1770. Baton Rouge: Louisiana State University Press, 1976.
Pitot, James. Observations on the Colony of Louisiana from 1796 to 1802. Baton Rouge and London: Louisiana State University Press, 1979.

Robin, C. C. Voyage to Louisiana: 1803 – 1805. Translated by Stuart O. Landry, Jr. New Orleans: Pelican Publishing Company, 1966.

Willie, Leroy E. Spanish and Natives of Louisiana who Served under General Don Bernardo de Galvez in his Campaigns Against the British. God Country Heritage, 1996.

Wood, Minter. Life in New Orleans in the Spanish Period. Reprinted from The Louisiana Historical Quarterly, vol. 22, no. 3, July 1939.

Woodward, Jr., Ralph Lee, ed. Tribute to Don Bernardo de Galvez. Baton Rouge and New Orleans: The Historic New Orleans Collection, 1979.

http://www.canaryislands-usa.com/cifec/losislenos.html

http://www.sonhex.dk/fandi.htm

AFRICANS
Ayensu, Dinah Ameley. The Art of West African Cooking. Garden City, New York: Doubleday & Company, Inc., 1972.

Bennett, Jr. Lerone. "The First Black Governor." Ebony, November 1986, 116.

Carter, Elva Jewel. "Toward Better Understanding: A brief history of the Negro in America including outstanding Negroes in Louisiana," 1975, vertical file, East Baton Rouge Parish Goodwood Library, Baton Rouge, Louisiana.

Christian, Marcus. "Demand By Men of Color For Rights in Orleans Territory." Negro History Bulletin Volume 36 No. 3 (March 1973): 54-57.

Crété, Liliane. Daily Life in Louisiana: 1815-1830. Translated by Patrick Gregory. Baton Rouge and London: Louisiana State University Press, 1978.

Durusau, Mary. "You may not know Leadbelly, but you know his songs."

Ferstel, Vicki. "1867 school for black children recognized." State Times, 22 May 1990, 3 (B).

Funk & Wagnalls Standard Reference Encyclopedia, 1969 ed. Vol. 9. "Emancipation Proclamation."

Hall, Gwendolyn Midlo. Africans in Colonial Louisiana: The Development of Afro-Creole Culture in the Eighteenth Century. Baton Rouge: Louisiana State University Press, 1992.

Harris, Jessica B. The Welcome Table: African-American Heritage Cooking. New York: Simon & Schuster, 1995.

Herskovits, Melville J. The New World Negro. Bloomington: Indiana University Press, 1966.

Hultman, Tami. The Africa News Cookbook: African Cooking for Western Kitchens. New York: Penguin Books, 1985.

Keasler, Jack. "Remembering Leadbelly."

Lanker, Brian. I Dream A World: Portraits of Black Women Who Changed America. New York: Stewart, Tabori & Chang, 1989.

Longone, Jan. "Early Black-Authored American Cookbooks." Gastronomica (February 2001): 96-99.

McDonald, Roderick A. The Economy and Material Culture of Slaves: Goods and Chattels on the Sugar Plantations of Jamaica and Louisiana. Baton Rouge and London: Louisiana State University Press, 1993.

Mills, Gary B. and Elizabeth S. Melrose. Natchitoches, Louisiana: The Association for the Preservation of Historic Natchitoches, 1973.

Paige, Howard. Aspects of Afro-American Cookery. Southfield, Michigan: Aspects Publishing Co., 1987.

Pena, Christopher G. Phone Interview. June 2004.

Richard, C. E. Louisiana: An Illustrated History. Baton Rouge: The Foundation for Excellence in Louisiana Public Broadcasting, 2003.

Sandler, Bea. The African Cookbook. New York and Cleveland: The World Publishing Company, 1970.

Searing, James F. West African Slavery and Atlantic Commerce: The Senegal River Valley, 1700-1860. Cambridge: Cambridge University Press, 1993.

Taylor, Joe Gray. Eating, Drinking, and Visiting in the South. Baton Rouge and London: Louisiana State University Press, 1982.

Taylor, Joe Gray. "Negro Slavery in Louisiana." Ph.D. diss., Louisiana State University and Agricultural and Mechanical College, 1951.

Thum, Marcella. Exploring Black America: A History and Guide. New York: Atheneum, 1975.

Van der Post, Laurens. Recipes: African Cooking. New York: Time-Life Books, 1970.

Vincent, Charles. Black Legislators in Louisiana During Reconstruction. Baton Rouge: Louisiana State University Press, 1976.

Vincent, Charles. The Louisiana Purchase Bicentennial Series in Loulslana History: Volume XI The African American Experience in

Louisiana Part B From the Civil War to Jim Crow. Publication of the Center for Louisiana Studies University of Louisiana at Lafayette. Lafayette, Louisiana: The Center for Louisiana Studies, 2000.

Wilson, Ellen Gibson. A West African Cook Book. New York: M. Evans and Company, Inc., 1971.

Wilson, Mary Tolford. "Peaceful Integration: The Owner's Adoption of His Slaves' Food." The Journal of Negro History XLIX (April 1964): 116-27.

http://afroamhistory.about.com/library/weekly/aa092300a.htm

http://ame2.asu.edu/sites/voodoodreams/marie_laveau.asp

http://chnm.gmu.edu/revolution/d/335/

http://mo.essortment.com/henriettedelill_rqbj.htm

http://nutrias.org/~nopl/info/louinfo/admins/bore.htm

http://www.ac-amiens.fr/college60/delaunay_gouvieux/codenen.htm

http://www.afgen.com/aboutgos.html

http://www.afgen.com/gospel1.html

http://www.africanamericanmuseum.org/events.htm

http://www.africanamericanmuseum.org/exhibitions.htm

http://www.allsands.com/History/People/marielaveaubio_aar_gn.htm

http://www.csicop.org/sb/2001-12/i-files.html

http://www.fortbutler.org/Pena%20Battle.htm

http://www.haiti-usa.org/historical/index.php?cp=0

http://www.haiti-usa.org/historical/index.php?cp=2

http://www.haiti-usa.org/historical/index.php?cp=3

http://www.haiti-usa.org/historical/index.php?cp=4

http://www.haiti-usa.org/historical/index.php?cp=6

http://www.haiti-usa.org/historical/index.php?cp=8

http://www.haiti-usa.org/historical/index.php?cp=22

http://www.haiti-usa.org/historical/index.php?chapter=012

http://www.likesbooks.com/neworleans.html

http://www.nathanielturner.com/livesandtimesofquadroons.htm

http://www.negrospirituals.com/

http://www.nps.gov/ncro/anti/emancipation.html

http://www.princeton.edu/~mcbrown/display/rillieux_biography.html

http://www.swagga.com/voodoo.htm

http://www.thelavinagency.com/college/ernestgaines.html

GERMANS
Blume, Helmut. The German Coast During the Colonial Era 1722-1803. Destrehan, Louisiana: The German-Acadian Coast Historical and Genealogical Society, 1990.

Deiler, J. Hanno. The Settlement of the German Coast of Louisiana and The Creoles of German Descent. Baltimore: Genealogical Publishing Co., Inc., 1969.

Falgoust, Glenn. "Determined Germans: The Price They Paid For La Louisiane." Sauce Piquante, Vol. 2, Issue 8, 6.

Forsyth, Alice D. German "Pest Ships," 1720-1721. New Orleans: Genealogical Research Society, 1969.

Giraud, Marcel. The Louisiana Purchase Bicentennial Series in Louisiana History. Vol. 1, The French Experience in Louisiana. Publication of the Center for Louisiana Studies, ed. Glenn R. Conrad. Lafayette: University of Southwestern Louisiana, 1995.

Hark, Ann and Preston H. Barba. Pennsylvania German Cookery: A Regional Cookbook. Allentown, Pa.: Schlechter's, 1956.

Hazelton, Nika Standen. The Cooking of Germany. New York: Time-Life Books, 1969.

Kondert, Dr. Reinhart. "Louisiana's German Pioneers: The Early Years (1720-1732)." New Orleans Genesis 22 (April 1983): 135-142.

Le Conte, Rene. "The Germans in Louisiana in the Eighteenth Century," Louisiana History, 8 (1967): 67-84.

Monteleone, Diana. "German-Americans." Center for Cultural and Eco-Tourism, University of Louisiana Lafayette, August 15, 2002.

Nau, John Frederick. The German People of New Orleans, 1850-1900. Leiden: E. J. Brill, 1958.

Oubre, Elton J. Vacherie: St. James Parish, Louisiana. Thibodaux, La.: Oubre's Books, 2002.

Robichaux, Jr., Albert J. German Coast Families: European Origins and Settlement in Colonial Louisiana. Rayne, La.: Hebert

Publications, 1997.

Saxon, Lyle. "German Pioneers in Old New Orleans." The American-German Review VII (February 1941): 28-29.

Taylor, Joe Gray. Louisiana: A Bicentennial History. New York: W. W. Norton & Company, Inc., 1976.

Voss, Louis. Louisiana's German Heritage: Louis Voss' Introductory History. Edited by Don Heinrich Tolzmann. Bowie, Maryland: Heritage Books, Inc., 1994.

http://www.enlou.com/communities/minden.htm

http://www.enlou.com/markers/germantown.htm

http://www.ohwy.com/la/g/grmnclmu.htm

http://www.stepintohistory.com/states/LA/Germantown_Colony.htm

ENGLISH
Bailey, Adrian. Recipes: The Cooking of the British Isles. New York: Time-Life Books, 1969.

Battle of New Orleans Sesquicentennial Celebration 1815-1965. Final Report of the United States Congress of the Battle of New Orleans Sesquicentennial Celebration Commission. Washington, D.C.: 1965.

Butler, Louise. "West Feliciana: A Glimpse of its History." The Louisiana Historical Quarterly 7 (January–October 1924): 90-120.

Calloway, Colin G. New Worlds for All: Indians, Europeans, and the Remaking of Early America. Baltimore and London: The Johns Hopkins University Press, 1997.

Carter, III Samuel. Blaze of Glory: The Fight for New Orleans, 1814-1815. New York: St. Martin's Press, 1971.

Casey, Powell A. Louisiana at the Battle of New Orleans. Eastern National, 2002.

Davis, Edwin Adams. Plantation Life in the Florida Parishes of Louisiana, 1836-1846 as Reflected in the Diary of Bennet H. Barrow. New York: Columbia University Press, 1943.

Garmey, Jane. Great British Cooking: A Well-Kept Secret. New York: Harper Perennial, 1992.

Garvey, Joan B. and Mary Lou Widmer. Louisiana: The First 300 Years. New Orleans: Garmer Press, Inc., 2001.

Huber, Leonard V. The Battle of New Orleans: New Orleans As It Was In 1814-1815. New Orleans: The Louisiana Landmarks Society, 1994.

Hutchins, Thomas. An Historical Narrative and Topographical Description of Louisiana and West-Florida. Gainesville: University of Florida Press, 1968.

Hyde, Jr., Samuel C. Pistols and Politics: The Dilemma of Democracy in Louisiana's Florida Parishes, 1810-1899. Baton Rouge and London: Louisiana State University Press, 1996.

Jean Lafitte National Historical Park and Preserve, Chalmette Battlefield Unit, National Park Service film, U.S. Department of the Interior, Chalmette, Louisiana.

L'Ami Des Lois, February 18, 1815.

L'Ami Des Lois, February 21, 1815.

L'Ami Des Lois, Saturday, March 18, 1815.

L'Ami Des Lois, April 4, 1815.

Louisiana Gazette, February 21, 1815.

Nichols, C. Howard. Louisiana's Florida parishes: a bibliography. Center for Regional Studies: Southeastern Louisiana University, 1983.

Pickles, Tim. New Orleans 1815: Andrew Jackson crushes the British. Oxford, United Kingdom: Osprey Publishing, 2003.

Reeves, Miriam G. The Felicianas of Louisiana. Baton Rouge: Claitor's Book Store, 1967.

Remini, Robert V. Andrew Jackson and the Course of American Empire, 1767-1821. New York: Harper & Row, Publishers, 1977.

Rowland, Dunbar, ed. Mississippi Provincial Archives 1763-1766: English Dominion: Letters and Enclosures to the Secretary of State from Major Robert Farmar and Governor George Johnstone. Vol. 1. Nashville, Tenn.: Press of Brandon Printing Company, 1911.

Sauer, Carl O. Seventeenth Century North America. Turtle Island: Berkeley, 1980.

Savelle, Max. Empires to Nations: Expansion in America, 1713-1824. Minneapolis: University of Minnesota Press, 1974.

Scott, Richard E. "Late 19th Century Sunday Menu." New Orleans, La.: Herman-Grima House, 2004. Faxed.

Skipwith, H. East Feliciana, Louisiana Past and Present: Sketches of the Pioneers. New Orleans: Hopkins' Printing Office, 1892.

Volo, James M. and Dorothy Denneen Volo. Daily Life on the Old Colonial Frontier. Westport, Connecticut and London: Greenwood Press, 2002.

Willie, Leroy Ellis. The History of Spanish West Florida and the Rebellion of 1810: and, Philemon Thomas, patriot. General Philemon Thomas Chapter of Baton Rouge: Louisiana Society of the Sons of the American Revolution, 1991.

Word, Ola Mae. Reflections of Rosedown. Lynchburg, Va.: Rosedown Plantation and Gardens.

http://www.inetours.com/New_Orleans/Garden_District.html

http://www.tour-new-orleans.com/garden-district.htm

ITALIANS
Baiamonte, Jr., John V. "Immigrants in Rural America: A Study of the Italians of Tangipahoa Parish, Louisiana." Ph.D. diss., Mississippi State University, 1972.

Gardner, Joel, ed. A Better Life: Italian-Americans in South Louisiana. American-Italian Federation of the Southeast, 1983.

Giordano, Paul Anthony. "The Italians of Louisiana: Their Cultural Background and Their Many Contributions in the Fields of Literature, the Arts, Education, Politics, and Business and Labor." Ph.D. diss., Indiana University, 1978.

Margavio, A. V., and Jerome J. Salomone. Bread and Respect: The Italians of Louisiana. Gretna, LA: Pelican Publishing Company, 2002.

Orso, Ethelyn. The St. Joseph Altar Traditions of South Louisiana. Lafayette: The Center for Louisiana Studies University of Southwestern Louisiana, 1990.

Pupella, Eufemia Azzolina. Sicilian Cookery: The Best Recipes of the Regional Cookery. Florence, Italy: Casa Editrice Bonechi.

Riviere, Mary Ann. From Palermo to New Orleans. 1987.

Robichaux, Jr., Albert J. Italian-American Roots: The Civil Registration of Births, Marriages, and Deaths in the Town of Alia on the Island of Sicily Volume I 1851-1861. Rayne, LA: Hebert Publications, 1994.

Root, Waverley and the editors of TIME-LIFE BOOKS. The Cooking of Italy. New York: Time-Life Books, 1968.

Sandel, Elias W. & Mary E. From Italy to the United States: Tangipahoa Parish, Louisiana. E. Sandel, 1993.

Scarpaci, Jean Ann. Italian Immigrants in Louisiana's Sugar Parishes: Recruitment, Labor Conditions, and Community Relations, 1880-1910. New York: Arno Press, 1980.

Warren, Karen. Feast of St. Joseph: Labor of Love by the Faithful. Hammond: Center for Regional Studies Southeastern Louisiana University, 1982.

http://www.muffoletta.com/history/

http://www.redhotjazz.com/odjb.html

http://www.sec.state.la.us/archives/italian2001/italian2001-commerce.htm

CREOLES
Falgoust, Glenn. "King Creole: Louisiana's 'Created' Aristocracy." Sauce Piquante, September 1999, 6.

ADDITIONAL SOURCES
Addison, Jeff. Phone Interview. July, 2004.

Amato, P.J. Phone Interview. July, 2004.

Ancelet, Barry Jean; Edwards, Jay; and Pitre, Glen. Cajun Country. Jackson and London: University Press of Mississippi, 1991.

Baudier, Roger, Sr. A General Review of Origin and Development of the Baking Industry in Old New Orleans, 1722-1892. New Orleans: Roger Baudier, Sr., 1953.

Bienvenu, Marcelle, ed. The Picayune's Creole Cook Book. New Orleans: The Times-Picayune Publishing Corp., 1987.

Bluysen, Judith. Cajun: A Culinary Tour of Louisiana. New York: Rizzoli International Publications, 2002.

Bourgeois, Lillian. Cabanocey: The History, Customs and Folklore of St. James Parish. Gretna: Pelican Publishing Company, 1957.

Boyle, Christopher C. "Collapse of the Georgetown Rice Culture." www.ego.net/us/sc/myr/history/decline.htm. 1996.

Bradshaw, Jim. "Rice Industry Turned Jefferson Davis Prairie Green." The Lafayette Daily Advertiser. (October 28, 1997) Lafayette, Louisiana.

Bradshaw, Jim. "South Louisiana Rice Farming Began in Earnest in the 1880s." The Lafayette Daily Advertiser. (March 24, 2004) Lafayette, Louisiana.

Brennan, Ella and Dick. The Commander's Palace New Orleans Cookbook. New York: Clarkson N. Potter, Inc., 1984.
Brennan, Pip, Jimmy and Ted. Breakfast at Brennan's and Dinner, Too. New Orleans: Brennan's Inc., 1994.

Brown, Helen Evans and Philip S. Breakfasts and Brunches For Every Occasion. Garden City: Doubleday & Company, Inc., 1961.

Brown, Mitchell. "Norbert Rillieux." Faces of Science: African Americans in the Sciences. www.princeton.edu/~mcbrown/display/rillieux.html. 1995-2000.
Burton, Nathaniel and Lombard, Rudy. Creole Feast; 15 Master Chefs

of New Orleans Reveal Their Secrets. New York: Random House, 1978.

Cabildo Online Project http://lsm.crt.state.la.us/cabildo/cab8.htm.

Chase, Leah. The Dooky Chase Cookbook. Gretna: Pelican Publishing Company, 1990.

Chesser, Jerald W., CEC, CCE. The Art & Science of Culinary Preparation. St. Augustine, Florida: The Educational Institute of the American Culinary Federation, Inc., 1992.

Collin, Rima and Richard. The New Orleans Cookbook. New York: Alfred A. Knopf, Inc., 1980.

Colt, George Howe. "Ghosts of the Mississippi." www.travelandleisure.com. March 2004.

Creech, Howard. "Traveling the First Gold Coast: Louisiana's Great River Road." www.epinions.com, May 12, 2002.

Cudney, D.W. and Elmore, C.L. "Common Purslane." UC IPM Online. www.ipm.ucdavis.edu/PMG/PESTNOTES/pn7461.html. University of California Statewide Integrated Pest Management Program. October, 2003.

Cunningham, Lynn. "Pride, tradition are leavening in N.O. baker's French bread." Times-Picayune. (December 12, 1988).

Daigle, Rev. Jules O. A Dictionary of the Cajun Language. Ann Arbor, Michigan: Edwards Brothers, Inc., 1984.

Davidson, Alan. Oxford Companion To Food. Oxford and New York: Oxford University Press, 1999.

DeMers, John. Arnaud's Creole Cookbook: Memoirs and Recipes from the Historic New Orleans Restaurant. New York: Simon & Schuster, 1988.

DeMers, John. "Save Our French Bread" New Orleans (Food: September 1991).

Distefano, Joey. "The Village and Jack Saban's." Phone Interview. Baton Rouge: August, 2004.
Dupaigne, Bernard. The History of Bread. Harry N. Abrams, Inc., 1999.

Encyclopedia of Foods: A Guide to Healthy Nutrition. San Diego: Academic Press, 2002.

Fitzgerald, Waverly. "Twelfth Night." School of the Seasons website. www.schooloftheseasons.com/twelfthnight.html. 2004.

Folse, Jerry. "Remembering Mary Ferchaud." The Enterprise. March 5, 2003.

Folse, John D. Hot Beignets and Warm Boudoirs: A Collection of Recipes from Louisiana's Bed and Breakfasts. Gonzales: Chef John Folse & Company, 1999.

Folse, John D. Louisiana Sampler: Recipes from Our Fairs and Festivals. Gonzales: Chef John Folse & Company, 1996.

Folse, John D. Plantation Celebrations: Recipes from Our Louisiana Mansions. Gonzales: Chef John Folse & Company, 1994.

Folse, John D. and Walker, Craig M. Something Old and Something New: Louisiana Cooking With a Change of Heart. Gonzales: Chef John Folse & Company, 1997.

Fontenot, Mary Alice and Landry, Julie. The Louisiana Experience. Baton Rouge: Claitors Publishing, 1983.

Garrett, Thomas. "Louisiana's rice mill is oldest in America." The Baxter Bulletin Online. www.baxterbulletin.com/news/stories/20030730/localnews/551228.html. July 30, 2003.

Galatoire, Leon. Galatoire's Cookbook. Gretna: Pelican Publishing Company, 1994.

Gore, Laura Locoul with commentary by Norman and Sand Marmillion. Memories of the Old Plantation Home and A Creole Family Album. Vacherie, Louisiana: The Zoe Company, Inc., 2000.

Gleason, David King. Plantation Homes of Louisiana and the Natchez Area. Baton Rouge and London: Louisiana State University Press, 1982.

Guste, Roy F., Jr. Antoine's Restaurant Cookbook. New Orleans: Carbery-Guste, 1978.

Guste, Roy F., Jr. The Restaurants of New Orleans. New York: W.W. Norton & Co., 1982.

Hammond, Rhonda. "Doing Honor to the Dead." Term Paper for Culinary 279: Cajun & Creole Cuisine, Chef John Folse Culinary Institute, Nicholls State University, Thibodaux, Louisiana, 2003.

Hanger, Kimberly S. A Medley of Cultures: Louisiana History at the Cabildo. New Orleans: Louisiana Museum Foundation, 1996.

Hearn, Lafcadio. Creole Cook Book. Gretna: Pelican Publishing Co., 1990.

Holliday, Daryl. "Andouille Sausage." Term Paper for Culinary 279: Cajun & Creole Cuisine, Chef John Folse Culinary Institute, Nicholls State University, Thibodaux, Louisiana, 2003.

Jenkins, Steven. Cheese Primer. New York: Workman Publishing Company, 1996.

Johnson, Phil, ed. <u>New Orleans Chef's Cookbook</u>. Gretna: Pelican Publishing Co., 1988.

Kafka, Barbara. <u>Soup: A Way of Life</u>. New York: Artisan, 1998.

Kane, Harnett. <u>The Bayous of Louisiana</u>. New York: William & Harrow, 1944.

Kelley, Mary Palmer. <u>The Early English Kitchen Garden: Medieval Period to 1800 A.D.</u> Columbia, South Carolina: Garden History Associates, 1984.

Keyes, Frances Parkinson. <u>All This is Louisiana</u>. New York: Harper Brothers Publishers, 1950.

Kilbourne, Kathy. "Vietnamese Folklife in New Orleans." Louisiana's Living Traditions. Louisiana Division of the Arts, 1999. www. louisianafolklife.org/LT/Articles_Essays/creole_art_vietnamese_folk. html.

Labensky, Sarah R. and Hause, Alan. <u>Oncooking: a Textbook of Culinary Fundamentals</u>. Upper Saddle River, New Jersey: Pearson Education, Inc., 2003.

Laborde, Errol. "French bread-an endangered species." <u>New Orleans</u>. (May, 1996).

Lambert, Paula. <u>The Cheese Lover's Cookbook and Guide</u>. New York: Simon & Schuster, 2000.

Lamonica, Dianne. "Louisiana is Rich in Christmas Tradition." CC Supp. December 1, 1972.

Litwin, Sharon. "Fourth generation on the rise." <u>Times-Picayune</u>. New Orleans (May 24, 1987).

Maguelonne, Toussaint-Samat. <u>History of Food</u>. Cambridge, Massachusetts: Blackwell Publishers, Inc., 1996.

Marmillion, Norman. Phone Interview. July, 2004.

McCaffety, Kerri. <u>St. Joseph Altars</u>. Gretna: Pelican Publishing Company, 2003.

Miester, Mark. "Good To The Last Drip." <u>Gambit Weekly,</u> (December 17, 2002) www.bestofneworleans.com/dispatch2002-12-17/cover_ story.html.

Montagné, Prosper. <u>The New Larousse Gastronomique</u>. New York: Crown Publishers, Inc., 1977.

Monteleone, Diana C. "Irish-Americans." University of Louisiana at Lafayette Center for Cultural and Eco-Tourism, 2001. http://ccet. louisiana.edu/03a_Cultural_Tourism_Files/01.02_The_People/Irish_ American.htm.

Oubre, Elton J. <u>Vacherie, St. James Parish, Louisiana: History & Geneology</u>. Thibodaux, Louisiana: Elton J. Oubre, 2002.

Owens, Maida. <u>Swapping Stories: Folktales from Louisiana.</u> (excerpt) University Press of Mississippi and the Louisiana Division of the Arts, 1997. "Swapping Stories: Louisiana's Traditional Cultures." www.lpb. org/programs/swappingstories/culture.htm.

Patout, Alex. <u>Patout's Cajun Home Cooking</u>. New York: Random House, 1986.

Poche, Robert. Phone Interview. July, 2004.

Regent, Nancy. "A Simple Celebration." The Morning Advocate. December 14, 1995. Baton Rouge.

Rognvaldardottir, Nanna. "Eggnog." www.whatscookingamerica.net/ Eggnog.htm.

Romero, Virginia. "Hungarian Folklife in the Florida Parishes of Louisiana." Louisiana's Living Traditions. Louisiana Division of the Arts, 1999. www.louisianafolklife.org/LT/Virtual_Books/Fla_Parishes/ book_florida_hungary.html.

Root, Waverly and de Rochemont, Richard. <u>Eating in America: A History</u>. New York: Ecco Press, 1981.

Saxon, Lyle, Dreyer, Edward, Tallant, Robert, eds. <u>Gumbo Ya Ya, Folk Tales of Louisiana</u>. Gretna: Pelican Publishing Company, 1988.

Smith, Andrew F. "History of Soup." Culinary Education Center. www. cheftalk.com/content, 2004.

Smith, John. "Cheesemaking in Scotland-An Early History." www. ebs.hw.ac.uk/SDA/cheese1.html. Scottish Dairy Association, 1995.

<u>Soups</u>. Alexandria, Virginia: Time-Life Books, 1979.

Stall, Gasper J. <u>Buddy Stall's Crescent City</u>. Louisiana: Gasper J. "Buddy" Stall, 1995.

Stall, Gasper J. <u>Buddy Stall's Louisiana Potpourri</u>. Gretna: Pelican Publishing Company, 1991.

Stall, Gasper J. <u>Buddy Stall's New Orleans</u>. Gretna: Pelican Publishing Company, 1990.

Starbird, Ethel A. "The Bonanza Bean: Coffee." <u>National Geographic</u> (March, 1981) www.nationalgeographic.com/coffee/ax/frame.html.

Stobart, Tom. <u>The Cook's Encyclopedia, Ingredients and Processes</u>. New York: Harper & Row, 1981.

Stradley, Linda. "History and Legends of Ice Cream." www. whatscookingamerica.net. 2002-2004.

Taggart, Chuck. "What is Absinthe?" www.gumbopages.com/food/ beverages/absinthe.html.

Tannahill, Reay. Food In History. New York: Crown Publishers, Inc., 1989.

Trager, James. The Food Chronology. New York: Henry Holt & Co., 1995.

The Good Cook: Salads. Chicago: Time-Life Books, Inc., 1981.

Vincent, Jennifer. "Andouille." Term Paper for Culinary 279: Cajun & Creole Cuisine, Chef John Folse Culinary Institute, Nicholls State University, Thibodaux, Louisiana, 2003.

Ware, Carolyn. "Croatians in Southeastern Louisiana: Overview" The Louisiana Folklife Program. Louisiana Division of the Arts, 1999. www.louisianafolklife.org/LT/Article_Essays/main_misc_croatians_s_ la.html.

Werlin, Laura. The New American Cheese. New York:Stewart, Tabori and Chung, 2000.

Zerangue, Kevin. "Sorrento Boucherie Festival." Term Paper for Culinary 279: Cajun & Creole Cuisine, Chef John Folse Culinary Institute, Nicholls State University, Thibodaux, Louisiana, 2002.

"A Rumination on the Invention of Soup." www.soupsong.com/ 2mar02.html.

"Eggnog-History." www.indepthinfo.com/eggnog/history.shtml. 1999-2004.

"Ratafia: for any palate, any time." www.abvwines.com/ratafia.html Alexis Bailey Vineyard.

"Sugar at LSU." www.lib.lsu.edu/special/sugar/sugar.html.

http://en.wikipedia.org/wiki/cocktail.

www.canadaegg.ca.

www.commanderspalace.com.

www.holsteincow.htm.

www.konriko.com.

www.riceweb.com.

www.ricefestival.com.

www.rootsweb.com/~larapide.

www.senate.gov/pagelayout/senators/one_item_and_teasers/ louisiana.htm.

www.stratsplace.com/rogov/joys_ratafia.html.

www.usda.gov.

www.watersheds.org.

www.worldjerseycattle.com

Index

Note: Page numbers in **bold** indicate recipe photographs.

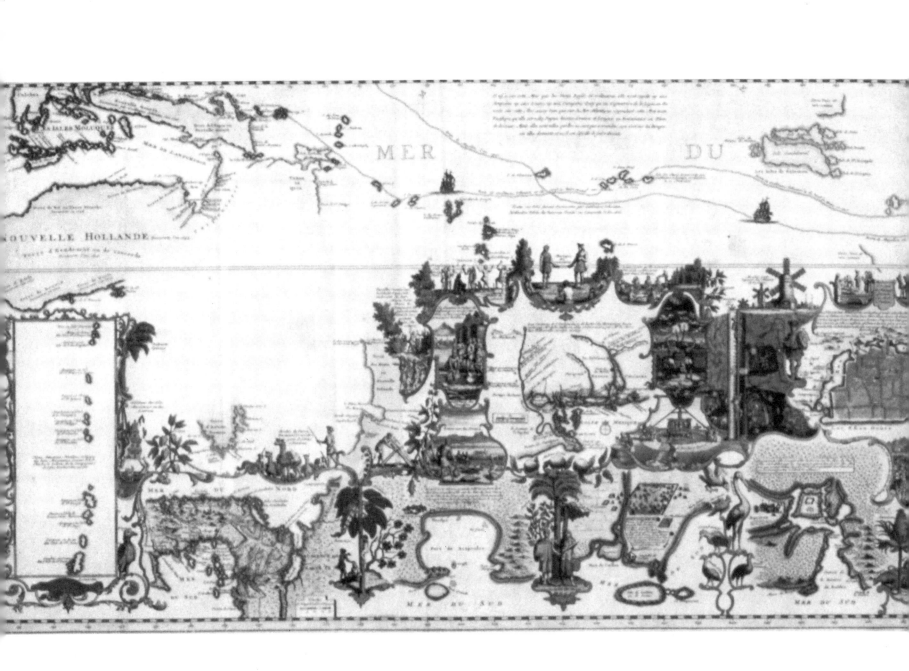